The Psychology of Cognition

This comprehensive, cutting-edge textbook offers a layered approach to the study of cognitive neuroscience and psychology. It embraces multiple exciting and influential theoretical approaches such as embodied cognition and predictive coding, and explains new topics such as motor cognition, cognitive control, consciousness, and social cognition.

Durk Talsma offers foundational knowledge which he expands and enhances with the coverage of complex topics, explaining their interrelatedness and presenting them together with classic experiments and approaches in a historic context. Providing broad coverage of world-class international research, this richly illustrated textbook covers key topics including:

- Action control and cognitive control
- Consciousness and attention
- Perception
- Multisensory processing and perception-action integration
- Motivation and reward processing
- Emotion and cognition
- Learning and memory
- Language processing
- Reasoning
- Numerical cognition and categorisation
- Judgement, decision-making, and problem-solving
- Social cognition
- Applied cognitive psychology

With pedagogical features that include highlights of relevant methods and historical notes to spark student interest, this essential text will be invaluable reading for all students of cognitive psychology and cognitive neuroscience.

Durk Talsma is a professor in the Department of Experimental Psychology, Ghent University, Belgium. His research interests include selective attention, multisensory integration, visual short-term memory, and event-related potential methodology.

'Although there exist very many introductory textbooks on psychology, this book stands out. This is the single best introduction to psychological science in existence. The author enlivens the text with concrete examples, interesting anecdotes, and historical excursions. All of this radiates a love for the field and a love for science.'

– **Eric-Jan Wagenmakers,** *Department of Psychological Methods, University of Amsterdam, Amsterdam*

'This is a hefty volume. It has to be — it is nothing less than a comprehensive and up-to-the-minute review of research in cognitive psychology. Talsma combines breadth of coverage and approachable style with nuance, depth of knowledge and historical context to satisfy newcomers to the field and the most demanding expert. This will become an instant classic and an indispensable resource for everyone interested in human cognition.'

– **Paul M. Corballis, PhD,** *Professor, School of Psychology, University of Auckland, New Zealand*

The Psychology of Cognition

An Introduction to Cognitive Neuroscience

Durk Talsma

Routledge
Taylor & Francis Group

LONDON AND NEW YORK

Cover image: © Getty Images

First published in English in 2023
by Routledge
4 Park Square, Milton Park, Abingdon, Oxon, OX14 4RN

and by Routledge
605 Third Avenue, New York, NY 10158

Routledge is an imprint of the Taylor & Francis Group, an informa business

First published in Dutch as *De psychologie van denken en doen: van hersencel tot hogere cognitie* by Owl Press, 2020

British Library Cataloguing-in-Publication Data
A catalogue record for this book is available from the British Library

Library of Congress Cataloging-in-Publication Data
Names: Talsma, Durk, author.
Title: The psychology of cognition : an introduction to cognitive neuroscience / Durk Talsma.
Other titles: Psychologie van denken en doen. English
Description: Abingdon, Oxon ; New York, NY : Routledge, 2023. | First published in in Dutch as De psychologie van denken en doen: van hersencel tot hogere cognitie by Owl Press, 2020. | Includes bibliographical references and index. |
Identifiers: LCCN 2022055143 (print) | LCCN 2022055144 (ebook) | ISBN 9781032333625 (hardback) | ISBN 9781032333618 (paperback) | ISBN 9781003319344 (ebook) | ISBN 9781032479217
Subjects: LCSH: Cognitive psychology. | Cognitive neuroscience. | Consciousness. | Social perception,
Classification: LCC BF201 .T36 2023 (print) | LCC BF201 (ebook) | DDC 153--dc23/eng/20230206
LC record available at https://lccn.loc.gov/2022055143
LC ebook record available at https://lccn.loc.gov/2022055144

ISBN: 9781032333625 (hbk)
ISBN: 9781032333618 (pbk)
ISBN: 9781003319344 (ebk)
ISBN: 9781032479217 (eBook+)

DOI: 10.4324/9781003319344

Typeset in ITC Slimbach Std
by KnowledgeWorks Global Ltd.

Access the Support Material: www.routledge.com/9781032333618

Contents

Contents

Contents

Contents

Foreword

If anybody would have asked me, at the start of my tenure as an assistant professor in cognitive psychology, if I would ever write an introductory textbook on cognitive psychology, my answer would probably have been a resounding no. After all, there are many high-quality textbooks on the market, and for a long time I was convinced that it would be extremely difficult, if not impossible, to match the quality of an already existing textbook. Moreover, within academic psychology, textbook writing is often considered to be inferior to writing original research papers.

The fact that this book is nevertheless here has a number of special reasons. The first reason is that over ten years of teaching the courses Introduction to Cognitive Psychology I and II at Ghent University made me that the existing books also had their limitations. In summary, these boil down to the fact that many of the existing textbooks were a little light on theory, while those that were sufficiently rooted in theory were too advanced to be suitable for an introductory course. Moreover, I was increasingly struck by the fact that the great majority of textbooks are extremely fragmented in their coverage of the most important cognitive processes, resulting in my observation that the bigger picture – that is, how all these functions are interrelated – remained underexposed. Finally, I became increasingly aware of the fact that many exciting new and emerging topics were not very well covered in existing material.

For these and other reasons, I began to entertain the idea of releasing a set of lecture notes as supplementary material to an existing textbook. To the best of my memory, I initially coined this idea in early 2017, and after sketching out a number of different approaches, the project would most likely have come to a complete standstill if it hadn't been for the fact that Sophie Vanluchene, publisher at OWL Press, convinced me to publish a Dutch language textbook for my Introduction to Cognitive Psychology courses. After I had committed myself to that project, I instantly knew that I wanted to take an approach that would emphasise the interrelation between the many aspects of human cognition while discussing each topic from state-of-the-art theoretical perspectives, wherever possible.

Moreover, a secondary aim in writing this textbook was that it should spark students enthusiasm for the field. After all, science is a human endeavour that is as much characterised by human ingenuity as it is by human fallacies. Science is an idiosyncratic activity that is sometimes characterised by a high degree of anarchy, despite the strict quality control procedures. Ideas may clash, discussions may become overheated, and methodological blunders may occasionally result in groundbreaking insights. There is a story behind almost any research question that has ever been asked, and some of these stories sparked my initial enthusiasm for the field. By including some of these stories, I hope to pass some of this enthusiasm on.

In retrospect, the writing of this book turned out to be an incredible adventure. Even though it is more than 30 years since I was an undergraduate psychology student myself, and more than 10 years since I started as a lecturer in cognitive psychology, it sometimes feels like I never learned as much about the field as I did while working on this book. After drafting an initial outline, an extensive literature search followed, which frequently resulted in many interesting, exciting, or unexpected results.

Consider, for example, the topic of action and action control. Although it was right from the start the plan to cover this topic extensively, it was only during the writing of the corresponding chapters that I realised how important this topic really is and how much we have learned about the complex processes that form the basis of human motor behaviour, as well as those processes involved in translating visual sensory information into visually guided actions. The same holds for the predictive coding theory, which I predominantly knew from the visual perception and multisensory integration literature, but which is now strongly intertwined with almost every domain in cognitive psychology imaginable. The underlying statistical principles, as outlined by Bayes theorem, are currently so prominently present in almost every domain of cognitive psychology that they deserved to be prominently featured in an appendix.

This book was originally published in Dutch, and for the production of the Dutch edition, I would like to thank the following people. First and foremost, I would like to thank Sophie Vanluchene for motivating me to start this project and for sharing her insights while writing the Dutch language edition of this book. In a similar vein, I would like to extend my appreciation to the entire OWL Press team for making the Dutch edition a reality. As such, I would like to thank, Nils de Malsche, Joni Verhulst, Pauline Scharmann, Jeroen Wille, Stephanie Philipaerts, Davine Peleman, Wannes Swings, Greet Van Looy, and the Crius Group.

For the English edition, I would also like to thank several people, most notably Ceri McLardi for making this edition a reality, as well as Emilie Coin, Tori Sharpe, and Khyati Sanger, who were all actively involved in the project, in guiding the translation process and making the accompanying website a reality. I would also like to express my gratitude to Suzanne Pfister and her team at KnowledgeWorks Global, and Laurie Fuller at Taylor & Francis for making the production of this book such a smooth process.

Obviously, I would also like to thank all my colleagues at the Department of Experimental Psychology for their support and encouragement during the entire project. In particular, I would like to thank the following people specifically: Marc Brysbaert, as an author of the largest Dutch language introductory textbook in psychology (and of several other internationally published titles), you were a major source of inspiration and I strongly value your encouragement to pursue this project, as well as your practical guidelines. Frederick Verbruggen, as my neighbour at the department, you were always available and willing to discuss the sometimes trivial but pressing issues that I might encounter while working on a specific part, and as a forerunner in the new renaissance of experimental methods and replication, you indirectly contributed a lot to both the introductory and the closing chapters of this book. Rob Hartsuiker, not only were your comments on the initial outlines of my language chapters invaluable, but I also have fond memories of our frequent lunchtime discussions about life in and outside of academia. Guy Vingerhoets, I would like to thank you for your valuable comments on Chapters 1 and 2 and your frequent interest in my progress. Tom Verguts, your valuable comments on Chapters 1 and 11 were really helpful in making those parts more accessible. Likewise, I really appreciated your frequent interest in my progress. Michel Quak and Raquel London, I would like to thank you for the inspiring discussions that we had over the years, which have indirectly also contributed to the existence of this book. I could not have wished for better PhD students. Finally, I would like to thank Nico Boehler and Ruth Krebs; I appreciate the many discussions we had over the years, and your literature suggestions for Chapter 11 where much appreciated.

In addition, I would also like to thank many colleagues from other universities for their constructive feedback and helpful discussions. Hedderik van Rijn and Ritske de Jong: I would like to thank you for your constructive feedback on the initial outline and the many helpful discussions at the start of this project. I would also like to thank Monicque Lorist for offering a place to work during my frequent visits to Groningen while working on the manuscript. I would like to thank many colleagues for reviewing specific sections or chapters: Eric-Jan Wagenmakers (Bayesian inference), Bernhard Hommel (Chapters 1, 3–5), Edward de Haan (Chapters 1–6), Sander Nieuwenhuis (Chapters 1 and 2), Marit Ruitenberg (Chapter 3), Stefan Van der Stichel (Chapter 4), Eveline Crone (Chapters 5 and 24), Niels Taatgen (Chapter 5), Sebastiaan Mathôt (Chapter 10), Pieter Medendorp (Chapter 10), Manon Mulckhuyse (Chapter 12), and Hein van Schie (Chapter 10). Moreover, I am much indebted to my friends and colleagues Elger Abrahamse, Guido Band, Johan Braeckman, Roshan Cools, Floris De Lange, Jacob Jolij, Leon Kenemans, Peter Klaver, Mark Nieuwenstein, Chris Olivers, Pieter Roelfsema, Heleen Slagter, Jan Theeuwes, Erik van der Burg, Miriam Keetels, Rob van der Lubbe, Nienke van Atteveldt, Freddy van der Veen, Jean Vroomen, and Johan Wagemans for their support, encouragement, and willingness to comment on specific issues.

Finally, I would like to thank my family and friends for their patience. The writing process was sometimes marked by extensive periods of hyper-focus, and many social activities have suffered from this. I hope that we can soon catch up! Last but not least, I would like to express my sincere thanks to one special person, without whose continuous support and encouragement this project would never have taken off: Juliette, not only your help in editing figure labels and illustrations has been instrumental, your comments on the readability of the main text and your continuous support have been crucial factors in the realisation of this book. It is for this reason this book is dedicated to you!

Ghent, October 2022
Durk Talsma

To Juliette

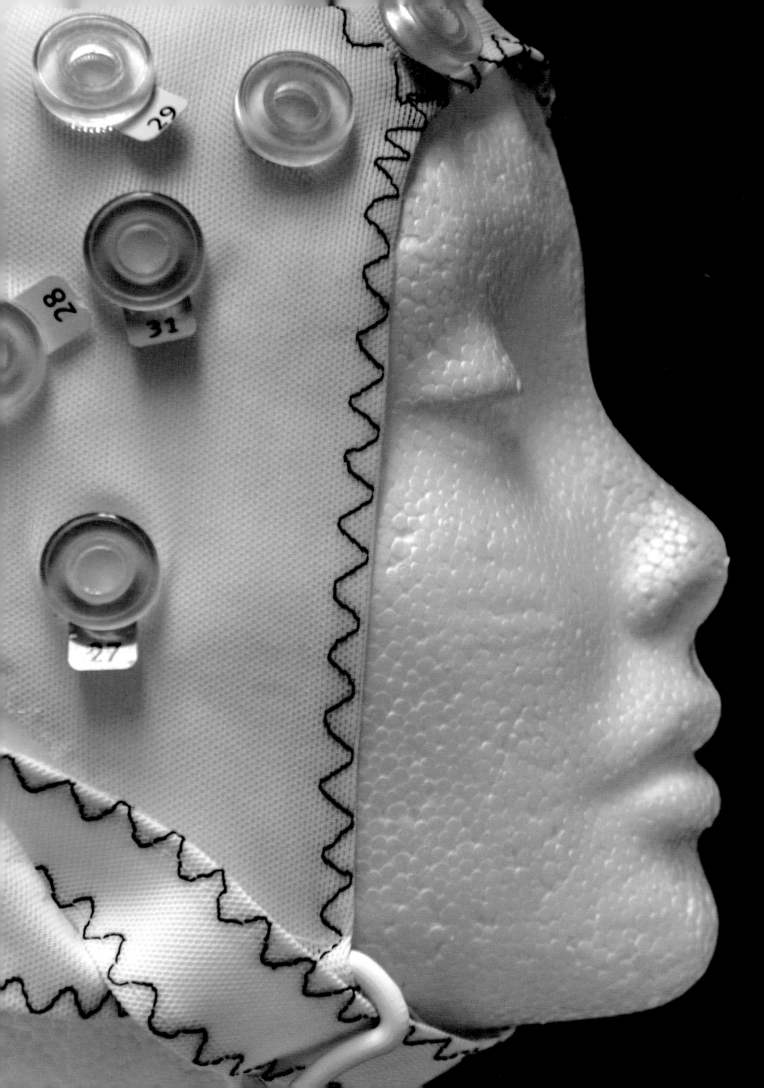

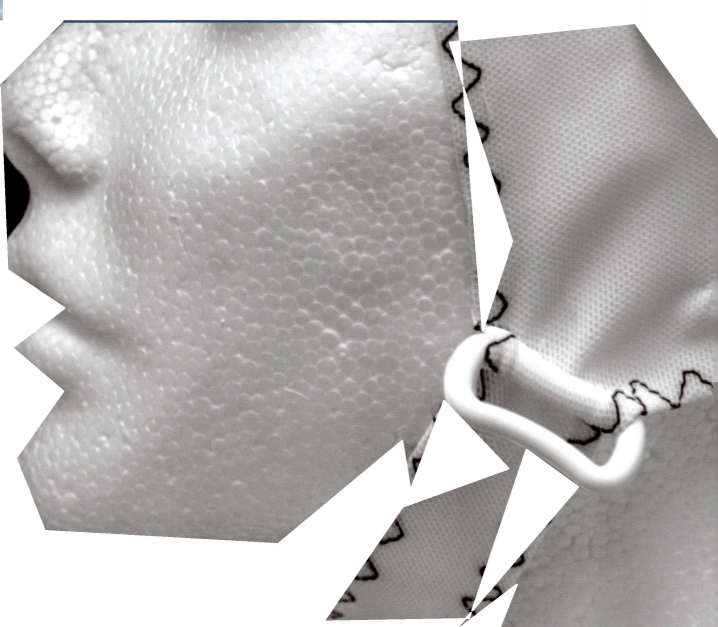

PART 1

Introduction

CHAPTER 1

Cognitive psychology: history and development of a discipline

1.1 INTRODUCTION

Ideas about the nature of the human 'soul' are presumably as old as humanity itself. Already in 387 BCE, for example, the Greek philosopher Plato argued that the brain is the seat of logos, the rational part of the soul (Crivellato & Ribatti, 2007). Even earlier, approximately around 400 BCE, another Greek philosopher, Empedocles, addressed questions involving visual perception (Siegel, 1959). Empedocles presumed that we perceive our environment because our eyes carry an internal fire that cause objects to light up (fig 1.1a). Empedocles' theory that our eyes emit rays of light, which has become known as the **emission theory**, turned out to be grandiosely incorrect; however, it did form the basis of much groundbreaking work in the fields of light and optics.

Eventually, around the years AD 1011–1012, the Arabic mathematician, physicist, and astronomer Ibn al-Haytham (in the West, known as Alhazen) noticed Empedocles' error, after an intensive study of the properties of light. Alhazen proposed that visual sensations come about because the light that is reflected by objects in our environment is immitted into our eyes (Smith, 1998). Based on this, Alhazen formulated an alternative theory, which is known as the **immision theory**. To this day, the immision theory forms the basis of everything we know about the workings of the human eye (fig 1.1b).

According to the **associationist theories of thought**, the resulting sensory impressions would be merged one way or another. Combined with already existing memories and ideas, associations between sensations and thoughts would be formed, which would serve as a basis for complex mental representations of our environment and abstract concepts. Although the roots of these associationist theories can be traced back to the era of Plato and Empedocles, they became more influential by the end of the 17th century, when the British philosopher and physician John Locke added a new chapter, entitled 'Of the associations of ideas', to his book *An essay concerning human understanding* (Bullard, 2016). Locke's ideas were further developed by the Scottish philosopher

David Hume (1739). Hume described, in his *A treatise of human nature*, how the proximity of individual sensory impressions, in time and in space, would influence the formation of sequences of thoughts and ideas. In Hume's work, associations were therefore mainly introduced as a way of describing how ideas could form, without specifically describing the processes involved in the formation of associations.

Studies investigating these processes emerged towards the end of the 19th century, based on the work of, among others, the Russian physiologist Ivan Pavlov, and the American psychologist Edward Thorndike. Pavlov's studies specifically centred around how two independent stimuli could become associated with each other. For this, he introduced the concept of **classical conditioning**. Meanwhile, Thorndike (1898) aimed to determine how the consequences of specific choices can affect the way associations form. As such, he was one of the first to study the process of **operant conditioning**. Operant conditioning describes how a reward can strengthen spontaneously formed associations, while a punishment can weaken them. This way, Thorndike's work was an important precursor for the eventual discovery of **shaping**; that is, the process of constantly refining behaviour through the application of specific rewards and punishments.

Both the immision theory and the associationist theories of thought strongly imply that information flows in just one direction through the brain. According to these views, our eyes are passive receptors that transmit information to the brain, where it is analysed at progressively higher levels of abstraction, without any information flowing in the opposite direction. As such, our eyes are presumed to register signals from our environment, which, combined with inputs from other senses, form a train of associations that is eventually converted into an action. A similar view has dominated cognitive psychology for the better part of the 20th century. This view is problematic, however, for two important reasons. The first problem is that it implies that humans are intrinsically passive information processors, whose actions are solely triggered by external stimuli. Such stimulus-driven responses are reflecting a

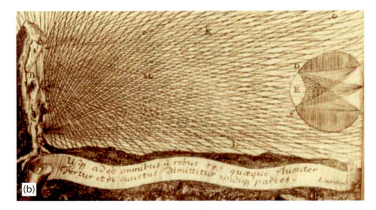

Figure 1.1 (a): Greek philosophers initially believed that our eyes emit a form of radiation that would highlight the objects in our environment that we perceive. (b): visual perception, as envisioned by Ibn al-Haytham (Alhazen) around the year AD 1011, that describes how light reflected by an object is projected into our eyes.

type of processing that is known as **bottom-up processing**. The second problem is that the sole reliance on bottom-up processing prevents us from explaining a large number of mental phenomena. Examples of these unexplainable phenomena include dreams, hallucinations, and mental imagery. All of these examples imply that we are capable of generating visual or auditory sensations that do not involve input from our senses.

Contemporary explanations for cognitive processes are, therefore, to a large extent, based on the idea that our brains are actively constructing models of our environment. The human brain is continually active, day and night. As such, it not only creates an internal model (or **representation**) of our environment, but it is also involved in simulating the outcomes of events that have yet to take place (Thakral, Benoit, & Schacter, 2017). According to the currently influential **predictive coding** framework (Friston, 2010), these models (see fig 1.2) are generating predictions about our environment. Based on

past experience, we know what to expect in our living rooms when we get home, and just before entering, the sensory parts of our brain are updated with these prior experiences in such a way that we hardly process our sensations at all.

The latter is an example of **top-down processing**. One crucial aspect of the predictive coding framework is that evidence for the internal models is collected by continuously comparing the predictions made by the model with sensory input from the environment, and by correcting the model on the basis of the resulting **prediction error**. Imagine, for example, our surprise when we discover that a burglar has ransacked our living room.

Thus, while our eyes are indeed light receptors, we do actually generate and maintain a mental representation of our environment because our brains are actively scanning it for evidence. We direct our eyes, for example, at locations where our brain expects to find relevant information. According to the predictive coding theory, the information that our eyes pick up is hardly processed at all, as long as it is in good agreement with our internal model. It is only when there is disagreement that the resulting prediction error indicates that the internal model needs to be adjusted.

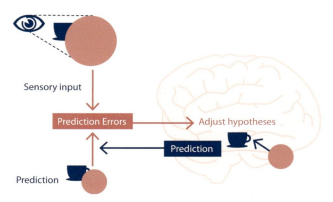

Figure 1.2 According to state-of-the-art theoretical frameworks, our brain generates internal models of our environment based on the input it receives from our senses. These internal models predict what sensory inputs should be expected. Strong discrepancies between the actual input and the model's predictions will be used to adjust the internal model.

Despite these recent developments, association is still considered to be an important concept in modern cognitive theories. For instance, cognitive psychologist and Nobel prize laureate Daniel Kahneman argues in his international bestseller, *Thinking, fast and slow*, that the formation of associations plays a crucial role in many cognitive processes. This is consistent with contemporary neuroscientific research data, which indicate that our conceptual knowledge is represented in interconnected networks. Accordingly, the activation of one concept implies that comparable concepts that are stored in our memories will also be activated via a string of associations.

One of the best examples illustrating the formation of associations can be found in the **priming effect** (Meyer & Schvaneveldt, 1971). Priming occurs when the processing of a stimulus can be influenced by a previously presented stimulus. Suppose that we are to decide whether NURSE is an existing word or not. When we have just been exposed to a related word, such as DOCTOR, our responses tend to be faster compared to when we had been exposed to an unrelated word, such as PIZZA.

Despite the robustness of these priming effects, it is still up for debate how strongly the underlying association processes can influence our behaviour in daily life. Some theorists argue that chains of associations have far-reaching influences in the sense that they affect our daily behaviours. It has been argued, for example, that thinking about older people makes us walk more slowly; that forcing our lips into a smiling expression makes us feel happier; that resisting the urge to eat a cookie causes us to loosen our grip on a handle (because such an action exhausts our will power); or that the presence of a box in our environment makes us more creative, because we literally are thinking 'out of the box'. Each of these findings has been reported at least once in the literature. Back in 2011, even Kahneman accepted most of these claims at face value. We will return to whether this was justified later on in this chapter, and again towards the end of the book, in Chapter 23.

According to Kahneman, associations are omnipresent, because they allow us to efficiently retrieve relevant information from our memories and to use this information to make predictions about future outcomes. As such, associations can be considered to be part of the aforementioned top-down predictive processing. Although these associative predictions typically yield feasible solutions to a given problem in daily life, these solutions are frequently inaccurate or **biased**.

According to Kahneman, there are two types of processes involved in human cognition. At the suggestion of Stanovich and West (2000), Kahneman labelled the first of these processes as **System 1**. System 1 involves rapid, unconscious, associative processing. This type of processing typically yields a quick and effortless solution to a problem. These solutions, however, are subject to biases and irrelevant aspects of the problem definition. Thus, in situations where a solution that is provided by System 1 will not suffice, it is possible to obtain more accurate solutions by recruiting additional mental processes. Examples of these situations include solving logical puzzles, or engaging in complex reasoning.

The additional processes that supplement System 1 are supposed to originate from **System 2**. In contrast to System 1, the solutions that are provided by System 2 are much less sensitive to biases, resulting in much-improved solutions. This improvement, however, comes at the cost of a strongly increased demand on our limited mental processing power. Consequently, when utilising System 2 processing, attention has to be focused on the task at hand. This distinction between automatic and controlled processing, as implied by Kahneman's System 1 and System 2 subdivision, is one essential aspect of human cognition that we will encounter specifically in Part 8, 'Higher cognition'.

1.2 WHY COGNITIVE PSYCHOLOGY?

Once, in the late 1980s, a poster reading, 'To err is human, but to foul things up completely requires a computer' was posted on one of the walls in my high school math class. One of the main reasons why I still remember this poster is that it beautifully illustrates two uniquely human traits. First, as a society, we have been inventive enough to develop advanced technologies. Despite its sophistication, however, our technology is still too coarse to operate without human intervention. As humans, we are able to flexibly assess the essence of a given problem, whereas computers approach the same problem according to strictly defined logical rules, frequently resulting in suboptimal, or even completely incorrect, solutions (Gigerenzer & Gray, 2017). Understanding the flexibility that is so unique to human thought is thus one of the major challenges of cognitive psychology.

Secondly, the poster illustrates that we make errors and that these errors can occasionally have disastrous consequences (specifically in a high-tech environment), and it is, therefore, crucially important that we develop protocols to mitigate the consequences of these errors to a bare minimum. Consider, for example, the aviation industry, which has had an immense impact on the development of our species in the past century. Even though aviation technology approaches the limits of our current technology, air travel is one of the safest forms of transportation around. This unprecedented level of safety is, among other things, related to the considerable amount of effort that has been invested in the development of safety protocols.[1] One aspect of these protocols is that they aim to prevent the limitations of our cognitive abilities from resulting in erroneous actions.

Because of these safety protocols, a single mistake or error rarely results in a disaster anymore. Nowadays, serious accidents typically occur due to an accumulation of errors. Errors that are each in their own right not fatal, but which may have fatal consequences when combined. For example, on August 14, 2005, an aircraft operated by the Greek company Helios Airways crashed en route from Larnaca

Figure 1.3 This particular Helios Airways Boeing 737 would crash a few months after this picture was taken, because all the passengers and crew members passed away due to oxygen starvation. This accident occurred due to the accumulation of a sequence of human errors, each of which in its own right would not have been fatal.

to Athens, after crew and passengers lost consciousness due to oxygen starvation (see fig 1.3).

This fatal crash could be attributed to the fact that during a routine ground inspection, just prior to the flight, the automatic cabin pressure regulator was switched off. During various phases of a flight, pilots need to complete a checklist to ensure that this type of error is noted and corrected. On this fatal day, however, the problem went unnoticed, resulting in the escape of cabin air during take-off and climb. Even this should not have been fatal, because the dropping cabin pressure automatically activates an alarm signal. This signal was, however, incorrectly interpreted by the pilots, resulting in the continual escape of air, the loss of consciousness of all on board, and the eventual crash near Athens after the plane ran out of fuel (Dekker & Woods, 2010).

This example illustrates that it is crucially important to discover why these types of error occur. Obviously, this is only possible by understanding how we humans function and by determining what our limitations are. Why did the crew miss these important warning signals? Was it because their occurrence is extremely rare? The switch in question is almost never placed in the 'off position' after all . . . Were the pilots confusing this particular warning with a different one? Were the crew members distracted during a crucial phase of the flight? To answer these questions, it is essential that we know under which conditions we can distinguish different types of signals from each other, and when they lead to confusion. It is equally important to know how much information we can process and what the consequences of mental overload can be.

The fatal airplane crash only illustrates one aspect of cognitive psychology. In addition to the importance of work safety, studying human cognition has yielded many

important insights. Next, I will present a few more examples to illustrate how cognitive psychology has contributed to a better understanding of how we function in our daily lives.

Consider, for example, why millions of individuals regularly participate in lotteries. After all, probability theory shows that the expected utility of a lottery is negative; that is, we are expected to lose more money than we are expected to gain. As we will discuss in later chapters, an important reason for this is that statistical probabilities are typically not represented objectively in our brains, resulting in the fact that we tend to overestimate them when they are small.

How is it possible that we sometimes fail to find the solution to a simple problem, while we have no trouble finding one for a complex problem? As we will cover in more detail in Chapter 19, the answer to this question is related to a phenomenon that is described by the German term **einstellung**: when we set up ourselves to solve complex problems, we tend to overlook the simple solutions to easy problems.

Why are we often distracted by trivial activities, when we would be much better off focusing on an important task at hand? Here we are dealing with the phenomena of **attention** and **cognitive control**. If the associative processes that we introduced earlier would run their course, we would automatically respond to the most salient information, which would be detrimental to completing important tasks that require the suppression of such automatic responses. Suppressing these impulses is possible, as we will see in Chapters 4 and 5, but this requires considerable effort.

Other examples involve phenomena that could historically only be 'understood' by reverting to 'spiritual' or 'paranormal' explanations (i.e., that could not be explained at all). Currently, we know that many of our cognitive processes are reconstructive; that is, our brains attempt to reconstruct a consistent representation of our environment (and our position in that environment) on the basis of sparsely available information. We are typically unaware of these reconstructive processes when they operate in a normal waking condition. Sometimes, though, for instance, when we experience a visual illusion, we may note that our cognitive processes generate a representation that conflicts with reality. In more extreme cases, these reconstructions can manifest themselves as dreams (Llewellyn, 2016) or hallucinations (Horga, Schatz, Abi-Dargham, & Peterson, 2014; Powers, Kelley, & Corlett, 2016a; Schmack, Rothkirch, Priller, & Sterzer, 2017). These types of conscious experiences were, until relatively recently, considered to be inaccessible to empirical studies; however, they have fascinated

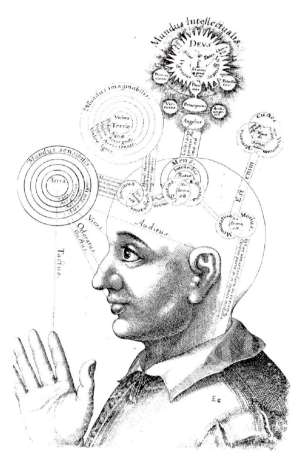

Figure 1.4 An illustration of the concept of 'consciousness', by the 17th-century illustrator Robert Fludd. Recent studies imply that consciousness is related to the integration of information, and that reconstructive processes are a major correlate of consciousness. Reconstruction of information stored in our memories can result in mental imagery. Uncontrolled or incorrectly controlled reconstructions can result in dreams while we are asleep or in hallucinations while we are awake.

humankind for centuries (see fig 1.4). Since the mid-20th century, cognitive psychology and its related fields have given us fascinating insights into human mental functioning and have yielded a wealth of practical and fundamental knowledge.

1.3 COGNITIVE PSYCHOLOGY: WHAT'S IN A NAME?

Since its inception, the field that is now known as cognitive psychology has been known under a variety of names. In Anglo-Saxon countries, the term **psychonomics** was used to identify the scientific field of research that studies phenomena such as perception, attention, memory, language processing, thought, reasoning, and problem-solving. This term emphasises the quantitative nature of the field: measuring, determining and explaining the laws underlying

human behaviour, as opposed to the traditionally more descriptive qualitative character of psychology. In some parts of the world, the field was initially known as **experimental psychology**, but this name was largely dropped in the 1950s, because other disciplines within psychology were also conducting experimental research. Since the mid-1990s, the names psychonomics and experimental psychology have been dropped to a great extent, in favour of cognitive psychology. Cognition refers to our ability to acquire knowledge and process information. Although the term has already been around since the 1950s, its popularity is strongly related to the rise to prominence of **cognitive neuroscience** in the 1990s.

1.4 COGNITIVE PSYCHOLOGY AS A SCIENTIFIC DISCIPLINE

What distinguishes cognitive psychology as a scientific discipline from other forms of psychology is a strong focus on the basic processes underlying thought and action, on the one hand, and a strong focus on experimental methods, on the other. Even though cognitive psychology can occasionally use other scientific methods as well, such as quasi-experimental designs or correlational methods, most of the studies conducted within the discipline have a very strong experimental focus.

Scientific research is typically based on a cycle involving several distinct stages. The cycle typically starts with a collection of incidental observations and the formulation of a possible explanation for these observations. This explanation is known as a theory. Based on this theory, we can then make predictions about conditions that we have not yet observed. In other words, we can formulate specific hypotheses. Now, we can design an experiment that aims to disprove our theory: when the results of our experiment are consistent with the theory, we have no reason to suspect that anything is wrong with it. When the results are inconsistent, however, we will either have to adjust our theory, or to reject it altogether. For reasons that will be discussed in greater depth in Chapter 19, it is impossible to 'proof' a theory: as long as we find no conflicting evidence, the theory remains plausible. This does not exclude the possibility, however, that there might be future results that will conflict. Although a theory becomes more plausible the more results we find that are consistent with it, it remains the case that (at least in principle) a single experiment yielding conflicting results would be sufficient to overthrow it.

In practice, however, a single experiment will almost never be able to provide direct evidence, either in favour of a specific theory or against it. It is only on the basis of a large number of studies, each using different approaches and methods, that we can form a consistent explanation of a specific process or phenomenon. This is an example of **converging operations**: different methods and approaches, each with their own strengths and weaknesses, converging to results that are consistent with each other, allow us to find a consistent interpretation of a given cognitive process. In contrast to what is commonly depicted in the popular press, a single scientific study is, therefore, typically not very informative. This is one of the reasons why the scientific literature is extremely extensive. A simple literature search, for example, using Google Scholar, yields more than seven million hits for the search term 'attention' alone.[2] This example illustrates that the literature that is discussed in this book is only the proverbial tip of the iceberg. The selection is not random, however, but based on the impact that the selected papers had on the field.

1.5 A BRIEF HISTORY OF COGNITIVE PSYCHOLOGY

1.5.1 THE FOUNDATION OF PSYCHOLOGICAL LABORATORIES

The year 1879 is generally considered to mark the start of psychology as a scientific discipline (see fig 1.5 and Box 1.1 for a timeline of major developments). In that year, Wilhelm Wundt founded the first official psychological laboratory at the University of Leipzig, in Germany. Wundt built upon a foundation that was established by earlier physiologists from Leipzig, namely Ernst Heinrich Weber and Gustav Theodor Fechner. Weber and Fechner made use

Figure 1.5 Prominent pioneers who have contributed towards the establishment of psychology as a scientific discipline. Top row (left to right): Wilhelm Wundt, Ernst Heinrich Weber, and Gustav Fechner. Bottom row (left to right): Jules Van Biervliet, Gerard Heymans, William James, and James McKeen Cattell.

of **psychophysical** methods to determine the physical laws underlying visual perception. Using such methods, Weber, for example, established that the smallest difference in size between two objects that we can still reliably perceive is linearly dependent upon the size of these objects themselves. This relation is now known as the Weber fraction.

Wundt specifically focused on questions related to the essence of a conscious experience. Partially related to Wundt's productivity, the end of the 19th century saw a booming German school of experimental psychologists. This school rapidly expanded to other countries, as a consequence of Wundt's many international doctoral students. In the United States, for example, a former student of Wundt, James McKeen Cattell, was the first to obtain a full professorship in psychology, even though many consider the philosopher William James (1842–1910) to be one of the founding fathers of American psychology. Likewise, Belgium's first psychological laboratory at Ghent University was inspired by a visit from its founder, the philosopher Jules Van Biervliet, to Wundt's lab in the academic year 1890–1891 (Nicolas & Ferrand, 1999). In 1892, this was followed by the foundation of the first psychological laboratory in the Netherlands, at the University of Groningen, by Gerard Heymans, who was, among others, inspired by Fechner.

Research in these labs was not limited to just studying mental processes, however. Cattell, for example, was interested in individual differences and in the development of psychological tests to measure these differences. Wundt also conducted cultural psychology studies, while Heymans was involved in the study of parapsychological phenomena. The core theme of the German school, which would subsequently become known as 'structuralism', consisted of determining the structure of a conscious experience. To do so, Wundt and his colleagues frequently used a method known as **introspection**. Introspection requires participants to describe a subjective experience in a structured way, and it was predominantly used by one of Wundt's former students, the British psychologist Edward Titchener. Even though introspection is still used in a much-limited form,[3] the method proved to be insufficient for obtaining the much sought-after essence of a conscious experience, despite the strict protocols that Titchener and his colleagues developed.

1.5.2 BEHAVIOURISM

Due to these insufficiencies, research involving mental processes was heavily criticised, specifically in the United States. This criticism culminated in a paper entitled 'Psychology as the behaviorist views it', by John B. Watson, in 1913. Watson argued that psychology should be, first and foremost, the study of human behaviour, and that this should be studied under strictly controlled conditions, comparable to the way **ethologists** study animal behaviour.

Box 1.1 An overview of important developments

400 BCE: the Greek philosopher Plato argues that the brain is the seat of the rational human soul.

1011: Alhazen's work on determining the basic properties of light fundamentally changes our understanding of the human eye.

1700: publication of John Locke's 'On the association of ideas'.

1868: the Dutch professor Franciscus Cornelis Donders publishes a method to measure the timing of mental processes.

1879: foundation of the first psychological laboratory by Wilhelm Wundt in Leipzig.

1926: discovery of the human electroencephalogram (EEG) by the German psychiatrist Hans Berger.

1935: the American psychologist John Ridley Stroop discovers that naming the colour in which words are printed may be slowed down when word meaning interferes with the to-be-named colour.

1940–1945: James Gibson's observations, while supervising the training of pilots during World War II, results in the formulation of his direct perception theory.

1953: the American neurosurgeon William Scoville carries out an experimental operation on the then 27-year-old Henry Molaison. From that moment on, Molaison is unable to form new memories.

1954: the American and Canadian neuroscientists Herbert Jasper and Wilder Penfield discover the existence of different rhythms in the EEG, relate these to different mental states, and develop a surgical procedure to counter epilepsy.

1954: the British psychologist Donald Broadbent presents his early selection theory of attention.

1956: the American psychologist George Miller publishes his influential paper 'The magical number seven on the capacity of our short-term memory'.

1968: the American psychologists Richard Atkinson and Richard Shiffrin present an influential model of short-term memory.

1969: publication of Saul Sternberg's additive factors method.

1973: the American Israeli psychologists Daniel Kahneman and Amos Tversky publish about biased statistical intuitions.

1974: the American psychologists Barbara and Charles Eriksen publish about the effects of interference during a letter discrimination task.

1974: the British psychologists Alan Baddeley and Graham Hitch publish the first version of their working memory model.

1980: Anne Treisman and Garry Gelade publish their feature integration theory about the role of attention during visual search.

1981: Roger Sperry shares the Nobel prize for physiology with David Hubel and Torsten Wiesel for their groundbreaking work in the field of neurophysiology.

1990: the discovery of an error detection mechanism in the brain, by the German Michael Falkenstein and the American Bill Gehring.

1990: start of the 'decade of the brain' in the United States of America.

1992: the American neuroscientists Joseph LeDoux describes how emotions can influence our behaviour.

1994: the American cognitive psychologist Michael Posner suggests the possible existence of two networks in the brain that are involved in controlling attention.

1995: the Australian philosopher David Chalmers identifies which aspects of consciousness can, and which aspects cannot, be studied empirically.

1999: Rajesh Rao and Dana Ballard publish a paper describing the predictive processes involved in the visual system.

2002: Daniel Kahneman receives the Nobel prize in economics for his cognitive psychological studies on judgement and decision-making.

2005: publication of Karl Friston's 'A theory of cortical responses', which introduces a generic theory of brain function based on prediction and error minimisation.

2011: beginning of the replication crisis in psychology, resulting in a methodological renaissance.

2015: start of a wide-spread application of the predictive coding framework in various subdomains of cognitive psychology.

2020: the worldwide Covid-19 pandemic forces many researchers to switch to online experiments.

Since it is impossible to speculate about internal mental states in animals, Watson argued, psychologists also should refrain from doing so. The only thing that we can control, according to Watson, is the **stimulus** that we present, and the only thing that we can measure is a participant's **response** to that stimulus. Watson considered internal cognitive processes to be a black box that we cannot observe. According to behaviourists, psychology should therefore limit itself to describing stimulus-response associations and to determining the laws describing these associations.

Despite the fact that behaviourism has been somewhat successful in describing learning processes, specifically those related to classical and operant conditioning, the behaviourist approach fell short in describing the full range of human behaviours in terms of stimulus-response associations. In cases where it turned out to be impossible to explain how a specific stimulus resulted in a specific response, it became necessary to define intermediate stages. In such cases, a stimulus was believed to not directly evoke an observable response. Instead, it was believed to trigger an intermediate internal response, which in turn was believed to generate an internal stimulus. This internal stimulus would then evoke the observable response. In essence, these intermediate responses and stimuli were concealed descriptions of mental processes. The allowance of this type of internal process not only allowed psychologists to covertly consider mental processes again, but it also marked the end of behaviourism as an important discipline in psychology.

1.5.3 THE COGNITIVE REVOLUTION

A turning point was reached in the mid-1950s, when a number of important developments took place. For example, Edward Tolman (1948) published influential studies on spatial navigation and introduced the concept of a **cognitive map**; George Miller (1956) published his influential article 'The magical number seven' on the capacity of short-term memory; Allen Newell and Herbert Simon were developing an influential computer model in the field of problem solving, named 'general problem solver' (see Newell, Shaw, & Simon, 1958); Bruner, Goodnow, and Austin (1956) published their first study on concept formation from a cognitive psychological perspective; and Noam Chomsky presented his theory on language. Together, these developments resulted in a drastic shift in focus that is frequently referred to as the cognitive revolution.

It should be noted, though, that the transition from structuralism, via behaviourism, to cognitive psychology was in reality a lot less abrupt than historians traditionally suggest. Many research questions that were posed before the 1950s were in essence already of a cognitive nature. For example, in 1935, the American psychologist John Ridley Stroop became interested in the automatic processing of words. Likewise, in 1945, the American biologist

Herbert G. Birch became interested in whether insight was involved in problem solving. These are only two examples of influential cognitive studies that were conducted up until the end of the Second World War. They illustrate, however, that the interest in cognitive phenomena never disappeared completely during the heydays of behaviourism, even though cognitive psychology came to fruition only later. For this reason, it might be more justified to consider the aforementioned developments to be part of a cognitive evolution, which accelerated rapidly in the 1950s, than to consider it to be a full-fledged revolution.

Regardless, it is certainly the case that the 1950s were characterised by a strong increase in interest in cognitive processes. Why specifically the 1950s? There are a number of possible reasons for this. Obviously, the influence of behaviourism was waning. Additionally, the Second World War had sparked the development of digital computers to a point where the first generally useable systems became commercially available. These computers began to serve as a metaphor for human information processing (see fig 1.6). They could process information in a flexible way because the instructions they were to carry out were stored in programmes (very rudimentary ones according to present-day standards though).

The development of digital computers also marked the introduction of a distinction between **hardware** and **software**. According to the most explicit version of the previously described **computer metaphor**, human information processing can be equated to software, while the brain can be equated to the hardware that is running the software. The metaphor is based on the idea that human information processing consists, in essence, of symbol manipulation: we process information that can be perceived, stored and manipulated in a symbolic form (see Box 1.3 for a formal definition of information processing). Symbol manipulation processes can, in principle, be executed independently of the underlying hardware,

Figure 1.6 The Electronic Numerical Integrator and Computer (ENIAC) was one of the first programmable digital computers. The availability of this type of computer contributed to a renewed interest in cognitive processes.

suggesting that cognitive processes would also be unrelated to the neural systems carrying them out.

Consequently, models of cognition that were developed in the latter half of the 20th century were strongly inspired by this computer metaphor. These models often resembled flow charts that depicted the order in which different processes occurred. An important point of debate during this period was whether cognitive processes were strictly serial or not. More concretely, this debate focused on whether consecutive processing stages in a cognitive process operated in discrete stages, where one process needed to be completely finished before the next one could be started, or whether they could operate more or less in parallel. Another important development in this period addressed to what degree cognitive processing operated automatically or in a controlled fashion. Processing is assumed to be automatic when an answer to a problem can be retrieved immediately, independently of the complexity of a stimulus or task. Controlled processing, in contrast, operates under the control of attentional processes. This type of processing is affected by task or stimulus complexity. Specifically in the 1970s, much research was devoted to addressing this question (Schneider & Shiffrin, 1977; Shiffrin & Schneider, 1977).

In the decades that followed, during the 1970s and 1980s, several, now classic, studies laid a foundation for our current knowledge of human cognition. To mention just a few: Philip Johnson-Laird (1994) developed a theory of mental representations; Daniel Kahneman and Amos Tversky determined how judgements and decisions can be affected by a host of cognitive biases (Kahneman & Tversky, 1972, 1982a, 1982b; Tversky & Kahneman, 1973); Alan Baddeley and Graham Hitch (1974) formulated a first draft of their influential working memory model, and Michael Posner's (1980) ideas about the neural basis of attention still form a major cornerstone of research in this area.

1.5.4 THE RISE OF THE COGNITIVE NEUROSCIENCES

The cognitive revolution from the mid-20th century initiated an extremely productive approach to studying human cognition, which is still very influential to this date. Many empirical findings from the latter part of the 20th century are still relevant, and many theoretical models are still leaving their mark on cognitive psychology. The pure experimental psychological tradition began to lose its influence in the 1990s, however, in favour of an approach that allowed combining experimental studies with the recording of brain activity. Around the same period, the influence of the computer metaphor started to wane. There are a number of reasons for this waning influence and the simultaneous rise of the cognitive neurosciences, as we will discuss in more detail next.

One major reason why the computer metaphor lost much of its initial appeal is related to the fact that many theorists began to notice an increasing discrepancy between tasks at which computers excel and tasks at which humans excel. While computers have traditionally been very efficient in tasks that we typically describe as 'higher cognition', such as arithmetic and formal logic, humans are typically far superior in recognising faces, analysing visual information, or finding a route through a complicated maze; skills that we typically describe as 'basic cognition'.

The more 'basic' a cognitive skill is, however, the harder it typically is to let a computer perform it efficiently.[4] To illustrate this, computers were already capable of solving complex numerical or logical problems during the mid-20th century. It was not until the mid-1990s, however, that a computer could beat a reigning world champion chess grandmaster, and it was not until around 2015 when the first autonomously operated cars, using a computer-based artificial visual system, were allowed to drive unsupervised on the road (and even then, only under strict conditions). One of the consequences of this realisation is that we can observe an inverse trend. For instance, many **machine learning algorithms** are currently based on principles that are inspired by neurobiology (Schmidhuber, 2015).

In addition to the realisation that the 'basic' cognitive functions are extremely complex, it also became increasingly clear that these functions cannot be separated from their important task of controlling our bodies. Most, if not all, of our cognitive functions have likely developed because they have given us an evolutionary advantage; they allow us to find food and water, to move around, to fight with a potential adversary, or to flee from them. From this realisation, we can derive the second reason why the computer metaphor has lost much of its initial influence: cognitive functions are inherently intertwined with the control of bodily functions, suggesting that the 'software' of the mind cannot be considered independently from its 'hardware'. This realisation has led to an influential school of thought, known as **embodied cognition**, which describes how cognitive processes are (at least in part) driven by the interpretation of signals that are generated by our bodies (Clark, 1999).

The third reason why the computer metaphor lost its influence is related to the rise of the cognitive neurosciences, which allowed us to directly study the relation between brain and cognition. The cognitive neurosciences came to full fruition in the 1990s, when newly developed techniques made it possible to measure activity in the living brain and to relate this activity to specific psychological processes. It should be said, however: this development did, in fact, already started in the 1950s and can even be traced back to the behavioural neurology literature from the 19th century. It is after all too much of a simplification

Figure 1.7 Example of a digital 'average response computer' from the late 1950s. These specialised devices allowed for the analysis of EEG signals. (photo: Barlow, 1997)

to state that before the 1990s cognitive brain research did not exist. Techniques for relating brain activity to cognitive processes were already available since the start of the cognitive revolution and resulted in the development of a research field that is known as **psychophysiology.**

Important lines of research within the field of psychophysiology focused, for example, on the influence of cognitive processes on heart rate (Van der Veen, Van der Molen, & Jennings, 2001), skin conductance (Barry, 1975), and pupil diameter (Kahneman, Onuska, & Wolman, 1968). Perhaps the most influential development in psychophysiology, however, consisted of the introduction of **electroencephalography** (EEG; see fig 1.7) to cognitive research. EEG recordings have been extremely influential in the development of the cognitive neurosciences. In particular, they contributed substantially to our knowledge of attention (Hillyard & Galambos, 1967; Hillyard, Hink, Schwent, & Picton, 1973; Näätänen, 1970; Walter, Cooper, Aldridge, McCallum, & Winter, 1964) during the 1960s and 1970s.

Partially influenced by these electrophysiological studies, the 1980s were marked by a renewed interest in the relation between brain and cognition. Consequently, a number of American scientific societies pleaded for an increase in funding for cognitive neuroscientific research. These efforts came to fruition by the end of the 1980s, when the American congress agreed to increase their budget for the neurosciences. This agreement was officially ratified on July 18, 1990, by President George Herbert Bush, when he declared the 1990s to be the Decade of the Brain.

1.5.5 A MULTIDISCIPLINARY APPROACH

By the first decade of the 21st century, the previously described developments facilitated a change in the approach to studying human behaviour. By exploiting the new opportunities that the neurosciences had to offer, the last decade

of the 20th century and part of the first decade of the 21st century were marked by a strong focus on the localisation of brain function, using a variety of brain scanning techniques. Even though this approach is still being used to date, more recent approaches in neuroscience have shifted from the pure localisation of brain functions to determining how specific brain areas are involved in cognitive processes and, more specifically, how multiple brain areas collaborate in implementing these processes. This new approach is also characterised by a strong multidisciplinary focus, in which cognitive psychologists, cognitive neuroscientists, computer scientists, linguists, physicists, and philosophers collaborate in multidisciplinary teams.

1.5.6 A NEW ROLE FOR EMOTION AND CONSCIOUSNESS

A second development, which more or less coincided with the rise of the cognitive neurosciences, consisted of a renewed interest in the role of emotion and consciousness in human cognition. Influenced by behaviourism and the computer metaphor, cognitive psychologists have traditionally been reluctant to study these aspects of human cognition. Around the turn of the century, interest in the role of cognition in emotion regulation processes began to increase, in part driven by the development of cognitive models for emotion regulation (Davidson, 2000; Gross, 1998) and also in part driven by the increased realisation that cognitive processes and the regulation of bodily functions are intrinsically intertwined (Clark, 1999).

One of the reasons for a renewed interest in consciousness was the realisation that the techniques that allowed us to relate brain activity to cognitive processes could also be used to study the relation between brain activity and conscious awareness. These developments were foreshadowed by a number of influential philosophical works, of which *Consciousness explained*, by the American philosopher and cognitive scientist Daniel Dennett (1991), is probably one of the most well-known. A second important development heralding a renewed interest in consciousness, consisted of the paper 'Facing up to the problem of consciousness' in which the Australian philosopher David Chalmers (1995) describes which aspects of consciousness can be studied empirically, and which ones cannot (see Chapter 4 for more details on this).

1.5.7 A NEW APPRECIATION FOR ACTION AND ACTION CONTROL

For almost more than a century after psychology was founded as a scientific discipline, most cognitive research focused on topics such as perception, attention, memory, language, and higher cognition, while – ironically – the most basic form of psychology hardly received any attention at all from psychologists. Action and action control form the basis of our behaviour, yet these topics were mostly ignored by psychologists until the late 20th century. Apart from a limited number of sports psychologists, this field of research was, until that time, almost exclusively the domain of the movement sciences. Since the beginning of the 21st century, however, our understanding of action and action control has increased dramatically, sparking a renewed interest in this domain for psychologists.

1.5.8 A REPLICATION CRISIS IN PSYCHOLOGY

In September 2011, the first symptoms of a crisis in the field of psychology as a scientific discipline began to emerge. The Dutch social psychologist Diederik Stapel was forced to resign from his academic position after revelations that he had fabricated the data for at least 55 scientific papers. Even though the 'Stapel affair', as it would be known, is one of the most extreme – and exceptional – cases of academic fraud,[5] it did indirectly contribute to a growing realisation that the established methods of scientific conduct were susceptible to human bias and that these biases could seriously distort the conclusions that were reached in scientific papers. The main problem was that freedom to choose between different analysis methods can result in results that appear to be more consistent with the researchers' hypothesis than they really are. Let us see how that can be possible.

1.5.8.1 Scientific Research: An Ideal Scenario

Ideally, science aims to objectively describe the general principles underlying a specific phenomenon. As described earlier, this is typically accomplished by iterating through a loop consisting of a number of discrete steps. This process starts by formulating a hypothesis that is based on a number of observations. The next steps consist of designing an experiment to verify whether the hypothesis holds or not. The results of the experiment can subsequently form the basis of additional hypotheses, and we can design new experiments to test these. A problem with this approach, however, is that, for a number of reasons that we will discuss next, it did not work properly until very recently.

1.5.8.2 Scientific Research: Problems

One of the reasons why the aforementioned scenario is problematic is that the results need to be published in a scientific journal before they will be officially recognised, and these journals scrutinise each contribution before publishing them. Obviously, studies containing gross errors will be rejected. Journals may also reject studies for other reasons, however.

One major reason for rejecting studies is related to statistical power, or – in other words – our level of confidence that

the published results are really meaningful. Suppose we want to determine whether peoples' responses are faster in the morning than in the evening. To do so, we conduct a simple study where, at two different moments during the day, we require our participants to respond as fast as possible to a letter that appears on a computer screen (see Box 1.2 for an explanation of the rationale behind this approach). We find a mean reaction time of 450 ms for the morning condition, and 470 ms for the evening condition. Intuitively, we might be tempted to conclude that we are indeed faster in the morning than in the evening, but how certain are we of that conclusion? Could it be that a random number of excessively slow responses in the evening condition are distorting our measurements? To determine this, we need to make use of statistical tests to ascertain that there really is a difference. To do so, we take the following approach: due to the limitations of our statistical analysis techniques, we have to start by assuming that there is no difference between our conditions. That is, we assume that we are equally fast in the morning and in the evening and that any observed difference in our data is due to random noise. This is our **null hypothesis**, and we try to determine how likely this null hypothesis is, given what we have just observed. Just a very few excessively slow responses in the evening condition do not give us any reason to reject the null hypothesis, while evening responses that are consistently slower than morning responses will.

When our statistical techniques indicate that we may reject the null hypothesis, we may conclude that there really is a difference between the morning and evening conditions, and we have a statistically **significant** result. Based on a somewhat arbitrary rule, a critical value of 0.05 is typically used as a cut-off. In other words, when the probability that our observed result is coincidental is less than 0.05, we consider it to be significant.

In contrast, when the probability of a coincidental finding is higher than 0.05, we may not reject the null hypothesis, and, now we have found a **null result**. In this case we have a problem because we still do not know anything: we did not find evidence that is strong enough to conclude that there is a difference between our morning and evening conditions. The absence of evidence, however, does not imply that we have evidence for the absence. (Think about that!) It might still be the case that there really is a difference between our conditions, but that our techniques were not sensitive enough to detect it. This problem is one reason why many studies reporting null results are rejected by scientific journals.

But, even when we do have a significant effect, we still might have a problem. There might, after all, still be a small chance that even this result is actually coincidental. For this reason, it is crucially important that studies are replicated, preferably by an independent team of

Box 1.2 Mental chronometry: A study of reaction times

The realisation that cognitive processes are not instantaneous, but take time instead, formed the basis of one of the most important breakthroughs in the study of human cognition. It followed from Hermann von Helmholtz' pioneering work on determining the speed of neural impulses. The first successful attempt at measuring the speed of human responses was carried out by the Dutch physiologist Franciscus Cornelis Donders (see Draaisma, 2002). Donders (1868) applied a method that is very simple in its essence: in collaboration with his student, Johan Jacob de Jaager, he attached electrodes to the left and right foot of a participant, allowing him to apply low intensity electric shocks. These shocks would also start a chronometer. The participant was then instructed to move his hand towards the direction of the shock, causing the interruption of an electric circuit that would stop the chronometer.

The participant was instructed upfront as to which foot the shock would be applied. Therefore, the reaction time that was recorded reflected the participant's perception of the shock and his response to it. In a second condition, the shock was randomly applied to either the left or the right foot, requiring the participant now to also decide to which side his hand needed to be moved, before actually moving it. Donders and De Jaager noted that the reaction time was now larger, and they attributed this increase to the additional step that needed to be taken: deciding whether to move the hand left or right. The approach introduced by Donders and De Jaager is now known as the **subtraction method**: the timing of one psychological process (in this example reflected as choosing between left or right) is determined by recording the reaction times when the process of interest is invoked (i.e., making the actual decision and moving the hand) and by recording them in a nearly identical experiment where it is not invoked (i.e., just moving the hand). The duration is then determined by subtracting the mean reaction times in the second condition from the mean reaction times in the first.

Even though the subtraction method can be used to determine the timing of various psychological processes, it has an important limitation. More specifically, the method always requires two different tasks, and it is nearly impossible to design pure tasks, that is, tasks that are completely identical except for the demand on the one process that we are interested in. To circumvent this problem, the subtraction method was largely superseded by an improved version of it in the 1950s and 1960s. This improved method is known as the **additive factors method** (Sternberg, 1969). One of the major changes is that this newer method consists of only one task that activates all cognitive processes of interest. The timing of one specific cognitive process is now estimated by manipulating the complexity of the corresponding component of the task.

We can, for example, present a set of four randomly chosen letters, and require participants to memorise those letters. After a few seconds, we present another letter (the so-called **test stimulus**) and participants are required to indicate whether or not this letter was part of the initial set, by giving a 'yes' or 'no' response as quickly as possible. Now, we can determine the effects of memory load by instructing participants to memorise either only a subset of these letters (for example only one or two) or the full array. The more stimuli the participants have to remember, the longer it takes for them to respond to the test stimulus. Likewise, we can estimate the effects of duration on memory performance by presenting the test stimulus after either two or four seconds. Finally, we can estimate the effects of visual perception on memory performance by partially masking the test stimulus with a noise pattern. Because it is possible to manipulate each of these factors independently, this method also allows us to study whether the different processes influence each other. It may be expected that noisier stimuli take more time to process, but is this dependent on memory load? If this is the case, we might expect that the effect of embedding a stimulus in noise will be greater under high memory load than under low memory load.

To obtain reliable estimates of responses, we need to consider the fact that our measurements can be distorted by a host of irrelevant factors. For instance, it is possible that participants may blink just when a stimulus is presented, or that they are momentarily distracted by an irrelevant thought, or by an unexpected movement of the experimenter. To mitigate these disturbing factors as much as possible, we aim to increase the reliability of our measurements by repeating them several times, and by averaging our measurements for each condition. Each individual measurement in our experiment is known as a **trial**.

One major assumption of this approach is that the average reaction time across a number of trials is an estimate of the timing of the process that we are interested in, while the variation in the individual responses is just noise. Even though this assumption is generally valid, we should consider whether this is always the case. Suppose that we are required to make an important decision. In this case, the time it takes to make this decision is strongly determined by how fast we gather evidence for the different options. Therefore, the speed of gathering information will be reflected in the variation of our reaction times. One method that takes advantage of the distribution of reaction times is the so-called drift diffusion model (Ratcliff & McKoon, 2008). In this model, the variance of reaction times is used as an estimate of the speed of gathering information for specific choices.

researchers. Until recently, psychological research has been faced with a blatant lack of **replication**. One reason for this lack of replication is that scientific research has been increasingly influenced by commercial motives in the past decades. Many scientific journals are actively trying to maximise their impact. As an inadvertent side effect, they may only publish original research that yields relatively remarkable findings. In addition, the career prospects of many young scientists are increasingly driven by their ability to publish original and innovative results.

Due to this selective publication and hiring policy, there is an elevated risk that the scientific literature is contaminated by 'remarkable' findings that are actually completely coincidental. To illustrate this, imagine that we found no evidence whatsoever that we are faster in the morning than in the afternoon. But did we use the right experiment? For this reason, we decide to use a complete battery of cognitive tasks. Out of the 20 experiments that we run, 19 yield a null result, but, in one case, we find a statistically significant effect. Now, we might be tempted to believe that this experiment is the correct one, and we decide to publish it. Bear in mind, however, that our previously established criterion for significance is set to 0.05, implying that there is actually a likelihood of 1/20 or less that our results are still coincidental. Therefore, we should expect approximately 1 out of 20 experiments to yield a significant result by chance. In statistics, this is known as the **multiple comparison problem**. For this reason, publishing only the results from the one experiment that yields a significant result is a thoroughly bad idea. To give readers of the published study a fair idea, the 19 null results from the other studies should also have been included in the paper. And, of course, the study should have been replicated.

Due to the aforementioned culture of selective publication, this inclusion of null findings and replication typically does not happen, resulting in many null results being stuck away in a **file drawer**. This lack of replication and transparency is not only problematic because it obscures the interpretation of the literature, but also because it affects the career perspectives of individual researchers. The pressure to find remarkable results may have the unintended side effect of researchers using **questionable research practices** that push the results of their statistical test just below the 0.05 threshold.[6]

Kahneman (2011), in *Thinking, fast and slow*, described a number of rather bizarre priming effects that had just appeared in the literature, but subsequently failed to be replicated. Initially, Kahneman accepted these results without much criticism because they were consistent with his views on cognition. As such, Kahneman himself might have become the victim of the very same **confirmation biases** that he so eloquently described in his book. Shortly after publication of *Thinking, fast and slow*, however, a

number of studies were published that failed to replicate the aforementioned priming effects. As a consequence, it was Kahneman who, becoming aware of a problem in psychology, sent out a mass email to hundreds of colleagues, urging them to initiate a massive replication attempt. Kahneman wrote in his email:

> For all these reasons, right or wrong, your field is now the poster child for doubts about the integrity of psychological research. Your problem is not with the few people who have actively challenged the validity of some priming results. It is with the much larger population of colleagues who in the past accepted your surprising results as facts when they were published. These people have now attached a question mark to the field, and it is your responsibility to remove it.

Based on these initial replication attempts, Kahneman's email, and an intense discussion that followed, the importance of replication has again been recognised in the past decade. We, cognitive scientist, are humans, and as such we are also sensitive to every bias imaginable; yet, we are also very creative in developing procedures that should prevent us from becoming the victims of our own biases. Inspired by the aforementioned developments, a great number of initiatives have recently been started with the aim of safeguarding the quality of the scientific process. One of the most important – and difficult – tasks that lays ahead in this respect will consist of separating the robust findings from the coincidental ones.

The previous section may have given a somewhat depressing view of the state of the art in psychology. This impression needs nuance, however. Even though there certainly are problems, one might have gotten the impression that psychological research is conducted by sloppy scientists who need to be reprimanded for their mistakes. Yet, this is not the case, for a number of reasons: firstly, as already mentioned, many initiatives have been launched that aim to prevent the problems described earlier from ever occurring again (see also the closing remarks in Chapter 24). Secondly, results that turn out to be incorrect will eventually lose their impact. And, the fact that conclusions turn out to be incorrect retrospectively should never result in damage to the reputations of the scientists involved in the original publication, as long as the original research was conducted in good faith. Scientific research should always be conducted in an open environment where ideas and results can be shared freely. This freedom should also encompass the right to investigate ideas that retrospectively turn out to be incorrect. But, likewise, science should also be marked by the freedom to criticise these ideas.

Finally, at the start of the new decennium, the field of psychology was hit by the sudden outbreak of a major pandemic. Just like the rest of society struggled to come to terms with a changed reality, cognitive scientists needed to adapt their methods, for example, by accelerating the switch from laboratory studies to online experiments that participants could engage in from the safety of their homes. The pandemic, however, also brought new opportunities for research. How can human beings be motivated to voluntarily participate in worldwide vaccination programmes (Chevallier, Hacquin, & Mercier, 2021), and why do others perceive Covid-related information as fake news (Pennycook & Rand, 2021)? Addressing questions like these will probably remain a mainstay in cognitive psychology programmes in years to come.

1.6 THE FOUNDATIONS OF COGNITIVE PSYCHOLOGY

At present, the cognitive sciences are based on a multidisciplinary approach to which many important disciplines contribute. In the remainder of this book, I will specifically focus on the contributions from experimental behavioural research, computational modelling, cognitive neuropsychology, and the cognitive neurosciences. Next, I will briefly introduce these disciplines.

1.6.1 EXPERIMENTAL BEHAVIOURAL RESEARCH

The first important foundation of cognitive psychology consists of experimental behavioural research. For many years, cognitive research consisted almost exclusively of behavioural experiments that were conducted in strictly controlled conditions, using healthy volunteers as participants. This tradition has yielded many ingenious experiments that have resulted in a wealth of knowledge about many of the basic processes underlying cognition, such as attention; perception; memory; and higher cognitive processes such as thinking, reasoning, and decision-making. Behavioural studies have either exploited the fact that mental processes take time (see Box 1.2) or the fact that errors in the processing of information (see Box 1.3) results in a very systematic variation in the errors that we make in processing these stimuli (see Box 1.4).

One major challenge in experimental behavioural research consists of developing 'pure' tasks. Most of our mental activities utilise a mix of different processes, making it difficult to interpret the results of an experiment. Suppose, for example, that we want to determine how well we are able to suppress a response that we have already started preparing. To answer this question, we can design an experiment that requires us to respond as quickly as possible to a stimulus. To do so we can, for example, present an image of a little green figure, and our task is to

respond as quickly as possible with our left hand when this figure is pointing leftward, and with our right hand when it is pointing rightward.

Sometimes though, a little red figure rapidly replaces the green one. This indicates that we are not allowed to respond, so we have to abort the response that we were already preparing. When the red figure appears immediately after the green one, this is typically not a problem. When it is presented very late, however, we will notice that it is almost impossible to withhold from responding. Thus, by systematically varying the time between the appearance of the two figures, we can determine at which point we are just capable of withholding our response.

This experiment, which is known as the stop-signal task, forms the basis of many studies in the field of response inhibition (Verbruggen & Logan, 2008). However, to correctly interpret the results of these types of experiments, we need to be aware of the fact that several additional factors can affect them. For instance, will the presentation of a second figure influence the processing of the first one? Will we hold back on preparing a response when we are aware that we might occasionally be required not to respond? To exclude these possibilities, we need to run a number of **control experiments**. For instance, we could opt to present a tone as the stop signal, instead of a little red figure. We could also reward participants for fast responses, to mitigate the problem of slower response preparation, allowing us to study the effects of motivation on the stopping process.

One major strength of experimental behavioural research is its versatility. Many of the most influential theories in cognitive psychology have been developed on the basis of this type of research. The field of cognitive neuropsychology (see Section 1.6.3) could only be established, for example, after theories that originated from behavioural research had indicated which neuropsychological conditions were of theoretical importance. Likewise, cognitive theories form the basis for most developments in the cognitive neurosciences.

Despite the aforementioned contributions, we should also identify some limitations. For instance, human behaviour can differ considerable between daily life and laboratory settings. Data that are obtained in a controlled experiment may therefore not readily generalise to an everyday setting. If this is the case, the experiment has a limited ecological validity.

A second limitation is that we are typically only capable of measuring the time it takes to respond, and to determine whether this response is correct or not. For this reason, the resulting reaction time and accuracy measurements provide only indirect information about the underlying cognitive processes. Another limitation is that theories are often only described in relatively generic terms, thus creating the risk of making them too vague to allow the generation of useful predictions for follow-up studies.

Box 1.3 Information, compression, prediction, and complexity

One major characteristic of cognitive psychology is that it considers human beings to be information processors. In this respect, it is remarkable that few introductory textbooks in this field formally define what **information** actually is. Although we can, in most cases, get away with an intuitive understanding of what information is, it is essential to provide a more formal definition for an understanding of the finer nuances of some recent developments.

One of the most frequently used formal definitions of information was formulated by the American mathematician Claude Shannon (1948). Shannon was employed by the Bell Telephone Company and was involved in optimising the limited capacity of the telephone networks. Put differently, his work involved determining how a signal could be reliably transmitted across a noisy communication channel. Shannon's work has had a far-reaching impact, ranging from enabling the Voyager space probes to reliably transmit information back from the far reaches of our solar system to the development of the compact disc, digital video streaming, cell phone technology, and – last but not least – the internet. Currently, Shannon's work is increasingly relevant for cognitive psychology, so a brief introduction is in order.

Shannon describes information from the context of a collection of possible messages that a sender can transmit across a noisy communication line to a receiver, who can decode these messages. Shannon thus always poses the presence of a sender, a transmission line, and a receiver. In this context, information is defined as the amount of uncertainty that is removed by a single transmission. Therefore, information is related to the number of messages that the sender and receiver can exchange and the probability that is associated with each message. This may still sound rather abstract but can be illustrated using a simple example.

Suppose that we have an app that receives the weather forecast for the coming day. In Western Europe, where it might be equally likely to rain, freeze, be overcast, or sunny, this app is most likely much more informative than in the Sahara Desert, where, apart from the occasional sandstorm, it is sunny almost every day. Now, suppose that the app receives a transmission once a day that corresponds to the expected weather. For Western Europe, there is much uncertainty before the code is received, because each type of weather is equally likely. Upon receiving the transmission, all uncertainty is taken away (assuming, for the sake of argument, that the app is perfectly reliable). In the

Sahara, there is much less initial uncertainty, however, because it is extremely likely that the transmission will decode as 'sunny'. Occasionally, however, it may decode as 'rainy', and, in this case, the message will be highly informative (and surprising), because this message is associated with a very low probability in the Sahara. Because the message itself is transmitted only very infrequently in the Sahara, a typical communication here will be – on average – much less informative than one in Western Europe.

Shannon (1948) showed that the uncertainty that is removed by each communication is dependent on the relative probability of it being sent: the lower this probability, the greater its surprisal. From this perspective, information becomes a random variable that has an expected value equal to the information entropy. Entropy generally refers to the level of uncertainty in a system, and the definition of information entropy, as introduced by Shannon, is equivalent to the classic statistical definition of entropy that the physicist Ludwig Boltzmann developed in thermodynamics. Shannon found that the average amount of information transmitted per communication can be expressed as the following equation, which is also known as the Shannon information function, or Shannon entropy:

$$H = -\sum_{i=1}^{n} p_i log_2 (p_i)$$

Here, H represents the average amount of uncertainty that is removed by each communication (expressed in the unit **bit**); p_i the probability that the communication consists of message i; $log_2(p_i)$ the binary logarithm of this probability; and n the size of the set of possible messages. Suppose that we have five possible weather scenarios (sunny, cloudy, rainy, frosty, and stormy) and that the probability of each message is 0.2. In this case, we find that H = 2.32 bit. Now, suppose that for the Sahara the probability for 'sunny' is 0.9, and the probability for each of the other messages is 0.025, in which case we would find that H = 1.04 bit.

The beauty of the Shannon information function is that we can also apply it to other forms of information processing that are not directly associated with physical transmission systems, such as telephone lines. When we are about to toss a coin, for example, ending up with 'heads' or 'tails' is equiprobable. The uncertainty that is taken away after the toss equals to H = 1 bit. Likewise, the information that is obtained after throwing a clean dice equals to H = 2.58 bit.

(Continued)

Box 1.3 (Continued)

This formal definition of information is also useful in cognitive psychology. Recent work in consciousness, for example, relates conscious experience to the selection of one mental representation from the unimaginably high number of representations that our brain contains. According to Tononi (2004), the actual selection of one of those representations is thus marked by an excessive reduction of uncertainty, making a conscious experience extremely informative (see Chapter 4 for an in-depth discussion). Similar principles can be found in the predictive coding framework, in the sense that uncertainties in our internal mental representations can be reduced by processing sensory information (see Chapter 2). The mechanisms involved in this also conform to Shannon's principles.

Returning to the example of our weather app, however, we are still faced with a system that needs to receive a code in order to successfully decode the weather forecast. This gives the impression that we still need to transmit the same amount of information, regardless of whether we are in Western Europe or in the Sahara. The developers could decide to update the app, however, such that it only needs to change its forecast when it receives a code. When it does not, it just repeats the prediction of the previous day. This way, we only need to send a code when the actual weather changes, and, specifically for the Sahara, we find that we need to send codes at a much-reduced rate, allowing us to utilise the freed bandwidth on our transmission line for other purposes. Now, we have introduced a limited form of **prediction**/predictive coding (unless informed otherwise, we predict that weather remains the same) and **data compression** (only transmit deviations from this prediction) in our app.

Suppose, however, that the weather changes each day, in a highly predictive pattern. For our current app, this is not an improvement, because we are back to square one in the sense that we still need to send a code once a day. For this reason, version 3.0 of the app uses an algorithm to forecast the weather on the basis of the pattern of the last few days. With this version, we are approaching the most ideal situation, because we now only need to send a code when the actual weather deviates from the predicted pattern, reducing the number of codes that we need to transmit to a bare minimum. Data compression is now maximal. This type of data compression is frequently utilised in many digital communication systems. For example, when saving a digital photograph, or transmitting it across the internet, it is useful to predict the value of each pixel, on the basis of the adjacent pixels (because they typically have similar values), and only transmitting the deviations from the prediction, as this substantially reduces the amount of information that needs to be transmitted.

When we have highly regular changes (such as the hypothetical weather pattern just described), complexity of the information is considered to be much lower than when the changes are highly irregular. But what exactly determines the **complexity** of information? This deceptively simple question was not addressed until the 1970s, however, when three mathematicians, the American-Argentinian Gregory Chaitin, the Russian Andrey Kolmogorov, and the American Ray Solomonoff, independently proposed a similar solution. The essence of their definition is that complexity is related to compressibility. In this case, complexity is formally defined as the shortest computer programme one can write that is capable of reproducing the original sequence of symbols.

What do we mean by this? Suppose we have a regular alternation between sunny and rainy weather, which we can denote as: r, s, r, s, r, s, r, s, r, s, r, s, r, s, r, s, r, s, r, s, r, s, r, s. We can simply rewrite this as the much shorter sequence: *13 × (r, s)*. Compare this to the following completely random sequence: s, r, s, s, s, s, s, s, r, s, s, r, s, r, r, r, r, r, s, r, r, r, r, s, s, r. This sequence cannot easily be rewritten into a shorter notation, implying that it has a much higher complexity than the first sequence. In cognitive psychology, the complexity of information is currently a major feature of theories describing how we form representations of categories and how we deal with rules and exceptions in categorisation (see Chapter 20).

Finally, the results from a specific experiment, or experimental paradigms, are often very specific, implying that they do not readily generalise to other experiments or paradigms. This is an example of **paradigm specificity**. One intrinsic danger of paradigm specificity is that the experimental paradigm itself is no longer used as a tool to study a cognitive process, but that it becomes the focus of research itself. In other words, in such a situation, new studies are more strongly motivated by a desire to study the limitations of the paradigm than to understand the underlying cognitive processes.

1.6.2 COMPUTATIONAL MODELLING

The second important foundation of cognitive psychology consists of computational modelling. **Computational models** are computer programmes that emulate intelligent

Box 1.4 Signal detection theory

Signal detection theory is a method that allows us to detect the difference between useful, informative patterns and meaningless patterns of noise. In the case of living organisms, we refer to these patterns as stimuli, and in the case of machines, as a signal. The origin of signal detection theory can be traced back to the development of radar during the Second World War (Marcum, 1960), as a means of detecting meaningful information in noisy radar images. In psychology, signal detection theory is frequently used to determine how we can perceive stimuli at, or near, our perceptual thresholds. According to the theory, observers play an active role in this process. In practice, the application of signal detection theory boils down to presenting a sequence of trials in which the stimulus of interest is either present or absent. The participant's task is to indicate whether or not this is the case. Based on the answers given and whether or not the stimulus was actually present, we can subdivide the trials into four different categories: (1) hits (stimulus is present and detected), (2) misses (stimulus is present but not detected), (3) false alarms (stimulus is absent and incorrectly reported as present), and (4) correct rejections (stimulus is absent and correctly reported as absent).

Obviously, we could try to calculate the participant's detection ability on the basis of a number of accuracy measures, such as the **hit rate**. This is done by dividing the number of hits by the total number of trials where the stimulus is actually present. In a similar vein, we can calculate the proportion of false alarms, by dividing the number of false alarms by the total number of trials on which the stimulus was absent. Even though these measures might be interesting in their own right, they are of limited value when we have to compare results across conditions. An experimental manipulation may result in an increase in the hit rate, but it is often impossible to determine what causes this: is it because participants are better at detecting the stimulus, or is it because they shift their response criterion? A change in response criterion can be caused, for example, because participants expect the stimulus to occur more frequently in one condition than in another,

causing them to respond 'present' more frequently in one condition than in another. To paraphrase, a change in response criterion might reflect that a participant is more 'trigger happy'.

In a study that we conducted at the University of Twente some years ago, we expected that participants would be more sensitive to detect a change in direction of a moving stimulus when this change was accompanied by an auditory signal (Staufenbiel, van der Lubbe, & Talsma, 2011). We presented an array of moving dots, and on 50% of all the trials, one of these suddenly changed direction. Fifty per cent of these direction changes were accompanied by a short tone. In addition, on 50% of all the trials where no direction change took place, a short tone presented at a random moment.

Based on previous literature, we expected that the presentation of the tone would have a positive effect on our ability to detect direction changes, but we also considered the possibility that the tones would make participants more trigger happy. A shift in response criterion would, in this case, result in an increase in the false alarm rate. But what should we expect in case of an increase in sensitivity? Would the false alarm rate go down, would it remain the same, or would we still expect a slight increase? On the basis of separate analyses of these accuracy measures, this is nearly impossible to determine.

Signal detection theory provides a solution for this, by introducing new quantities that combine information across trial types (hits, misses, false alarms, and correct rejections). One of these quantities, known as d′ (pronounced: dee prime), represents sensitivity, while another quantity, β (pronounced: bèta), represents the response criterion. By comparing these quantities across conditions, it can now easily be determined whether a change in accuracy is due to a change in sensitivity or due to a shift in response criterion. In our study, we found that sounds indeed affected sensitivity positively, while it had no significant effect on the response criterion.

---

behaviour. In this respect, they are comparable to artificial intelligence. An important distinction must be made here, however, because an artificially intelligent computer programme typically operates on the basis of principles that bear little or no resemblance to human cognitive processes. By contrast, computational models aim to solve problems in ways that are comparable to human cognition. A computational model can define the exact specifications of a theory,

and predict behaviour in novel circumstances. Typically, these models are either implemented as **production rule systems** or as **neural networks**.

1.6.2.1 Production Rule Systems

Computational models were originally most frequently implemented as production rule systems. Such models consist of long sequences of IF… THEN … rules, the so-called production rules. An example of such a rule would be IF light equals red, THEN press brake. The rules thus indicate what the programme should do when specific conditions are met. In addition to the production rules, these types of models are also equipped with a working memory that temporarily stores information. One important aspect of production systems is their capacity to generate new production rules when the programme encounters new conditions. This way, the model is capable of learning. One of the most prominent computational models that is based on production rules is the **General Problem Solver**, a programme that was developed to evaluate human problem-solving strategies (Newell & Simon, 1972). Currently, this approach has been largely abandoned in favour of a neural network approach.

1.6.2.2 Neural Networks

Neural networks (also known as 'connectionist' networks) consist of simple units (or nodes) that are connected with each other (see fig 1.8). A node is simply a variable that can represent a specific activation level. Within a network, information is represented as an activation pattern that is distributed across these nodes. Each node is connected to one or more other nodes and the activation of each node spreads via these connections to the connected nodes. How the activation spreads is determined by the weight of each connection. More specifically, each connection has a positive or negative weight, allowing it to activate or to inhibit the receiving node. Neural networks are often, but not always, organised in layers. The first of these layers is typically the input layer, which encodes a stimulus in the form of an activation pattern. Additionally, neural networks typically have an output layer which represents the 'answer' of the network to the stimulus. Finally, it is possible to have one or more intermediate layers that transform the input pattern into an output pattern.

Currently, neural networks form the core of many machine learning algorithms. This type of algorithm may, for example, be used in face recognition technology in photo-editing software. In this case, the input layer consists of the individual pixels comprising a photograph, while the output layer consists of a single node that is activated

above a specific threshold when a face is present in the photo, while it remains below this threshold when there is no face. If we assume that the activation level of each node can vary between 0 and 1, a white pixel will result in a full activation of the corresponding input node, whereas a black pixel will leave it fully inactive.[7] When a face is present, the activation of the output node should exceed the threshold of 0.5, whereas it should remain below this level when there is no face present.

One important aspect of neural networks is that it needs training. The weights of the connections between the nodes are initially unspecified, resulting in random behaviour of the network. In this state, the network is not capable of recognising faces. Training a network consists of presenting a large set of photos and adjusting the weights of the connections each time the network makes an erroneous classification. These adjustments can be made on the basis of different methods. For instance, **backpropagation** determines the difference between the correct output and the given output and then calculates how all the weights of the network need to be adjusted to achieve a slightly better match between the input stimulus and the response.

An alternative method for training neural networks is based on the application of **genetic algorithms**. Here the network also starts out with un-initialised weights. A number of variants of this network are made, however, each containing slight variations of the weights between the nodes. Now, the variant yielding the best performance during training will be used as the basis for the next generation of networks: again, a number of variations are spawn from this network and the one yielding the best performance will be used as a basis for yet another generation. This way, the network slowly evolves towards a system that can perform a classification task with a high level of accuracy.

1.6.2.3 Cognitive Architectures

Computational models such as the aforementioned general problem solver and the neural network–based machine learning algorithms are examples of relatively specialist computational models. In addition to these, there is a class of computational models, known as **cognitive architectures**, that aim to implement generic cognitive functionality.

One of the most successful cognitive architectures is the Adaptive Control of Thought-Rational (ACT-R) model, which was initially developed by John Anderson at Carnegie Mellon University in the 1970s. ACT-R originated from the merging of two of Anderson's earlier models – Adaptive Control of Thought (ACT) and Rational Analysis (RA) – making the name of the current model a concatenation of the former two. ACT-R is a software package capable of simulating a large number of cognitive

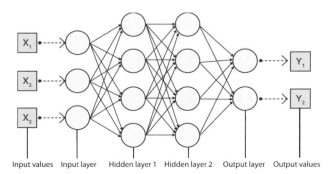

Figure 1.8 A schematic overview of a neural network.

Input values   Input layer   Hidden layer 1   Hidden layer 2   Output layer   Output values

functions (Anderson, Fincham, Qin, & Stocco, 2008). The most recent version of ACT-R, 7.27.7, was released in July 2022 as a freely downloadable open-source software package.

The package itself is written in the LISP programming language and consists of seven modules that are inspired by findings from cognitive psychology and the cognitive neurosciences. Four of these modules are specifically relevant for implementing cognitive task performance. These are the retrieval, imaginal, goal, and procedural modules. The retrieval module is involved in tracking which information should be retrieved from memory for subsequent use. The imaginal module transforms the representation of a problem in such a way that solutions can be facilitated. The goal module stores the goals of each task, and the procedural module makes use of production rules to determine which actions need to be carried out. The remaining three modules are involved in perception and motor control. It is important to note that ACT-R is a function library, that is, a collection of functions that an application programmer can use to write a programme. Thus, when researchers intend to use ACT-R to study the execution of a specific task, they can write their own programme to implement this task, based on the building blocks that ACT-R provides.

ACT-R represents an impressive attempt at building a generic theoretical framework of human cognition, which can be used to explain a wide variety of human behaviours. This generic applicability makes the theory flexible. This flexibility, while being a strength, could also be considered a weakness, however, because it limits the opportunities for disconfirmation, which is – as we have discussed earlier – a major cornerstone of the scientific endeavour.

1.6.3 COGNITIVE NEUROPSYCHOLOGY

The third major foundation of cognitive psychology consists of cognitive neuropsychology. This field studies behaviour that is expressed by brain-damaged patients. Typically, these patients' brains are lesioned, that is, they are structurally damaged due to illness or accident. Cognitive neuropsychology assumes that we can learn a great deal about normal cognition by studying brain damage.

Over the years, this assumption has been validated in many studies. Until the 1960s, for example, we knew very little about human memory, and believed that memories were diffusely distributed across our brains. A major breakthrough came, however, after a patient had a large area of his brain, known as the hippocampus, surgically removed to deal with the consequences of intractable epilepsy (Chapter 13). After the operation, the patient, who became famous in the neuropsychological literature as HM, was no longer capable of storing new memories, despite the fact that his existing memories had remained more or less intact. As a consequence, many existing notions about human memory had to be revised completely.

Because cognitive neuropsychologists study the brain, we might be tempted to believe that they are also specifically interested in neural processes. This is not necessarily the case, however. The main goal of neuropsychology is not so much to study the brain itself. Instead, it uses brain pathology as a means to understand cognitive processes (Coltheart, 2010).

1.6.3.1 Assumptions

Understanding cognitive processes on the basis of brain damage necessitates that a number of assumptions are being met. **Functional modularity** assumes that the cognitive system consists of many independent functional modules, each one being domain specific. Domain specificity implies that each module only responds to a specific class of stimuli. The additional assumption of seriality states that each module is activated in a strictly serial order, implying that there is little interaction between modules. The assumption of **anatomical modularity** states that each functional module is localised in a specific dedicated brain area. The third assumption is that the functional architecture is uniform across individuals. In other words, it is assumed that each individual has access to the same cognitive functions, and that these functions are localised in approximately the same brain areas across individuals. The fourth assumption, **subtractability**, states that brain damage only affects one or more specific modules, or connections between modules, and that patients are unable to develop new modules to compensate for the damaged ones.

Although these assumptions have allowed us to interpret a large variety of neuropsychological disorders, it should be noted that some of these assumptions can be questioned. Firstly, there is currently still no strong evidence for functional modularity. Even though neuropsychologists have found evidence for modularity, the strict assumption of functional modularity is hard to reconcile with recent findings in the neurosciences, which suggest that cognitive processes operate in a much more parallel fashion than previously assumed. The implication of the latter findings is that cognitive functions are far less modular than previously assumed.

1.6.3.2 Dissociations

How can we understand cognitive processes on the basis of brain damage? One of the most important methods we have at our disposal, in this respect, consists of finding dissociations. We can determine the existence of a dissociation when a patient's performance is normal on one task but significantly impaired on a different task. Suppose that a patient performs normally on a word-naming task but is

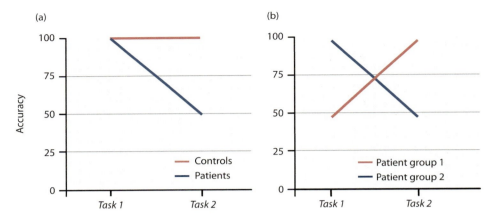

Figure 1.9 Examples of (a) a single and (b) a double dissociation.

strongly impaired on an arithmetic task (see fig 1.9a). We might suspect, on the basis of this result, that this patient has a specific deficiency for mental arithmetic, but can we be sure of this? A major problem here is that we cannot exclude that other factors might have influenced our results. Maybe the arithmetic task was more difficult than the word-naming task, with our patient no longer being able to compensate for this increased difficulty in a way that a neurotypical control can. In this particular case, we have found a dissociation between linguistic and arithmetic performance, but on the basis of this particular dissociation, we cannot yet conclude that our patient's difficulties are specifically related to arithmetic.

The latter conclusion can only be reached by finding a **double dissociation**. This type of dissociation can be found by comparing the results from two patients with different types of deficits. Suppose we find a second patient who performs normally on the arithmetic task but shows a deficit on the word-naming task. Now we can exclude generic differences, such as task difficulty. We can genuinely conclude that we have found substantial differences between linguistic and arithmetic task performance, which justify the conclusion that the two tasks selectively activate independent cognitive modules (see fig 1.9b).

Although the double dissociation method is frequently used to determine the modularity of the mind, the method can be criticised as well. For example, Chater (2003) states that the method can overestimate the mind's modularity. To use Chater's example: if we were to know nothing about the human digestive system, we might falsely conclude that we have two different digestive systems, one for peanuts and one for prunes, because some people have allergies for peanuts, but not for prunes, whereas others have allergies for prunes, but not for peanuts. In this case, we have found a double dissociation supporting this conclusion. In reality, however, both are digested by the same system, and the allergies are caused by subtle biochemical differences across individuals. In theory, it

would thus also be possible that damage to small and relatively specialised modules might result in the dissociation between the linguistic and arithmetic performance in our preceding example, while both processes employ the same overall cognitive process, such as attention or memory. In this respect, the British neuropsychologist Tim Shallice distinguishes between statistical dissociations and absolute dissociations. An absolute dissociation is characterised by a complete and absolute dissociation between tasks, whereas a statistical dissociation is characterised by relatively small differences in task performance. According to Shallice, absolute dissociations are indicative of modularity, whereas statistical dissociations are far less so.

1.6.4 COGNITIVE NEUROSCIENCES

The fourth major foundation of cognitive psychology consists of the cognitive neurosciences. Like cognitive neuropsychology, this field aims to understand cognitive processes by studying the living brain. In contrast, however, the cognitive neurosciences are not so much using the brain to understand cognition as they are aiming to understand the interaction between brain and cognition.

1.6.4.1 Functional Aspects of the Healthy Living Brain

Our knowledge of brain functions has been rapidly expanding since the beginning of the second half of the 20th century, when a large number of techniques were developed that allowed us to study the brain in a **non-invasive** manner. This was either done by recording the electromagnetic signals that the brain emits, allowing us to track changes in brain activity on a millisecond-by-millisecond basis, or by measuring regional changes of blood flow in neural tissue, allowing us to determine with an accuracy of a few cubic millimetres where in the brain changes in activation take place. By relating these changes in brain activation to behavioural outcomes, we can obtain new insights into cognitive processes.

1.6.4.2 Techniques

One of the first new techniques that was introduced in the early 1990s is positron emission tomography (PET). This technique allows the measurement of glucose uptake in different brain areas, allowing us to determine where in the brain activity increases in response to cognitive activities. During a relatively short period of time in the 1990s, PET contributed substantially to our knowledge about, among other things, attention (Corbetta, Miezin, Dobmeyer, Shulman, & Petersen, 1991) and visual perception (Kosslyn, 1999). Since then, PET has lost much of its initial popularity, due to the fact that its application is relatively cumbersome and expensive. Nevertheless, it is still used to address specific research questions.

One of the reasons that the use of PET has been on the decline is that it has largely been superseded by another technique, known as functional magnetic resonance imaging (fMRI; see Box 2.2). This technique is also capable of measuring brain metabolism as a proxy for brain activity, thus allowing us to determine which brain areas are activated in relation to a cognitive process.

Two other techniques have contributed to the rise of the cognitive neurosciences in this period: magnetoencephalography (MEG) and transcranial magnetic stimulation (TMS). The magnetoencephalogram is the magnetic counterpart of the EEG. Each electric current produces a corresponding magnetic field, which allows a magnetometer to measure the same activity as the EEG, at least in principle. MEG has a considerable advantage, however, because the magnetic fields are not distorted by the scalp, as is the case for EEG (see Box 2.3). For this reason, the sources of electromagnetic activity can, in principle, be localised more accurately with MEG than with EEG. It is a misconception, however, to assume that MEG is always superior to EEG (Srinivasan, Winter, & Nunez, 2006). In practice, MEG is capable of recording from sources of brain activity that cannot be readily measured with EEG and vice versa.

Even though MEG is currently still used quite regularly, it has never been considered to be a substitute for EEG. In fact, EEG is used far more frequently than MEG. One of the most important reasons for this is cost-efficiency. Magnetometers are highly sensitive to electromagnetic noise, requiring them to operate at extremely low temperatures and to be shielded from the earth's magnetic field. This results in significant construction and maintenance costs. Furthermore, to take full advantage of MEG's strengths, a detailed three-dimensional model of each participant's brain, dura, and skull is required, which, in turn, requires a detailed MRI-scan and a labour-intensive reconstruction process, resulting in significant additional costs.

TMS is also based on magnetism, but in contrast to the previously discussed techniques, TMS manipulates brain activity, as opposed to measuring it. TMS is based on the fact that a specially designed magnetic coil is capable of focusing a short but intense magnetic pulse at a specific brain area, allowing it to temporarily disrupt the normal operation in this area. Then, the way the targeted area is involved in the execution of a cognitive task can be experimentally determined.

1.6.4.3 Spatial and Temporal Resolution

Each of the techniques discussed earlier has a specific number of advantages and disadvantages. Which technique is best suited to address a specific research question is therefore dependent on several factors. In addition to practical considerations, such as costs and availability, one of the most important considerations is the **spatial** and **temporal resolution** of the technique in question (Churchland & Sejnowski, 1994). Spatial resolution relates to the accuracy of determining where in the brain changes in activation occur, whereas temporal resolution relates to the accuracy of determining when such a change occurs (see fig 1.10 for an overview of the spatial and temporal resolution of a number of different techniques). Which technique is most suitable depends to a large extent on the research question at hand.

1.6.4.4 Applicability and Limitations

Over the past 30 years, our current arsenal of neuroimaging techniques has provided a wealth of new knowledge and insights. Partly due to this success, we should be weary of over-reliance on these techniques, as we need to remain cautious of a number of limitations of these techniques. One limitation is that all techniques, with the exception of TMS, are correlational in nature. That is, these techniques are capable of establishing a relation between cognitive processes and brain activity, but cannot determine the causality.

The second important limitation that most techniques are still lacking fully developed statistical analysis techniques. In neuroimaging studies, the problem of multiple comparisons can be even more problematic than the 1 out of 20 problem we illustrated earlier in this chapter. In fMRI, for example, the brain is subdivided in a huge number (~1,000,000) of small volumes, known as voxels, of about 1 mm^3 each. When we determine for each of these voxels independently whether there are significant differences in activation between conditions, the probability of coincidental finding increases considerably. This was demonstrated rather dramatically by Bennett, Baird, Miller, and Wolford (2009), who found a statistically significant activation in one voxel of the brain of a dead Atlantic salmon, while it was supposed to be classifying human faces in an MRI scanner. Obviously, it is impossible (or to be more scientifically accurate; extremely unlikely) that a salmon is capable of doing so, let alone a dead one! And this was exactly the point of the experiment: the observed activation must necessarily be coincidental. For this reason, Bennet et al. argued that it is of crucial importance to correct for this type of coincidental results. Although some techniques are currently available to do so, researcher

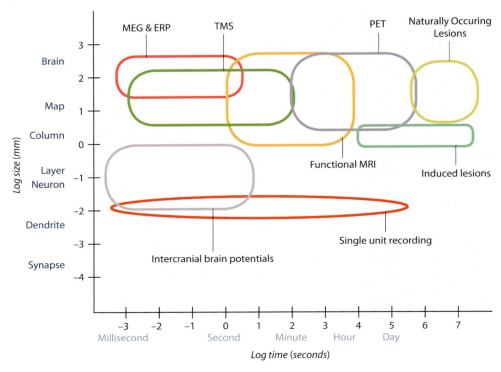

Figure 1.10 An overview of the spatial and temporal resolution of the most commonly used techniques for recording brain activity.

freedom is still considerable, leaving the door open for coincidental findings to penetrate the literature.

1.7 OUTLOOK AND ORGANISATION OF THIS BOOK

The overarching aim of this book is to provide an overview of the state-of-the-art in cognitive psychology and its related fields. This will be done on the basis of nine parts, starting with the basic functions and progressively discussing more complex, higher-order processes. Here, I deliberately chose not to follow the standard format that many other textbooks use, because it does not emphasise the interaction between the different topics and underexposes important emerging topics such as consciousness and action control. Most of the currently available books start with a fairly detailed overview of the individual sensory modalities, which is then followed by chapters on attention and memory, before delving into the higher cognitive processes, such as thought, reasoning, problem-solving, and language. Chapters on consciousness and emotion appear to be added as an afterthought, and important themes such as action control and multisensory integration are completely absent.

To emphasise the interrelation between various cognitive processes, this book follows a layered approach instead. After a short introduction of the most important neural mechanisms of the brain in Chapter 2. Chapter 3 follows

with a discussion of how ever increasingly complex neural structures allow us to produce complex actions, and how these mechanisms allow us to learn these actions. Then, Chapters 4 and 5 cover how we can consciously control our actions as a function of our task goals, and how we can select relevant information for further processing. Chapters 6 through 8 provide an in-depth discussion of our most prominent sensory modalities. Here, I not only cover the basic functions of these modalities, in their own right, but also discuss how attention can regulate the flow of information in these senses. Chapters 9 and 10 focus on integration. More specifically, Chapter 9 focuses on how our brain combines sensory input across different sensory modalities, while Chapter 10 focuses on the interrelation between perception and action. It is increasingly recognised that emotional and motivational processes play an important role in cognitive psychology. This topic is covered in Chapters 11 and 12. These chapters focus on the reciprocal relation between cognition, emotion, and motivation.

From Chapter 13 onward, the book follows a somewhat more traditional approach. Chapter 13 covers the architecture of memory, while Chapter 14 focuses on the dynamic short-term memory systems that are involved in learning, forgetting, and the manipulation of information that is temporarily stored in working memory. This chapter builds upon some ideas that were already introduced in Chapter 3. Chapter 15 describes the involvement of our memory in a host of everyday (and not so everyday!) activities. Here, I also focus on the importance of personal, autobiographical memory for the development of a person's identity.

Chapters 16 through 18 discuss one of the most important cognitive skills that we have, which has given us a unique position within the animal kingdom: our ability to communicate through language. Language can serve as a means of handing us an almost limitless number of mental representations, and to manipulate these representations directly. We can use these representations to solve a wide range of reasoning problems, which sometimes requires us to convert an abstract description into a concrete visualisation. In most cases, we are required to transform this representation. In Chapters 19 through 22, I discuss the nature of these representations, how they arise in our minds, how we can manipulate them, and what kind of errors typically occur in the process.

One final important aspect of human cognition is that we are not alone in this world. We are social beings, who spend a considerable amount of time interacting with fellow members of our species. Effective interaction with others requires us to interpret their intention. Chapter 23 discusses the cognitive aspects of social interaction. Finally, Chapter 24 focuses on applied cognitive research and specifically focuses on the practical aspects of human cognition on the work floor. Human error is a core theme of this chapter. Finally, in this chapter we also look forward and briefly speculate about some exciting developments that lay ahead.

1.7.1 FOUR GENERAL PRINCIPLES

One major aim is to discuss various aspects of cognitive psychology from four generally applicable principles. These principles are association, adaptation, integration, and prediction.

1.7.1.1 Association and Control

The first general principle focuses on the distinction between automatic associative processing and controlled processing. The distinction between these two forms of processing can be identified in a great number of cognitive phenomena. These may range from making choices in simple attention or memory tasks (Schneider & Shiffrin, 1977; Shiffrin & Schneider, 1977; Treisman & Gelade, 1980) to complex reasoning and decision tasks (Kahneman & Tversky, 1972; Tversky & Kahneman, 1973). In many cases, associative process can immediately provide an answer, which often may be wrong, or at least strongly biased. In these cases, a cognitive control process is required to generate the correct answer, or at least to verify the answer that was provided by the automatic process.

1.7.1.2 Adaptation and Compensation

The second general principle is that our behaviour is adaptive. We humans are capable of learning, and we are capable of adjusting our behaviour when circumstances require it. This may hold from simple behaviour, such as simple actions, to complex decisions, opinions, and beliefs. This flexibility is essential for our survival and plays an important role in learning and memory processes. On the other hand, much behaviour is initiated to maintain a stable internal state, resulting in compensatory behaviour in response to changes in our environment. Many motivational processes play an important role in maintaining a stable internal state. At lower levels of processing, we find many systems that are specifically evolved to maintain internal stability, by compensating for our own actions (see Chapters 3, 6, and 10).

1.7.1.3 Integration and Competition

The third general principle is that cognitive processes are integrative and competitive. As observers, we continually integrate different aspects of our environment, like images, sounds, smells, and other sensory information. In addition, we seamlessly integrate these percepts with the actions that we need to carry out. (If you have ever played a game of basketball, you would probably agree.) Integrating many sources of information is, therefore, an important aspect of human cognition; one that is strongly tied to consciousness (Tononi, 2004). On the other hand, we are often required to process multiple objects. Interestingly, the neural representations of separate objects do not integrate with each other. Instead, we often find them to be competing with each other. This competition is of crucial importance when we need to select one specific action from a number of alternatives, or when we need to attend to one specific object (while ignoring the others) when we perceive multiple objects.

1.7.1.4 Prediction and Correction

The fourth, and currently most influential, theoretical framework in cognitive psychology is that of predictive coding. This framework, as already introduced in the beginning of this chapter, is based on the idea that our brains produce a model of our environment that is corrected on the basis of our sensory input (Friston, 2010). Specifically, when a strong mismatch between the internal model and the incoming sensory information is detected (such as in the case of an unexpected event), the resulting prediction error will be used to update the model. This happens, for example, when we are about to cross the road and a car unexpectedly enters our field of vision. In this case, the car signals a strong prediction error, which results in an update of the model. In contrast, when there are no unexpected events, the model correctly predicts the sensory input, and consequently the input is hardly processed at all.

The predictive coding framework is also one of the most universally applicable frameworks, which is capable of explaining how our brains detect violations in the regularity of auditory (Näätänen, 2007) and visual (Stefanics, Kremlacek, & Czigler, 2014) sequences, or why the auditory centres of our brains respond less strongly to sounds that we produce ourselves (Horvath, 2015) compared to other sounds. It can also explain why we cannot tickle ourselves (Blakemore, Wolpert, & Frith, 2000), and it plays an important role in the interpretation of speech signals (Di Liberto, Lalor, & Millman, 2018). Each of these topics will be discussed in depth in the following chapters.

1.8 IN CLOSING

More than 120 years of empirical research in psychology has provided a wealth of knowledge on human cognitive functions and behaviour. New facts and theoretical insights have changed our ideas about cognitive psychology drastically. The influx of ideas from computer sciences, neuropsychology, the cognitive neurosciences, and cognitive psychology draw a picture of human cognition as being a very active process. Our brains are continuously active in integrating the information that reaches us through various senses with the information that is already stored in our memory, and it aims to use this information to predict the future. These predictions are continuously updated on the basis of new information that is collected by our senses.

Despite these developments, psychology (and, most notably, cognitive psychology) is still a very young science. Even though we have established several general principles, we are still a long, long way from the development of a grand unified theory of cognition that is capable of explaining a great many aspects of cognitive psychology. Theories of cognitive psychology are currently still domain specific, that is, most theories are only capable of explaining a very specific subsection of the human psyche. This is one of the reasons why we will discuss a large number of theories in the chapters to come.

The fact that we have this many theories is a frequent complaint among students taking an introductory course in cognitive psychology. This is often amplified by the fact that none of the theories presented appears to fully explain all the phenomena at hand. Even though this wealth of theories may initially appear to give the impression of a forest where we can no longer see through the trees, it is also a sign of the vitality of the field. Many students are often left wondering which theory is correct and which one is not. Even though some theories have already been outright rejected, it is often impossible to give a straight answer to this question. The reason is that many theories are developed to explain specific aspects of human behaviour. Therefore, it is possible that a theory that is well suited to explain one subfield is less equipped to explain another.

A good example of this is discussed in Chapter 18, where we discuss models of speech production. Two of these models, the spreading activation model (Dell, 1986) and the WEAVER++ model (Levelt, Roelofs, & Meyer, 1999), each attempt to explain the same process. However, the first model specifically attempts to do so on the basis of speech errors, whereas the second model specifically aims to explain word production times, thus resulting in two slightly different approaches to the same topic.

In addition, it is important to realise that the theories discussed in the remaining chapters often describe cognitive processes at different levels of description. To illustrate this point, we can take an example from popular mechanics. To explain how a car works, we can assume that there are different systems and each performs a specific task. We have an electric motor for propulsion, a battery to provide the necessary energy, wheels to enable guidance and fluent contact with the ground, and brakes to enable a timely stop. This is an explanation at the systems levels. When we make specific assumptions about the function of each component, we can adequately formulate an explanation at the systems level, without needing to explain how each component itself works. We can, however, attempt to explain the workings of the motor, by assuming the presence of magnetic coils, copper wires, and by assuming that each of these components has a specific function. At the molecular level, we can try to understand the principles of attractive and repulsive forces, and so on. As long as we assume that the motor is a power source, we do not need to know the details of its operation to understand what its function is in a car. Even more so, the details of one system are typically completely unrelated to the system as a whole.[8]

For theories of cognition, a similar principle can be identified. Some theories aim to describe human cognition at the systems level, while other theories aim to provide a detailed description of a specific component. Taken together, the full range of human behaviour is enshrouded by a patchwork of different theoretical models (Muthukrishna & Henrich, 2019). The challenge is therefore not so much to determine which theory is correct and which one is not, but rather to understand how these theories are connected. If you have not completely succeeded by the end of this book, don't worry: I started this adventure in 1990 and I am still learning every day.

1.9 SUMMARY

Despite the fact that cognitive psychology is still a relatively young science, it is rooted in a tradition going back at least 2500 years that seeks to find answers concerning the nature of the human soul. Associationist theories of thought aimed to explain how associations between perception and thought formed the basis for the emergence of new thoughts and memories. Although this school has formulated a number of influential ideas concerning human functioning, its approach is, in essence, bottom-up driven, which implies that humans are passive agents who predominantly respond to external stimuli. In contrast to this approach, current approaches of human cognition pose that our brains are continuously active and create an internal representation of our environment, and that perception mainly serves the purpose of updating this representation. The predictive coding framework supports this approach.

Cognitive psychology focuses on the scientific study of the basics of human thought and behaviour. This approach encompasses topics such as action control, perception, attention, consciousness, cognitive control, and memory. In addition, higher cognitive functions, such as thought, reasoning, and problem-solving, are among the topics that are encompassed by cognitive psychology. Knowledge about human cognition can be applied in a broad number of areas, one of which is safety.

The scientific discipline of cognitive psychology was established around the mid-20th century and was initially strongly inspired by the emerging field of computer sciences. Currently, cognitive psychological research is mostly conducted in an interdisciplinary context, involving collaborations between neuropsychologists and cognitive neuroscientists, along with computer scientists who build computational models of human behaviour. Neuropsychologists aim to understand cognition through the study of brain damage, while cognitive neuroscientists aim to relate brain activity directly to cognitive processes.

The cognitive neurosciences provide a host of techniques, including EEG and MEG, to measure electrical brain activity, and PET and fMRI to measure changes in metabolism in the brain.

NOTES

1 Even though flying is considerably safer than driving, many more people are afraid of flying than of driving. This is mainly due to the fact that the occasional plane crash that does occur receives an enormous amount of attention. In contrast, the continuous daily stream of fatal traffic accidents worldwide receives hardly any attention. As a consequence, our intuitive assessment of the relative frequencies of car and plane crashes is strongly biased.

2 The search term yielded 7,350,000 hits on January 24, 2023, to be precise. To give you an idea how large a body of literature this is, if we assume that a single paper, when printed on A4-format, has a thickness of about 2.5 mm, this would result in a pile of literature that could fit a bookshelf that is about 18.4 km long.

3 Current studies on consciousness, for example, present letters against a noisy background, such that the letters are hardly discernible. When participants report for about half of the presentation that they cannot perceive the letter, the letter is presented at the **subjective perceptual threshold**. This type of subjective report is a form of introspection. These introspective reports can be used to compare brain activity that occurs when the stimulus is consciously perceived, with activity occurring when it is not consciously perceived.

4 This phenomenon is known as Moravec's paradox, after artificial intelligence researcher Hans Moravec, who, together with his fellow computer scientists Rodney Brooks and Marvin Minsky, discovered that higher cognitive functions are much easier to emulate by a computer than basic cognitive functions.

5 Scientific fraud is highly exceptional but has occurred in almost every discipline imaginable: notable examples include the 'cold fusion' studies of the late 1980s, the fraudulent claim that vaccines would cause autism, and the American company Theranos, which claimed that they could carry out any type of blood analysis from a mere pinprick of blood.

6 Apart from the Stapel affair and a few other cases of outright fraud, in most of these cases, there is no intention of deliberate manipulation or deceit. Instead, researchers typically have some freedom in choosing between alternative methods of analysing their data, and this freedom may result in trying out different approaches and holding on to those that yield the results that are the most consistent with the hypotheses.

7 This example is based on grayscale images; for colour images, this should be repeated for each colour channel.

8 The idea that we can understand operations at the systems level on the basis of explanations at the smallest level of description is an example of the fallacy of reductionist thought.

FURTHER READING

Eyesenk, M. W., & Keane, M. T. (2020). *Cognitive psychology: A student's handbook*. Hove, UK: Psychology Press.

Glass, A. L. (2017). *Cognition: A neuroscience approach*. Cambridge, MA: Cambridge University Press.

Kahneman, D. (2011). *Thinking, fast and slow*. New York: Farrar, Strauss, and Giraux.

CHAPTER 2

The brain

2.1 INTRODUCTION

Before you continue to read, let's try the following exercise: compile a list of all the activities that you are currently involved in. Obviously, you are reading these these sentences and attempting to comprehend their meaning. That is, you are perceiving an array of abstract symbols and relating the meaning of these symbols to information that is stored in your memory. You are moving your eyes along the words printed on these pages and checking whether the one grammatical errors that you just encountered – which forced you to skip back to an earlier part of the text – was truly an error. In the meantime, you might have become aware that another word in this paragraph was printed twice, making to decide to reread the entire paragraph once again, realizing that top-down expectations fooled your eyes...

While doing so, you might be listening to music, which you may perceive without it really entering your conscious awareness. You may also be suppressing distracting background noises from outside. Every once in a while, your activities might be interrupted by an incoming message on your cell phone, while in the background you are digesting the remains of a light snack. While its nutrients find their way to your stomach, your digestive system is stimulated to convert them into energy. Meanwhile your heartbeat and blood pressure are adjusted according to the needs of your body. When you feel thirsty you will stand up and walk to the kitchen to pour yourself a glass of water. During all these activities, small contractions of your muscles ensure that you maintain your position. Your muscles also enable you to walk to the kitchen without collapsing.

All of these activities are executed in parallel and controlled by the most complex structure in the known universe: our brain. Contained within a volume of a little more than 1 litre, we find approximately 100 billion **neurons**, and about ten times as many **glia cells** (Herculano-Houzel, 2009). Our brains are continuously active, day and night, and they are involved in regulating our most basic bodily processes and every higher cognitive process

imaginable. Even when we are inactive, our brains are still continually processing information (Raichle et al., 2001). Despite the fact that there is still much to learn about the details of many brain functions, the cognitive neuroscientific revolution that started in the 1990s has yielded a wealth of knowledge in this area. Our increased understanding of brain function allows us to study the relation between brain and behaviour in much more detail than we previously believed to be possible. Thus, a basic understanding of the neurosciences is essential for coming to grips with the state of the art in cognitive psychology. For this reason, we start with a concise description of the brain's most important structures and functions, which are relevant for understanding the next chapters.

2.2 NEUROPHYSIOLOGY

2.2.1 NEURONS

2.2.1.1 Anatomy

Neurons are normal cell bodies that have developed a very specific property. By means of a complex electrochemical process, they are capable of passing signals to each other. A neuron consists of a **soma**, one or more **dendrites**, and one **axon** (see fig 2.1). The dendrites and the axon are also known as the extensions of a neuron. The soma, or cell body, is anatomically comparable to any other cell in the body and contains the internal organelles that keep the cell alive. Dendrites are thin extensions that branch off from the soma. Due to this branching, they are sometimes referred to as a dendritic tree. Axons consist of a single extension that is typically longer and thinner than a dendrite. In contrast to dendrites, axons do not branch, except for their ends, which are known as the terminal. Axons transmit electric pulses that are generated on the dendrites, which then travel via the soma and the axon to another neuron. Each axon is connected to a relatively small number of adjacent neurons. As such, an axon is part of a neuronal circuit. In some extreme cases, one axon can be connected to as many as 10,000 other neurons.

DOI: 10.4324/9781003319344-3

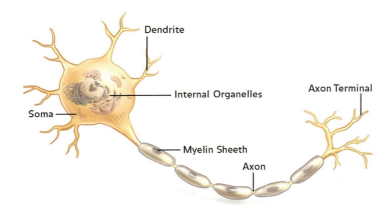

Figure 2.1 Cross section of a neuron. The cell body (soma) is comparable to other cell types and contains the organelles regulating the cells' functions. These include the nucleus, ribosomes, Golgi apparatus, and mitochondria. Dendrites are extensions branching off the soma, which receive impulses from other neurons. The axon is a singular extension that is involved in passing an electric impulse to another neuron. At the axon's end, known as the terminal, these impulses are passed on to an adjacent neuron.

2.2.1.2 Electric Potentials

Figure 2.2 illustrates one of the most basic neural mechanisms, which is the generation of an **action potential**. The cell membrane of a neuron is typically an electrical insulator. It contains a mechanism, however, which pressures electrically charged sodium ions out of the cell, while pressuring charged potassium ions into the cell. This displacement of ions takes place in a ratio of three sodium to two potassium ions, which ultimately results in a net potential difference of approximately -70 millivolts between the inside and the outside of the cell membrane. This is known as the cell's **resting potential**. The resting potential will be disrupted when the cell membrane temporarily depolarises. When this happens, the membrane will open ion gates as soon as the depolarisation reaches a critical threshold of -55 millivolts, allowing sodium ions to flow back into the cell, and potassium ions to leave it. Consequently, the cell membrane depolarises rapidly, and even temporarily overshoots to a positive potential difference of +40 millivolts. After the depolarisation, the cell repolarises, and in doing so even overshoots its resting potential temporarily. During this overshooting, the cell is hyperpolarised, causing it to be temporarily blocked from depolarising again. During this phase, the cell is known to be in its **refractory period**.

The initial depolarisation occurs at one specific location of the cell membrane and spreads out to neighbouring areas, which, in turn, also depolarise. This process can be compared to a sequence of falling dominoes: a local depolarisation triggers the depolarisation of neighbouring areas, forcing the start of a chain reaction. Via this mechanism, the spiking electric potential travels across the soma and traverses the length of the axon. This spike is known as an action potential. Because the action potential is a local phenomenon that triggers adjacent areas of the cell to generate an action potential of their own, its transmission speed is approximately 1 metre per second, which

(a)
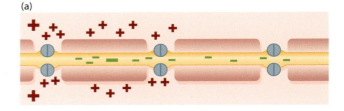

(b)
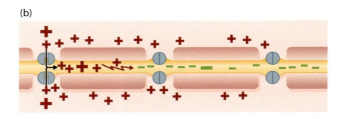

(c)
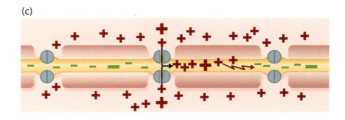

Figure 2.2 The action potential mechanism: when a part of a cell membrane depolarises (a, left), ion channels open (b, left). As a consequence, positively charged sodium ions flow inward, while negatively charged potassium ions flow outward, resulting in a further depolarisation of the cell membrane. The sodium ions flowing into the cell spread along the inside of the cell membrane, causing a further depolarisation of adjacent areas (b, middle). Consequently, ion channels at these adjacent locations open, resulting in a further in and outflux of sodium and potassium ions. This way, the action potential traverses the cell membrane or the axon (c, middle). When the axon is shielded by a sheath of myeline (illustrated by pink blocks in the figure), the depolarisation only takes place at the unshielded nodes of Ranvier, causing the action potential to jump from node to node (c, middle to right), thereby dramatically speeding up the transmission of the action potential.

is considerably lower than that of an electric current in electrically conductive materials, such as copper wires.

Long axons are frequently shielded by an isolating sheet of myeline. Myeline is a white substance that covers parts of the axon. Because of the isolating properties, the action potential can only be evoked in those areas that are uncovered, that is, at the so-called nodes of Ranvier. Consequently, the transmission speed of the action potential is much greater in myelinated axons, because the action potential now jumps from node to node. When the action potential reaches the terminal of the axon, it will stimulate the release of a chemical substance known as a neurotransmitter, which will, in turn, affect the polarisation of an adjacent target neuron.

2.2.2 SYNAPSES

Because the terminal of an axon is not directly connected with the target neuron, action potentials can only indirectly affect the target neuron. The axon terminal and the receiving target neuron are separated from each other by a small gap of about 19.3 nanometres (see fig 2.3). Upon arrival at the terminal, the action potential stimulates the release

of neurotransmitters. These neurotransmitters change the chemical balance of the receiving cell, thereby causing the resting potential to increase or decrease. When the neurotransmitter causes the resting potential of the target cell to increase (that is, to decrease the negative potential difference), the probability that this cell will generate an action potential increases, because its resting potential gets closer to the critical -55 millivolts threshold. This is an example of an **excitatory** neurotransmitter. In this case, the receiving cell generates an **excitatory postsynaptic potential** (EPSP). When the neurotransmitter causes a decrease of the resting potential (that is, an increase of the negative potential difference), the probability of the receiving cell generating an action potential decreases. In this case, the receiving cell generates an **inhibitory postsynaptic potential** (ISPS), and the neurotransmitter is **inhibitory**.

2.2.3 NEUROTRANSMITTERS

Neurotransmitters are molecules that enable the transmission of messages between neurons. They are released from the axon's terminal and bind to specific receptors at the target neuron. A direct consequence of this binding is a

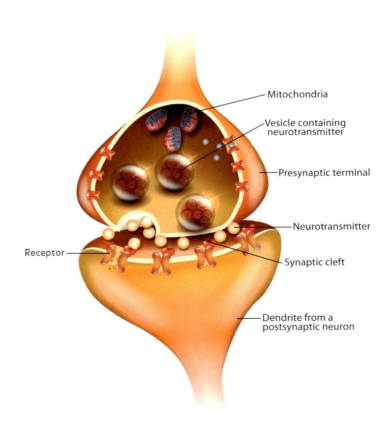

Figure 2.3 The synapse. The terminal of an axon is separated from an adjacent neuron by a tiny gap. The terminal contains vesicles filled with neurotransmitters. An action potential stimulates the release of these neurotransmitters into the synaptic cleft. Here, they increase or decrease the depolarisability of the receiving cell.

33

change in the resting potential of the target cell. In other words, they cause the aforementioned postsynaptic potentials. Some neurotransmitters do so directly by affecting the ion channels in the target cell's membrane, in which case their effect is **ionotropic**. Other neurotransmitters have a more indirect effect because they trigger a biochemical change in the target cell's membrane that can have a prolonged effect on the cells' postsynaptic potential. These neurotransmitters have a **metabotropic** effect. After their release, the neurotransmitters are eventually either broken down or reabsorbed by the releasing axon. The biochemical effects of binding to a receptor, the speed of breakdown or **reuptake** determine to a large degree the effects of a neurotransmitter. More than 100 different types of neurotransmitters have been identified.

Some well-known examples of neurotransmitters are endorphin, dopamine, acetylcholine, and serotonin. The effects of most psychopharmaceuticals, and the effects of illicit drugs, are due to the fact that they are biochemically related to neurotransmitters, and therefore affect their natural functions. Neural functions that are based on the operation of specific neurotransmitters are frequently identified by a name that is derived from the transmitter in question. Examples of these, as will be discussed later in this book, are the dopaminergic system or the serotonergic system.

2.2.4 CLASSIFICATION OF NEURONS

Although almost every neuron is characterised by the properties just described, there are many different types of neurons, and they can differ considerably in appearance. For this reason, neurons can be classified into different categories (see fig 2.4). For instance, **unipolar neurons** are

characterised by the fact that they have only one extension; an extension that can serve either as an axon or as a dendrite. This type of neurons is not very prominent in humans, as it is predominantly found in insects. **Bipolar neurons** have two extensions: a dendrite and an axon. **Multipolar neurons** have one axon and multiple dendrites. **Anaxonic neurons** are characterised by the fact that their axon cannot be distinguished from their dendrites. Finally, **pseudo-unipolar** neurons are characterised by the fact that one extension can function either as an axon or a dendrite.

Multipolar neurons can be further divided into two subtypes, which are both named after one of the most prominent pioneers in neuroscience, the Italian neuroscientist Camillo Golgi (see Box 2.1). Golgi I cells are characterised by extremely long axons, which make them ideally suited for mediating the communication among distant brain areas. Golgi II cells are, by contrast, characterised by much shorter axons. For this reason, they are more prominently involved in local communication. Golgi I cells can be further subdivided into **pyramidal** cells (which are named after the characteristic triangular shape of their soma), Purkinje cells (very large cells that are predominantly present in the cerebellum [see Section 2.3.5]), and anterior horn cells.

Neurons can be further subdivided on the basis of their function. **Afferent neurons**, also known as sensory neurons, send signals from the body's tissues and internal organs to the central nervous system. **Efferent neurons**, also known as motor neurons, send signals from the central nervous system to the tissues and organs. Finally, **interneurons** connect various parts of the central nervous system with each other.

2.3 BRAIN ANATOMY

2.3.1 NAVIGATING THE BRAIN

Obtaining a good insight into the brain's anatomy requires familiarising yourself with a number of new terms that we use to navigate its structures (see fig 2.5). Just like we can describe the location of our homes on a map using terms like north, east, south, or west, we have specific terms to indicate the location of specific brain structures. Since the brain is considerably more complex than a map, we also need more terms to localise these structures. In the following sections, we introduce the most important terms. Note that these terms are not specific to the brain but can be used in the context of other body parts as well. Here, however, we will specifically introduce these terms in the context of brain anatomy.

Firstly, we can view the brain on the basis of three orthogonal anatomical cross sections, or planes. The **sagittal plane** is vertical and intersects the brain from

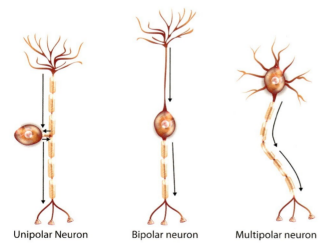

Unipolar Neuron   Bipolar neuron   Multipolar neuron

Figure 2.4 Examples of different types of neurons. Unipolar neurons (left) are characterised by the fact that they only have one extension that serves both as an axon and a dendrite. Bipolar neurons (centre) have one axon and a dendritic tree. Multipolar cells (right) have multiple extensions, including one axon and multiple dendritic trees.

Box 2.1 Golgi and Cajal: pioneering rivals of neuroscience

Scientific progress is driven by a multitude of ideas that are formulated by individual researchers, sometimes resulting in situations where different and sometimes strongly conflicting ideas are defended by their proponents. These ideas are typically formulated on the basis of ever-increasing innovations in research methods and more refined experiments. For this reason, it frequently happens that existing ideas have to be refuted or at least refined, making a scientific theory hardly ever 'definitive'. A scientific theory is typically developed from a relatively simple, and intuitively attractive, idea. Although it happens that this idea is outright incorrect, it is frequently the case that it initially appears to be plausible, but that it needs refinement when more precise observations become available. Sometimes an idea that initially appeared to be plausible needs to be rejected when better research methods become available.

Even when an old idea is no longer supported by the data, however, it can still take a long time before its influence has completely vanished. Science is a human endeavour, and older, established scientists may still be defending their ideas ferociously, even after new experiments have invalidated them over and over again.

One striking example of this is the controversy among two rivalling pioneers of neuroscience at the beginning of the 20th century, namely the Italian neuroscientist Camillo Golgi (1843–1926) and his Spanish rival Santiago Ramón Cajal (1852–1934). Until the end of the 19th century, studies of the central nervous system were hampered by the fact that individual neurons were hardly distinguishable from each other. In 1873, however, Golgi discovered a method which allowed him to highlight a random selection of neurons and their extensions. To do so, he stained the neural tissue with silver nitrate. This procedure coloured the affected neurons black, thereby contrasting them with the unaffected tissue. This discovery established Golgi as one of the most prominent neuroscientists in Europe, and resulted in a wealth of new insights into the nature of neural tissue. One of Golgi's most important observations was that neurons are characterised by complex extensions. These are the extensions that are currently known as axons and dendrites. Based on his still-limited observations, Golgi concluded that the extensions form a complex web of interconnected cells, in which information could freely flow. Golgi named this web the reticulum.

Golgi received much praise and recognition for his staining methods, and while his reticulum theory became our dominant view of neural functions, a relatively unknown neuroscientist from Spain, Santiago Ramón Cajal, was refining Golgi's method. Cajal succeeded in staining individual neurons with an unprecedented level of precision and, using his refined method, reached a conclusion that diametrically opposed Golgi's. Cajal had observed that axons from one cell terminated in an area that was known to contain dendrites from an adjacent cell. The adjacent cell was not coloured, however, implying that the two cells in question could not be part of one common reticulum. From this, Cajal concluded that neurons were individual units that were separated from each other by a physical barrier. With this, Cajal had laid the foundation for the discovery of the synapse. Even though Cajal had no way to directly observe the synapse, he deduced its existence from the fact that the axon of a stained cell could terminate in the proximity of the dendrites of an unstained cell.

Although Cajal's observations were revolutionary, they initially raised little awareness. After his first results were predominantly published in Spain, Cajal later attempted to publish his work in French to make his results better known to the rest of Europe's scientific community. Golgi's idea of the reticulum was dominating the prevailing consensus on neural function, however, resulting in little recognition of Cajal's ideas. The few researchers who had read them were distrustful. In an attempt to gain more recognition, Cajal turned to the German Anatomical Society, where he presented his drawings at the society's annual meeting in Berlin, while allowing the attendees to verify them using a microscope that he had borrowed for the occasion. Cajal was mostly ignored, and the few visitors who did show some interest were mostly disparaging about his work.

A turning point was reached, however, when Cajal decided to single-handedly convince the Swiss neuroanatomist Albert von Kölliker to have a look. Von Kölliker was one of the most prominent neuroanatomists in his time and in his wake, a number of interested attendees followed, curious to see what Kölliker's response would be to that strange Spanish fellow. After Cajal had patiently explained his work, and following his own observation, Kölliker realised the importance of Cajal's work and in the years to come, he promoted Cajal's ideas. The idea that neurons are independent units, which pass neural signals to each other, is known as the neuron doctrine. This doctrine is, to this day, our dominant vision about neural communication.

In 1906, both Golgi's and Cajal's contributions to neuroscience were recognised; they both received the Nobel prize for their groundbreaking work. Golgi, however, was never able to give up the idea of a neural reticulum. Allegedly, Golgi and Cajal never spoke with each other during the award ceremony.

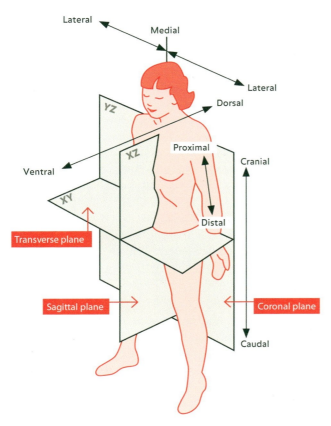

Figure 2.5 An overview of the most important anatomical terms that we use for navigating in the brain.

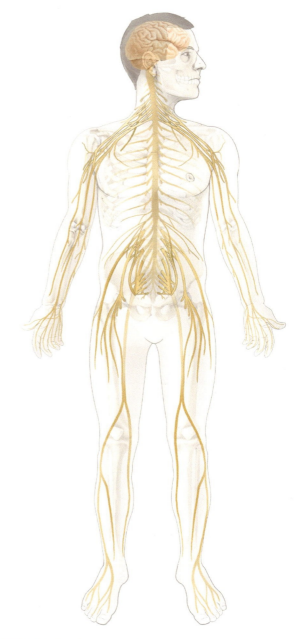

Figure 2.6 A schematic overview of the nervous system.

front to back. The **coronal plane** is also vertical and intersects the brain from left to right. Finally, the **transverse plane** is horizontal and perpendicular to the first two planes.

Additional terms can be used to describe relative positions in neuroanatomy. **Ventral** refers to the underside (or stomach side) of an animal, whereas **dorsal** refers to the backside.[1] **Anterior** indicates that the relative position of a structure is to the front side of a reference structure, and **posterior** indicates that it is to the back side of the reference structure. The terms **superior** and **inferior** indicate that a structure is above or below a reference structure, respectively. **Lateral** indicates that the structure is located to the (left or right) sides of the brain, while **medial** indicates that it is located in the middle, near the central sagittal plane.

2.3.2 GLOBAL ORGANISATION

The brain is part of an extensive network of fibres running through an individual's entire body. This network is known as the nervous system (see fig 2.6). The brain is the central hub in this network, where all incoming **afferent** (sensory) signals are being processed, and from where all outgoing **efferent** (motor) signals are projected to the body. The nervous system can be subdivided into a **central nervous system** and a **peripheral nervous system**. The central nervous system comprises the brain and the spinal cord, while the peripheral nervous system includes all the nerve fibres that we find in the rest of the body. The peripheral nervous system can be further subdivided into a **somatic nervous system** and an **autonomic nervous system**. The somatic system consists of nerves that transmit sensory information from the body to the brain and motor commands from the brain to the body. The autonomic nervous system regulates the

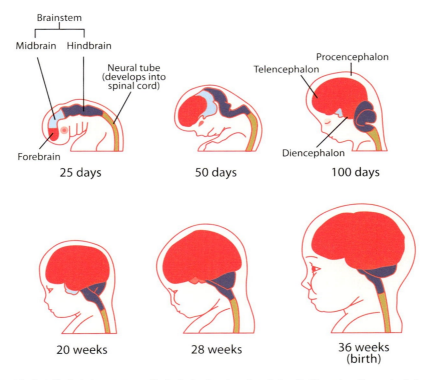

Figure 2.7 The development of the foetal brain during pregnancy. The brain develops from three bulges that form along the most anterior part of the neural tube. These bulges develop into the hindbrain, midbrain, and forebrain.

functions of internal organs and is, among other systems, involved in controlling heart rhythm and the functions of the digestive system.

At the most global level, the organisation of the brain can be best understood from a developmental perspective (see fig 2.7). During pregnancy, the nervous system develops from the so-called neural tube. This is a tube-shaped group of cells that develops during the first weeks of pregnancy. It forms the basis of the **spinal cord**. At the anterior end of the neural tube, three bulges start to grow, from which the basic building blocks of the brain start to develop, that is, the hindbrain, the midbrain, and the forebrain. During further development, these bulges will expand and further divide into additional nuclei, which will eventually develop into a full-grown brain.

2.3.3 THE SPINAL CORD

The spinal cord, which is part of the central nervous system, is located inside the spinal column. It enables communication between the brain, on the one hand, and the sensory organs and muscles of the body, on the other. One exception to this rule is the communication with the sensory organs and muscles that are located in the head, which is subserved by the **cranial nerves** (see Section 2.3.4).

The spinal cord consists of several segments (see fig 2.8). At the dorsal side of each segment, bundles of axons enter the spinal cord; one bundle on the left side and one on the right. These bundles, also known as nerves, transmit information from the sensory organs to the spinal cord. The soma of the neurons that comprise the

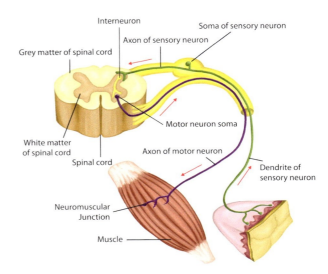

Figure 2.8 A schematic representation of the spinal cord. Sensory neurons are connected to the dorsal root ganglia at the dorsal side. The nerve endings of the motor system leave the spinal cord on the ventral side.

37

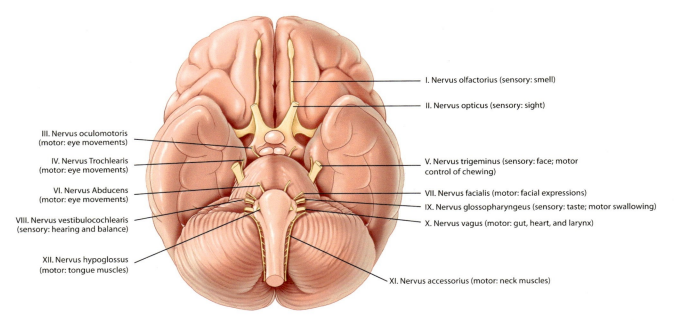

Figure 2.9 Schematic representation of the 12 cranial nerves. These nerves are involved in the transmission of sensory information from the face to the brain and of motor information from the brain to the face. The tenth cranial nerve, the nervus vagus, is involved in regulating autonomous bodily functions.

sensory nerves are located in the **dorsal root ganglia**, which are clusters of neurons located just outside the spinal cord.

On the ventral side, bundles of axons from the motor system (that is, the motor nerves) leave the spinal cord; again, one bundle on the left side and one on the right. In contrast to the sensory nerves, the soma from the motor neurons are located inside the spinal cord. The inner part of the spinal cord is composed of grey matter. This grey matter is formed by the soma and dendrites of all the neurons that comprise the spinal cord. The outside consists of white matter, which is formed by the myelinated axons of these neurons.

2.3.4 CRANIAL NERVES

The sensory signals that are generated in our heads, along with the motor commands that are transmitted to our facial muscles, are transmitted via the cranial nerves (see fig 2.9). These 12 nerves are involved in the transmission of visual information from the eyes to the visual cortex, of auditory information from the ears to the auditory cortex, and from somatosensory receptors in the skin to the somatosensory cortex. In addition, the cranial nerves are involved in controlling eye movements and the pupil reflex, along with controlling mouth and tongue movements, and neck and shoulder movements. Finally, the cranial nerves are involved in controlling the parasympathetic operation of the internal organs. Axons from the

tenth cranial nerve, known as the **nervus vagus**, leave the brain at the medulla oblongata (see Section 2.3.5) and project to the parasympathetic ganglia that control the function of, among other things, the heart, lungs, and intestines (see Chapter 3).

2.3.5 THE HINDBRAIN

The hindbrain (see fig 2.10) develops from the first bulge of the neural tube and is composed of the medulla, the pons, and the cerebellum. The medulla, also known as the medulla oblongata, is an extension of the spinal cord, as it is located right above it. Important functions of the medulla include the control of autonomous bodily functions, such as breathing, heartbeat, and digestion. The medulla, pons, and parts of the midbrain (see Section 2.3.6) are collectively known as the brainstem. The major pyramidal neural pathways from each side of the brain cross each other in the medulla, such that the left side of the brain is connected to the right side of the body and vice versa. This crossing of the neural fibres is also known as decussation.

The pons is located anterior and ventral relative to the medulla, and it is also involved in the control of various autonomous functions. Pons is Latin for 'bridge'. This name can either refer to the fact that the pons forms a bridge between the spinal cord and the rest of the brain (pons varolii) or to the fact that it connects to the cerebellum (pons cerebelli). The cerebellum is a large cauliflower

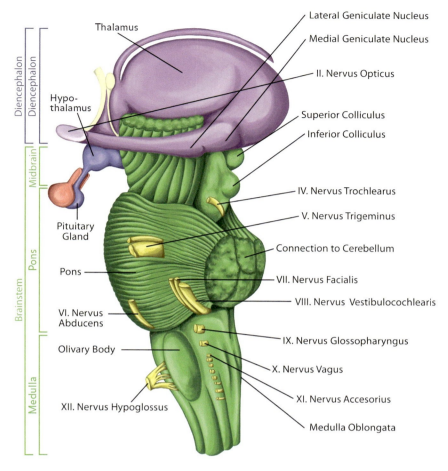

Figure 2.10 Schematic representations of the midbrain and hindbrain, two structures of the forebrain (the thalamus and the hypothalamus), along with the cranial nerves II–XII.

structure that plays a major role in the fine adjustment of motor commands. More recently, it has also been identified as being involved in a host of other cognitive functions that are related to the processing of rewards (Wagner & Luo, 2020).

2.3.6 THE MIDBRAIN

As the name already implies, the midbrain forms the central part of the brain. In mammals, it is a relatively small structure (see fig 2.10). During pregnancy, it develops from the second bulge of the neural tube. The upper part of the midbrain is formed by the **tectum**. The posterior end of the tectum is marked by two pairs of small bulges; these are the **inferior colliculus** and **superior colliculus**. The superior colliculus plays an important role in the regulation of attention and in the programming of eye movements to locations where we expect to detect important information. In addition, this brain area plays an important role in the integration of auditory and visual information. The inferior colliculus is located just below the superior colliculus and

this structure is involved in the transmission of auditory signals to the forebrain.

The **tegmentatum**, located below the tectum, controls eye movements and pupil size, amongst other things. The neural fibres that connect the spinal cord and the hindbrain to the forebrain also pass through the tegmentatum. Several other structures are located below the tegmentatum, including the **reticular formation**. This is a complex bundle of neural fibres which extend from the spinal cord, via central parts of the hindbrain, into the midbrain. Extensions from this bundle project, amongst other areas, to large parts of the forebrain, where they play an important role in the regulation of attention and arousal. This part of the reticular formation is known as the **ascending reticular activating system** (ARAS). In addition, the reticular formation contains a set of descending neural projections that connects to the spinal cord. These descending projections play an important role in integrating motor commands, mediating autonomous functions, modulating pain sensations, and regulating blood circulation in the thalamus. Finally, the **substantia nigra** is an important midbrain structure worth mentioning, as it has been shown that dysfunctions of this structure are related to Parkinson's disease.

2.3.7 THE RETICULAR ACTIVATION SYSTEM

Because it is strongly interconnected with the rest of the brain, the reticular formation is very effective in regulating a person's general level of awareness and in transitioning the state of consciousness between sleep and wakefulness. Its functions are related to selective attention, allowing the brain to temporarily enter states of hyper alertness.

One nucleus of the reticular activation system in particular, the locus coeruleus, is important for regulating the brain's state of alertness (Nieuwenhuis, Aston-Jones, & Cohen, 2005). The locus coeruleus is a small nucleus that is located in the pons. It is involved in the production of the neurotransmitter noradrenaline. The locus coeruleus projects to widespread areas of the brain. It has been argued that it plays an important role in cognitive control processes, because the noradrenergic projections temporarily increase the brain's alertness when additional cognitive processing is required.

2.3.8 THE FOREBRAIN

During pregnancy, the third bulge of the neural tube branches into three additional bulges (see fig 2.7). The dorsal side eventually becomes the **prosencephalon**, while the ventral side eventually become the **diencephalon** and the **telencephalon**. Collectively, these bulges eventually form the **cerebrum**, the largest structure of the human brain. The cerebrum consists of the **cerebral cortex** (literally meaning: 'shell around the cerebrum', also known as 'cortex', or 'neocortex') and several subcortical areas (that is, areas below the 'shell'), including the **thalamus**, the **basal ganglia**, the **pituitary gland**, the **olfactory bulb**, the **hypothalamus**, the **hippocampus**, and the **amygdala**. The latter four areas, together with a part of the cortex that is known as the **anterior cingulate**, are also known as the limbic system. The cerebrum consists of two equally sized hemispheres; one on the left side and one the right side. Each hemisphere is organised in such a way that it predominantly receives input from the contralateral (opposite) side of the body, while also controlling muscles on the contralateral side of the body. The two hemispheres are connected via a thick bundle of neural fibres that is known as the **corpus callosum**.

2.3.8.1 Thalamus and Hypothalamus

The diencephalon develops into the thalamus and the hypothalamus, while the prosencephalon and telencephalon collectively form the rest of the cerebrum. The thalamus forms the central structure of the forebrain. Its shape resembles two intertwined avocados, one in each hemisphere. The thalamus is considered to be the central switchboard of the brain: most sensory information is relayed via the thalamus before it is projected to a dedicated area of the cortex. The cortex itself can influence this transmission, by relaying information back to the thalamus, with the effect that specific information can be prioritised. This mechanism presumably plays an important role in selectively attending to specific sources of information, while ignoring others. Because the thalamus has connections with almost every part of the cortex, it is involved in coordinating the brain's activity. As such, it can be considered to be some sort of pacemaker or switchboard that is involved in synchronising the activation of large parts of the cortex. This function of the thalamus is most likely related to the integration of complex forms of information and modulating overall states of conscious awareness (Tononi, 2004).

The hypothalamus is a small area that is located ventrally to the thalamus. It is connected to major parts of the forebrain and midbrain, and it is involved in the regulation of emotions, specifically so for aggression and sexual behaviour. Moreover, the hypothalamus controls **hormone** production in the pituitary gland. Hormones are chemical substances, similar to neurotransmitters, that are involved in controlling many bodily functions. The pituitary gland is located inferior to the hypothalamus and strongly impacts many functions in large parts of the body, because the hormones it produces are released into the bloodstream and distributed across the entire body.

2.3.8.2 Basal Ganglia and the Striatum

The basal ganglia are formed by a group of three notable subcortical nuclei: the **caudate nucleus**, the **putamen**, and the **globus pallidus** (see figs 2.11 and 2.12). The caudate nucleus and the putamen are part of a structure that is known as the dorsal striatum. These structures are localised laterally relative to the thalamus, and they are strongly connected to various parts of the cortex, more specifically the frontal cortical areas. The basal ganglia play an important role in the planning of sequences of actions (see Chapter 3). Apart from the dorsal striatum, we can also identify a ventral striatum, which is composed of the **nucleus accumbens** and a part of the olfactory bulb. The dorsal striatum is believed to play an important role in skill learning (see Chapters 3 and 13), while the ventral striatum regulates goal-driven behaviour and evaluates rewards (see Chapter 11).

2.3.8.3 The Limbic System

The limbic system is predominantly composed of five brain areas, namely the olfactory bulb, the hypothalamus, the hippocampus, the amygdala, and the anterior cingulate cortex.

(a)

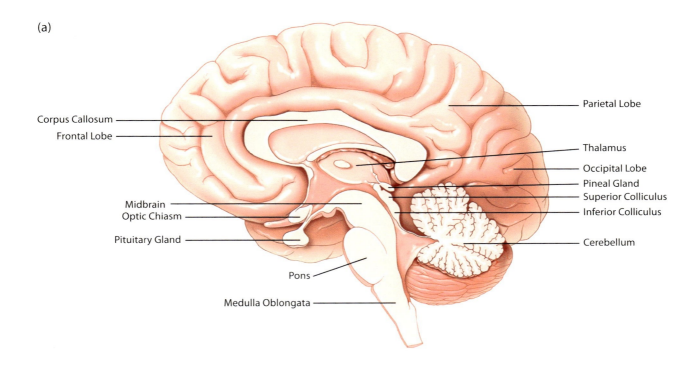

Corpus Callosum

Frontal Lobe

Midbrain

Optic Chiasm

Pituitary Gland

Pons

Medulla Oblongata

Parietal Lobe

Thalamus

Occipital Lobe

Pineal Gland

Superior Colliculus

Inferior Colliculus

Cerebellum

(b)

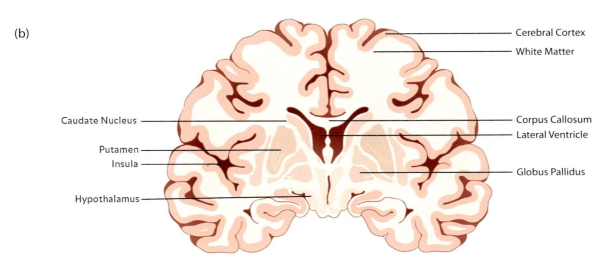

Caudate Nucleus

Putamen

Insula

Hypothalamus

Cerebral Cortex

White Matter

Corpus Callosum

Lateral Ventricle

Globus Pallidus

Figure 2.11 A sagittal (a) and coronal (b) cross section of the brain.

These areas are involved in the regulation of emotions and motivation, as well as in the consolidation of memories. The olfactory bulb is localised in the inferior anterior part of the cerebrum, and it receives direct input from the chemical receptors that are located in the nasal cavity. This direct input, combined with the fact that the olfactory bulb is part of the limbic system, may be among the main reasons why odour perception is almost always accompanied by an affective response. The hippocampus is a large seahorse-shaped structure that is localised posteriorly between the thalamus and the cortex. This structure plays an important role in storing new memories. Finally, the anterior cingulate cortex is an important brain area that was traditionally considered to be part of the limbic system, although it is, from an anatomical perspective, part of the cortex. This area plays an important role in emotion regulation and in many cognitive processes, including the detection and processing of errors (Bush, Luu, & Posner, 2000).

The limbic system derives its name from the fact that the brain areas introduced in the preceding paragraph form the border (Latin: *limbus*) between the cerebrum and the brainstem. Due to the wide variety of functions that these areas are involved in, the limbic system is currently much less considered to be a unit than it was originally believed to be.

(a)

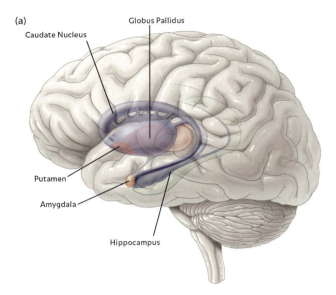

(b)

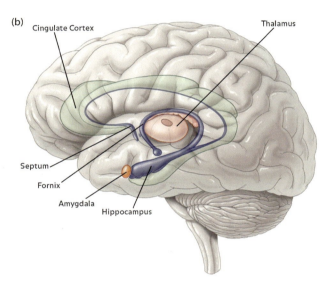

Figure 2.12 A schematic overview of the subcortical nuclei of the forebrain. (a) Basal ganglia and (b) limbic system.

2.3.8.4 The Neocortex

The cortex (see fig 2.13) is the structure that most of us would immediately identify as 'the brain'. From an evolutionary perspective, this part of the brain was most likely the last to develop, and, for this reason, it is also referred to as the 'neocortex'. The cortex folds like a shell around the rest of the brain and has a total surface area of approximately 1,800 mm² (Swindale, 1998). To fit this large surface into the limited volume of the skull, the cortex is characterised by deep ridges and bulges; these are the so-called **sulci** and **gyri**. The outer layers of the approximately 2–3 mm-thick cortex are marked by a greyish colour, due to the dense concentration of neurons that are involved in many of the important cortical functions. For this reason, this part of the cortex is also known as **grey matter**. The deeper layers are characterised by a more whitish colour, which results from the fact that it contains mostly myelinated axons. For this reason, this part of the brain is also known as **white matter**. Remarkably, the

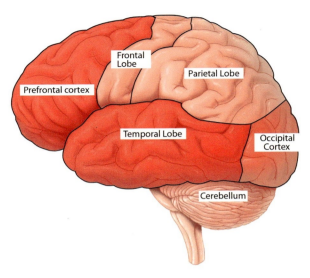

Figure 2.13 A lateral view of the brain. The neocortex and the cerebellum are prominently visible. The neocortex can be subdivided into the occipital, temporal, parietal, and frontal lobes.

distribution of grey and white matter is opposite to that of the spinal cord, where the inner layers are formed by grey matter and the outer layers by white matter.

The cortex itself can be subdivided into four **lobes**. The **occipital lobe** is located to the back of the brain and is predominantly involved in the processing of visual information.

The temporal lobe comprises the inferior lateral part of the cortex. Here, we find, among other things, areas that are involved in the processing of auditory information, along with areas that are involved in the processing of spoken language. The left temporal lobe is predominantly involved in the processing of linguistic content, while the right temporal lobe is predominantly involved in the processing of the **prosodic** (intonation, rhythm, etc.) and emotional content of spoken language. In addition, the temporal lobe is involved in the processing of visual information, more specifically in the recognition of shapes and objects. Finally, it plays a role in the processing of motivational and emotional content.

The parietal lobe is localised anterior and superior with respect to the occipital lobe, and superior relative to the temporal lobe. This lobe is, amongst others, involved in generating a spatial representation of a person's external environment and in providing visuospatial information to the motor systems, such that we can adequately integrate visual and other sensory information into actions. To the anterior side of the parietal lobe, we find the **somatosensory cortex**. This part of the cortex receives input from the tactile senses. It is also believed to generate an internal model of the body.

The parietal lobe is separated from the **frontal lobe** by a deep groove, known as the central sulcus. The frontal lobe occupies the largest part of the cortex. Along the central sulcus, we find the motor cortex, which is involved in the coarse planning of a person's motor actions. The area anterior to the motor cortex is known as the prefrontal cortex. This part of the brain is involved in many of the processes that are commonly known as 'higher cognition', such as decision-making and reasoning, along with controlling which information we should temporarily retain in memory.

The aforementioned lobes can be further divided into more specific areas, which are typically described on the basis of their specific location within a lobe. For instance, within the frontal lobes, we can identify the prefrontal cortex, which can be further divided into, amongst other areas, the dorsolateral prefrontal cortex (i.e., the dorsal and lateral part of the prefrontal cortex) and the ventromedial prefrontal cortex (i.e., the ventral and medial part of the prefrontal cortex). Similar subdivisions can be made within the other lobes, such as the parietal lobe. Some of these areas will be introduced in the remaining chapters, where applicable.

Although the macrostructure of the left and right cerebral structures is approximately the same, there are some differences in the way the two hemispheres are organised, and these differences form the basis for hemispheric specialisation. Of all the cognitive functions, language ability is the one that is most clearly lateralised (see Box 2.2 for some persistent myths about lateralisation). Important brain areas associated with language processing, such as Broca's and Wernicke's areas, are generally found in the left hemisphere. Although it was originally believed that the lateralisation of the language areas was related to hand preference, it is now becoming increasingly clear that these two forms of lateralisation occur independently of each other. For other cognitive functions, too, evidence has been found for a certain degree of lateralisation.

Box 2.2 Six persistent myths about the brain

Despite the enormous progress in unravelling the brain's mysteries that marked recent decades, public knowledge of brain function is still shrouded in a number of persistent myths. For example, the 2014 science fiction thriller *Lucy* presented a superhuman individual, played by Scarlett Johansson, who was able to achieve a tenfold increase in brain power, because she was able to tap into resources that are inaccessible to normal individuals. The movie's plot is based on a popular myth that claims that we only utilise 10% of the brain's power. Similarly, a quick search for topics related to creativity and human development on social media channels such as YouTube yields an overwhelming amount of material that is based on the faulty assumption of a dichotomy between the left and right hemisphere. According to this myth, the left hemisphere is analytical and the right hemisphere holistic and creative. Moreover, the myth presumes that there is a conflict between these two forms of processing. In this box we explore a number of persistent myths about the brain, identify how they started, and argue why they are incorrect.

Myth 1. We only use 10% of the brain's capacity.

The idea that we only use 10% of the brain's capacity is one of the most persistent myths. What started this myth is not exactly known, but we can identify a number of possible sources. Allegedly, in 1907, William James commented that we only use a small proportion of our full mental capacity, after which a journalist apparently misinterpreted him by writing that we only use 10% of our brain's capacity. Another possible origin of the myth can be found in the fact that the ratio of neurons to glia cells is about 1/10. One hypothesis, by now refuted, stated that glia cells were proto-neurons that could potentially develop into neurons.

Moreover, it originally appeared that lesions in large parts of the cortex (see Boxes 5.1 and 12.1) had a

negligible impact on our behaviour, which solidified the impression that the affected brain areas had no function. Based on advancing insights, we now know that glia cells do have their own specific functions and that the 'functionless' brain areas actually do have very important functions. Moreover, from an evolutionary perspective, it is highly implausible that the brain would develop into the complex, energy hungry organ that it is today, if it operated at only a small fraction of its capacity. Based on these arguments, we can safely debunk the 10% myth. Why is it still popular then? One likely reason is that the idea is perpetuated by a blooming industry of self-help and management gurus who find a willing ear for this myth among their clients. Specifically, when they advertise the promise of a secret method for unlocking the supposedly inaccessible capacity.

Myth 2. Our left hemisphere is analytical, and our right hemisphere is holistic.

One persistent myth is that our left and right hemispheres operate in two completely different modes. According to the myth, the left hemisphere is analytical and the right hemisphere holistic. An additional myth is that some individuals are 'left brainers', that is, analytical, rational, and scientifically inclined, whereas others are 'right brainers', that is, creative and artistically inclined. Moreover, according to the myth, the two hemispheres are entangled in a perpetual conflict, in which the left hemisphere tends to dominate the right hemisphere (at least when you are right-handed).

One aspect of the myth is correct though: there is a certain level of hemispheric specialisation. Linguistic abilities tend to be associated with functions in the left hemisphere, while visuo-spatial functions are associated with the right hemisphere. It is, however, a complete myth that the two hemispheres process

(Continued)

Box 2.2 (Continued)

information in completely different ways, let alone that they are in conflict with each other. Finally, no evidence has been found to suggest a relation between the degree to which a hemisphere has been developed and an individual's preference for analytical or creative thinking. So, what is the origin of this myth?

The fact that there is a certain level of specialisation, combined with two early 20th-century ideas, might have given rise to the myth. The first idea, that of a conflict between the hemispheres, was popularised by practitioners of psychoanalysis in the early 20th century, who based their claim on the now completely debunked idea that the human psyche predominantly consisted of a massive amount of suppressed and conflicting urges. The second idea that has given rise to the notion of conflicting hemispheres is related to early studies of **split-brain patients** (Sperry, 1968). Since these patients' two hemispheres are disconnected from each other, it could occasionally be observed that they gave apparently conflicting answers. More recently, a more consistent picture of the brain has emerged, however, in which separate brain areas are considered to be part of a collaborative network. The myth is still popular, however, because it is frequently used in self-help management books as a Deux Ex Machina that has the potential of turning even the stiffest office clerk into a creative wonder boy, simply by unlocking their 'right-brain potential'.

Myth 3. After birth we can no longer generate new neurons.

This myth presumably originated from the fact that for many years we could not establish that the brain actually does generate new neurons after birth. It wasn't until 1998 that a Swedish team of researchers succeeded in determining that hippocampal neurons continue to develop well into adulthood (Eriksson et al., 1998). In 2014, this finding was replicated for the **striatum** (Ernst et al., 2014), and, in the same year, it was shown that neurogenesis, that is, the production of new neurons from stem cells, can affect memory (Akers et al., 2014). Even though neurogenesis is most likely not very abundant, it becomes increasingly clear that neural tissue can regenerate in a regular and controlled fashion.

Myth 4. Drinking alcohol kills off neurons.

One persistent myth is that each alcoholic beverage kills off a few thousand neurons. This idea was probably proposed to explain the symptoms of alcohol intoxication, at a time when the mechanisms of neural communication were still unknown. Currently, we know that these symptoms are caused by the fact that alcohol disrupts neurotransmitter functions. The Danish neurologists Jensen and Pakkenberg (1993) were the first to debunk the myth by comparing tissue samples from the brains of deceased alcoholics with those from a non-drinking control group. Jensen and Pakkenberg found no difference in neural density in the brain samples from the two groups. Excessive doses of alcohol can cause permanent tissue damage, specifically among young children or foetuses. Also, combined with unhealthy diets, prolonged drinking can induce a severe memory problem in adults, known as Korsakov's syndrome. In low to moderate doses, however, alcohol is unlikely to structurally damage mature brains.

Myth 5. Male brains are more suitable for mathematics, female brains for empathy.

There are subtle anatomical differences between male and female brains. For instance, the hippocampus, which is involved in the formation of memories, is generally somewhat larger in women than in men, whereas the amygdala, which is involved in emotions, is, in general, somewhat larger in men, compared to women. Despite these anatomical differences, differences in academic performance are more strongly related to cultural influences than to intrinsic differences in ability. In one remarkable study, men and women were asked to solve complex mathematical problems (Spencer, Steele, & Quinn, 1999). When participants were exposed to the stereotype that women are generally worse in math than men, it turned out that female participants' scores were indeed lower than the male participants' scores. This difference disappeared, however, when participants were informed that on average men and woman tended to score equally well on the test.

Myth 6. Solving puzzles is good for your memory.

One equally persistent myth that, for the record, is enthusiastically perpetuated by a large industry of game developers, is that solving puzzles has a beneficial effect on the brain, and that it improves a host of cognitive functions, specifically those related to working memory. The somewhat sobering answer, however, is that solving puzzles is only beneficial for (surprise!) the ability to solve puzzles. Pillai et al. (2011) found that frequent puzzle-solving activities appeared to delay the onset of Alzheimer's disease, but cautioned that this effect appeared to be only temporary. Even though solving puzzles can have a positive effect on cognitive functions, the key issue here is transfer: does the improvement of one cognitive skill transfer to a completely different domain? As it turns out, this transfer is rather limited and the claims in favour of transfer are, in most cases, either strongly exaggerated or, in many cases, rather far-fetched (Boot & Kramer, 2014).

2.3.9 ORGANISING PRINCIPLES OF THE CORTEX

2.3.9.1 Layers and Columns

The neurons making up the cortex are organised in a complex but systematic manner, consisting of layers and columns (see fig 2.14). The 2–3 mm thick cortex consists of six layers that can be distinguished from each other on the basis of the type of neurons and the type of connections with other cortical or subcortical areas. In addition, groups of neurons are organised into distinctive vertical columns which are perpendicular to the cortical surface and which can be distinguished from each other on the basis of their functional specialisation (Feldmeyer, 2010). The basic unit of such a column, the so-called microcolumn, consists of approximately 100 vertically connected neurons, spanning the six layers of the cortex. The organisation of each microcolumn is mostly uniform across the entire cortex. Every microcolumn consists of a number of target neurons that receive input from subcortical structures, such as the sensory or motor nuclei of the thalamus. These neurons are typically found in layers 4 and 5. A different group of target neurons receives input from other parts of the cortex. These neurons are mostly found in layer 3, many of them receiving interhemispheric input, thereby facilitating the communication between the left and right hemispheres. Local circuits connect neurons that are located within a microcolumn with each other. Finally, output neurons in layer 6 transmit information to the thalamus. Individual microcolumns can be interconnected, thus forming a full-fledged column.

2.3.9.2 Thalamic Synchronisation

Another major organising principle that we can find in the cortex is related to the fact that large areas of the cortex have reciprocal connections to the thalamus (Llinás, 2003; Llinás, Ribary, Contreras, & Pedroarena, 1998). As discussed previously, layers 4 and 5 of the cortical column receive input from the thalamus, while the same column projects its output to the thalamus from layer 6. Because the connections from the thalamus are projecting to large cortical areas, the thalamus can simultaneously activate a massive number of cortical neurons (see fig 2.15).

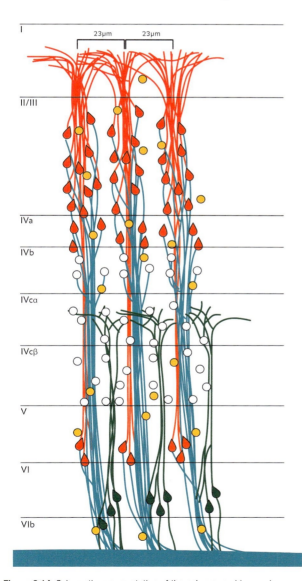

Figure 2.14 Schematic representation of the column- and layer-wise organisation of neurons within the cortex. (source: Mountcastle, 1997)

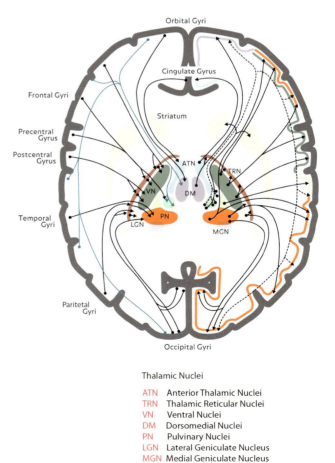

Thalamic Nuclei

ATN   Anterior Thalamic Nuclei
TRN   Thalamic Reticular Nuclei
VN   Ventral Nuclei
DM   Dorsomedial Nuclei
PN   Pulvinary Nuclei
LGN   Lateral Geniculate Nucleus
MGN   Medial Geniculate Nucleus

Figure 2.15 A schematic representation of the connections from the cortex to the thalamus (left half of the figure) and from the thalamus to the cortex (right half of the figure). (source: Ward, 2011)

Consequently, the firing patterns of neurons in layers 4 and 5 are largely synchronous, and this synchronous activity spreads throughout the entire cortical column. Ultimately, this causes the postsynaptic potentials of the involved neurons to synchronise. Because most neurons in a column have similar orientations, this synchronous activation results in a summation of all the individual electrical potentials, resulting in the fact that a net electrical potential difference exists that fluctuates at a rhythm that is driven by activity in the thalamus. The resulting electrical potential is strong enough to penetrate the skull and the dura, such that it can be measured from the scalp by using a pair of electrodes, manifesting itself as the electroencephalogram (EEG; see Box 2.3).

Its widespread connections make the thalamus an ideal candidate for synchronising the activation in widely distributed brain areas. Presumably, these **thalamo-cortical connections** play an important role in the integration of information from specialised modules, because they facilitate the information exchange between these modules (Tononi, 2004). Expanding upon this idea, it has also been suggested that the thalamus is critically involved in conscious awareness of this information (Ward, 2011).

Box 2.3 Electroencephalography

Two of the most peculiar properties of the brain are that neurons in the neocortex are organised into columns of similar orientation, and that large groups of neurons fire in simultaneous bursts. These two properties contribute to the fact that the electrical potentials that are elicited by each individual neuron are collectively strong enough to penetrate the skull, where they can be measured. This electrical brain activity was first recorded in 1924, in the form of an **electroencephalogram (EEG)**, by the German psychiatrist Hans Berger, although he published his findings only five years later (Berger, 1929).

Berger discovered that the EEG fluctuates with a certain regularity, at a frequency of about 10 Hz. This rhythm, the first one that was discovered in the EEG, is currently known as the alpha rhythm. Further important developments took place after the Second World War. In the 1950s, Penfield and Jasper (1954) discovered that transient spikes in the EEG signal were important predictors of epileptic seizures. In addition, it was found that alpha waves were strongly related to a person's level of wakefulness: in general, pronounced alpha waves are associated with a relaxed state of mind. Moreover, during this period, several other rhythms were discovered. The delta rhythm (<3 Hz) is predominantly present among young children, whereas adults elicit these waves mainly during deep sleep. The theta rhythm (3.5–7.5 Hz) is predominantly present in young children up to 13 years of age, whereas in adults they can also be found during sleep. The beta rhythm (14–30 Hz) is normally present in alert adults, and their presence has been related to an individual's level of alertness. Finally, the gamma rhythm (30–80 Hz) is strongly related to higher cognitive functions.

Even though the study of these rhythms has taught us a lot about the brain's dynamics, and has been specifically instrumental in understanding sleep, it had until recently taught us very little about cognition. To do so, we have to dig deeper into the EEG signal.

In addition to the spontaneously produced waves, the brain also generates an electric potential in response to an external event in the environment, such as a flash of light, a sound, or a touch of the skin. This was noted for the first time in the 1960s, when the American neurophysiologist Grey Walter and his colleagues noted that EEG signals were characterised by a negatively shifting electric potential when participants expected a stimulus to appear (Walter et al., 1964). In a similar fashion, other cognitive processes (i.e., making a decision or detecting an error) and motor processes (pressing a button) resulted in small changes in the electric potentials that the brain produces (Picton, Lins, & Scherg, 1995).

It is believed that the EEG signal, as it is measured, consists of a mix of spontaneous brain activity and activity that is evoked by a cognitive process. The latter part is typically too small to be noticed in the EEG recording, but it can be extracted relatively easily by repeatedly presenting the event that evokes the response, such as presenting a stimulus. Suppose we repeatedly present a flashing light for a grand total of 100 times. Now we can extract 100 epochs of EEG activity that directly follow the presentation of each flash and calculate an average EEG signal from these 100 responses. Because the spontaneous EEG fluctuates randomly from presentation to presentation, it will eventually cancel out in the averaging process. The EEG activity that is evoked by the flash will be more or less constant from presentation to presentation, which is why it will become visible as the average response to the flash.

By applying this procedure, we are eventually left with an **event-related potential** (ERP). ERPs are typically

(Continued)

Box 2.3 (Continued)

composed of several characteristic positive and negative waves, which are known as components. These components can be classified by their polarity, and the **latency** at which the component reaches its peak amplitude. For instance, the P300 is a positive peak that reaches its maximum amplitude approximately 300 ms after the presentation of the evoking stimulus. Likewise, the N400 is a negative peak with a latency of 400 ms after stimulus presentation. Sometimes, a rank order is used instead of a latency. For example, P1 is used to describe the first positive peak in the ERP.

ERPs have provided many new insights into a large number of cognitive processes, ranging from attention and perceptual processes to the processing of errors, to language processing. One major strength of the ERP method is that it allows us to track neural processes with a millisecond accuracy. The **temporal resolution** of EEG is therefore very high. A known limitation, however, is EEG's limited **spatial resolution**: in neurotypical participants, EEGs are recorded on the outside of the head, requiring the electrical potentials to penetrate the skull. Because the skull distorts the distribution of the electrical potentials significantly, it is impossible to determine exactly where in the brain they originated. Despite these limitations, it is possible to estimate these locations via advanced statistical models (Tzovara, Murray, Michel, & De Lucia, 2012).

A second limitation of the ERP method follows from the assumption that the evoked potentials are more or less constant from trial to trial. Moreover, it is currently still unclear what the exact neural basis of ERPs is. Initially, it was believed that ERP activity was evoked by an external stimulus. Thus, it was believed that it resembled additional activity that was mixed in with the ongoing spontaneous brain activity. Alternatively, it is possible that ERPs reflect changes in this spontaneous activity (Makeig et al., 2002). According to the latter view, spontaneous brain activity tends to synchronise with the presentation of a stimulus, causing this activity to remain present after signal averaging. It is still an open question how ERPs are generated; however, the synchronisation hypothesis emphasises the fact that neural processes are dynamic, causing a shift in electrophysiological research, from ERPs to the study of cortical **oscillations**.

In this context, oscillations are rhythmic patterns of cortical activity. Modern electrophysiological research focuses, among other areas, on determining how different neural rhythms are involved in cognitive processes and how these rhythms are interrelated (Dustman & Beck, 1965; Palva & Palva, 2007; VanRullen, 2016). This type of research has contributed to our understanding of the role of consciousness in cognition (Hunt, 2011).

One specific application of this technique is based on the fact that oscillations can be induced by repeatedly presenting a stimulus at one specific frequency (for instance, by repeatedly presenting it at a rate of 8 per second). This presentation results in EEG-activity at the same frequency, resulting in a wave that is known as the steady-state evoked potential (SSEP), or in case of a visual stimulus as a steady-state visual evoked potential (SSVEP). The amplitude of this SSEP is typically enlarged when it is attended, allowing us to use this technique to study how stimulus processing is affected by attention.

Despite the fact that EEG research is among the oldest methods available for studying the brain, it is one of the most frequently used methods, and one of the most dynamic and innovative methods available for studying the relation between brain and behaviour. EEG research is not only strongly represented in fundamental brain research but also frequently used in applied research, including lie detection and brain–computer interfaces (see Chapter 24). Both fields take advantage of one specific property of the P300 ERP component. The P300 is relatively easy to record and is relatively pronounced when evoked by a stimulus that bears special relevance to the observer.

Lie detection techniques take advantage of this property by presenting a series of images, including one that bears relevance to a crime scene, such as a photo of a murder weapon, to a suspect. When a suspect recognises the weapon, this results in an increased amplitude of the P300 component. Although proponents of this technique claim that this method is exceedingly effective, its reliability is currently not high enough to be used as evidence in a court case. For instance, it has been shown that training in using specific cognitive strategies allows participants to control the amplitude of their P300 wave (Rosenfeld, Soskins, Bosh, & Ryan, 2004).

The principles just described can be used in a more straightforward fashion in the design of a brain–computer interface. When brain lesions prevent effective communication, patients can use a system where a sequence of letters is presented. Whenever a letter is presented that the patient wants to select, an enlarged P300 is detected, which can be decoded using a computer. This way, the patient can formulate a message by selectively thinking about different letters. Likewise, the patient can instruct the computer to perform a certain action.

2.4 FUNCTIONAL CHARACTERISTICS OF THE BRAIN

2.4.1 HIERARCHICAL NETWORKS

Major parts of the brain are characterised by hierarchically organised circuits. These circuits can, among other things, be found in the sensory and motor pathways of the brain. In the sensory systems, they are composed of chains of neurons that send information upward to the brain. Originating from the sensory receptors, these signals pass through a chain of relay centres to the primary sensory cortices. For the motor system, these pathways consist of downward projecting chains of neurons that pass information from the brain, again via a chain of relay centres, to the muscles.

Information can be passed with high levels of accuracy in such a hierarchically organised chain. The principles of convergence and divergence are important in controlling the precision of this information. Convergence involves a large group of neurons at one level communicating with a smaller group of neurons at the next level, whereas divergence involves a small number of neurons at one level communicating with a larger group of neurons at the next level. Both principles are involved in effectively filtering and amplifying specific signals. An additional advantage of these principles is that they make the network resilient against damage. Damage to parts of the circuit can be compensated for by the redundancy that is built into the circuit.

2.4.2 ORGANISATION OF NETWORKS

How are the individual networks interconnected? According to Bullmore and Sporns (2012), there are two important principles involved in regulating energy consumption and spatial organisation in the brain. These are the principles of cost reduction and efficiency. Costs, in terms of energy use and brain volume, would be minimised when networks are composed of a limited number of relatively short connections. An efficient brain, on the other hand, would consist of a large number of connections, across short and long distances. These two principles conflict with each other, however, because an efficient organisation would come at the cost of a high energy consumption and an extensive volume, and vice versa. As a consequence, the brain has developed an optimal compromise between these two principles, in the sense that it is reasonably efficient in terms of organisation, while keeping costs, in terms of energy consumption and brain volume, at bay. As a consequence, neural organisation principles have evolved that are marked by networks consisting of separate modules that are interconnected via hubs. These hubs correspond with brain areas that have been identified to be involved in higher cognition and conscious awareness (see Chapters 4 and 5). The hubs themselves can be subdivided into two separate subtypes, known as "rich club" and "bow tie" hubs. Rich club hubs are characterised by the fact that they are richly interconnected with other brain areas, whereas bow tie hubs are characterised by two or more peripheral areas that are interconnected via a central hub (Markov et al., 2013).

2.4.3 FEEDFORWARD AND FEEDBACK CONNECTIONS

Finally, neural networks are hierarchically organised in the sense that the areas involved in perceptual analysis along with those involved in motor control can be subdivided into primary, secondary, and associative areas. The areas that are involved in perceptual analysis are typically located in the posterior parts of the brain, whereas the areas that are involved in task performance and the maintenance of a mental representation are typically localised in the anterior parts of the brain (Fuster, 2007). These networks are connected with each other via a number of intermediary networks that form increasingly more abstract representations of a person's environment. Feedforward connections link a network to a higher level of representation, whereas recurrent (or feedback) connections link to a lower level.

2.4.4 HEBBIAN LEARNING

One important property of the brain is its ability to learn. The brain can accomplish this through a principle known as **Hebbian learning**, named after the famous Canadian neuroscientist Donald Hebb. The principle states that the efficiency of a synaptic connection increases when a presynaptic cell repeatedly stimulates a postsynaptic cell (Hebb, 1949). Even though the Hebbian learning principle is frequently summarised with the expression 'What fires together, wires together', this summary is not completely accurate. One important condition for the increase in activity (and thus the connection between the cells) is causality, requiring the presynaptic cell to fire slightly earlier than the postsynaptic cell.

According to Hebb, the neurons that are connected according to these principles form networks that are known as **cell assemblies**. Presently, this term mostly refers to groups of neurons that are involved in the execution of specific actions, or cells that represent a specific concept.

2.4.5 DEFAULT MODE ACTIVITY

The last type of network that we need to discuss was discovered more or less by accident around the turn of the century. Raichle et al. (2001) reported the existence of an extensive network of brain areas that became less active during the execution of a mental task compared to a resting state. This network, which involved areas in the ventro medial prefrontal cortex and the posterior cingulate cortex, was discovered because neuroscientific studies at the time typically compared brain activity during task execution with baseline levels of activation, while participants were resting. Because the underlying assumption in much

fMRI research at the time was that brain activation should increase during task performance (see Box 2.4), Raichle et al. were surprised to find that mental tasks could actually cause a decrease in activation in the aforementioned areas. Because the identified areas appeared to be more active during rest than during a task, it was hypothesised

Box 2.4 fMRI: images of the brain

The foundation for one of the most influential brain imaging techniques was laid down towards the end of the 19th century by an Italian physiologist named Angelo Mosso (1846–1910). Mosso was the inventor of a device that allowed him to measure blood pressure differences in the brains of patients with brain injuries (Lin, Gao, & Fox, 2012). The greater this pressure difference, the stronger the blood flow in a specific area. Mosso's most famous observation concerned a 37-year-old farmer named Michele Bertino, who had suffered a serious skull fracture that exposed parts of his brain. While measuring Bertino's blood pressure differences, Mosso discovered a pulsation that increased in amplitude whenever Bertino was executing a mental task, such as listening to the sound of a church bell or engaging in mental arithmetic. Interestingly, this increase was found only in the brain, and not at a control position at the hand, which made Mosso conclude that the increase in blood flow was specific to the brain, presumably because the mental task required additional oxygen and glucose.

The British physiologists Roy and Sherrington (1890) have expanded upon this idea and concluded that the increase in activity in a specific brain area is associated to a regional increase in blood flow. **Functional magnetic resonance imaging** (fMRI) is a technique that takes advantage of this principle to measure brain activity. Magnetic resonance imaging (without the prefix 'functional') allows us to make detailed images of the brain. Even though it is intuitively attractive to equate an MRI scan with a three-dimensional photograph of the brain, this analogy is, strictly speaking, not correct. MRI measures the density of specific molecules in the brain, from which a computer reconstructs a three-dimensional image.

To do so, participants are positioned in a strong magnetic field which causes (a part of) the nuclei of the atoms that comprise the body's tissues to spin in a direction that is parallel to the magnetic field lines. Then, a brief radio frequency pulse is directed at the participant's brain, causing a disturbance in the atom's orientation, causing the spinning atoms to wobble. The wobbling atoms tend to realign themselves again with the magnetic field (note that this explanation is

somewhat simplified; a quantum physicist might point out that it does not exactly work this way). In doing so, they produce a radio signal in themselves which can be detected by a receiver that is placed outside the scanner. These radio signals are fed into a computer that converts the spin information into a location and an intensity. The location of the spinning atom can be determined because a gradient is introduced into the magnetic field. This gradient will force the affected atoms to spin at frequencies that vary in function of their location: the stronger the magnetic field, the higher the spinning frequency, and thus the frequency of the radio signal they emit. The frequency of the radio signal that is received is therefore location-dependent, allowing a signal analysis technique known as Fourier Transformation to convert the mix of radio frequencies into a density map.

A high-resolution MRI scan can take about ten minutes to complete. Even though this allows us to obtain extremely detailed images of the brain, such an acquisition time is way too long to measure short-lived changes in regional blood flow in the brain. To work around this, we can also obtain sequences of somewhat courser snapshots that only require about one second or less to complete, allowing us to track changes in blood flow with an approximate one-second resolution. Initially, much fMRI research focused on determining which brain areas were active in a given task. More contemporary research, however, has shifted its focus to determining the dynamic interactions among various cognitive processes (Bolton, Morgenroth, Preti, & Van De Ville, 2020).

In an experimental setting, fMRI can be used to measure the brain's blood flow while participants are involved in an intense mental task, which lasts for a couple of minutes. These data can then be compared to a control condition where the participants are resting. We can now mark every brain area where the blood flow was significantly higher during task performance with a colour, resulting in a statistical activation map of the brain. Next, we can superimpose this activation map on a detailed anatomical scan, to allow a relatively easy visual inspection.

(Continued)

Box 2.4 (Continued)

Although fMRI allows us to precisely determine where activation levels change in function of a mental task, it is difficult to determine the time course of these changes: the brain's metabolic response is relatively slow, and the scans are taken at a rate of approximately one per second. In other words, the spatial resolution of fMRI is high, but its temporal resolution is low. This problem of low temporal resolution was specifically true for traditional fMRI methods, where participants were required to conduct one specific task for a block of several seconds and then another task during another block lasting several seconds. Using this approach, the fMRI signals were aggregated across an entire block. This so-called **block design** has subsequently been supplemented by an **event-related design**, where trials from different conditions are presented in a random order. Because participants now switch between conditions much more frequently, the temporal resolution can be increased from tens of seconds to a few seconds or less.

In addition to the limited temporal resolution, there are a number of additional limitations known to fMRI. Collecting accurate data requires participants to lay still inside a narrow tube, which makes participation relatively exhausting, and unsuitable for claustrophobic participants. In addition, fMRI scanners are relatively noisy when they are in operation, requiring participants to wear ear protection. This makes the scanning procedure somewhat less suitable for studies using auditory stimuli, even though in recent years some procedures have been developed to mitigate this problem.

Despite these limitations, the fMRI technique has been extremely successful in the past decennia. As such, it has provided an invaluable contribution to our understanding of the neural basis of most cognitive processes. fMRI has been at the forefront of the maturation of the cognitive neurosciences, and it is currently still one of the most frequently used techniques to study the living brain.

---

that they are involved in activities that we typically engage in while resting, such as contemplating our lives, thinking about others, or imagining our futures (Andrews-Hanna, Smallwood, & Spreng, 2014). Because the network is mainly active when we are not engaged in specific tasks, it is known as the **default mode network**.

Since its discovery, it has been found that the default mode network is likely to consist of three interconnected networks (see fig 2.16). The first network is considered to be the core of the system and comprises a network of frontal and temporal cortical areas that are involved in self-referential processes, that is, processes that are related to thinking about ourselves, evaluating our values in life, and recollecting personal (autobiographical) memories. The second network is considered to be a subsystem and consists of a network of dorsal medial areas that are (in interaction with the core) involved in positioning ourselves in social situations along with imagining somebody else's perspective and evaluating this perspective. The third network is also considered to be a subsystem and consists of a medial temporal network. This network also operates in interaction with the core, and it is mainly involved in the processing of personal autobiographical memories. These memories will not only be retrieved but also used as input for the generation of possible future scenarios (Andrews-Hanna et al., 2014; Thakral et al., 2017). The default mode network does not operate independently of the rest of the brain, however. Uddin, Kelly, Biswal, Castellanos, and Milham (2009) reported a complex interaction between parts of

the default mode network and task-specific networks. Finally, in a recent literature review, Yeshurun, Nguyen, and Hasson (2021) argued that the default mode network is not only involved in self-referential processes, but that it also plays a crucial role in social processes that represent a social environment that is shared between the individual and others.

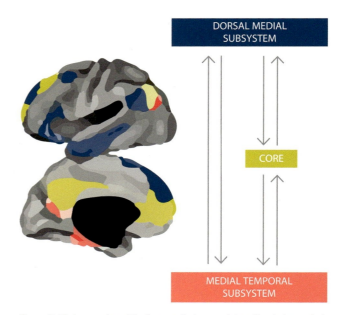

Figure 2.16 An overview of brain areas that are mainly active during periods of rest. This default mode network is presumed to consist of a core and two subsystems. (source: Andrews-Hanna et al., 2014)

2.5 OUR PREDICTIVE BRAIN

Now that we have introduced the most important anatomical and physiological principles, we will revisit the influential theoretical framework that we already briefly introduced in Chapter 1. The predictive coding framework has the potential to explain a host of functions, ranging from simple acts, such as moving our hands, to processing language, to understanding the intentions of others (Adams, Shipp, & Friston, 2013; Clark, 2013; Friston, 2010; Friston, Adams, Perrinet, & Breakspear, 2012; Hobson & Friston, 2014; Kilner, Friston, & Frith, 2007; Lupyan & Clark, 2015; Rao & Ballard, 1999; Shipp, Adams, & Friston, 2013). As we already briefly introduced in the previous chapter, the framework is based on the notion that our brains create an internal **generative model** of our environment. A generative model is like an internal simulation of our environment that is actively generated by the brain. This model is continually corrected on the basis of sensory input that we perceive via our eyes, ears, touch, taste, smell, along with the internal sensory organs that monitor the state of the body.

A key feature of the predictive coding framework is that it is hierarchically organised. Accordingly, higher-order representations generate predictions with respect to what should be expected at lower levels in the hierarchy. Even though the basic premises for the predictive coding framework were formulated in the early 21st century, some ideas that form the inspiration for it can be traced back all the way to the pioneering days of psychology, in the late 19th century. For example, Helmholtz (1860) already coined the idea that internal mental representations can strongly influence our perception.

2.5.1 THE HIERARCHICAL BRAIN

The idea of multiple, hierarchically organised levels of representation is consistent with an overwhelming amount of neuroscientific evidence. Consider, for example, the motor system. It is believed that the intention to make a movement starts to take shape in a part of the frontal lobe that is known as the premotor area (Jeannerod, 1994). Subsequently, the planning of the intended movement occurs in the primary motor cortex, on the basis of input from the anterior cingulate cortex and the parietal cortex. Here, the anterior cingulate cortex is mainly involved in choosing between different alternative responses, while the parietal cortex contains a spatial representation of our environment. Input from the parietal cortex thus adjusts a person's action plan on the basis of perceived changes in their environment. Further fine-tuning of the action plan then takes place in a host of subcortical nuclei, including the basal ganglia and the cerebellum, where eventually the precise motor commands are generated that are controlling the muscles.

For visual perception, we can identify a similar hierarchy. The visual cortex can, for example, be subdivided into a number of anatomically distinct areas that are more or less specialised in processing specific aspects of the visual information stream (see Chapter 6). The primary visual cortex, where the initial processing of visual information takes place, is specifically associated with representing basic properties of a visual scene. For instance, neurons in this area respond to specific patterns of light, or to lines at specific orientations (Hubel & Wiesel, 1962, 1979), while neurons at higher levels in the hierarchy respond to progressively more complex and abstract properties. In other words, the higher a brain area is in the hierarchy, the more complex the property are that neurons in this area respond to. As such, areas have been identified where neurons respond to colour (Goddard, Mannion, McDonald, Solomon, & Clifford, 2011), motion (McKeefry, Watson, Frackowiak, Fong, & Zeki, 1997), complete shapes or objects (Zoccolan, Kouh, Poggio, & DiCarlo, 2007), faces (Kanwisher, McDermott, & Chun, 1997), or even categories of stimuli (Kourtzi & Connor, 2011).

Auditory perception also proceeds along similar lines. The auditory cortex can be subdivided into a primary area, where basic sound properties, such as pitch and intensity, are represented (Pantev, Hoke, Lütkenhöner, & Lehnertz, 1989), and an array of higher-level areas representing progressively more complex properties of sounds, such as tone sequences (Kaas, Hackett, & Tramo, 1999), vocalisations (Petkov et al., 2008), complex natural or environmental sounds (Griffiths & Warren, 2002), or even the syntactic structure of language (Humphries, Love, Swinney, & Hickok, 2005; see Chapter 17).

2.5.2 BOTTOM-UP VERSUS TOP-DOWN PROCESSING

Classic theories of cognition have excessively focused on bottom-up processing. This excessive focus, however, has frequently created more problems than it has solved. Explanations that are exclusively based on bottom-up processing have had great difficulty explaining how we can effortlessly recognise objects, despite the wide variety of viewing conditions that introduce variations in size, lighting, viewing angle, or context. Moreover, bottom-up driven models of cognition have significant difficulties in explaining how the specialised output from different visual areas, which are specialised in processing colour, motion, or shapes, can be combined into a unified integrated percept of a person's environment.

Many of these problems can be resolved by considering the role of top-down processes, and by assuming that these processes generate ever more specific and more concrete predictions at progressively lower levels in the hierarchy. The basic idea here is that the highest levels of the cortical hierarchy actively generate internal models of our environment, which predict what should be represented one level below. This lower level, in turn, generates predictions for what should be represented at the next level, and so on. If we approach cognition from this perspective, our senses become part of an error-correction mechanism, which does nothing more than adjust the representation at the lowest levels in the hierarchy by detecting the mismatch between prediction and reality. Based on this prediction error, the representation at the lowest level of the hierarchy will be updated. The updated representation will now also push its prediction error one level up the hierarchy. The final result is an interactive cascade of top-down and bottom-up processes, in which a stream of predictions is generated by top-down processes which are continuously corrected by a stream of bottom-up driven prediction errors.

One key feature of a predictive coding mechanism is that it is an extremely data efficient mechanism. The mathematical foundations of the framework are, after all, strongly rooted in the data compression techniques that are employed in signal analysis (see Box 1.4). To illustrate this, consider the case where we want to transmit a digital photograph across a data network. In this case, we can – to a large degree – predict the value of a given pixel from the value of its neighbours. After all, sharp deviations between two adjacent pixels are indicative of an edge, while most surfaces are more or less uniformly coloured. For this reason, it is typically more efficient to transmit only the deviation from the expected value across the network than to transmit the raw pixel value. This approach is therefore also the basis of many lossless audio or image transmission protocols, such as live video streams. In these cases, the information that is sent upstream consists of deviations from the prediction, or – in other words – the prediction error. In neural systems, we can consider these prediction errors to be a proxy for the real sensory information that is being processed (Friston & Feldman, 2010).

2.5.3 BAYESIAN PRINCIPLES

How can the brain possibly use these predictions to generate internal models of our environment? To answer this question, we need to briefly introduce Bayesian inference. Bayesian inference, named after the British Presbyterian minister, statistician, and philosopher Thomas Bayes (1701–1761), describes how probability estimates should be adjusted in light of new evidence (see the Appendix for

a more formal description). According to Bayes theorem, the probability of a certain outcome can be estimated on the basis of a priori knowledge. When new evidence becomes available, however, our a priori estimate needs to be adjusted on the basis of this evidence, resulting in a new a posteriori estimate. In Bayesian terms, our a priori estimate is known as a 'prior' and the new a posteriori estimate as a 'posterior'. The result of this estimation process can be expressed as a **probability density function**. This function describes the likelihood that a specific event (Y) will occur as a function of an observed variable (X).

Although it is currently still unclear how concepts are represented in our brains, we can try to illustrate the probability density function using a simplified example. Suppose that we are presenting an object, while we are recording the observers' brain activity in an area that is known to be involved in object recognition. For the sake of our example, a strong increase in activity in this area corresponds with the perception of a porcelain coffee mug, while a lower level of activity corresponds to the perception of a plastic cup.[2] The neural activity in this area is, in other words, indicative of the representation that is currently active: the closer the actual activity is to one of the peaks of the curves, the more likely it is that the corresponding object is perceived, relative to the other object. Via recurrent connections to lower levels, the corresponding details of the dominant representation will be activated, and this process will cascade all the way down to the bottom of the hierarchy.

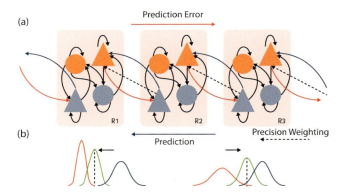

Figure 2.17 The neural basis of predictive coding. (a) Predictions are generated at all levels of the cortical hierarchy, here schematically represented as three levels: low (R1), intermediate (R2), and high (R3). Each of these levels is associated with a specific brain area. Predictions are passed from the higher levels to the lower levels, where they are compared to actual sensory input. The mismatch between prediction and input will be passed, in the form of a prediction error, to the higher levels. The effectiveness of these prediction errors is regulated by weighting the estimated precision of the prediction error. Triangles represent pyramidal neurons; circles represent inhibitory interneurons. (b) The influence of precision of the Bayesian inference method. The curves represent the probability density functions of a sensory signal (see Appendix). On the left, we find a highly reliable sensory signal (red) having a strong positive impact on the reliability of the Bayesian posterior (green), compared to the prior (blue). The impact of less reliable percept (right) has a negative impact on the posterior. (source: Seth, 2013)

Now, suppose that we are entering a room containing a coffee mug. Because we have never been in this room before, we have no prior expectation of it. Our initial scan of the room results in a visual impression of the outline of a coffee cup, but since we had no prior expectation, the visual signal will be passed on, in the form of a prediction error, which eventually results in the activation of our hypothetical object recognition brain area. Based on this initial sweep of activation, it cannot distinguish between the two alternative representations, namely that of the porcelain mug or the plastic cup. The plastic cup representation would, however, generate predictions at lower representation levels that are clearly inconsistent with the actual input, such as a dull white object with ribs and a thin surface. In contrast, the porcelain mug representation would generate predictions that are more in agreement with the actual input, such as the presence of a handle, a thicker wall, and a shiny surface. Because the 'porcelain mug' predictions are more consistent with the actual input, compared to the 'plastic cup' predictions, their prediction error is also smaller. As a consequence, the evidence shifts in favour of the porcelain mug. Neural activation in the hypothetical object recognition area will therefore shift towards the level representing the porcelain cup; consequently, this is the representation that becomes dominant.

From a predictive coding perspective, most cognitive processes can be conceived of as mechanisms involved in reducing uncertainty in the internal representation. For instance, attending to specific features of an object is believed to increase the weight that is given to the corresponding prediction errors, with the effect that the corresponding aspects of a relevant object are represented with a higher level of certainty (Seth, 2013). Expressed in Bayesian terms, this implies that the probability density function becomes sharper (see fig. 2.17). To illustrate this, when you are supposed to meet a friend at a busy festival, you will most likely attend to your friend's face and/or specific clothes that your friend will be wearing. The consequence is that you activate a strong representation of your friend, with the effect that each person you encounter, before meeting your friend, yields a strong prediction error. When you finally meet your friend, his or her representation will be strongly activated, facilitating immediate recognition.

Note that the preceding sections have predominantly related predictions to top-down processing, and prediction error processing to bottom-up processing. Recently, Teufel and Fletcher (2020) have argued that while this notion is not necessarily incorrect, it might be incomplete. They argue that regularities that are embedded in the environment, such as for example all the orientation cues in a visual scene, may also be considered as a form of prediction and that any predictive coding theory must account for these types of bottom-up predictions.

Clark (2013) identifies several phenomena where the predictive coding framework's explanatory power outshines the classical theories. Next, we will introduce two examples of these phenomena, namely delusions and hallucinations, on the one hand, and mental imagery on the other.

2.5.3.1 Hallucinations and Delusions

In recent years, we have seen the emergence of an impressive amount of literature that successfully explained key mechanisms of hallucinations and delusions (Allen, Laroi, McGuire, & Aleman, 2008; Corlett, Krystal, Taylor, & Fletcher, 2009; Fletcher & Frith, 2009a). According to Clark (2013), we must start with a normal, but unexpected, situation if we want to understand these abnormal functions. Imagine attending the performance of an illusionist, who suddenly – and unexpectedly – tricks us into believing that an elephant has appeared out of nowhere. Apparently, this experience is difficult to explain on the basis of a predictive coding mechanism. Since we had no a priori expectation of the elephant, it would require an extremely strong error signal for us to activate the representation of the elephant. Under the right circumstances, however, that is, in the presence of a strong visual signal and a strong precision weighing of the error signal, we can adjust our internal representation such that it becomes consistent with our sensory input (much like the way we recognised the coffee mug in our previous example). A strong mismatch between our a priori expectation and the real-world sensory data may thus result in a major update of our model, and the actual updating may be accompanied by a subjective feeling of surprise.

We can, however, also imagine a situation where the actual sensory input cannot result in an adequate internal representation. This may occur, for instance, when we have no representation of the actual input yet. Now, our sensory information needs to be embedded into a new internal model, which can presumably only be forged by a slow process of repeated exposure (as is the case during learning). According to Fletcher and Frith (2009a), this process can be of crucial importance for our understanding of hallucinations and delusions. Two different but related mechanisms may be involved here, with each of them manifesting their own deficiencies. A deficiency in the perceptual mechanisms may be responsible for inducing hallucinations, while another deficiency at the higher levels of the hierarchy may allow these distorted perceptions to enter the internal representations, thus allowing the formation of dysfunctional convictions and thoughts.

A link between these two mechanisms can be found by assuming that they are both involved in matching incoming sensory stimuli to top-down predictions. It is important to note that this matching process is modulated by a precision weighting mechanism. The more confidence the brain has in the accuracy of the incoming signal, the stronger the weight that is given to the prediction error. From this perspective, it is interesting to consider the consequences of an error in this precision weighting mechanism; specifically so when the error signals are false and weighed too strongly (Fletcher & Frith, 2009a). Deficiencies in the slow metabotropic neurotransmitter systems (such as the dopaminergic, serotonergic, and acetylchonergic systems), along with deficiencies in the synchronisation across local neural populations, may contribute to an incorrect weighting of the error signal. Consequently, the brain areas higher up in the hierarchy are flooded with incorrect error messages, resulting in a forced adjustment of the higher-order mental representations, which no longer correspond with the actual sensory input.

The process now runs the risk of becoming self-reinforcing: the new generative models that are now out of tune with reality send bogus predictions back to the lower areas, such that the new sensory predictions data are now modelled on the basis of hopelessly incorrect priors. These false percepts and bizarre convictions will now form an isolated self-reinforcing mechanism. Comparable mechanisms may also explain how hallucinogenic drugs can temporarily induce the symptoms of hallucinations and delusions.

2.5.3.2 Mental Imagery

A second, but somewhat less dramatic aspect of human cognition can also be explained by these predictive processes. It concerns the interplay between cognition, memory, perception, and **mental imagery**. One crucial feature of all these processes is that they are generative. That is, higher-level predictive mechanisms (i.e., retrieving a memory or imagining a hypothetical situation) generate activation in lower-level brain areas (revisualising a memory or imagining an upcoming exam for example). The predictive coding mechanism is not only capable of learning to recognise objects from sensory input, but it can also generate these percepts itself by activating the lower-level neurons via predictions that are derived from activated higher-order representation. We currently have an enormous amount of evidence consistent with the idea that generating a mental image activates the visual areas in our occipital cortex (Kosslyn, 1999; Kosslyn, Ganis, & Thompson, 2001; Reddy, Tsuchiya, & Serre, 2010). The generative models that are capable of learning to represent – say – a cat are, according to the logic of the predictive coding mechanism, also capable of generating the same activation patterns that correspond to the actual perception of a cat, via a top-down cascade of predictions, and – presumably – by inhibiting the error correction signals from our senses.

In a similar vein, internal generative models can also explain how information from multiple senses interacts (see Chapter 9 for an elaborate discussion). Vetter, Smith, and Muckli (2014) showed, for example, that the presentation of sounds, along with requiring participants to imagine these sounds, influenced activation in the visual cortex. One particularly interesting aspect of this study was that the activation patterns in the visual cortex corresponded to the higher-order semantic aspects of the sounds. Different categories of sounds, such as child play versus aircraft taking off, resulted in considerably different activation patterns in the visual cortex, whereas different samples of the same categories (for example, two different instances of busy traffic) did not. These results strongly suggest that the sounds that were presented activated a higher-order mental representation, which resulted in the generation of a mental image of the corresponding visual scenes, such as children playing, aircraft taking off, or a busy intersection.

2.5.4 CONCLUSIONS

The predictive coding framework, as introduced here, offers a wealth of possibilities for explaining a wide variety of empirical findings, ranging from perception and action control to the impact of attention and background knowledge on our thoughts and actions, to hallucinations and delusions. Because Bayesian principles can naturally explain the statistical uncertainty that is intrinsic to a mental representation, predictive coding has occasionally been referred to as a grand unifying theory of brain function. We need to be cautious, however. The exact mechanisms underlying the mechanism just outlined are still not fully known, and it is also not yet clear how many of the wide variety of cognitive functions that we will introduce in the next chapters will be compatible with a predictive coding account. For this reason, predictive coding will not yet be substituted for the classic cognitive theories that have been developed to explain specific aspects of human behaviour.

2.6 IN CLOSING

The human brain is presumably one of the most complex structures in the known universe, and therefore it may not come as a surprise that this chapter only covers a tiny bit of our current knowledge about it. The current introduction should provide sufficient information, however, to allow you to relate the psychological functions that we introduce next to the current state of affairs in cognitive neuroscience. Some additional details about specific neural processes will be introduced in the next chapters, where relevant (for instance, details of the motor system in Chapter 3; higher cognitive functions in Chapters 4 and 5; and perceptual systems in Chapters 6, 7, and 8).

2.7 SUMMARY

Neurons form the most important communication units of the brain, being cells that are specialised in transmitting messages to each other by way of an electrochemical process. In addition to a soma, they consist of one or more dendrites and a single axon. The terminal of an axon is connected to another neuron via a synapse. Neurons are normally electrically charged. The discharge of a neuron results in the generation of an action potential. At the axon terminal, the action potential triggers the release of neurotransmitters. Neurotransmitters can increase or decrease the polarisation of a receiving neuron, thus reducing or increasing the probability that it will generate an action potential itself.

The nervous system consists of a central brain and a peripheral nervous system regulating the flow of information to and from the body. The peripheral nervous system consists of a somatic nervous system and an autonomic nervous system. The autonomic nervous system regulates, among other things, internal organ functioning, and consists of a sympathetic and parasympathetic nervous system. The somatic nervous system consists of a sensory part and a motor part.

The brain itself is composed of the hindbrain, midbrain, and forebrain. The hindbrain is predominantly involved in regulating autonomous bodily functions, such as heart rate, breathing, and the activation of our internal organs. The midbrain is, among other things, involved in regulating our level of arousal, and it includes important nuclei that are involved in programming eye movements, integrating auditory and visual information, and transmitting auditory signals to the cortex.

The forebrain is composed of several important nuclei that collectively form the cerebrum. The cerebrum consists of two, approximately equally sized hemispheres. The outer layer of the cerebrum is known as the cerebral cortex; this is the part of the brain that is mostly associated with higher cognitive functions. The cortex can be subdivided into four lobes that are characterised by specialised functions. In addition to the cortex, the cerebrum consists of a several subcortical nuclei. Of these, the thalamus plays an important role in establishing the communication between large areas of the cortex. The cortex itself is characterised by a layer and column structure.

Functionally, the brain is characterised by different types of neuronal networks. The reticular activation system is involved in the general state regulation of the brain and in regulating the level of awareness. Communication in the brain takes place on the basis of an interaction between higher and lower order networks. Higher-order representations generate predictions that are projected, via recurrent connections, to lower-order networks where they are combined with actual sensory input. The brain is adaptive because Hebbian learning principles allow that the strengths of the connections between neurons can be dynamically adapted.

Large parts of the brain are spontaneously active during our normal waking lives, and a part of this activation is reduced when we focus on a task. This spontaneous activity has been related to everyday thoughts about ourselves, others, and reflecting upon our past and future.

The predictive coding framework stipulates that our brains are actively generating an internal representation of our environment along with the possible ways in which we can interact with this environment. According to the framework, the internal models are updated on the basis of sensory input, which is used as an error signal that informs the models of how they should be updated. This takes place in a hierarchically ordered system where the higher levels generate predictions for the lower levels, and where the lower levels are correcting the higher ones, based on actual sensory input.

NOTES

1 These anatomical terms are generic across species, resulting in a correspondence between 'top side' and 'back side'. Because we humans have assumed an upright position during the course of our evolution, this correspondence is somewhat lost for our species. The top side of the human brain is still considered to be dorsal, in order to describe the brain in terms that are consistent with those of other species.

2 It is more likely that a representation is formed by the activation *pattern* in a neuronal network, instead of the activation *level*. The precise details of this mechanism are still not known, however, and for the sake of our example, activation level will suffice.

FURTHER READING

Banich, M. T., & Compton, R. J. (2018). *Cognitive neuroscience*. Cambridge, MA: Cambridge University Press.

Churchland, P. S., & Sejnowski, T. J. (1992). *The computational brain*. Cambridge, MA: The MIT Press.

Bloom, F. E., & Lazeron, A. (1988). *Brain, mind, and behavior*. New York, NY: W.H. Freeman and Company.

Kalat, J. W. (2019). *Biological psychology* (13th ed.). Boston, MA: Cengage Learning, Inc.

Kandel, E. R., Schwartz, J. H., & Jessell, T. M. (2012). *Principles of neural science*. Norwalk, CT: Appleton & Lange.

Verstynen, T., & Voytek, B. (2014). *Do zombies dream of undead sheep? A neuroscientific view of the zombie brain*. Princeton, NJ: Princeton University Press.

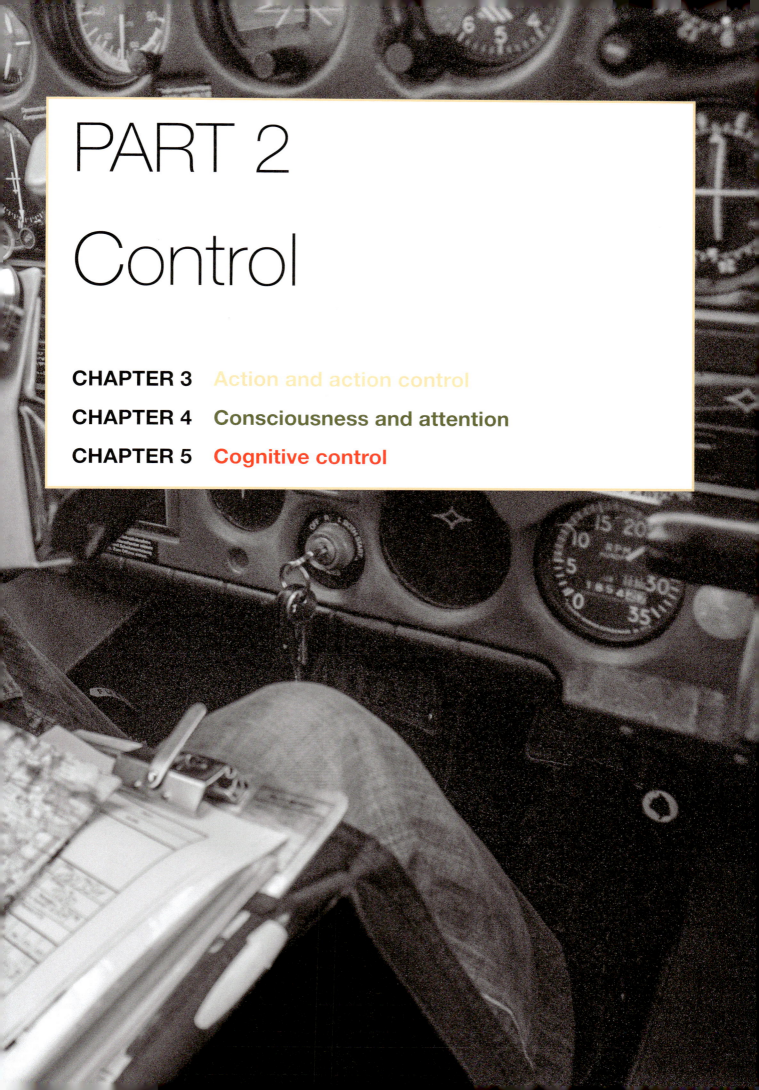

PART 2
Control

CHAPTER 3
Action and action control

3.1 INTRODUCTION

Why do we have a brain? Which evolutionary advantage has driven the development of a hypercomplex organ such as the brain? While trying to address these questions, we may encounter a number of deeply philosophical answers. Our brain not only allows us to make complex decisions, but it also allows us to consider the perspectives of others and provides us with a sense of morality. Although these abilities certainly contribute to our everyday activities, our intellectual capacities would be completely useless if we were unable to act upon them! The somewhat sobering answer is, therefore, that the brain has most likely evolved because it allows us to move. According to the British neuroscientist Daniel Wolpert and his colleagues, the main purpose of the brain is to convert sensory information into action (Wolpert, Doya, & Kawato, 2003).

Many of our cognitive faculties are therefore related to our motor system and our ability to regulate our internal states. One important aspect of this is that we are not only capable of executing actions but also of learning skills and of flexibly adapting ourselves to ever-changing circumstances. At the beginning of Chapter 2, we encountered an impressive list of activities that our brains are involved in, and it may not come as a surprise that the majority of items on this list are related to the regulation of bodily functions, including controlling our muscles and regulating the activities of our internal organs.

Despite the importance of action and action control, cognitive psychology has traditionally been based on an information-processing approach, which was characterised by the fact that mental processes were decoupled from the body. This began to change in the early 1990s, when a new movement emerged that became known as **embodied cognition**. This movement emphasised the interrelation between bodily functions and cognition. As such, the embodied cognition movement diametrically opposed the traditional decoupling between cognition and its biological basis. Consequently, it advocates that human cognition arose from a set of functions that were specifically engaged in controlling the body (Clark, 1999). Details of this approach are further discussed in

Chapter 11, where we introduce the cognitive processes that are involved in controlling the body's needs.

3.2 INTERNAL REGULATION

One important task of the brain involves the regulation of several internal bodily states, such as blood pressure, respiration, heart rate, activating the digestive system, and controlling all of the other internal organs. Most of these regulatory functions are carried out autonomously by nuclei in the brainstem. With the exception of respiration, we cannot control these functions consciously; they are controlled by the autonomic nervous system.

3.2.1 THE AUTONOMIC NERVOUS SYSTEM

The autonomic nervous system consists of neurons that transmit information to the heart, intestines, and other internal organs, along with neurons that receive information from these organs. The autonomic nervous system can be subdivided into a sympathetic part and a parasympathetic part (see fig 3.1).

3.2.1.1 Sympathetic Nervous System

The sympathetic nervous system prepares our internal organs for situations that require us to act. It consists of two chains of **ganglia** that are located to the left and right outside of the spinal cord. These ganglia receive input from axons that originate inside the spinal cord itself. The ganglia of the sympathetic nervous system are strongly interconnected, causing them to operate in unison. Axons extending from these ganglia stretch out to the internal organs, which they can prepare for a fight or flight response: heart rate and respiration will increase, while activity of the intestines will decrease.

3.2.1.2 Parasympathetic Nervous System

Functions of the parasympathetic nervous system are largely contrary to those of the sympathetic nervous system. Parasympathetic activity causes a slowing of heart rate

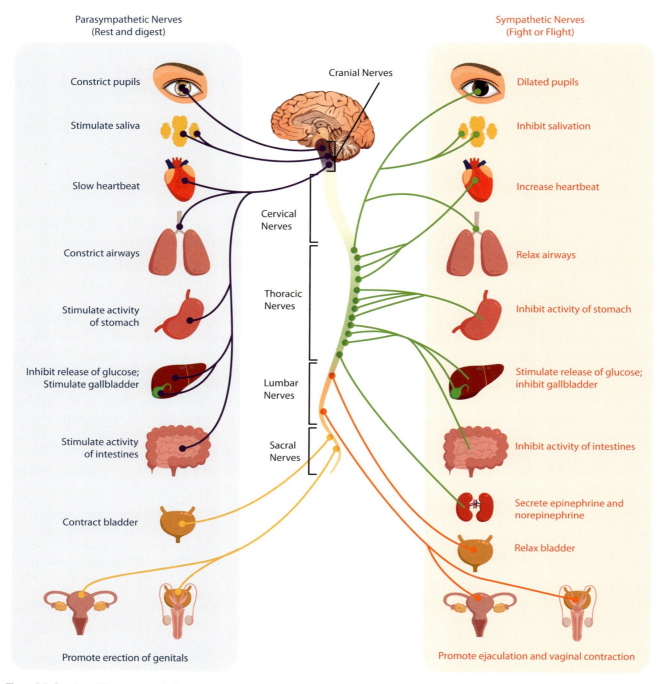

Figure 3.1 Overview of the parasympathetic and sympathetic nervous system. Parasympathetic activity is regulated via the tenth cranial nerve, which is connected to ganglia close to the internal organs, and via the sacral part of the spinal cord. Sympathetic activity is mainly controlled through two chains of ganglia that are located to the left and right of the spinal cord.

and respiration, while stimulating the digestive activities of the intestines. In contrast to the sympathetic nervous system, which operates as a unit, the parasympathetic nervous system is characterised by a much looser organisation. Relatively long preganglionic nerves stretch from the spinal cord to the parasympathetic ganglia, which are located relatively close to the internal organs themselves. The parasympathetic nervous system is also known as the cranio-sacral system because it is controlled by the cranial nerves and the sacral part of the spinal cord.

3.2.2 THE ENDOCRINE SYSTEM

In addition to the direct control of the internal organs by the sympathetic and parasympathetic nervous systems, there is an indirect control loop that operates by releasing hormones (see fig 3.2). **Hormones** are molecules with a signalling function, which are released by the hormone-producing glands. One of the most important hormone-releasing glands in the brain is the pituitary gland. Hormones released here regulate, among other things, growth, blood

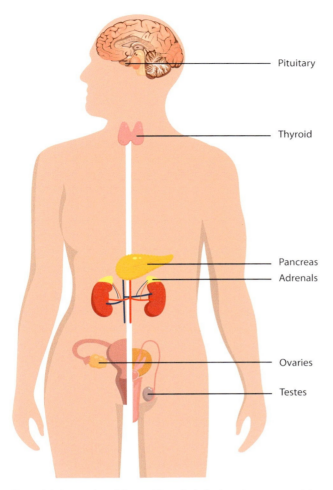

Figure 3.2 An overview of the most important glands and organs comprising the endocrine system.

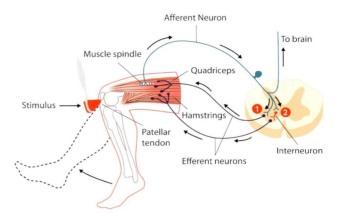

Figure 3.3 Illustration of a reflex arc: muscle spindles, detecting the stretching of a muscle, generate a response in an afferent (sensory) neuron. This afferent activity is then transmitted to both the brain and to an efferent neuron that simulates the contraction of the quadriceps (1). Moreover, via an inhibitory interneuron (2) an effent signal is generated that causes the hamstring to relax.

pressure, reproduction, and metabolism. Although hormones are chemically similar to neurotransmitters, their effects can be markedly different. Because hormones are released into the bloodstream, their effect is typically slower, longer lasting, and affecting larger parts of the body, in comparison to neurotransmitters.

3.3 REFLEXES

Reflexes are probably the most basic form of a motor action that we can identify. Consider, for example, the knee tendon reflex. Here, a gentle tap on the tendon just below the kneecap will typically result in an automatic extension of the lower leg. This reflex is the result of a mechanism that is normally involved in maintaining our balance. Tension in the knee tendon causes the muscles or the upper thigh to stretch. This stretching then generates a sensory neural impulse that is projected to motor neurons located in the spinal cord, which will, in turn, cause this muscle to contract. Another example is the automatic retraction of the hand after touching a hot surface. This type of reflex is automatically initiated by a relatively simple sequence of neurons that is known

as a **reflex arc** (see fig 3.3). Most reflexes consist of relatively simple sequences involving a sensory neuron, a motor neuron, and an interneuron that connects the sensory neuron to the motor neuron.[1]

Most reflexes are triggered automatically by changes in the environment. The knee tendon reflex is a consequence of a change in the length of the upper leg muscle, resulting in a corrective response that is aimed at maintaining a constant length. As such, this reflex helps us to maintain our position without the need for constant monitoring or conscious effort. Other examples include the pupillary light reflex or the accommodation reflex of the eye. The **pupillary light reflex** regulates pupil size as a function of the amount of light entering the eye, while the **accommodation reflex** changes the shape of the eye lens as a function of the distance to the stimulus that we fixate on.

3.3.1 CLASSICAL CONDITIONING

Reflexes are examples of **unconditioned responses**. The term 'unconditioned' is based on a translation error from the Russian physiologist Ivan Pavlov's original text. Pavlov was initially interested in the digestive system of dogs, which required him to develop a method for collecting the bodily fluids involved in digestion. Coincidentally, he noticed that dogs were already beginning to salivate when they saw the assistant responsible for feeding them. This observation resulted in a series of studies that would determine the rest of Pavlov's career. In one of the most well-known experiments, Pavlov presented the sound of a metronome shortly before the dog was fed. After a number of repetitions, the sound of the metronome itself was already sufficient to stimulate the release of saliva, due to the association that was formed between the ticking of the metronome and the expectancy of food (see fig 3.4).

Pavlov described the release of saliva that resulted from the presentation of food as an 'unconditional' reflex,

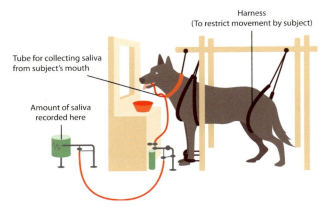

Figure 3.4 An example of the experimental setup that Pavlov used for his famous classical conditioning experiments.

because this reflex occurs always, without being dependent on other conditions. 'Unconditional' was erroneously translated from the original Russian text as 'unconditioned'. Likewise, the same erroneous translation was applied to the stimulus evoking reflex, which became the **unconditioned stimulus**. Pavlov further described the response to the metronome as the conditional reflex and the metronome itself as the conditional stimulus. Due to the same translation error, this reflex and stimulus have become known as the **conditioned response** and **conditioned stimulus**, respectively.

3.3.1.1 Forward, Backward, and Simultaneous Conditioning

Conditioning can be established using different methods. **Forward conditioning** is comparable to how Pavlov established associations between the metronome and the expectancy of food. In this case, the conditioned stimulus will be presented just before the unconditioned stimulus. **Simultaneous conditioning** involves the simultaneous presentation of both stimuli, whereas **backward conditioning** requires the conditioned stimulus to be presented after the unconditioned one. The effect of the latter is actually the reverse of forward conditioning, because the conditioned response is weakening. This weakening is probably due to the fact that the unconditioned stimulus now serves as a signal to indicate that the unconditioned stimulus will not be presented anymore.

3.3.1.2 Higher-order Conditioning

Higher-order conditioning involves multiple steps, in which initially a neutral stimulus is associated with an unconditioned stimulus, as in the classic example of the metronome becoming associated with food. When this stimulus is conditioned, a second stimulus, such as a flash of light, is paired with the conditioned stimulus, so that the latter stimulus will also evoke the conditioned response.

3.3.1.3 Extinction

Extinction involves the repeated presentation of the conditioned stimulus, without presenting the unconditioned stimulus. After a number of repetitions, the conditioned response

tends to weaken and eventually disappear. This gradual weakening of the conditioned response is known as **extinction**.

3.3.1.4 Relapse from Extinction

Despite the fact that the conditioned response eventually diminishes when the unconditioned stimulus is no longer paired with the conditioned one, extinction is often not complete. Reconditioning, after a period of extinction, will typically occur more rapidly compared to the initial conditioning process. This is known as reacquisition of the conditioned response.

In addition, the context in which conditioning occurred can be a major factor in establishing a relapse of extinction. For example, returning to the original environment where the conditioning originally occurred, after a period of extinction, automatically triggers a relapse. Extinction therefore plays an important role in a host of behavioural therapies aimed at reducing maladaptive associations, as might happen in anxiety or posttraumatic stress disorders.

3.3.2 OPERANT CONDITIONING

Similar to classical conditioning, operant conditioning involves the learning of new behaviours. In contrast, however, operant conditioning involves the selective rewarding or punishing of specific behaviours. While classical conditioning involves the modification of reflexes, operant conditioning involves the modification of spontaneous, operant behaviour (see fig 3.5).

Research involving operant conditioning often builds upon the pioneering work of Edward Thorndike, who observed how cats could escape from a puzzle box. The puzzle box was constructed by Thorndike in such a way that a cat could escape from it by pulling an array of levers. Thorndike observed that cats were learning via a trial-and-error process, in which their actions became increasingly more effective upon each successive attempt. Based on these observations, Thorndike formulated his famed law of effect, which states that behaviour yielding positive outcomes has

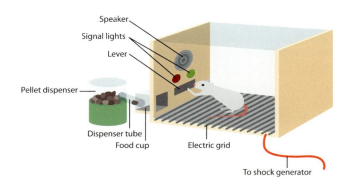

Figure 3.5 Example of a Skinner Box. Rats that are locked in a cage can be signalled, via a speaker or lightbulb, that an electric shock is imminent, which they can avoid by pressing a lever. Successful actions can be rewarded with a food pellet.

a greater probability of being repeated, while behaviour yielding negative outcomes tends to extinguish.

The law of effect forms the basis of operant conditioning. The selective reinforcing of desired behaviour and the omission of reward for undesired behaviour is known as reinforcement. In animals, reinforcement can be used to teach them specific behaviours. The training of pets, for example, is based on this principle. When an animal spontaneously displays a specific type of behaviour that roughly matches the desired behaviour, it will be rewarded. Over time, the criteria for rewarded behaviour becomes increasingly strict. To illustrate, when teaching a dog to sit properly, we can start by rewarding any type of behaviour that roughly corresponds with sitting. In the next phase, only real sitting behaviour is rewarded, and finally, we only reward the dog when it sits quickly, for example within three seconds. The latter is an example of **shaping**, a technique that can be used to train animals into performing very complex (and on occasion even bizarre, cf Box 3.1) behaviours.

Box 3.1 Project Orcon: B.F. Skinner's bizarre bomb

In 1943, the Second World War was raging. Allied air forces were continually carrying out strategic bombings of Nazi-controlled German territories. Although the main objective was to target the German war industry, technological limitations at that time prevented those bombardments from being carried out with any reasonable level of precision. Present-day missiles can be guided to their targets using a combination of GPS, laser technology, and advanced computer systems. During World War II, none of these technologies existed, however, resulting in the use of a brute-force strategy known as carpet bombing. This involved a complete squadron of bombers flying over a predetermined area, while dropping as many bombs as possible, in the hope that one or more would hit the intended targets. This tactic eventually resulted in the mass destruction of many civil areas, and innumerous loss of life.

One of the most bizarre solutions to this problem was proposed by the well-known American behaviourist Burrhus Frederic Skinner. Skinner, known as a radical behaviourist, was convinced that all actions are ultimately driven by stimuli in the environment and that learning is determined by the consequences that these actions have. Choices that have a positive outcome will be reinforced, according to Skinner, while choices that have negative outcomes will quickly extinguish. This principle forms the basis for **reinforcement learning** and is one of the foundations of operant conditioning. Skinner studied the principles of operant conditioning predominantly in pigeons.

When Skinner observed a flock of pigeons fly past one day, he imagined the possibility of employing them in a weapons guidance system. The idea was as follows: Skinner would train pigeons such that they would recognise a specific target and start pecking a button as long as the target remained in sight. The nose cone of the bomb would be equipped with a small cockpit, in which three pigeons would be placed (see fig 3.6). As long as the target remained in view of all three pigeons, they would continue to peck. The idea was to attach cables to the pigeon's heads, which would transfer the head motions to a steering mechanism, which would continue to align the bomb with the target, on the basis of the pigeons' head movements. Skinner had not foreseen an escape mechanism, so that for the unfortunate pigeons it would turn out to be a suicide mission.

Skinner approached a research committee of the American armed forces with this idea, code named Project Pigeon. Even though the committee members were understandably sceptical about the idea, they nevertheless awarded Skinner a start-up credit of $25,000. Skinner succeeded in training pigeons to respond to specific targets, and he built a small cockpit for the pigeons (see fig 3.6). Despite these efforts, the American air force eventually lost its confidence in the project, causing its cancellation on October 8, 1944.

In 1948, after the end of World War II, the project saw a brief rejuvenation under the name Project Orcon, where it was supervised by the American navy. In 1953, the project was definitively cancelled when the reliability of electronic guidance systems was sufficient, making Skinner's pigeon project superfluous.

Figure 3.6 The prototype of a cockpit for B.F. Skinner's pigeon-guided bomb.

3.4 HABITUATION AND SENSITISATION

Pavlov described reflexes as being unconditional, but this turned out not to be entirely correct: when the evoking stimulus is repeated, the resulting response can gradually change. **Habituation** refers to a gradual weakening of the response to a weak stimulus, while **sensitisation** refers to the increasing of a response to a strong stimulus.

Moreover, in the late 1950s, the Russian neuroscientist Evgeny Nikolaevich Sokolov (cited in Pribram, 1960) discovered that an organism will initially respond strongly to a change in its environment. This orienting response will habituate after the repeated presentation of the same stimulus. Sokolov demonstrated that this habituation could not possibly be a consequence of fatigue, because every change in a repetitive sequence of stimuli, even as small as a tiny change in illumination of a light source, resulted in a dishabituation of the orientation response. This effect implies that a neural model, that is, a representation of the environment, is formed by the central nervous system, against which every deviation from the sequence is tested.

3.5 THE MOTOR SYSTEM

Although the reflexes described earlier can also be found in humans, their roles are rather limited in our daily lives. To move ourselves through a complex, continually changing world, we need to be able to adapt ourselves in a flexible manner and assert voluntary control over our actions. To adequately navigate through the world, we need to recruit every cognitive system that we have at our disposal and integrate information across multiple cognitive domains. For instance, we need to have an adequate mental representation of our environment. We are therefore not only required to recognise objects, but we also need to be able to represent the relative spatial positions of these objects. In addition, we need to be able to predict where objects are located now and to which location they might move at some point in the future. In other words, we need to perceive our environment.

Based on the mental representation that we extract from our perceptions, we need to predict how we need to act in order to achieve a specific goal. Consider, for example, the simple act of drinking coffee. For this, we first need to determine the location of the cup, and how it is oriented on the table. Then we need to plan the trajectory that our hand has to move, in order to pick up the cup. The muscle or group of muscles that we will eventually use to perform the actual movement is known as an **effector system**. To follow the planned trajectory for reaching the cup, we need to generate thousands of motor commands to ensure that these effector systems are given the right instructions. While we are making the movement, thousands of

additional motor commands are being passed from the brain to the spinal cord ganglia, which ensure that our fingers are graciously wrapping themselves around the cup's handle, while grabbing it with exactly the right amount of force. Based on an estimate of the cup's weight, yet another few thousand motor commands guide our hand in the direction of our mouth. While the cup approaches the mouth, yet more neural impulses are projected along the cranial nerves, which ensure that our mouth opens, allowing the coffee to flow through our throat in an efficient and controlled way.

We typically perform the great majority of actions, such as these, without conscious awareness. Having the intention to drink coffee is typically already sufficient to initiate the sequence of motor commands required to perform this action. Our example only illustrates a relatively simple act that we conduct all by ourselves. In daily life, we often perform actions in collaboration with somebody else, requiring us not only to control our own actions but also to consider the intentions of the other. To do justice to the complexity of these processes, we will return to them in two further chapters. The remainder of this chapter discusses the basic mechanisms of human motor processing and our ability for learning skills. Then, the role of perception in controlling our actions will be discussed in Chapter 10, while acting in a social context is discussed in Chapter 23.

3.5.1 NEURAL PATHWAYS

The movements that our brains are planning need to be transferred to the muscles that are eventually involved in executing them. This transfer involves the motor pathways of the brain. The planning of movements is organised in a hierarchical fashion, where the global pattern of the motion is planned by several cortical areas, while details of the action plan are fine-tuned by a variety of subcortical areas. There are two important motor pathways connecting the brain with the muscles: the lateral pathway and the medial pathway (see fig 3.7).

The lateral pathway consists of neural fibres that originate from soma that are located in the primary motor cortex. From here, the fibres cross from one side of the body to the other in the medulla. This lateral path is predominantly involved in the control of fine motion, involving the muscles of our limbs, specifically the distal muscles of our hands, lower arms and legs, and our feet. In contrast, the medial path is mainly involved in controlling muscles of our trunk, and upper arms and upper legs. The medial path is not as strongly lateralised as the lateral path, projecting to both the ipsilateral and contralateral sides of the body. The main tasks of this pathway involve controlling our body's position, and bilateral movements, such as standing upright, walking, bowing, and turning.

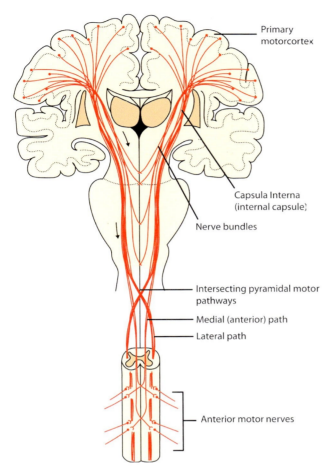

Figure 3.7 An overview of the neural pathways involved in motor control.

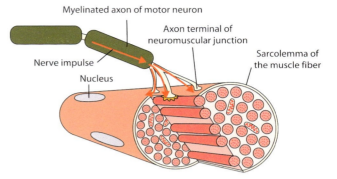

Figure 3.8 Schematic illustration of a human muscle. The neuromuscular junction forms the connection between the muscle and the peripheral nervous system.

3.5.2 MUSCLES

Eventually, all of our movements are carried out by our muscles. Muscles consist of fibres that are capable of contracting. These contractions are caused by an electric impulse that is delivered by a motor neuron. The soma of the motor neurons that are eventually connected to the muscles are localised in the ventral part of the spinal cord.

A typical motor neuron is connected to multiple muscle fibres, ranging from three fibres per neuron for muscles involved in fine motor control to hundreds of fibres per neuron for muscles involved in heavy lifting tasks, such as the leg muscles that are involved in maintaining an upright position. A motor neuron and its associated muscle fibres is known as a **motor unit**. The synapse between motor neurons and the connecting muscle fibres is larger and more specialised, compared to regular synapses, and it is known as the neuromuscular junction (see fig 3.8).

Muscle contraction is associated with electrical activity, which we can measure relatively easily by attaching an electrode to the muscle. We can then use the resulting electromyogram (EMG) to determine when motor commands activate the muscles (see Box 3.2). This is particularly useful for the recording of partial responses. A response is partial when the muscles are activated, but without actually moving the corresponding limb. Recording such partial responses can be useful, for example, in determining how conflicting information can result in the activation or suppression of incorrect responses, in the absence of the actual occurrence of these responses. Moreover, in many cases covert muscle responses can be amplified by applying transcranial magnetic stimulation (TMS; see Box 3.3) to parts of the cortex involved in motor control.

3.5.3 BRAIN AREAS INVOLVED IN MOTOR CONTROL: FROM INTENTION TO ACTION

The planning and execution of a movement is only possible through the coordinated activity of a large array of cortical and subcortical brain areas (see fig 3.9). Initially, an intention is formed in the frontal cortical areas, on the basis of sensory information that these areas receive from the parietal, occipital, and temporal areas (Hesslow, 2002). This intention translates into an action plan, which is shaping up in the cortical motor areas. Then, the action plan is fine-tuned, and possibly adjusted on the basis of changes in the environment. These adjustments are typically done by the subcortical areas.

3.5.3.1 Cortical Areas

The cortical motor areas of the brain are mainly involved in the planning of movements. Of all the areas involved in motor control, the primary motor cortex is perhaps the best known. It is, however, a fallacy to assume that this is also the only cortical area that is involved in motor control. Even more so, it is specifically for this area, still relatively unknown what its exact role in motor control is. While some studies suggests that the primary motor cortex is predominantly involved in planning, other studies suggest that it is mainly involved in controlling an action (Scott,

65

Box 3.2 The electromyogram

Movement scientists and psychologists interested in the details of our human motor behaviour have a wide range of techniques at their disposal, ranging from a kinaesthetic arm, to analysing the effects that a task might have on maintaining balance, to the precise measurements of the movements of individual fingers during a grasping motion, to the measurement of the activation of individual muscles. The latter is frequently done by employing **electromyography**, that is, by recording electrical muscle activity.

Experiments related to electromyography can be traced back to 1660, when the Italian physicist Francesco Redi discovered the existence of a highly specialised muscle in an electric eel, by showing that it produced electricity. In 1849, the German physiologist Emil Heinrich du Bois-Reymond showed that all muscles produce electricity when they contract. This activity is the result of the accumulated activity of all the individual action potentials that cause the muscle to contract (Denny-Brown, 1949), and it can be displayed as an **electromyogram (EMG)**. Throughout the first half of the 20th century, the accuracy with which this electric activity could be measured steadily improved.

Initially, it appeared to be problematic to distil useful information from the EMG, because the summation of the individual action potentials results in a relatively noisy high-frequency signal. Before the general availability of affordable computers, it was customary to plot this signal either on paper or on an oscilloscope, which limited the options for signal processing. Presently, it is customary to digitally record the EMG, allowing many more complex digital signal processing algorithms to be applied to the EMG. To extract useful information, the first step is typically to rectify the signal; that is, to invert all negative values, so that they become positive ones. Then the resulting signal is low pass filtered, such that all the individual peaks are smoothed. The processed signal now gives a much-improved estimate of the average change in muscle activity as a function of time. Based on this, it is now possible, for example, to determine the onset of muscle activity and to relate this to specific task parameters. For example, when a task evokes two conflicting responses, we can now determine whether the motor system evoked activity in the response hand that should not be used. Likewise, we can determine whether trials on which a response should be withheld will nevertheless evoke a motor response. In specific situations, the EMG may be used in combination with a TMS pulse (see Box 3.3), which stimulates specific areas of the motor cortex.

Although most cognitive psychological research involving electromyography focuses on the lower arm, to measure the control of the index finger, there are many other muscles that can be targeted. Facial muscles, for example, can be used to measure the emotional response to affective stimuli (Dimberg, 1990; Tamietto & de Gelder, 2010; Tamietto et al., 2009). In addition, electromyography is frequently used in biofeedback (Chesney & Shelton, 1976). Here, the signal is visualised, or converted to an auditory signal, while the participant is instructed to reduce the signal as much as possible through the use of relaxation techniques.

Currently, the EMG is frequently used in combination with other techniques, such as EEG or transcranial magnetic stimulation (TMS), allowing researchers to relate the activation of the central nervous system with that of the periphery of the body.

2000). In addition to the primary motor cortex, several other areas are involved in the planning of movements, such as the premotor cortex, the supplementary motor cortex, the frontal eye fields, the inferior frontal cortex, the anterior cingulate cortex, and the parietal cortex.

Each of these areas has its own specialised function. The premotor and supplementary motor cortices, along with the frontal eye fields, are typically involved in specifying, preparing, and initiating a response. The anterior cingulate cortex is involved in selecting between different response alternatives and monitoring whether an action was accurately executed. Finally, the spatial properties of our environment are represented in the parietal cortex. This brain area is actively involved in integrating spatial information into our movements and in adjusting these movements when changes in the environment are detected. In addition to these tasks, the parietal cortex is involved in linking patterns of motion to meaning, for example when interpreting gestures.

3.5.3.2 Subcortical Areas

In addition to the aforementioned cortical areas, a host of subcortical areas is involved in controlling movements. These areas include the cerebellum and the basal ganglia. In contrast to the cortical areas, the subcortical areas are not so much involved in the planning, but more so in the execution, of a movement. The **cerebellum** is a relatively large cauliflower-like structure that is part of the midbrain. This structure plays an important role in motor coordination, specifically with regard to the timing and planning of

Box 3.3 Intervening in the living brain: transcranial magnetic stimulation

Transcranial magnetic stimulation (TMS) is a technique that allows us to temporarily influence the processing of a small part of the cortex, by delivering a strongly focused intense magnetic pulse. This type of stimulation allows us to draw causal inferences between brain functions and cognitive processes. TMS is applied via a coil that is capable of generating a brief magnetic pulse. The shape of the coil focuses the magnetic field, allowing it to target a very specific predetermined brain area, while being delivered from the outside of the scalp. Thus, TMS is considered to be a **non-invasive technique**.

The magnetic field disrupts the electric currents in the targeted area, resulting in a temporary change in its functionality, typically disrupting it. Ideally, one would like to compare the effect of a TMS pulse with a condition in which no pulse is applied. In practice, this is difficult to achieve, however, because the application of TMS is accompanied by a notable clicking sound. In addition, the magnetic field tends to contract the facial muscles. For this reason, TMS studies frequently use a control condition in which the pulse is applied to a cortical area that is not involved in the task of interest. In this case, it may be expected that the task is affected in the experimental condition, but not in the control condition.

By manipulating the time window between stimulus presentation and TMS pulse application, we can determine when the targeted area is involved in the task at hand. For example, Cracco, Cracco, Maccabee, and Amassian (1999) found that our ability to detect letters was most strongly impaired when the TMS pulse was delivered at about 80–100 ms after the presentation of a target letter, relative to conditions where it was delivered earlier or later. It thus appears that the targeted area is mostly active shortly after the presentation of the letter.

The application of a TMS pulse has occasionally been compared to the induction of a temporary lesion. This comparison is not entirely accurate, however, because the effect of the pulse can vary, depending on its strength, the precise area that is targeted, and the exact manner of stimulation. Whereas the effect of a single pulse typically results in a temporary deactivation of the targeted area, the repeated stimulation often has the opposite effect, resulting in hyperactivation.

One of the major advantages of TMS is that it is a causal technique. In contrast to the other neuroimaging methods that allow us to infer correlational links between neural activity and cognitive processes, TMS allows us to determine whether a specific cortical area is necessary for specific behaviour. Despite this advantage, TMS is also limited by several factors. Firstly, the effects of TMS are complex, and the exact effect of magnetic stimulation is still not very well understood. Although it is assumed that one single pulse temporarily disrupts ongoing activity, the effects of a repeated pulse are typically much more complex. For example, Allen, Pasley, Duong, and Freeman (2007) found that repetitive stimulation of the visual cortex in cats resulted in a long-lasting increase in spontaneous brain activity, whereas the activity that was evoked by visual stimuli decreased by about 60%.

In addition, while the TMS pulse typically has a negative impact on behaviour, it can occasionally also be positive. The latter might happen because the TMS pulse targeted a brain area that would normally have an inhibitory effect on the behaviour under investigation. Moreover, the application of TMS is somewhat limited because the magnetic pulse can only reach the cortex, or parts of the cerebellum, because these areas are close to the scalp. A related limitation is that TMS cannot be applied over areas of the scalp that contain muscles, because the magnetic pulses can cause painful contractions of these muscles. Finally, there are some safety concerns; despite many precautions, the application of TMS pulses has incidentally resulted in epileptic seizures.

Despite these limitations, TMS has recently been very successful in uncovering how many brain functions and behaviour relate to each other. One particularly successful area involves studying the influence of cognitive processes on the motor system. For this, parts of the motor cortex are stimulated, resulting in a disinhibition of the covert responses that participants typically make while processing conflicting information. The disinhibition allows these responses to manifest themselves as electric muscle activity that can be measured using an EMG (see Box 3.2). Examples of such use of TMS can be found in studies on speech perception. These have shown that listening to speech sometimes results in a covert activation of the muscles involved in speech production (see Chapter 17). Another example involves tasks in which participants are preparing a response that has to be aborted (Chapter 5). Although participants are typically able to do so, we can nevertheless observe that residual motor commands are generated. Although these commands are typically too weak to trigger an overt response, they frequently result in small residual muscle contractions. The application of a TMS pulse can amplify these.

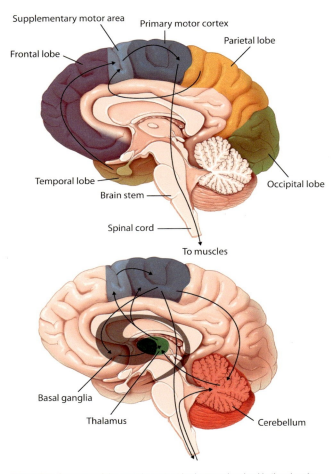

Supplementary motor area
Primary motor cortex
Parietal lobe
Frontal lobe
Temporal lobe
Brain stem
Spinal cord
To muscles
Occipital lobe

Basal ganglia
Thalamus
Cerebellum

Figure 3.9 Overview of the most important brain areas involved in the planning (top) and the coordination and execution (bottom) of movements.

individual movements. Damage to the cerebellum therefore strongly impacts the finer nuances of movements, causing them to become coarse and clumsy.

The basal ganglia are also strongly involved in motor control. Damage to these areas greatly impacts the smoothness of motions. Patients with Parkinson's or Huntington's disease, for example, are characterised by difficulties with initiating voluntary motions, presumably because the impaired functioning of the basal ganglia results in a stronger inhibition of the motor cortex. In addition, patients with Parkinson's disease are often displaying involuntary tremors. In contrast, Huntington's disease is often characterised by hyperkinesia, that is, by an excessive mobility.

3.6 THE MOTOR CORTEX

The primary motor cortex is characterised by a somatotopic organisation, that is, the anatomical organisation of the motor cortex is such that it represents a map of our body. Evidence for this map was found by electrically stimulating parts of the motor cortex, which resulted in the contraction

of specific groups of muscles (Penfield & Rasmussen, 1950). Since this map represents a distorted body, it is sometimes referred to as the homunculus (see fig 3.10).

3.6.1 CORTICAL PLASTICITY

Recent studies have shown, however, that the somatotopic maps only represents the anatomical organisation of the motor cortex to a certain degree. Even though the motor cortex is coarsely subdivided into areas representing the major body parts, such as arms, legs, or face, the microstructure of this brain area is characterised by local circuits that are much more diffuse (Sanes & Donoghue, 2000).

Based on refined microstimulation techniques that were developed after Penfield and Rasmussen's pioneering work, it was found that tiny changes in the position of the stimulating electrode would result in completely different motion patterns. When this method was employed in cats, to determine how specific body parts were represented in the motor cortex, it was found that the maps were much more diffuse and overlapping with areas representing other body parts, compared to the original findings (Stoney, Thompson, & Asanuma, 1968). Additionally, it has been reported that specific neurons from the motor cortex were associated with the control of multiple muscles (Buys, Lemon, Mantel, & Muir, 1986).

In addition to the aforementioned diffusion, the motor cortex is also characterised by a large degree of plasticity. Animals with a well-developed motor cortex are typically characterised by a large degree of flexibility in their behaviour. This flexibility can be attributed to an intrinsic flexibility of the cortex, suggesting that the architecture of the cortex can be dynamically adapted, depending on the circumstances. Ziemann, Muellbacher, Hallett, and Cohen (2001) found evidence for such a dynamic adaptation in the representation of the human biceps, as a consequence of training. Participants were required to execute a simple ballistic arm movement. When this exercise was accompanied by the administration of a neuromodulator (that is, a neurotransmitter-like substance that modulates the effect of neurotransmitters in the motor cortex), the cortical area representing the biceps increased significantly. Likewise, using magnetoencephalography, Elbert, Pantev, Wienbruch, Rockstroh, and Taub (1995) found an increase in the cortical representation of the fingers of the left hand among nine musicians (more specifically, six violinists, two cellists, and one guitarist) who had on average close to 12 years of experience playing their instruments.

Although such cortical plasticity is generally beneficial to the organism, extensive plasticity can also have detrimental consequences. For example, Pantev, Engelien, Candia, and Elbert (2001) describe the clinical condition of **focal hand dystonia**. This condition, which has frequently been reported among trained musicians, can also be described

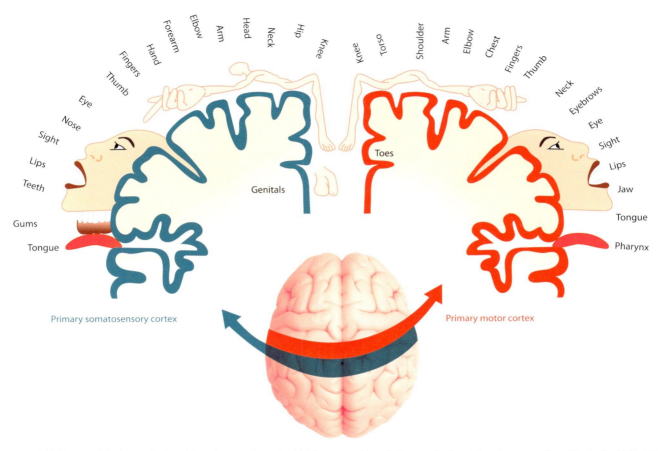

Figure 3.10 The somatotopic organisation of the primary motor cortex (right), compared to a similar organisation of the primary somatosensory cortex (right; see also Chapter 8). At the macroscopic level, both cortices are characterised by an organisation that is marked by the fact that specific parts of the cortex represent specific body parts.

as occupational hand cramp. It is characterised by a dyscoordination of the hand that results from the fact that the representations of different body parts begin to overlap and interfere with each other, due to excessive cortical plasticity. Individuals diagnosed with focal hand dystonia are frequently characterised by excessive muscle activity, which is often accompanied by an excessive application of force.

Focal hand dystonia can result from the intense rehearsal routines of musicians, which cause the cortical representation of the underlying muscles or muscle groups to expand (Candia et al., 1999; Elbert et al., 1998; Lederman, 1988). Consequently, the cortical areas representing the most frequently used fingers may start to overlap, causing the neural circuits to interfere with each other. Obviously, this can be disastrous for the future career of the affected musician.

Notice though that cortical plasticity is not unique to the motor cortex. Among blind individuals, it has been found, for example, that the parts of the visual cortex have become sensitive to tactile stimuli when reading in braille (Cohen et al., 1997). Likewise, a similar form of plasticity has been found in auditory cortex (Pantev et al., 2001; see Chapter 7).

3.6.2 MOTOR EQUIVALENCE

One of the most remarkable properties of our motor system is that we can achieve similar goals in many distinctly different ways, that is, by using different effector systems. In addition, we can employ one specific effector system for achieving multiple goals. This type of flexibility is known as **motor equivalence** (Hebb, 1949; Lashley, 1930). A striking example of motor equivalence is the fact that we can not only write our own name using a pen that we hold in our hand, but also when we hold it in our mouth or using our toes. Remarkably, our handwriting is reasonably comparable, regardless of the medium that we use for writing: the characteristics of individual letters are similar, despite being written on paper with a pen, on a blackboard using chalk, or in the sand using our foot (Wing, 2000).

Kelso et al. (1998) studied motor equivalence by measuring responses from the motor cortex using magneto-encephalography (MEG) (see Box 3.4). Participants were required to perform a simple task consisting of a finger movement. More specifically, they were required to either stretch or bend their finger to the beat of a metronome. In a second condition, they were required to perform the same action but now syncopated, that is, off beat. During these actions, activity from the motor cortex was

Box 3.4 Magnetoencephalography

In 1865, the renowned Scottish physicist James Clerk Maxwell published a discovery that would have a lasting effect on our society. He found that electric and magnetic fields manifest themselves as wave functions that traverse space at the speed of light. He showed that light, electricity, and magnetism are manifestations of the same phenomenon. Moreover, Maxwell formulated the equations describing the exact relation between electricity and magnetism. In essence, Maxwell found that each electric current generates a magnetic field that is oriented perpendicular to the current flow, and that each magnetic field generates an electric current in a conductive medium. This discovery foreshadowed the discovery of the electromagnetic spectrum and resulted in the development of electrical engineering and subsequently in the development of electronics. The electrical generator, radio, induction motor, and wireless cell phone charger are but a few of the direct results of Maxwell's discovery.

Maxwell's discovery is also relevant for neuroscience because the electric currents of the brain will also generate corresponding magnetic fields. Although these fields are extremely weak, they can be detected using specialised sensors. The resulting magnetoencephalogram (MEG) is remarkably similar to the electroencephalogram (EEG), but also differs in a number of important ways. The MEG was first recorded in 1968, by physicist David Cohen at the University of Illinois, in the USA. These recordings were obtained by using a copper induction coil. Induction refers to the fact that a changing magnetic field evokes an electric current in a metallic conductor. It is the principle that forms the basis of electric generators and modern cooking plates. Induction coils have one significant problem, however, which is the fact that they are extremely sensitive to external disturbances, such as the magnetic field of the earth, electric cables in nearby walls, passing trams, or the ignition systems of cars in an underground parking lot. In addition, they are also sensitive to electrostatic noise produced by the coils themselves.

To eliminate these problems, the initial recordings took place in an electromagnetically shielded chamber, but even the most stringent shielding turned out to be insufficient to properly measure the weak signals that the brain was producing (how weak these signals actually are is something that we will discuss later). For this reason, a different type of sensor is currently used, which is known as a **superconducting quantum interference device (SQUID)**. A precise discussion of the physical properties of a SQUID is beyond the scope of this book, however, it is relevant to note that SQUIDs are superconductive.

Super conduction occurs at extremely low temperatures (close to the absolute zero), when conductive materials lose their remaining electric resistance completely. Consequently, the electromagnetic noise that the sensors would normally produce is also reduced to an absolute minimum. For this reason, SQUIDs are extremely suitable for recording the extremely weak magnetic fields that our brains produce.

Initially, MEG was recorded using just a single SQUID, which was positioned at different positions above the scalp across different recording sessions. This required rerunning entire experiments for each position, resulting in MEG being an excessively labour-intensive process. For this reason, manufacturers of MEG scanners started integrating multiple SQUIDs into one system. Modern-day MEG scanners can be composed of up to 300 separate SQUIDs, which are mounted on the inside of a thermally isolated Dewar vessel, such that they surround much of the participants' heads. Superconductivity can be achieved by filling the vessel with liquid helium.

The electric currents that form the basis of the EEG (see Chapter 2) will, according to Maxwell's laws, also generate a weak magnetic field. To give an impression of how weak these signals are, we need to introduce the unit of magnetic field strength, the Tesla (T). A permanent loudspeaker magnet typically produces a magnetic field of about 1 to 2.5 T, whereas a refrigerator magnet produces a field strength of about 5 mT (or 5×10^{-3} T). The earth's magnetic field has a strength of about 3.2×10^{-5} T, while signals that our brains produce are in the order of about 100 femtotesla (100×10^{-15} T: or 10^{-13} T) to about 1 picotesla (10^{-12} T). In other words, the MEG signals are about 100,000,000,000,000 (one-hundred thousand billion) to 10,000,000,000,000 (ten-thousand billion) times as weak as a loudspeaker magnet and up to 10,000,000 (ten million) times as weak as the earth's magnetic field. The fact that we can nevertheless record these signals, may be considered an enormous achievement.

We can visualise Maxwell's equations using the right-hand rule. This is a simple rule of thumb, literally, to grasp the relation between electric currents and magnetic fields. Open your right hand somewhat, such that your fingers are still slightly bent, and stretch your thumb as much as possible. Now, your thumb represents the direction of the electric current flow, while your fingers represent the direction of the magnetic field lines, circling around the current. From this example, it follows that magnetic fields that are generated by neural sources that are mainly parallel to the surface of the scalp can be measured best with MEG. These sources cannot easily

(Continued)

Box 3.4 (Continued)

be picked up using EEG, making EEG and MEG complementary techniques. Considering that the magnetic field strength rapidly decreases with distance to its source, MEG is mainly limited to recording neural sources that are located directly below the scalp. A considerable advantage of MEG is that the magnetic fields are not distorted by the scalp, making MEG, in principle, a technique that is better capable of localising brain activity than EEG is. For this reason, MEG has not only a very good temporal resolution, but it also has a reasonable spatial resolution (albeit, still not as good as fMRI).

The requirement to cool the SQUIDs to temperatures close to absolute zero requires intensive maintenance and a frequent resupply of liquid helium. In addition, the SQUIDs still need shielding from external magnetic sources, requiring the equipment to be placed in dedicated electrically shielded rooms. For these reasons, MEG is expensive. In addition, participating in an MEG experiment is in some ways less comfortable than participating in an EEG experiment. Because the sensors are fixed to the scanner itself, participants are required to avoid moving during a recording session. In addition, the noise-sensitivity of the scanner prevents the use of much of the equipment we typically use in an experiment (computer screens, headphones, response-boxes, etc.), requiring specific precautions for allowing stimuli to be presented and responses to be collected.

Recently developed sensor types, such as the spin exchange relaxation free (SERF) magnetometers are potentially much less sensitive to magnetic interference and might therefore be promising for future MEG research. Experimental MEG scanners, which are based on SERF sensors, are much smaller because there is no need to cool them. For this reason, the sensors can be attached to the participants' head. At the moment of writing, these scanners are still in the initial stages of development, though (Koshev et al., 2021).

---

recorded using MEG. The recorded motor responses correlated strongly with the speed of the finger movement, regardless of the specific instruction (bending, stretching, on beat, or off beat). This result implies that the motor cortex is mainly involved in the coding of higher-order aspects of the motion, such as speed and direction, while the control of the individual muscles is relegated to the periphery of the motor system. Motor equivalence thus implies that actions are coded at a relatively abstract level of description that lies beyond the specific control of the relevant effector systems.

3.7 MOTOR CONTROL

Now that we have introduced the major neural mechanisms involved in regulating our motor systems, the next question is how we can control our actions. A related question that follows from this is how we can transfer our intentions into actions. What is involved in the coordination of individual muscles, and how can we flexibly adapt our behaviour when the circumstances in our environment change? These questions will be addressed in the following sections.

3.7.1 FROM INTENTION TO ACTION

The first question is how an intention, for example, our wish to make coffee, results in a coordinated series of actions that effectively results in moving ourselves to the kitchen, taking a coffee filter, folding it, grabbing a pack of coffee, pouring a few scoops of coffee in the filter, and filling the can with water. An influential framework describing this relation between intention and action is known as the **ideomotor theory** (Shin, Proctor, & Capaldi, 2010). This framework is based on the idea that actions are defined by their observable consequences. More specifically, the ideomotor theory presumes that imagining the effect of an action may trigger its actual execution. The activation of an action may take place internally. For example, when we imagine a fresh cup of coffee, this may result in the execution of the sequence of actions just described. In addition, our actions may also be triggered by external factors, for example, by observing how the action is performed by others.

The term 'ideomotor action' was first proposed by the British physiologist William B. Carpenter (1852), when he proposed that a reflex-like action of the cerebrum could manifest itself not only as a physical change in the brain but also in the form of muscle activity. Carpenter's ideas were inspired by Thomas Laylock (1878), who observed that fear of water, among patients suffering from rabies, resulted in a reflex-like response that was not only triggered by the presence of water itself but also at the suggestion of water. Around the same time, the German philosopher and educator Johann Friedrich Herbart (1825) developed ideas that were comparable to those of Carpenter. Adding to the earlier ideas, Herbart presumed that ideomotor actions were not limited to reflexes, but that learning was also involved. William James (1890) described ideomotor actions as a sequence of movements that followed upon the mere act of thinking about these movements. Thus, James assumed the existence of a direct relation between a thought and an action. According to James, the automatic execution of an action was only prevented because we frequently have multiple, competitive thoughts and ideas, among which one must be selected before we can act.

Although the idea of ideomotor action became largely unpopular towards the beginning of the 20th century, it has never been abandoned completely. Clark Hull (1931), for example, introduced the concept of **anticipatory goal reactions**, which he described as $R_G - S_G$, that is, representations for the goal reaction (R_G) and the resulting proprioceptive stimulus (S_G). According to Hull, however, ideas should not necessarily precede actions. Action could, according to Hull, be the consequence of the sensory feedback that follows an anticipated response. This way, Hull argued, ideomotor actions equate to ideas.

3.7.1.1 Greenwald's Ideomotor Theory

The first modern variant of the currently accepted ideomotor theory was coined by Anthony Greenwald (1970). Greenwald's theory is an extension of James' original ideas, but now formulated in more testable terms. More specifically, Greenwald identified three stages, namely Stimulus (S) – Response (R) – Effect/Sensory feedback (E). These three stadia follow each other in a fixed sequence, within a limited time frame. For instance, when we execute a specific action, this will result in action-specific feedback, which will always result in unique S-R-E triplets, such as S_1-R_1-E_1, S_2-R_2-E_2, S_3-R_3-E_3, and so on. Repeated exposure to these triplets will strengthen the associations between them. A consequence of these associations is, according to Greenwalt, a conditioned anticipatory image of the response feedback. In other words, by repeatedly executing a specific action, and by observing its consequences, we learn to recognise the consequences of these actions, and link them to the stimulus that is associated with this action.

3.7.1.2 Theory of Event Coding

Currently, one of the most influential ideomotor theories is the Theory of Event Coding, as formulated by Hommel, Müsseler, Aschersleben, and Prinz (2002). This theoretical framework is based on the idea that internal mental representations are shared by perceptual and motor processes. Different properties of an object are encoded by highly specialised brain systems. How these properties are bound together into a single unified representation is known as the **binding problem** (see also Chapter 6). Treisman and Schmidt (1982) and, subsequently, Kahneman, Treisman, and Gibbs (1992) described how perceiving an event automatically results in the binding of all the individual codes representing this event. Kahneman et al. argued, moreover, that these representations are also automatically bound to abstract semantic knowledge, thus resulting in the creation of an **object file**. These object files represent, according to Kahneman et al., not only the object that we perceived itself

but also how this object was perceived within a specific context. The central concept in the theory of event coding is the **event file**, which is a more generic version of an object file, in the sense that it not only represents the perceptual and contextual properties of an object but also the motor codes that are associated with it (Hommel, 2009).

Such autonomous links between perception and action are nicely illustrated by the Simon Effect. J. Richard Simon (1990) found that irrelevant, directional information is automatically encoded in our responses. In a typical **Simon task**, stimuli are used that are characterised by two specific dimensions, such as colour and location (for example, a red or a blue dot that can appear at either the left or right side of a computer screen). Participants are required to respond on the basis of one specific dimension, the task-relevant dimension, while ignoring the other, task-irrelevant, dimension. The required action itself has no correspondence with the task-relevant dimension but does so with the task-irrelevant dimension. For example, participants have to ignore the location of the stimulus while responding as quickly as possible on the basis of the colour of the stimulus. For example, they need to make a left-hand response to a red stimulus, and a right-hand response to a blue one. Although the location of the stimulus is completely irrelevant, it nevertheless affects participants' response times, resulting in relatively slow responses to red stimuli appearing on the right side of the screen and blue stimuli appearing on the left. Thus, although the location of the stimulus is completely irrelevant, it still affects our responses, facilitating responses that are compatible with it, and inhibiting responses that are incompatible with it.

3.7.2 MOTOR PROGRAMMES

Imagine being on a bicycle, waiting in front of a red light. When you anticipate the light turning green, you are typically able to respond relatively quickly. One of the main reasons for this is that while anticipating, you are already generating a motor programme. This programme encompasses the sequence of actions that are required to start riding: releasing the brakes, lifting your right leg from the ground, making a downward movement with your left leg, and so on. This motor programme can already be generated before the actual action is required. As such, motor programmes form a basis for motor cognition (see Section 3.10), because we cannot only use these motor programmes for the actual execution of an action but also to evaluate the eventual consequences of an action.

Response time studies have contributed considerably to our knowledge of motor programmes. Typically, this is done by observing what happens just before an action needs to be executed. This is the **motor anticipation** stage. Motor anticipation involves a collection of processes that are executed while preparing a motor programme. These processes are executed after the stimulus that triggers the action has appeared, but before it is actually executed. During this stage, electromyographic recordings (see Box 3.2) can be used to record muscle activity. During the initial stages of motor anticipation, this activity is hardly measurable, but gradually increases as the preparation of the response continues. This observation is evidence for the idea that mental processes are involved in the preparation of a response and that this involves two stages: a planning stage and an execution stage. In addition, it is found that the time required for planning is dependent on the complexity of the required action: the more complex it is, the more preparation time is required.

The preparation of a motor response manifests itself as a slow build-up of EEG activity in the brain. This activity manifests itself in a slowly increasing negative electrical potential that is known as the **readiness potential** (Kornhuber & Deecke, 1965). This potential is one of the few physiological signals that is also widely known by its original German name *Bereitschaftspotential*. This electric potential appears to be generated by the motor cortex, and in part by the supplementary motor areas. In addition, prefrontal cortical areas have been found to be involved in generating the readiness potential (Singh & Knight, 1990). Anticipation of a motor response is reflected not only in the readiness potential but also in activation of the parietal cortex, the thalamus, and the cerebellum (Decety, Kawashima, Gulyás, & Roland, 1992).

3.7.3 GLOVER'S PLANNING CONTROL MODEL

The British cognitive psychologist Scott Glover (2004) developed a model to describe how visual information can be used to prepare a movement. According to Glover, two systems are involved in this process, namely a planning system and a control system. The planning system is predominantly used to initiate a movement. It is involved in selecting an object, in determining how this object should be grabbed, and in computing the timing of all the movements. In doing so, the planning system is influenced by the goals of the actor, the nature of the target object, the visual context, along with a host of other cognitive processes. Because the planning system is required to integrate information from a wide variety of different sources, and because it is under wilful, conscious control, it is relatively slow. Planning is dependent on visual representations that are formed in the inferior parietal cortex and on motor processes in the frontal lobes and basal ganglia. Here, the parietal cortex is mainly involved in integrating object-related information into the motor processes, such that we can manipulate objects.

In contrast, the control system is mainly used during the execution of a movement. It is involved in ensuring that the movements are accurate and that corrections are implemented through visual feedback. As such, the control system is believed to be affected only by the visual properties of objects, and not by the surrounding context. This results in the control system being relatively fast. The control system is believed to operate on the basis of visual representations that are formed in the superior parietal cortex, combined with motor representations that are formed in the primary motor cortex and the cerebellum.

3.7.4 MOTOR CONTROL

As just described, Glover (2004) presumes that motor control is guided by visual feedback. Although visual feedback is important, it is not the only form of feedback that is involved in motor control. Davidson and Wolpert (2005) coin the idea that predicting the future state of the motor system is also essential for the successful planning of an action, because there is inevitably a delay between the initiation and the execution of an action. To illustrate, imagine lifting a bucket filled with water with a relatively well-known weight. There are, in principle, two different ways in which we can adjust the tension of our muscles to maintain a constant height or a constant motion. For example, when we move our arms away from us, we will need to keep applying more and more force to keep the motion constant. Likewise, when we fill the bucket with water, we will need to steadily increase our grip. These adjustments typically occur instantaneously, without delay. When we need to adjust our grip due to an unexpected circumstance, for instance because it was much lighter than expected, or when we are unaware that it is leaking water, adjustments will have to be made via somatosensory feedback. This type of adjustment is not instantaneous, however, but applied with a delay.

Because motor programmes can instantaneously adapt to expected changes, it is assumed that they involve **forward models** that predict the consequences of a motor action. Such forward models are presumably based on **efference copies** of the generated motor commands, that is, an internal copy of the outbound motor command which can be combined with visual input (see Chapter 10) to predict the consequences of an action. For this reason, forward models are predictive. In addition to these predictive forward models, we can also identify **inverse models**. The latter appear to be engaged when we have to adjust our actions due to unexpected changes in the environment, such as the aforementioned leaking bucket.

Evidence in favour of forward models has predominantly been obtained via psychophysical, electrophysiological, and, to a lesser extent, neurophysiological studies. Psychophysiological studies typically record the force that is required to keep an object firmly between the tips of our fingers. For this, we need to apply a force that is sufficient to prevent the object from slipping through our fingers.

When the object's behaviour is unpredictable, we need to adjust our grip on the basis of tactile feedback from our fingertips. This feedback will inevitably be processed with a delay, resulting in the observation that our grip adjustments will be somewhat delayed with respect to changes in the object.

When the object is behaving predictably, however, we can estimate the required grip force on the basis of a forward model, resulting in instantaneous adjustment. Likewise, when the force required changes on the basis of our own actions, we typically find that there is no delay between the force that is required and the actual force that is applied. These anticipatory adjustments are among the strongest pieces of evidence for forward models (Flanagan & Wing, 1997; Johansson & Cole, 1992; Kawato, 1999).

Additional evidence for forward models comes from deafferented individuals. Deafferentation can be a consequence of a neuropathological condition that affects the sensory pathways. Nowak, Glasauer, and Hermsdorfer (2004), for example, report the case study of GL, a patient whose myelinated sensory nerve fibres had deteriorated to the point that she lost all somatosensory input from her neck, trunk, and limbs (even though she could still experience sensations of pain and temperature). When GL was required to grasp objects, her grip was much stronger than that of a control group. The key observation was, however, that the force she exerted was modulated by the anticipated changes in motion-induced torque. This implies that such modulations are based on a forward model. Despite our limited knowledge about the neurophysiological basis of these forward models, it has been suggested that models describing the dynamics of the object being manipulated are stored in the cerebellum (Kawato et al., 2003). This suggestion was based on the fact that areas within the cerebellum were selectively activated during a task that required participants to adjust their grip.

Finally, we should discuss one interesting finding that appears to be at odds with the notion of forward models. After all, forward models suggest that self-generated actions automatically result in an adjustment of our grip force. In a study by Nowak and Hermsdörfer (2003), however, participants were learning to lift a container filled with water, which eventually resulted in the application of a precisely adjusted amount of force (see fig 3.11). After they had learned this, participants were required to drink half of the water, and then to lift the container again. The question here was whether the self-generated action of drinking the water was sufficient for the internal model to adjust the amount of force required for lifting the now much lighter container. It turned out that this was not the case: participants still applied the original amount of force, as if they were lifting a completely filled container. This result implies that the participants still expected to lift the full amount of weight.

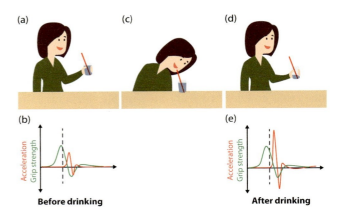

Figure 3.11 Participants trained in lifting a container of water (a) exerted a precisely measured amount of force (b). After drinking half of the container's content (c), they still exerted the same amount of force (e) as if the container was still full, while lifting it (d). Data from Nowak and Hermsdörfer (2003). (source: Davidson and Wolpert, 2005)

3.7.5 EYE AND HEAD MOTIONS

Before continuing, try to gently press one of your fingers against the edge of your left eye, near the temple. What did you notice? If all went well, you might have noticed that your environment started to move and, when you kept both eyes open, that you were temporarily seeing double. By pressing against your eye, you displaced it, which you perceived as motion of your environment. As we will see in more detail in Chapters 6 and 10, we make thousands of eye movements every day, without being aware of it, and – more remarkably – without noticing any instability in our visual perception. The latter observation is remarkable, given what we just experienced. Apparently pressing against our eyeballs results in visual instability, while our visual perception remains extremely stable when we move our eyes voluntarily. How is this possible? The main reason is that the forward models (just discussed) are also involved in eye movements. Although we typically are not required to adjust our muscle tension while moving our eyes, a large assembly of neural mechanisms needs to be informed about their actual position, so that the visual signals that are being picked up by the eyes can be seamlessly integrated with a pre-existing mental representation of our external environment.

Sommer and Wurtz (2002) found, on the basis of single cell recordings in monkeys, that neurons in the medial dorsal thalamus transmit a copy of the eye movement commands to the frontal eye fields. The latter brain areas are located in the frontal lobes and are involved in the preparation of eye movements. In this particular context, the efference copy is also known as a **corollary discharge signal**. This signal is used to update a forward model of the eyes' position, while the eye movement is executed. The thalamic neurons that are involved in this process were already activated before the actual execution of the eye movement, which implies that they are related to the motor commands themselves, as opposed to the feedback signals that follow the movement. Interestingly, when the corollary discharge signal was suppressed, the execution of the saccade itself was unaffected. The suppression did affect, however, the next saccade, suggesting that the internal model of the actual eye position was updated incorrectly, resulting in subsequent saccades that are erroneous.

Similar results have been reported for head movements. For example, in studying macaques Roy and Cullen (2001) found that an efference copy of the motor commands controlling the neck muscles is also used to cancel out the effects of self-generated head movement signals. More specifically, vestibular neurons that are normally involved in maintaining our balance (see Chapter 8) and in determining the rotation speed of our head during passive motions, were inhibited during active, self-initiated head movements.

3.7.6 OPTIMAL-FEEDBACK CONTROL

The Canadian neuroscientist Stephen Scott (2004) has proposed an **optimal-feedback control** mechanism that can be seen as an extension of the aforementioned control mechanisms. The central tenet of the optimal-feedback control mechanism is that our motor behaviour, the mechanical properties of our limbs, and the neural control mechanisms form a union that collectively determine our actions (see fig 3.12). Here, motor behaviour refers to the way a limb or body part moves while executing an action. This movement results from the combined actions of the neural circuits controlling the movement and the mechanical properties of our limbs. After all, the mechanical properties impose limits on the movements. For example, the way in which our skeleton is organised affects the way in which muscle tension can be converted into motion. Specifically, in movements involving multiple joints, the relation between muscle tension and motion becomes non-linear. Forces inducing motion in one joint can automatically induce motion in other joints. To illustrate this, try fully stretching your right arm. Now try to rotate your lower right arm upwards. Due to this action, the centre of gravity of your right arm changes, requiring

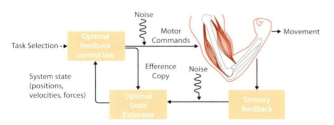

Figure 3.12 Scott's (2004) optimal-feedback control model. According to this model, motor control results from a combination of forward models, sensory feedback from the involved muscles, and the physical properties of the body. (source: Scott, 2004)

you to relax your shoulder muscles somewhat in order to keep your upper arm in its initial position. Despite these complexities, these movements are typically very smooth, allowing our hands to travel to their target positions in relatively straight lines.

Already by the mid-20th century, the American psychologist Paul Morris Fitts (1954) had described the way in which our limbs approach a target using an elegant law that still bears his name. **Fitts' law** states that the time needed to execute a rapid movement to a target location can be described as a function of the ratio between the distance to the target location and its radius. Fitts' law applies to simple movements, such as pointing to, or physically touching an object, with our hands or fingers. Harris and Wolpert (1998) have described a mechanism that can explain why such movements adhere to Fitts' law. Their optimal-feedback control mechanism combines information from forward models with sensory feedback in such a way that deviations from the optimal trajectory are rapidly detected and corrected (see also Wolpert, Gahahramani, & Jordan, 1995). According to Scott (2004), the primary motor cortex plays an important role in this feedback-driven control mechanism. Supporting this view, neurons in this area have been found to respond rapidly to perturbations of limb positions (Wolpaw, 1980).

3.7.7 PREDICTIVE CODING AND MOTOR CONTROL

Finally, what is the difference between the forward predictive models, as proposed by Davidson and Wolpert (2005), and the generative models that are central to the predictive coding framework? A crucial question here is whether the notion of a forward model can be unified with the key assumptions of the predictive coding framework. Although both approaches postulate an internal model, Friston (2011) emphasises that forward models differ fundamentally from the generative models that are postulated by the predictive coding framework. Friston argues, however, that the classic forward models can be made compatible with the predictive coding framework through a relatively small modification in the underlying mathematical implementation (see fig 3.13). In essence, this modification consists of adding the prediction error processing mechanism that was originally missing in the classic forward model.

Adams et al. (2013) noted that the descending neural signals, from the primary motor cortex to the periphery of the body, strongly resemble the top-down recurrent pathways connecting the higher levels of the visual cortex with the lower ones (see Chapters 2 and 6 for more details on these pathways). In the visual areas, these pathways are assumed to relay predictions to the lower-level areas. Based on this similarity, Adams et al. (2013) argue that the descending signals in the motor system are not motor commands, but predictions. According to Adams et al., these

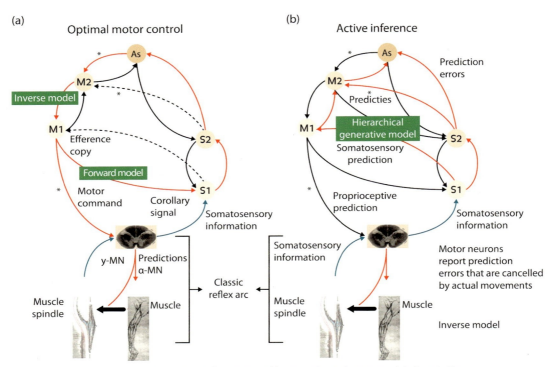

(a) Optimal motor control

(b) Active inference

Arrows marked with * differ in terms of functionality in the two models depicted here.

Figure 3.13 Forward versus generative models. (a) According to classic theories, motor control operates on the basis of a combination of forward and inverse models. (b) A nearly identical model can be achieved by adding a prediction error processing mechanism to these models. M1, M2, S1, and S2 refer to the primary and secondary motor and sensory cortices. As refers to the prefrontal association cortex. (source: Adams et al., 2013)

predictions reflect the state of our body that our brain expects it to be in. Again, this assumes the involvement of a predictive coding mechanism, because the somatosensory feedback signals from our body (see Chapters 8 and 10) and our eyes (Chapter 10) generate the prediction errors that then are relayed back, via ascending connections, to the motor cortex.

From this perspective, human motor behaviour is the result of processing these somatosensory and visual prediction errors. According to Adams et al., the descending motor signals do not represent commands that instruct our bodies what to do. Instead, Adams et al. assume they represent the expected state that our body should be in. Whenever a mismatch between the expected state and the actual state is detected, the mismatch is resolved via a prediction error processing system. This results in the activation of local neural circuits in the periphery of the body. On the one hand, this activation results in an adaptation of muscle tension, which ultimately results in motion. On the other hand, it results in the generation of a feedback signal that signals the mismatch and passes it on to higher levels in the motor system. From this perspective, the simple reflexes that we introduced at the beginning of this chapter are possibly part of a larger mechanism that is involved in minimising prediction errors. Moreover, such a prediction error minimalisation mechanism is capable of explaining many of the aforementioned effects of classical conditioning (Pezzulo, Rigoli, & Friston, 2015). After all, the expectancy of a specific stimulus may be sufficient

to generate a prediction to which the body responds automatically.

Expecting the body to be in a specific state would, according to the predictive coding theory, automatically trigger the adjustments in muscle tension necessary to align it with the expectation. Interpreted this way, the mere thought of an action would indeed result in the automatic execution of it.

3.8 PROCEDURAL LEARNING

3.8.1 SKILLS

According to Logan and Crump (2009, p. 1296), 'a world-famous rock guitarist, legendary for his dazzling speed and virtuosity, was once asked how he played so quickly. He said, "They asked me what I was doing, and I said I don't know. Then I started looking and it got confusing."' This example shows that learning a complex motor skill, such as playing the guitar, is largely an implicit process. In contrast to learning lists of words or memorising the capitals of each European country, which are examples of declarative processes, we have no conscious access to the motor programmes that we have acquired while learning the skill in question. This makes the learning of a motor skill a prototypical example of an **implicit learning**

process. Implicit learning processes are also known as **procedural learning**.

Cleeremans and Jiménez (2002) define implicit learning as a process that allows us to detect regularities in our environment. This takes place without having the intention to do so and without being consciously aware of it. Thus, implicit learning proceeds in such a manner that the resulting knowledge is hard, if not impossible, to describe verbally. More specifically, Reber (1993) has argued that implicit learning is characterised by the following five properties: (1) it is hardly affected by age or level of cognitive development; (2) implicit learning skills are unrelated to IQ; (3) it is not related to dysfunctions affecting explicit learning processes; (4) implicit learning is less affected by individual differences than explicit learning; and (5) implicit learning processes can be found among many different species.

3.8.1.1 What Constitutes a Procedure?

When we define a procedure as 'knowing how', we end up classifying a considerable amount of knowledge under this definition (Knowlton, Siegel, & Moody, 2017). For instance, every bit of knowledge that forms the basis of our perceptual and motor skills can be considered to be procedural, specifically so after an intense amount of training. Actions such as placing an autograph, or driving a car with a manual transmission system, are difficult to describe verbally, but are easy to execute under the right conditions. Other examples of 'knowing how' are less clearly procedural. For instance, learning the rules of a game might include a declarative phase, consisting of the explicit application of the rules, which might be followed by a more procedural phase, consisting of developing strategies to beat one's opponent. While the rules themselves are easy to verbalise, the underlying strategies or algorithms might be far less suitable for verbalisation, allowing them only to be acquired through intense training. In daily life, many procedures consist of a combination of explicit and implicit knowledge.

From the preceding description, it may already follow that implicit learning processes are not limited to acquiring motor skills. Learning to detect regularities in sequences or to classify visual patterns can also be considered to be forms of implicit learning (Leggio & Molinari, 2015). These aspects of procedural learning will be discussed in more depth in Chapters 13 and 14 (memory) and Chapter 20 (categorisation). In the following sections, we will predominantly focus on the processes involved in learning motor skills.

In addition to learning procedures and skills, we should also consider the formation of habits (Packard & Knowlton, 2002). The latter is an example of the gradual formation of stimulus-response associations. The idea that stimulus-response associations can be formed gradually was already promoted in the early 20th century by Clark Hull. Hull (1943) believed that all forms of learning could be reduced to such stimulus-response association. Although later work has refuted this idea, habit formation is a classic example of a situation where it does happen. Habits can be formed by routinely executing the same action over and over again. To illustrate, when we take the same route to the university every day, the habit of driving to work may eventually form. This habit may eventually be disconnected from its original goal, resulting in a situation where we might take the wrong turn when, on a Saturday, we are not driving to work but heading to the city centre. Compared to the learning of rules or skills, habit formation might be a less outspoken example of procedural learning. Nevertheless, habits are procedures in the sense that specific circumstances can trigger a specific action. Moreover, habits are often inaccessible to conscious awareness (Bayley, Frascino, & Squire, 2005).

3.8.1.2 Motor versus Cognitive Procedures

As detailed earlier, procedural learning involves motor skills and cognitive skills, suggesting a large degree of overlap between these two forms of learning (Rosenbaum, Carlson, & Gilmore, 2001). Nevertheless, substantial differences can be identified. Motor actions, for instance, always need to be planned on the basis of the geometry of our environment. In addition, motor skills are often critically dependent upon specific effector systems. It is, for example, almost impossible for musicians to switch their left and right hands while playing an intricate solo. However, even in these cases, a certain level of motor equivalence is still possible. On a guitar, for example scales can be played on different positions of the neck, allowing a certain degree of freedom in the actual execution. Finally, motor control is almost always dependent on feedback from the visual or proprioceptive systems.

The acquisition of cognitive skills is characterised by a less strict distinction between planning and execution. For instance, a game of chess can be played regardless of whether the pieces are moved using your left or right hand, or even by reporting the moves verbally. In addition, executing a cognitive skill is much less dependent on the instantaneous integration of feedback from the environment. The brain areas that are involved in learning motor skills are therefore different to those involved in learning cognitive skills. Despite these differences, however, some commonalities can be identified as well. Motor behaviour is instantiated via a rough action plan that will subsequently be transformed into actual muscle movements. These action plans are somewhat similar to the cognitive plans that are formed when learning a cognitive skill. Additionally, both skills share the property of not being readily transferable to a different context. For instance, mastering a programming language has typically no influence on one's everyday reasoning skills (Pea & Kurland, 1984).

3.8.1.3 Properties of Procedural Learning

Based on the definition of a procedure as 'knowing how', we can define procedural learning as 'learning how'. Starting from this definition, we can define scientific studies on procedural learning as a discipline that aims to determine how 'learning how' differs from 'learning that'. Put differently, the discipline does not focus so much on the skill itself, but instead aims to determine how this skill has been acquired. Because the learning process remains implicit, one cannot rely on verbal reports. Instead, the learning process needs to be studied by determining how task performance changes as a function of time. Because we have no conscious access to the learning process itself, we are facing a situation where we make progress on a task, without being consciously aware of it.

Since procedural knowledge is marked by a lack of flexibility, we can only apply procedural knowledge within the domain in which we have acquired the skill in question. Learning to type, for example, does not make us a better pianist. Even more so, even experienced drivers may initially experience difficulties while driving in an unfamiliar car model. In this respect, procedural knowledge is markedly different from consciously acquired **declarative knowledge** (see Chapter 13). Another marked property of procedural knowledge is that it is extremely difficult to execute only one part of a procedure. Finally, it has been found that procedural learning is typically still intact in patients with **amnesia** (Cohen & Squire, 1980). This fact, combined with the fact that the execution of mental tasks does typically not interfere with practicing motor skills, suggests a clear dissociation between procedural and declarative knowledge.

Despite this dissociation, it is unlikely that our declarative and procedural memories are completely separated. Learning to switch gears in a car with manual transmission, for example, requires us to know what a clutch and a gearbox are, and what their purpose is. Thus, we may assume that learning a skill always requires a certain level of declarative knowledge. This initial body of declarative knowledge forms a basis from which we gradually learn the procedures required to perform the skill in question. Additionally, procedural knowledge may sometimes interfere with declarative knowledge. As discussed earlier, we can habitually drive to a location that we did not intend to go to. Likewise, declarative

knowledge may interfere with procedural knowledge. For instance, many athletes or musicians are familiar with the phenomenon of choking under pressure, that is, the failure of successfully executing a skill when attention is too strongly focused on the performance (Baumeister, 1984).

Given the occurrences of these interactions between procedural and declarative knowledge, we can now ask where and when they occur. One possibility is that this occurs during the execution of a task, and that the precise nature of the interaction is dependent on which type of knowledge is accessible. For example, while driving a well-known route, we may be able to do so exclusively on the basis of our procedural knowledge. In contrast, driving to an unknown location may require us to make use of declarative knowledge in the form of a route description. Thus, when situations prevent us from taking advantage of our procedural knowledge, declarative knowledge may be used as a backup.

For the domain of work-related skills, the Danish human factors expert Jens Rasmussen (1983) has distinguished three different levels of task performance, that he identified as the skill-based, rule-based, and knowledge-based performance levels (see fig 3.14). According to Rasmussen, task performance is skill-based when a task can be completed solely on the basis of procedural knowledge. This is, for instance, the case while driving a well-known route or while performing a well-practiced guitar solo. Outside the motor performance domain, skills performed at this level may be found, for example, among medical experts inspecting X-ray images (see Chapter 22 for more details).

Rule-based performance consists of a combination of declarative and procedural knowledge. This type of

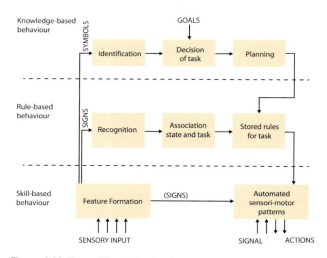

Figure 3.14 Three different levels of task representation according to Rasmussen (1983).

performance might be observed, for instance, when an unexpected obstacle along a well-known route requires us to deviate. In a similar vein, musicians frequently combine declarative and procedural knowledge during improvisations: the individual phrases of the solo are stored as procedural knowledge, while the manner in which they are combined is based on declarative knowledge. Here, the declarative rules describe how the procedural skills are sequenced in the right order.

Knowledge-based skills are typically employed when a task needs to be completed solely on the basis of declarative knowledge. This might be the case among medical specialist needing to formulate diagnoses for difficult, challenging cases (Mylopoulos & Regehr, 2007b). Considering that our procedural memory is less sensitive to distraction than our declarative memory (Foerde, Knowlton, & Poldrack, 2006a), skill-based performance, and to a lesser degree rule-based performance, is more resilient against distraction than knowledge-based task performance.

3.8.2 TASKS

3.8.2.1 The Mirror Trace Task

One of the first tasks that was ever employed in studies of procedural learning required participants to trace the outlines of an object, while patients monitored their own hand movements via a mirror. This mirror trace task was used by Milner (1962) to establish a dissociation between declarative and procedural knowledge (see Chapter 13). The successful completion of this task requires participants to invert the existing associations between visual information and motor commands. Initially, participants will pause frequently and deviate from the correct path. After some practice, however, they succeed in tracing the target object with a much higher efficiency (Gabrieli, Corkin, Mickel, & Growdown, 1993). In Milner's original study, it was found that a well-known amnesia patient, Henry Molaison (see Box 13.1), was capable of learning this task within a time span of just a few days, despite not remembering the learning experience itself. Similarly, the ability for procedural learning remains intact, not just in amnesia patients but also in patients with Alzheimer's disease (Gabrieli et al., 1993).

3.8.2.2 The Pursuit Rotor Task

Another task that is frequently used in procedural learning studies is the pursuit rotor task (Knowlton et al., 2017). Here, participants need to position a stylus on a small plate (of approximately 2 cm in diameter) that is mounted on the edge of a turntable. The rotation speed of this turntable can be adjusted to manipulate the difficulty of this task. Here, motor learning corresponds with an increase in the relative amount of time in which the participant succeeds in keeping the stylus positioned on the plate. Initially, most participants' movements are highly irregular; however, they gradually become smoother. Neuropsychological studies have found that the basal ganglia, in unison with the motor cortex and the supplementary motor cortex, strongly determine one's performance on this task. Patients with **Huntington's disease** and **Parkinson's disease** typically display impaired performance on this task (Harrington, Haaland, Yeo, & Marder, 1990; Heindel, Butters, & Salmon, 1988).

3.8.2.3 The Serial-Reaction Time Task

One of the most basic methods for studying implicit learning makes use of the serial-reaction time task (Nissen & Bullemer, 1987). As illustrated in Figure 3.15, in a typical version of this task, four positions are marked on a computer screen. On each trial, a stimulus will appear at one of these positions and it is the participant's task to respond as quickly as possible by pressing a button that corresponds with this position. Unknown to the participants, the stimuli will be presented in a complex repetitive order. At the end of the experiment, a new sequence will be presented, also unknown to the participant. During the experiment, participants' responses gradually become faster, until the new sequence is presented, when responses become markedly slower again (Shanks, 2010). When finished, participants typically report not being aware of the presence of hidden sequences. Again, patients with Huntington's disease (Knopman & Nissen, 1991) and Parkinson's disease (Jackson, Jackson, Harrison, Henderson, & Kennard, 1995)

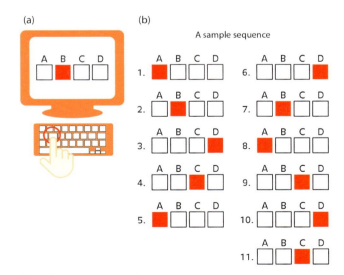

Figure 3.15 The serial-reaction time task. (a) Four positions are marked on a computer screen, each corresponding to a specific key. When one of these positions lights up, the participant is required to press the corresponding key as rapidly as possible. (b) Example of a sequence. (source: Knowlton et al., 2017)

are frequently characterised by impaired performance on this task.

Now, is it really the case that participants are unaware of the hidden sequence? To address this question, Wilkinson and Shanks (2004) gave their participants 1,500 trials, distributed across ten blocks of trials, and reported a strong decrease in mean reaction time across these blocks. Following this, a test for explicit learning was administered that was based on a **process dissociation procedure**. This procedure was initially developed by Jacoby (1991) to differentiate between implicit and explicit learning. It involves participants performing a task that consists of a series of repeating stimuli. In one condition, the inclusion condition, participants are encouraged to report their best guess of the next stimulus, while in another condition, the exclusion condition, they are encouraged to not guess the next stimulus. If sequence learning is completely implicit, participants should not be able to verbally report what they have learned, nor should they be able to use this information in their guesses. Thus, if learning is completely implicit, participants' reports should be approximately equal in both the inclusion and exclusion condition. If learning is at least partially explicit, however, it may be expected that participants' reports differ somewhat between the two conditions.

Wilkinson and Shanks' (2004) process dissociation procedure consisted of a block of trials in which participants were required to self-generate a number of responses. In the inclusion conditions, participants were required to mimic the sequence that was used in the original experiment as closely as possible, whereas in the exclusion condition, they were required to generate sequences that did not match the ones used in the main experiment. Wilkinson and Shanks found that in the inclusion condition, the generated sequences matched the original ones more closely than in the exclusion condition. This implies that participants had at least some degree of explicit knowledge of the sequences they had learned.

3.9 CHUNKING

3.9.1 CHUNKING AND SEQUENCE LEARNING

3.9.1.1 The Discrete Sequence Production Task

A second way of studying sequence learning processes is based on the **discrete sequence production task** (Abrahamse, Ruitenberg, de Kleine, & Verwey, 2013; Verwey & Eikelboom, 2003). This task is based on the serial reaction time task in that participants are also required to respond as quickly as possible to sequences

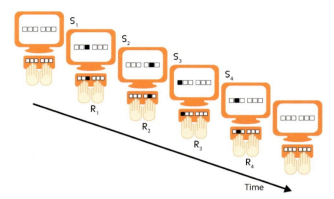

Figure 3.16 Illustration of the discrete sequence production task. Shown here is a sequence consisting of four responses (R₁–R₄) to a series of four stimuli (S₁–S₄). (source: Abrahamse et al., 2013)

of stimuli. Here, participants are required to place four to eight fingers on specified positions on a keyboard. A corresponding number of markers, frequently in the form of small squares, is presented on a computer display, such that each marker corresponds with one finger (see fig 3.16). As soon as one of the markers lights up, participants are required to press the corresponding key. After this, the next stimulus, consisting of the lighting up of the next marker, will be presented. A typical sequence consists of two fixed series of three to seven stimuli, resulting in the execution of two sequences of key presses. Typically, these sequences are presented in a random order. The implication of this approach is that, after practice, the task can be reduced to a simple two alternatives choice task, because participants need to determine which of the two sequences should be executed first.

The discrete sequence production task is characterised by two specific properties that are of interest here. Firstly, the task typically starts with a practice phase, consisting of approximately 500–1,000 repetitions per sequence, in which the building blocks of the task are formed, that is, motor sequences that can be considered a unit. Such a unit is known as a **motor chunk** as it is considered to be a set of motor commands that can be executed in one go (Pew, 1966; Verwey, 1996). After practice, the properties of these chunks can be studied in a subsequent test phase, in which they will be compared with new, unpractised sequences that serve as a control condition. When the practised sequences are executed more effectively, that is, more rapidly and with fewer errors, it can be concluded that they have been learned.

This task consists of spatially defined stimuli that are visible throughout the entire practice phase. In addition, they are directly linked to specific keys. In some variants of the task, participants are explicitly instructed what the sequence is and this sequence is explicitly associated to one specific stimulus (Rosenbaum, Inhoff, & Gordon,

1984). For instance, participants could be instructed to respond with their little (P), ring (R), middle (M), or index (I) finger of their left hand. Using this scheme, participants can, for example, be instructed to produce the sequence I-P-M-I-P-M. This sequence consists of two repetitions of a three-response sequence. Alternatively, they could be instructed to produce the sequence M-P-R-I-R-P, which consists of one repetition of a six-response sequence. Each of these sequences can now be linked to one specific stimulus (for instance, I-P-M-I-P-M to the letter O and M-P-R-I-R-P to the letter X). When one of these letters is presented on a computer screen, participants are required to produce the corresponding sequence as rapidly as possible.

Although the discrete sequence production task bears some resemblance to the serial reaction time task, there is one significant difference: although the serial reaction time task involves implicit learning, the responses cannot be broken down into discrete sequences. For this reason, chunks cannot be formed in the serial reaction time task (Jimenez, Mendez, Pasquali, Abrahamse, & Verwey, 2011). In contrast, one of the main goals of the discrete sequence production task is to study this chunk formation process. To do so, it is necessary to avoid common, well-practised motor sequences, such 12344321 or 12123434, as these correspond too closely to the layout of a numeric keypad.

3.9.1.2 Results

When we examine the execution of a given six-stroke key sequence, we can observe two typical results. Firstly, we can observe an initial phase that is marked by the initiation of the sequence. This is marked by an initial response time (that is, the time it takes before the first key stroke is executed) that is somewhat larger than the response times of subsequent keystrokes in the sequence. This extended initial reaction time is believed to reflect the selection and initiation of the relevant sequence. For longer sequences, it is typically found that this initial reaction time is also relatively long, suggesting that during this period the relevant responses are loaded into a motor buffer. It should be noted, however, that the degree of increase of this initial response time is reduced with practice. The latter result implied that practice results in a more efficient representation of a motor chunk.

Secondly, relatively long sequences, consisting of more than four keypress combinations, are typically characterised by a relatively long reaction time, approximately in the middle of the sequence. This implies these sequences are broken up into shorter chunks, with the extended reaction time in the middle representing the loading of a new chunk. More specifically, it possibly represents a higher cognitive process that is either involved in the processing of the next chunk in the sequence (Verwey, 2010) or in

the strategic dissection of the sequence (Wymbs, Bassett, Mucha, Porter, & Grafton, 2012).

3.9.2 NEURAL BASIS OF CHUNKING AND SEQUENCING

Verwey, Lammens, and van Honk (2002) combined the discrete sequence production task with TMS (see Box 3.3). They stimulated the supplementary motor cortex for 20 minutes using repetitive TMS, which resulted in a reduced excitability of this brain area. If the supplementary motor cortex is involved in the selection of individual elements of a known sequence, it should be expected that TMS would induce a general slowing while participants reproduce the sequence. If, on the other hand, this brain area is specifically involved in the preparation of an entire chunk, it should be expected that TMS would specifically affect the initiation of the sequence, but not the production of subsequent elements. Verwey et al. found that TMS had a negative impact during the learning phase. Here the production of each element was slowed down, implying that the supplementary motor cortex is involved in the processing of each individual element, suggesting that the concatenation of each element into a chunk had already taken place at an earlier stage.

Ruitenberg, Verwey, Schutter, and Abrahamse (2014) used a similar approach but stimulated the presupplementary motor cortex. This stimulation specifically affected the selection and initiation of a motor chunk. Thus, these results are consistent with the idea that the presupplementary motor cortex is involved in the planning of a motor programme.

Further evidence for the hypothesis that chunks are already formed at an early stage in the motor hierarchy is provided by an fMRI study by Wymbs et al. (2012). These authors found that the production of motor chunks is associated with an extensive network of brain areas that includes the putamen and a left hemisphere fronto-parietal network. Participants were required to produce sequences consisting of 12 key presses, while their brain activity was recorded. The exact sequence that was to be produced was presented visually, in the form of a sequence of musical notes. Here, the highest note corresponded with the little finger and the lowest one with the index finger. Based on the time that elapsed between two successive responses (the **inter key interval**), it could be determined how participants segmented these individual responses into chunks. Again, the same logic as described earlier was used: longer response times were taken as an indication of a boundary between two chunks. Wymbs et al. found an increase in activation in the bilateral putamen – a constituent of the basal ganglia – that was associated with the concatenation of two chunks. Likewise, activation in the fronto-parietal networks was associated with the segmentation, that

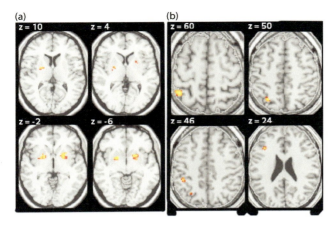

Figure 3.17 Brain activity associated with chunk formation. (a) Activation in the putamen was associated with the concatenation of individual motor elements. (b) Activation in the intraparietal sulcus and the dorsolateral prefrontal cortex was associated with the segmentation of motor elements. (source: Wymbs et al., 2012)

is the subdivision, of the 12 responses into two to four chunks of approximately three to six responses each (see fig 3.17).

The latter result is consistent with a TMS study by Robertson, Tormos, Maeda, and Pascual-Leone (2001). These authors found that repetitive TMS stimulation of the dorsolateral prefrontal cortex resulted in participants being less capable of learning sequences in a serial reaction time task. They also found, however, that this effect was limited to tasks employing spatial information, as is typically the case in serial reaction time tasks. Therefore, Robertson et al. concluded that the dorsolateral prefrontal cortex is mainly involved in converting the spatial position of the stimulus into an action that is required to be executed.

3.10 MOTOR COGNITION

The final topic in this chapter concerns **motor cognition**. We started our introduction of motor control by introducing the concept of embodied cognition, that is, the idea that our cognitive faculties have developed as a method of optimising our bodily functions. Motor cognition thus implies that we cannot decouple our cognitive functions from those involved in regulating our bodies. It follows that we are also unable to decouple cognition from motor functions (Clark, 1999; Wolpert et al., 2003). Thus, motor cognition refers to the idea that cognition is embedded in motor processes. The central idea behind motor cognition is that our motor systems are not only involved in the preparation and execution of an action, but that they are also involved in evaluating the consequences of possible actions and in evaluating somebody else's intentions. This suggests that human motor processing and cognition are

strongly intertwined, and it would be beyond the scope of this chapter to discuss all the details of this relation here. After all, it becomes increasingly clear that the motor system is involved in a wide range of cognitive functions. For this reason, we will only provide a brief introduction here, focusing on the interrelation between the major topics, while details will be discussed in the following chapters, where relevant.

3.10.1 SIMULATING ACTION

As discussed earlier, the motor system is not only involved in executing an action but also in imagining an action, or, put differently, in simulating an action (Sobierajewicz, Jaskowski, & Van der Lubbe, 2019). In a similar vein, the German neuroscientist Germund Hesslow (2002) has argued that these simulations will manifest themselves as conscious thought. According to Hesslow, this may happen in the form of internal (covert) speech, which bears all the characteristics of real speech, except for the fact that the eventual motor commands generating the required muscle and tongue moments are not generated.

Evidence for this idea stems from a TMS study, where stimulation of the motor cortex resulted in a disruption of inner speech (Aziz-Zadeh, Cattaneo, Rochat, & Rizzolatti, 2005). In this study, participants were required to count, either overtly or covertly, the number of syllables of a given word. In both the covert and overt conditions, reaction times were longer when the motor cortex was stimulated using TMS, implying that the motor cortex is critically involved in the counting process. This suggests that the motor cortex is involved in generating thoughts. This idea is consistent with an older finding suggesting that it is involved in the understanding of speech (Liberman, Cooper, Shankweiler, & Studdert-Kennedy, 1967). Evidence for the latter idea was also provided by a TMS study, in which a part of the motor cortex representing the tongue was stimulated. As a consequence, a significant increase in articulatory movements was found while participants listened to words that required strong movements of the tongue (Fadiga, Craighero, Buccino, & Rizzolatti, 2002).

According to Hesslow (2002), conscious thoughts can also manifest themselves in the form of mental imagery of actions or the consequences of these actions. This idea has two major implications. Firstly, it implies that our motor system is involved in mental imagery. There is indeed a substantial amount of evidence for this idea (see Chapter 4). Secondly, it suggests the existence of a strong relation between motor processes, perception, and cognition. For mental imagery, it has already been shown that it involves the visual system (Klein et al., 2004; Kosslyn, 1999; Kosslyn et al., 2001). As we will discuss in more detail next, evidence for a relation between perception and action can be found in two different forms, namely, in the form of a body model and in the integration of perceptual and motor representations.

Motor simulations are also believed to be active when we interpret the actions of someone else, for instance when we see another person dancing (Cross, Hamilton, & Grafton, 2006). The idea that we use our motor systems in these mental simulations forms one of the major foundations for the field of motor cognition (Jeannerod, 2001).

3.10.2 THE BODY MODEL

Our primary somatosensory cortex, which is the part of the neocortex where our bodily sensations, such as touch, pressure, temperature, and pain, are represented, is marked by an anatomical organisation that roughly corresponds with that of the primary motor cortex (see Chapter 8). Originally, it was believed that these somatosensory representations were formed solely on the basis of pure, bottom-up driven, afferent input from the senses. Recently, this view has been revised quite drastically. The German neuroscientist Michael Brecht (2017) proposed, for instance, that the somatosensory cortex hosts a representation of our body that can be used to simulate behaviour and to evaluate the consequences of these simulated actions (see Chapter 8). In addition, Brecht suggests that this model can also be used to evaluate the consequences of real actions.

3.10.3 PERCEPTION–ACTION INTEGRATION

Chapter 6 provides in-depth coverage of the visual system and discusses the contributions of the Canadian neuroscientist Melvyn Goodale and his British colleague David Milner. Goodale and Milner (see, for example: Goodale & Milner, 1992, 2006; Milner & Goodale, 2008) reported the existence of two different visual systems, namely one system that is involved in the recognition of objects and a second system that is involved in the perception of motion and the integration of visual information into an action plan. The latter system, known as the **perception-for-action system**, is therefore mainly involved in aligning our motor actions with a continuously changing environment, on the basis of information that is picked up by our visual system (see Chapter 9 for more details on perception–action integration).

3.10.4 MOTIVATION, EMOTION, AND SOCIAL COGNITION

The last major theme of motor cognition that we discuss here concerns the relation among motivation, emotion, and social interaction. The importance of the motor system in these aspects of cognitive psychology was first acknowledged by the discovery of the mirror neuron system in monkeys. **Mirror neurons** were originally found in the monkey ventro-medial premotor cortex (see Chapter 23). These neurons were characterised by the fact that they not only responded when the monkeys were required to perform an action themselves, but also when they observed an experimenter performing the action. A human equivalent of the mirror neuron system is not only believed to be involved in learning through imitation (Rizzolatti & Fabbri-Destro, 2010) but also in the understanding of the intentions (Gallese, Keysers, & Rizzolatti, 2004; Kohler et al., 2002; Umilta et al., 2001) or the emotions of someone else.

Finally, emotion and motivation research have a long-standing tradition of establishing a relation between bodily responses and cognition. This tradition originates from work conducted by William James (1884), Carl Lange (1885), Walter Cannon (1927), and (more recently) Antonio Damasio (1996). A central theme in these authors' work is that physiological responses (sweating, changes in heart rate, tremors) are not the consequences of emotions, but that emotions are experienced because we detect the physiological reaction of our body to an emotional stimulus (see Chapter 12). On a somewhat related note, motivation is related to our bodies need to regulate their internal states (see Chapter 11). Consequently, it appears to be of crucial importance that sensory signals transmitted from the body are integrated into our cognitive processes.

3.11 SUMMARY

Since the start of the early 1990s, there has been a growing realisation that cognitive functions arose from an evolutionary need to control the movements of the body and to regulate its internal states. This realisation forms one of the core assumptions of the embodied cognition movement.

Internal regulation is mainly carried out by autonomous systems in the brainstem, which communicate with the body via the sympathetic and parasympathetic nervous systems. In addition, internal regulation is mediated by hormones that are secreted by the endocrine system.

Reflexes form the most basic patterns of motion that we can identify. They are automatic responses to external stimuli, which are mediated by local circuits, that do not the brain. Reflexes can be learned through conditioning. Classical and operant conditioning are the two most well-known forms of conditioning. Unconditional reflexes are malleable, however, as they can either habituate or sensitise, depending on the nature of the stimulus. Novel stimuli typically evoke a strong response that is known as the orienting response.

The motor system that is involved in voluntary motion is characterised by a complex network of cortical and subcortical brain areas. Moreover, a large number of perceptual brain areas are involved in coordinating movements. Cortical brain areas are mainly involved in the planning of motion, whereas subcortical areas are mainly involved in the coordination of movements.

It is still not entirely clear what the exact role of the primary motor cortex is. Whereas some studies suggest that this brain area is involved in the planning of movements, other studies suggest that it is predominantly involved in controlling them. On a relatively course scale, the primary motor cortex represents a map of the body. On a more fine-grained scale, however, this map is considerably more ambiguous, as representations of different body parts tend to overlap somewhat. Moreover, the primary motor cortex is characterised by a large degree of plasticity. Practicing specific skills can increase the size of the areas related to the body parts in question and these organisational changes have been related to the acquisition of motor skills (Strick, Dum, & Rathelot, 2021). Extreme practice can result in impairments in motor control due to overlapping body representations.

The ideomotor theory describes how an intention can be converted into an action. This theory is based on the idea that thinking about the consequences of an action may result in the automatic execution of that action. The execution of the action itself has traditionally been believed to involve the execution of a motor programme. Such a programme needs to be planned before it can be executed. Different mechanisms have been identified that are involved in ensuring that the action is executed according to plan and in correcting any deviations from this plan. Forward models ensure that the actual output from the motor system is adjusted on the basis of expected changes. These models ensure, for example, that we adjust our muscle strength when we expect an object to change weight. In addition, they are also involved in compensating for changes in our sensory input, as a consequence of head and eye movements.

Forward models are supplemented by sensory feedback. Collectively, these sources provide the input for an optimal control mechanism capable of efficiently correcting deviations from a planned trajectory. Despite some similarities, optimal control mechanisms appear to be incompatible with the basic principles of the predictive coding theory. Relatively minor changes in the underlying mathematical implementation can make these models compatible, however. According to the predictive coding framework, the motor system does not generate motor commands. Instead, it assumes that the output of the motor system is a set of predictions. These predictions describe the state of the body that the brain expects it to be in. Deviations from the predictions result in both an error signal and a corrective muscular action that brings the body closer to its predicted state, thus minimising the prediction error.

One major characteristic of the motor system is its ability to learn. The way the motor system learns is a specific case of a more general form of learning that is inaccessible to our consciousness, known as procedural learning. Procedural learning involves the detection of regularities in our environment. Motor learning can be studied using a number of different tasks, including the mirror trace task, the pursuit rotor task, the serial reaction time task, and the discrete sequence production task.

The discrete sequence production task is also frequently used to study the formation of motor chunks. Studies based on this task have established that the basal ganglia and the prefrontal cortex play important roles in the generation of a motor chunk.

Motor processes are an intrinsic part of human behaviour. The scientific study of these processes has seen a strongly renewed interest in the last decennia. It is currently believed that motor processes are not only involved in the execution of motion, but that they also play a pivotal role in many other cognitive functions. A newly evolving field studying these relations between motor processes and cognition is known as motor cognition. This field studies, among other things, the involvement of the motor system in the simulation of actions, in perception and action integration, the interpretation of body states in emotional and motivational processes, and in the interpretation and understanding of the actions of others.

NOTE

1 Although the example refers to single neurons, this is somewhat misleading. In reality, even the simplest reflex arches consist of hundreds of neurons operating in parallel and thousands of synaptic connections between these neurons.

FURTHER READING

Abernethy, B., Hanrathan, S. J., Kippers, V. MacKinnon, L. T., & Pandy, M. G. (2005). *The biophysical foundations of human movement*. Stanningly: Human Kinetics.

Clark, A. (2015). *Surfing uncertainty: Prediction, action, and the embodied mind*. Oxford: Oxford University Press.

Rosenbaum, D. A. (2009). *Human motor control*. London: Elsevier.

Scott-Kelso, J. A. (1982). *Human motor behavior: An introduction*. New York, NY: Taylor & Francis Group.

Schmidt, R. A., & Lee, T. D. (2008). *Motor learning and performance: From principles to application*. Stanningly: Human Kinetics.

CHAPTER 4
Consciousness and attention

4.1 INTRODUCTION TO CONSCIOUSNESS

What is consciousness? Most likely, this question is already as old as the phenomenon itself. Famous ancient Greek philosophers such as Plato and Aristotle are known to have written extensively about the nature of consciousness and perception. Given this fascination, it appears to be somewhat surprising that the empirical study of consciousness did not come to fruition until the late 20th century. Despite some initial attempts by the German structuralists of the late 19th century, the general consensus was that consciousness was inaccessible to empirical methods, resulting in the fact that questions regarding consciousness remained almost exclusively in the domain of philosophy.

This situation gradually changed in the mid-1970s. Around that time, the Austrian-born American psychologist George Mandler (1975) introduced a differentiation between slow, serial, and limited-capacity conscious processing, on the one hand, and rapid, parallel, extensive processing, on the other. Since then, the arsenal of available research methods has steadily increased. For example, consciousness can be studied by investigating the effects of traumatic brain injury. In addition, changes in conscious awareness can be attributed to psychiatric conditions, mental illnesses, or drug use. Other studies have employed the use of ambiguous **bistable images**[1] (Leopold & Logothetis, 1999) by relating changes in the perception of these images to changes in brain activity.

4.2 CONSCIOUSNESS AND PHILOSOPHY

To fully understand the position of consciousness studies in the cognitive neurosciences, we need to start by investigating how our ideas about consciousness are rooted in philosophy. A number of influential schools of thought on consciousness can be found in both ancient Greek and modern Western philosophy. Of these, monism and dualism are among the most prominent schools of thought. Dualism assumes that a separation exists between a materialistic body and non-materialistic soul, whereas monism presumes the existence of only one essence, be it either materialistic or non-materialistic.

4.2.1 DUALISM

The idea of a distinction between a physical body and a non-physical soul can be traced back to ancient Greece. For example, both Plato and Aristotle believed in the existence of multiple souls. More specifically, they believed in a nutritive soul that was shared between plants, animals, and humans; a perceptive soul that was shared between animals and humans; and a faculty of reason that was unique to humans. It is the French philosopher and mathematician, René Descartes (1596–1650; fig 4.1), however, whose dualistic view of mind and body is perhaps the best known. Descartes lived at the end of an era when religious dogmas imposed by the Catholic church had held much of Europe's intellectual progress hostage. These dogmas slowly began to loosen their grip, resulting in the start of the Enlightenment. During this period, a new scientific world view began to dominate Western thinking. This view also implied that the human body should be considered to be a machine that operated on the basis of the newly discovered laws of physics. Moreover, it implied that our lives are completely deterministic, that is, if the body acted solely on the basis of the laws of physics, there should be no room for free will. To circumvent this problem, Descartes argued in favour of a distinction between a materialistic body, identified by Descartes as *res extensa* and a non-materialistic soul, identified as *res cogitans*. Descartes argued that *res cogitans* was not bound to the laws of physics and that it was capable of controlling *res extensa* by exchanging messages with it. Descartes believed that the nervous system was composed of a set of hydraulic vessels that were capable of transmitting messages across the body. According to Descartes, the exchange of information between *res cogitans* and *res extensa* took place in the pineal gland. Here, he believed, *res cogitans* would be able to exert pressure on the hydraulic nerve vessels. In a similar vein, it would be able to detect messages from the body by registering the subtle pressure changes arriving in the pineal gland. Descartes attributed this role to the pineal

DOI: 10.4324/9781003319344-6

Figure 4.1 The French philosopher and mathematician René Descartes is generally considered to be one of the major proponents of a dualistic vision of consciousness.

gland due to its unique location: it is one of the few brain structures that has no duplicate. Currently, we know that the pineal gland is involved in the production of the sleep hormone melatonin. Although it is thus somewhat involved in regulating our state of conscious awareness, the idea that the pineal gland is the epicentre of the soul has long since been disproven.

4.2.1.1 A Cartesian Theatre

Descartes' dualism, and thus the postulation of a soul, suffers from several other fundamental problems. One major problem is that the introduction of *res cogitans* implies a violation of the law of conservation of energy. That is, the initiation of a movement from a non-material soul implies the spontaneous creation of energy. The second problem is that the introduction of *res cogitans* also implies the existence of an internal observer in our heads. The American philosopher Daniel Dennett (1991) compares this situation with that of an observer in a theatre, which he – somewhat ironically – describes as the Cartesian Theatre (see fig 4.2). More specifically, Dennett states:

> *Cartesian materialism is the view that there is a crucial finish line or boundary somewhere in the brain, marking a place where the order of arrival equals the order of 'presentation' in experience because **what happens there** is what you are conscious of. [...] Many theorists would insist that they have explicitly rejected such an obviously bad idea. But [...] the persuasive imagery of the Cartesian Theatre keeps coming back to haunt us – laypeople and scientists alike – even after its ghostly dualism has been denounced and exorcized.*
>
> – Dennett (1991, p. 109),
> *Consciousness Explained (emphasis added)*

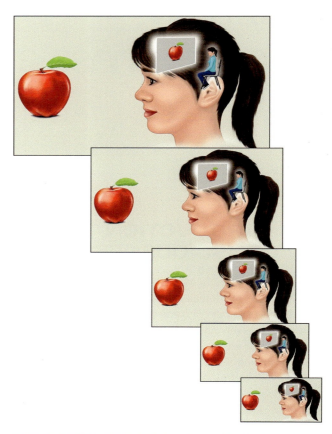

Figure 4.2 Graphical depiction of Dennett's Cartesian Theatre. One implication of Descartes' dualism is that it postulates an observer in our heads. Such an observer is also known as a homunculus. Introducing a homunculus as a means of explaining consciousness poses a problem, because this homunculus also requires an explanation, which can only be done by posing yet another homunculus inside the homunculus. Consequently, nothing is explained, as each homunculus requires an infinite regress of homunculi.

4.2.1.2 The Homunculus Problem

Dennett thus argues that dualism implies an observer in our heads: it suggests a sweet spot in our brains where every piece of information is brought together and where conscious awareness arises. Thus, a conscious observer must be present according to Dennett. A major problem with this explanation, however, is that it postulates a conscious observer whose consciousness also requires explanation. For this reason, one also needs to explain the observer by postulating a conscious observer inside it, which we can, in turn, only explain by postulating yet another observer inside its head, thus resulting in an infinite regress of observers inside observers. As a consequence, we can never really explain consciousness, but rather move its explanation into an infinitely deep level of homunculi (see fig 4.2).

4.2.2 MONISM

In contrast to dualism, monism is based on the idea that only one fundamental substance exists in nature. Within monism, we can distinguish rather markedly different views about the nature of this substance, however. These views vary from materialism, which basically states that matter is the only fundamental substance in existence, to solipsism, which states that our own mental world is the only thing that exists (or to be maybe even more correct, that only *my* mental world exists).

4.2.2.1 Materialism

According to philosophical materialism (not to be confused with economic materialism), matter is the only fundamental substance that exists in nature. According to this vision, mental processes and consciousness would arise from the interactions between the fundamental building blocks of matter, such as electrons, atoms, and molecules. As such, this view is comparable to the way physicists explain apparently non-materialistic phenomena, such as electricity, magnetism, or gravity, by focusing on the interactions between fundamental particles.

4.2.2.2 Idealism

Philosophical idealism – again, not to be confused with the ethical principle of idealism – states that the fundamental property of reality is in essence mental, that is, constructed by mental processes. This position arose from the perceived limitations of being able to know reality from a materialistic perspective. According to philosophical idealism, consciousness is not only the origin of material existence but also a necessary requirement. Idealism suggests that consciousness creates matter and that it defines its properties. As such, idealism's position is completely opposite to that of materialism.

4.2.2.3 Solipsism

Solipsism is an extreme variant of idealism which is based on the premise that our own mental world is the only one that we can be certain of. The external world, along with the mental worlds of others, would, according to this vision, not necessarily exist in reality. Instead, they are believed to be merely a projection of our own mental world.

4.2.2.4 The Identity Position

The identity position is a relatively mild variant of materialism which assumes that mental processes can be classified into different categories; each of which are related to physical processes in the brain. As such, the identity position is useful in explaining how physical processes give rise to mental processes. This position is currently most widely accepted among cognitive psychologists and cognitive neuroscientists.

4.2.3 EASY PROBLEMS AND THE HARD PROBLEM OF CONSCIOUSNESS

One of the main reasons why empirical scientists have traditionally shied away from consciousness research is that conscious experiences are by definition subjective in nature, thus requiring almost exclusively introspective methods. Already

in the early 20th century, Wundt and Titchener encountered many problems in their attempts to use introspection to study consciousness. To avoid these problems, the Australian philosopher David Chalmers (1995) proposed a radically different approach. This approach is based on a strict distinction between what Chalmers describes as the **hard problem of consciousness** and the 'easy problems'. The hard problem, according to Chalmers, relates to the subjective qualitative experience of consciousness. Questions involving these subjective experiences, such as 'what is the essence of the colour red', or 'is my experience of red the same as yours' relate to the contents of our consciousness. Lewis (1929) describes these contents as **qualia**. According to Chalmers, qualia are subjective by definition and therefore inaccessible to empirical studies.

Despite this limitation, Chalmers' distinction leaves open many other interesting questions that are accessible to empirical enquiry. These questions, known as the **easy problems**, include, for example, how we can discriminate or categorise stimuli, how we respond to them, how we can integrate information, how we can report our internal mental state and how we can gain access to it, how we can focus our attention, voluntarily control our behaviour, or what the difference is between being asleep or awake (Chalmers, 1995). Related to this, we can also aim to find a neural correlate of consciousness; that is, which neural processes are necessary for the evocation of a conscious experience?

4.3 WHAT IS CONSCIOUSNESS?

Given the aforementioned distinction between hard and easy problems, we can at least aim to explain parts of our conscious experience. Before doing so, it will be necessary to repeat the question stated earlier: what is consciousness? To illustrate the difficulty of addressing this question, let us consider two widely different cases of maladaptive states of consciousness.

4.3.1 THE REMARKABLE CASE OF KENNETH PARKS

One early morning in March 1987, the then 23-year-old Canadian Kenneth Parks (see fig 4.3) stepped into his car, drove 20 kilometres to the home of his parents-in-law, killed his mother-in-law, and left his father-in-law seriously wounded. Then he drove to the police station to turn himself in. All that Park apparently remembered from the incident was that he was screaming for help at the police station, stating: 'I believe that I killed people … look at my hands!'

When Parks arrived at the police station, his arms were seriously injured and the tendons in his wrists were

Figure 4.3 In 1987, the Canadian Kenneth Parks was acquitted of murder on the basis of reasonable evidence that he was sleepwalking while attempting to murder his parents-in-law.

partially severed. Parks, who had turned himself in, declared that he had been asleep during the incident and unaware of his actions. Because he had acted as an automaton, he pleaded not to have been responsible for his actions. Although Parks' pledge was initially received with scepticism, his EEG turned out to be highly irregular and his statements remained highly consistent, despite considerable pressure from his interrogators. Based on his medical reports it was considered likely that Parks had been sleepwalking during that peculiar night, and on the basis of this, he was acquitted of murder.

The Kenneth Parks case illustrates an important intuition that we have about consciousness, namely that conscious experience is related to free will, intentionality, and control over our actions. Consciousness and volition are thus important terms that have far-reaching consequences in our judicial system. As we will discuss in more detail later, we can ask ourselves, however, whether free will or volition even exist and whether consciousness is actually involved in the control of our actions.

The Parks case shows that, in principle, it is possible to perform a complicated series of coordinated actions while being asleep. For similar reasons, Chalmers (1999) argues that consciousness is not required for intentional control, by introducing the concept of the **philosophical zombie** as a thought experiment. According to Chalmers, philosophical zombies are people just like you and me, that are in no way distinguishable from normal humans. They undertake the same activities, and when we ask the zombies whether they have a consciousness, they will acknowledge so. Their actions and answers, however, are generated by a complex unconscious cognitive system. To

some degree, this experience may be familiar,[2] and this begs the question whether consciousness is really necessary for controlling complex actions.

4.3.2 ONE OR MORE CONSCIOUSNESSES?

4.3.2.1 Micro-, Macro-, and Unified Consciousness

A second example illustrating the complexity of our consciousness revolves around where our consciousness resides in the brain. Is there a single consciousness, or is our daily experience characterised by a conglomerate of multiple consciousnesses? Zeki (2003) proposes that consciousness is strongly related to the integration of information in the brain. As we will discuss in more detail in Chapter 6, different aspects of visual information, such as colour, position, shape, and motion, are each processed in different parts of the brain that collectively make up our visual system. According to Zeki, becoming aware of just a single feature of a stimulus, such as its colour, is related to a state of micro-consciousness. In a similar vein, Zeki identifies a macro-consciousness, which he associates with becoming aware of an entire object. According to this view, connecting the individual micro-consciousness's would result in the emergence of a macro-consciousness. Different individual properties of a stimulus would, according to Zeki, continuously reconnect with each other, giving rise to a continuous stream of micro- and macro-consciousnesses. This collection of micro- and macro-consciousnesses would then be integrated into a united consciousness. The latter would be our unified conscious awareness.

4.3.2.2 Split-brain Patients

Another approach to whether we have one or more consciousnesses arises from studies on **split-brain patients** (see fig 4.4). Split-brain patients have the connections between their left and right hemispheres, the corpus callosum, severed. In most cases, this is due to a surgical procedure that aims to limit the impact of severe epileptic seizures. After the operation, these patients mostly function normally, suggesting that the operation typically has minimal negative consequences. It is only during very specific tests that anomalies in their behaviour manifest themselves. For example, after presenting a photograph in patients' right visual field and then asking them to describe the photo we will typically observe that the patients have no trouble whatsoever to do so. It is only upon presenting a photograph in the patients' left visual field that we will typically observe the patients' having difficulties in trying to describe the photo. Because the language centres of the brain are typically lateralised in the left hemisphere of the brain, they no longer have access to the visual information which is now processed in the right hemisphere. Consequently, the patients will typically report not having seen anything. Should we

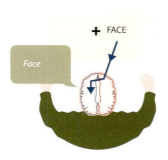

Figure 4.4 Research involving split-brain patients is frequently used to study the nature of consciousness. Is it just the left hemisphere that is conscious of a stimulus because it is capable of verbally describing it? Are both hemispheres aware of the stimulus? Or could there be something else going on here?

ask the patients to draw the stimulus, however, we will typically observe that they have no problem doing so.

The question is: which of these two actions are associated with consciousness? Is it the responses from the left hemisphere that reports not having seen a stimulus? Is it the response from the right hemisphere that was capable of drawing the stimulus? Do both exist in parallel, or could there be a different explanation, involving only a single unified consciousness?

The literature is currently still strongly divided about this point. For instance, based on the finding that both the left and right hemispheres are capable of responding to stimuli, each in their own way, Sperry (1968) argued that these patients have two consciousnesses. Sperry assumed, however, that the left hemisphere is dominant, due to the fact that it hosts the linguistic centres of the brain. Consequently, Sperry argued that the right hemisphere hosts a secondary consciousness. In contrast, Gazzaniga (2013) has argued in favour of a unitary consciousness that is localised in the left hemisphere. This consciousness acts, according to Gazzaniga, as an interpreter that strives to generate consistent interpretations for the different sensations that are processed by both the left and right hemispheres.

The aforementioned dichotomy has been criticised by Pinto, de Haan, and Lamme (2017). According to these authors, many of the cues hinting at a dual consciousness in split-brain patients can to some degree also be found in neurotypical controls. In addition, a theory of dual consciousness in split-brain patients should also be capable of explaining why these patients appear to experience hardly any aversive effects of their operation in everyday life. Finally, an increasing amount of evidence suggests that, despite the bisection of the corpus callosum in split-brain patients, communication between the hemispheres is still possible via several additional subcortical nuclei. Based on these arguments, Pinto et al. propose that consciousness

is unitary, but that split-brain patient's ability to integrate information has been impaired. They compare a split-brain patient's experience with watching a poorly mastered movie where the sounds and images are no longer synchronised. Even though we would still have a unified conscious experience of the movie, there is an increased awareness that it is presented via separate channels.

4.3.3 LEVELS OF CONSCIOUSNESS

To what degree can we identify different levels of consciousness? Many studies imply that our consciousness can be in different global states. Examples of these are the various post-comatose states, epileptic seizures, effects of anaesthesia, or sleep. Laureys (2005), for instance, proposes that consciousness involves two important components, that is, the degree of awareness of ourselves and our environment on the one hand, and our level of vigilance, or wakefulness, on the other (see fig 4.5).

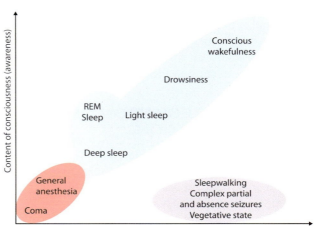

Figure 4.5 The classic approach to levels of consciousness. (source: Laureys, 2005)

Bayne, Hohwy, and Owen (2016), on the other hand, argue that the state of our consciousness cannot be expressed as a simple level, but that it involves multiple dimensions, most notably a local and a global state of consciousness. Here, the local state of consciousness corresponds to the specific contents of a conscious experience, for example our visual perception, mental imagery, bodily sensations, affective experiences, or thoughts. In contrast, the global state of consciousness corresponds to several other factors, such as our state of vigilance, or the various post-comatose states (vegetative, minimally conscious state, etc.). Bayne et al. (2016) argue that specific global states can exert a non-linear influence on the individual cognitive processes that are associated with specific local states, such as attentional control, memory functioning, verbal skills, or action control. Because specific global states (for example, REM-sleep related dreaming, or a mild propofol sedation) can selectively influence specific aspects of our local consciousness, it is, according to Bayne et al., impossible to rank these global states into a singular 'level' of consciousness.

4.4 FUNCTIONS OF CONSCIOUSNESS

A variety of answers can be given as to which function consciousness subserves, and many researchers strongly disagree with each other on this. Consciousness can, for example, be associated with the perception of our environment, be involved in social communication and understanding another's intentions, be involved in controlling our actions and intentions, allow us to reflect on situations that are not directly related to the here and now, and be involved in the processing of information.

In discussing the Kenneth Parks case, we already noticed that much controversy has already arisen over the role that consciousness supposedly plays in controlling our actions. Indeed, several studies have already shown that a large number of complex actions can be executed outside of our conscious awareness (Hassin, 2013). Thus, in the following sections, we will introduce some functions that consciousness might possibly subserve.

4.4.1 THE INTEGRATION OF INFORMATION

Many researchers argue that the integration of information might be one of the most important functions of cognition. Tononi (2004), for example, suggests that conscious awareness corresponds to a system's capacity to integrate information. According to Tononi, conscious awareness results from the formation of an informative pattern of activation that is generated when multiple sources of information are integrated. The more complex this information

patterns becomes, the higher the state of consciousness would become, according to this idea.

Consequently, Tononi and Edelman (1998) argue that consciousness is related to the complexity of the information that is being processed. They propose that two aspects of information processing are related to consciousness. Firstly, they argue that each conscious experience forms a coherent unity. Secondly, these experiences are highly differentiated, in that we can experience a large number of conscious states within a relatively short time frame. The idea that consciousness appears to be an integrated unit is consistent with the subjective impossibility of breaking down such experiences into their constituent parts. For example, when perceiving a red coffee mug, it is impossible to perceive the colour red independent from the object. The unity of our conscious experience also manifests itself in our inability to execute more than one task simultaneously. Indeed, this is only possible for simple, well-practiced tasks that no longer require conscious awareness. Additionally, we are typically limited to making just one decision every few hundreds of milliseconds (Pashler, 1984), and, in a similar vein, we are limited to perceiving only a single visual scene at the time, as is exemplified by the phenomenon of **binocular rivalry** (Leopold & Logothetis, 1999; for more details, see Section 4.6.1.2).

Even though conscious experiences are unified, it should also be noted that consciousness is also highly differentiated. For instance, within just a fraction of a second, we can recognise an almost limitless number of visual scenes. This implies that the number of conscious states that we can experience at any one given moment approximates the total amount of information that is stored in our brains. The conscious state that we actually do experience, however, is only one out of this impressive number of possible states. Therefore, the state that we do experience is of special importance, because the information it represents involves our thoughts, actions, and decisions.

Tononi and Edelman (1998) emphasise the importance of consciousness with the following thought experiment. Suppose we have a photosensitive receptor that beeps whenever a light is switched on or off. We also have a human operator performing the same task. Why is the differentiation between light and dark associated with a conscious experience in humans, while this is not the case for the photosensitive receptor? According to Tononi and Edelman, the crucial difference is that differentiating between light and dark is the only thing that the photoreceptor is able to do. In contrast, for the human operator, the experience of complete darkness and full illumination are just two out of an enormous repertoire of potential experiences. Thus, for humans, selecting one of these states is associated with an enormously rich increase in information, while this is not the case for the photoreceptor. It is, according to Tononi and Edelman, for exactly this reason that conscious awareness is related to such rich increases in information.

According to Tononi (2004), a conscious experience should correspond with an increase in coordinated brain activity, because it reflects the integration of various sources of information. Massimini et al. (2005) reported results from a combined EEG/TMS study that are consistent with this hypothesis. In their study, a TMS pulse was administered over the right premotor cortex that triggered an EEG waveform, which spread out across large sections of the cortex in awake participants. The same pulse, when applied while the participant was asleep, only triggered local activity that remained in the vicinity of the premotor cortex (see fig 4.6). The larger, more distributed, response

during wakefulness was considered to be a consequence of increasing levels of integration of information being carried out by the thalamo-cortical circuits.

Sasai, Boly, Mensen, and Tononi (2016) found further evidence for this hypothesis by asking experienced drivers to either listen to navigation instructions or to a radio programme during a driving task. The EEG activity that was recorded during this task was characterised by a higher level of **functional connectivity** when listening to the navigation instructions, as compared to listening to the radio. Functional connectivity is a measure of synchronicity between different brain areas. This measure can be obtained by determining to what degree EEG signals that are measured on different parts of the scalp

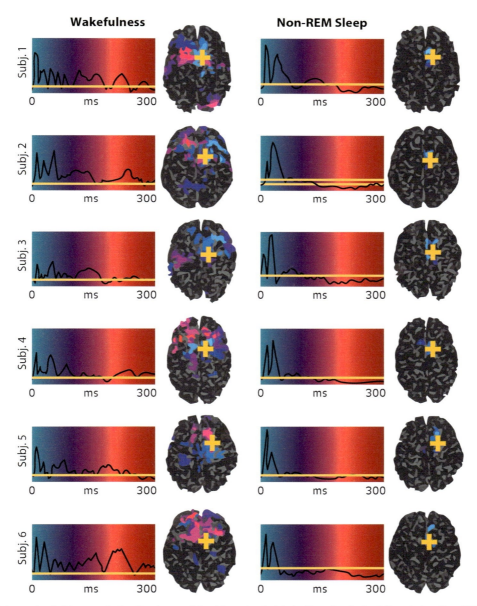

Figure 4.6 Effects of sleep and wakefulness on the functional connectivity of the cortex. A global pattern of cortical activity, as induced by a TMS pulse spreads across large parts of the cortex during wakefulness (left), while a similar pulse administered during sleep only triggers local cortical activity. Each row in the figure represents the data from a single participant. The black line presents the global field power of the cortical activity. The precise location where this activity became statistically significant is overlayed on an MRI image. The different colours in the overlays correspond to the time scales in the graphs. (source: Massimini et al., 2005)

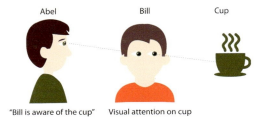

Abel   Bill   Cup

"Bill is aware of the cup"   Visual attention on cup

Figure 4.7 The necessity for conscious representations according to the social communication theory of consciousness. The central tenet of this theory is that consciousness is a necessary requirement of putting ourselves in the position of somebody else. (source: Graziano and Kastner, 2011)

show similar activation patterns. The stronger the similarity, the stronger the evidence that the underlying brain areas communicate with each other. The increase in connectivity that was found while listening to the navigation instructions suggests that information from this task was integrated with the driving task.

4.4.2 SOCIAL COMMUNICATION

According to Humphrey (2002), consciousness mainly subserves a social function. We humans are social animals, who have lived in social communities for several millennia. To successfully live in a social group, it is crucial that we are able to predict, understand, and manipulate the behaviour of others. According to Humphrey, this is much easier when we are able to imagine ourselves being somebody else. According to this interpretation, self-awareness is mainly a consequence of being able to understand another human being.

A similar idea was formulated by Graziano and Kastner (2011). These authors propose that the neural mechanisms that provide us with information about the intentions of others are the same mechanisms that provide self-awareness. According to this idea, awareness is strongly related to **social perception**. To illustrate, suppose that we have two persons, Abel and Bill. Bill takes a coffee mug from a table and Abel observes Bill (see fig 4.7). Abel constructs

a mental representation of Bill's mental state, based on the mechanisms of social perception. One crucial aspect of this mental representation is the assumption that Bill is aware of the mug. Graziano and Kastners assume that the same neural mechanisms that make Abel suspect that Bill is aware of the mug, also ensure that Abel is aware of Bill.

According to Graziano and Kastner, the temporoparietal junction is involved in this form of social awareness. Indeed, stimulating this brain area using a TMS pulse appears to limit our ability to switch between representing ourselves and representing somebody else (Sowden & Catmur, 2015).

4.4.3 THE CONTROL OF ACTIONS

One of the presumed functions of consciousness involves the wilful control of our intentional actions. As already discussed in the Kenneth Parks case, consciousness is typically associated with free will. We can question, however, whether this is really the case. For example, Wegner and Wheatley (1999) found that we frequently experience the illusion of free will, even when we have no control over our actions at all. For instance, when the interval between an action and a randomly occurring event is relatively small, we typically tend to attribute this event to our own actions.[3]

Wegner and Wheatley studied this phenomenon by requiring participants to move a cursor along different objects and to direct it towards a specific object at a predetermined time. Unbeknownst to the participants, however, the cursor was controlled by a confederate of the experimenter, who was able to move the cursor to a specific object. Either thirty or five seconds before or one or five seconds after the confederate had stopped the cursor, participants were instructed to move the cursor to a specific object. When participants were given this instruction either one or five seconds before the confederate stopped the cursor, they frequently believed that they had stopped the cursor themselves (see fig 4.8). This implies that participants had a strong illusion of control.

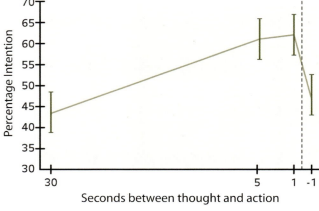

Figure 4.8 An experimental study on the illusion of control. Left: the experimental setup that Wegner and Wheatley (1999) used to study intentionality. Right: participants were required to indicate whether they believed that it was their own action that stopped the motion of a cursor. The degree to which they believed that this was the case was the most pronounced when the cursor was stopped either one or five seconds before their own action by a confederate. (source: Wegner and Wheatley, 1999)

4.4.3.1 The Illusion of Control

In 1983, the American neuroscientist Benjamin Libet and his colleagues published the results from a remarkable experiment (Libet, Gleason, Wright, & Pearl, 1983). Libet et al. asked their participants to flex their fingers and/or the wrist of their right hands. Participants were encouraged to do this spontaneously and note the position of the hands on a clock at the moment when they first felt the urge to do so (see fig 4.9). This way, the experimenters were able to determine the exact moment when participants first became consciously aware of their intention to exert a movement (Haggard, 2008).

In addition, Libet et al. used EEG recordings to measure activity in the motor cortex. To this end, they employed the **readiness potential** (Kornhuber & Deecke, 1965). As discussed in Chapter 3, this is a slowly increasing negative potential that has a maximum over the motor cortex. It typically reaches its peak amplitude at the moment an action is executed. By determining at which point in time this component began, Libet and his colleagues were able to determine when preparatory action started to develop in the motor cortex. Remarkably, it was found that the motor cortex was already active at about 500 ms before the execution of the response, while participants reported their conscious intention to move only 200 ms before the action. This result thus suggests that the motor cortex was already active for 300 ms before participants became aware of their intention to response,

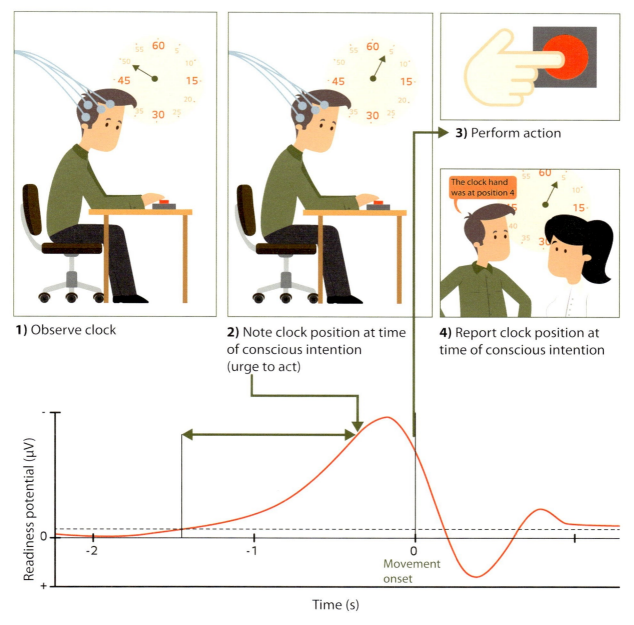

1) Observe clock

2) Note clock position at time of conscious intention (urge to act)

3) Perform action

4) Report clock position at time of conscious intention

The clock hand was at position 4

Readiness potential (μV)

-2   -1   0
Movement onset

Time (s)

Figure 4.9 Schematic depiction of the Libet et al. (1983) study. Participants were required to execute a manual response as soon as they felt the urge to do so. They were required to report the time at which they first noticed this urge. Physiological recordings showed that even before the urge was noted, the motor cortex was already activated. (source: Haggard, 2008)

thus questioning the common notion of consciousness as the initiator of a free will.

It should be noted, however, that it is a rather difficult challenge to measure the exact timing of conscious intentions. For example, Banks and Isham (2009) showed that such time estimations can be strongly affected by one's perception. When participants observed their own hand movements through a closed-circuit video system that had a 120 ms built-in delay, they reported decision times that were delayed by about 44 ms, compared to when they observed their hands directly. Moreover, it has recently been argued that the readiness potential may not be a suitable correlate of conscious intentional free will (Schurger, Hu, Pak, & Roskies, 2021). To avoid this type of problem, it is typically preferable not to focus on the timing aspect, but on the type of decision that is being made. Soon, Brass, Heinze, and Haynes (2008) used this approach in an fMRI study. Here, participants were free to choose whether to make a movement with either their left or their right hand. Activation patterns in the frontopolar cortex that were indicative of the movement that was going to be made could be observed as early as seven seconds before the onset of the movement, suggesting that the brain can already start to prepare a given movement seconds before its actual onset.

4.5 REPORTING CONSCIOUS EXPERIENCES

Consciousness is typically associated with subjective experiences. For this reason, it appears to be crucial that we are able to report these experiences. This might not always be the case, however, as we will discuss in the following sections.

4.5.1 THE VEGETATIVE STATE

One striking dissociation between consciousness and our ability to report conscious experiences was first reported in 2006. In that year, a group of British neuroscientists, led by Adrian Owen, reported the results of a study involving a 23-year-old female patient who was in a persistent vegetive state (Owen et al., 2006). In July 2006, the patient in question had suffered major brain injuries in a traffic accident. Five months later, she was still unable to respond to external stimuli, despite exhibiting a relatively normal sleep-wake cycle. Owen et al. used fMRI to determine to which degree this patient's brain was still able to respond to external stimuli. To this end, they initially compared the patient's brain activity that was evoked by spoken sentences with those that were evoked by meaningless speech fragments. Activation in the middle and superior temporal gyri, as evoked by the linguistically meaningful stimuli, was comparable to a similar pattern of activations that was evoked by a group of neurotypical control participants. This result implies

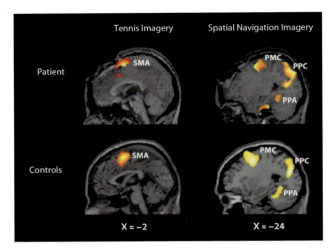

Figure 4.10 fMRI scans of a female patient in a persistent vegetative state (top) in response to instructions to imagine playing a game of tennis (left) or navigating her own home (right). The patterns of neural activity that were elicited by those tasks are comparable to those elicited by a control group (bottom). (source: Owen et al., 2006)

that the patient was capable of processing language, despite the absence of overt behavioural responses.

Although these results are indicative of a certain degree of conscious awareness, they are insufficient to allow the conclusion that she was fully aware. To do so, a second experiment was designed that targeted her mental imagery capacities.

In one condition, the patient was asked to imaging playing a game of tennis, while in another condition she was asked to imaging traversing a route through her own home (see fig 4.10). During the tennis-imagery assignment, a significant increase in brain activity was found in the supplementary motor areas, while the imaginary walk through her home resulted in a significant increase in parahippocampal activation, in addition to increases in the posterior parietal cortex and the premotor cortex. These patterns of activation were highly comparable to those found in a group of healthy volunteers that served as a control group. The correspondence between patient and the control group's patterns of brain activation not only shows that the patient was complying with the instructions, but also implies that the patient voluntarily cooperated with the researchers, which in turn implied an intentional, conscious action.

4.5.2 GAPS IN OUR CONSCIOUS EXPERIENCE

It does not require a vegetative state, however, to lose our ability to report conscious experiences. While awake, we frequently encounter situations in which we are no longer capable of reporting experiences. Consider, for example, the case of driving along a well-known route and not remembering having any conscious experience of having already passed long stretches of the route and not being fully aware where you actually are. In such cases, we can wonder, however, whether we really had no conscious experience of the situation, or that we have no memory of it. Many studies have shown, however, that stimuli can still be processed to very high levels, despite having no conscious experience of them.

4.5.3 BLINDSIGHT

One remarkable case of perception without awareness was first reported during the First World War. Many British soldiers were reported to be blind due to a shot wound damaging their primary visual cortex. These soldiers were treated by George Riddoch, an army physician, who noted that they were still able to respond to motion in the visual field that they reported to be blind in (Riddoch, 1917). Riddoch thus provided the first evidence for a dissociation between visual awareness and access to visual information. This phenomenon was later dubbed **blindsight** (Weiskrantz, 1986). Blindsight patients appear to have lost the ability to report visual experiences, despite being able to point to visual stimuli or to interact with them (see fig 4.11).

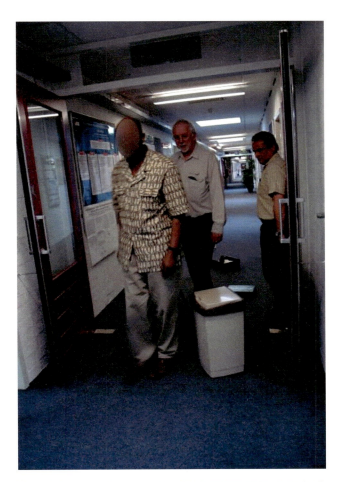

Figure 4.11 A blindsight patient walks along a hallway, while unconsciously avoiding all objects that have been placed there. (based on data from de Gelder et al., 2008)

4.6 NEURAL CORRELATES OF CONSCIOUSNESS

Insights into consciousness can be gained by manipulating the conscious perception of stimuli, while recording the changes in neural activity in functions of these changes. The following sections will discuss a number of methods that can be utilised to accomplish this.

4.6.1 PARADIGMS FOR INVESTIGATING CONSCIOUSNESS

The study of the types of problems that were labelled 'easy' by Chalmers (1995) requires methods that allow us to manipulate participants' conscious awareness of these stimuli. Most of these methods are based on a procedure that allows participants to either consciously or unconsciously perceive a stimulus, or which allows awareness of a stimulus to alternate between conscious and unconscious perception. One problem that is intrinsic to this procedure is that it always relies on participants' subjective reports and the fact that these reports can be influenced by a variety of factors, such as limitations in attention span, an inability to report the stimulus, or limitations in recalling the stimulus. Despite these problems, several paradigms have been developed and successfully applied in consciousness studies.

4.6.1.1 Masking

One effective way of limiting the conscious experience of a stimulus is to use a masking procedure. In general, there are two ways in which stimuli can be presented without gaining access to participants' awareness. In one version, stimuli are presented with extremely short durations (e.g., <16 ms). After such a **subliminal** presentation (see, for example, Mulckhuyse, Talsma, & Theeuwes, 2007), they are replaced with a mask that consists of a random pattern of dots or lines. After presentation, participants are asked to give a description of the stimuli, and these descriptions can be compared to those obtained in a condition where the stimuli are not presented subliminally. There is one problem with this method, however; it involves a comparison between stimuli that are presented under two physically different conditions. For this reason, it is typically better to present stimuli in such a way that participants report only being aware of them in 50% of all trials. This can be achieved by presenting the stimulus at the **perceptual threshold**, for instance by fine-tuning the presentation times and the degree of masking. This way, we can subdivide all stimuli into two categories, namely one category of stimuli that were consciously perceived and one category of stimuli that were not. Now, the neural responses to the two classes of stimuli can be used to detect awareness-related neural activity (Fahrenfort, Scholte, & Lamme, 2007).

Figure 4.12 Wittgenstein's rabbit-duck illusion is considered to be one of the earliest examples of a bistable image.

Another method of presenting stimuli at the perceptual threshold consists of degrading their image quality or reducing their contrast. According to Merikle, Smilek, and Eastwood (2001), we can distinguish two different thresholds using this method. By progressively degrading the stimuli, we eventually reach a point where participants are no longer able to report the contents of the stimuli. At this point, we have reached the **subjective perceptual threshold**. At this level of degradation, we can force participants to make a decision about the stimulus, and we will typically observe that they are still able to do so well above chance. For instance, consider presenting the digit '5'. When it is degraded to such a degree that participants are not capable of perceiving the stimuli consciously, we may conclude that we are below the subjective perceptual threshold. Now we require the participant to choose between two options. For instance, 'make a left-hand response when you believe is it a "3" and a right-hand response when you believe it is a "5"'. Typically, we would observe responses that are well above chance, implying that even without conscious awareness, participants are still able to collect enough information to make an informed choice. Reducing performance levels to chance would require an even further degradation, at which point the **objective perceptual threshold** is crossed.

4.6.1.2 Binocular Rivalry

A second method of studying consciousness involves bistable images. Examples of this type of stimulus involve the Necker cube, the rabbit-duck illusion, or a multitude of drawings that can be interpreted in multiple ways (see fig 4.12). One special case of bistable perception consists of presenting a different image to each eye (see for example fig 4.13). When we view Figure 4.13 through a set of anaglyphic 3D goggles, we are aware of only one of the two images, but also know that our conscious awareness

would slowly alternate between the two images, yet we would never perceive both of them at the same time. This phenomenon, the slow alteration between the two images is known as binocular rivalry (Logothetis & Schall, 1989). We can take advantage of this phenomenon to study the relation between changes in awareness and brain activity by presenting these images and instructing participants to report when their awareness shifts from one image to the other and by recording their brain activity (Britz, Pitts, & Michel, 2011).

4.6.1.3 Continuous Flash Suppression

A third method is known as **continuous flash suppression**. This method also takes advantage of the fact that a different image can be presented to each eye. Here, however, only a single meaningful stimulus is presented to one eye, while a continuously flickering noise pattern is presented to the other eye. Such patterns typically result in the suppression of conscious perception of the meaningful stimulus (Tsuchiya & Koch, 2005).

4.6.1.4 Distraction

Finally, an oft-used method consists of drawing attention away from a stimulus of interest. In a now classic study, Simons and Chabris (1999) showed participants a video of a ball game, requiring them to count how many times the white team passed the ball. In doing so, participants frequently failed to notice a person in a gorilla suit crossing the scene in the middle of the clip. This phenomenon, known as **inattentional blindness**, implies that much of the information that we perceive does not reach our conscious awareness when we do not attend it.

4.7 THEORIES OF CONSCIOUSNESS

During the past decennia, many new theories of consciousness have been developed. Despite the fact that Chalmers (1995) argued that it is intrinsically impossible to develop a unified theory that is able to explain the phenomenon of consciousness, Chalmers' identification of the easy problems has resulted in a sprawl of theoretical frameworks in the past 25 years. Many of these frameworks are at least capable of explaining some of the processes that consciousness is involved in. In the next section, we will consider a number of these perspectives.

4.7.1 QUANTUM PHYSICS

One of the major obstacles that theoreticians of consciousness face is the problem of free will. To circumvent this, many have attempted to integrate theories of consciousness with ideas that originated in quantum physics. The Australian physiologist Sir John Eccles (1992), for instance, introduced the concept of psychons. According

Figure 4.13 Example of a binocular stimulus. When seen through an anaglyphic goggle, 'Red' will be presented to the left eye and 'Blue' to the right.

to Eccles, psychons would be formed in converging bundles of dendrites that sprout from the pyramidal neurons in layer 1 of the cortex. Eccles assumed that qualia arise in these psychons via interactions at the microscopic (quantum) level in the synaptic cleft. Comparable ideas have been generated by Hameroff (1998), who proposed that quantum interactions could occur in the microscopic structure of dendrites, causing the response of a neuron not to be deterministic, but probabilistic instead, thus allowing a free will.

Because superficially quantum mechanical processes appear to ignore the classic laws of physics, they have given rise to many pseudoscientific ideas, including the notion that quantum mechanical processes could yield a uniform connectedness within the cosmos. This idea is then typically used to explain how the brain, which consists of individual neurons, could give rise to a unitary consciousness. Moreover, the famous uncertainty principle of quantum mechanics would provide a convenient way to circumvent determinism. There are several fundamental problems with this assertion, however, and by extension with all theories of consciousness that are based on quantum physics. The first problem is that quantum interactions only manifest themselves at (sub)atomic scales as purely stochastic processes. These phenomena do not scale up to the levels at which neural processes manifest themselves. Moreover, the uncertainty principle describes a methodological limitation as opposed to a fundamental property of nature, making it an ill-advised substitute for free will. Finally, one might wonder how much our will is worth when it is purely driven by the random flip of a subatomic particle.

Strictly speaking, the introduction of quantum physics in theories of consciousness is nothing more than a modern form of Cartesian dualism in disguise. The introduction of a quantum influence on neural functions bears a strong resemblance to the mind–body interactions that Descartes assumed to take place in the pineal gland. Similar to the way in which Descartes assumed that the pineal gland would enable the interaction between *res cogitans* and *res extensa*, modern quantum dualists assume an interaction between a non-materialistic consciousness and a materialistic body. Again, following the analogy of classic dualism, nothing is really explained.

4.7.2 INTEGRATIVE THEORIES

Integrative theories state that consciousness plays an important role in the integration of information. According to these theories, domain-specific information can be processed by specialised modules. This type of processing can take place automatically, without the need for consciousness. Consciousness comes into play, however, when information needs to be integrated across different modules.

Both Ward (2011) and Tononi (2004) define consciousness as the capacity of a system to integrate information. This integrative capacity depends on the system's ability to form a 'dynamic core', that is, a complex, continuously changing pattern of interactions between the various elements that contribute to the system. Such a dynamic core is characterised by enormous complexity, that is, by the extremely large number of possible states that it can represent. The thalamo-cortical system, that is, the extensive network of neural connections between the thalamus and the cortex, represents a possible neurobiological implementation. Details of this mechanism are discussed in more detail later in the chapter.

4.7.2.1 Global Workspace Theories

One specific example of such an integrative theory was proposed by Baars (2005). According to his **global workspace theory**, the early stages of stimulus processing do not depend on conscious perception (see also Baars & Franklin, 2007). Instead, consciousness is believed to occur as a result of the integrated activation of several specialised processing units during the later processing stages (see fig 4.14).

There is indeed much evidence to support this assumption: Lamy, Salti, and Bar-Haim (2009) instructed their participants to locate a target stimulus and to report how aware they were of this stimulus. In the event-related potentials (ERPs) evoked by these stimuli, two clearly differentiable components could be identified. The amplitude of the early P2 component did not vary as a function of the degree of awareness of the target stimulus, whereas the amplitude of the later P300 component did. On average, the amplitude of this component was greater when participants were aware of the stimulus than when they were unaware of it. In addition, Lamy et al. found that this P300 component was characterised by a relatively diffuse scalp distribution, implying that a large number of brain areas were involved in its generation when the stimulus was consciously perceived. When the stimulus was not consciously perceived, the P300 component was much more concentrated over the central parietal cortex.

When a stimulus is expected, top-down processes may accelerate access to conscious awareness. Melloni, Schwiedrzik, Muller, Rodriguez, and Singer (2011) found evidence for this idea in a study where participants had to judge the visibility of letters that were presented amidst random noise while ERPs were measured. When participants expected to see a letter, the difference between a seen and an unseen letter manifested itself in an ERP effect at around 200 ms after the onset of the letter. When participants were not expecting a letter, this ERP effect only manifested itself about 300 ms after the presentation of the letter. Despite this difference, however, Melloni et al. also found that early processing of the letters did not differ between seen and unseen letters and that expectation had no effect on these early stages of processing.

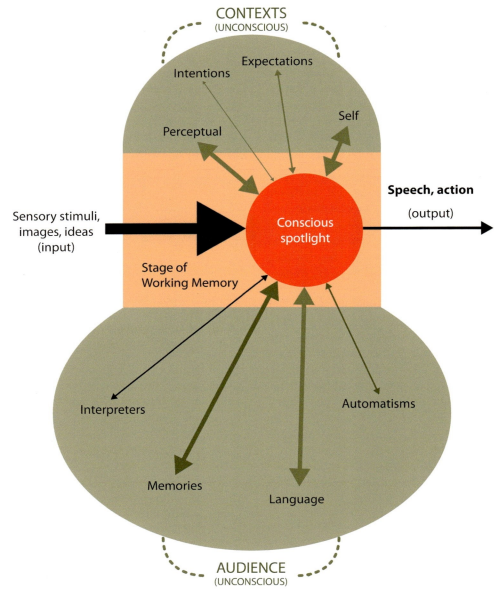

Figure 4.14 A graphical representation of the global workspace theory. (source: Baars and Franklin, 2007)

Thus, the latter finding implies that the early stages of processing are largely unconscious, and that awareness may therefore occur only from about 200 ms after the presentation of the stimulus.

Melloni et al.'s findings are consistent with the global workspace theory, which predicts that consciousness is only involved when information must be integrated across different modules. According to Baars and Franklin (2007), this would take place at a late stage of processing and would involve widespread synchronised activation of a large number of brain areas. A combination of top-down and bottom-up processes would trigger a large-scale synchronisation of brain activity, making the information from the different specialised modules available globally, resulting in a conscious experience. In addition, the theory assumes that the specific brain areas associated with conscious experience will vary according to the content of the conscious experience.

A neural implementation of the global workspace theory has been developed by Dehaene and colleagues (Dehaene & Changeux, 2011; Dehaene & Naccache, 2001; Dehaene, Changeux, Naccache, Sackur, & Sergent, 2006), which they labelled as the global neuronal workspace theory. Although the precise pattern of activation may vary depending on the nature of the information being integrated, Dehaene and Naccache (2001) emphasise the role of the dorsolateral prefrontal cortex and the anterior cingulate cortex in awareness. In a similar vein, Dehaene and Changeux (2011) identify the prefrontal, cingulate and parietal areas as being involved in conscious awareness.

These areas are believed to play a central role in synchronising activation between different brain areas and thus facilitating the sharing of information between these areas. A final assumption of the global workspace theories is that there is a strong link between attention and conscious awareness. According to this idea, attention is used to select the information that we become aware of (Baars & Franklin, 2007).

4.7.2.2 Neural Correlates of Integration

The global neuronal workspace hypothesis predicts that awareness is associated with an increase in global, coordinated activation in a network of brain regions covering a large part of the cortex. Evidence for this hypothesis has been provided by Rodriguez et al. (1999) and by Melloni et al. (2007). For instance, Rodriguez et al. (1999) recorded the EEG at 30 locations on the scalp, while participants were shown black-and-white drawings of faces. These faces could either be presented upright or they could be rotated 180°. When they were rotated, they were no longer recognisable as a face, despite the fact that their basic properties remained the same. The coherence in the EEG activity that followed the presentation of the stimulus was calculated for the Gamma band (i.e., oscillations in 30–80 Hz range). Coherence is a metric for the degree of synchronisation between different brain areas. A recognisable face resulted in a high level of coherence between distant brain areas, at around 360–540 ms after stimulus onset, while this was not the case for the stimuli that were not recognised as a face.

Melloni et al. (2007) found similar results based on a study in which a word was presented subliminally, which participants had to compare to a subsequent word that was also presented subliminally. In all cases, these words were presented for 33 ms and then masked. The intensity of the mask was manipulated, however, which affected participants' ability to consciously perceive the words. Here, it was found that conscious perception resulted in an increase in gamma band activity, however, this activation already started around 40 ms after presentation of the stimulus.

4.7.3 SIMULATION

Hesslow (2002) argues that conscious thought represents the simulation of behaviour and perception. Hesslow's idea is, in fact, based on the classical philosophical ideas of David Hume (1739) and his Associativist successors (Bain, 1868). Bain, for instance, suggested that thinking is in fact a covert or 'weak' form of behaviour, except that the body is not activated in the process. As such, Bain argued that thinking is a restrictive form of speech or action. This idea, which was also central to behaviourism, could be refuted when it turned out that participants were still able to think after they had been paralysed by the administration

of curare (Smith, Brown, Toman, & Goodman, 1947). A complete refutation of Bain's ideas is probably premature, however, as we shall argue next.

4.7.3.1 Simulation of Behaviour

As already discussed in the previous chapter, our intention to act involves a cascade of a hierarchical interactions between the frontal lobes and other cortical areas. Activity in the sensory cortices is projected via intra- and subcortical pathways to the supplementary and premotor cortex, from which ultimately the primary motor cortex is signalled. Here, the signals that control our muscles are generated. Relatively complex movements, such as grasping, require the precise sequencing of a large group of muscles, a process that is controlled by the more anterior regions of the motor cortex. In the prefrontal cortex itself, only the most basic aspects of behaviour are coordinated. At every level, the frontal cortex interacts with the basal ganglia, where the final movement commands are precisely shaped.

The idea that behaviour can be simulated implies that the motor structures that prepare the initiation of a movement can be activated while its actual execution is suppressed by the motor cortex itself. There is now an overwhelming amount of evidence supporting this idea (Jeannerod, 1994; Jeannerod & Frak, 1999; Kosslyn et al., 2001).

There are, for example, some remarkable similarities between simulated movements and actual movements. The time taken to simulate a movement is very similar to the time taken to perform the actual movement (Decety, Jeannerod, & Prablanc, 1989). Ingvar and Philipson (1977) found that activation of the premotor areas of the frontal cortex increased both when participants had to imagine a hand movement and when they actually performed the hand movement. The activation of the primary motor cortex only increased when they actually performed the movement, however. Although there are some differences between actually performing and imagining a movement, several studies have subsequently shown that the premotor and supplementary motor areas are activated while imagining a movement (Deiber et al., 1998; Lotze et al., 1999; Rao et al., 1993), which implies that there is a strong relationship between thinking and doing.

4.7.3.2 Simulation of Perception

The idea that we can simulate perception, in the form of mental imagery, has also been suggested by Hume (1739), and was again made more explicit by 19th-century philosophers (Bain, 1868; James, 1890). More direct evidence for this idea is quite recent, however (Farah, 1988; Kosslyn, 1999; Kosslyn et al., 2001). **Mental rotation** requires participants to compare two objects, while one of the objects is rotated relative to the other. Here it is often found that participants' decision time is linearly dependent on the angle of rotation between the two objects (Shepard &

Metzler, 1971), as if participants had to mentally rotate one of the objects in an analogous manner before they could be compared.

In addition, many studies have found that the instruction to generate a mental representation activates the primary visual cortex (Kosslyn et al., 2001). Many patients with a visual cortex dysfunction also lose their ability to generate mental representations (Farah, 1988). A final piece of evidence for a link between mental representation and the visual system comes from patients with **hemineglect**. Hemineglect patients are characterised by their inability to detect visual stimuli. In most cases, their left visual field is affected. Bisiach and Luzzatti (1978) described hemineglect patients who were also characterised by severe problems in generating mental representations involving the visual field that was associated with their brain damage. When these patients, who were natives of Milan, were asked to describe the famous Piazza del Duomo, they described only the buildings on their right side. Then, when asked to imagine themselves standing on the opposite side of the square, they again described only the buildings on their right-hand side. Thus, in the latter condition, they described the buildings they initially failed to describe, while failing to describe those buildings they did mention initially.

4.7.3.3 Anticipation and Awareness

It is a plausible assumption that perceptual simulations arise because we anticipate performing certain actions. Indeed, what we perceive is often driven by our own actions: visual input changes as a function of the position of our head or eyes, and tactile stimulation is often caused by the fact that our hands manipulate objects. The consequences of these actions are often predictable. Hesslow (2002) assumes that the brain mechanisms involved in preparing an action are linked in an associative way to the perceptual mechanisms. This link would be established in such a way that activation of the preparatory mechanisms results in sensory activity that is similar to the activity that would occur if the action was actually performed. According to Hesslow's simulation theory, consciousness is the result of these active simulations: the internal simulations create an internal representation that is very similar to the experiences that people normally associate with consciousness.

4.8 SLEEP AND DREAMS

One of the most remarkable and, at the same time, most mysterious aspects of our lives is that our state of consciousness dramatically changes on a daily basis. During sleep, our normal conscious state disappears and our ability to respond to external stimuli is drastically reduced. During a normal night, we enter several sleep stages, including REM and non-REM sleep. Our normal daytime vigilance is

maintained by activation of the reticular formation. While falling asleep, our arousal level slowly decreases under the influence of adenosine, a substance that reduces the effectiveness of this arousal regulation mechanism.

During REM sleep, activation in the pons, the limbic system, and parts of the parietal and temporal cortex increases. Simultaneously, activation of the primary visual cortex, the motor cortex, and the dorsolateral prefrontal cortex decreases. During REM sleep, the EEG is characterised by a typical pattern known as PGO waves (pons-geniculate-occipital waves). After sleep deprivation, these waves can also occur during periods of non-REM sleep, or even while awake. The latter occurrence may be accompanied by behaviour that is indicative of hallucinations. During typical REM sleep, neurons in the pons inhibit the motor neurons in the spinal cord that control the main muscles in our body. Interestingly, when this part of the pons was damaged in cats, they exhibited behaviours during REM sleep that indicated they were reacting to their dreams, such as chasing imaginary prey or jumping up in fright.

4.8.1 DREAMS

We spend parts of our sleep cycle dreaming. Dreams are a state of consciousness that are characterised by highly visual, colourful experiences and are often dynamic (i.e., involving moving images), while objects or persons from our everyday lives often appear in them. Sound is also represented in dreams, as are occasionally tactile or olfactory experiences (Nir & Tononi, 2010). Also, our personal interests and drives, along with personal dispositions such as specific fears, are frequently represented in dreams. The normal experience is that we ourselves actively participate in our own dreams. In these respects, the experience of a dream is very similar to the experiences of daily waking life.

An important difference between dreaming and waking is that we often wake up being surprised by our own dreams, indicating that we had not consciously decided to dream a specific dream. Moreover, we frequently experience a sense of loss of control over our actions while dreaming. In addition, dreams often consist of separate scenes that appear to follow each other naturally and logically during the dream itself but which, upon subsequent reconstruction, often turn out to be very inconsistent.

Converging evidence, from different fields of study, now support the idea that dreams are very similar to mental imagery processes, in the sense that brain activation spreads in a top-down fashion (Pezzulo, Zorzi, & Corbetta, 2021). According to this idea, activation in the higher-order emotional and cognitive processing centres, for example those area reflecting our active thoughts or memories (Schwartz, 2003), spreads to lower-order perceptual areas. Here, the concepts and emotions form a mental representation that, since it cannot be corrected by actual sensory

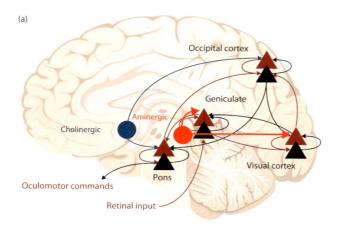

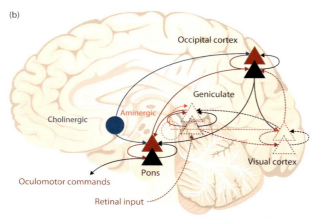

Figure 4.15 The neural basis of dreams, based on the principles of predictive coding. (a) During the normal waking state, internal predictions are corrected on the basis of an active inference mechanism. (b) Absence of the neurotransmitter serotonin during sleep results in a decreased postsynaptic sensitivity of the superficial pyramidal neurons, resulting in a progressively reduced ability for visual signals to propagate through the visual cortex. As a result, perception is now dominated by the predictive recurrent connections. (source: Hobson and Friston, 2012)

input, manifests itself as a dream (Hobson & Friston, 2014; Kok & de Lange, 2015). Figure 4.15 illustrates the possible neural basis of this mechanism. Here, the PGO waves are believed to be a neural correlate of the mechanism that blocks the processing of retinal information, so that the visual cortex only receives information from the internal generative models (Gott, Liley, & Hobson, 2017; Hobson & Friston, 2012).

4.9 CONSCIOUSNESS AND CORTICAL SYNCHRONISATION

4.9.1 CORTICO-THALAMO-CORTICAL CIRCUITS

Llinas, Ribary, Contreras, and Pedroarena (1998) argue that the thalamus forms a hub that is capable of allowing any cortical area to communicate with any other cortical area. These authors therefore argue that consciousness is the result of the intrinsic activity of these thalamo-cortical circuits. Consistent with an assumption of the predictive coding framework (Clark, 2013; see Chapter 2), Llinás and Paré (1991) propose that consciousness is the result of internal neural activity that is modulated by input from the senses, as opposed to consciousness being produced by the senses. Several studies have found evidence for a link between cortico-thalamic connections and consciousness. Ferrarelli et al. (2010), for example, found a strong decrease in cortical connectivity following a midazolam-induced loss of consciousness. This result is consistent with those from Massimini et al. (2005), discussed earlier, which also reported a decrease in cortical connectivity during sleep.

4.9.1.1 Thalamic Dynamic Core Theory

Ward (2011) takes this idea even one step further and suggests that conscious experiences themselves arise in the thalamus. A conscious experience, according to Ward's dynamic core theory, arises because the thalamus, through its massive cortico-thalamo-cortical connections, receives many neural signals back from the cortex, which are highly synchronised and rich in information. According to this hypothesis, the cortex generates the contents of our consciousness, while the thalamus is the critical locus where this content is experienced. The idea that the thalamus is the locus of conscious experiences is supported by the fact that anaesthesia acts on thalamic functions (Alkire, Haier, & Fallon, 2000) along with the fact that many coma patients in a vegetative state often have extensive thalamic damage.

4.10 ATTENTION

When you hear the term **attention**, you will probably immediately have an intuitive idea what it means: the term is so well established in our language and culture that we use it several times a day. One of the founding fathers of American psychology, William James (1890), even stated that everyone knows what attention is:

> *Everyone knows what attention is. It is the taking possession by the mind, in clear and vivid form, of one out of what seem several simultaneously possible objects or trains of thought. Focalization, concentration, of consciousness are of its essence. It implies withdrawal from some things in order to deal effectively with others and is a condition which has a real opposite in the confused, dazed, scatter-brained state which in French is called distraction, and Zerstreutheit in German.*
>
> - William James (1890)

According to James, attention involves directing our mental processes to a single task: directing and focusing our mental capacities on a task prevents us from being distracted. Attention causes thoughts that are not task-relevant to be suppressed, so that our consciousness can concentrate fully on what is relevant. Despite (or perhaps due to) the fact that everyone has an intuitive notion of what attention entails, it is very poorly defined as a scientific concept. Therefore no one really knows what attention is. Precisely because attention is formulated from an intuitive idea, there are many different cognitive processes that we can somehow qualify as attention. For this reason, we first need to give an overview of the different forms of attention that we can identify.

As James already noted, when we focus our attention on something, we are in a state of controlled processing. When we need to focus on a complex task for a prolonged period of time, for example, solving a puzzle, attention helps us to stay focused. This is known as focused attention. During task performance, we sometimes need to selectively focus attention on specific sources of information while ignoring others. This is an example of **selective attention**. In other cases, for example when we have to perform two tasks simultaneously, we have to divide our attention.

In all of these cases, we direct our attention voluntarily to the task or the stimulus we are processing. This is known as of top-down controlled **endogenous attention**. It can also happen that – while we are strongly focused on one task – a salient external stimulus captures our attention. For example, think of a situation where you want to cross a busy street and fail to notice an approaching car. The honking car will then automatically capture your attention; this is an example of bottom-up driven **exogenous attention**.

4.11 A TAXONOMY OF ATTENTION

Although William James represents our intuitions quite well, more than 130 years after the publication of his seminal work, our intuitive notion poorly reflects the current state of cognitive research. Ironically, it is precisely because the term 'attention' describes these intuitions so well that it has become such a broad concept that can somehow be involved in almost any cognitive process. Attention is thus becoming a catchall term, describing a multitude of processes that are somehow related to the selection or the regulation of cognitive processes.

Initially, this was not the case, however. At the start of the cognitive revolution, research questions involving attention were quite specific. During the heyday of the computer metaphor, there was a growing realisation that information had to be selected at some stage for further processing and the question was when this selection took place. The prevailing view at the time was that information processing was predominantly bottom-up and the

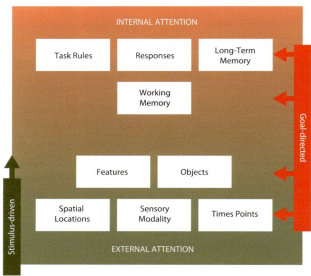

Figure 4.16 A taxonomy of attention. Internal and external attention are at opposite ends of a continuum, while the boxes on this continuum represent a process on which attention can act. Goal-driven, top-down controlled endogenous attention is here assumed to influence both internal and external processes, while stimulus-driven, bottom-up exogenous attention is primarily concerned with external attention. (source: Chun, Golomb, and Turk-Browne, 2011)

questions that were addressed concerned the moment at which information was selected. Attention was conceived as a filtering mechanism and the question was where in the processing pipeline that filter was situated. Was it early (Broadbent, 1954), late (Deutsch & Deutsch, 1963), or was it a more gradual and conditional process (Treisman, 1964a)?

In recent years, however, it has become increasingly clear that selection processes play a role in almost all domains of cognitive psychology, so that the term 'attention' itself has become very generic. Attention is believed to be involved in selecting relevant stimuli, in visual search processes, in selectively listening to a conversation in a crowded environment, in retrieving information from memory, and in regulating all the tasks we are currently engaged in. To frame this, a clear and concise taxonomy of attention is necessary (see fig 4.16). The taxonomy that we discuss next is largely based on a proposal from Chun et al. (2011).

4.11.1 THE BASIC FUNCTIONS AND PROPERTIES OF ATTENTION

4.11.1.1 Limited Capacity
Attention is necessary because the environment offers many more stimuli than we can process at any one time. We can only perform one action at a time or retrieve a limited set of memories at any given moment, so we are forced to select from all available options. Attention is therefore limited in capacity: it acts as a filter that separates relevant

from irrelevant information. Attentional processes have evolved to direct our limited processing capacity towards those resources that should be given the highest priority.

4.11.1.2 Selection

From the fact that we have limited processing capacity, it follows that attention must necessarily be selective. For decades, the question of how attention selects relevant information and ignores irrelevant information has been an important driving force behind attention research. Selection is therefore a core function of any form of attention. Almost every situation that requires selection involves multiple stimuli that compete for selection. The role of attention is to bias this competition in such a way that only the most relevant stimuli are processed (Desimone & Duncan, 1995).

We find examples of this kind of selection process in many different domains. For example, we can only perceive a very small part of our environment in detail and therefore have to continuously select where to focus our eyes. We also find similar selection processes in the auditory domain. For example, when talking to someone at a noisy party, we have to select the speech signal and suppress irrelevant background noises (Cherry, 1953). Higher-order cognitive processes also require selection: choosing between two alternatives or retrieving one out of several possible memories are examples of this kind of selection process.

4.11.1.3 Modulation

When a stimulus, event, or memory is selected, attention will also help to determine how the selected event should be processed further. Here, attention regulates the extent to which a stimulus is processed, how quickly and accurately a task is performed, and whether its performance will be remembered later. As we will discuss in more detail in the following chapters, attention can affect the processing of sensory stimuli at various stages of processing and even modify the qualia of the perceived stimuli (Carrasco, Ling, & Read, 2004). The main consequence is that relevant items can be processed with a higher priority than non-relevant items. For this reason, there is a strong similarity between selection and modulation. The most important difference, however, is that selection involves several items competing with each other, with only one item being processed further, whereas modulation involves the regulation of the processing of the selected item itself.

4.11.1.4 Vigilance

Vigilance is related to the modulatory function of attention. We can define modulation as the immediate influence of attention on the processing of a stimulus, whereas vigilance mainly refers to our ability to keep attention focused on one specific task for a prolonged period of time. In this respect, vigilance is similar to sustained attention. Our cognitive processes do not always function at peak level

but fluctuate with a certain regularity in terms of intensity and efficiency. It follows that task performance is generally not constant either. We should therefore also be able to relate variations in task performance to fluctuations in the efficiency of the neural mechanisms that regulate our vigilance. Indeed, it has been found that neural activation in brain areas involved in this regulation is a good predictor of the efficiency of processing this stimulus; for example, how well we remember a stimulus (Otten, Henson, & Rugg, 2002) or how well we can prepare to perform a task (Weissman, Roberts, Visscher, & Woldorff, 2006).

The ability to concentrate for long periods on a single task is essential for a wide range of everyday activities, from focusing on reading a textbook (or writing one...), to detecting defects in in the manufacturing of car tyres, to screening baggage at airports (Wolfe, Horowitz, & Kenner, 2005).

4.11.2 ATTENTION IS NOT A UNITARY FUNCTION

Now that we have introduced some of the important functions of attention, we can turn to the question whether all of these functions are subserved by a single underlying mechanism, or whether attention is an umbrella term for a number of different, independently operating, but functionally related, processes instead. For example, is a visual stimulus selected by the same process as a task instruction? Are visual search processes guided by the same processes that regulate selective listening? The answer to these questions is most likely a resounding no! There is no single attentional process, but rather a collection of neural and cognitive processes that operate in concert, while higher-order executive functions (see Chapter 5) are involved in coordinating the system as a whole.

4.11.3 EXTERNAL AND INTERNAL FOCUS

The first distinction we can make is between external and internal attention. External attention is defined as attention to sensory input. Sensory input is characterised by specific properties, such as location or timing. This information is specific to each sensory modality (e.g., visual or auditory). Attention can be directed not only to specific properties of objects in our environment, for example, the location or colour of a stimulus, but also to an object in its entirety. For example, we can attend to the white colour of a coffee cup, but also to the cup as a whole. Moreover, attention can influence the processing of each of these aspects. Internal attention, on the other hand, refers to the selection and modulation of internally generated information, such as the contents of our memory (see Chapter 14), task goals that we need to keep track of, or the selection of a specific response to a stimulus. Interestingly, this distinction between external and internal attention is already reflected in William James' quote. What James describes as taking possession of the mind by objects is, in fact, a description of external attention, whereas trains of thought refer to internal attention.

4.11.4 EXTERNAL FOCUS

External attention in itself can be further subdivided according to a number of criteria. Firstly, attention can be focused on one or more sensory modalities (Talsma, Doty, & Woldorff, 2007). Next, attention can be directed, independent of the modality, to specific locations or moments in time. Attending to each of these aspects requires its own specific processing mechanisms. Finally, across modalities, location, and time, attention can be directed to specific stimulus features (e.g., the colour of a visual stimulus or the pitch of an auditory stimulus) or even to entire objects.

4.11.4.1 Modalities

We perceive the world around us through our eyes, ears, and the senses of smell, taste, and touch. Although the information from these senses can be integrated at a fairly early stage (see Chapter 9), the senses themselves operate more or less independently of each other and we may focus our attention specifically on only one or on a limited subset of senses. A relatively extreme example of this is when we close our eyes to fully focus ourselves on a particularly beautiful piece of music, or when we seek out a quiet spot to enjoy a beautiful sunset. However, even without shutting off the actual input of one of our senses, we can direct our attention specifically to one sensory modality at the expense of another. For example, when we are instructed to attend to visual stimuli, this results in an increase in sensitivity of the neural systems in the visual cortex, which enables us to detect smaller differences in contrast (Tootell et al., 1998). In a similar way, attention to auditory stimuli can increase the sensitivity of the auditory cortex (Woldorff et al., 1993), which enables us to detect fainter sounds and to discriminate smaller differences in pitch. Similar effects have also been found for the other sensory modalities.

Naturally, the signals from our various senses must converge at some point to form an internally consistent representation. Where this convergence takes place is still an important question, and it is equally unclear what the role of attention is in this process. Although the different sensory systems exchange information with each other early on in processing (see Chapter 9), a consistent multisensory representation probably only emerges at higher levels in the cortical hierarchy (Talsma, 2015). Based on a representation that we form of our surroundings, we can link corresponding signals from the various sensory modalities together. Attention to a particular location thus not only improves the processing of visual signals coming from that location but also the auditory (Eimer & Schöger,

1998; Talsma & Kok, 2002) or tactile signals (Eimer, Van Velzen, & Driver, 2002).

4.11.4.2 Spatial Attention

Attention that is focused on a specific location in our environment is known as **spatial attention**. Spatial attention enables us to process information at specific locations in our environment with a higher priority. In this respect, spatial attention is an example of the limited capacity of attention. Although spatial attention is primarily linked to our visual modality, it can be found in other modalities as well. Spatial attention is often compared to a searchlight or zoom lens (see Chapter 6): the location in our environment that we attend to comprises the proverbial spotlight, enabling us to better process information from this location. Although this metaphor is intuitively appealing, we will see in the following chapters that it is somewhat oversimplified.

Spatial attention is also important for the programming of eye movements. Several studies have found that just prior to making an eye movement to a given location, attention has already shifted to this location. According to the influential **premotor theory of attention**, these shifts of attention are crucial for selecting new locations on which to fixate next (Rizzolatti, Riggio, Dascola, & Umilta, 1987). Indeed, it has been found that there is often a strong link between attention and eye movements (Schall & Thompson, 1999). Attention and eye movements are not completely locked to each other; however, we can direct our attention to a given location without actually moving our eyes.

Finally, we cannot only focus our spatial attention in an endogenous, voluntary manner. Attention can also be captured exogenously by salient stimuli. Although these stimuli can sometimes be relevant, such as the approaching car from our earlier example, there are also many other cases where they turn out to be irrelevant, as is the case with the blue flashing lights of an ambulance that passes us on the opposite side of a four-lane motorway. In such situations, attention also plays an important role in preventing us from being distracted by these stimuli (Folk, Remington, & Johnston, 1992; Slagter, Kok, Mol, Talsma, & Kenemans, 2005).

Distraction can occur when salient stimuli capture our attention. Although it is not yet completely clear which stimuli or aspects of a stimulus are most effective in capturing our attention, it is at least assumed that the sudden appearance of a stimulus (Theeuwes, 2004), the emotional salience of a stimulus (Phelps, Ling, & Carrasco, 2006), and the novelty of the stimulus (Yantis & Egeth, 1999) are important contributing factors. Other factors, such as motion, may also be involved. In particular, looming stimuli tend to be very effective in capturing our attention.

4.11.4.3 Temporal Attention

In addition to locations, attention can be directed to specific points in time: stimuli that we expect to occur at specific moments in time can be processed with greater priority, even when these stimuli overlap with other stimuli in space (Coull & Nobre, 1998). Just as our spatial attention is limited in capacity, we can also only process a limited number of objects within a given time frame. In other words, the amount of information we can process concurrently is limited, and attention helps to select what is the most relevant. To investigate the temporal aspect of attention, visual information is typically presented in rapid succession. For example, when a series of pictures is presented, participants are still able to identify target stimuli when the pictures are presented at a rate of eight to ten pictures per second.

Our ability to retain information is considerably more limited, however. This becomes apparent when participants have to identify not one but two target stimuli. Here, a consistent finding is that participants' ability to process the second target stimulus can be severely impaired when it is presented shortly after the presentation of the first one (Shapiro, Arnell, & Raymond, 1997). In many cases, this is investigated by having participants detect two letters that are interspersed between a series of digits that are presented in rapid succession. Detecting the first digit will generally not be a problem, but the ability to detect the second digit is severely impaired when it follows shortly after the first digit (see fig 4.17).

This remarkable lack in our ability to detect the second target stimulus is known as the **attentional blink**. Interestingly, there is typically no attentional blink when

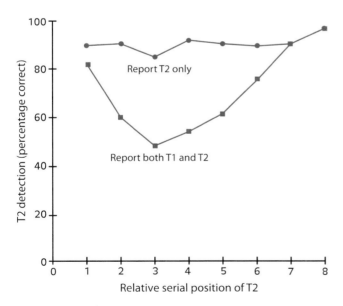

Figure 4.17 An example of the attentional blink. The figure shows the average accuracy with which participants can identify a second target stimulus (T2) in a set of irrelevant distractors, as a function of the relative position of this stimulus to a previous target stimulus. Task performance is significantly reduced when this target stimulus is presented shortly after the first one, and improves as more distractors are presented in between the first and second target. Note that performance is barely reduced when the first and the second target stimulus immediately follow each other (relative position 1). When there is no need to identify the first target stimulus, there is no reduction in performance related to reporting the second target stimulus. (source: Shapiro, Arnell, & Raymond 1997)

the two target stimuli are presented immediately after each other; instead, it appears that there needs to be at least one distractor between the two target stimuli for the attentional blink to occur. Moreover, the fact that this phenomenon represents a limitation in our attention, and not a fundamental shortcoming in our visual perception, is shown by the fact that the attentional blink only occurs when the first target stimulus is relevant. When we are allowed to ignore the first target, we also have no limitation in processing the second target. The exact reason why we miss this second stimulus is still unknown, and it is a topic of extensive discussion in the attention literature. We have evidence suggesting that we are able to detect the second stimulus but are unable to consciously report it (Luck, Vogel, & Shapiro, 1996; Marois, Yi, & Chun, 2004; Shapiro, Driver, Ward, & Sorensen, 1997). This suggests that the stimuli may be selected, but that we fail to memorise them.

4.11.4.4 Properties and Objects

Finally, we can focus our attention not only on sensory modalities, locations, or specific time points but also on entire objects, or on specific properties of these objects. This can be done independently of modality, space, or time. For example, when we attend to our favourite pet, we can do so by attending its shape, its movements, or the sound of its barking. Similarly, we can attend to a television set by focusing on its location, its shape, or the sounds it makes.

Besides attending to complete objects, we can also attend to individual properties. Properties are defined in this case as modality-specific stimulus dimensions, such as colour, shape, pitch, sweetness, or temperature. Highly salient stimulus properties of objects, for example, one red tulip in an otherwise completely green meadow, a crying baby, or an unexpectedly hot cooker can immediately focus our attention on the object in question.

4.11.5 INTERNAL ATTENTION

The external attention processes we just discussed mainly involve the selection and processing of sensory information. We also have a multitude of cognitive processes at our disposal that are involved in regulating our internal mental environment. Similar to the processing of external stimuli, these internal processes have a limited capacity. As discussed in later chapters, we are limited in the number of items we can hold in our working memory, limited in the number of tasks we can perform simultaneously, and limited in the number of concurrent responses we can generate at any given time. Therefore, an important function of our internal control mechanisms involves selecting between the different response alternatives. These internal attention processes are also known as cognitive control processes. What follows is a brief overview of the most important processes and the extent to which these processes correspond to and differ from external attention, while the details of these processes will be the topic of Chapter 5.

4.11.5.1 Response and Task Selection

When we have to make two choices or responses in rapid succession, we find that the second response is often delayed (Pashler, 1984). This is specifically so when the second response should normally be made within half a second after the first response. A consistent finding here is that the closer the two choices are made to each other, the more the second response is delayed. Several experiments have implied the existence of a central processing bottleneck, which is independent of the sensory modality in which the task is presented, or the type of task that is to be performed. This suggests the presence of a central decision-making process that can only be allocated to one task at a time. A second task can therefore only be continued after the decision process has finished processing the first task.

In addition to a capacity limitation in response selection, we are also limited in our efficiency to switch between tasks. After switching to a new task, we are typically slower than when we have to repeat the same task (Rogers & Monsell, 1995). These task switching costs increase as the time we have been given to switch to a new task decreases. This suggests that switching to a new task requires preparation. However, even with very large amounts of preparation time, we remain relatively slow in picking up the new task. This implies that we must actually perform the new task before we have completely switched to it. In other words, our flexibility in switching between different tasks is limited (Monsell, 2003).

Both response and task selection are clearly internal processes but share the basic properties of attention as just defined: they are capacity-limited and solve this capacity problem by selecting one of several possible alternative options and by prioritising neural activity that corresponds to the processing of the selected item. Moreover, it takes effort to sustain these tasks (Braver, Reynolds, & Donaldson, 2003).

4.11.5.2 Long-term Memory

As we will discuss in more detail in Chapters 13 and 14, we can distinguish between long-term memory, where our memories are stored more or less permanently, and working memory, which we use to store information temporarily. Not all of our experiences are stored in long-term memory, and internal attention plays an important role in selecting the information that is stored. The more we attend to a specific memory, and the deeper we process it, the better it tends to be consolidated in long-term memory (Craik & Lockhart, 1972). Deeper processing involves the formation of associations between the memory itself and a context that is formed by information that is already present in memory. Since this process is also limited in capacity, attention plays

a major role in selecting the relevant information, in modulating the processing of this information, and in sustaining the formation of associations.

In addition to processing new information, the occasional retrieval of existing memories can help to retain them in long-term memory. Since the amount of information in long-term memory is extremely large and since we can only recall a limited number of situations at a given time, attention is also strongly involved in selecting the exact memory that we retrieve.

Retrieval of memories is typical in many of our everyday tasks. For example, when we have to describe the way to the supermarket to someone, we have to retrieve the relevant details of the route from long-term memory and describe them in the correct order. Again, capacity is limited here: we only have to select the relevant memories from all possible memories and report them in the right order. Different memories may compete with each other for retrieval, as is shown by the fact that when one memory is successfully retrieved from memory, related memories are forgotten more quickly. Here, forgetting is caused by strengthening the associations with the retrieved memory, while weakening those with the unretrieved memory (Anderson et al., 2004).

4.11.5.3 Working Memory

Information that we need to remember temporarily is stored in working memory (see Chapter 14). Our working memory also enables us to form and manipulate mental representations. This can either be done by using information from our long-term memory or by retaining sensory information that is no longer physically present (D'Esposito et al., 1995; Smith & Jonides, 1999). Because the information that is stored in working memory needs to be kept active, it has been proposed that attention is involved in doing so. Notice, however, that working memory is at the intersection of internal and external operations, because it also plays an important role in retaining information that was still present just moments earlier. For example, consider remembering instructions someone gave you a few seconds earlier, or a random quote that you happened to see on a poster somewhere (Backer & Alain, 2014). In other words, the information that ends up in working memory is, to a large degree, determined by those aspects of the external environment that we attend.

In addition to the fact that external attention can determine what information is stored in working memory, working memory itself can influence external attention. An inward focus of attention, for instance, may result in external stimuli being processed with a lower priority (Talsma, Wijers, Klaver, & Mulder, 2001). Moreover, remembering specific locations in our environment may also affect the way we process the external world, since our attention is focused on those locations (Awh & Jonides, 2001; Corbetta

& Shulman, 2002). Similar results have been found for the processing of shapes (Downing, 2000).

Again, selection is necessary because the capacity of working memory is limited. An interesting feature of working memory is that the internal representations are related to the external visual modalities: visuo-spatial information and auditory-phonological (speech: see Chapters 7 and 17) information appear to be remembered separately. The capacity of visual working memory is limited to about four objects, and that of auditory working memory to about seven, depending on the precise phonological properties of the stimuli. The maintenance of representations is also influenced by internal attentional processes, which control the information that is stored in working memory and which are also involved in maintaining these internal representations.

4.12 BIASED COMPETITION

From the preceding overview, it will be clear that the concept of attention is so diverse that we can ask ourselves whether a unified theoretical framework can be devised to encompass all the diverse aspects of attention. Despite the varieties in functions discussed earlier, the answer to this question, does turn out to be yes!

The British psychologist John Duncan and colleagues (Desimone & Duncan, 1995; Duncan, 1996; Duncan, Humphreys, & Ward, 1997) developed the **biased competition theory** to do so. This theory describes attention as a competition between multiple inputs and representations; this competition can take place at any stage of processing. After all, in everyday life, we often perceive several objects simultaneously. Consider for example a scene of an outdoor party where we are about to unbox a present while an aeroplane passes low overhead. Both objects compete for our attention, and both can elicit a wide range of behaviours. For example, we look towards either the box or the aeroplane, stretch to point at one of them, or pronounce the name of the object. Moreover, at various levels in the processing hierarchy, our brain encodes a large set of internal properties for each object, such as its colour, location, or shape, and these properties are also in competition with each other for processing resources (see fig 4.18).

In its simplest form, the competition manifests itself between the physical properties. The most salient properties will win the competition and capture our attention. In other words, a strong bottom-up signal will be processed quickly and efficiently. For example, if a glass breaks at the party, the sound of this will be in competition with the other sounds present, and because of its saliency, it will win the competition. Such competition also applies to other sensory modalities.

Figure 4.18 The activation of multiple brain systems in response to competing visual inputs. Each input allows us to perform multiple actions, such as looking at or pointing at an aircraft, unwrapping a gift, or uttering the objects' name. Attentional mechanisms are involved in both the selection of the objects we perceive and in selecting the different actions appropriate to that object. (based on Duncan, 1996)

The competition can also be influenced (biased) by top-down processes. Desimone and Duncan (1995) argue that attention is an **emergent property** of several neural functions that jointly resolve the competition for perceptual processing and control of our behaviour. The competition arises because it is impossible to respond to all sensory inputs, so we must prioritise specific stimuli. In the example of the broken glass, the competition is mainly influenced by the salience of the stimulus; therefore, the selection is exogenous or, put differently, driven by bottom-up processes. When we set ourselves the goal of reading a book, when we are hungry or suffer from a spider phobia, however, stimulus processing may be biased by our internal goals. As a result, the book, the pepper steak, or the spider, respectively, are processed with greater priority, even though the physical properties of these stimuli may be less salient than those of competing stimuli. In this latter case, the selection is endogenous, or put differently, affected by top-down processes.

Competition can occur at all levels in the processing of a stimulus. As we will discuss in more detail in Chapter 6, the basic properties of a visual stimulus are processed in the occipital cortex. At this level, competition will be mainly bottom-up, because the salience of (for example) a specific colour strongly influences the competition. The outcome of this competitive selection process then affects the processing in the higher-order, more anterior brain areas, where more complex features of the stimulus are processed. Thus, for example, a highly salient red colour can influence the selection of any objects that have this colour. At the end of this processing pathway, top-down aspects, such as relevance or task goals, will play an increasingly important role in the selection process. It is important to note that these task goals can also indirectly influence competition at lower levels. For instance, when we are looking for a red object, the attribute red will be processed with a greater priority than other colours, so we are biased to selectively detect red objects.

The biased competition theory states not only that competition occurs at different levels of cognitive processing, but also that the final selection is based on the integration across all these levels. For this reason, it should not be surprising that a wide range of brain areas contribute to the final selection. Based on a single cell recording study in monkeys, Moran and Desimone (1985) found that two stimuli that fell into the same receptive field of a neuron were in competition with each other for the neural response of the cell. When one of the two stimuli was a relevant target stimulus and the other one an irrelevant distractor, Moran and Desimone found that the cell responded mainly to the relevant stimulus and not to the irrelevant one. Assuming that such competitive processes occur along the entire processing path of the stimuli, we can imagine attention as a control mechanism, selectively adjusting the processing of a stimulus based on a combination of our internal task goals and the external salience of the stimulus itself. The result of the competition is that one stimulus is selected for further processing. A similar mechanism is also involved in selecting one specific action to be executed.

Evidence for the role of competition in attentional processes is currently abundant. We will discuss some of the results relevant to this in more detail in the chapters on perception, but one result is worth highlighting here, which is the phenomenon of **extinction** (de Haan, Karnath, & Driver, 2012). Extinction is a specific form of the previously discussed attentional dysfunction hemineglect. Extinction patients typically do not show any neglect symptoms when only one stimulus is presented, even when this stimulus is presented in the affected visual field. However, when an additional stimulus is presented in the intact visual field, they are no longer able to perceive the stimulus in the damaged field. This is probably due to competition with the stimulus presented in the intact visual field.

Interestingly, Vuilleumier, Schwartz, Clarke, Husain, and Driver (2002) found that although extinction patients were barely aware that stimuli were presented in the damaged visual field, they did process these stimuli to some extent. When two stimuli were presented simultaneously (one in the damaged visual field and one in the intact visual field), their patients showed little sign of recognition for the stimuli presented in the damaged visual field. When these stimuli were subsequently used in a highly degraded form in a recognition test, the patients had almost no difficulties recognising them compared to a similar set of figures, which they had not seen before. These results

suggest that the initial processing of the stimuli that were presented in the affected field is not impaired in itself, but that the competition primarily results in a limitation in gaining conscious awareness of the stimulus.

This conclusion is supported by ERP results that were reported by Di Russo, Aprile, Spitoni, and Spinelli (2008). These researchers found that the initial processing of a stimulus that was presented in the affected visual field did not differ from that of a stimulus presented in the unaffected visual field. More specifically, the early latency ERP components were similar regardless of whether a stimulus was presented in the affected or in the unaffected visual field. Differences in processing manifested themselves only after approximately 130 ms, as evidenced by differences in the longer latency ERP components.

4.12.1 BIASED COMPETITION AND PREDICTIVE CODING

It is interesting to try and reconcile the biased-competition model with the predictive coding framework. At first, the two theories seem incompatible, as they would predict opposite effects. Indeed, the biased-competition model predicts that we will process information that is relevant to the organism (the information that we attend and expect) with a higher priority, whereas the predictive coding framework predicts that we will be especially active in processing unexpected information. Evidence for such a dissociation between attention and expectation has indeed been reported (Kok & de Lange, 2015; Kok, Jehee, & de Lange, 2012).

Spratling (2008), however, presents a computational model that is based on a predictive coding principle which is able to emulate the functions of biased competition, implying that the apparent discrepancy between the two theoretical frameworks is not a fundamental obstruction for unifying the two ideas. In the predictive coding framework, the effects of competition can possibly be explained by the precision weighing mechanism (see Chapter 2). For relevant and salient stimuli, the prediction error is assigned a greater weight than for other stimuli, thus reducing the uncertainty in the mental representation of relevant stimuli.

4.13 ATTENTION REGULATION

4.13.1 NEUROBIOLOGICAL ATTENTION MODELS

Both Posner (1980) and Corbetta and Shulman (2002) have proposed models in which two different networks are involved in the regulation of attention. The models they propose differ in detail, but both assume that one network is involved in goal-directed, or endogenous, attention, while the other is involved in stimulus-driven, or exogenous, attention.

4.13.1.1 Posner's Cueing Task

The original dissociation between endogenous and exogenous orienting of attention was proposed by the American cognitive psychologist Michael Posner (1980), based on a series of experiments using a cueing task (see fig 4.19). This task requires participants to respond as quickly as possible to a target stimulus that is presented on the left or to the right side of a screen. Although this location is chosen randomly, the stimulus is preceded by a cue, which either endogenously or exogenously directs the participant's attention to one of these locations. The **endogenous cue** consists of a meaningful instruction which informs the participant at which location the stimulus is most likely to appear. Because this type of cue has a symbolic meaning, it is also referred to as a **symbolic cue**. Originally, the symbolic cue consisted of an arrow pointing to the direction where the target was most likely to appear, but since arrows have been shown to direct attention in a reflexive, exogenous way (Tipples, 2002), currently more abstract types of cues are used (e.g., the letters 'L' or 'R' to direct attention to the left or right locations respectively).

Posner found that when the arrow indicated the correct location, that is, the location where the target stimulus actually appeared (i.e., when the cue was valid), participants were able to respond relatively quickly. When the arrow pointed in the wrong direction (i.e., when the cue was invalid), participants were relatively slow. Sometimes the cue did not provide any meaningful information at all, and then the reaction time was somewhere between those of the valid and invalid cues. Posner could explain the speedup that was caused by the valid cue by assuming that attention had already been directed to the location where the stimulus was expected. The relatively slow reaction times to the invalidly cued stimuli were indicative of the fact that participants had to reorient their attention before they could process the target stimulus. According to Posner, this reorientation consists of three different stages. First, attention needs to be disengaged from the location where the attention is already focused, then it needs to shift to a new location where the stimulus has actually appeared, and finally, it needs to be reengaged to the stimulus at that location.

The second type of cue that Posner (1980) used did not consist of a symbolic instruction, but of a brief flash at the location where the target stimulus would appear shortly afterwards. This type of cue, known as an **exogenous cue**, was found to direct attention as well, but the results were somewhat different from those that were obtained using symbolic cues. More specifically, when the cue and the target stimulus were presented within rapid succession, that is, with an interval of about 100–300 ms, Posner found that processing of the target stimulus was facilitated when it appeared at the same location as the cue. However, when the time interval between the cue and the target stimulus was more than 500 ms (up to about 3000 ms), Posner found that response to the target stimulus was actually slower. Posner and Cohen (1984) described this phenomenon as **inhibition of return**. Inhibition of return implies that attention is resistant to salient stimuli that repeatedly attempt to capture attention. When a salient stimulus captures attention, the attentional mechanism inhibits this location after about 300–500 ms to prevent the organism from being forced to continuously attend to it.

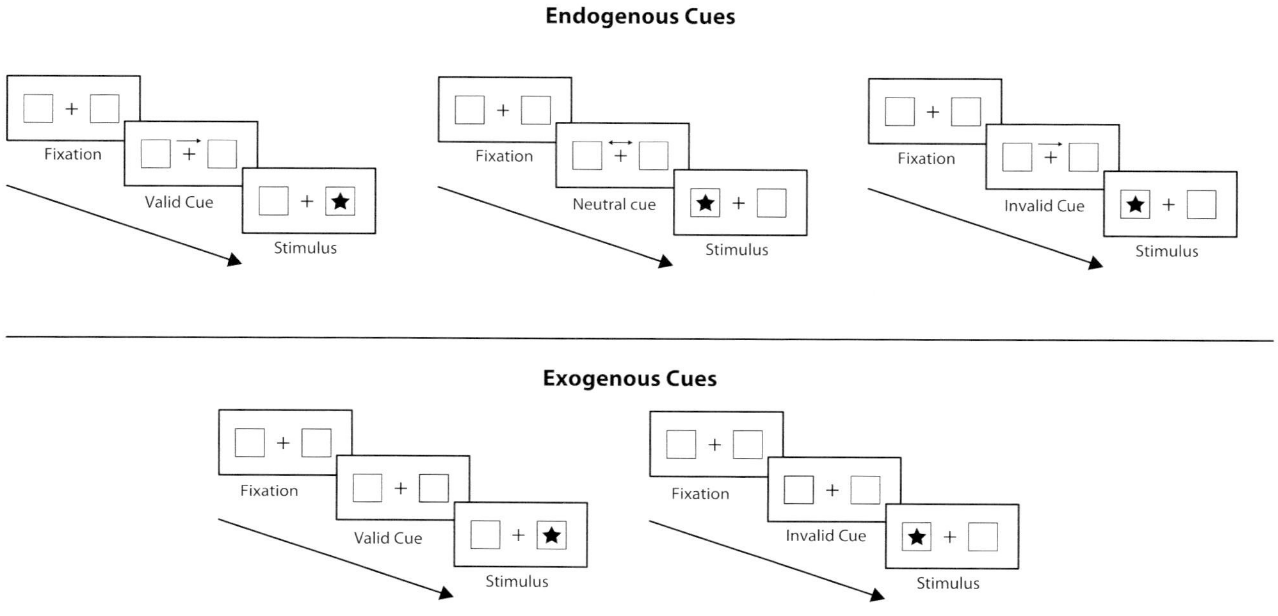

Figure 4.19 An example of the selective cueing paradigms developed by Posner (1980).

4.13.2 ANTERIOR AND POSTERIOR ATTENTION NETWORKS

Ten years after Posner's original findings were published, he and neuroscientist Steve Petersen reported the first results of an investigation into the neural mechanisms of attention (Posner & Petersen, 1990). Using the then newly developed **positron emission tomography (PET)** technique (see Box 4.1), Posner and Petersen identified a large number of brain areas involved in the control of attention. Most of these areas were part of two networks, the anterior and posterior attentional networks. For each of these networks, they identified specific functions. The anterior network was believed to be involved in the detection of relevant target stimuli, whereas the posterior network was believed to be involved in the orientation of attention. In addition, Posner and Petersen identified a third network that was thought to be primarily involved in vigilance.

Box 4.1 Positron emission tomography and the start of the neuroimaging revolution

In Box 2.2 we introduced Angelo Mosso's discovery of pulsations in the blood vessels surrounding the brain that result from mental activity. Mosso's discovery, and its further elaboration by Roy and Sherrington (1890), not only inspired the development of fMRI, it also forms the basis for the use of positron emission tomography (PET) in the cognitive neurosciences. Like fMRI, the PET scanning technique is based on the principle that an increase in brain activation is associated with a regional increase in blood flow. In PET, however, this increase in blood flow is measured by injecting a radioactively labelled tracer into the bloodstream.

Traditional PET neuroimaging studies used the radioactive ^{15}O oxygen isotope (that is, an oxygen atom consisting of eight protons and seven neutrons). This isotope has the same chemical properties as the stable ^{16}O isotope, which is most commonly found in nature. It can bond to two hydrogen atoms and form a water molecule. ^{15}O is an unstable isotope, however, which has a half-life of about two minutes. This means that after about two minutes, half of all ^{15}O isotopes have decayed to ^{15}N (and after another two minutes, half of the remaining ^{15}O isotopes have decayed, etc.). The isotope decays because one proton in the oxygen nucleus emits a positively charged positron, thus changing into a neutron (which incidentally also changes the chemical properties of the atom, because it changes from an oxygen atom into a nitrogen atom, however, that is not relevant right now).

A positron is basically the same as an electron, except that it has a positive electrical charge, whereas an electron has a negative charge. For this reason, an electron is matter and a positron is antimatter. The positron will almost immediately collide with an electron and the two particles will annihilate each other, emitting two gamma photons that depart in opposite directions.

PET is based on the principle that radioactively labelled water (i.e., water consisting of the ^{15}O isotope) is injected intravenously into the upper arm of the participant. After injection, it reaches the brain within seconds, where it crosses the blood-brain barrier. Then it predominantly flows to those parts of the brain where the blood flow is the highest. During the few minutes that the water is radioactive, participants perform a task, and the PET scanner can determine which parts of the brain show the highest density of radioactively labelled water. To do so, radioactive decay is measured by a ring of gamma detectors that is placed around the participant's head. When two detectors simultaneously detect a pulse of gamma rays, it can be calculated at which location a positron and an electron have annihilated each other, and the resulting data can be plotted in the form of a density map. After each administration of a dose of O^{15}-labelled water, a recording session will be started, which will take a few minutes, and during this session, a single condition of a task will be presented. A second condition must be presented during another recording, because the information on blood flow accumulates throughout the session.

The use of PET in neuroimaging is thus limited to the block designs. This is a considerable disadvantage compared to fMRI. In addition, the total measurement time within a PET scan session is limited. When using ^{15}O, each session only takes about two minutes, because the injected radioactive material is then too diffusely distributed throughout the body to provide reliable measurements. Before the next session can start, the remaining radioactive material must have decayed sufficiently, which means that there must be at least 15 minutes between each session. Taking part in a PET scan session therefore consists mainly of waiting, while being in an uncomfortable position with the head stuck in a fixed position inside the scanner, making it impossible to move, and with an infusion in the arm (personal experience of the author). To overcome some of these problems, fludeoxyglucose (^{18}F), a form of glucose in which a radioactive isotope of fluor is used as a tracer,

(Continued)

Box 4.1 (Continued)

has subsequently been used more frequently. The main advantage of ^{18}F is its higher half-life of 20 minutes, which allows significantly longer scans per session.

The health risk associated with PET is very minimal. The dose of radioactivity administered during one experiment (about 14 mSv) is about five times the typical annual dose of radioactive radiation a human receives from natural sources. There is a small increased risk for laboratory staff, however, because they have to work with the radioactive materials on a daily basis. Therefore, protective clothing is mandatory for the operating staff. A cyclotron is required to produce the radioactive isotopes. These characteristics combined make PET very expensive to use.

Despite the aforementioned disadvantages, PET was particularly successful for a relatively short period in the first half of the 1990s and produced some particularly influential results. After the maturation of MRI scanners, however, PET research has largely been superseded by fMRI, a technique that has considerably fewer disadvantages and a much better temporal resolution. Nevertheless, PET is still used because it also has some unique properties. Instead of water or glucose, it is also possible to radioactively label substances that bind to specific neurotransmitter receptors, for example, the dopamine D1 or D2 receptors (two variants of dopamine), making it possible to determine fairly precisely the density of these receptors in the brain.

In a retrospective, Petersen and Posner (2012) look back on their original model and propose some adjustments. New evidence has shown that the frontal brain regions are mainly involved in maintaining task goals and in voluntarily switching attention. This network is therefore primarily an executive system, whereas the posterior network is more involved in automatic, exogenous orientation.

4.13.3 FRONTOPARIETAL NETWORKS

Based on a meta-analysis of neuroimaging studies, Corbetta and Shulman (2002) proposed a neurobiological model of attention regulation that is based on the distinction between Posner's endogenous and exogenous forms of attention (see fig 4.20). This model identifies a goal-directed, or top-down, attentional system that consists of a network of frontal and parietal cortical brain regions. This system is related to the regulation of expectations, knowledge, and goal-directed actions. As such, it is involved in directing attention to specific locations by processing information from symbolic cues. This network is also known as the dorsal attention network and includes areas in the intraparietal sulcus and the superior frontal cortex.

In addition, Corbetta and Shulman (2002) identified a ventral network which is mainly involved in the exogenous, bottom-up focusing of attention. The latter network consists mainly of areas in the temporoparietal cortex and the inferior frontal cortex of the right hemisphere, and it is mainly involved in the detection of relevant stimuli, especially when these are salient or unexpected. Corbetta and Shulman hypothesised that this ventral network may function like an electric circuit breaker, in that it can interrupt the activity of the goal-directed system when an unexpected but salient and potentially relevant stimulus presents itself.

Corbetta and Shulman's (2002) model describes how two different forms of attention can interact. Under normal circumstances, the goal-directed network is involved in selecting stimuli that are relevant and in directing attention to those locations where these stimuli are found. If, however, we only had a goal-directed attentional network, we would be extremely inflexible. For this reason, the exogenous attention network can interrupt the goal-directed system when a situation arises that demands our

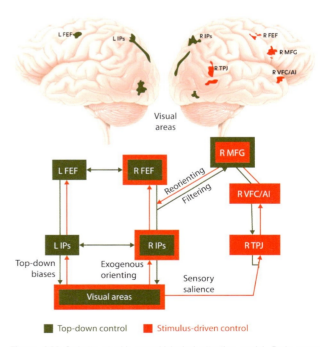

Figure 4.20 Corbetta et al.'s neurobiological attention model. Brain areas involved in top-down control are shown in green; areas involved in stimulus-driven bottom-up control in red. FEF: frontal eye fields, IPs: intraparietal sulcus, MFG: middle frontal gyrus, VFC: ventral frontal cortex, AI: anterior insula, TPJ: temporoparietal junction. (source: Corbetta, Patel, & Shulman, 2008)

attention, such as immediate danger, threats, or otherwise salient stimuli.

The next question is how these two systems can interact. Corbetta et al. (2008) argue that, on the one hand, signals from the top-down system aim to inhibit the representations of distractor information that is present in the bottom-up system, so that our attention remains focused on the selected target. On the other hand, when stimuli are detected that are not goal-relevant, the bottom-up system will attempt to interrupt the goal-oriented attention system so that attention can be directed on the new stimuli. In other words, the two attention networks are in competition with each other.

4.13.3.1 Top-down versus Bottom-up: Shared or Independent Neural Substrates?

Is there a complete separation between the networks involved in top-down and bottom-up control of attention, or is there some overlap? The answer to this question appears to vary considerably depending on the research method used (Talsma, Coe, Munoz, & Theeuwes, 2010). In fact, fMRI studies using block designs (see Box 2.2; Chapter 2) found a strong overlap between brain areas involved in top-down and bottom-up attentional control, whereas fMRI studies using event-related designs (Box 2.2) reported a dissociation between top-down and bottom-up brain areas. To circumvent these problems, Talsma, Coe, et al. (2010) used an event-related fMRI design and an experiment in which top-down and bottom-up attentional processes could be manipulated independently (see fig 4.21). In this study, a

mask consisting of a digital representation of the number 8, outlined by a border consisting of a combination of a circle and a diamond, was presented at four positions on a screen (see fig 4.21a).

Just before this mask changed into a stimulus, a distractor could be presented that consisted of a salient colour change of one of the four stimuli (the singleton; see fig 4.21b). The participant had to ignore this distractor and detect a stimulus that then appeared either at one of the four positions (the search condition) or at all four positions (the non-search condition). This stimulus consisted of either a regular letter 'C' or a mirrored letter 'C', and the participant's task was to report which of the two was displayed by pressing a button. The rationale for this manipulation was that participants in the search condition had to invoke the top-down attention control mechanism, whereas in the non-search condition they did not have to do so. Similarly, the bottom-up attentional control mechanism was only activated in the condition in which the distracting singleton was presented. This study confirmed that different networks are involved in top-down and bottom-up regulation of attention, but at the same time found evidence for a neural mechanism that is shared by both forms of attention control.

The Corbetta and Shulman (2002) model is mainly based on studies that have investigated the role of attention in visual perception. According to the model, the top-down attention network is able to selectively influence the processing of specific properties of a stimulus, so that these properties are processed with a higher

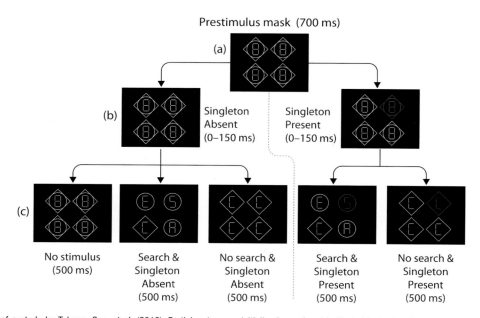

Figure 4.21 Outline of a study by Talsma, Coe, et al. (2010). Participants were initially shown four identical objects, in which, over time, a target stimulus was presented, of which the participants had to indicate whether this was the letter 'C' or a mirrored 'C'. Depending on the specific task, they either had to search for this stimulus or not, in addition to which they were distracted on some trials by an irrelevant but salient stimulus (represented here as a singleton).

priority (note that a similar idea was coined by Posner & Dehaene, 1994). Although Corbetta and Shulman do not go into full detail about how this prioritisation comes about, the idea is compatible with older ideas that suggest that the frontal and parietal brain regions can send biasing signals to different parts of the visual cortex in order to selectively prioritise the processing of relevant stimulus features (Brunia, 1999; Gitelman et al., 1999; LaBerge, 1990). Moreover, Corbetta and Shulman's model is also consistent with the biased competition theory of attention, in that the proposed biasing signals represent a neural implementation of the biasing processes posited by this theory.

4.14 A DISTINCTION BETWEEN ATTENTION AND CONSCIOUSNESS

Although attention and consciousness are related, there has been a long-standing debate on whether attention and consciousness are manifestations of the same process or not. Baars (1997) argues that attention and consciousness are strongly related, and that attention is needed to select the information that we eventually become aware of. According to this interpretation, attention can be compared to selecting a television channel and consciousness to the image that appears on screen.

4.14.1 ATTENTION WITHOUT AWARENESS

The idea that attention is necessary before we can become aware of a stimulus sounds plausible, but many researchers object to this assumption. Koch and Tsuchiya (2012), for example, argue that attention and awareness can manifest themselves independently of each other. According to Koch and Tsuchiya, attention can affect behaviour outside of consciousness. Jiang, Costello, Fang, Huang, and He (2006), for example, presented photographs of nude men and women to participants' non-dominant eye. These photos could not be consciously observed because masking noise patterns were presented to the dominant eye. After the participants had completed a task using this noise pattern, a new stimulus was presented. This stimulus was presented either to the dominant or the non-dominant eye, and again, participants had to perform a task. Performance on the latter task depended on attention. If attention was already focused on the location of this stimulus, performance was higher than if attention was focused elsewhere.

The crucial finding was that the photographs affected the participants' attention. Heterosexual men's attention was captured by the invisible female nudes, and heterosexual women's attention was captured by the invisible male nudes. The fact that non-consciously perceived photos can capture attention implies that attention can operate independently of consciousness. The results can possibly be explained by the emotional valence of the stimuli (see Chapter 12). Troiani, Price, and Schultz (2014) found that unconsciously perceived fearful faces resulted in activation of the amygdala (see fig 4.22). This activation was associated with activation of brain areas involved in the attentional network.

The conclusion that unconsciously perceived stimuli can capture attention also follows from a similar – but admittedly less sexy – experiment by Naccache, Blandin, and Dehaene (2002). In this study, participants had to decide as quickly as possible whether a number that was presented was larger or smaller than 5. Just prior to the presentation of this target stimulus, another digit was presented subliminally, and this digit could either be compatible (e.g., both digits smaller than 5)

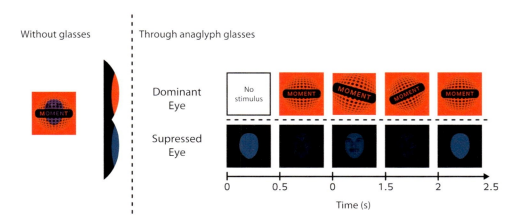

Figure 4.22 Fearful faces presented through anaglyph glasses (3D) resulted in unconscious perception. Left: an example of a stimulus as it would be perceived without glasses. Right: the stimuli as perceived through anaglyph glasses. Words were presented to the dominant eye, while faces were presented to the non-dominant eye. (source: Troiani et al., 2014)

or incompatible (e.g., first digit smaller than 5, second digit larger than 5) with the target digit. Compared to a control condition in which no additional digit was presented, responses were faster in the presence of the subliminal digit, but the degree to which the response was facilitated depended on the congruency. They were more strongly facilitated when both congruent than when they were incongruent, again showing that subliminal stimuli can capture our attention.

4.14.2 CONSCIOUSNESS WITHOUT ATTENTION

Baars (1997) also assumes that attention must precede awareness, and this assumption, too, has been received with much scepticism. Some theorists argue that awareness is not dependent on attention (Koch & Tsuchiya, 2007, 2012), whereas others argue exactly the opposite (Bor & Seth, 2012), namely that conscious awareness must precede attention. Arguments in favour of the idea that attention is necessary for conscious awareness are often based on the phenomena of **inattentional blindness** and **change blindness**. As we will discuss in more detail in Chapter 6, these phenomena describe how we can sometimes notice particularly large changes in visual scenes only when we attend to them (Hollingworth & Henderson, 2002; Landman, Spekreijse, & Lamme, 2003; Simons & Chabris, 1999; Simons & Rensink, 2005). This obviously implies that attention is necessary for consciousness.

In contrast, Koch and Tsuchiya (2007) identified several situations where awareness can occur without attention. For instance, when observing natural scenes, we can quickly become aware of the essence of a scene without attending them. Cohen, Alvarez, and Nakayama (2011) investigated whether this is actually the case by giving participants an attention-demanding task. Participants were presented with a rapidly paced series of letters and numbers and their task was to count how many numbers they had seen. During the presentation of these stimuli, a series of continuously changing checkerboard patterns were presented in the background. Unexpectedly, one of these patterns was replaced by a picture of a natural scene, depicting an animal or a vehicle. Under these conditions, only 23% of the participants could immediately identify the object in the picture and half of the participants even reported being unaware of the fact that a picture had been shown. Upon completion of the digit-counting task, participants were instructed to attend to the background, and now they could correctly classify the scenes in 93% of cases. This result therefore suggests that attention is required for the processing of natural scenes.

Lamme (2003) states, however, that although we can become aware of a stimulus, we won't be able to respond to them without attending them (see fig 4.23). According to Lamme, we can be aware of a large number of stimuli. Without directing our attention to one of these stimuli, we cannot access it, and our conscious experience quickly disappears again. This short-lived and fleeting conscious experience is known as our **phenomenal awareness**. In addition, Lamme identified a more robust form of consciousness, known as **access awareness**. It is only after we focus our attention on a conscious experience that we can report it. At that point the experience has become part of our access awareness.

Let's illustrate this distinction between phenomenal and access awareness with a simple example. Suppose we spend an entire day at home, finishing a writing assignment. Now, our attention is predominantly focused on our computer and our conscious experiences are mainly made up by the topics that we are writing about. These conscious experiences form our access awareness. Meanwhile, we may become aware of all kinds of events happening around us: a car passing by in the street, music playing in the background, or a faint beep coming from the kitchen. Without focusing our attention on the beep, we cannot describe what it is. The beep is part of our phenomenal awareness, and our conscious experience of it fades away when we start writing again. When we are about to get up and grab ourselves a coffee, we notice that the beeping sound is caused by the door of the fridge that was left open: we have now focused our attention on the beeping sound, and we are able to describe it. It has now become part of our access awareness.

4.14.2.1 A New Interpretation of Attention and Awareness

Lamme (2003, 2004, 2006a, 2006b, 2010) argues that attention and awareness should be defined in terms of their neural mechanisms, instead of the classical folk-psychological terms that are still prevalent in psychology. This argument is primarily based on results from studies involving visual awareness (see also Lamme & Roelfsema, 2000). Here it was found that the presentation of a visual stimulus results in a rapid automatic processing of this stimulus in the visual cortex (see Chapter 6 for details). Processing begins in the primary visual cortex and quickly spreads to the higher cortices. This form of processing is described by Lamme as the feedforward sweep and lasts approximately 100–150 ms. This feedforward sweep is, in most cases, followed by recurrent processing. This recurrent or top-down processing takes place in the form of feedback from the higher to the lower areas in the visual cortex, causing extensive interactions between the different areas.

According to Lamme, it is this recurrent processing that determines the emergence of awareness. Lamme (2006a)

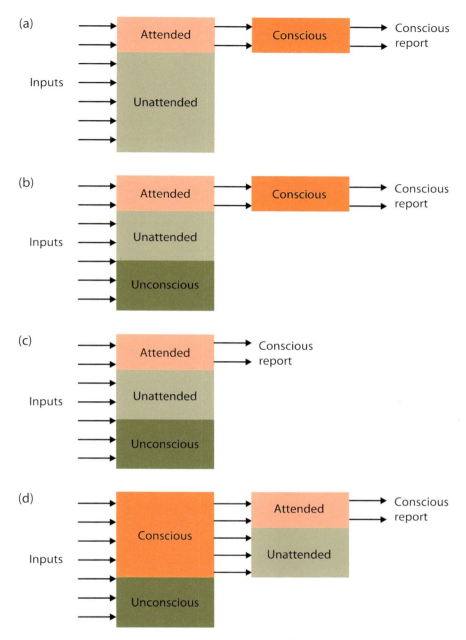

Figure 4.23 Four possible relations between attention and consciousness according to Lamme (2003). (a–c) The classical view that assumes that attention precedes consciousness. (d) An alternative view that assumes that consciousness precedes attention. In the latter case, only stimuli that are attended can be consciously reported. According to Lamme, these stimuli enter our access awareness. We can be aware of unattended stimuli, but they enter our phenomenal awareness and cannot be reported.

argues that becoming fully aware of a visual stimulus involves three stages (see fig 4.24). The first stage consists of the feedforward sweep. According to the principles of the biased competition mechanism, attention can selectively influence the processing of a specific stimulus at this stage. This allows us to automatically respond to a stimulus without becoming aware of it. During the second stage, localised recurrent processing will emerge. Localised recurrent processing integrates the individual properties of the stimulus, resulting in phenomenal awareness. Thus, we become aware of a stimulus but we cannot yet report it. Finally, in the third stage, widespread recurrent processing is in full swing, resulting in stimuli entering our access awareness. At this stage, recurrent processing involves an extensive network of brain areas, including the frontal and/or the language areas of the brain. Extending recurrent processing to these latter brain areas is facilitated by attention, because the biasing processes enhance the representation of a specific stimulus. Nevertheless, the emergence of a stable representation in

(a) The feedforward sweep

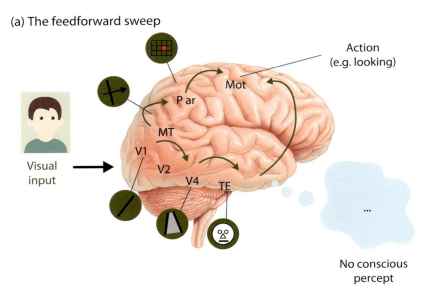

Action (e.g. looking)

No conscious percept

(b) Localised recurrent processing

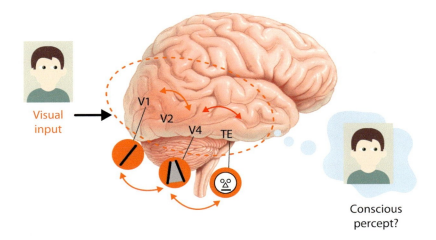

Conscious percept?

(c) Widespread recurrent processing

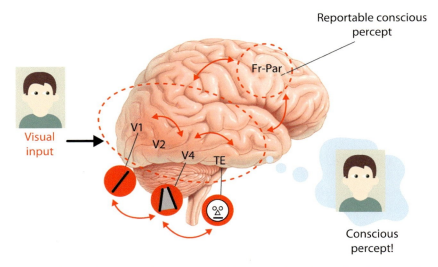

Reportable conscious percept

Conscious percept!

Figure 4.24 The role of feedforward and recurrent processing in our awareness of a stimulus. (a) As long as there is only forward processing, there can be no awareness. (b) Forward processing is immediately followed by localised recurrent processing. There may now be a conscious experience, but it cannot yet be reported. (c) When widespread recurrent processing is involved, the stimulus can be reported consciously. (source: Lamme, 2006a)

our access awareness is, according to Lamme, solely due to recurrent processing.

Evidence for the idea that awareness is related to recurrent processing is found in an ERP study of Fahrenfort et al. (2007). These authors presented masked and unmasked stimuli, and for each of those stimuli, participants were instructed to decide whether they contained a specific object. In the masked condition, participants performed at chance level, which is a clear indication that they were unable to perceive the stimulus. The ERPs in the unmasked condition were characterised by a series of components that are characteristic for the visual processing of a stimulus (see Chapter 6), namely the P1 (appearing 80–110 ms after stimulus onset), the N1 (110–140 ms), and the N2 (180–305 ms). In the masked conditions, the initial P1 component was still intact, whereas the subsequent N1 and N2 components were strongly reduced in amplitude. Since these later components possibly reflect the effects of recurrent processing, their absence in the masked condition, combined with the fact that participants were no longer able to consciously perceive the stimuli, strongly imply an important role for recurrent processing in the emergence of a conscious visual experience.

More direct evidence for the hypothesis that recurrent processing is related to conscious perception was reported by Koivisto, Railo, Revonsuo, Vanni, and Salminen-Vaparanta (2011) based on a TMS study. These authors presented natural scenes, and participants had to decide whether they contained an animal. The study exploited the fact that visual processing initially starts in the primary visual cortex, then spreads to the more laterally localised higher visual areas, after which information is projected back to the primary visual cortex via recurrent connections. Koivisto et al. used a TMS pulse to disrupt recurrent processing in the primary visual cortex after information processing had already started in the lateral visual cortex. The effect of this disruption was a significantly reduced performance on the decision task.

A similar result was found by Boyer, Harrison, and Ro (2005). Again, recurrent processing in the primary visual cortex was disrupted by means of a TMS pulse, which resulted in simulated blindsight. More specifically, participants were no longer aware of a visual stimulus but were nevertheless still able to report specific properties of these stimuli.

4.15 IN CLOSING

At first sight, attention and consciousness appear to be two comparable and strongly related functions. Yet their differences are greater than we might initially think. These differences are perhaps also underlined by the way attention and consciousness have been treated in academic studies over the past century and a half. Whereas attention was considered to be a phenomenon that everyone knew what it was, to paraphrase William James (1890), it appears more appropriate to state that, to this day, no one really knows what attention is. In contrast, consciousness was so elusive that, apart from the German structuralists of the late 19th century, few researchers dared to venture into tackling the problem of consciousness until Chalmers' (1995) influential essay.

At present, we see the emergence of an opposite trend: while more and more researchers are focusing on consciousness and conscious experiences, doubt about the usefulness of attention as a scientific concept is ever increasing (Anderson, 2011). The British cognitive neuroscientist Vincent Walsh (2003), for instance, describes attention as psychology's 'weapon of mass explanation'. Due to the multiplicity of definitions that are derived from intuitive ideas, attention is increasingly becoming a catchall term, and the question arises whether it would not be useful to redefine attentional processes in terms of biasing, competition, expectation, precision weighting, and cognitive control. Despite these objections, it still makes sense to continue to use the term 'attention', as long as we are aware of its specific limitations, and despite these limitations, our knowledge of attentional processes has grown extremely rapidly over the last century.

4.16 SUMMARY

Consciousness has fascinated mankind for as long as humanity has existed. Although consciousness was originally the exclusive domain of philosophy, empirical research has increasingly focused on it since 1995. Essential questions are whether consciousness is unitary and how consciousness emerges in the brain. René Descartes introduced the distinction between body and mind in his dualistic world view. Although dualism provided an opportunity to maintain the concept of free will, it also appears to have introduced a number of essential problems, making it of limited explanatory power. The main objection to dualism is that it introduces a homunculus, which does not explain the problem of consciousness, but merely passes it on to the next homunculus.

The currently most widely accepted position is that conscious experiences are the result of brain activity. In 1995, David Chalmers distinguished between the hard problem of consciousness and the easy ones. He argued that only the latter are accessible for empirical research.

Is conciousness localised or is it the result of global coordinated activation of the brain? Is there a relationship between consciousness and intentional behaviour? Do we have free will? Are there different levels of consciousness? Various ideas have been formulated about the function of consciousness. Some researchers have related consciousness to perception, others to social functions or to the intentional control of our actions. Finally, others point out that consciousness is strongly associated with the integration of information. Mental simulation of actions, the ability to evaluate the consequences of actions, has also been considered as an important function of consciousness. The latter function can be extended to the evaluation of not only one's own actions but also to the evaluation of the actions of another.

Brain research suggests that thalamo-cortical circuits play an important role in awareness. A conscious state is associated with a high degree of synchronisation between various widespread brain areas. Electrophysiological and neuroimaging studies suggest that we have much less intentional control over our own actions than we believe we have, suggesting that we do not have free will. However, most studies in this area have focused on relatively simple actions, and it is not yet clear whether, and if so how, these results can be extrapolated to more complex actions and decisions. In some cases, neuroimaging results, can be used to determine whether a comatose patient still has conscious experiences or not.

Various experimental procedures have been developed to measure the neural correlates of conscious experience. For this purpose, bistable images, blindsight, binocular rivalry, continuous flash suppression, or distraction can be used.

Many theories of consciousness are based on the idea that consciousness is associated with the integration of information. The two main groups of theories in this area are the global (neuronal) workspace theories and the dynamic core theories. Some researchers have attempted to base theories of consciousness on quantum physics, but most of the predictions of these models are either non-falsifiable or have been falsified. In essence, the link between quantum physics and consciousness is a modern form of Cartesian dualism.

Sleep is an example of an altered state of consciousness that we still know relatively little about. Part of our sleep cycle is characterised by the occurrence of dreams. Recent neuroscientific evidence suggests that dreams are caused by processes similar to those of mental imagery. The muddled, inconsistent nature of dreams can be explained by a defective control mechanism or the absence or impaired functioning of the prediction error correction mechanism of our sensory modalities during sleep.

Attention can be regarded as a selection mechanism that can manifest itself in a multitude of different ways. Attention prioritises the processing of some stimuli, memories, or thoughts at the expense of others. It can be directed externally to stimuli in the environment, or internally to representations in memory, thoughts, or task goals. In addition, attention plays a role in vigilance: sustaining a specific task for an extended period of time and staying alert. When considering external attention, the multitude of different aspects of our environment on which our attention can be focused is almost overwhelming: spatial locations, visual objects, specific characteristics of an object such as colour or shape, specific conversations, pitch, or full sensory modalities. In addition, strikingly salient stimuli can grab our attention.

The enormous variety of attentional processes may be explained in a relatively straightforward manner by the biased-competition theory of attention. According to this theory, different stimuli are in constant competition with each other for limited processing capacity. Attention can adjust the outcome of this competition at all levels of processing, by giving more or less priority to specific properties of a stimulus. The biased-competition theory is compatible with the predictive coding framework. Neurobiological models of attention specify how this prioritisation is implemented in the brain, involving networks of brain areas in the frontal and parietal cortex.

To what extent are attention and consciousness manifestations of the same process? Some theorists argue that attention is a necessary condition for awareness, but others dispute this. Unconscious perception can influence attention, but it is less clear to what extent awareness of a stimulus can occur without attention. Lamme argues that awareness and attention are manifestations of two different neural processes: attention is associated with feedforward processing and awareness with recurrent processing.

NOTES

1 An image is bistable when it can be interpreted in two different ways. One of the simplest examples of a bistable image is the Necker cube, that is, a two-dimensional representation of a cube that can be interpreted in two different ways. We either match the front of the cube to the square on the bottom-left or the square on the top-right. Although we can interpret the cube in both ways, and can even flexibly switch between these two representations, we are never able to perceive both variants simultaneously.

2 A well-known example is driving. Many experienced drivers report, while driving along known routes, not having had conscious experience while traversing long sections of these routes. At least they report not having a conscious recollection of this experience.

3 Presumably, the renowned humanistic psychotherapist Carl Rogers was once persuaded to join a duck hunt. After a long wait, an opportunity for shooting a duck presented itself and Rogers' friends gave him ample opportunity to go for it. Exactly at the moment when Rogers fired a shot, however, another hunter a few 100 metres away, also fired a shot. While both hunters went out to claim the shot duck, Rogers aptly articulated what both hunters presumably thought: 'You feel that this is your duck' (Epstein & Joker, 2007).

FURTHER READING

Edelman, G. M., & Tononi, G. (2001). *A universe of consciousness: How matter becomes imagination*. New York, NY: Basic Books.

Seth, A. (2021). Being you: A New Science of Consciousness. London: Faber & Faber Ltd.

Styles, E. A. (1997). *The psychology of attention*. Hove: Taylor & Francis.

CHAPTER 5
Cognitive control

5.1 INTRODUCTION

Suppose you are walking down a busy shopping street on a Saturday afternoon: although you have a deadline for a statistics class assignment, you have to run into town for an errand. As you find your way through the crowd, your mind remains focused on the assignment, going over every step you have taken and trying to work out why the code you have written is giving incorrect results. While deeply focused on the problem, you are suddenly distracted by the unexpected meeting with a friend who captures your attention. Together you decide to go for a coffee. Once you find yourself sitting on a terrace, you are seduced by the attraction of a chocolate cake that is on special offer. Do you give in to your impulse to enjoy yourself or do you stick to your intention to keep dieting?

If you recognise aspects of this example, you have experienced cognitive control, that is, the ability to coordinate your thoughts and actions according to your internal goals (Koechlin, Ody, & Kouneiher, 2003b). Cognitive control involves several functions, which together enable us to respond flexibly to our environment. For example, it involves the ability to divide our attention in such a way that we can seemingly perform two tasks at the same time, or at least flexibly switch between different tasks, such as avoiding people in a busy crowd and solving a logical problem at the same time. A second aspect of cognitive control is that it enables us to resist impulses, such as eating a calorie-rich cake. This is an example of inhibitory control. Cognitive control processes also play a key role in performing complex cognitive tasks, such as reasoning or solving a complex equation. In particular, cognitive control processes retrieve problem-specific information from memory, and they are involved in the manipulation of this information. In other words, cognitive control processes are strongly tied to our **working memory**. A final important aspect of cognitive control processes is that they are involved in detecting and processing any error that we might make in such a way that we can flexibly adapt our behaviour when making the error, in order to prevent us from making the same error again later.

5.2 EXECUTIVE FUNCTIONS

5.2.1 THE NATURE OF EXECUTIVE FUNCTIONS

5.2.1.1 Dysexecutive Syndrome

Cognitive control is closely related to the concept of **executive functions**. The latter type of functions has primarily been identified in neuropsychology, in describing the behavioural changes in patients with damage to their frontal lobes (see Box 5.1). In general, these patients have many difficulties functioning in their everyday lives, although they often score normally on IQ tests and typically perform almost normally on a wide range of standard cognitive tasks. In particular, it is their performance on tasks requiring cognitive control that is impaired.

According to Baddeley (1996), these patients are characterized by a **dysexecutive syndrome**. This syndrome involves a wide variety of cognitive deficiencies (see fig 5.1), such as impaired performance in inhibiting responses, in inferring and generating rules, in switching between different **task sets**, or in writing fluently (Godefroy et al., 2010). These deficiencies can lead to a variety of problems. For example, Ardila and Surloff (2006) found that a dysexecutive syndrome can have consequences for writing skills. Not only do patients with a dysexecutive syndrome miss the ability to stay focused on producing a long text for an extended period of time, they also often lack the ability to organise complex ideas and represent them coherently (see Chapter 18 for more details on writing and organising texts).

Stuss and Alexander (2007) criticise the notion of a dysexecutive syndrome, however. In their view, it implies that damage to the frontal lobes affects all executive functions. Stuss and Alexander accept that this may be so in exceptional cases, in particular when patients have extensive damage to their frontal lobes; however, they argue that this is typically not the case. For this reason, Stuss and Alexander focused on patients with limited damage to the frontal lobes and have, on the basis of this, identified three specific functions related to cognitive control.

DOI: 10.4324/9781003319344-7

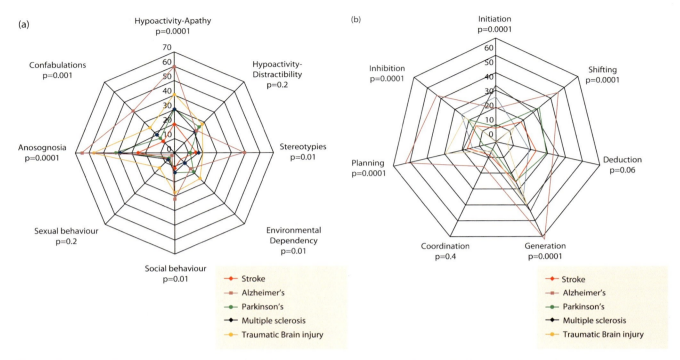

Figure 5.1 Overview of the relative occurrence of specific behavioural (a) and cognitive issues (b) in stroke, Alzheimer's disease, Parkinson's disease, multiple sclerosis, and traumatic brain injury. (source: Godefroy et al., 2010)

Box 5.1 Walter Freeman's brutal psychosurgery practices

At the start of the 20th century, our knowledge of the brain was still very rudimentary, to put it mildly. This lack of knowledge, combined with a very limited understanding of the human psyche, resulted in an extremely poor treatment of psychiatric patients. The most common method was to simply put them away in asylums – madhouses – where they were often housed under appalling conditions and subjected to questionable treatments.

One of the most controversial treatments was that of **psychosurgery**. The first psychosurgical procedures were conducted in Switzerland around 1880 and they started to become commonplace in the 1930s under the influence of the Portuguese neurosurgeon Egas Moniz. The procedure introduced by Moniz involved removing parts of the frontal lobes, using a procedure that Moniz named **leucotomy**. Unlike other parts of the brain, such as the visual cortex or the somatosensory cortex, the prefrontal cortex did not appear to have any significant function in those days, and surgical interventions in this part of the brain appeared to have little or no negative effects on a patient's behaviour.

One of the most fanatical proponents of psychosurgery was the American neurologist Walter Freeman, who had been influenced by Moniz's work (Caruso & Sheehan, 2017). Freeman performed his first leucotomy in 1935, with the assistance of neurosurgeon James Watts.

Freeman had recruited Watts to join his practice because Freeman did not have a licence to perform surgeries himself. A year after this first surgery, Freeman, along with Watts, conducted his first **frontal lobotomy** on Alice Hood Hammatt, a housewife from Topeka, Kansas, who had been diagnosed with depression. A lobotomy involved severing all connections between the prefrontal cortex and the rest of the brain, with the main effect of eliminating many of the patient's symptoms. The day before her operation, Hammatt decided to withdraw from the procedure, but despite her opposition, Freeman convinced her to undergo the treatment. By 1942, Freeman and Watts had already completed around 200 of these operations.

Despite this high number, Freeman was dissatisfied by his perceived lack of progress. Frustrated by his inability to perform the surgeries himself, he started looking for an alternative way to carry out the procedure. Inspired by the work of an Italian doctor, Amarro Fiamberti, he found a way to sever the connections to and from the prefrontal lobe via the eye sockets. The bones at the top of the skull are relatively thin and easy to pierce with a sharp object. This immediately simplified the procedure considerably: Freeman found a sharp object in the form of an ice pick, and he simply tapped it through the bone above the eyeball using a small hammer, after which a few rough movements destroyed the brain

(Continued)

Box 5.1 (Continued)

tissue between the prefrontal cortex and the rest of the brain. An additional advantage was that this new procedure did not require an operating licence, and therefore allowed Freeman to perform the procedure himself (see fig 5.2). Patients were not anaesthetised but were put into a state of shock by means of **electroconvulsive therapy**. The new procedure was known as **transorbital lobotomy**. Watts did not approve of this new procedure and terminated his collaboration with Freeman.

After the development of the transorbital lobotomy, Freeman travelled across the United States (according to some unconfirmed rumours in a van known as the 'lobotomobile') performing and promoting transorbital lobotomy in various psychiatric facilities. During this period (roughly between 1946 and 1952) Freeman personally conducted approximately 4000 lobotomies. Of these, 19 involved minors, including four-year-old children. Approximately 2500 of these procedures were performed using the ice pick; the remainder were traditional prefrontal lobotomy surgeries that Freeman performed himself despite his lack of qualification.

Freeman's most infamous patient was Rosemary Kennedy, the late US President John F. Kennedy's sister. In her youth, Rosemary was plagued by various mental health issues, including intense mood swings that resulted in rebellious behaviour. Kennedy senior, back then US ambassador to Great Britain, was troubled by his daughter's unpredictable behaviour and, at the advice of his physician, requested Freeman have her lobotomised. The operation was an epic failure that destroyed young Rosemary's life forever. After the operation, she had the intellectual capacity of a two-year-old and, as a result, spent the rest of her life in various psychiatric institutions.

Despite the criticism that Freeman had to endure, his popularity continued to grow, and he was able to continue his business for many years. Nevertheless, the outcome of almost all of Freeman's operations were similar: although some of the patients' initial symptoms disappeared, they were all suffering from significant side effects. After the operation, they became inactive and lethargic. Many reported losing part of their identity.

Eventually, the negative results and publicity surrounding Rosemary Kennedy's botched lobotomy began to wreak havoc on Freeman. Slowly but steadily, the media began to portray psychosurgery as a method that was primarily used by psychiatric institutions to silence troubled patients. The latter was superbly portrayed by Jack Nicholson in the 1975 classic movie 'One Flew over the Cuckoo's Nest'. This development, combined with the introduction of the clinical use of chlorpromazine (Thorazine) in 1955 and negative publicity about the death of a patient during treatment (while posing for a photograph, Freeman lost control of the ice pick, fatally injuring a patient), resulted in a gradual decline in Freeman's activities.

The only positive thing to come out of this dark page in the history of psychiatry is that we came to understand,

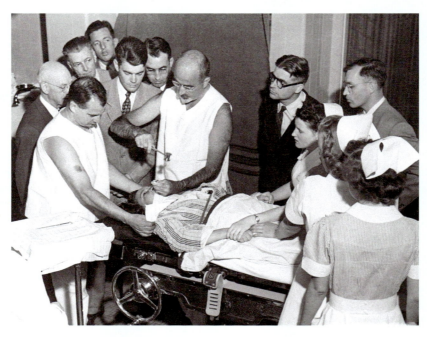

Figure 5.2 Walter Freeman demonstrating his transorbital lobotomy procedure.

(Continued)

Box 5.1 (Continued)

in a shocking way, how incredibly important the prefrontal cortex is to our functioning. Freeman's methods have created a stigma around psychosurgery that exists to this day. Yet, psychosurgical procedures are still performed, albeit in a much more subtle way – and with much more positive results. Examples include **deep brain stimulation**, where a depth electrode is inserted into the brain that is capable of regulating neural functions. This stimulation is successfully used,

for example, in the treatment of Parkinson's disease symptoms, obsessive-compulsive disorder, and epilepsy. Studies on its effectiveness in treating chronic pain and depression are ongoing.

Ironically, Freeman, the man who had been performing unlicensed operations for years, died on the operating table in 1972 due to complications from cancer treatment.

The first function they identified is 'task setting'. This function relies mainly on planning processes and the establishment of stimulus-response relationships. The second function is 'monitoring', that is, a function involved in monitoring one's own task performance and adjusting it on the basis of processing errors; limited monitoring results in impaired performance and an overall increase in errors. The third function is 'energisation'. This function is mainly involved in maintaining attention or concentration. An impairment of this function results mainly in a slowing down of task performance.

Each of these functions is associated with a specific area of the frontal cortex. Moreover, Gläscher et al. (2012) identified an additional component of executive functions, namely a function that is involved in determining the value of a reward. This function was identified on the basis of results that were obtained using the **Iowa gambling task**. In this task, participants are presented with four stacks of cards, and they must choose a card from each of the stacks. Each card indicates whether they have won or lost a sum of money. The cards are organised in such a way that some stacks occasionally result in a huge profit, but often also in a moderate loss, so that the net expected **utility** (i.e., return) of these risky stacks is negative. The other stacks regularly result in small profits, and occasionally in a small loss, so that the expected utility of these stacks is positive.

Most participants gradually learn that there are good stacks, which typically yield a net profit, and bad stacks, which typically yield a net loss. Patients with executive dysfunctions, however, tend to consistently choose from the bad stacks, seemingly because they continue to be attracted by the occasional huge profit. Gläscher's key finding was the identification of two separate networks of brain regions, namely a cognitive control network and a valuation network. The cognitive control network included the dorsolateral prefrontal cortex and the anterior cingulate cortex and was associated with response inhibition, conflict monitoring, and task switching. The valuation network included the orbitofrontal, ventromedial, and frontopolar cortices. This network has connections with the limbic system and is involved in emotion and value-related decisions.

5.2.1.2 Executive Functions: Unity and Diversity

Miyake et al. (2000) investigated the separate components of executive functions that can be identified by comparing the performance of neurotypical participants across nine different tasks. Three of these tasks required inhibiting an automatic response to a stimulus. Three other tasks mainly involved switching between different tasks, and the third set of three tasks required participants to keep updating their working memory. Miyake et al. analysed participants' performance using a statistical technique known as confirmatory factor analysis. In short, this technique involves investigating the extent to which variations in task performance are clustered in three factors: inhibition, task switching, and updating. In other words, do participants who, for example, score lower on the inhibition tasks also score lower on the switching tasks and/or the updating tasks? Or is their performance on the latter two tasks not correlated with their performance on the inhibition tasks? It was found that within each cluster, performance on the individual tasks correlated strongly, implying that executive functions can be divided into an inhibition, task switching, and updating component. Moreover, it was found that these three components themselves also correlated somewhat with each other. The latter implies that the three components partly overlap, suggesting that all three functions are related to each other in some way.

5.2.2 EXECUTIVE FUNCTIONS IN THE BRAIN

Based on the aforementioned results, Miyake and Friedman (2012) developed a unity/diversity framework for executive functions (see fig 5.3). This framework is based on the idea that each executive function consists of a common part and a unique part. The common part is what is shared with all other functions, whereas the unique part is specific to each function. According to Miyake and Friedman (2012), all executive functions have in common that they are involved in actively maintaining task goals and goal-related information, and that they use this information to efficiently control lower levels of processing. Friedman et al. (2008) tested this idea and found additional evidence for the unity/diversity

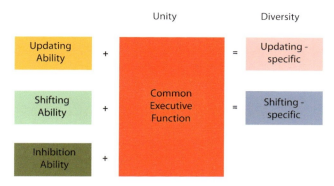

Unity   Diversity

Figure 5.3 An overview of the classification of executive functions according to Miyake and Friedman (2012).

framework. A key finding of theirs was that after the variance that was common to the functions was explained, there was no unique variance left for the inhibition function. In other words, the inhibition function correlated almost completely with the other executive functions, which might imply that inhibitory functions can also be described by other cognitive processes (for more details, see the following section).

Neuroimaging results are reasonably consistent with the unity/diversity framework. Collette et al. (2005), for example, found that all three functions that were identified by Miyake et al. (2000) were associated with activation of a unique part of the prefrontal cortex; a finding that is consistent with the diversity notion. In addition, all three functions were associated with shared activity in other brain regions, such as the left lateral prefrontal cortex, a finding that is consistent with the unity notion.

Hedden and Gabrieli (2010) found similar results but focused on the inhibition and task switching functions. Several brain regions, including the dorsolateral prefrontal cortex, the anterior cingulate cortex, and the basal ganglia, were strongly associated with both functions. Other areas, including the right ventromedial prefrontal cortex and the bilateral temporoparietal junction, were more strongly associated with the inhibition function than with the task switching function. In other words, there was overlap between the two functions, but also diversity, particularly with respect to the inhibition function.

Although the functions that were identified by Stuss and Alexander (2007) differ from those identified by Miyake et al. (2000), there is also some overlap. For example, task setting and monitoring, along with inhibition and task switching, all encompass crucial aspects of cognitive control. Stuss (2011) stresses the importance of the three functions identified by Stuss and Alexander (2007) and adds a fourth one – a function he describes as metacognition/integration. According to Stuss, this function has a coordinating role in the sense that it orchestrates other cognitive functions, including the energetic, motivational, emotional, and executive functions to perform novel complex tasks. According to Burgess, Simons, Dumontheil, and Gilbert (2007), damage to the frontopolar prefrontal cortex disrupts these integrative functions.

Note, however, that although there is some overlap in the individual functions identified by different research groups, there is currently no consensus on what an optimal classification of these functions would be. In addition, there are no clear criteria that make a cognitive function 'executive'. Despite these limitations, the current state of the art provides a good starting point for further research on these key cognitive control processes.

5.3 INHIBITORY CONTROL

5.3.1 INHIBITION AS A PSYCHOLOGICAL PROCESS

5.3.1.1 The Concept of Inhibition in Neuroscience

The preceding discussion of executive functions already shows that the inhibition function is potentially problematic. One reason for this is that the term **inhibition** is poorly defined in psychology (see fig 5.4 for an overview of the many uses of the term). The term has a clear definition in neuroscience, where it is used to denote the processes that reduce the firing rate of a neuron, or a neural circuit (Aron, 2007). In psychology, the term 'inhibition' is also frequently used to describe a subset of the processes that are part of cognitive control mechanisms. More specifically, it refers to processes that allow us to ignore unwanted stimuli, task sets, responses, memories, or emotions.

Historically, in neuroscience, the term 'inhibition' can be dated back to the 19th century. Here, inhibition has several meanings, which may relate to the outcome of behaviour, neural circuits, the firing rate of individual neurons, or the functioning of enzymes. At the behavioural level, for example, inhibitory processes play an important role in the simple reflex arc (see Chapter 3). Likewise, inhibition is involved in the operation of cortical systems. In Chapter 2, for example, we discussed how inputs in layer 6 of the cortex project to the reticular nucleus of the thalamus. These projections use the neurotransmitter GABA (gamma-aminobutyric acid) and they are inhibitory.

5.3.1.2 The Concept of Inhibition in Psychology

In contrast to neuroscience, the term 'inhibition' is ill-defined in psychology. Early theories of mental processes relied on inhibition to explain a very wide variety of phenomena, such as the mental development of a child (the cerebral cortex would develop to suppress impulses from the subcortical nuclei), the phenomenon of extinction after conditioning (inhibition would develop when the unconditioned stimulus is no longer accompanied by a conditioned response), or the repression of memories ('psychic repression': Sigmund Freud's long refuted idea that unpleasant memories of abuse would be excluded from conscious experience by an active inhibition mechanism). It is thus

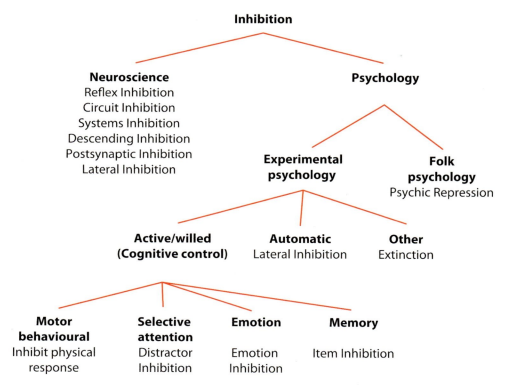

Figure 5.4 An overview of the use of the term 'inhibition' in psychology and neuroscience. (source: Aron, 2007)

the question whether the use of the concept of inhibition is still meaningful in psychology.

In experimental psychology, the term 'inhibition' is still frequently used, however, and here it can have several meanings (Aron, 2007). An important distinction can be made between inhibitory processes that are automatic and processes that are active/volitional. An example of automatic inhibition is the process of **lateral inhibition** of several conflicting response representations. The phenomenon of lateral inhibition was first described as a neural process on the retina of the eye, where it was found that interneurons tend to inhibit the input of neighbouring neurons (see Chapter 6). Such competition is also common at more abstract levels of representation. For example, multiple visual stimuli may compete for processing resources (i.e., biased competition; see Chapters 4 and 6), just as multiple activated word representations in our lexicon (Chapter 17) or multiple alternative motor actions (this chapter; see also Chapter 3) might do. In all cases, multiple alternative representations are activated. At the same time, each representation seeks to actively inhibit the competing representation, and it can do so more effectively the stronger it is activated. In the end, there is one representation that becomes the eventual winner. This is the representation that is ultimately selected. Active/volitional forms of inhibition include suppressing an irrelevant response, stimulus, or memory.

In the field of cognitive control, the concept of inhibition is often used to explain a wide variety of experimental findings.

These findings include, for example, the extent to which we ignore visual and auditory distracting stimuli, suppress unwanted memories or negative emotions, or prevent ourselves from performing incorrect actions. The latter form of inhibition relates not only to manual actions but also, for example, to speech errors (see Chapter 18) or eye movements. In neuropsychology, dysfunctional inhibitory control is also frequently considered to explain impulsivity, perseveration, mania, obsessions, attention disorders, aggression, post-traumatic stress disorders, and impaired decision-making.

5.3.1.3 Inhibition and Cognitive Control

Although there is no single definition of inhibition in psychology, the preceding discussion makes it clear that mental representations or processes might need to be processed at a lower priority in one way or another. This becomes clear when we take a closer look at selective attention. After all, it might very well be possible that without inhibitory processes, our conscious awareness would be completely overloaded with irrelevant information. Likewise, without any regulatory mechanism, we would never be able to suppress unwanted impulses. Tipper (2001) argues, for example, that in many cases, visual input can automatically trigger specific actions (thus bypassing our awareness), but that regulation of these actions is necessary. If this were not the case, we would have no choice but to react haphazardly to whatever visual input we perceived at any given moment. We must, in other words, have the ability to resist this impulse to react, or to allow irrelevant information to enter our consciousness at all. Thus, we can distinguish between behavioural inhibition and cognitive inhibition.

Cognitive inhibition refers to both the suppression of previously activated cognitive representations or processes and to the removal of irrelevant actions from the focus of our attention or awareness. In addition, it relates to resisting interference from attentional processes or representations. Behavioural inhibition, on the other hand, relates to the control of excessive behaviour, such as resisting temptations, delaying immediate gratification, suppressing motor actions, and controlling impulses.

5.3.1.4 Arguments against the Need for Inhibition

Although the phenomena just described make it plausible that there is such a thing as inhibition, there are also a number of important arguments against the notion of inhibitory control. One of the first arguments is that, from a computational perspective, it is very inefficient for the waking brain to actively suppress most ongoing processes. It is also conceivable that, by default, activation levels in the brain are low, and that, by contrast, only those signals that are relevant are amplified (Hillyard & Anllo-Vento, 1998; Miller & Cohen, 2001; Miller & D'Esposito, 2005). Data from Egner and Hirsch (2005) strongly suggest, for example, that in case of conflict the selection of stimuli takes place by amplifying the relevant response, as opposed to inhibiting the irrelevant ones (see fig 5.5).

A second objection to the concept of inhibition is that it is limited in explaining the deficits observed in neuropsychological patients. Consider the following example, taken from Nieuwenhuis and Yeung (2005). Suppose that one day a glass of water accidentally spills on your computer, causing a short circuit that results in the appearance of randomly coloured spots on the screen. In such a case, you would not readily conclude that the damaged circuit represents a 'colour inhibition system'. A more accurate conclusion would be that the damaged circuit, the video card, initially performed very detailed calculations, resulting in meaningful colours. After the damage, however, it only produces random patterns. Damage to the dorsolateral prefrontal cortex typically results in an inability to inhibit undesired behaviour, yet we must be careful to conclude that this area is a centre of inhibitory control. Analogous to the video card example, it is equally well possible that the dorsolateral prefrontal cortex is involved in a very complex form of information processing. Damage to this area can also result in changing meaningful behaviour into random forms of behaviour that manifest themselves as an inability to inhibit impulses.

Kimberg and Farah (1993) implemented a neural network model to mimic patients performance on the **Stroop task** and the **Wisconsin card sorting task**, by simulating frontal lesions. They found that an increase in interference from irrelevant items could be simulated by simply weakening the associations between items in working memory.

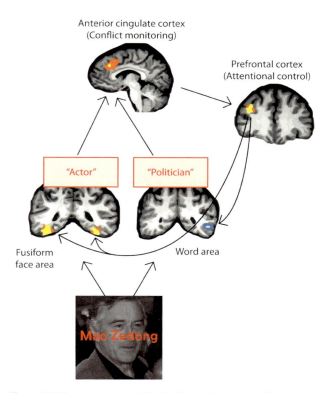

Figure 5.5 Example of a conflict situation in Egner and Hirch's study. Participants were required to classify faces as 'actor' or 'politician'. The automatic processing of the conflicting word could result in an erroneous classification. Egner and Hirch found strong evidence that this conflict was resolved by boosting the processing of facial information and not by inhibiting the processing of the conflicting words. (source: Nieuwenhuis & Yeung, 2005)

Such weakened connections may also explain why young children might have difficulties in suppressing specific choices, without resorting to inhibitory processes.

5.3.2 RESPONSE INHIBITION

The discussion so far shows that the concept of inhibition has lost some of its meaning and that we might be better off explaining some of the cognitive control processes on the basis of other, more specific, mechanisms, such as conflict detection (discussed in more detail later in this chapter), degraded memory representations, or top-down biasing mechanisms. Yet, there are still some specific situations in which the concept of inhibition remains meaningful. For example, there is a general consensus that humans are able to inhibit a motor response once it has been prepared, if they are given sufficient time to do so.

5.3.2.1 The Stop-Signal Paradigm

Our ability to inhibit a prepared action is often investigated using the **stop-signal paradigm** (Logan & Cowan, 1984). Here, participants need to perform a primary task, which often requires them to respond with their left or right hands, as quickly as possible, depending on a specific stimulus that is being presented (see fig 5.6a). This is the so-called go stimulus, which is occasionally followed by a signal indicating that they should withhold their response. This is the stop

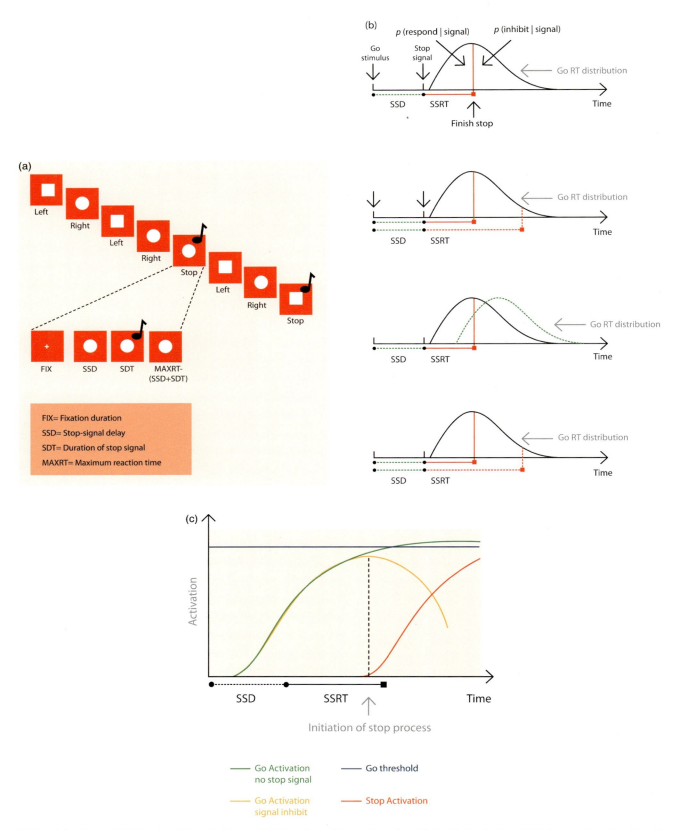

Figure 5.6 Schematic representation of the stop signal paradigm. (a) A possible sequence of stimuli. Participants have to respond as quickly as possible with their left hands when presented with a square and with their right hands when presented with a circle. A tone acts as a stop signal, indicating that they should inhibit their response. (b) By varying the time interval between the presentation of the stimulus and the stop signal, the time required to inhibit a response can be estimated. (c) The assumed interplay between the activation of response preparation and the inhibition of this response. (source: Verbruggen & Logan, 2008)

signal. The stop-signal paradigm is well-suited for determining how far into the preparation we can still inhibit a response. This is done by manipulating the time between the presentation of the go stimulus and the stop signal. When the stop signal follows the presentation of the go stimulus immediately, we can still easily inhibit our response, because we are still in the early stages of preparing it.

In contrast, if we present the stop signal very late in the preparation phase, for instance, just before we are about to respond, it is impossible to stop. This is like a traffic light turning orange just before approaching an intersection. The stop-signal paradigm uses a probabilistic approach in which the time interval (the **stimulus onset asynchrony**; **SOA**) between the go stimulus and the stop signal is varied systematically. By determining the proportion of successfully inhibited responses as a function of this SOA, we can estimate the minimal stop time (that is, the **stop-signal reaction time**; **SSRT**).

Initially, response inhibition was considered to be a competition between two independent processes: the go process, involved in the preparation of a required response, and an independently operating inhibitory process that was initiated by the presentation of the stop signal. As these processes were considered to operate independently of each other, a **race model** (Logan & Cowan, 1984) was therefore used to determine which of the two processes was the fastest (see fig 5.6b). More recent models, however, assume that the go process, and the inhibitory process are interactive, in the sense that the stopping process actively inhibits the go process (Verbruggen & Logan, 2008).

5.3.2.2 Neural Mechanisms

De Jong, Coles, Logan, and Gratton (1990) reported that two inhibitory mechanisms are possibly involved in stopping a response, namely a central and a peripheral one. To do so, they combined a stop-signal paradigm with event-related potential (ERP) and electromyographic (EMG) recordings. ERPs associated with response inhibition showed a frontocentral positive component that appeared approximately 300 ms after the onset of the stop signal. Moreover, the latency of this ERP component was independent of the SOA of the stop signal. Interestingly, this component emerged only after inhibitory effects on muscle activity had already been observed in the EMG signal. Therefore, De Jong et al. hypothesised that a second inhibitory mechanism is inhibiting the transmission of signals from the central to the peripheral motor structures.

Aron and Poldrack (2006) used fMRI in combination with the stop-signal paradigm and found that both cortical and subcortical neural mechanisms are involved in response inhibition. They found that successful inhibition of a response was related to activation of the inferior frontal cortex and the subthalamic nucleus; the latter being part of the basal ganglia. In addition, the strength of activation in these areas correlated with the efficiency of the stopping process.

5.3.2.3 Attention

Bekker, Kenemans, Hoeksma, Talsma, and Verbaten (2005) found evidence for the possible involvement of attention in response inhibition. Auditory stop signals were used in a stop-signal paradigm, and ERPs evoked by this auditory stop signal were characterised by a frontocentrally distributed N1 component that is typical of auditory processing. As we will discuss in more detail in Chapter 7, the amplitude of the N1 component is typically larger when participants attend the evoking stimuli. In the Bekker et al. study, a distinction was made between successfully and unsuccessfully stopped responses. More specifically, it was found that trials in which participants' responses were successfully stopped, the N1 component was relatively large, implying more attention was allocated to the stop signal, compared to unsuccessful stop trials (see fig 5.7).

Boehler et al. (2009) found similar results using MEG recordings. Adding to these findings, however, they not only studied the neural response to the stop signal but also the one to the go stimulus. Here they found that a larger initial sensory response to the go stimulus was associated with more efficient execution of the response, whereas a larger response to the stop signal was associated with more efficient inhibition. Since these studies, there has been overwhelming evidence for a relationship between attention and response inhibition (Gomes et al., 2012; Janssen et al., 2018; Knyazev, Levin, & Savostyanov, 2008; Langford, Krebs, Talsma, Woldorff, & Boehler, 2016).

5.4 CONFLICT, INTERFERENCE, AND ERRORS

Response inhibition almost always involves a conflict: in the stop-signal paradigm described earlier, we have a response that is in an advanced stage of preparation that must be inhibited. Thus, we have a conflict between the execution of the response and its inhibition. In other tasks, such as the **anti-saccade task** or the Stroop task, a dominant response must be suppressed in favour of a non-dominant response. Because the dominant and non-dominant responses are in competition for selection, these conflict situations often result in a relatively large number of errors.

A classic example of competition involves the Stroop effect. In 1935, John Ridley Stroop described how word meaning could interfere with a colour naming task. This was specifically the case when the meaning of a word conflicted with the colour in which it was printed (e.g., the word 'red' printed in green). This interference manifested itself as an increase in the total time that participants needed to name the colours of a sheet filled with these conflicting words, compared to a condition where there was no conflict. Stroop attributed this effect to the fact that the automatic activation of word meaning had to be inhibited.

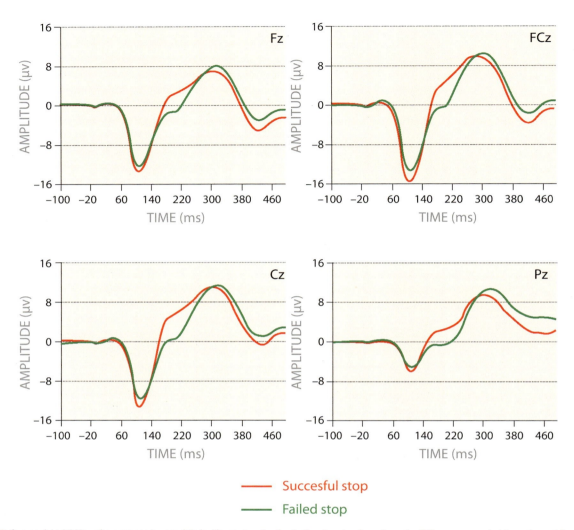

Figure 5.7 Successful inhibition of a response is associated with greater attention to the stop signal, as shown by ERP measurements (shown here at four different scalp locations over the frontal and parietal lobes). The amplitude of the N1 component of an ERP evoked by an auditory stop signal was found to be, on average, larger in trials in which the participant was successful than in trials in which the participant was unable to stop. The amplitude of this component is associated with attention to this stimulus. (source: Bekker et al., 2005)

Another particularly influential experimental paradigm for investigating the effects of these kinds of conflicting processes is the **Eriksen flanker task** (Eriksen & Eriksen, 1974). In the original version of this task, participants are presented with a stimulus that is located centrally on a display. This stimulus is the letter 'H' or 'S', and participants are required to report as quickly as possible which letter is presented. The stimulus is flanked, however, on both the left and right side, by other letters, which are either congruent with the central letter (e.g., 'SSSSS' or 'HHHHH') or incongruent (e.g., 'SSHSS' or 'HHSHH'). In the incongruent condition, participants are generally much slower and they typically make many more errors, compared to the congruent condition. Moreover, the effects of a previous trial often continue to affect the current trial. For example, participants are slower in processing a congruent trial when the previous trial was incongruent than when the previous trial was also congruent. Later versions of the task have also used arrows instead of letters (e.g., '← ← →← ←' or '→ → → → →'), in

which the participant has to indicate to which direction the central arrow is pointing.

5.4.1 CONFLICT MONITORING

Botvinick, Braver, Barch, Carter, and Cohen (2001) developed an influential neurobiologically plausible computational model for **conflict monitoring**. This model assumes that the detection of conflict plays an important role in the recruitment of cognitive control processes. These control processes then seek to resolve the conflict by modulating the strength of specific stimulus-response associations. More specifically, they strengthen relevant associations while weakening irrelevant ones. To do so, the conflict monitoring model presumes an important role of the anterior cingulate cortex. This brain region is involved in both cognitive control processes and in signalling response conflicts (Bush et al., 2000).

Botvinick et al. validated their model by simulating a number of classic conflict tasks, including the Eriksen

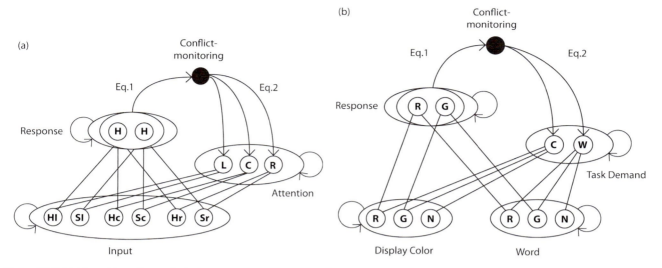

Figure 5.8 Botvinick et al.'s conflict monitoring model. (a) An example of the processes involved in the Eriksen flanker task, in which participants are required to decide whether a centrally presented letter is either an 'S' or an 'H'. L = left, C = central, R = right, S = 'S', H = 'H'. (b) A similar example of the processes involved in the execution of a Stroop task. R = red, G = green, N = neutral, C = colour, W = word. (source: Botvinick et al., 2001)

flanker task and the Stroop task. Figure 5.8a illustrates the processes that, according to the model, are involved in the detection and resolution of conflict situations in a flanker task. The input level shows the different possible inputs, each of which is associated with a specific response, thus creating a conflict between the 'H' and 'S' response in the case of incongruent trials. The activation of both response codes is signalled by the conflict-monitoring module, which is associated with activation of the anterior cingulate cortex. This activation, in turn, triggers feedback to an attention module, which can selectively influence the representation of the inputs, thereby reducing the conflict between the response alternatives. A similar mechanism regulates behaviour during the execution of the Stroop task (see fig 5.8b).

5.4.2 ERRORS

5.4.2.1 Post-error Slowing

A particularly consistent finding is that participants are, on average, slower in responding to the next trial after they just made an error. It is not yet exactly clear what this **post-error slowing** effect represents. One possible explanation is that it represents a strategic attempt to prevent further errors. Another explanation, however, is that errors involuntarily capture attention, and that the delay on the next trial reflects an attempt to resolve the issues that gave rise to the error. Notebaert et al. (2009) found that attention may play a role in this. In their first experiment, participants were required to identify the colour of a stimulus as quickly as possible, and they were given feedback on their performance. On average, participants were slower after receiving negative feedback, that is, feedback informing them that they had made an error. In a second experiment, participants were required to do the same task, but now the feedback was

replaced by an occasional meaningless auditory stimulus. Even after these trials, participants were found to be slower on average, implying that attention to infrequent events was already sufficient to negatively impact task performance.

5.4.2.2 The Neural Basis of Error Detection

Around 1990, research groups in both Germany and the United States discovered independently of each other that the brain detects errors more or less automatically. In Germany, Michael Falkenstein's research group was interested in the question of how efficiently letters could be identified when they were presented both visually and auditorily. For this purpose, participants were presented a letter and they had to press a corresponding key as quickly as possible. While performing this task, EEGs were recorded, and ERPs were extracted from these EEGs. More speciffically, an analysis technique was used, in which the ERPs were calculated with respect to the onset of the response. Falkenstein et al. compared the ERPs elicited by correct and incorrect responses and they found that the incorrect-response ERPs were marked by a negative component that appeared almost instantly after the response. This component was not present in the correct-response ERPs (Falkenstein, Hohnsbein, Hoormann, & Blanke, 1991).

Around the same time, Bill Gehring completed his doctorate at the University of Illinois in the United States. He was investigating the conflicts that were induced by irrelevant flankers in a flanker task (Eriksen & Eriksen, 1974). Also in Gehring's experiment, ERPs were calculated relative to the response, and here, too, a negative deflection could be identified in the ERP, immediately after the error (Gehring, Goss, Coles, Meyer, & Donchin,

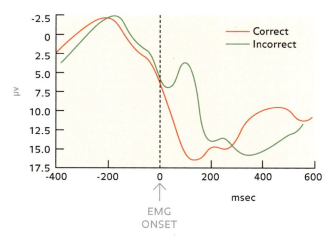

Figure 5.9 The error-related negativity (ERN) reported by Gehring et al. Approximately 100 ms after the onset of the electromyogram (EMG), which reflects the actual initiation of a response, a negative peak can be observed with an incorrect response, which is not present with correct responses. Negative voltages are plotted upwards. (source: Gehring et al., 1993)

1993) (see fig 5.9). Further information on the background of this discovery is detailed in Gehring, Goss, Coles, Meyer, and Donchin (2018).

The aforementioned error signal is due to its simultaneous co-discovery known by both its German designation, error negativity (N_e: Falkenstein), and its American designation, error-related negativity (ERN: Gehring). The importance of this discovery was slowly but steadily realised in the next few years. An important reason for this is the fact that the N_e/ERN can be linked to the functionality of the anterior cingulate cortex. Subsequently, Botvinick et al. (2001) hypothesised that the N_e/ERN is not so much an error detection mechanism, but that it reflects the activation of their proposed conflict detection mechanism (described earlier in the chapter). They modelled the ERN by including an activation threshold for responses in their model. More specifically, low activation thresholds are associated with easily triggered responses, which typically result in fast responses. In this case, conflicting response codes (for example incongruent flankers or conflicting word meanings) may easily trigger an incorrect response. This erroneous response is then also detected by the brain, resulting in an increase of the response threshold on a subsequent trial. Such an increase makes the model less sensitive to errors, but it also increases response times.

5.5 TASK SWITCHING AND MULTITASKING

5.5.1 DIVIDED ATTENTION

In our daily activities, we are often occupied with a multitude of different tasks. While at work or studying, various events, such as a WhatsApp message, a status update on Facebook, or an urgent phone call, demand our attention,

but also within our work or study, we are regularly distracted by a multitude of deadlines that must all be met, or by various tasks that we must perform simultaneously. Ophir, Nass, and Wagner (2009) used a questionnaire to determine the extent to which people are multitaskers in everyday life and found that individuals who scored high on this scale were relatively easily distracted. Ophir et al. concluded that individuals who attend to different media sources simultaneously develop a breadth-based cognitive control style. More specifically, this means that they are not selective in directing their attention. Individuals scoring low on multitasking, on the other hand, tend to have very strong top-down control over their focus of attention. This conclusion is consistent with results from Cain and Mitroff (2011), who found that individuals scoring low on multitasking are better capable of ignoring distracting information in a focused attention task.

5.5.2 DUAL TASKS

Ostensibly, we are flexible in tackling multiple tasks, but to what extent are we really able to perform more than one task at a time? A standard method in cognitive psychology to investigate this question involves the use of dual tasks. Here it is first determined how these tasks are performed separately, and then these performances are compared to a condition where these tasks are performed simultaneously.

5.5.3 FACTORS INFLUENCING DUAL TASKING

A large number of studies conducted in recent years have shown that there are several factors that determine the extent to which we can or cannot perform two tasks simultaneously. Task similarity is one of these factors. For example, Treisman and Davies (1973) found that two tasks interfered more strongly when both tasks made use of the same sensory modality (e.g., when both tasks required the detection of visual stimuli or the detection of auditory stimuli), than when each task involved a different modality.

In addition, the two tasks may also share a response modality; for example, a button press. McLeod (1977) found that this also affected the extent to which participants could perform dual tasks. In this study, participants were engaged in a tracking task, in which they had to try to use a joystick-like controller to keep a dot as closely as possible to a specific target. This task was combined with a tone identification task. One group of participants had to indicate whether they heard a high or a low pitched tone by pressing a button, while the second group could do so by verbally reporting them. Performance on the tracking task was lower in the button-press group than in the vocal-response group.

A third factor that can contribute is practice. Spelke, Hirst, and Neisser (1976) discuss the effects that intensive practice had on two volunteers: Diane, a PhD student in biology, and John, a student at Cornell Hotel School. John and Diane trained for an hour every working day for 17 weeks in being able to read stories and write down dictated words simultaneously. Although they initially found it extremely difficult, after just six weeks of training they were able to combine the two tasks efficiently. Their reading performance was just as efficient in the dual task condition as in a single task condition (i.e., when they just had to do this task). Although these results suggest that exercise can greatly improve our ability to multi-task, we should be very careful about generalising these results. One reason for this is that Spelke et al. focused on the accuracy with which the tasks were performed, but accuracy may be much less sensitive to interference from a second task than reaction time (Lien, Ruthruff, & Johnston, 2006). In addition, the reading task gave both participants considerable freedom of choice, in the sense that they could decide when to switch their attention from the reading task to the dictation task, which may have further limited the amount of interference.

Task difficulty is also a determinant of our ability to perform two tasks simultaneously. Sullivan (1976) used a **shadowing task**, in which participants were required to repeat an auditory message presented to one ear (see Chapter 7). At the same time, they had to detect target words presented to the other (non-shadowed) ear. When the primary shadowing task was made more difficult, which was done by reducing the redundancy of the contents of the shadowed message, fewer target words were detected in the non-shadowed message.

Segal and Fusella (1970) found that task similarity has a greater effect on our ability to combine tasks than the difficulty of a task in itself. In this study, participants had to imagine visual or auditory scenes and simultaneously detect visual or auditory stimuli. The accuracy of detecting these cues was much lower when the imagining task relied on the same modality as the one in which the stimuli were to be detected, compared to the condition in which detection and imagining each relied on a different modality.

5.5.4 COGNITIVE BOTTLENECK THEORY

As already discussed, specific conditions allow two tasks to be performed without interference (Spelke et al., 1976). In Spelke et al.'s study, however, participants were flexible in how they could perform the tasks, and when they could perform them. When this flexibility is removed, we may be able to detect more subtle forms of interference that would otherwise go unnoticed. The most effective way of detecting this interference is by conducting an experiment in which participants are given two tasks to perform within a very short timeframe. This is typically done by presenting

two stimuli in quick succession that each require their own response. Participants must respond to each of these stimuli as quickly as possible. When the two stimuli are presented simultaneously, performance on both tasks is usually lower than when each stimulus is presented separately. When the stimuli are presented shortly after each other, however, participants are usually only slower in responding to the second stimulus; an effect that is known as the **psychological refractory period** (PRP). As the time interval between the two stimuli is increased, the delay decreases. The name of the effect is based on the analogy with a hyperpolarised neuron, which is temporarily refractory. In a similar way, it was originally believed that the cognitive system was also temporarily refractory after a stimulus was processed.

This explanation has been firmly refuted, however. So, what causes this temporary delay? Most classical explanations are based on the idea that the processing of a stimulus involves three stages: (1) perception; (2) central processing, for example, deciding which response to give; (3) preparation and execution of the response. Welford (1952) assumed that there was a limitation at the central processing stage; a phenomenon he described with the term **central bottleneck**. According to Welford, cognitive processes are limited to making one decision at a time. This restriction thus prevents multiple cognitive decision processes from being active simultaneously (Pashler, 1984; Pashler, Harris, & Nuechterlein, 2008). As a result, a decision process related to a second task will have to wait while a decision on an earlier task is still in progress (see fig 5.10), resulting in an increase of the reaction time to the second task. Strobach, Liepelt, Pashler, Frensch, and Schubert (2013) found that intensive practice can reduce the PRP effect, but not eliminate it completely.

One of the predictions that follows from the central bottleneck theory is that the early perceptual processing of the

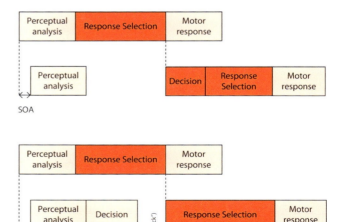

Figure 5.10 Two examples of delayed response times due to a central bottleneck. When two tasks are presented shortly after each other, the response to the second task is relatively slow, because the decision processes that are still ongoing for the first task block the execution of the second task. (based on Pashler et al., 2008)

stimulus is not delayed, but that the central decision-making processes are. Evidence for this prediction was found in an ERP study of Hesselmann, Flandin, and Dehaene (2011). These authors found that the latency of the P300 component, which is associated with central decision processes, corresponded to the reaction time to a second stimulus in a PRP experiment. The earlier ERP components, which are associated with perceptual processing of a stimulus, were not delayed, however.

5.5.5 CENTRAL CAPACITY AND RESOURCES

The next question is: why is there a central bottleneck? One view, which has been dominant in the attention literature for many years, considers attention as a limited-capacity mental resource (Kahneman, 1973). According to this idea, selectively focusing attention on a specific stimulus implies allocating part of our precious mental resources to the processing of that stimulus, at the expense of the processing of other stimuli (see fig 5.11). According to this view, attention can be conceived of as a type of mental fuel, of which there is a limited supply. For this reason, it must be allocated selectively to specific cognitive tasks. Although Kahneman argued that capacity is limited, he also proposed that we have some flexibility, in the sense that an increase in arousal can temporarily free-up additional resources. Cognitive theories that aim to explain attention from this idea of resources are known as **resource theories**.

According to Kahneman's (1973) central capacity theory, there is one central resource that attention can flexbally allocate to any given task. According to this idea, the

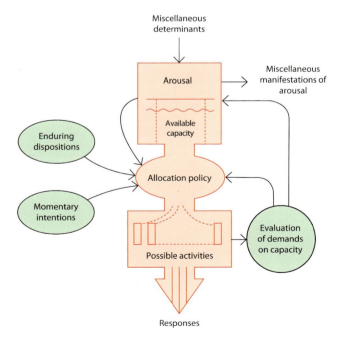

Figure 5.11 Kahneman's (1973) central capacity model.

extent to which two tasks can be performed simultaneously thus depends strongly on the extent to which the different tasks make use of this resource. Based on such an assumption, we can, for example, explain why talking on the phone has a negative impact on our driving performance, since both tasks claim our cognitive resources.

5.5.5.1 Dual Tasks and Interference
Bourke, Duncan, and Nimmo-Smith (1996) investigated the extent of the interference that occurs when dual tasks make a claim on a shared central resource. They used four different tasks for this purpose: (1) a task in which participants had to generate a random sequence of letters; (2) a prototype learning task, in which participants had to learn to identify a prototype of a certain stimulus category on the basis of observing several instances of this category (see Chapter 20 for more details on this procedure); (3) a manual task, which consisted of tightening a screw on a bolt several times in a row; and (4) a task that consisted of detecting a specific target tone. Participants performed two of these tasks simultaneously, after it was emphasised that one of the two tasks should be given more priority. Bourke et al. (1996) hypothesised that the task that relied the most heavily on the central resource (i.e., the random letter generation task) would interfere the most with the other tasks, whereas the task that relied least on it (i.e., the tone detection task), would do so the least. Broadly speaking, this was also what Bourke et al. found, regardless of whether the task was prioritised compared to the task with which it was paired.

Hegarty, Shah, and Miyake (2000) also used dual tasks, however, their results were inconsistent with the idea of a central resource. In an earlier study, they had already found that a paper-folding task required more central capacity than a task that involved comparing two figures. The paper-folding task required participants to imagine the effect of poking a hole in a folded piece of paper. Hegarty et al. therefore hypothesised that a second task, the generation of random numbers, would interfere more when performed concurrently with the paper-folding task than when it would be performed concurrently with a figure comparison task. Hegarty et al.'s results were completely contrary to this expectation, as the strongest interference effects were found in the figure comparison task. Based on these results, they argued that this was probably caused by the fact that the figure comparison task placed a greater demand on response selection processes, since participants had to choose which of two test figures most resembled a target figure.

5.5.5.2 Limitations
Although the central resource theory has been reasonably successful in explaining some important empirical results, it also has some significant caveats. First, the notion of a

central resource might be based on a circular argument. After all, we can explain dual task interference by assuming that the interfering tasks share a resource. But how can we determine what this resource is? By determining that there is dual task interference! In other words, assuming the existence of a shared resource merely involves reformulating the existing problem instead of explaining it. A second criticism is that evidence for the existence of a central capacity limit is not very informative about the nature of the resource (Bourke et al., 1996). Finally, interference can occur as a result of response selection (Hegarty et al., 2000), as a result of task similarity (Segal & Fusella, 1970) or as a result of a limitation in central processing capacity, allowing resources to take many guises.

A somewhat related criticism is that the central resource theory implicitly assumes that all participants are likely to follow the same strategy; an assumption that is probably incorrect. For instance, Lehle, Steinhauser, and Hübner (2009) trained participants to follow either a serial or a parallel strategy while performing a relatively simple dual task (determining whether digits were even or odd; two digits were presented shortly after each other and participants had to report the decision with their left hand for the first digit and with their right hands for the second digit). Heart rate was used as a measure of mental effort (see fig 5.12), and it was found that participants using a serial strategy performed better but that they found the task more demanding than those using a parallel strategy. The higher effort reported by participants in the serial condition was consistent with an increase in heart rate observed in these participants.

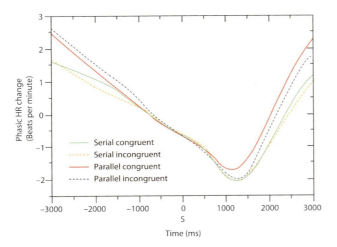

Figure 5.12 Time course of phasic heart rate during the performance of a dual task (see text for details). Participants who used a serial strategy showed a greater decrease of their heart rate than participants who used a parallel strategy. Congruent: a task condition in which the response to the second task is congruent with that to the first task (e.g., both numbers even). Incongruent: a task condition in which the responses to the first and second tasks were incongruent with each other (e.g., first task even, second task odd). "S" marks the time of stimulus onset. (source: Lehle et al., 2009)

5.5.6 COGNITIVE RESOURCES: A SOUP STONE?

The Israeli cognitive psychologist David Navon (1984) criticised the use of cognitive resources, arguing that they contribute nothing to theory development. One of Navon's criticisms is that cognitive resources are either ill-defined or not defined at all. In general, resources resemble either a limited set of communication lines, storage locations in memory, or mental energy. The list of possible interpretations can be divided into two different classes: units and commodities. Units are, for example, long-term memory, or communication lines. These units can only represent one state, or at least a very limited number of states at a time, implying that they can only be used in a limited number of tasks. Commodities are, on the other hand, represented by mental effort, or the availability of working memory. While units can be used by multiple tasks, commodities are specifically allocated to one process.

Navon compares this to traffic. Fuel is a commodity that is linked to one driver: after all, a litre of fuel is allocated to one car and cannot be shared with another driver. Units, such as the road network, are shared by all drivers, and in case of limited capacity (i.e., a traffic jam) the different processes (cars) have to wait for each other. The problem with this imprecise definition of a resource is that it remains unclear which aspects of a task will affect dual task performance. As a result, identifying whether interference occurs between two tasks is often the only way to conclude that two tasks must share a resource, or that there is a limited supply of resources. The danger of this approach, as already noted, is that it can lead to circular reasoning, where the occurrence of an interference is used as an explanation for the occurrence of this interference.

For this reason, and inspired by an old Russian folk tale, Navon (1984) compares cognitive resources to a theoretical soup stone. According to the story, there was once a rascal who taught a fool how to make a delicious soup. 'All you have to do', said the rascal, 'is to throw this stone into boiling water. But, if you want to improve the taste, you have to add some vegetables; some meat will make the soup really delicious and adding some vermicelli, salt, and pepper won't hurt either, of course...'.

The bottom line of the story is, of course, that the stone does nothing at all! Similarly, we can also ask what the theoretical contribution of cognitive resources is. Although the concept of cognitive resources has certainly been useful in formulating initial theories on dual-task performance and cognitive control mechanisms, the concept has largely been abandoned in recent decades, in favour of theories where the underlying cognitive processes are much more clearly defined.

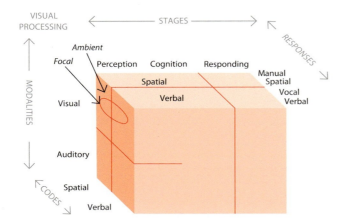

Figure 5.13 Wickens (2008)'s multiple-resource model.

5.5.7 MULTIPLE RESOURCES

The American cognitive psychologist Christopher Wickens (2008) has proposed an extension of the previously described central-bottleneck model. He argues that our cognitive processing system consists of various processing mechanisms that operate independently of each other. Wickens also uses the term 'resources' to describe these mechanisms, however, in his definition, they have a different meaning than in the central-resource model. More specifically, Wickens' multiple-resource model identifies four independent dimensions (see fig 5.13):

1. The processing stages: these consist of the successive stages of perception, central processing, and response.
2. The processing codes: the processing stages use either a spatial or a verbal code depending on the specific task.
3. Modalities: perception processes can use visual or auditory sources.
4. The response type: responses can be manual or verbal.

In addition to these four properties, Wickens (2008) distinguished between focal and ambient visual processing. Focal visual processing is used for object recognition, whereas ambient visual processing is mainly involved in orientation and motion detection.

Wickens (2008) states that interference depends on the degree of similarity between the two tasks in any of these aforementioned dimensions. In other words, tasks that use different resources can be performed more easily together than tasks that share one or more resources.

Wickens' (2008) multiple resource theory is consistent with findings from many dual task studies. The previously described studies showing that stimulus and response similarity leads to reduced dual-task performance (McLeod, 1977; Treisman & Davies, 1973) are, for example, consistent with Wickens' assumption that tasks that share these peripheral features can be less effectively performed together than tasks that are each characterised by a different peripheral feature. The results of these studies are therefore more compatible with Wickens' multiple-resource theory than with the central-resource theories discussed earlier.

Although the multiple resource theory is consistent with several empirical findings, it should also be mentioned that it is too simplistic in some ways. The successful performance of dual tasks often requires a high degree of coordination and organisation, and these aspects are not described by the theory. In addition, the theory does not describe which cognitive processes are specifically involved in the performance of the different processing stages between stimulus and response.

5.5.8 THREADED COGNITION

Salvucci and Taatgen (2008) introduced in their **threaded cognition theory** the idea that multiple cognitive processes can be carried out independently of each other without necessarily causing interference. This is done in a manner similar to how several computer programmes can run simultaneously on a multitasking operating system. It is only when the different programme threads have to use the same hardware that one programme will have to halt its execution for the time that the other programme occupies this device. The same principle applies to threaded cognition. When, for example, two tasks depend on visual perception, the second task will only be able to start when the processing of the first task has advanced sufficiently. In threaded cognition theory, the term 'resource' is used to refer to all cognitive processes and structures that a task can call upon. This includes, for example, the visual system, long-term memory, the motor system, and working memory. Figure 5.14 illustrates how two different tasks can interfere with each other (Borst, Taatgen, & van Rijn, 2010).

In dual-task conditions, various cognitive resources can be the cause of interference. As such, threaded cognition theory differs strongly from the previously discussed central-bottleneck theory. Moreover, an important feature of the model is that there is no general executive function that controls the different processes. Instead, it assumes that the various processes all operate autonomously. Each

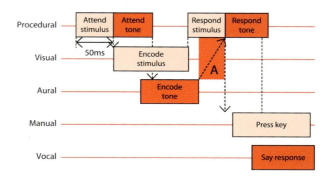

Figure 5.14 An example of how two tasks can be interwoven with each other according to the threaded cognition model. (source: Borst et al., 2010)

processing thread autonomously controls its access to the cognitive resource it needs. According to the model, this is done in a greedy but polite manner. Gaining access is greedy because the processing thread allocates the resource to itself as soon as it is available, and it is polite because the resource is released again as soon as it is no longer needed.

In this respect, the threaded cognition approach differs from other cognitive control models, such as the working memory model (Baddeley & Hitch, 1974), which do assume that an executive control process (see Chapter 14) exists which regulates access to resources. The absence of such an executive mechanism allows various task goals to be active simultaneously. In this respect, the threaded cognition idea is somewhat similar to the multiple-resource model of Wickens (2008). A major difference, however, is that the threaded cognition model has been developed into a computational model, which enables it to make very specific predictions that can be tested empirically.

One specific prediction of the threaded cognition model is that each cognitive resource can only be used by one process at a time. Nijboer, Taatgen, Brands, Borst, and van Rijn (2013) tested this hypothesis by having partici-pants perform a dual task. In the main task, they had to per-form an arithmetic task in which two numbers had to be subtracted from each other. Moreover, participants had to type the answers onto a keypad. In the difficult task, digits had to be carried over (memorised), while in the easy task this was not necessary. Therefore, the difficult task required working memory and an attentional focus, whereas the easy task did not. The second task was either a tracking task that required a manual response or a working memory demanding counting task.

Nijboer et al. (2013) expected that performance on the easy subtraction task would decrease especially when com-bined with the tracking task, because both tasks involve visual and manual cognitive resources. In addition, the difficult subtraction task might be expected to interfere mainly with the counting task, because both tasks involve working memory. Their results were consistent with this hypothesis. Borst, Buwalda, van Rijn, and Taatgen (2013) found a similar result. They also examined an additional prediction of the theory, namely that task performance can improve when additional cues are available that can help with task performance. This prediction was tested by giving participants a visual cue during the difficult sub-traction problems. This cue helped them to indicate when to start memorizing the digit that was to be carried over. This visual cue significantly improved task performance when the subtraction task was combined with a second task that also relied on working memory.

Threaded cognition theory also predicts that we are gen-erally better at multitasking than we typically assume (Salvucci & Taatgen, 2008). Switching between two tasks takes time, but studies examining task switching processes almost always require participants to switch tasks according to a predetermined schedule (see more on this later), which may artificially restrict our ability to switch. In reality, we may be much more flexible in switching between tasks when we can choose ourselves when to switch to a new task and when we can make use of external cues to do so (Borst et al., 2013). Janssen and Brumby (2010) investigated to what extent this is actually the case. Here, participants were engaged in a simulated driving task and had to type in an 11-digit telephone num-ber, which they had memorised beforehand. They had to give the highest priority to either the driving task or to the number task. Participants were flexible in doing so, which was demonstrated by the fact that both tasks were performed better when prioritised. Furthermore, when the driving task was prioritised, participants were found to be more likely to switch their attention away from the number task. They had initially been taught to type the number in two **chunks**: initially the first five numbers and then the last six. When they had to give priority to the driving task, they switched after only three digits, implying that they switched more frequently back to their primary task.

Although these results imply that we can flexibly adapt our task performance to the circumstances, it also appears that this is not always the case. In the previously discussed study of Nijboer et al. (2013) participants could choose which task they wanted to perform as a secondary task after each trial, allowing them to learn which tasks were best combined. One-third of the participants showed no signs of learning, while the remaining participants also needed many trials before they consistently made the optimal choices (see fig 5.15).

Threaded cognition theory is able to generate very specific predictions, which, moreover, are largely consistent with empirical findings. However, the theory also predicts that two tasks can be performed independently of each other, without the need for coordinating processes. This predic-tion, however, is inconsistent with a substantial body of literature that stresses the need for executive functions.

5.5.9 TASK SWITCHING

In our everyday lives, we frequently have to alternate between different tasks. Consider the following example: while you are studying, you receive a message from a fellow student asking whether you can remember the assignment for a specific course for the coming week. As you put down your book, you reply to the message, turn to your computer to look up the specific email that describes the assignment, forward it, grab your cell phone again to inform your classmate that you have forwarded the assignment, and pick up the book again. Each of these tasks requires a specific configuration of men-tal processes, or in other words, a task set (Monsell, 2003).

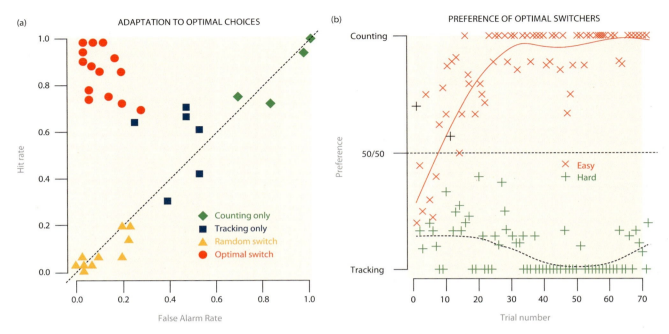

Figure 5.15 Adaptation to interference. (a) The sensitivity of each participant, grouped according to a clustering of their personal task switching behaviour. Optimal switchers (red) make few errors, characterised by a high proportion of hits and few false alarms, so they cluster in the upper left corner of the graph. (b) The switch preferences of the optimal switchers during the experiment. These participants learn during the experiment that on easy trials it is advantageous to switch to the counting task and on difficult trials to the tracking task. (source: Nijboer et al., 2013)

Such task sets are partially initiated by external stimuli (i.e., a cell phone message or the assignment), but each of these stimuli allows alternative actions: you can choose not to answer the message, you can tell your fellow student to figure it out for himself, or you can answer it anyway. You can forward the assignment, or you can paraphrase it. In other words, cognitive control is needed to choose the right action, to prevent us from being led by impulsive actions.

5.5.9.1 Essential Features of Task Switching

The previous example shows that each stimulus is associated with multiple alternative responses. Moreover, each action can be described at different levels of abstraction. Eating a sandwich, for example, can be described as 'putting a piece of toast in your mouth' or as 'providing my body with nutrients': both descriptions refer, in principle, to the same action. To avoid conceptual confusion, it is necessary to remain consistent in the level of abstraction at which we describe a task if we are to adequately describe tasks and task switching processes. In the task switching literature, this is usually done at a relatively low level, where the task is described as performing the appropriate action. We can now ask how the appropriate task set is selected.

In most cases, we can prepare ourselves to perform a complex action without knowing exactly what to do. For example, we can prepare ourselves to name an image without knowing exactly what kind of image we are about to see. When the object is shown, however, it will automatically result in the retrieval of its name and the production of

speech signals, without any further intentional actions. The sequence of actions takes the form of a prepared reflex (Hommel, 2000) or an ideomotor action. From this, we can define a task set as a complex pattern of actions that we have learned through intensive practice, and which is now stored as a chunk in our procedural memory (see Chapter 3). The more we have practised a task set, the easier it is to perform it. In some cases, we can even execute task sets with such ease that we do so involuntarily. For example, we involuntarily read roadside billboards or recall the names of people who pass us in the hallway. The classic laboratory variant of this is the famous Stroop task (Stroop, 1935), where the automatic word meaning interferes with another task. The efficiency with which we can perform a task thus depends on a complex interaction between our goal-driven intentions and the ease with which tasks can be carried out.

Thus, our cognitive control processes must balance our goal-driven control mechanisms, to ensure that ongoing tasks are not constantly interrupted by distractors. Yet, we must also retain enough flexibility to deviate from a goal when necessary. To investigate how we can achieve this flexibility, we need to be able to experimentally induce a task switch and ensure that participants can prepare for this switch.

5.5.9.2 The Task Switching Paradigm

To do so, we typically rely on the task switching paradigm (Jersild, 1927). Here, participants are initially trained to perform two simple tasks that can be done on the basis of a limited set of stimuli such as numbers or letters. In the first task, participants must determine whether a given number is

140

discriminate between two letters by responding as quickly as possible with their left or right hand respectively. In the other task, they have to determine whether a number is greater or smaller than five and also report this by a response with the left or right hand. Thus, each task requires attention to be focused on a different aspect of the stimulus and its classification is also based on a different criterion.

After the training, participants are presented with one stimulus at a time, and they are instructed to perform one of the two tasks. The exact task that needs to be performed is instructed on a trial-by-trial basis. There are various methods by which this can be done. In all cases, however, the same task must sometimes be performed on two or more consecutive trials, while at other times, a different task must be performed compared to the previous trial. This method enables us to determine whether additional demands have been placed on cognitive processes after a task switch. Moreover, it can also relate the effects of brain damage or pharmacological interventions to the ability to switch between tasks. Based on this paradigm, several robust findings have been reported, which we will discuss in more detail later in the chapter.

5.5.9.3 Mix, Switch, and Residual Switch Costs

Various studies have shown that switching between two tasks always comes with a cost, as evidenced by longer reaction times and an increase in the proportion of errors following a switch (Monsell, 2003). In other words, there is a **task switching cost** (see fig 5.16). These switching costs can be reduced when participants are informed in advance about the task switch and given a sufficient amount of time to prepare for it. They can be reduced even further when participants can predict the task change, yet they can never be completely eliminated, even when participants are given a long time to prepare for a switch (Rogers & Monsell, 1995).

In addition to these switch costs, we can identify a mix cost. Although participants quickly show improved performance after a task switch, reaction times are always greater compared to what we would find when only one task needs to be performed during a block of trials. The effects described earlier imply that there are both short-term and long-term costs associated with task switching.

The reaction time delay that occurs during a task switch implies that a reconfiguration of the task set must take place (Monsell, 2003). This reconfiguration may involve

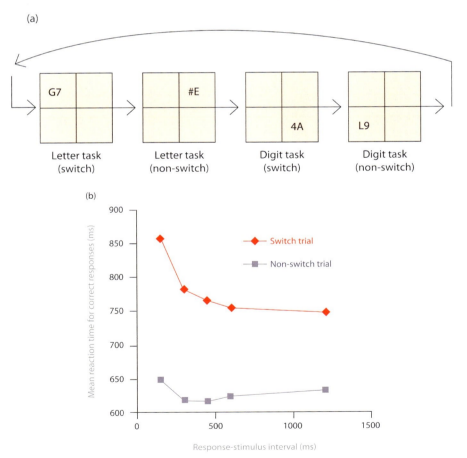

Figure 5.16 Example of a task switching paradigm and the residual switching cost. (a) A possible sequence of trials in which participants have to perform either a letter discrimination task or a number discrimination task. The position of the stimuli indicates which task has to be performed (top is letter task and bottom is number task). These positions move in a fixed order. (b) Average reaction times after a task change or a task continuation as a function of the interval between the response to the previous stimulus and the presentation of the next. (source: Monsell, 2003)

switching attention to a new aspect of the stimulus, deciding what to do, and deciding how to do it. In addition, delays may also occur as a result of having to inhibit those elements from the previous task set that are no longer relevant. The fact that switch costs can be reduced when participants are sufficiently prepared is consistent with the idea that this reconfiguration can take place under voluntary, endogenous control, before the new stimulus appears.

The existence of residual switch costs is intriguing, however. Why are we still slower immediately after a task switch, even when we have been given ample time to prepare for it? Rogers and Monsell (1995) assume that part of the task reconfiguration can only proceed after it has been triggered exogenously, that is, after the next stimulus is presented. An alternative explanation is provided by De Jong (2000). According to his *failure to engage* hypothesis, there is no distinction between endogenous and exogenous task reconfiguration. In most cases we fully succeed in preparing, but on a small proportion of trials we fail. An analysis of the distribution of reaction times on individual trials (see Box 1.1) suggests that this is indeed the case (De Jong, 2000; Nieuwenhuis & Monsell, 2002). But why do we sometimes fail to reconfigure our task set? One possible answer to this question is that we need to retrieve the new task goal or task rules from memory and that sometimes we fail to do so (Mayr & Kliegl, 2000; Sohn & Anderson, 2001).

A further remarkable finding is that it often takes us more effort to switch to a dominant, more practiced task than to a less dominant, less practiced task (Cohen, Dunbar, & McClelland, 1990). In the Stroop task, for example, naming the colours of the words is much less practised than reading the words themselves. When participants had to switch from naming the colours to naming the words, this resulted in much higher switch costs than when participants had to switch from naming the words to naming the colours. This effect is probably the result of having to inhibit the dominant task more strongly while performing the non-dominant task, and the extra-long switching costs are the result of having to let go of this inhibition.

5.6 AUTOMATIC VERSUS CONTROLLED PROCESSES

An important feature of tasks that require cognitive control is that they cannot be performed automatically. But what exactly distinguishes automatic from controlled processes? A consistent finding in dual-task scenarios is that task performance often improves dramatically after intense practice. It is generally believed that through practice, a task can be automated and that it therefore no longer needs the supervision of a cognitive control process.

In two seminal studies in the mid 1970s, the American cognitive psychologists Richard Shiffrin and Walter Schneider have made an important contribution to the distinction between automatic and controlled processes (Schneider & Shiffrin, 1977; Shiffrin & Schneider, 1977). They concluded that controlled processes are characterised by limited capacity, require attention, and that they can be flexibly adapt to changing circumstances. In contrast, Shiffrin and Schneider concluded that automatic processes are unlimited in capacity, independent of attention, and inflexible. An automatic process, once learned, is difficult to change.

In Schneider and Shiffrin's (1977) study, participants had to memorise sets of one to four letters. This so-called **memory set** was then followed by a search display, also consisting of a set of one to four letters. Now, participants were required to decide as quickly as possible whether an item in this display matched with an item from the memory set. The crucial manipulation in this study involved the choice of stimulus material. In one condition, Schneider and Shiffrin used a **consistent mapping**, in which only consonants were used for the memory set and only digits for the distractors in the visual search displays. Thus, when there was a consonant in the display, participants automatically knew that it had to be part of the memory set. In the second condition, Shiffrin and Schneider used a **varied-mapping**, in which consonants and digits were used in both the memory set and in the visual search displays, making it impossible to automatically determine whether the item was part of the memory set or not.

The use of this mapping had a particularly strong effect on response times (see fig 5.17). In particular, for the varied mapping condition, it was found that both the memory set size and the number of items in the search displays affected

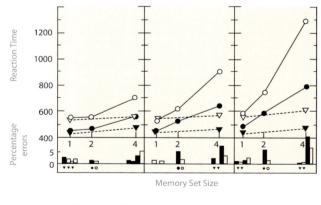

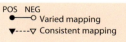

Figure 5.17 Response times of a memory search task, as a function of the number of items in the memory set, the number of items in the search display, and the type of mapping. POS: positive trials, that is, trials requiring a 'yes' response (an item from the memory set was actually present in the search display). NEG: negative trials, that is, trials requiring a 'no' response (none of the items from the memory set was present in the search display). In the varied-mapping condition, there was a strong increase in response times depending on both the size of the memory set and the size of the search display. For the consistent-mapping condition, this was much less prominent. (source: Schneider & Shiffrin, 1977)

the response time, while in the consistent-mapping condition this was much less the case. Based on these results, Schneider and Shiffrin (1977) argued that the former condition required controlled processing. More specifically, it required each element in the search display to be serially compared with an item in the memory set. For the consistent-mapping condition, Schneider and Shiffrin argued that an automatic process can evaluate all the items in the display in parallel. We are able to do that because years of practice have taught us to rapidly distinguish numbers from letters.

In a follow-up study, Shiffrin and Schneider (1977) investigated to what extent practice can affect the automatisation of task performance. To do so, they introduced a new consistent mapping, which consisted of the consonants B through L as items that could appear in the memory set and the consonants Q through Z as items that could appear as distractors in the search displays. This is similar to the distinction between digits and consonants that Schneider and Shiffrin (1977) had used as a consistent mapping, but with the difference that our ability to distinguish these groups of letters as two different categories not so strongly developed. Using these stimuli, Shiffrin and Schneider found that task performance improved considerably after approximately 2100 trials, the point at which the participants were able to automatically distinguish the two groups of letters as different categories.

The automatisation was also characterised by a high degree of inflexibility, however. Shiffrin and Schneider (1977) demonstrated this by reversing the mapping halfway through the experiment. After the first 2100 trials, the participants had to perform another 2100 trials with the reversed mapping. This reversal had a disastrous effect on task performance, and participants required approximately 1000 trials before their performance returned to their initial level at the start of the experiment.

5.6.1 DICHOTOMY OR GRADUAL DIFFERENCES?

5.6.1.1 Arguments in Favour of Gradual Differences

Since the publication of Shiffrin and Schneider's studies, the strict distinction between automatic and controlled processes has been questioned by several researchers. One of Shiffrin and Schneider's assumptions is that automatic processes operate in parallel and do not require attention. This would also imply that the reaction times in their consistent-mapping conditions should be flat; that is, they should not be affected by the size of the memory set or the number of items in the search display. This was not the case, however. Although reaction times were indeed much less affected than in the varied-mapping condition, they still showed a small increase that depended both on the size of the memory set and on the number of items in the search display.

Based on the Stroop effect (Stroop, 1935), it was also was assumed that word naming is an automatic process which is not influenced by attention. Kahneman and Chajczyk (1983) found, however, that this is not the case. They presented a colour word next to a solidly coloured surface and required participants to name the colour of this surface. Using this configuration, the Stroop effect was much less pronounced than when the colour and the word were in the same position.

Aside from these reaction time effects, it is also problematic that Shiffrin and Schneider's approach is descriptive rather than explanatory. For example, Shiffrin and Schneider do not elucidate which factors determine whether a process is automatic or controlled. For this reason, Moors and De Houwer (2006) have argued that we should identify which properties underly automaticity.

Moors and De Houwer eventually identified four unique properties that determine the degree of automaticity. More specifically, they argued that processes can be automatic when they are goal independent, unconscious, efficient, and fast. Moors and De Houwer also argue, however, that this does not imply that not all of these properties are necessary for a process to be automatic. Moreover, these properties are not dichotomous in the sense that they are present or not. Instead, Moors and De Houwer argue that they vary on a more or less continuous scale. This implies that every task can be automated to a greater or lesser degree. For example, a task may be relatively fast or slow, or may only be partially executed consciously. According to this view, processes are therefore not fully automatic or controlled, but rather graded. This also explains why training can have an effect on task performance, because it can gradually influence the efficiency of a process, allowing a process to become increasingly automated.

5.6.1.2 The Neural Basis for Automatisation

Jansma, Ramsey, Slagter, and Kahn (2001) used fMRI to investigate how neural processes change when tasks are automatised. To do so, they used a task that was similar to the one used by Schneider and Shiffrin (1977). Automatic processing was associated with a reduced activation in brain areas that are associated with working memory (see Chapter 14), more specifically its executive component. Notably, Jansma et al. found that activity in the dorsolateral prefrontal cortex, the right superior prefrontal cortex, the right frontopolar cortex, and the supplementary motor areas decreased as the task became more automated.

Poldrack et al. (2005) reported a similar decrease in the dorsolateral prefrontal cortex as a result of practice when participants performed a serial reaction time task (see Chapter 3) under dual-task conditions (see fig 5.18). The latter result is representative of most findings on task automatisation. For example, in a literature review Saling and Phillips (2007) discussed several studies that report automatisation being associated with a decrease in cortical activation. Moreover, sometimes this decrease is associated with an increase in the activation of subcortical nuclei, such as the basal

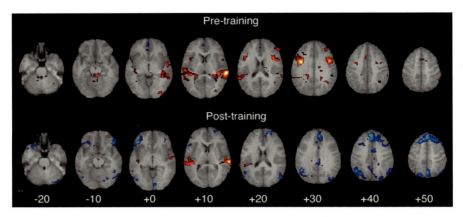

Figure 5.18 FMRI results of a study on the effects of practice on the execution of dual tasks. Practice resulted in a decrease in activation in the dorsolateral prefrontal cortex. Red-yellow areas mark brain regions where there was a significant increase in activation when a serial reaction time task was combined with another task, compared to a condition in which this task was performed alone. Blue areas mark a significant decrease. (source: Poldrack et al., 2005)

ganglia. These results imply that the shift from controlled to automatic processing involves replacing flexible cortical control with simple direct control from the basal ganglia.

5.6.2 INSTANCE THEORY

The American cognitive psychologist Gordon Logan and his colleagues (for example: Logan, 1988; Logan, Taylor, & Etherton, 1999) have presented a comprehensive model of the development of automatisation. According to their **instance theory**, automatic processes can be fast because they operate by retrieving a previous solution from memory. When we perform a novel task, we are limited by a lack of knowledge, so these tasks must be performed under the control of an attentional mechanism. As we become more practiced, however, attentional processes are no longer needed because the retrieval of a solution is immediate and efficient. Moreover, the execution then bypasses our consciousness because a direct association between the stimulus and the appropriate response has been established. According to Logan et al. (1999), however, the extent to which a task can be automated depends on specific conditions.

5.7 INTERPRETING AND FOLLOWING INSTRUCTIONS

Curiously, one of the most essential and widely used cognitive functions has been largely ignored by cognitive psychologists for many years, namely, our ability to follow instructions. The fact that we can follow instructions from others is crucial in everyday life. Without the ability to interpret and act on instructions that are given by others, we would be severely limited in our ability for social interaction; what's more, we would even be limited in our ability to perform the most basic actions. Our ability to carry out instructions is also crucial to just about every cognitive psychology study ever conducted. Yet until recently, however, many cognitive psychologists have taken this ability for granted.

Brass, Liefooghe, Braem, and De Houwer (2017) aptly illustrate this in a review article by discussing a study of Nakahara, Hayashi, Konishi, and Miyashita (2002). This study discusses the fMRI results of a macaque that had learned to perform the Wisconsin card sorting task. These results were very similar to those obtained in humans, leading to the conclusion that monkeys and humans perform the task in a similar way. A few years later, the study was heavily criticised, however, by Roepstorff and Frith (2004). These authors argued that it is impossible to compare the results across different species, for the simple reason that humans can generally perform the task after only a short instruction – and with minimal training – whereas for other animals it takes years of training, requiring them to learn the desired task through a carefully designed process of shaping.

The question, then, is how it is possible that humans can so easily perform tasks based on instructions, while animals have so much difficulty doing so. Of course, one important aspect involves our unique human ability to gain direct access to abstract concepts through language (Lupyan & Bergen, 2016). Language allows us to directly convert these concepts into an instruction that we can carry out. Brass et al. (2017) have argued that our linguistic abilities are a necessary but insufficient criterion for instruction following. After all, following instructions not only requires our ability to understand these instructions, but also our ability to convert them into behaviour (see fig 5.19). To illustrate: most of us will be able to interpret a recipe for baking a cake, but that does not guarantee that we will be able to successfully carry out the instructions.

5.7.1 AUTOMATIC INFLUENCES OF INSTRUCTIONS ON BEHAVIOUR

Let's start by investigating the simplest form of instruction following, that is, the automatic execution of an instruction. After all, there are many situations in which instructions

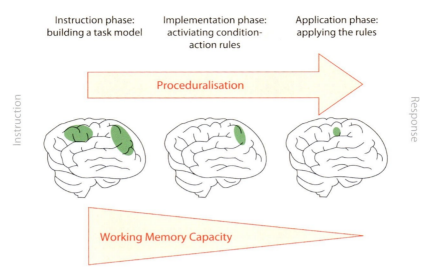

Instruction phase: Implementation phase: Application phase:
building a task model   activiating condition-   applying the rules
                         action rules

Proceduralisation

Working Memory Capacity

Figure 5.19 A model for converting an instruction into an action. (source: Brass et al., 2017)

have a very direct and automatic impact on our behaviour. Already by the late 19th century, evidence had been found in favour of the notion of a **prepared reflex** (Hommel, 2000). The basic idea behind the prepared reflex is that participants prepare themselves for a task by putting themselves in a state that allows the task to be performed efficiently. Although preparation for the task is voluntary, requiring effort, its execution (i.e., translating the stimulus into a response) is more or less automatic once it has been prepared.

We can, however, only conclude that instructions automatically exert their influence on behaviour when a specific set of conditions is met (Meiran, Pereg, Kessler, Cole, & Braver, 2015a). First, we need to ensure that the stimulus-response mapping that is to be learned cannot be automated. In other words, the stimulus-response mapping must be new on every trial. That is, on every trial, the task that we need to execute when presented with a given stimulus must be completely new. In an even more extreme case, we can also resort to mappings that we never need to execute. The reason for this condition is that if tasks can be automatised, we can argue that it was the earlier execution that created the mapping, rather than the instruction. Moreover, we need to ensure that the task instruction contains at least two different stimulus-response mappings, to avoid participants simply preparing to perform a specific response, rather than establishing a more general mapping between all possible stimuli and all possible responses.

One of the most common ways to investigate prepared reflexes consists of introducing interference via task instructions. There are several ways of doing this. One way consists of the previously described Eriksen flanker task (Eriksen & Eriksen, 1974). With some modifications, this paradigm can also be used to study the mapping of instructions. Cohen-Kdoshay and Meiran (2007), for example, gave participants a new set of stimuli with a new pair of category-response mappings. In one block of trials, participants either had to

respond with the left hand when a digit was even, and with the right hand when it was odd, or (alternatively) they had to respond with the left hand when the digit was greater than five and with the right hand when the digit was less than five. In the actual experiment, only a limited subset of these instructions was actually used. The others acted as distractors. An important finding by Cohen-Kdoshay and Meiran (2007) was that they observed clear effects of flankers on those stimuli that never required a response.

A second method to study the effects of the automatic processing of instructions stems from dual tasks (De Houwer, Beckers, Vandorpe, & Custers, 2005; Liefooghe, Wenke, & De Houwer, 2012; Waszak, Wenke, & Brass, 2008). The basic idea here is to give specific task instructions for one task and then test whether these instructions affect the performance on another task, even when they are irrelevant. For example, Waszak et al. (2008) instructed participants to switch between responding to the shape or the colour of a stimulus. During the instruction phase, four colours and four shapes were associated with left- and right-hand responses. In addition, there were two additional colours and two additional shapes of stimuli that were not linked to a response. During the task, participants had to switch between the shape task and the colour task.

The crucial manipulation in the experiment was that during the execution phase, only two of the four instructed colours and two of the four instructed shapes were used as relevant dimensions. The other two were only used when the dimension in question was irrelevant (e.g., red stimuli were used only when the participant had to judge the shape of the stimulus, despite the fact that the colour red was also associated with a response). In addition, the colours and shapes that were not associated with a response were sometimes also used in the irrelevant dimension (e.g., a blue stimulus, while the participant had to judge the shape of the stimulus). This way, it was

145

possible to investigate whether associating a response with a specific stimulus dimension, via an instruction, could cause interference. Waszak et al.'s results showed that when a given feature was associated with a specific response via instruction, it could cause interference, even when the associated response never had to be executed.

5.7.2 GOAL NEGLECT

One of the first indications that following instructions goes beyond simply understanding the instructions comes from patients with prefrontal cortex injuries. In these patients, we can sometimes find a dissociation between 'knowing' and 'doing'. For example, Brenda Milner (1963) already found that frontal **leucotomy patients** performed incorrect actions, which were accompanied by verbal reports indicating that the patients did intend to perform the correct action. According to the Russian neuropsychologist Alexander Luria, this dissociation between knowing and doing can neither be caused by a lack of understanding of the instruction nor by a motor deficit.

To explain this dissociation between knowing and doing, Duncan and colleagues introduced the concept of **goal neglect** (Duncan, Burgess, & Emslie, 1995; Duncan, Emslie, Williams, Johnson, & Freer, 1996). Goal neglect is defined by three properties: (1) it reflects an extreme failure to follow task rules; (2) task performance is limited mainly by the complexity of the task rules and not by the complexity of task execution; (3) the failure cannot be explained by difficulties with remembering the task rules.

Duncan et al. (1996) were the first to investigate goal neglect by using a letter monitoring task (see fig 5.20). Here, participants are shown two numbers or letters, with one

Figure 5.20 The letter monitoring task, as used by Duncan et al. (1996). (source: Brass et al., 2017)

character presented on one side of the screen and the other character presented on the other side. Before executing the task, participants are instructed which side of the display is relevant and they are required to read out loud the letters that are presented there. Numbers on the relevant side and all characters on the other side should be ignored. After a number of trials, participants are instructed either to switch to the letters on the other side of the screen or to continue reading the letters on the same side as they started. Duncan et al. (1996) found that some participants did not switch to the other side when instructed to do so, although they were able to repeat the instructions they were given at the end of the experiment. This failure to follow the instruction can be considered a form of goal neglect.

In a follow-up study, Duncan et al. (2008) investigated the effects of task difficulty on goal neglect. In their first experiment, the number of stimuli that participants had to monitor was increased. Interestingly, this manipulation had no effect on goal neglect. In their second experiment, participants were required to perform an additional task together with the monitoring task. Now, they did find an effect on goal neglect, but only when the primary and the secondary task were introduced simultaneously. When the second task was introduced later, the additional load of this task had no effect on goal neglect. Thus, these results suggest that it is mainly the complexity of the internal representation of the task that is formed during the processing of the instructions that influences goal neglect. In other words, when we are faced with too much information at once, there is an increased risk that our limited capacity will prevent us from processing this information into a **task model**. A task model is an internal representation that we store in working memory, containing all the relevant facts, rules, and task requirements that are necessary for performing a task.

Bhandari and Duncan (2014) have extended the concept of goal neglect in several important ways. Their first observation is that goal neglect is strongly related to the extent to which we can group complex task instructions into chunks. When this can be done, each of the chunks can be executed on its own with relative ease. The more efficiently this chunking can be done, the less likely it is that goal neglect will occur. Secondly, Bhandari and Duncan found that goal neglect depends only on the complexity of the task itself, and that it is independent of a possible secondary task: making a second task more complex did not affect the degree of goal neglect on the main task. Finally, Bhandari and Duncan found that when participants were beginning to apply a new task rule, their performance was often unstable. It always took a few trials before participants found a stable strategy. The latter implies that we actually need to run through the internal task model a few times before it actually stabilises.

Although the studies discussed here imply that goal neglect depends primarily on the instructional phase and the construction of the task model, it is also possible that difficulties with implementing the task model contribute to goal neglect (De Jong, Berendsen, & Cools, 1999). Here, implementation refers to the planning process that precedes the actual performance of the task. De Jong et al. (1999) emphasised the importance of individual differences in implementing specific elements of the task model. Although participants are, in principle, perfectly capable of implementing the task model, they will occasionally fail to do so because it is difficult. When it is not necessary to implement all elements of the task model, there is also an elevated risk that the implementation will not be a complete success (McVay & Kane, 2009).

5.7.3 A DISSOCIATION BETWEEN KNOWING AND DOING: NEUROIMAGING EVIDENCE

The aforementioned data on goal neglect, along with the corresponding data on prefrontal cortex damage, are already indicative of a clear dissociation between knowing and doing (Duncan et al., 1995; Duncan et al., 2008; Milner, 1963). More recently, we have also seen a growing body of evidence for this idea from the cognitive neurosciences (Cole, Bagic, Kass, & Schneider, 2010; Dumontheil, Thompson, & Duncan, 2010; Everaert, Theeuwes, Liefooghe, & De Houwer, 2014; Hartstra, Kühn, Verguts, & Brass, 2011; Ruge & Wolfensteller, 2010).

One way of investigating the relationship between instruction and motor activity is by using ERP recordings. A specific ERP component, known as **lateralised readiness potential (LRP)**, is particularly suitable for this purpose. The LRP is a difference wave that is obtained by subtracting the EEG signals measured above the left and right motor cortex from each other. To illustrate, preparing a response with our left hand will result in greater activation of the right motor cortex, compared to the left. By tracking this relative activation, in the form of the difference between left and right motor cortex EEG activity, we can estimate how quickly the motor cortex responds to an instruction. The LRP thus reflects the stronger activation of the contralateral motor cortex. Although the LRP is normally evoked by an actual action, it can also be evoked by a prepared response that is not actually performed. In classic interference tasks, such as the flanker task, it is often found that LRPs are larger for congruent stimuli than for incongruent ones (Eimer, 1995).

Meiran, Pereg, Kessler, Cole, and Braver (2015b) conducted an EEG study in which participants had to perform a **go/no-go task**. In this type of task, participants are required to respond only when a stimulus meets specific characteristics. In the Meiran et al. study, participants were instructed to respond with one hand when the stimulus was a specific target letter and with their other hand when it was any other letter. Moreover, they were instructed to respond only when the letter was green. The first trials following this instruction were red, which meant that participants should never respond on these initial trials. These trials were included to

determine whether they nevertheless evoked activation in the motor cortex. Meiran et al. found that this was indeed the case. The observed LRPs were quickly attenuated, however, as more trials were presented. Taken together, these results imply that stimulus-response coupling can result in the automatic activation of the instructed motor response.

fMRI studies have also found that instructions can result in the automatic formation of stimulus-response associations. For instance, Brass, Wenke, Spengler, and Waszak (2009) used a dual task similar to the one employed by Waszak et al. (2008), in which participants had to switch between responding to the shape of a stimulus and its colour. As described earlier, in this task two colours and two shapes were associated with a response that was never executed, and there were also two shapes and colours that were not associated with a response. A key finding of this study was that a network of brain regions including the anterior cingulate cortex, the presupplementary motor areas, the frontal cortex, and the parietal cortex was involved in inhibiting a conflicting instruction. This network was strongly associated with the processing of conflicting information. It was activated more strongly when the irrelevant stimulus property was associated with a (never to be executed) conflicting response than when the irrelevant stimulus property was not associated with a response (see fig 5.21).

5.8 IN CLOSING: COGNITIVE CONTROL, ALWAYS BENEFICIAL?

Cognitive control is necessary to focus ourselves and to enable us to achieve our goals. But, we may finally ask, is cognitive control always beneficial? Amer, Campbell, and Hasher (2016) argue that this is not necessarily the case (see fig 5.22)! Cognitive control processes do indeed have a beneficial effect on various tasks. Because we can focus better and because we are less likely to be distracted by irrelevant information, cognitive control generally allows us to perform better on academic tasks. One consistent finding in the literature is that cognitive control processes become weaker with age. Consequently, a huge industry, targeting the ageing population, has developed that aims to stimulate cognitive control processes.

It should be noted, however, that there are many tasks where distraction can actually be beneficial. Consider implicit learning processes, for example, where a diminished cognitive control can aid us in detecting regularities in seemingly random patterns. We can find a good example of this in newborn children, who learn to detect structure in complex visual and auditory stimuli this way. A similar process is involved in the way children learn a new language: too much cognitive control can be detrimental to learning a

(a)

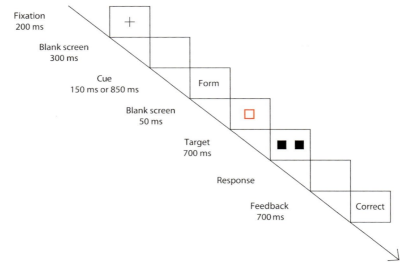

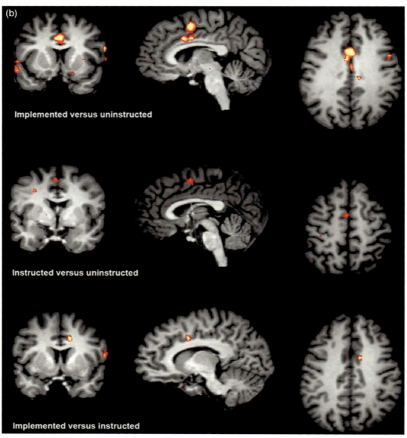

Figure 5.21 (a) Set-up and results of an experiment in which participants had to alternate between responding to the colour or the shape of a stimulus. Some stimulus-response combinations were part of the instruction set but were never presented in practice. (b) fMRI results showed increased activation in a network of brain areas, including the anterior cingulate cortex, the presupplementary motor areas, the frontal cortex, and the parietal cortex. Activation in this network was associated with inhibition of conflicting instructions. (source: Brass et al., 2009)

language, because the statistic regularities that underlie the grammatical structures are less easily detected.

Another case is problem-solving. Reduced cognitive control enables us to abandon a failing strategy sooner. Creative solutions are often associated with reduced activation of the prefrontal brain areas. Even more so, creativity often requires combining various elements into an innovative solution, and the narrowed attention span that often results from a high degree of cognitive control is therefore very unfavourable here. Note, however, that creativity is often considered to be a process that consists of two stages: a generative component and an evaluative component. The generative component has been discussed previously: it is the component that results in new ideas. The evaluative component, however, is necessary to test the new ideas for usefulness, and this is precisely a process that can benefit from cognitive control.

Amer et al. (2016) conclude that although older individuals can also benefit from a certain degree of cognitive control, especially when it comes to performing tasks that depend on selective attention, their reduced cognitive control also offers unique opportunities. Precisely because older people have accumulated a great deal of knowledge and experience throughout their lives, reduced cognitive control can actually enable them to discover new patterns in this knowledge (see Box 5.2).

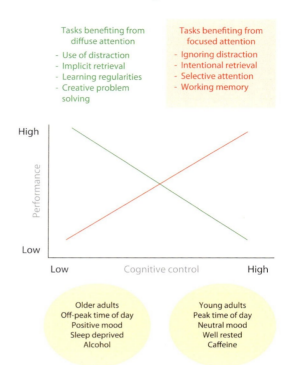

Figure 5.22 Schematic representation of the advantages and disadvantages of cognitive control. (source: Amer et al., 2016)

Box 5.2 Cognitive control across the lifespan

We now have overwhelming evidence to show that the frontal lobes play an important role in cognitive control. Since the frontal lobes are among the last brain areas to fully develop and since they are also among the first brain areas to show signs of degeneration with increasing age, it is plausible that we might observe significant changes in our cognitive control functions across our lifespans.

Rubia et al. (2006) report a wide variety of studies showing that, compared to children, adults are characterised by a stronger activation of their prefrontal areas while performing a wide range of tasks requiring cognitive control, such as the stop-signal paradigm, the go/no-go task, or the Stroop task. Behaviourally, the ability to exert cognitive control also systematically increases with the age of developing young children (Tottenham, Hare, & Casey, 2011).

Knowing that cognitive control processes steadily improve during development, we may wonder what exactly happens during puberty. This stage of our lives, which is situated roughly between the ages of 10 and 15, is characterised by significant physical and hormonal changes. Puberty partly overlaps with adolescence

(10–22 years), during which phase we not only undergo physical changes but also mature socially. Since the prefrontal cortex continues to develop until approximately 20 years of age, which is considerably longer than any other part of the cortex, we may wonder whether this relatively slow development plays a role in the sometimes considerably risky behaviour that is exhibited by adolescents (Steinberg, 2007).

Luna, Padmanabhan, and O'Hearn (2010) review a large body of fMRI studies that have attempted to investigate the relationship between cognitive control and prefrontal brain activity. These authors also note that most cognitive control functions increase during childhood, but that these functions are not yet optimally effective at the start of adolescence. The corresponding brain activation patterns are somewhat inconsistent, in the sense that some areas become more activated during adolescence, while other areas become less active. Luna et al. conclude that the age-related increase can be interpreted as a reflection of the increase in cognitive control, while the decrease can be interpreted as an increase in the efficiency with which the control processes operate, thereby requiring less brain activation.

(Continued)

Box 5.2 (Continued)

These authors note, however, that caution is needed when interpreting these differences. Especially when comparing different age groups, the possibility remains that differences in brain activity may not only reflect structural differences in cognitive skills but also strategic differences. For example, adults may make more use of verbal strategies (especially in tasks that make strong demands on working memory), which means that the patterns of brain activity evoked by a cognitive task may change with age. Another possible explanation for some of the inconsistencies in the results discussed by Luna et al. is that most of the studies they discuss were conducted in the early days of fMRI research and may therefore have been limited by sample sizes that are too small. More recent studies, based on much larger samples, do show fairly consistently that the increase in cognitive control during adolescence is mediated by the prefrontal cortex (Satterthwaite et al., 2013).

According to Steinberg (2007) the risk-taking behaviour that is exhibited by many adolescents results from a sharp increase in impulsive behaviour due to the onset of puberty and a relatively deficient cognitive control mechanism (which should control these impulses) that is not fully developed until the age of 18. Steinberg notes that risky behaviour occurs mainly in a social context: adolescents who are alone display much less risky behaviour than adolescents who are in the company of friends. Crone and Dahl (2012) also conclude that the development of affective and social functions is probably more important than the mere fact that cognitive control functions are developing too slowly. Whatever the exact cause of the behavioural changes we often observe in adolescents, based on current developments in cognitive neuroscience, we are slowly but surely beginning to grasp the underlying mechanisms. Much work remains to be done, however, before we can definitively answer this question.

Also with ageing, we often find changes in our cognitive abilities. Although cognitive ageing is often accompanied by impairments in memory functioning, we also find that oftentimes older adults have more difficulties focusing their attention. Attentional control appears to weaken with age and we also become less flexible in switching tasks with advancing age. An influential hypothesis, which was very popular in the 1990s, is that ageing is associated with increased inhibitory control deficiencies, and that older adults are therefore more likely to be distracted by irrelevant stimuli. The prefrontal cortex is also believed to be involved in this form of cognitive decline (West, 1996). There is indeed some evidence that inhibitory control deteriorates earlier than, for example, working memory functions (Sweeney, Rosano, Berman, & Luna, 2001). Braver and Barch (2002) suggest that cognitive ageing primarily results from a deterioration of the dopaminergic system projecting to the prefrontal cortex. According to Braver and Barch, this system is, among others, involved in generating and maintaining task goals (see also: Braver, 2012). One consequence is that with increasing age we should become less able to hold on to these goals.

Of course, ageing involves many more changes to the brain than just the deterioration of the prefrontal functions as outlined earlier (Reuter-Lorenz & Park, 2014). This implies that the idea that cognitive ageing can be primarily attributed to a deterioration of cognitive control functions is too one-sided. In addition to a massive loss of neurons, the formation of **amyloid plaques**, changes in brain volume, and changes in connectivity, a wide range of other changes contribute to the phenomenon of cognitive ageing. However, a wide range of processes also make the brain resistant to ageing. These include biological processes, such as the recruitment of new brain areas for existing cognitive functions, or changes in connectivity between different brain areas. But also, psychological processes such as intellectual activity, education, fitness, and the continued exercise of higher cognitive skills contribute to the retention of many crucial cognitive functions.

5.9 SUMMARY

Cognitive control processes play an important role in how we can flexibly adapt our behaviour to changing environmental conditions. These processes enable us to direct behaviour in such a way that task goals are achieved. Moreover, they allow us not to be distracted by impulses from the environment, and to flexibly coordinate different tasks. Executive functions play a crucial role in these processes.

These functions are, among other things, involved in task switching, inhibition, and updating working memory. Neural circuits in the prefrontal cortex, particularly in the dorsolateral prefrontal cortex, the anterior cingulate cortex, and some temporal and parietal areas are involved. Some patients with brain injuries are characterised by specific impairments of these executive functions. These patients are often characterised by difficulties in planning activities, and performing gambling tasks.

A key concept in the cognitive-control literature is inhibitory control. Inhibitory control describes the processes involved in suppressing unwanted stimuli, task sets, emotions, or memories. Although the necessity of the concept of inhibition is still debated in experimental psychology, there is at least one form of inhibition that is universally accepted: response inhibition. Response inhibition involves aborting a motor response that is being prepared. A common paradigm for investigating response inhibition is the stop-signal paradigm. This paradigm is based on the idea that response preparation and response inhibition are two independent processes that compete with each other.

Response inhibition is associated with conflict: it is assumed that two processes compete with each other, with the winner ultimately determining whether a response is generated or not. The degree of conflict can be experimentally manipulated by using a flanker paradigm. Influential cognitive models assume that the degree of conflict that is experienced determines whether cognitive control processes are necessary. According to these models, such conflicts are identified by the anterior cingulate cortex, which can then engage attention and control processes. Conflict may also result in errors. One observation is that people tend to react more slowly after making an error. The brain appears to detect errors automatically, and this process is reflected in an ERP component known as the ERN. Producing an error may result in an adjustment of the response threshold, which reduces the chances of errors on future occasions; however, it also slows down responses. In addition, errors also capture attention.

A second key concept is multitasking and task switching. When we have to perform two tasks simultaneously, we are slower and more prone to making errors than when we perform these tasks separately. It was originally believed that the performance of a dual task was limited by a central capacity limit. Later models, however, suggest that performance is also limited when tasks require the use of peripheral resources, such as perception or response modalities. Most theories assume that multiple tasks are performed under the supervision of a central executive function, which coordinates the allocation of resources. An exception to this is the threaded cognition model, which assumes that tasks can proceed unsupervised.

In addition to multitasking, much research has focused on task switching. The processes involved in switching between a set of tasks are studied by using the task switching paradigm. One of the most striking findings is that task switching always comes at a cost: the performance of the new task is slower than that of a previous task. Although these costs can be mitigated when participants are given time and opportunity to prepare, they never completely disappear. A possible explanation for these switch costs is that we sometimes fail to recall the new task rules.

In some cases, we can perform tasks more or less automatically, whereas in other cases they always require cognitive control. In a classic experiment by Shiffrin and Schneider, it was found that tasks employing a consistent mapping can be automated, whereas tasks employing a varied mapping always remain under cognitive control. There is, however, probably no strict distinction between controlled and automatic processes. Practising a task will result in knowledge about the action to be performed, which can be efficiently retrieved from memory. In case of new tasks, or tasks where such automation is not possible, the supervision of a cognitive control process will always be necessary. Automation is generally accompanied by a decrease in the involvement of cortical brain areas and an increase in subcortical ones.

A specific aspect of cognitive control involves dealing with instructions. Understanding and implementing an instruction requires language skills, but that is not enough. The verbal instructions must also be converted into a task set. Complex instructions are sometimes characterised by the phenomenon of goal neglect: a failure to carry out the task rules. Especially with complex task instructions, a discrepancy can arise between knowing and doing.

Based on the available cognitive control literature and the popular interpretation of these findings, the suggestion is sometimes made that more cognitive control is always better. However, some researchers argue that this is not necessarily the case. Cognitive control processes have a positive effect on a wide range of tasks, because we have a better focus, are less easily distracted, and can switch more flexibly. Amer, Campbell, and Hasher (2016) argue, however, that there are also many activities where distraction can be beneficial. For example, distraction can help in gaining insight in complex patterns, help in learning a second language, or assist in finding creative solutions. Older adults, in particular, in whom cognitive control processes are generally impaired, may therefore excel at these tasks, especially in discovering patterns in the knowledge and experience they have acquired throughout their lives.

FURTHER READING

Braver, T. (2015). *Motivation and cognitive control*. London, UK: Routledge.

Crone, E. M. (2018). *The adolescent brain: On brain development in the unique period of adolescence* (2nd ed.). Amsterdam: Prometheus.

Egner, T. (2017). *The Wiley handbook of cognitive control*. Chichester, UK: John Wiley and Sons.

PART 3

Perception

CHAPTER 6
Visual perception

6.1 INTRODUCTION

Imagine getting up very early in the morning to attend a lecture. It is still dark outside when you leave your home and on your way to the lecture hall you observe a remarkable phenomenon. Starting from the dark, the world around you slowly changes from a dark grey black and white environment to a colourful one, especially when it is a beautiful sunny winter or spring morning.

The fact that we perceive the world at night in blurry grey tones is so obvious that we hardly ever think about it. Consider, however, taking a photograph at night: under low light conditions, we get a result that is unrealistically colourful – and often unrealistically sharp. The reason for this is that our human visual perception utilises different receptors for day and night vision. One type of receptor is involved in coding colour and detail, while the other is especially light sensitive, however, it cannot represent colour and it is low in detail. A camera, however, only has one sensor, which works in both low and high light conditions, effectively producing the same result, regardless of how much light is available.

6.2 A TRUE IMAGE OF THE WORLD?

In our daily waking life, we are constantly aware of our surroundings: our eyes, like a camera, objectively perceive the environment and project a particularly colourful and true representation of reality to our brains. At least, that is what we typically believe to be happening, but in the remainder of this chapter we will discuss why this is not the case. Upon closer inspection, we have to conclude that the conscious representation of our environment is closer to an illusion than to an adequate representation of reality. The camera analogy, as just illustrated, thus only applies to a very limited extent.

6.2.1 VISIBLE LIGHT: A LIMITED WINDOW ON THE OUTSIDE WORLD

Why does our visual perception not produce an adequate representation of our environment? To address this question, we must first establish exactly what our eyes perceive.

Visible light is part of an enormous spectrum of electromagnetic waves, known as the **electromagnetic spectrum** (see fig 6.1). An electromagnetic wave can be defined by its wavelength and its corresponding frequency of vibration. The full electromagnetic spectrum includes wavelengths ranging from megametres (= million metres) to picometres (= 1/1,000,000,000,000 metres) and beyond. Visible light is formed by those wavelengths that the receptors in our eyes are sensitive to: about 400–700 nanometres (1 nanometre = 1/1,000,000,000 metres). Out of this enormously broad spectrum, we can thus only perceive an extremely small cross section.

Secondly, we should be aware of the fact that colours do not exist as such in the environment; they are constructed by our brains. Our eyes contain three different types of receptors, known as cones, that are involved in colour vision. Each type of cone is selectively sensitive to a specific range of wavelengths. The signals transmitted by the cones are combined into a representation that results in our subjective experience of colour. Moreover, we can only perceive these colours when there is a sufficient amount of light. In the dark, we can still perceive our environment, but now we do so on the basis of another receptor type, known as rods. These rods are very sensitive to light but are not colour-selective, so that at night we only perceive the world in shades of grey (see fig 6.2). Moreover, the density of these rods on the retina is much lower (see more on this later in the chapter) than the density of cones, which implies that we are limited in perceiving details in the dark.

6.2.2 EYE MOVEMENTS

Moreover, even during the day, our eyes are capable of perceiving details in only a very small region of our visual field, which extends to about 2–3 degrees of arc. To put this into perspective, this is about the width of our thumb at arm's length. Yet during our waking life we have the subjective experience of continuously perceiving our entire environment. This illusion arises because we are constantly scanning our environment, making several thousands of eye movements every day. Those

DOI: 10.4324/9781003319344-9

The Electromagnetic Spectrum

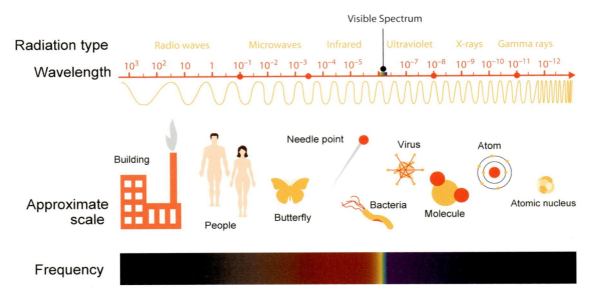

Figure 6.1 An overview of the electromagnetic spectrum. The classification of different forms of radiation as a function of wavelength is shown at the top of the figure. The reference objects at the bottom reflect the order of magnitude of the corresponding wavelengths. Our eyes can only perceive a very limited part of this spectrum – the visible spectrum.

parts of the environment on which our eyes are not fixated are believed to be filled in by predictions generated by the brain (Friston et al., 2012).

6.2.3 THE CAMERA ANALOGY

Based on the preceding, we can already conclude that the often-heard analogy that our eyes are like a camera, which faithfully records what happens in the outside world is false. In Chapter 4 we have already discussed the philosophical arguments against this idea (Dennett, 1991). In this chapter, we will see further arguments against this camera metaphor

and discuss how visual information is processed into a mental representation. To do so, we must first consider the basic functionality of the eye and the visual system.

6.3 THE NEURAL BASIS OF VISUAL PERCEPTION

Our visual experiences are produced by a complex series of processing steps that can be traced from the eye to several brain regions involved in forming higher-order mental representations of the environment. In general, this system is hierarchically organised. The lower levels, early in the

Figure 6.2 A night scene observed through a digital camera. On the left is the scene as captured by the camera, on the right is an edited version that matches the image as closely as possible to the subjective experience of the photographer. (source: The Goldilock Project)

processing stream, process details of a visual scene, such as the position and orientation of lines. In contrast, higher-order properties of objects and concepts are represented at the higher levels and at later stages of processing. Yet, despite this organisation, we are surprisingly quick in determining the essence of a scene (Thorpe, Fize, & Marlot, 1996), suggesting that our brains can very rapidly access high-level visual information.

The fact that our brains can process these higher-level types of visual information has puzzled vision scientists for decades. One of the main reasons for this is that the visual system has traditionally been studied from a bottom-up perspective that predominantly considered the forward, bottom-up, processes in the visual system. Before proceeding to discuss the further details of the visual system, note that we will initially also focus on this bottom-up perspective. We proceed in this way because this is how the visual system has initially been studied. Note that this perspective is not necessarily incorrect, but that it is incomplete. Indeed, all visual pathways are characterised not only by forward projections from the primary to the higher processing centres, but also by a massive amount of backward (recurrent) projections. Historically, vision scientists have been struggling to understand the significance of these recurrent projections; however, currently it is becoming increasingly clear that they are involved in generating predictions about the expected visual input. As such, the importance of these recurrent projections is detailed after the introduction of the main functionality of the forward projections.

6.3.1 THE EYE

All forms of visual perception originate in our eyes. The eye is a spherical organ; the front consists of semi-transparent tissue, known as the cornea, which allows light to enter (see fig 6.3). This light is then focused by a convex lens and projected onto the retina, which is located at the posterior end of the eye.

6.3.2 THE RETINA

The retina consists of a layer of tissue that hosts the photoreceptors. Here, we can identify two types of receptors, the cones, which are tuned to specific wavelengths of light, and the rods, which are very light sensitive but unable to distinguish between different wavelengths (see fig 6.4). Note that these photoreceptors are not evenly distributed across the retina. More specifically, the cones are highly concentrated in one location directly behind the eye lens, a location known as the **fovea**, whereas the rods are much more scattered around the periphery. Curiously, the photoreceptors are located at the posterior end of the retina away from the light, such that light has to penetrate the retinal tissue before it can stimulate them. Output from the photoreceptors is not transmitted directly to the brain but passes through a series of intermediate steps. This implies that some degree of preprocessing of the optical signal already takes place inside the retina.

From the photoreceptors, the optical signal first passes through a layer of **bipolar** and **horizontal cells** and then through another layer of **amacrine cells** and **retinal ganglion cells**. Here, the optical signal is pre-processed before it is transmitted to the brain. The horizontal cells connect multiple light receptors and cause neighbouring cells to inhibit each other's activation. The result of this process is the enhancement of local contrasts, in a process known as **lateral inhibition**. Bipolar cells connect directly to the photoreceptors and to the horizontal cells, which in turn connect to the retinal ganglion cells, which ultimately transmit the signal to the brain. Finally, amacrine cells connect several retinal ganglion cells, integrating the information from different photoreceptors.

The output of the retinal ganglion cells is transmitted via a bundle of neural fibres known as the optic nerve (also known as the second cranial nerve). The area where this bundle leaves the retina does not contain any photoreceptors. At this location we are effectively blind: it is the retina's blind spot. Yet, under normal circumstances, we do not notice this blind spot because the brain automatically fills in the missing information through predictive processes (Komatsu, 2006).

6.4 NEURAL PATHWAYS FROM THE EYE TO THE CORTEX

The distinction between rod and cone receptors marks the beginning of a dichotomy that persists more or less throughout the remainder of the visual system

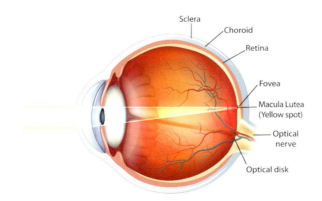

Sclera
Choroid
Retina
Fovea
Macula Lutea (Yellow spot)
Optical nerve
Optical disk

Figure 6.3 Cross section of the human eye. Light entering the eye from the front is refracted by the cornea and the eye lens and is focused on the retina at the back of the eye. The resulting retinal image is encoded by a series of receptors and transmitted to the brain in the form of neural impulses. The amount of light that can enter the eye is regulated by a variable-sized pupil.

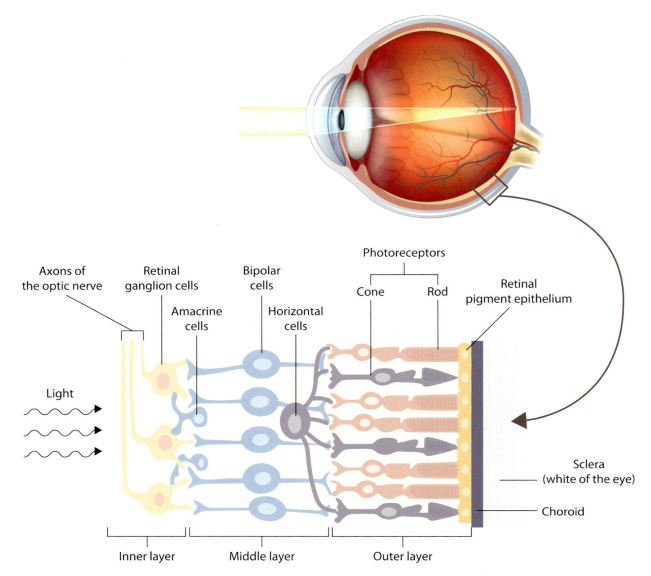

Figure 6.4 Cross section of the retina. The choroid layer to the right marks the back of the eye. Here, the retinal pigment epithelium prevents light from leaving the back of the eye. The next layer consists of the photoreceptors. There are two types of photoreceptors: cones for colour vision and rods for dim-light vision. These photoreceptors stimulate the horizontal cells, bipolar cells, and the amacrine cells. These cells in turn stimulate the retinal ganglion cells, which project the optical information to the cortex.

(see fig 6.5). All retinal output is projected by the optic nerve to a number of subcortical brain areas, before eventually reaching the primary visual areas in the occipital cortex. In one of these subcortical nuclei, the optic chiasm, some of the neural pathways cross, so that output from the right side of each eye is ultimately projected to the right visual cortex and output from the left side of each eye is projected to the left visual cortex. Because the image on the retina is rotated 180 degrees, the consequence of this projection is that visual information is processed by the hemisphere that is contralateral relative to the location where it is perceived.

The retinal ganglion cells project the visual signal to the lateral geniculate nucleus; one of the thalamic nuclei. From here, information is projected to the primary visual cortex along the optic radiation. The geniculate nucleus

also projects to the superior colliculus, and through the colliculus to the pulvinar. The superior colliculus is involved in programming eye movements and in integrating visual and auditory input (see Chapter 9).

Although output from the cones and rods share the same neural pathway that projects the neural output from the eye to the cortex, within these pathways, we can distinguish two visual systems, each largely involved in processing the output from one of these receptors. More specifically, input from the cones is projected primarily to neurons in the parvocellular layer of the geniculate nucleus (Goodale & Milner, 1992). Neurons in this part of the geniculate nucleus are relatively small. This so-called **parvocellular pathway** is sensitive to colour and fine detail. Input from the rods, on the other hand,

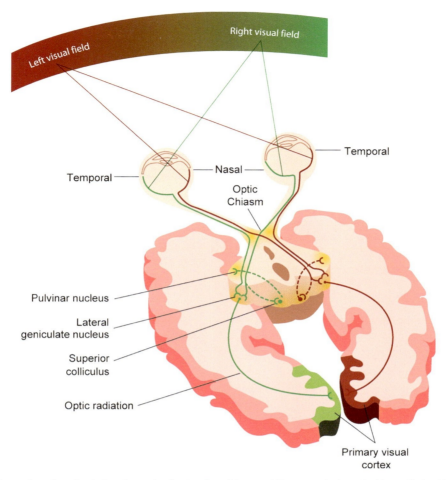

Figure 6.5 The visual pathways from the retina to the primary visual cortex. Part of the neural fibres cross in the optic chiasm. All visual information is projected to the left and right lateral geniculate nuclei. From there, the visual signal is projected onward to the primary visual cortex. Part of the visual signal is also projected to the superior colliculus.

projects mainly to neurons in the magnocellular layer of the geniculate nucleus. These magnocellular neurons are relatively large and widely branched, and the **magnocellular pathway** is particularly sensitive to motion information.

Although there is some crosstalk between the parvo- and magnocellular pathways, the distinction between these neural pathways does reflect the start of two more or less distinct visual systems, each involved in quite dramatically different functions and, remarkably, each also seemingly operating relatively independently of each other. That is, we can identify a **vision-for-perception system**, which is primarily involved in recognising objects, and a **vision-for-action system**, which is primarily involved in processing spatial relationships, motion information, and the visual guidance of our own actions (Milner & Goodale, 2008). Although recent studies suggest that there is a stronger overlap between the vision-for-perception and vision-for-action systems than originally assumed (Rossetti, Pisella, & McIntosh, 2017), the distinction as originally formulated by Milner and Goodale (2008) is still a good starting point for discussing the basic processes of visual processing.

6.5 INITIAL PROCESSING: VISUAL CORTEX

Neurons in the lateral geniculate nucleus project to the visual cortex, which consists of a number of areas in the

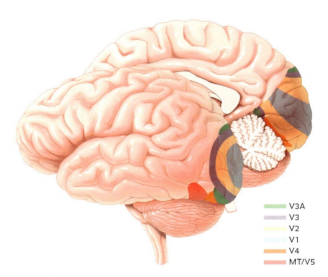

Figure 6.6 Schematic overview of the visual processing areas in the brain.

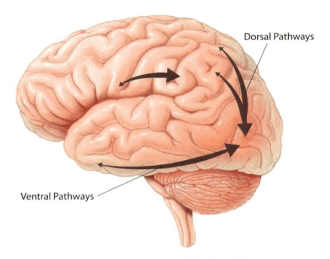

Dorsal Pathways

Ventral Pathways

Figure 6.7 Schematic illustration of the dorsal and ventral pathways in the brain. After the primary visual cortex, the processing of visual information takes place along two different routes in the brain. The dorsal route is mainly involved in processing motion encoding spatial positions, and integrating visual information into motor actions. The ventral route is mainly involved in recognising colours and shapes, and in identifying objects and faces.

occipital cortex (see fig 6.6). In these areas, the primary and secondary processing of the visual input takes place, with initial processing mainly occurring in the primary visual cortex. This is the most occipital part of the cortex, also known as area V1 or striate cortex, because of the striped appearance of this part of the cortex. After V1, further processing takes place along two specialised pathways, each associated with different forms of processing (see fig 6.7).

After V1, the parvocellular pathway is primarily associated with a **ventral route**, which projects through the visual area V4 to the inferotemporal cortex. This pathway is mainly involved in object, shape, and colour recognition. The magnocellular pathway is primarily associated with a **dorsal route**, which projects to the posterior parietal cortex. This pathway is strongly involved in the processing of position and motion information. It is involved in the processing of the location of objects as well as in processing how we can use this information while manipulating objects. Although the parvocellular pathway is primarily associated with the ventral pathway and the magnocellular pathway with the dorsal pathway, we must emphasise that this separation is not complete. Both pathways converge in the primary visual cortex and some parvocellular neurons project, for example, onto the dorsal pathway (Parker, 2007).

6.5.1 PRIMARY VISUAL CORTEX (V1)

The primary visual cortex (V1) processes the basic properties of light. Neurons in the primary visual cortex respond to stimuli presented at specific locations on the retina but not at others: as such, neurons are characterised by a **receptive field** (Hubel & Wiesel, 1962). When we map the receptive fields of V1, we see that there is a direct correspondence between the location on the retina being stimulated and the location in

V1 that is activated: this is the **retinotopic map**. V1 is also characterised by different types of neurons. Simple cells either respond more strongly when light falls into the cell's receptive field or more weakly. Complex cells respond to higher-order properties of stimuli, such as the specific orientation of lines or to motion. These complex cells are characterised by relatively large receptive fields, and they receive input from groups of simple cells (Hubel & Wiesel, 1979).

6.5.2 SECONDARY VISUAL CORTEX (V2)

The primary visual cortex transmits information to the secondary visual cortex (V2), which further processes this information and transmits it to higher visual areas. In addition, the connections between these visual areas are reciprocal, that is, the higher-level areas are also connected to lower-level areas. The functionality of V2 is similar to that of V1, in that neurons respond mainly to relatively simple stimulus properties such as the orientation of lines and spatial frequencies. An important distinction is that V2 appears to be composed of only complex cells, and that V2 cells also respond to more complex properties of stimuli, such as the orientation of illusory contours, binocular disparity,[1] or the difference between object and background.

6.5.3 VENTRAL AND DORSAL ROUTES

After V2, processing takes place in the higher-level visual areas V3 to V5. From V2 onwards, the dorsal and the ventral pathways are becoming increasingly segregated (Ungerleider & Haxby, 1994). Area V3 is part of the dorsal pathway and receives input from V2 and V1 that mainly originates from the magnocellular pathway. Area V3 is believed to be primarily involved in the processing of motion information.

Area V4 is part of the ventral pathway and also receives input from areas V2 and V1. This input originates from both the magnocellular and parvocellular pathways. Neurons in area V4 are sensitive to orientation, spatial frequencies, and colour, along with complex object properties such as geometric shapes. Neurons in V4 project to two further areas in the inferior temporal cortex: both the magnocellular and parvocellular pathways project to the posterior inferior temporal cortex, whereas a second neural pathway consisting mainly of parvocellular output projects to the more anterior inferior temporal cortex.

6.6 FURTHER PROCESSING: FUNCTIONAL SPECIALISATION

The British neurobiologist Semir Zeki was among the first to study the neuronal activation patterns in area V4 and found that this area responded mainly to colour information. This finding was one of the reasons for Zeki to propose the idea of **functional specialisation** (Zeki, 2001), that is, the idea that each area in the visual cortex is involved in only one or at least in only a limited number of tasks, such as processing shape, colour, or motion.

6.6.1 SHAPE PROCESSING

Several brain areas are involved in shape processing. These areas include V1–V4 and the inferior temporal cortex. Neurons in higher regions respond to increasingly complex and abstract shape properties, from simple on and off responses in V1 to more complex responses to line orientations in V1 and V2, to full stimulus categories (such as body parts or tools) (Kourtzi & Connor, 2011) or 3D representations (Yamane, Carlson, Bowman, Wang, & Connor, 2008) in the inferior temporal cortex.

6.6.2 COLOUR PROCESSING

In addition to Zeki's work, several other studies have found evidence for the assumption that area V4 is involved in colour processing. Goddard et al. (2011), for example, used fMRI to investigate the role of V4 in colour perception. When participants were asked to watch movie fragments, they found an increase in V4 activation when these fragments were shown in colour compared to when they were shown in black and white.

Neuropsychology has also contributed significantly to our understanding of the involvement of V4 in colour vision. **Achromatopsia** is a neuropsychological condition in which patients lose their ability to perceive colours after a traumatic brain injury. The first reports of achromatopsia date back to the late the 19th century (Zeki, 1990). A more systematic investigation was reported by Bouvier and Engel (2006), however, who conducted a **meta-analysis**, based on 38 case studies. An important aim of this analysis was to determine to what extent the individual lesions overlapped in the individuals included in the meta-analysis. Despite considerable variability in the nature of the lesions, a high degree of overlap was found in an area around V4.

Bouvier and Engel argued that three conditions must be met before V4 could be considered the colour centre of the brain. First, colour vision should be limited to just this one visual area; second, colour vision should be the only function that it performs; and third, colour vision should not depend on processes in higher-order visual areas. The results of Bouvier's and Engels' meta-analysis indicate, however, that the region damaged in almost all patients comprised two visual areas, which were also partly involved in spatial perception (see fig 6.8). Since most patients discussed had retained a residual ability to perceive colours, it is likely that other brain areas are also involved in colour perception. Consistent with the observation, evidence has been found that V1 and V2 are also partially involved in the processing of colour information (Wade, Brewer, Rieger, & Wandell, 2002), thus arguing against the idea of full-blown functional specialisation.

Using optical imaging techniques in a study on macaques, Tanigawa, Lu, and Roe (2010) found that V4 is involved in processing both colour and orientation, but that these two functions were each related to different regions within V4. Conway, Moeller, and Tsao (2007) used single-cell recording techniques in macaques and found neurons in area V4 that were selectively sensitive to colour. These neurons were found in specific colour-sensitive clusters, the size of a few millimetres in diameter, which the authors described as **globs**. Cells within a glob were sensitive to colour and to some extent also to shape, but not to luminance. Interestingly, however, the cells located between globs were not selectively sensitive to colour. Roe et al. (2012) argue, therefore, that V4 is not a colour centre of the brain, but rather that is should be considered to be a central hub within the visual system which regulates the coordination of various perceptual processes, and also plays an important role in the regulation of visual attention (see Section 6.11).

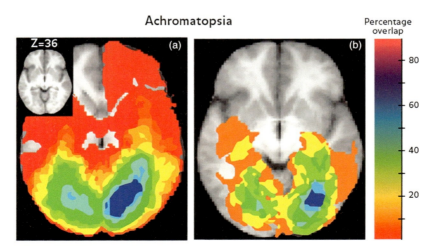

Figure 6.8 (a) Overlap of all lesions found in achromatopsia patients. (b) Overview of lesions specific to achromatopsia. (source: Bouvier and Engel, 2006)

6.6.3 MOTION PROCESSING

Motion is predominantly processed in V5, an area that is also known as the middle-temporal gyrus (MT). McKeefry et al. (1997) found that activation in this area increased as a result of perceiving moving stimuli. Moreover, Salzman, Britten, and Newsome (1990) used a technique known as **microstimulation**, using a microelectrode to electrically stimulate specific areas in the cortex. Here they found that this affected rhesus monkeys' ability to detect motion.

Beckers and Zeki (1995) showed that short **transcranial magnetic stimulation (TMS)** pulses directed at visual areas V1 and V5 could temporarily deactivate these areas (see fig 6.9). Deactivation of area V5 resulted in a sharp

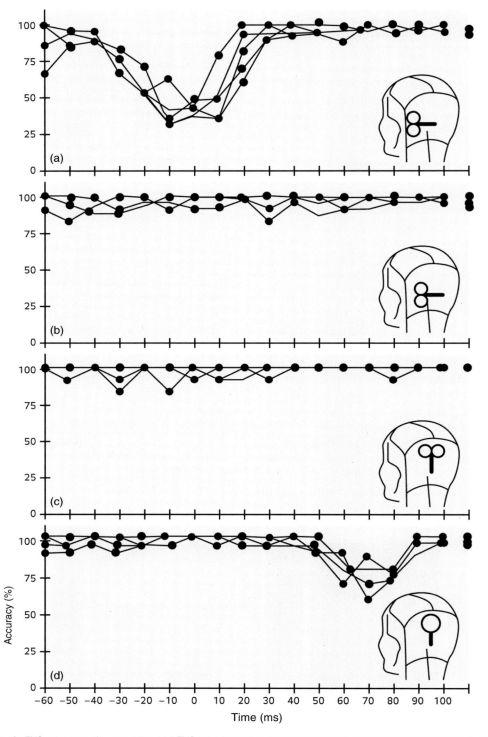

Figure 6.9 The effects of a TMS pulse on motion perception. (a) A TMS pulse focused on area V5 impaired the ability to detect the direction of a moving stimulus. (b) Stimulation of an area outside V5 had no effect on motion detection. (c) A control condition without TMS stimulation. (d) Stimulation of V1 had a small effect on the ability to detect motion. (source: Beckers & Zeki, 1995)

decrease in the ability to perceive motion. When V1 was targeted, a similar small reduction in participants' ability to perceive motion was found. The same pulse, however, had no effect on the participants' ability to discriminate fine letters. From the latter we can deduce that the TMS pulse had no effect on visual perception per se, but that it specifically affected the ability to detect motion. Similar results were found by McKeefry, Burton, Vakrou, Barrett, and Morland (2008), who showed that stimulation of V5 by a TMS pulse resulted in a reduced ability to detect differences in the speed of moving stimuli.

Further evidence for the involvement of V5 in motion perception comes from **Akinetopsia** patients. Zihl, Von Cramon, and Mai (1983) reported the case of LM, a 43-year-old female patient who was admitted to the hospital in 1978 following a cerebral haemorrhage. The haemorrhage resulted in lesions, including in the mid-temporal gyrus. Although LM performed normally on most neuropsychological tests, she had a deficiency perceiving motion.

These results demonstrate a strong involvement of V5 in motion perception. Note, however, that V5 is not the only brain area involved in the processing of motion information. Patients with damage to the medial superior temporal cortex (area: MST) are also frequently characterised by severe deficits in their ability to perceive motion. Typically, these patients have difficulties with avoiding moving objects and persons crossing their paths. For this reason, MST is believed to play an important role in the integration of perception and action (Vaina, 1998). We will explore this aspect of motion perception further in Chapter 10.

Using MEG, Anderson, Holliday, Singh, and Harding (1996) showed that area V5 is not only involved in the detection of motion but also to some extent in the processing of contrast and spatial frequencies. Moreover, in humans it appears to be the case that areas in V3A and the intraparietal sulcus are more sensitive to motion than areas in V5 (Orban et al., 2003). Based on these results, it appears that although V5 is highly involved in the processing of movement information, area V5 is by no means the motion processing centre of the brain, again undercutting the idea of full-blown functional specialisation in the visual system.

6.6.4 THE BINDING PROBLEM

The notion that the visual system consists of specialised regions for colour, shape, and movement processing that forms the basis for Zeki's (2001) functional specialisation theory is inconsistent with our everyday visual experience, which is characterised by unity and consistency. Functional specialisation, in contrast, should be expected to produce an incoherent patchwork of visual impressions. The implication of this inconsistency is that the specialised modules somehow all contribute to this experience and that the results of the higher-order visual processes are reassembled into a coherent perceptual stream. From a traditional bottom-up perspective, the aggregation of the results of the different modules is problematic, because there appears to be no mechanism that could combine the output of the different modules (see fig 6.10). For this reason, the mystery of how these separate sources of information are bound together is known as the **binding problem** (Singer & Gray, 1995; Treisman, 1996).

The binding problem can possibly be solved when we assume that cortical specialisation is much less strict than Zeki originally assumed. It follows from the previous description that V4 is not the colour centre of the brain and that several areas contribute to colour perception. It is also true for motion perception that, although specialisation

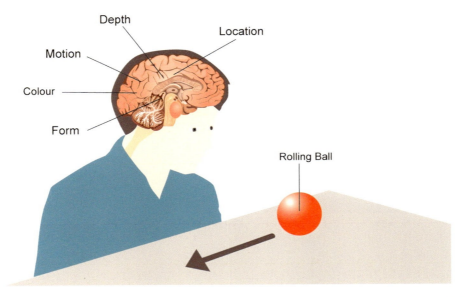

Figure 6.10 Illustration of the binding problem: when we perceive a rolling ball on a board, the result is a coherent percept, despite the fact that depth, motion, shape, colour, and location cues selectively activate specific brain areas.

is stronger here, it involves several areas. In a literature review, Kourtzi, Krekelberg, and van Wezel (2008) discussed various studies indicating that the brain areas discussed earlier contribute actively to the integration of shape, colour, and motion information. These authors assume that the integration takes place at various levels in the cortex, and that recurrent processing, that is, the feedback from the higher to the lower brain areas, plays a crucial role in binding the individual features together.

The integration of the individual stimulus properties is often accompanied by an increase in high-frequency oscillations in the cortex, which can be measured using EEG (Tallon-Baudry & Bertrand, 1999). According to the **synchronisation hypothesis**, the perception of an object results in a large-scale activation of the visual cortex and a high level of synchronisation across the different visual areas. This increase in synchronisation is related to awareness of the object as a whole (Melloni et al., 2007; Rodriguez et al., 1999), and it is assumed to be related to the binding of the individual properties of this object (see fig 6.11; see also Chapter 4).

Synchronisation can also be observed when separate elements are presented, which, when combined, may form an **illusory figure** (Senkowski, Röttger, Grimm, Foxe, & Herrmann, 2005). It is important to emphasise here that the idea of neural synchronicity is in itself too simplistic to fully explain the binding problem. The processing of a visual stimulus involves a large number of stages across many brain areas. This makes it implausible that an extremely high degree of synchronicity can be achieved. In addition, the visual system must be able to distinguish between multiple objects that are presented simultaneously. Therefore, Guttman, Gilroy, and Blake (2007) suggest that it is not so much the precise synchronicity that is important, but rather that different objects are characterised by different patterns of neural activity, with each object being characterised by a unique pattern of activation.

Finally, it is important to realise that the binding problem is only a problem when we limit ourselves to explaining visual processing from a strictly bottom-up perspective. Viewed from a predictive coding perspective, our conscious perception arises from the predictions that are generated by an internal model (Friston, 2010). According to this perspective, the processing of individual stimulus properties therefore merely involves resolving the

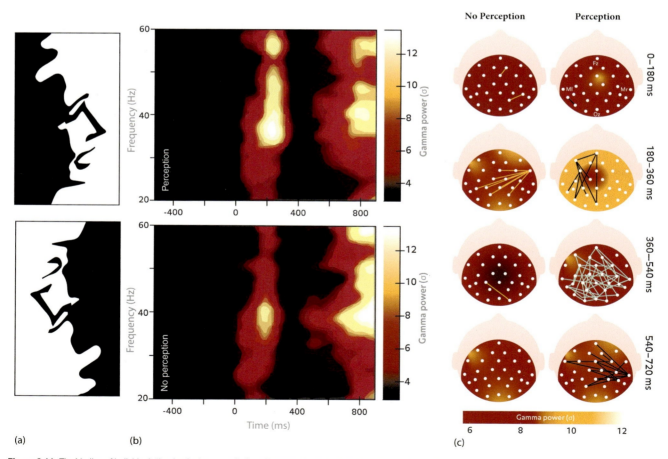

(a) (b) (c)

Figure 6.11 The binding of individual stimulus features results in an increase in synchronisation between different cortical areas. (a) Line drawings could be interpreted either as a face (top) or as a meaningless collection of lines (bottom). (b) The emergence of a percept results in an increase in oscillations in the frequency band between approximately 6 and 20 Hz, around 200 ms after stimulus presentation. (c) This increase is furthermore characterised by an overall increase in cortical synchronisation in the gamma band (40-80 Hz). Lines connecting electrode pairs indicate that there was a significant degree of synchronous activity between these pairs. (source: Melloni et al., 2007)

prediction error that arises when a prediction that is fed back from the higher-order representations to the lower-order areas, via recurrent connections, turns out to be incorrect. Interpreted this way, Hohwy (2007) argues that the binding problem does not need to be solved, because the problem spontaneously dissolves itself.

6.7 FURTHER PROCESSING: TWO VISUAL SYSTEMS

6.7.1 TWO SYSTEMS

What is the main function of visual perception? The most intuitive answer to this question will probably be that it enables us to generate a conscious representation of our environment. From an evolutionary perspective, however, we may identify a much more important function of vision, namely the fact that it enables us to respond appropriately to changes in our environment (see also Chapter 3 for a similar argument about the brain itself). David Milner and Melvyn Goodale (see fig 6.12) argue that there are two distinct visual systems, each of which performs its own task, namely a vision-for-perception system and a vision-for-action system (see for example: Goodale & Milner, 1992; Milner & Goodale, 2008). The idea that we have two separate visual systems is, among other things, based on the previously discussed distinction between the magnocellular and parvocellular pathways, and on the

Figure 6.12 British neuroscientists David Milner (a) and Melvyn A. Goodale (b).

functional specialisation of the ventral and dorsal pathways (Mishkin, Ungerleider, & Macko, 1983).

The idea of a dichotomy between two visual systems has its roots in the late 1960s when it was discovered that the superior colliculus and other subcortical areas are involved in the processing of visual information (Schneider, 1967). According to Schneider, these subcortical pathways would enable animals to localise objects, whereas the evolutionarily newer cortical pathways would be mainly involved in identifying these objects. This idea was further developed by Ungerleider and Mishkin (1981) with the identification of the dorsal and ventral pathways in the brain. Ungerleider and Mishkin thus related the distinction between a visual system for object recognition and location processing to the two separate cortical pathways, establishing the current characterisation of the ventral and dorsal pathways as a 'what' and a 'where' system, respectively.

6.7.2 DORSAL: VISION FOR ACTION

Although at present there is little discussion about the existence of the ventral and dorsal pathways, during the early 1990s, Goodale and Milner began to doubt whether the two pathways really represented object and location processing, as was previously assumed. The reason for their doubt was based on two observations. The first of these came from the study of a patient, DF, with severe **visual agnosia** (that is, the inability to recognise objects), due to carbon monoxide poisoning. Milner et al.'s (1991) main interest, however, was not so much focused on DF's deficiencies but on what she still could do. Although she performed very poorly on object recognition tasks, she was still able to manipulate the objects that were shown to her without any difficulties.

The second observation was made by a group of Japanese researchers, led by Hideo Sakata. These researchers built on the work of American physiologist Vernon Mountcastle and colleagues. Mountcastle, Lynch, Georgopoulos, Sakata, and Acuna (1975) had already discovered a number of different classes of neurons in a brain area that would later be identified as the dorsal stream. A specific subclass of the neurons they had found did not fit the classical idea that the dorsal stream was mainly involved in the processing of locations. Interestingly, work by Taira, Mine, Georgopoulos, Murata, and Sakata (1990) had shown that these neurons were in fact associated with the encoding of the shape of objects. These neurons were, however, not so much involved in the recognition of objects, but rather in the visual guidance of hand movements. In particular, they appeared to be involved in the matching of hand movement patterns to the shapes of the objects in question. Thus, the dorsal stream appears to be not so much involved in the processing of spatial locations, but rather in determining how these spatial positions and shapes of an object are used while interacting with them. Details of this aspect of the dorsal stream are discussed in more detail in Chapter 10.

6.7.3 VENTRAL: VISION FOR PERCEPTION

The distinction between the dorsal vision-for-action system and the ventral vision-for-perception system is further supported by observations in patients with **optic ataxia**. Optic ataxia (also known as Bálint's syndrome, in honour of its discoverer, the Hungarian neurologist Rudolf Bálint) is a syndrome that is characterised by patients' difficulties in pointing to or grasping objects and by damage to the parietal cortex.

Thus, while damage to the ventral pathway results in a specific inability to recognise objects, damage to the dorsal pathway results in a specific inability to manipulate them (Goodale & Milner, 1992). Goodale and Milner (2006) suggest that the ventral vision-for-perception system is primarily involved in generating abstract representations of our environment. These representations are not only immediately accessible but may also be used on future occasions. According to Goodale and Milner, the ventral system allows us to generate mental representations that allow us to think about the world and recognise and interpret future input. In contrast, Goodale and Milner argue that the dorsal vision-for-action system operates entirely in real time, instantaneously controlling the actions we perform. Therefore, this system allows us to move through the world with fluid and effective movements. Its instantaneity, however, prevents us from being aware of it.

6.7.4 TWO SYSTEMS: IN CONCLUSION

Although the distinction between a vision-for-action system and a vision-for-perception system has been very influential, offering a good explanation for many perceptual processes, we may take a moment to consider whether such a distinction is really necessary. Firstly, recent research has suggested that two visual systems may not be sufficient to explain the full complexity of the visual system, with the result that models with three or even four or five different functional systems have been proposed to explain a variety of functions, such as visually guided reaching or grasping, awareness of self-initiated actions, or processing of time-related information (Battelli, Walsh, Pascual-Leone, & Cavanagh, 2008; Grol et al., 2007; Jackson et al., 2009; Kravitz, Saleem, Baker, & Mishkin, 2011; Sincich, Park, Wohlgemuth, & Horton, 2004). In addition, it is difficult to explain how two independently developed systems can interact with each other.

De Haan and Cowey (2011) therefore argue that there is not so much a clear distinction between a ventral vision-for-perception system and a dorsal vision-for-action system, but rather that the diversity of our visual skill set has developed more or less in parallel throughout the evolution of our species. According to this view, colour vision would have developed independently and more or less in parallel with object recognition, motion perception, and with our ability to use visual input to guide our actions. If this is the case, we should consider the visual system to be a patchwork of more or less overlapping and interacting visual systems rather than a clear separation between a vision-for-action and a vision-for-perception system. According to de Haan and Cowey (2011), such an approach is much more capable of explaining how the different visual systems interact than two separate systems that are assumed to have arisen independently of each other.

6.8 COLOUR PERCEPTION

What is the added value of perceiving colours? After all, we are perfectly capable of perceiving the world through grey tones, as is simply shown by one glance at a black and white photo. One evolutionary advantage of colour vision, however, is that certain objects can become more salient in comparison to the background, giving these objects a better chance of being noticed.

As already discussed in the introduction to this chapter, colour is primarily a property that the brain adds to our mental representation of the outside world. The perception of colour arises by combining the output of three different light receptors, each being selectively sensitive to a different part of the electromagnetic spectrum.

6.8.1 TRICHROMATIC COLOUR PERCEPTION

According to the trichromatic theory, colour perception arises because most stimuli activate two or more colour receptors. The colour we perceive would then be the result of the relative stimulation of each of these receptors. Many forms of colour blindness are consistent with this idea. One of the most common forms of colour blindness is **dichromacy**, in which case one type of colour receptor is missing.

The fact that we have three types of colour receptors is probably due to an evolutionary coincidence. The selective sensitivity of three different receptors probably represents a good compromise between efficiency and richness in visual representations. Other species are sometimes characterised by a larger or smaller number of colour receptors.

6.8.2 OPPONENT PROCESS THEORY

Although the trichromatic theory just described can explain some basic aspects of colour perception, it has difficulties explaining the existence of **negative afterimages**. For example, look at the black dot in Figure 6.13 for one minute and then immediately look at a white surface. What do you see now? If the image fades, you can try to hold it for a while by blinking.

In 19th century, the German physiologist Ewald Hering (1878) tried to explain these negative afterimages by supposing that three types of oppositional processes operate in our colour vision system. He proposed that the first opponent process produces green when stimulated in one way and red when stimulated in another way. Similarly, the second opponent process should result in the perception of blue or yellow and the third opponent process in the perception of white or black. According to Hering, an afterimage is created when exposure to a colour activates one specific component of the opponent process system, which inhibits the opposing component. When the stimulus is removed, this inhibition ceases and the hitherto inhibited component can be temporarily activated more strongly, resulting in a negative afterimage.

Physiological evidence for opponent processes has been found by, among others, De Valois and De Valois (1975), who discovered the existence of opponent cells in the geniculate nucleus of monkeys. These cells showed an increase in activation following stimulation with one specific wavelength of light, and a decrease in activation following stimulation at other wavelengths. For

example, for red-green cells this change took place half-way between the red and green parts of the spectrum and for blue-yellow cells between the blue and yellow parts of the spectrum. The opponent process theory also predicts that it will be impossible to see blue and yellow or red and green together. That is, colours such as reddish-green or bluish-yellow would be impossible to perceive. This has indeed been found in a study by Abramov and Gordon (1994), in which participants had to indicate what percentage of blue, green, red, or yellow they saw when they perceived specific colours.

6.8.3 DUAL PROCESS THEORY

Although the opponent process theory can successfully explain several crucial aspects of colour perception, the theory itself is difficult to reconcile with the trichromatic colour theory, which explains several other aspects of our colour perception, as discussed earlier. The trichromatic colour theory and the opponent process theory are therefore both only partially correct, but they can be easily reconciled in the dual process theory, which was developed (in 1957) by Leo Hurvich and Dorothea Jameson, during their work for the Eastman Kodak photographic laboratory. According to this dual process theory, signals coming from the three colour receptors are combined before being projected to the opponent cells (see fig 6.14). More specifically, the signals are combined in the following way: an achromatic channel combines the activity of the medium (green) and long (red) wavelength receptors. Then there is a blue-yellow channel, which contrasts the combination of the medium (green) and long (red) wavelength receptors with that of the short

Figure 6.13 Example of a negative colour stimulus. (source: Goldilock Project)

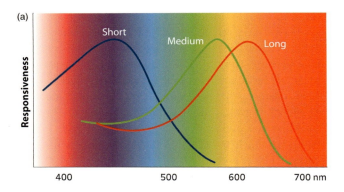

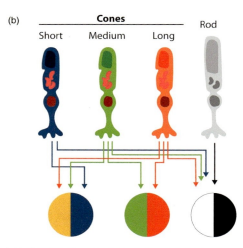

Figure 6.14 Overview of the early stages of colour coding. (a) The sensitivity to the three colour receptors as a function of the wavelength of light. (b) Three different combinations of these receptors result in the contrasts yellow-blue, green-red, and light-dark respectively.

(blue) wavelength receptors. Finally, there is a red-green channel, which contrasts the medium (green) and long (red) wavelengths.

The dual process theory is well able to combine the trichromatic and opponent colour theories. Moreover, it is consistent with neurophysiological data that have demonstrated the existence of horizontal cells, which combine the output of the individual receptors. Nevertheless, it is becoming increasingly clear that the theory is too simplistic in several respects (Solomon & Lennie, 2007). For example, there is considerable individual variation in the distribution of different colour receptors, but this appears to have a negligible influence on our ability to distinguish colours. In addition, the distribution of colour receptors across the retina is quite random (Roorda & Williams, 1999). This random distribution appears to be problematic, as it reduces the effectiveness of the opposing connections. One conclusion must therefore be that basic colour processing is much more complex than the theories that we previously discussed assume. Thus, there is currently a growing awareness that the visual cortical areas play a very important role in colour perception.

6.8.4 COLOUR CONSTANCY

One of the psychological aspects of colour perception that cannot be adequately explained by the theories described earlier is the phenomenon of **colour constancy**, that is, the phenomenon that objects appear to have a uniform colour, despite a particularly high degree of variation in lighting conditions. This phenomenon implies that a colour, as we perceive it, is not only dependent on the perceived light frequencies but also on how we interpret this colour. The latter suggests that we also consider the context in which a colour is perceived.

Colour constancy is important because it contributes to a stable representation of our environment. If we did not perceive colours as constant, the internal representation of an object could change dramatically under varying lighting conditions, which would impair our ability to recognise them.

Granzier, Brenner, and Smeets (2009) studied colour constancy under natural conditions. Here, participants were initially shown pieces of paper which all had similar uniform colours. After learning to name these colours, they had to recognise them in a wide variety of locations, both indoors and outdoors, which differed drastically in terms of the lighting conditions. The crucial finding of this study was that the participants were able to name 55% of the colours correctly. This result is remarkable, given the similarity of the colours and the huge variation of lighting conditions used in the experiment.

6.8.4.1 Retinex Theory

Edwin Land developed a theory, known as Retinex, which attempts to explain colour constancy via the interplay between retinal and cortical processes (Land, 1986; Land & McCann, 1971). According to Land, colour perception results from determining to which degree a surface can reflect light of different wavelengths and by comparing the outcome of this process to that of adjacent surfaces. In other words, the theory assumes that we make use of local colour contrasts. Foster and Nascimento (1994) found evidence for this idea. They noted that the ratio of excitability of the different colour receptors (cones) is an important factor in this process. We can best illustrate this principle of **cone-excitability ratios** by the following example. Suppose we have two different light sources and two different surfaces (each with a different colour). For the cones that are sensitive to long wavelengths (in other words, red), we can find the following result: if we find for the first surface that the first light source excites these cones three times more than the second light source does, then we will find exactly the same ratio for the second surface. In other words, the ratio of excitability of a specific colour receptor is not influenced by the light source, but by the illuminated surface, and this property can contribute to colour constancy. Although the cone-excitability ratio

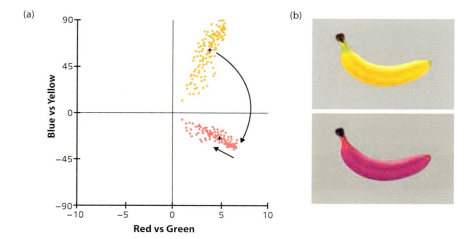

Figure 6.15 Colour adjustments of different types of fruit. (a) Participants had to adjust the colours of familiar fruits by adjusting the proportions of the red vs. green and the blue vs. yellow contrasts in such a way that the colour became a neutral grey. (b) Familiarity with a specific fruit colour often resulted in an overcorrection. (source: Hansen et al., 2006)

can explain elementary colour constancy to some extent, it is still limited in explaining colour constancy in complex visual scenes. For this reason, Brainard and Maloney (2011) proposed an **equivalent illumination model**. According to this model, colour detection involves two stages. The first stage consists of determining the cone-excitation ratios, as just described. This stage provides a general impression of the colour of each surface. The second stage then consists of comparing the actual colour signal to the perceived colour signal on the basis of Bayesian inference principles (Brainard et al., 2006). The result of this comparison is the perceived colour.

These results are consistent with some of Zeki's (1983) earlier findings showing that neurons in area V4 are selectively responsive to the colour of a surface but not to the colour of the light source. Neurons that responded to red surfaces, under a red light, no longer responded when the red surface was replaced by a green, blue, or white surface, even when the dominant colour of the light reflected from the surface was still red.

A second important factor contributing to colour constancy is the global colour contrasts. Global colour contrast compares the colour response of a specific surface with the colour response of the entire visual scene, in a way similar to how a modern digital camera determines the white balance of a scene. A final important factor contributing to colour constancy involves reflected highlights from shiny surfaces. When this information is removed from a scene, the colour constancy drops significantly.

6.8.4.2 Familiarity and Expectation

The theoretical models described up to this point are largely bottom-up driven. Note, though, that top-down processes also play a crucial role in colour constancy. For example, based on prior experience, we know that bananas are yellow and oranges orange. To determine the effects of

familiarity, Hansen, Olkkonen, Walter, and Gegenfurtner (2006) showed photographs of various types of fruit, after which participants had to adjust the colour balance in such a way that they appeared to be grey (see fig 6.15). The result was that the participants overcompensated: when the banana was objectively grey, it still appeared yellow to the participants, so they gave it a light blue colour.

6.9 DEPTH PERCEPTION

One of the most striking capabilities of the visual system is its ability to form a three-dimensional representation of our environment. Our ability to estimate depth is obviously essential when interacting with our environment. Without it, we would have many difficulties grasping objects or navigating our environment. The question now is: how can we create a full-fledged three-dimensional representation from the two-dimensional images that are projected onto our retinas?

According to Ernst and Bülthoff (2004) such a representation arises from the combination of various visual and other cues. From a (Bayesian) predictive coding perspective, each cue can be regarded as an a posteriori estimator that can sharpen the internal a priori representation (see Appendix). Since each sensory cue is characterised by an intrinsic margin of error, the best estimate can be obtained by combining several cues. Yet, some cues may conflict with each other. For example, while watching a movie, both of our eyes perceive the same image, which results in a two-dimensional sensation, whereas other cues, such as perspective, illumination, or occlusion (the fact that some objects are covered by others), result in an impression of depth. One of the most important depth cues we encounter in everyday life is motion. Because motion perception is so crucial, and due to the role it plays in the coordination of our motor skills, motion perception will be discussed further in Chapter 10. Here, we will thus focus on the discussion of static cues and the role of these cues in depth perception. Depth cues can be subdivided into monocular, binocular, and oculomotor cues.

6.9.1 MONOCULAR CUES

Monocular cues require only one eye, although they can be processed with both eyes. These cues are effective because our environment, even when viewed with only one eye, still contains a certain amount of depth information. These cues are sometimes known as pictorial cues because painters and photographers use them with great effectiveness to create depth in a two-dimensional image. One of the cues that can be used for this purpose is linear perspective: parallel lines of objects that disappear into the distance seem to converge. This convergence creates a strong illusion of depth, but can also, when exaggerated, result in an unnatural image (see fig 6.16). This exaggerated perspective is common in photography when an extreme wide-angle lens is used, which increases the convergence of the lines. One of the masters in the use of linear perspective was the Dutch-Flemish painter Johannes Vredeman De Vries. Todorovic (2009) used his work to investigate under what circumstances linear perspective produces a natural image and when it appears exaggerated. One of the factors that plays an important role here is distance. When viewed up close, Vredeman De Vries's sketches result in a natural looking image, whereas when viewed from a distance they appear unnatural.

Texture is another important monocular cue. Most objects in our environment are characterised by surfaces with a certain pattern, such as the grain of a wooden table, a repeating pattern on a tiled floor, gravel paths, or grass fields. The perceived frequency of this texture is an important distance cue: the finer the pattern, the greater our distance from the object. In addition, objects that disappear into the distance, such as roads or lawns, are characterised by a texture gradient (Gibson, 1979). Sinai, Ooi, and He (1998) found that participants were very good at estimating distances when a surface had a uniform texture, but that they overestimated distances when the texture was interrupted.

Other monocular cues are formed by shadows and interposition. Shadows imply the presence of three-dimensional objects. Interposition is the phenomenon that objects in the foreground partially cover objects that are further away from the observer. Moreover, when we know the size of a given object, we can use this information to estimate the distance to this object. The fact that we can be easily misled by this, however, was demonstrated in an intriguing study from the early 1950s. Ittelson (1951) allowed participants to observe playing cards through a

Figure 6.16 An example of the exaggerated perspective of a wide-angle lens. (source: Goldilock Project)

peephole that limited their vision to just one eye. Playing cards of different sizes were all displayed at a distance of 2.28 metres, but the perceived distance was greatly influenced by the actual size of the card. Cards that were twice as large were estimated to be much closer, while cards that were only half as large were estimated to be about twice as far away. Finally, a final strictly monocular depth cue is formed by the motion parallax. Objects that are close to an observer appear to move faster than objects that are further away. Rogers and Graham (1979) found that this motion parallax, even when it was the only cue, could result in adequate distance estimates.

6.9.2 BINOCULAR CUES

Binocular cues take advantage of the fact the each of our two eyes perceives the world from a slightly different perspective. Probably the best-known binocular cue is **binocular disparity**; this is the phenomenon that an object is perceived by each eye from a different position. The closer the object is to the observer, the greater the disparity. Held, Cooper, and Banks (2012) found that binocular disparity and blur both contribute to depth perception (see fig 6.17).

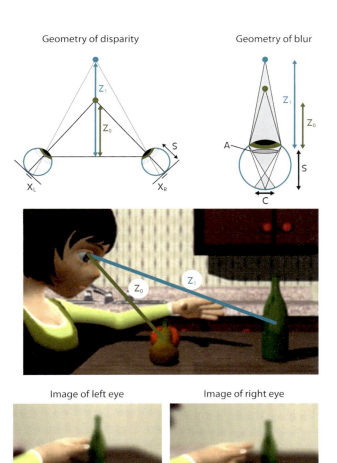

Figure 6.17 The relationship between binocular disparity and blur. (source: Held et al., 2012)

Objects that are located in front of or behind the fixation point are blurred and this blur can also be used as a distance cue. Binocular disparity is particularly effective near the fixation point, while blur is particularly effective as a depth cue for objects that are further from the fixation point.

Binocular disparity results in the phenomenon of **stereopsis**. Stereopsis is particularly effective for objects that are close to the observer. Since the discrepancy between the eyes decreases rapidly as objects get further away, stereopsis also quickly becomes ineffective as a depth cue for objects located at a greater distance.

6.9.3 OCULOMOTOR CUES

Finally, oculomotor cues are formed by accommodation of the eye lens and by vergence. Vergence describes the phenomenon of the two eyeballs turning towards each other when observing objects that are close to the observer. Depth cues that are based on accommodation are formed as the eye lens bulges when we fixate on nearby objects. However, the effectiveness of divergence and accommodation is limited because we can only fixate on one object, so these cues are necessarily limited to one object.

6.10 OBJECT AND FACE RECOGNITION

The higher-order visual brain regions along the ventral pathway are involved in object and face recognition. Do object and face recognition processes involve the same visual process or can they be dissociated from each other? Most evidence today suggests the latter. For instance, research involving neuropsychological patients has revealed a dissociation between face and object recognition processes. More specifically, object recognition is mainly associated with the anterior inferior temporal cortex, whereas face recognition is mainly associated with the **fusiform face area** and a host of other face-specific brain areas.

Every day we effortlessly recognise thousands of objects. Because we do this seemingly instantly, we greatly underestimate the complexity of this process. The complexity only became clear when computer scientists started developing software for object recognition. Even the most advanced robotic computer systems that are equipped with artificial vision can only do a fraction of what the human mind can do without any effort. To get an appreciation of the complexity of this process, try making a list of all the problems we have to overcome while recognising an object.

To illustrate, suppose you need to identify an everyday object, such as a corkscrew. This object is three-dimensional, and we can observe it from every possible angle. So, we need to be able to recognise a three-dimensional representation based on an infinite number of different possible viewing angles. In addition, the corkscrew may be in a kitchen cupboard, surrounded by, and partly hidden behind, other objects. Yet in everyday life, we are hardly affected by these obstacles and almost always recognise the object instantly. The size and specific design also play a role. We can perceive the corkscrew at different distances, which effectively means that the size of the projection of the object on the retina can vary enormously. This variation will almost never affect our estimate of an object's size when we perceive it. Finally, we may be dealing with a designer corkscrew, which differs greatly in shape from the basic models. In this case, too, we almost never have any difficulty in recognising the object.

6.10.1 PATTERN RECOGNITION

Before we take up the challenge of investigating how we can recognise three-dimensional objects, we should start by considering a somewhat simpler problem, in which humans are also many times more efficient than computers, namely recognising two-dimensional patterns. Pattern recognition is a skill that we also use many thousands of times a day. When we read, for example, we are converting line patterns into letters and words. Although this task is relatively simple when we read printed text, we only begin to appreciate the complexity of our pattern recognition process when we are confronted with the billions of different handwritings in the world, all of which we can decipher with more or less effort.

6.10.1.1 Global and Local Processing

Several researchers have observed that for objects and patterns alike, we typically first recognise their coarse essence and only then the finer detail (Hegdé, 2008; Navon, 1977; Thorpe et al., 1996). For example, Thorpe et al. presented two photos of natural scenes and instructed their participants to move their eyes as quickly as possible towards the photo that contained an animal. It turned out that the participants were already able to make this eye movement within 150 ms, which implies that the essence of those photos was already detected within that short time span.

Navon (1977) drew a similar conclusion based on a series of experiments in which participants were required to make decisions about letters. The stimuli used by Navon consisted of large letters that were composed of smaller ones (see fig 6.18), such as a large letter H that was composed of small letters S. Navon's participants had to respond to either the large 'global' letter or the small 'local' letters. There were two types of stimuli in the experiment: congruent ones, where the large letter and the small letters matched (e.g., a global H composed of local H's) or incongruent ones (e.g., a global H composed of local S's). When participants had to respond to the local letters, their response time was significantly increased

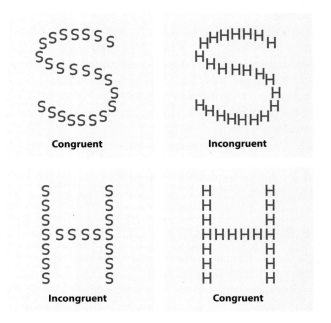

Figure 6.18 An example of the type of stimuli used by Navon (1977).

when the large letter was incongruent, compared to when it was congruent. When they had to respond to the global letter, however, there was no influence of the local letters, suggesting that the global letter interfered with the local letters, but not the other way around.

6.10.1.2 Spatial Frequencies

How does the coarse-to-fine processing of visual information proceed? Interestingly, some of the primary visual cortex neurons turn out to be selectively sensitive to a specific **spatial frequency**. Low spatial frequencies represent coarse information, such as light or dark surfaces, whereas high spatial frequencies primarily represent details, such as edges and contours (see fig 6.19).

Low spatial frequencies are assumed to be projected rapidly to higher-order cortical areas via the magnocellular pathway, whereas high spatial frequencies are projected in a slower fashion by the parvocellular pathway. Musel et al. (2014) found evidence for the idea that these spatial frequencies play a role in recognising visual scenes. In this study, participants were shown images consisting of a sequence of different spatial frequencies displayed in rapid succession for 150 ms. This sequence could either go from coarse to fine or from fine to coarse. In the coarse-to-fine sequence, participants were able to decide more quickly whether a scene involved an interior or an exterior compared to the fine-to-coarse sequence. Flevaris, Martinez, and Hillyard (2014) used the Navon task to find that this preference for coarse to fine processing is relative and task-dependent. In their study, the neural response to local letters was greater than the one to global letters when participants had to identify the local letters.

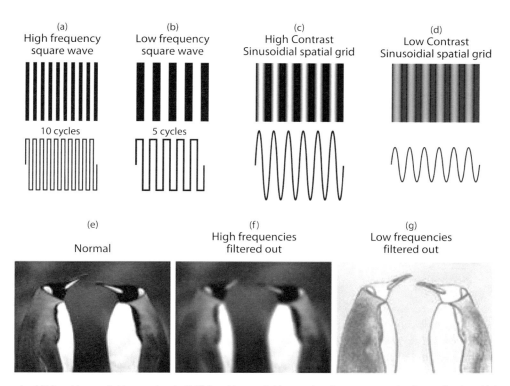

Figure 6.19 An example of high and low spatial frequencies. (a–b) High and low spatial frequencies of square waves; (c–d) same for sinusoidal waves; (e) a normal, unprocessed photograph; (f) the same picture represented in just the low spatial frequencies; (g) the same image, but now in just the high spatial frequencies.

6.10.2 PERCEPTUAL ORGANISATION

6.10.2.1 Gestalt Principles

The next question is how we segment a visual scene into individual objects. One of the first attempts to describe this process came from the German gestalt psychologists at the beginning of the 20th century. This group of psychologists, whose famous pioneers included Kurt Koffka, Wolfgang Köhler, and Max Wertheimer, formulated a fundamental principle known as the **Law of Prägnanz**. This law states that what we observe is generally the simplest of all possible configurations. Specific examples of this law are formed by the principle of proximity, which describes how visual elements that are close to each other tend to be grouped together; the law of similarity, which describes how similar elements are grouped together; and the law of good continuity (see fig 6.20).

6.10.2.2 Figure-background Segregation

Although the gestalt laws are relatively simple, and deal with relatively simple line elements, the principles are found in many everyday visual scenes and play an important role

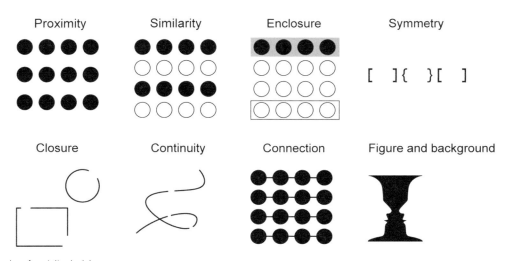

Figure 6.20 Examples of gestalt principles.

in the way we recognise objects in everyday life (Wagemans et al., 2012). In addition to these descriptive laws, gestalt psychologists have also attached great importance to figure-background segregation. Part of the visual field is recognised as the figure and the rest is background. Various factors determine what is perceived as the figure and what as the background. Relatively small convex surfaces, however, are often identified as figures (Wagemans et al., 2012).

The gestalt psychologists assumed that the figure is rapidly segregated from the background, which would imply that this process would not be influenced by attention. Although it has been shown that the figure-background segregation can indeed take place without attention when the figures are relatively simple (Kimchi & Peterson, 2008), Vecera, Flevaris, and Filapek (2004) have shown that attention can play a role in figure-background segregation. These authors presented two separate visual regions, each of which could be interpreted either as a figure or as background. When a cue had directed attention to one of the two regions, that region was interpreted as a figure and the other region as background.

Gestalt psychologists also assumed that the figure-background processes are innate and thus not dependent on previous experience or learning. This assumption also turns out to be incorrect. Barense, Ngo, Hung, and Peterson (2012) tested amnesia patients (see Chapter 13) and neurotypical control participants using a task in which they had to identify a figure on the basis of known and unknown patterns. The control participants performed better on this task when familiar patterns were shown, while the amnesia patients' performance did not differ between the two types of patterns. This result implies that figure-background segregation is not just based on basic perceptual principles, but that prior experience does play a role.

6.10.2.3 Perceptual Organisation in Natural Scenes

The gestalt principles are based on relatively simple and abstract visual elements. Geisler, Perry, Super, and Gallogly (2001) investigated whether these principles also apply to natural images. They used photographs of flowers, rivers, trees, and so on to determine how participants identified these objects. Two additional principles were identified that had not been formulated by the gestalt psychologists: (1) adjacent segments of a contour tend to have similar orientations; (2) segments further apart tend to have widely different orientations.

Palmer and Rock (1994) also identified an additional grouping principle, not yet described by gestalt psychologists, which they labelled **uniform connectedness**. This principle describes how each connected region with uniform visual properties (such as colour, texture, or brightness) is perceived as a single perceptual unit. Palmer and

Rock found that this principle played a more prominent role than the gestalt principles in processing natural scenes, especially when different gestalt laws conflicted.

6.10.3 OBJECT RECOGNITION

The next question is how we can generate a mental representation of our environment on the basis of visual information. One of the conditions for the successful creation of such a representation is that we are able to process objects in a meaningful way, such that we are able to recognise them.

6.10.3.1 Computer Vision

One of the most influential theories on object recognition from the early 1980s was formulated by the British neuroscientist David Marr (1982), who passed away prematurely in 1980. Marr's most influential work, 'Vision: A Computational Investigation Into the Human Representation and Processing of Visual Information', was published posthumously in 1982. Marr identified three stages at which visual information can be represented. He described the first stage as the primary sketch. According to Marr, this stage represents a two-dimensional description of the scene. Here, information about the position of light sources is represented, as well as information about edges, contours, and global shapes. Marr considered this representation to be viewpoint dependent.

Marr described the second stage as the 2.5D-sketch. Here, according to Marr, depth information is added to the sketch. This would be done by analysing information about lighting (position of light and shadows), texture, movement, and binocular disparity. This representation was not yet fully three-dimensional but did contain the necessary cues to generate a three-dimensional representation. Like the primary sketch, this 2.5D-sketch was assumed to be viewpoint dependent.

Finally, the third stage was supposed to consist of a full 3D representation. At this stage, the complete three-dimensional forms of objects were fully described, as well as the mutual positions of the individual objects. According to Marr, this representation was independent of the observer's viewing point.

6.10.3.2 Recognition by Components

Although Marr described a model that could possibly explain how a three-dimensional representation could be formed from two-dimensional information, he was unable to describe how that representation was created, due to his unexpected passing in November 1980. His work has inspired several researchers to continue the development of object recognition theories, however.

One of these researchers is the American vision scientists Irving Biederman. According to his recognition-by-components theory (Biederman, 1987) objects can be recognised because they are composed of basic geometric shapes that Biederman identified as **geons** (geometric icons). Biederman estimated that there are about 36 such geons, including blocks, cylinders, and spheres. Because we can combine these geons in so many different ways, we can, according to Biederman, identify an almost infinite number of forms from a relatively small number of geons, just like we can represent an infinite number of words from a limited number of letters.

According to Biederman, object recognition takes place in a number of discrete stages. First, the edges of objects are identified in the two-dimensional representation. After that, it is determined how the visual objects should be segmented in order to determine the surfaces of an object. Two different processes are believed to play an important role here. The first is to determine concave parts of a surface; the second process is to identify its edges. The information gathered can then be used to determine how a geon corresponds to these properties. For example, a cylinder consists of curved edges with two parallel lines connecting these edges.

An important property of a mental representation of an object is that it is ultimately viewpoint-independent. Biederman and Gerhardstein (1993) found evidence for this assumption. In their study, participants were shown images of pairs of objects (e.g., of a desk lamp and a torch). At a later stage, they were again shown pairs of images and had to decide whether the combination of objects had been presented before. The crucial manipulation in this study was that sometimes images were used in which one of the objects had been replaced by another of the same category (e.g., a round desk lamp by a rectangular one), while in other trials the same objects were used, but from a different viewing angle. Participants were efficiently able to recognise the previously shown combinations of objects, regardless of the viewing angle.

One limitation of this study is that Biederman and Gerhardstein used images of familiar objects. In contrast, Tarr and Bülthoff (1995) used novel objects that participants had not been exposed to before. Now, object recognition was found to be viewpoint dependent, indicating that prior experience is an important factor for determining whether object recognition is viewpoint dependent or not. Vanrie, Béatse, Wagemans, Sunaert, and Van Hecke (2002) also found that viewpoint independence is not universal. In their study, participants were shown two objects that were rotated relative to each other. Here, the participant's task was to indicate whether the two objects were identical or not. There were two different dimensions on which the two figures could differ (see fig 6.21). In the invariant condition, one of the bars on the figure was slightly bent relative to the reference object; whereas in the rotation condition, one of the bars was rotated 90 degrees along the axis about which the figure itself was

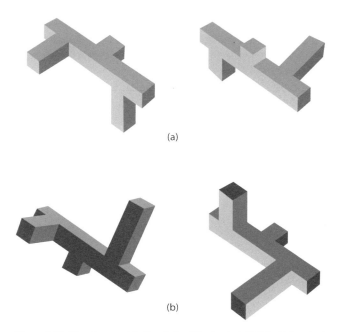

(a)

(b)

Figure 6.21 Stimuli as used in the study of Vanrie et al. (2002): (a) invariant condition, (b) rotation condition.

rotated. Participants were considerably slower in the rotation condition than in the invariant condition, suggesting that viewpoint dependency can be selective.

6.10.3.3 Recognition by Top-down Prediction

An important limitation of Biederman's recognition-by-components theory is that it is primarily bottom-up driven and that it is therefore limited in explaining the effects of experience and context discussed earlier. For this reason, more recent theoretical developments aim to account for the influences of top-down processes in object recognition. Bar et al. (2006) have proposed an adapted version of Biederman's theory, in which a distinction is made between detailed bottom-up processing of visual input and a more generic top-down influence. According to Bar et al., detailed information is represented in the high spatial frequencies. This information is largely processed in a bottom-up manner, involving the ventral pathway of the visual system. At the same time, however, information from the low spatial frequencies is projected via the dorsal magnocellular pathway to the orbitofrontal cortex. Here, the information contained within the signal will activate a large number of candidate objects, which roughly correspond in shape to the objects present in the scene. Simultaneously, the low-frequency information will activate the possible context in which these objects are perceived. Based on this combined activation, an expectation is created which, on the basis of top-down feedback, via recurrent neural connections, adjusts and limits the possible interpretation of the detailed information at the lower cortical levels. According to this interpretation, prediction is therefore also an important aspect of object recognition (Spratling, 2017).

One of the consequences of top-down influences in object recognition is that expectation is important for object recognition. Evidence for this assumption has been provided by several studies. For instance, Goolkasian and Woodberry (2010) used ambiguous figures, that could either portray an Inuit or a Native American (dubbed the 'Eskimo/Indian' illusion by Goolkasian and Woodberry) or the word liar or a face of a person wearing sunglasses (dubbed 'liar/face' illusion) (see fig 6.22). When they primed participants with concepts related to Inuits, such as pictures of snow, participants were more likely to see the Inuit. In contrast, when a tomahawk was used as a prime, participants were more likely to recognise the picture as a Native American. The same applied to the liar/face illusion. Here, the use of written words resulted mainly in the recognition of the written word 'liar', whereas the presentation of faces resulted mainly in the recognition of the face.

Lupyan and Ward (2013) also manipulated participants' expectation while they had to try to recognise stimuli that were made invisible using the **continuous flash suppression** method. Here, either a circle, a square, or a figure that was an intermediate between the two, was presented. Participants' task was to indicate which figure was shown. Prior to the presentation of the object, a cue was given that was either valid, invalid, or not informative about the object the participants were seeing. These cues effectively increased the participants' sensitivity and consequently their accuracy.

Eskimo/Indian

"Liar"/Face

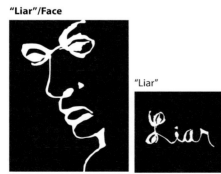

Figure 6.22 The 'Eskimo/Indian' and 'liar/face' illusions. (source: Goolkasian & Woodberry, 2010)

6.10.3.4 Object Representation in the Visual System

The inferior temporal cortex is believed to play an important role in representing objects (Leopold & Logothetis, 1999). This brain area is part of the ventral pathway and receives input from both the magnocellular and parvocellular pathways. How are objects represented here? After all, we can perceive objects under a wide variety of viewpoints, illuminations, orientations, and sizes. The question, in other words, is how objects can be represented under these variable viewing conditions.

Two important principles are involved in this: selectivity and tolerance (Ison & Quiroga, 2008). Neurons that respond very strongly to a specific object, but hardly at all to other objects, are known as strongly selective. Likewise, neurons that always respond to an object, regardless of lighting, orientation, or size, have a very high tolerance. If neurons in the inferior temporal cortex were characterised by a high degree of tolerance, this would be consistent with the idea that object recognition is viewpoint independent. Note, however, that we have to be careful with this conclusion, because the occurrence of high-tolerance neurons could also be explained by the idea that these neurons receive input from a very large number of viewpoint-dependent neurons, that is, from low-tolerance neurons (Hayward, 2012).

The question is therefore whether neurons in the inferior temporal cortex can be characterised as high or low tolerant. To address this question, Logothetis, Pauls, and Poggio (1995) presented familiar objects to monkeys while recording the responses from neurons in this brain area. Most neurons were viewpoint dependent, that is, they were maximally responsive for one given viewpoint compared to any other viewpoint. Booth and Rolls (1998), however, found that some neurons were characterised by high tolerance and others with low tolerance. The monkeys involved in this study were initially allowed to play with some of the objects. Booth and Rolls then took pictures of these objects and presented them to the monkeys while measuring neuronal activity in the inferior temporal cortex. Here, they found that 49% of the neurons responded only to specific viewpoints and only 14% of the neurons responded viewpoint-independently.

Although these viewpoint-independent neurons are a minority, their role should not be underestimated. Booth and Rolls (1998) found that there was probably enough information in these viewpoint-independent neurons to differentiate between the objects that they had used in their study.

Zoccolan et al. (2007) studied the relationships between selectivity and tolerance and found a moderate negative correlation between selectivity and tolerance. This implies that some neurons respond to many different objects, regardless of orientation, viewpoint, size, or lighting. Other neurons respond very selectively to specific objects and under very specific conditions. Why is this correlation negative? Perhaps this is related to the enormous range of visual tasks we have to perform, which can vary from very precise fine-grained discriminations to very coarse categorisations. Different degrees of representation are therefore believed to be encoded by different neurons in the inferior temporal cortex.

These results imply that a small proportion of cells in the inferior temporal cortex is extremely selective to very specific concepts. Some theorists have taken this concept to extremes, suggesting that specialisation can be extended to one specific cell representing one concept. Consider a cell with such a high selectivity and tolerance that it only responds to, say, your grandmother. This cell would therefore represent the concept of 'grandmother'. Is it likely that such a grandmother cell actually exists? The answer is no. If that were the case, damage to this cell would immediately damage all representations related to your

grandmother. It is more likely that highly specific and tolerant cells are part of a network in which the concept of grandmother is represented, without the cell itself being crucial to this concept (Quiroga, Reddy, Kreiman, Koch, & Fried, 2005).

6.10.3.5 Object Recognition and Predictive Coding

The development of object recognition theories is indicative of the ever-growing realisation that top-down processing is of crucial importance in human cognition. While the original gestalt theories, as well as Marr and Biederman's ideas were still largely based on bottom-up processing, later theoretical approaches (Goolkasian & Woodberry, 2010; Lupyan & Ward, 2013; Spratling, 2017) increasingly recognise the importance of top-down processes in object recognition, as discussed earlier (see fig 6.23).

The question whether predictive coding is involved in object recognition was addressed by Summerfield et al. (2006). They presented pictures of different categories of

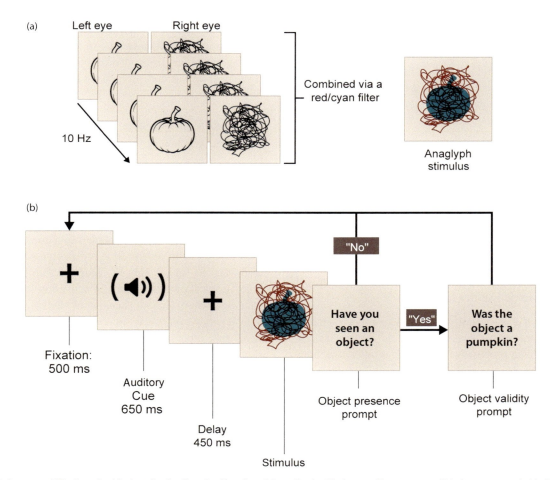

Figure 6.23 Lupyan and Ward's method for investigating the role of top-down information in object recognition processes. Objects were presented to the left eye and were masked by a continuously changing pattern of lines presented to the right eye. (a) Illustration of the procedure used to present the different stimuli to each eye; (b) the sequence of events within a trial. Prior to each visual stimulus, an auditory cue was presented that was either associated with this stimulus or not. This auditory cue influenced the recognition of the visual stimulus. (source: Lupyan and Ward, 2013)

objects, consisting of faces, houses, and cars. In one condition, participants were instructed to decide whether the object was a face or not and, in another condition, they were required to decide whether the object was a house or not. This manipulation induced a 'faces' prediction in one condition and a 'houses' prediction in the other condition. The stimuli were degraded, so that it was not immediately clear what kind of object was shown. Activation in the medial frontal cortex corresponded to the activation of the prediction that was generated while participants were deciding whether an object was a face or not. It was found that making this decision was associated with an increase in top-down connectivity from the frontal cortex to the face-specific areas in the visual cortex (the fusiform face area; see Section 6.10.4.2). This activation is consistent with the idea that there is a match between the predicted and observed evidence for the presence of faces.

6.10.4 FACE RECOGNITION

Recognising faces is one of the most important tasks performed by the visual system. Every day we easily recognise people on the basis of their faces. When we think of someone, we usually get an immediate mental image of their face and the features that make it unique to us. In this respect, faces play a much more important role than other physical characteristics of an individual. In fact, we are so accustomed to this that we even tend to recognise faces in all sorts of everyday objects. For this reason, face recognition is assumed to be a specialised form of object recognition, based on, at least in part, specialised modules.

6.10.4.1 Are Faces Special?

How does face recognition differ from regular object recognition? One important difference is that face recognition appears to be strongly rooted in holistic processing. The individual properties of faces are processed to a large degree in parallel. One of the consequences of this is that face recognition is fast; a familiar face can be recognised within half a second (Bruce & Young, 1986).

Evidence for the idea that, compared to other forms of object recognition, face recognition is more strongly based on holistic processes stems from studies that have examined the **face inversion effect** (Bruyer, 2011; McKone, Kanwisher, & Duchaine, 2007). This effect describes how faces that are presented upside down are much more difficult to recognise than faces presented in a regular orientation. For regular objects this effect is generally much smaller.

Further evidence that face recognition is a special form of visual processing comes from the **part-whole effect**. This effect describes the phenomenon that it is easier to

recognise a feature of a face when it is part of a face than when it is presented as a separate feature. For example, Richler, Cheung, and Gauthier (2011) used compound faces that that consisted of an upper and lower half that could or could not be from the same face. Participants had to judge whether the top halves of two consecutively presented faces were the same or not. Interestingly, they were less accurate when the lower halves of the faces were different, which implies that the participants were processing the faces as a whole and that they were not able to process only the upper parts.

6.10.4.2 The Fusiform Face Area

Several studies have found evidence for the existence of a specialised brain area involved in face recognition. This area, the fusiform face area, is located in the ventral temporal cortex. Several neuroimaging studies have found that this area is activated more strongly by faces than by other objects (Downing, Chan, Peelen, Dodds, & Kanwisher, 2006; Kanwisher et al., 1997). Gainotti and Marra (2011), however, found that in addition to the fusiform face area, other areas are involved in face processing, including an area in the occipital cortex (Atkinson & Adolphs, 2011). Gainotti and Marra argue, therefore, that face recognition is not performed by just one area, but by a network of different areas instead. Damage to these areas also often results in a neuropsychological impairment in face recognition, which we will discuss next.

6.10.4.3 Prosopagnosia

Some neuropsychological patients are selectively impaired in processing faces. Their condition is known as **prosopagnosia**. Prosopagnosia is a heterogeneous condition, in which the exact symptoms can vary from patient to patient. Although some prosopagnosia patients can still process facial information, this information might no longer reach their conscious awareness. This was shown by Simon et al. (2011), who reported the results of a prosopagnosia patient, PS, who was no longer able to recognise familiar faces. Yet brain scans showed evidence of activation in the fusiform face area when familiar faces were shown. This was not the case, however, for unfamiliar faces. These results thus imply that processing of familiar faces is still taking place subconsciously, but that this information no longer reaches consciousness.

Could it be that prosopagnosia results from a deficiency in distinguishing fine nuances? After all, most studies of object recognition require participants to make a relatively coarse discrimination between categories, whereas face recognition mainly relies on detecting the finer nuances within a category. Busigny, Joubert, Felician, Ceccaldi, and Rossion (2010) addressed this question by studying a prosopagnosia patient, GG. GG was asked to recognise specific objects within a select number of categories, namely birds, boats, cars, chairs, and faces. Compared to neurotypical control participants, GG performed about equally well on all categories except faces (see fig 6.24), implying that the deficiency is specific to faces and that it cannot necessarily be generalised to other forms of fine discrimination.

6.10.4.4 The Expert Hypothesis

The previously described and refuted hypothesis that prosopagnosia is related to a deficiency in the processing of fine visual details is a specific case of a more general theoretical approach which proposes that face recognition relies mainly on fine, detailed visual analysis, of which we have acquired a high level of expertise during our lifespan. Based on this hypothesis, Diamond and Carey (1986), have argued that face recognition is not a special process, but that it can be fully explained by expertise. Gauthier and Tarr (2002) also argue that our ability to recognise faces is mainly due to an enormous amount of expertise that we have acquired during our lifespan. According to their expertise hypothesis, the brain regions involved in face recognition are also involved in recognising other objects for which we have developed a high level of expertise. As such, the fusiform face area could be considered to be an area of expertise, as opposed to a face processing area. According to this idea, expertise should result in an increased level of holistic processing. We find this type of expertise, for example, in holistic pattern recognition processes, which we have identified in experienced chess players or medical experts (see Chapter 22).

There is currently no unequivocal evidence for the expertise hypothesis, however. If face recognition is primarily related to expertise, we should also find an inversion effect for non-face objects. Diamond and Carey did find this in dog experts who had to recognise photos of different dog breeds. Wallis (2013) reported the results from a computational model for object recognition. After training, this model was capable of simulating some effects that are usually associated with face recognition, such as the inversion effect and the part-whole effect. The model's behaviour in this respect is consistent with that of human medical experts, who are capable of extremely rapidly detecting tumours, in a way that is consistent with holistic processing (Kundel, Nodine, Conant, & Weinstein, 2007). In addition, chess experts were found to show increased activation in the fusiform face area when recognising chess positions (Bilalic, Langner, Erb, & Grodd, 2010), which is consistent with the idea that this area is a centre of expertise.

McKone et al. (2007), however, review several studies that are less consistent with the expertise hypothesis. Some studies found small associations between fusiform face area activation and expertise. The largest effects of expertise were found outside the fusiform face area, however, which implies that the relationship between expertise and the fusiform face area is limited. Moreover, Rossion and Curran (2010) found relatively small inversion effects among car experts who had to recognise pictures of cars. Nevertheless, they did find a correlation between the degree of expertise and the magnitude of the inversion effect. The latter result implies that expertise may contribute to recognition but that it is probably not all-important.

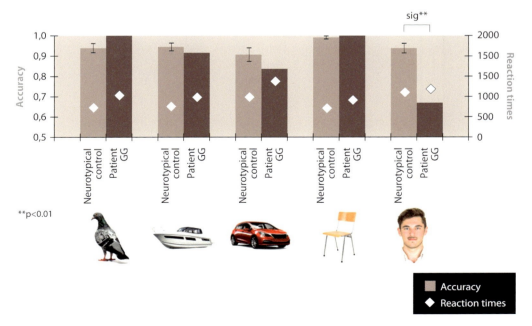

Figure 6.24 The performance of prosopagnosia patient GG, compared to neurotypical control participants on five different object recognition tasks. (source: Busigny et al., 2010)

6.10.4.5 A Model for Face Recognition

Bruce and Young (1986) describe an extensive theoretical model for face recognition (see fig 6.25). This model consists of eight different stages, namely:

1. *Structural encoding.* At this stage, various descriptions and representations of a face are generated.
2. *Analysis of facial expressions.* This stage is involved in inferring the emotional state of another (see also Chapter 23).
3. *Speech analysis.* Speech perception (Chapter 17) is promoted by interpreting lip movements (Chapter 9).
4. The analysis of specific facial characteristics.
5. Identification of invariant face features.
6. Person identification.

7. *Name retrieval.* Identifying the name of the person.
8. *A cognitive system.* Here general background knowledge affects face recognition.

The model predicts that there should be significant differences between recognising known and unknown people. After all, specific components of the model, such as name retrieval and face recognition, can only contribute to the identification of a known person. The ability to identify unknown persons is very important in eyewitness testimony. In a study in which Dutch and British participants were instructed to classify photographs of two well-known Dutch celebrities (who were largely unknown to the British participants), Jenkins, White, Van Montfort, and Burton (2011) have, however, convincingly shown that we are

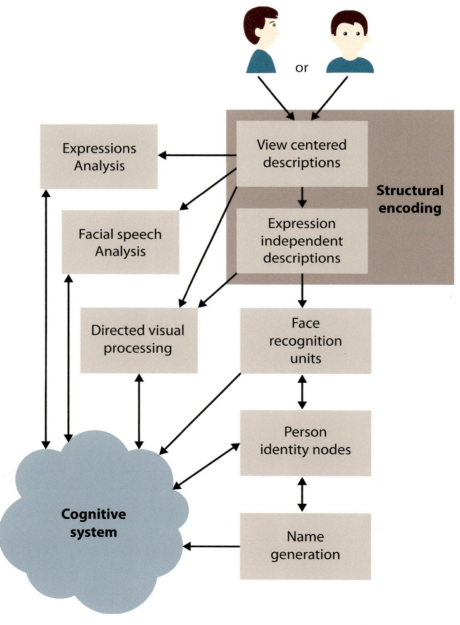

Figure 6.25 Bruce and Young's (1986) face recognition model.

considerably worse at identifying unknown than known people (see Chapter 15 for more details).

In addition, the Bruce and Young model also predicts that the identification of emotions and the recognition of a facial expression occur independently from the identification of a person. According to the model, identification mainly involves recognising more or less stable features of a face, while the recognition of emotion and facial expression mainly involves the identification of features that are variable. Consistent with this idea, Haxby, Hoffman, and Gobbini (2000) have argued that the processing of variable and stable facial features should involve separate brain areas. Fox, Hanif, Iaria, Duchaine, and Barton (2011) found evidence for this idea: patients with damage to brain areas associated with face recognition experienced no difficulties recognising facial expressions. In contrast, patients with damage to the superior temporal sulcus had no difficulties recognising faces but did have so for recognising facial expressions, suggesting the involvement of two neural pathways in face and expression recognition. The two pathways are not completely independent however, as studies have shown that in some tasks, information about a person's identity can influence recognition of facial expressions (Fitousi & Wenger, 2013).

6.11 VISUAL ATTENTION

In our daily lives, our eyes take in much more information than we can consciously process. In Chapter 4, we discussed how we are able to select information that is relevant to our current goals through the deployment of attention. Then, in Chapter 5, we discussed how attention is regulated by cognitive control or executive functions (Corbetta & Shulman, 2002; Miyake et al., 2000; Posner, 1980). In the following sections, we will discuss how these control processes can affect the processing of visual information. An important debate in the visual attention literature focuses on whether we select information based on spatial locations, or whether we select whole objects, or possibly use a combination of these two selection mechanisms. Another prominent question is what role attention plays in visual search processes. That is, how do we find an object that we are looking for amidst a large number of irrelevant objects? Finally, what happens when we overlook something? We will elaborate on these questions in the following sections.

6.11.1 COVERT VERSUS OVERT ATTENTION

Behaviourally, attention can manifest itself in various ways. Suppose we are sitting in a café and notice that at the table next to us a young couple is arguing intensely. Because we do not want them to notice us, we stoically keep looking straight ahead. Under these conditions, our attention is focused on a different location than our eyes. This is an example of **covert attention**. Although this example shows that it is possible to disengage attention from your eye position, in most normal situations our eyes will simply follow our attention. The latter is known as **overt attention**.

6.11.2 NEURAL MECHANISMS

In a literature review, Gilbert and Li (2013) discuss the possible mechanisms that may be involved in top-down controlled selective attention. Gilbert and Li conclude that top-down biasing signals are projected throughout the cortex via a series of descending recurrent projections. Thalamic nuclei play an important role in transmitting these signals from the control areas of the brain to the visual areas (see fig 6.26). These recurrent connections can selectively alter

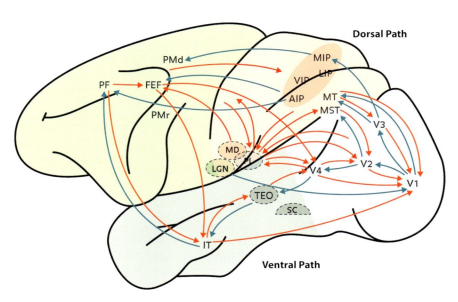

Figure 6.26 A schematic overview of the descending recurrent pathways (red) that may be involved in the regulation of top-down controlled selective attention. (source: Gilbert and Li, 2013)

the response thresholds of neurons along these processing pathways (see also Chapter 4), allowing attention to selectively enhance neural sensitivity to relevant stimulus features and weaken their sensitivity to irrelevant stimulus features.

6.11.3 SENSORY GAIN

Numerous ERP studies have found indications that visual attention can indeed affect the sensitivity of specific neuronal populations in the visual cortex (Eason, 1981; Eason, Harter, & White, 1969; Luck et al., 1994; Talsma, Mulckhuyse, Slagter, & Theeuwes, 2007; Talsma, Slagter, Nieuwenhuis, Hage, & Kok, 2005; Van Voorhis & Hillyard, 1977). In this type of studies, participants are shown a series of simple visual stimuli, such as letters. They are

required to keep their eyes fixated at a central point, while these stimuli are presented randomly to the left or right of this fixation point (see fig 6.27). The participant's task is to attend to one of these two locations (e.g., left) and to respond to specific properties of this stimulus (e.g., respond only when a number was presented, instead of a letter). Thus, the stimuli presented on the left are attended, whereas those presented on the right are unattended. With some regularity, participants are instructed to shift their attention to the opposite side. Consequently, the stimuli that were initially attended are now unattended and vice versa. During the task, the EEGs are recorded, which allows the extraction of ERPs that are evoked by the stimuli. Now it is possible to compare ERPs across these two conditions: that is, when the stimuli were attended versus when they were unattended.

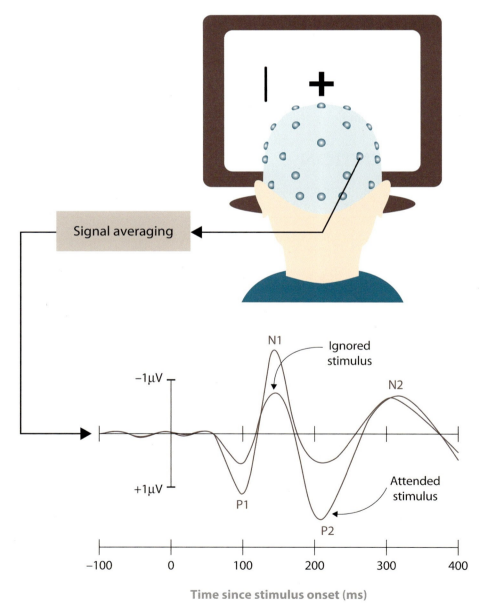

Figure 6.27 Illustration of a typical sensory gain experiment. Visual stimuli presented in one visual half-field, here the left, evoke a contralateral ERP. The amplitudes of the early components of this ERP are larger when this stimulus is attended than when it is unattended. (source: Hillyard et al., 1998)

The crucial finding of these studies is that the amplitude of some of the early ERP components, in particular the P1 and the N1, are larger when the stimuli are attended than when they are unattended. This P1/N1 amplitude enhancement effect can be observed predominantly over the posterior brain regions that are contralateral to the location of the stimuli. This increase in amplitude suggests that neurons with receptive fields corresponding to the relevant location respond more sensitively when a stimulus is actually presented at this location. For this reason, this effect was initially interpreted to reflect a **sensory gain mechanism** (Hillyard, Vogel, & Luck, 1998). That is, it was believed to be reflecting the increased sensitivity of those visual neurons that were responsive to the attended stimulus feature. Based on source localisation techniques, it has been suggested that the sensory gain effect is most likely to originate from the secondary or extrastriate visual cortex.

Although the amplitude increases of the P1 and N1 components were initially considered to be a unitary gain effect (Eason et al., 1969), later studies have found a dissociation by showing that the amplitude of the P1 component mainly reflects the suppression of irrelevant information, while the N1 amplitude mainly reflects the enhancement of relevant information (Luck et al., 1994; Talsma, Mulckhuyse, et al., 2007; Talsma et al., 2005).

The latter result was obtained by using a symbolic cueing task (Posner, 1980; see Chapter 4). Here, ERPs were evoked by a target stimulus, which was preceded by a valid, an invalid, or a neutral cue. The crucial result of these studies was that the P1 amplitude was specifically smaller for invalidly cued targets compared to neutral or validly cued trials (while the P1 amplitude in the latter two conditions did not differ from each other). On the other hand, the N1 component was specifically enlarged for validly cued trials compared to neutral or invalidly cued targets. These results thus suggest the existence of two distinct mechanisms: suppression of the processing of unattended stimuli was reflected in the reduced P1 amplitude, whereas the facilitation of the processing of relevant stimuli was reflected in an increase of the N1 amplitude.

These P1 and N1 effects suggest that attention can selectively affect the processing of visual information. Neurons that have receptive fields corresponding to the attended location would, under the influence of top-down biasing mechanisms, become selectively more sensitive and thus process stimuli at these locations with greater priority. At what stage of visual processing, and in which brain areas, does attention affect the processing (Posner & Gilbert, 1999)? The ERP results described earlier suggest that this happens in the secondary visual areas. fMRI studies (Somers, Dale, Seiffert, & Tootell, 1999) as well as single-cell recordings in primates (Roelfsema, Lamme, & Spekreijse, 1998) have, however, already shown that

activation in the primary visual areas can be affected by attention, suggesting that attention can even affect the very early stages of visual processing.

These results are difficult to reconcile with the ERP findings mentioned earlier. Both the localisation and the timing of the P1 (˜120 ms after stimulus presentation) and N1 (˜180 ms) suggest that these components are generated in the secondary visual areas and not in V1. Thus, the V1 effects found with fMRI must either be due to recurrent processing (see Chapter 4) or manifest themselves in a way that is not, or only with great difficulty, observable with ERPs. It is possible, however that some effects of V1 processing can be measured with EEG, as some effects of attention have been observed on the C1 component. The C1 is a component that is most likely generated in V1, which typically precedes the P1, and there are currently some studies that report that the C1 amplitude can be modulated by attention (Kelly, Gomez-Ramirez, & Foxe, 2008; Rauss, Pourtois, Vuilleumier, & Schwartz, 2011). This would indeed suggest that attention can influence our visual processing at a very early stage.

6.11.3.1 Zoom Lens versus Searchlight

Now that we have detailed how we can focus our attention on specific locations, we can ask what effect attention may have on visual processing. Posner (1980) compared visual attention to a searchlight shining on the environment. Stimuli that fall within the searchlight are attended. Eriksen and St. James (1986) have taken this idea one step further and have represented visual attention as a zoom lens that can be focused on the environment and whose size can be adjusted, if necessary. One of the consequences of their model is that we can either focus our visual attention strongly at one specific location or we can diffuse our attention across the entire visual field.

Laberge (1983) found that this is indeed the case on the basis of the following experiment. Participants were shown a series of five letters and were required to either decide whether this series formed a word or whether the central letter belonged to a specific category. In the first condition, attention would be fairly diffusely distributed over the word, and, in the second, it would be strongly focused on the central letter. To test whether this was actually the case, Laberge occasionally presented a second, so-called probe stimulus. This probe stimulus consisted of four plus signs and one digit. These symbols appeared at the same locations as where the letters would normally appear. The location of the digit was random, however. Here, participants had to decide whether the digit in question was a seven and then respond as quickly as possible when it was. The pattern of reaction times evoked by this probe corresponded to Laberge's expectation. When the probe stimulus was further away from the centre, the reaction time became larger, but this was only the case in the letter condition, where attention was strongly focused. In the word condition, where attention was divided across all possible locations, reaction times were similar for all probe positions.

6.11.4 ONE OR MORE SEARCHLIGHTS?

Awh and Pashler (2000) found that visual attention is not limited to a single spotlight. When they instructed participants to attend to two locations, it was found that the participant's performance in detecting stimuli at these locations was high. However, when a stimulus was presented at a location that was between the two locations, the task performance was suddenly much lower, suggesting that the intermediate location was not attended.

6.11.4.1 Locations or Objects?

Although the results just discussed suggest that visual information is selected on the basis of locations, it is questionable whether location is the only form of selection. Indeed, currently a growing body of literature shows that selection can also take place on the basis of objects. For example, O'Craven, Downing, and Kanwisher (1999) conducted an fMRI study in which houses and faces were presented at overlapping positions on a computer screen. The reason for using houses and faces as stimuli is that they selectively activate specific brain areas. Faces activate the fusiform face area, and houses activate the **parahippocampal place area**. When participants were instructed to attend to the faces, activation in the fusiform face area increased, and when they were instructed to attend to the houses, activation in the parahippocampal place area increased. Because the two stimuli overlapped in space, we cannot explain this effect on the basis of a theory that assumes selection on the basis of location. Thus, we can select objects even when they partially overlap with another object.

Now that we have seen that selection can be based on location as well as on objects, we can ask what role these two forms of selection play. Egly, Driver, and Rafal (1994) investigated this question by using a variant of a cueing task. Participants were required to detect a target stimulus that could appear at one of four possible locations. Each of the four locations where the target could appear was connected to one other location via a rectangular bar, causing the two locations to become part of an object. The target was preceded by an exogenous cue, which could be valid or invalid. Importantly, when the cue was invalid, it could either be presented inside or outside the object of which the target stimulus was a part. Detection of targets was slower on invalidly cued trials compared to validly cued trials. This was specifically so when the cues were presented outside of the object where the target stimulus

appeared. This result thus implies that we are more effective at switching our attention within an object than at switching between objects.

Andersen, Fuchs, and Müller (2010) used EEG recordings to investigate the role of attention. They used a special characteristic of the EEG. By repeatedly presenting a stimulus, the EEG will synchronise with the presentation frequency of the stimulus, resulting in a steady state visual evoked potential (SSVEP). For example, if we repeat a stimulus 12 times per second, we will observe an oscillation of 12 Hz in the EEG. When we present several streams of stimuli, each at a different frequency, we can measure different SSVEPs (see fig 6.28). Interestingly, the amplitude of the SSVEP varies with attention. When attending to one of the two stimulus streams, the amplitude of the oscillation evoked by this stream increases.

Andersen et al. exploited this property by presenting two blinking dot patterns at two different locations: at each location, one red pattern and one blue pattern was presented. Because each pattern blinked at a unique frequency, it was possible to track the neural response to each of these patterns. When participants were required to attend to the blue stimulus on the left, the amplitude of the SSVEP that corresponded with the frequency of this stream increased. Interestingly, the amplitude of the SSVEP that corresponded with the blue stimulus stream on the right also increased, implying that object-based attention causes an early facilitation of the relevant stimulus properties.

Marshall and Halligan (1994) also found evidence for object-based attention in a study involving hemineglect patients. These patients had to draw a jagged contour that ran through the centre of their visual field. In one condition, this contour was part of an object located in their intact hemifield. In this case, the patients had no difficulties in reproducing the contour. When the exact same contour was part of an object that was in the damaged hemifield, they did have difficulties doing so. This result implies that the location of the contour is associated with the object in question and that its perception is strongly influenced by this.

6.11.4.2 Attention to Non-spatial Characteristics of a Stimulus

ERP studies have shown that, in addition to locations and complete objects, we can also focus our attention on non-spatial properties of a visual scene, such as colours (Anllo-Vento & Hillyard, 1996; Lange, Wijers, Mulder, & Mulder, 1998; Slagter, Kok, Mol, & Kenemans, 2005) or textures (Heslenfeld, Kenemans, Kok, & Molenaar, 1997; Talsma & Kok, 2001). In ERP studies, non-spatial attention processes are often investigated by using a procedure similar to the one used for spatial attention (see Section 6.11.3). The main difference is that now two different stimuli are

(a)

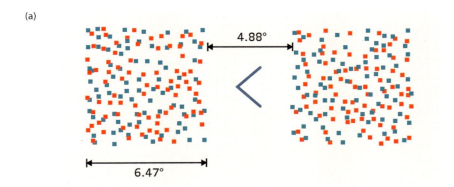

(b)

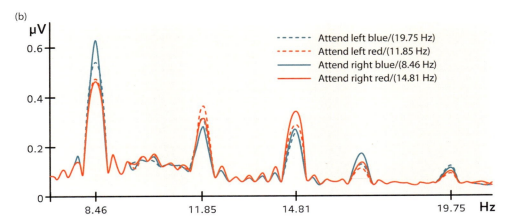

Figure 6.28 A method of measuring the effects of visual attention by repeating a stimulus pattern at a fixed frequency. (a) Dot patterns are presented in the left and right visual field. Each combination of colour and location flashes at a different frequency. (b) The flash frequency of each stimulus is reflected in the power spectrum of the EEG. (source: Andersen et al., 2010)

used, which differ on only one feature (e.g., colour or texture difference). These two stimuli are presented, at random, one after the other, at one location.

The rest of the procedure is the same as for spatial attention: participants have to selectively attend to one of the two stimuli and detect an occasional deviant stimulus. Again, for each stimulus, two ERPs extracted, one for the condition in which it was attended and the other for the condition in which it was unattended. The ERPs evoked by these stimuli are often quite different from those of the spatial experiments, however. For non-spatial attention it is found that the attended stimuli evoke a positive potential over the frontal scalp and a negative potential over the occipital scalp. The occipital negative potential is believed to reflect the selection of individual stimulus characteristics (Potts & Tucker, 2001), whereas the frontal positive potential is believed to represent the selection of the object as a whole (Kenemans, Smulders, & Kok, 1995).

6.11.5 VISUAL SEARCH

The attention effects discussed earlier mainly relate to situations where the object that we attend is already known. In everyday life, however, we spend a considerable amount of time searching for objects. These visual search processes operate on the basis of a template of the object that we need to find, that we have activated in our memory, and that we try to match with an object in our environment.

6.11.5.1 Feature Integration Theory

Before reading any further, take a look at Figure 6.29. Try to find the deviant stimulus in the left display as quickly as possible. No doubt you did not have much trouble with this. Now try to find the deviant stimulus in the right display. This task is probably more difficult. Why is that? According to the influential **feature integration theory** (Treisman & Gelade, 1980), the difference in difficulty is caused by the fact that in the left display the deviant is defined by only one feature, while in the right display the deviant is defined by a conjunction of features that is unique, while the features themselves are not unique. According to Treisman and Gelade, the individual properties of an object are processed quickly and in parallel, while we need to combine all individual properties into complete objects through a slow, attention-demanding process.

In their original model, Treisman and Gelade argued that this binding of the separate elements is driven by the location of the stimulus. They believed this because in the early 1980s it was assumed that visual attention could only be focused on locations; an assumption that, as we have already discussed, was later shown to be incorrect. For this reason, the model was updated to allow attention to operate through other aspects of objects as well (Treisman, 1998). Treisman and Gelade (1980) tested crucial assumptions of their original model by having participants search for deviant items, as illustrated in Figure 6.29. Each display could or could not contain a deviant target stimulus, and the participants' task was to press a button as quickly as possible to indicate whether this was the case. When the deviation was defined by one feature and when the deviant target stimulus was actually present in the display, the search time was not affected by the number of visual elements in the display; this is indicative of a parallel search process. Because the stimulus in such a situation appears to pop out of the display, this it is sometimes referred to as a **pop-out effect** that is the result of a **feature search** process. When, however, the deviant was defined by a combination of features, the response times increased more or less linearly with the number of elements in the display, indicating that participants now had to perform a serial search. This is also known as a **conjunction search**.

A number of important limitations to the feature integration theory have led various theorists to propose alternative models. One problem is the fact that Treisman and Gelade did not assume that the nature of the deviant stimulus feature was important. Duncan and Humphreys (1989), however, emphasise that this is the case. For example, a letter E is more difficult to detect in a field consisting of letters F than when this E is placed in a field containing the letters O. These properties can also result in the fact that we do not consider many distractors when we search conjunctively. For example, when we search for a blue circle, we will only consider the blue stimuli.

6.11.5.2 Guided Search

Wolfe (2003) states that there is no strict distinction between parallel and serial processes. Evidence against the strict distinction between serial and parallel processes has indeed been found. Thornton and Gilden (2007), for example, analysed the results of 29 different search tasks and found evidence for serial processing in only a minority of the tasks. For this reason, the **guided search model**, by Wolfe, Cave, and Franzel (1989), assumes that the differences in efficiency are rather gradual. According to Wolfe et al. there is an initial scan of the display, which results in an activation map. The most likely properties that could possibly constitute the sought-after stimulus are marked on this activation map. The closer each feature resembles that of the sought-after object, the greater the activation at that location on the map. Thus, the objects that receive the highest activity will be attended this way. This approach is consistent with a computational model for visual attention developed by Itti and Koch (2001) (see fig 6.30).

The studies discussed earlier typically use displays in which the target stimulus can appear at any location, making the search essentially a random process. This situation is not very consistent with real life, where our searches are often guided by our top-down background knowledge. When we look for our keys, we will usually not look at the sky, but always limit our search to plausible locations.

For this reason, Ehinger, Hidalgo-Sotelo, Torralba, and Oliva (2009) analysed eye movement patterns of people searching natural scenes and found that participants tended to fixate on locations that were relevant, such as footpaths or cars, while they tended to ignore regions that were not relevant (trees, the sky). To reconcile these results with the guided search model, Wolfe, Vo, Evans, and Greene (2011) proposed a dual-path model. According to this model, a selective path with limited capacity is

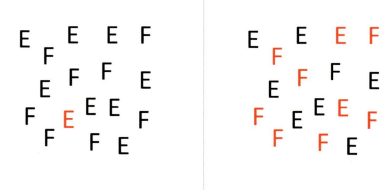

Figure 6.29 Examples of displays used during visual search tasks. In which display can you most quickly find the anomalous element?

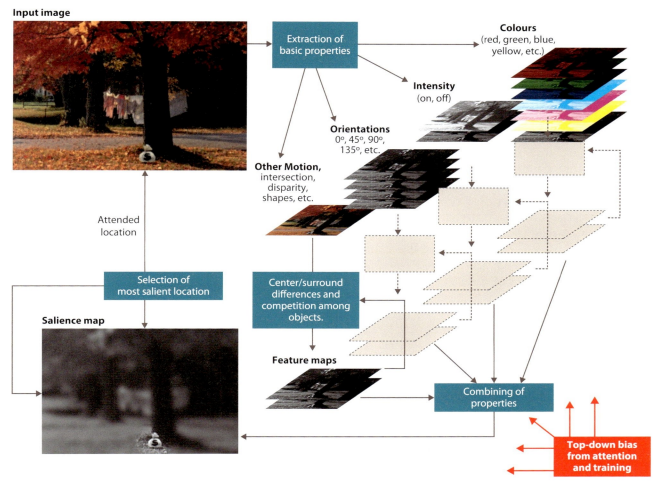

Figure 6.30 A computational model for visual attention. (source: Itti and Koch, 2001)

involved in processing details of a scene and a non-selective path is involved in processing its essence.

Wolfe, Alvarez, Rosenholtz, Kuzmova, and Sherman (2011) reported that finding targets in a natural setting is faster compared to finding the same targets when they are presented in a random display. This result is consistent with the idea that a non-selective path guides the search process to the most relevant locations, thus effectively reducing the set of potentially relevant items. Vo and Wolfe (2012) found evidence that is consistent with this idea. When participants had to search for specific items, for example, a jar in a kitchen, they mainly looked in the locations where they believed they could find it, while other locations were hardly fixated.

Finally, one remarkable finding is that we can also learn to search for invisible items! Chukoskie, Snider, Mozer, Krauzlis, and Sejnowski (2013) presented an invisible target stimulus and instructed participants to fixate on it. When they fixated on the correct location, they were rewarded with a tone indicating that they had found the correct location. The location where the invisible stimulus was presented was not random, however, but limited to a number of possible locations in the top left corner of the screen. Chukoskie et al. found a strong learning effect. At the beginning of the experiment, the fixations were randomly distributed across the screen, but after a few trials they started to cluster in the location where the participants expected the target to be.

6.11.5.3 The Texture Tiling Model
An important criticism of the previous models is that they may place too much emphasis on attention. Both the feature integration theory and the guided search model assume an initial parallel processing of the individual stimulus features. For some features this assumption is questionable, because our visual system is only capable of perceiving a small part of the visual field in detail. Therefore, Rosenholtz, Huang, and Ehinger (2012) argued that it is not so much attention but perception that limits visual search processes. When the visual information is detailed enough to capture attention, as is the case when we have to find a T amidst a field of rotated letters L, this is usually sufficient, but in the case of fine discriminations in natural scenes, this is often not the case.

6.11.6 THE INFLUENCE OF IRRELEVANT STIMULI

6.11.6.1 Perceptual Load

What is the effect of irrelevant stimuli? The British-Israelian cognitive psychologist Nilli Lavie has done important work to address this question. Her perceptual load theory (Lavie, 1995, 2005; Lavie, 2010) states that the extent to which we can be distracted by irrelevant stimuli depends on two factors: perceptual load and cognitive load. According to Lavie's theory, we are less likely to be distracted under a high perceptual load because the large amount of information we have to process forces us to focus all our cognitive processes on the task, whereas under a low perceptual load there is more capacity left to process additional stimuli. Cognitive load, however, has the opposite effect. Under a high cognitive load, we are actually more quickly distracted, because we are less capable of recruiting cognitive control processes that prevent distraction.

6.11.6.2 Attentional Capture

Theeuwes (1992) investigated how top-down and bottom-up processes can interact. Participants were presented displays such as those shown in Figure 6.31, in which they had to search for an object with a unique shape (fig 6.31: top left) or a unique colour (fig 6.31: top right) and report whether the line segment contained in this object was horizontally or vertically oriented. On some trials, a distractor was presented. For example, when participants had to search for a unique shape, an object with a unique colour could be presented (fig 6.31: bottom left) and when they had to search for a unique colour, an object with a unique shape could be presented (fig 6.31: bottom right).

Theeuwes (1992) found that complete shielding from the distractors was not possible, even after intensive practice. The objects with a unique shape interfered with the search for objects with a unique colour and vice versa, suggesting that these objects automatically captured attention, a process known as **attentional capture**. In a follow-up study, Theeuwes, Kramer, Hahn, Irwin, and Zelinski (1999) investigated the effects of attentional capture on eye movement patterns. Here, participants were initially shown six uniformly shaped objects. The task-relevant target stimulus was revealed by removing some image elements from one of these objects, while the other objects similarly changed to irrelevant distractors. Such an offset of elements did not result in an automatic capture of attention, so participants had to actively search for the relevant stimulus (a 'C' or a mirrored 'C'). Shortly after the stimuli were revealed, an additional stimulus appeared at a new location, which was able to capture attention (see fig 6.32a for the sequence of events within a trial). The results showed that participants were typically unable to suppress eye movement towards the irrelevant stimulus. The results implied that participants programmed two different saccades in parallel: one saccade to the task-irrelevant distractor and one saccade to the task-relevant target stimulus (see fig 6.32b for an overview of the results).

6.12 VISUAL PERCEPTION AND AWARENESS

Most of the literature discussed in the previous sections relates to conscious perceptual processes. As discussed at the end of Chapter 4, there are, however, several situations in which visual information is processed without it reaching our awareness. As such, we have already been introduced to the phenomena of blindsight and hemineglect. These phenomena illustrate the fact that visual awareness is limited in capacity. The question is, however, to what extent unconsciously perceived stimuli can still influence our behaviour.

6.12.1 SUBLIMINAL PERCEPTION

One of the most talked-about forms of unconscious perception is the phenomenon of subliminal perception. A stimulus is subliminally perceived when it is presented too briefly to reach conscious awareness. In most cases, a presentation time of about 16 ms (one cycle of the 60 Hz refresh cycle of a monitor) is followed by the presentation of a masking stimulus, which is sufficient to prevent the stimulus from entering our awareness. This method has gained a certain level of notoriety, because in 1957 an unsuccessful market researcher named James Vicary claimed that subliminally presenting the advertising messages 'Drink Coca-Cola' and 'Eat popcorn' during a feature film resulted in a spectacular

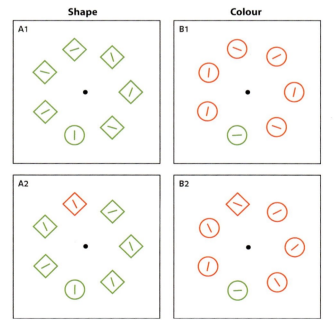

Figure 6.31 Examples of the types displays used by Theeuwes (1992).

(a)

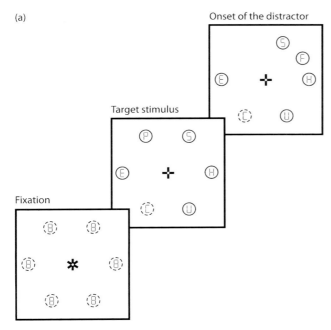

(b)

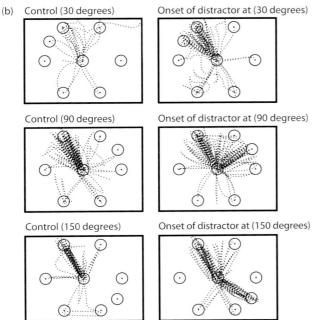

Figure 6.32 Setup and results from a study by Theeuwes et al. (1999). (a) The sequence of events within a trial. Initially, six objects consisting of a digital representation of the number 8 were presented, which were surrounded by a circle. Subsequently, each of these objects changed into a unique letter. Participants had to detect the letter 'C' as quickly as possible. This letter was the only one that was presented within a circle that did not change colour. The presentation of this target letter was sometimes immediately followed by the presentation of a highly salient but irrelevant distractor. (b) Eye movement patterns: when the irrelevant distractor was presented, a significant number of eye movements were directed towards this distractor. (source: Theeuwes et al., 1999)

increase in sales of these products during the film's intermission. The results proved to be impossible to replicate and Vicary later admitted to making them up.

Although subliminal perception does not appear to have an effect on our consumer behaviour, subliminal stimuli do appear to have an effect on a number of more basic cognitive processes. For example, Naccache et al. (2002) found that subliminally presented numbers could affect numerical judgements (see also Chapter 4), while subliminally presented emotional pictures could also unconsciously capture attention (Öhman & Soares, 1994).

6.12.2 GAPS IN OUR PERCEPTION

The subliminal perception described here is created in an artificial situation that we will not often encounter in everyday life. Even in more mundane situations, however, it appears that we perceive much less than we often believe. A simple example is a friend asking you what you think of her new haircut. If at that moment you have to admit that you do not know what she is talking about, you are probably experiencing one of the phenomena of **change blindness** or **inattentional blindness**.

6.12.2.1 Change Blindness versus Inattentional Blindness

Both change blindness and inattentional blindness are phenomena related to the fact that we sometimes fail to perceive important changes in our environment, and, in both cases, attention often plays an important role. Despite these similarities, there are also a number of important differences between the two phenomena (Jensen, Yao, Street, & Simons, 2011), as we will outline next.

One of the most common problems in feature films is the so-called continuation error: when the scene switches between two different camera positions, it often turns out that props are not in the same place, that a wound on an actor's face changes position, or that some other noticeable change takes place. Sometimes these continuity errors can be significant. For example, in the James Bond movie 'Diamonds Are Forever', Bond drives into a narrow alley at the beginning of a scene with his car balancing sideways on two wheels, only to emerge again at the other end of the alley, but this time balancing on the other two wheels. The mistake, which was probably caused by someone not paying attention during production, is now known as one of the greatest continuation errors in film history. Yet most people did not notice it when the film first hit the theatres in 1971 because they did not pay attention to this detail. Not noticing this type of change is an example of change blindness.

Change blindness often involves memory: an earlier scene must be actively compared with a later scene. When we do not know exactly what to look for, the instruction to detect the change becomes particularly difficult (Simons & Rensink, 2005). So, what causes change blindness? One of the possible causes is the fact that our attention is usually focused on just a limited part of the visual scene; the part where we expect the most relevant information, so that other parts, where the change usually occurs, are not noticed. Rensink, O'Regan, and Clark (1997) found evidence for this explanation. They presented pictures where a change had been introduced that was either close to the most interesting locations or in a peripheral location. In the latter case, it took on average much longer (10.4 seconds) to detect the changes than in the former case (2.6 seconds). This finding suggests that peripheral elements of the scene are not attended and are therefore not, or only sparsely, represented. Rensink et al. (1997) and Simons and Levin (1997) assume that this is an example of a sparce representation, that is, a representation that consists of just a limited amount of superficial features.

Other researchers, however, hypothesise that we do initially form a detailed representation, but this representation quickly decays unless attention maintains it. Evidence for the latter hypothesis is provided by a study by Landman et al. (2003). Here, participants were initially shown displays depicting a series of abstract figures. After a short interval, they were shown a new display, which was either identical to the original display or in which one of the figures had changed. Participants had to indicate whether they had noticed a change. Performance on this task was generally quite low unless participants were given a cue that indicated which object might be changing. Importantly, this cue could also be presented after the first display had already been removed. The participants evidently still had a detailed representation of the stimuli in their memory, which they could maintain by still focusing their attention on it.

Further evidence for the role of attention was found in a study by Hollingworth and Henderson (2002). They presented pictures of natural scenes, for example, a living room or a kitchen, while participants' eye movements were recorded. Because in natural situations attention is usually directed covertly, eye positions can be used as a proxy for the location where attention is directed. While the participants were freely looking at a given scene, it was replaced by a modified version, in which one object was replaced by another. There were two types of change: in a token change, an object was replaced by another object of the same category (e.g., a notebook was replaced by another notebook). In a type change, an object was replaced by an object of a different type (e.g., a notepad was replaced by a floppy[2] disk).

Hollingworth and Henderson (2002) found that changes were detected much more when the object in question had been fixated once just before the change. They also found that type changes were noticed more than token changes. This makes sense since type changes are often more dramatic than token changes. Finally, they also found that the more time elapsed between the last time the changed object was fixated and the change, the less frequently the change was detected. The latter result is more compatible with the trace decay explanation than with the sparce representation explanation since each fixation was assumed to refresh the representation, after which it would start to decay again.

6.12.2.2 Inattentional Blindness

The phenomenon of inattentional blindness can also be illustrated by an example from a Hollywood movie. The original Star Wars movie 'Episode IV: A new Hope', contains a scene where a group of stormtroopers guarding the Death Star seeks to arrest the droids R2D2 and C-3PO. In that scene, one of the stormtroopers bumps with his head into the door. Again, most people failed to notice this at first because their attention was focused elsewhere. The major difference with change blindness, however, is that in this case we do not have to compare two different scenes and that detecting the remarkable event suddenly becomes trivial when we know what to attend to.

How remarkably strong the effect of inattentional blindness can be was convincingly demonstrated by Simons and Chabris (1999). They showed participants a short video of two teams, one dressed in white and the other in black, playing a ball game. The participants' task was to count how many times the players of the white team passed the ball to each other. After the video, they were asked if they had noticed anything unusual. Most participants were unable to report that, halfway through the video, a person in a gorilla costume had walked into the video, stood still for a while in the middle of the scene, punched himself in the chest and then walked away again.

What exactly causes inattentional blindness? According to Jensen et al. (2011) the extent to which we notice an unexpected object or event depends strongly on the extent to which it is able to capture attention. Two factors are important here: the similarity between the unexpected objects and the task-relevant stimuli, and the available processing capacity. For example, Simons and Chabris (1999) found that the gorilla was detected much more rapidly when participants had to attend to the black team, instead of the white team.

6.13 IN CLOSING

In this chapter, we have introduced some of the most complex cognitive processes we know, namely visual perception and visual attention. From research spanning more than a century, we begin to understand how visual perception arises and how different theoretical perspectives can be reconciled. This research has unravelled the existence of a hierarchical system of cortical networks comprising neurons with progressively larger receptive fields, which also represent progressively more complex aspects (see fig 6.33).

An important finding is that these networks are in competition with each other (Serences & Yantis, 2006) and that this competition plays out across all levels of the processing hierarchy (see also Chapter 4). Applied specifically to visual attention, such a model can explain how top-down,

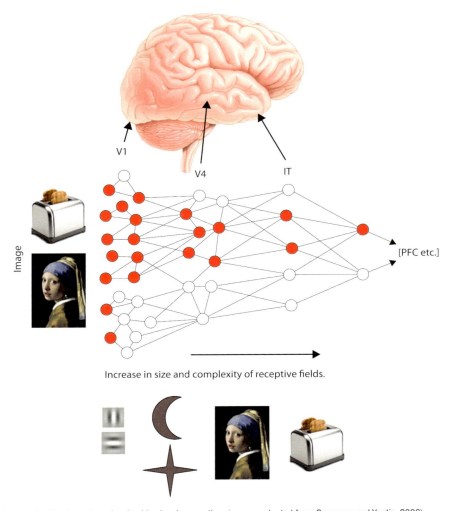

Figure 6.33 A hierarchical network of brain systems involved in visual perception. (source: adapted from Serences and Yantis, 2006)

and bottom-up controlled attention processes can interact. The saliency of an external stimulus will have an effect on the strength with which this stimulus is represented. At the same time, goals and intentions are involved, which in turn can influence the priority of other stimuli. Visual search processes can be affected in this way because the specific properties of the sought-after stimulus are given higher priority, and this can also explain why a variety of different stimulus properties can be attended to, such as location, colour, movement, or even entire objects. Each form of attention induces a bias at a different level in the cortical hierarchy.

6.14 SUMMARY

Human visual perception is based on several different receptor systems that convert electromagnetic radiation into neural impulses. The eyes are the starting point for the route that these neural impulses take through the brain. Two different receptors in the retina of the eye are involved in converting light into a neural signal: the rods and the cones. These receptors provide input for the magnocellular and parvocellular pathways respectively. These two pathways converge in the primary visual cortex. This part of the cortex contains neurons that are sensitive to basic properties of a stimulus. After this primary visual area, more complex processing takes place in the higher cortical areas: V2 through V5. These areas are more or less selectively sensitive to specific information, such as colour, shape, and movement. From these areas, visual information is projected to the higher regions along two different routes. The ventral route is mainly involved in recognising shapes and objects, whereas the dorsal route is mainly involved in encoding locations and integrating this location information into our motor actions.

The idea that the visual system is broken up after the primary visual cortex, with specialised cortical areas involved in different aspects of the analysis of the visual signal, appears to create a fundamental problem: the binding problem. This problem can be resolved by assuming the existance of a predictive coding mechanism since the specialised processing can then rather be seen as solving a specific prediction error initiated from higher cortical areas.

Milner and Goodale's work has given rise to the idea that there are two separate visual systems: one for perception and another for integrating visual information into our motor actions. Evidence for this dissociation has been found in patient studies. Patients with visual agnosia have difficulties recognising objects, but relatively little difficulty grasping or otherwise interacting with them. Patients with optic ataxia, on the other hand, still have a relatively intact ability to recognise objects, but have significant diifuclties pointing to or grasping objects. Milner and Goodale argue that the vision-for-action system operates in real time, is impervious to illusions, and is ephemeral. In contrast, the vision-for-perception system has greater visual memory, is more susceptible to illusions, and is more persistent.

Colour is a property that arises in our mental representation by combining information from three different wavelengths of light. Three different types of cones are sensitive to long, medium, and short wavelengths. An evolutionary advantage of colour perception is that specific objects become more salient. Different theories can each explain specific aspects of colour vision, such as the negative-negative colour after-effect. One aspect of colour vision that is still not fully understood is the phenomenon of colour constancy. A number of factors, such as cone-excitability ratios and equivalent exposure models, are involved in establishing colour constancy. Top-down influences, such as familiarity with an object and expectation may also regulate colour constancy.

Depth perception is based on a combination of several different cues. These cues can be roughly divided into monocular cues, binocular cues, and oculomotor cues. Monocular cues are linear perspective, blur, texture, shadow, interposition, known size, and the motion parallax. The best-known binocular cue is formed by binocular disparity, which results in the phenomenon of stereopsis. Finally, oculomotor cues are formed by the accommodation of the eyeball and by vergence.

Object recognition takes place mainly in the anterior inferior temporal cortex, whereas face recognition is mainly associated with the fusiform face area. Effortless object recognition is one of the greatest achievements of the visual system, given the enormous variety of objects that we can recognise and the large variation of viewpoints per object. Various studies show that the analysis of visual scenes takes place on the basis of a global-to-local progression. Thus, we are very quickly able to recognise the global essence of a scene, whereas the analysis of details takes much longer. The analysis of spatial frequencies appears to play an important role here. Information from low spatial frequencies is rapidly projected to the frontal cortex, whereas detailed information from high spatial frequencies takes much longer.

Before objects can be recognised, they must first be identified in the visual scene. In part, this can be done via the figure-background segregation and grouping processes proposed by the gestalt psychologists. These principles were later supplemented by a number of other principles for natural scenes, including the principle of uniform connectedness.

Several theorists have initially aimed to explain object recognition processes on the basis of bottom-up principles. Although these theories have had some success, they turned out to be unable to explain the influence of top-down processing. More recent updates, such as Bar's model, hypothesise that information encoded in low spatial frequencies activates top-down predictions related to candidate object selection on the one hand and to contextual information generation on the other. Studies using ambiguous figures, or the masking of the conscious perception of objects, have shown that top-down predictions play a significant role in object recognition. Neurons in the inferior temporal cortex are selectively sensitive to specific objects or classes of objects. The specific tolerance and selectivity of these neurons varies, allowing a greater variety of objects to be encoded.

Face recognition is a special form of object recognition. Based on double dissociations, it has been established that object and face recognition processes are probably modular. Evidence for the idea that faces are special comes from the part-whole effect and the face inversion effect. These effects suggest that faces are processed in a more holistic way. A number of brain regions, including the fusiform face area and an occipital face area, are involved in face processing. Evidence for the idea that face recognition is primarily the result of highly developed expertise is not unequivocal.

Bruce and Young describe a comprehensive model for face recognition. This model assumes independent processing of facial expressions and of person identification. The model predicts that we have less trouble recognising the faces of familiar people than unfamiliar ones.

Visual attention plays an important role in regulating the flow of visual information and can be directed overtly or covertly. Top-down regulation is driven by task goals, whereas bottom-up regulation takes place because salient visual stimuli attract attention. ERP research has established that salient stimuli are prioritised in neural processing by increasing the sensitivity of the neurons encoding the salient feature of the stimulus.

Some researchers imagine visual attention as a proverbial searchlight or zoom lens, which can be focused on specific parts of a visual scene. This searchlight can increase or decrease in size depending on the task and can even be directed at multiple locations at once. Although it was originally believed that attention could only be directed to spatial locations, more recent studies show that attention can also be directed to entire objects, even when they (partially) overlap. Other aspects of an object can also attended.

In visual search, we need to detect relevant objects in a visual scene. It was originally believed that visual search processes could be divided into a parallel feature search process and a serial conjunctive search process. Later theories make a less strict distinction between these forms. The salience of the different features of the stimulus to be detected plays an important role in the search process. Influences of context and background knowledge are now believed to constrain the potential locations where we can search. We should be careful not to put too much importance on the role of attention, because in many everyday situations, visual acuity can be a much greater constraint than our attentional capacity.

Salient but task-relevant stimuli can have a major influence on visual attention. A high perceptual load results in less distractibility, whereas a high cognitive load results in greater distractibility, because fewer cognitive control processes are available. Theeuwes and colleagues found that even a high level of top-down control could not prevent irrelevant stimuli from capturing attention. In many cases, this even resulted in an involuntary eye movement towards this distractor.

Visual information that is not consciously perceived can still influence behaviour. Subliminal perception involves the brief presentation of a stimulus. When we can no longer consciously perceive a stimulus, we can often still make informed decisions about it.

In many everyday situations, we often miss important information. This phenomenon is described as change blindness or inattentional blindness. These phenomena can be explained by the fact that attention can only be focused on a limited amount of information, which means that we quickly miss information that we do not attend.

NOTES

1 Because our two eyes perceive the world slightly differently because they are each in a different position, they also send a slightly different image to the brain. The closer an object is to us, the greater the difference. This difference is known as binocular disparity, and it is one of the bases for our ability to perceive depth.

2 A clear indication that this study was conducted at the turn of the century.

FURTHER READING

Ditzinger, T. (2014). *Optical illusions: A journey through the world of visual perception*. The Hague: Scientific Library.

Friedenberg, J. (2013). *Visual attention and consciousness*. New York, NY: Taylor & Francis Group.

Wade, N. J., & Swanston, M. T. (2013). *Visual perception: An introduction*. Hove, UK: Psychology Press.

Yantis, S. (2000). *Visual perception: Essential readings*. Hove, UK: Psychology Press.

CHAPTER 7
Auditory perception

7.1 INTRODUCTION

If we were to be asked which of our sensory system we consider to be the most important one, it is highly likely that we would answer that it is our visual system. Nevertheless, we should not underestimate the importance of our auditory system. Imagine, for instance, what the consequences of a sudden hearing loss would be. Not only are we no longer able to enjoy music, but we are also severely limited in our ability to engage in a conversation. Listening to speech is a skill that not only manifests itself during conversations, it also plays a central role in our education, and in a variety of cultural manifestations. Without our hearing capabilities, there would be no concerts, lectures would no longer make sense, and personal tutoring would become considerably more complicated. In addition, we would need to be much more aware of potential dangers in our environment. For instance, we would not be able to notice a honking motorist while crossing a busy street. Even more so, we would no longer be able to notice possible threats, ranging from possible thunderstorms to a faint crackling in the bushes while hiking in a forest. In short, our lives would change dramatically if we had to do without our hearing capacity.

Our auditory system is remarkable. It can detect subtle changes in air density with frequencies ranging from about 20 to 20,000 Hz. In terms of intensity, audible sounds may be caused by anything from a subtly falling leaf to a jet fighter departing with full afterburners. The loudest sounds that we can still tolerate are about a trillion times as intense in terms of power as the quietest sounds we can still perceive. Because we can perceive different frequencies simultaneously, we are able to interpret the combination of these frequencies, so that we can, for example, distinguish between the low 'E' tone on a guitar and the rumbling sound of a distant thunderstorm. We can also delineate the dynamic changes in these frequencies and use them, for example, to understand speech or to interpret rhythmic patterns in a piece of music.

7.2 SOUND

Physically, sound is defined as a vibration, which travels as an observable pressure wave through a conductive medium. In most cases, sound travels through the air, however, it can also travel through liquids, such as water, or solids, such as wood or metals. We can experience sound travelling through these alternative media by, for example, swimming under water or by placing our ear against a metal surface.

Sound is created by an oscillating source. The oscillation is characterised by two different basic properties. The amplitude (or strength) of the oscillation determines the intensity of the perceived sound, whereas the rate (or frequency) of the oscillation, expressed as the number of cycles per second (Hz), is related to its perceived pitch. In natural environments it is rare for us to encounter pure tones, that is, tones that consist of just one frequency. In contrast, a natural sound source tends to produce a range of different frequencies. When the mix of these frequencies is completely random, the resulting auditory signal is noise. In contrast, when the frequencies have fixed proportions to each other, a harmonic sequence is produced, and we typically perceive the resulting acoustic signal as a musical tone.

In addition, we are able to identify numerous transient changes in a sound source, which will also affect the properties of the perceived acoustic signal. These transient changes are essential for understanding speech (see Chapter 17), and they also play a critical role in distinguishing different musical instruments from each other. For example, a short sharp onset, which is followed by a rapid extinction, is characteristic of a drumbeat, while a sustained tone, with a large series of harmonic frequencies, characterises an electric guitar.

From a physical perspective, sound intensity is defined as the average energy that a sound wave projects each second onto an area of 1 m^2. Since energy is denoted with the unit joule (J), the unit for sound intensity is J/s×m^2. Because J/s equates to power [expressed by the unit Watt (W)], sound intensity can also be denoted as W/m^2. The lowest sound intensity that we can still perceive is around 10^{-12} W/m^2 (= 0.0000000000001 W/m^2). At the other end of the scale, sounds that we start to experience as unpleasantly loud have an intensity of about 1 W/m^2.

Our auditory system can therefore process intensity differences with a range of approximately 10^{12}. Moreover, our subjective experience of sound intensity is logarithmically related to physical intensity. Due to this relation, the

DOI: 10.4324/9781003319344-10

unit W/m² is unpractical in describing sound intensity differences. For this reason, we prefer to use a relative metric, known as the decibel (dB) scale. The zero point on this scale, the reference value, is defined as the lowest intensity level that people can still perceive. The dB scale is logarithmic and defined in such a way that a tenfold increase in power corresponds to an increase of 10 decibels. A 10 dB sound is therefore ten times as intense as the reference value, whereas a sound of 20 dB is 100 times as intense as the reference value.

7.3 ANATOMY AND FUNCTIONING OF THE EAR

The ear can be divided into an outer ear, a middle ear, and an inner ear (see fig 7.1). The outer ear consists of the auricle. This is the part that we typically identify as our 'ear' in our everyday life, however, in reality it is only a very small part of our auditory system. The auricle changes and reflects sound waves, in such a way that it amplifies them and facilitates the localisation of sound sources. The waves then pass through the auditory channel, and eventually reach the **eardrum** at the end of the channel. The eardrum is part of the middle ear and vibrates at the same frequencies as the sound waves that hit it.

The eardrum is connected to three small bones, the malleus, the incus, and the stapes (also known as hammer, anvil, and stirrup, respectively). These three bones are connected to the oval window and amplify the vibrations of the eardrum. The oval window forms the separation between the middle ear and the inner ear. The inner ear consists of two structures: the vestibular organ (also known as the labyrinth: see Chapter 8) and a small snail shell-shaped structure filled with fluid, which is known as the **cochlea** (see fig 7.2). The cochlea consists of three fluid-filled ducts; the scala vestibuli, the scala media, and the scala tympani. Vibrations from the oval window are passed on to the liquid in these ducts. These vibrations set the auditory receptors, which consist of small cilia, in motion.

How are the different frequencies that comprise a sound wave encoded by these cilia? There may be multiple answers to this question. According to the frequency encoding theory, neurons connected to the cilia fire at the same frequency as that of the perceived sound. A 20,000 Hz sound wave should therefore produce 20,000 action potentials per second. A major problem with this explanation, however, is that a neuron's **refractory period** (see Chapter 2) is about 1/1000 of a second, thus theoretically limiting its firing frequency to a maximum of 1000 Hz. In practice, the maximum firing frequency of a neuron is even further limited to around 1 Hz. For this reason, the frequency encoding theory appears to be unable to adequately explain pitch perception.

Alternatively, the place encoding theory proposes that the perceived frequency is determined by the location of the cochlea that is stimulated. This explanation is similar to the way in which the sound box of a guitar amplifies the tones it produces. The strings of a guitar produce tones that are dependent on their length and thickness. These tones are transmitted via a bridge to the sound box, which will resonate with the strings and thus cause a large mass

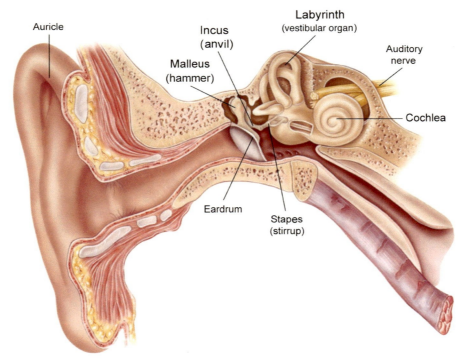

Figure 7.1 Anatomy of the ear. The auricle, part of the outer ear, reflects sound waves through the ear canal to the middle ear, where they cause the eardrum to vibrate. These vibrations are transmitted to the cochlea via the malleus, the incus, and the stapes. The cochlea contains cilia that convert the vibrations into neural impulses.

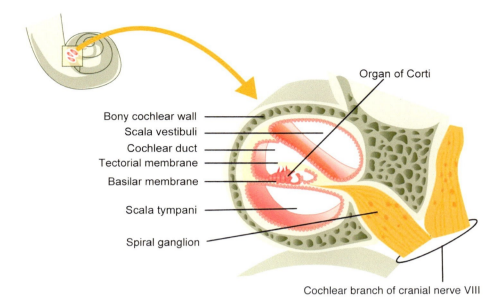

Figure 7.2 Cross section of the cochlea.

of air to vibrate. However, the resonance of the box is not uniform: some frequencies are more effective than others. To minimise this problem as much as possible, the box is designed so that its cross section is variable, causing the larger parts to resonate with the lower frequencies and the smaller parts with the higher frequencies. This is also the case with the cochlea. Due to variations in cross section and stiffness of the cochlea, different locations are selectively sensitive to different frequencies. The cochlea is, in other words, **tonotopically** organised. Again, this explanation is not without problems. If frequency

separation was solely based on the tonotopic organisation of the cochlea, we would expect to find that human pitch discrimination would be relatively course, disallowing us to make the fine frequency discriminations that cause us to detect a poorly tuned guitar or a poor vocal performance.

We can combine both explanations, however, to achieve a better understanding of frequency encoding. Although individual neurons can fire up to once per second, populations of neurons can encode higher frequencies (see fig 7.3). This is based on the principle that each

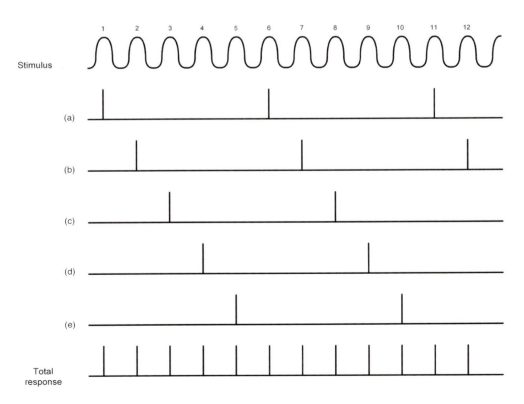

Figure 7.3 The principle of population coding.

wave top can only activate a subset of neurons. The combined firing frequency of all these neurons together, however, is equal to the frequency of the sound wave (Rose, Brugge, Anderson, & Hind, 1967). Up to frequencies of about 4,000 Hz, this mechanism can adequately explain how we can distinguish tones. In everyday practice, this is also the tonal range that we use the most for fine pitch discriminations (see also Box 7.1); for example, the highest note on a piano has a frequency of 4,224 Hz.

Box 7.1 Auditory masking and the rise of online music streaming

In 1982, the introduction of the compact disc (CD) sparked nothing less than a revolution in the music industry. Until then, sound was stored as an analogue signal on a physical medium. In most cases, this was done either as a groove that was cut into a vinyl record or as a magnetic track on a tape. On CDs, however, the audio signal is stored in the form of a series of Pits and Lands that is scanned by a laser beam and converted into numbers. Playback consists of reading 44,100 numbers, or samples (each containing 16 bits of information) per second for each channel. Together these samples describe the audio signal. A digital converter then transforms the samples into an analogue audio signal that can be amplified and reproduced using loudspeakers. A CD offered various technical advantages over traditional vinyl LPs or analogue cassette tapes, including a relative insensitivity to physical defects. Moreover, they also stored the information in a considerably more compact form. Limitations in computer technology of the early 1980s of the 20th century resulted in the signals being stored in an uncompressed format.

With the increase in computing power and the development of a formal description of information complexity (see Box 1.3), it eventually became technologically possible to compress and decompress digital audio signals in real time. It remained problematic, however, that the compression techniques yielded only a limited advantage: audio signals are typically complex and rich in information, so that gains in terms of storage space were relatively limited. From the mid-1990s onwards, it became technically possible to play music straight from the hard disk of a personal computer. Nevertheless, the problem remained that most computers in those days only had a relatively limited amount of storage space. In addition, the data files containing music were still too large to be sent via the extremely limited capacity of the internet of the 90s. For these reasons, CDs remained the most popular medium for storing and playing music.

Already at the time when CDs rose to prominence, however, a small German research project managed to report a major breakthrough that would eventually lead to the development of modern audio players and online music streaming. The project in question had set itself the goal of sending music over a telephone line, which made it necessary to compress the audio signal much further than the recently developed compression techniques allowed. To achieve such dramatic compression rates, information had to be removed from the signal, and the challenge was to remove as much information as possible without degrading the quality of the signal too far. The successful solution to this problem was based on a psychoacoustic model of the human auditory system. As is the case with the visual system, we typically hear much less than we assume. More specifically, loud sounds in a specific frequency band will mask sounds in the adjacent frequency bands. In addition, our hearing is also not equally sensitive to all frequency bands: we are particularly sensitive to frequencies from 2 to 4 kHz. This implies that we only need to have a high-quality sound representation in this frequency band.

The application of this psychoacoustic model has resulted in an algorithm that is able to reduce the size of an audio file to about 10% of its original size, without any apparent loss of quality. Although the algorithm has never been used to transmit music over a telephone line, it has become world famous after it was chosen to encode audio signals that were linked to digital videos. This video standard was developed by the Motion Pictures Experts Group (MPEG), and the name of the audio encoding was derived from it: MPEG-layer 3. After this standard was introduced in 1992, it was also more and more frequently used as an independent audio format, where it gained fame under the name MP3. From the late 1990s onward, in part related to the development of this standard, more and more independent media players would become available to play MP3 files. In addition, portable CD players and car stereo systems were also given the ability to play data CDs containing MP3 files, increasing the effective playback time of a CD by a factor of ten.

A more compact data format also made it possible to store music online, which has caused the online streaming and digital downloading of music to take off since the first decade of the 21st century. A remarkable development is that at the same time, the vinyl LP is making a huge comeback. Due to the combination of a renewed interest in physically buying music on LP and streaming online, it seems that the CD is going to be the big loser in this story.

Yet, we can still observe much higher frequencies; up to about 20,000 Hz. These higher frequencies are observed based on the differences in stiffness and width of the **basilar membrane** of the cochlea. The basilar membrane is part of the partition between the scala tympani and the scala media. This membrane is stiff and narrow at the base of the cochlea (where it resonates at the highest frequencies), and wide and limp towards the end, near the apex of the cochlea, where it resonates at low frequencies.

7.4 AUDITORY NEURAL PATHWAYS

The auditory neural signals pass through several subcortical nuclei before arriving at the auditory cortex (see fig 7.4). First, the auditory signal is projected to the cochlear nucleus, which is part of the medulla (see Chapter 2). From the cochlear nucleus, the signal is projected onward to a second nucleus in the medulla, known as the superior olive complex (also known as the superior olivary nucleus). At the cochlear nucleus, the auditory information is split in such a way that it is projected to both the ipsilateral and contralateral superior olive. From here, the information is projected forward to the inferior colliculus in the midbrain. The colliculus then projects the auditory information onward to the medial geniculate nucleus of the thalamus, and from there it is finally forwarded to the primary auditory cortex.

Auditory and visual signals intersect at a few points along this trajectory. The inferior colliculus processes auditory signals while the nearby superior colliculus processes visual input. The proximity of these two nuclei allows the possibility that there may already be some interaction between the visual and auditory modalities at this level (see Chapter 9 for a further discussion of multisensory interactions). Next, the signals intersect in the thalamus: here the auditory signals are processed by the medial geniculate nucleus, while the visual signals are processed by the lateral geniculate nucleus. In addition to the ascending projections discussed here, the auditory system is, just like the visual system, characterised by descending projections. These descending projections are involved in projecting modulatory signals back to the earliest stages of auditory processing, allowing us to adapt our auditory processes to current circumstances based on attention, expectations, or context.

7.4.1 AUDITORY LOCALISATION IN THE BRAINSTEM

One of the major challenges that our auditory system faces is sound localisation. For the auditory system this is a much greater challenge than it is for the visual system, because the location of a sound cannot be derived directly in the way that the visual system can derive this based on gaze position and the part of the retina that is stimulated. Nevertheless, being able to adequately localise sounds has very likely provided a great evolutionary advantage, with the consequence that the auditory system has developed a very robust sound localisation system. Part of this localisation process is already carried out in the brainstem, where the input from both ears is combined. Since our ears are on opposite sides of our body, they will each process sounds that originate from a given source slightly differently.

For example, a sound that originates from our left reaches our left ear just a little earlier than our right ear, causing

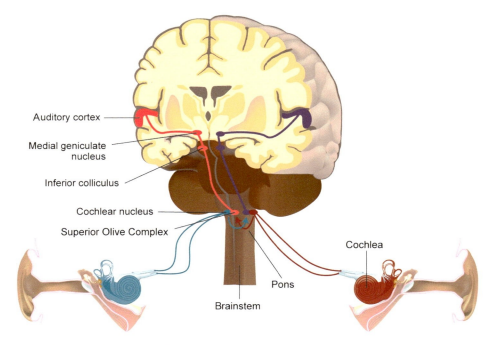

Figure 7.4 The auditory neural pathways from the inner ear to the primary auditory cortex.

an **interaural time difference**. This temporal difference is typically smaller than a millisecond. Moreover, the sound that reaches the first ear is also slightly more intense than the sound that reaches the second ear, because our head partially blocks the path of the sound wave to the second ear. This volume difference is known as the **interaural intensity difference**. In addition to these differences, we use several additional, more complex cues to determine the location of a sound source. These cues are, among others, based on the shape of our heads and ears. More specifically, the specific shape of our ears causes sounds

coming from below to be perceived slightly differently than sounds coming from above.

Many processes involved in sound localisation are already carried out at the earliest stages of sound processing that take place in the brainstem. More specifically, research in barn owls has established that a major part of the localisation process is carried out by the superior olive (Konishi, 2003). Neurons in this area receive input from both the left ear and the right ear (see fig 7.5) and can detect the aforementioned interaural time differences by being

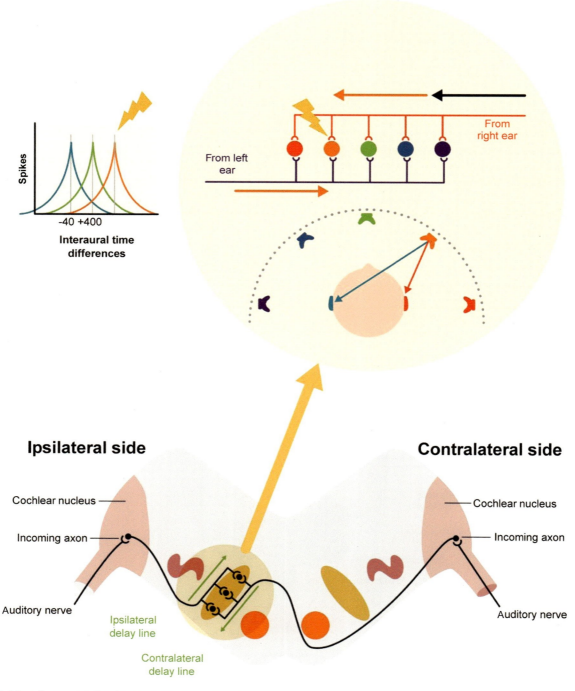

Figure 7.5 Schematic representation of the interaural delay lines in the superior olive, which are involved in decoding spatial information in the auditory signal.

connected via delay lines. These delay lines create a map of the spatial locations of our ambient sounds. Further steps in the processing of the auditory signal make use of the spatial information that is thus obtained. For example, the inferior colliculus contains a spatial map of our acoustic environment, which can be combined with the similar map of our visual environment that exists in the superior colliculus. From an evolutionary perspective, it makes sense for auditory spatial information to be calculated at such an early stage, because it allows us to respond quickly to auditory warning signals.

7.5 THE AUDITORY CORTEX

The aforementioned subcortical pathways eventually project to the auditory cortex, which is located in the temporal lobe. Most of our knowledge about the auditory cortex has been obtained from animal studies, including primates. Although a sufficient amount of research is also carried out in humans, it is difficult to measure auditory cortex activity directly in humans. One of the main reasons for this is

that fMRI techniques are difficult to combine with auditory stimulation, because fMRI scanners are noisy, forcing participants to wear ear protection, which limits our options to work around the scanner noise.

Moreover, working with naturalistic sounds poses additional problems in fMRI research. Due to the intense magnetic fields generated by the scanner, it is impossible to use loudspeakers in the vicinity of the scanner. Instead, either special fMRI-compatible headphones should be used, or the sounds should be produced outside the scanner and presented to the participant by means of an acoustic transmission system. Due to these challenges, which are also complicated by the fact that the participant is laying still in a very narrow tube, it is particularly difficult to present natural-sounding spatial sounds. Nevertheless, studies involving humans are consistent with animal studies and converge into a consistent view of the anatomical organisation of the auditory cortex (Recanzone & Sutter, 2008).

The auditory cortex can be roughly divided into three regions (see fig 7.6), known as the core, the belt (which surrounds the core), and the parabelt [which surrounds the belt (Hackett & Kaas, 2004; Romanski & Averbeck,

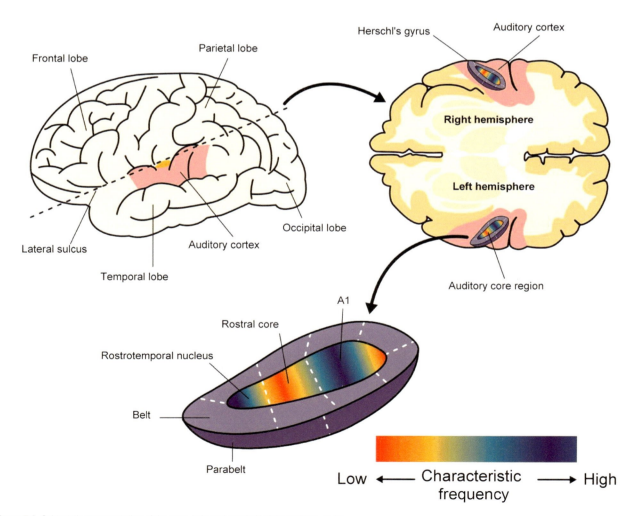

Figure 7.6 Schematic representation of the core, belt, and parabelt of the auditory cortex.

2009)]. The core itself can be subdivided into the primary auditory cortex (A1; also known as **Herschl's gyrus**) and the areas that are located anteriorly relative to the primary auditory cortex. These are the rostral and rostro-temporal fields. The core receives input from the medial geniculate nucleus of the thalamus, while the belt receives input mainly from the core. The parabelt mainly receives input from the belt. Although this sequence assumes a hierarchical organisation, the belt and the parabelt also have also been found to receive input directly from the medial geniculate nucleus.

7.5.1 TONOTOPIC ORGANISATION

All three areas in the core of the auditory cortex (A1, the rostral, and the rostrotemporal fields) are organised according to a tonotopic map. A tonotopic map is similar to the retinotopic map in the visual system, with the main difference being that a tonotopic map predominantly represents pitch. Here, specific areas in the core represent the individual frequencies of the auditory spectrum. Neurons in nearby areas are characterised by similar receptive fields. Unlike the receptive field of the visual system, these receptive fields are not sensitive to specific locations, but to specific pitches. In general, the closer the match between a presented sound and the receptive field of the neuron, the stronger the neuron will fire.

When we plot the relationship between the pitch of the presented sound and the activity of the neuron, we obtain a **tuning curve**. Note that the characteristics of these tuning curves vary across different parts of the core of the auditory cortex. In area A1, neurons are generally characterised by relatively narrow tuning curves, implying that neurons are very selective to specific pitches, while in the belt and the parabelt the tuning curves are much broader. In addition, neurons in the primary auditory cortex respond mainly to pure sounds, that is, to sounds that consist of only a single pitch, while neurons in higher-order regions respond predominantly to more complex sounds.

7.5.2 PRIMARY AUDITORY CORTEX: PITCH AND FREQUENCY

Although the primary auditory cortex appears to respond predominantly to pure tones, we must note an important caveat here. Pitch and frequency are related to each other, but they are not the same. For instance, Pantev et al. (1989) have described a clear distinction between these two aspects of sound perception. To illustrate, a clear example of the ambiguous relation between pitch and frequency can be found in the phenomenon of the missing fundamental. Typically, a tone consists of a fundamental frequency (for example, the standard 'A' at 440 Hz)

and a series of harmonics that are each a multiple of the fundamental frequency (e.g., 880 Hz, 1320 Hz, 1760 Hz, etc.). Subjectively, we perceive this mix as a single tone corresponding to the standard 'A'. If we omit the 440 Hz, fundamental frequency, we essentially still hear the same 'A' tone, as if the fundamental frequency is still there. Based on this phenomenon, we can turn to the question how exactly pitch is represented.[1]

To address this question, two radically opposing hypotheses have been proposed. Initially, Hermann Von Helmholtz (1862) proposed that tones were ordered according to frequency in the auditory system and represented in spatially distinct areas of the auditory cortex. Although Von Helmholtz's theory was consistent with the tonotopic organisation of the auditory cortex that we have already introduced, it had difficulties explaining the missing fundamental phenomenon.

Thus, a more elaborate explanation of pitch perception is based on the idea that pitch is related to the temporal structure of the auditory stimuli. More specifically, this idea assumes that the greatest common denominator of the periodicity of all harmonic frequencies together equates to the period of the fundamental frequency. The American computer scientist Joseph Licklider (1956) attempted to explain this phenomenon on the basis of the assumption that pure tones are processed by the same cortical areas as complex tones with the same temporal structure. Pantev et al. (1989) did indeed find evidence for this hypothesis. They used magnetoencephalography and compared activity in the auditory cortex that was evoked either by simple tones or by complex harmonic tones of the same fundamental frequency. The main finding was that both complex and simple tones activated the same areas in the auditory cortex. This result suggests that pitch processing has already taken place in one of the subcortical relay nuclei, through which the auditory signal had passed before reaching the auditory cortex.

7.5.3 BELT AND PARABELT: COMPLEX SOUNDS

Non-human primate studies have reported that damage to the belt and parabelt does not impair the ability to recognise isolated sounds. In contrast, it is the ability to distinguish complex patterns, such as sequences of tones, that is impaired (Kaas et al., 1999). Other studies in monkeys have shown that neurons in the lateral belt areas are specifically sensitive to vocalisations (Petkov et al., 2008; Romanski & Averbeck, 2009). Moreover, neurons in the belt are more sensitive to top-down attentional influences, compared to neurons in the core. It thus appears that, similar to the visual cortex, the auditory cortex is marked by a hierarchical organisation in which progressively more complex properties of a stimulus are represented at progressively higher levels in this hierarchy.

In humans, it is assumed that the belt and the parabelt areas correspond to an area known as the planum temporale, which is involved in speech processing. More specifically, the left planum temporale is mainly activated by speech signals, while both the left and the right planum temporale are also activated by other complex sound patterns, such as music and natural sounds (Griffiths & Warren, 2002), implying that this area is involved in recognising higher-order aspects of sounds.

7.5.4 'WHAT' AND 'WHERE' PROCESSING IN THE AUDITORY CORTEX

Separate neural pathways have been identified for the processing of spatial and non-spatial auditory properties (Kaas & Hackett, 1999; Rauschecker, 2015; Rauschecker & Scott, 2009). It has been shown that spatial information is mainly processed by the more caudal, posterior areas of the auditory cortex, while non-spatial information is processed by the more rostral, anterior parts of the auditory cortex (see fig 7.7). The non-spatial properties of auditory stimuli consist of combinations of frequencies – and changes in these frequencies – that enable us to identify a sound as a particular object, for example a voice, a church bell, a telephone, or a guitar. The specialised processing of spatial and non-spatial information is thus roughly equivalent to the visual 'what' versus 'where' distinction that we have already introduced in the previous chapter.

Further evidence for a distinction between the processing of 'what' and 'where' properties come from studies focusing on the anatomical projections of the auditory cortex to other brain areas. The caudal auditory cortex projects, among others, to brain areas involved in the processing of spatial information and the integration of this information

into our actions. These areas include the parietal cortex and the frontal eye fields (see Chapters 9 and 10). The rostral auditory cortex, on the other hand, projects mainly to association areas in the temporal cortex and the orbitofrontal regions (Hackett & Kaas, 2004). Single cell studies in monkeys have provided further evidence for this distinction. Increases in activity in the lateral belt areas were recorded while monkeys were listening to calls from their kin. Moreover, neurons in the anterior part of the belt mainly responded to the specific type of call, while neurons in the posterior part of the belt mainly responded to the location of the call (Tian, Reser, Durham, Kustov, & Rauschecker, 2001).

In humans, too, evidence has been found for the distinction between what and where in the auditory cortex. Ahveninen, Jääskeläinen, et al. (2006) used a combination of fMRI and MEG while participants heard a vowel that was presented from an unknown location. After this, another vowel was presented. This second vowel could either be identical to the first, or it could be another vowel presented from the same location, or the same vowel presented from a different location. When the two items were presented from different locations, this resulted in a stronger activation in the posterior regions of areas A1 as well as in the superior temporal gyrus. This result suggests that these areas are specifically sensitive to the location of a sound. In contrast, the anterior parts of A1 as well as the superior temporal gyrus responded more strongly when another vowel was presented from the same location, suggesting that these areas are especially sensitive to the type of sound. Finally, it was found that administering a TMS pulse over the posterior auditory cortex mainly impaired the ability to localise a sound, while a TMS pulse over the anterior auditory cortex mainly had a disruptive effect on the ability to identify a sound (Ahveninen et al., 2013).

7.5.5 CORTICAL PLASTICITY OF THE AUDITORY CORTEX

The auditory cortex is also characterised by a high degree of plasticity. For example, Pantev, Oostenveld, Engelien, Roberts, and Hoke (1998) recorded MEG responses to piano tones in musicians. They found that the amplitude of the cortical response to these tones was increased by about 25% compared to a control group that had never played a musical instrument. Moreover, they found that the amount of magnification correlated with the number of years of experience that the musicians had.

7.5.5.1 Tinnitus

Although cortical plasticity is a mostly adaptive process, yielding predominantly positive effects, maladaptive forms of adaptation can also occur (Elgoyhen, Langguth, De Ridder, & Vanneste, 2015). Shore, Roberts, and Langguth (2016) for instance, argue that maladaptive plasticity may be

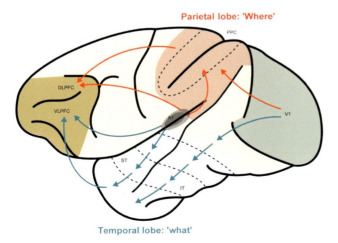

Figure 7.7 The ventral and dorsal pathways in the auditory system. PPC: posterior parietal cortex, DLPFC: dorsolateral prefrontal cortex, VLPC: ventrolateral prefrontal cortex, A1: primary auditory cortex, V1: primary visual cortex, ST: superior temporal lobe, IT: inferior temporal lobe. (source: Rauschecker and Scott, 2009)

linked to the onset of **tinnitus**. Tinnitus is a form of phantom perception, which often manifests itself in the form of a continuous beep. It also frequently occurs in a multitude of auditory pathologies (Jestreboff, 1990). The most frequent cause of tinnitus is hearing loss, due to aging or prolonged recreational exposure to high sound volumes. Although most occurrences of tinnitus are characterised by a continuous beep, other phantom percepts have been reported, such as continuous hearing of insect sounds, bells, running water, or even multiple sounds at the same time (Shore et al., 2016).

The fact that tinnitus is not caused by changes in the peripheral auditory system is evidenced by the fact that **deafferentation** of the auditory nerves does not cause the symptoms of tinnitus to disappear. In some cases, this procedure may even strengthen them (Blasco & Redleaf, 2014). Shore et al. identify a number of factors associated with tinnitus, including plastic changes at the brainstem level, and increased connectivity between the auditory cortex, the frontoparietal attention networks, the sensorimotor networks, and the networks involved in memory and emotion (see fig 7.8).

Hullfish, Sedley, and Vanneste (2019) have attempted to explain tinnitus using the predictive coding framework. These authors make a distinction between acute and chronic tinnitus. They hypothesise that acute tinnitus is caused by increased sensory precision in the auditory channels. Chronic tinnitus, on the other hand, is caused by a change in predictive processes, according to Hullfish et al.. This change, combined with a reduced afferent input from the auditory system, would result in a change in perception.

7.6 BASIC AUDITORY PROCESSING

7.6.1 AUDITORY ERPs

Much research on basic auditory processing employs electrophysiology. In audiological studies, short intense stimuli are sometimes used to evoke an acoustic reflex (also known as the **stapedius reflex**). This reflex is caused by an automatic contraction of a middle ear muscle in response to the sound. EEG can also reflect the transmission of auditory signals through the brainstem. This can be observed by presenting a short sound, which evokes five specific peaks in the EEG. These peaks are known as the auditory brainstem responses (Picton, Hillyard, Krausz, & Galambos, 1974).

Cognitive psychology studies investigating auditory perception focus mostly on auditory ERPs. A simple auditory ERP is characterised by a number of distinct components, including P1, N1, P2, and N2 (Fonoaryova Key, Dove, & Maguire, 2005; Picton et al., 1974). The P1 peaks approximately 50 ms after the onset of an auditory stimulus and the amplitude of this component is associated with the

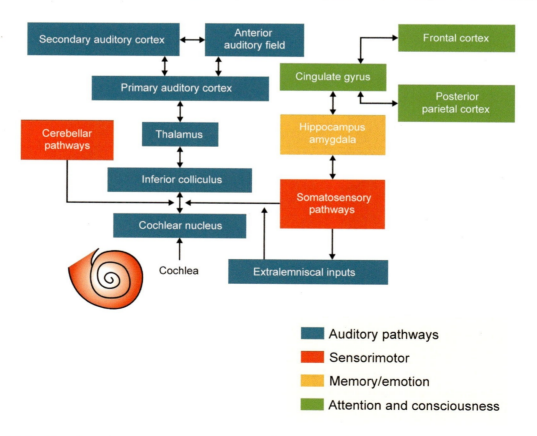

Figure 7.8 An overview of the main neural connections involved in the generation of tinnitus. (source: Shore et al., 2016)

inhibition of auditory information. The P1 amplitude is often recorded using a **sensory gating** paradigm. Here, two clicks are presented in quick succession, and a typical finding is that the amplitude of the P1 following the second click is reduced in amplitude, compared to the P1 following the first click. This finding implies that the processing of the second click is inhibited. The P1 component is likely to be generated by multiple brain regions. Using **intercranial EEGs**, Korzyukov et al. (2007) found a possible source of the P1 in the temporal cortex. The gating mechanism, however, was more strongly associated with activation in the frontal lobes. The N1 component often co-occurs with the P2, resulting in the fact that they are sometimes also denoted as the N1/P2 complex. Note, however, that Crowley and Colrain (2004) have report that the P2 can be evoked independently of the N1. Moreover, the amplitude of the N1 component is sensitive to attention (Woldorff et al., 1993).

The auditory ERP components just described are likely to be generated in, or near, specific areas of the auditory cortex (Hari, Aittoniemi, Jävinen, Katila, & Varpula, 1980). Interestingly, their amplitude is typically the largest over the frontal and central parts of the scalp. In other words, auditory ERPs are characterised by a frontocentral scalp distribution. The reason why the amplitude of these components is not maximal directly over the brain areas where the component is generated is that the neural generators in the auditory cortex are located in a sulcus and thus partly tangentially oriented relative to the scalp. As a consequence, their electric fields project onto the more distant frontal and central parts of the scalp. Because MEG is well suited to measure activity from tangential cortical sources (see Box 3.4; Chapter 3), MEG is a relatively popular technique for studying auditory processing (Hari et al., 1980).

7.6.1.1 Auditory ERPs and Self-Generated Sounds

A remarkable finding is that auditory ERPs are typically reduced in amplitude when the evoking sounds are self-generated (Mifsud, Beesley, Watson, & Whitford, 2016). Hungarian perception scientist János Horvath (2015) has discussed possible explanations for this phenomenon. The currently most-accepted explanation is based on the concept of forward models (see Chapter 3). It assumes that a self-generated action generates a **corollary discharge signal** that is projected to the sensory cortices. Evidence for this explanation is rather scarce, however, as it is mostly based on studies involving schizophrenia. In schizophrenic patients, the amplitude of the auditory N1 component has been found to be reduced (Ford & Mathalon, 2012), and since schizophrenia patients are believed to have an impaired capacity of generating forward models (Frith, Blakemore, & Wolpert, 2000), this observation would be consistent with the idea that self-generated actions attenuate auditory processing. It has also been found that the lateralisation of the **readiness potential** tends to correspond with the

attenuation of the N1 component (Ford, Palzes, Roach, & Mathalon, 2014). The latter finding implies that individuals with a stronger willingness to act are also characterised by a greater attenuation of auditory processing.

7.6.2 MISMATCH DETECTION

One of the most robust findings in the field of auditory perception is that the auditory cortex is particularly sensitive to the violation of expectations in auditory patterns. This was first reported in the form of the **mismatch negativity**, that is, a negative ERP component that occurs when an auditory stimulus deviates in some way from other stimuli in the sequence. As we will discuss in detail next, this mismatch negativity can be evoked by a wide variety of deviations in stimuli or stimulus patterns.

7.6.2.1 The Mismatch Negativity

The existence of the mismatch negativity was first reported by Näätänen, Gaillard, and Mäntysalo (1978). In their study, participants were presented a series of tones, which were delivered randomly to their left or right ear. Most of the tones were identical, but occasionally a slightly deviant tone was presented. The participant's task consisted of counting the deviant stimuli that were presented to one ear. During the experiment, EEGs were recorded, and the ERPs that were evoked by the deviant stimuli were characterised by a negative potential that manifested itself at about 150 ms after stimulus onset and lasted a few hundred milliseconds. This mismatch negativity can be visualised by subtracting the ERP response to the standard tone from an ERP response to the deviant tone, thus accentuating the difference between the standard and the deviant stimulus (see fig 7.9).

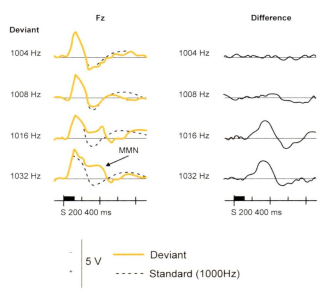

Figure 7.9 Illustration of the mismatch negativity, as recorded by an electrode on the forehead. (source: Näätänen, Paavilainen, Rinne, and Alho, 2007)

In a literature review, Näätänen et al. (2007) argued that the mismatch negativity reflects the brain's automatic response to any change in auditory stimulation that can be subjectively noted. In addition, they also discussed how the mismatch negativity can be evoked by more abstract forms of changes in auditory stimulation, such as grammatical errors in our primary language. The mismatch negativity typically starts around 150 ms after the onset of the deviant stimulus, however, this onset becomes shorter as the deviation increases. An important precondition of the mismatch negativity is that the brain must have been given the opportunity to form a representation of what the standard is. In addition, the response is largely automatic: the mismatch negativity is detected even when participants do not attend the evoking stimuli (but, see: Woldorff, Hillyard, Gallen, Hampson, & Bloom, 1998, for results that did show that the mismatch negativity can be manipulated by attention).

Although most studies on the mismatch negativity have used relatively simple stimuli, such as beeps, it can also be evoked by changes in complex stimuli, such as speech sounds. It can even be evoked by stimuli that deviate from a relatively abstract rule, such as the repetition of an identical tone in a sequence of descending tones. Most likely, there are two intracranial processes that contribute to the generation of the mismatch negativity. The first process is localised in the bilateral supratemporal cortex. This process is presumably involved in the early stages of deviance detection. The second process is primarily localised in the right frontal cortex and is presumably involved in exogenously focusing attention on the auditory deviance.

Because ERPs are often sensitive to the physical properties of a stimulus, current mismatch negativity studies typically evoke it by using a stimulus that is used as the standard in one condition and as the deviant stimulus in another condition. For example, consider a tone of 1000 Hz that is presented in the first condition as a deviant stimulus between a series of tones of 1100 Hz. In the second condition, this is reversed; the 1000 Hz tone is now the default. The mismatch negativity can now be calculated by calculating only the ERP response evoked by the 1000 Hz tone and by comparing these ERPs across the two conditions.

7.6.2.2 The Neural Basis of the Mismatch Negativity

Traditionally, two alternative explanations have been proposed for the mismatch negativity: the adaptation hypothesis and the model adjustment hypothesis. The model adjustment hypothesis assumes that the mismatch negativity is the result of modifying an internal model of the auditory input. This model would be stored in memory and adjusted upon the detection of an irregularity. The adaptation hypothesis, on the other hand, assumes that there is a much simpler neural mechanism, namely the adaptation

of auditory cortex neurons to a changing sound pattern. Garrido, Kilner, Stephan, and Friston (2009) postulate that both theoretical explanations could possibly be united in the predictive coding framework.

Wacongne, Changeux, and Dehaene (2012) took a similar approach and developed a computational model to describe the neural basis of the mismatch negativity. This model, which is based on the predictive coding framework, postulates that in layers 2 and 3 of the auditory cortex, predictions are generated from a memory trace. Furthermore, a mechanism for processing prediction errors was proposed to exist in layer 4 of the auditory cortex. The predictions generated in layers 2 and 3 are then believed to be compared with the actual sensory input projected from the thalamus to the auditory cortex. The difference between the predicted and the actual inputs is then assumed to be determined in layer 4. The model of Wacongne et al. calculates the electrical potentials that would arise from the activation of the prediction error mechanism.

Simulation results that were generated by the model were then compared with the results of an MEG study in which the mismatch negativity was evoked using an auditory **oddball paradigm**. In this paradigm, a regular sequence of stimuli is presented, which is occasionally interrupted by the presentation of a deviant stimulus (the oddball). The onset and the time course of the actual mismatch negativities elicited by the oddball paradigm corresponded well with the simulation results. In addition, Wacongne et al. simulated a number of other conditions that would evoke a mismatch negativity, for example, when a stimulus is omitted from the sequence. Again, when our brain does not expect stimuli to be omitted from a sequence, it will generate a mismatch negativity. This observation implies that the mismatch negativity is indeed mainly caused by the processing of prediction errors. Deviations in the duration of the stimuli were also modelled and predicted to evoke a mismatch negativity; a prediction that was confirmed by the empirical results.

7.7 AUDITORY SCENE ANALYSIS

Obviously, auditory perception is not limited to simple beeps and the localisation of those beeps. In everyday life, we are confronted with a complex spectrum of sounds, ranging from traffic and other environmental noise in a busy city to a variety of natural sounds in a forest (birds chirping, crackling branches) to busy conversations in a large auditorium to the sound of radio, television, or HiFi equipment in our living rooms. The study of the processes that allow us to recognise and distinguish these individual sounds in our natural environment is known as **auditory scene analysis**.

7.7.1 BASIC PRINCIPLES OF AUDITORY SCENE ANALYSIS

One of the problems that our auditory system is confronted with is that the mix of auditory signals that reaches our ears is particularly ambiguous (Pressnitzer, Suied, & Shamma, 2011). A major problem here is that an auditory signal is, in essence, one-dimensional. That is, the sound waves that reach our ears consist of nothing more than a sequence of vibrations that progress over time. To interpret this mix, our auditory system needs to generate a spatiotemporal reconstruction of this environment based on the information contained in this signal. The problem is, of course, that any compression of the eardrum can be caused by one or another other sound source, and the crucial question is how these sources can be distinguished from each other.

Bregman (1990) presumes that auditory scene analysis can be broken up into two distinct subproblems. The first problem is time-bound and is described by the term 'vertical organisation'. This description is derived from the way in which different frequencies of an acoustic signal are represented in a spectrogram (see fig 7.10). A spectrogram represents the frequencies that are present in the signal at a given time. In this case, vertical refers to the frequency axis of the spectrogram. At any given time, the auditory scene analysis process must determine the energy distribution over the different frequencies and, based on this, attempt to determine their source.

This can be done, for example, through the analysis of harmonic information. The occurrence of harmonic frequencies can be an indication that they originate from the same source. Note, however, that the auditory system must also be able to identify sounds that are not completely periodic and therefore not capable of generating

perfect harmonies (a muted tone on a guitar, for example). For this reason, the system must have some built-in tolerance for imperfect harmonies. Other principles that can contribute to grouping different frequencies include the onset (Hukin & Darwin, 1995), the location (as determined by interaural time differences; as already described) of a sound (Darwin, 2008), or other regularities in the auditory spectrum (Roberts & Bailey, 1996).

The second subproblem is known as the 'horizontal organisation' and is related to the temporal axis of the spectrogram. The source of a sound can be present across extensive periods of time, but it does not necessarily need to be continuously active. Consider, for example, a series of footsteps that we attribute to one sound source. Here, we typically do not need to reorganise our percept for every single footstep. Multiple discrete sounds all belonging to the same source are known as a stream. Melodies are a very clear example of a stream. The cues that we collect with respect to the horizontal organisation follow the principle of plausibility. That is, we consider the likelihood that multiple sounds belong to the same stream. For instance, because it is unlikely that two individual sounds coming from the same source will differ drastically in timbre, pitch, and location in a short period of time, we tend to group similar sounds that follow each other over time together into a stream. Perceptually similar sounds are thus grouped together, while perceptually dissimilar sounds are segregated from each other.

More recently, a drastically different organisational principle for auditory scene analysis has been proposed (Elhilali, Ma, Micheyl, Oxenham, & Shamma, 2009; Shamma, Elhilali, & Micheyl, 2011). According to these theorists, there is only one simple organisational principle

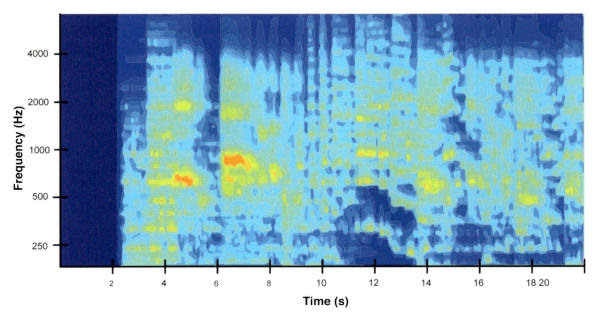

Figure 7.10 Example of a spectrogram. (source: Pressnitzer et al., 2011)

that determines how auditory streams are formed. This would be done on the basis of multiple parallel neural channels, each representing a different aspect of sound, such as periodicity, location, or temporal or spectral modulation. The problem with auditory scene analysis is that these different channels have to be bound together. According to this view, the problem of auditory scene analysis is comparable to the **binding problem** of visual perception (see Chapter 6). The temporal coherence between channels can possibly determine which channels should be bound together into a stream and which channels should be separated from each other.

Pressnitzer et al. (2011) also argue that top-down influences play an important role in auditory scene analysis. Familiarity with sounds (Agus, Thorpe, & Pressnitzer, 2010; Bregman, 1990; McDermott, Wrobleski, & Oxenham, 2011), attention (Thompson, Carlyon, & Cusack, 2011), and visual processes (Suied, Bonneel, & Viaud-Delmon, 2008) have been reported to affect the segmentation of auditory information into multiple streams.

7.7.2 AMBIGUITY

In combining different cues, the auditory system must be able to handle ambiguities. Pressnitzer et al. (2011) argue that studying these ambiguities can be useful for gaining crucial insights into the auditory scene analysis process. They propose to use auditory **bistable** illusions for this purpose. Such illusions may be conceived as the auditory counterpart of the visual bistable illusions that we have already introduced in Chapters 4 and 6, such as the face-vase illusion, the Necker cube, or the rabbit-duck illusion.

Although the use of bistable stimuli is considerably less prominent in the auditory sciences than it is in vision sciences, some auditory stimuli are bistable and are therefore potentially suitable for investigating auditory scene analysis. A surprisingly simple auditory stimulus already appears to be bistable. When we take two pure tones of different frequencies, and play them in an alternating repetitive pattern, they can be observed as either one melody or as two intertwined melodies (see fig 7.11). Another bistable auditory stimulus, described by Pressnitzer et al.

(2011), consists of repeating a simple sequence of words, such as the series 'life life life'. When presented repeatedly, the sequence tends to alternate between 'life life life' and 'fly fly fly' for most listeners.

How can such bistable stimuli be used to investigate auditory scene analysis processes? One possibility is to relate the subjective changes in perception, as reported by participants, to changes in neural processes. Note that this is similar to the way bistable visual stimuli are used in vision sciences (Leopold & Logothetis, 1999).

Studies using such bistable auditory stimuli aim to find a neural correlate for the change in perception. Since the physical input remains constant, these changes must be related to a change in the grouping of the stimuli. Based on this procedure, it has been shown that these changes can occur at various stages of auditory processing. For example, Gutschalk et al. (2005) found, on the basis of MEG results, that the subjective shift from one stream to two streams and vice versa corresponded to a change in activation of the secondary auditory cortex. Likewise, Cusack (2005) used a paradigm similar to that of Gutschalk and found fMRI results suggesting that the change in perception was associated with activation in the intraparietal sulcus. This area is located near the auditory cortex, and it is involved in multisensory processing (see Chapter 9). Kondo and Kashino (2009) were specifically interested in the moment when the change in perception occurred and were able to relate this change to changes in activation in both the primary auditory cortex and the auditory transmission nuclei in the thalamus.

A number of studies have even reported that the formation of auditory streams may already take place in the cochlear nucleus, which is the first relay station after the cochlea (Micheyl, Tian, Carlyon, & Rauschecker, 2005). It should be noted, however, that this is most likely only the case for very simple stimuli. More complex stimuli, such as speech, may be segmented at much higher levels, possibly even involving the frontal cortex (Kondo & Kashino, 2007). Thus, to summarise, these results imply that auditory stream formation is a complex process that takes place at multiple levels in the auditory processing pathways.

Figure 7.11 Example of a bistable audio stream. (a) Sequences in which the consecutive tones do not differ much in pitch, causing them to be perceived as one auditory stream; (b) sequences in which the consecutive tones differ considerably in pitch, causing them to be perceived as multiple streams. Bistable streams are at the intersection between these two examples. (source: Pressnitzer et al., 2011)

7.8 MUSIC PERCEPTION

Our ability to perceive and to produce music appears to be a uniquely human feature. As such, it is comparable to our language skills. Although, historically, much less cognitive research has been devoted to the study of music than to language, music, and the cognitive sciences are strongly intertwined (Pearce & Rohrmeier, 2012).

It is not yet clear what the potential evolutionary advantages of music might have been. Nevertheless, the role of music does appear to extend beyond its pure emotional experience, since specific brain areas appear to be dedicated to the perception and processing of music. An important difference with language perception is that music is not a symbolic representation of our environment, but instead exists in its own right (Besson & Friederici, 2005). To understand the exact role of music, we would need to have a formal definition of music, and this is currently still lacking. Traditional music theory aims to describe the fundamental rules of music. In practice, however, this often boils down to an extremely limited set of rules that are mainly focused on the genre that the rules in question aim to describe (Purwins et al., 2008). Music theory should therefore be considered more as a guideline than as a formal description of the processes involved in music perception.

7.8.1 BASIC PROCESSES OF MUSIC PERCEPTION

Our understanding of the perceptual processes involved in music has taken giant leaps forward since the mid-19th century (Helmholtz, 1862). Ever since von Helmholtz's influential work, we have been able to identify key aspects, such as perceptual thresholds, pitch, loudness, and timbre, and to describe the interactions between these aspects. For instance, extending the tonotopic organisation of the auditory cortex, as described earlier, a clear distinction between pitch and time-based representations has been found (Justus & Bharucha, 2001). More specifically, representations of harmonic and rhythmic patterns are believed to be formed in the secondary belt areas, and the integration of the individual patterns into an overall musical representation has been found to take place in the parabelt.

Koelsch and Siebel (2005) argue that music perception involves several specific neural and cognitive processes (see fig 7.12). According to Koelsch and Siebel's model, perception starts with the analysis of elementary properties of the acoustic signal, such as pitch, chroma, timbre, intensity, and roughness. Based on Gestalt principles, these individual properties are then believed to be integrated into melodies and rhythmic patterns and stored in an auditory memory. This initial analysis is then followed by a more detailed analysis of the harmonic intervals. Here, different types of chords (minor, major, etc.) are identified, based on the underlying relationships of the tones forming a melody or a chord. At the same time, a more detailed analysis of temporal intervals takes place. These analyses of harmonic and temporal intervals are likely to occur independently of each other, as a double dissociation has been found between these forms of processing.

In addition, Koelsch and Siebel (2005) hypothesise that syntactic analysis plays a major role in music perception. Almost every form of music is characterised by a specific organisation of perceptual elements, which can be structured on the basis of syntactic regularities (Koelsch, 2005). For example, the relationship between a chord and

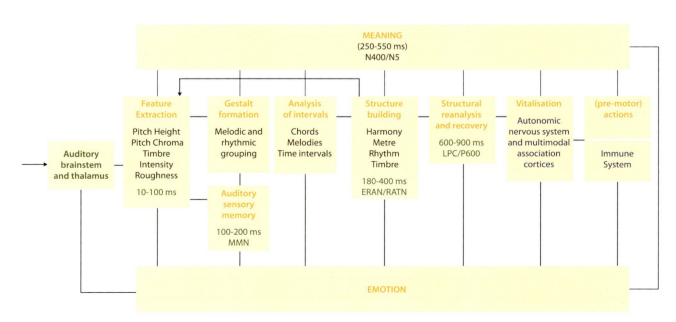

Figure 7.12 An overview of the most important processes of music perception. (source: Koelsch and Siebel, 2005)

the preceding harmonic context can be used to determine a chord's function. Similar processes are probably involved in the processing of rhythm and metre. This is probably done automatically, and the processes involved are also active in people who have received little to no formal musical training. Koelsch and Siebel (2005) argue that this form of syntactic processing is of the same level of complexity as the syntactic processing of language (see Chapter 17). Koelsch et al. (2004) hypothesise that the result of these syntactic processes in music perception is crucial for the processing of meaning and emotion in music. Structurally irregular events, such as irregular chords, can trigger affective emotional responses, such as surprise. Later stages of syntactic processing may be necessary when a reanalysis, or correction, of the mental representation is necessary.

In one of the last stages of music processing, the body is affected through a process that Koelsch and Siebel (2005) describe with the term 'vitalisation'. Vitalisation involves the activation of the autonomic nervous system. In addition, it is involved in integrating musical and non-musical information. Here, non-musical information includes the associations that are linked to a piece of music, along with the emotional and physical responses to the music. This integration process presumably involves multimodal association areas in the parietal cortex. These areas are probably also involved in musical awareness (Block, 2005). Thus far, the effects of music on the autonomic nervous system have mainly been recorded using heart rate and skin conductance measurements, along with subjective reports of goosebumps and chills.

These bodily reactions can have an effect on the immune system and the motor system. For instance, music perception can influence motor preparation processes in musicians (Drost, Rieger, Brass, Gunter, & Prinz, 2005a; Drost, Rieger, Brass, Gunter, & Prinz, 2005b). For pianists, listening to piano pieces can evoke activity in the premotor cortex (Haueisen & Knösche, 2001). In addition, it is very common for music to evoke the tendency to tap, sing, or dance along (Cannon & Patel, 2021). It appears that the induction of such actions by music is linked to neural impulses in the reticular formation, and that they are related to the enhancement of arousal. These forms of expression underscore the social importance of music (see also: Leman & Maes, 2014, for a literature review).

7.8.1.1 Harmony and Dissonance

One of the basic processes in music perception is the perception of harmony and dissonance. Harmony is experienced when three or more tones are presented simultaneously that have a specific mathematical relationship to each other in terms of frequency (as discussed previously). Consonant, or harmonic, tones sound pleasant and stable, while dissonant tones sound unpleasant and unstable. Why exactly some relationships sound pleasant and others do not

is a question that has occupied musicians, music theorists, and music psychologists for centuries. Historically, two dominant views on this question have been provided: Von Helmholtz (1862) hypothesised that dissonance was experienced because the individual tones could affect similar parts of the basilar membrane, causing interference. Tonal theories, on the other hand, sought to explain dissonance based on violations of the harmonic principles underlying Western music.

Johnson-Laird, Kang, and Leong (2012) propose a dual mechanism that is based on a combination of both of the aforementioned principles. Their dual theory assumes that there are three principles involved in determining the degree of dissonance in a chord. The first of these states that chords based on a major scale are less dissonant than chords based on a minor scale, which in turn are less dissonant than chords that are based on another scale. The second principle states that chords based on a major triad are less dissonant than chords that are not. Finally, the third principle assumes that chords made up of intervals of thirds are less dissonant than chords that are not. Together, these three principles – the use of the diatonic scale, the central role of the major triad, and the construction of chords of thirds – are all applicable to tonal music. According to Johnson-Laird et al. (2012), these three principles are nested together in the previously described order, and collectively determine the relative dissonance of a chord. The authors also emphasise that the context in which a chord is heard can also affect the perceived dissonance. Therefore, they assume that tonal chords (i.e., chords that conform to the previously described principles) sound more consonant in a tonal sequence than in a sequence that is random.

These principles describe the relative dissonance based on harmonic theory. It should be noted, however, that different chords, for example CGBD and CDEG, can belong to the same class. Both chords belong to a major scale, are consistent with the major triad, and can be constructed indirectly from the rule of thirds. To explain differences in dissonance within this category, the roughness score that is based on Von Helmholtz (1862) principles can be used. More specifically a roughness score can be calculated using an algorithm developed by Parncutt (1989). Based on this algorithm, CGBD will obtain higher roughness score than CDEG, so CGBD should be sounding more dissonant than CDEG. Thus, Johnson-Laird et al. (2012) assume that the harmonic class to which a chord belongs mainly determines the degree of dissonance, while within the same class the roughness score further determines the degree of dissonance.

To test this hypothesis, Johnson-Laird et al. (2012) required participants to evaluate all 55 chords that can be constructed on the basis of three tones, as well as a representative sample of 48 chords that can be based on four tones, on their perceived roughness. Consistent with the hypothesis, the authors did indeed find that the participants' ratings represented a mix of harmonic category and roughness.

7.8.1.2 Music and Predictions

Koelsch, Vuust, and Friston (2019) argue that music perception is an active process. While listening to music, we continuously make predictions about what will happen next (Pearce & Wiggins, 2012). Because almost all musical genres are based on predictable regularities, such as the rhythmic structure and the construction of melody lines, music is an ideal tool to test the predictive coding framework. Actively focusing attention on music reduces uncertainty about the predictions that we make (Rohrmeier & Koelsch, 2012). Nevertheless, there are many irregularities in music; for example, in the form of rhythmic deviations or irregular chords. Koelsch et al. hypothesise that the processing of these irregularities is only to a limited extent influenced by top-down predictions, because additional higher-order predictive mechanisms are involved in processing them. These higher-order predictions consist of predictions about the expected uncertainty. Koelsch et al. (2019) illustrate this mechanism by using two examples of irregularities in

music, involving the perception of rhythm and the perception of harmony.

In most forms of music, rhythm is based on a regular beat. This beat often induces a tendency to tap along with it. A beat is typically divided into a metre, which is filled with equally distributed and differently accentuated beats (Palmer & Krumhansl, 1990), which generate an a priori context in which the progression of a musical piece is framed. Note, however, that music can contain various elements that can violate the expectations created by the metre. An example of this is syncopation, that is, musical accents that are offset with respect to the beat. Interestingly, it is exactly this type of syncopation that makes us want to move, especially when it occurs repetitively. Given a constant tempo, Witek, Clarke, Wallentin, Kringelbach, and Vuust (2014) found an inverted U-shaped relationship between the degree of syncopation, the tendency to move, and the pleasure people derive from music. Koelsch et al. (2019) hypothesise that the subjective experience of Grooviness can be explained by the product of syncopation and the precision that is attributed to the prediction error that is generated by syncopation (see fig 7.13).

The inverted U-shape of Groove

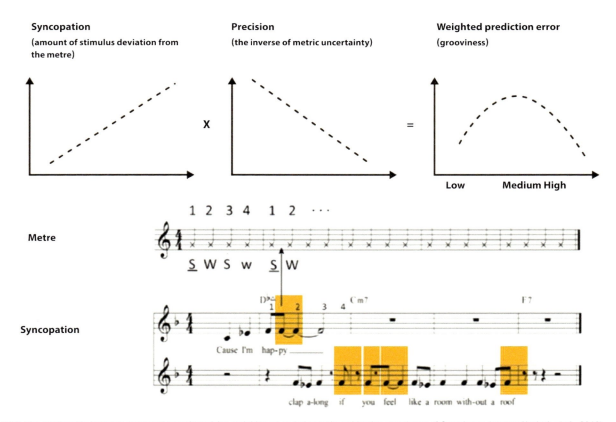

Figure 7.13 The relationship between syncopation and precision weighing as an index to the subjective experience of Grooviness. (source: Koelsch et al., 2019)

Similar expectancy violations take place during the perception of harmony. Consider, for example, the beginning of Mozart's 31st Symphony. Here, the last note in the sequence can be predicted on the basis of our familiarity with the major scale. We can predict this note with a high degree of precision, given the context. Later on, the same passage is repeated, but modified in such a way that the last note falls outside of the scale, making it unpredictable, typically resulting in a variety of emotional responses, such as surprise, anticipation, and tension. This type of musical expectancy violation typically evokes an ERP component that is similar to the mismatch negativity but more specific to musical violations (Fiveash, Thompson, Badcock, & McArthur, 2018; Lagrois, Peretz, & Zendel, 2018; Sun, Liu, Zhou, & Jiang, 2018; Vuvan, Zendel, & Peretz, 2018; Zhang, Zhou, Chang, & Yang, 2018). When musicians listen to two different chord sequences, one ending in a regular harmony and the other in an irregular harmony, the latter will evoke such a mismatch negativity. This does not happen, however, when the listeners are informed that the chord sequence will end in an irregular harmony.

Koelsch et al. (2019) explain these findings by assuming that predictions are generated at two different levels (see Fig. 7.14). First-order predications generate an expectation about the sequence, while second-order predications are involved in processing the precision of these predictions. By adjusting this precision downward, no prediction error will be generated in case of syncopated rhythms or violations of the harmonic expectation.

7.8.1.3 Music Perception and Prosody

Many people are able to recognise complex musical structures, even when they have limited musical training. This finding suggests that our ability to process music is innate. Some researchers suggest that these musical skills are an important prerequisite for the processing of language. For instance, young children acquire much knowledge about word boundaries and learn to identify phrases on the basis of prosodic cues (Jusczyk, 1999). As we will discuss in more detail in Chapter 16, **prosody** consists of rhythm, emphasis, and intonation. These prosodic cues can be seen as the musical part of a speech signal, since they include a melodic component, as well as metre, rhythm, and timbre. In addition, in some tonal languages, the meticulous coding of tonal relationships between different phonemes (units of speech sound; see Chapter 17) plays an extremely important role. Also in non-tonal languages, the analysis of prosody plays a very important role in correctly decoding the meaning of the speech signal. This last aspect will be discussed in more detail later in this chapter.

7.8.2 MUSIC AND AUDITORY SCENE ANALYSIS

Auditory scene analysis processes are also crucial for music perception (Pressnitzer et al., 2011). Musical auditory scenes are possibly among the most complex we have to deal with in everyday life, due to the extremely high number of sound sources comprising the scene. In addition, one or more of the principles that we normally use for auditory

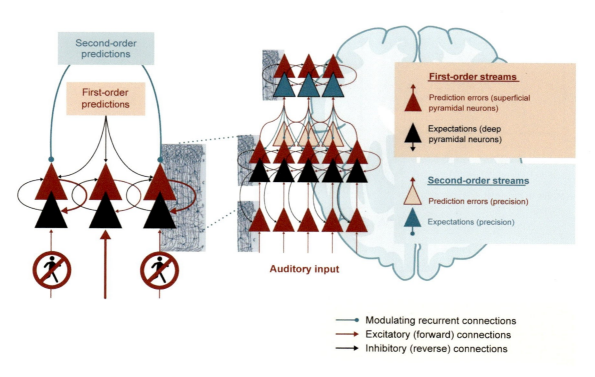

Figure 7.14 A proposed hierarchical mechanism of prediction error processing in music perception. (source: Koelsch et al. 2019)

scene analysis can be violated while processing music. For example, the aforementioned principle of vertical organisation describes how a series of tones forming a harmonic series originates from the same source. This principle can be easily violated in music. This is the case, for example, when the composer decides to have different instruments play a harmonic sequence. A good example of this is 'Das Musikalisches Opfer' by Johann Sebastian Bach. Bach is believed to have acquired the basic melody from Frederick the Great, then Emperor of Prussia, of which Bach made a polyphonic canon, where six different melody lines are intertwined.

7.8.2.1 Melody

An important organisational principle, which is based on auditory scene analysis, is formed by **voice leading**. Voice leading describes the progression of the individual voices or instruments in time. Proper use of voice leading provides clearly distinguishable melodies. In case of Bach's 'Musikalisches Opfer', the voices clearly comply with several auditory scene analysis principles, such that the individual melodies remain clearly distinguishable (Huron, 2001). Synchronous harmonic intervals are avoided, for example, to avoid confusion between the different voices. Moreover, the individual melodies consist of relatively small harmonic steps, to promote auditory stream formation.

While the Bach example described here is a good example of a clear stream separation, music perception can also involve the fusion of different voices into one indistinguishable whole. In early church music, for example, all voices are merged. Likewise, the way in which several instruments in a symphony orchestra merge into each other illustrates the use of musical fusion.

7.8.2.2 The Shepard Tone

In 1964, Roger Shepard, a researcher affiliated with the American Bell Telecom Laboratories, published a procedure to generate a series of tones that violate the transitivity of relative pitches. Put differently: Shepard (1964) managed to generate a series of tones of which a tone consisting of higher frequencies was sometimes perceived as lower than a tone consisting of lower frequencies, and vice versa. The resulting sequence has become known as the Shepard tone in honour of its developer. The Shepard tone consists of ten sinusoid components, each differing an octave from another, and consisting of different amplitudes (see fig 7.15). The frequency of each of these components is continuously modulated, creating the illusion of a continuously increasing pitch. As their frequencies increase, the highest frequency waves decrease in amplitude and are replaced by lower frequency waveforms that gradually increase in amplitude. As a consequence, the tone remains stable over longer periods of time resulting in the illusion of a tone that continuously rises in pitch.

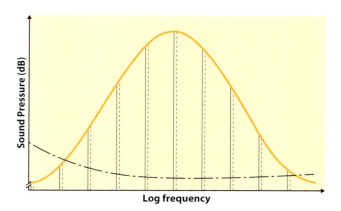

Figure 7.15 Example of a Shepard tone. (source: Shepard, 1964)

7.8.2.3 Missing Fundamental Frequency and Melody Invariance

Houtsma and Goldstein (1971) reported that the perception of melodies is based on the integrated processing of information from both ears. These authors instructed participants to recognise musical intervals, on the basis of synthetic tones that were composed of two randomly chosen harmonics. Although the fundamental frequency was omitted from these tones, participants were nevertheless capable of detecting the fundamental frequency and to use this in determining what musical interval was presented. In one condition, both harmonics were presented binaurally, while in a second condition, each ear was presented a different harmonic. The latter manipulation had no influence on the perception of the fundamental frequency. Consequently, it also did not impair participants' ability to estimate the intervals.

7.8.2.4 Tone Deafness

Although most people have no difficulties recognising melodies, about 4% of the population is estimated to have **amusia**, or tone-deafness (Hyde & Peretz, 2004). Tone-deafness is characterised by a selective limitation in the processing of melodies. Individuals with tone-deafness typically possess normal language skills, including a normal ability to recognise lyrics and also a normal ability to process intonation. In addition, it appears that these individuals have far fewer difficulties with processing rhythmic information than with melodies. Amusical individuals therefore seem to have a selective disability in processing melodies in terms of scales.

7.9 THE NEURAL BASIS OF SPEECH RECOGNITION

7.9.1 SPEECH SIGNALS

Speech consists of a complex set of acoustic signals. To get an appreciation of this complexity, a speech signal can be transformed into a spectrogram. As can be seen in

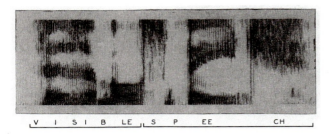

V I S I B LE S P EE CH

Figure 7.16 A spectrogram of a speech signal.

Figure 7.16, strong voice-activated frequency bands can be identified, which are known as formants. Here, vowels are generally represented by three formants, which are numbered in order of increasing frequency. The first formant thus represents the lowest frequency band. These formants are relatively constant while the pronunciation of a vowel is ongoing. Consonants, on the other hand, are mostly reflected as rapid changes in the frequency spectrum. Finally, an important property of a speech signal is that there is typically a weak correspondence between the acoustic energy of the speech signal and boundaries between words. Thus, in speech signals, two consecutive words frequently morph directly into each other, while the middle of a word can sometimes be characterised by a low amount of acoustic activity.

7.9.2 ANATOMY

Since the early 21st century, much research has focused on unravelling the neural basis of speech recognition. The initial analysis of speech signals was found to take place in the auditory cortex. As discussed earlier, the auditory cortex is characterised by a hierarchical organisation in which neurons in the nucleus predominantly respond instantaneously to simple tones, while neurons in the belt regions show somewhat delayed responses to spectrally more complex stimuli (Kaas & Hackett, 2000). The core of the auditory cortex is therefore supposed to process the elementary properties of an acoustic signal, while the belt and the parabelt areas mainly respond to higher-order properties of sounds (Rauschecker & Scott, 2009).

Okada et al. (2010) investigated how sensitive the auditory cortex is to variations in acoustic signals that are related to intelligible and non-intelligible speech. They found that the core of the auditory cortex is indeed very sensitive to variations in the basic properties of these signals, while areas in the bilateral anterior superior temporal sulcus are mainly sensitive to speech intelligibility and much less so to the individual variations within the signal. The latter areas are therefore characterised by acoustic invariance. Such acoustic invariance is observed even more strongly in the bilateral posterior superior temporal sulci in both hemispheres. Thus, Okada et al. conclude that the activation in these latter areas reflects a representation at the phonological level. This

conclusion is consistent with the idea of a hierarchical representation of information in the auditory cortex.

More evidence for such a hierarchically organised speech recognition system has been reported by Humphries et al. (2005). These authors found that part of the anterior temporal cortex, and specifically so the left supratemporal sulcus, is more strongly activated by sentences than by word lists, implying that this area primarily represents the syntactic structure of a sentence. The result was obtained using fMRI, while participants were instructed to listen to stimulus material where both syntactic structure and prosody were manipulated independently. Here, participants were presented either normal sentences, sentences where the word order was mixed up, or lists of individual words. In addition, each of these lists was pronounced either with a normal prosody or with an ultra-flat prosody. The prosodic cues predominantly affected the activation of the dorsal parts of the anterior temporal lobe; more specifically, in a bilateral region along the superior temporal gyrus.

7.9.2.1 Speech Recognition and Music

Earlier in this chapter, we introduced the idea that the processes involved in the perception of music may also play a role in the processing of prosody. Rogalsky, Rong, Saberi, and Hickok (2011) argue that there are even more similarities between speech recognition and music perception by arguing that speech recognition processes share specific neural mechanisms with the processes involved in music processing.

Rogalsky et al. conducted a study in which participants were presented phrases, scrambled phrases, or melodies. Using fMRI, they found a significant overlap among brain areas involved in language and those involved in music processing, predominantly in the bilateral superior temporal cortices. In addition, however, a significant amount of non-overlap was found. More specifically, sentences mainly activated the ventrolateral areas, while melodies mainly activated the more dorsomedial areas. In the overlapping areas, subregions could also be identified that were specifically sensitive to either music or language. Areas specifically sensitive to the higher-order integration of sentences were found in a network of activation patterns in the bilateral temporal lobe. These areas were identified by comparing the activation patterns evoked by sentences with the patterns evoked by scrambled sentences. The areas that represented sentence integration processes were not activated by melodies, however, suggesting that the latter network is specifically involved in language processing.

7.9.2.2 Physiology

Next, we can turn to how auditory information is segmented into a speech signal. As discussed, there is currently an increasing amount of evidence suggesting a hierarchical organisation of the auditory cortex, in which neurons in higher regions encode increasingly complex properties of a stimulus. According to Giraud and Poeppel (2012), neural **oscillations** in the auditory cortex play an important role in speech recognition. These oscillations are ubiquitous in the brain, and they are in many ways related to cognitive processing. They can, for example, separate streams of information by coordinating the timing of neural action potentials. Recent findings have shown that oscillations in the delta, theta, and gamma bands of the EEG are dynamically following the various rhythms present in a dynamic speech signal. According to Giraud and Poeppel, these rhythms are essential for segmenting the continuous speech signal into individual packets of information.

An acoustic speech signal is characterised by the fact that organisational principles can be identified at different time scales. Transient cues at high frequencies (~30–50 Hz) are usually associated with the finer nuances of the speech signal, such as formant transitions (e.g., /ba/ vs. /da/), while information at about an order of magnitude slower (~4–7 Hz) represents the acoustic envelope of the speech signal. The latter timescale corresponds roughly to the speed at which syllables are pronounced. Information at the level of individual phrases is related to a rhythm of about 1–2 Hz. Intonation and prosody also roughly correspond to this time scale. Giraud and Poeppel (2012) argue that the three timescales correspond to the EEG low gamma (25–35 Hz), theta (4–8 Hz), and delta frequencies (1–3 Hz), respectively, and that

this correspondence may form a link between neurophysiology, neural computation, acoustics, and psycholinguistics (Ghitza, 2011).

If speech analysis is mediated by activation in these frequency bands, it would follow that the intelligibility of speech is limited when one of these rhythms is disrupted. Ghitza and Greenberg (2009) found evidence for this hypothesis, using synthetic speech. They generated artificial sentences that they then played at three times their normal speed. The effect of this manipulation was a sharp decrease in intelligibility. When a pause was inserted after each word, however, so that the total duration of the sentence was back to its original length (while the words were still pronounced three times as fast), the intelligibility of the sentence increased sharply again. It should be noted, however, that the breaks had to be regularly divided across the sentence, such that the rhythm at sentence level corresponded to that of the original sentence.

Giraud and Poeppel (2012) developed a speech perception model that is characterised by five different neural processes. These processes are involved in the decoding of speech information from the rhythmic structure of the speech signal (see fig 7.17). According to the model, the acoustic signal triggers a series of neural pulses in layer 4 of the auditory cortex. These neural pulses affect the phase of the spontaneous theta and gamma rhythms in the auditory cortex (step 1), causing these rhythms to follow the pattern of the stimuli (step 2) and coupling the

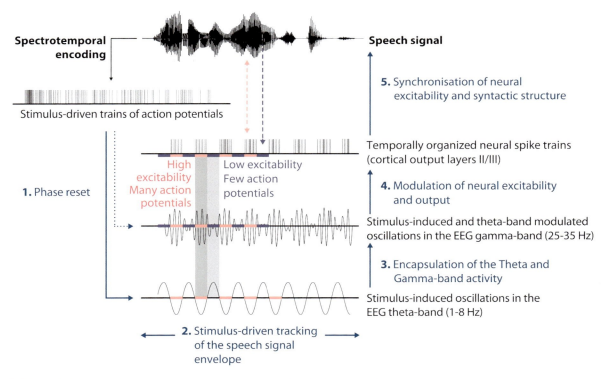

Figure 7.17 The role of neural oscillations in speech recognition (see main text for details). (source: Giraud and Poeppel, 2012)

theta and gamma band signals (step 3). This coupling can then modulate the original neural pulse train (step 4), creating a stronger correspondence between the neuronal excitability and the content of the acoustic signal.

After being modulated this way, the speech signal is then further interpreted on the basis of predictions that are generated by the context in which a conversation takes place (Peelle & Sommers, 2015; Sohoglu, Peelle, Carlyon, & Davis, 2012). In addition, auditory speech recognition is controlled by visual information (van Wassenhove, Grant, & Poeppel, 2005).

7.10 AUDITORY ATTENTION

How do we recognise what one person is saying when others are speaking at the same time? With this question, the British cognitive scientist Edward Colin Cherry (1953) introduced the famous **cocktail party problem** more than 65 years ago. Obviously, attention is involved in selecting the auditory stream that we aim to follow and in ignoring all other auditory streams (Fritz, Elhilali, David, & Shamma, 2007; Lee, Larson, Maddox, & Shinn-Cunningham, 2014). The fact that we are not perfectly able to filter out all unattended information is evident, for example, from the phenomenon that we may suddenly hear someone mention our name at a party. In Chapter 4, we have already been introduced to the general selection mechanisms that regulate both the top-down and bottom-up control of attention. Therefore, the following sections will introduce the specific mechanisms involved in the regulation of auditory information streams.

7.10.1 ATTENTION AS A FILTER

Listening to one specific voice is a particularly complex process and requires us to solve various problems (McDermott, 2009). As discussed earlier in this chapter, auditory processing starts by segregating the auditory signal. Here, one specific source must be extracted from the mix of sound sources, which we then attend to. Segregating an auditory signal is generally much more complex than segregating a visual signal, because the sound sources overlap considerably. This process becomes particularly complex in the analysis of speech signals (see Chapter 17 for further details).

7.10.1.1 The Dichotic Listening Task

To investigate auditory attention processes, Cherry (1953) developed a **dichotic listening task**. In this task, headphones present a different auditory message to each ear (see fig 7.18), while a listener is instructed to attend to only one message. To ensure that participants actually comply with this instruction, Cherry developed a procedure that is known as **shadowing**. Here, participants are instructed to repeat the attended message out loud. Using this task, Cherry found that participants separated the two different auditory streams on the basis of the physical properties of the signals, such as the speaker's gender, the intensity of the voice, or the speaker's location. When, for example, Cherry presented two messages from the same voice to each ear, listeners found it particularly difficult to select one of the two messages based solely on the content of the message.

Initially, Cherry (1953) found that not much information was retained from the ignored message. For example, listeners frequently failed to notice that the ignored message

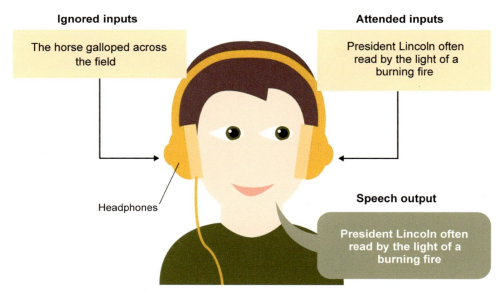

Dichotic Listening Task

Ignored inputs

The horse galloped across the field

Attended inputs

President Lincoln often read by the light of a burning fire

Headphones

Speech output

President Lincoln often read by the light of a burning fire

Figure 7.18 Example of a dichotic listening task.

was in a foreign language or even that it was played backwards. Physical changes, however, such as the presence of a pure tone, were almost always noticed. Likewise, Moray (1959) reported that non-attended signals were hardly processed. Participants could barely remember words presented in the unattended message, despite the fact that they had been presented 35 times.

7.10.1.2 Historical Theories of Auditory Attention

The aforementioned findings can be explained by assuming that there is a bottleneck in auditory processing, and much of the early attention literature focused on the question of where that bottleneck was located. The British psychologist Donald Broadbent (1954) argued that attention acts as a filter that is situated at the earliest stages of auditory processing. This filter would select auditory information based on its physical characteristics. According to Broadbent, all auditory information would be temporarily stored in a sensory buffer and quickly degrade, unless it was attended. Moreover, Broadbent argued that attentional selection of information thus occurs early on in the processing stream.

Broadbent's model failed to explain a number of crucial observations, however, including the fact that a person can suddenly detect their own name in an otherwise unattended conversation. It also had difficulties explaining results reported by Allport, Antonis, and Reynolds (1972). These authors found that participants were very well capable of shadowing an auditory stream, while simultaneously performing a secondary task, such as viewing complex visual scenes or reading a musical score. To explain these findings, Treisman (1964b) proposed a less extreme variant of an early selection model. According to Treisman's attenuation model, listeners attempt to process as much auditory information as possible. It is only when our processing capacity is exceeded that the processing of irrelevant information is attenuated. Top-down processes are believed to play an important role in the processing of auditory stimuli. For example, Treisman (1960) found

that during a shadowing task, listeners would occasionally repeat a word that is presented in the non-attended channel. This happened specifically when the word in question matched the context of the attended message. Deutsch and Deutsch (1963), on the other hand, argued that selection takes place at much later stages. According to their model, all stimuli are fully processed, but it is only the most relevant stimuli that determine how we will respond to them.

7.10.1.3 Effects of Attention on Auditory Processing

Direct evidence for early selection in auditory processing was found in a classic ERP study from Hillyard et al. (1973). These authors found that ERP components associated with the early processing of stimuli are affected by attention. In this study, participants were required to detect deviant stimuli, while selectively attending one of two simultaneously presented streams of short tones. Each of these streams was presented at a different location. It was found that the amplitude of the early N1 component was larger for the attended than for the unattended tones, suggesting that attending to a specific location affected the early processing of auditory stimuli. In a follow-up study (see fig 7.19), which used magnetoencephalography, it was found that the magnetic counterpart of this N1 originated in the auditory cortex (Woldorff et al., 1993).

In addition to location, attention can also be directed to pitch. For example, Talsma and Kok (2001) presented a stream of tones with a high or low pitch. Here, participants were instructed to specifically attend to only one of the two pitches. ERPs that were evoked by the attended tones were characterised by a negative electrical potential that started about 180 ms after stimulus presentation.

Finally, Ahveninen, Jaaskelainen, et al. (2006) found that attention could not only affect the processing of specific locations or pitches of an auditory stimulus but also their phonetic properties. This influence of attention could be traced back to the anterior 'where' and the posterior

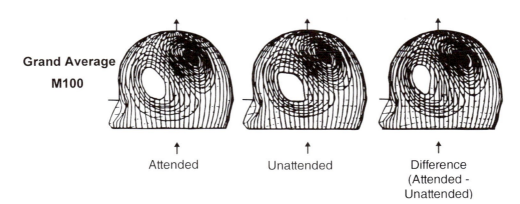

Figure 7.19 The brain's magnetic response to attended and unattended auditory stimuli. Left: attended; middle: unattended; right: the difference between these two conditions. The amplitude of each of these responses has been normalised, to allow better comparison of the magnetic field distributions. In reality, the field strength was larger for the attended than for the unattended condition. (source: Woldorff et al., 1993)

217

'what' pathways in the auditory cortex. Note that this observation is consistent with the previously discussed distinction between the processing of spatial and object-oriented properties of stimuli in the auditory cortex (Kaas & Hackett, 1999; Rauschecker, 2015; Rauschecker & Scott, 2009; Warren & Griffiths, 2003).

7.10.1.4 The Orienting of Auditory Attention

The results discussed earlier show that attention can influence both spatial and non-spatial aspects of auditory information processing. Are these forms of attention regulated by the same control system, or are different control systems involved? The currently existing evidence is mostly consistent with the latter. For example, it appears that the bilateral premotor and inferior parietal areas are more strongly activated when participants perform a sound localisation task, compared to a recognition task (Mayer, Harrington, Adair, & Lee, 2006). In addition, the frontal eye fields are also more active while attending to a location compared to attending a specific pitch (Degerman, Rinne, Salmi, Salonen, & Alho, 2006). Recent MEG, EEG, and fMRI studies have suggested that the networks involved in controlling auditory spatial attention are the same networks as those controlling visuospatial attention (Diaconescu, Alain, & McIntosh, 2001; Smith, Davis, et al., 2009). Taken together, these results imply that attending to locations is a process that is shared with the visual system (see also Chapter 9), but that focusing attention on pitch or phonetic properties is a specialised function of the auditory system.

For visual attention (see Chapters 4 and 6), it has been found that switching between different locations is controlled by networks in the parietal cortex. An increasing number of studies suggests that the same networks are involved in switching attention between different auditory streams. For example, Shomstein and Yantis (2006) found that the posterior parietal cortex became more active when participants were instructed to switch their attention from one ear to the other (where a male and a female voice were presented respectively).

Salient auditory stimuli can also automatically capture attention. The resulting exogenous (automatic) switch of attention is reflected in a host of electrophysiological effects, such as the mismatch negativity, the novelty P300, and the reorienting negativity (Escera & Corral, 2007). As discussed earlier, the mismatch negativity reflects the automatic pre-attentive detection of an anomalous stimulus. The novelty P300 is a positive ERP component that is evoked at about 300 ms after the appearance of a novel and salient stimulus. It is characterised by a maximum amplitude over the frontocentral scalp (Combs & Polich, 2006). Finally, the reorienting negativity (Schröger & Wolff, 1998) is a late negative ERP component that is associated with the reorientation of attention after a distracting auditory stimulus has been evaluated.

7.10.2 OBJECT-BASED AUDITORY ATTENTION

The studies discussed thus far show that auditory attention can not only be focused on locations or pitch but also on entire objects. A striking problem in auditory attention research, however, is that it is particularly complex to define what an auditory object is (Shinn-Cunningham, 2008). After all, sounds that we hear cannot always be attributed to objects that we perceive in a visual scene. Moreover, specific sounds can be linked to multiple objects, as is the case with the multiple voices of a choir. Finally, the listener's expectation can also influence the link between sound and object. The cognitive processes that play a role in identifying objects form the basis for the previously discussed auditory scene analysis. Next, we turn to how attention can influence these auditory scene analysis processes.

Shinn-Cunningham (2008) argues that the auditory object-based attention processes are very similar to the processes involved in visual object-based attention (see fig 7.20). As for visual attention, there is a competition between different object representations, which takes place at all levels of processing (Desimone & Duncan, 1995; Duncan, 1996; see Chapter 4). Competition between two different object representations arises mainly from the similarity between the two signals. This is the case, for example, when you simultaneously hear two different male speakers both expressing something similar. In such a case, the two different auditory streams will no longer be distinguishable. If they are made sufficiently distinguishable and if the listener is informed about this distinction, it might, however, be possible to selectively focus one of the two streams via the deployment of top-down attention. When the listener is not familiar with these properties, or when one of the two auditory currents is significantly more salient than the other, the top-down selection of attention may fail (Conway, Conway, & Bunting, 2001).

7.10.3 AUDITORY SEARCH

Analogous to the visual search process, we may sometimes have to search for the source of specific sounds. Consider, for example, the situation in which a mother tries to locate her crying child in a crowd on the beach, or in which we try to detect a hissing leak in a bicycle tire. Gamble and Luck (2011) used ERPs to determine the neural basis of these auditory search processes. In their study, two sounds were presented simultaneously, and participants had to indicate which of these two sounds was a pre-defined target sound. Gamble and Luck found a negative ERP component that was observed mainly anteriorly and contralaterally relative to the location of the sound that had to be found. The ERP component, labelled N2ac, was considered to reflect the focusing of attention on the location where the relevant sound was presented.

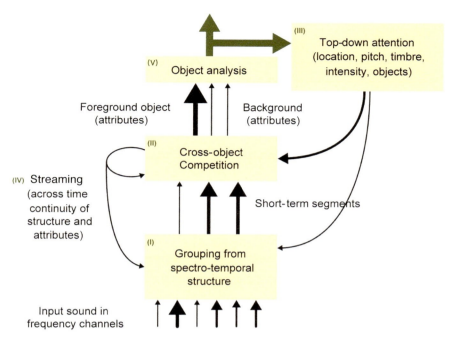

Figure 7.20 A conceptual model of the processes involved in the formation of auditory objects and the role of top-down and bottom-up attention in these processes. (source: Shinn-Cunningham, 2008)

In a follow-up study, Gamble and Woldorff (2015) investigated which neural processes are specifically involved in auditory search. This study also used ERPs, while participants were required to detect one specific tone in a series of tones that were presented randomly to the left or to the right of the participants. Here, Gamble and Woldorff found that the relevant stimulus could already be detected at about 60 ms after presentation of the tone, but that attention only shifted to the relevant location at about 120 ms after its presentation, suggesting that attentional capture by a tone is a two-stage process.

7.10.4 INATTENTIONAL DEAFNESS

As with visual perception, we process much less auditory information than we usually assume (see also Box 7.1). For auditory processing, this is referred to as inattentional deafness. Dalton and Fraenkel (2012) found evidence for this phenomenon by designing an auditory version of the original gorilla study by Simons and Chabris (1999; see Chapter 6). Participants heard an auditory scene in which four people (two men and two women) were preparing a party, while they were regularly moving around the room (fig 7.21). Half of the participants were instructed to listen to the conversation of the men and the other half to the conversation of the women, with the aim of answering a number of questions about the conversations afterwards. Unknowingly to the participants, an additional male actor walked through the scene who repeated the phrase 'I'm a gorilla' a number of times. Most of the participants who were instructed to attend to the female voices did not notice the 'gorilla' voice.

Raveh and Lavie (2015) reported that inattentional deafness is influenced by perceptual load. These authors not only manipulated the auditory load but also the visual load, and found that increasing visual load also contributed to the phenomenon of inattentional deafness. Dehais et al. (2014) reported that inattentional deafness due to perceptual load can contribute significantly to the fact that pilots can sometimes miss important auditory warning signs.

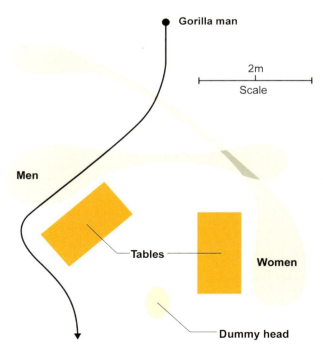

Figure 7.21 A schematic overview of the auditory scenes that were constructed by Dalton and Fraenkel. (source: Dalton and Fraenkel, 2012)

7.11 SUMMARY

Hearing forms the basis of our auditory perception system. Sound consists of vibrations that move through a medium like a pressure wave. A sound wave is characterised by two properties: amplitude and frequency. A typical sound consists of a mix of different waves. Sound can vary in intensity from 0 to 120 decibels and frequencies from about 50 to 20,000 Hz are audible. The auditory system can be divided into the outer, middle, and inner ear. The eardrum vibrates in response to the sound waves and converts this vibration into a mechanical movement of cilia in the cochlea. A combination of resonance and tonotopic organisation of the cochlea ensures a very accurate encoding of frequencies.

Auditory information is projected via the auditory nerve and is routed through a number of subcortical nuclei, namely the cochlear nucleus, the superior olive, the inferior colliculus, and the medial geniculate nucleus of the thalamus before reaching the primary auditory cortex. These projections are reciprocal: in addition to the ascending projections, there are also a large number of descending projections that send modulating signals back to the periphery.

Auditory localisation is based on determining interaural time and intensity differences. Part of this localisation process already takes place in the superior olive, which already creates a spatial map of auditory locations at the level of the brainstem. This spatial map is most prominent in the inferior colliculus.

The auditory cortex is characterised by a tonotopic organisation and can be divided into three main regions: the core, the belt, and the parabelt. The core can be further subdivided into the primary auditory cortex and areas anterior to it. The core is especially sensitive to the basic properties of sound, and it is tonotopically organised. The belt and the parabelt are relatively sensitive to complex properties of sound, such as vocalisations and sequences of tones. In humans, these areas are also linked to the processing of speech and other complex sounds, such as music or natural ambient sounds.

In the auditory system, too, a distinction has been found between the processing of spatial and non-spatial information. The caudal, posterior areas are mainly involved in the processing of spatial information and the rostral, anterior areas in the processing of non-spatial information. The auditory cortex is characterised by a high degree of plasticity. The cortical representation of music-related information is greater in musicians than in non-musicians. In the case of hearing loss, cortical plasticity can result in a maladaptive process, which manifests itself in the form of tinnitus.

Electrophysiological studies have yielded much of our knowledge about the basics of auditory processing. The presentation of simple tones results in a characteristic series of auditory electrophysiological potentials. Some of these potentials, such as the N1, are sensitive to attention, and others, such as the mismatch negativity, to violations of expectations. Self-generated stimuli result in a decrease in amplitude of these components.

A major challenge for the auditory system consists of separating the complex mix of auditory signals into identifiable auditory streams. The study of these processes is known as auditory scene analysis. Auditory scene analysis can be broken down into two different subproblems, known as the problems of vertical and horizontal organisation. The problem of vertical organisation describes how different frequency bands that occur simultaneously can be separated from each other, while the problem of horizontal organisation focuses mainly on the question of how events that are separated in time can be divided into separate auditory streams.

Studies on auditory stream formation often use bistable sound patterns; that is, series of tones that can either form part of one melody or that appear to consist of two separate melodies. Depending on the nature of the stimulus, the changes in perception may be related to alterations in activation in the cochlear nucleus, the auditory cortex, or the frontal and parietal cortical networks.

Auditory processing processes play an important role in the perception of music. Recent studies suggest that there are strong links between music and speech perception. Representations of harmonic and rhythmic patterns are formed in the secondary auditory cortex. The processing of these patterns presumably takes place independently of each other. The integration of these elements can be described in terms of a syntactic analysis, in which the interrelationship of the individual elements is determined. Violations of expectation play an important role in evoking an emotional response. In addition to the purely auditory processing and evocation of emotion, music can also exert an influence on the body. The latter happens in the form of a reaction of the immune system as well as in the tendency of the body to move along to music; that is, to dance to it.

Two processes appear to be involved in the perception of dissonance in harmonies: the harmonic principles underlying Western tonal music and the extent to which different tones both stimulate the same parts of the basilar membrane. Predictive processes play an important role in music perception; both in the perception of harmony and in the perception of rhythm. The degree to which there is a deviation from a fixed metre can result in a more pleasant perception of rhythm, which can be described as a groove. The relationship between the pre-dictability of the beat and the Grooviness of the rhythm can be described by means of an inverted U-curve. A note that does not fit into the context of an earlier melody will also generate a violation of expectation and evoke an emotional response.

The processes involved in the analysis of melody and rhythm may also play a role in the perception of speech. Rhythmic and melodic patterns that indicate the course of the sentence and the word boundaries influence the neural response. As such, they possibly contribute to the segmentation of the speech signal into individual words. The principles underlying auditory scene analysis pro-cesses may also play a role in the perception of melodies. The processes of voice and fusion describe how different sound sources are either kept separate and experienced as separate melodies or merge into a harmonious whole.

The experience of melody is not limited by the absence of the fundamental frequency. Even when separate har-monic frequencies are each presented to a different ear, we are still able to detect the fundamental frequency. Some individuals have been identified as being tone-deaf. These individuals lack the ability to adequately distinguish small pitch differences.

Speech recognition is one of the most important functions of the auditory system. Neural oscillations play an important role in the analysis of the speech signal. These neural oscillations dynamically follow the rhythms present in the speech signal. Here, higher frequencies are associated with the processing of the finer nuances of the speech signal, while the lower frequencies are mainly involved in the analysis at the word or sentence level.

What auditory information we do or do not perceive is regulated by auditory attention mechanisms. Auditory attention can be focused on pitch, location, or objects. Initially, auditory attention was considered to be a filtering mechanism and it was discussed whether the selection took place at early or late stages of processing. Many results have been obtained by using the dichotic listening task, in which participants are required to shadow one of two auditory messages. Evidence for early selection was found on the basis of ERP research.

Currently, attention is no longer so much considered as a filtering mechanism, but rather as the result of a competitive mechanism, in which the representations of different stimuli are in competition with each other for further processing. Salient stimuli have an advan-tage in this competition and can therefore automatically capture attention. Top-down mechanisms can, however, influence the competition, giving task-relevant stimuli a greater chance of winning the competition. Although this biased competition model was initially developed for visual selective attention, the principles can also be applied to auditory stimuli. As with visual stimuli, we can also miss auditory information when attention is not focused on it. This phenomenon is known as inatten-tional deafness.

NOTE

1 It's not an entirely correct assertion that we would not hear any differences between these tones: even though the perceived pitch does not change with removing the fundamental frequency, the timbre of the tone does change. Many people describe sounds with a missing fundamental as 'tinny'. The fact that we still hear the same tone, explains why music played through small speakers is still recognisable, even though the lack of a large bass speaker does cause the sound to be less rich.

FURTHER READING

Celesia, G. G., & Hickok, G. (2015). *The human auditory system: Fundamental organization and clinical disor-ders (handbook of clinical neurology 129)*. Amsterdam, the Netherland: Elsevier.

Eggermont, J. J. (2019). *The auditory brain and age-related hearing impairment*. Amsterdam, Netherland: Elsevier.

Hallam, S., Cross, I., & Thaut, M. (2016). *The Oxford handbook of music psychology*. Oxford, UK: Oxford University Press.

Levitin, D. J. (2008). *This is your brain on music: The sci-ence of a human obsession*. New York: Paw Press.

Yost, W. A., & Watson, C. S. (2016). *Auditory processing of complex sounds*. Hove, UK: Routledge.

CHAPTER 8
Mechanical perception

8.1 INTRODUCTION

Mechanical perception encompasses the processing of all the signals that are produced by the body. Our mechanical senses respond to pressure, bending, or other deformations of a receptor. As such, mechanical perception includes pain, somatosensation, motor feedback, and other bodily sensations. The vestibular system, which regulates our balance, is also considered to be part of the mechanical senses. Strictly speaking, auditory perception could also be classified as a form of mechanical perception, since the receptors in our ears are also triggered by mechanical responses to air vibrations. Due to the complexity of the auditory system, however, it was covered separately in the previous chapter.

Although mechanical perception is covered here as the last chapter in the perception theme, we should be careful not to suggest that mechanical perception is subordinate to our visual or auditory perception. On the contrary: being deaf or blind, we can still survive in modern society, albeit with some adjustments. If we were to lose our mechanical perception, however, our chances of survival would be significantly reduced. For instance, without our vestibular system, we would not be able to perform any actions, as we would always lose our balance; without tactile perception, we would not be aware of the dangers of cold, heat, stretching of the skin, or we could fall victim to pressure ulcers. Without feedback from our muscles, we would not be able to control our motor actions; without pain sensations we could fatally injure ourselves or be forced to ignore the symptoms of serious diseases. Without interoception, that is, the perception of our internal body signals, we would not be able to signal feelings of hunger, thirst, or physical fatigue, with potentially dramatic consequences. Moreover, it has recently been argued that, in addition to these functions, interoception is crucially involved in the establishment of self-awareness (Quigley, Kanoski, Grill, Barrett, & Tsakiris, 2021).

8.2 BALANCE AND BODY POSITION

As you continue to read, try moving your head up and down. Will you be able to keep reading? Now try again while holding your head still but moving the book up and down using your hands. Are you still able to keep reading? Why are you still able to do so in the first situation, and not in the second? It is because our vestibular system registers every movement of our heads and sends a compensatory signal towards the oculomotor system, such that our eyes always remain focused on the same target. The vestibular system not only detects the head's position, but also its acceleration, and thus regulates balance. Under normal circumstances, the corrective actions that are regulated by the vestibular system are fully automatic and unconscious. Each day we make thousands of head movements, however, they hardly affect our visual perception at all. It is only under extreme circumstances that we become aware of signals from the vestibular system, such as when performing a pirouette or during a roller coaster ride.

8.2.1 THE VESTIBULAR ORGAN

The vestibular organ consists of three semi-circular channels, which are oriented in three orthogonal planes and filled with a viscous fluid. A head movement in a specific direction causes the fluid in one or more of these channels to flow, stimulating hair cells on the inside of the channels. This stimulation triggers action potentials that are projected, via the eighth cranial nerve, to the brainstem and the cerebellum. An interesting feature of the vestibular organ is that its size is about the same for all species. For example, whales are ten million times as massive as mice, but their vestibular system is only five times as large (Squires, 2004).

8.2.2 BALANCE AND POSTURE CONTROL

Information from the vestibular organ is processed by a host of brain areas involved in maintaining balance and controlling posture (fig 8.1). Unlike other cortical areas that specialise in the processing of sensory information, the processing of vestibular information is not restricted to one specific area. Instead, vestibular functions are spread across multiple brain regions (Guldin & Grüsser, 1998). The right hemisphere in particular is assumed to play an important role in the processing of vestibular information

DOI: 10.4324/9781003319344-11

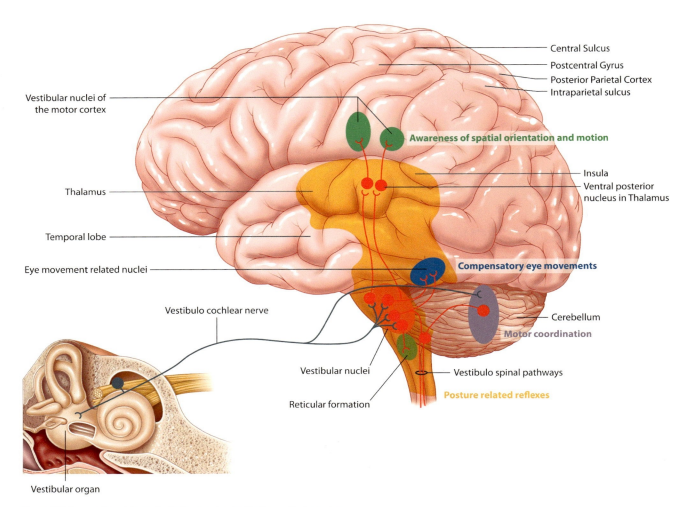

Figure 8.1 An overview of the major brain areas involved in the vestibular system.

(Dieterich et al., 2003). Specific cortical areas that appear to be involved in the processing of vestibular information include the insula, the posterior parietal cortex, the intraparietal sulcus, the temporal lobe, and vestibular nuclei in the motor cortex. These areas are connected via subcortical projections that also involve the cerebellum (fine regulation of motor responses), the inferior colliculus (compensatory eye movements to stabilise gaze control), and the ventral posterior nucleus of the thalamus.

Indovina et al. (2005) found evidence to suggest that the vestibular system contains an internal model for body orientation. This was specifically the case for the posterior insula of the right hemisphere. This internal representation is believed to be formed by the integration of information from different senses, including visual information. More specifically, Indovina et al. found that this part of the insula was activated not only by vestibular information but also by visual motion that was related to acceleration. This finding implies that for proper processing of body orientation, vestibular information needs to be integrated with other sources of information. It is believed that the angular gyrus, which is an area bordering the parietal and temporal cortex, plays an important role in this integration.

Patients with damage to this area have difficulties with integrating the information from different senses (see Chapter 9). For instance, Blanke, Ortigue, Landis, and Seeck (2002) describe an interesting case study: electrical stimulation of the angular gyrus disrupted the normal functions of this brain region. Each time this area was stimulated, the patient reported an out-of-body experience, as if she was observing her body from a different location. Blanke et al. argue that this experience results from an impairment in integrating the vestibular sensations with the visual and auditory percepts.

8.3 SOMATOSENSATION

8.3.1 SOMATOSENSORY RECEPTORS

The skin contains a large number of different types of **somatosensory receptors** (see fig 8.2). Although it was initially believed that each receptor had a specific function (Iggo & Andres, 1982), later studies have shown that the receptors operate in conjunction with each other

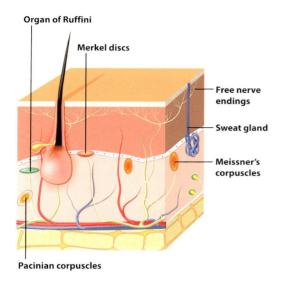

Organ of Ruffini

Merkel discs

Free nerve endings

Sweat gland

Meissner's corpuscles

Pacinian corpuscles

Figure 8.2 Schematic overview of the most common somatosensory receptors in the skin.

(Paré, Smith, & Rice, 2002). Each receptor presumably contributes to different forms of somatosensory experiences. Of these somatosensory experiences, the sense of touch and pain, along with the perception of cold and heat are the most well-known. These experiences are mainly recorded by receptors that are located in the skin (see also Box 8.1). In addition, we also receive numerous signals from our internal organs and from our muscles. These receptors encode the degree to which our muscles contract, or our joints move. The sensory feedback that these receptors produce about the state of a body is essential for motor coordination (see Chapters 3 and 9).

Somatosensory receptors can range from very basic to extremely complex. In its simplest form, a somatosensory receptor consists of a free nerve ending; that is, an unmyelinated axon located just below the surface of the skin. Stimulation of this receptor results in the

Box 8.1 Why can't you tickle yourself?

It's a well-known fact that you can't tickle yourself. Why is that? Before we can address this question, however, we will first have to ask what tickling actually is and why someone else can actually tickle us. Why does tickling arouse an irresistible laughter response, while the person being tickled usually does not find it pleasant to be tickled at all? The famous evolutionary biologist Charles Darwin hypothesised that there was a link between tickling and humour, as he considered humour to be the tickling of the mind (see Wattendorf et al., 2013). Later studies hypothesised that the laughter response that results from tickling is one of the building blocks of humour (see e.g., Hall & Allin, 1897). Unfortunately, these ideas turned out to be incorrect, because no connection between tickling and humour could be established: most people do not like to be tickled and certainly not by a stranger. When a joke makes us laugh, another joke has a stronger tendency to cause us to laugh again. When we are being tickled, however, the chances of us laughing at a joke do not change (Harris, 1999). All that tickling and humour appear to share is the final motor response (Harris & Christenfeld, 1997).

Wattendorf et al. (2013) assume that the laughter response that is due to tickling is a primitive form of vocalisation, mediated by the limbic system. Based on fMRI results, they did indeed find evidence for the involvement of the limbic system in the tickle-induced laughter response. At the somatosensory level, we must make a distinction between a caress and an itch (Zotterman, 1939). Both sensations are the result of a slight activation of the somatosensory receptors; however, the sensation of a caress is mainly projected to the brain by the somatosensory receptors, whereas the itching sensation is mainly due to a slight activation

of either pain receptors or of itch-specific receptors (Schmeiz, Schmidt, Bickel, Handwerker, & Torebjörk, 1997). When a tactile response is very light, it results in a neural response consisting of only a few action potentials. So why does such a subtle response result in a laughter response? There is currently no clear answer to this question, but there are a few possible reasons.

One of those reasons is anticipation. Carlsson, Petrovic, Skare, Petersson, and Ingvar (2000) report that a caress can evoke an anticipatory response that is so strong that it can in itself result in the activation of the primary somatosensory cortex. In addition, tickling is associated with sympathetic and emotional arousal (Bachorowski & Owren, 2006; Szameitat, Darwin, Wildgruber, Alter, & Szameitat, 2011). Because tickling often involves relatively vulnerable body parts, the laughter response can be considered an evolutionarily primitive response to potential threats.

Of course, the question remains why you can't tickle yourself. Part of the answer is related to anticipation: the effectiveness of tickling is in part related to the fact that you can't predict exactly when the tickling will start. In addition, stroking yourself also has the side effect that your own motor system produces an efferent copy of your motor actions, which compensates for the sensory consequences of your own actions (Blakemore, Frith, & Wolpert, 1999). Blakemore et al. (2000) argue that it is precisely for this reason that you cannot tickle yourself. In an experiment in which participants could either tickle themselves directly, or via a robotic arm, which conveyed the caressing sensations with an adjustable time delay, they found that participants increasingly experienced a tickling sensation as the time interval between their own action and the effect of the robotic arm increased.

opening of potassium channels in the axon membrane, thus creating an action potential (Price et al., 2000). These simple receptors are mainly involved in the perception of pain, heat, and cold. Other receptor types are slightly more complex. For example, **Organs of Ruffini** are surrounded by supporting tissue, which stimulates the nerve when this tissue is stretched. These receptors are therefore sensitive to the stretching of the skin. Similarly, **Meissner's corpuscles** are surrounded by supporting tissue that is sensitive to sudden movement of the skin and to low-frequency vibrations. **Pacinian corpuscles** are surrounded by non-neural tissue, which modifies the function of the nerve ending. As a result, these receptors are specifically sensitive to high-frequency vibrations of the skin. These receptors are shaped like an onion. The neuronal membrane is located in the core. The shell-shaped layers of tissue surrounding the nucleus allow only large sudden changes or high-frequency vibrations to stimulate this neuron.

Specific chemicals can also affect receptor functions. For example, heat receptors are affected by capsaicin, a substance present in chili peppers. For this reason, peppers get a hot taste. Cold receptors react similarly to menthol and to a lesser extent also to mint (McKemy, Neuhausser, & Julius, 2002).

8.3.2 NOCICEPTIVE RECEPTORS

A specific category of receptors that we have not yet discussed is pain receptors. As we will discuss later in this chapter, pain perception is the result of a complex interaction between top-down and bottom-up processing. The peripheral signals projected from the body to the brain are known as nociceptive signals, and pain is the result of the interpretation of these nociceptive signals. **Nociception** involves no fewer than three different systems: a system for sharp, acute pain, a system for burning pain, and a system for painful coldness (Craig, Krout, & Andrew, 2001). Considering how complex pain sensations are, it is remarkable that nociceptive signals are recorded by the most basic receptors we have discussed here, the free nerve endings.

Most axons that transmit nociceptive signals to the brain are not myelinated, making the transfer of pain signals relatively slow. Thicker and faster axons project sharp, acute nociceptive sensations, whereas thinner, slower axons project the dull sensations that are typically felt as an after-effect of acute pain. The axons that project the body's nociceptive sensations to the spinal cord release two different types of neurotransmitters: a mild nociceptive signal that results in the release of glutamate, while intense signals result in the release of glutamate and substance P. Substance P plays an important role in encoding the severity of pain, as shown in a study of mice that lack substance P receptors. These mice responded to intense pain stimuli as if they were mildly painful stimuli (De Felipe et al., 1998).

8.3.3 THE CENTRAL NERVOUS SYSTEM

Somatosensory experiences are projected from the skin to the brain via the cranial nerves (for the head) or the spinal cord (for the rest of the body). Each spinal nerve is connected to a specific area of the body. The area to which a nerve is connected is known as the **dermatome**. From the spinal cord, somatosensory information is projected to the brain via clearly defined neural pathways. Here we find two separate pathways: one for the sense of touch and one for pain. These pathways project to the somatosensory nuclei in the thalamus and from there to different areas of the primary somatosensory cortex in the parietal lobe. Two parallel, strip-shaped regions in the somatosensory cortex respond specifically to superficial tactile stimulation, whereas two other areas respond specifically to deep pressure and movement of joints and muscles. This finding implies that at least two separate neural pathways project to the primary somatosensory cortex. In each strip, specific areas of the somatosensory cortex correspond to specific locations of the body (see Section 8.3.4.1).

8.3.4 THE SOMATOSENSORY CORTEX

8.3.4.1 The Homunculus

An important assumption in neuroscience is that the sensory cortices, and in particular the somatosensory cortex, are characterised by a sensory map (see fig 8.3). For the visual cortex we have already introduced the retinotopic map, and for the auditory cortex the tonotopic map. For the somatosensory cortex we find a similar organisation, but here it has traditionally been believed that the map reflects the body.

This body map, which is similar to the way the primary motor cortex is organised, was first proposed by Canadian neuroscientists Wilder Penfield and Edwin Boldrey, based on electrical stimulation of specific locations of this part of the cortex (Penfield & Boldrey, 1937). After stimulation, patients were asked what sensations they experienced. Based on these results, the somatosensory cortex was considered to be a purely bottom-up driven system that was mainly involved in the reception and processing of sensory stimuli. As consequence, many other important properties have been largely overlooked, such as the fact that the somatosensory cortex is strongly connected to the motor cortex. Over the past half-century, however, a growing body of literature has provided evidence for the idea that the somatosensory cortex is also involved in motor processes (Gioanni & Lamarche, 1985; Matyas et al., 2010).

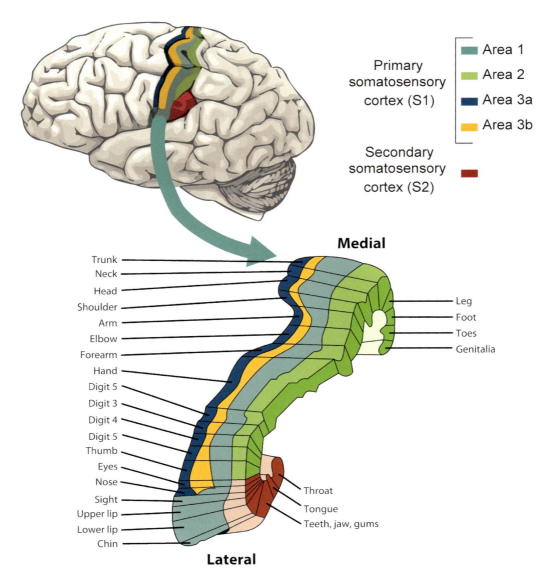

Figure 8.3 Organisation of the somatosensory cortex.

8.3.4.2 Criticism of the Homunculus

In recent years, the idea of the somatosensory cortex as a homunculus, or body map, has been increasingly criticised. The central tenet of this criticism is that the idea of such a map is naïve; that is, that it only represents the afferent inputs from the sensory receptors. Moreover, the original map, as devised by Penfield and colleagues was compiled almost exclusively on the basis of externally triggered signals (i.e., sensations perceived on the body, such as touches). Areas in the somatosensory cortex that represent, for example, joints or sensations from our internal organs were mostly ignored. An additional problem was that the idea of a sensory map does not allow for a link with cognitive processes. A somatosensory map that is created on the basis of a purely bottom-up driven process is limited in explaining how bodily sensations can contribute to mental processes such as thoughts or emotions. Finally, this model also does not explain how the link between a representation of our body and the perception of sensations comes about.

8.3.5 A BODY MODEL OF THE SOMATOSENSORY CORTEX

Based on the criticism of the sensory map just described, the German neuroscientist Michael Brecht (2017) has proposed an intriguing functional extension to the classic somatosensory cortex. According to Brecht, the somatosensory cortex represents a complete body model. Brecht has based this idea on the fact that the somatosensory cortex is characterised by a particularly complex organisation of cortical layer 4. According to Brecht, the somatosensory cortex would have two important functions. Firstly, if would be involved in generating an active representation of the body, and secondly, it would be involved in performing simulations of bodily functions.

The body model would, according to Brecht (2017), be represented in layer 4 of the somatosensory cortex and develop on the basis of both genetic information and inputs from somatosensory and other senses. According to this idea, the body model is the result of active neural computational operations and not the result of the passive projections of the somatosensory senses that the more traditional homunculus model assumes.

Part of the evidence for a body model can be found in a patient with Alzheimer's disease. This patient had damage to the somatosensory cortex. More specifically, she had difficulties with tasks that involved her own body. For example, she had difficulties getting dressed and answering questions such as 'show me your elbow' or 'point to your knee', even though she had no trouble pointing to other objects in her environment. When she had to point to her elbow, she usually responded by touching her wrist and arm and suggesting that her elbow must be somewhere in that area. In general, she responded as if her body map was extremely blurry (Sirigu, Grafman, Bressler, & Sunderland, 1991).

The second function that Brecht (2017) attributes to the somatosensory cortex is that it performs simulations of bodily functions. These simulations would be implemented as animations that are carried out in layer 4 of the somatosensory cortex, based on inputs from layer 6 (see fig 8.4). According to Brecht, these types of simulation would be similar to the way in which a flight simulator mimics the behaviour of an aircraft. The simulations would be used for mental preparation processes and/or the practicing of actions. Moreover, they could be used to

make our behaviour adaptive by mentally evaluating the various bodily functions.

An important feature of this body model is that it can be animated. In other words, according to Brecht, the model is able to walk, sit, stand, laugh, cry, and perform a large number of physical actions, without the body itself having to perform these actions directly. In that respect, the mental simulation model can be considered to be an avatar of the real body. For example, if you need to throw a ball, you will probably first mentally simulate this action, and the idea is that this simulation is performed in layer 4 of the somatosensory cortex. According to the model, the parameters that represent all relevant aspects of the body are represented in this layer of the cortex, based on both a genetically encoded physical representation and on the basis of practice.

According to Brecht, the body model is based on active neural calculations, and the central function of the somatosensory cortex consists of keeping the model active. Moreover, the results of the simulations that the body model performs can serve as input for other mental operations. The idea that the somatosensory cortex is involved in mental simulations is consistent with other ideas about the involvement of mental simulations in perceptual processes (Hesslow, 2002). Moreover, it is consistent with the idea of mental simulations in motor (Cross et al., 2006; Jeannerod, 2001) or in memory retrieval processes that

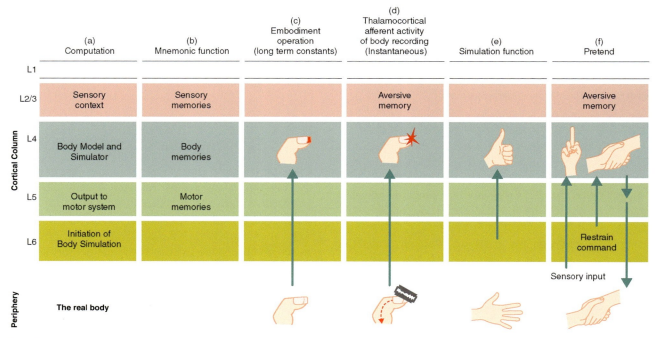

Figure 8.4 A schematic overview of the functions that layers 1 to 6 of the somatosensory cortex perform according to Brecht's body model. (a) The basal computations that are assumed to be carried out in each individual cortical layer. (b) The mnemonic functions of the body model and their implementation in specific cortical layers. (c) Long-term operations of the body that have to be represented – illustrated here by a growing fingernail. (d) The transformation of afferent inputs via cortico-thalamic circuits, exemplified here by the sensation caused by the innervation of a fingernail by a sharp object. This sensation can result in an aversive memory. (e) Simulation: while in reality the hand is in a stretched position, layer 4 can simulate a thumbs up gesture, (f) behaving as if, that is, the actual execution of a bodily simulation. In reality, an outstretched hand from an aversive individual is reciprocated by a friendly gesture. The natural response to the sensory input and aversive memories are inhibited in favour of a more friendly gesture. (source: Brecht, 2017)

involve the hippocampus (Lee & Wilson, 2002; Wilson & McNaughton, 1994). In addition, the idea of an active mental simulation is also consistent with the predictive coding framework. A basic assumption of the body model is that sensory input is compared with an internal expectation (Shipp et al., 2013) so that this input can be processed efficiently. It should be noted, however, that Brecht assigns more functions to the body model than just the prediction of sensory input in the sense that Brecht's body model is also capable of simulating alternative consequences of bodily actions.

8.3.6 PLASTICITY

Similar to the previously discussed motor, visual, and auditory cortices, the somatosensory cortex is characterised by a high degree of plasticity. In a literature review, Feldman and Brecht (2005) discuss a large number of factors that contribute to this plasticity. Among other factors, peripheral lesions, passive sensory experience, and training of sensory tasks are associated with the occurrence of structural changes in the somatosensory cortex. Much research on somatosensory plasticity is based on the study of the representation of rodents' whiskers. Sensory experience, especially early in life, results in a high degree of plasticity in the area in the somatosensory cortex where these hairs are represented. In humans, exercise has been found to affect the plasticity of the somatosensory cortex (Kerr et al., 2008). For example, Chinese Tai chi meditation trainees were found to have developed an increased tactile sensitivity to, among other things, their fingertips. Likewise, it has been found that training in musicians results in a sharp increase in their tactile sensitivity (Ragert, Schmidt, Altenmüller, & Dinse, 2004).

In humans, the effects of plasticity are also found after **deafferentation** (Kaas et al., 2008). Deafferentation occurs when the axons in the brainstem are no longer able to regenerate after an accident, preventing the brain from receiving sensory information from the body. One of the most observed consequences of such a condition is that cortical projections of other body parts, often originating from the face, invade the affected parts of the somatosensory cortex, resulting in a maladaptive plasticity, and in the perception of phantom sensations (Draganski & May, 2008).

8.3.7 PHANTOM LIMBS

One of the more striking consequences of cortical plasticity can be found in patients who have either lost a limb or at least lost the neural connections between a limb (or body part) and the brain. In these cases, it is frequently reported that the patient still reports feeling the body part in question (Hunter, Katz, & Davis, 2003); that is,

Figure 8.5 Illustration of the mirror-box illusion; a commonly used method of investigating phantom sensations.

they report experiencing a **phantom limb**. Hunter et al. examined 13 patients who had undergone an amputation of their arm. Twelve of these patients reported feeling a spontaneous, non-painful sensation in the amputated arm. In addition, seven patients reported feeling a mirror sensation; that is, when their intact arm was stimulated with a slight tactile stimulus, they reported feeling this stimulus not only in that arm but also in their amputated phantom arm. The latter effect was reported in particular when the patients saw their intact arm through a mirror, giving them the illusion that this was in fact their intact arm (see fig 8.5).

Phantom limb sensations are probably a consequence of the plasticity of the cortex, and it may be similar to the mechanism that causes focal hand dystonia (Pantev et al., 2001) in trained musicians (Chapter 7). Ramachandran, Rogers-Ramachandran, and Stewart (1992) described two patients showing massive cortical reorganisation after amputation of their arms and one patient showing similar effects after the amputating of a finger. These patients reported that slight touches of body parts that were at a relatively large distance from the amputation zone resulted in clearly localisable sensations in the phantom limb. One interesting finding was that stimulation of parts of the face also resulted in phantom sensations. The latter result is clear evidence for cortical plasticity, because the face and arms are represented in adjacent areas of the cortex. In addition, the reported phantom sensations were not random, but followed a clearly defined spatial pattern. More specifically, there was a one-to-one correspondence between the location on the face that was stimulated and the location on the phantom limb where this sensation was felt. Most phantom sensations were reported on the hand, and predominantly so on the thumb and little finger. Ramachandran et al. found that this reorganisation can manifest itself relatively rapidly: one patient reported experiencing these phantom sensations within four weeks after the amputation.

8.4 INTEROCEPTION

The term 'interoception' describes the perception of our bodily processes (Craig, 2003). In this respect, we must distinguish between the sensations of temperature, itching, and pain, which are considered to be exteroceptive functions, on the one hand, and the less-explicit sensations of hunger, thirst, and motor feedback signals from the muscles that form the interoceptive signals, on the other. Although Vaitl (1996) also classifies the exteroceptive functions among the interoceptive functions, Craig (2002) argues that the neural basis of the interoceptive system is strictly separated from that of the exteroceptive system. Interoception plays an important role in emotion and motivation (see Chapters 11 and 12 for further details).

Vaitl (1996) makes a further distinction by subdividing interoceptive functions into proprioceptive and visceroceptive functions. Proprioception involves the processing of signals that determine our posture, based on signals from receptors in the skin and joints. Visceroception, on the other hand, includes signals that originate from the internal organs. Most visceroceptive signals are generated by receptors whose soma are located in the ganglia of the sympathetic part of the autonomic nervous system. These signals are projected from the autonomic nervous system to the brainstem, hypothalamus, and amygdala. Only a small percentage of the total afferent input to the brain, however, is visceroceptive; about 2% of all input has been found to be involved in visceroceptive perception.

The main function of these visceroceptive afferent inputs is to ensure that the body maintains a stable internal state (see also Chapter 11). Moreover, visceroceptive perception is involved in the perception of our posture. Information from the kidneys, in combination with the observation of the distribution of body fluids in the cardiovascular system, plays a particularly important role here. Finally, interoception plays a decisive role in determining the direction of gravity. This is achieved by combining information from receptors in the joints, tendons, muscles, and skin.

8.4.1 VISCEROCEPTION

Most research on visceroception involves three different systems: the cardiovascular system, the respiratory system, and the gastrointestinal system. Studies involving cardiovascular interoception primarily focus on how perceived changes in blood pressure may influence behaviour. Blood pressure is regulated by a number of different systems, including the baroreflex. The baroreflex is a rapidly signalling mechanism which can trigger near instantaneous changes in blood pressure by regulating heart rate and contracting blood vessels, and by increasing their peripheral resistance. This is mainly achieved through the activation of baroreceptors, that is, mechanical receptors in the carotid artery and the aortic arch. Baroreceptor activation can also affect motor and cognitive functions. For instance, it has been found that a high degree of baroreceptor activity is associated with a reduced effectiveness of autonomic reflexes in the spinal cord, and with changes in the perception of pain (Rau, Elbert, Geiger, & Lutzenberger, 1992).

8.4.2 INTEROCEPTION, FEELINGS, AND PREDICTIVE CODING

Damasio and Carvalho (2013) argue that feelings are the results of a mental process evaluating the state of the body (see fig 8.6). This involves the processing of physiological needs (such as hunger), tissue damage (pain), sensations of optimal functioning (well-being), threats (fear or anger), or specific social interactions (compassion, gratitude, or love). Damasio and Carvalho, proposed the existence of a neural body map, where all the bodily signals are related to physiological parameters. This process is believed to maintain the body's internal balance. As such, the body map is believed to function as a monitor that registers where deficiencies occur. Although such deficiencies can, in principle, also be corrected using relatively simple mechanisms, Damasio and Carvalho argue that a subjective component, that is, a sense of feeling, evolved on top of these basic mechanisms because it provides an intrinsic benefit. Feelings of pain, hunger, or thirst force an organism to attend to the needs of the body. Moreover, the processing of subjective feelings may also play an important role during learning processes.

Critchley, Wiens, Rotshtein, Ohman, and Dolan (2004) concluded that the insula, somatomotor, and cingulate cortices are involved in the interpretation of bodily responses (see also Singer, Critchley, & Preuschoff, 2009 for a similar conclusion). Participants in the Critchley et al. study were instructed to assess the timing of their own heartbeat. The accuracy of their estimates corresponded to activation of the right anterior insula. Seth (2013) discusses interoception from the predictive coding framework. He proposes that the anterior insula is important for comparing an expected response of the body with the actual one. The detection of a mismatch between these two is a prerequisite for triggering an emotional response in Seth's model. Thus, according to Seth, emotional responses are generated by such an active top-down prediction mechanism. This mechanism not only predicts the causes of a particular bodily reaction, but it also generates our emotional state based on this expectation.

8.5 PROPRIOCEPTION

Proprioception refers to the perception of the position of the body and its movements (Hillier, Immink, & Thewlis, 2015). Already in the first half of the 19th century, Sir Charles Bell (a Scottish physician who became famous

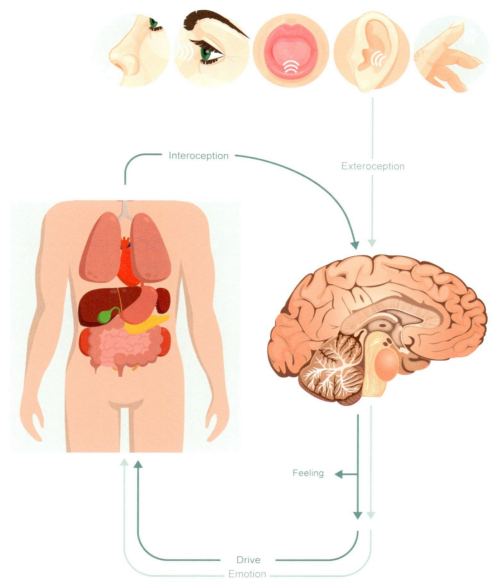

Figure 8.6 The relationship between interoception, exteroception, emotion, and motivation, according to Damasio and Carvalho (2013).

for discovering the difference between motor and sensory nerves) described this type of perception as the sixth sense (McCloskey, 1978). Proprioception arises from feedback produced by muscle spindles and the Golgi tendon organs (Fallon & Macefield, 2007). These receptors detect changes in muscle length and the rate of contraction. Thus, motion is detected by determining the relative contraction of different muscles and by determining the ratio of activity of the agonist and antagonist (for example, the biceps and triceps of the upper arm). In addition, receptors in the skin are involved in the detection of movement and position (Proske & Gandevia, 2012), for example, by measuring the stretching of the skin. Finally, our joints contain sensors that are involved in encoding body position. For example, organs of Ruffini are involved in measuring pressure on the joints. These receptors are mainly involved in detecting acceleration and deceleration.

The receptors just described are not only stimulated when we actively perform a movement but also when a body part is moved passively. This receptor activity is integrated with the efferent signals generated by the motor system (see Chapter 3). Together, these signals produce a series of mechanical sensations that are not only involved in perceiving the current position of the body but also in producing, predicting, and simulating a specific action of a joint. Finally, they are involved in determining the amount of force needed to hold or change a position.

8.5.1 A BODY REPRESENTATION

Longo and Haggard (2010) found evidence for an internal body model that is involved in determining body posture. They argued that information about the position of the individual joints is not sufficient to efficiently integrate all the aforementioned proprioceptive signals. After all, an implicit model of the body, in which the interrelationship between the joints and the individual receptors is encoded, is necessary to form an adequate representation of our body's position (see also, Longo, 2022). To illustrate: if we want to know whether we can reach the top shelf in the kitchen, it is not enough to have access to information about our individual joints, we also need to have a representation of our body's size. Longo and Haggard developed a method for systematically investigating this body representation. They did this by instructing participants to indicate where in an external reference frame ten specific positions were located. These positions were marked on the participants' hand, which was then hidden from view. After hiding the hand, participants were instructed to estimate the position of the marked locations in the now empty space. Longo and Haggard found that participants used an internal body representation. Interestingly, this representation was systematically biased (see fig 8.7). More specifically, the bias in the model corresponded to the extent to which specific parts of the hand were represented in the classical Penfield and Boldrey (1937) homunculus.

Artificial stimulation of a muscle can also result in a change in body representation (de Vignemont, Ehrsson, &

Haggard, 2005). De Vignemont et al. instructed blindfolded participants to hold their left index fingers with their right hands. Presenting a vibrating stimulus to the right biceps resulted in the subjective sensation that the left index finger became longer, while presenting the same stimulus to the right triceps resulted in the subjective sensation that it was shrinking. The relative length of the finger is measured using the following method. Two positions on the index finger and two positions on the forehead were stimulated using a tactile stimulator. Participants were then required to indicate on which part of the body (forehead or index finger) the two locations were further apart (see fig 8.8).

8.6 NOCICEPTION AND PAIN

Suppose that while crafting, you cut yourself with a pair of scissors, a knife, or a hacksaw. Without being aware of it, you continue to focus on your work until you find a trace of blood running along your finger. Now, slowly but steadily, you become aware of a very sharp and biting pain. In contrast, it is also possible that you perceive a painful sensation when you observe someone else suffering in

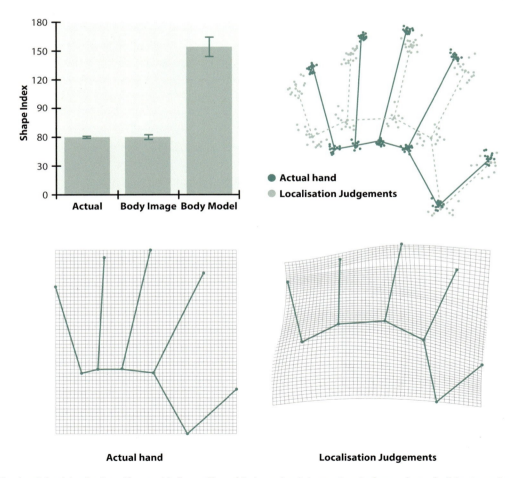

Actual hand

Localisation Judgements

Figure 8.7 Results of participants' estimates with respect to the positions of their own hands in an external reference frame. Participants used an internal model of their own body to make these estimates. (source: Longo & Haggard, 2010)

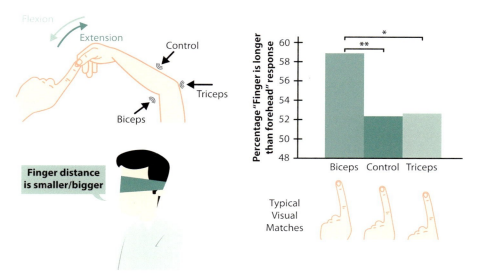

Figure 8.8 When participants were instructed to estimate the relative distance between two locations on their left index finger, this estimate was influenced by stimulating the right biceps or triceps. (source: de Vignemont et al., 2005)

pain, or that you suffer from a persistent chronic pain in your back. Although your back may have been injured in the past, the physical damage has already been healed, yet the painful sensation is still there.

These examples illustrate that pain perception is a complex process. On the one hand, there may be tissue damage without raising awareness, yet there may also be a pain sensation without a direct physical cause. More generally, pain is a negative affective sensation that can be both interoceptive and exteroceptive. Pain perception can manifest itself in many different forms and can be influenced by various factors. To fully encompass all the facets of a painful sensation, we must distinguish between nociception and pain. Nociception is used to denote the neural signals that are registered by pain receptors, whereas the term 'pain' is used to describe the resulting subjective experience. The latter is the result of cognitive processes affecting the nociceptive input. Earlier in this chapter, we introduced the most important nociceptive receptors and the main neural pathways that project the nociceptive signals to the brain. We also introduced the distinction between different types of pain: acute sharp pain, burning pain. and painful coldness. Given the complexity of the pain sensation, the International Association for the Study of Pain (IASP) has developed a classification system to describe the different forms of pain (Woolf et al., 1998). Woolf et al. propose the existence of three major pain categories; that is, transient pain, pain due to tissue damage, and pain due to damage to the central nervous system.

8.6.1 TYPES OF PAIN

Transient pain is strongly associated with the abrupt activation of a nociceptive receptor, which occurs without any tissue damage. An example of this is a pinprick that does not damage the skin. Pain that does result from tissue damage can be caused by sensitisation of the nociceptive receptors, by the recruitment of additional nociceptive receptors, or by the summation or amplification of these nociceptive signals. Finally, pain that is due to damage to the central nervous system can be caused by the nociceptive axons being stimulated in locations that are not associated with the location of the nociceptive receptor. This may happen for a number of reasons, including deafferentation, the disinhibition of interneurons, or the structural reorganisation of the central nervous system.

In everyday practice, we typically make a distinction between acute pain and chronic pain, although Woolf et al. (1998) argue that this distinction is not indicative of the underlying mechanisms. Nevertheless, acute pain mainly corresponds to transient pain along with pain that is due to tissue damage. Pain that lasts longer than three months is described as chronic pain. Chronic pain occurrence has been reported in about 20% of the adult population, particularly in women and the elderly (Breivik, Collett, Ventafridda, Cohen, & Gallacher, 2006). It is particularly problematic to treat chronic pain. Although chronic pain often starts with tissue damage or inflammation, it can become chronic due to the sustained activation of the descending projections from the brain that modulate the nociceptive signals (Porreca, Ossipov, & Gebhart, 2002). This sustained activity may be the result of maladaptive changes in nuclei in the medulla.

8.6.2 PAIN MEMORIES

A painful experience, such as touching a burning stove – or grabbing an electric fence – can result in a one-time intense experience, which we will most likely not forget for the rest of our lives, and which results in a strong resistance to ever performing this action again. According to Ji, Kohno, Moore, and Woolf (2003), these painful experiences directly trigger a sensitisation process (see Chapter 3), thus forming very strong pain memories. The formation of these pain memories is probably a reflection of one of the essential evolutionary survival functions of pain.

8.6.3 PAIN AND AWARENESS

Pain is a conscious experience that involves the interpretation of nociceptive inputs (Bob, 2008). These inputs are modulated by memories, along with emotional, pathological, genetic, and cognitive factors. Consequently, the resulting pain experience is not the direct result of the nociceptive input, and a painful experience may also not be directly related to its essential protective function. This is particularly so for chronic pain. Our responses to painful events are also modulated by what is appropriate or possible in a given situation. The subjectivity of pain is also evident from its official IASP definition: 'An unpleasant sensory and emotional experience associated with, or resembling that associated with, actual or potential tissue damage'.

Although the subjective nature of pain is a major hurdle for many pain studies, the last two decades have seen reasonable success in uncovering the mechanisms involved in the perception of pain. One of the central findings is that pain can be regulated through central (top-down) and peripheral (bottom-up) mechanisms.

8.6.3.1 Neural Mechanisms

In a literature review, Tracey and Mantyh (2007) provide an overview of the most important processes involved in pain awareness (see fig 8.9). Nociceptive information is projected to the brain via three different ascending tracts: (1) a spinothalamic tract to the thalamus, (2) a spinoreticular and (3) spinomesencephalic tracts to the medulla and brainstem. Each of these tracts serves a different purpose. The projections to the brainstem play a particularly important role in the integration of nociceptive signals with homeostatic, arousal-regulating, and autonomic processes. In addition, these projections play a role in communicating the nociceptive signals to the forebrain, where the pain sensation is believed to be perceived. The brainstem is believed to play an important role in mediating the experience of this perception. Finally, the thalamic tracts are most likely involved in the perception of chronic pain (Di Piero et al., 1991).

Bastuji, Frot, Perchet, Magnin, and Garcia-Larrea (2016) also found evidence for the existence of separate mechanisms being involved in pain awareness. They studied the neural mechanisms of pain perception based on **intercranial EEG** recordings. In this study, transient nociceptive stimuli were administered by using a short but intense laser pulse. EEGs were recorded in 16 different brain regions, including the insula; the parietal, prefrontal, and cingulate cortices; and the hippocampus and limbic system. Based on these data, Bastuji et al. found three waves of activation at various stages of (pre)conscious processing of the stimulus. Preconscious activation was recorded in the posterior insula, operculum, mid-cingulate cortex, and amygdala. Activation in the anterior insula, the prefrontal cortex, and the posterior parietal cortex started later and developed simultaneously with the awareness of, and the voluntary response to, the stimulus. Responses in the hippocampus

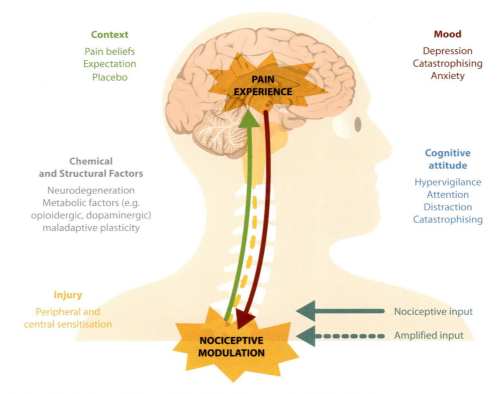

Figure 8.9 An overview of the main factors that contribute to the perception of pain. (source: Tracey and Mantyh, 2007)

and two additional areas in the cingulate cortex developed even later, and these areas remained active long after the patients became aware of the stimulus. The nociceptive inputs reached the sensory and limbic areas in the brain more or less simultaneously. According to Bastuji et al. (2016), the activation in the frontoparietal brain regions is related to awareness of the nociceptive stimulus, while the later responses are associated with encoding the pain sensation in memory, with self-awareness (i.e., the realisation that the stimulus may be a threat to the self), and the modulation of the pain sensation.

8.6.3.2 The Pain Matrix

Because pain is a complex multifaceted subjective experience, the processing of nociceptive stimuli involves a large and diffuse network of brain regions. Melzack (1999) initially described this activation pattern as the pain 'neuro-matrix', however, at present it is mostly known as the **pain matrix**. In essence, this pain matrix consists of a lateral and a medial component. The lateral component is considered to

be the sensory and descriptive component, and the medial component is considered to be the affective, cognitive, and evaluative component (Albe-Fessard, Berkley, Kruger, Ralston, & Willis, 1985). It should be noted, however, that various factors might influence how each brain area contributes to the pain matrix. These factors include, among others, attention, mood, or the nature of the injury. For this reason, the pain matrix is a relatively loosely defined concept. Based on a meta-analysis, however, Apkarian, Bushnell, Treede, and Zubieta (2005) were able to identify several brain areas that play an important role in the experience of acute pain, including the primary and secondary somatosensory cortices, the insula, the anterior cingulate and the prefrontal cortices, and the thalamus (see fig 8.10). In addition to these areas, the basal ganglia, cerebellum, amygdala, hippocampus, and areas in the parietal and temporal cortices can also be activated, depending on the specific conditions.

As discussed, chronic pain is in many cases no longer associated with tissue damage. Instead, it appears to be the

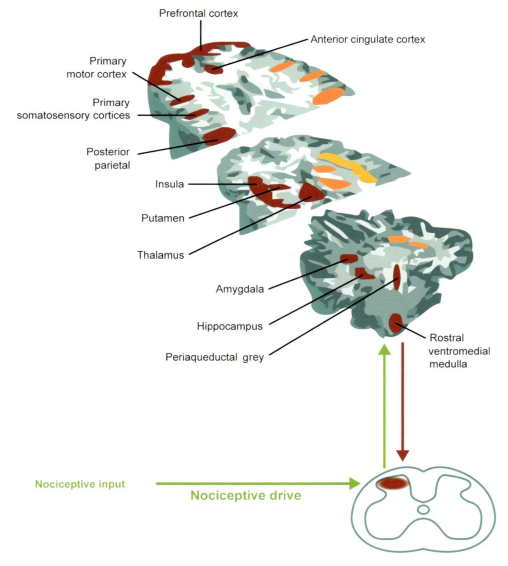

Figure 8.10 An overview of the brain areas involved in the perception of acute pain. (source: Tracey and Mantyh, 2007)

result of a maladaptive pain regulation mechanism. Tracey and Mantyh (2007) argue that neural mechanisms that fall outside the classical pain matrix are involved in the perception of chronic pain. Baliki et al. (2006) found evidence for this by investigating the relationship between brain activity and the intensity of spontaneous chronic back pain in 11 patients. In patients with back pain, the spontaneous chronic pain typically fluctuates, and the researchers were able to identify two different phases that they denoted as sustained and increasing pain. The intensity of sustained pain correlated with activation of the medial prefrontal cortex. This brain region is associated with the processing of negative emotions (see Chapter 12), the processing of conflicting responses (see Chapter 5), and the detection of adverse outcomes (see Chapters 11 and 21). Increasing pain, on the other hand, mainly activated the brain areas that are part of the pain matrix. This result implies that the perception of chronic persistent pain is strongly associated with the emotional evaluation of this sensation.

Given the diffuse nature of the pain matrix, Tracey and Mantyh (2007) argue that pain perception is mainly related to the integration of activity in a large number of brain regions, in which the interaction between top-down and bottom-up driven processes play a particularly important role. Legrain, Iannetti, Plaghki, and Mouraux (2011) also emphasise the diffuse nature of these processes and argue that the network traditionally described as the 'pain matrix' is not so much involved in the processing of pain, but rather that it is a network involved in the processing of salient sensory events. According to Legrain et al., this network would be mainly involved in detecting events that may threaten the integrity of the body, while the sensory channel with which this event is detected is of minor importance.

The main task of the 'pain matrix' would therefore consist of constructing a representation of the body and the peripersonal space around the body. Peripersonal space is defined as a multisensory representation of the space directly surrounding the body. More specifically, it is the space in which we can move our limbs under normal circumstances; where we can manipulate objects and where we can expect any threats to the integrity of our bodies to happen. Legrain et al. therefore assume that the pain matrix represents a defence system that alerts us to potentially harmful events. From this point of view, the network traditionally considered as pain matrix would not so much be involved in the processing of nociceptive sensations, but rather in selecting an appropriate action to avert the potential threat.

8.6.3.3 Attention and Context
Several studies have provided evidence for the idea that attention is highly effective in regulating pain perception (Legrain, Crombez, & Mouraux, 2011; Levine, Gordon, Smith, & Fields, 1982; Miron, Duncan, & Bushnell, 1989; Villemure & Bushnell, 2002). fMRI and electrophysiological studies have provided evidence for the idea that attention and distraction

can modulate the neural activity that is triggered by nociceptive stimuli (Bantick et al., 2002; Lagrain, Guérit, Bruyer, & Plaghki, 2002). For example, Van der Lubbe, Buitenweg, Boschker, Gerdes, and Jongsma (2012) found that selective attention could influence ERP responses that were evoked by electric shocks. Participants were given either a single shock or a series of five shocks to the left or right index finger. Before the stimulus was presented, they were instructed to attend to one of the two fingers and to respond when a deviant stimulus was presented to the attended finger. The two components of the nociceptive ERP, the N100 and the N150, were larger in amplitude when the stimulus was presented to the attended finger compared to the non-attended finger. Although it is not yet fully understood how attention can modulate these nociceptive activations, one possibility is that it is done via the previously discussed descending projections (fig 8.11). Since the mid-20th century, this descending system has been known to facilitate or inhibit nociceptive processing (Hagbarth & Kerr, 1954).

Ploghaus, Becerra, Borras, and Borsook (2003) found that pain perception can be influenced by expectations, as illustrated by the well-known placebo effect. Likewise, a PET study by Petrovic, Kalso, Petersson, and Ingvar (2002) found that placebos could affect the activation of the rostral anterior cingulate cortex in a way that was similar to opioid painkillers. Based on this finding, Wager et al. (2004) tested the hypothesis that placebos produce analgesic effects by changing expectations. Participants were conditioned to expect a painful stimulus. Placebos reduced the activation of the brain areas traditionally associated with pain processing. In addition, they were associated with an increase in activation of the prefrontal cortex during the anticipation of a painful stimulus. These results are consistent with the idea that activation of the prefrontal cortex may stimulate the release of opioids into the brainstem.

8.6.3.4 Emotions and Mood
Pain may have an impact on negative moods (Price, 2000). It is believed that this is caused by the fact that pain is generally more intense than other somatosensory experiences, that it is persistent and diffuse, and that the nociceptive stimuli for some forms of pain summate across time. In addition, for both acute and chronic pain, our mood may have a significant impact on the perception of pain and on our ability to cope with it. For example, anticipating a pain stimulus may strongly impact how pain is experienced. To a certain degree, this anticipation is adaptive. For example, as a child, we learned not to touch hot cooking pans and not to stick our fingers in a hot candle flame. However, for chronic pain patients, pain experiences can become maladaptive and result in anxiety and avoidance reactions. Fairhurst, Wiech, Dunckley, and Tracey (2007) found for neurotypical adults that the extent to which a painful event is anticipated correlated positively with the intensity of the reported pain. This enhancement of the pain experience was partially mediated

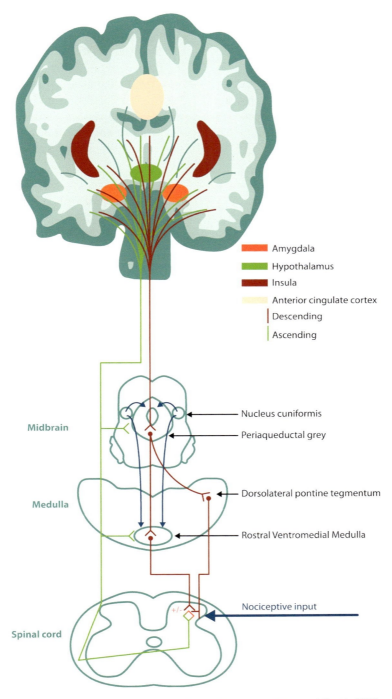

Figure 8.11 Overview of the descending modulatory projections involved in pain regulation. (source: Tracey and Mantyh, 2007)

by activation in the ventral tegmentum, the entorhinal cortex, and parts of the descending modulatory pain system.

Depressive symptoms are also frequently associated with pain experiences. Although this association has been shown to exist, it is not yet clear whether there is a causal relationship. It is unclear whether depression causes the pain experiences or vice versa, or whether there may be an underlying cause for both. A relatively limited number of studies have attempted to identify the neural mechanisms that mediate the relationship between pain and depression (Giesecke et al., 2005; Neugebauer, Li, Bird, & Han, 2004).

For example, Giesecke et al. (2005) found that activation of the amygdala and the anterior insula differed greatly between fibromyalgia patients with and without depression (see Section 8.6.6 for a discussion of fibromyalgia).

Another negative cognitive and affective state that may strongly impact pain experiences is catastrophising. Catastrophising is characterised by focusing on pain-related symptoms, **ruminating** about pain, feelings of helplessness, and pessimism about pain-related outcomes (Edwards, Bingham, Bathon, & Haythornthwaite, 2006). Gracely et al. (2004) found, also in a group of fibromyalgia patients, that catastrophising over pain was strongly related to an increase in activity in brain areas related to the anticipation of pain (medial frontal cortex, cerebellum), attention to pain (dorsal anterior cingulate cortex, dorsolateral prefrontal cortex), emotional aspects of pain (areas related to the amygdala), and motor control. These results imply that catastrophising affects pain perception by focusing attention, anticipation of pain, and increasing the emotional response to pain.

We may wonder whether pain-related activation of these 'emotional' brain areas has an impact on tasks that require emotional decisions. Apkarian et al. (2004) found that chronic pain patients' performance on the Iowa gambling task (see Chapter 5) was impaired, compared to neurotypical control participants, implying that the emotional impact of pain can also affect our everyday functioning.

8.6.4 PAIN AND PREDICTIVE CODING

Earlier in this section, we already introduced the mechanisms involved in modulating pain perception through expectation. Ploghaus et al. (2003) argue that these mechanisms form the basis of the placebo effect. Büchel, Geuter, Sprenger, and Eippert (2014) aimed to further explain placebo effects on the basis of the predictive coding framework. According to Büchel et al., the ascending and descending pain systems operate like a prediction machine. According to this view, the pain experience is not perceived passively, based on the nociceptive signals, but actively, since the brain generates inferences based on previous experiences and expectations.

Analgesia is a condition where the pain experience is completely suppressed. Although placebos can reduce pain sensations, there is no complete suppression. For that reason, the effects of placebos are described with the term 'hypoalgesia'. Büchel et al. (2014) argue that placebo effects are the result of a Bayesian inference process that is based on combined top-down a priori expectations and bottom-up driven nociceptive signals (see fig 8.12). It is not only the intensity of the expectation that plays a role here but also the precision of the expectation. Büchel et al. describe how this model can explain the effects of acute pain, and its mediation by placebos.

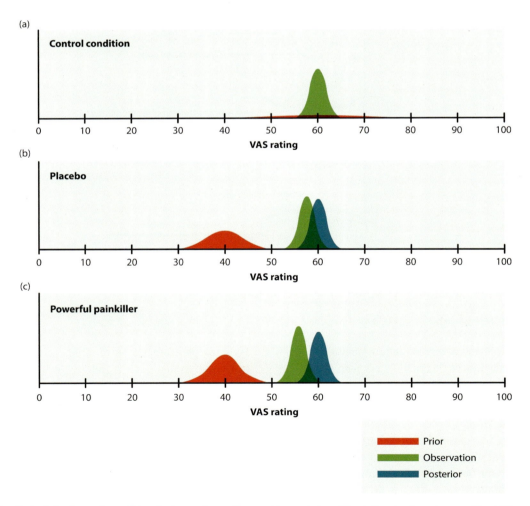

Figure 8.12 The effects of placebos on the precision of pain experiences. Compared to a control condition, both a placebo and a powerful painkiller can modulate the a priori expectation of pain, causing the actual nociceptive stimulus to be perceived as less intense. (source: Büchel et al., 2014)

Both the ascending and descending pain systems are characterised by many recurrent connections, which makes the idea that these pain systems are part of a predictive mechanism plausible. For example, recent fMRI (Ritter, Franz, Dietrich, Miltner, & Weiss, 2013) and electrophysiological studies (Johansen, Tarpley, LeDoux, & Blair, 2010) have found evidence that the descending system is also involved in the transmission of nociceptive stimuli. In addition, opioid neuromodulators, which are involved in the reduction of pain sensations, have also been found to modulate the ascending pain system. In summary, these results suggest that a dichotomy of the pain system in a pain-responsive (ascending) and pain-modulating (descending) system is too simplistic and there is a much stronger interaction between these two systems than was initially assumed (Millan, 2002).

Evidence for Bayesian integration (see Appendix) of a priori expectations and physical nociceptive stimulation comes from studies that manipulate the expected intensity of a nociceptive stimulus by using a cue. Lorenz et al. (2005) used two different levels of pain intensity and presented a cue to inform participants which of the two intensities they could expect. They found that the relatively weak nociceptive stimuli were perceived as more painful – and strong stimuli as less painful – when preceded by an invalid cue. Pain expectation is not only modulated by the intensity of the stimulus but also by the precision of the expectation. Brown, Seymour, Boyle, El-Deredy, and Jones (2008) used different pain intensities, which were cued with either a high or low degree of certainty (that is, in one condition, the proportion of cues that was valid was much higher than in another condition). The perceived intensity of the nociceptive stimulus depended on the predictive value of the cue. This observation is consistent with the principles of Bayesian integration; that is,

high-intensity stimuli were perceived as more painful the greater the predictive value of the cue. These results are consistent with other data implying that pain perception is better explained by a Bayesian model than by simpler models (Yoshida, Seymour, Koltzenburg, & Dolan, 2013).

8.6.5 PHANTOM PAIN

As already discussed, dissecting the afferent connections of a body part can result in the perception of a phantom limb. Although phantom limbs are experienced regularly in such cases, sometimes, the phenomenon can manifest itself as **phantom pain**. Phantom pain can be extremely intense and perceived to originate from an amputated body part. In addition to the pure phantom pains, there may also be residual pains that are experienced in intact body parts that are in close proximity to the amputation.

Phantom pain can manifest itself in many ways (Flor, Nikolajsen, & Staehelin Jensen, 2006), ranging from simple short-term shooting pains to prolonged intense episodes in which the patient has an intense experience of the missing body part (see fig 8.13). The intensity of the pain is usually more intense in the more distal parts of the amputated body part, and the sensation can take all sorts of forms, from a stabbing or a throbbing pain to burning sensations. Feelings of cramping in the amputated limbs have also been reported.

There are several factors that can contribute to the development of phantom pain. Both pre- and postoperative factors can influence the onset and intensity of the phantom pain, and it can sometimes be difficult to distinguish between these forms of pain, especially in the initial phase after surgery. In Western Europe and North America, most amputations are related to chronic vascular

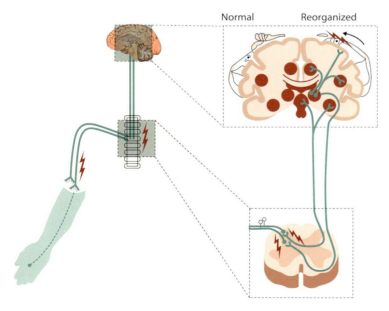

Central changes
- Unmasked
- Sprouting
- General disinhibition
- Remodeling of sensory map
- Loss of neurons and neuronal functions.
- Denervation
- Alteration in neuronal and glial activity
- Sensory-motor and sensory-incongruence

Peripheral changes
- Structural changes in neurons and axons
- Ectopic impulses
- Ephaptic transmission
- Sympathetic Afferent Coupling
- Down- or up-regulation of neurotransmitters
- Alterations in channels or in transduction molecules
- Selective loss of unmyelized fibers

Figure 8.13 A schematic overview of the mechanisms involved in phantom pain. (source: Flor et al., 2006)

disease, and patients are therefore often relatively old and characterised by a long history of chronic pain prior to amputation. In other parts of the world, amputations are frequently a consequence of war traumas. It is therefore an interesting question whether phantom pain develops differently in traumatic pain patients compared to chronic pain patients. Although this question has not yet been answered, it has been established that the likelihood of developing phantom pain is greater when an amputation occurs during adulthood than during childhood.

8.6.5.1 Peripheral Changes

After amputation, a swelling forms at the end of the remaining body part, the stump, where the axons of the deafferent nerves start to grow again. This outgrowth results in a **neuroma**, that is, a cross-linked mass of axons that can no longer reconnect with the tissue of the amputated body part. Stimulation of this neuroma, for example by tapping against it, can result in a phantom pain experience. The neurons in the stump are characterised by atypical activation patterns. This atypical activity cannot be the only explanation for phantom pain, however, because the pain can be present soon after surgery, when the neuroma has not yet developed.

Another possible cause of phantom pain can be found in the dorsal root ganglia (see Chapter 2). In the absence of regulation by normal input from the intact part of the body, neurons in these ganglia can spontaneously fire and this activity can possibly be enhanced by the neural impulses that originate from the neuroma. Moreover, this activation can also be reinforced by sympathetic activation. The latter mechanism could explain the fact that most patients experience an increase in phantom pain at the time of emotional distress.

8.6.5.2 The Spinal Cord

Local anaesthesia of the stump results in a decrease in phantom pain in only half of all cases, suggesting that an even more central mechanism is involved. Evidence that the human spinal cord is involved in the development of phantom pain was obtained when it was found that a number of patients who were normally not experiencing phantom pains began to experience them after receiving a spinal cord anaesthetic. Although it is not yet clear how this came about, it is possible that a mechanism similar to that involved in the processing of inflammatory pain is involved. Increased activation of receptors sensitive to inflammatory pains typically results in a lasting increase in the sensitivity of dorsal spinal cord neurons. This increase in sensitivity is known as central sensitisation, and may also be triggered by nerve damage, for instance following an amputation.

The loss of direct stimulation from the peripheral nervous system may also trigger a downregulation of opioid receptors, causing a disinhibition of the central pain receptors.

Finally, the loss of normal peripheral stimulation may result in a massive degeneration of the axons that normally project from the amputated limb to the spinal cord. As a consequence, the freed-up space in the spinal cord may become occupied by axons that originate from adjacent, healthy body parts.

8.6.5.3 Brainstem, Thalamus, and Cortex

A final set of changes may occur in the brain itself. Neural tissue in the brainstem, the thalamus, and in the cortex, is reorganised following an amputation. It is not yet clear how these changes is related to each other. It is clear, however, that a massive reorganisation takes place in the primary somatosensory cortex as a result of an amputation. For example, animal research has shown that the amputation of a finger can trigger the part of the cortex that previously represented the amputated finger to be invaded by axons from the surrounding areas.

Similar results have been found following a dorsal rhizotomy, that is, a procedure in which part of the dorsal spinal nerves is damaged. For example, it has been found that the representation of the jaw took over the entire representation of the hand and arm. This cortical reorganisation may explain why phantom sensations can be triggered by the stimulation of adjacent body parts. The invasive axons can interfere with the still rudimentary representation of the original body part and can therefore trigger a phantom sensation. Ramachandran, Rogers-Ramachandran, Stewart, and Pons (1992) managed to find a one-to-one relationship between the location on a patient's cheek where they stimulated and the location of a sensation on the patient's phantom hand. This observation suggests that a topographical remapping is taking place.

Note, however, that reorganisation is not necessarily limited to an invasion from adjacent areas. It has also been found that phantom pain in the arm could be triggered by stimulation of the toe. Since the somatosensory representations of the arm and toe are far apart in the cortex, we must conclude that other mechanisms are also involved in cortical reorganisation. More recent studies have shown that the reorganisation can change greatly with time (Halligan, Marshall, Wade, Davey, & Morrison, 1993). For instance, neuroimaging studies have found that among patients with an arm amputation, somatosensory cortical areas that represent the mouth progressively invaded the region that previously represented the arm. Moreover, it was found that the degree of invasion from the mouth areas was related to the degree of pain experienced in the phantom arm.

8.6.5.4 Motor Feedback

In addition to the primary somatosensory cortex, the frontal and parietal cortices are also likely to contribute

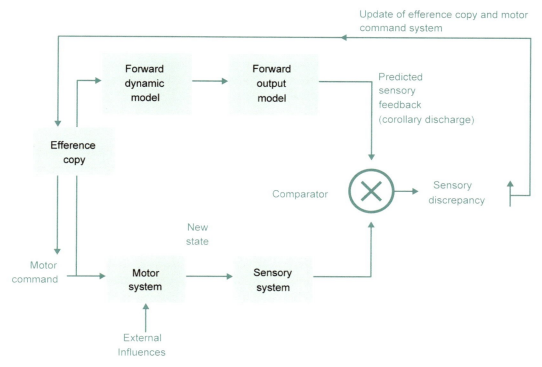

Figure 8.14 A schematic overview illustrating the role of efference copies of the motor signal on phantom pain. (source: McCabe et al., 2005)

to the experience of phantom pain. The suggestion is that pain in a phantom limb may be caused by an incongruence between motor intention and sensory feedback (see fig 8.14). McCabe, Haigh, Halligan, and Blake (2005) found evidence for this hypothesis by having participants perform actions in which they observed one-half of their body through a mirror, creating the illusion that the limb perceived in the mirror was their real amputated limb. When the real arm had to make movements that were incongruent with what the participants observed, they reported a number of symptoms that are related to pain, such as numbness, prickling, or even real pain sensations.

Another phenomenon that occurs regularly with phantom pain is **telescoping**. This is the phenomenon in which patients with phantom pain regularly report that their phantom limb is significantly shorter than their original limb was; in some extreme cases they may even report it to be smaller than the stump. Although telescoping was originally considered to be the result of adaptation, more recent studies have shown that telescoping is actually associated with increases in phantom pain.

8.6.5.5 The Pain Memory Hypothesis
Some studies have found that the phantom pain experienced bears a strong relation to the pain that was experienced before the amputation. Presumably, the memory of this pain is implicitly stored. In individuals with chronic back pain, the duration of painful episodes appears to be related to the size of the somatosensory cortical area representing the back. The enlarged areas are believed to represent the pain memory. When such a pain memory is stored

in the somatosensory cortex, the invasion of axons from neighbouring somatosensory areas can stimulate this pain representation again following an amputation. This may result in the subjective experience of a phantom pain which is very similar to the pain that was originally experienced. Indeed, a number of studies have shown that there is a strong link between the duration of chronic pain before surgery and the likelihood of phantom pain developing (Nikolajsen, Ilkær, Krøner, Christensen, & Jensen, 1997).

If should be noted, however, that although the relationship between pain memory and the development of phantom pain has been clearly demonstrated for chronic pain, the results are more ambiguous for traumatic pain. It is possible that in this case pain memories are formed as a result of the surgical procedures or the trauma that gave rise to the amputation. However, studies on the effects of peripheral and central pain suppression, during and after surgery, have not yet been able to provide a clear answer.

8.6.5.6 Implications for the Treatment of Phantom Pain
Most of the traditional treatments of phantom pain are largely ineffective. These treatments consist of the administration of painkillers, antidepressants, or stimulants. The problem with these treatments is that their impact on the aforementioned mechanisms is negligible. Given the impact of cortical plasticity in the development of phantom pain, behavioural treatment methods that capitalise on this plasticity are of potential interest. The use of **myoelectric prostheses** is particularly promising in this context. A myoelectric prosthesis is an electronically controlled prosthesis

that can be used to grab objects, which is controlled by decoding the electromyographic signals generated by muscles on the intact part of the amputated arm. The use of these types of prostheses is effective in counteracting cortical reorganisation, and may thus have a positive effect on preventing phantom pain by minimising the incongruence between motor signals and perception.

Patients who are not eligible for using prostheses can possibly benefit from behaviourally relevant stimulation of the stump. In one study, a two-week training, in which patients had to discriminate between different types of electrical stimulation of the stump, was found to significantly decrease the reported phantom pain sensations and to reverse the cortical reorganisation process (Flor, Denke, Schaefer, & Grüsser, 2001). A similar result was found with stimulation of the stump and mouth in patients with an amputated arm (Huse, Preissl, Larbig, & Birbaumer, 2001). Finally, the use of mirrors can trick the brain into believing that it perceives a real limb at the site of the phantom limb, which can also result in an effective treatment of phantom pain (Ramachandran & Rogers-Ramachandran, 1996).

In summary, phantom pain is a complex phenomenon that is probably caused by a multitude of factors that manifest themselves at various levels of processing in the peripheral and central nervous system. The plasticity of the cortex, which is so beneficial in normal life, probably plays an important role in the development of phantom pain. Behavioural techniques that capitalise on this plasticity have been shown to be more effective in mitigating phantom pain than traditional pharmacological treatments.

Sherman, Arena, Sherman, and Ernst (1989) argue that, in addition to the physiological mechanisms described earlier, psychological processes are involved in the regulation of phantom pain. Although Sherman et al. found no evidence that personality disorders or the need to gain control over one's own life contribute to the regulation of phantom pain, mood states such as anxiety or depression can contribute to the development of phantom pain. The onset and duration of phantom pain is affected by stress, exhaustion, and other psychological factors, in a manner similar to the way physical pain sensations are regulated.

8.6.6 FIBROMYALGIA

Fibromyalgia is a syndrome that is characterised by a generic chronic pain in muscles and joints that cannot be related to specific tissue damage or inflammation. In addition, fibromyalgia is characterised by an excessive sensitivity to pressure on specific muscles or tendon groups. Patients with fibromyalgia are characterised by a relatively low threshold for pain. Moreover, they frequently give high pain ratings to pain-inducing stimuli (Goldenberg, Burckhart, & Croffert, 2004). Neuroimaging studies have shown that fibromyalgia is related to changes in central neural system functions, which might be triggered by a genetic disposition (Bradley, Mckendree-Smith, Alarcon, & Cianfrini, 2002).

The pain sensations that are related to fibromyalgia might also affect cognitive processes. For example, Glass (2008) reports increased memory problems and impairments in dual-task performance in fibromyalgia patients. Moreover, Crombez, Eccleston, Van den Broek, Goubert, and Van Houdenhove (2004) have reported that fibromyalgia patients are hypervigilant with respect to nociceptive stimuli, compared to a control group consisting of lower back pain patients. In addition, the fibromyalgia patients also reported more intense pain sensations, more negative affect, and a higher degree of catastrophising over pain (see fig 8.15).

Van Damme, Legrain, Vogt, and Crombez (2010) proposed that an increased attentional focus to painful stimuli may be related to motivation and suggest that two possible mechanisms might be involved in this. On the one hand, a painful stimulus may happen to capture

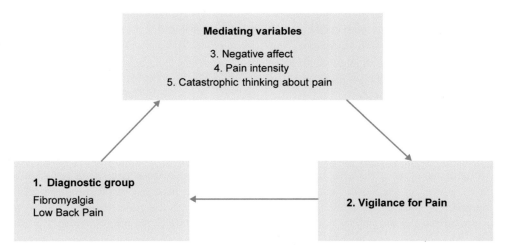

Figure 8.15 The relationship between fibromyalgia and vigilance, according to Crombez et al. (2004).

attention while performing a task, even when it is not task-relevant. On the other hand, attention to pain and pain-related information may be goal driven. Focusing attention on pain is particularly relevant when the task consists of controlling the pain. In the case of fibromyalgia, the latter aspect is particularly relevant, as the increased sensitivity to pain strongly motivates these patients to avoid painful stimuli.

Earlier in this chapter we introduced the pain matrix and the fact that it might consist of an alerting system warning the body of potential threats and selecting actions to avert them (Legrain, Iannetti, et al., 2011). According to this interpretation, fibromyalgia patients would be extra vigilant to events that take place in their peripersonal space. De Paepe, Crombez, Spence, and Legrain (2014) found evidence for this: visual stimuli presented in peripersonal space were detected earlier than visual stimuli presented further away from the body.

8.7 TACTILE PERCEPTION AND ATTENTION

As discussed in the previous two chapters, the cognitive processes related to visual and auditory perception are predominantly studied in a modality-specific fashion. Interest in the interaction between the various sensory modalities has only arisen relatively recently. Studies involving the tactile modality are somewhat of an exception here, however, because they have had a strong tradition of emphasising the interactions between tactile processes, on the one hand, and auditory and visual processes, on the other. For this reason, just before the start of the theme 'integration', it is appropriate to discuss some multisensory processes in which the tactile modality is involved. In the current section, we will therefore first introduce some basic effects of pure tactile attention and perception and then discuss how visual and tactile attention processes are related.

8.7.1 TACTILE PERCEPTION

The somatosensory cortex is crucial for our awareness of tactile stimuli. For instance, Palva, Linkenkaer-Hansen, Naatanen, and Palva (2005) presented brief tactile stimuli to the hand and found a clear relationship between awareness of these stimuli and activation of the somatosensory cortex. This relation between cortical activation and awareness is illustrated by an intriguing illusion. For instance, when we are briefly touched at two different locations on the hand, we will most likely experience it as one touch that we feel at the location halfway between the two locations that were actually touched. This condition typically results in activation of the primary somatosensory cortex that corresponds

to the location where this sensation is perceived and not to the actual locations that were stimulated (Chen, Friedman, & Roe, 2003).

This result implies that the primary somatosensory cortex represents the integrated activation of the afferent inputs. The latter conclusion is consistent with a remarkable tactile illusion that was reported by Geldard and Sherrick (1972) in the prestigious journal *Science*. Geldard and Sherrick found that when they tapped their participants (who kept their eyes closed) a few times on the fist, then a few times on the elbow, and finally a few times on the shoulder, this stimulation was experienced as a series of taps that moved across the length of the arm, as if a rabbit were hopping over it. This effect, which has since become known as the rabbit illusion, implies that the perception of touch is the result of integrating a series of stimuli across time.

Evans (1991) investigated to what extent we are able to distinguish tactile motion on the hand. To do so, he presented rotating motion patterns at two adjacent locations on the palm of a participant's hand (just below the fingers). The participant's task was to focus their attention at one of these locations and determine the direction of the rotation at that location. Evans found that participants were consistently faster and more accurate when the two rotational movements were congruent. This effect was only found, however, when the two patterns were both presented on the same hand. When the irrelevant pattern was presented on the other hand, there was no effect of congruence of the rotational movement (see fig 8.16). These results also imply that tactile information about adjacent areas of the skin is integrated.

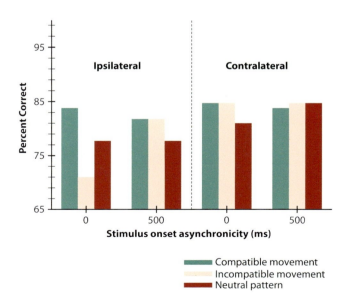

Figure 8.16 Results of a study in which participants had to detect the direction of a rotational movement on the palm of their hand, as a function of the presence or absence of a second, irrelevant rotational movement. (source: Evans, 1991)

Burton et al. (1999) used positron emission tomography to study the effects of tactile attention on the activation of the somatosensory cortex. Here, participants were instructed to touch two grid patterns with their index fingers, which were moved under their fingertips. They either had to passively feel these patterns, or they had to decide which of the two patterns was rougher. Blood flow to the secondary somatosensory cortex was increased in this task, compared to the passive condition. For the primary somatosensory cortex, however, no difference was found.

8.7.2 TACTILE ATTENTION

Attention can modulate activity in both the primary and secondary somatosensory cortices. For instance, activation in the primary somatosensory cortex was found to increase when tactile stimuli were attended (Krupa, Wiest, Shuler, Laubach, & Nicolelis, 2004). Interestingly, activation of the secondary somatosensory areas was found to be even more dependent on attention (Young et al., 2004).

Adler, Giabbiconi, and Muller (2009) concluded that the degree to which irrelevant tactile stimuli are still being processed depends, among other things, on perceptual load. This conclusion was based on the use of steady-state evoked potentials (SSEPs; see Box 2.3). The SSEP is an electric brain potential that is evoked by presenting a stream of repeating tactile stimuli. Here, these

stimuli were presented to the index finger of each hand. Participants were instructed to selectively focus their attention on one of these two fingers, and to report the presence of a deviant target stimulus presented within the attended stimulus stream. In one task, they simply had to detect this deviant stimulus, while in a second task, they had to discriminate between two different deviant targets stimuli. Adler et al. were interested in the amplitude of the SSEPs that were evoked by both the attended and unattended stimuli. It is well documented that attention enhances the amplitude of the SSEP, and this is considered to be an index of the level of processing of these stimuli. The key question that Adler et al. investigated was how the amplitude of the SSEPs that were evoked by the unattended stimuli varied as a function of task difficulty. They found that in the easy detection task, the SSEP amplitude was greater than in the difficult discrimination task (see fig 8.17). This result implies that participants in the difficult discrimination task had less capacity left to process the irrelevant stimuli.

8.7.3 VISUOTACTILE INTEGRATION AND ATTENTION

Spence and McGlone (2001) found that exogenous tactile attention can be focused on a specific location. They used a tactile version of Posner's (1980) cueing paradigm

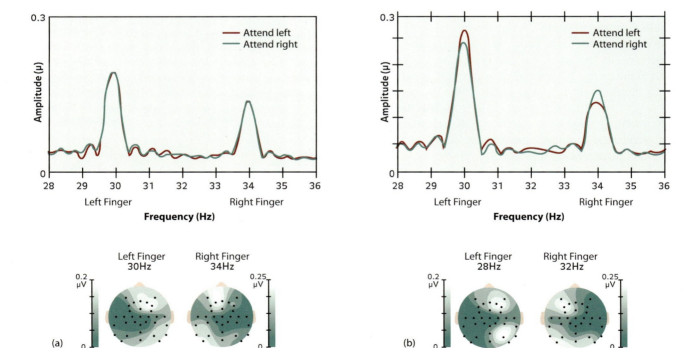

Figure 8.17 Results of a tactile-stimulus-detection-and-discrimination task. The amplitude of a steady-state evoked potential, which was triggered by an irrelevant stimulus, varied depending on the amount of attention to be focused on the relevant stimulus. (a) Results from the easy detection task; (b) results from the difficult discrimination task. (source: Adler et al., 2009)

(see Chapters 4 and 6), in which tactile stimuli were presented to the left or right index finger or thumb. Participants were required to report as quickly as possible whether the index finger or thumb was stimulated. These target stimuli were preceded by an exogenous cue which consisted of the stimulation of either the left or the right index finger and thumb. This cue was not predictive and could be presented either on the same side as the target stimulus or on the opposite side. Target discrimination was faster and more accurate when the cue was presented on the same side as the target stimulus.

Although these results show that attention to tactile stimuli can be focused on a specific location, we may wonder how this location is represented in the brain. A simple explanation would be that these locations are defined in terms of anatomical body coordinates. After all, the somatosensory cortex is characterised by a sensory map. We should also consider the possibility, however, that the spatial presentation of a somatosensory stimulus is encoded in an external reference frame. After all, when we perform manual tasks, we move our hands continuously, requiring us to update the representation of the position of our limbs based on visual input (see Chapter 10). Moreover, when we have to perform fine motor actions, such as tightening a screw, it would not be very cost-effective if we had to continuously switch between a reference frame that represents the object we want to manipulate and a reference frame that represents the positions of our fingers.

Eimer, Forster, and Van Velzen (2003) used ERPs to investigate the neural basis of these spatial tactile attention processes. Tactile stimuli were presented at one of the fingertips of participants' left or right hand. They were instructed to focus their attention on one of the two fingertips. On each trial, a visual cue (consisting of an arrow pointing left or right), indicated whether the left- or right-hand finger was to be attended, which was then followed by the presentation of a tactile stimulus. The crucial manipulation in this experiment was that in one condition participants crossed their hands so that their left hand was to their right and vice versa. The researchers were interested in the ERPs that were evoked by the cues.

Based on many visual attention studies, it had already been established that the orienting of attention to a specific location is reflected in two ERP components that are evoked by the cue. Both of these components are characterised by a negative electrical potential that is most pronounced over the hemisphere that is contralateral to the location indicated by the cue. A cue that is pointing to the left is thus characterised by a negative electric potential over the right hemisphere and vice versa (Eimer & Van Velzen, 2002; Harter, Miller, Price,

LaLonde, & Keyes, 1989; Talsma et al., 2005). The first of these components, the early directing attention negativity (EDAN) has a maximum amplitude over the posterior scalp, while the second component, the anterior directing attention negativity (ADAN), is characterised by a more anterior maximum.

If tactile stimuli were represented in an anatomically defined reference frame, we would expect that the EDAN and ADAN components would now be found to have an ipsilateral scalp distribution when participants had their hands crossed. In contrast, if these stimuli were represented in an external reference frame, we would expect that the EDAN and the ADAN should retain their contralateral maximum in the hands-crossed condition. Interestingly, however, Eimer et al. (2003) found a dissociation between the lateralisation of the EDAN and that of the ADAN. While the scalp distribution of the EDAN was not affected by the crossing of the hands, it was for the ADAN. According to Eimer et al., this finding implies that the posterior attention network, which is reflected in the EDAN, operates in an external reference frame, while the frontal attention network, which is reflected in the ADAN, operates in an anatomically defined reference frame.

It should be noted that crossing the hands can have a particularly negative impact on our tactile perception. For example, Yamamoto and Kitazawa (2001) along with Shore, Spry, and Spence (2002) found that crossing the hands has a particularly strong impact on our ability to estimate the order in which two tactile stimuli are presented. Participants received a tactile stimulus on their left and right hands in a rapid succession, and their task was to indicate which of the two hands was stimulated first. When their hands were crossed, participants were much less accurate than when their hands were uncrossed.

Some theorists have argued that we are not born with an external reference frame, but that it develops during early childhood, based on visual experience (Bremner, Mareschal, Lloyd-Fox, & Spence, 2008; Pagel, Heed, & Roder, 2009). It should be noted, however, that Eardley and van Velzen (2011) found that this is not necessarily the case. More specifically, they found in a group of early blind participants (that is, participants who had lost their complete eyesight within 18 months after birth) a result that was similar to the one already reported in the Eimer et al. (2003) study discussed earlier. Participants performed a similar task, with the exception that the visual cue was replaced by an auditory one. As in the previous study, Eardley and van Velzen found that the ADAN component differed between the crossed and non-crossed conditions. Moreover, they found that this component was delayed in the crossed condition

Uncrossed

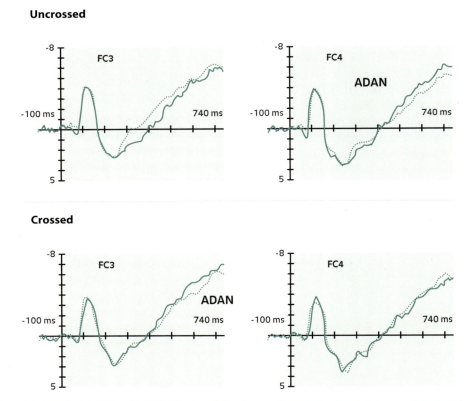

Crossed

Figure 8.18 ERPs were recorded over the left (FC3) and right (FC4) frontocentral scalp areas. The crossing of hands in a group of blind participants resulted in a shift in scalp distribution, and in a delay of the ADAN component. This component was associated with a frontal attention network that operates in a body-centred coordinate system. (source: Eardley and van Velzen, 2011)

(see fig 8.18). The authors interpreted the latter effect as a reflection of a conflict between the anatomical and external coordinate systems. The effects found in the blind participants group were similar to those found in the control group, which consisted of participants with normal vision.

8.8 VISUOTACTILE ILLUSIONS

When inputs from the visual and tactile modality are no longer in agreement with each other, a number of bizarre illusions can occur, which can give us valuable insights into the way our brains represent the world around us and our place in it. In the following sections we will consider two specific cases of such illusions in more detail, namely the rubber hand illusion and the effect of hand position.

8.8.1 THE RUBBER HAND ILLUSION

To create one of the most remarkable multisensory illusions, we just need a few simple tools. Two brushes, a table with a platform at the bottom, an artificial rubber hand, a

large kitchen knife, and an accomplice will suffice. First, we ask our participant to place his or her hand on the platform under the table, next, we place the rubber hand on the table, so that it is exactly aligned with the participant's own arm, so the participant's arm is hidden from view, while the rubber hand is still clearly visible (see fig 8.19). Now, we take the brushes and stroke both the rubber hand and the participants' own hand in synchrony. Here we make sure that the participant sees how the rubber hand is stroked. After we have done this for a few minutes, we ask our

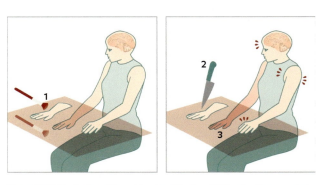

Figure 8.19 Illustration of the rubber hand illusion. (1) The simultaneous stroking of the real and a fake rubber hand; (2) the stabbing of a knife in the rubber hand; (3) the startled withdrawal of the real hand by the participant.

accomplice to enter the room with the kitchen knife and to stab it into the rubber hand . . .

It is extremely likely that the participant will withdraw his/her hand in shock when our accomplice stabs the rubber hand! Why is that happening? Botvinick and Cohen (1998) and also Armel and Ramachandran (2003) reported that the correspondence between the touch that we feel on our own hand and the touch that we see on the rubber hand implicitly force us to perceive the rubber hand as our own. For this reason, it is important that the brush strokes are applied simultaneously to both the participant's hand and the rubber hand: if this is not the case, it is much less likely that participants would consider the rubber hand to be their own. In addition, the rubber hand must also be in line with the participant's hand for the illusion to work.

Ehrsson, Spence, and Passingham (2004) used these properties to study the neural basis of this illusion. Indeed, participants reported that the illusion only occurred under the aforementioned conditions (compared to conditions where the brush strokes were either administered asynchronously or where the rubber hand was not aligned with participant's own arm). When participants reported experiencing the illusion, activation in the bilateral inferior parts of the precentral sulcus and the frontal operculum (an area adjacent to the premotor cortex) was observed. In addition, Ehrsson and colleagues found that the level of activation in the bilateral premotor cortex corresponded with the strength of the illusion, as reported by the participants. Finally, it was found that synchronous brush strokes, compared to asynchronous brush strokes, resulted in an increase in activation in the parietal cortex.

Ehrsson et al. suggested the existence of three neural mechanisms that are involved in the development of the rubber hand illusion: the first of these is multisensory integration (see Chapter 9), which involves inferring that the simultaneous visual and tactile information belongs to the same source. This integration involves processes in the parietal cortex. This is followed by a recalibration of the proprioceptive representation of the rubber hand, after which it is attributed to our own body. Ehrsson et al. has linked the latter two processes to activation in the premotor cortex.

8.8.2 THE PERIPERSONAL SPACE

The integration of visual and tactile information is also important in the formation of **peripersonal space**. This area surrounding the body is believed to be formed by the integration of visual, tactile, and nociceptive sensory stimuli. The perception of a tactile stimulus is always registered at a specific body location. We may wonder, however, how this stimulus is represented in our peripersonal space.

Is this done in a body-specific reference frame, or are these tactile sensations transformed, on the basis of visual information, into a global reference frame in which the position of our limbs is also encoded?

Eimer, Cockburn, Smedley, and Driver (2001) presented tactile stimuli. These stimuli were randomly presented to one of two hands. In addition, they presented visual stimuli, which were also randomly presented at locations to the left and right of the participant. When participants were required to detect deviant stimuli that were presented on one specific hand (e.g., left), they found that ERPs evoked by visual stimuli that were presented to the same location as the tactile ones were enlarged in amplitude, compared to the ERPs that were evoked by stimuli presented at the opposite location. In other words, when participants had to detect a tactile stimulus on their left hand, it also resulted in an increase in the amplitude of the ERP that was evoked by a visual stimulus in the left visual field. Similar results were found for the locations on the right side.

In a follow-up study, participants were required to cross their hands, so that the left hand was now on the right side of the peripersonal space and vice versa. Now it was found that detecting a tactile stimulus presented on the left hand (now located to the right of the participant) resulted in an enlargement of the visual ERP components that were evoked by a stimulus presented on the right visual field (and vice versa). These results thus imply that tactile sensory information is represented in a peripersonal coordinate system that can be flexibly updated on the basis of integrated visual and tactile information.

Làdavas (2002) discusses the neural mechanisms that may be involved in generating the peripersonal space. An important property of the peripersonal space is that it is limited to the area surrounding the body that can be reached (see fig 8.20). In monkeys, neurons in the putamen, along with neurons in the parietal and frontal lobes, have been found to respond to both visual and tactile stimuli, but only when these stimuli are within a specific distance of the body (Duhamel, Colby, & Goldberg, 1998; Iriki, Tanaka, & Iwamura, 1996; Rizzolatti, Scandolara, Matelli, & Gentilucci, 1981). These neurons are characterised by the following four properties.

1. The receptive fields for visual and tactile stimulation correspond to each other.
2. The visual receptive fields have a limited depth, which is limited to the direct space around the hand, arm, or head of the monkey.
3. The firing frequency of the neurons, due to visual stimulation, decreases as the distance between the visual stimulus and the cutaneous receptive field increases.
4. The visual receptive field is presented in a body-dependent coordinate system.

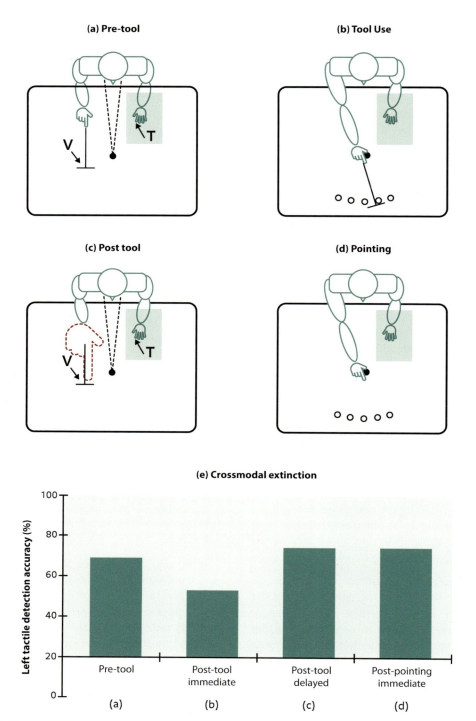

Figure 8.20 The extension of the peripersonal space by the use of tools. The sensitivity for a tactile stimulus (T) administered to the left hand could be affected by a visual stimulus (V) that was positioned outside of the peri-personal space, near the right hand, immediately after participants had used a rake to move an object. This effect was due to cross-modal extinction. When participants merely pointed to the object, the cross-modal extinction effect could not be found, implying that tool use temporarily extends peripersonal space. (source: Làdavas, 2002)

Evidence has been found, showing visual and tactile stimuli share a coordinate system around the hand region (di Pellegrino, Làdavas, & Farne, 1997; Làdavas, di Pellegrino, Farne, & Zeloni, 1998). In these studies, patients with right hemisphere damage exhibited a specific form of visuospatial neglect known as extinction (see Chapter 4). Extinction patients are normally still able to perceive visual stimuli in their contralesional visual field. Their difficulties emerge, however, when an additional visual stimulus is presented in the ipsilesional field (Bartolomeo, Thiebaut de Schotten, & Chica, 2012). A similar effect can be found for tactile stimuli. Làdavas et al. (1998) found that a visual stimulus presented to the ipsilesional field also resulted in the extinction of a tactile stimulus in the contralesional field, to the same extent as a tactile stimulus in the ipsilesional field could accomplish this. Interestingly, this effect was found only when the visual stimulus was presented near the patient's body, suggesting that the shared representation only existed in peripersonal space.

8.9 SUMMARY

Mechanical perception is defined as all forms of perception that are triggered by receptors that respond to pressure, bending, or other types of distortions. The importance of mechanical perception is often underestimated; however, it is of crucial essence for our survival.

The vestibular system is involved in determining the direction of gravity, determining the position of the head, and coordinating head and eye movements. This system consists of the vestibular organ in the middle ear and several cortical areas. The the cortical areas consist of a conglomerate of different brain regions, which are involved in the integration of various sensory inputs, including vestibular, tactile, proprioceptive, visual, and auditory signals, which jointly determine the position of our body in space.

A great variety of receptors with specific functions are involved in mechanical perception. Well-known receptor types include the organs Ruffini, Meissner's corpuscles, and Pacininian corpuscles. Most receptors are triggered by tissue deformations; however, the presence of specific chemicals can also affect receptor function. Tissue damage is signalled by nociceptive receptors, which consist of free nerve endings.

Somatosensory stimuli are transmitted to the brain via the somatosensory and cranial nerves. The area of the body from which a nerve is transmitting information is known as a dermatome. Eventually, the stimuli reach the somatosensory cortex, a brain area that is characterised by a sensory map, which is also known as the homunculus. Initially, the somatosensory cortex was predominantly seen as a passive receiver of somatosensory input.

Both the passive nature of the somatosensory cortex and the homunculus concept were later heavily criticised. Recent findings suggest a much more active role for the somatosensory cortex, resulting in the hypothesis that this area actively represents a body model. This body model is not only believed to be involved in integrating somatosensory input into our current body state but also to be used for the simulation of yet to be executed actions and alternative 'what if' scenarios.

The somatosensory cortex is characterised by a great level of plasticity: both mental and physical training can affect the functional organisation of the somatosensory cortex. In extreme conditions, the plasticity of the somatosensory cortex can result in phantom sensations. This is specifically the case after the amputation of a body part. Although it is not yet completely clear what causes these phantom sensations, a plausible hypothesis is that sprouting neural connections of adjacent body parts innervate the non-functional neural tissue of the amputated body part.

Interoception describes the perception of processes that take place in one's own body. This includes the sensations of hunger, thirst, and feedback from the motor system. These interoceptive functions can be further subdivided into proprioceptive and visceroceptive. Most research on visceroception involves the cardiovascular system, the respiratory system, and the gastrointestinal system.

Interoceptive perception can be explained on the basis of the predictive coding framework. An optimal state regulation is based on comparing an ideal optimal (predicted) state and the current state. The detection of a mismatch between these two states can be related to functions of the anterior insula, which can act as a comparator between the predicted state of the body and the actual body state.

The perception of the position and movements of our joints is known as proprioception. Based on receptors in muscles, tendons, joints, and the skin, an internal representation of the position of the joints is formed. The information from the individual joints is integrated into an internal body model. This internal representation is used to determine the position of a body in external space.

Pain is one of the most complex mechanical sensations that we know. The pain perception system can be subdivided into an ascending and a descending system, in which, according to classical pain theories, the ascending system is involved in the perception of nociceptive signals, and the descending system in regulating of the pain experience. Various types of pain are distinguished on the basis of their origin: transient pain, pain due to tissue damage, and pain due to damage to the central nervous system. A painful experience can be enough to produce a lasting memory. Strong pain memories can be formed on the basis of primitive neural mechanisms, such as sensitisation.

Chronic pain can often arise from tissue damage, but it can persist due to maladaptive processes in the descending regulatory system, causing pain sensations to persist even after the original tissue damage is no longer present. Pain is therefore also a conscious interpretation of the nociceptive signals, and this interpretation is influenced by a multitude of factors. Nociceptive signals are projected to the brain via various ascending projections. Each of these projections fulfils a different purpose in generating pain awareness, the realisation that the stimulus can pose a threat to the body, and the modulation of the response.

Traditionally, the network of pain-related brain areas was described as the 'pain matrix'. However, the precise involvement of the areas concerned depends on the situation; some forms of pain processing appear to be associated with brain areas that are not traditionally part of the pain matrix, while areas that are involved also perform non-pain-related functions. Based on these observations, it is now believed that the pain matrix is not so much related to the processing of pain perception, but that it forms a multisensory threat detection system that is involved in preserving the integrity of the body.

Attention plays an important role in the modulation of pain perception. Distraction can result in a reduction of electrophysiological responses that are evoked by nociceptive signals. In addition, the subjective intensity of a nociceptive stimulus can be influenced by context, for example by the administration of placebos. Placebos result in lower pain expectations and an increase in the release of opioids into the descending modulatory pain regulation system. In addition to the influences of attention and context, a clear relationship between pain perception and mood has been reported. Negative moods can increase sensitivity to nociceptive stimuli. Ultimately, a sustained negative mood can contribute to the development of chronic pain.

Recently, it has been shown that there is a stronger interaction between the ascending and descending pain systems than was initially assumed. These interactions are consistent with the idea that the pain-processing brain regions are part of a predictive system. The extent to which expectation, and in particular the precision of this expectation, influences the intensity of a nociceptive stimulus is consistent with the principles of Bayesian inference.

Phantom pain can occur after severe damage to a body part, for example, following an amputation. This pain sensation can occur through various mechanisms, located in the peripheral and central nervous systems. A second serious pain condition is fibromyalgia. Fibromyalgia syndrome is characterised by chronic generic pain in muscles and joints. Fibromyalgia patients are particularly sensitive to potential threats in their peripersonal space.

Tactile perception can be strongly influenced by attention; integrative processes play an important role in this. Tactile precepts are partly encoded in a body-specific coordinate system and partly in an external visuospatial coordinate system. Visuospatial processes also play an important role in the rubber hand illusion. This interaction probably takes place because the visual and tactile inputs are encoded in peripersonal space.

FURTHER READING

Aberšek, B. (2018). *Problem-based learning and proprioception*. Cambridge, UK: Cambridge Scholars Publishing.

Gallace, A., & Spence, C. (2014). *In touch with the future: The sense of touch from cognitive neuroscience to virtual reality*. Oxford, UK: Oxford University Press.

Hertenstein, M. J., & Weiss, S. J. (2011). *The handbook of touch: Neuroscience, behavioral, and health perspectives*. Heidelberg: Springer Verlag.

Ramachandran, V. S., & Blakeslee, S. (1998). *Phantoms in the brain: Human nature and the architecture of the mind*. New York, NY: William Morrow and Company.

PART 4

Integration

CHAPTER 9
Multisensory integration

9.1 INTRODUCTION

In everyday life, we are constantly integrating all the information that we receive from our senses: from a soft thud that we hear when a cup of coffee hits a wooden tabletop in the early morning, to the slow changes in engine sounds as our car changes speed during our daily commute, to the fusion of sounds and images of a movie that we watch in the evening. In all of these cases, we perceive visual and auditory information through separate senses, yet we take it for granted that these signals correspond to each other.

It is typically only when this correspondence is disrupted that we become aware of the fact that we perceive sounds and images as separate signals. Suppose that while taking a walk in the countryside we observe a farmer who is busy maintaining a fence. To this end, he drives a pole into the ground with a sledgehammer. Each time he hits the pole, we notice that the sound is about one second late. This delay is caused by the fact that the speed of sound is significantly slower than the speed of light, so that the distance between us and the farmer causes the sound to reach us much later than the image. We can actually use this information for distance determination. For example, when we are caught by a thunderstorm, we can use this delay to estimate how far away it is, by counting the number of seconds between the flash of lightning and the sound of the thunder (fig 9.1). When thunder and lightning coincide, you know you'd better seek shelter![1]

Other examples of the disruption of synchronicity can be found in modern technology. In some countries, such as Germany, it is customary to dub foreign language films, which typically disrupts the synchronicity between lip movements and speech. Additionally, we can also identify a multitude of technical problems (poor mastering of DVDs, or problems with online streaming) that can cause a temporal delay in one of the two channels (image or sound), again resulting in an asynchronous perception.

Thus, awareness of the fact that we perceive image and sound separately typically occurs only when their synchronicity is disrupted. This phenomenon implies that there is a high degree of correspondence between the different sensory modalities. In the previous chapter we introduced some aspects of this correspondence, as many facets of tactile perception and tactile attention can be influenced by visual perception. Moreover, we have discussed how tactile, nociceptive, and visual signals that are observed in peripersonal space are integrated with each other. Apart from these limited cases, the previous chapters have introduced our sensory modalities independently from each other, thus incorrectly suggesting that they also operate largely independently. This suggestion is not justified, however, because the visual and auditory modalities also strongly interact with each other. The purpose of this chapter on multisensory processing is, therefore, to provide an overview of the main processes underlying these interactions and to discuss the main consequences of these interactions for the generation of internal mental representations.

Until about 1990, research on multisensory interactions was sporadic (notable exceptions are McGurk & MacDonald, 1976; Stein & Arigbede, 1972; Urbantschisch, 1880; Welch & Warren, 1986). Consequently, the most important developments in the field of multisensory processing did not happen until the 1990s. Since then, however, research investigating the neural basis of multisensory interactions has taken a giant leap forward.

Research on multisensory interactions is often approached from different perspectives, ranging from the study of basic physiological processes to behavioural observations (Alais, Newell, & Mamassian, 2010; Angelaki, Gu, & DeAngelis, 2009; Budinger, Heil, Hess, & Scheich, 2006; Nagy, Eordegh, Paroczy, Markus, & Benedek, 2006a; Pouget, Deneve, & Duhamel, 2002; Stein & Stanford, 2008; Ursino, Cuppini, & Magosso, 2014a). We will elaborate on these different perspectives in more detail in the following sections.

9.2 THE NEURAL BASIS OF MULTISENSORY PERCEPTION

The fact that we experience information that is coming from different senses as internally consistent is backed-up by a large number of scientific studies showing the existence

DOI: 10.4324/9781003319344-13

Figure 9.1 A thunderstorm is one of the few examples of a natural phenomenon where image and sound are out of sync.

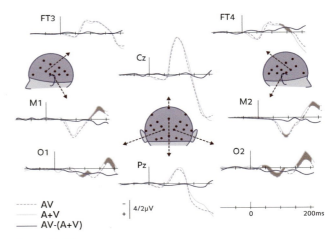

------ AV
——— A+V
——— AV-(A+V)

$-\ |\ $4/2μV
$+\ |$

0   200ms

Figure 9.2 ERP evidence showing that multisensory interactions can occur shortly after stimulus presentation. For electrodes placed over the occipital cortex, it was found that the neural response to an audiovisual stimulus deviated as early as 40 ms after its presentation compared to conditions in which the auditory or visual stimulus was presented alone. This deviation is represented by the shaded area between the [A + V] and AV curves. The thick curve shows the time course of this difference. (source: Giard and Peronnet, 1999)

of **multisensory integration**, that is, the process whereby information from two or more senses is combined to form an internally consistent mental representation. Integration typically occurs when information from the different senses is congruent (Stein et al., 2010).

9.2.1 ASSOCIATIONS

One limitation of studying the individual sensory systems independently of each other is that it implicitly promotes the idea that our senses also operate independently of each other. According to this idea, multisensory representations would only be formed after the primary processing steps have been fully completed. For example, in a now classic textbook, Bloom and Lazeron (1988) argued that **association areas** in the parietal cortex integrate somatosensory information with auditory and visual information that is projected from the occipital and temporal lobes. As such, the parietal cortex would form a spatial representation that allows us to navigate in our environment (see Chapter 10). Although the parietal cortex is indeed involved in the generation of spatial representations, we should emphasise the idea that the association areas would be the key centre of multisensory integration is largely incorrect. First and foremost, it is incorrect because it has been found that multisensory interactions occur much earlier than the aforementioned model implies.

Evidence for an extremely early integration of auditory and visual information was reported, for example, by Giard and Peronnet (1999). These authors used ERPs to study how visual and auditory stimuli integrate. This was done by presenting random sequences of visual, auditory, and audiovisual stimuli. Here, an audiovisual stimulus was simply defined as the simultaneous presentation of the auditory and visual stimulus. Next, the ERPs that were evoked by the auditory (A) and visual (V) stimuli were summed [A + V] and compared with the ERPs that were evoked by the audiovisual (AV) stimulus. Using this approach, the multisensory effects were expressed as the

difference of these two ERP responses (AV – [A + V]). The earliest effects reported by Giard and Peronnet were found to be as early as 40 ms after stimulus presentation (see fig 9.2).

9.2.2 SUBCORTICAL ACTIVATIONS

One of the first studies to examine the neural basis of multisensory integration reported the existence of multisensory neurons in a subcortical brain region known as the superior colliculus. Stein and Arigbede (1972) used a single cell recording technique, in which a depth electrode can be very precisely positioned, to record the electrical activity of a single neuron. Based on these recordings, Stein and Arigbede identified neurons that responded to both visual and auditory stimuli. More interestingly, however, is what happened when the visual and auditory stimulus were presented simultaneously. Although both stimuli were independently able to trigger the firing of these neurons, their response to an audiovisual stimulus was significantly stronger than what was expected based on the sum of the auditory and visual stimulus when presented separately. Multisensory responses that are larger than the sum of the responses evoked by unisensory stimuli are denoted as **super-additive responses**.

The degree to which neurons exhibit super-additive responses depends on three principles. First, the visual and auditory stimulus must be presented near simultaneous. Super-additive responses are the most pronounced when the auditory and visual inputs are presented within a time window of about 250 ms, and specifically so when the auditory stimulus is presented at about 50 ms after the visual stimulus. Second, the neurons' firing rates tend to be the highest when the visual and auditory stimulus are presented from approximately the same location. Taken together, these observations have resulted in the formulation of the principles of spatial and temporal proximity. When the spatial and/or temporal proximity principle is violated, we will typically not observe any super-additive responses. Even more so, we may observe the opposite, that is, a sub-additive response. In this case, the neuron's response to a multisensory stimulus is smaller than that to a unisensory stimulus (Stein & Stanford, 2008), a phenomenon that is known as multisensory depression.

There is a third principle, which is known as the **law of inverse effectiveness**. This principle describes how the super-additivity of multisensory neurons decreases as the response to the individual auditory or visual inputs becomes larger. To illustrate, consider hearing a dog barking in the distance (fig 9.3). Because the dog is far away, its sound is weak, resulting in a weak auditory response in our superior colliculus. When we also happen to see the dog, however, the added stimulation, resulting from the image of the dog will cause our collicular responses to increase considerably. Now, consider the scenario where the dog is approaching us. As it moves closer, its barking becomes louder and louder with the result that the amplification that results from the multisensory interaction will gradually become weaker. It is still not entirely clear what mechanism is causing this effect. While some researchers have argued that it may be a statistical artefact (Ernst & Banks, 2002), it is also possible that it increases the effectiveness of multisensory stimuli when the individual signals are weak.

The latter is the case when the dog is far away. In this case we may benefit more from combining sound and vision when it is far away than when it is nearby.

9.2.3 CORTICAL INVOLVEMENT IN MULTISENSORY INTEGRATION

In addition to the superior colliculus, several cortical areas have been identified as having multisensory properties. One specifically important brain area that was initially identified in cats is the anterior ectosylvian sulcus. This is a part of the association cortex that receives inputs from the visual, auditory, and somatosensory cortices (Stein & Stanford, 2008). Activation in this brain region has been shown to modulate the responsiveness of neurons in the superior colliculus.

In monkeys and in humans, a diffuse network of brain areas is related to multisensory integration (see fig 9.4). For example, specific areas in the macaque auditory cortex have been found to be sensitive to the integration of lip movements and vocalisations (Ghazanfar, Maier, Hoffman, & Logothetis, 2005). These results are consistent with previous fMRI findings in humans, suggesting that the superior temporal sulcus (STS) is involved in the integration of auditory and visual speech signals (Calvert, Campbell, & Brammer, 2000). In the latter study, it was found that brain activation was increased following the presentation of congruent audiovisual speech fragments, compared to incongruent fragments.

9.2.3.1 Direct Connections between the Sensory Cortices

The early multisensory integration effects discussed previously are clearly not compatible with the original idea that auditory and visual inputs are only integrated after processing in the visual and auditory cortices has been fully completed. The fact that auditory and visual information integrates very rapidly implies that the various sensory systems are much more intertwined than we initially assumed. Budinger et al. (2006) found evidence for this idea based on animal studies. More specifically, axons in the auditory cortex of Mongolian gerbils were stained (see Box 2.1) and could be traced back to several cortical and subcortical nuclei, including the visual nuclei of the thalamus and nuclei in the multisensory association cortices. In humans, fMRI studies have also shown that tactile stimuli can activate the auditory cortex (Foxe et al., 2002). In primates, similar results have been found for the visual cortex (Falchier, Clavagnier, Barone, & Kennedy, 2002). This area was found to receive projections from the belt and parabelt areas of the auditory cortex. These results imply that visual information is also projected to the auditory cortex, and that processing in the auditory cortex can also be influenced by processes in the multisensory association areas.

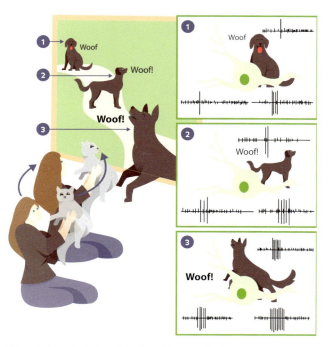

Figure 9.3 An illustration of the law of inverse effectiveness. Based on Stein and Stanford (2008). The right depicts the response of a superior colliculus neuron. When auditory and visual responses are weak (1), the firing rate of this neuron is relatively strong. Increasing the strength of the input signals (2–3) hardly affects the output firing rate.

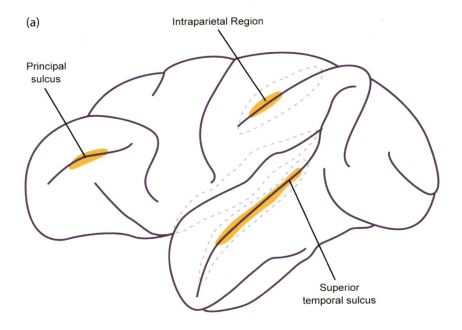

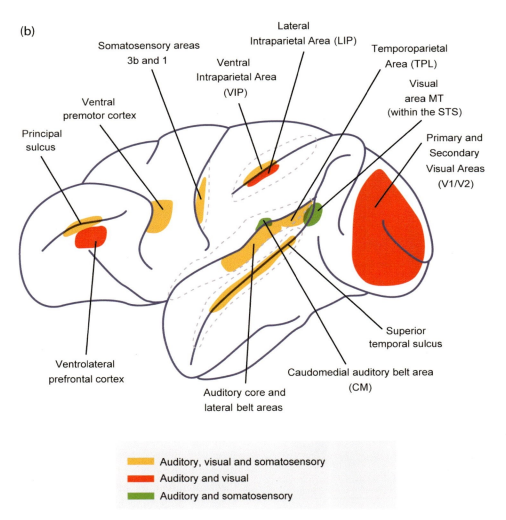

Figure 9.4 An overview of multisensory integration areas in the neocortex. (a) Areas that were traditionally marked as multisensory; (b) additional brain areas that have been identified as having multisensory properties. (source: Ghazanfar and Schroeder, 2006)

Further evidence for the idea that our sensory cortices are interconnected comes from studies showing that the visual cortex of blind people can be activated by input from other sensory modalities (Alais et al., 2010). For example, Kujala et al. (1995) found that blind individuals' visual cortices were activated during an auditory discrimination task. Moreover, Sadato et al. (1996) and Goyal, Hansen, and Blakemore (2006) found a similar visual cortex activation on the basis of tactile stimulation. In both studies, the visual cortex was activated during Braille reading. Finally, Burton, Snyder, Diamond, and Raichle (2002) reported activation of the visual cortex when blind participants were generating verbs on the basis of auditorily presented nouns.

9.2.3.2 Multisensory Association Areas

The existence of direct connections between the sensory cortices, combined with evidence that the primary sensory cortex receives neural projections from the higher-order multimodal association regions, corroborates the idea that the different sensory modalities are much more closely intertwined than initially assumed. For this reason, we could question the concept of unisensory cortex altogether. Indeed it has been argued that the entire neocortex is in essence multisensory (Ghazanfar & Schroeder, 2006).

Ghazanfar and Schroeder (2006) provide an overview of all the cortical areas involved in multisensory processing and discuss the functional role of each of these areas (see fig 9.4). In addition to the direct connections between the sensory cortices described earlier, they identify, among others, the superior temporal sulcus, the intraparietal sulcus, and the frontal and prefrontal areas. Of these areas, the superior temporal sulcus is involved in the detection of audiovisual congruence. In addition, it is involved in the processing of **biological motion**, such as vocalisation, or the act of tearing a piece of paper apart. Barraclough, Xiao, Baker, Oram, and Perrett (2005) found that the activity of a proportion of neurons responding to this type of movement was modulated by the presence of sound. This modulation was only found, however, when the sound was congruent with the motion.

The intraparietal sulcus is part of a larger network that is involved in coordinating motor actions based on multisensory information (see Chapter 10). Within the intraparietal sulcus, two specific areas can be identified to be involved in multisensory integration. The first region, the lateral intraparietal region (LIP) was originally believed to be involved in the processing of just visual information. Later studies have shown, however, that this area not only receives visual input but also information about eye position along with auditory information (Andersen, Snyder, Bradley, & Xing, 1997). How neurons in this area respond depends on the type of actions that the organism needs to conduct, suggesting that area LIP is involved in integrating different sources of information during response preparation.

The second area, the neighbouring ventral intraparietal region (VIP) receives input from visual, auditory, somatosensory, and vestibular projections. The responses of the multisensory neurons in this area are also task dependent. Jointly, these two areas are believed to represent a multisensory map of our environment. Finally, the temporoparietal junction, which is an area situated approximately between the parietal and temporal lobes, is also believed to contain a multimodal representation of our environment (Leinonen, Hyvärinen, & Sovijärvi, 1980). This area mainly contains neurons with receptive fields representing the head and shoulder regions of the body. For this reason, it is believed to be involved in controlling the orientation of the head.

Finally, Ghazanfar and Schroeder (2006) describe a number of multisensory responses in the frontal and prefrontal cortices. The interactions observed in these areas appear to represent the higher-order aspects of multisensory integration. For example, when monkeys were taught to form associations between high- and low-pitched tones, on the one hand, and between two colours, on the other, neurons in the prefrontal cortex were found to respond to both the visual and the auditory stimuli (Fuster, Bodner, & Kroger, 2000). Finally, evidence has been found to indicate that the ventrolateral prefrontal cortex is involved in the integration of the visual and auditory components of vocalisations. Again, whether or not these signals were integrated depended on the congruence of both signals.

In summary, based on the aforementioned results, we can conclude that multisensory integration processes can occur at multiple levels in the processing hierarchy of the brain. In a later section, we will discuss the precise role of each of these areas in the integration process. Before we can do that, however, it is necessary to first discuss some essential behavioural effects of multisensory integration. These effects often manifest themselves in the form of illusions.

9.3 AUDIOVISUAL ILLUSIONS

The multisensory interactions discussed so far are mainly driven by properties of the stimuli; that is, the strongest neural responses to multisensory stimuli can be observed when the individual inputs are consistent with each other and appear to be generated by a common cause. By contrast, we can observe the most pronounced multisensory effects behaviourally when there is a slight discrepancy between the inputs, in which case they manifest themselves as multisensory illusions. Research into multisensory integration in humans has therefore been strongly influenced by the study of these illusions. Striking examples of these illusions occur when auditory and visual inputs are presented from different locations, or when speech sounds and lip movements are de-synchronised. The resulting illusion is most likely the brain's attempt to generate a representation that is internally consistent, despite the conflicting inputs. Based on this assumption, audiovisual illusions can be roughly divided into two categories. The first category consists of illusions where the auditory input is made consistent with the visual input, whereas the second consists of exactly the opposite: here the visual input is adjusted to make it consistent with the auditory input.

9.3.1 THE MCGURK EFFECT

The **McGurk effect**, named after the original discoverers McGurk and MacDonald (1976), is an audiovisual illusion that arises when the sound of a syllable no longer corresponds with the observed lip movements (see fig 9.5). The illusion was accidentally discovered when John MacDonald, at the time a research assistant in Harry McGurk's lab, was creating stimulus material for a study on the development of language perception in young children. MacDonald had instructed a technician to edit a videotape of an actor, such that on the audio track one phoneme was substituted with another. When McGurk and MacDonald reviewed the tape, however, they heard neither the newly substituted phoneme nor the original one, but – to their surprise – a third phoneme. The McGurk effect is best observed when the syllables /ba-ba/ are pronounced, while the lip movements correspond to the syllables /ga-ga/. The result of this combination is that we tend to perceive /da-da/.

The McGurk effect probably arises because the brain aims to minimise the conflict between the visual and auditory inputs. Although it was originally believed that the McGurk effect is omnipresent when audiovisual speech signals conflict, it was later found that the strength of the McGurk effect depends, among other things, on the specific syllables that are presented. For example, the combination of /ba/ and /ga/ typically yields quite a strong effect, while other combinations do not, or hardly, induce the illusion at all (Basu Mallick, Magnotti, & Beauchamp, 2015). According to Basu Mallick et al., this can possibly be explained by the fact that some lip movements, such

as /da/ and /ga/, can be easily confused with each other, whereas /ba/ is much more distinctive. Thus, the lip movement corresponding to /da/ can easily be interpreted as /ga/ by a conflicting sound, while this is much less easily the case with the lip movement corresponding to /ba/.

In addition, large individual differences in one's susceptibility to the illusion have been reported (Basu Mallick et al., 2015; Nath & Beauchamp, 2012). Although it is not yet completely clear what the neural basis of these individual differences is, it appears that the superior temporal sulcus plays an important role in the integration of visual and auditory speech signals, as discussed earlier. Nath and Beauchamp (2012) found that McGurk stimuli activated this brain region, and the stronger this activation was, the more sensitive participants were to the illusion.

The McGurk effect was initially considered an automatic response, that is, an effect that always occurs when we observe McGurk stimuli. It was later found, however, that our sensitivity to the illusion can decrease when we have to perform an attention-demanding secondary task (Alsius, Navarra, & Soto-Faraco, 2007; Alsius, Navarra, Campbell, & Soto-Faraco, 2005). Moreover, Young, Fruhholz, and Schweinberger (2020) discuss how perceiving faces and voices involves more than the automatic integration of lip movements and sounds. These authors propose a model in which the integration of voice and face information involves several levels of processing, including structural analysis, speech analysis, and the analysis of affect.

9.3.2 THE VENTRILOQUIST ILLUSION

Perhaps the most famous audiovisual illusion is named after a well-known theatre act. The **ventriloquist illusion** is modelled after the famous act in which a puppeteer manages to speak without producing any lip movements, while simultaneously mimicking these movements using a hand puppet (Connor, 2000). The act induces the illusion that it is the puppet who speaks instead of the puppeteer. Although the illusion is mostly known from the theatre, we also encounter it many times in our daily lives. For example, when watching a movie on television or in a cinema the sound is most likely presented through speakers that are set up next to the screen. Our subjective experience, however, is that the location of the sounds that we hear match with their on-screen sources.

How exactly does this illusion arise? Bertelson (1998) argued that the conflict between the visual and auditory senses forms the basis for the illusion. To further investigate this, Bonath et al. (2007) used ERP and fMRI recordings. They used an experiment in which a short tone was presented by one of three loudspeakers which were located centrally (right in front of the participant) or five degrees of arc to the left or right of the participant, respectively. Simultaneously, a flash of light was presented, using a light

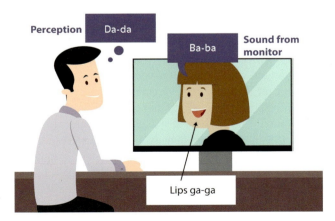

Figure 9.5 Illustration of the McGurk effect. When lip movements do not correspond to the sound that is actually presented, we typically perceive a different sound altogether.

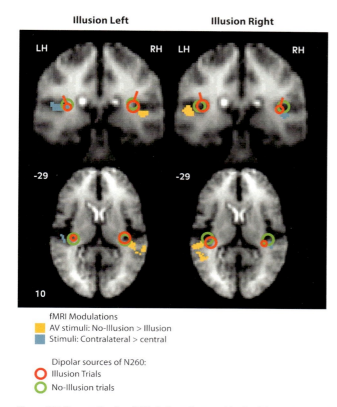

Figure 9.6 The results of an fMRI study on the neural basis of the ventriloquist illusion. When the illusion was experienced, an increase in activation in the contralateral auditory cortex was observed. The red and green circles indicate the locations in the auditory cortex where the observed ERP activity was most likely generated. This activity was also stronger on the contralateral side of the brain when the illusion was experienced. (source: Bonath et al., 2007)

emitting diode (LED) that was located at ten degrees to the left or right of the participant (see fig 9.6). The participants' task was to determine the location from which the sound was presented. The crucial manipulation in the experiment consisted of a condition where the tone was presented from the central location, while the visual stimulus was presented from either the left or right location. When participants experienced the ventriloquist illusion, their judgements would be biased towards the locations of the light. The experiment was set up in such a way that in

some trials the participants were experiencing the illusion and on others they were not, while using physically identical trials across these conditions. Using this set-up, Bonath et al. were able to determine which neural processes were affected by the illusion.

In trials where no illusion was experienced, ERPs associated with processing in the auditory cortex were bilaterally distributed across the scalp. This result suggests that both auditory cortices are involved in the processing of this stimulus. In contrast, when the illusion was experienced, the scalp distribution of the auditory ERP shifted to the contralateral hemisphere (relative to the side where the tone was experienced). The scalp distribution of these ERPs already suggests that the relocalisation of the sound occurs at very early stages of auditory processing and that it involves the auditory cortex. The spatial resolution of ERPs is too low, however, to provide conclusive evidence about the involvement of the auditory cortex. For this reason, additional fMRI recordings were made, which were highly consistent with the EEG findings in that they showed an increase in activity in the auditory cortex in response to the sound. This activation was bilateral when the illusion was not experienced but lateralised when it was. Taken together, these results suggest that the spatial information of the visual stimuli can already influence the neural processes in the auditory cortex.

9.3.3 TEMPORAL ORDER/ SIMULTANEITY JUDGEMENT TASKS

Much research on audiovisual integration in humans is conducted using tasks in which two stimuli, one visual and one auditory, are presented in quick succession. The relative onset of the stimuli, known as the **stimulus onset asynchrony (SOA)**, is then systematically varied, so that with a variable delay either the auditory or the visual stimulus is presented first (see fig 9.7).

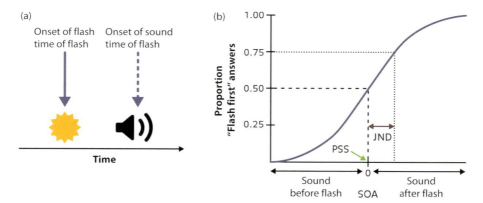

Figure 9.7 An illustration of a temporal order judgement task. (a) A flash of light and a tone are presented with a variable onset. (b) A schematic overview of the method to calculate the point of subjective simultaneity (PSS) and the just noticeable difference, based on the proportion of 'flash first' responses in function of the actual time difference between the two stimuli (based on Chen and Vroomen, 2013).

Participants can be instructed to report which of the two stimuli was presented first, making this a **temporal order judgement task**. In this case, participants' accuracy is calculated as a function of the stimulus onset asynchrony. This method can be used to determine the minimum temporal difference that is required to perceive the two stimuli as two separate events (in more technical terms, this is known as the **just noticeable difference**). The same method can also be used to determine when we subjectively experience the two stimuli as being simultaneous (see fig 9.7); this is the point of **subjective simultaneity**. Notice, however, that these estimates be affected by the participants' response strategies: when faced with uncertainty, they may be strongly biased towards one type of response. For example, they may always indicate that the auditory stimulus is first when they are uncertain; a tendency which may also strongly bias the estimates of simultaneity.

To avoid this problem, it is possible to simply instruct participants to indicate whether or not they experience the two stimuli as simultaneous, as is done in a **simultaneity judgement task**. There is also a disadvantage of this task, however, because it is no longer possible to determine what the perceived order of the stimulus is. In addition, this task is also susceptible to bias, because participants may differ in their strategies. For example, some participants may only report that the two stimuli are not presented simultaneously when the stimulus onset asynchrony is very large.

9.3.4 TEMPORAL VENTRILOQUISM

The ventriloquist illusion manifests itself not only in a spatial shift of the auditory stimulus, but it can also be observed as a temporal shift of the visual stimulus. In a literature review, Chen and Vroomen (2013) reported findings that show how the presentation of a short tone can influence the subjective timing of a visual stimulus. When such a tone is presented immediately after a visual stimulus, participants frequently report that the flash appeared later than it actually did. This effect is most likely due to the fact that the temporal resolution of our auditory system is higher than that of our visual system. Again, the brain aims to resolve the temporal conflict between the visual and auditory modalities by adjusting the subjective timing of the visual modality to that of the auditory one.

9.3.5 ADDITIONAL FLASH ILLUSION

The observation that auditory stimuli are able to affect the timing of our visual experience is also evidenced by the **additional flash illusion**. Shams, Kamitani, and Shimojo (2000) presented a series of flashes of light, and participants were instructed to report how many flashes they saw. In some trials, these flashes were accompanied by a series of tones, which were completely irrelevant. The crucial manipulation in the experiment, however, was that on occasion one flash was presented that was surrounded by two tones. As a result of this manipulation, participants frequently reported seeing two flashes, instead of one.

9.3.6 BOUNCE-PASS ILLUSION

Sekuler, Sekuler, and Lau (1997) found another remarkable effect of sound on our visual perception: they presented two small circles on a computer screen that moved towards each other. When these circles overlapped, they could either briefly pause or continue to move without interruption. In some trials, a short click was presented at one of the three specific moments: either 150 ms before or after the time of overlap, or exactly coinciding with it. Participants were instructed to report whether they experienced the two circles as passing each other or whether they experienced them as colliding and then bouncing back. When the click coincided with the overlap, participants generally reported that they experienced the stimuli as colliding and bouncing back. However, when the click was presented at one of the other two moments (or when it was absent altogether), they mainly reported that the stimuli passed each other.

9.4 SYNAESTHESIA

In addition to the audiovisual illusions discussed earlier, the interaction between the senses is evident from the phenomenon of **synaesthesia**. Synaesthesia is the phenomenon where the perception of a specific stimulus results in conscious sensory experiences that are typically not associated with the stimulus in question (Grossenbacher & Lovelace, 2001). For example, in some individuals, a letter can evoke a colour sensation, where each letter is associated with its own unique colour. A synaesthetic experience is involuntary, in the sense that it is automatically evoked and is not the result of a learned association or a strategy. A relatively small proportion of the population has a synaesthetic experience on an almost daily basis, and many synaesthetes are generally surprised to realise that most people do not experience these additional sensations.

Interestingly, synaesthetic experiences are not limited to one sensory system, as in the letter-colour example. For example, Grossenbacher and Lovelace (2001) describe the experiences of a synaesthetic woman who experienced the sound of her crying baby as an unpleasant yellow colour. Synaesthetic experiences are generally unidirectional. For example, sound can result in a colour experience, however, a coloured stimulus will not

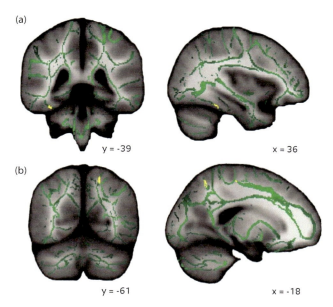

(a)

y = -39   x = 36

(b)

y = -61   x = -18

Figure 9.8 A schematic overview of the main white matter tracts in the brain, as revealed by diffusion tensor imaging. The tracts highlighted in yellow mark those that have stronger connectivity in synaesthetes compared to neurotypical controls. (a) Results for the right inferior temporal cortex; (b) results for the left parietal cortex and bilateral frontal cortex. (source: Rouw and Scholte, 2007)

necessarily result in an auditory experience (Mills, 1999). Typically, the sensations that are evoked consists of simple stimulus properties, such as a colour, a location, or a combination of these properties. It is almost never the case that higher-order sensations, such as objects or faces, are evoked.

Based on studies using **positron emission tomography (PET)**, Paulesu et al. (1995) have shown that synaesthetic colour experiences corresponded with a stronger activation of brain areas in the extrastriate visual cortex while synaesthetes were listening to spoken words. This result suggests that the synaesthetic colour experience arises from feedback from higher-order areas in the brain, without the involvement of the primary visual areas. Rouw and Scholte (2007) used a special MRI scanning technique known as **diffusion tensor imaging (DTI)** to investigate the neural basis of synaesthesia. With this technique it is possible to determine the connectivity between brain areas (see fig 9.8). Rouw and Scholte found that synaesthetes who perceived colour sensations while reading specific **graphemes** were characterised by a higher degree of connectivity in the right inferior temporal cortex and in the left parietal cortex and bilateral in the frontal cortex. These results suggest that synaesthetic experiences are caused by stronger connectivity between the brain areas specialised in processing the triggering stimulus and those involved in processing the synaesthetic experience.

How synaesthetic sensations are experienced appears to vary considerably across individuals. In case of letter-colour synaesthesia, for example, some synaesthetes report that the synaesthetic colour fills the evoking letter, whereas others describe the synaesthetic colour as being projected onto a virtual plane, which is located at arm's length from them, without being linked to the letter itself. Still others report that the colour sensation appears only in front of the mind's eye without being linked to a specific location.

Although synaesthesia is not strictly a multisensory phenomenon, it is highly informative about the way sensations are formed in the brain. Seth (2014) aims to explain synaesthesia on the basis of the predictive coding framework. According to Seth, modality-specific predictions are generated from one common generative model. For example, the concept 'dog' will generate predictions matching a visual representation of a dog as well as predictions matching the corresponding barking sounds (see also Talsma, 2015, for a comparable idea that will be discussed later in this chapter). Under normal circumstances, this predictive model will form representations that are congruent with each other, but in the case of synaesthesia that is not the case. The reason for this is that, according to Seth, under normal circumstances the possible causes of a perceptual representation are also coded in the generative model. As a result, a wide range of inconsistent modality-specific percepts are typically not predicted by the generative models. With synaesthesia, however, this is not the case, resulting in the generation of auditory and visual percepts that are inconsistent with each other.

9.5 COMPUTATIONAL MODELS

Visual and tactile stimuli are required to be integrated into an internally consistent reference frame, as was already discussed in Chapter 8. Pouget et al. (2002) have developed a computational neural network model that can explain how these transformations can be performed in a biologically plausible way. Their model contains two main elements: **basis functions** and **attractor dynamics**.

Basis functions consist of linear combinations of non-linear functions yielding a powerful set of functions to compute the mathematically complex transformations between different reference frames. The output of these functions results in the approximate alignment of the different sensory input in the target coordinate system. According to Pouget et al., the remaining mismatch is solved by the attractor dynamics mechanism. This mechanism yields inferences based on the transformed inputs. The transformations with the smallest degree of statistical uncertainty weigh the heaviest in the final matching process.

In a review of the literature, Ursino, Cuppini, and Magosso (2014b) discuss different computational approaches to describe the integration of multisensory information in the brain. More specifically, they identify three main types of models: (1) a statistical approach based on Bayesian inferences; (2) biologically inspired models; and (3) models of semantic memory (see Chapter 13) in which the meaning of concepts is defined by the combination of sensory and motor properties. We will discuss these models next.

Various computational models aim to explain multisensory integration processes based on Bayesian inference models. Alais and Burr (2004) discuss how the ventriloquist illusion can be explained using such an approach. A key feature of their model is that it takes the relative precision with which auditory and visual signals can be located into account. Interestingly, participants' estimates of the location of the visual and auditory input converge with each other when they believe that these inputs have a common cause. In contrast, when participants believe that these inputs originate from different sources, the convergence is much smaller, or does not even exist at all (Bresciani, Dammeier, & Ernst, 2006; Roach, Heron, & McGraw, 2006; Shams, Iwaki, Chawla, & Bhattacharya, 2005; Wallace et al., 2004).

Bayesian models thus take the relative precision of the inputs into account, along with the relative probability that these inputs originate from the same source. Based on these principles, Rowland, Stanford, and Stein (2007) developed a model that was capable of simulating superior colliculus responses that were observed when cats were orienting themselves to a light source in the vicinity of a conflicting auditory stimulus.

9.5.1 SEMANTIC MEMORY

In addition to the aforementioned principles, there is another factor that affects multisensory integration: the detection of congruence. Consider, for example, the ventriloquist illusion. For the most basic version of the illusion, we can conclude that spatial and temporal proximity are the major factors contributing to the illusion. It is the simultaneous appearance of a flash of light and a mismatch in location that drives the illusion.

For the classic theatre act, however, there are many more contributing factors. Here we also need to detect that the lip movements of the doll and the verbal expressions of the ventriloquist are congruent. It is unlikely that is to happen solely on the basis of establishing temporal simultaneity. It is necessary that we derive semantically congruent information from both the speech signals and lip movements. A further complicating factor is that, in our daily lives, we frequently perceive a huge amount of visual and auditory signals simultaneously, where we have to determine which signals belong together and which ones

do not. After all, we should only integrate those auditory and visual signals that come from the same object, while we should not integrate the signals that come from other sources. For example, when we have a conversation with our partner, we need to integrate the lip movements with his/her voice, and not with a voice that we happen to hear on the radio at that moment. The detection of semantic congruence is most likely to play an important role in this process, implying that our **semantic memory** (that is, our memory for concepts and facts) is also closely involved in the integration of audiovisual inputs.

As we will discuss in more detail in Chapter 13, there are currently two different views on how semantic memory is organised. According to the first view, known as the amodal view, semantic memory consists of a network of amodal symbols (Fodor, 1983; Johnson-Laird & Shafir, 1993). In this case, 'amodal' implies that concepts are represented in an abstract manner, disconnected from the peripheral 'superficial' visual, auditory, tactile properties. According to this view, modal percepts are first transformed into amodal symbols that represent our knowledge in semantic memory. One of the consequences of this view is that thinking about objects implies the use of these symbols, a process that does not involve the original modal representations.

The second, currently more accepted view, is based on the **embodied cognition** approach and on the idea that semantic memory employs the same neural representations that we also use for perception or for actions (Barsalou, 2008; Borghi & Cimatti, 2010; Gallese & Lakoff, 2005; Gallese & Sinigaglia, 2011). As will be further elaborated in Chapter 13, the latter view is increasingly supported by empirical evidence (Pulvermüller, 2005; Pulvermüller, Lutzenberger, & Preissl, 1999). According to this view, the various modal representations of a concept influence the integration of the different modalities.

A possible implementation of this idea was presented by Ursino and colleagues (Ursino, Cuppini, & Magosso, 2013; Ursino et al., 2014). Figure 9.9 illustrates their auto-associative model. According to this model, low-level stimulus features can integrate into more complex concepts via convergence zones. Convergence zones are formed by neural populations that are responsive to multiple individual properties of the concept (for example, a neuron in a convergence zone of the concept 'hammer' responds not only to the abstract concept but also to the visual image of a hammer, or to the ticking sound of a hammer on metal). According to a similar process, multiple concepts can converge into semantically complex, hierarchically organised concepts. An important feature of the model is that the connections between the different layers in the hierarchy are bidirectional, allowing more complex concepts to be activated from the lower modal properties, while activating the higher-level abstract concepts can also activate the lower levels.

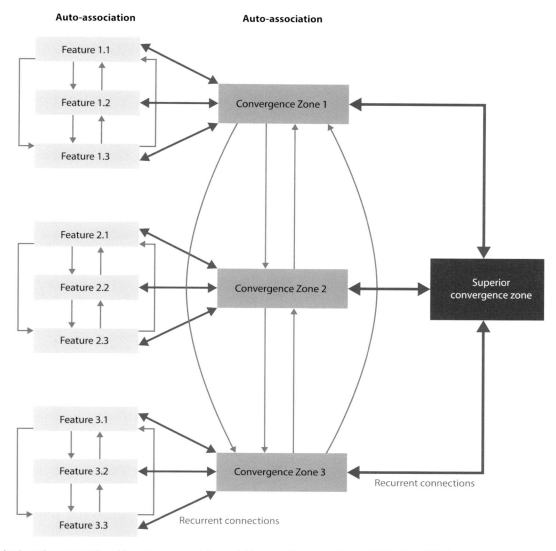

Figure 9.9 A schematic representation of Ursino's auto-associative model for semantic memory. (source: Ursino et al., 2014a)

9.6 TOP-DOWN INFLUENCES ON MULTISENSORY PROCESSING

With the exception of Ursino's model, the effects of multisensory integration described in the previous section are mainly driven by properties of the stimuli; that is, they are predominantly bottom-up. In addition, several additional top-down principles have been identified, as we will discuss next.

9.6.1 THE MODALITY APPROPRIATENESS HYPOTHESIS

The **modality appropriateness hypothesis** states that in situations where two sensory modalities are stimulated at the same time, the one with the highest accuracy will dominate the multisensory integration process (Welch & Warren, 1980). To illustrate, consider the ventriloquist effect. Here, the spatial resolution of the visual modality is higher than that of the auditory modality. For this reason, we tend to adjust the location of the sound to that of the lip movements. Similarly, for the temporal ventriloquist illusion, we will observe that the timing information of the visual stimulus is adjusted to the auditory signal.

9.6.2 THE UNITY ASSUMPTION

The **unity assumption** refers to the extent to which we believe that two sensory stimuli are related to the same object or event. For instance, Lewald and Guski (2003) found that participants' estimates of whether auditory and visual inputs have a common cause depended on the temporal and spatial proximity of the two inputs. That is, the more similar the locations were, the more likely participants were to report that these stimuli had a common cause. In addition to these bottom-up factors, top-down influences were also found to be involved: in a literature review, Chen and Spence (2017) identify the major factors that contribute to the unity assumption, and report the following:

1. Semantic congruence. Auditory and visual inputs are semantically congruent when they communicate similar meanings. A visual impression of a dog and the sound of a barking dog, as well as the correspondence between speech and lip movements, are examples of semantically congruent stimuli.
2. Cross-modal correspondences. Cross-modal correspondence is the phenomenon of inputs presented to each modality sharing statistic regularities. Examples include the associations between visual spatial frequencies and auditory pitch, or the Bouba-Kiki phenomenon. The latter phenomenon describes how the sound 'Bouba' is mainly associated with round visual shapes, while 'Kiki' is more often associated with sharp corners.[2]

The predictive coding theory can explain the unity assumption in terms of an a priori expectation affecting the integration of the individual inputs. Based on our everyday experiences, we expect lip movements to be in sync with a speech signal just like we expect dogs to bark. Expressed in Bayesian terms, the unity assumption can be equated to a Bayesian prior that can strongly affect the integration of the individual sensory inputs (Ernst, 2007; Sato, Toyoizumi, & Aihara, 2007; Shams & Beierholm, 2010). Thus, the Bayesian approach expresses the unity assumption in terms of certainty that we have about the correspondence of the auditory and visual inputs. The stronger the prior, the more likely it is that both inputs will be interpreted as a unit. Again, we can see this reflected in the ventriloquist effect. Both the temporal synchronisation of the auditory and visual signals, and the semantic congruence strengthen the assumption of unity, reinforcing the prior belief that the signals have a common origin. This belief in turn influences the spatial processing of the sound, causing it to be perceived as originating from the same location as the visual source.

Evidence showing that the assumption of unity can influence audiovisual perception was found in several classical studies, in which participants' a priori belief was explicitly influenced by the experimenter. This was done, for example, by informing participants that the inputs of different modalities either did or did not have a common cause (Welch & Warren, 1980). For instance, Welch (1972) instructed his participants to point to a specific target location without them being able to observe their own hand. Critically, Welch induced a deviation in the participants representation of their own hand by using a procedure that is essentially a precursor to the rubber hand illusion (see Chapter 8). At the end of the pointing procedure, participants were given the illusion that they saw their own finger, however, the finger they actually saw was Welch's, and it was slightly displaced relative to that of the participant. This displacement resulted in an adjustment of the participants pointing behaviour, suggesting that they corrected for the illusory displacement. Crucially, however, this correction was smaller in the group that was informed about the fact that the finger position was manipulated than in the group that was not informed about this displacement.

Yet, not everybody adapts equally in all situations. For instance, Radeau and Bertelson (1974) studied adaptation using the ventriloquist effect. Participants were briefly exposed to simple audiovisual stimuli, in which the location of the visual stimulus did not match the location of the auditory stimulus. After they had been exposed to these stimuli, they were required to locate the stimuli by pointing to them. In this pointing task, either only the sound or the light was presented. Although participants were not aware of the fact that the locations of the light and sound were misaligned, this mismatch did have an effect. More specifically, localisations of the sounds were biased towards the direction of the light and localisations of the light were biased towards the direction of the sounds. The degree of adaptation was the same, however, regardless of whether participants were told that the stimuli had a common cause, had a different cause, or even when they were not given any information about a possible common cause.

Using a temporal order judgement task, Parise and Spence (2009) found that cross-modal correspondences could influence the unity assumption. They used a large or a small circle as a visual stimulus and a high- or low-pitched tone as the auditory stimulus. All four possible combinations of visual and auditory stimulus were used (large-low, large-high, small-low, and small-high). It was found that the just noticeable difference was larger for the congruent pairs (large-low, small-high) than for the incongruent pairs (see fig 9.10). This result implies that participants are more likely to perceive congruent inputs as a unit, allowing them to integrate the inputs across larger temporal differences.

9.7 CALIBRATION

When an auditory signal lags behind the visual one, we typically begin to notice this at sufficiently large stimulus onset asynchronies. One interesting question is whether we can adapt to such asynchronies. Vroomen, Keetels, de Gelder, and Bertelson (2004) addressed this question by using the aforementioned temporal order judgement task. The crucial manipulation in their experiment was that participants were exposed to a series of sounds and flashes, which were presented with a constant time difference relative to each other. A few minutes of exposure had an effect on the extent to which participants were able to determine which stimulus was presented first on the temporal order judgement task. More specifically, the point of subjective

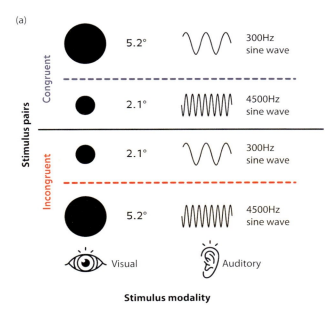

(a)

Stimulus pairs

Congruent

5.2° — 300Hz sine wave

2.1° — 4500Hz sine wave

Incongruent

2.1° — 300Hz sine wave

5.2° — 4500Hz sine wave

Visual   Auditory

Stimulus modality

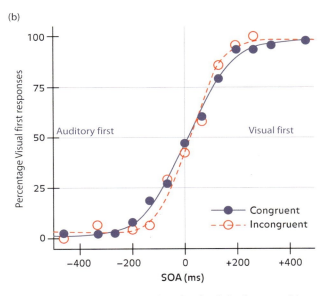

(b)

Percentage Visual first responses

100

75

50

25

0

Auditory first

Visual first

—●— Congruent
—○-- Incongruent

−400   −200   0   +200   +400

SOA (ms)

Figure 9.10 Experimental set-up and results of a study of cross-modal correspondences. (a) Participants were performing a temporal order judgement task, using large or small circles for the visual stimulus and high or low tones for the auditory stimuli. (b) Results for the congruent (large-low or small-high) and incongruent (large-high or small-low) input pairs. Congruent pairs are more likely to be perceived as a unit, as evidenced by the flatter curve, which implies that the temporal order of the two inputs can only be observed at greater stimulus onset asynchronies. (source: Parise and Spence, 2009)

simultaneity shifted towards the asynchrony to which the participants had been exposed. Similar results have been reported by Fujisaki, Shimojo, Kashino, and Nishida (2004). Moreover, Fujisaki et al. extended these findings by showing that exposure to a series of asynchronous stimuli had an effect on the aforementioned bounce-pass illusion. When participants were exposed to sequences where the auditory stimuli were lagging behind the visual ones, it was found that the most effective bounce illusion occurred when the evoking tone was also delayed.

9.7.1 ADAPTATION TO AUDIOVISUAL ASYNCHRONY

Although the results discussed so far imply that audiovisual integration processes can adapt to asynchronous stimuli, Van der Burg, Alais, and Cass (2013) argue that these results also imply that the adaptation process is slow, since the previously discussed studies always required a few minutes of adaptation. Although the fact that we can adapt is theoretically interesting, it is, from an evolutionary perspective, implausible that adaptation would be such a slow process, according to Van der Burg et al. After all, prolonged periods of continuous exposure to asynchronous multisensory stimuli almost never happen in natural environments. In contrast, in our daily lives, we typically have to deal with only brief occurrences of asynchronous multisensory exposures, as was already exemplified at the beginning of this chapter. For this reason, Van der Burg et al. wondered how rapidly audiovisual integration processes can adapt to asynchronous stimulation. To address this question, they used a simultaneity judgement task.

The rationale for using this task is this: if we can quickly adapt to audiovisual asynchrony, then the effect of an asynchronously presented stimulus pair should influence our judgement of the next trial. For example, if we take a trial where the auditory stimulus is presented after the visual one, and if we adapt to the asynchrony, this implies that on the next trial we are more likely to observe a similar asynchrony as simultaneous. Van der Burg et al. (2013) found that this is indeed the case, implying that we can rapidly adapt to asynchronous audiovisual inputs. Our subjective sense of simultaneity is, in other words, continuously recalibrated based on the actual input.

9.7.2 SINE WAVE SPEECH

A second form of calibration involves lip reading. Earlier in this chapter, we introduced the McGurk effect, which describes how a conflict between visual lip movements and auditory speech sounds can result in a completely new percept. What happens, however, when the auditory information is ambiguous? For example, sounds are ambiguous when they are equally likely to match with two or more **phonemes** (i.e., the basic units of speech; see Chapters 7 and 17). When these ambiguous sounds are combined with visual lip movements, we tend to interpret the sound in a way that matches the lip movement. This recalibration of the phonological categories is probably due to the fact that the brain aims to minimise the discrepancy between the visual and auditory inputs (Bertelson, Vroomen, & De Gelder, 2003).

Vroomen and Baart (2009) used an artificial auditory signal to investigate the effects of phonological calibration. In this signal, known as **sine wave speech** (Remez, Rubin, Pisoni, & Carrell, 1981), the natural richness of a

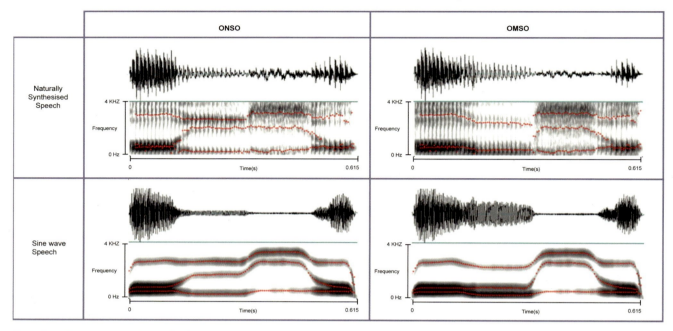

Figure 9.11 Example the /ONSO/ and /OMSO/ speech fragments and their sine wave equivalents. (source: Vroomen and Baart, 2009)

speech signal is substituted by three sinusoids, which follow the central tenet of the original signal. Sine wave speech is interesting because most untrained listeners do not recognise it as speech, but rather describe it as 'whistles or bleeps from a cheap sci-fi movie'. When listeners are informed that the signal is derived from speech, however, they will typically begin to recognise it as speech. Even more so, they tend to understand what is actually being said.

Based on this selective ability to understand sine wave speech, Vroomen and Baart (2009) made a distinction between non-speech mode (in which participants do not recognise sine wave stimuli as speech) and speech mode (in which participants do recognise it as speech). This difference between speech mode and non-speech mode was used to investigate to what extent sine wave speech can be influenced by visual lip movements. To this end, two speech fragments (/ONSO/, /OMSO/ and various ambiguous intermediate forms thereof) were converted to sine wave speech (see fig 9.11). Participants were first trained to distinguish between the two fragments just mentioned. Then, half of the participants, namely those who were put into speech mode, had to classify it as /ONSO/ or /OMSO/ while the group that was not put into speech mode simply had to designate the distinction as category 1 or category 2. After this, the ambiguous intermediate forms were combined with lip movements that corresponded either to /ONSO/ or to /OMSO/. Participants' perception of these fragments was influenced by the lip movement; however, interestingly enough, this only happened when they were put into speech mode. This result thus suggests that integration with the lip movements occurred only

when participants were able to recognise the sine wave sounds as speech.

Stekelenburg and Vroomen (2012) aimed to determine the neural mechanisms behind this effect by combining sine wave variants of /ONSO/ with lip movements that corresponded either to /ONSO/ or to /OMSO/. For participants who were put into speech mode, the combination /ONSO/OMSO/ resulted in a mismatch negativity (see Chapter 7), whereas for participants who were not put into speech mode, this was not the case, again suggesting that the mismatch between visual and auditory inputs could only be detected when the sounds were recognised as speech.

9.8 CROSS-MODAL ATTENTION

To what extent are these multisensory effects further influenced by higher cognitive processes? In the previous chapters we have discussed how attention can selectively modulate the processing of sensory information (visual, auditory, or tactile), but we have not yet considered whether this modulation occurs independently for each sensory modality, or whether attention affects multiple sensory modalities in parallel.

9.8.1 INTERMODAL ATTENTION

Consider the following scenario. We stand in front of an intersection with the intention of crossing a busy street. We closely attend to the traffic approaching us from the left.

Now what is happening in our attentional systems? Is it the case that while our visual attention is focused on the left that we are also more sensitive to sounds coming from the left, or is our auditory perception not affected by where we visually attend? One of the major problems involved in addressing this question is that we need to create a situation where sounds are irrelevant, while we are still able to measure the effects of attention on the processing of these sounds. We cannot solve this problem by giving participants a task involving these sounds, because then they would no longer be irrelevant. A good workaround for this problem is to use ERP measurements. Since the effects of attention on visual, auditory, and tactile ERPs are well documented (Hillyard et al., 1998; Näätänen, 2008), they are ideally suited for studying the effects of visual attention on auditory processing and vice versa.

9.8.1.1 Spatial Attention

Eimer and Schöger (1998) took advantage of this approach by presenting streams of visual and auditory stimuli (consisting of the letter W and low-pitched tones). These stimuli were randomly presented to either the left or right hemifield of the participant. Participants were instructed to focus their attention on one specific stimulus combination (e.g., visual stimuli presented on the left) and to respond only to stimuli in the designated channel that differed slightly from the standard. These deviant target stimuli were presented infrequently and consisted of either the letter M or of a high-pitched tone.

In this study, Eimer and Schröger were interested in whether focusing visual attention on a specific location affected the processing of auditory stimuli and vice versa. The ERP results showed that this was indeed the case. For example, when attention was focused on visual stimuli presented in the left hemifield, the attention-sensitive ERP components evoked by auditory stimuli presented from the same locations were larger in amplitude, compared to the condition where visual attention was focused at the opposite location. For the visual stimuli, a similar effect was found when attention had to be focused on one of the auditory stimuli. Interestingly, however, Eimer and Schöger (1998) only found these results when the difference between left and right was clearly distinguishable and when the locations of the visual and auditory stimuli were tightly matched.

9.8.2 CROSS-MODAL LINKS

The ERP results described in the previous section are consistent with those from behavioural studies conducted around the same time. Spence and Driver (1996) used a cross-modal variant of Posner's (1980) symbolic cueing paradigm. In this study, target stimuli, consisting of a flash of light or a short tone, were presented in either the left or the right hemifield, and slightly above or below the horizontal meridian. Participants then had to determine as quickly as possible whether the stimulus was presented above or below the meridian. The stimuli were preceded by a cue, which indicated whether the stimulus would appear in the left or right hemifield (see fig 9.12).

Spence and Driver found that responses to stimuli that were preceded by a valid cue were typically faster than those that were preceded by an invalid cue; even when participants did not know in advance whether the target stimulus would be auditory or visual. Moreover, when

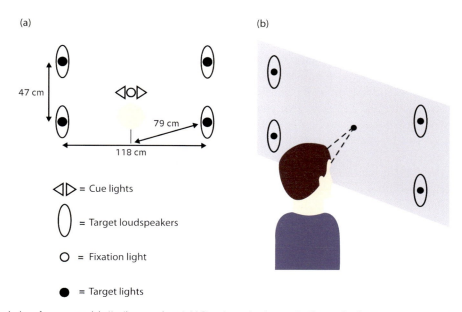

Figure 9.12 Schematic design of a cross-modal attention experiment. (a) By using a visual cue, attention can be directed to the left or right side, after which either a visual stimulus or an auditory stimulus appears at one of the four possible locations. (b) Three-dimensional representation of the arrangement shown in (a). (source: Driver and Spence (1998) and Spence and Driver (1996))

participants expected a target stimulus at a particular location in one specific modality, a corresponding shift of attention to the other modality was found, as shown by a relatively rapid identification of the corresponding stimulus in that modality. Although the latter result suggests the existence of a cross-modal link between visual and auditory attention, it also turned out that attention could be split between the visual and auditory modalities. When participants expected visual stimuli on one side and auditory stimuli on the other side, it was found that in both cases they were able to efficiently detect these stimuli.

In summary, these results suggest that top-down controlled attention can be focused in parallel on both visual and auditory features of an object, suggesting that the processing of our sensory modalities is linked in a flexible manner (Driver & Spence, 1998). Spence and Driver (1997) found similar results, based on a series of experiments using exogenous cues (see Chapter 6). The main difference was that exogenous auditory cues were able to capture visual attention, whereas the exogenous visual cues were not able to do so for auditory attention.

9.8.3 SPREADING OF ATTENTION

The aforementioned studies have mainly focused on spatial intermodal attention. But what about object-based cross-modal attention? Busse, Roberts, Crist, Weissman, and Woldorff (2005) found in a combined ERP and fMRI study that visual attention can selectively influence the processing of auditory inputs. Busse et al.'s experiment is illustrated in Figure 9.13. A series of visual stimuli was presented in a random order in the left or right visual field, while participants selectively focused their attention on one of these two locations. On half the trials, a tone was presented simultaneously with the visual stimulus, so that it coincided with either the attended visual stimulus or with the unattended one. The ERP activity evoked by these tones showed clear differences between the tones that coincided with the attended visual stimuli and the tones that coincided with the unattended visual stimuli. More specifically, when the tones coincided with an attended visual stimulus, their ERPs were characterised by a prolonged negative potential difference. The fMRI results suggested that this potential difference originated from a neural generator in the auditory cortex. Busse et al. argued that the pairing of a visual and an auditory stimulus will result in visual attention spreading to the auditory aspects of the object that is attended.

Talsma, Doty, et al. (2007) suggested that the negative ERP component that Busse et al. (2005) observed is the result of a deeper processing of the auditory component, as if it is fully attended. Evidence for this idea was found by comparing the ERP results from a spreading of attention

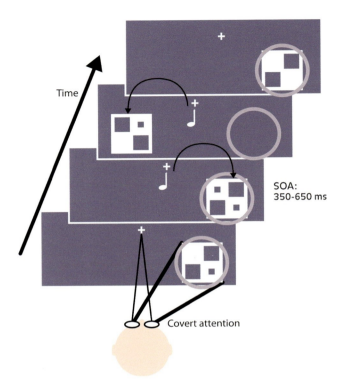

Figure 9.13 Schematic overview of an experimental set-up to investigate the effects of attention on multisensory objects. Irrelevant tones could be paired with attended or non-attended visual stimuli. (source: Busse et al., 2005)

condition (similar to that of Busse et al.) with those that were obtained in a classic auditory attention condition. Both conditions yielded highly similar ERP results, thus implying that the auditory component is indeed processed more fully when it is part of an object of which the visual component is attended.

9.9 ATTENTION AND MULTISENSORY INTEGRATION

In the previous section, we learned that attention processes are not limited to a single sensory modality, but that attention allows us to be selective across multiple modalities. Next, we can turn to whether attention may then also affect the integration of multisensory information.

This question has been discussed intensely. Given the previously discussed principles of proximity (spatial and temporal) and inverse effectiveness, we could make a point that integration is strictly determined by these stimulus properties and not by top-down influences such as attention. Also, audiovisual illusions, such as the McGurk effect or the ventriloquist illusion were initially believed to be insensitive to attention, which contributed to the assumption that multisensory integration is an automatic process that is not modulated by attention.

9.9.1 NO ROLE FOR ATTENTION

Bertelson, Vroomen, and colleagues used the ventriloquist illusion to test whether attention can affect multisensory integration. In their studies, the ventriloquist illusion was implemented in a computer task in which tones were presented. Participants had to indicate from which location each tone was presented by pointing in that direction. When visual stimuli were presented together with the tones, they could affect participants' localisation judgement. More specifically, the approximate pointing direction shifted towards the visual stimulus. In addition to this task, a small visual target stimulus was presented, either on the left or right side of the screen, which occasionally changed shape. When such a change occurred, participants had to report this change instead of reporting the direction of the sound (Bertelson, Vroomen, De Gelder, & Driver, 2000). The rationale behind the latter manipulation was that participants were required to focus their attention endogenously on the target to perceive its shape change. As a result, attention was selectively directed to the left or the right.

Now, if attention did affect the ventriloquist illusion, we would expect to see a systematic shift in participants' location estimates. However, this was not found, and Bertelson et al. concluded that attention did not affect audiovisual integration. In a follow-up study, Vroomen, Bertelson, and De Gelder (2001) investigated whether exogenous attention could influence the ventriloquist illusion. To this end, a similar set-up was used, but the small visual target stimulus was replaced by a large salient stimulus that was presented shortly before the audiovisual stimuli, thus capturing attention. Again, no effect on the localisation task was found. Based on these results, it appears that there is no influence of attention on audiovisual integration.

9.9.2 ATTENTION AFFECTS MULTISENSORY INTEGRATION

Despite the conclusion that attention would not affect multisensory integration, there are several reasons to argue otherwise. One argument is that attention and multisensory integration serve similar purposes, in the sense that both processes contribute to clarifying a mental representation of the environment by reducing ambiguities in our perception. Therefore, it is plausible that attention and integration would influence each other. Indeed, ERP results provided evidence for this (Talsma & Woldorff, 2005). Here participants were presented with a series of visual, auditory, and audiovisual stimuli, consisting of simple grid patterns, tones, or a combination of the two. These stimuli were presented at random to the left and right of the participant. The participant's task was to attend to one of the two locations and to detect an occasional target stimulus at that location. The participant's attention was therefore always focused on either the left location or the right location. During the task, ERPs were recorded, and the multisensory interactions were estimated by applying the [AV – (A + V)] method described earlier in this chapter. This resulted in two datasets: one where the stimuli were attended to and one where they were not. The main finding was that the multisensory interactions occurred earlier when the stimuli were attended than when they were not.

Nevertheless, the ERP effects that were observed still occurred significantly later than the earliest effects reported by Giard and Peronnet (1999), as discussed earlier. One possible explanation for the difference is that the ERP methodology in the Talsma et al. study was not sensitive enough to detect the earliest effects when stimuli are presented in the periphery of our gaze. Senkowski, Talsma, Herrmann, and Woldorff (2005) provide some evidence for this assertion, based on the analysis of oscillations in the EEG gamma band (40–80 Hz). More specifically, they found that the amplitude of these oscillations was increased when multisensory stimuli were attended and that this effect already occurred at about 50 ms after stimulus presentation. More evidence was provided in a follow-up study to Talsma and Woldorff (2005), where stimuli were presented centrally. Here, an effect of multisensory integration was found in the early time window of about 50 ms of the ERPs. Moreover, this effect was also modulated by attention (Talsma, Doty, et al., 2007).

Around the same time, work from a Spanish research group was published which also concluded that attention could affect multisensory integration, but based on a different approach (Alsius et al., 2005; Alsius et al., 2007). In this case, the McGurk effect was used. Participants were presented with video clips of a face that pronounced a single syllable. These video clips were manipulated in such a way that there was a mismatch between the lip movements and the audio signal, causing the McGurk effect. Participants were instructed to repeat what they had heard. In addition, participants were required to do a secondary task, which consisted of presenting drawings and sounds. These were presented simultaneously with the presentation of the syllable. Occasionally, one of these stimuli could be repeated. If that happened, participants were required to respond as soon as they detected it. Performing this second task had a strong detrimental effect on participants sensitivity to the McGurk effect, which also implies that guiding attention away from the McGurk stimuli by a second task impacts multisensory integration. These results are consistent with fMRI results from Fairhall and Macaluso (2009), who reported an increase in activation in the superior temporal sulcus, the superior colliculus, and the visual cortex when attention was focused on a congruent combination of lip movements and speech signals (see fig 9.14).

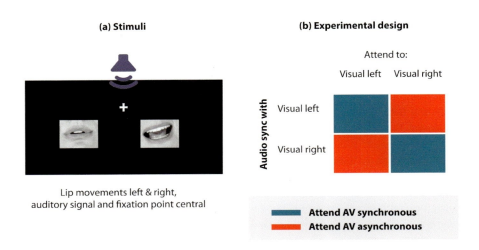

(a) Stimuli

Lip movements left & right,
auditory signal and fixation point central

(b) Experimental design

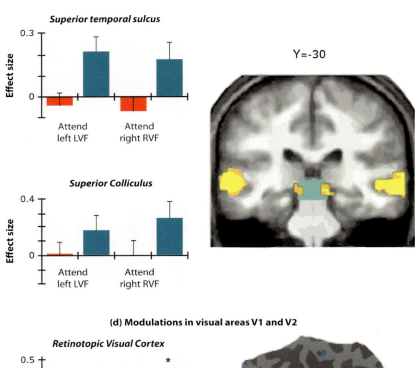

(c) Modulations at various processing stages

Superior temporal sulcus

Superior Colliculus

Y=-30

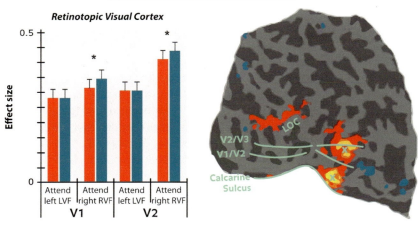

(d) Modulations in visual areas V1 and V2

Retinotopic Visual Cortex

Figure 9.14 Experimental design and results of an fMRI study on the effects of attention on the processing of congruence of audiovisual stimuli. (a) Speech fragments could be combined with synchronous or asynchronous lip movements. (b) Schematic overview of the experimental design. (c) Attention to synchronous lip movements resulted in an increase in activation in the superior temporal sulcus and the superior colliculus. (d) A similar increase in activation was found in the right visual cortices V1 and V2. (source: Talsma, Senkowski, Soto-Faraco, and Woldorff (2010), based on results from Fairhall and Macaluso (2009))

9.9.3 MULTISENSORY INTEGRATION AFFECTS ATTENTION

Although the results discussed so far imply that attention influences multisensory processing, evidence suggesting exactly the opposite effect was published around the same time (Van der Burg, Olivers, Bronkhorst, & Theeuwes, 2008, 2009). Van der Burg et al. (2008) used a visual search task (see fig 9.15), in which participants were required to detect one deviant target stimulus in a display that was filled with red and green coloured diagonal lines. The target was either a horizontal or a vertical line. At pseudo-random moments, one or more of these lines switched colours. The time required to detect the target increased more or less linearly

(a) Search Display

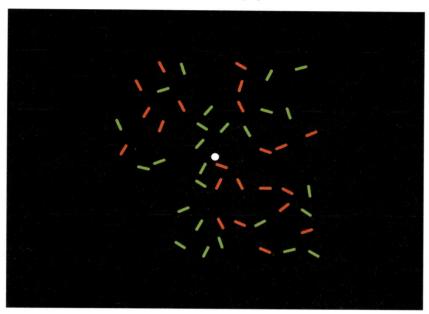

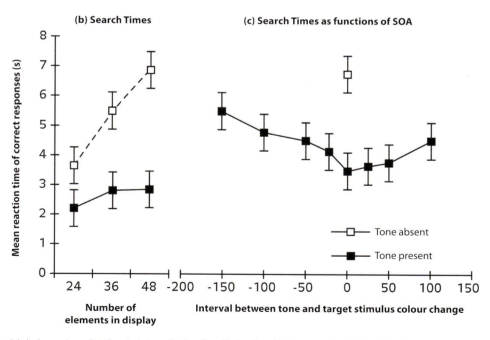

Figure 9.15 Experimental design and results of a study investigating the effects of multisensory integration on attention. (a) Participants were shown displays consisting of random diagonal line elements, in which they had to detect a deviant (horizontal or vertical) target stimulus. The lines could change colour at semi-random moments. (b) Results. When the colour change of the target stimulus was accompanied by a short tone, the search time was hardly affected by the number of irrelevant lines in the display (the set size). When no tone was presented, search times were affected by set size. (c) Results of a control experiment, in which the time between the colour change of the target stimulus and the tone was manipulated. The search time was shortest when the tone was presented 50 ms after the colour change. This time course is consistent with the idea that the line and the tone are integrated with each other. (source: Talsma, Senkowski, et al. (2010), based on results from Van der Burg et al. (2008))

with the number of elements in the display. According to Treisman and Gelade (1980), this implies the presence of an attention-demanding serial search process (see Chapter 6).

When, however, a tone (Van der Burg et al., 2008) or a tactile stimulus (Van der Burg et al., 2009) was presented when the target stimulus switched colour, it was detected almost immediately. Now, the search time was no longer dependent on the number of elements in the display, allowing us to deduce that attention is immediately captured by the target stimulus. This observation was also consistent with most participants' subjective experience that the sound made the visual target stimulus pop out of the display. Given that it was a pip that caused the visual stimulus to pop out, Van der Burg et al. aptly named their result the 'pip and pop' effect.

To ensure that the pip and pop effect was caused by multisensory integration, and not because the auditory or tactile stimulus simply alerted the participant that a colour change of the visual target stimulus had occurred, several control studies were conducted. For example, in one study the tone was replaced by the flashing of a visual halo around the display, but no facilitation of search time was found. In addition, the stimulus onset asynchrony between the target stimulus and the sound was manipulated. Here, it was found that participants benefited the most from the auditory stimulus when it was presented about 50 ms after the visual colour change. This interval is consistent with previous findings showing that audiovisual integration is most efficient when the auditory stimulus is presented at about 50 ms after the visual one (Lewald & Guski, 2003). Instead, a warning account would predict that the auditory of tactile stimuli would be most efficient when it would precede the colour change. Thus, both findings argue against an alerting account.

9.9.3.1 Individual Differences

A number of studies that were based on the previously discussed pip and pop experiment have reported finding significant individual differences in our ability to integrate audiovisual stimuli. Van der Burg, Talsma, Olivers, Hickey, and Theeuwes (2011) used a modified version of the experiment to determine to what extent the sounds indeed capture our attention and whether this is driving the multisensory integration process. Using ERPs, they observed a multisensory integration effect that occurred already at 50 ms after the appearance of the target stimulus effect. Moreover, the magnitude of this effect correlated with task performance: the better the participants were able to detect the audiovisual target stimuli, the greater the physiological response was.

Van den Brink et al. (2014) used diffusion tensor imaging (see Section 9.4), to determine whether there is a neural basis for these individual differences. For each participant, connectivity estimates were obtained for their auditory and visual neural pathways. In a separate session, each participant then completed the pip and pop task. Then the

connectivity of each participants' neural pathways was correlated with their performance on the pip and pop task. The results of this analysis showed that connectivity in the earliest stages of the auditory pathways (see Chapter 7), in particular the connections between the cochlear nucleus, the auditory thalamus, and the primary auditory cortex, were predictive of the extent to which participants were able to integrate auditory and visual stimuli, thus showing that fundamental anatomical differences may be related to our ability to integrate audiovisual information.

9.9.4 THE SALIENCE FRAMEWORK

The previous results imply a paradox: on the one hand, attention appears to facilitate multisensory integration, yet, on the other hand, multisensory integration appears to facilitate attention. We can most likely resolve this paradox, however, when we consider the fact that the various experiments described earlier are characterised by differences in salience of the stimuli they employed. Moreover, the extent to which different stimuli compete for processing resources may also play an important role in the interaction between attention and multisensory integration.

Talsma, Senkowski, et al. (2010) present a theoretical model that describes how attention and multisensory integration can influence each other. In essence, the model predicts that when the individual auditory and visual inputs are not very salient and when the competition is strong, attention is needed to facilitate the integration process. If, however, the competition is limited, salient stimuli (such as the tones in the Van der Burg et al. study) can pre-attentively integrate with a less salient stimulus in another modality (e.g., the target stimulus in Van der Burg et al.) in order to increase the salience. Finally, if there is no competition at all, multisensory integration can occur pre-attentively.

9.10 PREDICTIVE CODING AND MULTISENSORY INTEGRATION

Earlier in this chapter, we discussed computational models that aim to describe multisensory integration processes from a Bayesian inference perspective. According to the principles of Bayesian optimal integration, precision of the information affects the extent to which a sensory modality contributes to the final outcome of the integration process. More specifically, the higher the precision, the more this input affects the integration. Expressed in Bayesian terms, the steeper the posterior probability density function, the stronger it affects the prior (see fig 2.17, Chapter 2, and Appendix for more details on Bayesian inference). By applying this principle, Ernst and Bülthoff (2004) were able to explain the modality appropriateness hypothesis. Likewise, Angelaki et al. (2009) have concluded, on the basis of a literature review, that the detection of our own motion is also based on the integration of multisensory vestibular and visual cues, and that the way these cues are integrated can be explained by these Bayesian principles.

Given that the predictive coding framework is largely consistent with the principles of Bayesian optimal integration, it is plausible that many multisensory integration processes are affected by the brain's predictive processes. Note, however, that the predictive coding framework postulates an internal model that generates modality-specific predictions, which are corrected by sensory input. In contrast, Bayesian optimal multisensory integration is believed to operate on the basis of direct interactions between two sensory systems. That is, the models describing these processes assume that the senses directly correct and update each other's representations, without necessarily assuming that this is based on an overarching generative model. However, the mathematical principles on which these updates are based are similar to those of the predictive coding framework.

Given these similarities, is it possible to reconcile the two approaches? The short answer is: most likely (Talsma, 2015)! As discussed, multisensory integration effects can be found at various levels in the brain's processing hierarchy. This argument is partly based on the fact that various theorists assume that multisensory integration is an intrinsic property of the brain (Ghazanfar & Schroeder, 2006; van Atteveldt, Murray, Thut, & Schroeder, 2014). If this is the case, it follows that progressively higher levels of processing can also lead to progressively more complex multisensory interactions. For example, Ghazanfar and Schroeder (2006) describe in an already extensively discussed literature review several of these findings. For instance, the multisensory properties of the primary sensory cortices involve spatial and temporal proximity, while higher-order areas involve more complex stimulus properties: the superior temporal sulcus, for instance, is involved in the detection of semantic congruence. Similarly, the parietal areas represent a multisensory spatial map, while the frontal and prefrontal areas are mainly involved in the processing of conceptual information.

The complex set of results that has been discussed so far fits nicely with the predictive coding framework. For instance, if we assume that the internal models generate predictions about our environment, then we can also assume that they are not limited to predictions for the visual system, but that they also involve our auditory, somatosensory, proprioceptive, and nociceptive senses. Moreover, we may safely expect that the predictions for these senses will be internally consistent; when you expect to cut yourself, this will result in a prediction of feeling pain and seeing blood.

Moreover, these predictions are likely to be influenced by our knowledge and expectations: for example, our level of command of a foreign language affects the intelligibility of speech and the mere knowledge that a complex

auditory signal is actually a speech signal boosts its intelligibility, as we have already discussed (Remez et al., 1981; Stekelenburg & Vroomen, 2012; Vroomen & Baart, 2009). This way, visual information can influence the interpretation of auditory information. For example, when reading along with a text that is read to us aloud, what we read strongly influences what we hear. Here too, the integration of visual and auditory information takes place via an internal generative model, in which the modality with the least ambiguity (the written text) most strongly influences the processing of the modality with the highest ambiguity. This integration is also likely based on an internal generative model. A model is formed on the basis of the visually presented text, and this generates predictions for the auditory modality.

These predictions are most likely supplemented by conceptual knowledge, as illustrated by the following example. Suppose we go for a walk in the countryside, and we expect to encounter a cow. This expectation will activate the concept of 'cow', but it will not only activate the abstract properties of the concept but also the visual and auditory representation that we have formed during prior encounters with cows. Activating the concept presumably corresponds with activity in the frontal and prefrontal lobes (Ghazanfar & Schroeder, 2006). When our visual system detects that the cow is about to start mooing, this indirectly generates the prediction of a cow sound, by activating the relevant auditory representation. The semantic congruence between image and sound is encoded by the supratemporal sulcus (Calvert et al., 2000; Ghazanfar & Schroeder, 2006; Ghazanfar, Maier, Hoffman, & Logothetis, 2005).

Such an internal generative model, which generates predictions for both the visual and auditory perceptual systems, can explain a wide range of multisensory effects. Thus far, we have implicitly assumed, however, that the visual and auditory predictions are generated independently of each other: we have assumed that they both arise independently of each other from a generic representation, but that there is no direct mutual influence yet. This model does, therefore, not yet explain the contributions of the direct neural connections between the different sensory systems that we have identified earlier in this chapter. Although somewhat speculative, it is plausible that these direct connections give the various sensory systems additional input, which can ensure that inaccuracies in the perception of temporal and spatial information are quickly corrected by combining their inputs (Talsma, 2015). Evidence for this idea is slowly but steadily becoming available. For example, Mercier et al. (2013) showed that the oscillations of the background electrocorticogram (that is, EEGs registered by **intercranial** electrodes) in the visual cortex can be affected by auditory stimulation. Moreover, Mercier et al. were able to record ERPs, which were triggered by auditory stimuli, in the visual cortex.

Evidence that internal models are involved in audiovisual integration processes is becoming increasingly readily available. For example, we might expect that auditory information should indirectly generate predictions that result in activation of the visual cortex. Evidence for the idea that the basic processing processes in the visual cortex can be affected by top-down processes or by other sensory modalities is discussed by Clark (2013). For example, implicit multisensory associations can influence speech recognition (von Kriegstein & Giraud, 2006). Similarly, expecting a stimulus to appear in one sensory modality can already cause the other sensory modalities to become more active (Langner et al., 2011).

Additional evidence for the hypothesis that predictive models are involved in multisensory processing was reported in a study that we already briefly introduced in Chapter 2 (see fig 9.16). Vetter et al. (2014) presented sounds of different categories, such as children playing or airplanes taking off. Each sound category resulted in a distinctive activation pattern in the visual cortex. According to Vetter et al., this result implies that sounds activate a mental representation that generates predictions in the visual cortex, eventually resulting in a mental representation of the scene. In a follow-up, Vetter et al. also explicitly instructed participants to imagine these kinds of scenes, and this resulted in similar activation patterns in the visual cortex, suggesting a similar involvement of generative internal models.

Similar results have been reported in two studies by Berger and Ehrsson (2013, 2014), in which some of the classic audiovisual illusions described earlier in this chapter were used. Berger and Ehrsson (2013), for instance, used the bounce-pass illusion. In one condition, however, the presentation of the sound was replaced by an instruction to imagine it. This instruction, like the real sound, resulted in an increase in the proportion of bounces reported. Similarly, Berger and Ehrsson (2013) reported that mentally representing a specific phoneme influenced the perception of an ambiguous lip movement and that mentally representing a visual stimulus at a specific location influenced the localisation of a sound.

The neural basis of the latter effect was further investigated by Berger and Ehrsson (2014). Here, participants were instructed to imagine a circle at a specific location, after which a sound was presented. This sound could be presented either in sync with the imagined stimulus or at a time when the participant did not imagine anything. Consistent with Berger and Ehrsson's earlier result, it was found that imagining resulted in an altered perception of the location of the sound. Based on fMRI recordings, it was now also determined that the extent of this ventriloquist illusion – which was caused by an imaginary stimulus – correlated with activity in two brain regions, namely the superior temporal sulcus and the auditory cortex.

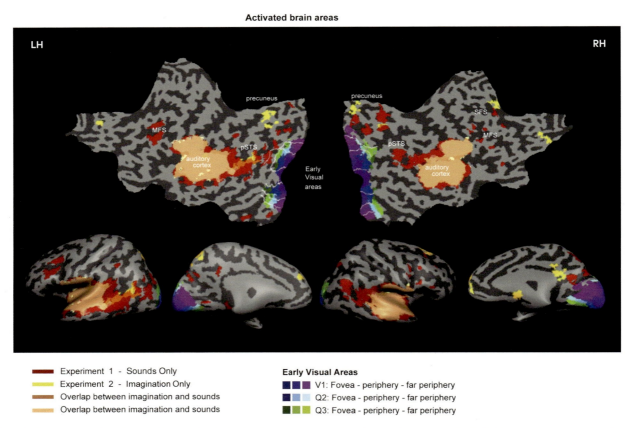

Activated brain areas

Experiment 1 - Sounds Only
Experiment 2 - Imagination Only
Overlap between imagination and sounds
Overlap between imagination and sounds

Early Visual Areas
V1: Fovea - periphery - far periphery
Q2: Fovea - periphery - far periphery
Q3: Fovea - periphery - far periphery

Figure 9.16 Results of an fMRI study investigating the effects of auditory processing on the activation of the visual cortex. Both the presentation of specific categories of sounds and the instruction to participants to imagine these sounds resulted in category-specific activation patterns in the visual cortex. (source: Vetter et al., 2014)

9.11 MULTISENSORY INTERACTIONS ACROSS THE LIFESPAN

Although multisensory interactions are an essential part of our everyday cognitive functions, most evidence seems to indicate that the cognitive processes underlying multisensory integration are not innate and take several years to fully develop. In addition, it increasingly appears to be the case that anomalies in (multi)sensory integration processes underlie a number of well-known mental conditions, of which schizophrenia and autism spectrum disorder are probably the best known. In this last part of the multisensory integration chapter, we will discuss some recent insights into the (atypical) development of multisensory integration.

9.11.1 DEVELOPMENT

Murray, Lewkowicz, Amedi, and Wallace (2016) have described multisensory processing as a balancing act across the lifespan (see fig 9.17). According to Murray et al., the balance consists of the brain being able to carefully select which stimuli should be integrated with each other and which ones should not. They argue that multisensory processes can be divided into two different categories. One category operates in the short term and is related to basic stimulus properties, such as the previously discussed temporal and spatial proximity, while the other category operates in the long term and mainly relates to learned associations. According to Murray et al., the latter category of processes spans across our entire lifetime. In other words, we are constantly learning new audiovisual associations that we can use in the integration process. Although multisensory processing as we discuss next, develops relatively late, our ability to do so remains intact throughout our lifespan. Even more so, older individuals appear to be even better at it than young adults.

Multisensory processing does not appear to develop until late childhood. For example, Ross et al. (2011) report that

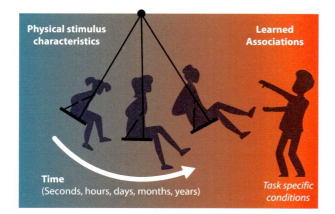

Figure 9.17 The balance between basic principles that manifest themselves in the short-term and long-term, lifelong learned associations in multisensory integration. (source: Adapted from Murray et al. 2016)

our lip reading ability does not start to develop until we are approximately 10 or 11 years of age. A similar result was reported for the rubber hand illusion (Cowie, Sterling, & Bremner, 2016). Cowie et al. found that children up to the age of 10 locate the position of their hand much more on the basis of visual information (and thus much less on the basis of proprioceptive information) than adults. As a result, when they do not see their own hand, they also do not integrate its position with their own body and therefore become less sensitive to the illusion.

Musacchia, Arum, Nicol, Garstecki, and Kraus (2009) used ERPs to investigate the effects of hearing loss on audiovisual integration processes. To do so, they presented recordings of a speaker who pronounced the syllable /bi/. On separate trials, either only the sound was presented, or only the image of the lip movement, or the image and the sound simultaneously. In the simultaneous audiovisual (AV) condition, it was found that the P1 and N1 components of the evoked ERPs were smaller than what was found when the unisensory visual and auditory ERPs [A + V] were combined. This amplitude difference was interpreted as a marker of audiovisual integration, and it was larger in a group of older adults than in a group of young adults. Interestingly, this increase in integration did appear to reflect a compensation for hearing loss, as older adults with hearing loss showed a less pronounced integration effect than older adults without hearing loss.

9.11.2 ATYPICAL DEVELOPMENT

In recent decades, the idea that dysfunctions in perceptual processes play an important role in mental conditions has become increasingly influential. Much research in this area focuses on the relationship between audiovisual integration, on the one hand, and autism spectrum disorder and schizophrenia, on the other.

9.11.2.1 Schizophrenia

Schizophrenia is a neuropsychiatric disorder characterised by a complex pattern of symptoms, including, among others, impaired affect, abnormal thoughts, paranoia, and hallucinations. The symptoms of schizophrenia often manifest themselves for the first time around early adolescence. Stone et al. (2011) have reported anomalous multisensory integration effects in ERPs that were obtained in a group of patients diagnosed with schizophrenia. Their (AV – [A + V]) effects were much more pronounced compared to neurotypical control participants. Ross et al. (2007) found similar results for audiovisual speech perception. Here, schizophrenia patients were impaired at discriminating ambiguous phonemes on the basis of visual lip movements than neurotypical control participants.

9.11.2.2 Autism

Autism, also known as autism spectrum disorder (ASD), is a neuropsychiatric disorder which often manifests itself during early childhood. It is characterised by difficulties in social communication and restrictive (repetitive) behavioural patterns and limited interests and activities. Russo et al. (2010) presented auditory (A) and tactile (T) stimuli (simple tones and tactile vibrations) while participants watched a silent movie. Multisensory (AT) stimuli consisted of the simultaneous presentation of the auditory and tactile stimuli. In the ERPs of children with ASD, multisensory integration effects [AT – (A + T)] were found to be smaller than those of neurotypical controls. Children with autism are also frequently characterised by abnormal processing of temporal information from audiovisual stimuli. For example, using a temporal order judgement task, Kwakye, Foss-Feig, Cascio, Stone, and Wallace (2011) found that children with ASD could integrate auditory and visual inputs across a greater time window than normally developing children could. This is consistent with findings from other studies (Foss-Feig et al., 2010). Brandwein et al. (2013) found that children with ASD are impaired in processing audiovisual stimuli compared to neurotypical control children. Taken together, these results suggest

abnormal development of multisensory processing in individuals with these conditions.

Both Schnitzler and Gross (2005) and Uhlhaas and Singer (2006) hypothesise that the disrupted multisensory integration processes along with the symptoms of autism and schizophrenia are markers of an underlying neural deficit. More specifically they suggest that natural electrical oscillations in the brain are disrupted. Presumably, these oscillations are involved in the formation of associations, and disruptions in that process can result in the formation of incorrect associations. More recent theories hypothesise that the symptoms of autism and schizophrenia can be explained by disruptions in the predictive models in our brains or by a disruption in the processing of the prediction errors (see Chapter 24 for more details on this). One implication for multisensory integration is that disruptions in these mechanisms could result in excessive under or over integration of multisensory information. More research in this area is still needed, however.

9.12 SUMMARY

The study of multisensory processing aims to explain how our different senses interact with each other. In everyday life, we process information from different senses almost completely automatically, and the integration of these information streams is largely unconscious. In our natural environment, the information provided by the different senses is typically congruent, but when this is not the case, we may notice these discrepancies.

Historically, the different sensory systems, or sensory modalities, have been studied independently of each other, giving rise to the incorrect idea that they also largely operate independently of each other. Moreover, it has given rise to the suggestion that the integration of multisensory input occurs late in the processing stream. Originally, it was believed that multisensory interactions occurred in the association areas of the cortex, based on inputs from the sensory cortices.

Since the turn of the century, neuroimaging and electrophysiological studies have substantially contributed to our understanding of the neural basis of these multisensory interactions. Animal studies have found evidence for the involvement of the superior colliculus in multisensory integration processes. Neurons in this brain region respond more strongly to audiovisual inputs than to visual or auditory inputs, when the auditory and visual components of such a stimulus meet a number of specific conditions. These properties are defined by the spatial and temporal proximity principle and by the law of inverse effectiveness.

In addition, ERP and neuroimaging studies have identified a large number of cortical brain areas to be involved in

multisensory processing. The primary sensory cortices receive direct input from other sensory systems. In addition, the supratemporal sulcus plays a role in the detection of multisensory congruence. Parietal brain areas are involved in the formation of a multisensory cognitive map of our environment. Finally, the prefrontal cortex is involved in the formation of multisensory associations and the processing of higher-order properties of a multisensory stimulus.

Discrepancies between auditory and visual inputs can result in audiovisual illusions. The McGurk effect is an illusion in which a discrepancy between a heard phoneme and a lip movement results in hearing an entirely different phoneme altogether. Our sensitivity to the McGurk effect depends on which phonemes are used. In addition, there are strong individual differences in our sensitivity to the illusion. The ventriloquist illusion consists of mis-locating a sound, based on conflicting visual input. The illusion reflects altered processing in the auditory cortex.

Many studies on multisensory integration employ a temporal order judgement task or a simultaneity judgement task. In both types of tasks, a visual and an auditory stimulus are presented in quick succession, and participants are instructed either to decide which of these two stimuli was presented first, or whether or not the two stimuli were presented simultaneously. Based on these tasks, it has been established that there is also a temporal ventriloquist effect, in which the timing of a visual stimulus is affected by the presence of an auditory stimulus. The additional flash illusion is another example of how our visual perception can be altered by an auditory stimulus. Finally, the bounce-pass illusion occurs when two visual stimuli cross each other's path while a sound is played at the moment they overlap each other. Now a strong illusion arises that the two stimuli collide and bounce back in opposite directions.

Synaesthesia is the phenomenon that some individuals form strong associations between the sensory modalities. The best-known example of this is grapheme-colour synaesthesia, in which letters are associated with specific colours. The experience of perceiving a colour when a letter is presented is accompanied by an increased activation of the visual cortex. Synaesthetes are characterised by stronger connections between different brain regions.

Computational models attempt to explain multisensory integration processes based on the principles of Bayesian inference. These models can explain the basic principles of multisensory integration by assuming that information with a higher precision is more strongly weighted in the integration process.

The detection of semantic congruence involves semantic memory. This implies that modality-specific representations of concepts are stored in our semantic memory. Ursino's auto-associative model was developed to explain how these representations are stored. The model explains how the individual sensory properties of a concept can converge into an abstract representation. Some features of multisensory integration are top-down driven. The modality appropriateness hypothesis describes how the information with the highest precision weighs most heavily in the integration, while the assumption of unity describes how our prior conviction that two inputs have a common origin influences the integration process.

Exposure to asynchronous auditory and visual input results in a recalibration of the audiovisual integration mechanism. Consequently, asynchronous stimuli are better integrated after a period of exposure than synchronous stimuli. Although it was initially believed that recalibration was a slow process, recent studies have found evidence for a rapid recalibration process, which can occur after just one trial. A specific synthetic form of speech is particularly suitable for the study of multisensory

phenomena. Sine wave speech is initially unintelligible as speech to untrained participants, but after they are informed that it is a speech signal, they will recognise it as such. Participants who are put into speech mode integrate these sine wave speech signals with visual cues in a way that participants who are not put into speech mode do not.

The orienting of selective attention does not appear to be limited to one specific sensory modality. The expectation that a visual stimulus will appear in a specific location also makes us more sensitive to the processing of an auditory stimulus at that location and vice versa. When visual and auditory inputs are part of a single audiovisual object, visual selective attention can also influence the further processing of the auditory input. Evidence for these attention effects has been obtained on the basis of behavioural and electrophysiological studies.

The answer to the question of whether attention plays a role in multisensory integration is complex and multifaceted. Although initially evidence against a role of attention in multisensory integration was found, more recently more and more evidence is becoming available showing that there are interactions between attention and multisensory integration. On the one hand, attention appears to be able to affect the integration processes, but on the other hand, multisensory integration also appears to affect attention. This apparent paradox can be resolved by considering the salience and uniqueness of the individual inputs.

The complex interactions associated with the integration of audiovisual percepts can possibly be explained by the predictive coding framework, in which hierarchically organised concepts generate predictions for the expected input in our individual modalities. This idea is consistent with the idea that multisensory integration does not appear to be innate but that it develops through experience that continues to accumulate throughout the life course. Abnormalities in these developments appear to be strongly related to specific mental disorders, including autism and schizophrenia. Disruptions in the neural oscillations involved in the integration of multisensory information may underlie both the abnormalities in the integration process and (part of) the symptoms of autism and schizophrenia.

NOTES

1 As we will discuss further on in this chapter, we are inclined to observe time differences between auditory and visual stimuli that are on the order of 250–350 ms as simultaneous. Since the speed of sound is about 300 metres per second, which corresponds to a distance of less than 100 metres!

2 If you appreciate the Disney movie 'The Lion King', you may notice that the names of the skinny meerkat 'Timon' and the chubby warthog 'Pumbaa' are consistent with this association.

FURTHER READING

Ho, C. & Spence, C. (2017). *The multisensory driver: Implications for ergonomic car interface design.* Hove, UK: Taylor & Francis Group.

Murray, M. M., & Wallace, M. T. (2011). *The neural bases of multisensory processes.* Hove, UK: Taylor, and Francis Group.

Stein B. E. (2012). *The new handbook of multisensory processing.* Cambridge, MA: MIT Press.

Stokes, D., Matthen, M., & Biggs, S. (2014). *Perception and its modalities.* Oxford, UK: Oxford University Press.

CHAPTER 10
Perception-action integration

10.1 INTRODUCTION

Imagine playing a game of frisbee on a beautiful summer's day at the beach. While your feet try to keep their grip in the loose rough sand, you keep a close eye on your partner who is busy throwing the frisbee at you with a graceful swing. As it spins towards you, your need to take a few steps to the side to catch it. Halfway, a sudden gust of wind causes the frisbee to change its course and you quickly have to take a few extra steps to enable you to catch it. This movement brings you dangerously close to a few other guests at the beach. Therefore, you must quickly make some extra adjustments to ensure that you do not end up on one of their towels. After you catch the frisbee, you look for your partner and you gracefully throw it back in her direction.

This simple example illustrates some key aspects of the theme of this chapter, namely how we can generate action plans on the fly, based on sensory input and, when necessary, flexibly adjust them. A simple task such as catching a frisbee requires the online processing of visual input, so that we can generate action plans and adjust them when the circumstances require it. To do this adequately, we must be able to perceive motion and use the motion information to estimate future outcomes; for instance, we must determine when the frisbee will contact our hands.

In addition, we must continuously update the representation of our body and its position in our environment. Here, head movements and information coming from the vestibular system plays an important role (Taube, 2007). The successful completion of an action also depends on integrating this representation into our action plan. Finally, after catching the frisbee, we need to throw it back again. Performing this deceivingly simple action requires us to estimate the distance and direction of our throw. We need to consider the weight and aerodynamic properties of the frisbee, and, based on this, we must exert a very precisely determined force. We convert these estimates into a very complex combination of motor commands to our individual muscles. While we are doing all of this, we have to process the tactile feedback signals from our feet and use

this to estimate the properties of the rough sand we stand on. Ultimately, these estimates allow us to exert just the right amount force to move in it, without tipping over.

10.2 DIRECT PERCEPTION

As already discussed in Chapters 3 and 6, there is a strong relation between our visual and our motor systems. This relation was already implied in 1909 by the Hungarian neurologist Rudolf Bálint, when he described a patient with bilateral damage to the parietal lobes. When shown objects, this patient had specific difficulties pointing at them or grabbing them. On the other hand, he had no trouble touching parts of his own body after they had been touched by the researcher. Based on these findings, Bálint concluded that this patient had a specific problem with his visuomotor skills, that is, with the integration of visual information into an action plan.

A second important development in the study of the perception and action integration took place during World War II and was driven by the American psychologist and vision scientist James Gibson. Gibson's ideas were ignored for a long time, however. Until about the mid-1990s, the dominant idea was that visual perception is mainly involved in object recognition. In contrast, Gibson proposed that the major function of visual perception is that it allows us to navigate through the external world (Gibson, 1950). Recognising objects requires a lot of cognitive processing power, as we have already discussed in detail in Chapter 6. Gibson argued that object recognition is only of limited use for our interactions with the outside world. Instead, Gibson believed that our visual system has evolved by and large because it allows us to respond quickly and flexibly to our ever-changing and occasionally unpredictable environment. Gibson proposed a **direct perception theory**, which bears some similarities to Goodale and Milner's (1992) vision-for-action system (see Chapter 6). Gibson considered his theory to be an ecological theory, in the sense that it emphasised the interaction between an individual and their environment. He hypothesised that visual information was processed 'directly', in the sense

DOI: 10.4324/9781003319344-14

that the relationship between light patterns and actions was not mediated by retinal, neural, or mental images. The information packed in the beam of light that reaches the eye would be directly converted into actions, according to Gibson. This process was described by Gibson as the pick-up of information.

Gibson's direct perception theory is based on the assumption that light that falls on our eyes contains all the information that we require to move through our environment. Gibson defined this pattern of light as an **optical array**. According to Gibson, this optical array would contain unambiguous information about the layout of different objects. The information encoded in the optical array would consist of textures and optical flow patterns, along with information about how objects could be used (an aspect of visual processing that was defined by Gibson as an affordance).

10.2.1 OPTICAL FLOW

The roots of Gibson's (1950) seminal work can be traced back to the time when Gibson was the director of the American training institute for fighter pilots, during the Second World War. In this capacity, he was developing tests for prospective pilots. As such, he became interested in the question of which visual cues pilots use while performing manoeuvres, particularly during take-off and landing. One of the main factors Gibson identified is the optical flow field (see fig 10.1). An optical flow field is formed by the changes in the pattern of light that we perceive due to motion in our visual environment. Suppose we observe the landing of an aircraft from the cockpit.[1] What we observe is that the point that we are moving towards, the beginning of the runway, does not appear to move, while the remainder of the visual environment appears to move away from this **expansion point**. The expansion point is therefore one of the invariant properties of the optical array. The greater the distance of an object from this expansion point, the faster it appears to move away from

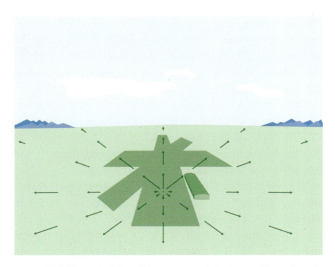

Figure 10.1 The optical flow field as proposed by James Gibson. (source: Gibson, 1950)

it. Wang, Fukuchi, Koch, and Tsuchiya (2012) showed that attention can be captured by the expansion point, suggesting that it is indeed a critical point for the processing of motion.

10.2.2 AFFORDANCES

A second important invariant is formed by the potential usability of objects. Gibson hypothesised that we can directly observe the possible ways in which an object can be used, an aspect of visual processing that Gibson described using the term **affordance**. Affordances are, in other words, usage properties that an object allows or disallows. For example, a ladder allows you to climb on it, a hammer allows you to hit something, and a chair allows you to sit on it. Gibson hypothesised that affordances are encoded as possible actions. Importantly, Gibson argued that these possible actions are encoded by the environment, instead of being represented in our minds. It should be noted, however, that affordances do not cause behaviour, in the sense that the mere presence of an object triggers a mindless action; they simply allow behaviour (Withagen, de Poel, Araújo, & Pepping, 2012). Moreover, each object can be associated with multiple affordances, with each of them selectively influencing our behaviour, depending on our mood. For example, a tomato may have the affordance of edibleness when we are hungry, but it may get the affordance of a projectile when we're angry.

Gibson himself did not attempt to identify which processes were involved in determining what types of uses an object affords. He simply stated that the perceptual system is capable of learning. After practice, Gibson argued, it can be expected that an individual is better able to orient, to listen, and to perceive. Despite this lack of specification, the idea of affordances has gained a lot of support. For example, Pappas and Mack (2008) used subliminally presented photographs of objects so that they would not gain access to conscious awareness. Still, the objects were able to prime the motor programmes that were associated with the object's typical uses. This result thus suggests that the potential usages of an object are automatically activated when it is observed.

Wilf, Holmes, Schwartz, and Makin (2013) also found that affordances are triggered automatically. They presented photographs of either a graspable object (e.g., a lollipop) or of an ungraspable object (e.g., a road sign) that was similar in shape to the graspable object (see fig 10.2). Participants were instructed to lift their hands from a platform and make a reaching movement with their arms, as soon that the photo appeared. Wilf et al. found that when a graspable object was shown, participants started this reach movement earlier than when a non-graspable object was shown. From these results, they concluded that the affordance of graspability can facilitate a rapid activation of the motor system.

Since Gibson's pioneering work, other theorists have also incorporated the affordance concept into their work. For example, Barsalou (2009) developed a simulation framework

Non-graspable	Graspable	Non-graspable	Graspable

Figure 10.2 Examples of images of graspable and non-graspable objects. (source: Wilf et al., 2013)

In addition, Gibson was one of the first to emphasise the crucial importance of motion perception. As such, he was very influential in emphasising the importance of a vision-for-action system. How important this concept actually was, was recognised only years later, on the basis of, among others, Goodale and Milner's (1992) work.

Despite these successes, however, Gibson's work is also marked by some limitations. For instance, Gibson himself made no attempt to identify the underlying mechanisms of his model. In a way, Gibson's ideas were also, in many ways, too simple. Subsequent research has shown that key aspects of motion perception are much more complex than Gibson originally believed. A further limitation is the abolishment of internal mental processes, since it has turned out to be impossible to reduce object recognition processes to the analysis of a set of invariant visual properties. In everyday life, visual scenes are far too complex for that. Recent ideas about object recognition therefore acknowledge the ever important influence of top-down processing and internal representations (Lupyan & Ward, 2013). Finally, Gibson assumed a very simple relationship between perception and motion. As we will discuss next, however, in reality many more sources of information contribute to our interaction with the external world than Gibson originally assumed.

to explain how the motor system is activated when we try to understand the meaning of a concept. Indeed, more and more evidence is accumulating to show that concepts are represented hierarchically in **semantic memory** (see also Chapter 9 for a brief introduction of this idea, and Chapter 13 for a further elaboration). According to Barsalou, semantic memory not only stores the abstract meaning of a concept but also its practical properties, such as the associated motor actions, along with the verbal, visual, auditory, and other sensory representations of the concept (Mayberry, Sage, & Lambon Ralph, 2011; Pobric, Jefferies, & Lambon Ralph, 2010a, 2010b). This new vision of semantic memory, which we will discuss in more detail in Chapter 13, may explain why not only the perception of an object itself can trigger an affordance, but also a verbal description of that object.

10.2.3 EVALUATION

Despite the fact that it was slow to take off, Gibson's ecological approach can be considered to be a particularly successful theoretical framework. Although Gibson himself did not specify the underlying mechanisms that bring about the relationship between perception and action, he has successfully identified several key aspects of our visual system and outlined their involvement in action plans. One of the important developments was that Gibson emphasised the importance of natural scenes as visual stimulus material.

10.3 MOTION DETECTION

Gibson's work on motion perception was seminal in that it argued for a direct connection between perception and action, a connection that essentially bypassed the higher-order object recognition mechanisms of the brain. The limitations of his work, however, stemmed largely from the fact that Gibson did not have the ability to determine how motion information is encoded in the visual system. One discipline that has contributed significantly to our understanding of motion detection is psychophysics. Nakayama (1985) and Burr and Thompson (2011) give a comprehensive overview of the research on motion detection that has been carried out in this discipline. By the early 1980s, the first evidence showing that a brain area in the mid-temporal gyrus (MT) played an important role in the perception of movement became available (Albright, 1984; Albright, Desimone, & Gross, 1984; Zeki, 1980). This work was consistent with the previously described case study of a female patient, LM, by Zihl et al. (1983), who had been diagnosed with motion blindness (**akinetopsia**) due to bilateral damage in the MT area (see Chapter 6).

It was, among others, these findings that paved the way to propose the existence of a separate visual system that is involved in the detection of motion. Rudiments of this idea can also be found in the previously discussed distinction between the parvocellular and magnocellular pathways, along with the closely related distinction between a dorsal and a ventral stream (see Chapter 6). Research into motion perception also came to full fruition due to the availability

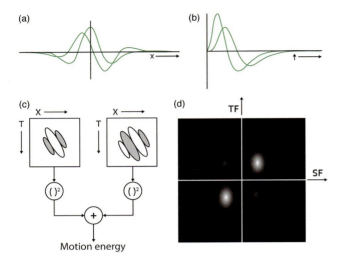

Figure 10.3 Schematic representation of a motion detector. Contrasting different spatial (a) and temporal frequencies (b) results in an estimation of kinetic energy (c). The different components of the resulting motion vectors can be displayed in a two-dimensional heat map representing the motion components (d). (source: Burr and Thompson, 2011)

of affordable personal computers in the 1980s, which made it a lot easier to animate stimuli. Against this backdrop, the year 1985 marked a turning point, as the big questions concerning motion detection could finally be addressed. How is directionality coded? How sensitive are the motion detectors of our visual system? How is speed coded?

One of the initial findings from the resulting research programmes was that motion parameters can be relatively easily retrieved by decomposing a frame into a series of spatial frequencies (see Chapter 6 for more details on spatial frequencies), after which the results of this analysis

are compared across different frames. The result of this comparison is a direction vector (fig 10.3).

10.3.1 ILLUSORY MOTION

Before reading any further, take a quick look at Figure 10.4. What do you observe? Why do we experience motion when inspecting this figure? Different explanations are possible for this phenomenon. According to Weiss, Simoncelli, and Adelson (2002), illusory motion results because the visual system attempts to determine the speed of visual objects. Weiss et al.'s model assumes that temporary changes in the stimulus' intensity may occur due to motion being detected in parts of the image. Consider for example filming a tree. Here the motion of the leaves in the wind would result in a continuous change in the intensity of the pixels that correspond to those leaves.

In addition to these actual changes, however, our perception of a scene is also affected by noise. Weiss et al.'s model assumes that speed estimates are made on the basis of the observed changes in intensity. This would be accomplished through a predictive Bayesian inference process (see Appendix). Here, the motion estimation process is not only influenced by the actual input but also by the noise. The subjective perception of motion is thus based on the combination of an a priori assumption of motion and the actual observation of change. The resulting a posteriori probability distribution function represents, in other words, the probability of observing motion, given both the assumption of motion and the actual observations. Weiss et al. found that their model was able to explain illusory motion under many experimental conditions. One of their experiments is illustrated in Figure 10.5: here a rhombus

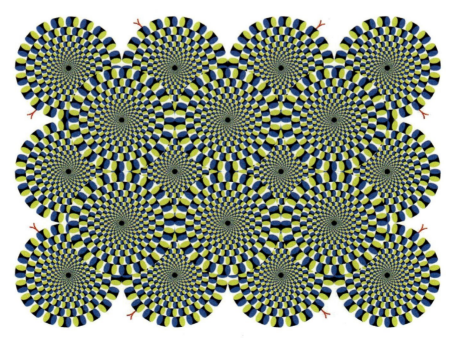

Figure 10.4 An example of a stimulus with illusory motion. (source: Fermuller, Ji, and Kitaoka, 2010)

was used as a stimulus, which slowly changed its shape from thin to thick [panels (a)–(c)], resulting in illusory motion to the right.

Fermuller et al. (2010) argue that temporal filtering is another key factor determining the perception of motion in static images such as those shown in Figure 10.4. According to Fermuller et al., eye movements contribute significantly to experiencing illusory motion. Motion is deduced by filtering the fluctuations in retinal input over time. The filtering is thus based on the currently available information and on the information that was available in the past. If our eyes remained perfectly fixated on a static image, no change would be detected, and thus no motion would be perceived. In practice, however, we always make numerous micro-saccades, resulting in imperfect

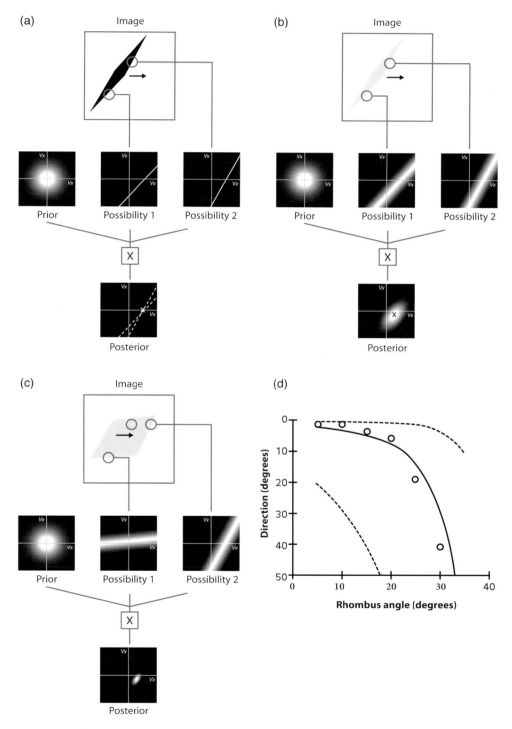

Figure 10.5 A computational model for illusory motion based on Bayesian principles. (a–c) Description of the posterior probability distribution for a motion vector describing a rhombus that (a) moves to the right, (b–c) changes shape. (d) Empirical results for the subjectively experienced direction of motion as reported by one representative participant for a deforming rhombus. (source: Weiss et al., 2002)

fixations and constantly changing input on the retina. For specific spatial frequencies, these microscopic changes in eye position can interfere with the motion detection mechanisms, causing the subjective impression of motion that in reality is not there.

10.3.2 BIOLOGICAL MOTION

In 1973, the Swedish psychophysicist Gunnar Johansson reported the results of a study that showed how humans are particularly sensitive to a very specific type of motion. To show this, Johansson (1973) made use of the point light method. A research assistant was equipped with a series of lights that were placed at strategic locations on the body (see fig 10.6). Next, the assistant performed several movements that were filmed in complete darkness. Johansson found that observers were able to recognise most of these movements using as few as six points of light. Later studies showed that exposing participants to fragments of biological motion lasting only 200 ms, was already enough to distinguish specific types of human motion (Johansson, von Hofsten, & Jansson, 1980). The fact that complex human motion can be processed this rapidly on the basis of very limited amounts of information implies that human

biological motion can be detected much more efficiently than other types of motion.

What is so special about recognising biological motion that we are so good at it? Much evidence supports the conclusion that we are better at detecting biological motion than at detecting other forms of motion. Moreover, we are also better at detecting human motion than at detecting biological motion that corresponds to movements typical to other animal species (Shiffrar & Thomas, 2013). One possibility is that we often interact with other humans in our daily lives, making the recognition of biological motion particularly effective. There might be at least two reasons for this. The first is that biological motion is the only type of motion that we can actually execute ourselves. Based on data collected in a group of patients with Asperger's syndrome, Price, Shiffrar, and Kerns (2012) found evidence for a relationship between motor skill and the ability to recognise biological motion. Asperger's syndrome is often characterised by significant problems with social communication and with motion skills. The fact that we can produce biological motion ourselves could therefore also be a reason that we can also recognise this type of motion in others.

A second reason is that in everyday life we often need to determine the intentions of others. One of the processes we use for this is **mind reading**. As we will discuss in more detail in Chapter 23, mind reading involves assessing another person's intentions and/or emotional states based on their expressions. Consistent with the hypothesis that the ability to recognise biological motion plays a major role in this process, Atkinson, Dittrich, Gemmell, and Young (2004) found that human observers were very well capable of deducing emotions from point light displays. Their participants were specifically capable of recognising fear, sadness, and happiness. Further evidence for the involvement of social factors stems from individuals diagnosed with autism spectrum disorder. These individuals often have a specific deficit in their ability to detect biological motion, while their ability to recognise other forms of motion is typically intact.

10.4 PERCEPTION-ACTION CYCLES

10.4.1 CORTICAL HIERARCHY

In the previous chapters we have already been introduced to the hierarchical organisation of the brain. This hierarchy is characterised by another feature, which has been extensively discussed by the American neuroscientist Joaquín Fuster (2004). Fuster identified a remarkable dichotomy in the structure of our nervous system, namely the fact that the posterior structures are mainly involved in perceptual

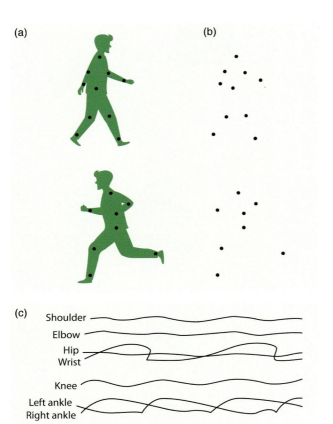

Figure 10.6 Illustration of the point light method. (a) An assistant wearing lights on the joints was filmed in a dark environment. (b) Impression of the resulting light patterns. (c) Typical motion patterns of the individual lights, while the assistant walked from left to right. (source: Johansson, 1973)

Figure 10.7 Portrait of Vladimir Betz.

functions, whereas the anterior structures are mainly involved in motor functions. This dichotomy, which was first noted by the Russian neuroanatomist Vladimir Betz[2] (1874; see fig 10.7), is the most pronounced in the spinal cord. Here, the anterior (ventral) neural bundles are formed by the efferent descending nerves that project the motor commands to the body, while the posterior (dorsal) bundles are formed by the afferent ascending nerve fibres that project the somatosensory signals to the brain (see Chapter 2).

For the cerebral cortex, we can – with a little stretch of the imagination – make a similar distinction. The distinction holds when we include the mental representations that are obtained through the senses as 'sensory' representations, and when we can classify the executive task sets as 'motor representations'. This way, the executive areas in the prefrontal cortex will also become part of this hierarchical organisation. Adding to this idea, we now have an overwhelming amount of evidence suggesting that the executive areas in the lateral part of the frontal cortex are hierarchically organised. The motor cortex and the premotor areas constitute the lowest level of this hierarchy. The more anterior part of the prefrontal cortex contains a large number of areas that represent progressively more complex and more abstract aspects of an action (Fuster, 2004).

Evidence for such a hierarchical organisation was found by Koechlin, Ody, and Kouneiher (2003a). These authors instructed participants to respond to visual stimuli of varying complexity. The response to each stimulus depended on two factors: the physical stimulus properties and the instructions participants were given. Prior to the presentation of a stimulus, a cue gave specific instructions on how to respond to it. Koechlin et al. were interested in to what extent the cues providing the instruction would activate the anterior (caudal) and posterior (rostral) prefrontal cortices and the premotor cortex. They found that the posterior prefrontal cortex is primarily involved in processing the cues, whereas the anterior prefrontal cortex is mainly

involved in processing the context in which the cue was presented. Finally, Koechlin et al. reproted that the premotor cortex is involved in processing the stimulus itself.

According to Fuster (2004), the organisation of the prefrontal cortex is best understood by assuming that the frontal areas are part of a representational map to which all cortical areas contribute (see fig 10.8). This representational map describes how neural networks are distributed across the cortex, with each of those networks representing very specific forms of knowledge. The knowledge represented in these networks is acquired through life-long experience and stored in long-term memory (see Chapter 13). According to Fuster, the representational map plays a major role in the emergence of **perception-action cycles**. The perception-action cycle represents a circular stream of information from the environment to the sensory areas and from there via the motor areas back to the environment, from where it flows back to the sensory areas.

According to this view, memory traces are formed from the primary cortical areas and stored along progressively higher areas in the hierarchy. Here, the primary sensory regions form the lowest levels in this hierarchy, where our primary perceptual experiences are represented. The more complex aspects of a memory are captured in the higher association areas of the cortex. It is believed that the hippocampus and the amygdala play an important role in consolidating these memories, although the mechanisms behind this are still not fully understood.

Similar to how our perceptual memories accumulate in the posterior parts of the cortex, so, according to Fuster (2004), do the executive memory traces in the anterior parts of the cortex. Here we can also distinguish a hierarchy involving the basic primary cortices and the higher order association areas. According to this scheme, the motor cortex generates and integrates the motor commands that are initiated by the higher areas, such as the speech production centres of the brain. These higher levels also involve the premotor cortex, which represents the movements defined by the current goal of an action and the intended trajectory of a movement. The highest levels, finally, are represented by the nuclei of the prefrontal cortex, which represent the more complex schemes and plans for a goal-directed action.

10.4.2 PERCEPTION-ACTION CYCLES

For any kind of adaptive behaviour, we are required to process a continuous flow of perceptual information and to translate this into a stream of actions. The effects of actions require new visual inputs, creating a continuous cycle of perceptual and action signals. This continuous flow of information is believed to occur at all levels of the hierarchy (Fuster, 2004): simple actions require direct feedback

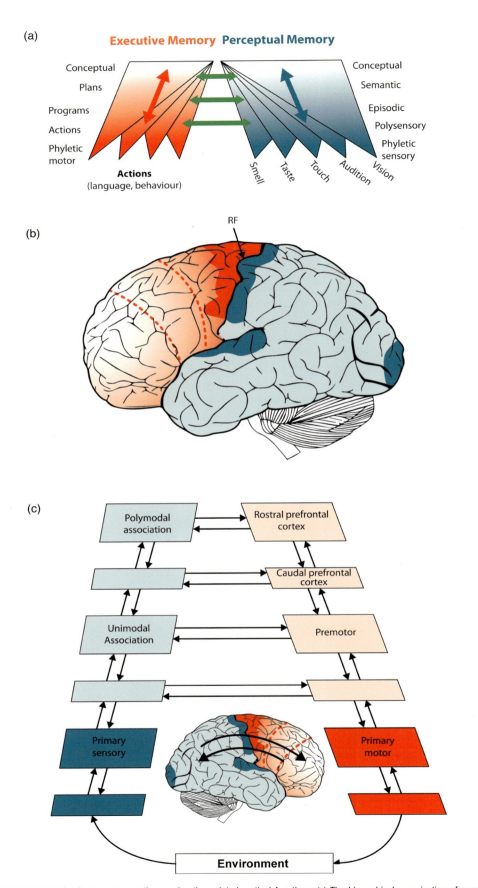

Figure 10.8 The hierarchical distinction between perception- and action-related cortical functions. (a) The hierarchical organisation of executive and perceptual memory and its relation to motor and perceptual systems. (b) Anterior brain regions are mainly associated with executive processes, and posterior brain regions with perceptual processes. (c) The continuous interaction between the executive and perceptual areas gives rise to perception-action cycles. (source: Fuster, 2004)

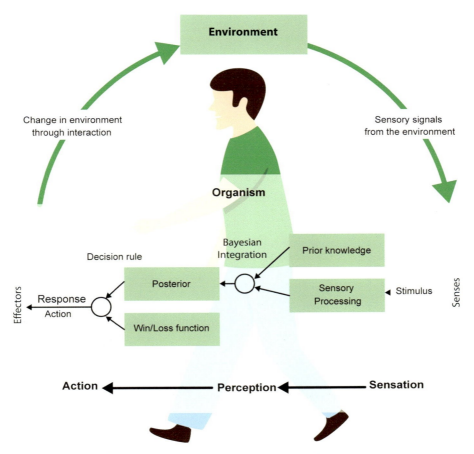

Figure 10.9 A perception-action cycle based on Bayesian principles. (source: Ernst and Bülthoff, 2004)

based on basic perceptual signals, and more complex, goal-directed actions require feedback from more complex representations, including previous experiences and memories. These complex representations can then influence the motor representations in the anterior parts of the brain.

Ernst and Bülthoff (2004) argue that the perception-action cycles just described are consistent with a Bayesian (predictive coding) framework. According to these authors, our background knowledge (i.e., the 'memory traces' in Fuster's, 2004, model, described earlier) forms a Bayesian prior, which can be combined with the actual sensory input, to form an a posteriori presentation. The latter can be combined with a gain/loss function that influences a decision rule, to select a motor action (see fig 10.9). The involvement of the latter function implies that our actions are not only controlled by sensory input but also by emotional and motivational processes, as we will discuss in the next two chapters.

10.5 VISUALLY GUIDED ACTION

As already illustrated in the first part of this chapter, our visual system has a very important function; it allows us to integrate the constantly changing flow of visual impressions into our actions. Even simple actions, such as taking a walk or grabbing a coffee cup, employ our visual system to guide our actions. How can we do this?

10.5.1 VISUOMOTOR INTEGRATION

As already discussed, Gibson (1950) identified our ability to perceive motion as one of the crucial properties of the visual system. It is also crucial in perception-action integration, since motion represents the temporal flow of information, thus allowing us to anticipate changes in our environment. For this reason, Gibson identified motion perception as a crucial prerequisite for performing an action. This idea is consistent with the vision-for-action system that we introduced in Chapter 6 (Goodale & Milner, 1992, 2006; Milner & Goodale, 2008). According to Milner and Goodale, the vision-for-action system is primarily associated with the magnocellular pathway, which is predominantly driven by the light-sensitive rods, and mainly projects to the dorsal pathway. This dorsal pathway projects to the posterior parietal cortex, a brain region that supposedly represents a cognitive map of our immediate environment (Tolman, 1948) that is continuously updated on the basis of visual information. As discussed in Chapter 9, subsequent studies have also found evidence suggesting that the spatial maps can be updated on the basis of other sensory information (Ghazanfar & Schroeder, 2006).

Evidence that the posterior parietal cortex is involved in visually guided actions was found by Van der Werf, Jensen, Fries, and Medendorp (2010). They recorded MEG activity while participants were preparing either to reach to a specific location or look at that location. When they prepared to reach, this resulted in an increase in synchronised high-frequency activity in the medial posterior parietal cortex. Preparing a saccadic eye movement resulted in a similar increase in activity, but now in a slightly lower frequency band, in the more central parts of the posterior parietal cortex. These results imply that different modules in the parietal cortex are involved in the planning of the different effector systems (eyes, hands).

The results from the Van der Werf et al. (2010) study are consistent with those from earlier studies implying that neurons in the parietal cortex are involved in the integration of visuomotor information. For instance, Mountcastle and colleagues found neurons in the parietal cortex that they initially had difficulties with classifying (see Chapter 6). However, these were later found to encode how our motor system can manipulate objects (Taira et al., 1990). Medendorp, Goltz, Crawford, and Vilis (2005) found further evidence for the involvement of the posterior parietal cortex in visuo-motor integration. Their fMRI results showed an increased activation in posterior parietal cortex nuclei while participants either had to make an eye movement to a specific target location or to point to this target location with their hands.

Wolpert et al. (1995) argue that the integration of sensory and motor information is based on an internal forward model. This forward model is similar to the internal simulations (Davidson & Wolpert, 2005) or body models (Brecht, 2017) that we discussed in Chapters 3 and 8 in the context of the planning of movements and the simulation of bodily functions. These forward models are formed not only on the basis of an efference copy of the motor commands but also on the basis of visual information and proprioceptive information.

To illustrate how these models operate, let us start with the simplest scenario possible: suppose we move one of our arms, without having access to any visual information about this motion. Next, we can conceive three possible scenarios for getting information about the current status (i.e., the position and speed) of our arm. First, we can use information from our proprioceptive senses; second, we can use the integrated motor output, that is, the set of motor commands that has been projected to the muscles; and finally we can use a combination of the two.

Wolpert et al. tested which of these scenarios is most plausible, by requiring their participants to move their arm twice, while they were in a completely dark environment. These movements had to be performed under three different conditions: once with a cooperating external force, once with an opposing external force, and once without assistance. The internal representation of the movement was estimated by asking participants to estimate the position of their arm after the movement. Wolpert et al. found that participants systematically overestimated the distance their arm had moved. This overestimation increased under the influence of the cooperating external force, and it decreased under the influence of the opposing force. The latter result implies that the forward internal model of the hand is not generated solely on the basis of the motor output. Interestingly, however, Wolpert et al. found that the overestimation was not constant, but that it fluctuated as a function of the distance the arm had travelled. These fluctuations could be best explained by a model in which the information of the motor output and the proprioceptive sensory input is combined, that is, when they were integrated.

10.5.2 OPTIMAL FEEDBACK CONTROL

In Chapter 3, we introduced the optimal feedback control mechanism for motor control (Scott, 2004). This model describes how movements can be updated through continuous sensory feedback. This feedback includes not only visual information but also sensory feedback from the skin, muscles, and joints. The optimal feedback control mechanism uses these signals to make small online adjustments to the required muscle strength. The model thus assumes the use of an inverse model. Inverse models are involved in situations which require us to adjust our grip, for example, when holding objects. These grip adjustments occur in response to small changes in the tactile feedback provided by sensory input from the fingertips. According to the model, these feedback signals are integrated with the motor commands in the primary motor cortex.

According to the optimal feedback control mechanism, visual information is similarly integrated into the motor commands (Saunders & Knill, 2003). In a follow-up study, Saunders and Knill (2004) investigated whether motion or position information is used as input for the feedback mechanism. Here, participants were shown a virtual version of their own finger using a mirror system (see fig 10.10), and their task was to move this virtual finger to a specific target location. At the start of the movement, the position and speed of the virtual finger matched the participant's own finger. When the virtual finger was temporarily hidden from view, however, its position and/or direction of motion was manipulated. This was done in such a way that the participants either did or did not have to adjust their motor programme to reach the intended target. Saunders and Knill found that all perturbations resulted in corrections of the hand's trajectory, even when the perturbation resulted in a new trajectory that did not require any corrections. Based on these results, they concluded that both position and motion information is used as feedback.

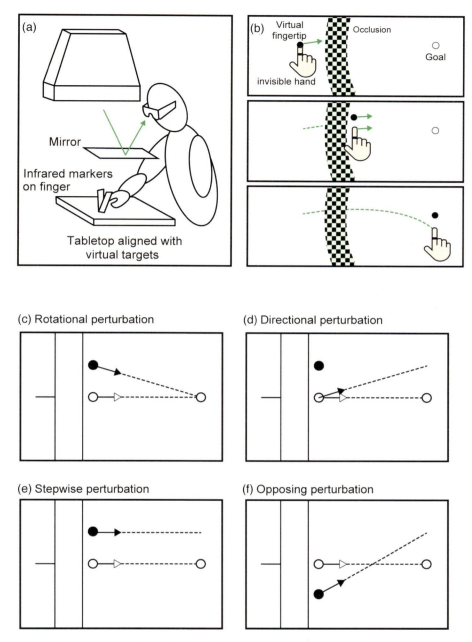

Figure 10.10 Schematic overview of an experimental method to investigate perception-action integration. (a) Participants have to perform a movement with their hand, which is hidden from view. Feedback is projected onto a mirror via a monitor. (b) Example of how the visual feedback can be perturbed. (c)–(f) Examples of the possible perturbations of the feedback. (source: Saunders and Knill, 2004)

Because there is always a certain level of imprecision in our ability to localise a visual stimulus, Körding and Wolpert (2006) argue that the sensory feedback signals are weighed using a Bayesian inference mechanism. Thus, the effectiveness of sensory feedback should also fluctuate with the precision of our observations (McGuire & Sabes, 2009). For example, playing a game of tennis would require us to estimate where the ball will land. Since our visual system does not provide perfectly reliable information about the speed of the ball, its landing point cannot be perfectly predicted either. An estimate of the noise in the visual signal will allow us to estimate the probability for different locations.

We can combine this information with the information obtained from earlier games. After all, based on previous experience, we know that the probability of the landing point is not uniformly distributed over the field, but that it shows a clear peak at the edges of the field. This distribution forms the a priori distribution (in Bayesian terms: 'the prior'). During each action, this a priori information is combined with the online estimate to determine the a posteriori probability.

Körding and Wolpert (2004) found evidence for such a Bayesian weighting mechanism by systematically manipulating the precision of the sensory feedback they gave. Participants were required to perform a reaching movement, during which the trajectory of their hand was recorded. As in the Saunders and Knill (2004) study, the participants' real arm was hidden from view, while their hand's position was marked by a cursor. This cursor became invisible as soon as the participant started moving. Moreover, the now invisible cursor was displaced somewhat. To hit the target, the participant's had to compensate for the displacement. This could be done on the basis of limited visual feedback: when the finger was halfway along the trajectory, feedback about the position of the finger was given by briefly showing the cursor. The precision of this feedback varied, however. In some trials, the cursor was displayed as a clear dot, representing the exact position of the finger, while on others it was shown as a diffuse cloud of points that represented the position of the finger only approximately. The extent to which participants used the feedback provided by the cue was best explained by a Bayesian integration mechanism that combined the a priori expectation and the accuracy of the feedback.

10.5.2.1 Motor Control and Eye Movements

Crawford, Medendorp, and Marotta (2004) review several studies that have investigated hand-eye coordination. These studies imply that eye movements are involved in selecting what is relevant in a visual scene. When performing actions based on this visual information, we thus find complex interactions between all the effector systems that are involved in this process. Both our eyes and hands must be guided on the basis of visual information. Crawford et al. (2004) conclude from their review that eye movements and other motor actions are likely to have a common neural basis, and that eye movements are initiated according to the action to be performed.

One of the fundamental problems in coordinating eye and hand movements is the fact that delays in information processing are inevitable. For example, when we want to grasp a moving target, we have to do so on the basis of the image projected on the retina. Although grasping motions can be coordinated by an internal model, the problem is how we should deal with changes in the direction of motion of the object that we want to grasp. When we start to track the object, visual information processing is interrupted after every saccade or update of our head position, disrupting the spatial relationship between our visual system and the external world. Consequently, a new model can only be generated when our eyes are fixated on a new location. Updating an internal model would therefore be so slow that we would only be able to grasp very slowly moving objects by means of extremely slow movements (O'Regan & Noë, 2001).

An additional problem here is that, in many cases, saccadic eye movements cause the target of our action to be moved from the centre of our field of vision to the periphery (where we can only form a much less-detailed representation). In more extreme cases, the target may even disappear from our field of view altogether. In addition, updating an internal model after each new fixation is a particularly costly operation in terms of the transformations between the different coordinate systems that would have to be carried out after each saccade. For this reason, Duhamel, Colby, and Goldberg (1992) argued that our internal models are not continuously updated after each eye movement, but that only those representations relevant for future actions are preserved. According to Duhamel et al., this can either be in the form of a representation that is independent of eye movements, or in the form of an adaptation to an internal model.

Some theoretical models assume that the eye-hand coordination system can make egocentric and allocentric representations of the environment, depending on factors such as the sensory information available, constraints imposed by the task, the visual background, and the context in which a task is performed (Battaglia-Mayer et al., 2000; Hayhhoe, Shrivastava, Mruczek, & Pelz, 2003; Hu & Goodale, 2000). An assumption here is that for simple tasks, for example, reaching for or pointing to an object, it will suffice to use a simple egocentric, viewpoint-dependent system (McIntyre, Stratta, & Lacquaniti, 1997; Vetter, Goodbody, & Wolpert, 1999), whereas for more complex tasks, it is necessary to use an allocentric coordinate system.

Henriques, Klier, Smith, Lowy, and Crawford (1998) found evidence for this assumption by using a task in which participants were required to focus on a briefly flashing target stimulus, then turn their eyes away and point to the location of the target stimulus in the dark (see fig 10.11). If participants represented the location in a non-retinal coordinate system, it might be expected that the subsequent eye movement would have no effect on the pointing direction. If, however, this location was represented in a retinal coordinate system, we might expect that an echo of this eye movement could be found in the pointing direction. Henriques et al.'s results are consistent with the latter hypothesis: an eye movement away from the location of the target stimulus resulted in a systematic bias in the location that the participants pointed at.

The aforementioned results mainly concern the two-dimensional monocular orientation of objects. Successfully grasping or reaching for an object would require us to form a three-dimensional representation of the location of the target object (Crawford et al., 2004). To successfully

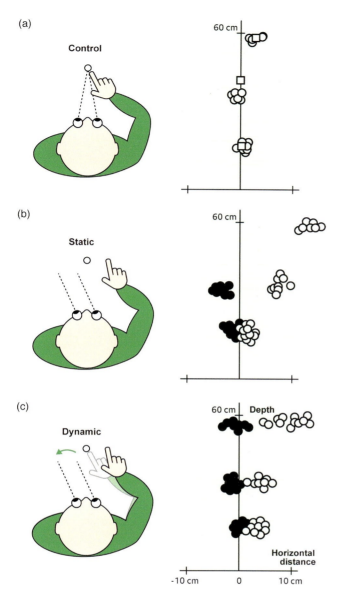

Figure 10.11 Illustration of the relation between eye moments and pointing behaviour. (a) A control condition in which participants could continue to look directly at the target they had to point at. (b) A condition in which they had to look away from the target location before pointing to it. (c) A condition in which they first had to look at the target location, then look away, and then point. The right column shows the position of the fingers in the horizontal plane. Target stimuli were presented at distances of 2 m, 42 cm, and 15 cm from the participant. Both the static (b) and dynamic (c) conditions resulted in a systematic deviation from the viewing direction. White circles represent the finger positions for a viewing direction to the left and black circles those for a viewing direction to the right. (source: Crawford et al. 2004)

create such a representation, we need to use binocular cues. Van Pelt and Medendorp (2008) noted that this is done primarily on the basis of vergence cues from the two eyes (see Chapter 6 for a discussion of depth cues).

Since we have two eyes, each at a different position in our head, we need to consider how these eyes are used as a reference point during motor planning. In case of objects located at distances at which we can manipulate

them, vergence is significant, since each eye is pointing in a slightly different direction. The classic interpretation is that the direction to an object is determined by the combination of information from both eyes. In other words, according to this interpretation, we would have a virtual cyclops eye in the middle of our heads, right between the two eyes (Ono & Barbeito, 1982; Ono, Mapp, & Howard, 2002), which would be used as a reference point. Although this idea has been disputed (Erkelens & van Ee, 2002), the idea that we normally use one central point of reference is confirmed by the analysis of errors that we make during a visually guided reaching movement. These errors are characterised by an elliptical distribution around the target object, with one of the axes of the ellipse pointing in the direction of a fixed point on the head (McIntyre et al., 1997).

10.5.2.2 Development of a Motor Plan

Just determining the three-dimensional position of a target object will not suffice for performing a reaching movement, however. To do so, we first need to integrate visual information with the hand position. It was originally believed that we could do this by transforming the retinal coordinates into a body-centred coordinate system. This would be done in two stages, by first serially combining all sensory signals and then comparing these body-centred coordinates with the coordinates of the hand (Flanders, Tillery, & Soechting, 1992; McIntyre et al., 1997). Using single cell recording techniques, Bueno, Jarvis, Batista, and Andersen (2002) found, however, that the coordinate systems would be integrated at a much earlier stage.

Bueno et al. (2002) also found evidence that, when the hand is not visible, the coordinates of the hand position are inferred on the basis of proprioceptive signals, which are then converted to a coordinate system that is based on the viewing direction. This finding implies that a reaching movement can be performed instantaneously because only the relative positions of the hand and the target object has to be considered in this coordinate system. This type of direct transformation would, in principle, be possible because translational vector operations are independent of a reference frame (see Box 10.1). In practice, however, the eyes and other body parts such as the head, mainly rotate during a reaching movement, so that, as discussed in Box 10.1, a systematic deviation should be found which depends on the coordinate system used.

10.5.2.3 Eye-Head-Shoulder Coordination

This reference problem becomes even more pronounced when we have to consider the position of our heads and shoulders. If the head, the eyes, and the shoulders were all rotated around the same point, the problem of geometrical

Box 10.1 Reference frames and transformations

Studies on perception-action integration aim to understand how visual information can be used to guide our actions. To properly understand the processes that are involved in this, it is necessary to briefly introduce a few key concepts from geometry that we need to formally define: motion and position. As discussed by Crawford, Henriques, and Medendorp (2011), position and motion can be mathematically represented as a vector. For our current purpose, we can think of a vector as a three-dimensional arrow, with a tail that coincides with the null vector (also known as the reference point) and a head that coincides with a target location. To have a meaningful reference point, it must be defined within a coordinate system. A coordinate system consists of a reference frame and a set of coordinate axes.

To describe movements, we can define the reference frame as a rigid body to which we can relate the relative position or orientation of the object of interest. In neuroscience, two different types of reference frames are commonly used, namely the egocentric and the allocentric one. Egocentric reference frames are defined relative to a specific body part, such as the retina, the eye, the head, or the torso. Allocentric reference frames, on the other hand, are defined relative to an external object. Studies on motor control often employ a relatively stable reference frame. For example, in eye movement studies, the head is frequently used as a reference frame, while the torso is frequently used as a reference frame for studying head or arm movements.

A given reference frame can then be used to define the coordinate axes. These axes are used to define the components of the vector that describe the position and motion of the body part in question. In doing so, it is important to distinguish between positions/translations on the one hand and orientations/rotations on the other, because these two aspects of motion are described by fundamentally different mathematics. More specifically, vectors defining translations and positions are additive. In other words, the order of operations does not impact their outcome. To illustrate: suppose we are in an American city, and we want to move three blocks to the north and four blocks to the east. It does not matter whether we first go north and then to the east, or whether we first go to the east and then to the north. In both cases, we end up at the same destination.

Rotations and orientations, however, are not additive. The mathematics of rotations is not linearly additive, which results in the fact that the final outcome of a series of operations can be strongly affected by the order in which the operations are applied. Again, to illustrate: if you fall flat on your face and then turn a full quarter of a circle around your own body axis, this results in a different position than when you first turn a quarter of a circle around your body axis and only then fall flat on your face. (Be careful when trying this at home!) A problem in the study of visually guided actions, however, is that almost all movements of our body parts are defined by rotations, while many internal models for perception-action integration are based on translations.

transformations would be trivial. Unfortunately, they are not. The rotation of our head results in a translation of our eyes, relative to the shoulders. Not compensating for this translation during a reaching movement should therefore result in a systematic deviation in this movement (see fig 10.12).

Henriques, Medendorp, Gielen, and Crawford (2003) found that this is indeed the case. Here, participants were required to reach a predetermined target location, while keeping their heads in different positions. They were able to perform this task accurately as long as they could keep their eyes focused on the target. When their gaze was averted from the target, however, this resulted in a systematic error that depended on the head's position.

Based on the aforementioned results, Crawford et al. (2004) assume that there are still two stages, but that the results of Bueno et al. (2002) can be explained by

assuming that the initial internal representation is formed on the basis of ocular coordinates. Then, the error that occurs due to eye and head rotations can be used to adjust

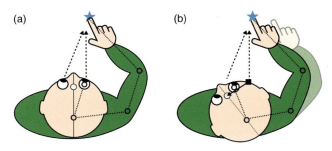

Figure 10.12 Schematic representation of the systematic error that would result from not compensating for a head movement. (a) When the head is not rotated, pointing accuracy is high. (b) Rotating the head to the left while continuing to fixate a target stimulus shifts the cyclopean eye slightly rightward and backward. Not compensating for this would result in a systematic pointing error. (source: Crawford et al., 2004)

the motor programme during both the planning and the execution of the movement.

10.5.2.4 Grasping

Most of the results discussed so far in this section concern pointing or reaching for a certain target object. But what about grasping an object? Grasping requires a complex series of motor actions and a fine analysis of the surface of the object to be grasped. In anticipation of grasping an object, we adjust our grip based on expected properties, such as size, shape, hardness of the material, and weight. An efficient grasp requires us to encode the location of the object, along with its size and position, and to efficiently convert these coordinates into a pattern of finger and wrist movements.

As discussed in earlier chapters, the parietal cortex is believed to play an important role in generating an internal spatial representation of our environment. Although it initially was believed to be mainly involved in generating a higher-order representation along with generating awareness of our environment, it increasingly appears to be the case that nuclei in the parietal cortex are also involved in generating the spatial transformations involved in grasping movements (Crawford et al., 2004; see also Taira et al., 1990, as discussed in Chapter 6). In particular, neurons in the anterior intraparietal cortex have been found to encode the size, position, shape, and orientation of graspable objects (Gallese, Murata, Kaseda, Niki, & Sakata, 1994; Taira et al., 1990). These neurons are maximally active when, under visual guidance, a grasping movement is made towards a specific object.

10.5.2.5 Interactions between Grasping and Reaching

A grasping movement appears to consist of three general components, namely the displacement, the rotation, and the opening of the hand. It is assumed that all three components rely on the same visual representation of the orientation of the object (Mamassian, 1997). Marotta, Medendorp, and Crawford (2003) found evidence for this by studying the torsion of the upper and lower arm while participants were performing a combined reaching and grasping movement. More specifically, participants were required to grasp a rectangular bar that was mounted on a wall in front of them. From trial to trial, the orientation of this bar was manipulated systematically. The hypothesis here was that if reaching and grasping movements were coordinated independently of each other, hand orientation would be mainly controlled by the upper arm. It was found, however, that both the upper and lower arm contributed to the orientation of the hand.

Various neuroimaging studies have shown that both reaching and grasping involve the parietal cortex, but that these two processes can be differentiated on the basis of the specific nuclei that are activated in this area

(see Vingerhoets, 2014, for a literature review). Reaching requires us to integrate the location of an object with our body's position, whereas grasping requires the matching of the position of our hand with the shape of the object we want to grasp. Both types of actions result in bilateral activation of the posterior parietal cortex, however, this activation is more prominent over the contralateral hemisphere. Grasping and reaching movements are essential for tool use. Tool use can be investigated by studying their actual use, by depicting their uses, or by mentally imagining the use of a tool. The dorsal and medial parietal cortices appear to be involved in the online monitoring of grasping actions, while the functional, goal-oriented use of objects appears to involve the inferior lateral parietal cortex.

10.5.2.6 A Neural Model for Perception-Action Integration

Crawford et al. (2011) provide an overview of the most important brain areas that are involved in visually guided actions (see fig 10.13). These authors make a distinction between the encoding of the goals of an action and the encoding of the sensory and motor actions themselves. In this context, task goals consist of encoding the positions of objects that we want to fixate or grasp, whereas sensory or motor encoding consists of representing the actual eye or hand position. The dissociation between the neural code of the target position from the neural code of the sensory representation of a stimulus can be investigated by using the **anti-saccade task**. In this task, the goal is to make an eye movement to a location that is opposite to that of the stimulus (Munoz & Everling, 2004). The posterior parietal cortex is selectively sensitive to the target direction in anti-saccades, and this target direction can be dissociated from the actual saccade direction.

As discussed in Chapter 6, the dorsal vision-for-action system is believed to operate on the basis of an egocentric coordinate system. Single-cell studies of the receptive fields of neurons in the posterior parietal cortex and the superior colliculus imply that this coordinate system is centred around the eye and oriented around the gaze direction (Andersen & Buneo, 2002; Colby & Goldberg, 1999). Exactly which coordinate system is used appears to depend on the specific task that is to be performed. When, for example, the target stimulus is somatosensory, the posterior parietal cortex appears to be capable of switching to a body-centred coordinate system (Bernier & Grafton, 2010).

In contrast, the ventral vision-for-perception system is assumed to operate in an allocentric coordinate system (Goodale & Milner, 1992), that is, a coordinate system that is defined with respect to an external reference frame. Moreover, it has been found that the more time is allowed for an action the more the brain makes use of such an allocentric system (Glover & Dixon, 2004;

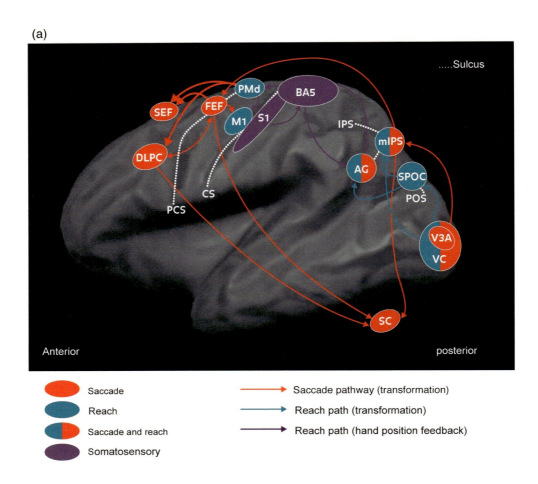

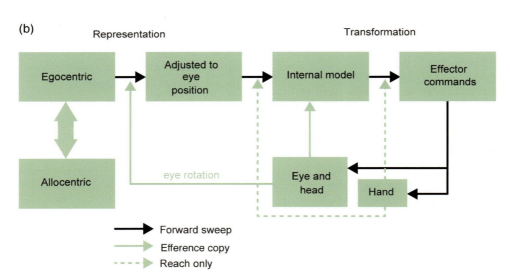

Figure 10.13 (a) An overview of the main brain regions involved in visually guided grasping and reaching movements. (b) Schematic overview of the interaction between the neural mechanisms involved in grasping and reaching. (source: Crawford et al., 2011)

Goodale & Haffenden, 1998; Obhi & Goodale, 2005), presumably because these allocentric representations are more stable. An important consequence of the difference between egocentric and allocentric coordinate systems is that a continuous transformation must take place between these systems.

Single-cell recording studies in primates have provided a growing body of evidence indicating that this transformation takes place involves a **remapping** process. Remapping is the process by which an internal forward model updates the receptive fields of each relevant neuron, after an eye movement has taken place (Duhamel et al., 1992).

In monkeys, evidence for such a remapping process has been found in almost every part of the brain that is involved in the coordination of eye movements (Crawford et al., 2011).

10.5.2.7 In Conclusion

As shown by the preceding sections, the interaction between perception and action is extremely complex. Crawford et al. (2004) have argued that some of these complex and sometimes inconsistent results can be explained by assuming that eye movements are made as a function of the goal of the action. According to this view, the oculomotor system is slaved to the motor system. Because eye movements are made as a function of a grasping or reaching movement, some of the complexity that would otherwise be required to convert three-dimensional positions from a gaze-specific coordinate system to a body-oriented system can be avoided. Conversion is, however, necessary to convert an egocentric coordinate system to an allocentric one.

Recent studies focus on determining what the exact role of the parietal cortex is in sensorimotor integration. Medendorp and Heed (2019), for instance, argue that it is involved in optimal feedback control. According to this view, this part of the brain is continuously involved in integrating sensory input with predictions of this input. These predictions would, according to Medendorp and Heed, be based on the output of internal forward models. Thus, according to this view, the forward models generate a prediction of the sensory consequences of an action. For example, when we throw a ball, the forward model of this throw will predict the visual consequences of this throw. In other words, the throw results in an estimate of the ball's trajectory, in the form of a visual representation represented in the posterior parietal cortex. This prediction is then integrated with the actual sensory input.

10.5.3 MULTISENSORY INTEGRATION

In recent decades, it has become increasingly clear how information from multiple senses is combined and used to control motor processes. To optimally execute an action, it is necessary to combine information from various sensory modalities. A number of studies have therefore found evidence for the involvement of multisensory integration processes in motor control (Crevecoeur, Munoz, & Scott, 2016; Nagy, Eordegh, Paroczy, Markus, & Benedek, 2006b; Sober & Sabes, 2003).

For example, Sober and Sabes (2003) investigated to what degree visual and proprioceptive signals contribute to the planning of a movement. In their study, participants were instructed to place their arms on a frictionless sled that was placed on a table. This allowed participants' arms to move freely in two dimensions. Then, the participants were instructed to make a movement to a specific target location (see fig 10.14), while their arm was hidden from view. Information about the hand's position was given by projecting a dot onto the table at the beginning of a trial. The position of the dot could be manipulated by projecting it either at the actual hand's position, or by projecting it 5 cm away from it. After participants initiated a movement, the dot disappeared. Sober and Sabes found that the dot was mainly used for planning the direction of movement, whereas the actual motor commands were mainly based on proprioceptive feedback. When incorrect visual feedback was given, the initial direction of movement showed a systematic bias which corresponded strongly to the initial visual information. This bias was corrected during movement, however. Sober and Sabes concluded from these results that the human motor system can switch flexibly between visual and proprioceptive information, depending on which source of information is available.

Crevecoeur et al. (2016) reached a similar conclusion using a set-up that was similar to that of Sober and Sabes (2003). Here, participants had to make an eye movement to a specific target location. This task had to be performed under three different conditions, which Crevecoeur et al. identified as the mechanical condition, the mechanical and visual condition, and the visual condition. In the mechanical condition, participants had to try to follow the position of their finger with their eyes while making an arm movement. The arm movement was disrupted by an external force that was applied to the sled. In the mechanical and visual condition, participants had to perform the same task, but now the position of the finger was marked by a visual dot that was projected on the table. Finally, in the visual condition, participants only had to follow the position of the dot without making any arm movements. The results of this study showed that while the eye movements that were based on visual information were more accurate, eye movements that were based on the mechanical feedback could be initiated much faster. The results in the mechanical and visual condition could be explained on the basis of a Bayesian combination of visual and mechanical information.

10.5.4 DIRECTION AND STEERING

The motion patterns that moving objects project onto the retina provide a rich source of information for detecting a multitude of properties of moving objects, such as the direction of motion. This information enables us to successfully navigate through our environment. The optical flow field can be decomposed into a large number of basic patterns, for example, radial, circular, translational, and shifting patterns (Helmholtz, 1858; Koenderink, 1986).

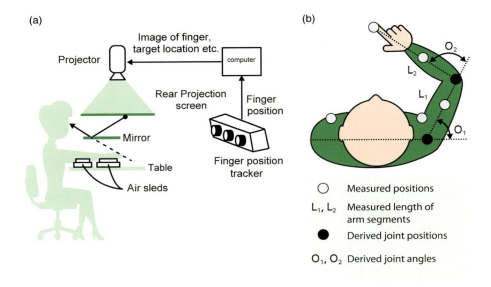

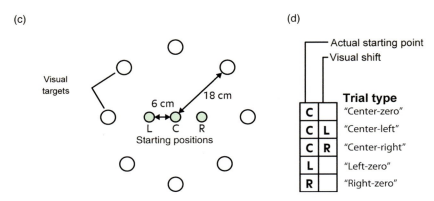

Figure 10.14 The experimental set-up used by Sober and Sabes (2003). (a) Schematic overview of the experimental set-up. (b) The main positions on the upper body that were tracked. (c) Simplified representation of the task: from one of the starting positions, participants had to move their finger to one of the target circles. (d) Schematic overview of all possible starting points: when the hand departed from the central starting position, visual feedback could be given to falsely suggest that the starting position corresponded to the left or right location. (source: Sober and Sabes, 2003)

By the early 1990s, we began to understand how these patterns contribute to our ability to determine changes in our environment, when several neurons had been identified that were selectively sensitive to specific flow patterns. Notably, these neurons were found in the medial superior temporal (MST) cortex of the macaque brain. Moreover, Britten and van Wezel (1998) reported that electrical stimulation of these neurons can bias monkeys' judgements of motion direction.

What is the influence of our own movements on determining motion direction? Warren and Hannon (1988) investigated this question by using simulated motion information. To do so, they produced two films, consisting of moving dot patterns. Both films produced the motion patterns that someone moving in a specific direction would observe. The difference between the two films, however, was that one contained a rotating optical flow component, while for the other film, participants had to produce this rotating component themselves by making

an eye movement (see fig 10.15). The same optical information was present in both conditions, yet the difference was the presence of additional extraretinal information (that is, information that is not intrinsic to the flow pattern, but added by the participants' eye movement) in the second condition. This extraretinal information did not affect the participants' ability to determine the direction of the motion pattern. The latter result implies that we can, in principle, determine directional judgements based on retinal flow information alone.

Later studies, however, do imply that extraretinal information may nevertheless affect our ability to navigate: Wilkie and Wann (2003a), for instance, showed participants animated motion patterns in scenes of fast walking, cycling, or slow driving, from the perspective of an actor. Here, participants were required to fixate on a target location that was offset from the direction of motion. The offset between target and the movies' direction motion affected participants estimates of this motion direction.

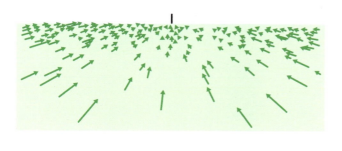

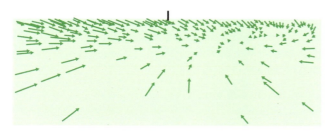

Figure 10.15 Visual impression of the visual motion patterns employed by Warren and Hannon (1988).

In a follow-up study, Wilkie and Wann (2003b) instructed participants to navigate along a computer-generated path and found that this was most accurately done when their viewing direction was not restricted.

10.5.5 THE ROLE OF MOTION INFORMATION

Gibson already assumed that the optical flow information is crucial for determining the direction of our motion. Hahn, Andersen, and Saidpour (2003), however, found that this is not necessarily the case. They presented photographs of natural scenes in fairly close succession, with the camera moving between the two shots. When these photos were shown 50 ms apart, participants perceived apparent motion, whereas this was not the case when the interval between the two photos was 500 ms. In the latter case, participants were still able to detect the direction in which the camera moved. However, the smaller the distance the camera had moved between the two successive shots, the less accurate the participants were. This was not the case for the 50 ms condition, however, where accuracy was not affected by distance.

Snyder and Bischof (2010) assumed that, when motion information is not available, we can derive directional information from the retinal displacement of objects. Objects that are closer to the direction of motion are to a lesser degree displaced than objects that are further

away from it. Although Snyder and Bischof found evidence for this assumption, they also found that retinal displacement was of limited use, particularly when following curved paths.

Taken together, these results imply that determining motion direction involves two mechanisms: the extraction of motion information when it is available and the use of other cues when it is unavailable.

The previous results are limited to the rather simple situation where we have to assess motion direction along a straight path. Wilkie and Wann (2006) argue that these assessments are of limited use when we have to move along a curved path. According to Wilkie and Wann, path determination, that is, identifying future points along the path, is much more efficient in these cases. To test this, they showed participants an animation of motion along a curved path (see fig 10.16). Participants had to make estimates of the current direction of motion and of the path. In this case, they were more accurate in estimating the path (average deviation of 5 degrees) than in estimating the direction of motion (average deviation 13 degrees).

The results from the Wilkie and Wann (2006) study imply that when we are moving along a curved path, we focus on specific points along that path. As shown in Figure 10.16, we use another alternative to the future path, in that we focus on specific points when steering along a curved path (Wilkie et al., 2010). These points are known as **tangential points**, or the points where the direction of motion of the path appears to invert. In a simulated driving task, Land and Lee (1994) found that the eyes were predominantly fixated on these points. It is likely that many drivers choose these points because they are clearly identifiable and because the curvature of the road can be easily determined on the basis of the difference between the direction of motion and the direction of the tangential point.

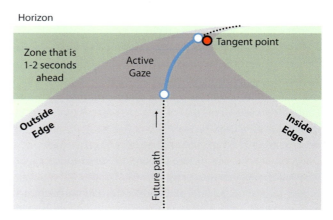

Figure 10.16 Impression of motion information, direction, and points along a path. (source: Wilkie, Kountouriotis, Merat, and Wann, 2010)

Therefore, the use of tangential points typically yields more accurate steering performance. Indeed, when participants were explicitly instructed to use the tangential points, while driving on a cloverleaf intersection of a German motorway, their steering performance was more accurate than when they were explicitly instructed not to use them (Kandil, Rotter, & Lappe, 2009).

A more specific analysis of the data from Land and Lee (1994) suggests, however, that the tangential point may not be as important as was initially believed. Although participants initially focus on this point, a more detailed analysis of the eye movement patterns shows that participants initially fixate on this point when approaching a turn, but that they fixate on more specific points along the future trajectory when entering the turn (Lappi, Pekkanen, & Itkonen, 2013). Moreover, drivers' actual viewing behaviour may depend on specific circumstances. For instance, when the tangential point is not visible, we tend to use the future path, and this is also the case when we are given specific instructions, for example, to stay in the middle of the road (Wilkie et al., 2010).

10.5.6 TIME TO CONTACT

In many situations, it is necessary to determine when an object is going to hit us. Consider, for example, a ball that is thrown towards us or a situation where we are walking towards a wall. In principle, we can calculate the time remaining before we make contact by dividing an estimate of the distance to the object by the estimated speed at which the object is approaching us. In practice, however, this is problematic because both distance and speed estimates are not directly available, which would make any calculation extremely error prone.

Lee (1976) argued that there is no need to estimate speed and distance, because when an object approaches us, we can estimate the time of contact from the physical properties of the object itself. According to Lee, we can infer this time directly from the size of the retinal projection of an object, by dividing this by its degree of expansion. This ratio was defined by Lee as the parameter **tau**. Lee's approach is similar to Gibson's in that he assumes that information about the time to contact can be derived directly from the available optical flow patterns. Savelsbergh, Whiting, Pijpers, and van Santvoord (1993) examined the extent to which the degree of expansion could affect our time-to-contact estimates. They did so by using a balloon that could inflate or deflate while swinging on a pendulum. Participants had to grab this balloon at the end of the swing. When the balloon became smaller – which corresponds to a longer time to contact – the participants' grasp started later than when the balloon remained at a constant size. Although these results are consistent with Lee's predictions, the delays reported by Savelsbergh et al. were much smaller than what was predicted on the

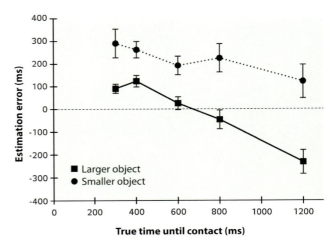

Figure 10.17 The influence of the size of an object on the estimated time to contact. (source: Hosking and Crassini, 2010)

basis of the tau mechanism alone. The result thus implies that factors other than tau also contribute to the estimation of time to contact.

Hosking and Crassini (2010) found indeed evidence for the contribution of such additional factors. Participants had to estimate the time to contact of known objects such as a tennis ball or a football at their normal size or of a manipulated size (e.g., a tennis ball the size of a football). In addition, Hosking and Crassini used unknown objects. Their results showed that participants were strongly influenced by the known size of an object. This was particularly the case with an extremely small tennis ball, which resulted in a strong overestimation of the time to contact (see fig 10.17). In addition to this known size, binocular disparity (see Chapter 6) plays an important role in estimating the time to contact. Rushton and Wann (1999) used a virtual reality environment in which participants were required to catch a ball. In the virtual environment, tau and binocular disparity could be manipulated independently of each other. The key finding of this study was that the estimated time to contact consisted of a weighted combination of tau and binocular disparity.

Lee used tau in particular to describe the braking behaviour of drivers. To do so, Lee introduced an additional parameter: **tau over time** (also known as tau-dot), which represents the decrease in tau as a function of time. As long as tau over time is greater than tau, there is still enough time to brake. Lee argued here that drivers aim to achieve a constant change in tau during braking. Some evidence for this idea was obtained by Yilmaz and Warren (1995). They asked participants to brake in a driving simulation task. Most participants showed a gradual decrease in tau, but not all: some participants showed quite abrupt braking behaviour.

Although Lee's (1976) approach has been very influential, Tresilian (1991, 1999) has identified some important limitations of tau. For example, tau does not consider any acceleration of the object itself. Moreover, tau is based on the expansion of the retinal projection of an object, so the time to contact is defined as the contact with the eye. In most cases, however, we want to be able to stop well before an object hits our eye. After all, if we relied entirely on tau, every braking action would result in a head-on collision! Finally, Tresilian notes that tau is only effective for spherical objects. For this reason, Tresilian (1999) argues in favour of another approach, in which tau is only one of the factors we use to determine the time to contact.

10.6 MOTOR IMAGERY

Since the late 20th century, an increasing amount of evidence has been reported to show that motor processes are involved in mental imagery (Jeannerod, 1995). These results suggest that when we have to make mental images of situations involving our limbs, or when we have to imagine performing actions with utensils, we involve our motor system. For example, when we have to imagine how to grab a coffee cup, or how to tighten a screw, we are supposed to perform this task by mentally simulating the corresponding actions.

The idea that motor actions can be simulated mentally is supported by results showing that both the actions themselves and the mental imagery of these actions activate similar brain areas (Lotze & Halsband, 2006). Jackson, Lafleur, Malouin, Richards, and Doyon (2001) argue that this form of **motor imagery** can be used to rehearse motor actions without actually performing them. As such, practicing motor actions can be contrasted with learning them. During the actual implicit learning of an action (see Chapter 3), it is absolutely necessary that the action is performed, while it is not necessary that it is already sufficiently practised. In contrast, motor imagery is only effective when the action itself has already been sufficiently practised. Studies on the use of motor imagery in trained athletes and musicians reported positive correlations between the degree of use of motor imagery and task performance in their domain of expertise (Driskell, Copper, & Moran, 1994; Pascual-Leone et al., 1995).

Vingerhoets, de Lange, Vandemaele, Deblaere, and Achten (2002) found that motor processes are also crucially involved in mental imagery processes. In their study, participants were required to perform a mental rotation task. They were shown two images of an object, one of which showed the object rotated relative to the other, and they had to decide whether the two images represented the same object or not. Two different sets of images were used, namely one set involving hands and one set involving utensils (see fig 10.18). The fMRI results of this study were consistent with those of previous studies on mental rotation processes. Activation of the bilateral parietal lobule and the visual extrastriate cortex was associated with mental rotation. These activation patterns were found for

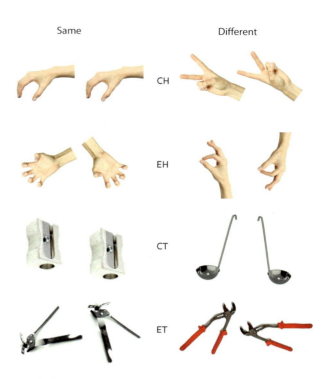

Figure 10.18 Examples of stimuli used in a mental rotation task. (source: Vingerhoets et al., 2002)

the images of hands as well as those of utensils. However, a differentiation was found between utensils and hands. Indeed, hands activated the bilateral premotor areas, whereas utensils only activated the left premotor area. This result implies that participants in the hand condition imagined both hands in a simulated mental rotation, whereas in the utensil condition they only used their right hands to mentally manipulate the object.

10.7 ATTENTION

An increasing number of studies is now reporting that attention plays a crucial role in perception and action integration. Indeed, selective attention processes are involved in the selection of information that is relevant for any task that we perform. Most of the objects that we encounter in our daily lives allow for multiple actions, making attentional or cognitive control processes necessary for determining which action to perform.

According to the influential **premotor theory** of attention (Rizzolatti et al., 1987), spatial attention is even a consequence of activation in the motor system. More specifically, the theory assumes that attending to a specific location is a consequence of planning a goal-directed action, such as reaching, or planning an eye movement, towards a target stimulus. The premotor theory is based on four central elements that describe the possible role of the motor system in the control of attention (Smith & Schenk, 2012). First, the theory assumes that spatial attention is the result of activation of neurons in the spatial cortical maps that are involved in action planning. In other words, selective attention and motor planning are assumed to use the same neural circuits, thus equating selective attention to motor planning. Second, the theory assumes that the activation of these neurons is dependent on preparing a specific action, so that spatial attention is a consequence of planning these actions. Third, it assumes that different spatial maps can become active, depending on which effector system (e.g., arms or eyes) is involved in the planned action. Thus, according to the theory, spatial attention can in principle be caused by any effector system. Finally, despite the fact that in principle any effector system could be involved in directing attention, Rizzolatti et al. (1987) assign special significance to the oculomotor system.

10.7.1 ATTENTION AND EYE MOVEMENTS

One of the most basic forms of perception-action integration can be found in the oculomotor system. We typically make thousands of eye movements each day, allowing us to focus our eyes on the most informative, salient, or unexpected aspects of our visual environment. But what determines what we fixate? After all, before we make an eye movement to a relevant location, we must have determined that this location is interesting enough to fixate. In Chapter 6 we discussed how attention can, in principle, shift to specific locations in a manner that is independent of our eye movements. This is known as covertly orienting our attention. This covert orientation enables us to determine, prior to executing the actual eye movement, whether the information at this location is of sufficient interest.

The observation that spatial attention can be oriented independently of eye movement may at first seem problematic for the premotor theory. This is not necessarily the case, however, because the premotor theory assumes that it is the preparation of an action that is essential for attention and not the actual execution of the action itself. According to this view, covertly orienting attention is thus equivalent to planning an eye movement without actually performing it. The idea that planning an eye movement is necessary for the endogenous orientation of attention was first put forward and then rejected by Klein (1980). Participants in Klein's study were engaged in a dual task. In the primary task they were required to make a saccade to a specific target location, while in the second task they were required to detect an infrequently occurring probe stimulus. Klein expected that participants would be faster in fixating the target location when it matched the location of the stimulus belonging to the secondary task. This acceleration would be due to the fact that focusing attention on the probe stimulus resulted in planning a saccade to this location. Klein did not find this effect, however. Proponents of the premotor

theory argue, however, that Klein's results are difficult to interpret because it is not clear which strategy participants use when preparing a response.

An alternative way to demonstrate a link between attention and the motor system is to study patients who have an impairment in their oculomotor system. The results of these studies are not univocal, however. For example, Rafal, Posner, Friedman, Inhoff, and Bernstein (1988) studied patients whose oculomotor control system was impaired by a progressive neurological disorder. These patients were significantly impaired in their ability to focus their attention exogenously while their ability to orient their attention endogenously remained largely intact. This result is remarkable, because the ability to make voluntary eye movements was particularly impaired in these patients. Henik, Rafal, and Rhodes (1994) found similar results in patients with lesions in the frontal eye fields. These patients were also characterised by difficulties with initiating saccades, while their ability to endogenously orient their attention remained intact.

Finally, Sereno, Briand, Amador, and Szapiel (2006) report the results of a patient with a lesion in the superior colliculus, who had difficulties with both reflexive eye movements and with the exogenous orientation of attention. This implies that exogenous attention is linked to oculomotor control. Although this patient was not explicitly tested for his ability to orient attention endogenously, there were indications that he had preserved his ability to remain focused at a location that was cued endogenously.

Craighero, Carta, and Fadiga (2001) report results that do imply a direct link between the oculomotor control system and spatial attention. Their patients were characterised by a degeneration of the sixth cranial nerve, which restricted the movement of one eye. These patients alternated between performing an endogenous attention task with their impaired eye and their intact eye. Endogenous attention was impaired when the task was performed with the impaired eye but not when performed with the intact eye. A subsequent study by Smith, Rorden, and Jackson (2004) reported an endogenous and exogenous attention study in a patient, AI, who had had both eyes completely paralysed since birth. Because of this condition, AI had never been able to make voluntary eye movements. AI was able to orient attention endogenously without difficulty, although she had a slight deficiency in her ability to orient attention exogenously. In addition, AI's behaviour showed no signs of inhibition of return (Smith, Jackson, & Rorden, 2009). Similar results were found in a study by Gabay, Henik, and Gradstein (2010) in a patient with a chronic condition that restricted the movement of one eye (known as Duanes retraction syndrome). In this patient, too, a small limitation in exogenous orientation was found, but no limitation in endogenous orientation.

These results imply that the endogenous orientation of attention is not dependent on the oculomotor system. Four of the five studies described here report no deficits in the ability to orient attention in an exogenous manner. The fact that patients cannot perform eye movements still leaves open the possibility that they can plan this movement, however, so these patient studies provide relatively weak evidence against the idea that motor preparation processes are involved in the orientation of attention. Ideally, therefore, a critical test for premotor theory should be under conditions where both preparation and execution of saccades are impossible.

Craighero, Nascimben, and Fadiga (2004) designed an ingenious experiment to test whether orienting attention is impaired when participants cannot prepare eye movements towards a stimulus of interest (see fig 10.19). In one condition, participants sat directly in front of a computer screen, as is the case in most classic attention studies. In a second condition, however, they were seated at a 40-degree angle to the screen, so that they had to maximally deflect their eyes to the left in order to fixate on the display. This way they were still able to prepare saccades to the nasal side of the display but no longer to the temporal side (see fig 10.19). Consistent with the premotor hypothesis, in this condition participants were still able to execute an endogenous shift of attention to the nasal side, but no longer to the temporal side.

Smith and Schenk (2012) note, however, that although Craighero et al. (2004) studied endogenous attention, they may have used cues that captured attention exogenously. Although the cues they used were presented at the fovea, they were not central: the cues consisted of lines that could be presented directly to the left or to right of the fixation point. Here, the location of the cue corresponded to the location that the participant was supposed to attend to. For this reason, the participants did not have to interpret the symbolic meaning of the cue, allowing attention to be cued directly, in an exogenous fashion. For this reason, Craighero et al. may have found no cueing effect for stimuli that fell outside the range of the oculomotor system.

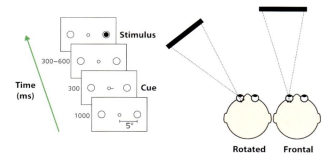

Figure 10.19 Illustration of a selective attention task. In one condition, participants had to perceive stimuli at an angle, which might prevent them from moving their attention further to the periphery. (source: Craighero et al., 2004)

10.7.2 A CRITICISM OF THE PREMOTOR THEORY

Smith and Schenk (2012) argue that there is little evidence for a direct relationship between the endogenous orientation of attention and the programming of eye movements, and that the relationship between attention and eye movements that does exist is mainly limited to the exogenous orientation of attention. For this reason, they propose an alternative to the premotor theory. The core of this alternative framework is that the relationship between attention and eye movements is mainly limited to exogenous orientation of attention. Moreover, Smith and Schenk propose that this relationship can be explained by the biased-competition model of attention (see Chapter 4), as originally proposed by Desimone and Duncan (1995). According to this view, different sensory inputs compete with each other for a representation in the sensory and motor systems of the brain, with the most salient stimuli being represented the most strongly. The competition between these representations is integrated across the sensory and motor systems, so that the different systems converge to one representation. This representation is the winner, in the sense that it gains access to our higher cognitive systems, allowing it to be consciously perceived and making it accessible to the motor system. As discussed in Chapter 4, this competition can be influenced (biased) by top-down factors, such as task goals, so that physically weaker stimuli can still win the competition.

During the presentation of an exogenous cue, its sudden appearance can dramatically increase the salience of the cued location, thus inducing a strong bias (in both the visual system and in the oculomotor system) to process information at this location. If for some reason, however, the ability to represent this location is impaired in the oculomotor system, the appearance of the cue can no longer induce the aforementioned bias. This disruption may be due, for example, to a lesion in the oculomotor system, or because the cued location is outside the action range of the oculomotor system. The lack of bias will then ensure that stimuli that appear later at the cued locations are not processed with a higher priority than stimuli that appear at other locations.

In case of an endogenous cue, however, participants know that the cue will predict with some degree of accuracy where a stimulus will appear. They can then use this knowledge to prioritise this location in a manner that bypasses the oculomotor system. Therefore, lesions in the oculomotor system are unlikely to affect the top-down (endogenous) orientation of attention. When the top-down biases are in competition with biases originating from the oculomotor system, the relative strength of the different biases will determine which locations capture attention. In particular, when both systems operate at the same location, the top-down cognitive and the bottom-up driven oculomotor biases may reinforce each other. According to this view, planning an eye movement to a specific location without actually executing it may facilitate planning an attentional shift to this location, however, it is not necessary for executing an endogenous shift of attention. Thus, the motor preparation of an eye movement may increase the likelihood that a specific location will be attended, but it does not guarantee that this will happen.

10.7.3 ATTENTIONAL REMAPPING

Earlier in this chapter, we encountered the problem of transformation between coordinate systems in perception-action integration. This problem is particularly relevant when we make eye movements, and it illustrates one of the most important aspects of the complexity of the relation between perception and action. In a now classic article, Walls (1962) argues that the ability to move our eyes arose because it gave us the evolutionary advantage of a stable field of vision. Every time we move our heads we make a compensatory eye movement, which helps to keep the environment stable. In a similar way, our eyes can follow moving objects. For example, when we are on a train our eyes follow the objects that pass us by. These field-of-view stabilising reflexes compensate for more than 90% of the movement patterns that would otherwise disrupt a stable image on the retina (Ferman, Collewijn, Jansen, & Van Den Berg, 1987; Skavenski, Hansen, Steinman, & Winterson, 1979). Thanks to these eye movements, we are protected against a serious loss of visual acuity and sensitivity (Murphy, 1978; Westheimer & McKee, 1975).

Paradoxically, however, eye movements also introduce the most violent disruptions of visual stability imaginable. However, when we make a saccadic eye movement, we typically do not notice this disruption at all. Moreover, under normal circumstances, we do not notice any difference in our visual experience before and after the saccade. In fact, in daily life, we are hardly aware of the fact that we are making saccades, even when we are performing visually guided actions (Cameron, Enns, Franks, & Chua, 2009).

How can we have such a stable visual experience, given the enormous amount of eye movements that we make every day and the corresponding changes in retinal input that result from these movements (see fig 10.20)? Nowadays, many researchers assume that these disruptions are prevented by a predictive remapping system (Melcher, 2011). Duhamel et al. (1992) introduced the term 'remapping' to describe the enormous changes in receptive fields that can be observed in the parietal cortex of monkeys following an eye movement. Duhamel et al. found that many parietal neurons responded in advance to a stimulus that would be brought into their receptive field by an upcoming saccade.

Since Duhamel et al.'s (1992) results were published, several studies have found effects of remapping in behavioural data (Hunt & Cavanagh, 2011; Mathôt & Theeuwes, 2010, 2011; Melcher, 2009; Rolfs, Jonikaitis, Deubel, & Cavanagh, 2011) and in ERP data (Parks & Corballis, 2008, 2010; Talsma, White, Mathôt, Munoz, & Theeuwes, 2013). For example, Mathôt and Theeuwes (2010) investigated the extent to which attention is influenced by saccadic eye movements. Here, participants were instructed to make a saccade to a specific location. The location in question was marked by the appearance of a stimulus. Along with this stimulus, an additional irrelevant, but salient and attention capturing, exogenous cue stimulus appeared. Then, 30 ms after the participants initiated their eye movement, a probe stimulus was presented, which remained onscreen for 100 ms.

The crucial manipulation in this experiment consisted of manipulating the exact location where the probe stimulus appeared. In the first condition, known as the spatiotopic condition, it appeared at exactly the same location on the screen as where the exogenous cue had appeared. In the second condition, known as the retinotopic condition, the location of the probe shifted along with the eye movement, so that it eventually appeared at the same retinal coordinates as where the exogenous cue had appeared before the eye movement. This manipulation allowed investigating the question to which extent attention moves along with the predictive remapping process: if attention is remapped after an eye movement, we might expect that participants would be better able to detect the probes in the spatiotopic condition. If, on the other hand, attention is not remapped, we might expect that the probes would be more easily detected in the retinotopic condition.

Mathôt and Theeuwes (2010) found, however, that for attention only partial predictive remapping occurs. Indeed, both the probes that were presented at the original spatiotopic positions and those presented at the original retinotopic locations were better detected than those presented at a neutral control location. In a follow-up study, a similar experimental design was used, but now also ERP recordings were added (Talsma et al., 2013). In this study, a cue was used to indicate a specific location that participants had to memorise. The rationale for this manipulation was that it required the participants to keep their attention focused at this location (see Chapter 14). Once participants had memorised the location, they were required to move their eyes to a new location. Shortly after the completion of this eye movement, a probe stimulus was flashed with the aim of evoking an ERP response.

As discussed in Chapter 6, the amplitudes of two early visual ERP components, the P1 and the N1, are affected by attention, which allowed us to use the

(a)

(b)

Fixation 1   Fixation 2

(c)

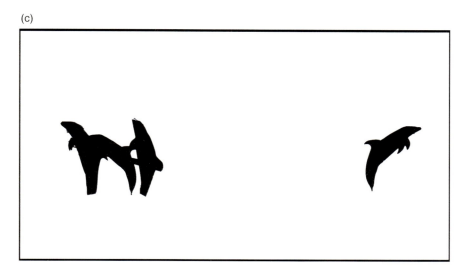

Figure 10.20 In everyday life, we experience our visual environment as stable, despite an enormous amount of disruptive eye movements. (a) A visual scene; (b) the part of the scene that we could perceive in two successive fixations; (c) the stable mental representation that we form after integrating the information we gather during the two fixations. (source: Mathôt and Theeuwes, 2010)

aforementioned probe stimulus to determine the extent to which attention remained focused on the originally cued location after a saccade was made. The ERP results showed that the amplitude of the P1 component was greatest when the probe stimulus was presented at a location that corresponded to the retinotopic coordinates of the memorised location. This result implies that attention initially moves along with eye. Thus, the remapping of attention is not fully predictive, but is still partially performed after a saccade.

10.8 SUMMARY

James Gibson hypothesised that visual motion is crucial for guiding actions. According to his direct perception theory, we are directly able to derive crucial information from retinal flow patterns, without the need for complex cognitive processing. Gibson identified the expansion point as an important indicator of motion direction. Moreover, Gibson assumed that potential uses of objects are automatically activated by merely perceiving them; a property he described with the term 'affordance'. Affordances are not only dependent on the object itself but also on the internal state of the observer. Evidence for the existence of affordances has been obtained from studies in which people performed grasping movements in response to images of graspable and non-graspable objects. Recent theories suggest that affordances are stored in semantic long-term memory in the form of action codes.

In perception-action integration, motion detection is crucial for the successful execution of an action. Psychophysical studies conducted over the past decades have provided many insights into how motion information can be decoded in the brain. Based on these studies, different types of motion have been identified. Simple forms of motion can be explained well by assuming detectors based on spectral analysis. Higher-order motion is partly illusory and dependent on attention. These forms of motion can be explained in part by assuming that the brain is trying to minimise a prediction error caused by micro-saccades and changes in luminance. Biological motion, and in particular human motion, is a special form of motion in the sense that we are particularly sensitive to this form of motion. Our sensitivity is possibly related to the fact that we can also perform this type of motion ourselves or that it is crucial for recognising the intentions of another individual.

In order to efficiently carry out a goal-directed action, it is necessary to process a continuous stream of perceptual signals from the environment. Since our actions also influence the environment, a continuous perception-action cycle is generated. Both the perceptual and the motor systems in the brain are characterised by a hierarchical organisation. According to Fuster, the internal representations of perception and action influence each other at every level of this organisation. To use visual information efficiently when performing a motor action, perceptual information must be transformed between different coordinate systems. The posterior parietal cortex appears to play an important role in this process. This brain region is believed to contain a spatial map of the environment, which is formed on the basis of visual, tactile, and auditory information. In addition to integration with other sensory information, perception-action integration also involves internal feedback from our muscles and joints. This feedback is combined with an internal forward model of the motor commands to determine the current position of the body. Feedback from the visual system and the internal sensory representation is weighted via Bayesian principles to produce an optimal estimate of the body's position.

Eye movements are crucially involved in the integration of visual information into motor actions. Systematic deviations in hand position, which are the result of an eye movement during the pointing of a specific target location, imply that motor actions are in principle encoded in a retinotopic coordinate system. This interpretation is complicated by a number of additional factors, however, including the fact that we usually use two eyes and that head movements can induce a translation of the eye position. These factors often result in pointing errors, which can be used to further update the hand position. When making a grasping movement, additional factors, such as the orientation of the target object and the expected properties of the material, must also be considered.

The vision-for-action system appears to operate by predominantly using an egocentric coordinate system, however, it can switch to an allocentric system when tactile stimuli are involved. The vision-for-perception system appears to operate mainly on the basis of an allocentric coordinate system. Switching between the different coordinate systems appears to involve a remapping process. Remapping involves a shift of the receptive fields of visual neurons as a function of eye position.

When determining the direction of motion, we can do so on the basis of a number of different visual cues. The optical flow patterns on the retina are important for this, as are cues from eye and head movements. Although the ability to detect motion has a positive effect on the accuracy of direction determination, we are also able to determine in which direction an image has moved by comparing two static images. When navigating along a curved path, we often use a number of specific reference points. One of these points is the tangential point. When this point is not available, we rather use the future path, and also when we approach the tangential point, we often switch to another reference point.

In order to come to a full stop in time for an obstacle, it is necessary to estimate the time remaining until we come in contact with this object. Lee hypothesised that this time can be estimated from the ratio between the retinal projection of this object onto the retina and the degree of expansion of this projection. Although this ratio, tau, is probably one factor on which we base our estimate of time to contact, recent research has shown that tau alone is not sufficient and other factors are also involved.

Many visual tasks involve motor imagery processes. This is the case, for example, in mental rotation tasks where two different hand positions or two different utensils have to be compared. This form of motor imagery can also be used to rehearse certain motor skills. It is, however, a condition that the motor action has already been practised in such a way that the motor programme for it is present.

Selective attention is also involved in perception and action integration. According to the premotor theory, a shift of attention is caused by preparing an eye movement to a new location. Here, attention would precede a saccade as a result of the activation of neurons in the spatial maps that are involved in planning a motor action. Although several studies have found evidence for a link between eye movements and shifts in attention, the conclusion that preparing an eye movement is a prerequisite for preparing a switch of attention may be too premature. Several neuropsychological studies have found this link for exogenous shifts of attention but not for endogenous shifts. This discrepancy between exogenous and endogenous attention shifts can possibly be explained by the biased competition framework for visual attention.

Spatial attention is influenced by eye movements. Saccadic eye movements are accompanied by a predictive remapping of attention, allowing attention to remain focused on the original spatiotopic position after the eye movement. However, this remapping is not complete: behavioural studies have shown that objects at the original retinotopic positions can also be better discriminated after performing a saccade. ERP results are consistent with this finding.

NOTES

1 To experience this yourself you no longer have to follow expensive pilot training: there are numerous examples of cockpit videos you can easily find on YouTube.
2 Betz's most groundbreaking contribution to neuroscience was the discovery of the large, triangular pyramidal cells (see Chapter 2) and the discovery that these neurons play an important role in motor functions.

FURTHER READING

Cutsuridis, V., Hussain, A., & Taylor, J. G. (2011). *Perception-action cycle: Models, architectures, and hardware.* Heidelberg: Springer Verlag.

Glencross, D. J., & Piek, J. P. (1995). *Motor control and sensory motor integration: Issues and directions.* Amsterdam: Elsevier.

Noë, A. (2004). *Action in perception.* Cambridge, MA: The MIT Press.

PART 5

Emotion and Motivation

CHAPTER 11

Motivation and reward

11.1 INTRODUCTION

Suppose you are working on a particularly difficult assignment that is part of your academic degree. Your first attempt to find a solution has failed miserably and you are not sure what to do next. You consider your options: do you want to stop with the assignment, or do you want to try again? Quitting has a positive short-term consequence in the sense that you can save yourself a lot of effort, but, on the other hand, there are many negative long-term consequences: you may not be able to complete the course; or even to obtain your degree, and your chances of a successful career will be dramatically reduced as a consequence. Eventually, you decide to have another go at the problem and although it is not immediately successful either, the new experience gives you courage to keep working on it and eventually you find the right solution. Your perseverance is rewarded with a nice final grade.

This example illustrates the complex interaction between motivation, cognition, and reward. Intrinsic motivation, such as the motivation to obtain a diploma, can be important for engaging in many cognitive activities, while the successful performance of these actions can result in a reward. Cognitive control processes (see Chapter 5) are also crucially involved in motivation: our ability to not give in to impulsive behaviour plays a crucial role in the implementation of the goals that we have set based on our intrinsic motivation. Finally, the reward that can result from intrinsically motivated actions can then serve as an extrinsic motivator to hold on to our intrinsic motivations and encourage us to engage in those actions that are consistent with these motivations.

11.2 AN EVOLUTIONARY PERSPECTIVE

In a literature review, Duchaine, Cosmides, and Tooby (2001) discuss how various cognitive functions could have arisen through natural selection during the evolution of our species. According to these authors, all the basic cognitive functions that we have discussed so far have probably developed because they offered some evolutionary advantages

(see also Gallistel & Gibbon, 2000). However, most of these functions are involved in the collection of knowledge and information. According to Duchaine et al., these functions would be useless if they could not be linked to motivational systems that could generate adaptive choices and behaviour in our evolutionary ancestors.

An important implication of Duchaine et al.'s (2001) argument is that our cognitive functions do not so much serve information processing. Rather their ability to process information is a by-product of numerous developments that increase our chances of survival by providing our bodies with the necessary nutrients, by allowing reproduction, and by facilitating cooperation with others (see fig 11.1). This implies that many neural processes are related to supplying the body with its basic needs such as maintaining the balance of bodily fluids (Parsons et al., 2000), maintaining social relationships (Chevallier, Kohls, Troiani, Brodkin, & Schultz, 2012), and producing offspring (Both, Everaerd, & Laan, 2007).

One consequence of realising that cognitive functions developed because they gave our bodies an evolutionary advantage is that cognitive functions can no longer be considered to operate separately from the body, as was originally proposed by advocates of the **computer metaphor**. Around the turn of the century, this realisation contributed greatly to the development of the **embodied cognition approach**, which we already discussed briefly in earlier chapters.

Although we should realise that not all cognitive processes require embodiment (Clark, 1999), there are at least two closely related aspects of human cognition that are closely tied to the processing of bodily signals. Emotions, or states of mind, are related to feelings (Craig, 2004), and most theories in this field are based on the central assumption that emotions are strongly related to the interpretation of bodily signals, such as an accelerated heartbeat, increased blood pressure, perspiration, or tremors (see Chapter 12). These bodily signals can either directly (by satisfying a bodily need) or indirectly (through emotions) affect our motivated behaviour. The idea that we perceive emotions on the basis of bodily reactions is a clear example of how a

DOI: 10.4324/9781003319344-16

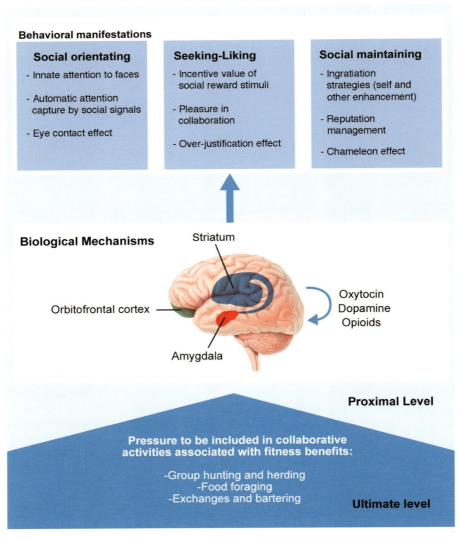

Figure 11.1 A model of social motivation according to Chevallier et al. (2012).

state of mind can be affected by perception (see Chapter 8). This influence can also be indirect, for example through music (Chanda & Levitin, 2013) or the visual arts. Finally, most activities in our daily lives take place in a social context and in many cases they involve emotions that can influence our behaviour (see Chapter 23). Also in this case, the interpretation of one's own body signals often plays a crucial role in the processing of these emotions (Goldman & de Vignemont, 2009).

The aim of the current theme – motivation and emotion – is to discuss the most important relationships between emotion, motivation, and cognition. Because motivation and emotion are strongly related, it is almost impossible to completely separate these two concepts. Later in this chapter, we will see that emotions are strongly embedded in recent theories of motivation. After all, emotions are assumed to drive thoughts (e.g., 'This is a good thing') that in turn guide behaviour (Todd, Miskovic, Chikazoe, & Anderson, 2020). A central theme in this chapter is that motivational processes interact with cognitive control

processes and thus regulate behaviour. Given the strong emphasis on cognitive control, it is recommended that you briefly review Chapter 5 before continuing to read.

Although the core assumptions from the Duchaine et al. (2001) article have stood the test of time, much has changed in our thinking about the involvement of motivational processes in human cognition in more than 20 years since its publication. Before we can begin to discuss these recent developments, however, it is necessary to address some historical ideas and to correct the main misconceptions that have arisen from them.

11.3 MOTIVATIONAL THEORIES IN A HISTORICAL CONTEXT

There is a general consensus that motivational processes serve the survival of both the individual and the species. They are crucial for regulating an organism's internal state:

that is, they are involved in ensuring an optimal balance of nutrients and fluids. In addition, it is very important for our survival that our activity level remains optimal so that we can respond adequately to threats. Finally, to ensure the continuation of our species, we must ensure that we reproduce ourselves.

11.3.1 GENERAL PHYSIOLOGICAL PRINCIPLES

Berridge (2004) discusses several basic principles that underlie state regulation processing in an organism and form the basis for motivational processes. The two key concepts that are linked to these processes are **homeostasis** and **drives**. Homeostasis refers to the maintenance of a stable internal state. In a motivational context, the concept of homeostasis can be traced back to the physiologist Walter Cannon's (1932) work. Homeostatic processes are typically described in terms of control systems that aim to maintain the internal physiological state at a fixed set value. To achieve this, the current state is continuously compared to a target value, and, if a deviation is detected, the system strives to bring the state back to this value. This way any physiological parameter, such as body temperature, fluid level, blood pressure, blood acidity, glucose level in the brain, or energy reserves, can be regulated.

11.3.1.1 Homeostatic Motivation

Every homeostatic system includes a target value, a detection mechanism, and a correction mechanism that reduces the difference between the current state and the target value. In this respect, **homeostatic motivation** can be compared to the way a thermostat works in a modern home: it measures the actual temperature in the living room and compares it to a set value; if the temperature deviates too much from this value, the thermostat signals a heater or cooler to bring it closer to the set value. This setup involves a negative feedback loop, in which the action of the system reduces the difference between the actual and the target value. A built-in tolerance ensures that the system can be inactive for significant periods of time without having to switch continuously between heating and cooling, preventing the temperature from continuously oscillating around the target value (see fig 11.2).[1]

For biological systems, it is extremely important that the homeostatic mechanism ensures that the state of the system remains within a narrow margin, as deviations that are too large can become life-threatening. Low levels of body fluids, for example, trigger a hormonal response that activates the sensation of thirst and stimulates drinking behaviour. Similarly, we can assume that the body has specific target values for physiological parameters related to hunger, such as body weight, glucose levels in the blood, or metabolic activity (Berthoud, 2002; Friedman, 1997).

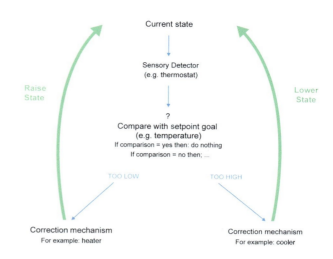

Figure 11.2 The principle of homeostatic regulation. (source: Berridge, 2004)

For homeostatic mechanisms to function correctly, it is important that there are target values and error-detection mechanisms to detect any deviation from these values. For intake-related motivation, such as hunger or thirst, this is easy to imagine, and with some effort it is also possible to imagine that such mechanisms exist for other motivational systems, such as sex or aggression. In the latter cases, it can be assumed that a crucial regulatory factor, such as the amount of sex hormones or steroids in the blood, reaches an excessive level after long periods of abstinence or pent-up aggression. The expression of sexual or aggressive behaviour would then bring hormonal levels back to their optimum value.

11.3.1.2 State Regulation without Homeostatic Mechanisms

Although homeostasis appears to play an important role in the maintenance of our internal state, we also need to consider the possibility that regulatory processes involve other, non-homeostatic mechanisms. This is the case, for example, when the mechanism involved does not operate on the basis of a target and an error detection mechanism. Such a form of state regulation operates on the basis of an anticipatory mechanism. Examples of these mechanisms can be found in anticipatory eating or drinking, that is, eating or drinking even before the internal state begins to deviate from the optimal value (Weingarten, 1983). These anticipatory actions may be initiated via associations with other types of behaviour: for example, a feeling of thirst may be activated at dinner even before the intake of food has stimulated the withdrawal of water from our blood plasma. Similarly, during our lifetimes we will consume many meals before a physiological deficiency is detected. In these cases, there is no homeostatic regulation. Thus, the question is whether such anticipatory regulatory mechanisms involve the same neural processes as the homeostatic mechanisms.

11.3.1.3 Settling Point Regulation and Illusory Homeostasis

Internal balance can also be achieved when two opposing forces balance each other out. There are many examples of this in our environment. Consider, for example, sea water levels in the oceans. These levels have been more or less constant for centuries without any active monitoring of the sea level, comparison with a target value, active replenishment of the oceans, or extraction of water from them. Sea levels are more or less constant as a result of the Earth's energy balance, which implies that the inflow of water into the oceans (from rivers, melting polar ice, etc.) equals the outflow (from evaporation). These different forces have reached an equilibrium that is known as a **settling point** (see fig 11.3). Such settling points can sometimes be surprisingly stable, as in the case of sea levels. Settling points can also change, however, when the balance between the different forces changes. For example, sea levels are likely to rise in the decades to come as a result of global warming, and as the opposing forces find a new balance, they will reach a new settling point.

A biological example of such regulation by opposing forces is body weight. The bio-psychologist Robert Bolles has argued – somewhat provocatively – that hunger and eating behaviour have no homeostatic basis and that body weight settles at a point that is only marginally stable. Taking this idea further, we can observe that obesity (for example, due to damage to the ventromedial hypothalamus, a leptin deficiency, or some other neural change) is not the result of a change in a target value but rather of an altered balance between different forces.

According to Bolles, the settling point is not only determined by internal appetite but also by the external availability and palatability of food and by other factors, such as the need to exercise. Anecdotal evidence for this idea comes from the fact that obesity has increased considerably in recent years.

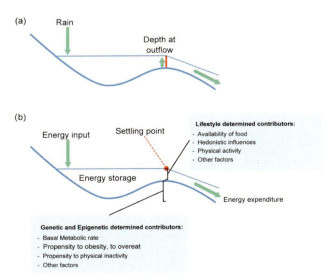

Figure 11.3 State regulation via the settling point principle. (a) Example of the depth of a river; (b) a comparable principle involving the energy balance of the human body.

This increase can hardly be attributed to a change in an internal target value; rather, it is due to a sharp increase in the availability of cheap junk food, a cultural acceptance of regular snacking between meals, and a society that promotes a lack of exercise and sports. The consequence of these changes is that in many individuals the balance of forces has shifted to a higher settling point. On the other hand, aphagia (i.e., difficulties with swallowing) or low body weights due to lateral hypothalamic lesions or dietary medication may result from a disruption of forces in the opposite direction.

Finally, it should be noted that the distinction between homeostasis and settling point mechanisms is, in practice, less strict than the preceding description would suggest. Walter Cannon himself never described the self-regulating mechanisms in terms of fixed targets and negative feedback mechanisms, but rather in terms of opposing reflexes that resulted in a more or less stable state. The formal definition of homeostatic mechanisms is derived from cybernetics (i.e., control theory) in mechanical engineering and computer science, where the concepts of target value, target/ state equation, and negative feedback loops were common. These concepts were later introduced into biology, as the idea that a machine could achieve a stable internal state based on an internal target value made it very attractive to assume that the brain operated in a similar way.

11.3.1.4 Allostasis

The direct counterpart of homeostasis is **allostasis**. Allostasis does not so much describe the self-regulating processes that lead to stability, but rather the processes that lead to changes. In the most extreme sense, allostasis can involve **positive feedback loops**. Positive feedback occurs when an initial response to a change contributes to even larger subordinate response to this change. A good example of this is when an electric guitar (or the microphone of a clumsy lecturer...) picks up the sound of a connected loudspeaker, which then feeds this sound back to the loudspeaker, causing the whole system to reverberate. In neuroscience, positive feedback mechanisms can often be found in physiological responses to long-term stress exposure (Lee, Kim, & Choi, 2015). In this case, the **hypothalamic-pituitary-adrenal (HPA) axis** responds more and more strongly to a repeated series of stressors (see fig 11.4), which may, in extreme cases, even result in damage to brain structures such as the hippocampus or the amygdala.

In other cases, allostasis describes changes in processes that are normally considered homeostatic. Consider, for example, an addict who continues to take drugs to counteract the effects of abstinence (Koob & Le Moal, 2001). Initially, normal functioning is achieved without drugs, but when withdrawal symptoms begin to occur (e.g., because the body produces fewer natural endorphins as a result of the use of opiates), the user will have to take larger quantities of the drug just to keep the withdrawal symptoms away. In this case, no positive feedback loops are involved: the

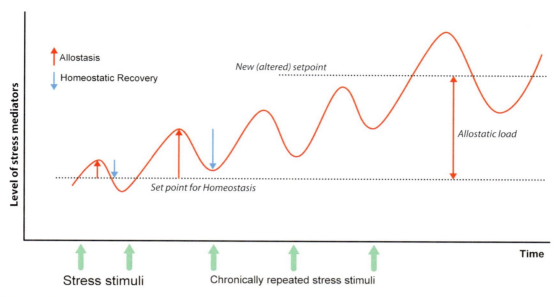

Figure 11.4 The influence of allostatic stress mechanisms on the activation of the regulation of the HPA axis.

decay into a state of withdrawal is the result of the natural downregulation of neurotransmitter receptor sensitivity, based on negative feedback mechanisms.

11.3.1.5 Drives

Now that we have become acquainted with the most important regulatory mechanisms, let us take a moment to consider the concept of a drive. How can we best define a drive? To answer this question, let's imagine ourselves as a pure behaviourist scientist trying to explain behaviour in terms of mere stimulus-response relationships. Imagine that we want to consider all the factors that have an effect on our willingness to drink water (see fig 11.5). Abstinence from water is one of those factors, but overheating, eating dry (and salty) food, or the injection of a solution of sodium chloride will also stimulate our willingness to drink. In addition to our willingness to drink, we are also motivated to do other things as a function of these factors. For example, we are willing to work for a sip of water, to take a sip of a bitter-tasting liquid

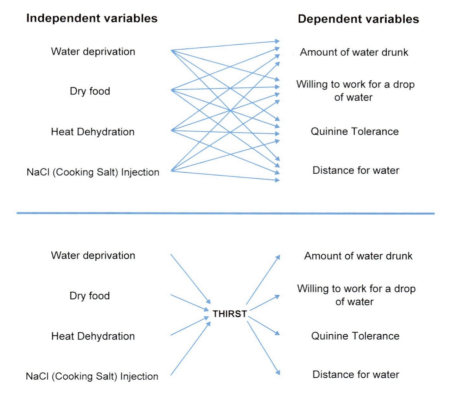

Figure 11.5 The concept of a drive as an intervening variable, illustrated here using the concept of thirst, to explain complex stimulus-response relationships. (source: Berridge, 2004)

(such as a quinine solution), or to travel a long distance to get to the water. As diehard behaviourists, we would have to establish a complex relationship between every dependent and independent variable. Now, if we want to explain each of these underlying relationships – and find an underlying neural mechanism for each relationship – we quickly find ourselves lost in a jungle of complex relationships, which prevents a simple explanation. It is therefore better to introduce an **intervening variable**, in the form of thirst, which is much better able to describe the complex relationship between the independent variables and the dependent variables. We can think of this intervening variable as a drive.

There is one danger inherent to defining drives this way, however, and that is that it can result in a circular argument. For example, we can explain why you are currently reading this chapter, by assuming that you have an incentive to read about cognitive and neuroscientific concepts that relate to motivation. The problem with this 'explanation', however, is that it merely repeats what we have just observed, namely that you are reading a chapter about motivation. Such a circular argument is not an explanation! Yet we can define drives very well without having to resort to circular arguments.

In essence, we can avoid these types of circular arguments if we can use our definition of a drive to make new predictions about behaviour that go beyond merely describing the types of behaviour that we already know. To illustrate this using our water intake example: if we have already determined that saltwater injections induce thirst because they make a rat drink, then we can also expect to observe other behaviours that are related to thirst but that we have not yet observed. For example, we might also expect

rats to become more tolerant of quinine or expect a rat to press harder and more frequently on handles that allow it to obtain drops of water. When these predictions can be confirmed, we have validated the drive construct and it is therefore no longer circular (Berridge, 2004).

11.3.2 EXPECTATION AND REWARD

Although the physiological mechanisms discussed here already enable us, in part, to explain motivated behaviour, we are still limited to the regulation of internal states. Yet there are still many processes that we cannot explain with this approach. For example, it has been found that rats, when they have to cover a certain distance to obtain a reward, run faster as the size of the reward increases. If on a given trial the reward is suddenly doubled, the result will be that on the next trial the rat will suddenly run significantly faster (Crespi, 1942). Since we can rule out that we have reinforced the running behaviour itself, this effect implies, according to Crespi, that the rat has formed an internal expectation of the reward, was positively surprised by the increase in reward, and that it has therefore created an expectation that there will be a large reward again following the second run. Besides forming an expectation, we may also expect that affective responses play an important role here. According to this idea, motivation is aimed at achieving hedonistic goals; that is, goals that elicit an affective response.

11.3.2.1 Opponent Processes
Solomon and Corbit (1974) have introduced a useful model to explain the impact of hedonic stimuli on behaviour (see fig 11.6). According to this **opponent-process**

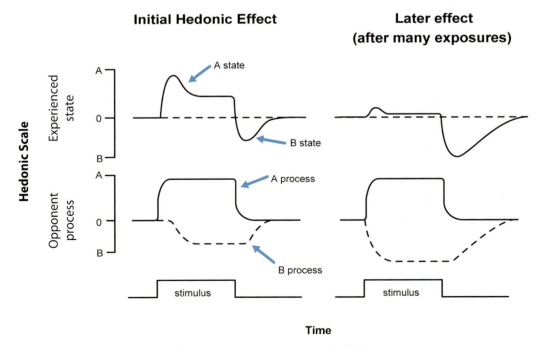

Figure 11.6 Illustration of Solomon and Corbit's (1974) opponent-process model. (source: Berridge, 2004)

model of motivation, hedonic stimuli will not only evoke their own hedonic neural response but also an opposite response with an opposite hedonic valence. This opponent process follows the initial hedonic response, which was evoked by the stimulus itself. When the stimulus was pleasant, the opponent process is unpleasant and vice versa. The idea behind this opponent-process approach is that the brain strives for a stable internal state, and in that respect, Solomon and Corbit's idea is related to the basic principles of homeostasis. More specifically, the concept of their opponent-process theory is based on the opponent-process theory of colour perception, which we have already introduced (see Chapter 6).

This principle of opposing processes is best illustrated by the effects of the drug heroin. According to the opponent-process theory, the stimulus (heroin) will initially evoke a pleasant hedonic response in the reward circuits of the brain (the A reaction), resulting in a pleasant affective state (the A state). However, the A reaction will result in an opponent (negative) B process, which results in a negative experience (the B state). This B state on its own would be unpleasant, but combined with the heroin-induced A state, the result is only a weakened A state. An important aspect of Solomon and Corbit's theory is that with repeated use, the B reaction becomes stronger and stronger, while the A reaction remains unchanged. The unpleasant B process therefore becomes stronger and longer lasting, with the result that eventually there is a sustained B state which is no longer compensated by an A state. This is the case with withdrawal symptoms. The end result of this process is the build-up of a drug dependency.

For unpleasant stimuli, Solomon and Corbit assume that exactly the opposite phenomenon would occur. Here, a painful stimulus, such as an electric shock, would trigger a negative A process, resulting in a negative A state. This negative state then triggers a positive B response. For example, a painful stimulus may stimulate the release of opioids, which may not only diminish the effects of the pain but may, if repeated, also result in a pleasurable B state when the direct effect of the painful stimulus has worn off. Such a mechanism could possibly explain the effect of a runner's high (the euphoric state often reported by runners after intense workouts).

Although the opponent-process theory provides a useful framework for explaining many motivational processes, there are a number of limitations to the idea. It has been found, for instance, that not every A process automatically triggers a B process, and when it does, the B process does not always turn out to be the most important motivator for behaviour. Although withdrawal symptoms are strong, they are surprisingly often not the main reason why addicts continue to use heroin (Shaham, Shalev, Lu, de Wit, & Stewart, 2003).

11.3.3 LORENZ'S HYDRAULIC-DRIVE MODEL

We have already been introduced to the idea of drives as an intervening variable. If, however, we want to go beyond simply describing drives in terms of intervening variables, we must be able to explain more complex aspects of motivated behaviour. For example, why will a stimulus sometimes elicit motivated behaviour and sometimes not? Or why will a greater variety of behaviours occur as the motivational drive increases? Possible answers to these questions can be found in the **hydraulic-drive model**, which was formulated by the well-known ethologist and Nobel Prize winner Konrad Lorenz (see Berridge, 2004).

Lorenz proposed an interaction between the strength of an internal drive and the strength of an external stimulus (see fig 11.7). When the internal drive is low, a strong stimulus is needed to trigger behaviour. In contrast, when the internal drive is high, a much weaker stimulus will suffice. The motivated behaviour that results from the combination of internal drive and external stimulus can, according to Lorenz be compared to a valve in a hydraulic system. Opening the valve will cause liquid to flow out of the vessel. Likewise, the motivated behaviour will result in a decrease of the internal drive.

When the internal drive is extremely high, we might occasionally observe a spontaneous outburst of motivated behaviour even without the presence of a stimulus. Lorenz identified this spontaneous reaction as **vacuum behaviour**. A well-known example of vacuum behaviour is observed in canaries living in captivity. When they do not have access to building material during the nesting

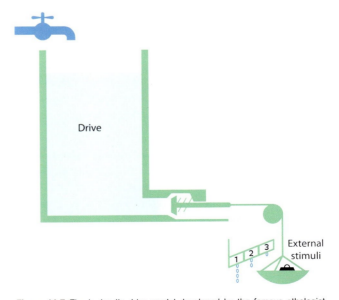

Figure 11.7 The hydraulic-drive model developed by the famous ethologist Konrad Lorenz. (source: Berridge, 2004)

season, they become increasingly restless. Eventually, this can result in a situation in which they use their own feathers as building material.

Although the hydraulic-drive model can explain the interaction between internal drives and external stimuli (or the lack thereof in the case of vacuum responses), it is also marked by several significant limitations. First of all, the model suggests a rather abrupt outbreak of motivated behaviour, which in reality is rather rare. In addition, in real life we hardly ever find any situation in which the motivated behaviour actually reduces our internal drive. There are many situations in which behaviour actually sustains internal drives, or even strengthens them. This type of motivated behaviour is nicely illustrated by the cocktail party phenomenon. When, for example, you take a few peanuts or appetisers at a party, out of politeness and without any actual motivation to eat, and you soon feel the urge to eat a few more, and before you know it you may find that the entire bowl is empty.

Lorenz's hydraulic-drive model has also never been very popular in the cognitive neurosciences because it is not very informative regarding the underlying neural mechanisms. Despite these shortcomings, the model provides an interesting framework for describing behavioural data related to the build-up of a drive, the prevention of expressing that drive, and the interaction between internal motivators and external stimuli.

11.3.3.1 Drive Reduction and Reward

Finally, one aspect of the concept of drives is still relevant to discuss, and that is the relationship between drive reduction and external reinforcement. Drive reduction was originally considered to be the most important function of reward processing (Hull, 1943; Miller & Kessen, 1952). If motivated behaviour is the result of a drive, then we may assume that satisfying the need that underlies this drive should be sufficient to reduce this behaviour. This idea is seemingly so obvious that for many years researchers simply assumed it to be true. The idea is so powerful that some researchers – as Berridge (2004) dryly notes – write about it today as if they still believe in it. Unfortunately, the idea is not correct!

In the 1960s, the first pieces of evidence against the idea of drive reduction regulating motivated behaviour appeared. The first source of evidence is somewhat anecdotal and comes from a patient named Tom (Wolf & Wolf, 1949). As a nine-year-old boy, Tom suffered permanent damage to his oesophagus as a result of accidentally swallowing extremely hot soup. The resulting burn permanently closed his oesophagus and blocked the passage of food to his stomach. For this reason, it was decided to surgically insert a gastric fistula, through which food was passed directly into Tom's stomach. Although Tom did not

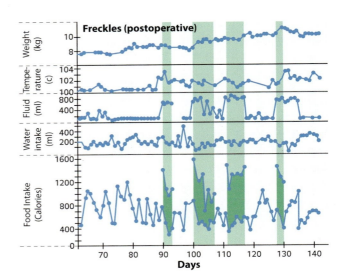

Figure 11.8 Post-operative data from one of the dogs ('Freckles') involved in a study on the effects of intravenous feeding on eating behaviour. Shaded areas show the periods when Freckles was fed intravenously. (source: Turner et al., 1975)

actually have to eat to satisfy his need for food, he insisted on putting his food in his mouth first and chewing it before feeding it into his stomach. When he was asked why he did this, Tom replied that otherwise his appetite would not be satisfied.

Animal studies also found that drive reduction was not a sufficient explanation for motivated behaviour. When dogs were intravenously fed with their daily nutrient requirement, their normal eating behaviour was not affected. When given the opportunity, they still ate their normal portion of food, resulting in them rapidly becoming obese (see fig 11.8). Yet the dogs continued to eat (Turner, Solomon, Stellar, & Wampler, 1975). This result shows that homeostatic drives were not the reason that these dogs ate, and also that their motivation to eat was not reduced by the physiological drive reduction that came from intravenous feeding. Miller and Kessen (1952) found a similar result. In their study, rats had to run through a maze. For a reward, they were given a shot of milk, which was either given intravenously or which they could drink. When the rats could drink the milk, they quickly learned to run towards their goal, whereas when the milk was administered intravenously, they were much slower.

The most convincing evidence against drive reduction, however, came from studies that used direct electrical stimulation of the brain (see Box 11.1). Based on the principle of drive reduction, researchers initially also expected that stimulating brain areas associated with the processing of rewards would result in a decrease in motivated behaviour. James Olds (1973) originally expected that an electric stimulus would cause an animal to react as if it were hungry, in other words that it

Box 11.1 James Olds and the accidental discovery of the nucleus accumbens

One of the most sensational discoveries in the field of motivation and reward was made by the American cognitive psychologist James Olds (1922–1976). Olds' career is a fascinating story of the growth and development of an exceptionally creative mind. Born in Chicago, Olds already proved to have a special talent for experimental psychological questions when he was still a young student, which earned him several prominent publications in his student days. During his psychology studies at Harvard – and strongly influenced by the book *The Organisation of Behaviour* (1949) by one of the great pioneers of learning psychology, Donald Hebb, Olds began to develop a keen interest in motivation. Both his early Harvard work and the influence of Hebb's ideas made him one of the first psychologists in the world to realise that neural processes should be the basis for psychological theories. By the time he received his doctorate, Olds was a neuroscientist at heart, although his training in this field was still lacking. Olds therefore decided to specialise further in this field, and to do so at one of the few locations where, at the time, the link between psychology and neuroscience was already commonplace: McGill University in Canada. There, Olds obtained a position in Hebb's laboratory.

Once he arrived at McGill, Olds was largely given a free reign to pursue his own ideas. Together with Peter Milner, Olds began testing a new theory describing a link between positive reinforcement and activation of the reticular system in the brain. To establish this link, Olds and Milner made their own depth electrodes and implanted them in rats, with the aim of electrically stimulating the reticular formation. The hypothesis they tested was that electrical stimulation should reinforce the rats' operant behaviour. The rats were required to manoeuvre through a maze and at specific locations in the maze their reticular formation would be stimulated. Olds and Milner were expecting that the reinforcement evoked by the stimulating current would encourage the rat to return to this location.

The experiment would have been a complete failure had it not been for an ingenious mistake by Olds. During the preparation phase, he had accidentally misplaced an electrode, such that it did not end up in the reticular formation, but in the basal forebrain (Shizgal, 2001). None of the rats, Olds and Milner tested, showed any evidence of reinforcement, but there was something unusual about this one rat that Olds had prepared. After stimulation, the rat kept returning to the location where the stimulation had taken place. In the resulting article, 'Positive reinforcement produced by electrical stimulation of septal area and other regions of rat brain', Olds described this finding, as well as how rats can be stimulated. Olds and Milner (1954) describe both this finding and the finding that rats who can stimulate themselves by pressing a pedal continue to do so at an excessively high rate. The article in question has become one of the most influential papers in the reward literature. Afterwards, Olds and Milner managed to establish that the brain area in which Olds' electrode had accidentally landed was the nucleus accumbens. Because of the excessive degree of self-stimulation that they had observed in rats, Olds and Milner formulated the hypothesis that the nucleus accumbens is the pleasure centre of the brain.

This fabulous accidental discovery was the start of a long research project, which has resulted in an enormous improvement in our understanding of motivational processes. One important conclusion that we now have to draw is that Olds and Milner's original interpretation, that the nucleus accumbens is the pleasure centre of the brain, is wrong! Numerous studies have shown that this area of the brain is stimulated by activities that its owner no longer enjoys or that are downright destructive to the individual. These include the continued use of drugs, compulsive gambling – or the excessive checking for social media likes(!). For this reason, the nucleus accumbens is nowadays regarded more as a brain area that is activated by immediately rewarding impulses.

would act as a drive-inducing stimulus. Therefore, Olds hypothesised that this stimulus had aversive properties. In other words, if the electrical stimulus stimulated eating behaviour, then, according to the drive reduction hypothesis, we might expect this stimulus to act as a punisher. Along similar lines, an electric stimulus that would stop eating behaviour would be regarded to act as a reward.

It turned out, however, that the drive-reduction hypothesis was incorrect, because most often the exact opposite results were found. The brain areas where electrical stimulation induced eating behaviour were almost always associated with reward processing (Valenstein, Cox, & Kakolewski, 1970). This result implies that reward is not related to drive reduction. Reward should therefore be considered an independent motivational factor, characterised

Box 11.2 Fact or fiction: reward and addiction

Although many of the theories and empirical findings written in this chapter are based on reward processing, the usefulness of the reward concept in cognitive psychology is not beyond criticism. For example, the American psychologist and addiction specialist John D. Salamone (2006) wrote a particularly sharp critique of the concept of reward in the journal *Addiction Biology*. Salamone's criticism focuses on the popular use of the word 'reward' in the context of addiction. This criticism focuses on the fact that in reports on addiction problems, rather generalising remarks are often made that link the drug in question to the dopaminergic system. Typically, the release of dopamine, or the prevention of its reuptake, is equated to receiving a reward. Although it is indeed often correct that drugs act on the dopaminergic systems of the brain, Salamone believes it is too simplistic to equate this process with subjective terms such as 'pleasure', 'hedonism', or 'reward'.

For this reason, the addiction literature is marked by a clear trend away from these terms in favour of more objective descriptions of the impact of dopaminergic changes on reinforcement learning (Wise, 2004) or

self-insight into the addict's problem (Goldstein et al., 2009). Although Salamone acknowledges that the term 'reward' has some value in describing the global principles of addiction, or in classifying a particular group of substances, he also argues that the term 'reward' is seriously deficient in describing the processes underlying addiction. On the one hand, the term 'reward' is too generic, because it lumps different processes together. On the other hand, it is too specific, because it only focuses on one aspect of addiction, namely the motivational aspect, while dopamine also plays a role in stress, learning, compulsivity, motion control, and schizophrenia.

Therefore, there is currently a growing realisation that addiction is considerably more complex than the simple idea that suggests that dopamine is a reward agent. Factors such as reinforcement, motivation, learning, habit formation, compulsivity, and effort are crucially involved in addiction (Rushworth, Walton, Kennerley, & Bannerman, 2004; Salamone & Correa, 2012). The bottom line is that reward does play a role, but it is only one of the many factors that contribute to addiction.

by specific brain mechanisms. The search for the neural mechanisms behind reward processing is therefore currently an important focus of cognitive neuroscience (see also Box 11.2).

11.3.3.2 Hedonic Rewards

The aforementioned results forced researchers to seek a new explanation for the role of rewards in motivated behaviour. Ultimately, this would result in the notion that motivation was primarily a response to an **incentive**. Before this notion could be established, researchers first had to be convinced of the idea that a hedonic reward is just what it is: its hedonic properties directly induce behaviour, without contributing to drive reduction. In a classic study, Young (1966), for example, found that rats change their behaviour purely on the basis of the hedonic properties of a stimulus.

Sheffield (1966) reported similar results: rats drank large quantities of nutritionless water that was diluted with saccharin. Moreover, male rats were prepared to perform tasks in order to gain access to a female partner for a brief copulation. This happened even when there was no time for ejaculation, which, according to the prevailing theory, would be necessary to reduce the sex drive. Sheffield refused to introduce hedonic concepts into his theory,

however, and tried to explain his results on the basis of a drive-induction concept. According to Sheffield, taste or sexual sensations induce the very drive that prompts behaviour; a concept that was inconsistent with most drive-reduction theories. Ultimately, both views would be proven to be incorrect.

A major problem with all classical motivation theories is that they attempt to explain behaviour in terms of internal drives. A breakthrough came when Pfaffman (1960) succeeded in interpreting all of Young and Sheffield's results in terms of hedonic sensory rewards, without resorting to the drive concept. Pfaffman's conclusion was that the neural response to the taste of sweetness to sexual or other hedonistic stimuli is rewarding and motivating in itself, without requiring a drive reduction mechanism.

11.3.3.3 Incentive-based Motivational Concepts

One of the consequences of rejecting the idea that motivation is tied to drive reduction was that it opened the development of theories that are focused on incentives. One of the first attempts to explain motivation in terms of incentives can be found in the Bolles-Bindra-Toates theory (Bindra, 1974, 1978; Bolles, 1972; Toates, 1986). Based on a literature review, Robert Bolles identified several failed attempts to explain motivation in terms of drive reduction. He argued that individuals are motivated by the expectation of an incentive. Bolles described these expectations, which were formed by learning to expect a hedonic reward, as S-S* associations. More specifically, this meant that a predictive neutral stimulus (S), such as a light, became associated with a hedonic reward (S*), such as food, through repeated pairing of these stimuli. In terms of classical conditioning, S was the conditioned stimulus and S* the unconditioned stimulus (see Chapter 3). Having established this, Bolles was not yet able to explain, however, why an S-S* expectation would induce motivated behaviour.

For this reason, the Canadian neuropsychologist Dalbir Bindra rejected the idea that the expectation itself was the main factor driving incentive-based motivation. Instead, Bindra hypothesised that the learned association not only evokes the expectation of a reward but also leads the individual to perceive the conditioned stimulus itself as a hedonic reward. If this is the case, then one would have to expect that a person will always respond to a conditioned stimulus as if it were a reward, regardless of their internal physical state. This is highly unlikely, however. After all, we are less likely to drink when we are hungry and more likely to do so when we are thirsty.

This implied that physiological signals from our bodies are also involved in motivated behaviour. To account for these signals, Frederick Toates proposed an adaptation to the concepts introduced by Bolles and Bindra. According to Toates, the physiological signals can modulate the rewarding value of an incentive: the stronger the body signals a deficit, the greater the rewarding value of an incentive becomes. According to this interpretation, the physiological signals are therefore not directly involved in inducing motivational behaviour but regulating the hedonic impact of the reward. Ultimately, then, there is a complex three-way interaction between the physiological state, the conditioned stimulus, and the learned association with the unconditioned stimulus. Tasty food, refreshing drinks, and other rewards are all examples of hedonic incentives whose value can be modulated by a physiological deficit. The motivational value of the image or smell associated with these incentives may then be modulated by the learned association with the reward itself (Berridge, 2004).

The way in which the hedonic value of an incentive can change is related to the concept of **alliesthesia** (Cabanac, 1979). This concept refers to a change in sensation, or more specifically, a change in the pleasure that a sensation evokes. For example, we give higher ratings to the pleasure of eating sugar when we are hungry than when we are satiated. Although the pleasurable effect changes, the subjective experience of sweetness remains the same. Toates (1986) suggested that alliesthesia

underlies the change in the hedonic impact of stimuli that we have already discussed: when we are not thirsty, the hedonic value of a refreshing drink will be weaker and consequently its image on a billboard will also have a much weaker impact. Likewise the smell of freshly baked bread will also have a weaker impact when we are not hungry.

11.3.3.4 Liking versus Wanting

A final aspect of hedonic rewards is the distinction between 'liking' and 'wanting'. According to Bindra and Toates' original formulation, hedonic stimuli should be both liked and wanted. However, this is not always the case (Berridge, 2004). Based on neurophysiological research, we can make a distinction between liking and wanting (Salamone & Correa, 2012). Here, liking can be equated with the sensory hedonic impact of a stimulus, whereas wanting is more strongly related to the motivational impact of a stimulus. Why are two different mechanisms involved in the processing of these aspects? Berridge (2004) hypothesises that the mechanisms involved in 'wanting' were the first to appear in the evolution of our species, as they brought about goal-directed behaviour, without directly involving a hedonic experience. According to Berridge, subsequent mechanisms evolved in the form of a 'liking' mechanism. The latter mechanism is based on the hedonic value of the stimulus. In most cases, wanting and liking both serve the same purpose, but it is important to know that they can be dissociated under specific circumstances.

Liking can occur without wanting and vice versa. For example, liking without wanting can occur as a result of a suppression of the mesolimbic dopaminergic system. Dopamine suppression results in individuals having almost no motivation to seek incentives, such as those obtained from food, sex, drugs, and so forth (Brauer, Goudie, & de Wit, 1997; Ungerstedt, 1971).

In contrast, wanting without liking, can be produced in rats by various neural manipulations. Electrical stimulation of the hypothalamus, for example, can stimulate eating behaviour. This behaviour is usually not accompanied by the typical hedonic reactions that normally follow the taste of food. Berridge and Valenstein (1991) found, for example, that such electrical stimulation resulted in an aversive facial expression when a rat drank sugar water – as if the water tasted bitter.

Based on the developments of the past 50 years or more in the area of research on motivation, we may therefore conclude that motivational processes are much more complex than originally assumed and that, as a result, there is also a strong interaction between motivational and cognitive processes. The exact nature of this interaction will be elaborated upon in the following sections.

11.4 THE NEURAL BASIS OF MOTIVATIONAL PROCESSES

11.4.1 THE ROLE OF THE ANTERIOR CINGULATE CORTEX

Holroyd and Yeung (2012) suggest that the anterior cingulate cortex plays the role of motivator in the execution of goal-directed, motivated behaviour. This is illustrated by the phenomenon of **akinetic mutism**. Akinetic mutism is a neurological condition characterised by a strong reduction in spontaneous behaviour or even its complete absence, while all motor skills are still intact. Patients affected by this condition are often still capable of performing actions but lack the initiative or the will to do so. The condition is often linked to lesions in the anterior cingulate cortex (Devinsky, Morrell, & Vogt, 1995; Németh, Hegedüs, & Molnár, 1988). Based on these observations, neurologists have traditionally hypothesised that the anterior cingulate cortex acts as a motivator for goal-directed behaviour (Devinsky et al., 1995). This interpretation is consistent with more recent ideas suggesting that the anterior cingulate cortex has a global energetic function that can accelerate responses, induce effort, and increase arousal.

Although the idea that the anterior cingulate cortex plays a role as a motivator is interesting, it is problematic for two reasons. The first reason is that the explanation relies on computationally ill-defined terms such as effort and energy. The second problem is that most recent theories of anterior cingulate cortex do not ascribe a motivational role to this brain region but assume that it is primarily involved in decision-making and in regulating cognitive control processes (see Chapter 5). More specifically, it was suggested that the anterior cingulate cortex is involved in regulating the strength of top-down cognitive control, in response to the amount of conflict experienced (Botvinick et al., 2001).

Holroyd and Yeung (2012) have placed the role of the anterior cingulate cortex in a broader perspective. Their basic idea is that the anterior cingulate cortex is mainly involved in the selection and retention of options. Here, options are defined as extended context-specific sequences of actions aimed at specific goals. According to Holroyd and Yeung, these sequences are learned through a process of **reinforcement learning**. From this perspective, the anterior cingulate cortex may be involved in regulating cognitive control, while it still allows us to explain why damage to this area results in difficulties with the initiation of motivated, goal-directed behaviour. To explain the latter, we may assume that the capability of selecting and retaining options is impaired.

A key aspect of Holroyd and Yeung's (2012) theoretical approach is that the learning of complex actions involves a hierarchical form of reinforcement learning (Botvinick, Niv, & Barto, 2009). Using this mechanism, complex goals are achieved because specific options represent different possible action sets, with each set consisting of different primitive actions (see fig 11.9). For driving,

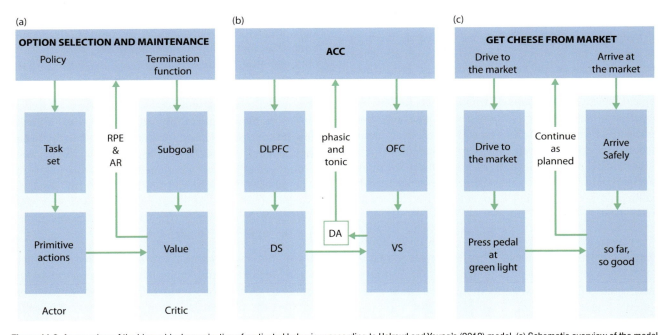

Figure 11.9 An overview of the hierarchical organisation of motivated behaviour according to Holroyd and Yeung's (2012) model. (a) Schematic overview of the model. (b) The neural implementation of the actor and the critic. (c) A concrete example of the processes involved in the execution of a real-world task. RPE = reward prediction error; AR = average reward; ACC = anterior cingulate cortex; OFC = orbitofrontal cortex; DLPFC = dorsolateral prefrontal cortex; DS = dorsal striatum; VS = ventral striatum; DA = midbrain dopaminergic system. (source: Holroyd and Yeung, 2012)

such an action set would consist of the individual actions necessary to operate the car, such as turning the ignition key, releasing the hand brake, clutching, shifting gears, accelerating, steering, and so on. An option consists of the sequence of actions that takes the driver to a specific destination, for example a specific supermarket. A crucial factor here is that each option does not just consist of the given action set, but of all possible action sets that can be used to get you to the supermarket from any destination.

According to Holroyd and Yeung's view, options are defined by the target state (the supermarket), any initial state that triggers the option (hunger, car availability, etc.), and the action sets that can be used to make the transition from the initial state to the target state. The chosen action set is also known as the policy. This hierarchical form of reinforcement learning is computationally efficient because it allows us to regulate behaviour at the level of options, rather than at the level of individual actions.

Botvinick et al. (2009) discussed how hierarchical reinforcement learning may be implemented in the brain. A key feature of their work is that the concept of options is closely related to that of **task sets**, as defined in the cognitive control literature (see Chapter 5). These task sets could be composed by the prefrontal cortex (Sakai, 2008). Holroyd and Yeung (2012) assume, however, that the anterior cingulate cortex also plays an important role in this process. In doing so, Holroyd and Yeung propose an approach that they designated as the actor-critic model. In this model, cognitive control is split into two parallel operating modules; one for selecting actions (the actor) and one for monitoring task performance, that is, the critic (Botvinick et al., 2009; Niv, 2009).

According to Holroyd and Yeung (2012) the anterior cingulate gyrus is involved in coordinating the various options. Specifically, they hypothesise that this brain region is involved in selecting and holding on to the options, while the dorsolateral prefrontal cortex and the motor structures in the dorsal **striatum** execute them. According to this view, these areas form the actor, while the orbitofrontal cortex and the ventral striatum form the critic. According to this view, the critic would be mainly involved in evaluating the degree to which the goal state is achieved.

The proposed framework is consistent with known functions of the aforementioned brain regions. For instance, the dorsal striatum implements the actor's policy by initiating specific actions, such as stopping a car in response to a red traffic light, while the ventral striatum acts as a critic by evaluating whether the actions to be performed will result in a reward or not, for example by signalling that stepping on the accelerator at a red traffic light is a form of maladaptive behaviour (Shohamy, 2011). The dorsolateral prefrontal cortex facilitates the execution of the selected option by sending biasing signals to the dorsal striatum, which indicate whether the current policy should be maintained. These biasing signals are particularly important when the policy is not yet fully learned by the dorsal striatum, or when it is inconsistent with learned behaviour, as is the case when driving on the other side of the road in a foreign country. Finally, the orbitofrontal cortex provides the ventral striatum with information about the abstract task goals. This information ensures that the basal ganglia can learn in a flexible way and that this learning depends not only on the direct physical consequences of an action (such as the pain resulting from a car accident) but also on the goal-related outcomes (such as the fact that a red traffic light implies braking).

While the preceding framework has been successful in explaining many aspects of goal-directed behaviour, it also has several limitations (Holroyd & Yeung, 2012). In particular, it is limited in explaining how we are able to perform particularly complex sequences of actions – such as driving to the supermarket and successfully returning with a full bag of groceries – since the computational load increases non-linearly with the number of steps required for an action. In addition, the framework does not specify how the dorsolateral prefrontal cortex implements tasks, nor how the orbitofrontal cortex can determine which goal is appropriate for a given task. These problems may be overcome if we assume that some of these functions are performed by the anterior cingulate cortex, based on the principles of hierarchical reinforcement learning. If we assume that reinforcement learning takes place in a hierarchical manner, the computational load on systems such as the dorsal striatum is considerably reduced. Moreover, the anterior cingulate cortex can learn to associate different values with options via standard reinforcement learning. According to this view, the anterior cingulate cortex would be involved in deciding which task to perform and in instructing the dorsolateral prefrontal cortex to implement this task.

11.4.2 THE INTERACTION BETWEEN MOTIVATION AND COGNITION

The fact that Holroyd and Yeung's (2012) model is based on the principles of reinforcement learning implies that rewards are important in motivated goal-directed behaviour. In a literature review, Braver et al. (2014) have identified the effects of motivation and reward on various cognitive functions involved in attention, memory, and decision-making processes (see also: Locke & Braver, 2008; Maddox & Markman, 2010; Pessoa, 2009; Pessoa & Engelmann, 2010; Shohamy & Adcock, 2010). The neural basis for this interaction between emotion, motivation, and cognition can be found in a network of neural systems consisting of the prefrontal cortex, the already discussed anterior cingulate cortex, the dopaminergic system in the midbrain, and a number of subcortical structures, including the basal ganglia and the hippocampus (see fig 11.10).

In recent decades, two different lines of research have strongly impacted our understanding of motivational processes. The first of these has focused on the development of a computational framework for reinforcement learning (Berridge, 2007; Daw & Shohamy, 2008; McClure, Daw, & Read Montague, 2003; Niv, Daw, Joel, & Dayan, 2007). This framework assumes that the current and future motivational values of events are used by the brain as learning signals. These learning signals then serve to induce biases in decision-making processes.

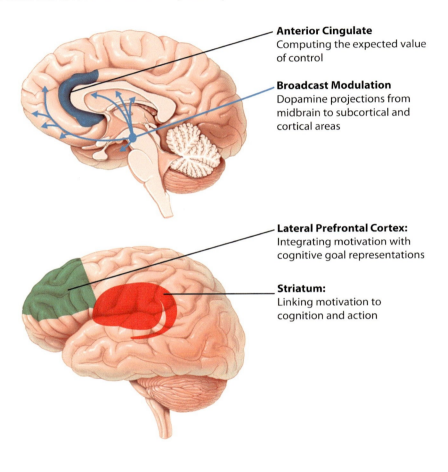

Anterior Cingulate
Computing the expected value of control

Broadcast Modulation
Dopamine projections from midbrain to subcortical and cortical areas

Lateral Prefrontal Cortex:
Integrating motivation with cognitive goal representations

Striatum:
Linking motivation to cognition and action

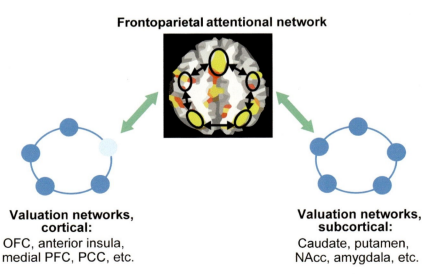

Frontoparietal attentional network

Valuation networks, cortical:
OFC, anterior insula, medial PFC, PCC, etc.

Valuation networks, subcortical:
Caudate, putamen, NAcc, amygdala, etc.

Figure 11.10 The neural basis of motivated, goal-directed behaviour according to Braver et al. (2014). OFC = orbitofrontal cortex; PFC = prefrontal cortex; PCC = posterior cingulate cortex; NAcc = nucleus accumbens.

The second line of research focuses mainly on the social, affective, and personality perspectives. As such, there is a strong focus on the question of what type of goals people strive for and what internal and external factors can influence the pursuit of these goals. Studies that were part of this second line of research reported two surprising findings. First, it was found that the explicit motivational value of a goal is often only weakly indicative of the actual pursuit and implementation of this goal (Gollwitzer, 1999). Unconscious processes may affect the pursuit of these goals by influencing the perceived motivational value of their outcomes (Custers & Aarts, 2005). Second, goal pursuit was found to occur at specific stages and time courses, so that goal-directed behaviour may fluctuate over time, depending on the nature of the task and the feedback received.

11.4.3 COGNITIVE CONTROL AND REWARD

As discussed in the previous section, reward is crucially involved in linking motivation to cognition. In cognitive neuroscience, motivation is strongly related to the expected outcome of a decision. A central question is thus how this expected outcome is represented by neural mechanisms. To address this question, most studies in this area use a cue with an extrinsic incentive value. This cue signals, in other words, whether specific rewards can be obtained with a certain action. In most cases, the reward consists of a small amount of money that can be earned by performing an action.

This type of research makes extensive use of the monetary incentive delay (MID) task (Knutson, Fong, Adams, Varner, & Hommer, 2001). Here, participants must perform a relatively simple task, such as responding quickly to a briefly presented visual target stimulus. Before this stimulus is presented, participants are informed by a cue whether they can earn a reward if they respond within a given time window. Here, the time window in which participants can respond is usually dynamically adjusted so that only a portion of the trials in which the participants can earn a reward are actually rewarded. This paradigm is often used to study cue-related activity in brain areas linked to motivation. Here, the expected outcome of an action is considered to be a proxy for the actual motivational process.

A second method that is widely used involves studying the effects of fluctuations in incentives on invested effort. An example of this approach is the incentive-driven coding paradigm. Here, cues are used to indicate which incentive is linked to the successful memorisation of a specific stimulus. The reward itself is only given during a subsequent memory test (Adcock, Thangavel, Whitfield-Gabrieli, Knutson, & Gabrieli, 2006; Wittmann et al., 2005). This paradigm has not only been used to investigate the effects of incentives on memory performance, it has also been applied to study sustained activity in motivation-related neural circuits.

Krebs, Boehler, and Woldorff (2010) used this method, for example, to investigate the effects of reward on the Stroop task (see fig 11.11). Here, participants had to name the print colour of various colour words. Some colours, such as green and blue, were associated with a reward, whereas the other colours (i.e., red and yellow) were not. For the colours that could potentially be rewarded, performance was generally improved, as indicated by shorter reaction times and lower error rates. In addition, it was found that the negative effects of conflicting information from the word meaning were less pronounced when the word was related to a non-rewarded colour. When the word meaning was related to a rewarded colour, however, interference was larger.

Similar results were found by Padmala and Pessoa (2011), using a conflict task. Here, pictures of houses or buildings were shown, over which the words 'HOUSE' or 'BLDNG' were projected. Participants had to indicate by pressing a button which type of picture (house or building) they saw, while ignoring the meaning of the word. Prior to the presentation of the stimulus, a cue indicated whether or not they could be rewarded for a rapid correct response. Both the results from Krebs et al. (2010) and those from Padmala and Pessoa (2011) imply that the prospect of a reward strengthens the processing of task-relevant stimulus features, whereas incongruent information related to a reward, even when not task-relevant, may actually interfere with the task.

These results suggest that rewards can influence selective attention processes. Krebs, Boehler, Roberts, Song, and Woldorff (2012) examined the extent to which the processes that are involved in processing a reward and selective attention processes share a neural substrate. fMRI data were collected while participants were engaged in a variant of Posner's (1980) symbolic cueing task. Here, a target stimulus was presented to the left and right of the fixation, consisting of a circle with a gap at the top and bottom. The participants' task was to detect which of these two openings (top or bottom) was the larger. Prior to the presentation of this target, a cue indicated which of the two locations participants were required to focus on in order to discriminate the target stimulus. In addition, the cue also indicated whether the target stimulus would be easy (a clear difference between the two gaps) or difficult (a small difference between the gaps), and whether the response to the trial in question could be rewarded or not. The cues activated a network of brain areas, consisting of the midbrain, the dorsal striatum, and the frontoparietal areas.

Moreover, the prospect of a reward was associated with additional activation of the ventral striatum, posterior

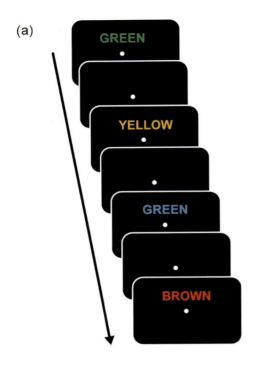

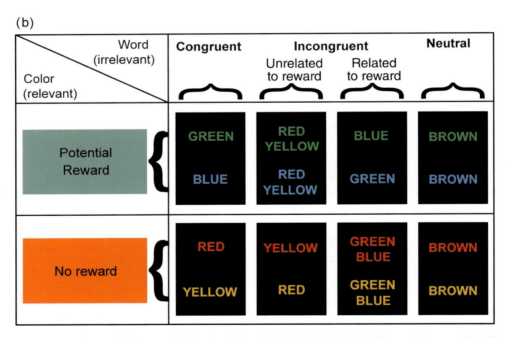

Figure 11.11 The method used in a study of the effects of reward on the Stroop task. (a) Participants had to decide as quickly as possible which colour a word was printed in. (b) If participants performed well on naming the colours green and blue, they received a small financial reward. Similar performance on naming red or yellow was not rewarded. (source: Krebs et al., 2010)

cingulate, and occipital lobe, while task difficulty was associated with activation of medial and dorsolateral frontal regions. An additional network of brain regions, including areas in the midbrain, caudate nucleus, thalamus, and anterior mid-cingulate gyrus was involved in the additional recruitment of neural processes in situations where a difficult task could result in a favourable outcome. These results suggest that the latter cortico-striatal-thalamic network is involved in the integration of attention- and reward-related processing.

Chapter 5 already discussed how cognitive control processes can adjust those features of a task that are relevant to the current goal (Botvinick et al., 2001). Verguts and Notebaert (2009) argue that these processes strengthen the associations between the task-relevant properties of a stimulus. Since rewards are also supposed to strengthen these associations (Waszak & Pholulamdeth, 2009), it is plausible that motivated behaviour in earlier trials in an experiment affects the processing of subsequent trials. Braem, Verguts, Roggeman, and Notebaert (2012) investigated whether this is the case by using a flanker paradigm. In this task, responses to 25% of all trials could be rewarded. Braem et al. found that responses to congruent trials were faster than responses to incongruent trials. Interestingly, on the trials that were rewarded, a clear effect of the previous trial could be identified, particularly on the congruent trials. It turned out that the response to these trials was relatively slow when the previous trial was incongruent.

Van Steenbergen, Band, and Hommel (2012) investigated the effects of gains and losses on the degree of conflict adaptation. In an EEG study, participants had to respond as quickly as possible to the central stimulus of a flanker task. In contrast to Braem et al. (2012), van Steenbergen et al. did not reward specific trials, but instead randomly informed participants that they had won or lost a small amount of money. Despite the fact that this feedback was unrelated to a participant's performance, van Steenbergen et al. found that task performance during the trial that followed these wins or losses was indeed influenced by this feedback. Wins resulted in a lower degree of conflict adaptation, implying that after a win, participants were more distracted by the task-irrelevant features of the previous trial, whereas losses were characterised by a higher degree of conflict adaptation. A frequency analysis of the EEG implied that losses were associated with an increase in activation in the anterior cingulate cortex, causing participants on the trial following a loss to focus their attention more on the central stimulus, to avoid being distracted by the flanker stimuli. In contrast, for gains, they found a decrease in anterior cingulate activity. This decrease was associated with a higher degree of attention on the irrelevant flanker stimuli.

11.4.3.1 Processing a Reward

At first glance, Braem et al.'s (2012) results appear to contradict those of van Steenbergen et al. (2012). There are a number of important differences between these two studies, however, that may explain these differences. In the Braem et al. study it was known in advance which trials could be rewarded, and awarding the reward was also performance related. In contrast, in the Van Steenbergen et al. study, rewards and losses were allocated at random and were not performance dependent. Thus, the differences indicate that the way in which we process a reward depends to a large extent on the task at hand.

Differences in the way participants process rewards were also reported by Yeung, Holroyd, and Cohen (2005). In this study, participants were engaged in a gambling task while their EEG was recorded. In one condition, participants

had no influence on the outcome of the gambling task: they had to start a roulette wheel by pushing a button, and the outcome determined whether a sum of money was lost or won. In a second condition, the participants did have an influence on the outcome. Here, they had to choose from four different response alternatives, and the choice could result in winning or losing a small amount of money. Yeung et al. were interested in the processing of the outcome of the gamble. To this end, ERPs following the feedback (the eventual announcement of whether the participant had won or lost) were computed. This **feedback-related negativity** shared some similarities with the error-related negativity that we discussed in Chapter 5, in the sense that it is a negative ERP component that is mainly found when an action or an outcome has negative consequences for the participant.

Yeung et al. (2005) found that this feedback-related negativity was present when the outcome of a gamble was negative, even when the participant had no choice (see fig 11.12). When participants did have a choice, similar feedback-related negativity was found, but it was significantly greater than when participants did not have a choice. Yeung et al. further found that the magnitude of feedback-related negativity correlated with participants' subjective engagement with the task. This correlation implies that feedback-related negativity is strongly influenced by motivational processes.

Choice

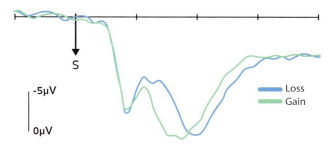

No Choice

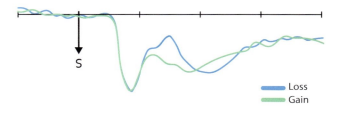

Figure 11.12 ERP results of a study on the processing of feedback. Participants involved in a gambling task received feedback after each trial. ERPs elicited by the feedback stimulus showed a negative deflection, regardless of whether the participant had a choice or not, although the amplitude of this feedback-related negativity was greater when the participant did have a choice. (source: Yeung et al., 2005)

11.5 REWARD AND ATTENTION

In Chapter 6, we discussed how attention plays a central role in visual search processes. One of the central issues we discussed there is how salient stimuli can automatically capture attention and automatically initiate an eye movement (Theeuwes, 2004; Theeuwes et al., 1999). In the studies discussed in Chapter 6, salience was entirely determined by the physical properties of a stimulus, however, such as a unique colour or a sudden onset. But what is the role of motivation in these processes? Stimuli that are associated with a reward may also be more salient than those that are not. Hickey, Chelazzi, and Theeuwes (2010a) found evidence for this idea. In their study, participants had to search for a unique target stimulus (a horizontal or vertical line inside a circle, within a display that otherwise consisted of lines inside a diamond-shaped figure), while being distracted by another salient deviant stimulus (a diamond in a different colour; see fig 11.13). ERPs evoked by the displays were characterised by an **N2pc** component when participants were rewarded for a rapid response.

This N2pc component is associated with the deployment of attention and it is marked by a negative potential across the scalp areas that are contralateral to the location where attention is being deployed (Eimer, 1996; Luck & Hillyard, 1994). The stimulus that evoked this N2pc component in the Hickey et al. study depended to a large degree on the previous trial. In half of all trials, the colours of the target and distractor stimuli switched: the colour that had previously been associated with the target stimulus now became the colour of the distractor and vice versa. When there was no colour change, the N2pc was evoked by the target stimulus; after a colour change, the N2pc was evoked by the distractor, but this only happened when the trial in question was associated with a reward.

A number of studies have shown that reward can directly influence the salience of stimuli (Bucker, Belopolsky, & Theeuwes, 2014; Failing & Theeuwes, 2014; Failing, Nissens, Pearson, Le Pelley, & Theeuwes, 2015; Hickey, Chelazzi, & Theeuwes, 2011; Theeuwes & Belopolsky, 2012). For example, Theeuwes and Belopolsky (2012) found that stimuli associated with a reward automatically captured eye movements. During an initial training phase, participants had to rapidly detect a horizontal or a vertical bar, which was presented in a display that also contained four circles and a triangle. Participants were instructed to make a saccade to the location of the bar as quickly as possible. They were informed that they could be rewarded depending on their performance. After each trial, participants received feedback indicating whether they had earned €0.01 or €0.10. In reality, however, the reward did not depend on the participants' performance but on the orientation of the bar. Following a correct saccade, for half of the participants a high probability of receiving the high reward was associated with the vertical bar, while for the other half of the participants is was associated with the horizontal bar.

Upon completing the training, another task followed in which the participants no longer received rewards. In this task, six red circles were presented initially, one of which changed into a grey circle after some time. Simultaneously with the colour change, an additional stimulus, consisting of a horizontal or a vertical bar, appeared. The participant's task was to make an eye movement towards the grey circle as quickly as possible. Previous studies (see Chapter 6) had already shown that the appearance of an additional distracting stimulus disrupts this task, because participants tend to saccade towards the distractor (Theeuwes et al., 1999). Theeuwes and Belopolsky (2012) aimed to determine what the exact influence of an associated reward was on this effect. They found that when the additional stimulus had been associated with a high reward during the previous training phase, it also tended to capture attention more strongly, compared to when it had been associated with a low reward.

Bucker et al. (2014) found similar results in a study in which information about a reward could directly influence the direction of a saccade. In this study, participants had to make an eye movement towards a grey dot. Simultaneously with this dot, a coloured dot appeared in the vicinity of the grey dot. This coloured dot was in itself task irrelevant, however, its colour signalled how much of a reward the participants could earn. Bucker et al. were interested in the extent to which the coloured dot could influence the direction of the saccade. The hypothesis was that when the target dot was flanked by a dot that signalled a high reward, this would influence the final eye position more strongly than when the flanking dot signalled a low reward. This was indeed what was found (see fig 11.14).

Using a similar paradigm, Failing et al. (2015) demonstrated that stimuli that signal a high reward can be strong distractors. Here participants had to make an eye movement to a target stimulus, and keep their eyes fixated on this stimulus for at least 100 ms. This study also presented an additional stimulus. Again, the colour of this stimulus indicated how much of a reward participants could earn. This time the stimulus was not only task-irrelevant, participants had to actively ignore it. If participants accidentally fixated on it during a trial, the trial was considered an omission and no reward was awarded! Although ignoring stimuli that signalled a high reward was actually beneficial to task performance, Failing et al. found that it was precisely in these trials that participants fixated on the distractors relatively often.

These results imply that stimuli associated with a high reward can capture attention in a relatively automatic way. Failing and Theeuwes (2014) showed in a more direct way

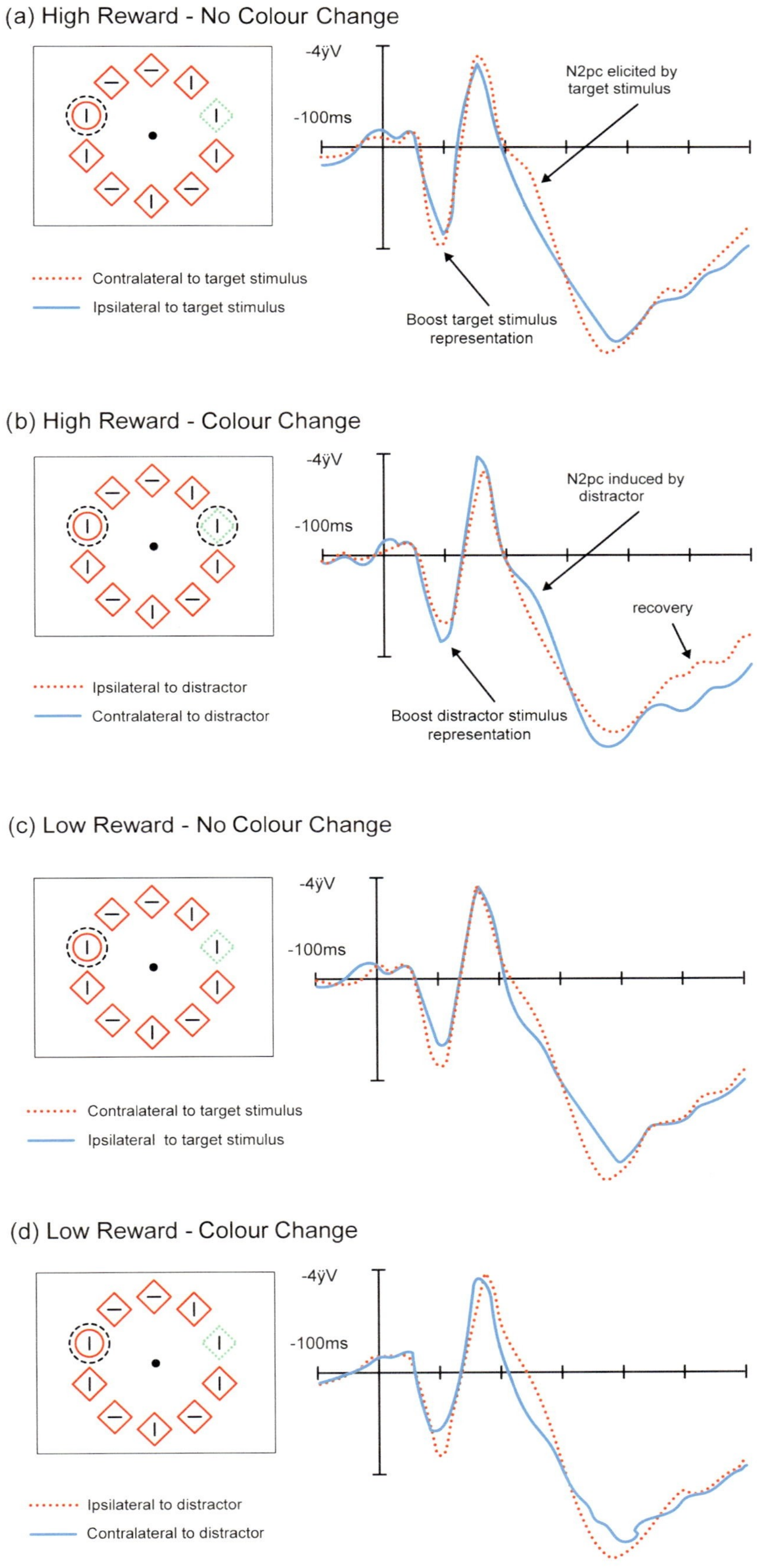

Figure 11.13 An experimental design and results of a study examining the effects of reward on attention. (a) Stimuli that are strongly rewarded immediately capture attention, as shown by the appearance of an N2pc component. (b) When the colour of the relevant stimulus and that of a distractor have been swapped, attention is captured by the distractor. (c–d) Similar results for a task condition where only a small reward was given. Here, the N2pc effects are less pronounced. (source: Hickey et al., 2010a)

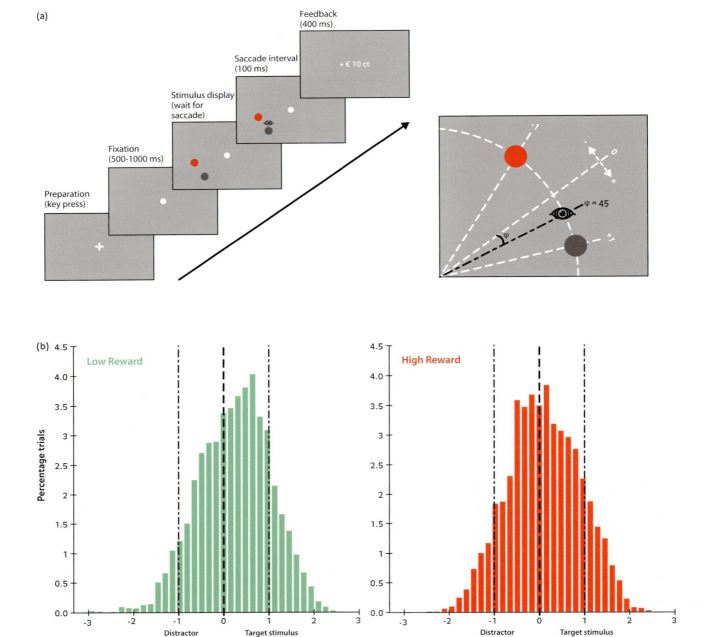

Figure 11.14 The effects of reward on viewing behaviour. (a) Participants were required to make an eye movement towards a target stimulus, which was flanked by a stimulus that had to be ignored. The colour of this stimulus gave an indication of the reward the participant could receive. (b) Stimuli that signalled a high reward had a greater influence on the final eye movement than stimuli that signalled a low reward. (source: Bucker et al., 2014)

that this is indeed the case. In doing so, they used a variant of Posner's (1980) exogenous cueing paradigm. Here, participants were required to detect a target stimulus that could appear in one of two possible locations. Prior to this stimulus, a cue was presented at both locations. One of these cues had previously been associated with a reward, while the other cue had not. Participants were faster at detecting the target stimulus when it appeared at the location where the cue associated with a reward was presented than when the target stimulus was presented at the other location.

Although the prospect of a reward can thus apparently affect visual perception and attention, Hickey, Chelazzi, and Theeuwes (2010b) found significant individual differences in the extent to which this can occur. In this study, participants took part in an experiment similar to the Hickey et al. (2010a) experiment just described. Now, a questionnaire was administered to each participant which determined the extent to which they were characterised by a personality trait of seeking reward. This was the behavioural inhibition scale/behavioural activation scale (BIS/BAS). Sensitivity to reward was estimated by calculating the degree of **reward priming**, that is, the degree to which participants were influenced by the prospect of a reward, even when better choices were available.

In the studies of Hickey et al. (2010a, 2010b), this was operationalised by the extent to which participants allowed their attention to be captured by a stimulus was associated with a reward on the previous trial, but no longer on the current one. It was found that this reward priming measure correlated strongly with a specific subscale of the BAS, namely the BAS_{drive} scale when there was a prospect of a high reward. These results imply that motivational processes can have a strong influence on perceptual and attentional processes, but in addition this influence can be mediated by personality traits.

11.6 AFFECTIVE SIGNIFICANCE

Pessoa (2009) has proposed a conceptual framework to describe the interaction between emotion, motivation, and cognitive control. Central to this framework is the concept of **affective significance**. Affectively significant items are those that have a positive or negative value for the organism. Also, in Pessoa's affective-significance framework, competition and conflict play important roles, with emotions and motivational processes influencing the competition between different stimulus and response alternatives (see fig 11.15). Pessoa identified two forms of competition: perceptual and executive competition. When, according to Pessoa, several stimuli are in competition with each other for further processing (see Chapter 4), this competition

can affect all levels of processing. Duncan (1996) already suggested that this competition can be biased at all levels of the processing hierarchy. According to Pessoa's framework, perceptual competition occurs when emotional stimuli can influence further processing (see also Chapter 12). In contrast, executive competition occurs when a stimulus has a potential impact on our task goals.

Moreover, Pessoa (2009) states that affectively significant items can evoke an emotional response and become more salient via this mechanism. As a result, these stimuli can act as motivators. Perceptual competition in the visual cortex can be biased because the emotional valence of a stimulus strengthens its perceptual representation (Vuilleumier, 2005). This strengthening is likely due to output from the amygdala, which is known to have neural projections to multiple cortical areas, including the visual cortex.

Emotional factors can influence executive control in two different ways. The first is that the enhanced sensory representations result in a stronger attentional bias. The second is that the affective significance of items is projected directly to the cognitive control systems of the brain. This involves, for example, the direct connections from the amygdala to the anterior cingulate cortex.

According to Pessoa (2009) the way in which an affective stimulus is processed depends largely on the degree of threat that is emanating from this stimulus. Stimuli with a negative valence and a low degree of threat result in a stronger bias to process these stimuli (Brosch, Sander, Pourtois, & Scherer, 2008; Whalen, 1998). These stimuli are likely to capture attention because they are ambiguous. This ambiguity then signals a stronger need to gather

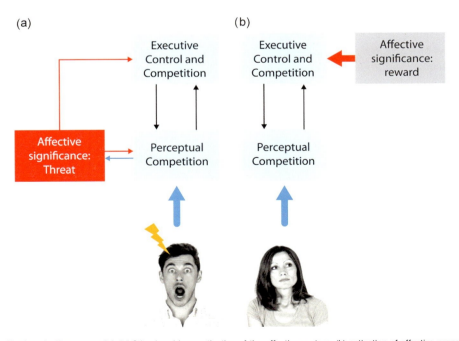

Figure 11.15 Pessoa's affective-significance model. (a) Stimulus-driven activation of the affective system; (b) activation of affective processes via reward mechanisms. (source: Pessoa, 2009)

more information about the stimuli in question. Although these stimuli are then assigned a higher priority, it is assumed that this additional information gathering takes place in the background, without having a strong impact on the processing of other stimuli, or on the cognitive control processes involved in task switching. The effects of these types of stimuli on behaviour are therefore also subtle, possibly difficult to replicate, and therefore only observable in people with a strong disposition for anxiety (Fox, Russo, Bowles, & Dutton, 2001).

In contrast, highly threatening stimuli are assumed to be processed with a high degree of priority. This prioritisation, unlike that of low-threat stimuli, does result in the mobilisation of additional processing power, so that the effects on behaviour are also considerably stronger (Lang, Davis, & Öhman, 2000). The most dramatic effect of processing such a threatening stimulus is that they are strongly prioritised, which triggers the attention process to start recruiting other executive functions. This eventually causes us to switch to processing the threat and inhibiting the processing of other, irrelevant stimuli (Bishop, 2007; Eysenck, Derakshan, Santos, & Calvo, 2007; Mathews & Mackintosh, 1998). Because these threatening stimuli require so much additional processing power and place a demand on the limited capacity of the cognitive control system, this implies that the processing of other stimuli is limited. Evidence for this comes from a study by Verbruggen and De Houwer (2007), who found that negative emotional stimuli increased the stop signal reaction time (see Chapter 5, for a discussion of this paradigm).

One way of investigating the effects of threat is by using a conditioning procedure in which a specific stimulus is associated with a mild electric shock. Lim, Padmala, and Pessoa (2008) instructed participants to perform a visual search task in which they had to detect the presence of the letter X in a series of letters. The perceptual load was manipulated by presenting the X in a display of uniform distractors (low load: e.g., OOOXOO) or amidst a random sequence of letters (high load: e.g., GFDXHF). These letter sequences were superimposed on images of faces.

Although the faces were task-irrelevant, some of the faces had been associated with an electric shock in an earlier phase. fMRI was used to record the activation of brain areas involved in processing threat-related information. For several brain areas, Lim et al. found a negative correlation between the degree of threat that was associated with the face and the performance on the letter detection task. A higher level of threat was reflected in a relative increase in activation of the anterior cingulate cortex after presentation of a threatening face. The degree to which this activation increased corresponded to a decrease in the letter detection task in the threat condition.

Pessoa (2009) assumes that at least three different neural mechanisms can be identified that are involved in the recruitment of executive functions during a threat (see fig 11.16). First, it is hypothesised that threats can regulate attentional control functions via the activation of the anterior cingulate cortex. The anterior cingulate cortex is involved in integrating the inputs from different neural systems, including systems involved in processing affective and motivational inputs (Bush et al., 2000). As such, it interacts with the anterior insula and orbitofrontal cortex (Barbas, 1995; see also Chapter 12). Moreover, as already discussed in Chapter 5, the anterior cingulate cortex is involved in detecting cognitive conflicts, in estimating the probability of making errors, in the monitoring of these errors, and in determining the relative costs and benefits of an action. Because of these properties, it can be expected that the detection of a threat may result in a reduced availability of executive functions for these other tasks. Because the anterior cingulate cortex is likely to represent the neural substrate that the updating, inhibition, and shifting functions have in common (Miyake et al., 2000; see Chapter 5), it may be expected that the activation of the anterior cingulate also activates these functions.

Second, it may be assumed that a threat can also have an effect on specific executive functions. Pessoa (2009) assumes that this happens via the activation of areas in the prefrontal cortex that are involved in specific executive functions. Although these areas may selectively recruit

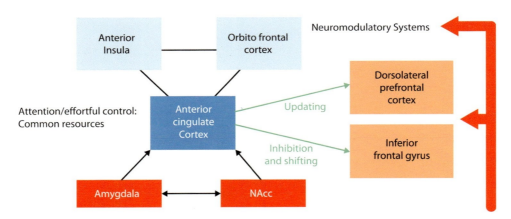

Figure 11.16 Overview of the neural mechanisms involved in the recruitment of executive processes. (source: Pessoa, 2009)

the updating or the inhibition and shifting functions, it is assumed that this recruitment occurs indirectly via the anterior cingulate cortex (see fig 11.16).

The exact influence of affective significance on task performance will depend on various factors, given the complex interactions outlined here. For example, an affective stimulus can improve task performance when it is relevant, because the affective valence results in additional attention to this stimulus. However, when the stimulus is task irrelevant, allocating attention to it will result in a reduction in task performance. In addition to the affective valence of a stimulus, the level of threat will also play a role here. Strongly threatening stimuli will capture more attention and recruit a considerable amount of processing power from other cognitive mechanisms. This can lead to a situation where these stimuli are processed in more detail, while the impact on task performance is still negative.

Third, threat can influence executive functions by inducing changes in mood. These changes presumably involve the ascending neural projections from the locus coeruleus and the ventral tegmentum (Heimer & Van Hoesen, 2006; Sarter & Bruno, 1999). At least two factors may contribute to such a change in mood, namely general factors, such as one's general mood or level of anxiety (Eysenck & Calvo, 1992), and specific factors, such as the prospect of a reward or incentive (Braver, 2012).

Pessoa (2009) hypothesises that motivation can affect task performance similar to the way threatening stimuli do, namely through the recruitment of executive functions and through the biasing of the processing of those stimuli that are relevant to obtaining a reward. In addition, motivation has two further effects on the recruitment of executive functions.

First, it is assumed to sharpen the impact of executive functions by predominantly boosting specific functions, instead of exerting a generic influence on the common part. For example, motivation can specifically influence the orientation and refocusing of attention, with the result that participants are more sensitive to detecting stimuli (Engelmann & Pessoa, 2007; Engelmann, Damaraju, Padmala, & Pessoa, 2009). In the Engelmann et al. studies, it was found that the sensitivity for detecting specific stimuli increased as a function of the incentive that was given. This increase in task performance correlated with an increase in activation of the fMRI responses in the visual cortex.

Second, motivation will affect the degree to which executive functions are deployed in a given task. Because multiple cognitive processes must be prioritised, a redistribution of these priorities may not only affect the processes involved in processing the reward but also other processes involved in processing a task, with a net result of reduced task performance. For example, when participants are rewarded for accurate and fast responses to go-trials while performing a **stop signal task**, this may result in a longer stop signal reaction time (Padmala & Pessoa, 2010). These results can be explained by the fact that participants who are rewarded focus their attention more strongly on the go stimuli and therefore process the stop stimuli less well (Bekker et al., 2005; Boehler et al., 2009).

11.7 SUMMARY

Since the late 20th century, there has been an increasing realisation that cognitive functions cannot be separated from the regulation of bodily functions, and that motivational and emotional processes play a key role in this. This realisation has led to a new movement in cognitive psychology known as embodied cognition. Motivated, goal-oriented behaviour is strongly influenced by emotions and by the interpretation of bodily signals. In addition, the processing of a reward plays a crucial role in motivated behaviour. The motivational processes manifest themselves by influencing perceptual, attentional, and cognitive control processes.

Research into motivational processes already has a relatively long history, dating back to much animal physiological research into basic state regulation processes. Historic motivation theories are therefore often based on physiological principles such as homeostasis and drives. Homeostatic motivation theories are based on the idea that an organism strives for an optimal state.

It might not be strictly necessary to include homeostatic mechanisms in these explanations. A competing idea uses the concept of settling points, that is, the balance that can be achieved between two or more opposing forces. These opposing forces might create the illusion of homeostatic regulation. A direct counterpart of homeostasis is allostasis. In contrast to homeostasis, allostatic processes do not strive for stability of an organism, but for growth and development. In some cases, however, allostasis can be a response to a disrupted homeostatic process, for example in the case of addiction.

Drives may be considered as an intervening variable between a variety of internal states and the possible actions that may follow. An example of such a drive is the concept of thirst. Although the danger of a circular argument lurks when defining drives, it is actually possible to define drives without resorting to circular arguments. This is especially possible when the definition results in specific predictions that have not yet been observed. A problem with the purely physiological motivation theories is that they cannot explain the effects of expectation.

The opponent-process theory of motivation states that every hedonistic stimulus not only evokes a hedonistic response but also a slower anti-hedonistic response, which becomes stronger and stronger after repeated exposure to the stimulus in question, with the result that it masks or overshadows the original hedonistic response. The opposing processes can be well illustrated by the effects of heroin addiction. When abstaining from the stimulus, only the anti-hedonistic reaction will occur, causing withdrawal symptoms to follow.

The ethologist Konrad Lorenz proposed a hydraulic model of motivation. A central feature of this model is that internal drives become stronger and stronger as long as no drive-reducing behaviour is displayed. The model can explain vacuum responses in animals well, but it is characterised by a number of other aspects of behaviour that it cannot explain. This is particularly the case when behaviour does not appear to be aimed at reducing the motivation, as is the case with excessive eating.

Originally, the processing of a reward was assumed to be related to drive reduction. However, an overwhelming amount of evidence now shows that this is not the case. Evidence ranges from an insistence to taste food without this being required for reducing nutritional deficiency, to studies showing that dogs continue to overeat after their stomachs are intravenously filled, to electrophysiological studies in rats which show that stimulating the reward centres of the brain actually results in an increase in the behaviour that this stimulation brings about.

Because these drive-reduction theories were deficient, a new explanation had to be found. This was done from the view that motivated behaviour followed as a response to an incentive. One of the first theories to be formulated on the basis of this principle was the Bolles-Toates-Bindra theory, which states that physiological signals can regulate the hedonic impact of a reward. The way in which this happens can be described with the term 'alliesthesia'. This concept describes the change in pleasure that a stimulus can evoke, as a function of the body's internal state.

To understand the full impact of a reward, however, it is necessary to make a distinction between 'liking' and 'wanting'. Here, liking equals the hedonic impact of a stimulus, whereas wanting equals its motivational impact. It is possible that this distinction arose from an evolutionary advantage that initially lacked the hedonic aspect.

Recent research on motivation suggests that the anterior cingulate cortex plays an important role in the execution of goal-directed behaviour. This brain area is probably involved in selecting and holding on to task goals, while other brain areas, including the striatum and areas in the prefrontal cortex, are involved in the precise execution of the actions required for these goals and in evaluating them. A hierarchical form of reinforcement learning plays an important role here.

In addition, recent studies indicate that rewards can strongly influence cognitive control processes. An important assumption in this work is that the current and future motivational values of events are used by the brain as learning signals, which in turn can influence decision processes. Here, motivation is strongly related to the expected outcome of a decision. Many studies conducted in this area make use of the monetary incentive delay task. Here, participants have to perform a relatively simple task, in which they are informed by a cue prior to the task whether they will receive a reward. Another frequently used approach is the incentive-driven coding paradigm.

The general pattern of results found with these tasks suggests that participants often become selectively better at processing the stimuli that are rewarded, or that irrelevant stimuli associated with a reward often interfere more strongly with task performance. Neuroimaging and electrophysiological studies suggest a strong overlap in the neural circuits involved in reward processing and those involved in the regulation of cognitive control processes. It is likely that the influence on cognitive control processes involves strengthening the associations between the stimulus and the relevant task properties. However, the precise influence depends on multiple properties, including the way in which a reward is given and the extent to which a participant can influence the outcome of an action.

Reward can not only influence higher-order aspects of task performance, such as the selection of task sets, but can also directly influence attention and perception. Participants continue to attend more to stimuli associated with a reward, even when those stimuli have become irrelevant distractors with a negative impact on task performance. In addition, participants also have a strong tendency to look at stimuli that signal a high reward, even when this looking behaviour results in missing out on the reward.

Behaviour is not only influenced by rewards but also by the affective significance of a stimulus. Here, the level of threat plays a particularly important role. Threatening stimuli require extra attention, especially when they are ambiguous, and cause a reallocation of cognitive control processes. As a result, threatening stimuli are processed with a higher priority, which may be at the expense of processing other tasks or stimuli.

NOTE

1 At least, that is the case with older thermostats; more modern, so-called modulating systems are capable of keeping the temperature constantly close to the target value, without a continuous oscillation: as the desired temperature gets closer to the target value, energy output of the heater decreases. We also find such modulating corrective actions in many biological systems, for instance in systems regulating blood pressure. Control of food and water intake, however, appears to be controlled on the basis of a built-in tolerance: after all, we are not constantly eating or drinking.

FURTHER READING

Braver, T. S. (2015). *Motivation and cognitive control*. Hove, UK: Routledge.

Dreher, J.-C., & Tremblay, L. (2009). *Handbook of reward and decision making*. Amsterdam: Elsevier.

Ryan, F. (2019). *The Oxford handbook of human motivation*. Oxford, UK: Oxford University Press.

Stellar, J., & Stellar, E. (2012). *The neurobiology of motivation and reward*. Heidelberg: Springer Verlag.

CHAPTER 12
Emotion and cognition

12.1 INTRODUCTION

One of the major shortcomings of the information-processing approach that originally triggered the cognitive revolution is that it did not consider a possible role for emotion in cognitive processes. After all, this approach regarded the computer as a metaphor for human information processing, and we can hardly imagine how computers can exhibit emotions. Moreover, properly manipulating the emotional state of a participant in an experimental setting has traditionally been problematic, so that in most cases participants were tested in an emotional state that was as neutral as possible. For these reasons, the interaction between emotion and cognition was largely ignored for a long time. Classic cognitive-psychological research can therefore be classified as **cold cognition**. The cold cognition approach implies that people perform tasks in a cold, rational manner, where they try to optimise task performance as much as possible.

Although several scientific studies on emotion had been conducted since at least the beginning of the 20th century, a renewed interest in the relationship between emotion and cognition began around the turn of this century (Davidson, 2000; Gross, 1998). In this new line of research, we can distinguish two main approaches: the first concerns how cognitive processes can influence our emotional experiences; the second, how emotions can influence cognitive processes.

12.2 EMOTION, MOOD, AND AFFECT

What is an emotion? To address this question, we must first distinguish between emotions, mood, and affect. **Emotions** are often short-lived moods that can vary greatly in intensity and, moreover, can often either be directly evoked by a specific event or be influenced by our interpretation or representation of this event. For example, the anticipation of an expected win or loss (or actual winning or losing of a sum of money) can result in strong emotions. A **mood**, on the other hand, is much more stable, and the specific cause of a particular mood is often less clear-cut. Despite these

differences, there is a strong interaction between emotion and mood: an emotion can turn into a mood or vice versa. In the remainder of this chapter, we will often use the broader term **affect** (or state of mind), which describes both emotion and mood. Positive affect refers to a range of positive emotions and moods, whereas negative affect refers to negative emotions and moods. Finally, the term **valence** refers to a continuous dimension that can vary from an extremely negative to extremely positive affect.

12.3 THE STRUCTURE OF EMOTIONS

Ideas concerning emotions have changed considerably over time. Historically, emotions have been defined as subjective conscious feelings, such as love, contempt, anger, jealousy, or despair. Because these subjective experiences are hardly accessible to empirical research (see Chapter 4), defining emotions in purely subjective terms is problematic. To circumvent this problem, we currently define emotions predominantly in terms of a composite of feelings, behavioural expressions, and physiological changes. As such, we can understand emotions as traits that enable us to adaptively respond to significant events in ways that promote our evolutionary success.

Traditionally, two influential classes of theories describing the structure of emotions can be identified, namely the categorical theories and the dimensional theories. Categorical theories assume that emotions are composed of a small set of independent basic emotions, which combined form a richer set of complex emotions. Dimensional theories, on the other hand, regard each emotion as a point on a multi-dimensional continuum. In addition to these two approaches, a more recent development is based on the idea that emotions are the result of predictive processes; an approach to which we will return briefly towards the end of the chapter.

12.3.1 THE CATEGORICAL APPROACH

Some researchers argue that we can distinguish a set of basic emotions, such as anger, sadness, joy, fear, disgust, and surprise (Izard, 2007). According to their categorical

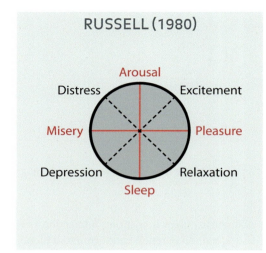

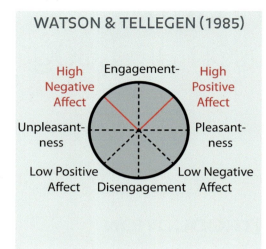

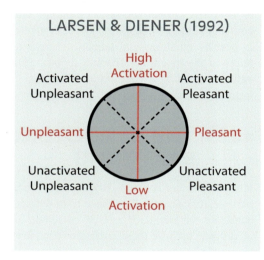

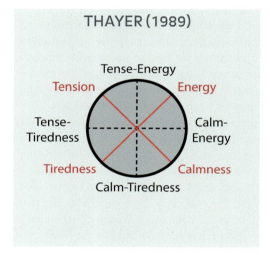

Figure 12.1 Examples of the different dimensional classifications of emotions. (source: Barrett and Russell, 1999)

approach, these basic emotions are considered to be innate, shared with other species, and expressed through specific physiological responses and facial expressions. Basic emotions are also found in several different cultures (Power & Dalgeish, 2008). How many basic emotions exist has not yet been firmly determined: estimates range from four to eight, with most researchers assuming the existence of five to six basic emotions. Complex emotions, on the other hand, are assumed to be learned, to vary from culture to culture and, to vary in terms of expression, and to be composed of response patterns that are based on combinations of the basic emotions.

12.3.2 DIMENSIONAL APPROACH

Other researchers view emotions as a point on a continuum that is defined by two or more orthogonal axes. Barrett and Russell (1999) have identified many different ways in which emotions can be classified according to this dimensional approach. For example, Russell (1980) proposes a classification according to the axes of misery-pleasure and arousal-sleep, while Watson and Tellegen (1985) propose

a classification according to the axes of positive affect versus negative affect. Although these researchers each propose different classifications, there is a high degree of agreement between these approaches, as Figure 12.1 shows. This dimensional approach is supported by a considerable amount of evidence. For instance, Baucom, Wedell, Wang, Blitzer, and Shinkareva (2012) found that the patterns of brain activity measured while participants viewed emotional pictures were consistent with the two independent dimensions of arousal and valence.

12.4 HISTORIC EMOTION THEORIES

Although the focus on the role of emotion in cognitive processes is relatively new, emotion research itself can boast a long tradition. Although there are considerable differences between the various classic theoretical approaches, they all assume that emotions arise from three processing stages: (1) the evaluation of sensory input; (2) the conscious

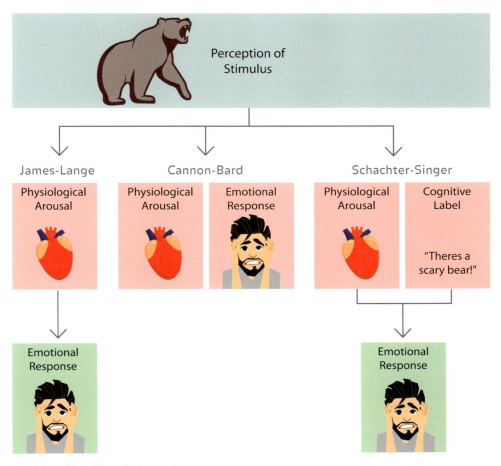

Figure 12.2 An overview of three different theoretical approaches.

(or unconscious) experience of a feeling; and (3) the expression of behavioural and physiological responses. The main differences between the classic emotion theories involve the order in which these processes operate and the interaction between them (see fig 12.2).

12.4.1 JAMES-LANGE FEEDBACK THEORY

One of the first emotion theories was formulated by the American pioneering philosopher and psychologist William James (1884). James' ideas with regard to emotion are based on the following question: 'Do we run away from a bear because we are afraid of it, or are we afraid of a bear because we run away from it? Although intuitively we would think that we run away because we are afraid of a bear, James followed the exact opposite reasoning. His interpretation of emotions was that the action of running away, combined with the physiological responses, such as sweating, increased heart rate and respiration, were the very triggers that brought about a fear response. James started from the assumption that there is a deterministic relationship between physical responses and emotion. Consequently, if these physical responses are absent, James argued, we experience no emotions.

At about the same time as James, the Danish physiologist Carl Lange put forward a similar theory (Lange, 1885). An important difference between the two theories is related to the importance that was attached to the individual physical signals. While James proposed that emotions could be triggered by a multitude of physiological signals, Lange attached particular importance to the cardiological functions. Lange was also less interested in our awareness of the emotional experiences. Despite these differences, the general approach proposed by James and Lange that physical reactions cause emotions is known as the James-Lange feedback theory.

12.4.2 CANNON-BARD THEORY

A few years after James and Lange, the physiologists Walter Cannon and Philip Bard published a critique of the original James-Lange theory (Cannon, 1927). Cannon and Bard's main criticism was that the responses of the autonomic nervous system were not sufficiently differentiated to evoke the wide variety of emotions that we can experience. A specific autonomic response, such as getting goose-bumps, can occur in combination with several emotions so that the occurrence of the response is in itself insufficient to evoke a specific emotion. Moreover, Cannon and Bard argued that the hormonal feedback mechanisms are too slow to explain the abrupt onset of an emotion. Experimental manipulation of these hormonal mechanisms also proved ineffective in evoking emotional responses. Cannon and Bard therefore proposed that the autonomic nervous system is primarily involved in regulating the body's flight or fight response, which coordinates bodily functions during an emotional response. This view is consistent with the arousal and activation axes that we already discussed when introducing the dimensional emotion models.

Cannon and Bard studied the effects of surgically severing connections between the cortex, the brainstem, and other subcortical areas on emotion processing in animals. They found that emotional responses were unaffected as long as the operation took place at levels higher than the diencephalon (i.e., the hypothalamus and thalamus). These results were consistent with studies that had shown that electrical stimulation of the hypothalamus elicited emotional responses in cats. Based on these results, Cannon and Bard proposed that emotional responses are processed by the diencephalon. These responses would then be projected both to the cortex, where they contribute to awareness of the emotional experience, and to the periphery of the body, where they are expressed in the form of physiological effects and behavioural changes.

12.4.3 THE SCHACHTER-SINGER THEORY

A similar idea was put forward by Stanley Schachter and Jerome Singer (Schachter & Singer, 1962). These authors also hypothesised that emotions are the result of the interpretation of physiological signals. Unlike the James-Lange and Cannon-Bard theories, however, Schachter and Singer assumed that although the emotion itself is evoked by a physiological response, the interpretation of this response is a cognitive process. According to the Schachter-Singer theory, the fact that we experience emotions is thus triggered by the interpretation of these bodily signals. The exact emotion we experience is the result of a cognitive evaluative process, according to Schachter and Singer.

12.4.4 DUAL PROCESS THEORY

One of the most influential theories describing how emotion can contribute to the recognition of danger is the dual process theory by the American neuroscientist Joseph LeDoux (1995). Perhaps you might have had the experience of being startled by an unexpected event, only realising later what it was that startled you. LeDoux's model can explain this experience from the idea that emotional valence of the visual signal is processed by two neural circuits. The first of these two consists of a slow operating circuit in which information from the thalamus is projected via the visual

cortex to the amygdala. The second is a fast-operating circuit that projects information from the thalamus directly to the amygdala. Why would there be two circuits? Most likely, the fast circuit allows us to respond extremely quickly to a threatening situation, which is essential for our survival (McFadyen, Dolan, & Garrido, 2020). The slow circuit, on the other hand, allows us to make a detailed representation of the emotional significance of the situation, which enables us to adapt our behaviour appropriately to the current situation.

Although the dual process theory is very influential and offers a good explanation for the phenomenon that an emotional response can occur before we become aware of the triggering stimulus, the theory also makes predictions that are not well supported by empirical findings. For example, the theory assumes that associating an affective response with a stimulus involves a specialised mechanism, so that the formation of this association is not influenced by extinction and **occasion setting**. Occasion setting is the process that links the association to very specific circumstances, implying that the emotion would be experienced specifically under those circumstances. Moreover, the formation of the association would not be influenced by competition from other stimuli in this case.

Lipp and Purkis (2005), however, found no evidence for a special mechanism that would be involved in the formation of these associations. In their study, neutral images of geometric shapes and neutral tactile stimuli were paired with a negative electric shock. However, the stimuli that were thus conditioned were subject to extinction, occasion setting, and competition. Moreover, it was found that the conditioning effects were only found when the participants were aware of the dependence of the relationship between the unconditioned stimulus and the conditioned stimulus.

12.4.5 SOMATIC MARKER THEORY

In the last decade of the last century, the American-Portuguese neuroscientist Antonio Damasio (1996) published a theory that bears some similarities to the James-Lange theory. Damasio's **somatic marker** theory is also based on the idea that emotional reactions result from the interpretation of our bodily responses to an emotional event. An important difference with the earlier James-Lange theory is that Damasio assigns an important role to the prefrontal cortex in recognising these emotions and in regulating our behaviour on the basis of these emotional signals (see Box 12.1). When we consider performing an action, we will experience an emotional response based on the expected outcome of this action. This expectation is based on previous experiences of performing similar actions. For example, speeding on the motorway may result in a fine. The negative experience of receiving a

Box 12.1 Phineas Gage: man, myth, and mystery

Few neuropsychological case studies have captured the public imagination as much as that of American railway worker Phineas Gage. On September 13, 1848, toward the end of a long working day, the then 24-year-old Gage filled a borehole with gunpowder. Gage was considered one of the best foremen and for this reason the Rutland and Burlington Railroad Company had hired him to prepare a particularly difficult stretch of track near Cavendish, Vermont, for the construction of a new railway. Gage's job was to carefully pound the powder with an iron rod, after which his assistants would fill the hole with sand and detonate it in a controlled fashion. At a crucial moment, however, Gage was distracted, possibly by his workmen loading rocks onto a cart, causing the rod to smash unintentionally onto the gunpowder, resulting in a fatal explosion.

This event would mark the last normal day of Gage's life, for the iron bar was thrown upwards by the blast and penetrated Gage's skull near his left jawbone and exited it at the top of his head. Miraculously, Gage not only survived the accident, but he was also standing upright again within minutes. He himself claimed never to have lost consciousness. What follows these events is a fascinating story of intrigue, speculation, myth, and mystery, regarding Gage himself, his behavioural change, the extent of his brain damage, and the dubious conclusions that are drawn from his case.

Although Gage is probably the most famous neuropsychological patient who ever lived, his life after the accident is surrounded by mystery. The canonical story about Gage is something like this: although Gage appeared to function normally after his accident, his personality had changed dramatically. From a well-respected railway foreman with a great sense of responsibility, he had turned into a vagabond, no longer capable of taking responsibility, and suffering from emotional outbursts. The lesson for neuropsychology was simple and straightforward: the brain areas destroyed by Gage's accident are crucially involved in the cognitive control of our behaviour and emotions.

It is unknown, however, which brain areas were damaged exactly, since the original reports of the physicians who were treating Gage were very vague about this. Although Gage's case study had already been standard material in many neuropsychology textbooks, 1994 witnessed a strong revival of interest in his accident. The Portuguese American neuroscientists couple Hanna and Antonio Damasio had developed a new theory about the relationship between emotion regulation and cognitive control, known as the somatic marker theory, which states that our conscious experience of bodily emotional signals results in the subjective experience of emotions and that the perception of these signals can also influence our decision-making behaviour. They suspected that the bilateral prefrontal cortex played an important role in this regulation and saw in the historical Phineas Gage an interesting case supporting their ideas.

The problem was that, in order to do this, the Damasio's needed to know exactly which brain areas were damaged. To get an idea of this, they developed a simulation of the accident on the basis of the recently developed MRI technique and Gage's preserved skull. Based on the holes in Gage's skull, they calculated the path that the iron bar had taken through Gage's brain; and based on the results, which were published in the prestigious scientific journal *Science* (Damasio, Grabowski, Frank, Galaburda, & Damasio, 1994), the Damasios and their colleagues concluded that the bilateral prefrontal cortex had indeed been damaged. The results of this remarkable simulation have become an icon of modern cognitive neuropsychology and adorn almost every textbook on the subject, making Phineas Gage the perfect textbook example of the behavioural change that results from prefrontal damage.

Unfortunately, however, the example is too perfect. When we consider the few historical facts, we must conclude that both Gage's remarkable behavioural change and the conclusion that the bilateral prefrontal cortex is involved in this behavioural change need nuance. In the first weeks after the accident, Gage was treated by a local physician, Dr John Harlow, who arrived a few hours after the accident (after Gage had already received emergency care from an anonymous doctor). Dr. Harlow saw Gage, still soaked with blood, staggering to his hotel room. At first, Harlow mainly tried to stop the bleeding. Gage remained, according to Harlow's report, conscious and in a rational state of mind. In the days that followed, however, his condition deteriorated dramatically: his brain began to swell, he began to lose his temper and finally a fungal infection developed in the wound. Gage consequently lost consciousness and appeared to be doomed. In the following weeks, Harlow managed to stop the swelling, however. While Gage's condition remained critical, Harlow slowly but steadily began to remove the bone fragments and close the wound.

In 1849, after Gage's physical medical condition had sufficiently recovered, he was invited to Harvard

(*Continued*)

Box 12.1 (Continued)

Medical School, by a certain Dr Henry Bigelow, for a formal medical evaluation. Bigelow regarded Gage primarily as a medical curiosity, and his evaluation of Gage is the only detailed medical account of Gage that is known to exist, besides Harlow's. Interestingly, Bigelow noted that Gage's 'physical and mental faculties recovered remarkably well'. The problem, however, is that at the time medical tests predominantly focused on sensory and motor skills, so Bigelow's conclusions are based mainly on the fact that Gage could still hear, see, walk, and talk. Bigelow, like his contemporaries, was convinced that the prefrontal lobes had no significant function and therefore he had paid little attention to them.

In contrast to Bigelow, Harlow had previously made some remarks on Gage's changed mental state, but even these remarks did not go much further than a few loose statements about the fact that the once decisive Gage had become an indecisive man who made many plans and gave them up again quickly. His respect for his former life values had disappeared and so had his business acumen. Harlow concluded that the balance between Gage's intellectual skills and his animal instincts was disturbed. Friends also remarked that Gage was no longer himself.

Following the accident and the changes in his behaviour, the railway company terminated its contract with Gage, and to make a living he travelled around New England exhibiting himself and his iron rod. He eventually found work as a coachman in New Hampshire. Although these accounts indicate that Gage had changed, the problem is that most of the descriptions are too vague to get a good impression of the exact nature of these changes. For example, how often did Gage have tantrums and what exactly was meant by 'balance between intellectual skills and animal instincts'? Unfortunately, no one who knew Gage before the accident left a detailed account of his change, which left the door wide open to a wide variety of myths. After the accident, therefore, the most fantastic stories began to circulate. For example, Gage is said to have repeatedly sold the exclusive rights to his skull to various prestigious medical institutions and to have swindled the money, or to have walked around with his iron rod still stuck in his head for another 20 years! Some described Gage as sexually apathetic, while others portrayed him as a licentious person with no sexual inhibitions. He was described as an emotional hothead, as well as a person lacking emotions.

One problem is that some of these caricatures have also penetrated the scientific literature. In his book *Descartes Error* (1994) Antonio Damasio describes Gage as a sociopath, a liar, and a braggart who also drank excessively; behaviour that, Damasio suggested, indicated that Gage had lost his free will, thus becoming a victim of his impulses. According to Damasio, this change was due to his dysfunctional prefrontal lobes.

Because the simulation of Gage's accident by Damasio et al. (1994) is still rightfully considered to be an ingenious feat, there is a significant risk of forgetting that in the last 25 years there has been a huge increase in computing power that allows us to make much more sophisticated models of Gage's skull. In 2012, neuroscientists Jack van Horn and his colleagues conducted a new study, using a highly refined reconstruction of Gage's skull, which they used to simulate the effects of millions of potential trajectories of the iron bar through Gage's head. Almost all of these trajectories were rejected because they would either fracture Gage's jawbone, explode his skull, or have other consequences that were inconsistent with the wounds in Gage's skull.

Based on the possible pathways that remained, Van Horn et al. (2012) concluded that it was highly unlikely that Gage had suffered bilateral damage, but that the initial damage was limited to the left hemisphere. According to Van Horn et al., the degree of grey matter damage would also have been relatively limited. White matter damage, however, would have been considerable according to Van Horn et al.'s estimate: about 11% of the important connections between the frontal lobes and other brain areas were estimated to be destroyed by the impact.

According to Van Horn et al. the behavioural change resulting from such an impairment could be similar to that observed in Alzheimer's patients. Although Gage's behaviour was initially described by Harlow as 'not comparable to that of dementia', we must consider the fact that Harlow only treated Gage in the first weeks after the accident and that the progressive degeneration of the dying brain tissue, in combination with the swelling and the fungal infection, may have led to a progressive degeneration of Gage's behaviour.

Remarkably, and in spite of the many speculations about the loss of his cognitive control functions, Gage left for Chile in 1852, only a year and a half after he started working as a coachman in New Hampshire, at

(Continued)

Box 12.1 (Continued)

the invitation of an American prospector who hoped to make his fortune during the Chilean gold rush. In Chile, Gage would continue to work as a coachman for a number of years, regularly travelling the steep mountain routes between Santiago and Valparaiso. Eventually, poor health forced him back to the United States in 1859. During the final year of his life, he lived with his family near San Francisco. After his health had somewhat recovered, he found work on a farm by the beginning of 1860. Here, a relatively stable period followed, until an intensive day of work in the spring of 1860 floored Gage. An epileptic seizure followed the next night. More seizures followed and a particularly severe one eventually proved to be fatal. Phineas Gage died on May 21, 1860, at the age of 36, 12 years after his near fatal accident.

In all likelihood, the Phineas Gage story would have ended here, had it not been for the fact that Dr Harlow had re-established contact with Gage's family. After interviewing the family, Harlow managed to convince Gage's sister Phebe to open Gage's tomb for the purpose of preserving Gage's skull. Phebe Gage agreed and with a small ceremony, in which even the mayor of San Francisco was present, Phineas Gage's skull was exhumed. After receiving it from the Gage family, Harlow wrote his final report on the Phineas Gage case, and it is this report that contains just about all the factual information about Gage's life, his mental state, and his trip to South America.

More than 150 years after Gage's accident, we can only speculate what exactly happened to Gage on the basis of the few pieces of information that we have. Nevertheless, the fact that Gage worked as a coachman in Chile for many years could be crucial to understanding the Gage case according to psychologist, historian, and Gage expert Malcolm Macmillan (2000). Driving a carriage required a complex set of skills, flexibility in planning and motor coordination to man the individual horses. In addition, Gage had to manoeuvre the coach on long routes through difficult mountain paths, where he had to be alert to unexpected circumstances, such as fellow road users or robbers. He was also responsible for collecting travel money from the passengers and taking care of the horses. The fact that Gage managed to carry out these tasks for many years is inconsistent with the image of an irresponsible bon vivant who could only react on impulse. Instead, it is more consistent with a man who had to undergo a tough rehabilitation process and who had partially recovered from his brain damage. Although he may not have had the insight and responsibility of the past, the environment in which he worked as a coachman offered him enough structure to not only function but also to facilitate his recovery.

fine can evoke an emotional response if, on a later occasion, we have the urge to speed again. This emotion then translates into a physical response, such as sweating or an increase in heart rate. These bodily reactions, the somatic markers, would under normal circumstances be interpreted by the ventromedial prefrontal cortex, and used to adjust our decision-making behaviour, thus avoiding reckless behaviour.

Damasio and colleagues observed that patients with damage to the ventromedial prefrontal cortex showed impairments in expressing and experiencing their emotions. Despite continued normal performance on a wide range of tests of their intellectual abilities, these patients also appeared to show a change in their decision-making behaviour, particularly with regard to risk-taking behaviour. Several studies have also shown that these patients show riskier behaviour on gambling tasks. According to Damasio, this risk-taking behaviour follows from the fact that these patients are unable to adequately read the emotional response that follows a risky decision.

A common method for investigating the effects of this type of risk behaviour employs the **Iowa gambling task** (see fig 12.3). As discussed in Chapter 5, this task involves participants choosing a card from one of four decks. Two of these decks offer the chance of a relatively large profit, but also incur regular solid losses. The other two decks

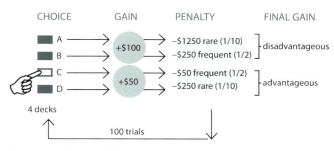

Figure 12.3 Overview of the Iowa gambling task. Participants have to choose a card from one of four decks. Two of the four stacks regularly result in high gains but are disadvantageous in the long run due to frequent high losses. The other two stacks result in lower gains, but also fewer high losses, making the long-term return higher.

do result in smaller gains, but here the losses are also very limited, so that the net gain of the latter two stacks is higher. Participants without prefrontal damage typically learn to choose cards from the latter decks pretty quickly. Patients with prefrontal damage can learn that choosing a card from the risky decks is often unsuccessful. When they consider choosing a card from this deck, however, they often do not exhibit the typical physical characteristics of increased arousal that neurotypical participants show (Bechara, Damasio, Tranel, & Damasio, 2005). As a result, prefrontal patients often persist in risky behaviour: the bodily signals that normally tell us that a certain choice is a bad idea are largely absent in prefrontal-damaged patients.

12.4.6 APPRAISAL THEORIES

Appraisal theories aim to explain emotional responses on the basis of the subjective value that we attach to those actions that provoke an emotional response. Cognitive processes are involved in evaluating this response. As such, appraisal theories assume that emotional responses are triggered when we begin to evaluate the relevance of changes in our environment that have the potential to affect our well-being (Brosch, 2013). Since the initial formulation of an appraisal theory by the American psychologists Richard Lazarus and Elizabeth Alfert (1964), numerous variants have been formulated. What most of these theories have in common is that each emotion is evoked by its own specific interpretation and appraisal process and that top-down processes are crucially involved in this (see fig 12.4). For example, anger involves blaming someone else for the situation that we are in, whereas sadness is more likely to be experienced when we have little control over the situation.

Most appraisal theories assume that the appraisal processes determine to a large extent which emotional state we will find ourselves in. The theories also assume that these appraisal processes result in additional emotional experiences, such as changes in our bodily sensations or our willingness to engage in actions. Cognitive appraisal processes may be both conscious and unconscious. Smith and Kirby (2009) distinguish between appraisal processes that are based on explicit conscious reasoning and processes that are based on the unconscious retrieval of memories. Appraisal based on conscious processes is generally slower, but also more flexible, compared to the unconscious processes.

Cognitive appraisal processes appear to be consistent across cultures. For example, Fontaine, Scherer, and Soranio Salinas (2013) report the results of a large-scale study conducted in 27 different countries. Participants from these countries were very good at classifying emotions based on appraisal patterns alone. Adding additional

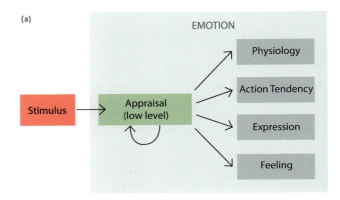

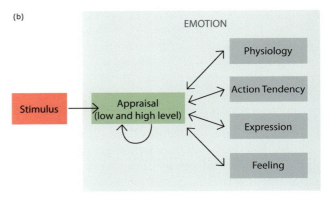

Figure 12.4 An overview of the processes involved in an emotional response. (a) There is an initial forward sweep, in which bottom-up driven appraisal processes result in the activation of a cognitive schema. (b) This initial sweep is followed by an elaboration process, in which cognitive appraisal processes interpret the emotional response. (source: Brosch, 2013)

components, such as bodily sensations or expressions of actions, had only a limited influence on the quality of the classification. These results suggest that cognitive appraisal is a vital component in determining one's emotional state.

12.4.6.1 Conscious Appraisal

In one of the first studies of appraisal processes, Speisman, Lazarus, Mordkoff, and Davison (1964) used film fragments involving several fear-inducing scenes. One scene involved an Aboriginal ritual where adolescent boys were given deep cuts in their penises. Another scene showed various accidents in a carpentry workshop. Cognitive appraisal processes were manipulated via the accompanying commentary track. For example, denial was induced when the commentator mentioned that the incisions were not painful and that the accidents were staged. In another condition, intellectualisation was induced by approaching the incision ritual from the perspective of an anthropologist (emphasising how important the ritual was to the members of the tribe) and prompting participants to view the workshop film objectively. In a control condition, no comments were made. Compared to this control condition, both experimental manipulations resulted in a strong decrease in stress responses as measured by, among others, heart rate and skin conductance responses.

Emotions can result from the combination of different appraisal processes. For example, Kuppens, Van Mechelen, Smits, and De Boeck (2003) found that four different factors can produce anger, namely obstructions to achieving a goal, holding another person responsible for a situation, dishonesty, and the degree of control over a situation. In addition, they found that none of these components was in itself necessary to experience anger: the experienced anger could be evoked by any combination of several of these factors. Similar results were found by Tong (2010).

Presently, most research on conscious appraisal processes is based on hypothetical scenarios in which participants have to identify themselves with somebody else. Smith and Lazarus (1993), for example, used such a scenario in which a student had performed poorly on an exam. Participants reported that this student would probably be angry if he blamed his low grade on an unhelpful teacher, but sad if he blamed the result on himself; for example, by starting assignments too late.

An important criticism of research with hypothetical scenarios is that the situation and the valuation processes are often manipulated simultaneously. Consequently, it is very difficult to know whether an emotional response is a direct result of the situation or a response to the evaluation of the situation. In order to circumvent this problem, Siemer, Mauss, and Gross (2007) used only one specific situation. Participants were asked to participate in an experiment about the role of emotions on cognitive task performance. The experimenter acted brusque, condescending, and extremely critical to the participant. Moreover, the participants' performance was rated very negatively. At the end of the study, the participants were asked to rate their own emotions and also to indicate how they had appraised the situation. The main finding of this study was that the intensity of self-reported emotions was strongly dependent on the cognitive rating of the situation. For example, the degree to which participants reported having control over the situation had a strong negative relationship with feelings of guilt and sadness, but not with anger.

An additional problem with hypothetical scenarios is that most participants experience little in the way of real emotions. To circumvent this problem, Bennett and Lowe (2008) investigated work-related incidents among nursing staff in hospitals. Anger and frustration were the most commonly reported emotions associated with the most stressful incidents, and these emotions were reasonably well predicted by the cognitive appraisal of the stressful situations in question. A major exception was sadness, as this emotion was fairly commonly used to describe a negative situation.

Most appraisal studies report correlations or associations between the cognitive appraisal processes and the emotions experienced, so they cannot infer any causal

relationships between the two. If, however, cognitive appraisal processes cause emotional reactions, then decisions about the appraisal should be made more quickly than decisions about the emotional experience itself. In practice, however, it is often the other way around. Decisions about the emotional experience are generally made more quickly than decisions about the cognitive appraisal of a situation (Siemer & Reisenzein, 2007). It is still possible, however, that the cognitive appraisal itself is determined very quickly, but that it takes a relatively long time before it can be made explicit and become accessible to consciousness. Siemer and Reisenzein (2007) found that cognitive appraisals did indeed become available sooner, when similar appraisals were required in quick succession, implying that in such cases awareness of our appraisal can be facilitated.

To address the question of whether cognitive appraisal processes can cause an emotional state, researchers manipulate the appraisal processes when participants are shown an emotional stimulus. Schartau, Dalgleish, and Dunn (2009) did so by showing films in which humans and animals experienced suffering. Some participants had first received cognitive appraisal training that helped them to experience a situation more positively. The effect of this training was a decrease in the experienced negative emotions, such as disgust, sadness, and physiological arousal, as indicated by skin conductance measures (see fig 12.5).

Similar studies have focused on the **interpretation bias** that some anxious individuals may exhibit. Individuals with an interpretation bias tend to interpret ambiguous situations negatively. The existence of this bias in

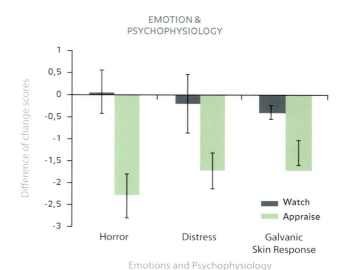

Figure 12.5 Results of a study of the effects of passive perception and emotional appraisal. Applying an appraisal strategy resulted in a significant decrease in ratings of experienced levels of horror and misery during the rewatching of emotional scenes, compared to a passive condition. Similar results were found for the skin conductance response. (source: Schartau et al., 2009)

individuals with an anxiety disorder suggests that their cognitive appraisals are often disproportionately negative. Training to reduce this bias often results in a decrease in perceived anxiety (Mathews, 2012).

12.4.6.2 Unconscious Appraisal

In addition to the conscious cognitive appraisal processes described here, there are also a large number of processes that can result in unconscious emotional responses. For example, Öhman and Soares (1994) found that unconsciously perceived photographs could elicit a fear response. They presented photos of spiders, snakes, flowers, and mushrooms to a group of spider-phobics and a group of snake-phobics. The pictures were presented **subliminally** and masked so that the participants were unaware of the pictures being shown. The spider-phobics showed an emotional response to the spider pictures, as measured by skin conductance recordings. The snake-phobics showed a similar emotional response to the snake pictures. In a follow-up study, Öhman, Flykt, and Esteves (2001) also found that participants with a snake phobia were faster at finding snake-related information in photos than participants without a phobia. A similar result was found for spider-related information for participants with a spider phobia. Thus, these results imply that an emotional disposition can influence attentional processes.

Tamietto and de Gelder (2010) studied the extent to which **blindsighted** patients (see Chapters 4 and 6) are still able to recognise emotions. Some of these patients were still able to recognise emotions, without being able to consciously describe them (Heywood & Kentridge, 2000). Tamietto et al. (2009) reported the results of two patients whose facial muscles responded to the emotional expression of faces that they were shown (see fig 12.6). More specifically, these patients were shown faces or physical expressions showing either a happy or a fearful emotion. Their facial muscles responded both when the stimulus was presented in the intact and in the damaged visual field.

In particular, Tamietto et al. were interested in the response of the zygomaticus major muscle, which is involved in laughter, and the corrugator supercilii, which is involved in frowning. They found that the zygomaticus was mainly activated when happy faces or expressions were shown, whereas the corrugator was mainly activated by anxious faces. Interestingly, these activation patterns were found both when stimuli were presented in the intact field and in the damaged visual field, implying that the emotional expression of the faces or expressions was still being processed in the damaged visual field. The activation of these facial muscles was also about 200–300 ms faster when the stimuli were presented in the damaged visual field than in the intact one. This result implies that emotional processing is faster when consciousness is not involved.

The conclusion that emotional stimuli are processed more efficiently outside our awareness is consistent with earlier findings from Jolij and Lamme (2005). These authors used transcranial magnetic stimulation (TMS) to induce affective blindness in neurotypical participants. Participants were shown displays on which four emojis were presented, surrounding a central fixation point. Three emojis showed a neutral expression and the fourth was a happy or an angry expression. The participants' task was to detect the emotion of the deviant stimulus and then to indicate whether this deviant stimulus was to the left or right of the fixation point. The stimuli were presented for 17 or 33 ms and during the presentation affective blindsight was induced via a TMS pulse.

Jolij and Lamme found a somewhat surprising result, namely that participants were less capable of recognising the emotion expressed by the stimulus the better they were trained in the task and also the longer the stimuli were presented. This result is particularly surprising because better training and longer presentation time were both associated with an increase in the participants' confidence in the task performance. Thus, we can conclude that awareness of the stimulus itself has a negative effect on the unconscious processing of its emotional content.

12.4.6.3 Appraisal: Limitations

Although the various appraisal theories are consistent with the previously discussed results, and also despite the fact that there is little discussion about the role of cognitive processes in emotion processing, there are some limitations to the appraisal approach that need to be mentioned. First, the assumption that cognitive appraisal is always necessary to elicit an emotional response appears to be too strong. The emotions that we experience often appear to be only partially explained by the value that we attach to a given situation. Appraisal theories therefore often exaggerate the importance of top-down processes at the expense of bottom-up processes (Ochsner et al., 2009). Second, appraisal theories often assume passive individuals who are alone when confronted with an emotional situation. Parkinson (2011) argued, however, that it is rare for us to encounter emotional situations in such a way. In the vast majority of cases, emotions arise in social situations, from interaction with others, and partly under the influence of the emotional responses of others. Third, most appraisal theories limit themselves to emotions related to the current situation, whereas in very many cases emotions are caused by past events or expected future outcomes. Finally, appraisal theories assume that emotions arise from cognitive appraisal processes. In practice, however, we see a much less clear-cut dividing line between cognition and emotion (McEachrane, 2009).

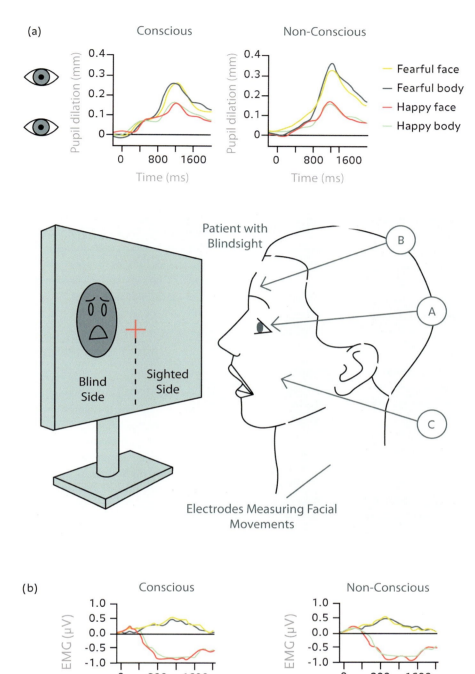

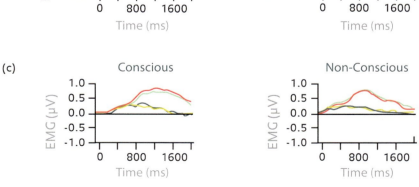

Figure 12.6 Effects of perceiving facial expressions among blindsight patients as reflected in pupil size and the tightening of two facial muscles. The main diagram shows the experimental setup and the locations of the physiological recording sites, highlighted with the letters a–c. Panels (a–c) show responses to stimuli presented in the intact hemifield (left) and blind-sighted hemifield (right). More specifically, panel (a) shows the effect of fearful and happy stimuli on pupil dilation; panel (b) shows the response of the corrugator supercilii muscle to these stimuli; and panel (c) shows the response of the zygomaticus major muscle. (source: Tamietto and de Gelder, 2010)

12.5 TOP-DOWN AND BOTTOM-UP PROCESSING

As already noted, the emphasis on top-down processes is a major limitation of most appraisal theories. The American psychologist Kevin Ochsner and colleagues (Ochsner & Gross, 2005; Ochsner et al., 2009; Ochsner, Silvers, & Buhle, 2012) therefore argue that emotional experiences depend on both top-down and bottom-up processes. The top-down component consists of the appraisal processes described earlier, while the bottom-up component consists of basic perception and attention processes (Ochsner et al., 2009). Ochsner and colleagues used fMRI methods to investigate the contribution of these processes. Participants were shown aversive or neutral images. In one condition, the bottom-up condition, they had to react to the pictures in the most natural way possible. In a second condition, the top-down condition, they had to interpret the neutral photos as if they were aversive.

The bottom-up condition showed that the amygdala was activated more strongly by the emotional stimuli than by the neutral ones. Moreover, this amygdala activation was strongly related to the degree of negative affect reported by the participants themselves. For the top-down condition, a different set of brain areas was found to be activated. Here, an increase in activation was found in the dorsolateral and medial prefrontal cortices; that is, brain areas that are usually associated with higher-order cognitive control processes. Increased activation was also found in the anterior cingulate and the amygdala. The degree of experienced negative affect was mainly related to the degree of activation of the medial prefrontal cortex. This area is associated with generating a cognitive representation of the meaning of a stimulus.

12.6 EMOTION REGULATION: THE INFLUENCE OF COGNITION ON MOOD

The theories discussed in the previous sections consider emotion regulation to be a single-stage process. That is, when we encounter a situation, an emotional response follows. In most cases, our experience does not stop at just experiencing the emotion, but we also attempt to do something with that emotion. For example, an authoritarian police officer approaching you in an unpleasant manner, evokes our anger. We can vent this anger in front of the officer and run the risk of receiving a large fine. Alternatively, we can pretend that everything is alright and covertly think to ourselves 'what an idiot'. In the latter scenario, we are regulating our emotions. **Emotion regulation** consists of activating a process that aims to regulate the intensity of an emotional experience, both in terms of intensity and duration (Gross, 2013).

Although it is intuitively appealing to distinguish between generating an emotional response and regulating it, in practice, this distinction is sometimes difficult to make (Gross & Barrett, 2011; Gross, Sheppes, & Urry, 2011). As discussed earlier, partially overlapping brain areas have been found that are involved in generating and regulating emotions (Ochsner et al., 2009), suggesting overlap between the generation and the regulation of emotions. Moreover, emotion-generating processes are partly self-regulating (Kappas, 2011). That is, emotion-generating processes can result in behaviour that changes the situation and ultimately the emotional response. Despite these limitations, however, it has become clear that we can explicitly regulate our emotional responses.

12.6.1 A PROCESS MODEL FOR EMOTION REGULATION

Gross and Thompson (2007) introduced an influential process model for emotion regulation. The basic processes involved in emotion regulation are shown along the horizontal line in Figure 12.7. The model assumes that the intensity of the emotion generally increases as we move from left to right along this line. Furthermore, the model assumes that emotion regulation strategies can operate at different points in time. For example, if we have to cycle to a lecture hall on a very cold rainy winter day, we may reduce the negative emotion evoked by the bad weather by deciding not to go. This is an example of emotion regulation at the situation selection stage.

In addition, if the plan not to go fails, we have a number of other strategies at our disposal. We can modify the situation, for example, by going, but using the weather forecast to decide not to leave home until the very last moment and to use the extra time to dress extra warmly, ride faster, and hope that the prospect of good weather will indeed come true. This is an example of situation modification. Another alternative might be to decide to play our favourite music extra loud and think about our upcoming holiday in warm Namibia while cycling. This is

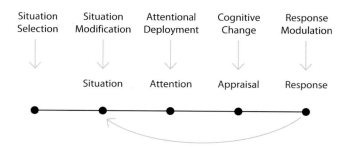

Figure 12.7 Schematic representation of Gross and Thompson's (2007) process model.

an example of attentional deployment. Alternatively, we can also apply cognitive reappraisal. By thinking about the negative outcome of alternatives ('That stupid bus is always late' or 'In this weather, the roads are full of traffic jams') and the positive consequences of our current actions ('It is really worth coming to class today; this lecture on emotion is really essential'), we can also change the negative valence of our emotions. This is an example of emotion regulation at the cognitive reappraisal stage. Finally, we can try to simply ignore the negative aspects of the situation: 'Don't nag and keep on cycling'. The latter is an example of response manipulation.

Response modulation is almost the complete opposite of situation selection. Whereas situation selection strategies all aim to prevent an emotional response from being evoked in the first place, response modulation is a strategy that focuses on the emotional response itself. What is the effectiveness of response modulation? It is a popular myth that giving in to aggressive tendencies has a positive effect. In practice, however, it often turns out that giving in to anger only makes the emotion stronger rather than lessening it: aggressive behaviour facilitates the retrieval of thoughts that continue to feed the emotional state (Bushman, 2002).

12.6.1.1 Attentional Deployment and Cognitive Change

Most emotion regulation strategies involve attentional development and cognitive change, for example by diverting attention from a negative situation or by emphasising the positive long-term consequences of a negative emotional situation. According to Sheppes et al. (2014), the intensity of an emotional response to an event tends to increase over time if the emotion is not regulated. Distraction is generally less cognitively demanding than reappraisal, which is why this strategy is often the initial response to controlling negative emotions. Although reappraisal is cognitively more demanding, it has the advantage of being more effective in the long run.

Based on this idea, Sheppes et al. (2014) aimed to predict when attentional distraction and cognitive change would be used the most. According to Sheppes et al., distraction would be used relatively frequently in intense negative emotional situations because distraction can regulate emotions before they reach their peak intensity. Reappraisal, on the other hand, would be used mainly in situations that we are likely to encounter repeatedly. The reason for this is that reappraisal can have a lasting effect across multiple encounters with similar situations.

These mechanisms suggest that all emotion regulation processes are explicit. However, this is not necessarily the case: Gyurak, Gross, and Etkin (2011) argue that emotion regulation can also be evoked implicitly. These implicit processes could be evoked automatically by the stimulus itself and proceed without entering our conscious awareness. Such an implicit regulation process would be evoked specifically when a specific strategy is used repeatedly.

12.6.1.2 Effectiveness

How effective are these emotion regulation strategies? Based on a **meta-analysis**, Augustine and Hemenover (2009) found a distinction between cognitive strategies and behavioural strategies, in which cognitive strategies turned out to be more effective than behavioural ones. Webb, Miles, and Sheeran (2012) also conducted a meta-analysis on a large number of studies that compared the effectiveness of different strategies. Strategies based on cognitive change generally had a moderate effect on emotions. In contrast, response-modulation strategies were only of limited effectiveness. Although strategies based on attentional enhancement did not show significant effects on their own, Webb et al. (2012) note that attentional-deployment is typically used as an umbrella term under which several specific strategies can be classified, such as 'distraction' or 'concentration'. These strategies can in themselves be further classified into different sub-strategies. Within these sub-strategies, those based on distraction were effective. Cognitive change could also be subdivided into different sub-strategies. For example, reappraising the situation proved more effective than reappraising the emotional response itself.

We should make one important comment on Webb et al.'s (2012) results. The effectiveness of a specific emotion regulation strategy is presumably highly situation dependent. For example, Troy, Shallcross, and Mauss (2013) found that participants with highly developed skills for reappraising an emotional situation suffered less from depression than participants with less well-developed skills in this area. They found this result by measuring not only the emotion regulation skills of their participants, but also the stress levels that recent negative life experiences had evoked in these participants and the extent to which they had reported having control over these experiences.

Troy et al. (2013), however, argued that this relationship between cognitive reappraisal and depression should only be found in situations where participants had no control over their stress levels. When they could control these, Troy et al. expected to find a different relationship between cognitive reappraisal and depression, because other strategies would be more effective in those types of situations. For example, strategies that focused more on solving the problem than on regulating the emotion, would be more effective in these situations. Consistent with their hypothesis, Troy et al. found a positive relationship between the intensity of stress levels and the degree of depression in participants when stress levels were highly controllable.

12.6.1.3 Brain Mechanisms of Emotion Regulation

In recent years, much has become known about the neural basis of emotion regulation strategies (Ochsner & Gross, 2008). Many strategies are based on cognitively demanding processes that are associated with prefrontal cortex activation. This activation is often related to a decrease in amygdala activation, a brain region that is strongly associated with emotional processing. Kohn et al. (2014) identified a large number of brain regions involved in emotion regulation on the basis of a meta-analysis (see fig 12.8).

Based on this analysis, Kohn et al. concluded that emotion regulation involves three stages. The first stage consists of the evaluation of emotions, and this is associated with activation of the ventrolateral prefrontal cortex. At this stage, the cognitive appraisal processes are probably initiated, in addition to signalling the need to initiate an emotional response. The second stage then involves the initiation of the regulation itself. This process involves the dorsolateral prefrontal cortex. Finally, the third process consists of executing the emotion regulation process. This involves a large number of brain areas, including the supratemporal gyrus, the supplementary motor cortex, and the angular gyrus (see fig 12.8).

Kohn et al.'s (2014) model suggests a strong relationship between emotion regulation processes and amygdala activation. Evidence for the idea that prefrontal cortical activity can influence amygdala functions was found by Lee, Heller, van Reekum, Nelson, and Davidson (2012). In their study, participants were required to use reappraisal strategies while viewing pictures with a negative emotional valence. fMRI was used to estimate for each participant the connectivity between the frontal areas and the amygdala. The resulting estimate was then related to the extent to which participants were able to regulate their emotional response, which was determined by measuring the skin conductance response to each picture. Lee et al. found a clear correlation between skin conductance and the degree of connectivity: the better the participants were able to regulate their emotional response, the higher the connectivity between the frontal areas and the amygdala appeared to be (see fig 12.9).

Sheppes and Gross (2011) aimed to determine when each emotion regulation strategy is the most effective. They assumed that the intensity of an emotional response to a threatening or unpleasant stimulus normally increases with time (see also: Sheppes et al., 2014). When a strategy requires little cognitive processing power, such as distraction, this aspect is not important. However, when it does, for example in cognitive reappraisal, it is important for the participant to apply the strategy as soon as possible (when the emotional response is still weak). Indeed, a literature review found that distraction is equally effective whether applied early or late (Sheppes & Gross, 2011). It was also

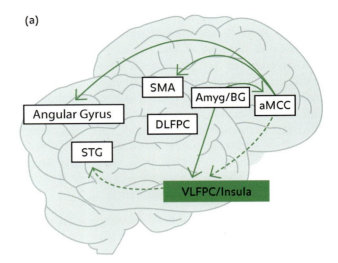

(a)

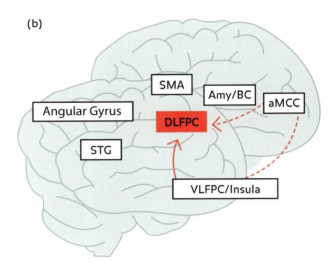

(b)

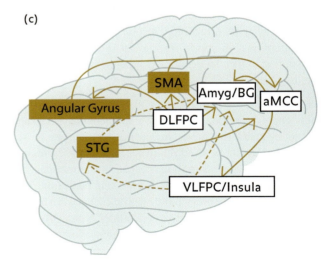

(c)

Figure 12.8 A model of emotion regulation. (a) The network involved in emotion evaluation; (b) the network involved in the regulation of emotion; (c) the network involved in the implementation of regulation. STG = superior temporal gyrus; SMA = supplementary motor area; BG = basal ganglia; DLFPC = dorsolateral prefrontal cortex; VLFPC = ventrolateral prefrontal cortex; aMCC = anterior medial cingulate cortex. (source: Kohn et al., 2014)

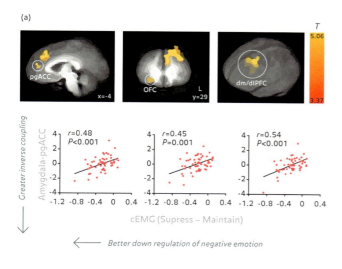

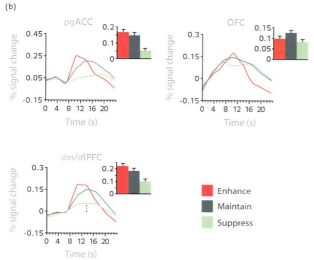

Figure 12.9 Correlations between amygdala-prefrontal cortex connectivity and the ability to regulate an emotional response. (a) Brain areas involved and their respective correlation with emotion regulation skill; (b) BOLD responses as a function of the type of regulation. pgACC = pregenual anterior cingulate cortex; OFC = orbitofrontal cortex; dm/dlPFC = dorsomedial/dorsolateral prefrontal cortex. (source: Lee et al., 2012)

found, however, that reappraisal was effective with low-intensity emotions but that it was counterproductive with high-intensity emotions.

12.7 THE INFLUENCE OF MOOD ON COGNITION

As already noted, most traditional cognitive studies have attempted to exclude the influence of emotion by having participants take part in experiments in an emotional state that is as neutral as possible. This approach stands in sharp contrast with everyday life, however, where we are frequently in a non-neutral state of mind while performing a cognitive task. Consequently, there are currently far too few studies available that have examined the influence of happiness, anger, sadness, or fear on our cognitive functioning.

Nevertheless, it is becoming increasingly clear that emotions do have an influence on our daily functioning, and we are slowly beginning to understand how this is happening.

To illustrate this, consider road rage, that is, the phenomenon whereby aggression results in reckless driving behaviour. Stephens and Groeger (2011) studied this using a driving simulator, where drivers were made angry by blocking them behind a slow-moving vehicle. Consequently, they started to show poor judgement by performing irresponsible overtaking manoeuvres and by recklessly driving towards dangerous situations. This example illustrates that emotions can influence our behaviour. The question we will try to answer in this section is how this can occur.

12.7.1 NETWORK THEORY

Bower (1981) was one of the first to explain the influence of mood on cognition with his network theory. This theory assumed that emotions are part of a **semantic network** in long-term memory (see Chapter 13 for further details on this network). Moreover, the theory is based on the following six assumptions: (1) emotions are represented as units or nodes in the network; these nodes are connected to related ideas, physiological systems, events, and expressions; (2) emotional material is represented in the network in the form of propositions or assumptions; (3) thoughts arise through the activation of these nodes; (4) the nodes can be activated by internal or external stimuli; (5) activation spreads to related nodes; (6) consciousness is formed by the network of nodes activated above a critical threshold.

The fifth assumption of the model is crucial for explaining the influence of emotions on cognition, because it describes how the activation of an emotion can activate the nodes or concepts related to this emotion. The model has generated a number of specific, testable hypotheses. For example, it predicted the **mood congruence** and the mood-state dependent memory effects. In addition, the model also predicts **thought congruence** and mood intensity. Mood congruence and the mood-state dependent memory effect mainly concern attentional and memory processes, whereas thought congruence mainly concerns decision processes. In the following sections, we will examine these effects more closely.

12.7.2 ATTENTION AND MEMORY

12.7.2.1 Attention

As discussed in detail in previous chapters, attentional mechanisms enable us to flexibly perceive and plan actions. The question here is to what extent attention can be influenced by different states of mind. Although the role of emotions in cognition has only become the focus of research in recent decades, it has inspired one of the earliest attentional theories. Easterbrook (1959) assumed that the number of stimuli that we can process was reduced when arousal or anxiety levels increased. In other words, the focus of attention would, according to Easterbrook, narrow under the influence of negative emotions. This narrowing would initially have a positive effect on task performance, because it would make us less susceptible to being distracted by irrelevant distractors. However, a further narrowing would have a negative effect because it would reduce our attention span to such an extent that we would no longer have sufficient capacity to process relevant stimuli. A strong negative emotion would, in other words, create a tunnel vision, according to Easterbrook.

Easterbrook's hypothesis has practical implications. It can explain, for example, why eyewitnesses often miss important details (see Chapter 15 for a detailed description of eyewitness memory). After all, testimonies of criminal events often happen under extremely stressful circumstances. In a similar way, anxious motorists are also less sensitive to peripheral information than non-anxious motorists (Janelle, Singer, & Williams, 1999).

What about positive emotions? According to Frederickson (2001), positive emotions can actually broaden our attentional focus. Her **broaden and build theory** describes how positive emotions can result in a broadening of the repertoire of thoughts and actions available to an individual. Frederickson argues that the narrowing of attention by negative emotions is necessary to increase decisiveness in threatening situations. However, when there is no threat, or any other negative situation, this decisiveness is not necessary, and positive emotions such as joy, curiosity, contentment, pride, or infatuation can be allowed to have a complementary effect. They stimulate the individual to become playful and creative, to explore, and to engage in self-development.

Vanlessen, De Raedt, Koster, and Pourtois (2016) assume, however, that there is no unambiguous relationship between positive mood and the broadening of attention. These authors argue that there is rather a balance

between internal and external attention (see Chapter 4), in which the combination of mood and the need for cognitive control jointly determines whether attention is focused internally or externally (see fig 12.10).

Along similar lines, Harmon-Jones, Gable, and Price (2011) argue that the theoretical approaches of both Easterbrook (1959) and Frederickson (2001) are too limited, in the sense that they only considered the emotional valence and not the **motivational intensity**. A positive emotion can be caused by listening to cheerful music (low motivational intensity) or by the prospect of obtaining a high grade on an exam (high motivational intensity). The same applies to negative emotions. These can be evoked by exposure to a tragic news item (low motivational intensity) or by exposure to a threatening situation (high motivational intensity).

Harmon-Jones et al. (2011) argue, therefore, that it is specifically the motivational intensity that influences the attentional state. More specifically, they hypothesise that both positive and negative emotions can result in a narrowing of attention when the motivational intensity is high, because this narrowed state of attention helps us to realise desired situations and to avoid undesired ones. When motivational intensity is low, however, attention may broaden because this state allows us to take advantage of new opportunities. Gable and Harmon-Jones (2010) found differential effects of disgust and sadness on attention: while disgust resulted in a narrowing of attention, sadness resulted in a broadening. These results are consistent with the idea that disgust is an emotion with a high motivational intensity, whereas sadness is an emotion with a low motivational intensity.

Similarly, according to Gable and Harmon-Jones (2011), positive emotions can also result in a narrowing of attention. They found evidence for this idea by manipulating the motivational intensity of positive emotions. Figure 12.11 illustrates the paradigm they used. Here, participants were either given a financial incentive before

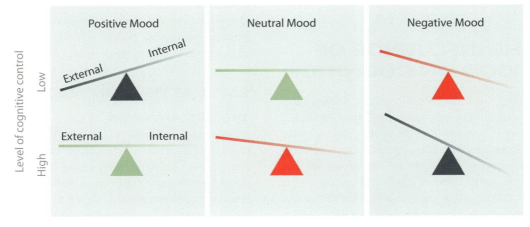

Figure 12.10 The balance between internal and external attention, mediated by cognitive control and mood. (source: Vanlessen et al., 2016)

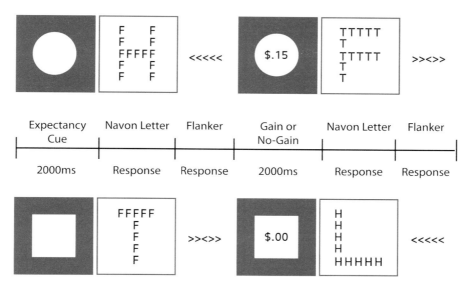

Figure 12.11 Overview of an experimental trial from the study by Gable and Harmon-Jones (2011).

starting a trial (if they responded faster than average, they got a reward; high motivational intensity) or they could be given an unexpected financial reward afterwards (low motivational intensity). In the main task, participants had to respond to the direction of the central arrow of an **Eriksen flanker task** (Eriksen & Eriksen, 1974).

Before performing this flanker task, participants were given a cue indicating whether they could receive a reward, and this cue was immediately followed by a stimulus from a **Navon task** (Navon, 1977). Navon stimuli consist of large letters that are composed of smaller ones (see Chapter 6). In the Gable and Harmon-Jones study, participants were instructed to detect as quickly as possible whether a letter T was present in these letters. This T could either be the global letter or the local letter. The relative speed with which the participants were able to detect either the global or the local T was used as a measure of the breadth of their attention.

Immediately after participants responded to the flanker stimulus, they were given another cue. This cue informed the participants whether or not they had won a sum of money, and this cue was again immediately followed by a Navon stimulus. Gable and Harmon-Jones (2011) found that positive emotions with low motivational intensity (unexpectedly earning a reward) resulted in a broadening of attention, which was reflected in a relatively fast response to the global T on the second Navon stimulus. However, high motivational intensity, which was induced by the first cue indicating that participants could earn a sum of money, resulted in a narrowing of attention.

Lee, Mirza, Flanagan, and Anderson (2014) hypothesised that emotional expressions may influence the way we process visual information. Fear is associated with pupil dilation, whereas disgust is associated with a contraction of the pupil. Pupil dilation can result in an increase in our ability to detect relevant stimuli, but at the expense of visual depth of field. Contraction of the pupil has the opposite effect. Lee et al. hypothesise that these features may have a function: fear would help us to detect objects or potential threats, whereas disgust would help us to better inspect the source of our disgust (such as spoiled food).

12.7.2.2 Memory: Mood Congruence

Emotions have different influences on learning and memory. For example, when we are sad or angry, this will mainly result in the retrieval of negative or unpleasant memories. When we are happy, however, this will mainly result in the retrieval of positive memories. This correspondence between our state of mind and the memories we retrieve is known as **mood congruity**. More specifically, mood congruity describes the effect that emotional material is best learned or retrieved when your current mood matches that of the material. This effect may also explain why negative moods sometimes persist in everyday life: a negative mood makes it easier to recall negative memories, which then maintain the negative mood.

Miranda and Kihlstrom (2005) found evidence for the mood congruence effect. They asked adults to recall memories from their early childhood or from more recent periods of their lives on the basis of pleasant, unpleasant, and neutral cues. The participant's mood was modulated by music. The retrieval of pleasant memories was facilitated by the positive mood and the retrieval of sad memories was facilitated by the sad mood. In general, autobiographical memories are found to have clear effects of mood congruence when the mood is positive. However, the results are much less unambiguous for negative moods (Holland & Kensinger, 2010). Also for non-autobiographical memories it was found that the effects of mood congruence are much clearer in a positive state of mind than in a negative state of mind (Rusting & DeHart, 2000).

Rusting and DeHart (2000) hypothesised that the lack of uniformity in mood congruence in negative states of mind could be explained by the idea that participants with a negative state of mind strive to improve this state by applying emotion regulation techniques. Indeed, they found that participants who claimed to be better at regulating their emotions showed less strong mood congruency effects than participants who were less capable of doing so.

The fact that mood not only has an effect on recall, but also on learning, was demonstrated by Hills, Werno, and Lewis (2011). Participants in whom a happy mood had been induced were better able to learn to recognise happy faces than sad ones. No significant effect was found for the participants in whom a sad mood was induced: overall, sad participants were better at remembering faces than happy participants.

12.7.2.3 Memory: The Mood-State Dependent Memory Effect

A second important effect of mood on memory is the **mood-state dependent memory effect** (see fig 12.12). This effect represents an improvement in our memory performance when our state of mind during retrieval matches our state of mind during learning. Here, it is also found that the effects are generally more unambiguous for positive states of mind than for negative ones (Ucros, 1989). Again, it is likely that people with a negative state of mind aim to improve it, which reduces the effects.

The mood-state dependent memory effect is also mainly found for memories that we actively retrieve ourselves. Eich (1995) argued that one's mood-state may influence memory to a lesser degree when one is presented with crucial information that can be used to retrieve a memory. It appears that the mood-state only impacts effortful learning and memory retrieval. Eich's argument is based on earlier results from Eich and Metcalfe (1989). In that study, participants were either required to read word pairs, such as river-valley, or to generate some of the word pairs themselves. In the latter condition, for example, they were shown the incomplete word pairs: river-v____. When participants had to generate the second word themselves,

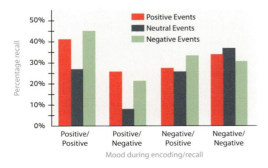

Figure 12.12 The percentage of correct recall as a function of mood during learning and retrieval. (source: Eich, 1995)

they were forced to process the stimuli more deeply. In this 'generate' condition, the mood-dependent memory effect was found to be much larger than in the 'read' condition.

Kenealy (1997) also found evidence for this idea. She gave participants a map, on the basis of which they had to learn a series of instructions that were required to give directions. The participants' mood was manipulated by music. One day later, participants were tested, and here, too, their mood was induced by music. The participants either had to try to spontaneously report as many of the learned instructions as possible or they had to do so on the basis of cues they were given. In the latter case, an outline of the map was used. One of Kenealy's key findings was that there was a mood-state-dependent memory effect during free recall, but not during cued recall. When the key positions on the map were cued, processing was less intense, so the impact of the participants' mood was negligible. Taken together, these studies thus show that both the depth of processing while memorising stimuli (Eich & Metcalfe, 1989) and while retrieving them (Kenealy, 1997) can affect the mood-dependent memory effect.

12.7.3 DECISION-MAKING PROCESSES

It is typically found that emotions can exert a strong influence on decision-making processes. For example, Angie, Connelly, Waples, and Kligyte (2011) concluded from a literature review that different states of mind have a significant effect on judgement and decision-making processes. These effects are particularly pronounced in decision-making processes. In this context, we need to make a distinction between **integral emotions** and **incidental emotions**. Integral emotions are triggered by the evaluation of the consequences of a decision, whereas incidental emotions are triggered by past events that are totally unrelated to the decision. In particular, negative states of mind are found to make participants risk-averse, while positive states of mind are found to make us more willing to make risky decisions.

Most studies on decision-making processes have focused on incidental emotions (Lench, Flores, & Bench, 2011). In these studies, participants must, for example, describe an emotional experience, after which they are then required to perform an unrelated task. In reality, however, our actions are often linked to our emotional states: we perform an action or make decisions that we hope will improve our negative states of mind. Damasio's (1996) somatic marker theory (discussed earlier) describes how emotions themselves may play an integral role in our decision-making behaviour. Indeed, according to the somatic marker theory, emotions are the result of arousal-related signals generated by our bodies in response to emotional events or decisions. These somatic markers can affect our decision-making processes if we are able to interpret them properly. **Interoception**, that is, the ability to interpret these signals consciously or unconsciously, is an essential process in this respect.

Indeed, Dunn et al. (2010) found evidence that somatic markers, and particularly the ability to interpret them, are possibly involved in decision-making processes (see Fig 12.13).

Dunn et al. used the already discussed Iowa gambling task (Bechara et al., 2005) and recorded participants' heart rates before they took a card from either the high-risk or low-risk stacks. When participants chose a high-risk card, this was often accompanied by an increase in heart rate. In addition, Dunn et al. determined how well the

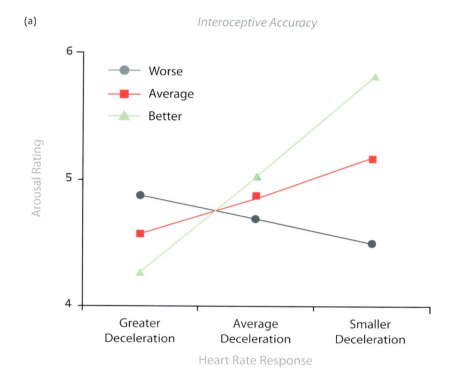

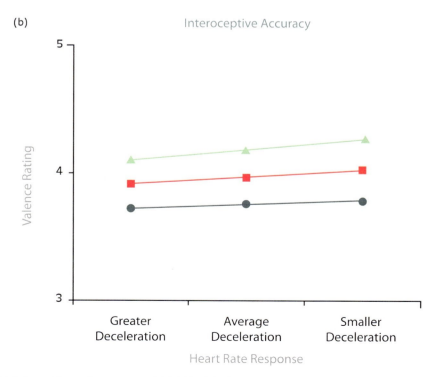

Figure 12.13 The relationship between interoceptive accuracy and risk-taking behaviour expressed as arousal (a) and valence ratings (b) shown for worse, average, and better interoceptive accuracy and three different levels of heart rate deceleration following a risky choice. (source: Dunn et al., 2010)

participants were able to interpret their own physiological signals. This was done by having them determine how many beats their hearts made in a specific time interval. Participants whose heartbeat increased more strongly generally made better choices than participants whose heart rates accelerated less. Moreover, participants who were able to interpret these signals well benefited the most from this. The perception of emotional bodily signals can thus strongly influence our choice behaviour.

12.7.3.1 Fear

Fear generally evokes risk-averse behaviour. For example, Lorian and Grisham (2011) administered the domain-specific risk-taking scale to patients with an anxiety disorder, a 30-item questionnaire that attempts to identify risky behaviour. These patients generally scored lower on this scale than neurotypical controls. Furthermore, Gambetti and Giusberty (2012) studied real-life financial decisions made by anxious and non-anxious individuals. This study also showed that anxious individuals took fewer risks than non-anxious ones. Raghunathan and Pham (1999) asked participants to choose between two possible jobs. The first of these offered a high salary but little job security, while the second job offered a lower salary but more security. Anxious participants were more likely to choose the more secure job compared to control participants. Sad participants, however, more often chose a job with less certainty.

12.7.3.2 Sadness

The Raghunathan and Pham (1999) study suggests a dissociation between fear and sadness. Although fear and sadness are both negative emotions, sadness also involves the absence of positive affect. As a result, sad participants experience their environment as unrewarding, causing sad participants to frequently make great efforts to obtain a reward. Consequently, they may be motivated to take greater risks, as risky choices are also often associated with greater reward.

Cryder, Lerner, Gross, and Dahl (2008) investigated this relationship between sadness and risk taking by studying the **misery-is-not-miserly effect**. This effect describes how sad individuals are willing to pay a higher price for a product than non-sad individuals. In the Cryder et al. study, participants had to indicate how much they were willing to pay for a trendy water bottle. Sad individuals were prepared to pay up to four times more for this bottle than participants in a neutral state of mind. Interestingly enough, an interaction was also found with self-focus, that is, the degree to which participants had focused their attention on themselves and their own situation: sad participants with a high self-focus were particularly willing to pay a lot for the bottle.

12.7.3.3 Anger

Anger generally results in an increased feeling of control over a situation, so we may also expect that when people are angry, they will take more risks. In the previously described driving simulation experiment (Stephens & Groeger, 2011), we have already discussed how angry drivers do indeed take more risks. Lerner and Keltner (2001) studied the effect of anger using the **Asian disease problem**. In this problem, which is used in many decision-making studies (see Chapter 21), participants have to imagine that an epidemic has broken out, and they have to choose between two alternative treatment programmes: one of these programmes offers a great deal of security while only saving a limited part of the population, while the other programme may be able to save everyone, but also carries a high risk that everyone will die. Anxious participants in Lerner and Keltner's study often chose the programme that offered a lot of certainty, while angry participants chose the high-risk programme more often. Gambetti and Giusberty (2012), as discussed earlier, also reported that, while that fearful participants made more conservative financial decisions, angry participants made more risky decisions.

These results appear to imply a fairly unambiguous effect of anger. Kugler, Connolly, and Ordonez (2012) suggest, however, that this effect is somewhat more complex. This study replicated the effect that angry participants are more willing to take risks than neutral or happy participants, when they act on their own. However, the opposite effect was found when participants had to collaborate. During a gambling task, each participant had to choose between a risky option and an option with no risk attached. In the latter case, the outcome was only determined by the participant's own choice and not by that of the partner. In the risky choice, the outcome was determined by the partner's choice. In this case, angry participants were much less willing to make the risky choice than fearful participants. This is probably due to the fact that, in this case, they relinquished part of their control in making the risky choice and that their aversion to losing control prevented them from making the risky choice.

12.7.3.4 Positive Affect

Back in Chapter 1, we already distinguished between a heuristic System 1 and an analytic System 2. Positive affect is primarily associated with an increase in the use of System 1 and a decrease in the use of System 2 processes (Griskevicius, Shiota, & Neufeld, 2010). Although many studies do not distinguish between different types of positive affect, a more detailed analysis suggests the existence of at least eight different forms of positive affect (Campos, Shiota, Keltner, Gonzaga, & Goetz, 2013). The extent to which these different variants of positive affect have an effect on cognition is not yet fully clear. Griskevicius et al. (2010) found that some forms of positive mood (amusement, satisfaction, enthusiasm) induced a more heuristic reasoning style: in these moods, it turned out to be easier to convince participants on the basis of weak arguments.

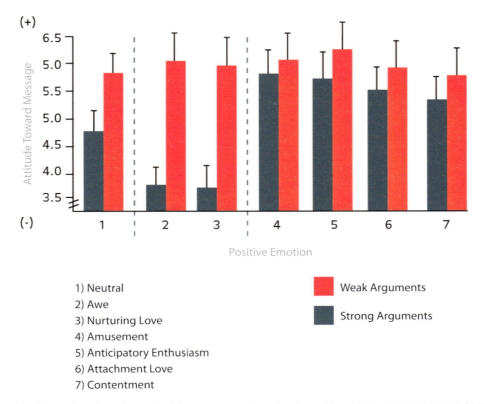

1) Neutral
2) Awe
3) Nurturing Love
4) Amusement
5) Anticipatory Enthusiasm
6) Attachment Love
7) Contentment

■ Weak Arguments
■ Strong Arguments

Figure 12.14 The extent to which participants can be convinced by weak arguments as a function of different positive emotions. (source: Griskevicius et al., 2010)

This was not the case however for other positive moods, such as admiration or caring love (see Fig 12.14).

De Vries, Holland, and Witteman (2008) argued that we are most satisfied with a decision when we can use our preferred reasoning strategy. In their study, participants were informed that a thermos flask was being raffled off among all the participants. The participants were then put into a positive or negative state of mind by means of a film clip from either the *Muppet Show* (joyful) or from *Schindler's List* (sad), after which they had to indicate which of the two thermos flasks they would prefer to win. One group was instructed to respond as quickly as possible, while a second group was instructed to evaluate the pros and cons of each of the two thermos flasks as carefully as possible. De Vries et al. found that happy participants were most satisfied with their choice when they could decide quickly, while sad participants were most satisfied with the more explicit deliberative decision.

Furthermore, de Vries, Holland, Corneille, Rondeel, and Witteman (2012) found that happy participants were more likely to use a less optimal gambling strategy than sad participants. In this study, participants could choose between two different gambles: (1) 50% chance of winning €1.20 and 50% chance of winning nothing or (2) 50% chance of winning €1.00 and 50% chance of winning nothing. Obviously, option 1 is the most rational choice under all circumstances. However, happy participants showed more signs of heuristic processing in that they

chose option 1 less consistently, but switched often – for example, after losing.

12.8 COGNITIVE BIASES

Most of the material we have discussed so far in this chapter relates to the relatively short-term effects of emotions. In this final section will discuss the long-term effects of mood on cognition. More specifically, we will focus here on the effects of anxiety and depression. A problem in studying these effects is that many individuals with an anxiety disposition also frequently suffer from depressive feelings and vice versa. In other words, there is **comorbidity**.

Despite this overlap, there are also many clear differences between an anxiety disorder and depression. Past losses, for example, are strongly associated with depression, whereas future threats are mainly associated with an anxiety disorder. Eysenck, Payne, and Santos (2006) found such a dissociation by using scenarios in which participants were informed of a negative event, such as a diagnosis of a serious illness. Each scenario had three different versions, which varied according to the time when the scenario took place: it could either be situated in the past, involve a possible future event, or a probable future event. Participants had to indicate how anxious or depressed each scenario would make them. Anxiety was mostly associated with future events, whereas depression was associated with the versions of the scenarios situated in the past.

a)

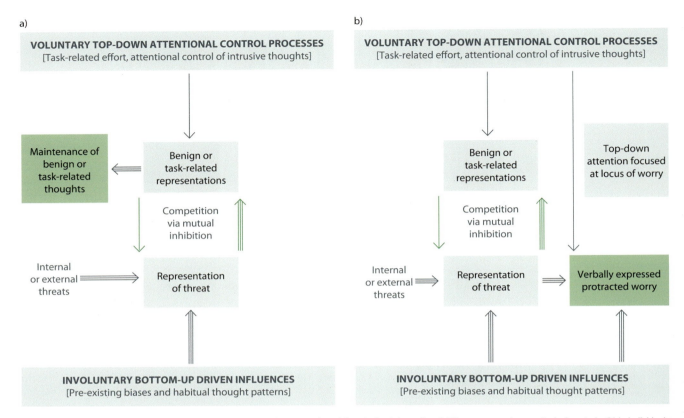

b)

Figure 12.15 The role of top-down and bottom-up processes in the processing of threatening information. (a) The processes in neurotypical controls; (b) in individuals who have a disposition to worry.

Further evidence for a dissociation between anxiety and depression can be found in the symptoms associated with them. For example, worrying about future events is a symptom of anxiety disorders (Hirsch & Mathews, 2012) (see Fig 12.15). In contrast, rumination, or constantly thinking about negative feelings and experiences from the past (Martin & Tesser, 1996), is common in depressed individuals.

12.8.1 BECK'S SCHEMA THEORY

The American psychiatrist Aaron Beck (1976) has played a particularly important role in the development of cognitive behavioural therapies for the treatment of anxiety and depression. His treatment is based on the idea that some individuals have a higher degree of vulnerability to these disorders than others, because they develop maladaptive **cognitive schemas** early in life. Cognitive schemas organise knowledge into clear structures (see Chapter 13) and, in the case of a depression, they can be dominated by an excessive amount of negativity. The negative cognitive trait therefore becomes evident in depressed individuals' self-image, their outlook on the world, and their future prospects. Maladaptive schemas in people with anxiety disorders, on the other hand, are characterised by a continuous perception of threat (both physical and psychological) and an exaggerated sense of vulnerability (Beck & Clark, 1988).

Beck and Clark (1988) hypothesise that these schemas will influence most cognitive processes. These processes include attention, perception, learning, and retrieving information from memory. In addition, schemas also produce biases in the sense that predominantly schema-consistent information is processed. Thus, individuals with an anxiety disposition mainly process information related to threats, whereas depressed individuals mainly process negative information. Although these schemas can exert a structural influence on the emergence of biases, Beck and Clark emphasise that these schemas only become active when someone is in a state of anxiety or depression. When they do become active, however, they can continue to selectively process negative information, thereby exerting a self-reinforcing effect. Cognitive therapies and cognitive behavioural therapies should therefore focus on reducing these biases. The following biases play an important role in this:

Attention bias: selective attention to threatening stimuli, when a threatening and a neutral stimulus are presented simultaneously.

Interpretation bias: the tendency to interpret ambiguous stimuli and situations as threatening.

Explicit memory bias: the tendency to recall mainly negative or unpleasant memories during memory tests that focus on conscious memories.

Implicit memory bias: the tendency to perform better when implicit memory tasks contain negative or threatening information, compared to neutral stimulus material.

Individuals characterised by these biases would be excessively alert to threats, perceive most situations as threatening, and believe that their experiences would be mostly unpleasant. Such individuals would have a strong disposition to develop a depression or an anxiety disorder. We must be careful not to lose sight of the underlying causal relation here: did the cognitive biases develop the disposition or did the disposition actually trigger the cognitive biases? This is to a large extent still an open question and subject to much ongoing research.

12.8.8.2 ATTENTION BIASES

Attention biases can be investigated with different tasks, for example the dot-probe task or the emotional Stroop task. In the dot-probe task, two stimuli are presented simultaneously on a computer screen (fig 12.16). In some trials, one of the two stimuli depicts a negative emotional situation (such as an aggressive dog), whereas the other stimulus is emotionally neutral. The degree to which attention is focused on these stimuli is determined by recording the speed at which a participant detects a dot that replaces one of the two stimuli. The assumption is that the detection rate is higher in areas of the visual field where attention is focused. An attentional bias can therefore be identified if the detection is consistently faster when the dot replaces the negative stimulus than when the dot replaces the neutral stimulus. The emotional Stroop task is similar to the regular Stroop task, but with the difference that the words used here are not colour names, but neutral or negative emotion words. Again, the task consists of naming the colour in which the words are printed and ignoring their meaning. An attentonional bias is associated with a longer naming time for the negative words, due to the fact that the meaning of these negative words nevertheless capture attention.

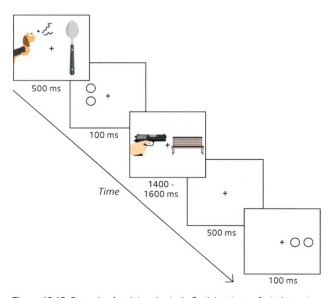

Figure 12.16 Example of a dot-probe task. Participants are first shown two stimuli, one of which is neutral and the other threatening. Then they have to decide as quickly as possible on which side of the display a dot is presented.

12.8.8.3 INTERPRETATION BIAS

Each day we encounter many situations that are ambiguous. For example, when someone ignores you, it can have several meanings: does that person dislike you or did they simply not notice you? Individuals with an interpretation bias will in such situations have a strong tendency to interpret the situation in a negative, threatening way. This interpretation bias is often found among anxious individuals. For example, Eysenck, MacLeod, and Mathews (1987) asked participants to spell aurally presented words. Some of these words were **homophones**. As we will discuss in more detail in the language chapters, homophones are formed by words that are spelled differently but have a similar pronunciation, such 'dye' and 'die', or 'pain' and 'pane'. The degree to which participants reported the negative emotional version of the spoken word correlated strongly with the degree to which participants were sensitive to fear. Walsh, McNally, Skariah, Butt, and Eysenck (2015), however, found that this interpretation bias was mainly present for potential social or intellectual threats, but not for physical threats.

12.8.8.4 MEMORY BIASES

Memory biases may play an important role in maintaining negative moods through relatively automatic (implicit) or controlled (explicit) processes. Williams, Watts, MacLeod, and Mathews (1997) argued that explicit memory bias is more common in depressed than in anxious individuals, whereas the opposite is true for implicit memory bias. Indeed, explicit memory bias was found relatively often in depressed individuals (Rinck & Becker, 2005). Moreover, implicit memory biases are also reported in depression (Phillips, Hine, & Thorsteinsson, 2010).

Mitte (2008), however, found no relationship between implicit memory biases and anxiety disorders. Although she did report effects of an explicit memory bias in patients with an anxiety disorder, the precise effect of this was strongly dependent on the nature of the memory test. For example, a relationship between anxiety and memory bias was reported for a recall test, but not for a recognition test.

The previously discussed results are inconsistent with the predictions made by Williams et al. (1997), since both depression and anxiety are associated with explicit memory biases. Clear differences were found, however, between individuals with depression and individuals with anxiety; in particular because the effect of the explicit memory bias is stronger in depressed individuals. These differences are consistent with the observation that depression, more than an anxiety disorder, is strongly associated with a focus on internal thoughts and memories. This internal focus is strongly associated with rumination, which makes the network of negative memories and emotions more accessible (Bower, 1981), which in turn may lead to a negative memory bias and the danger of reinforcing the rumination processes (Kuhn, Vanderhasselt, De Raedt, & Gallinat, 2012).

12.8.8.5 COMBINED COGNITIVE BIAS HYPOTHESIS

The preceding discussion could have given the impression that the four aforementioned cognitive biases are independent. Hirsch, Clark, and Matthews (2006) argue, however, that this is not the case. Their combined cognitive bias hypothesis assumes that the biases can influence each other. Hirsch et al. focused in particular on social phobias, that is, the excessive fear of social situations, and reported several studies that found that socially anxious individuals are characterised by multiple negative cognitive biases. For example, they often generate more negative mental images of themselves and they also tend to interpret social situations more negatively. Everaert, Koster, and Derakshan (2012) argue that such interactions can also be found in depression.

White, Suway, Pine, Bar-Haim, and Fox (2011) found that an attentional bias could evolve into an interpretation bias. They manipulated the attentional bias via a training procedure. As a result, participants had a stronger tendency to interpret ambiguous information as threatening. Amir, Bomyea, and Beard (2010) reported the inverse result. They applied a training procedure to reduce the interpretation bias, with the result that participants were able to focus their attention away from the threatening stimuli more easily.

Salemink, Hertel, and Mackintosh (2010) finally gave their participants a number of scenarios that were emotionally ambiguous, and instructed participants to imagine that they were in this situation. Participants were also instructed to imagine how the scenario would end. Afterwards, the participants were given training to reduce their interpretation bias or, on the contrary, to increase it. After this training, the participants had to remember the scenarios. They had to report specifically how they had ended. Training that promoted the negative interpretation bias resulted in verbal reports with stronger emotional undertones than the training that decreased the negative interpretation bias (see fig 12.17).

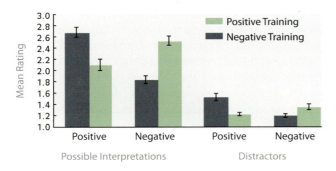

Figure 12.17 The effects of cognitive training on interpretation bias. (source: Salemink et al., 2010)

The aforementioned results imply that cognitive training can influence cognitive biases and that we can therefore gain control over these biases. Therefore, Joormann and colleagues (see for example Gotlib & Joormann, 2010; Joormann, Yoon, & Zetsche, 2007) argue as well that cognitive control processes may influence the extent to which biases can play a role in depressed individuals. For example, depressed individuals may have difficulties disengaging their attention from negative stimuli when there is deficiency in inhibitory control (Zetsche & Joormann, 2011). As a result, the negative stimuli are processed longer and more deeply, which ultimately results in a stronger representation of these stimuli in memory. The end result is that a memory bias is formed. De Raedt and Koster (2010) report evidence that depressed individuals are slower to disengage their attention from negative stimuli, compared to a control group. Besides depression, difficulties with attention regulation may also play a role in anxiety disorders. According to the attention control theory of Eysenck et al. (2007), anxiety reduces the efficiency of attentional regulation processes.

12.8.8.6 THE COGNITIVE VULNERABILITY HYPOTHESIS

Cognitive therapists hypothesise that individuals who suffer from one or more cognitive biases are more susceptible than others to developing an anxiety disorder or depression (Beck, 1976; Beck & Clark, 1988; Beck & Clark, 1997; Williams et al., 1997). According to this cognitive vulnerability hypothesis, major negative life events will have a relatively large impact on the well-being of individuals with cognitive biases. Lewinsohn, Joiner, and Rohde (2001) found evidence for this. They determined the degree of interpretation bias in a group of adolescents. Then, one year later these individuals were asked about the negative life events that had occurred in the preceding year. Participants who had experienced the most negative events and who had a strong interpretation bias were also most likely to develop a major depression (see fig 12.18). The probability of developing a depression was low among participants who had a low interpretation bias, however, even when they had experienced many negative events. In other words, cognitive vulnerability had a major influence on the extent to which negative events could bring about depression.

Similar results were reported by Cohen, Young, and Abela (2011). They recorded how children responded to negative events. Pessimistic interpretations of the consequences of these events were interpreted as correlates of an interpretation bias. The researchers then determined the extent to which actual negative events resulted in depressive symptoms. Many negative events resulted in a relatively strong increase in depressive symptoms, especially in

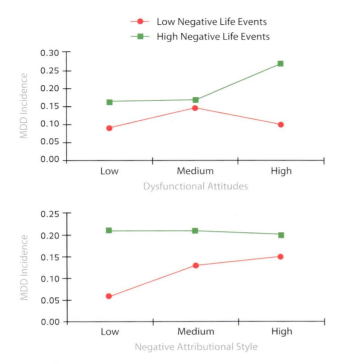

Figure 12.18 The relationship between emotional life events, cognitive biases, and the likelihood of developing major depression. (source: Lewinsohn et al., 2001)

cognitively vulnerable children, that is, children with a strong interpretation bias.

12.8.8.7 IN CLOSING

The relationship between cognitive biases and emotions is complex and not always straightforward. Nevertheless, we can draw a number of cautious conclusions. First, it has been shown that anxious and depressed individuals differ with regard to the specific biases they display. Individuals with an anxiety disorder are characterised by a relatively strong external focus, an attention bias, and, to a lesser extent, an interpretation bias. These biases are consistent with the idea that anxious individuals are primarily focused on detecting future threats. Although anxiety and interpretation biases also occur in depression, depression is more likely to be characterised by an internal focus and by memory biases; in particular, by an explicit memory bias. This pattern of results implies that individuals with depression are primarily internally focused on past events. This interpretation is consistent with the idea that depression is primarily associated with processing failed goals from the past and producing new goals.

The results discussed here are potentially of great therapeutic value. Although, as was argued at the beginning of this section, it is difficult to establish a causal relationship between cognitive biases and anxiety or depression disorders, a number of procedures have been developed to reduce cognitive biases through experimental procedures. For instance, **cognitive bias modification** attempts

to reduce attentional or interpretational biases through training (Hallion & Ruscio, 2011). For an attention bias, this is done, for example, by using a modified dot-probe task. In this task, the dot is always presented at the location of the neutral stimulus, which teaches the participant to stop paying attention to the threatening stimulus. For interpretation bias, this is done, for example, by presenting homographs (words with multiple meanings), which are followed by a word fragment that the participant must complete. For example, 'choke' can be presented as a homograph (meaning: 'to choke someone' or 'to regulate the fuel mixture'), after which the participant has to complete the word fragment ENG_N_ ('engine'). Through this task, participants learn to focus on the positive or neutral interpretation of words. Cognitive-bias modification is effective in reducing anxiety symptoms and, to a lesser extent, depressive symptoms.

12.9 IN CONCLUSION: EMOTIONS AS PREDICTIONS

Recent work from the American emotion expert Lisa Feldman Barrett (2017) suggests a fundamentally new interpretation of the concept of emotion. According to her **constructed emotion theory**, affective experiences are the result of the predictions generated by the brain. Barrett (2017) argues that the brain constructs emotions in the same way as it does for other perceptions by utilising the predictive mechanisms that we have already introduced in previous chapters. According to Barrett, **allostasis** is one of the most important functions of the brain. In the previous chapter, we were already introduced to the concept of allostasis as a counterpart to homeostasis. Barrett describes allostasis as the careful balancing of all the processes that enable an organism to grow, survive, and reproduce.

In Barrett's view, the neural circuits involved in processing **visceroceptive input** and motor coordination are also strongly involved in allostasis. According to Barrett, these circuits also generate the concepts that form the basis of the internal predictive models. Predictions that are then generated from these concepts are not only projected to the visceroceptive systems but are also included in the efferent copies of these signals that are projected to both the motor cortex and the primary sensory cortex. Here the generated concepts form the basis for an emotional response because they manifest themselves here as motor and sensory responses of the body to an emotional concept.

This description may still sound somewhat abstract; however, we can illustrate it via a relatively simple thought experiment. In the past, you have probably experienced different moments of happiness, ranging from lying in the grass on a beautiful summer day, to successfully completing an intense workout, to hugging a loved one, to winning a competition, to eating a large piece of chocolate cake. These examples vary widely, so the brain constructs a concept of 'happiness' to categorise and interpret all expected sensory and physical experiences. This expectation is constructed on the basis of Bayesian inference mechanisms, depending on the specific situation, and it serves the process of allostasis, that is, it allows the organism to grow and develop.

As the predictions spread throughout the brain, the incoming sensory signals allow prediction errors to be calculated, thus updating the internal model. This process

updates the viscero-motor and motor action plans, along with the internal sensory representations. In addition, the generative model also receives prediction errors from the amygdala and the cerebellum. Barrett (2017) assumes that the information received from the amygdala does not necessarily have to be emotional, but that the amygdala primarily signals uncertainty about the predicted sensory input, thus adjusting the inner state of the system, allowing it to develop. One of the consequences of the mechanism proposed by Barrett (2017) is that the subjective experiences of emotions are constructed as a result of the categorisation of motor and sensory responses linked to an affective experience.

12.10 SUMMARY

Since the early 21st century, there has been a renewed interest in the scientific study of the relationship between emotion and cognition. In contrast to the early cold cognition approach, which implied that people perform tasks in a rational manner, recent research has reserved a more prominent place for the role of emotions in cognitive processes. This research focuses on the question of which cognitive processes play a role in emotion regulation, on the one hand, and how emotions can affect cognitive processes, on the other.

In emotion research, we can distinguish between emotion, mood, and state of mind. Although these terms are related, they differ in terms of duration and intensity. The terms 'valence' and 'affect' are often used to describe the nature of a state of mind.

Traditionally, two different ways of classifying emotions have been developed. According to the dimensional approach, all emotions can be classified into two independent dimensions, while the categorical approach assumes that emotions can be divided into basic emotions (found in all cultures) and complex emotions, which are formed by a combination of two or more basic emotions.

According to a recent idea, emotions are the result of the awareness of the predictions generated by our brain and, in particular, the awareness of the consequences that these predictions will have for our body. Barrett assumes that emotions are generated on the basis of the same predictive principles as those involved in the generation of perceptions. The internal models involved in the processes that enable the organism to grow, survive, and reproduce continuously to generate predictions and emotions and, according to Barrett, are the result of the awareness of these predictions.

The idea that awareness of bodily sensations plays a central role in experiencing emotions is at the heart of most classical emotion theories, such as the James-Lange

feedback theory, the Cannon-Bard theory, and the Schachter-Singer theory. LeDoux's dual route theory assumes that there are two routes in the brain along which fear-related emotional information is processed. According to LeDoux, the amygdala plays an important role in signalling emotionally salient information.

Appraisal theories of emotion assume that emotional experiences are the result of a cognitive value determination process, which evaluates the potential consequences of changes in our environment. These processes can be divided into conscious and unconscious appraisal. Conscious appraisal can be influenced, for example, by taking a different perspective. In contrast, unconscious appraisal occurs automatically. For example, phobic individuals respond automatically to photographs showing the subject of their phobia, and emotional facial expressions were also found to be processed automatically in individuals with affective blindness. Although appraisal theories are influential, they are limited in the sense that they assume a strict unidirectionality, that is, that cognitive processes generate emotions, whereas nowadays there is also evidence that emotions can influence cognitive processes. Moreover, the idea that cognitive processes generate emotions places a strong emphasis on top-down processes. Ochsner and colleagues argue that emotional experiences are not just the result of top-down processes alone but are rather the result of an interaction between top-down and bottom-up processes. The top-down processes are shaped by appraisal, whereas the bottom-up component is the result of direct perception of the stimulus.

Emotion regulation describes how cognitive processes can adjust emotional responses. Gross and Thompson developed a process model for emotion regulation that consists of the following stages: situation selection, situation modification, attentional release, cognitive change, and response manipulation. Response manipulation is generally an ineffective strategy. Most cognitive emotion regulation strategies take place at the level of attentional deployment and cognitive change. These cognitive strategies are generally more effective than behavioural strategies. There are also differences in effectiveness between attentional development and cognitive change. The results of attention deficit are not univocal, because in this strategy a number of different, more specific sub-strategies can be classified.

The prefrontal cortex and the amygdala are important brain areas involved in emotion regulation. Three stages can be distinguished in regulation: evaluation, initiation of regulation, and implementation of regulation. However, since there are a relatively large number of specific strategies, a fairly large range of brain areas are generally identified as being involved in emotion regulation.

Besides the fact that cognition can influence emotion, emotions can also influence our cognitive processes. For example, anger and irritation can cause drivers to become more reckless. Bower suggested that emotions are part of the semantic network through which emotions can activate specific information. Based on this network theory, he predicted the occurrence of a number of specific effects, including the mood congruency effect, the mood-state dependent memory effect, and the thought congruency effect.

Positive emotions were originally thought to have a broadening effect on attention, whereas negative emotions would result in a narrowing of attention. Subsequent theorists, however, have qualified this simple relationship. Vanlessen et al. point out that cognitive control processes play a mediating role and hypothesise that there is more of an internal versus external focus of attention. Harmon-Jones et al. stress the importance of motivational intensity.

In memory, effects of mood congruence and mood dependent memory have been found. However, the latter effect is mainly found when participants voluntarily recall memories. When the relevant information is cued, there is no influence of mood anymore.

Negative emotions generally result in risk-averse decision-making behaviour, while positive emotions stimulate risk-taking behaviour. The extent to which we are prepared to take risks is, in part, regulated by our ability to interpret our body's interoceptive signals. People who were good at estimating their own heart rate generally performed better on the Iowa gambling task. The risk-averse behaviour for negative emotions applies specifically to fear. Sadness and anger, on the other hand, often result in an increased willingness to take risks. Reasoning processes are also influenced by emotion. Positive emotions, in particular, result in a greater willingness to accept weak arguments and to make greater use of heuristic processes.

Cognitive biases play an important role in anxiety disorders and depression. The development of maladaptive cognitive schemas plays a central role in this. When schemas are characterised by an excessive amount of negativity due to an excessive focus on potential threats and past losses, this results in cognitive vulnerability. These cognitive schemas can also influence the way we perceive the world and interpret and remember the past, resulting in a cognitive bias. The following biases can be distinguished: attention bias, interpretation bias, implicit memory bias, and explicit memory bias.

Attentional biases can be examined using the dot-probe task or the emotional Stroop task, whereas interpretation biases are examined using homophones. Memory biases play an important role in maintaining a negative state of mind by focusing strongly on internal negative experiences from the past. When the focus remains on these negative events, the danger of rumination arises: the process of endlessly ruminating on negative events from the past, keeping these negative representations activated.

Although these individual biases were initially studied separately, there is now a growing awareness that there is a strong interaction between the different biases. Cognitive control processes probably play an important role in the regulation of cognitive biases. The cognitive vulnerability hypothesis postulates that people with a strong cognitive bias are more susceptible to negative life events and therefore have a higher risk of depression. Cognitive bias modification training aims to reduce attentional or interpretive biases through experimental procedures.

FURTHER READING

Barret, L. F., Lewis, M., & Haviland-Jones, J. M. (2016): *The handbook of emotions*. London, UK: The Guilford Press.

Moore, S., & Oaksford, M. (2002). *Emotional cognition: From brain to behavior*. Amsterdam: John Benjamins Publishing.

Power, M., & Dalgeish, T. (2008). *Cognition and emotion: From order to disorder*. Hove, UK: Psychology Press.

PART 6

Learning and Memory

CHAPTER 13
The architecture of memory

13.1 INTRODUCTION

While visiting your parents and rummaging through some of your old belongings, you suddenly come across a box of old photographs from your high school days that you believed had been long lost. As you flip through the photos you notice that your fellow classmates look so much younger than you remember them. Seeing the photos makes you think back to your first years in high school. Your thoughts go back to that time and various memories come flooding back. As you browse the photos, the names of your classmates come back to you, and you remember the endless breaks that you spent with your group of friends. You remember the one boy you disliked so much and that one time when you were expelled from class – completely unfairly of course. What was the name of that annoying teacher again, and what subject was he teaching? You think of the good and the bad moments: that one moment when at the exam you were asked to do exactly what you had learnt, which gave you a very high mark. But then again, what topic was it? You think of the drawing lessons, where you always knew so quickly how to apply a certain technique, or of the swimming classes where despite your best intentions you never managed to master your hand and leg coordination. Until one day, without even realising what you were doing, you all of a sudden got it right.

The scenario sketched here illustrates the complexity of our memory: although we tend to believe that information once stored in our long-term memory is permanent, we find that it can be quite severely distorted, as illustrated by the fact that your classmates were so much younger than you remember them. All memories of personal episodes from your life, such as the memory of breaks, classmates, or specific incidents, are stored in your episodic long-term memory. However, these episodic memories are stored separately from the facts you learned at school. The latter memories are stored in your semantic memory and the fact that you cannot remember which subject that annoying teacher taught again implies that **semantic** and **episodic memory** are two separate memory systems.

Both memory systems are, however, part of an explicit, **declarative memory**. That is, a memory system storing those memories that we have explicit, conscious access to. In contrast, we can also identify **non-declarative memory**, that is, a memory system where, among other things, skills such as painting or swimming are stored. Unlike our declarative memory, we do not have conscious access to our non-declarative memory, and therefore we can only learn such skills by repeating them very often in a controlled way. Acquiring skills remains implicit, as shown by the example of the swimming lesson where you cannot remember how you learned to master a specific stroke.

13.2 THE ARCHITECTURE OF MEMORY

The first memory studies were published around the middle of the 20th century. In 1950, the American psychologist and behaviourist Karl Lashley published a report detailing his 30-year quest to find the locus of memories in our brain, also known as the **engram** (Lashley, 1950). Lashley originally believed that memory traces are stored at specific locations. He attempted to locate these memory traces by training rats to find their way through a maze and then inducing lesions in their cortices. Lashley hypothesised that when the part of the cortex where the memory of the maze was stored was damaged, the rat's ability to find its way through the maze would be greatly impaired. Despite the very extensive lesions that Lashley induced, he could find no evidence for this idea, and after a 30-year-long search Lashley concluded that memories are not stored in one specific location, but they are diffusely distributed across the cortex (fig 13.1).

More specifically, Lashley found that a lesion in a local part of the cortex had little effect on how the rats found their way through the maze, but that their performance declined gradually as larger parts of the cortex were damaged. To explain this effect, Lashley developed two new theories: known as the theories of **equipotentiality** and **mass action**. Equipotentiality describes the idea that each part of the cortex can contribute equally to storing a memory. Mass action refers to the idea that the speed of learning depends on the amount of cortex that is

DOI: 10.4324/9781003319344-19

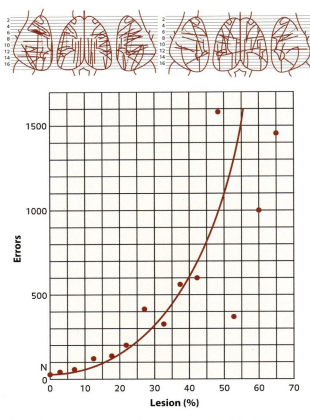

Figure 13.1 Results of Karl Lashley's search for the engram. Top: Even extensive cortical lesions did not prevent rats from finding their way through a maze. Bottom: The relationship between the percentage of cortex that was lesioned, and the number of errors made while rats were finding their way through a maze. (source: Lashley, 1944; Lashley & Wiley, 1935)

available. More specifically, Lashley and colleagues found that the impairments in the maze traversing tasks were proportionally related to the amount of cortex that was damaged, rather than the specific location of the lesions (see fig 13.1). Furthermore, Lashley et al. found that the lost skills could be relearned, but the time required to do so was also linearly dependent on the amount of damaged cortical tissue.

13.2.1 ARCHITECTURE VERSUS PROCESSES

At first glance, Lashley's findings, and his principles of equipotentiality and mass action, appear to be inconsistent with the observations reported by Scoville, Penfield, and Milner based on their observations of the famous memory patient HM (see Box 13.1). The latter observations suggested that there are indeed specific brain areas involved in the formation of memory traces. It is important to realise, however, that Lashley's experiments were primarily based on maze finding tasks, that is, tasks that may have depended upon a combination of explicit memories and implicitly learned skills. Moreover, Lashley focused mainly on the cortex, whereas HM's case studies involved the hippocampus, indicating that the latter brain region is primarily involved in the formation of new memory traces. This does not exclude the possibility that the memory traces themselves are formed in the cortex. It does imply, however, that memory trace formation occurs under the influence of the hippocampus.

Box 13.1 The success of Henry Molaison's failed brain surgery

On September 1, 1953, the American neurosurgeon William Scoville performed an experimental operation on the then 27-year-old Henry Molaison. Using a hand drill and a vacuum tube, he removed a part of Molaison's brain that is known as the hippocampus. As a seven-year old child, Molaison had suffered a severe skull fracture during a bicycle accident and he had suffered from severe epileptic seizures ever since. These seizures were so severe that they regularly led to blackouts and the loss of control of his bodily functions.

Scoville, at the time one of the best-known neurosurgeons in the United States, had an intuitive suspicion that the hippocampus, a brain structure that is part of the limbic system, was involved in the seizures. At the time, the limbic system was associated with emotion, but apart from that, not much was known about its functions. The operation was partly successful, in the sense that the epileptic seizures were drastically

reduced. Soon, however, Molaison turned out to have a much greater problem: he was no longer able to retain new personal memories, nor was he able to remember new facts, and his memories of the period up to a few years before the operation were also affected to a greater or lesser degree.

When Scoville realised the consequences of the operation, he notified the eminent memory expert Wilder Penfield. Penfield then commissioned a young PhD student, Brenda Milner, to examine Molaison. After an extensive study, Milner found that although Molaison could still retain information for several minutes, he forgot it as soon as his attention was focused elsewhere. New information could thus be retained briefly, however Molaison was no longer capable of permanently storing it. An important exception was Molaison's ability to learn new skills. When Milner asked him to recreate a star-shaped pattern, in which Molaison could only see his hand through a mirror, his

(Continued)

Box 13.1 (Continued)

performance was initially very poor. After several days of practice, however, Molaison's skill in performing this task greatly improved, despite the fact that each time he claimed never to have done it before.

Based on Milner's studies and those of several of her colleagues, who studied patient HM (as Molaison was known in the neuropsychological literature during his lifetime), our knowledge of human memory has been drastically revised (Squire, 2009). Before the fatal operation, human memory was considered a unitary system, involving the entire cortex; at present we can distinguish between long-term and short-term memory. **Long-term memory** can be divided into a declarative memory system, which stores our conscious memories, and a non-declarative or **implicit memory**, which stores procedures and skills that we have learned unconsciously.

Patient HM has never been aware of these developments. From his operation in 1953 until his death on December 2, 2008, he led a quiet life in a nursing home, where he spent his days rewatching film classics over and over again – each time for the first time. The quietness of his life was only interrupted by the occasional visit from one of the more than 100 neuroscientists who studied him. After his death, Molaison's brain was donated to science and reconstructed in minute detail. On the basis of this reconstruction, it was possible to ascertain exactly how Scoville had performed the operation. Surprisingly, part of Molaison's hippocampus had not been removed during the operation, and there was additional damage to parts of the frontal cortex. These are facts that require a critical reappraisal of the original results reported by Milner and colleagues. As a result, the remarkable case study of Henry Molaison continues to leave its mark on scientific understanding of memory.

Taken together, these findings already illustrate part of the complexity of our memory system. To gain a thorough understanding of this, it is necessary to make a distinction between memory architecture and memory processes. Here, **memory architecture** refers to the organisation of memory systems and the brain areas associated with it, whereas **memory processes** mainly refer to the cognitive operations involved in the formation of these memory traces, the retrieval of information from memory, as well as the manipulation of information that we need to remember temporarily for the performance of a multitude of cognitive tasks.

13.2.1.1 The Architecture of Memory

Canadian psychologist Brenda Milner's (1962, 1963) studies on HM showed, among other things, that we can distinguish between short-term and long-term memory (see Box 13.1). In long-term memory, we can further distinguish between information that we have conscious access to (general facts and personal memories) and information that we have unconsciously acquired based on the formation of associations (see also Chapter 3) and from practising skills (Henke, 2010). The further delineation of these memory systems will be the main topic of the remainder of this chapter.

13.2.1.2 Memory Processes

Memory processes are involved in storing and retrieving information, as well as manipulating information in a host of cognitive tasks. Many of these processes involve short-term memory. For example, how do we hold on to the numbers 2 and 21 and how to manipulate these numbers when

we want to multiply them. Moreover, much information is lost from memory. Discussing these memory processes will be the topic of Chapter 14.

13.3 AN OVERVIEW OF LONG-TERM MEMORY SYSTEMS

As the introductory example to this chapter shows, we have traditionally distinguished between declarative and non-declarative long-term memory (see fig 13.2). Moreover, declarative memory can be subdivided into episodic memory for personal memories and **semantic memory** for general factual knowledge. Non-declarative memory can, according to this approach, be further subdivided into several subtypes: habituation, classical conditioning, priming, and procedural memory. Habituation and classical conditioning represent relatively long-lasting changes in learned reflexes (see Chapter 3). Priming can also be categorised as a non-declarative memory process because the presentation of a stimulus results in the temporary activation of the **semantic network**, which temporarily facilitates access to related concepts in semantic memory. However, the effect of priming is generally only temporary and therefore this phenomenon will not be discussed here: see Chapters 17 (Language Perception) and 23 (Social Cognition) for further details.

Although the traditional division into declarative and non-declarative memory is intuitively appealing, there is

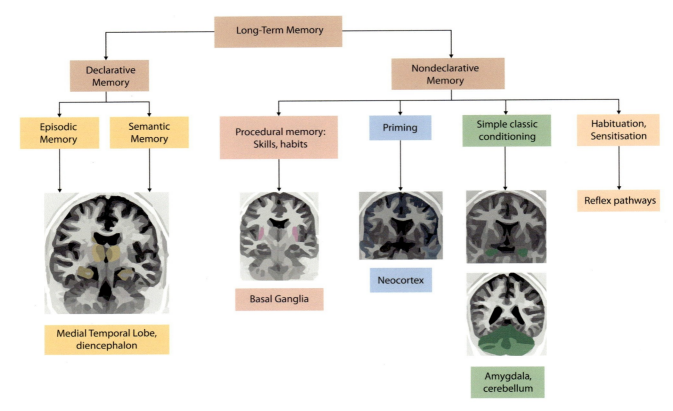

Figure 13.2 The traditional distinction between memory systems. (source: Henke, 2010)

an increasing realisation that this approach is incomplete and that it cannot be properly explained in terms of the underlying brain mechanisms (Cabeza & Moscovitch, 2013; Hannula & Greene, 2012; Hannula, Tranel, & Cohen, 2006; Henke, 2010). Despite these limitations, the current division is still highly influential and also useful. For this reason, we will first discuss the most important results on long-term memory in terms of declarative and non-declarative memory systems. It is important to keep in mind, however, that in the long run it is too simplistic. In particular, it is implausible to assume that each memory system has its own neural mechanism and that these neural mechanisms are strictly separated in terms of brain areas. For this reason, towards the end of this chapter, we will propose a classification based on processes rather than systems (Cabeza & Moscovitch, 2013; Henke, 2010).

13.4 AMNESIA

Much evidence for the distinction between different memory systems comes from amnesic patients. In feature films (see Box 13.2), **amnesia**, or memory loss, is relatively often caused by traumatic brain injury. Although that may indeed be one of the possible causes of amnesia, in reality there are several other causes. For example, amnesia can result from a bilateral stroke, as well as from chronic alcohol abuse. Because traumatic brain injury is often accompanied by a wide range of other cognitive deficiencies, research

into amnesia is preferably conducted using patients with **Korsakoff's syndrome**. This syndrome often occurs as a result of a vitamin B_1 (thiamine) deficiency caused by chronic alcohol abuse.

Although Korsakoff's syndrome results quite specifically in memory problems, here too there are problems that complicate the study of amnesia. After all, thiamine deficiency develops slowly, so that the onset of the amnesia is gradual. This makes it difficult to determine whether specific events took place before the onset of the amnesia or not. Moreover, the damage to the Korsakoff patient's brain is very diffuse. Although most of the damage appears to affect the medial temporal lobes and hippocampus, we can also find damage in the frontal lobes, which can cause various other cognitive deficiencies. These additional problems may hamper the interpretation of the patient's deficiencies.

There may also be considerable individual differences in the nature of the damage identified in Korsakoff's syndrome. Consequently, we may also find considerable variation in the exact nature of the amnesic symptoms. For example, in some cases, Korsakoff's syndrome is preceded by Wernicke's encephalopathy, a dysfunction that is characterised by confusion, lethargy, and a lack of attention (Fama, Pitel, & Sullivan, 2012). This makes it difficult to generalise the results across patients. Finally, studies involving Korsakoff's syndrome are unable to directly determine the impact of brain damage on long-term memory.

Box 13.2 Fact and fiction: the role of amnesia in film and literature

In the classic comic 'Asterix and the Big Fight', Obelix brings the famous Gaulish village from the Asterix comic book series into much trouble when he accidentally throws a heavy menhir onto Getafix, the druid. As a result, Getafix loses his memory and is unable to remember the recipe for the magic potion that is to protect the village from an attack by Roman soldiers. At the end of the story, Obelix has the luminous idea that a second blow from a menhir might cure the druid. However, just before Obelix's attempt to strike the poor druid again, Getafix accidentally concocts a potion that cures him; a potion so strong that his memory even survives the second blow from Obelix's menhir. A similar scenario can also be found in the Tintin album 'Destination Moon', in which Professor Calculus suffers from a serious form of amnesia after a fall, following an outburst of anger.

These scenarios, which give rise to a series of hilarious incidents in both stories, are classic examples of the use of amnesia as a plot device. The amnesia is often caused by a sudden onset of traumatic brain injury (a blow to the head) and typically takes the form of a retrograde amnesia. Obelix's idea of curing the amnesia with a second blow on the head is also classic. In reality, however, we know that this is not a recommended medical practice and fortunately Getafix's potion was so strong that it made him resistant to Obelix's second blow! Captain Haddock's idea of curing Professor Calculus by evoking an intense emotion is perhaps a little more sound from a scientific perspective. Indeed, when Haddock accidentally refers to the incident that evoked Calculus's anger in the first place, his memory returns miraculously easily; a hint to the fact that emotions can have a strong impact on our memory.

Yet amnesia, as portrayed in the Tintin album is also largely based on fiction. Traumatic brain injury resulting only in a sudden and complete amnesia is extremely rare in reality, if not impossible. Also, the fact that both the Asterix and Tintin stories depict an almost complete retrograde amnesia, while the victims are still able to store new memories, does not correspond to reality, where anterograde amnesia is mostly the dominant form of memory loss.

Hollywood has a long tradition of using amnesia as plot devices as well, dating back to at least 1915. In the movie 'Garden of lies', from that year, a doctor hires a new husband for a bride with amnesia – with predictable consequences – in the hope that he can help her recover her memory. British neuropsychologist Sally Baxendale (2004) discusses some of the characteristics of amnesia in movies. Unfortunately, there are only but a few movies that accurately portray the phenomenon. In reality, amnesia results most often from neurosurgery, infection, stroke, or alcohol abuse. In movies, it is typically caused by car accidents or armed robberies, while the real world causes of amnesia hardly ever play any significant role at all in movies. In addition, while in reality we might observe a limited form of retrograde amnesia around the period of the accident, a general complete retrograde amnesia, as it is often portrayed in films, is highly unrealistic.

In many movies, the protagonists have no trouble whatsoever forming new memories after their accidents, even though they typically have lost their complete set of autobiographical memories (and lost their identities in the process). Consider, for example, Jason Bourne, from the eponymous Bourne trilogy (2002–2016). Bourne, a special agent and assassin for the CIA, loses his autobiographical memory after a traumatic experience and has to take on his former employer without knowing who he is. Incidentally, the loss of autobiographical memory and identity appears to be an occupational hazard for assassins in Hollywood movies. For instance, the main protagonist from 'The long kiss goodnight', a secret agent with amnesia, slowly but surely starts remembering her own past (after receiving a blow to her head!).

Some forms of Hollywood amnesia are not even related to any scientifically justified neurological condition at all. Consider the main protagonist of 'Clean slate' (1994), for example, who is perfectly capable of storing new memories during the day, yet they are miraculously erased at night. A similar theme forms the major plot device in the movie '50 first dates', in which Adam Sandler tries to seduce Drew Barrymore. Barrymore, however, promptly forgets their meetings the next day due to a short-term memory problem. Although, as Baxendale (2004) wryly notes, many people would envy Barrymore's ability to forget an encounter with Adam Sandler, the movie appears to attribute this ability to traumatic brain injury rather than to the suppression of a traumatic experience in itself. Yet, traumatic experiences can also be the cause of amnesia in many movies. For example, Jason Bourne's amnesia is apparently caused by the shocking revelation that his intended victim was playing with his young son at the moment Bourne intended to kill him. Other traumatic experiences, such as the murder of a spouse or a shipwreck, can also cause amnesia in movies.

The recovery of amnesia in films, as already noted, is bizarrely often represented by a second blow to the head.

(Continued)

371

Box 13.2 (Continued)

This tradition can be traced back to 'Tarzan the tiger' from 1922. A second common method of curing a movie protagonist is via an encounter with a familiar object, as it is for example portrayed in the 2003 movie 'Saved by the bells'. Hypnosis or neurosurgery are also often proposed as possible cures.

Indeed, neurosurgery, or similar procedures, play a crucial role in movies in which the artificial manipulation of the protagonist's memory forms a central theme; a theme that is particularly well explored in science fiction. For example, in 'Eternal sunshine of the spotless mind', Jim Carrey has his memories of a failed relationship removed, with some highly unexpected consequences. In 'Men in black', the protagonists have to frequently remove memories of alien encounters from members of the population. Manipulating memories can also be used to keep ex-secret agents in check, as happened to Arnold Schwarzenegger in 'Total recall'. Finally, memories can be manipulated to give artificial life forms an identity, as portrayed in the classic movie 'Blade runner' or in its excellent sequel 'Blade runner 2049'. Reality, illusion, and the manipulation of memories – and particularly their philosophical consequences – are, incidentally, a recurring theme in the work of noted science fiction author Philip K. Dick, the original author of the short story on which 'Blade runner' is based.

Although these examples of amnesia can result in interesting stories, as neuroscientist or cognitive psychologist we often have to suspend a critical piece of professional knowledge to accept the credibility of the story. This is due to the fact that the scientific basis for most memory-related phenomena portrayed in movies is virtually non-existent. Yet there are some exceptions to this rule. The movie 'Se quen eres', from 2002, follows a patient with Korsakoff's syndrome, and

although the authors have taken some artistic liberty, it gives a fairly realistic picture of this syndrome.

'Memento', from 2002, also deserves a special recommendation. This movie is partly inspired by the case study of Henry Molaison. The main protagonist, Leonard (portrayed by Guy Pearce), has developed a severe form of anterograde amnesia after a robbery in which his wife was killed. Unlike many other movies, Leonard appears to have retained his identity as well as his memories from before his accident. His short-term memory functions extremely poorly, however, and when he is distracted for a moment, he immediately forgets new information. Moreover, the editing of the movie gives the viewer a very intimate experience of the life of an anterograde amnesia patient.

Ironically, the movie that most accurately portrays memory loss is not about a human, but about a fish! The animated movie 'Finding Nemo' (2003) introduces Dory, a fish with a serious memory problem. Although the cause of the memory problem is not given, the way in which Dory copes with her problems with learning and remembering new information, remembering names, as well as remembering what she is up to (and why!) is an extremely realistic representation of the problems that amnesia patients encounter in everyday life.

Incidentally, Hollywood also seems to be aware of the stereotyping of amnesia and the clichés are sometimes ridiculed, as is the case in the parody 'The Bourne identity crisis' (2003) or in the classic 'Groundhog day' (1990), in which the main character, played by Bill Murray, is the only person on Earth who does not suffer from amnesia, while the rest of the world does not seem to notice that they are reliving the same day over and over again.

For example, plasticity and the use of compensatory strategies have been found to alleviate some aspects of the memory problems (Fama et al., 2012).

Moreover, Korsakoff patients often suffer from an amnesic syndrome, which can be characterised by the following four symptoms: first, they typically have an **anterograde amnesia**, that is, a limitation in the ability to form new memories. This is the form of amnesia that was identified by HM (see Box 13.1). Second, they may also be characterised by **retrograde amnesia**. Retrograde amnesia is defined as a deficiency in remembering events that occurred before the onset of the amnesia. Third, their

short-term memory functions are still relatively intact, and fourth, their ability to learn (motor) skills is also still relatively intact.

Smith, Frascino, Hopkins, and Squire (2013) wondered whether anterograde and retrograde amnesia involve the same brain regions. They addressed this question by examining 11 patients with medial temporal lobe damage and found a strong correlation between the degree of anterograde and retrograde amnesia, suggesting that the same brain regions are involved in both forms of amnesia. It should be noted, however, that this correlation tends to be lower when additional brain areas are involved in the damage.

In summary, the study of amnesia patients has provided much knowledge about the architecture of memory. It has provided the basis for the distinction between short- and long-term memory. In addition, as we will discuss in more detail later, these studies have also provided the basis for the distinction between declarative (or explicit) and non-declarative (or implicit) memory.

13.5 DECLARATIVE MEMORY

Upon hearing the word 'memory', we typically tend to think of declarative memory; this is the memory system where both our personal memories and all the facts we have ever learned are stored. It turns out, however, that declarative memory is not a unitary system. Notably, the Canadian-Estonian memory researcher Endel Tulving (1972) has argued that personal memories and factual knowledge are two different forms of memory, which can be classified as episodic memory and semantic memory respectively.

According to Tulving (1972), episodic memory has a focus on the past, develops relatively late, and decays relatively early. Episodic memory is more sensitive to neural dysfunctions than other memory systems. According to Tulving, episodic memory enables us to mentally travel back in time, to relive our past experiences (see also: Tulving, 2002). Episodic memory is thus characterised by its ability to identify when and where specific personal events occurred in our lives. The episodic memories themselves are relatively limited in scope; in that they relate to relatively simple everyday events. These everyday memories can be combined,

however, to form autobiographical memories, as we will further elaborate in Chapter 15.

Semantic memory, on the other hand, is not bound to a specific time or place. According to Binder and Desai (2011), semantic memory is a repository of knowledge about the world. This knowledge is abstracted from personal experiences, a process involving a large network of neural systems (see fig 13.3). Semantic memory, however, is conceptual, in the sense that the knowledge contained in semantic memory is generalised and disconnected from the original experiences. Of course, there are similarities between semantic memory and episodic memory. For example, when you are gathering factual knowledge about cognitive psychology, these facts will initially be related to your personal experiences in attending specific lectures and/or specific courses, but as you learn more about cognitive psychology, the knowledge you gain will become increasingly independent of these specific experiences. In addition, our semantic knowledge can also influence our personal memories. For example, when we meet up with a friend to have a coffee, our memories will also be partly influenced by our general knowledge about these types of situations. As we will discuss later in this chapter, our personal experience is influenced by cognitive schemas that are driven by semantic knowledge.

Much of the evidence for the differences between episodic and semantic memory has been obtained by studying patients with brain damage (Greenberg & Verfaellie, 2010). Many of these studies have focused on the patient's ability to store new information after the onset of amnesia; in other words, they focused on the nature and extent of anterograde amnesia. For example, Spiers,

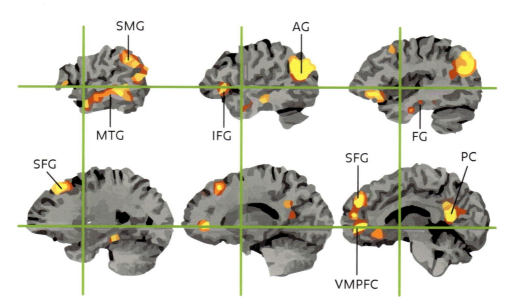

Figure 13.3 Brain regions involved in semantic processing. AG = angular gyrus; FG = fusiform gyrus; IFG = inferior frontal gyrus; MTG = middle temporal gyrus; PC = posterior cingulate gyrus; SFG = superior frontal gyrus; SMG = supramarginal gyrus; VMPFC = ventromedial prefrontal cortex. (source: Binder and Desai, 2011)

Maguire, and Burgess (2011) have reviewed 147 cases of amnesia in patients with damage to the hippocampus or the fornix. All of these cases involved episodic memory impairments, while there were significantly fewer semantic memory impairments. In all cases, the impairments reported were also limited to long-term memory, while short-term memory performance remained relatively intact.

Although these results already indicate that there is a dissociation between semantic memory and episodic memory, evidence for this would be even stronger if we could also identify patients whose memory difficulties were essentially limited to their episodic memory, while their semantic memory is essentially intact. Vargha-Khadem et al. (1997) report two case studies that may meet this criterion. These patients, Beth and Jon, had suffered brain damage to the hippocampus in early childhood (Beth at birth and Jon at age four). Both patient's memories for daily activities, such as television programmes, telephone calls, or remembering visual information were severely limited (see fig 13.4). Their semantic-memory performance was classified as normal, however, and both patients had a relatively normal school career.

Follow-up studies have shown, however, that Jon's semantic memory was not entirely without impairments (Gardiner, Brandt, Baddeley, Vargha-Khadem, & Mishkin, 2008), as his learning speed for specific facts involving geography, history, and other forms of knowledge was lower than average. Gardiner et al. suspected that Jon was able to compensate for his deficiency by spending much time repeating the material to be learned.

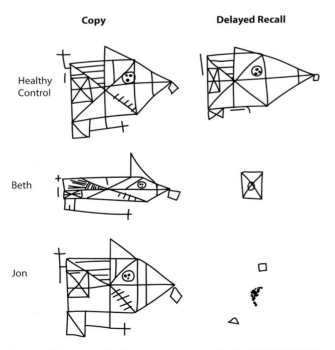

Figure 13.4 Jon and Beth's performance on a figure reproduction task. (source: Vargha-Khadem et al., 1997)

According to Vargha-Khadem et al. (1997), the fact that Jon and Beth have severe difficulties with their episodic memories, while their semantic memories are essentially intact, can be explained by assuming that episodic memory mainly involves the hippocampus, while semantic memory mainly involves the entorhinal, perirhinal, and parahippocampal cortices. Although the hippocampus is also involved in semantic memory in neurotypical adults, the early onset of hippocampal damage in Jon and Beth may have caused these hippocampal functions to be taken over by other brain areas.

Another possibility is that in most amnesia patients, the damage is not limited to the hippocampus, but that other adjacent areas are also affected. Some evidence for this idea has been obtained by Bindschaedler, Peter-Favre, Maeder, Hirsbrunner, and Clarke (2011). They reported the case study of VJ, a boy with severe atrophy of the hippocampus. Interestingly, however, the adjacent cortical areas were still intact. VJ's performance on semantic-memory tasks was in line with that of his peers, whereas his performance on episodic-memory tasks was severely impaired.

The studies we have reviewed so far report mainly deficiencies in the formation of new memories. However, some impairments in retrieving old memories, that is, memories that were formed before the onset of amnesia, have also been reported. For most patients, retrograde amnesia is much more severe for episodic than for semantic memories. Tulving (2002) describes the case study of KC, a patient who, at the age of 30, had suffered a severe brain injury following a motorcycle accident. KC was no longer able to recall personal events before the accident, while the semantic knowledge he had acquired before the accident was still reasonably intact. His general knowledge of the world was comparable to that of other people with a similar level of education as KC. Retrograde amnesia for episodic memories typically involves several years or more. Moreover, retrograde amnesia is often characterised by a gradient, where older memories are less severely affected than more recent memories (Bayley, Hopkins, & Squire, 2006). Retrograde amnesia for semantic knowledge, on the other hand, is limited, except for knowledge acquired just before the accident (Manns, Hopkins, & Squire, 2003).

These results mainly imply that brain damage affects episodic memory. Are there also patients who have mainly semantic memory problems? It appears that this is the case for patients with **semantic dementia**. These patients are characterised by a severe loss of their conceptual knowledge (Mayberry et al., 2011), while their episodic memories and most of their cognitive functions are still reasonably intact. For example, Adlam, Patterson, and Hodges (2009), asked a group of patients with semantic

The architecture of memory

dementia to report details about an event that happened 24 hours prior to their examination. They found that this group performed similarly to a control group. Semantic dementia is characterised by a degeneration of the anterior temporal lobes. As discussed earlier, the perirhinal cortex and the entorhinal cortex are most likely involved in the formation of semantic memories, while the anterior temporal lobes are probably involved in the semi-permanent storage of these memories.

Kopelman and Bright (2012) have discussed three different theories that aim to explain retrograde amnesia. According to the **consolidation theory**, the consolidation of episodic memories in the hippocampus is a long-term process. It is assumed that after a period of several years, memories are stored elsewhere, protecting them from hippocampal damage. This theory may explain the temporal gradient, however, the idea that consolidation takes years is implausible.

According to the **episodic-to-semantic shift theory**, episodic memories are gradually transformed into semantic memories, making them more robust against brain damage. In some circumstances, episodic memories can be transformed into semantic memories. Suppose you once visited an amusement park. Originally your memory of it was episodic, since you remember the details of the amusement park, such as the name, the location, and when the visit took place. Over time, however, you only remember that you visited a theme park, without being able to recall specific details. The episodic memory has now morphed into a semantic memory.

This change is known as **semanticisation** and implies that there is no sharp distinction between an episodic memory and a semantic memory trace. Evidence for semanticisation is provided by Harand et al. (2012). In their study, participants were shown 192 photographs, after which they were given a memory test, on two different occasions. The first of these was administered three days later and the second one three months later. For some photos, the participants still remembered the contextual information surrounding the photos on both occasions, whereas for other photos, this information was only available during the first memory test (fig 13.5).

The third, **multiple trace theory**, assumes that the hippocampus is always involved in declarative memory; both in consolidating the memories and in retrieving/reactivating them. Nadel and Moscovitch (1997) assume that the hippocampus acts as a pointer or index: the success with which a memory can be retrieved depends on the strength of the connections between the hippocampus (which is involved in retrieval) and the temporal lobes where the memory is stored. The more often this index is activated, the stronger the connections become, until at some point the connections become so strong that indexing via the

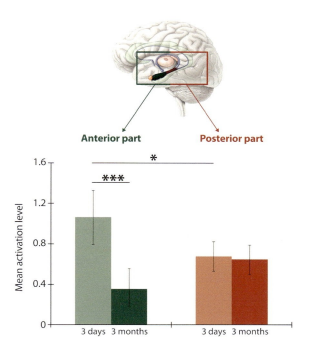

Figure 13.5 Hippocampus activation related to memories that were tested using the recall/know procedure. Stimuli that the participants remembered three months later showed a dissociation between anterior and posterior hippocampal activity. (source: Harand et al., 2012)

hippocampus is no longer necessary. It is important to note that episodic memories are often based on separate, one-off learning events, whereas semantic memory traces are often the result of multiple learning experiences, which implies that semantic memories can be retrieved much more rapidly and robustly.

13.6 EPISODIC MEMORY

13.6.1 THE PERMASTORE

Most episodic memories are forgotten over time, to a greater or lesser extent. There appear to be some exceptions to this rule, however. For example, Bahrick, Bahrick, and Wittlinger (1975) used photographs from high school yearbooks and asked former students to recall memories of their classmates based on these photographs. Most participants had remarkably good memories of their classmates, even after 25 years. In about 90% of all cases, they still recognised the names of their classmates, in addition to correctly associating the photos with their names. Their memory performance remained extremely high even after 50 years, although the recognition of names began to decrease over that period. Yet, participants memories were not perfect, as some distortions were observed. Most notably Bahrick, Hall, and Da Costa (2008) questioned former students about their study results. Distortions (typically consisting of overestimating one's own school grades!) appeared in the

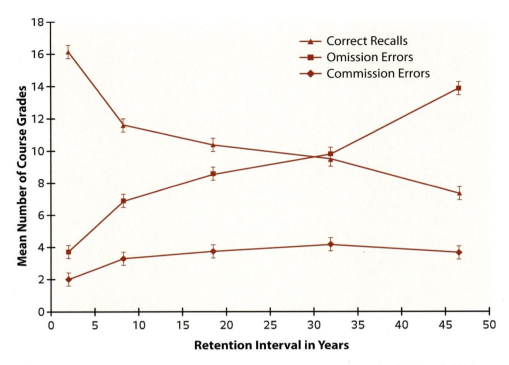

Figure 13.6 Memories of participants own school results as a function of the length of the retention interval. (source: Bahrick et al., 2008)

period immediately following the exam. After that initial period, the memories remained reasonably stable over the years, however (see fig 13.6).

To describe this semi-permanent storage of episodic memories, Bahrick (1984) introduced the term **permastore** to describe stable long-term memories. This term, which was inspired by permafrost, the permanently frozen ground in the polar regions, describes the particularly stable episodic memories that are very robustly encoded in memory.

13.6.2 RECOGNITION VERSUS REMEMBERING

The American psychologist Ulric Neisser (1984) has criticised the idea of the permastore, however. According to Neisser, there is no such thing as an exceptionally well-stored memory. Instead, he attributes these remarkably robust memories to the formation of a cognitive schema. Schemas are knowledge structures in which individual memories can be embedded. Bahrick (1984) originally reported that Spanish words could be recalled 50 years after learning them and argued that they were stored in the form of a permastore. According to Neisser, however, there is a simpler explanation for this exceptionally good memory performance. That is, in Bahrick's studies, participants had to recognise words. According to Neisser, cognitive schemas associated with the retrieval cues used in the recognition test contain enough information to positively influence the recognition processes, even when the original memory has already faded.

Neisser's (1984) critique thus highlights a crucial distinction in the way we retrieve episodic memories.

In episodic memory research, we can distinguish between recognition and recall. Recognition often involves the presentation of a series of items, where participants must indicate whether an item is new or whether it has already been presented once before. The investigation of recall, on the other hand, involves one of the following three methods: free recall, serial recall, or cued recall.

In free recall, participants are required to produce a list of the items that were memorised that is as complete as possible, while there are no restrictions on the order in which the items can be listed. In serial recall, participants are also required to produce a list of the items that were memorised, but here the items are to be listed in the order in which they were originally memorised. Finally, cued recall requires participants to produce an item on the basis of a cue that is provided. For example, when participants are learning word pairs, such as 'elephant – table', the cue 'elephant –???' can be used during the subsequent memory test, prompting participants to recall the item associated with the cue.

13.6.2.1 Recognition

Recognition can be divided into two different subprocesses, namely recollection and familiarity. According to Diana, Yonelinas, and Ranganath (2007) recollection is defined as the recognition of an item based on the retrieval of contextual details. Familiarity, on the other hand, is the process of recognising an item on the basis of perceiving the relative strength of the memory, but without retrieving specific details related to the context in which the item was initially encountered.

How can we clearly distinguish between familiarity and recollection? One way to do so is by applying the remember/know procedure (Migo, Mayes, & Montaldi, 2012). Here, participants have to indicate whether an item is new or whether it has been presented once before. When participants indicate that they remember items that are classified as 'old', this is considered to be recognition based on recollection. In contrast, when participants indicate that they know they have encountered an item before, this is considered to be recognition based on familiarity.

A question that logically follows from the distinction between recollection and familiarity is whether these two different forms of recognition are based on entirely different retrieval processes, or whether it simply reflects a difference in the strength of the memory traces. According to a meta-analysis conducted by Dunn (2008), results that are obtained with the remember/know procedure can be perfectly well explained by differences in memory trace strength. Based on ERP results, other researchers argue, however, that different mechanisms are involved. After all, if different mechanisms are involved, we might expect recollection to occur later than familiarity, because recollection involves the processing of more information. Several ERP studies have found evidence that this is indeed the case (Addante, Ranganath, Olichney, & Yonelinas, 2012). Familiarity could be related to a negative ERP component, the FN400, which peaked approximately 400–600 ms after the onset of the retrieval cue. Recollection, on the other hand, was associated with a positive component, known as the late positive complex, which peaked approximately 600–900 ms after the retrieval cue.

13.6.3 THE BINDING OF ITEM AND CONTEXT MODEL

Diana et al. (2007) proposed a theoretical model that can explain the distinction between familiarity and recollection (fig 13.7). According to their **binding of item and context model**, three specific processes contribute to recognition. According to Diana et al. the perirhinal cortex processes item-specific information. This process is sufficient for familiarity judgements, but not for recollection. Next, the parahippocampal cortex is assumed to receive information about the context in which the item in question has previously been encountered. This process is necessary, but not sufficient for recollection. The main reason for this is that the information about the item and the context must be integrated with one another. According to Diana et al., this integration, or binding, involves the hippocampus.

Diana et al. (2007) found evidence for their model in a meta-analysis, which showed that recollection was more strongly associated with activation of the parahippocampal cortex and the hippocampus than with activation of the perirhinal cortex. For familiarity, it was exactly the

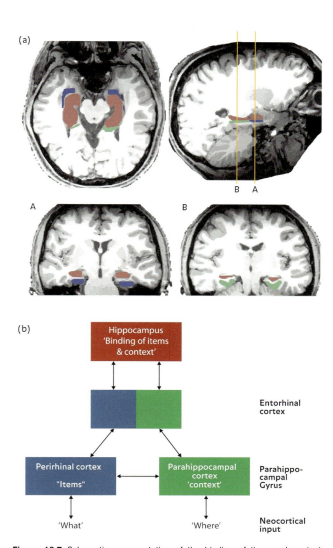

Figure 13.7 Schematic representation of the binding of item and context model. (a) Brain areas involved in the retrieval of items, context, and the formation of associations between item and context. The letters A and B mark the locations of the coronal cross sections. (b) Schematic representation of the interaction between these processes. (source: Diana et al., 2007)

other way a round. Similar results have been reported by de Vanssay-Maigne et al. (2011).

Note, however, that these neuroimaging results are correlational, making it difficult to show that hippocampal activity causes the binding between items and context. Moreover, it may be problematic that recollection is generally more difficult and requires more information processing than familiarity, so task difficulty may be a confound. Indeed, after controlling for task difficulty, Wixted and Squire (2011) found no significant differences in hippocampus activation between familiarity and recollection.

If, however, the hippocampus is involved in recollection, then neuropsychological studies of patients with hippocampal damage should also show that they have selective difficulties with recollection. Bowles et al. (2010) studied a group of amnesia patients whose hippocampus and amygdala had been surgically removed. These patients were significantly impaired in their ability to recognise items, while their familiarity judgements were not affected. These results are consistent with other neuropsychological studies, although some deficits in familiarity judgements have been reported as well (Skinner & Fernandes, 2007).

The previously discussed study by Addante et al. (2012) also reported that amnesia patients had difficulties with recollection, while their familiarity judgements remained reasonably intact. The FN400 component, which was related to familiarity, remained intact in amnesia patients, whereas the late positive complex, which was associated with recollection, was no longer present. According to the Diana et al. (2007) model, we would expect that patients with damage to the perirhinal cortex should be particularly impaired at making familiarity judgements. Bowles et al. (2007) and Bowles, O'Neil, Mirsattari, Poppenk, and Kohler (2011) tested this assumption in a patient, NB, who had a large part of her perirhinal cortex and part of the adjacent entorhinal cortex surgically removed. Her ability to recognise a wide range of materials was largely intact. For verbal materials, however, she had difficulties with familiarity judgements.

13.6.4 RECALL

To what extent does recall differ from recognition? Staresina and Davachi (2006) aimed to address this question by giving participants three different memory tests, namely an item recognition test (which is sensitive to familiarity), an associative recognition test (which is sensitive to recollection) and a free recall test. More specifically, their scanned encoding task consisted of the following sequence (see fig 13.8). First, during the encoding phase, participants were presented with combinations of colours and words, and they were instructed to imagine as clearly as possible whether the word and colour combinations were plausible or not. Then, during the subsequent memory tests, they either had to name as many of the presented words as possible (free recall) or decide whether a presented word was old or new (item recognition). The item recognition task was followed by a decision about the colour that was associated with the word in question. The fMRI data showed that associative recognition was related to an increase in activation in the bilateral hippocampus and in the left anterior inferior frontal gyrus compared to familiarity. For free recall, an even stronger increase in activation was found in these areas. Moreover, for free recall, an additional effect was found in the dorsolateral prefrontal cortex and the posterior parietal cortex (see fig 13.8). According to Staresina and Davachi, this increase in activation reflects the formation of associations between the words that were to be remembered and the colours that were paired with these words.

Another way of investigating recall is based on the remember/know procedure. Mickes, Seale-Carlisle, and Wixted (2013) used this procedure by presenting participants words, to which they had to respond by answering

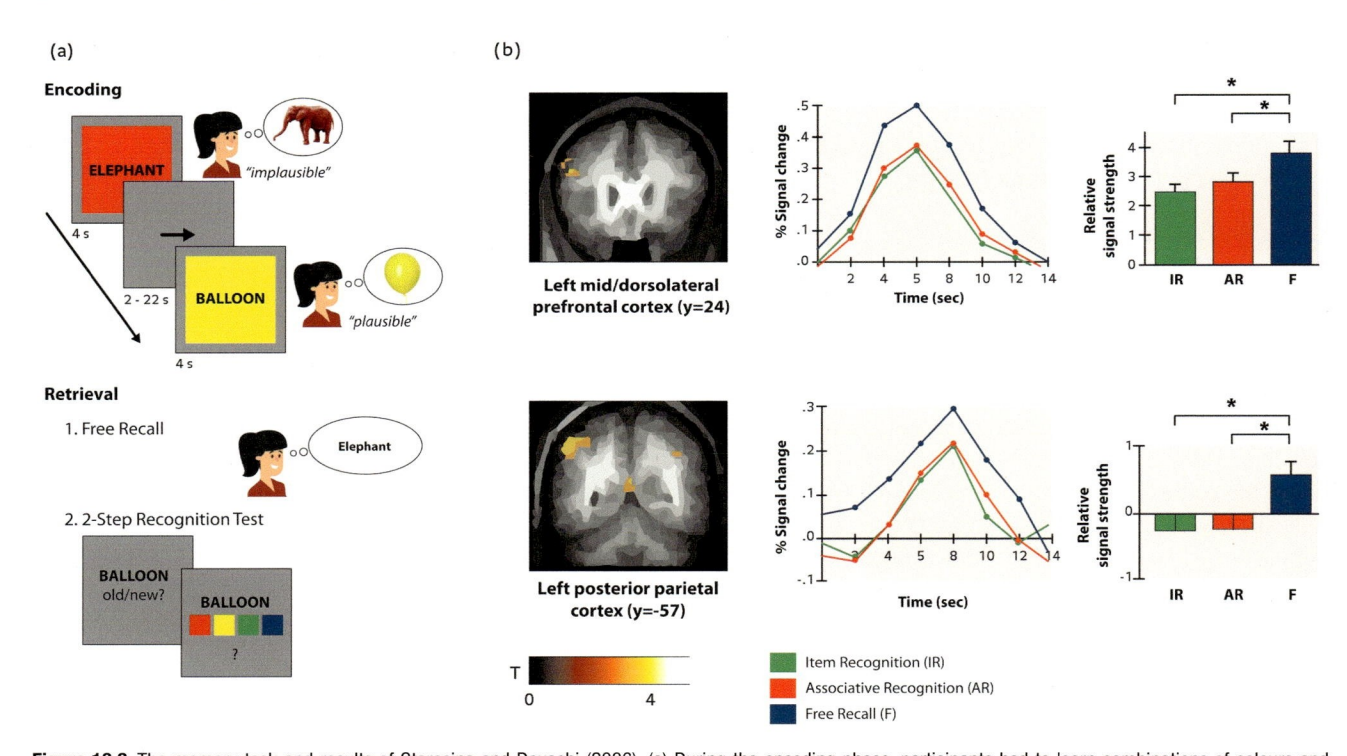

Figure 13.8 The memory task and results of Staresina and Davachi (2006). (a) During the encoding phase, participants had to learn combinations of colours and words and to imagine whether the combinations were plausible. During retrieval, they either had to name as many of the memorised words as possible (free recall), recognise given words (cued recall), or name the corresponding word based on a given colour (associative recall). (b) Results: free recall activated two areas in the left hemisphere more strongly than the other two forms of recall. (source: Staresina and Davachi, 2006)

an animacy question ('Is it a living or a dead object?') or a size question ('Is the object bigger than a shoebox?'). Then, for each word, participants had to give a 'remember' or 'know' answer and indicate which question was associated with each item. For more than half of the words, participants gave a 'remember' answer. Moreover, the questions associated with the words that the participants indicated as 'remembered' were reproduced more clearly than those associated with words that participants indicated as 'knowing'. These results also imply that, just as in recollection, recall involves stronger associations between the items and the context.

13.6.5 MEMORY AS A CONSTRUCTIVE PROCESS

The results just discussed imply that successfully retrieved memories are associative. Why is this? A popular misconception about episodic memory is that it resembles a video in the sense that it records complete episodes of our lives. The fact that associations are formed implies that this is not the case. For this reason, Schacter and Addis (2007) argue that episodic memory is fundamentally constructive rather than reproductive, making it prone to various forms of error and distortion. This constructive nature of episodic memory may explain why systematic biases can occur in the way we remember stories (see Chapter 16), why eyewitness testimony is highly susceptible to bias (Chapter 15), and why our personal recollections are sometimes significantly distorted.

Considering that our constructive memory is so susceptible to distortions, we may wonder why we are equipped with such a fragile memory system. Schacter and Addis (2007) suggests three possible reasons for this. First, it would require an enormous amount of processing power to store a semi-permanent and complete record of every experience. Second, from an evolutionary perspective, we have little to gain from storing detailed and mostly trivial memories. Third, and possibly most importantly, Schacter and Addis along with Addis, Wong, and Schacter (2007) argue that a constructive memory system allows us to use our episodic memories to imagine future scenarios. Imagining such scenarios is only possible if we can flexibly recombine elements from past memories. Both Barry and Maguire (2019) and Biderman, Bakkour, and Shohamy (2020) have argued that the hippocampus is involved in the recombining of memory traces.

One of the consequences of a constructive episodic memory system is that the ability to recall the essence of an experience increases during childhood (Brainerd, Reyna, & Ceci, 2008). This is, however, also marked by a general increase in sensitivity to false memories (see Chapter 15). For instance, Brainerd and Mojardin (1998) examined the extent to which children were sensitive to reconstruction errors in their episodic memories. To do so, children had to listen to sets of three different sentences, such as 'The coffee is hotter than the tea', 'The tea is hotter than the cocoa' and 'The cocoa is hotter than the soup'. Then the children were presented with several test sentences and they were required to decide whether they had heard these exact sentences before. The crucial manipulation here consisted of presenting sentences that had the same meaning as one of the originally presented sentences but used different wording, for example: 'The cocoa is cooler than the tea'. The false recognition of these sentences was greater in older than in younger children.

What about evidence for the hypothesis that episodic memory is used in constructing future scenarios? If this is the case, we should expect that brain regions involved in episodic memory are also activated when we imagine the future. Viard, Desgranges, Eustache, and Piolino (2012) have reported a meta-analysis of relevant studies. Most of these studies found an increase in hippocampal activation while participants imagined future scenarios. This was particularly the case when these scenarios were related to personal events. Moreover, the degree of hippocampal activation was related to the clarity and emotional and personal significance of the proposed scenarios.

Hippocampal activity is also typically greater during the imagining of future scenarios than during memory recall (Viard et al., 2012). Gaesser, Spreng, McLelland, Addis, and Schacter (2013) have argued that this additional activity results from constructing a coherent imaginary event. Based on this argument, they predicted – and found – that hippocampal activation would be greater when participants had to imagine a new scenario than when they had to reimagine a previously imagined scenario.

These results demonstrate a link between hippocampal activity and the construction of future scenarios, however, they do not yet demonstrate that the hippocampus is necessarily involved in this process. We would therefore have stronger evidence if we found that patients with hippocampal damage are not only limited in their episodic memory use, but also in their ability to imagine future scenarios. Hassabis, Kumaran, Vann, and Maguire (2007) found that this is indeed the case. Amnesia patients and neurotypical control participants were instructed to imagine future scenarios. The scenarios reported by the patients consisted of isolated fragments, devoid of detail and coherence. Similar results have been reported in literature reviews by Schacter, Guerin, and St. Jacques (2011) and by Addis and Schacter (2012).

Race, Keane, and Verfaellie (2011) identified two possible reasons why damage to the hippocampus results in a reduced ability to generate future scenarios. The first reason is that hippocampal damage results in a

Figure 13.9 Example of an image used by Race et al. to study constructive processes in patients with hippocampal damage. (source: Race et al., 2011)

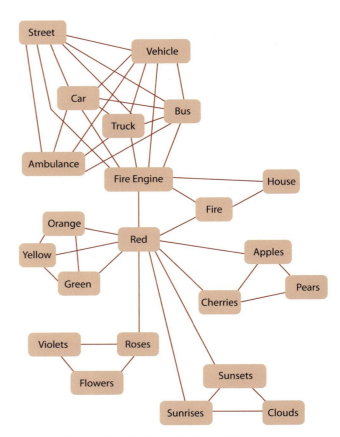

Figure 13.10 Illustration of Collins and Loftus's (1975) spreading activation model.

reduced ability to extract detailed information from episodic memory and thus a limitation in our ability to use this information in the construction of a scenario. The second reason is that hippocampal damage merely limits the patient's ability to describe these scenarios. To investigate this, Race et al. (2011) used pictures and asked patients with hippocampal damage to describe them (see fig 13.9). This implies that they did not have to retrieve information from memory. Under these conditions, the patients' performance was comparable to that of control participants, which rules out the possibility that they have a limited ability to describe situations. Thus, the available evidence appears to indicate that these patients are specifically impaired in retrieving the memory traces.

13.7 SEMANTIC MEMORY

Our knowledge is stored in semantic memory in the form of concepts. Most theories of semantic memory are based on the idea that every concept that we have ever learned is part of a semantic network. In this semantic network, related concepts are interconnected, so that the activation of one concept also results in the activation of related concepts.

One of the first models that was based on this principle was Collins and Quillian's (1969) hierarchical-network model. This model assumes that concepts are represented hierarchically in semantic memory. Although this model was very influential, several of its key assumptions turned out to be incorrect, so that Collins and Quillian's model failed to properly explain how we represent concepts (see Chapter 20 for details). This was specifically so for the hierarchical organisation proposed by Collins and Quillian.

Moreover, in a later study, Collins and Loftus (1975) argued that the original hierarchical organisation proposed by the Collins and Quillian model is not flexible

enough. For this reason, Collins and Loftus introduced their **spreading activation theory** of semantic memory. The basic premise of this theory is that semantic memory is organised on the basis of semantic relatedness, or semantic distance between concepts. Figure 13.10 illustrates a part of this organisation. The distance between two concepts indicates the strength with which these concepts are associated. For example, the concept 'red' is more strongly associated with 'orange' than with 'sunset'.

According to the spreading activation model, a concept will be activated as soon as you see, hear, or think about it. This activation then spreads to related concepts, with the concepts that are most strongly associated being activated the most, and the more distant concepts that are less strongly associated being activated to a lesser extent. This spreading activation model is well able to explain priming effects, such as those reported by Meyer and Schvaneveldt (1971) (see Chapters 1 and 17 for more details).

13.7.1 HIERARCHY OF CONCEPTS

Although most empirical studies appear to be more consistent with the associative spreading of activation model than with Collins and Quillian's (1969) hierarchical model, recent studies have shown that to a certain extent concepts in episodic memory are still somewhat hierarchically organised. This idea is consistent with the idea that categories are characterised by a graded structure (Barsalou, 1987). For example, when we see a picture of a chair and we are asked to describe the object, we can identify it as a chair, a piece of furniture, or a recliner. These answers imply a hierarchy. Rosch, Mervis, Gray, Johnson, and Boyes-Braem (1976) identified three levels in such a hierarchy: a superordinate level (e.g., furniture), a basic level (e.g., the chair), and a subordinate level (e.g., a recliner). Although we sometimes refer to the superordinate level or the subordinate level, we most often refer to the basic level when describing objects.

Rosch et al. (1976) asked participants to generate as many properties of concepts as possible for each of the three levels in the hierarchy. On the superordinate level, relatively few properties were mentioned, as this level is generally relatively abstract. For the other two levels, relatively many items were generated. For the lowest level, however, many similar properties were given for the different objects (e.g., a recliner shares many properties with an office chair). For the basic level, these properties were much more distinct. The properties at this level are shared much less with those of other members of the category (e.g., chairs and tables).

Apart from distinctiveness, the basic level is characterised by several additional special features. For example, all members of the basic level are characterised by sharing certain motor actions. All chairs are, for example, characterised by the fact that they can be sat on in a similar manner. This property is not shared with the way we interact with a table. Moreover, in a picture naming task, Rosch et al. (1976) found that participants used names most often at the basic level.

We will not always prefer to use the basic level, however. For example, experts often refer to objects at the subordinate level. For example, Tanaka and Taylor (1991) found that birdwatchers and dog experts used subordinate names much more often within the domain of their expertise than outside it. Likewise, Anaki and Bentin (2009) found that we use subordinate names much more for faces than for other objects. Here, participants were given a label on the subordinate, basic, or superordinate level, after which they had to decide whether the label matched a familiar face. Participants could make this decision much faster when it concerned subordinate labels than when it concerned basic level labels. Anaki and Bentin investigated whether this preference for subordinate labels was related to a specific expertise in recognising faces and reported evidence that it was not. For example, when participants were given labels to associate with famous landmarks, such as the Eiffel Tower or the Leaning Tower of Pisa, they also showed a preference for subordinate labels.

Although we generally prefer labels at the basic level, this does not mean that we are also the most efficient at processing this level. Prass, Grimsen, Konig, and Fahle (2013) instructed their participants to categorise images at either the superordinate level (animal or vehicle), the basic level (dog or cat), or the subordinate level (e.g., Siamese cat or Persian cat). Here, task performance was highest at the superordinate level and lowest at the subordinate level (fig 13.11). These results reflect the fact that categorisation at a more detailed level is more informative and therefore requires more detailed processing (Close & Pothos, 2012). This idea is consistent with results from Rogers and Patterson (2007), who studied patients with semantic dementia and found that these patients performed better at the superordinate level than at the basic level.

13.7.2 THE NATURE OF CONCEPTS

It was originally assumed that the concepts that are stored in semantic memory were abstract and thus decoupled from the sensory and motor representations. In addition, their representations would be stable in the sense that each individual would use the same representation of a concept regardless of the occasion in which it was used. Finally, different individuals would have a more or less similar representation of a concept. The concepts stored in semantic memory would, in other words, resemble abstract encyclopaedic descriptions. This interpretation is problematic, however, because it is far removed from the way we handle concepts in everyday life. For example, how could we use encyclopaedic concepts when describing the world we perceive around us in everyday life?

For this reason, Barsalou (2009) argues that all of these theoretical assumptions are incorrect. This is because in everyday life we hardly ever encounter just a single isolated concept, but rather interpret concepts in different contexts, so that the representation of a concept can vary greatly from situation to situation and be dependent on the goals we want to achieve. Consider the following example quoted by Barsalou. Traditionally, it was assumed that for the concept of a bicycle, it would suffice to activate the dictionary definition of a bicycle: 'vehicle with two wheels, one directly in front of the other, propelled by pedals'. Depending on our specific goal, however, other aspects of the concept bicycle will have to be activated, according to Barsalou. For instance, information about the tyres has to be activated when we need to repair them, while the saddle and pedals are much more important when we intend to ride a bicycle. Finally, the motor affordances (see Chapter 10) will also be activated when using the bicycle.

Barsalou (2009) aimed to explain the flexible use of concepts on the basis of his simulation theory, which assumes that our perceptual and motor systems are involved in the

(a)

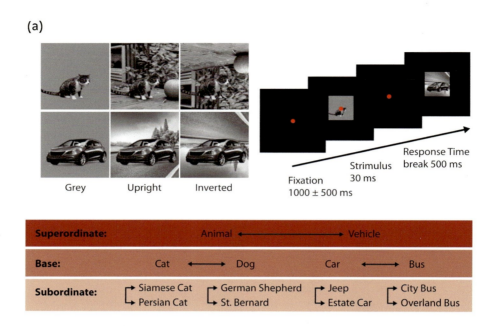

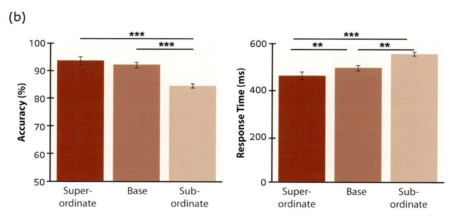

(b)

Figure 13.11 Experimental design and results of a study on the hierarchical organisation of semantic memory. (a) Participants were presented with images, which they had to categorise at either the superordinate level, the basic level, or the subordinate level. (b) Results: the more detailed the categorisation was, the longer the decision time and the less accurate the naming. (source: Prass et al., 2013)

processing of concepts. Currently, a progressive body of evidence supports this theory (see fig 13.12). For example, Wu and Barsalou (2009) found that the perceptual systems are involved in the processing of concepts. In their study, participants had to name as many properties as possible on the basis of a given noun. The properties reported by the participants were strongly dependent on the visual image that the noun had evoked. Likewise, Wang, Conder, Blitzer, and Shinkareva (2010) found, in a meta-analysis of neuroimaging studies, that concrete concepts activate the visual areas of the cortex, while abstract concepts do not.

Evidence for the activation of the motor system during the processing of conceptual information stems from several studies that have exploited the fact that different body parts, such as the tongue, the fingers, or the feet, produce specific activation patterns in the motor cortex when we move them. When participants were shown words that

were associated with movements of these body parts, corresponding areas of the motor cortex were activated (Hauk, Johnsrude, & Pulvermüller, 2004; Pulvermuller, 2013).

More direct evidence for the involvement of the motor system in the processing of action-related concepts comes from a study by Shebani and Pulvermüller (2013). Here, participants were required to process arm-related words such as 'grasping' or 'peeling', or leg-related words such as 'running' or 'kicking'. At the same time, they had to perform a tapping task using either their arms or their legs. The extent to which participants were able to subsequently report the words depended on the task and the type of words they had to remember. Indeed, memory performance was lower when there was a similarity between the words they had to remember and the body part they had to use to perform the tapping task. Similar evidence

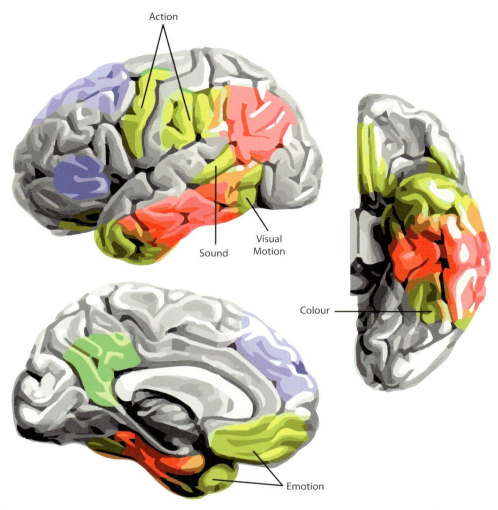

Figure 13.12 The representation of perceptual, emotional, and motor codes in semantic memory. (source: Binder and Desai, 2011)

was provided by a TMS study conducted by Pulvermüller, Hauk, Nikulin, and Ilmoniemi (2005). In this study, participants were required to decide whether sequences of letters formed a word or not (i.e., a lexical decision task: see Chapter 16), while different parts of the motor cortex were stimulated using TMS (see fig 13.13). Some of the words that were presented were arm or leg related. The arm-related words were processed faster when the arm-related part of the motor cortex was stimulated, while the leg-related words were processed faster when the leg-related part of the motor cortex was stimulated.

These results imply that both perceptual representations and action codes are part of the semantic network, and that the degree to which concepts are processed depends on the purpose for which they are used. These aspects of semantic memory are consistent with Barsalou's (2009) theoretical approach. Although Barsalou emphasises the dynamic aspect of semantic memory, we should note that this approach does not rule out the existence of a stable and abstract semantic core, as it was originally proposed (Mazzone & Lalumera, 2010).

How can we reconcile the dynamic approach from Barsalou's (2009) proposal with the notion of a stable and abstract semantic memory, as proposed by the classical approach (Collins & Loftus, 1975; Collins & Quillian, 1969)? Several theorists have proposed a **hub-and-spoke model**, in which the spokes are formed by various modality-specific representations that are associated with sensory and motor areas in the brain, while the hubs are formed by a stable modality-independent representations, in which all knowledge about a concept is integrated (Patterson, Nestor, & Rogers, 2007; Pobric et al., 2010b).

According to the model, the hubs are presumably stored in the anterior temporal lobes (Binder, Desai, Graves, & Conant, 2009). Indeed, patients with semantic dementia are likely to have damage in this area and they typically show significant losses of their conceptual knowledge (Patterson et al., 2007). For example, they can no longer identify concepts based on a given description (e.g., 'A striped animal from Africa') or they can no longer identify objects based on characteristic sounds, for example, that of a barking dog. As discussed earlier,

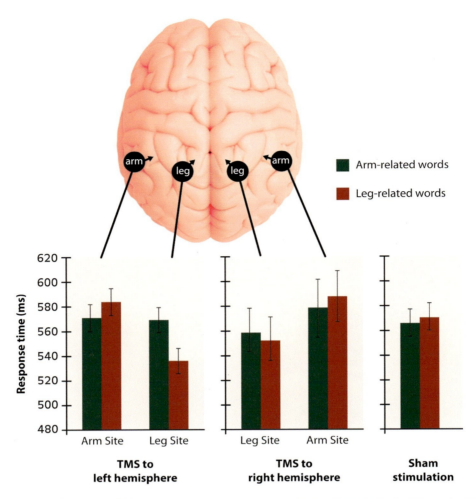

Figure 13.13 Results of a study of the impact of TMS on the ability to process arm- or leg-related words. A TMS pulse directed at the parts of the motor cortex representing the leg accelerated the processing of leg-related words. Stimulation of the arm-related parts of the motor cortex had a similar impact on the processing of arm-related words. (source: Pulvermüller et al., 2005)

Mayberry et al. (2011) have argued that semantic dementia is related to a progressive degeneration of hub-related information, blurring the boundaries between concepts.

According to Mayberry et al. this blurring should result in two specific problems for semantic dementia patients. First, they should have difficulties in identifying atypical members of a category (e.g., an emu is an atypical bird). Second, they should have problems in identifying non-members of a category that do share some visual features with the category (e.g., a butterfly that has some bird-like features). This is indeed what was found: regardless of whether concepts were presented in word or pictorial form, the semantic dementia patients showed specific difficulties with the identification of atypical members of a category and with the identification of pseudo-typical non-members (see fig 13.14).

Evidence for the existence of spokes comes from patients with category-specific deficits, or the fact that some patients have difficulties in processing specific categories of objects. For example, some patients have more difficulties with identifying living objects than with identifying inanimate ones. This deficiency is difficult to explain on the basis of the classical interpretation of semantic memory. Note, however, that living objects are often characterised by a greater overlap in contours, are more complex in terms of visual structure, and are characterised by complex motion patterns, relative to non-living objects. Thus we can assume that patients who have difficulties identifying living objects have more difficulties with the identification of these modality-specific features than with the fundamental distinction between living and non-living features (Marques, Raposo, & Almeida, 2013). Cree and McRae (2003) identified seven different patterns of specific deficits resulting from brain damage. Their patients differed on the specific properties of concepts they could no longer identify. The properties of objects that the patients had the most difficulty with were colour, taste, visual motion, and the objects' affordances, suggesting indeed a crucial role for these modality-specific features.

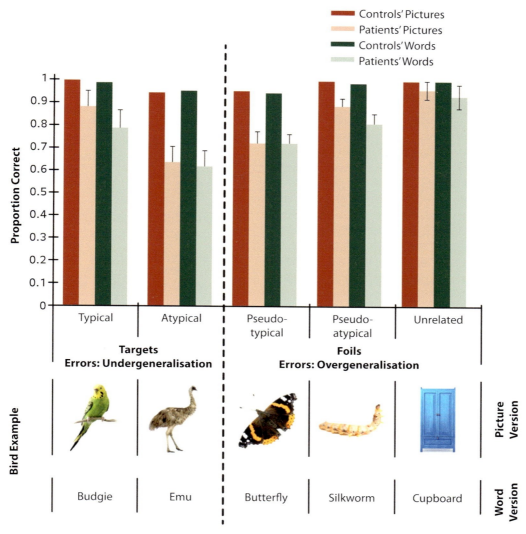

Figure 13.14 Compared to neurotypical controls, patients with semantic dementia were less accurate in classifying both atypical members of a category and pseudo-typical non-members of the category. (source: Mayberry et al., 2011)

13.7.3 SCHEMAS AND SCRIPTS

As already discussed, concepts are not a loose collection of items. In addition to the hierarchical organisation in a semantic network, they can be further organised into schemas. Schemas consist of well-organised chunks of knowledge about the world, events, people, or actions. Many of these schemas can take the form of a script. Such scripts contain information about the sequence of events and actions. A classic example of such a script is the restaurant script, which consists of the sequence: receiving the menu, ordering food and drinks, enjoying the meal, paying the bill, and leaving the restaurant (Bower, Black, & Turner, 1979).

Schemas and scripts play an important role in language comprehension, since we can use cognitive schemas to make inferences about those aspects of stories that are not explicitly described (see Chapter 16). Yet, they can also lead to (sometimes serious) distortions in our memories because ambiguous information is remembered in a way

that is consistent with our schema and not necessarily with the way an event actually happened. As we will discuss in more detail in Chapter 15, these intrusions of schema-related information can sometimes result in serious errors in eyewitness testimonies. In the present section, however, we will focus on the question of how concepts can be organised in such schemas.

Most knowledge about the organisation of semantic memory has been obtained from studying patients with brain damage. Bier et al. (2013), for example, studied how patients with semantic dementia were able to use scripts. These patients were asked what they would do if they had accidentally invited two guests for lunch. The corresponding script required them to get dressed to go out, go to the supermarket, buy food, prepare a meal, and clean up afterwards. One of the three patients was able to reproduce this sequence effortlessly, despite the severe difficulties semantic dementia patients often have with concept retrieval. The other two patients were also able to reproduce the sequence, albeit with some assistance. These results suggest that semantic dementia patients are specifically impaired at retrieving conceptual information, while their abilities to imagine goal-directed actions are still reasonably intact.

We can now turn to whether there are also patients who show the opposite pattern, that is, patients who have no difficulties with retrieving conceptual information from their semantic memory, but who do have difficulties planning goal-oriented actions. One of the first studies to identify such patients was published by Sirigu et al. (1995). These researchers found that while patients with prefrontal damage could generate as many actions as neurotypical control participants, their main impairment was in finding the right sequence of actions; they were unable to assemble the information in a script into an optimal sequence.

A more detailed study was conducted by Cosentino, Chute, Libon, Moore, and Grossman (2006). They tested patients with **frontotemporal dementia**, patients with semantic dementia, and neurotypical controls. These participants were presented with various scripts which contained either sequence errors or semantic errors. For example, a sequence error involved a story about fishing, in which the fish was put in the bucket before the fishing line was cast. A semantic error involved putting a flower on the hook instead of a worm. The frontotemporal dementia patients failed to notice many of the sequence errors (compared to both the semantic dementia patients and the healthy controls), while they had little trouble detecting the semantic errors. Thus, these results imply that the frontotemporal patients have a selective deficiency related to the sequencing of actions.

According to Farag et al. (2010) scripts are characterised by clusters (see fig 13.15). For example, the fish script can be broken down into a cluster related to the bait (opening a jar of worms, putting the worm on the hook, etc.), a cluster related to the casting of the fishing line (casting, monitoring, retrieving, etc.), and so on. Farag found that both semantic dementia patients and controls were better able to assess the order of events within a cluster than the order between clusters, whereas frontotemporal dementia patients had difficulties determining the order within

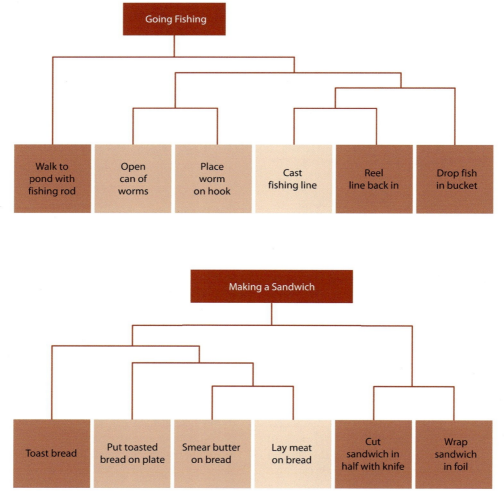

Figure 13.15 The clustering of sequences in a script. (source: Farag et al., 2010)

(a)

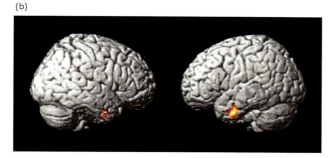

(b)

Figure 13.16 Brain regions showing increased levels of atrophy in two different patient groups, compared to neurotypical older adults. (a) Patients with progressive non-fluent aphasia. These patients, who were characterised by a relatively high degree of atrophy in the frontal lobes, had relatively severe difficulties with the sequencing of actions in a script. (b) Patients with semantic dementia and Alzheimer's disease. (source: Farag et al., 2010)

clusters as well as between clusters. The latter patients were characterised by damage to the inferior and dorsolateral prefrontal areas, whereas these areas were intact in patients who had no difficulties with sequencing such events (see fig 13.16).

13.8 NON-DECLARATIVE MEMORY

We have already introduced non-declarative, or implicit, memory in previous chapters. This type of memory does not manifest itself consciously, but in the form of learned skills and patterns we have learned to recognise. As discussed earlier, evidence for the distinction between declarative and non-declarative memory has been found in a large number of studies involving amnesic patients, who are often still capable of learning various skills (Hayes, Fortier, Levine, Milberg, & McGlinchey, 2012; Spiers et al., 2011). Tasks involving procedural memory can be very diverse and include the skills already discussed in Chapter 3, such as learning motor sequences, copying a mirror image, or tracking a rotating disk. Implicit skills, however, are not limited to the motor system and also include the ability to detect patterns in noisy stimuli, to read mirror writing, or to process artificial grammars.

To what extent are declarative and non-declarative memory dissociable? As discussed earlier, most amnesia patients are severely impaired in their declarative abilities,

whereas their performance on implicit tasks is virtually intact (Hayes et al., 2012; Spiers et al., 2011). For example, Tranel, Damasio, Damasio, and Brandt (1994) studied the procedural skills of 28 amnesia patients by using the pursuit rotor task (see Chapter 3). All patients were able to learn this task and performed at a level that was comparable to neurotypical controls. One patient was particularly notable. This patient, Boswell, had very severe damage to brain areas strongly associated with declarative memory, including the medial and lateral temporal lobes. Despite this damage, Boswell was able to learn the pursuit rotor task, and this skill was still intact after two years.

Cavaco, Anderson, Allen, Castro-Caldas, and Damasio (2004) have argued, however, that most tasks used to study implicit learning have little ecological validity. For this reason, they used a series of tasks that were more similar to tasks we perform in everyday life, such as weaving, or moving handles in a way similar to how machines are operated. Anderson et al. (2007) conducted a similar study in which amnesic patients had to perform a driving task. Both the results of Cavaco et al. and those of Anderson et al. indicate that amnesia patients are able to perform these tasks in a manner that is similar to neurotypical controls. This implies that there is a clear dissociation between declarative and non-declarative memory.

There is also evidence, however, to suggest that the separation between declarative and non-declarative memory is not as strict as these results imply. In a literature review, Hayes et al. (2012) reported the results of studies on patients with Korsakoff's syndrome. Hayes et al. found that most of these patients were characterised by normal performance on procedural tasks. Some patients, however, showed impaired performance on these tasks, which may indicate that some tasks also involve declarative memory and that the distinction between declarative and non-declarative memory is therefore not as strict as was originally assumed.

Evidence that declarative processes may be involved in implicit learning has also been found in studies using the serial reaction time task. In this task, participants are required to respond as quickly as possible to a stimulus that appears on a computer screen, using a finger that corresponds to the location where the stimulus appears (see Chapter 3). There is a hidden sequence behind the locations where the stimuli successively appear, which typically allows for progressively faster responses. Amnesia patients typically perform normally on this task. For neurotypical controls, it has often been found, however, that they do have some conscious knowledge of the hidden sequence (Gaillard et al., 2009).

These results imply that there may be some involvement of declarative memory in learning implicit skills. It has been reported that depending on specific circumstances, declarative memory may be involved in non-declarative memory tasks (Foerde, Knowlton, & Poldrack, 2006b; Spiers et al., 2011). A good example of this is provided by a task in which participants are instructed to interpret several indicators, to predict whether the weather will be sunny or not. Reber, Knowlton, and Squire (1996) found that amnesia patients were able to learn this weather prediction task as rapidly as neurotypical controls, which implies that this task involves implicit memory.

Foerde et al. (2006b) used this task as well but instructed their participants to perform this task either alone or concurrently with a secondary task. Task performance was similar in both conditions, but differences in patterns of brain activity implied that participants used different strategies in the single- and dual-task conditions. Indeed, in the single-task condition, task performance correlated with activation of the medial temporal lobe, a brain area associated with declarative memory, whereas in the dual-task condition it did not. Here, task performance correlated with activation of the **striatum**, a brain region that is associated with non-declarative memory (see fig 13.17). Similarly, Schwabe and Wolf (2012) found that the extent

to which the weather prediction task involved implicit memory was not constant. Stressed participants relied primarily on non-declarative memory for this task, as evidenced by an increase in striatum activation, whereas relaxed participants relied more strongly on declarative memory, as evidenced by hippocampal activation. Thus, the extent to which a task places a demand on implicit memory can depend on both external factors such as task load and on internal factors such as stress.

The aforementioned results imply that the traditional distinction between declarative and non-declarative memory is probably too simplistic, specifically the assumption that non-declarative memory processes rely on the striatum, whereas declarative processes rely on the hippocampus. Indeed, there is now ample evidence to support the assumption that skill learning relies on a complex neural mechanism involving both the striatum and the hippocampus. For instance, Albouy, King, Maquet, and Doyon (2013) discuss evidence related to motor sequence learning. One crucial finding is that the hippocampus is involved in the acquisition and storage of procedural memories.

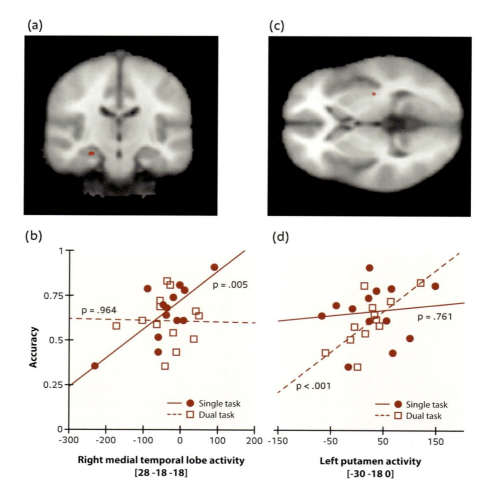

Figure 13.17 Results of a study using a weather prediction task, which was either performed in combination with a secondary task or not. (a–b) For the right medial temporal lobe, a correlation was found between accuracy on the weather task and activation of this brain region in the single task condition. For the dual-task condition, there was no significant correlation between activation and accuracy. (c–d) For the putamen, exactly the opposite was found. Here there was a correlation between task performance and activation in the dual task condition, but not in the single task condition. (source: Foerde et al., 2006b)

More specifically, it was found that various interactions occur between the hippocampal-cortical and the striato-cortical circuits. Although Albouy et al. identify the involvement of the hippocampus in these processes, they argue that this does not necessarily imply the involvement of declarative learning.

Robertson (2012) argues that there are functional connections between implicit and explicit memory. Evidence for this was reported by Brown and Robertson (2007), who gave participants a procedural motor task and simultaneously asked them to perform a declarative memory task consisting of learning a word list. Performance on the word-learning task was lower when the procedural task was performed simultaneously, implying that there may be an interaction between the two systems.

13.9 BEYOND THE DISTINCTION BETWEEN DECLARATIVE AND NON-DECLARATIVE MEMORY

The distinction between declarative and non-declarative memory has been regarded more or less as a given fact for several decades. It was made primarily on the basis of whether we have conscious access to the information that is stored in memory. In addition, a clear distinction was made between the neural systems involved in these memory systems. Conscious memories were believed to be primarily mediated by activation of the hippocampus, while unconscious memories were primarily associated with activation of the striatum. These assumptions have been very influential for many years and, as already discussed, they are reasonably well supported by empirical findings.

Since the beginning of the 21st century, however, several results have been found that are inconsistent with the strict distinction between declarative and non-declarative memory. For this reason, new theoretical models have been developed, as we will discuss next.

13.9.1 A BLURRED LINE BETWEEN IMPLICIT AND EXPLICIT MEMORY PROCESSES

Is the distinction between implicit and explicit memory as unambiguous as it was originally believed to be? Dew and Cabeza (2011) argue that this is not the case. Consider, for example, the word-completion task, that is, a task in which participants are required to learn a list of word pairs. We might assume this to be an explicit memory task. When this task is followed by a seemingly unrelated task in which

participants have to complete word fragments that are given to them, we can typically observe an implicit memory effect, because participants frequently complete the words by using the words from the pairs they had just learned. Since the participants were not instructed to use these words, this task can be qualified as an implicit memory task. Yet, participants who were aware of this link between the learned word pairs and the word completion task performed better than participants who were not aware of it (Mace, 2003), which implies that explicit memory is also involved. Similarly, autobiographical memory studies (see Chapter 15) have also found that the boundary between implicit and explicit retrieval is often not clearly defined (Uzer, Lee, & Brown, 2012). Although the memories themselves are explicit and accessible, their retrieval often occurs involuntarily and spontaneously.

The patterns of brain activity that are associated with implicit and explicit memories are also often ambiguous. As discussed earlier, explicit memory is traditionally associated with activation of the hippocampus, whereas implicit memory is associated with activation of the striatum. There is now increasing evidence, however, that this is not necessarily the case, as some of these studies suggest that implicit memory may also involve activation of the hippocampus (Albouy et al., 2013; Foerde et al., 2006b; Schwabe & Wolf, 2012). Moreover, it has also been shown that episodic memory, which is part of explicit declarative memory, may be related to activation of the striatum, or interactions between the striatum and the hippocampus (Sadeh, Shohamy, Levy, Reggev, & Maril, 2011).

A final problem with defining memory systems on the basis of whether or not the information is accessible to consciousness is that this definition is based on a property of human cognition that is, by definition, impossible to define empirically (Chalmers, 1995; see Chapter 4). For this reason, Ortu and Vaidya (2013) argue that basing a taxonomy of memory on criteria that include consciousness will hamper rather than facilitate scientific progress.

13.9.2 PROCESS MODELS

The aforementioned limitations have resulted in new theoretical memory models that have been developed in the past two decades. One major characteristic of these new models is that the traditional distinction between declarative and non-declarative memory has largely disappeared (Cabeza & Moscovitch, 2013; Dew & Cabeza, 2011; Henke, 2010). Next, we will discuss some of the major features of these models.

13.9.2.1 Henke's Process Model

Henke (2010) rejects the idea that consciousness is a relevant criterion for distinguishing between memory systems; instead, she advocates a process model, in which the most important differences between the individual memory systems are distinguished on the basis of the neural processes

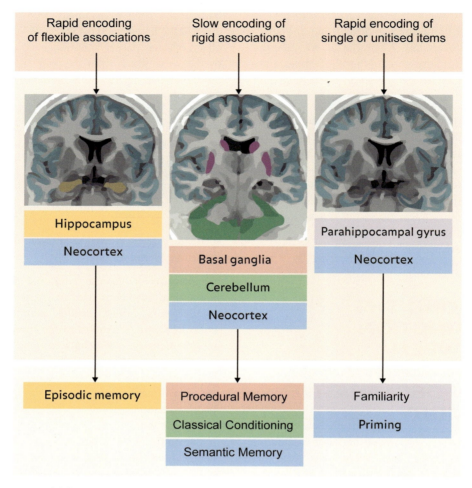

Figure 13.18 Henke's process model distinguishes memory processes on the basis of their underlying neural processes. (source: Henke, 2010)

involved (see fig 13.18). As such, Henke distinguishes three different memory processes. The first of these involves the rapid encoding of flexible associations. This process is mainly involved in episodic memory and depends on the hippocampus. Henke also hypothesises that semantic memory may also be dependent on this process. The second of these processes involved the slow encoding of rigid associations. This process is mainly involved in procedural memory, in semantic memory, and in classical conditioning processes. The basal ganglia (a group of subcortical nuclei that includes the striatum) and the cerebellum are involved in this process. Finally, the third of these processes involves the rapid encoding of single items. This process is involved in familiarity and priming and depends on the parahippocampal cortex.

Henke's (2010) model can explain why patients with hippocampal damage specifically have difficulties with their episodic memory. Interestingly, this fact has largely formed the basis of the traditional distinction between declarative and non-declarative memory. Note, however, that Henke's process model also makes several specific predictions that are inconsistent with this traditional distinction. For example, the model predicts that the encoding of flexible associations can be done both consciously and unconsciously, so that patients with hippocampal damage should have difficulties with both forms of encoding. In addition, and in contrast to the traditional approach, the model predicts that the hippocampus is not directly involved in familiarity judgements.

In a literature review, Hannula and Greene (2012) discuss several studies that provide evidence for the prediction that **relational learning**, that is, formation of new relationships between items and their context, can proceed beyond our conscious awareness. For example, Duss, Oggier, Reber, and Henke (2011) used a task in which participants were subliminally presented with pairs of faces and professions. After exposure to these stimuli, only the faces were presented, and the participants then had to answer a number of questions about them, such as level of education, income, and whether the person was regularly employed. The fact that participants were able to do this implies that they had unconsciously coded the association between face and occupation. Based on a similar task and using fMRI, Henke et al. (2003) found an increased activation of the hippocampus during the subliminal presentation of the face-occupation pairs.

They also found that the hippocampus was active during the retrieval of this information in the second phase of the task.

Ryan, Althoff, Whitlow, and Cohen (2000) investigated to what extent amnesia patients were able to form flexible associations. They used a task in which patients were shown different photographs of landscapes. Sometimes one of the original photographs was repeated, while in other cases a photograph was repeated in which certain objects had been moved to a different location. During the presentation of these photos, the patients' eye movements were recorded. Ryan et al. were particularly interested in how the patients looked at the manipulated regions. If the proportion of fixations in the manipulated region was greater than that in other parts of the photos, this would be an indication that the patients had noticed the displacement. A group of neurotypical controls fixated longer on the critical regions, implying that they had noticed the changes, whereas the amnesia patients did not, suggesting that they had not noticed the changes.

These results are similar to those of an earlier study by Hannula et al. (2006; see Chapter 14). Although most studies are consistent with the prediction that amnesia patients are not able to form flexible associations, there are some exceptions (Verfaellie, LaRocque, & Keane, 2012). In the Verfaellie et al. study, amnesia patients had to form verbal associations. They were given a category, after which they had to name four instances of this category. Verfaellie et al. found that the patients reported as many of these associations on an implicit memory test as the neurotypical controls.

The final prediction from Henke's (2010) process model is that the hippocampus is not necessarily involved in making familiarity judgements. Earlier in this chapter, we discussed how amnesia patients with hippocampal damage are still reasonably capable of making familiarity judgements, while they do have difficulties with recollection (Bowles et al., 2010). Although this result is consistent with Henke's prediction, it is not a typical finding: indeed, most results indicate that hippocampal amnesia patients do have difficulties with recognition, but that their familiarity judgements are also somewhat impaired, as discussed earlier (Skinner & Fernandes, 2007). This discrepancy with Henke's prediction can possibly be explained when we consider that the brain damage observed in amnesia patients is often very extensive, implying that adjacent areas, such as the perirhinal or parahippocampal cortex might also be affected. This assumption is consistent with results from Aggleton et al. (2005), who describe an amnesia patient whose brain damage was limited to the hippocampus and whose familiarity assessments were similar to those of neurotypical controls.

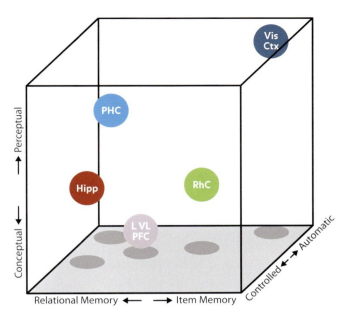

Figure 13.19 A classification of memory processes that is not based on the distinction between conscious or unconscious processing, but on the dimensions conceptual versus perceptual, controlled versus automatic, and relational versus item memory. (source: Dew and Cabeza, 2011)

13.9.2.2 Cabeza and Moscovitch's Component Framework

Cabeza and Moscovitch's (2013) component framework bears some similarities to Henke's (2010) model in that it emphasises the underlying neural processes rather than the classical taxonomy between conscious and unconscious processing. Cabeza and Moscovitch's approach is more flexible, however, in that it assumes that there is a wide variety of neural processes (as opposed to the three processes assumed by Henke) that can be combined with each other in a flexible manner depending on the specific goal. Considered this way, memory systems are formed by ad hoc coalitions of specific modules that can be recruited from task to task (Dudai & Morris, 2013).

The development of this model was motivated by the enormous amount of neuroimaging data indicating that brain areas traditionally assumed to be involved in one specific memory task can apparently be recruited to other tasks as well. In response to this observation, Dew and Cabeza (2011) proposed a theoretical framework that focuses on how different memory processes are related to specific brain areas (fig 13.19).

13.10 IN CLOSING

The last two decades have been characterised by a fundamental shift in our thinking about memory systems, in which the classical distinction between declarative and non-declarative memory is slowly being replaced by a process model approach. This approach is characterised by several strengths, as it is better capable of explaining several important empirical findings than the traditional approach. Despite these notable advantages, we are probably still far removed from the final stages of theoretical development in the field of human memory. While the process model approach is an important step forward, current models are often not yet specific enough to generate concrete predictions (Cabeza & Moscovitch, 2013).

A major challenge here will be to determine how the various neural processes are related to each other and how these processes interact with other functions. This work can also contribute significantly to our understanding of the functions of the hippocampus and in particular how this brain area contributes to other cognitive functions, such as perception, inference, imagining the future, or decision-making (Shohamy & Turk-Browne, 2013).

13.11 SUMMARY

Studies on memory began with the search for the engram, that is, the location in the cortex where specific memories were assumed to be stored. This fruitless search resulted in the formation of two new principles: that of equipotentiality and that of mass action. Although these principles initially implied that memory is distributed across the cortex in a diffuse manner, later studies have found evidence for neural specialisation. This was based in particular on the findings from the famous memory patient HM, whose hippocampus had been surgically removed, and who was consequently no longer capable of storing new memories in his long-term memory. These studies resulted in the traditional distinction between short- and long-term memory, with long-term memory being divided into declarative and non-declarative memory.

Declarative memory is characterised by the fact that memories are accessible to consciousness, and this type of memory can be subdivided into episodic and semantic memory. Studies in amnesic patients show that semantic memory is more robust than episodic memory. Non-declarative memory includes processes such as habituation and sensitisation, classical conditioning, priming, and procedural learning.

Much of our knowledge about memory systems is gained from the study of amnesia patients. Because traumatic brain injury often results in additional cognitive problems, memory research often involves patients with Korsakoff's syndrome, although the study of these patients is also not without additional problems. Amnesia is often characterised by a retrograde and an anterograde component.

Episodic memory is characterised by the storage of personal memories that are typically learned on the basis of a single experience. Therefore, they are bound to specific times and places. Partly because of this, episodic memories are often more fragile than semantic ones. Because details of a memory can be lost over time, episodic memories can gradually morph into semantic memories. Amnesia patients are typically characterised by episodic memory impairments, whereas semantic dementia patients are characterised by semantic memory impairments. Explanations for the course of amnesia, particularly the relative degrees of retrograde and anterograde amnesia, have been found in the form of the consolidation theory, the episodic-to-semantic shift theory, and the multiple trace theory.

Although some researchers assume that information stored in episodic memory is particularly robust, these memories sometimes appear to be very susceptible to decay. Two different processes have been identified that are involved in the retrieval of information from episodic memory, namely recognition and recall. In the case of recognition, a distinction can be made between recollection and familiarity. Recollection involves a connection between items and the context of this item.

Episodic memory is constructive. That is, memories are reconstructed from the individual memory traces when they are retrieved. The functions involved in this reconstruction can also be used for imagining future scenarios. In addition, these reconstructive processes result in people becoming sensitive to false memories. This sensitivity appears to increase with age. The hippocampus in particular appears to be involved in these reconstructive processes.

Semantic memory is formed by a network of interconnected concepts, where the activation of specific concepts results in the activation of related concepts through the principles of spreading activation. Originally, concepts were assumed to be organised in a hierarchical way. Although the original models aiming to describe this hierarchy generated predictions that were inconsistent with the empirical evidence, later results indicate that there is indeed a hierarchical organisation of concepts. Here, a basic level, a subordinate level, and a superordinate level can be distinguished. Although most concepts are named at the subordinate level, this is not always the case, for example in the case of experts, who often describe objects in the domain of their expertise at the subordinate level.

Initially, it was believed that concepts were represented in semantic memory in an abstract and amodal manner.

This idea has been surpassed by an increasing number of studies that have shown that perceptual and motor codes are also represented in semantic memory. For this reason, it is currently more common to think of semantic memory in terms of a hub-and-spoke model.

A final organisational principle that we can identify in semantic memory consists of schemas and scripts. These knowledge structures represent the underlying organisation of concepts. Scripts describe a sequence of actions. Neuropsychological studies indicate a double dissociation between patients who have a deficiency in the representation of semantic concepts and patients who have a deficiency in the sequencing of actions. Scripts often consist of clusters of action patterns.

Non-declarative memory is traditionally characterised by all processes that are not accessible to consciousness.

These include habituation and sensitisation, priming, classical conditioning, and procedural learning. This distinction was initially identified on the basis of studies with amnesia patients. However, more recent neuroimaging studies imply that the classical distinction is no longer tenable. There does not appear to be a strict separation between implicit and explicit memory, and the involvement of the underlying neural mechanisms also depends on specific task conditions.

To explain these results, recent theoretical models have abandoned the distinction between declarative and non-declarative in favour of a process approach. This approach identifies the underlying neural processes involved in different forms of memory encoding and/or retrieval and is potentially able to explain more empirical results than the traditional approach can. However, much research in this area is still ongoing.

FURTHER READING

Howes, M. B., & O'Shea, G. (2013). *Human memory: A constructivist view*. Amsterdam: Elsevier.

Loftus, G. R., & Loftus, E. F. (2019). *Human memory: The processing of information*. Hove, UK: Routledge.

Otani, H., & Schwartz, B. L. (2018). *Handbook of research methods in human memory*. Hove, UK: Routledge.

Tulving, E., & Craik, F. I. M. (2000). *The Oxford handbook of memory*. Oxford, UK: Oxford University Press.

CHAPTER 14
The dynamics of our memory

14.1 INTRODUCTION

Your exams are about to start, and you are deeply committed to mastering your courses. After much effort and with relentless repetition, you have finally managed to memorise a list of hopelessly intricate names of brain areas. Having succeeded, you put your anatomy course aside and you start applying an equation that is part of your statistics course. As you go over each step of the equation, you retrieve your mathematical knowledge while you try to remember what your professor told you about it in class. You try to imagine the curvature of the function that is described by the equation, and you check the result you obtain against a few examples. As you slowly begin to grasp the essence of the equation, you leave it to rest for a while and return to refresh your knowledge of brain areas. To your own dismay, you notice that you have already forgotten some of the names. Yet, you also notice that this second time around it takes you much less effort to relearn the list. After a few days of studying, questioning, and testing yourself, you begin to notice that you are mastering the material and that you can reproduce the names with increasing ease.

This example illustrates some key aspects of the dynamics of memory: learning new information is a gradual process of perceiving, repeating, and testing. The continuous repetition and retrieval of information is essential for the permanent storage of relevant information. In some cases, as illustrated by using the equation, it is not necessary to store everything permanently, as it is sufficient to keep the result temporarily active in your short-term memory. When you try to solve a problem, such as by applying a mathematical function to a specific example, you must also store the result of all the interim operations. The latter is an example of your working memory in action. Working memory is not only involved in remembering the intermediate results of an equation but also in keeping the ultimate goal of your studies in mind.

The dynamics of memory, as illustrated here, are essential for our everyday functioning and thus for our survival as individuals. Having learnt about the main structures and properties of human memory in the previous chapter, this chapter gives an overview of the main processes that make memory a dynamic system.

14.2 THE MULTI-STORE MEMORY MODEL

Milner's (1962) finding that Henry Molaison was only capable of remembering information for short periods of time, while he was unable to store new information permanently, underlined the need to distinguish between a short-term and a long-term memory system. Atkinson and Shiffrin (1968) acknowledged this need by developing their multi-store short-term memory model (see fig 14.1). According to Atkinson and Shiffrin's model, information would initially be stored in a sensory buffer. This buffer was believed to be modality-specific, that is, the model assumed the existence of separate buffers for the visual and auditory modalities. These buffers would be able to hold information for only a very short amount of time. In addition to these sensory buffers, the model also assumed the presence of a limited capacity short-term store and a long-term store with an almost infinite storage capacity. It was assumed that information remains unchanged for a long period of time in the latter store.

The basic principle of Atkinson and Shiffrin's model is that sensory information is initially stored in sensory buffers. Information that is attended would be transferred to a short-term store, where it would be processed more deeply. Some of this information would then be transferred from the short-term store to a long-term store. More specifically information in short-term memory would have to be kept active by a repetition process, which would prevent it from getting lost. Repetition would also ensure that information would eventually be encoded in long-term memory, via a slow consolidation process.

DOI: 10.4324/9781003319344-20

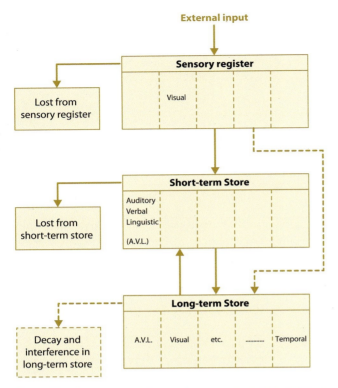

Figure 14.1 Atkinson and Shiffrin's (1968) multi-store memory model. According to Atkinson and Shiffrin, external input is first stored in a sensory register. Sensory information is briefly held in a short-term store, where it is kept active by repetition. Information in the long-term store is held there more or less permanently but may be distorted as a result of decay or interference. (source: Atkinson and Shiffrin, 1968)

14.2.1 SENSORY STORES

14.2.1.1 Sperling's Partial Report Studies

Atkinson and Shiffrin's (1968) model is based on several earlier findings showing that sensory information is briefly available for further processing. Sperling (1960), for instance, assumed that sensory information decays after approximately 500 ms. He reached this conclusion by presenting arrays of letters, varying in length from three to twelve, which participants had to memorise. In general, participants could on average not accurately reproduce more than four and a half letters. Yet they could nevertheless report having seen more letters than the ones they could remember correctly.

Thus, to determine whether the letters that the participants could no longer report were still accessible in one way or another, Sperling used a modified version of his experiment, in which a large number of letters were presented, which the participants had to memorise. The letters were now divided into rows and columns, however, after the displays were no longer visible, a tone was used to instruct participants to only report a subset of those letters, namely those that were listed in one specific column of the display (see fig 14.2). One of

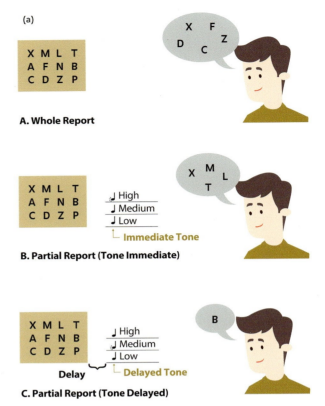

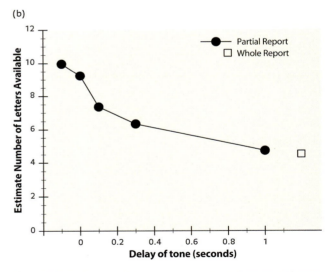

Figure 14.2 Sperling's partial report experiment. (a) Experimental design. Participants had to memorise a series of letters for subsequent reporting. Full report implies that participants had to report all the letters they had memorised. In the partial report condition, a tone indicated which row of letters had to be reported. For the delayed partial report condition, the same applied, but the tone was delayed, so that participants had to select the letters from their iconic memory. (b) The effect of the delay of the tone. The more the tone was delayed, the less successful participants were in naming the relevant letters. (source: Sperling, 1960)

Sperling's crucial findings was that participants were still able to report the correct letters very accurately when the tone was presented shortly after the removal of the display, but that their ability to do so decreased significantly with increasing delays of the tone. These results thus imply that visual information is still available for a short amount of time after the original displays have already disappeared.

14.2.1.2 Visual-sensory Memory

According to Sperling, visual information remained briefly accessibe in a visual-sensory memory buffer that is also known as **iconic memory**. Atkinson and Shiffrin (1968) assumed that iconic memory is preattentive, that is, it would not depend on attention, or be affected by attention.

Landman et al. (2003) found that representations in iconic memory could remain intact for 1500 ms, considerably longer than Sperling's estimates of iconic memory decay. In the Landman et al. study, participants had to memorise a display that was filled with eight grid patterns and then compare the contents of their memory to a new display that also contained eight grid patterns. In this new display, one of the patterns could deviate from the one in the memory set and participants' task was to simply indicate whether such a deviant pattern was present. A cue indicated which pattern they had to evaluate. The interesting manipulation in this experiment consisted of the timing of the cue. It could be presented while the first display was still visible, while second display was already shown, or at any time between the two displays. When the cue was presented during the presentation of the second display, participants' accuracy was slightly higher than 60%, suggesting that they remembered only part of the stimuli correctly. When the cue was already presented during the first display, their accuracy was almost 100%, implying that in that case the participants selected and remembered only one item.

What happened when the cue was presented between the two displays? As the cue was presented progressively later, the participants' accuracy slowly decreased; however, in all cases it was significantly higher than when the cue was presented during the second display (on average, about 80% correct). These results thus suggest that when visual information is only available in our iconic memory, we are able to select it and retain it in short-term memory.

14.2.1.3 Auditory-sensory Memory

Auditory-sensory memory is also known as **echoic memory** (Gardiner, 1983). Echoic memory is assumed to temporarily retain auditory information before attention can hold it in short-term memory. We have probably all experienced situations where someone started talking to us while we were involved in another activity. In situations like this, it frequently occurs that at the moment we are about to ask the other person to repeat his or her message, we realise what

was being said. The reason we can still recall the content of what had been said is that this information was still present in our echoic memory.

14.2.2 SHORT-TERM MEMORY

The modality-specific memory traces decay particularly rapidly when attention is not directed to them. Atkinson and Shiffrin (1968) assumed that this information can be retained for a longer period of time in a short-term memory buffer, where active repetition prevents it from decaying. The capacity of this short-term memory was believed to be extremely low. Note, however, that the question of what exactly the capacity of our short-term memory is, is far more complex than was initially assumed. Addressing this question has resulted in some of the most long-lasting debates among cognitive psychologists, as we will discuss next.

14.2.2.1 Memory Span

One of the first capacity estimates of short-term memory was given by George Miller (fig 14.3) in his influential paper 'The magical number seven, plus or minus two: some limits on our capacity for processing information' (Miller, 1956). Here, Miller described how participants can typically retain a maximum of five to nine letters or numbers, with an average of seven.

A progressive number of more recent studies have questioned this estimate of our **memory span** (see for example Diamantopoulou, Poom, Klaver, & Talsma, 2011; Gao et al., 2009; Luck & Vogel, 1997; Luria, Sessa, Gotler, Jolicœur, & Dell'Acqua, 2009; Olsson & Poom, 2005). For instance, Cowan (2000) warns against the danger of overestimation when considering only single items instead of meaningful chunks. Single items are much easier to remember when you can combine them into a meaningful chunk. For example, if you have to remember the letters C O G N I T I O N,

Figure 14.3 George Miller (February 3, 1920–July 22, 2012).

then we can consider these to be nine separate items, yet we can make a single word out of them. That is, we can **chunk** them into one meaningful unit. Although the concept of a chunk generally remains fairly vague, Mathy and Feldman (2012) argue that participants remember items by compressing them into the smallest possible number of items. In the example, given here that would be one word; while in the case of the letters T N T I B M U F O, the items could be reduced to three meaningful units (TNT, IBM, UFO).

When we need to memorize visual information, additional factors may influence our estimates of our working memory capacity. When memorising visual objects, we are often dealing with objects that may vary in complexity or level of abstraction. Both factors influence the capacity of short-term memory. For example, Gao et al. (2009) and Luria et al. (2009) found that we are better able to remember simple figures than complex ones. Along similar lines, Olsson and Poom (2005) found that the degree to which stimuli can be categorised or verbally labelled will also affect our ability to memorise them. For example, memorising a series of figures consisting of coloured geometric shapes, such as a blue triangle and a red plus sign, will be much easier than memorising a series of ellipses that are each coloured with a slightly different reddish-brown hue. Olsson and Poom found an estimated memory capacity of four items for the former type of figures and about one item for the latter type of figures.

14.2.2.2 The Serial Position Curve

In addition to the complications just discussed, not all relevant items are stored equally. For example, when we have to memorise a list of words, we may notice that the words we can still reproduce on a subsequent test are not a random selection from the list. Experiments in which participants were instructed to report all the words that they could still remember have shown that the words that participants reported were often the words from either the beginning or the end of the list. When we plot the probability of remembering a word correctly as a function of its position in the list, we get a typical curve (see fig 14.4), which is known as the **serial position curve**. The over-representation of words from the beginning of the list is known as the **primacy effect**, whereas the over-representation of words from the end of the list is known as the **recency effect**. Glanzer and Cunitz (1966) assume that the primacy and recency effects are caused by two different processes. According to these authors, the primacy effect occurs because the first items are already relatively well consolidated in long-term memory, because they could be rehearsed relatively often. In contrast, the recency effect was believed to occur because the most recent items are still relatively fresh and thus relatively strongly activated in short-term memory.

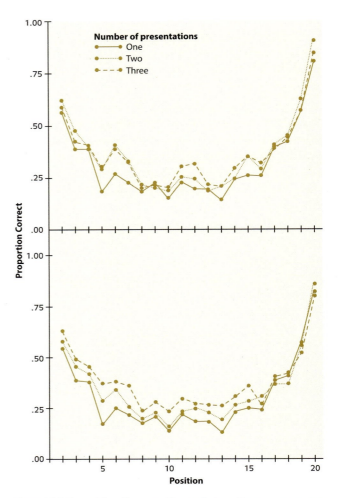

Figure 14.4 The serial position curve. The graph shows the average accuracy as a function of the position in the list originally learned. (source: Glanzer and Cunitz, 1966)

14.2.2.3 Memory Loss

The many studies by Milner and colleagues involving Henry Molaison's memory performance (Chapter 13) have already shown that amnesia can take specific forms. Although most amnesic patients develop long-term memory deficits, several important neuropsychological case studies have described patients with short-term memory deficits (Markowitsch et al., 1999; Warrington & Shallice, 1969). For example, Warrington and Shallice reported the results of patient KF, a 28-year-old male who had suffered a skull fracture over the parietal-occipital lobe in a motorcycle accident. KF showed normal performance on long-term memory tasks but was found to have a short-term memory span of only two.

Similarly, Markowitsch et al. (1999) discussed the results of their study of EE, a 44-year-old patient with normal intelligence. A large part of the left angular gyrus and the neighbouring white matter had been removed from EE's brain due to a tumour. As a result of this operation, EE had developed significant short-term memory problems, along with problems with translating numbers into number words. Interestingly, both EE's and KF's performance on long-term memory tasks was close to normal, giving further rise to the suggestion that short-term memory and long-term memory consist of dissociable modules.

14.2.2.4 Forgetting in Short-Term Memory

An important assumption we have made so far is that information in short-term memory decays spontaneously. Evidence for this idea was initially provided by Brown (1958) and by Peterson and Peterson (1959) in two very similar studies. In Peterson and Peterson's study, participants were required to memorise a sequence of three randomly selected letters, then count backwards from a given number and finally report the letters they had memorised. The main finding of these experiments was that the longer the participants had to count backwards, the less capable of reporting the letters they were. From this, Peterson and Peterson deduced that the memory traces automatically decayed as a function of time (fig 14.5). Brown found similar results from a task in which participants were presented with two sets of stimuli, both of which they had to read aloud, while they had to memorise one of them. This study also found that the interference caused by reading the other set aloud interfered with letter recall. Because the experimental approaches of Brown and Peterson are so similar, their experimental procedure is now known as the **Brown-Peterson paradigm**.

Nairne (2002) has rejected the explanation of trace decay, however. According to Nairne, forgetting in short-term memory is not so much caused by the gradual weakening of memory traces. Instead, Nairne proposes that interference with other memory traces is the major cause of decay: the cues that we can normally use to recall information from short-term memory would be lost due to interference caused by other tasks. Nairne, Whiteman, and Kelley (1999) tested this hypothesis by having participants memorize words instead of letters and, at the end of a trial, having them reconstruct the order of the words (instead of having them recall the words themselves). Participants had to retain these words while being engaged in a number naming task for 2 to 32 seconds. Under these conditions, Nairne and colleagues found a much lower decay rate, compared to a typical Brown-Peterson task.

14.3 WORKING MEMORY

The distinction between short-term and long-term memory has proven useful in identifying under which circumstances information remains in memory for prolonged periods of time, and under which circumstances it decays rapidly. Note, however, that the construct of 'short-term memory' fails to explain why we sometimes need to retain information for only short periods of time. In the past, we could use the flimsy excuse that short-term memory was useful for remembering telephone numbers, but since the introduction cell phones with number storage, that argument is no longer very convincing.

Yet, the relevance of short-term memory becomes very clear when we consider that the information that we need to temporarily remember serves many cognitive tasks that we perform on a daily basis. Because these tasks require us to actively remember various forms of information, the term 'short-term memory' has been largely abandoned in favour of **working memory** (Baddeley & Hitch, 1974). To emphasise the importance of working memory, consider the following:

> Although this skill [of temporarily remembering information] seems relatively simple and straightforward, it enables us to perform a wide variety of tasks and activities. Imagine you are walking along a busy street. You are hungry and want to buy a sandwich from the bakery across the street. To get there, you have to cross the street, enter the bakery, and buy the roll. To cross the street, you have to keep an eye on the traffic around you; cars are approaching from left and right and on the pavement, people are walking in all directions. You look to your left and see a car approaching; at the same time, you hear the siren of an ambulance approaching from your right. At this moment, you are actively trying to remember the car from the left, the ambulance from the right, the goal to buy a sandwich and the plan to cross the street, and to follow all these goals simultaneously. It is easy to see how a failing working memory would result in major problems in everyday life.
>
> (Quak, 2017)

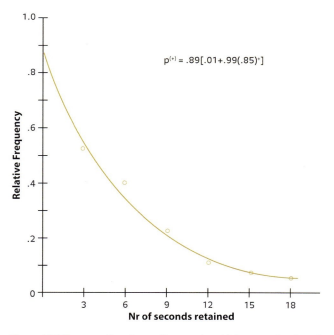

Figure 14.5 The proportion of correctly remembered letters as a function of the time they had to be retained. (source: Peterson and Peterson, 1959)

The idea that short-term memory is essential for many of our daily activities was first put forward by Baddeley and Hitch (1974). In doing so, they also noted that the information that is stored in working memory can be divided into two different types. On the one hand, we have **phonological** information that can be remembered in the form of a verbal/auditory code and, on the other hand, we have visual and spatial information (Baddeley, 1992). This distinction between auditory/verbal on the one hand and visual/spatial on the other, has been made on the basis of many dual-task studies that determined which types of tasks interfered with each other.

Robbins et al. (1996), for example, have investigated which factors influence our ability to play chess. As such, chess players were required to plan a move while simultaneously performing one of the following three tasks: (1) repeating the phrase 'see-saw' (a task that suppresses other phonological processes), (2) pressing keys on a numerical keypad repeatedly in a fixed order (a task involving visuospatial skills; or (3) generating random numbers (a task involving executive processes; see Chapter 5). Robbins et al. found that both the key-press task and the random number generation task affected chess performance, implying that chess skills rely heavily on both visuospatial memory processes and executive control processes, but not on articulatory/verbal memory processes.

Based on the aforementioned division into auditory/verbal and visual/spatial working memory and the observation that most complex tasks require some form of coordination, Baddeley and Hitch proposed a working memory model that originally consisted of the following three components (see fig 14.6).

1. A central executive. This system was assumed to control the operation of the other systems and to allow us to manipulate, retain, or update the contents of the working memory when necessary.

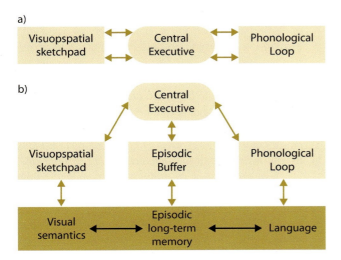

Figure 14.6 A schematic representation of the multicomponent working memory model. (a) The model was originally proposed by Baddeley and Hitch (1974). (b) The revised model. (source: Baddeley, 2000)

2. A phonological loop. This system was assumed to be involved in remembering auditory and phonological information.
3. A visuospatial sketchpad. This is the system that was assumed to handle the memorisation of visual and/or spatial information.

In addition to these components, in the year 2000, a fourth component was added to the model by Baddeley. This component is known as the episodic buffer and, according to Baddeley, it is involved in the temporary storage of integrated pieces of information, especially information related to personal events.

14.3.1 THE MAIN WORKING MEMORY COMPONENTS

14.3.1.1 The Phonological Loop

One of the first systems to be studied in detail was the phonological buffer. Baddeley, Thomson, and Buchanan (1975) hypothesised that the phonological loop is composed of two subsystems: a phonological store, where the words to be remembered are temporarily retained, and an articulatory loop, where the words are kept active through a subvocal repetition process. Larsen, Baddeley, and Andrade (2000) found that phonology impacted the recall of sequences of words. Participants' accuracy was 25% lower when they had to remember a list of phonologically similar words or letters, than when they had to remember dissimilar items. This effect, known as the **phonological similarity effect**, suggests that we use our (articulatory) speech production system while memorising words (see fig 14.7).

A second clue to suggest that we use speech processes in memorising words comes from the **word length effect** (Baddeley et al., 1975). This effect describes the relationship between word length and the number of words that we can memorise: the longer the words are, the fewer we can typically memorise. This suggests that the capacity of the phonological buffer is limited by the time it takes to repeat the words we need to remember (Mueller, Seymour, Kieras, & Meyer, 2003).

14.3.1.2 The Visuospatial Sketchpad

Just like the phonological buffer, the visuospatial sketchpad is limited in capacity. Under normal circumstances, it can store about four objects (Cowan, 2000; Vogel & Machizawa, 2004). According to Wheeler and Treisman (2002), we tend to memorise complete objects, as opposed to memorising their individual features, because attention binds the individual properties of objects, such as colour and shape, suggesting that attending to these objects is one of the main processes involved in retaining them.

Baddeley (2003) emphasises that we need to distinguish between visual memory on the one hand and spatial

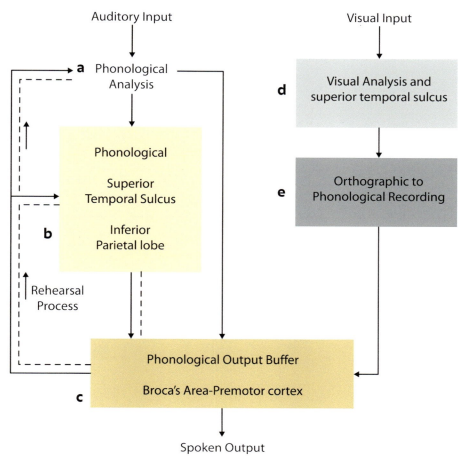

Figure 14.7 The articulatory loop and phonological buffer components of the working memory model. (source: Baddeley, 2003)

memory on the other (see fig 14.8). The capacity of spatial memory can be determined by using the Corsi block tapping task. In this task, a sequence of blocks is shown, after which the experimenter briefly taps two of them. Participants are then required to tap the blocks in the same order. Then, the sequence of blocks that are being tapped by the experimenter becomes progressively longer, up to the point where the participants fail to reproduce the sequence correctly. The visual counterpart of this task is the pattern-span task, in which participants are shown a matrix of cells, with a random selection of cells being filled. Participants are initially shown a 2×2 matrix and must then report which cells are filled. After that, increasingly larger matrices are shown, again up to the point where participants are no longer able to reproduce them correctly.

Della Sala, Gray, Baddeley, Allamano, and Wilson (1999) demonstrated a double dissociation between visual and spatial information. The Corsi task was influenced by spatial interference, whereas the pattern-span task was mainly influenced by visual interference. Klauer and Zhao (2004) found similar results. In their study, participants had to memorise spatial information (consisting of the geometric configuration of dot patterns) or non-spatial information (consisting of Chinese characters). In addition, as a secondary task, they were either engaged in a motion discrimination task or in a colour discrimination task. The key finding of this experiment was that the motion detection task interfered with pattern recall, whereas the colour discrimination task interfered with Chinese character recall. However, the motion detection task did not interfere with remembering the Chinese characters and the colour detection task did also not interfere with remembering the patterns, implying that there is a double dissociation between visual and spatial working memory.

To explain this distinction between visual and spatial memory, Logie (1995) proposed that visuospatial working memory is composed of two distinct subsystems, namely the **visual cache** and the **inner scribe**. Logie proposed that the visual cache holds information about the individual properties of a stimulus, while he assumed that the inner scribe is a mechanism that is involved in the processing of spatial information and in repeating this information in the visual cache. But how is visual information kept active, and what is repetition in visual memory? Unlike the articulatory repetition mechanism, it is not as intuitive to imagine how visual information is repeated. Awh

401

(a)

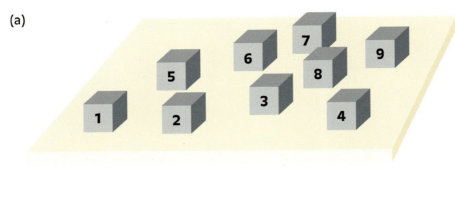

(b)

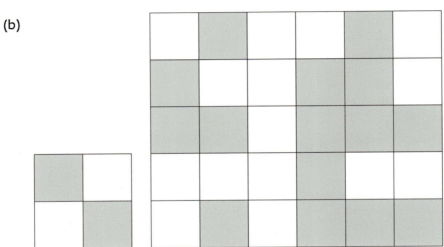

(c)

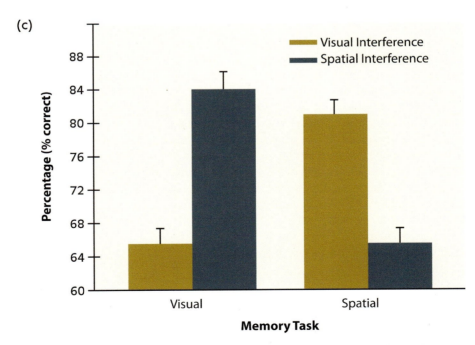

Figure 14.8 The distinction between visual and spatial memory can be identified by using two different tasks. (a) Schematic representation of the Corsi block tapping task. (b) The pattern span task. (c) The effects of visual and spatial interference on visual and spatial working memory tasks, respectively. (source: Baddeley, 2003)

and Jonides (2001) have, however, proposed an elegant solution for this, by suggesting that repetition occurs because attention is constantly shifting between the different objects that we need to memorise, thus repeatedly activating these stimuli and ensuring that they are kept active in memory.

How is visuospatial information stored in memory? In Chapter 6, we introduced the idea that the visual cortex might be involved in generating mental imagery (Kosslyn, 1999). We can extend this idea and consider whether the visual cortex is also involved in memorising visuospatial information. We investigated this question by recording ERPs when participants had to memorise simple geometric figures (Klaver, Talsma, Wijers, Heinze, & Mulder, 1999; Talsma et al., 2001). These figures were presented to either the left or the right visual hemifield, and we found a prolonged negative ERP component over the occipital cortex contralateral location of the stimulus that had to be memorised (see fig 14.9). This contralateral negative component remained present as long as the figure had to be memorised. Subsequently Vogel and Machizawa (2004)

showed that the amplitude of this component depended on the number of stimuli that have to be memorised. These results thus imply that the memorisation of visual objects is likely due to the fact that a representation of these objects is kept active in the visual areas of the brain.

14.3.1.3 The Episodic Buffer

The **episodic buffer** was later added to the working memory model because, according to Baddeley (2000), the original model still had trouble explaining some of the behaviours of patients with short-term memory deficits. These behaviours suggested the presence of an additional backup storage area, which Baddeley identified as the episodic buffer. More specifically, the need for this buffer was derived from the fact that visually similar items influence verbal recall in these patients, as well as the fact that word meaning was found to affect the recall of sentences and text fragments (Baddeley & Wilson, 2002). To explain these effects, Baddeley hypothesised that there was a third storage system where information was stored in an integrated manner.

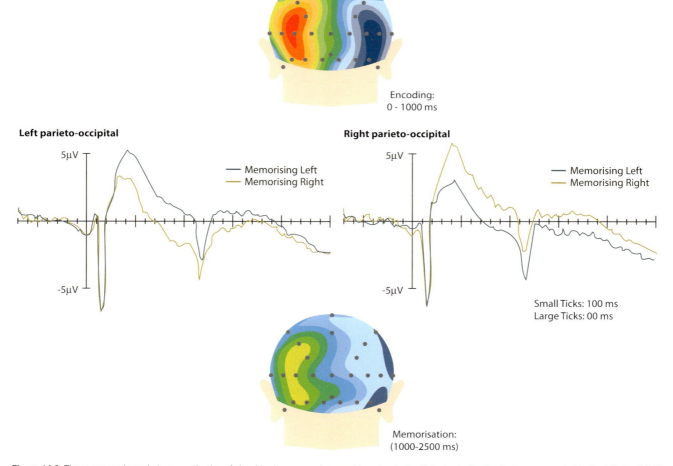

Figure 14.9 The correspondence between activation of visual brain areas and memorising visual stimuli. A visual stimulus that was presented in the left visual field resulted in a negative electrical potential across the right parieto-occipital scalp, both during visual processing and during the memorisation. A similar potential was found over the left scalp when a figure presented in the right visual field had to be memorised. (source: Klaver et al., 1999)

Baddeley hypothesised that the episodic buffer is a storage system that is characterised by limited capacity, where information from different sources can be integrated. The buffer is episodic because it is assumed to store integrated episodes that are limited to a specific time and to specific locations. In this respect, the episodic buffer is similar to the part of our long-term memory that stores the personal episodes of our lives – our episodic memory (see Chapter 13). The main difference with episodic memory, however, is that the episodic buffer is a temporary storage system, which may still be intact even in patients with severe damage to their episodic long-term memory (Baddeley & Wilson, 2002).

The episodic buffer is believed to be crucial for the transfer of information into long-term memory as well as in the retrieval of information from long-term memory. The system is considered to be a buffer in the sense that it acts as an interface between the other components of memory, specifically between the other two slave systems on the one hand and episodic long-term memory on the other.

14.3.1.4 The Central Executive

The **central executive** is the most central component in Baddeley and Hitch's (1974) working memory model. This component controls the flow of information into and out of working memory, and it also allows for the manipulation of the contents of working memory, for example, when we have to remember the intermediate results during a mental arithmetic task (see Chapter 21). Initially, Baddeley and Hitch (1974) kept the definition of the central executive intentionally vague. They recognised the need for a system that could regulate the flow of information to and from short-term memory, but in the early 1970s they did not yet have a clear idea of how this system was supposed to work.

Baddeley (1996) stated the following about this:

> It is probably true to state that our initial specification of the central executive was so vague as to serve as little more than a ragbag into which could be stuffed all the complex strategy selection, planning, and retrieval checking that clearly goes on when participants perform even the apparently simple digit span task.

In other words, the central executive was originally conceived as a module that would contain all the functions necessary to regulate the flow of information to and from working memory, depending on the requirements of any task at hand. Since its original formulation, several of these central executive functions have been defined more clearly. Many of these functions are similar to the executive functions that are involved in cognitive control processes, as already discussed in Chapter 5.

In an attempt to more clearly define the central executive, Baddeley (1996) initially identified four distinct processes: (1) the focusing of attention, or concentration; (2) the division of attention between multiple streams of information; (3) the switching of attention between multiple tasks; and (4) the establishment of a connection with long-term memory. Many of these functions have been identified in patients with impairments of their executive functions. As discussed in Chapter 5, these individuals were characterised as having a **dysexecutive syndrome** (Baddeley, 1996).

It should therefore not be surprising that the functions identified by Baddeley bear some resemblance to the executive functions that were proposed by Miyake et al. (2000). The latter authors identify inhibition, shifting, and updating as the three central components of executive functions. In the context of working memory, these functions also regulate the flow of information to and from memory, prevent the degradation of information in working memory, and also ensure that the memory contents can be updated if necessary.

14.3.2 WORKING MEMORY AND CONSCIOUS EXPERIENCES

Baddeley (2000) assumes that conscious experiences are crucial for the interaction between short- and long-term memory processes since these interactions involve the previously discussed episodic buffer. More specifically, the executive processes regulate which sources of information will be integrated with the episodic buffer. These sources can be perceptual, the other two slave systems, or long-term memory. Since the episodic buffer can integrate information from this many sources, it can be conceived as a global workspace where consciousness experiences might emerge (Baars & Franklin, 2003).

14.3.3 WORKING MEMORY CAPACITY

As already discussed, there is no one single method for determining short-term memory capacity. This problem becomes even more complicated when considering the additional requirements for working memory. After all, estimating short-term memory capacity only involves determining how many items one is capable of memorising. In contrast, working memory is more than just a passive short-term memory system. It is also capable of manipulating the contents of short-term memory. Working memory capacity estimates will therefore not only involve memory buffer size but also the possible limitations in our ability to manipulate information.

Despite these problems, there are several reasons why it is very important to develop reliable and valid methods for estimating working memory capacity. Most importantly, there are substantial individual differences in working memory capacity, and these differences appear to be related to a wide range of cognitive functions, including language, reasoning, and problem-solving skills. Next, we will take a closer look at some of the tasks used to estimate this capacity.

14.3.3.1 The Reading Span Task

One of the oldest methods used to determine working memory capacity was developed by Daneman and Carpenter (1980), and is known as the **reading span** task. This task requires participants to read a sentence and process its meaning. In addition, they are required to remember the last word of the sentence. Reading span is then determined via the following procedure. Participants are required to read a variable number of sentences, and the largest number of sentences for which they can still remember all the final words on at least 50% of all trials determines the reading span. Daneman and Carpenter assumed that part of working memory capacity had to be used for reading comprehension, while the remaining capacity could be used to retain the final words.

14.3.3.2 The Operation Span

The **operation span** is another task that has been widely used to estimate working memory capacity (Turner & Engle, 1989). Here, participants are presented with a series of items, each consisting of a simple arithmetic task and a word. For example, they are shown:

$$(9 / 3) - 2 = 6?\text{CHAIR} \ ;$$

and in addition to remembering the word, they have to verify whether the sum is correct. After a variable number of items, they are required to reproduce the final words. The operation span is then determined as the largest number of items for which the participant can still report all the words correctly. The operation span correlates significantly with the reading span.

14.3.3.3 The N-back Task

A third method of determining working memory capacity and manipulating working memory load involves the **N-back task** (see fig 14.10). The task was originally designed by Wayne K. Kirchner, an employee of the Minnesota Mining Company in the United States, to test how older workers could cope with rapidly changing information (Kirchner, 1958). The N-back task requires participants to process a series of stimuli. For each of these stimuli, it is their task to decide whether or not it is the same as a stimulus that was shown N positions earlier, where N represents an integer number. For example, if N = 2, participants must decide whether the current stimulus is the same as the one that was shown 2 positions earlier. The larger N becomes, the stronger the demands that are placed on working memory. Participants not only have to retain more stimuli, they also have to keep track of how many positions ago each of these stimuli was presented, and each time a new stimulus is presented, this information has to be updated for each stimulus that is still relevant.

14.3.3.4 Working Memory Capacity and Suppression of Irrelevant Information

Vogel and Machizawa (2004) reported a more direct measure of working memory capacity involving EEG recordings. Participants were shown a display of stimuli that

Verbal n-back

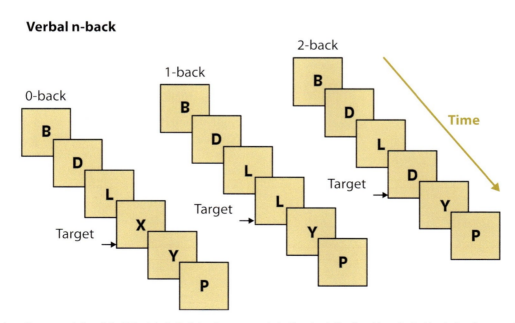

Figure 14.10 Schematic representation of the N-back task. Participants are presented with sets of stimuli and have to decide whether the current item is the same as an item that was presented N positions back. Left: example for N = 0; centre: N = 1; right: N = 2.

consisted of a collection of coloured blocks (see fig 14.11), of which they only had to memorize the items in one hemifield. The reason for this was that Vogel et al. could take advantage of the lateralised negative slow-wave in the ERP component that had been reported a few years earlier (Klaver et al., 1999; Talsma et al., 2001). They found that

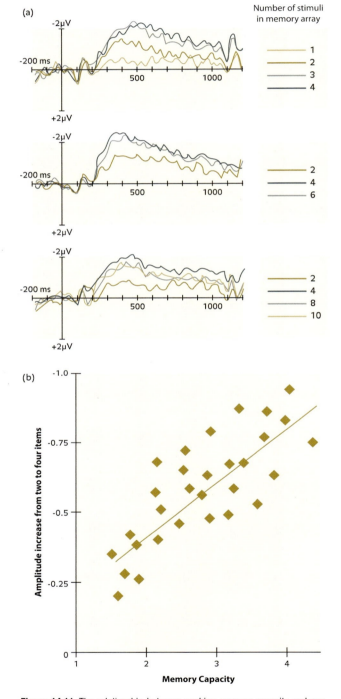

Figure 14.11 The relationship between working memory capacity and neural processing. (a) The results of three experiments showing the relationship between the amplitude of a contralateral negative brain potential and the number of items that were memorised. (b) The correlation between the estimated working memory capacity and the increase in amplitude of the negative potential. (source: Vogel and Machizawa, 2004).

this ERP component increased in amplitude with progressive numbers of stimuli that had to be memorised. This increase correlated strongly with individual memory capacity, but levelled off when working memory capacity was exceeded.

In a follow-up study, a similar task was used, but now the investigators not only varied the number of stimuli in the display, but they now also explicitly instructed participants to only memorise a subset of those items (Vogel, McCollough, & Machizawa, 2005). This was done using coloured stimuli. In a display containing red and blue stimuli, participants were instructed to only memorise the blue stimuli. A clear difference was found between individuals with low and high working memory capacities. For high-capacity individuals, the negative slow wave increased with the number of stimuli that had to be memorised, whereas for low-capacity individuals, it increased mainly as a function of the number of stimuli in the display, even when these additional stimuli were not required to be memorised and therefore only served as distractors. Vogel et al. (2005) thus concluded that working memory capacity is mainly determined by the extent to which we succeed in suppressing irrelevant information.

Gaspar, Christie, Prime, Jolicoeur, and McDonald (2016) reported results that are consistent with this conclusion. In their study, 55 students were tested for their working memory capacity using a change detection task that was similar to the one used by Vogel and Machizawa (2004). Here participants were engaged in a task that required them to decide as quickly as possible what the orientation of a line was. In doing so, they were sometimes distracted by a highly salient distracting stimulus that could be presented on the left or right side of the display. One of the properties of such a distracting stimulus is that it can also evoke an ERP component, which is considered to be an index of the degree to which attention is deployed to the evoking stimulus. This component, known as the **N2pc**, can be found over the posterior scalp, contralateral to the evoking stimulus.

In addition to the N2pc, an ERP component was identified that was associated with suppressing our tendency to focus attention on such a stimulus. This component was identified as the **distractor positivity (Pd)**. Gaspar et al. (2016) found a highly significant correlation (r = 0.59) between the amplitude of this Pd component and participants' working memory capacity.

14.3.4 OBJECTS, PROPERTIES, AND DETAIL

A final question related to working memory capacity is what exactly the right unit of capacity is. As already discussed, short-term memory capacity estimates can be strongly influenced by our ability to compress information into meaningful chunks. For visual working memory, we might also ask which elements are relevant in determining its capacity (Xu, 2010). Do we, for example, retain complete objects, individual parts of an object, or is capacity determined by the relevance of the material that has to be remembered? A point that is currently still strongly debated is to what extent the need to memorize specific properties of an object can influence working memory capacity.

Quak, Langford, London, and Talsma (2018) found, for example, that an increase in the number of features of a visual object that participants were required to remember did affect estimates of visual working memory capacity. Participants were shown one or more visual stimuli. These stimuli consisted of rectangles with a variable aspect ratio which were filled with a grid pattern with a specific colour, orientation, and grid thickness. Participants were instructed to memorise only one specific property of these stimuli (e.g., only the colour, orientation, or thickness of the grid or the aspect ratio of the figure itself) or a specific combination of these properties (e.g., colour and aspect ratio). The more features participants were required to memorise, the smaller the number of objects they could retain. During the study, EEGs were recorded as well. The stimuli that were memorised evoked a contralateral negative ERP component; however, the amplitude of this component depended only on the number of objects that had to be remembered and not on the number of relevant properties of a stimulus.

These results suggest that there is a subtle trade-off between the number of objects we can successfully memorise and the amount of detail that we need to retain for each figure. Van den Berg, Shin, Chou, George, and Ma (2012) have suggested that working memory does not have a fixed capacity, but that capacity can fluctuate dynamically depending on the precision with which we need to retain certain aspects of our environment. In the Van den Berg et al. study, a number of stimuli were briefly presented and participants had to memorise their colour. Afterwards, they had to report the colour of one of these stimuli by either selecting it from a limited set of candidate colours (i.e., make a relatively coarse selection) or they had to report the colour as accurately as possible by selecting it on a colour wheel. For the latter condition, capacity estimates for working memory were found to be much lower than for the first condition.

Similar results were found by Roggeman, Klingberg, Feenstra, Compte, and Almeida (2014). In this study, participants had to memorise the position of three or five items. Prior to the presentation of the stimuli, a cue was presented that indicated how many items participants could be expected to memorise (see fig 14.12). When the cue indicated '5', this was considered to be a 'boost' cue,

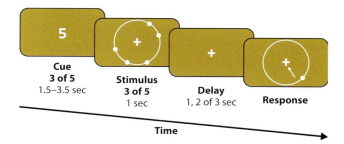

Figure 14.12 Experimental design of a study that examined the trade-off between working memory capacity and precision. When participants expected that were required to remember five items, this was done at the expense of the precision with which each item was represented. (source: Roggeman et al. (2014)

because this number was expected to exceed the capacity of participants' visual working memory. Roggeman et al. hypothesised that this cue would stimulate the participant to boost their working memory functions to memorise more items. However, this boost came at the expense of the precision with which the position of the items was represented, indicating a trade-off between precision and capacity.

In summary, it is unlikely that working memory capacity can be expressed in one unit. Rather, there is a flexible trade-off between capacity and precision which depends on the specific task requirements.

14.4 WORKING MEMORY REVISED

14.4.1 WORKING MEMORY AS AN EMERGENT PROPERTY OF THE BRAIN

Since its original conception, the notion of working memory has been criticised from various perspectives. Despite the successes of the original Baddeley and Hitch (1974) model there appears to be several issues with the concept of working memory. For example, what is a buffer and what is the neural implementation of such a buffer? Another significant limitation relates to the fact that the prefrontal lobes were assumed to be involved in almost all working memory functions. Postle (2006) discusses how, based on numerous single-cell studies in monkeys, an increasingly complex set of dissociations has been found for the selectivity of the prefrontal cortical neurons that are involved in working memory. These dissociations, combined with the ever-increasing trend for specialisation that can be observed in the development of Baddeley's model, have given rise to speculation about ever increasingly specialised modules in working memory.

At first sight, the idea of hyper-specialised modules also appears to be supported by additional empirical research.

For example, within the spatial domain of the inner scribe another dissociation between egocentric and allocentric working memory has been reported, and within egocentric working memory yet another a dissociation has been reported between motor memories related to tasks involving hands, eyes, and feet! There also appear to be further dissociations for the memorisation of manipulable and non-manipulable objects: for faces versus houses; for specific basic visual stimulus properties (spatial frequencies, colour, etc.); for phonological versus semantic properties; for the content of a stimulus versus its messenger; for pitch, timbre, and volume of auditory stimuli. In addition, it appears that we have specialised memory systems for touch, smell, and so on.

This extreme specialisation may lead us to question whether working memory is a meaningful concept, at least in the sense of specialised neural systems that do nothing but store and manipulate information. For this reason, Postle (2006) has argued that from an evolutionary perspective it is very unlikely that our brain has spontaneously developed all these functions just for remembering information. Posner therefore argues that it is far more likely that these specialised functions arose because, during the course of evolution, our brain succeeded in developing memory functions that are based on the reuse of other, more generic neural circuits. Just as the visual brain areas are involved in the generation of mental imagery, they may also be involved in the memorisation of visual information. As such, memorising visual information may consist of keeping visual information activated in visual cortex, even after this information is no longer physically present. Moreover, visual representations might also be reactivated by accessing information stored in long-term memory. Some evidence for this idea has already been discussed, as it was found that memorising visual objects corresponds to a slow negative ERP wave over the occipital scalp areas (Klaver et al., 1999; Talsma et al., 2001).

More direct evidence for the involvement of the visual cortex in working memory was obtained by Harrison and Tong (2009). These authors used fMRI while participants were shown grid patterns. The exact orientation of these grids had to be retained after they were no longer visible. By using a classification algorithm, Harrison and Tong were able to find a link between the activation pattern present in the primary visual areas and the specific orientation of the grid pattern that had been memorised.

In summary, these results imply that working memory is not a stand-alone module in the brain, but it is rather the result of a close interaction between attentional, perceptual, and long-term memory processes. How exactly these processes interact will be elaborated next.

14.4.2 ATTENTION, PERCEPTION, AND LONG-TERM MEMORY

The aforementioned concerns have been incorporated into a new approach to working memory, which emphasises the link between attention, perception, and long-term memory (Jonides et al., 2008; Oberauer, 2002; Olivers, Peters, Houtkamp, & Roelfsema, 2011). According to these models, attention is crucially involved in creating a representation in working memory.

14.4.2.1 Single Store Models
Jonides et al. (2008) argue that short-term and long-term memory can be combined into a single-store model that has the same functionality as working memory. One of the key assumptions of this approach is that short-term memory is formed by temporarily activating already existing representations in long-term memory. Jonides' model is based on a similar assumption that was already proposed by Cowan (1988). According to Cowan, there is only one type of representation for each object that we have to memorise and that is the representation that is already stored in long-term memory (see fig 14.13). Long-term memory representations can vary in their level of activation, however. According to Jonides et al. the activation levels of these long-term memory representations depend, among other things, on the recency of the memory trace and how frequently the event that is associated with the memory trace has occurred. The higher the memory trace is activated, the greater the likelihood that this long-term representation will be retrieved from memory. Moreover, a limited set of long-term memory representations can also be activated by attention. These representations are considered to be the focus of attention.

14.4.2.2 Single Store Models: the Role of the Hippocampus
While Atkinson and Shiffrin (1968) emphasised the differences between short- and long-term memory, proponents of single-store models emphasise the similarities between these two types of memories. They argue that there is insufficient evidence for the assumption that there are differences between the architecture of short- and long-term memory. If, however both short- and long-term memory share a common architecture, then how can we explain that amnesia patients have serious long-term memory impairments (see Chapter 13), while having an intact short-term memory? Jonides et al. (2008) argue that this is primarily due to functional differences that are specifically related to the involvement of the hippocampus. More specifically, amnesia patients would have specific difficulties with **relational learning**, that is, with binding specific items together, or relating these items to a specific

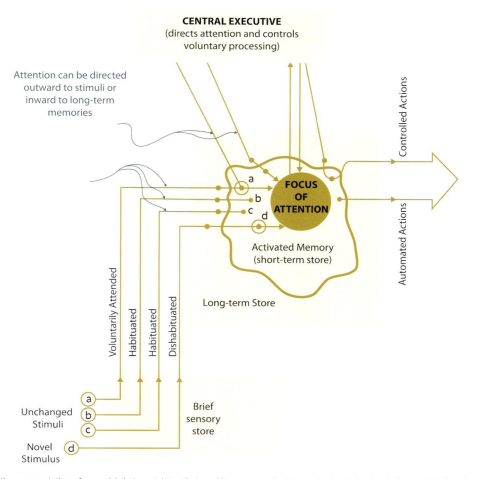

Figure 14.13 Schematic representation of a model that postulates that working memory is the result of an interplay between attention, long-term memory, and sensory systems. (source: Cowan, 1988)

context. According to this view, amnesia patients have no short-term memory impairments because most memory tasks do not involve the establishment of these kinds of relationships.

Hannula et al. (2006) found evidence for this idea (see also Chapter 13) in a study in which they presented scenes comprising computer-generated interiors (see fig 14.14). Each scene was repeated once, but only in half of all trials the repeated scene was identical to the previous one. In the other half, one item in the scene had been relocated (e.g., a chair moved to another corner of the room). Both amnesia patients with damage to the hippocampus and neurotypical controls participated in the experiment. Patients' accuracy was lower than that of the controls, even when they only had to remember the scene for a very short time, suggesting that amnesia patients had difficulties with encoding the relation between the item and the context.

Jeneson, Mauldin, Hopkins, and Squire (2011) note, however, that the study by Hannula et al. did not only examine relational memory but also invoked working memory.

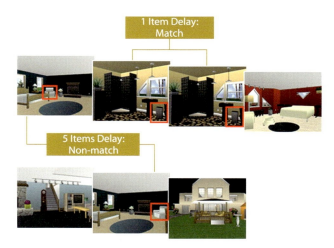

Figure 14.14 Stimuli used to study the effects of relational learning in short-term memory. (source: Hannula et al., 2006)

That is, participants in Hannula et al.'s study had to memorise multiple scenes simultaneously. According to the single storage models, this involves the activation of multiple long-term memory traces. When Jeneson et al.

used exactly the same procedure as Hannula et al., they replicated their results. When they presented only one scene at a time, however, the amnesia patients (who were also all characterised by hippocampal damage) performed at similar levels as the controls. Thus, these results imply that the hippocampus is not crucial for storing relational information per se, but that it is when the task involves long-term memory.

14.4.2.3 The Three-Component Model

The German-Swiss cognitive psychologist Klaus Oberauer (2002) also developed an influential working memory model that describes the relationship between attention, long-term memory, and perception. According to Oberauer, working memory consists of activating existing representations in long-term memory. We can probably best illustrate this relationship with an example. Suppose you are a bird watcher on holiday in an exotic forest area and you have set yourself the goal of observing all five rare bird species that live in this area. Obviously, you have an extensive knowledge about these birds in your long-term memory.

While walking through the forest you activate these representations. According to Oberauer, these representations define the contents of working memory. Among this collection of activated items there are a few items to which you have direct access (known as the **region of direct access** or **broad focus**), and within this subset there is then one item with the very highest level of activation. According to Oberauer, the latter item forms the narrow focus of attention and it is represented here by one particular bird that we are currently searching for. The remaining items, those to which you have immediate access, are formed by the birds that you might not be looking for directly but

which you might have a better chance of noticing when they happen to be flying by.

The essential difference between Oberauer's model just discussed and the classic working memory model by Baddeley and colleagues is that the former assumes that working memory is based on the activation of representations in long-term memory and therefore does not assume the existence of separate storage buffers. Models based on this principle are also relatively good at explaining why working memory can influence attention; an aspect that Baddeley's model is much less capable of doing.

In a literature review, Oberauer and Hein (2012) discuss several studies that have examined the relationship between attention, working memory, and long-term memory. The general conclusion of this review is that working memory models that are based on the activation of long-term memory representation can be more easily integrated in other cognitive processes than the traditional Baddeley and Hitch model. To illustrate, during mental arithmetic the activated part of long-term memory consists of the digits that we need to remember for the task at hand. For example, when memorising the number 324 and adding 12 to it, the digits 3, 2, 4, 1, and 2 become activated and each will be associated with its role (hundred, ten, unit). The more limited focus of attention serves to select one item or a chunk of items for the next cognitive operation. For example, attention would be focused on the digit that has to be modified in the next arithmetic operation.

14.4.2.4 The Region of Direct Access

Evidence for the existence of the broad focus or region of direct access was obtained in an experiment in which participants had to memorise words (Oberauer, 2005). As illustrated in Figure 14.15, participants were instructed to

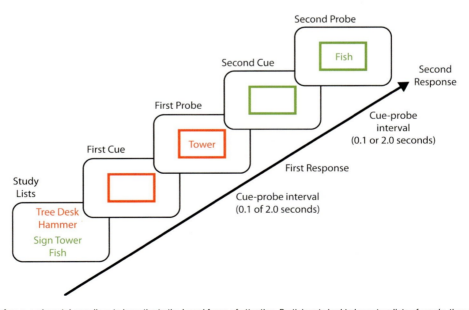

Figure 14.15 Outline of an experimental paradigm to investigate the broad focus of attention. Participants had to learn two lists of words, then flexibly switch between them during a subsequent memory test. (source: Oberauer and Hein, 2012)

410

memorise two short lists of words. These lists were each manipulated in terms of their length. After studying the lists, participants were subjected to two recognition tasks in succession. Each recognition task was preceded by a cue indicating which list was relevant for the task at hand. The results of this study showed that the length of the irrelevant list still affected the participant's reaction time when the probe word (i.e., the word for which the participant had to decide whether it was in the corresponding list or not) appeared within 100 ms of the presentation of the cue, but no longer when this probe appeared 2 seconds after the cue. This result suggests that the irrelevant list was removed from the broad focus within a time frame of two seconds.

A remarkable result, however, was that the irrelevant list was not completely forgotten. When a probe word was presented that was part of the irrelevant list, participants needed more time to reject it than when it was a randomly chosen word that was not part of any of the original lists. In fact, when the second recognition task was related to the list that had initially been irrelevant and contained a probe word that was part of this list, participants were able to recognise this word with a high level of accuracy. This phenomenon illustrates the function of the broad focus (or region of direct access): it allows us to switch efficiently between subsets of items that may become relevant at any given time.

14.4.2.5 The Narrow Focus of Attention

Evidence for the narrow focus of attention is provided by at least three different experiments. The first investigated the dynamics of retrieving information from memory. Studies of these dynamics have shown that the last item in a list of items that has been studied has a privileged status in working memory. For example, McElree and Dosher (1989) found that the last item in a list is accessed faster during a recognition task than any other item, implying that attention was focused on this item.

The second experiment concerns the dynamics of switching attention between items in working memory. Garavan (1998), for example, presented a random sequence of triangles and rectangles and instructed participants to keep track of how many objects of each category were presented. Consequently, in each trial, participants had to either update the same counter as they had on the previous trial (when an object of the same category was repeated) or they had to update a different counter (when they had to switch to a different object). After the presentation of each object, participants could indicate when they were ready to process the next object. They were approximately 300 ms slower in doing so after a switch, compared to a repetition, implying that the focus of attention was still on the object that was processed during the previous trial.

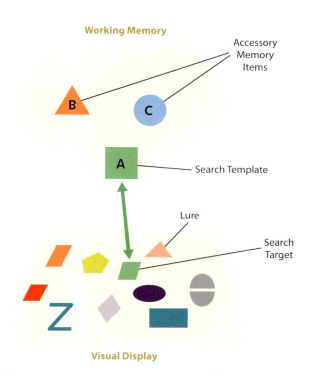

Figure 14.16 The relationship between visual search, attention, and working memory. (source: Houtkamp and Roelfsema, 2009)

Although the narrow focus of attention appears to be limited to just a single item, this is not necessarily the case. When two items are required for a cognitive operation, such as in adding two numbers, they may be selected simultaneously in the form of a chunk (Oberauer & Bialkova, 2009). Moreover, it has been found that when two items are so distinctive that they cannot possibly be confused, they can also occupy the focus of attention simultaneously (Gilchrist & Cowan, 2011; Oberauer & Bialkova, 2011).

The third experiment involves visual search tasks (see also Chapter 6). While searching for an item, participants should keep a template of the target object in working memory (see fig 14.16), as illustrated by the birdwatcher who kept a template of a specific bird activated. Participants should compare this template with every object they perceive until they encounter a stimulus that matches the template. It has been found that we typically only use one template (Olivers et al., 2011). For instance, when participants have to search for multiple target stimuli, their accuracy drops significantly (Houtkamp & Roelfsema, 2009), suggesting that participants typically only use a single template.

14.4.3 WORKING MEMORY: IN CONCLUSION

The ability to briefly hold and manipulate information in memory is one of the most essential cognitive skills that we have. Since the original formulation of Atkinson and Shiffrin's (1968) multi-store model, our ideas about short-term memory have changed dramatically. The introduction of multiple, independent systems involved in the storage of visuospatial and phonological information by Baddeley and colleagues was a significant step forward, in the sense that this model was able to explain the results of a large number of neuropsychological studies along with the results of a large number of dual-task studies. Yet, the working memory model proposed by Baddeley and colleagues is also problematic because it suggested the existence of a large number of separate memory buffers that are biologically implausible. Moreover, while there is much evidence that visuospatial phonological information is stored in the form of separate codes, recent studies also show that auditory and visual auditory codes may interfere with each other in short-term memory (Thelen, Cappe, & Murray, 2012; Thelen, Talsma, & Murray, 2015). Therefore, Quak, London, and Talsma (2015) conclude in a literature review that there are more interactions between visual and auditory working memory than we would initially have assumed on the basis of Baddeley's model.

These interactions between visuospatial and phonological working memory can, however, be explained by assuming the presence of a mechanism that operates on the basis of an internal model that is generated by activating existing representations from long-term memory through an attentional and/or predictive coding mechanism (Quak et al., 2015). Recent theoretical models attempt to describe this activation in terms of an internal attention process (Abrahamse, Majerus, Fias, & van Dijck, 2015; Chun et al., 2011; Cowan, 1988; Oberauer, 2002).

14.5 LEARNING AND FORGETTING

14.5.1 LEVELS OF PROCESSING

What determines how well we are able to remember new information? The Canadian cognitive psychologists Fergus Craik and Robert Lockhart (1972) hypothesised that the way we process information during learning is crucial for this. They argued that perceptual and attentional processes involved in learning are involved in determining which information is stored in long-term memory. As such, Craik and Lockhart have identified different levels of processing, which can vary from a superficial (or physical) analysis of the stimulus to a deep (or semantic) processing of it. For example, superficial processing consists of determining whether a specific letter appears in a word, while deep processing consists of processing the semantic meaning of a word. The deeper the level of processing, the more extensive, stronger, and more robust the memory trace would become, according to Craik and Lockhart. Originally, Craik

and Lockhart assumed that processing always proceeded in a serial fashion, from superficial to deep. In a later retrospective (Lockhart & Craik, 1990), however, they nuanced this idea and argued that processing can also often proceed in parallel.

Moreover, and in contrast to Atkinson and Shiffrin (1968), Craik and Lockhart (1972) argued that repetition does not automatically lead to improved long-term memory representation. They identified two different types of rehearsal. Firstly, the automatic repetition of a memory representation of a stimulus was described by Craik and Lockhart as **maintenance rehearsal**. Secondly, they identified a more elaborate, active form of rehearsal that they described as **elaborative rehearsal**. Elaborative rehearsal involves more deeply thinking about stimuli, forming associations, et cetera.

The idea that the level of processing has an effect on memory performance is consistent with several studies. For example, Craik and Tulving (1975) showed that the recognition of words depends on the task to be performed during learning (see fig 14.17). Participants were presented with a series of words that required them to perform one of three tasks: (1) determine whether the word was printed in upper or lowercase; this was designated the superficial graphical task; (2) determine whether the word rhymed with a given target word; this was designated as the intermediate level phonemic task; or (3) determine whether the word fits an empty position in a given sentence; this was designated the deep semantic task. After finishing the task, participants were then subjected to an unexpected recognition task. The depth of processing appeared to have a very large effect on memory performance.

Craik and Tulving (1975) used an unexpected recognition task because their aim was to study the effects of depth of processing on learning. If participants had been aware that they might be questioned afterwards, this might have affected memory performance. Although the results are consistent with the idea that deeper processing leads to better memory performance, we may question whether Craik and Tulving's idea that semantic processing is deeper than visual processing is correct.

After all, evidence for Craik and Tulving's (1975) hypothesis is not entirely consistent. Wagner, Maril, Bjork, and Schacter (2001) found, for example, that semantic processing resulted in greater activation of the left inferior frontal lobe and the left lateral and medial temporal lobes than perceptual processing. In this study, participants were presented with three words. In one condition, they only had to repeat these words, while in another condition they had to order these words by desirability. Park and Rugg (2008) found similar results on a memory task. In this study, pairs of words were presented. In one condition, participants had to indicate whether the two words had a

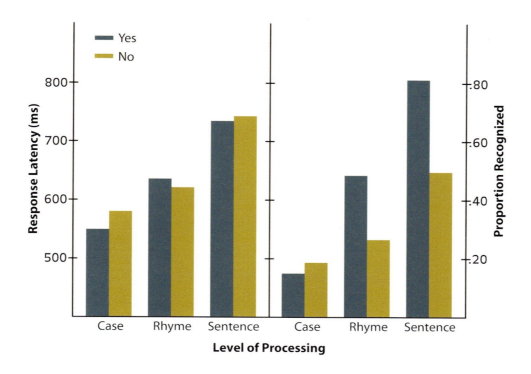

Figure 14.17 The effects of depth of processing on accuracy and reaction time. (source: Craik and Tulving, 1975)

semantic correspondence, while in another condition they had to determine whether the two words rhymed. Words from the semantic condition were generally more accurately recalled than those from the rhyming condition. However, Park and Rugg also found that successful retrieval of a word was associated with activation of the left ventrolateral cortex, regardless of the condition in which the word was presented. The latter result suggests that there is not an unambiguous relationship between the successful retrieval of a word and the way in which the word was originally presented.

14.5.1.1 Distinctiveness

Eysenck and Eysenck (1980) tested the hypothesis that word recall depends not only on the level of processing but also on the distinctiveness, or uniqueness, of the stimulus material. They took advantage of the fact that some English words are characterised by an irregular correspondence between their spelling and their pronunciation (a grapheme-phoneme correspondence; see Chapter 17). An example of such a word is the name Django, where the 'd' is silent. Participants had to pronounce words that were presented visually. In one condition, they were instructed to pronounce these irregular words as if they were regular, which gave the participants a much more distinct memory of these words, in comparison to the regular words. The result of this manipulation was that participants were much better at recognising the irregular words, implying that distinctiveness plays an important role in recalling information.

14.5.1.2 The Effect of Relevance

Morris, Bransford, and Franks (1977) argue that the extent to which memorised information can actually be retrieved depends on the relevance of the material during the memory test. In the Morris et al. study, participants were given lists of words, about which they either had to answer questions involving their semantic properties or decide whether they rhymed or not. This was followed by either a standard recognition test or a rhyme recognition task. In the latter task, participants had to select words from a list that rhymed with the words used earlier in the experiment.

For the standard recognition task, the classical effect was found that deep semantic processing resulted in better recognition than the superficial rhyme task. In the rhyme recognition task, however, the exact opposite result was found. Here the rhyme task resulted in better memory performance than the semantic processing task. According to Morris et al. (1977) these results are consistent with the **transfer-appropriate processing theory**. According to this theory, different forms of learning result in specific aspects of a stimulus being encoded in memory in a way that is task dependent. Whether these aspects are retrieved later depends on the relevance of the material stored. In the case of a rhyming task that was used by Morris et al. **phonological** information of words is stored, and this information is retrieved most efficiently when the new task also involves phonological information.

Initially, most of the studies on levels of processing used explicit memory tasks. It is, however, also plausible to assume that the depth of processing may affect implicit memory. Challis, Velichkovsky, and Craik (1996) set out to address this question. They did so by having participants learn lists of words, after which they had to perform several tasks: (1) assess whether the words were related to the participants themselves (self-assessments); (2) learn the words intentionally; (3) assess whether a word related to a living organism; (4) count the number of syllables; and (5) count the number of letters of a specific type. These tasks, in the order in which they are described here, require a progressively shallower level of processing. After the study phase, there were four explicit memory tasks and two implicit memory tasks.

For the four explicit memory tasks, it was found that performance generally improved as a function of depth of processing. One of the two implicit memory tasks consisted of answering a number of general knowledge questions, the answer to which was related to one of the previously learned words. The other implicit memory task consisted of completing word fragments, where a subset of the words that had to be completed had been used in the previously learned word list. The latter test did not show any effect on depth of processing. However, the general knowledge test did show a slight effect on depth of processing.

From a transfer-appropriate processing theory perspective, these results are plausible. The general knowledge test involves the processing of conceptual information, so it is likely that this type of knowledge can be influenced by the depth to which previous information has been processed. The word completion task, on the other

hand, is a task that involves mainly the superficial features of the words that had been learned, so it is unlikely that this task would be influenced by the depth of processing.

14.5.2 LEARNING BY RETRIEVAL

The studies reviewed so far in this chapter imply that memory traces are not only formed during encoding but also during memory retrieval. From this, it follows that regularly testing our knowledge should have a positive effect on our memory performance. Building on a long tradition of sporadic research into this so-called **testing effect** (Glover, 1989), Roediger and Karpicke (2006) found evidence that this is indeed the case. They did so by using a task in which participants had to study two short texts. In one condition, participants had to spend as much of their time as possible studying the text (the study-study condition), while in another condition they not only had to study the text but also to test themselves at regular intervals (the study-test condition). The result was that, although participants in the study-study condition were initially better at remembering the material, in the long run, testing (study-test condition) resulted in better memory performance (see fig 14.18).

14.5.2.1 The Testing Effect
Why does testing our own knowledge result in better memory performance? Pyc and Rawson (2009, 2010) investigated two possible explanations for this. According to the retrieval effort hypothesis, a difficult, but successful, retrieval from memory would result in better performance

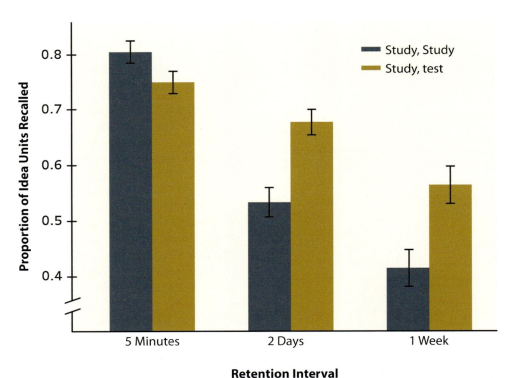

Figure 14.18 The effect of testing on memory performance. (source: Roediger and Karpicke, 2006)

than an easy retrieval. Pyc and Rawson (2009) tested this hypothesis by using word pairs of English–Swahili. During an initial study phase, participants were presented with a set of word pairs that they had to study. Then, during the test phase, they were presented with another set of words, and they were required to reproduce the correct translation. The difficulty of the task was manipulated by both varying the length of the time window in which an item had to be retrieved and by manipulating the number of items that had to be reproduced correctly. Pyc and Rawson (2009) found that higher task difficulty resulted in a better memory performance, which is consistent with the retrieval effort hypothesis.

Moreover, Pyc and Rawson (2010) argued that mediators may play an important role in the successful retrieval of information from memory. Mediators are associations between the items that are to be learned, whereby the associations can be strengthened during testing. Such mediators often form a connection between the phonology of a word in one language and the semantics of a word in the second, such as in the Swahili English word pair 'wingu–clouds', where the word 'airplane' can form a mediator. According to Pyc and Rawson, such mediators are effective because a given cue can activate the mediator, which in turn activates the target word.

They found evidence for the effectiveness of mediators using the Swahili–English word reading experiment just introduced, in which participants were explicitly asked to generate mediators and to report which mediators they had generated. Then, during the test phase, participants were either presented a cue alone, as had been done in previous studies, or they were given a mediator, or a combination of cues and mediators. This study also involved either a study-only phase or a study-plus-test phase before the final memory performance was tested. Results showed that participants performed better in the study-plus-test condition and that final memory performance was strongly influenced by the extent to which participants were able to retrieve mediators.

14.5.2.2 Learning and Prediction Errors

De Loof et al. (2018) identify prediction errors as a possible explanation for the effectiveness of the testing effect. According to the predictive coding framework, most information processing takes place when the brain makes a prediction error and tries to correct it. To investigate the role of predictions, De Loof et al. used a multiple-choice, Dutch-language variant of the aforementioned Swahili–English learning experiment. In this experiment, participants were presented with a Dutch word and four possible Swahili candidate words. Participants had to learn the correct translation by choosing from one of these alternatives. In half of the trials, participants had to choose from four options, while in the other half of the trials the number of options

was cut in half by cueing two out of the four options as the possible translations. Thus, each time a Swahili word was presented participant could choose from either two or four possible options. A correct choice was rewarded, while an incorrect one was not.

Without the participant's knowledge, however, there were several Swahili words associated with each Dutch word, which implies that the participants did not actually learn real Swahili words, and they could sometimes make choices that were not rewarded. For this reason, the prediction errors could be split into signed and unsigned prediction errors. Signed prediction errors indicate whether the outcome of the choice was better or worse than expected, whereas unsigned prediction errors simply indicated that the outcome was merely different than expected. The larger the signed prediction errors were, the better the participants were able to reproduce the learned word associations later.

14.5.3 FORGETTING

14.5.3.1 Ebbinghaus' Savings Method

Although information may remain present in long-term memory for a relatively long period of time, the current and previous chapters have already introduced some examples of memories that are being lost. Research into forgetting was already being conducted towards the end of the 19th century by the German psychology pioneer Hermann Ebbinghaus. In doing so, Ebbinghaus (1885) created lists of meaningless syllables. He would then study a list until he could fully reproduce it, after which he would note the time that it had taken him to learn the list. He then waited some time before studying the list again until he was again able to perfectly reproduce it. Ebbinghaus then noted again how long it had taken him to relearn the list. Finally, he calculated the percentage of time he had saved on the second learning attempt by dividing the time it had taken him to relearn the list by the time it had originally taken him to learn it.

Ebbinghaus repeated this procedure with different lists, and different intervals that ranged from 21 minutes to 31 days before re-learning the list. Ebbinghaus' main finding was that the proportion of time he was able to save decreased dramatically with increasing amounts of time between learning and relearning the list. Moreover, he found that this decrease was greatest in the first hour after the original learning. Because Ebbinghaus considered the time saved while relearning the lists to be the most important dependent measure, the procedure that Ebbinghaus developed is known as the savings method.

14.5.3.2 Forgetting Curves

The degree to which information is forgotten was expressed by Ebbinghaus (1885) as a reduction in the time saved in relearning. When we plot these savings as a function of

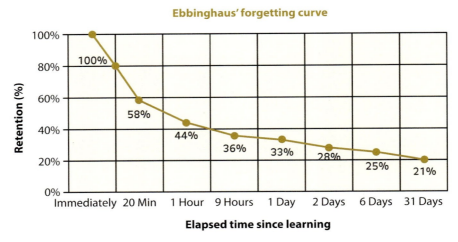

Ebbinghaus' forgetting curve

Figure 14.19 The forgetting curve, expressed as the decrease in the amount of time saved while relearning a word list. (source: Ebbinghaus, 1885)

the interval between learning and relearning, we obtain a forgetting curve (see fig 14.19). On the occasion of the 100th anniversary of the publication of Ebbinghaus' original findings, Rubin and Wenzel (1996) published an extensive literature review that largely corroborates Ebbinghaus' pioneering findings.

Why does information disappear from long-term memory, and is there any benefit to forgetting? Intuitively it may be an attractive idea that we would never forget anything; in reality it is often desirable that some memories disappear (see also Box 15.1). For example, it is no longer relevant to remember last year's class schedule, or the addresses of friends who have long since moved. In these cases, we need to update the contents of our memory and forget old information.

Forgetting can take place in both our explicit, declarative memory and in our implicit procedural memory. Although studies of forgetting in implicit memory are relatively limited, the results that are available do suggest that forgetting an implicit memory is much slower than forgetting a declarative memory (Tulving, Schacter, & Stark, 1982). The robustness of implicit memory has been convincingly demonstrated by Mitchell (2006). Participants who had volunteered in a study that was conducted by Mitchell 17 years earlier were shown fragments of images and were asked to recognise them. Some of these fragments had also been used in the original study. Participants were significantly better at recognising the images used in the original 1989 study, yet there was little explicit recollection. Some participants even reported not remembering that they ever participated in the original study.

14.5.3.3 Trace Decay

Probably the simplest explanation for forgetting is that the memory traces decay over time (Hardt, Nader, & Nadel, 2013). Despite the simplicity and plausibility of this explanation, the idea of memory trace decay was initially ignored

by most theorists. Hardt et al. argue, however, that each day we form massive amounts of trivial memories, which also requires a process that erases these memories. Spontaneous decay, according to Hardt et al. can perform this function very well, and it was hypothesised that this would mainly happen while we sleep. Trace decay is assumed to take place in the hippocampus, and this assumption is supported by several neuroimaging studies that Hardt et al. discuss in their literature review.

14.5.4 INTERFERENCE THEORY

Interference with other memories is also believed to contribute substantially to the forgetting of information. According to interference theory, there are two different types of interference that can contribute to the forgetting or the distortion of information in long-term memory. Proactive interference occurs when older information interferes with the newly learned material, and retroactive interference occurs when new material interferes with an already formed memory trace.

14.5.4.1 Proactive Interference

Proactive interference can occur when certain habits change, creating new stimulus-response associations. This is the case, for example, when we are used to the coffee always being in the top kitchen drawer, but then decide to put it in a different location after a kitchen redesign. Now when we are asked to make coffee, we tend to look for it in the old, and therefore wrong, location. Jacoby, Debner, and Hay (2001) argue that proactive interference can occur either because the correct response is relatively weak or because the incorrect response is relatively strong.

Bäuml and Kliegl (2013) argued that proactive interference is mainly related to the retrieval of information. They expected that proactive interference would be greatly reduced if participants forgot some of the learned material. To test this hypothesis, they had participants learn three

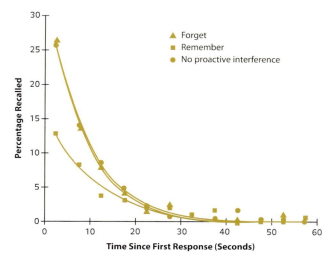

Figure 14.20 Accuracy as a function of time for conditions where a word list is actively forgotten or not. (source: Bäuml and Kliegl, 2013)

lists of words and then instructed them to remember as many words as possible from the last list they had learned. Under normal conditions, effects of proactive interference from the first two lists were found. In one condition, however, Bäuml and Kliegl (2013) instructed participants to actively forget the first two lists. This instruction resulted in a significant decrease in the amount of proactive interference (see fig 14.20).

Bergstrom, O'Connor, Li, and Simons (2012) used ERPs and found that proactive interference can be caused by both the automatic and controlled retrieval of information. The automatic processes were related to an early ERP component, which was followed by subsequent ERP activity that was associated with controlled activity. Similarly, using fMRI, Nee, Jonides, and Berman (2007) found that the ventrolateral prefrontal cortex and the anterior prefrontal cortex are involved in the processing of conflict that results from proactive interference (see fig 14.21). Additional evidence that proactive interference can be partially controlled was reported by Wahlheim and Jacoby (2013). They found that participants could become increasingly aware of proactive interference through practice, and thus spent more time learning the items that were sensitive to interference. Under these conditions, participants also focused more on actively retrieving the information, which also reduced proactive interference.

14.5.4.2 Retroactive Interference

Retroactive interference involves new information interfering with older information. For example, if we have learned to apply a specific mathematical equation and are then given a new equation that is based on similar principles, our knowledge about this new equation may interfere with the application of the original equation. Many people anecdotally experience how exposure to a second language can interfere with processing words in their first language. Misra, Guo, Bobb, and Kroll (2012) aimed to find empirical

evidence for these claims by studying bilingual participants who had Chinese as their native language and English as their second language. When these participants had to name images in their native language, they did so more slowly if they had named the same images before in their second language. ERP evidence suggested that they inhibited the words in their second language when naming the images in Chinese.

In general, retroactive interference is found to be strongest when the new material that has to be learned bears a strong resemblance to the old material. Dewar, Cowan, and Sala (2007) found, however, that this is not necessarily the case. In their study, participants had to learn words, after which they were exposed to various tasks during the retention interval, before having to perform a memory test. Dewar et al. found that the tasks in question induced a strong degree of retroactive interference, even when the tasks consisted of identifying differences between pictures or detecting tones. According to Dewar et al., retroactive interference can therefore occur for two different reasons: it can either be due to a high level of mental effort during the retention interval, or due to interference from similar stimulus material. Finally, Eakin and Smith (2012) found that retroactive interference can occur not only in declarative memory but also in implicit memory.

14.5.5 MOTIVATED FORGETTING

Traditionally, forgetting has always been considered to be a passive process, resulting from trace decay or interference. In many cases, however, it is no longer relevant to retain outdated information, and a certain degree of control over which information we choose to forget could therefore have an evolutionary benefit.

Recent memory research has focused on to what extent we are capable of forgetting information in a goal-directed manner. For this purpose, the procedure of **directed forgetting is often used**, that is, the forgetting of information in long-term memory via specific instructions. A common method of directed forgetting is the item method. Here, an item is presented, which is immediately followed by an instruction to either remember or forget this item. The 'forget' instruction most likely results in the selective repetition of those items that do need to be remembered, at the cost of the items that are required to be forgotten (Geraerts & McNally, 2008).

A another method that is widely used to study active forgetting of information is the think/no-think paradigm, which was developed by Anderson and Green (2001). Here, participants learn a list of word pairs. Then one of the words in the pair is used as a cue and participants are instructed to either think about the word that was associated with the cue, or to suppress it thinking about. When participants were instructed to suppress the words, they

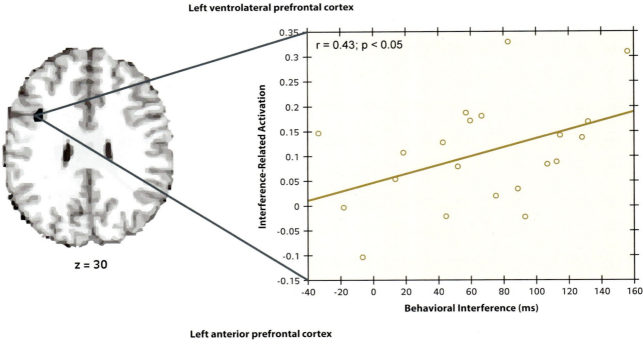

Left ventrolateral prefrontal cortex

r = 0.43; p < 0.05

z = 30

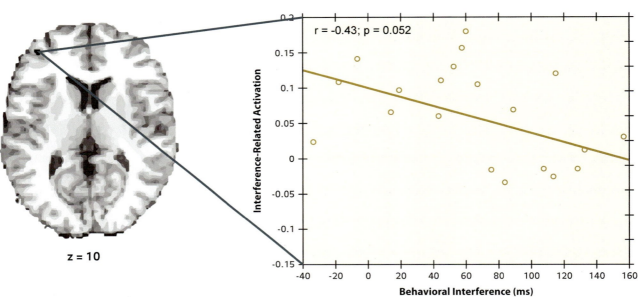

Left anterior prefrontal cortex

r = -0.43; p = 0.052

z = 10

Figure 14.21 The correlation between conflict, as induced by proactive interference, and activation of the ventrolateral and anterior prefrontal cortices. (source: Nee et al., 2007)

might be expected to have lower recall than when they were instructed to think about them. Moreover, active suppression should result in an even lower level of recall than if the participants had learned the words passively. This is indeed what was found.

14.5.6 CUE-DEPENDENT FORGETTING

We often assume that forgetting is a consequence of the weakening of a memory trace. In many cases, however, we are simply unable to remember something because the cues that are needed to retrieve the memory are no longer present. Memories that are seemingly forgotten often come back to us when someone gives us a relevant cue.

Tulving and Thomson (1973) argued that forgetting is often the result of a poor match between the contents of the memory trace and the information that is available during retrieval. Based on this idea, Tulving formulated his **encoding specificity principle**, which states that the probability of retrieving a memory will increase as a function of the overlap between the information available during retrieval and the information stored in memory. The encoding specificity principle is similar to the previously discussed transfer-appropriate processing theory that was developed by Morris et al. (1977). The main difference, however, is that Morris et al. mainly focused on the memorisation processes themselves, whereas Tulving mainly focused on the information that is already encoded in memory.

According to Tulving, we not only store information about a particular event but also information about the context of that event. According to the encoding specificity principle, information retrieval is easier when it takes place in the same context where it was learned. As discussed earlier (Chapter 12), this context can be internal, in the form of a mood-state, or external, in the form of the environment where information was learned.

Godden and Baddeley (1975) demonstrated the effectiveness of the external context in a rather dramatic manner. The participating volunteers were deep-sea divers who had to learn lists of words. Half of the participants had to learn these words on land (on the beach), while the other half had to learn these word lists at a depth of ten feet under water. They were then given a test that was either taken in the same environment as where the words were learned or in the other environment. Recollection was much better when the test was taken in the same environment, compared to the other environment. However, this effect was only found during a recall test. When a recognition test was used, no difference between the environments was found.

14.6 IN CLOSING

We started the previous chapter with a discussion of Karl Lashley's unsuccessful search for the engram and his conclusion that memory traces are distributed throughout the cortex. In this context, it is remarkable that we will conclude the present chapter by noting that in recent memory research, the concept of the engram has once again taken centre stage. According to recent neurobiological theories of memory, engrams are, however, defined as the physical representation of a memory in the brain (Dudai, 2012). Thus, according to this definition, engrams are comparable to memory traces. The question that most neurobiological models thus aim to answer is how these engrams are formed.

Nadel and Moscovitch (1997) argue that the hippocampus is involved in the rapid encoding of episodic memories (see also Chapter 13). According to Nadel and Moscovitch, this information is encoded sparsely in a distributed network of hippocampal neurons. According to this model, these neurons act as an index for cortical neurons that form a coherent network under the influence of hippocampal activation, which is the basis of the memory trace. The formation of such cortical memory traces under hippocampal control is known as consolidation. Murre (1996) developed

a computational model, known as trace-link, that mimics consolidation processes (see fig 14.22). Because the memory trace is reactivated in various contexts, this will result in a condition where the hippocampus keeps adding new memory traces to an already existing one.

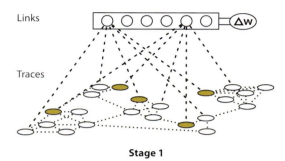

Stage 1

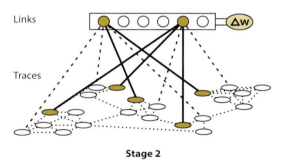

Stage 2

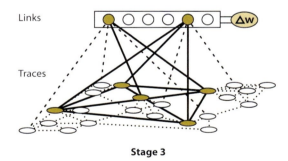

Stage 3

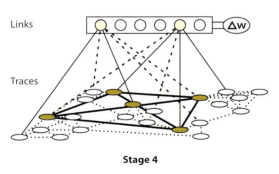

Stage 4

Figure 14.22 A schematic overview of the trace-link model. The hippocampus is assumed to maintain the connections between the cortical circuits that represent a memory trace, allowing the continued consolidation of these connections. When the memory traces are sufficiently consolidated, support by hippocampal activation is no longer needed. (source: Murre, 1996)

The final result of this process is the emergence of multiple memory traces that all share a part of the initial trace. Over time, multiple related memory traces may emerge, facilitating the extraction of factual knowledge. As such, information is integrated into a larger semantic network, which causes the factual information to become independent of the specific episodes related to the acquisition of our factual knowledge. Although the existence of consolidation processes is now fairly widely accepted, there is still much debate about the exact role that consolidation processes play in memory formation, and in particular whether consolidation processes remain permanently active. The basic idea is that new memories are bright but fragile, whereas old memories are faded but robust (Wixted, 2004).

Some theorists assume that consolidation processes remain perpetually active, and that the reactivation of a memory brings the memory trace back into a fragile state (Hardt, Einarsson, & Nader, 2010; Nadel, Hupbach, Gomez, & Newman-Smith, 2012). This reactivation would result in a process of reconsolidation, whereby the fragility of the memory trace allows us to update it. A process like this might explain why our personal memories may become severely distorted over time and why we are susceptible to false memories, as will be discussed in more detail in the next chapter. Interestingly, however, impairments of these consolidation and reconsolidation mechanisms may also result in memory erasure (Haubrich, Bernabo, Baker, & Nader, 2020).

14.7 SUMMARY

Our memory plays a crucial role in a wide variety of cognitive tasks. In particular, the ability to temporarily retain and manipulate information is essential for most high-level cognitive processes. Atkinson and Shiffrin developed an influential multi-store memory model based on the assumption that sensory information could be transferred from a sensory buffer to short-term memory and eventually into a long-term memory store via a repetition process. Evidence for the existence of sensory memories was found using partial report studies. Visual sensory memory is known as iconic memory and the auditory sensory memory as echoic memory.

Our short-term memory capacity is limited. Originally estimated at seven plus or minus two items, later estimates have been considerably lower and range from four items to just one item. Which items are remembered best in short-term memory depends on several factors, including the position of the item in the list of items to be remembered. Especially the first and last items are best remembered. Remembering items in short-term memory requires an active repetition process. When this repetition is interrupted, the items are quickly forgotten. It was originally believed that this was due to rapid decay of the memory traces. However, it is more likely that interference processes play a role in this.

Many cognitive tasks require us to do more than just temporarily memorise information. Information that is stored in memory must often also be manipulated. To better explain these activities, short-term memory is nowadays mainly conceived of as working memory. One influential working memory model was developed by the British psychologists Alan Baddeley and Graham Hitch. This modular working memory model consists of two slave systems, namely the phonological buffer and the visuospatial sketchpad. The information stored in these systems can be integrated with episodic information from long-term memory. According to the model, the latter involves an episodic buffer. Moreover, the model assumes that all systems are under the control of a central executive, which coordinates the functions of the slave systems.

Working memory capacity can be estimated using a host of cognitive tasks. Examples of these tasks involve the reading span task, the operation span task, and the N-back task. Low working memory capacity may be related to a relatively limited ability to filter out irrelevant information. In addition, working memory capacity may also be influenced by the need to remember detail: the more in detail stimuli have to be remembered, the smaller the number of items that can be retained.

Despite the successes of Baddeley and Hitch's working memory model, some recent findings are difficult to explain by this model. For this reason, it has been suggested that working memory is an emergent property of the brain, that is, working memory arises because other pre-existing cognitive functions can be used to retain and manipulate information. From this perspective, working memory can be conceived of as an activated part of long-term memory, with attentional processes playing an important role in determining which parts are activated and how this information is used.

Learning plays a crucial role in our lives and the formation of memories is closely related to learning processes. Craik and Lockhart initially assumed that the deeper a stimulus is processed, the better it is stored. Although this depth of processing certainly plays a role, a number of other factors also appear to contribute to the efficiency of the learning process. One of these factors is distinctiveness. Distinctive, unique, and distinguishable memories are remembered relatively well. Another contributing factor is the relevance of the memory. According to the transfer-appropriate processing theory, the way a stimulus is learned contributes to the way the stimulus can be used later. As a result, processing the relatively superficial features of a stimulus may result in better processing later when precisely these superficial features are relevant.

Regularly retrieving information also contributes to better recall. The testing effect describes how testing one's own knowledge after an initial study period results in better memory performance. A number of factors may contribute to this effect. First, a difficult but successful retrieval from memory may result in a stronger activation of the memory traces involved. Second, information retrieval may result in the formation of mediators, which can be used as an additional cue to retrieve the relevant information. Finally, the processing of prediction errors are also likely to be involved in the testing effect.

Besides learning, our memory is also characterised by the frequent forgetting of information. One of the first methods to study forgetting in long-term memory was developed by Hermann Ebbinghaus. His savings method consisted of determining how much time could be saved when relearning a list of syllables, compared to the time that was initially needed to learn the list. The degree to which information is forgotten as a function of time can be described by a forgetting curve.

There are several possible explanations for forgetting information from long-term memory. One of the simplest explanations is that of trace decay. Other processes may also be involved, however, in particular proactive and retroactive interference processes. Although forgetting was originally believed to be primarily a passive process, there is now increasing evidence that forgetting can also occur in a more controlled manner. A final factor that contributes significantly to forgetting information is that the cues that could activate the appropriate memory are no longer available. The coding specificity principle describes how the probability of correctly remembering a specific event depends on the overlap between information available in the memory trace and the information available during recall.

Consolidation processes play an important role in the recording of a memory. According to recent findings, the hippocampus is involved in the formation of networks of cortical neurons, which ultimately form the memory traces. When these memory traces are activated again, in a different context, new contextual elements are added to the memory trace. According to some theorists, the activation of a memory trace results in it being brought back into a fragile state, making it necessary to consolidate it again. This fragile state would allow an existing memory trace to be actualised on the basis of new information.

FURTHER READING

Baddeley, A., Eysenck, M. W., & Anderson, M. C. (2015). *Memory*. Hove, UK: Psychology Press.

Gathercole, S. E. (2013). *Models of short-term memory*. Hove, UK: Psychology Press.

Vallar, G., & Shallice, T. (2007). *Neuropsychological impairments of short-term memory*. Cambridge, UK: Cambridge University Press.

CHAPTER 15
Everyday memory

15.1 INTRODUCTION

Let's take a trip down memory lane. On September 11, 2001, two hijacked commercial airliners flew into the World Trade Center in New York City (see fig 15.1), a third one crashed into the Pentagon in Washington DC, while a fourth plane crashed somewhere in rural Pennsylvania. At that time, I was busy arranging a position as a postdoctoral researcher in the United States, and earlier that day, I had emailed a copy of my signed contract back to the United States from the University of Amsterdam. I heard about the disaster when I visited a friend and colleague at the developmental psychology department afterwards. To get more details about the news, we tried to access the Internet, but in the chaos that ensued it was impossible to access a news server. Back at my desk, while trying to break the news to my colleagues, I was told in disbelief not to be silly! My former PhD advisor, who had just started taking flying lessons, believed that the crash was a navigational error and muttered something about a misaligned navigation beacon. Slowly but surely, however, the news trickled in, and the rest of the day was dominated by the disaster that had just occurred. Once at home, it turned out that there was almost no television station that did not continuously repeat the images of the crash.

How is it that experiences such as these are still so strongly imprinted in our memory even decades later, while we forget other more mundane experiences after just a few days? In the previous two chapters we have mainly discussed how memory is organised, focusing on how we can store information, how we can use our memory for all kinds of cognitive tasks, and how we can learn new skills. In Chapter 13, we also discussed how personal memories are stored in episodic memory. Although we have discussed how these personal memories can be stored (and in part be reconstructed: Schacter et al., 2011), we have not yet discussed how these memories contribute to the development of identity, self-image, goals, and life story. One of the goals of the present chapter is to discuss this in more detail.

15.2 DIFFERENT APPROACHES TO MEMORY RESEARCH

The studies that were introduced in the previous two chapters focused on the questions of how memory is organised, how much information can be stored in memory, and how this information is stored. This traditional approach to memory research often uses arbitrary stimulus material, without regard to its relevance to the participant. In contrast, the everyday-memory approach focuses more on the relevance of the material that has been remembered and how we retain information for future goals and motives (Cohen, 2008). The latter aspect is also strongly reflected in **prospective memory**: a specific use of our memory that we use to keep track of things we still have to do. The traditional and everyday-memory approaches have both contributed significantly to our understanding of human memory, and the two approaches are therefore complementary. Before we begin a discussion of everyday memory, it is important to list the differences between the two approaches.

15.2.1 THE TRADITIONAL APPROACH

The traditional approach to memory research focuses on the amount and the type of information that can be retained or learned. For this reason, relatively arbitrary study material such as word lists or numerical sequences are typically used, and participants are required to memorise this material during the experiment. Learning is therefore intentional: participants are explicitly instructed to study the materials, yet the relevance of the materials to the participants is of a lesser concern here. Many studies focus on how many items can be remembered, how long these items can be remembered, and how accurately the learned material can be reproduced.

15.2.2 EVERYDAY MEMORY APPROACH

In contrast, the everyday memory approach mainly focuses on the relevance of the information that is retained. The

DOI: 10.4324/9781003319344-21

Figure 15.1 For many people, the terrorist attacks on the World Trade Center in New York City, on September 11, 2001, are a flashbulb memory.

study material in this type of research therefore often consists of older memories that have long been consolidated in long-term memory. The participants' motivation to hold on to these memories is strongly linked to their personal goals, and the learning process is therefore much more incidental compared to the traditional memory approach. For this reason, there is also a stronger focus on the relevance of the memories than on the capacity of our memory. An important measure in everyday memory research is the goodness-of-fit between the objective records of events and participants' subjective reports of them.

15.3 THE MALLEABILITY OF LONG-TERM MEMORY

An important distinction between the traditional approach to memory research and the everyday memory approach is the emphasis on this goodness of fit: in the traditional approach, accuracy is often the dependent measure of memory performance, whereas in the latter approach, the mismatch between a memory and the actual course of an event is often considered an intrinsic property of memory.

As we have discussed in Chapter 13, memory is often constructive (Schacter & Addis, 2007), and interference with other events can result in the distortion of a memory (Schacter et al., 2011).

A good example of such a goodness of fit approach is provided by a study of Marsh and Tversky (2004), who investigated how accurately students could relay stories to each other. Over a four-week period, students participating in the experiment voluntarily recorded stories as they passed them on to each other; they later rated these recordings for accuracy. About 42% of these stories were reported as inaccurate by the participants themselves. Of the stories that were labelled as accurate, another 36% contained distortions in the form of exaggerations or minimisations of relevant details. Similar results were found by Marsh, Tversky, and Hutson (2005) in a study involving the memory of emotions (see fig 15.2). Here, participants were shown video fragments involving violence. Afterwards, one group could share the emotions they experienced with another participant, similar to how one would share an emotional experience with friends. A second group was questioned about the details of the scene in a manner that was similar to how the police would interrogate a witness, and a third group was given an unrelated task. The group that had to share their emotions had, on average, a better memory of the emotions they experienced. However, this group also showed a greater distortion of their memories of the actual events.

The effect of this type of distortion on our personal memories was investigated by Dudukovic, Marsh, and Tversky (2004). They instructed participants to read a story and then to retell it three times. The retelling of the story had to be either as accurate as possible or as entertaining as possible. A memory test showed that the participants who had to retell the story as accurately as possible remembered more details than those who had to retell the story as entertainingly as possible.

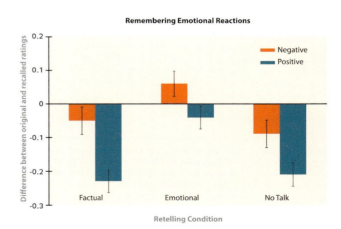

Figure 15.2 The accuracy of memory for emotions as a function of processing these emotions. (source: Marsh et al., 2005)

15.4 RESEARCH METHODS

15.4.1 DIARY STUDIES

One method of studying everyday memory involves the use of diary notes. A good example of this concerns a study by the Dutch cognitive psychologist Willem Albert Wagenaar (1986), who recorded his personal experiences for six years, according to four predefined criteria: what the event was, who were involved in the event, and where and when the event took place. In addition, the experience was rated on emotional intensity. Recollection of the memory was cued by an assistant, using either a single criterion or a combination of two or more, after which it was Wagenaar's task to retrieve the memory (see fig 15.3).

Wagenaar found that, in general, the 'what' cues were the most effective in retrieving a memory, followed, in descending order of effectiveness, by the 'where', 'who', and 'when' cues. The older the memory, the more difficult it became to retrieve, but with three cues, about half of the events were recalled by Wagenaar. Finally, the emotional intensity of the event correlated strongly with the likelihood of recalling it successfully.

15.4.2 LIMITATIONS OF DIARY STUDIES

Burt, Kemp, and Conway (2003) argue that diary studies are often appropriate for examining specific events but that they are of limited use when studying how memories of larger life episodes develop, since these events stretch out over periods spanning several days or more. Burt et al. had participants classify personal memories on the basis of diary entries or photographs of personal events; they found that this classification was often based on the aggregation of several single-day episodes into multi-day events. Moreover, each of these events could be related to one of several themes. For example, several episodes that took place in December could all be classified under the 'Christmas shopping' theme. Moreover, each episode was often related to multiple themes such as friendships, family, relationships, and so on. Burt et al. note that diary studies can also be a useful research tool in this context, but point out that, if the organisation of events into themes is not considered, the method may wrongly equate episodic memory with everyday memories.

15.5 AUTOBIOGRAPHICAL MEMORY

15.5.1 AUTOBIOGRAPHICAL VERSUS EPISODIC MEMORY

All the personal memories we have are combined into our **autobiographical memory**. As such, it is important to distinguish between autobiographical and episodic memory.

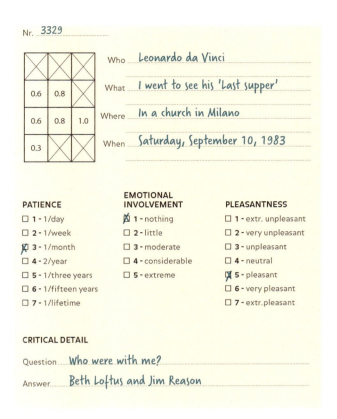

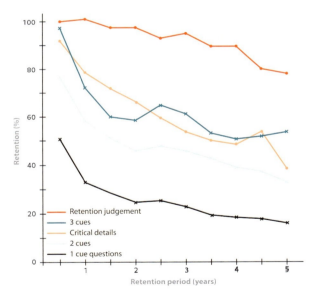

Figure 15.3 Example of a diary entry and the results of Wagenaar's diary study. (source: Wagenaar, 1986)

Autobiographical memory is strongly related to our personal life stories, whereas episodic memory is formed by individual events which are bound to specific locations and times. Since both types of memory are personal, there is necessarily some overlap between them. There are also considerable differences, however; autobiographical memory, for example, often includes the major events that can span long periods of time. These include, for example, our college days or our career paths. Episodic memory, on the other hand, contains relatively trivial everyday events. These specific episodic memories fade over time – unless they are salient in themselves – and morph into an autobiographical memory. Thus, episodic memories do typically not extend far back in time (see Box 15.1), whereas autobiographical memories can span years or even decades.

We have a growing amount of evidence from cognitive neuroscience indicating differences between episodic and autobiographical memories. For instance, Gilboa (2004) conducted a meta-analysis of studies on autobiographical and episodic memory and found that the retrieval of information from episodic memory was associated with activation in the right middle dorsolateral prefrontal cortex. In contrast, retrieval from autobiographical memory was associated with more activation in the left ventromedial prefrontal cortex. These differences suggest that the processes involved in the retrieval of episodic memory involve the monitoring of the accuracy of the information that is retrieved, whereas the retrieval of autobiographical memories involves checking the information for internal consistency and cohesiveness of the memories.

Box 15.1 Fact or fiction: does the perfect memory exist?

Wouldn't it be wonderful to never forget anything ever again? Never having to study for an exam, or having a perfect memory of our entire life, who wouldn't want that? Yet, never forgetting anything would also imply never losing a bad memory, or carrying around loads of information that has become obsolete. In neuropsychology, some remarkable case studies of individuals with a seemingly perfect memory have been reported. But is this really the case? Does a perfect memory really exist? Here we will take a closer look at two of the most remarkable cases of a seemingly perfect memory. They involve the Russian journalist Solomon Shereshevsky and the American author Jill Price.

One late afternoon in April 1929, the Russian journalist Solomon Shereshevsky visited the Academy of Communist Education in Moscow and asked for a memory specialist. He was referred to the then 27-year-old Alexander Luria. Luria would later become world famous as one of the founders of neuropsychology, but back then he was still at the early stages of his career. Shereshevsky was referred to Luria by his editor-in-chief after it turned out that Shereshevsky never took notes. When asked, Shereshevsky told his editor that he had no need to do so, because he remembered everything anyway. In response, the chief editor read a section from a newspaper and asked Shereshevsky to repeat it. When Shereshevsky repeated the whole section verbatim, the chief editor was convinced that there was something special about Shereshevsky's memory and referred him to Luria.

Shereshevsky, who would later become known as 'S' in the neuropsychological literature, was studied by Luria for many years. S was allegedly so desperate to lose some of his memories that he wrote them down, hoping that this would relieve his memory, as Luria wrote in his case study of S: The Mind of a Mnemonist (Luria, 1965). When that did not help, he set them on fire, hoping to get rid of his memories for good.

Although a perfect memory may seem appealing, Luria identified several problems that S encountered with his detailed memories. One of the problems in particular was S's inability to integrate the individual loose episodic memories into larger life themes. For S, every word and each thought was filled with an excessive amount of detail.

Although these anecdotes appear to give the impression that S was incapable of forgetting, this actually turned out not to be the case. In an article in The New Yorker, journalist Reed Johnson describes how he managed to track down some of Shereshevsky's relatives in Moscow, years after his death. Based on their testimonies, together with original notes from S, Johnson has managed to recreate an image of the historical Shereshevsky, which shows that his memory was not so perfect after all. The retrieval of Shereshevsky's memories was not so much the result of a photographic memory, but rather that of a lot of conscious effort and creativity. A nephew of Shereshevsky even described him as forgetful.

Shortly after his first visit to Luria, S quit his job as a journalist and started a career as a mnemonist. A career, by the way, which did not go exactly smoothly in the Stalin-ruled Soviet Union. For his performances, S had to train for hours on end to remember all the relevant material. Luria has also described a number of the mental tricks that were employed by S. Upon closer inspection, these tricks bear a strong resemblance to the standard mnemonic tricks that anyone can use to improve their memory performance. S often imagined a busy street in Moscow, and he mentally placed the various objects and people he wanted to remember along this imagined street. Although Luria was aware of S's use of mnemonic tricks, he was convinced that S started using them only later in life and that they were mainly an addition to his natural mnemonic talent.

(Continued)

426

Box 15.1 (Continued)

Luria also noted that S had an extreme form of synaesthesia (see Chapter 9) and suspected that the web of multimodal associations resulting from his synaesthesia was used by S to retain his memories. S was also particularly affected by these associations. Reading the newspaper resulted in scent sensations that interfered with his breakfast. These associations also hindered him as much as they helped him with his performances. He managed to remember long lists of words by turning them into sparkling multisensory impressions and weaving them into a story. But in order not to become overwhelmed during a performance, he had to control the flow of associations. So, it was not so much his ability to memorise long lists of words that made S's story special, but his ability to weave them into a story full of associations on the spot. So, it is probably not Shereshevsky's memory that is so special, but rather his lively and associative imagination.

By the way, towards the end of his life, Shereshevsky did find a method to destroy his memories: he started drinking heavily. In 1958, he died from complications of alcohol poisoning.

A few decades later, a new case study of a seemingly perfect memory caused a stir. In this case, it concerned a woman, the American author Jill Price, who was born in 1965 (Parker, Cahill, & McGaugh, 2006). Price is able to provide detailed information about any given day from her 14th birthday onward, including particularly obscure details. The term **hyperthymic syndrome** (academic Greek for 'special memory') has been coined for her condition. Jill Price also suffers from these detailed memories. In her own words, every day her whole life races through her head. What is special about Jill Price

is that it is only her autobiographical memory that appears to be so well developed. The rest of her memory performance is normal. Her performance at memorising word lists is average and she has difficulties remembering what all the keys on her key ring are for.

So why is it that Price's autobiographical memory is so well developed? Again, this particular achievement can probably be attributed to factors other than a well-developed memory. It is not that Price thinks about her own life every day because she remembers so much of it, it is more likely that she remembers so much of her life because she constantly, obsessively, thinks about her own life. She has written over 50,000 pages of diary notes in a super-small handwriting and has countless audio and video tapes and other memorabilia from her own past. These obsessive tendencies make her compulsively repeat her own life to herself.

Since the notable case study of Jill Price, a number of other cases of hyperthymic syndrome have been reported sporadically (LePort et al., 2012; LePort, Stark, McGaugh, & Stark, 2015). Almost all of the reported cases performed significantly better on autobiographical memory tasks, compared to a control group, and many of them exhibited obsessive-compulsive traits similar to those of Jill Price. These individuals were also found to perform average on standard memory tasks.

The bottom line is that there is no such thing as a perfect memory. The remarkable memory performances demonstrated by Solomon Shereshevsky and Jill Price can be attributed to the use of efficient mnemonic tricks or an obsessive-compulsive rumination on one's own life.

15.5.2 THE SELF-MEMORY SYSTEM

According to the British psychologists Martin Conway and his colleagues, autobiographical knowledge is crucial for the development of identity and self-image (Conway & Pleydell-Pearce, 2000; Conway, Pleydell-Pearce, & Whitecross, 2001). Through autobiographical memory, our personal memories can be linked to our public histories and this allows us to keep a track record of personal goals throughout our lives (see fig 15.4). Conway and Pleydell-Pearce (2000) introduced the **self-memory system**, which consists of two main components: an *autobiographical knowledge base* and the *working self*.

15.5.2.1 The Autobiographical Knowledge Database

According to Conway and Pleydell-Pearce, the autographic knowledge database consists of personal information that can be classified at three different levels of specificity. The first level includes periods that span our lifetime; periods defined by long-term situations, such as living with our partner, completing our studies or our career paths; the second level includes repetitive events, such as regular visits to a club or sports activity, or larger isolated events such as a holiday in Australia or Namibia. The third level includes event-specific knowledge. This type of knowledge is related to single events and corresponds to episodic memories.

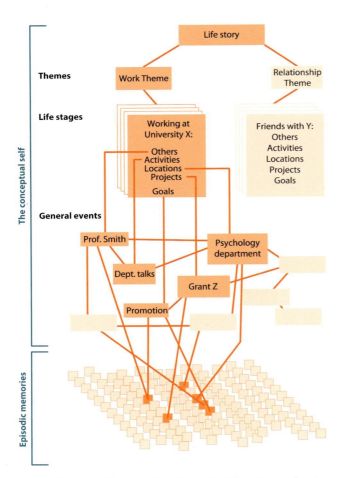

Figure 15.4 The hierarchical organisation of knowledge structures in autobiographical memory, according to Conway's self-memory system. (source: Conway, 2005)

15.5.2.2 The Working Self

The working self refers to our self-image, that is; what we will become in the future, and what our personal goals are. The goals of the working self will influence the autobiographical memories stored in the autobiographical knowledge database and thus influence the memories that we actually retrieve. Thus, according to this view, our autobiographical memories serve our self-image and reflect our successes and failures in achieving our self-established goals.

According to the self-memory system, there are two different ways to retrieve autobiographical memories: either by **generative retrieval** or by **direct retrieval**. Conway (2005) argues that generative retrieval involves combining the functions of the working self with knowledge from the autobiographical knowledge database. This form of retrieval generates autobiographical memories related to our internal goals. Generative retrieval is, according to Conway, an active effortful iterative process.

The generative retrieval processes operate as follows: when we are cued to retrieve an autobiographical memory, we will first try to relate the cue to an object or

situation from our personal environment. For example, the word 'bicycle' can make us think of our own bicycle at home and the fact that we have often ridden on it. The memory of bicycle rides can lead us to a specific location that we like to visit. When this place is found, very specific memories can follow. Direct retrieval, on the other hand, is the result of an involuntary retrieval triggered by an external stimulus. For example, hearing the word 'elephant' may instantaneously trigger memories of a holiday in Namibia.

15.5.3 OLFACTORY CUES AND MEMORIES

A well-known example of direct retrieval is often found in fragrances. The power with which olfactory cues are able to evoke memories is known as the **Proust phenomenon**, named after the French novelist Marcel Proust. In his novel *À la recherche du temps perdu*, Proust describes how the smell and taste of cupcakes dipped in tea brought back strong childhood memories that he had seemingly lost. Whether it is possible to actually bring back memories that have been completely lost will be discussed later in this chapter. It is a fact, however, that olfactory cues are often powerful in evoking memories.

For instance, Maylor, Carter, and Hallett (2002) found that olfactory cues were particularly effective in evoking autobiographical memories in groups of young and old adults. With olfactory cues, both groups were able to report about twice as many autobiographical memories than without these cues (see fig 15.5). One of the specific properties of the Proust phenomenon is that olfactory cues would

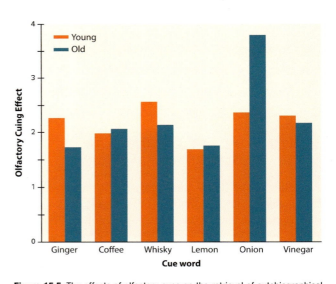

Figure 15.5 The effects of olfactory cues on the retrieval of autobiographical memories. Young and older participants were queried twice (after the presentation of one of the odour words) to retrieve autobiographical memories. On the second occasion, the corresponding odour was actually presented in half of the cases. The actual presentation resulted in approximately a doubling of the number of autobiographical memories retrieved. (source: Maylor et al., 2002)

trigger very old memories. Chu and Downes (2004) found that the memories triggered by these cues were often from the period when the participants were six to ten years old. These memories were considerably older than those triggered by verbal cues.

The question is why olfactory cues have such a strong effect on memory. One possible reason is that odour and taste cues are integrated with each other in the orbitofrontal cortex, which may contribute to the formation of strong autobiographical memories. A second reason is that we usually have relatively few odour-related autobiographical memories, so that the ones that do exist are much more distinct than those in other modalities. A third reason is that olfactory memories are less easy to be described in words, making them resistant to interference.

15.5.4 FLASHBULB MEMORIES

We typically have very strong and vivid memories of important, dramatic, and public events, or at least we think we do. The description of the events surrounding the terrorist attacks of September 11, 2001, in the United States with which this chapter began is a good example of such a memory. Other public events that are known to trigger this kind of memory are, for example, the disintegration of the Space Shuttle Challenger during its launch in 1986, Princess Diana's car accident while trying to evade paparazzi in 1997, or, more recently, the terrorist attacks in Paris in 2015, or the Russian invasion of Ukraine in February 2022.

Brown and Kulik (1977) introduced the term **flashbulb memories** for this type of memory. They hypothesised that memories that have possible consequences for us as individuals and that are experienced as surprising activate a special neural mechanism that is involved in storing these types of memory. According to Brown and Kulik, this mechanism would ensure that the details of the event are permanently recorded as a memory. This would include details about the informant (who delivered the news), the place where the news was heard, the events that took place while we were hearing the news, our own emotional state and that of others, and the consequences of the event for us as individuals.

Brown and Kulik emphasise that two factors are involved in the formation of flashbulb memories: surprise and potential consequences for the individual. Conway et al. (1994) used an unexpected turn in British politics to investigate how these factors contributed to the formation of a flashbulb memory. On November 28, 1990, former British Prime Minister Margaret Thatcher resigned unexpectedly after having held this position for more than ten years. For many British citizens, this was a very surprising turn in a short political struggle that could have had many consequences for their personal lives. Conway et al. found that for many people this event had resulted in a flashbulb memory. Of those surveyed, 86% reported still having a flashbulb memory 11 months after the event, and 26 months after the event the memories were still consistent.

15.5.4.1 Are Flashbulb Memories Special?

Are flashbulb memories really a special type of memory, or is there a mechanism that makes them appear to be special? Finkenauer et al. (1998) have argued that the formation of a flashbulb memory depends on several factors, including a person's emotional involvement in the event in question. However, these factors basically play a role in the formation of any personal memory, so it is possible that flashbulb memories are just intense variants of normal memories.

One crucial factor is that flashbulb memories are often repeated. Bohannon (1988) found, for example, that many people could still remember the details of the Space Shuttle Challenger accident because they repeated their own memories often. Another factor that comes into play here is the important role the media play in maintaining flashbulb memories. Repeated exposure to media can actively distort our own memories. For example, as many as 73% of American students who participated in a survey organised by Pezdek (2003) reported that they had witnessed the first plane crash into the World Trade Center tower on September 11, 2001. In reality, this was not possible, because on the day itself only a video of the second impact was available. In a similar fashion, many people are convinced that they have seen video recordings of Princess Diana's car crash, while in reality these recordings do not exist at all (Ost, Vrij, Costall, & Bull, 2002).

15.5.4.2 Liveliness

We can thus question whether we really remember the events related to flashbulb memories as well as we think we do. Talarico and Rubin (2003) investigated this question by asking 54 students at Duke University, the day after the September 11 attacks, to write down their most vivid memories of the attack. They also had to do the same for a more mundane event. Then, they also had to give each of these memories a vividness rating. The same students were tested again 7, 42, and 224 days later. The main results of this study were that the vividness ratings of the flashbulb memories remained high, while those of normal everyday memories decreased over time. The consistency of the flashbulb memories, however, also decreased systematically over time. The latter suggests that flashbulb memories are not essentially different from normal memories. The uniqueness of the events ensures that we remember them vividly, but not necessarily accurately (fig 15.6).

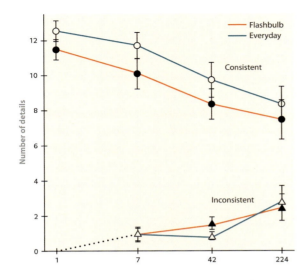

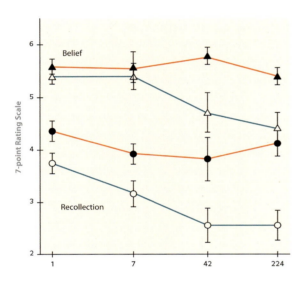

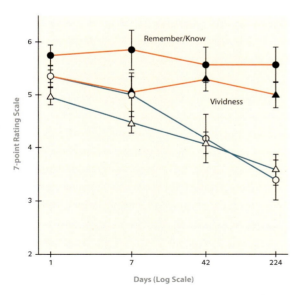

Figure 15.6 The relationship between vividness and accuracy of flashbulb memories, as a function of the number of days between the event and the moment of recall. (source: Talarico and Rubin, 2003)

15.5.5 MEMORIES ACROSS THE LIFESPAN

Our autobiographical memories consist of events that have happened throughout our lives. If we take a closer look at these memories, however, we typically find that they are not evenly distributed across our lifespans but that the distribution is characterised by a number of characteristic peaks and troughs. If we ask older people to write down their memories, we typically find that almost no memories are reported before the age of three, and that a large proportion of the memories that are reported stem from the period between the ages of 10 and 30. The absence of early age memories is known as **childhood amnesia** and the peak between ages of 10 and 30 as the **reminiscence bump**. According to Conway, Wang, Hanyu, and Haque (2005) these two phenomena can be found in at least five different cultures, namely in China, Japan, England, Bangladesh, and America, which suggests that it is a universal phenomenon (fig 15.7). But, why are our memories so unevenly distributed throughout our lives?

15.5.6 CHILDHOOD AMNESIA

What is the oldest personal memory you have? For most of us this will be a memory from approximately the age of three. How is it possible that we cannot remember anything before that age? Have episodes from the earliest phase of our lives never been stored, or is something else going on? In the following sections, we will discuss some possible explanations for childhood amnesia.

15.5.6.1 An Immature Brain
The brain is far from being fully developed at birth, and parts of the prefrontal cortex continue to develop even well into our early twenties. Particularly in the first years after

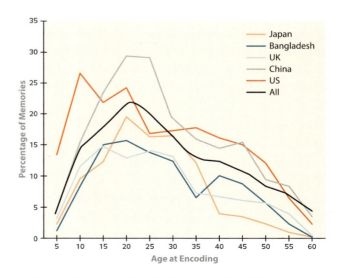

Figure 15.7 The distribution of spontaneous memories across the lifespan, shown for five different cultures. (source: Conway et al., 2005)

birth, our brains continue to develop rapidly. As discussed in the previous two chapters, the hippocampus is important for the consolidation of memories. This is one of the brain areas that still develops strongly after birth. One part of the hippocampus, known as the dentate gyrus, is not fully developed until about a year after birth, and also other parts of the hippocampus are characterised by major developments that continue until up to eight years after birth. The fact that the hippocampus is not yet fully developed could therefore explain why we cannot store memories in the first years of life.

Fivush, Gray, and Fromhoff (1987) reported, however, that children between 29 to 35 months of age are nevertheless able to report early childhood memories. They interviewed these children about their recent (< 3 months) and less recent (> 3 months) memories and found that young children could recount these experiences with ease and that – based on interviews with the parents – their memories were particularly accurate. Based on this finding, we must therefore conclude that we are indeed able to form autobiographical memories as young children, but that these memories are somehow lost again during the later stages of our lives.

15.5.6.2 Repression
One of the earliest ideas on child amnesia was formulated by the well-known Austrian psychiatrist and founder of psychoanalysis, Sigmund Freud. According to Freud, childhood amnesia is the result of the repression of threatening thoughts that are banished into the unconscious and consequently transformed into less harmful memories, known as screen memories. There are, however, several major problems with this idea: it is not falsifiable and it is also incapable of explaining why we are also unable to remember positive or neutral events from childhood. Moreover, much of Freuds' theorising was based on a framework that has no empirical basis at all (Crews, 2017).

15.5.6.3 The Cognitive Self
According to Howe and Courage (1997), children can only form autobiographical memories after a sense of self-awareness has been developed. Since autobiographical memories are by definition linked to the development of an identity, children's self-awareness, known as the **cognitive self**, could serve as a framework in which autobiographical memories can be organised.

15.5.6.4 Sociocultural Development
Fivush (2010) states that language and cultural development are crucially involved in the development of autobiographical memory. Language is important because it is a means of transmitting and recounting our autobiographical memories. Memories that are formed before our language skills are fully developed are therefore much more difficult to convert into verbal expressions later in life, according to Fivush. A second aspect that, according to Fivush, strongly contributes to the formation of early memories, is the mother's reminiscence style. Some mothers have a much stronger tendency to recall memories than others. In a study among 12-year-old children, it was found that children whose mothers had a more extensive reminiscence style had, on average, more access to early memories than children whose mothers had a less extensive reminiscence style (Jack, MacDonald, Rees, & Hayne, 2009).

15.5.6.5 Two-Stage Theory
Most theories assume a gradual decline in childhood memory during the first years of life. According to Jack and Hayne (2010), however, this assumption is incorrect: they found that young adults at the age of 19 had no memories at all from before their 23rd month after birth, and only a few loose memories from the first four to six years of their lives. Based on this, Jack and Hayne concluded that childhood amnesia is a two-stage process, in which there is absolute amnesia for the first two years of life and gradual amnesia for the remaining period until the sixth year of life. The authors hypothesise that the end of the period of absolute amnesia corresponds to the development of the cognitive self, while the gradual decline in amnesia is related to the development of language skills.

15.5.6.6 Neurogenesis
Finally, Akers et al. (2014) return to the immature brain to explain childhood amnesia. Contrary to popular myth (see also Box 2.2), our brains continue to sprout new neurons after birth. Although this process, known as **neurogenesis**, slows down dramatically after birth, there are still several brain areas, including the hippocampus, where neurogenesis continues for several years. Akers et al. managed to manipulate the degree of neurogenesis in the hippocampus of mice and found a relationship between this and the degree to which these mice responded afterwards to a previously conditioned stimulus: the stronger the neurogenesis, the weaker the conditioned response.

The continuous formation of new neurons in the hippocampus may explain why young children can initially store autobiographical memories but subsequently lose them again. According to this view, early memories would be encoded in the neural networks that are formed by the already existing neurons. As more neurons develop during the first years of childhood, they would also form new networks, which would then overgrow the early memory traces.

15.5.7 THE REMINISCENCE BUMP
The second striking fact regarding the distribution of our memories across the lifespan is formed by the reminiscence bump. When we ask older people to recall their

personal memories, we typically find that a significant proportion of these memories originate from the period between the start of adolescence and early adulthood, approximately between the age of 10 and 30 years (Rubin, Rahhal, & Poon, 1998).

15.5.7.1 The Life Script

According to Rubin and Berntsen (2003), we can explain this relatively high concentration of memories from that period by considering the concept of a **life script**. The life script comprises the essential stages that we expect to pass through in our lives, given the culture in which we live. According to Rubin and Berntsen, the life script gives structure to our life stories. As such, the life script can be regarded as an index for the stages of life where we might expect important changes to happen. Examples of these changes are moving out from our parents' home, attending college, falling in love, getting married, having children, and finding a job. The structure that the life script provides, together with the uniqueness of the memories that accompany the beginning of each new stage of life, make it easier to retrieve these memories.

An important prediction made by Rubin and Berntsen (2003) is that the reminiscence bump would be mainly comprised of positive, spontaneous memories, as it would mainly be the retrieval of these memories that would be facilitated by the life script. In a follow-up study, Berntsen, Rubin, and Siegler (2011) instructed older individuals to explicitly report their most positive and most negative memories. Most of their positive memories showed a reminiscence bump, whereas their negative memories were more evenly distributed across their lives. In terms of content, positive memories also corresponded strongly with the life script, such as having children, getting married, studying, or falling in love. Negative memories reported included things such as the death of a loved one, or life-threatening illnesses, which were not part of the life script.

15.5.7.2 Unexpectedness and the Feeling of Control

In addition to the life script, two other factors may contribute to the reminiscence bump. The first factor is the unexpectedness of the event. Although the memories that can be fitted into the life script are generally expected events, memories of unexpected events may also be characterised by a reminiscence bump. At first glance, this pattern is inconsistent with the life script explanation. However, the fact that these unexpected memories also show a reminiscence bump can be explained by assuming that strong autobiographical memories are linked to the development of our identity (Conway, 2005). Since our identity develops strongly during adolescence, it may be that this development facilitates the recollection of unexpected events during this period.

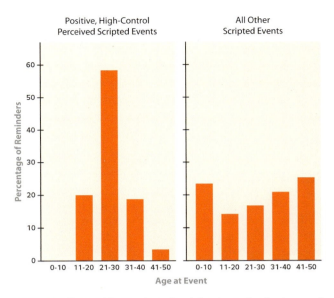

Figure 15.8 The reminiscence bump in relation to emotional valence and control. In particular, positive events over which we have control concentrate around the 20th to 30th year of life. (source: Glück and Bluck, 2007)

Finally, the degree of control that we have over a situation may also play a role in the development of the reminiscence bump. For example, Glück and Bluck (2007) recorded 3542 life events from 659 participants between the ages of 50 and 90. These participants had to rate each memory on the criteria of emotional valence, personal importance, and sense of control. Only the positive memories with a high sense of control showed a reminiscence bump. In summary, three factors contribute to the formation of the reminiscence hump: the development of one's own identity, the novelty of experiences or expected major changes in a stage of life, and the sense of control (fig 15.8).

15.5.8 THE NEURAL BASIS FOR THE RETRIEVAL OF AUTOBIOGRAPHICAL MEMORIES

How are autobiographical memories retrieved? Svoboda, McKinnon, and Levine (2006) found that the medial and ventromedial prefrontal cortices are almost always active during autobiographical retrieval, along with the lateral temporal cortex. Summerfield, Hassabis, and Maguire (2009) instructed participants to either retrieve autobiographical or non-autobiographical memories or to imagine fictional memories. Both real and fictional memories resulted in activation in specific areas in the dorsal and ventral medial prefrontal cortex, the retrosplenial cortex and parts of the parieto-occipital sulcus, suggesting that these areas are involved in relating the self to these events. However, recalling genuine autobiographical memories resulted in stronger activation of the ventromedial prefrontal cortex and the posterior cingulate cortex.

15.5.9 THE CABEZA AND ST JACQUES MODEL

Cabeza and St Jacques (2007) describe a theoretical framework for explaining the neurobiological basis of autobiographical memories. This framework consists of six processes: (1) search and controlled processing, (2) self-referential processes, (3) recollection, (4) emotional processing, (5) visual imagination, and (6) accuracy monitoring. In the following sections, we will introduce these six components in more detail.

15.5.9.1 Search and Controlled Processing

The processes related to search and controlled processing are associated with generative retrieval. Steinvorth, Corkin, and Halgren (2006) found more activation in the lateral prefrontal cortex during autobiographical memory retrieval than during semantic memory retrieval (e.g., 'What colour is Garfield's coat?'). Moreover, these areas remained more strongly activated for the entire period during which participants were retrieving the memory. The latter finding is consistent with the idea that the reconstruction of an autobiographical memory requires the continuous involvement of an active search process.

15.5.9.2 Self-referential Processes

Cabeza et al. (2004) manipulated self-referential processes by asking participants to take photographs of specific locations at the campus of Duke University. During an fMRI experiment, these photos were then used along with photos of similar locations taken by other Duke students participating in the experiment. When participants saw their own photos again, this was accompanied by an increase in activity in the medial prefrontal cortex.

15.5.9.3 Recollection

The hippocampus is involved in the retrieval of basic autobiographical memories. Gilboa et al. (2005) found that the loss of autobiographical memories in Alzheimer's patients was associated with damage to the hippocampus and medial temporal regions.

15.5.9.4 Emotional Processing

Autobiographical memories, more than other memories, are generally more associated with emotions and therefore they are also more strongly associated with amygdala activation. Buchanan, Tranel, and Adolphs (2006) found that patients with brain damage to the amygdala and the medial temporal lobes were more impaired in retrieving autobiographical memories than patients who only had damage to the medial temporal lobes. Daselaar et al. (2008) found that a memory retrieval initially resulted in amygdala activation and that the degree of this activation correlated with the emotional intensity of the memory, as reported by the participants.

15.5.9.5 Visual Imagination

Autobiographical memories are often particularly vivid because of the imagery that is associated with this type of memory. Evidence for the involvement of mental imagery in the generation of autobiographical memories was also found by Daselaar et al. (2008). These authors reported that the initial amygdala activation was followed by activation of the visual cortex. The degree of activation correlated with the vividness ratings reported by the participants.

15.5.9.6 Monitoring for Accuracy

The final process in Cabeza and St Jacques' model, the monitoring for accuracy, is believed to be a rapid and unconscious process that checks the accuracy of the retrieved autobiographical memories. Gilboa et al. (2006) found that patients with brain damage to the ventrolateral prefrontal cortex spontaneously produce false autobiographical memories, without intending to do so, thus suggesting a problem in the monitoring system.

The relation between the processes identified by Cabeza and St Jacques' model is shown in Figure 15.9. Their model is one of the first to provide a fairly complete picture of all the processes involved in the generation and retrieval of an autobiographical memory. The model can also explain why different brain injuries can lead to specific impairments in the processing of autobiographical memories. Although there is much evidence for the existence of the six processes just introduced, it is not yet clear how exactly they interact.

In a subsequent extension of the model, St Jacques, Kragel, and Rubin (2011) argue for the existence of four specific brain networks that are assumed to be involved

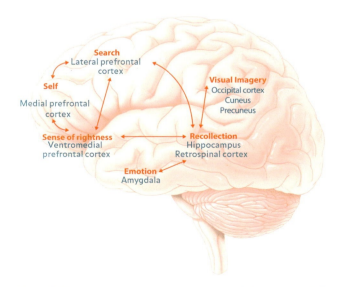

Figure 15.9 Schematic representation of Cabeza and St Jacques' (2007) autobiographical memory system.

433

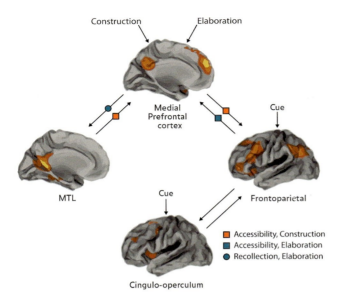

Figure 15.10 St Jacques et al.'s (2011) autobiographical memory model.

in the generative retrieval of emotional autobiographical memories (see fig 15.10). Here, a frontoparietal network is involved in the construction of autobiographical memories and controlled search processes. This network is assumed to process the cues that trigger the retrieval of a memory. Moreover, it is assumed to direct the search processes to the right information. St Jacques et al. found activation of a cingulo-opercular network, which they assumed to be involved in the reconstruction of the memory, and in goal maintenance (that is, in retaining why a memory is retrieved). A medial prefrontal cortical network appears to be involved in constructing the memory and elaborating on it. This network was also important for the self-referential process. Finally, a medial temporal network was also found to be involved in the construction and elaboration of autobiographical memories. The latter network was mainly linked to declarative memory and conscious processing of the memory. All four networks are, according to St Jacques et al. (2011), involved in the generation of autobiographical memories, whereas only the latter two networks are involved in their elaboration.

15.6 EYEWITNESS TESTIMONIES

15.6.1 THE FALLIBILITY OF MEMORY

We have already introduced the idea that memory is reconstructive, giving rise to the suggestion that the memories we retrieve are susceptible to distortion. In case of eyewitness testimonies, it is therefore extremely important that we are aware of the limitations of memory. Although the

problem of the unreliability of eyewitnesses was already a major theme of the 1957 Hollywood classic *Twelve Angry Men* (in which Henry Fonda has to save a young defendant from the death penalty by showing that several eyewitness testimonies cannot possibly be correct), it still appears that many judges and jurors are unaware of the frailty of our memories. For instance, Benton, Ross, Bradshaw, Thomas, and Bradshaw (2006) asked judges, jurors, and memory experts 30 questions related to eyewitness testimonies. Judges disagreed with the experts on 60% of the questions, and jurors even on 87% of the questions.

The consequence of these problems is that there have been a considerable number of criminal cases in which suspects have been found guilty on the basis of testimony that has been proven to be unreliable. One of the most high-profile cases is that of John Demjanjuk, a Ukrainian-born Soviet soldier turned German prisoner of war during the Second World War, whose identity was mistaken for someone else (see Box 15.2), but several other cases are known, such as a sensational incest case in the Netherlands in the early 1990s, or the infamous case of the American police officer Paul Ingram, which we will discuss later.

Some of the problems with eyewitness testimonies may be the result of **false memories** (see Section 15.7), but they may also have a less drastic cause. The testimonies can, for example, also be distorted by **confirmation bias**, that is, by our own goals or expectations. Consider, for example, Lindholm and Christianson (1998), who instructed Swedish students to watch videos of staged robberies in which a perpetrator inflicted serous wounds on a cashier using a knife. After watching the video, participants were shown pictures of eight men: four Swedes and four immigrants, and they had to decide whether one of these men was the perpetrator. Both Swedish students and students with an immigrant background were twice as likely to choose a photo of an immigrant than of a Swedish suspect.

According to the British psychologist Sir Frederic Bartlett (1932), we can explain the malleability of our memories by assuming that we try to fit new information into existing cognitive schemas (see also Chapter 16). These schemas are involved in structuring our knowledge, but this can also result in distortions of our memories, because they force us to reconstruct details of an event on the basis of what we believe to be true. Tuckey and Brewer (2003a), for example, found that for most people, the bank robbery schema describes a perpetrator as a darkly clothed male, having a getaway car with a driver. They showed participants a video of a staged robbery, which was followed by a memory test. Consistent with schema theory, participants remembered schema-relevant information better than schema-irrelevant information.

Following up on this, Tuckey and Brewer (2003b) investigated how eyewitnesses remembered ambiguous

Box 15.2 The Demjanjuk case

John Demjanjuk (born: Ivan) was an American automobile industry employee, who was born in 1920 in Ukraine. During the Second World War he fought for the former Soviet Union's Red Army. In 1942, during the Crimean Offensive, he was captured by German troops and placed in custody in a Soviet prisoner of war concentration camp. To escape the terrible living conditions, Demjanjuk volunteered to work as a camp guard for the German occupying forces. In 1952, he emigrated to the United States, where he obtained American citizenship in 1958 and got a job as a mechanic in a Ford car factory in Ohio.

That is about as much as we know about John Demjanjuk's early life. What follows can be read as an international spy novel with witnesses, memory experts, and secret service agents in leading roles. During the 1970s, information was leaked about the involvement of former Soviet prisoners of war in Nazi war crimes, and based on the testimony of a fellow prisoner, Demjanjuk was accused of being an infamous Treblinka camp guard known as Ivan the Terrible. In 1987, Demjanjuk's American citizenship was revoked, and he was extradited to Israel, where several Treblinka survivors identified him. On the basis of these testimonies, Demjanjuk received the death sentence in 1988 (fig 15.11). The American memory expert Elisabeth Loftus was invited to act as an expert witness, but she declined because of her Jewish background and the resulting potential conflict of interest. Instead, the

Figure 15.11 John Demjanjuk hears the death sentence pronounced against him during his trial in Jerusalem, on April 25, 1988.

Dutch cognitive psychologist Willem Albert Wagenaar acted as an expert.

Wagenaar immediately noticed a serious flaw in the procedure that the Israeli police had used to obtain the testimonies. They used a line-up, in which a series of photos was shown, including one of Demjanjuk, and the witnesses were asked to point out the photo depicting Ivan the Terrible. The Treblinka survivors remembered Ivan the Terrible as a balding man with a round face and a short neck – a description that was also somewhat applicable to Demjanjuk. Moreover, it was also the only photograph in the series that matched these characteristics, while Demjanjuk's photo was also slightly larger than the other photos. When Wagenaar presented the same photos to his students in Leiden, who had obviously never seen Ivan the Terrible before, they all picked out Demjanjuk's picture. On the basis of these findings, Wagenaar pleaded for acquittal, but he did so in vain.

In 1989, after the collapse of the iron curtain and before the death sentence had been executed, however, several new documents emerged from the KGB archives in former East Germany showing that Ivan the Terrible was actually someone else, a certain Ivan Marchenko. Based on this new information, Demjanjuk was acquitted in 1993, and five years later he regained his American citizenship. In 2004, however, it was revoked again, on the grounds that he had concealed his past as a camp guard when immigrating to the United States, and on the grounds that a copy of an identity card had turned up, which would have indicated that Demjanjuk had been a camp guard in the Sobibor concentration camp. For the latter case, the only evidence available actually consisted of this identity card, of which the authenticity has been seriously doubted. The card ended up in the hands of the American government via Russian connections, and because of Demjanjuk's past as a volunteer who had collaborated with the Nazis, it could have been forged to discredit Demjanjuk. In 2011, a German court sentenced him to five years in prison. Demjanjuk was released pending an appeal. He did not live to see the appeal or the prison sentence. Demjanjuk died on March 17, 2012, at the age of 91: in freedom, but without any nationality.

information. Participants watched videos of staged robberies, in which for half the participants some details had been made ambiguous. This was done, for example, by having the robber wear a ski mask, which made the robber's gender ambiguous. As predicted, the witnesses interpreted the ambiguous information in a schema-consistent way. Consequently, their memories were consistently distorted by the schemas even when the information from the schema did not correspond to reality.

15.6.1.1 Influencing by the Interviewer

In a now classic study, Loftus and Palmer (1974) showed participants a movie fragment of a traffic accident involving several cars. Afterwards, they had to answer various questions about the fragment. Some participants were asked: 'How fast were the cars going when they smashed into each other?' Other participants were given a slight variation of the question where 'smashed' had been replaced with a more neutral sounding word, such as 'collided', 'bumped', 'contacted', or 'hit'. The estimated speed was about 41 mph when the word 'smashed' was used, while the estimated speed was about 34 mph when one of the more neutral descriptions was used.

In a second experiment, one week later, the participants were again questioned about the accident. One of the questions now was whether they could remember whether broken glass had been present. In reality, this was not the case, but 32% of the participants who had been asked the non-neutral speed question answered that they had actually seen glass. For the participants who had been asked the neutral speed question, this percentage was considerably lower, namely 14%. The latter percentage was comparable to a group of control participants, who had not answered any questions about the car's speed. We can therefore conclude that our fragile memory can be distorted by changing just a single word.

15.6.1.2 Influence of the Situation

The Loftus and Palmer (1974) study just discussed shows how easily an eyewitness can be influenced by an interviewer. In addition, eyewitness accounts can also be influenced by the situation itself. For example, Lindsay, Allen, Chan, and Dahl (2004) showed videos involving a burglary in a museum. A day before the videos were shown, participants listened to a story that was either thematically similar to the burglary (a break-in at a palace) or not (a school trip to a palace). When the video and the story were thematically similar, participants made many more errors in reporting the details of the film than when they were not. This latter fact is important, because eyewitnesses in everyday life often also have prior experiences that may interfere with the memory of a crime. Similar results were found when participants had to read two stories (see fig 15.12) and answer questions about one of these stories. Suggestive questions related to the other story were relatively often incorrectly recognised.

It is clear that our memories can be strongly distorted. The next question is why this can happen. There are a number of theoretically plausible reasons for this. The first is that we may attribute a memory to the wrong source (Johnson, Hashtroudi, & Lindsay, 1993). A specific cue, for example, a question, can activate several memory traces that overlap with respect to the information they contain.

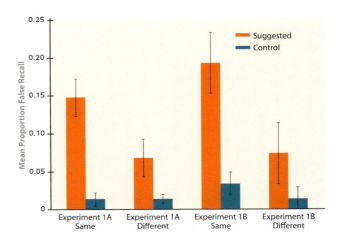

Figure 15.12 Results of a study on distorted memories. Suggestive questions, which referred to a story that participants had read previously were relatively often incorrectly answered. This was particularly the case when the stories were thematically similar. The results shown here relate to two experiments: Experiment 1A was conducted online, while Experiment 1B was conducted by students at Western University in Illinois, during a classroom session. (source: Lindsay et al., 2004)

This is most likely to happen when memories that stem from different sources are very similar.

A misattribution such as this can be avoided, however, when witnesses have to explicitly indicate the source of their memory. Prull and Yockelson (2013) found, for example, that participants' memories were clearly distorted when presented with misleading information. Participants were first shown a series of photos that told a story (e.g., someone coming home from grocery shopping and then going into the kitchen to prepare a meal). The pictures showed objects that we usually find in a kitchen, but also objects that we usually find in a workshop, such as a chisel, woodchipper, and so on. After these pictures were shown, participants were told a story that was essentially the same as the series of pictures, but in strategic places referred to another object: for example, a reference to a toaster was replaced by a reference to a blender. This manipulation resulted in participants being influenced by this misinformation. The crucial finding of this study, however, was that the distortions were relatively limited when participants were explicitly instructed to indicate the source (pictures or story) when reporting their memory. It is important to note, however, that these studies may exaggerate the fallibility of everyday memory. Many studies focused on the recollection of details and it is precisely in these details the distortion of memory can occur (Dalton & Daneman, 2006).

15.6.1.3 Expectation and Threat

Another factor that is involved in the distortion of eyewitness accounts is the emotional valence of the situation. Much research has focused on the phenomenon of **weapon focus**, that is, the observation that witnesses often focus their attention on weapons that are being used, often leaving other details unnoticed.

Loftus, Loftus, and Messo (1987) showed two groups of participants different film fragments. The first group was shown a fragment in which a person pointed a gun at a cashier and received a sum of money, while the second group was shown a fragment in which the person gave a cheque to the cashier and then also received a sum of money. The first group's eyes were more focused on the gun than the second group's eyes were focused on the cheque. After they finished watching the fragment, participants were questioned about details that were not related to either the gun or the cheque. The performance of the group that had watched the gun variant of the film was on average lower than that of the group that had watched the cheque variant.

This study shows that weapons can capture our attention, but the question is why. Is it because they are threatening, or because they are unexpected in most everyday situations? To show which of these two factors is more decisive, Pickel (1999) produced a series of videos showing a man approaching a woman while holding a handgun. The videos were designed to manipulate both threat level and the participant's expectation. To do so, the scenes either took place at a shooting range (expected) or at a baseball field (unexpected). In addition, the man could approach the woman with the weapon pointed downwards (low threat level) or he could approach her with the weapon pointed at her, while she retreated in fear (high threat level). Afterwards, participants had to give a description of the man. The results were clear: in the shooting range setting, where the weapon was expected, participants were much better able to describe the man than in the baseball field setting. Moreover, the level of threat did not have any effect on this (see fig 15.13).

Stress and anxiety can also affect the accuracy of eyewitness testimonies. For instance, Peters (1988) found evidence for this by making ingenious use of a situation in which students were being vaccinated. Two minutes after the injection their heart rate was measured, and

based on this the students were divided into two groups: one group whose heart rate was significantly increased by the vaccination (the high-reactive group) and one group whose heart rate was barely affected by it (the low-reactive group). Then, the students had to identify the nurse who had administered the injection. The low-reactive group was much better capable of doing so (59% correct) than the high-reactive group (31%). The group that considered the vaccination stressful also had a much lower memory performance. These results are consistent with those of a meta-analysis that was done by Deffenbacher, Bornstein, Penrod, and McGorty (2004). Thus, stress and anxiety generally have a negative effect on our memory performance.

15.6.2 PROBLEMS WITH THE IDENTIFICATION OF SUSPECTS

15.6.2.1 Face Recognition and Line-Ups

A common method of identifying a suspect involves the police asking a witness to identify suspects by selecting them from a group of people (see also Box 15.2). The identifications that are obtained this way are generally highly fallible. Valentine, Pickering, and Darling (2003), for example, examined the results of 640 eyewitnesses who tried to identify a suspect in 314 real line-ups. About 20% of them falsely identified a non-suspect. Of the remaining 80%, only half of them actually succeeded in successfully identifying the suspect; the other half did not identify anyone. Odinot, Wolters, and van Koppen (2009) studied the memories of 14 supermarket employees who had witnessed a robbery at close hand; they found a moderate correlation between the trust these witnesses had in their account and the accuracy of their testimony. Thus, eyewitnesses who are very confident in their identification tend to be slightly more accurate than those who are not so confident (Brewer & Wells, 2011).

The identification of a suspect generally relies on face recognition (see also Chapter 6). A problem with this, however, is that although a witness can recognise a face, they may not remember the context in which they saw it. For example, Ross, Ceci, Dunning, and Toglia (1994) asked participants to observe a film of an event in which either an innocent bystander or the perpetrator of a crime was visible. When innocent bystanders were visible, they were identified significantly more often in a subsequent line-up than any other random person. This effect is known as unconscious **transference**.

15.6.2.2 The Other-Race Effect

Another finding that is particularly relevant to eyewitness testimony involves the **other-race effect**. This effect relates to the fact that we identify faces of our own ethnicity better

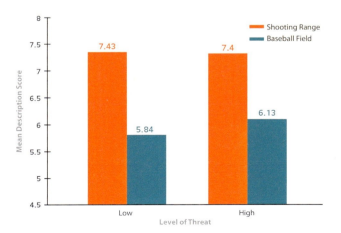

Figure 15.13 Results of a study of the effects of expectation and threat related to the weapon focus effect. (source: Pickel, 1999)

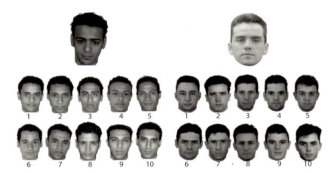

Figure 15.14 Illustration of the other-race effect. (source: Megreya et al., 2011)

Figure 15.15 A series of photographs of famous actor Robert De Niro. Some photos are much more representative of De Niro than others. (adapted from: Jenkins et al., 2011)

than faces of another ethnicity. One possible explanation is that we find it more difficult to remember the characteristics of faces from another ethnicity than those of a face belonging to our own ethnicity. This explanation is incomplete, however, for two reasons. First, Megreya, White, and Burton (2011) found that perceptual processes may also be involved. British and Egyptian participants were shown a target face and had to decide whether this target face was present in a set of ten other faces. This task made minimal use of memory processes because both the target face and the series with which they had to compare the target face remained in view continuously (see fig 15.14). Nevertheless, Megreya et al. observed an other-race effect. Second, Shriver, Young, Hugenberg, Bernstein, and Lanter (2007) found that the other-race effect was not limited to ethnicity, but that it can also be found for groups with which we do not identify. Shriver et al. presented white American university students with photographs of white persons in a poor environment and found that the advantage normally associated with recognising one's own ethnicity largely disappeared; this was probably due to the fact that these students did not associate the persons with a group with which they would normally identify.

15.6.2.3 Face Recognition and Familiarity

A third aspect of face recognition that is relevant for eyewitness testimonies is the fact that we are much less capable of recognising unfamiliar faces than familiar ones. Not many studies have reported this, however, because face recognition is often studied by using a more or less homogeneous set of photos that are typically taken on the same day. This typically results in a relatively good performance on face-recognition tasks, even when the photographs include strangers. Megreya, Sandford, and Burton (2013) found, however, that participants were much less able to match photos of strangers when those photos were taken across a period of a few months.

How bad we actually are at recognising unfamiliar faces was convincingly demonstrated in a study by Jenkins et al. (2011). Here, British participants were given the task of sorting photos of two well-known Dutch celebrities (Chantal Janzen and Bridget Maasland, who are relatively unknown in the United Kingdom) into separate piles. The British

participants sorted the photos into an average of seven to eight unique piles, suggesting they believed that the photos represented this many different individuals. These results are related to the fact that photographs of a single individual can vary considerably (see fig 15.15), making it extremely difficult to identify a person on the basis of a single photograph, as is often the case in a line-up. For this reason, Jenkins and Burton (2011) have argued that the information from several photos should be combined to create a more representative average face. Consistent with this idea, Jenkins et al. (2011) found indeed that computer algorithms for face recognition were much more accurate when using average faces than individual photos.

15.6.2.4 Memory and Ageing

You might already have suspected that eyewitness testimonies made by older individuals are less reliable than those made by younger people. This is indeed the case, as was shown in a study by Dodson and Krueger (2006). They showed a video clip to younger and older participants, who then had to fill in a questionnaire about the clip. The questionnaire was misleading, however, because it referred to events that were not shown in the video. For the older participants, this resulted in the creation of a relatively large number of false memories, compared to younger participants. What was worrying is that the older participants were also more confident that their false memory accounts were real than the younger participants.

15.6.3 IMPROVING EYEWITNESS TESTIMONIES

It follows from this discussion that there is a strong need to develop procedures that improve the reliability of eyewitness reports. In the next section, we will introduce two different approaches to this. The first approach concerns improving the performance of eyewitnesses during a line-up while the second approach involves the improvement of the interview techniques that are used to record eyewitness testimonies.

15.6.3.1 Adjustments to Line-Ups

There are two common procedures for a line-up. In a simultaneous line-up witnesses observe every potential suspect at the same time, whereas in a sequential line-up they observe them one at a time. Steblay, Dysart, and Wells (2011) conducted a meta-analysis of 72 studies focusing on the differences between simultaneous and sequential line-ups. When the perpetrator was present, they were on average identified in 52% of cases in the simultaneous line-up and in 44% of cases in the sequential line-up. When the perpetrator was not present, however, the simultaneous line-up resulted in relatively more false alarms (54%) than the sequential line-up (32%). The latter implies that eyewitnesses used a more conservative criterion in sequential line-ups than in simultaneous ones. Steblay et al. conclude that, in general, the sequential line-up is preferable to the simultaneous line-up. They argue that the small reduction in identifications when a perpetrator is present does not outweigh the drastic reduction in false identifications when the perpetrator is not present.

False identifications can be further reduced by explicitly giving witnesses an 'I don't know' option. The presence of this option was found to reduce false identifications even further, to only 12% (Steblay & Phillips, 2011). Finally, it is also possible to inform a witness that the perpetrator may not be present in the line-up. According to a meta-analysis by Steblay (1997), this option resulted in a 42% reduction in the number of false identifications, while the correct identifications, when the perpetrator was present, only decreased by 2%.

15.6.3.2 Improving Interrogations

Naturally, the police want to obtain as much information as possible from a witness statement. Cognitive psychologists have contributed significantly to this by developing the **cognitive interview** (Fisher, Geiselman, & Amador, 1989; Geiselman, Fisher, MacKinnon, & Holland, 1985). A cognitive interview is a structured procedure that is based on four rules to recount a memory as accurately as possible.

1. Mental reconstruction of the environment and all personal contacts experienced at the time of the crime.
2. Encouragement to report all details, including the less important ones.
3. Describing the incident in different orders, including, for example, in reverse chronological order.
4. Describing the incident from different perspectives, including those of other eyewitnesses.

The cognitive interview is effective because it is based on our current understanding of human memory. For example, the first two rules are based on Tulving and Thomson's (1973) encoding specificity principle (see Chapter 14). According to this principle, memory depends on the overlap between the context in which an event was perceived and in which it is remembered. The third and fourth rules assume that memory is complex, associative, and based on various sources of information. As a result, retrieving a memory is most efficient when it is done via different routes.

Although the cognitive interview has been around since about 1985, it has been continuously developed since its first inception (Memon, Meissner, & Fraser, 2010). One of those developments involves the establishment of a rapport between the interviewer and the witness. This can be done by minimising distractions, allowing the witness to tell their account slowly, allowing sufficient pauses between the answer and the next question, adapting the language to that of the individual witness, following up answers with interpretative comments, trying to allay the fears of the witness, and by avoiding judgemental and personal comments. In practice, the police often focus on the first two rules. The reason for this is often that a full cognitive interview can be very time-consuming.

15.7 FALSE MEMORIES

A consequence of the fact that autobiographical memory is constructive is that memories are susceptible to suggestion. In the most extreme cases, such suggestions can result in a false memory. One of the best-known examples of a false memory was given by Loftus, Coan, and Pickrell (1996). They succeeded in getting a 14-year-old adolescent named Chris to remember that he had once been lost in a shopping mall. With the help of his mother and older brother, the investigators gave Chris descriptions of three events that had taken place during his childhood. In addition, his older brother was also involved in the fabrication of one event that had never happened. For a five-day period, each day Chris was asked to write down facts that related to these events. If he could not remember any facts, he had to write that down too.

The false memory was introduced to Chris in a short paragraph describing how, when he was five years old, he got lost in a shopping mall in Spokane, Washington, and how he cried very hard when he was found by an elderly man who reunited him with his family. Over the five days, Chris began to report more and more details about this incident. Afterwards, he had to give each memory a rating ranging from 1 (not clear at all) to 11 (very clear). He gave the false memory a rating of 8, the second highest of the five ratings. Chris was then told that one of the events he had been given was false and then he was asked which one it was. In response, Chris selected one of the real events. In a later study, the same method was used more systematically involving 24 different participants, but with similar results (Loftus & Pickrell, 1995).

In a similar vein, Roediger and McDermott (1995) found that false memories could also be induced by just learning a list of words. Participants were given lists containing 12 words, such as 'bed', 'rest', and 'awake', which they had to study. Each word in the list was associated with one word that was not presented, such as 'sleep'. During an immediate free recall, the associated word was mentioned in 40% of all cases. Moreover, these words were recognised with a high degree of confidence during a subsequent test. In a second study, in which a larger set of words was used, the percentage in which the associated word was mentioned was even higher (55%) and participants incorrectly recognised this word about as often as they recognised the actual words that had been presented. Roediger and McDermott suggest that the spontaneous recall test facilitates the consolidation of the falsely remembered word, thus creating a false memory.

Patihis et al. (2013) investigated to what extent individuals with a superior autobiographical memory (see Box 15.1) are sensitive to false memories. Their hypothesis was that individuals with a particularly good autobiographical memory are less sensitive to intrusions of false memories, because the existing memory representations are much more robust than those of the average participant. Patihis et al. used a method based on that of Roediger and McDermott (1995). In addition, false information was presented in the form of photographs and fake news reports (see fig 15.16). Interestingly, the results showed, however, that individuals with superior autobiographical memories are actually more sensitive to false memories, compared to controls.

As with eyewitness testimony, the unreliability of autobiographical memory is of crucial importance in our judicial system. A controversial high-profile example of this involves Paul Ingram, a local chairman of the American Republican Party in the state of Washington. In 1981, Ingram was accused by his daughters of sexual abuse. After the initial indictment, the accusations were expanded even further as Ingram, a deeply religious individual, was also accused of being involved in satanic rituals, including the slaughter of 25 babies.

Figure 15.16 An illustration of the misinformation procedure to investigate false memories. (source: Patihis et al., 2013)

Initially, Ingram confessed to all accusations, until the American sociologist Richard Ofshe (1992) acted as memory expert. Ofshe set up a test consisting of fabricating an accusation. This accusation involved forcing his son and daughter to have sex with each other and it was presented to Ingram together with the other accusations. Eventually Ingram confessed to this accusation too and he even insisted that it had actually happened after Ofshe revealed the fabrication. Although Ofshe's method has been criticised by some proponents of the repressed memory movement (Olio & Cornell, 1998), the fact remains that Ofshe convincingly demonstrated how easy it is to manipulate individuals into falsely remembering incriminating events that never happened in real life.

The latter was also convincingly demonstrated by Shaw and Porter (2015). In their study, young adults were given the suggestion that between the ages of 11 and 14 they had committed a crime. Afterwards, by using suggestive interview techniques, a false emotional memory was induced, which could or could not be related to a crime. After three of these interviews, 70% of the participants were found to have a false memory of committing a crime. The false memories were similar in detail and vividness to real memories.

15.8 PROSPECTIVE MEMORY

All memory studies discussed so far have dealt with retrospective memory, that is, with memories that relate to the past. The final section of this chapter introduces prospective memory. Prospective memory includes the cognitive functions we use to formulate plans and promises, to store them, and to remember when either the time has come to carry them out or the right opportunity has arisen (Graf, 2012).

Prospective memory is crucial for many everyday actions, and its failure can have dramatic consequences. Einstein and McDaniel (2005) discuss, for example, the story of a father who forgot to drop off his son at day care, driving straight to work instead, and finding his child dead in the car at the end of the day. In a similar vein, they introduce the story of a patient who was still showing various symptoms of pain after a surgery, only to find out that the surgical staff had forgotten to remove a clamp from his body. These are all examples of prospective memory errors. Although such errors are often the result of a failure of memory, the social perception of this is often different. According to Graf (2012), errors in prospective memory are often attributed to lack of motivation or unreliability, whereas problems with retrospective memory are more likely to be attributed to poor memory.

There are several other differences between prospective and retrospective memory. While retrospective memory is

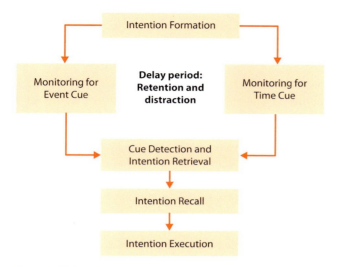

Figure 15.17 Schematic overview of the processes assumed to be involved in prospective memory. (source: Zogg et al., 2012)

about remembering facts, prospective memory is mainly about remembering to do something in the future. Retrospective memory is thus information-rich, whereas prospective memory is rather information-poor. In addition, research on prospective memory is generally the only discipline that is not so much concerned with memory itself, but rather with how we can apply memory to carry out future actions.

15.8.1 PROCESSES INVOLVED IN PROSPECTIVE MEMORY

Zogg, Woods, Sauceda, Wiebe, and Simoni (2012) have given an overview of the various processes that are involved in prospective memory (see fig 15.17). As the first step, they identified the formation of an intention. This intention is then linked to a specific cue; for example, we may decide to speak to a friend when we see them. Then there is a retention interval, that is, the interval between the formation of the intention and its execution. This period can take minutes, weeks, or even longer. During this period, we typically check the environment for cues that may result in executing our intention. When a relevant cue is detected, this results in the initiation of the corresponding intention. The intention is then retrieved from memory and executed.

15.8.2 TWO DIFFERENT FORMS OF PROSPECTIVE MEMORY

Relevant cues can be retrieved from memory in two different ways. First, we have a time-based prospective memory, which involves performing an action at a specific time. An example of this is attending a class that starts at a specific time. Second, event-based prospective memory is used when a specific action has to be performed when the right circumstances arise. An example of this is passing a message when you meet someone.

Experimental research on prospective memory typically involves giving participants a task that is unrelated to prospective memory, while they have to remember to perform a secondary task at some instance during the experiment. This secondary task must either be performed at a specific time or when the specific circumstances warrant it. Sellen, Louie, Harris, and Wilkins (1997) investigated prospective memory by having participants wear badges. These badges contained a button that had to be pressed either at a specific time (every two hours) or on a specific occasion (e.g., when the participant entered a specific room) over a two-week period. In addition, the participants also had to indicate when they were thinking about the task. Although the participants who were assigned to the time-based task thought about the task more often, compared to the participants assigned to event-based task, their performance was worse. The reason for this difference is that in the event-based task, the intention is more likely to be triggered by an external cue.

Time-based and event-based tasks thus differ considerably in terms of the strategy that is used. For time-based tasks, monitoring increases sharply the more the moment approaches that the task has to be performed. This is not the case for event-based tasks: here, participants continue to monitor their environment for relevant cues at a relatively constant rate (Cona, Arcara, Tarantino, & Bisiacchi, 2012).

Cona et al. (2012) used a task in which participants were periodically given a series of five letters. On each trial, participants had to decide whether or not the second and fourth letters in the series were the same. Moreover, they were given a second task. In the event-based condition, this task consisted of deciding whether the letter 'B', when it occurred, was in the second or fourth position in the sequence. In the time-based condition, a similar second task had to be performed, but at a fixed time, namely, every five minutes. During the task, EEG was recorded, and the ERPs that were evoked by the stimuli of the primary task were extracted from the EEG. The ERP activity evoked in a block of trials in which the participant had to perform the secondary task was compared to a block of trials in which he did not have to do so.

In the task blocks where the secondary task had to be performed, and thus where prospective memory had to be invoked, an increase in brain activity was found, which was reflected in a series of positive ERP components. This additional activity was found in both the time-based and the event-based condition. Cona et al. hypothesised that this activity was related to the retrieval of the task instructions. Additional activity was found in the event-based condition. Between 130 and 180 ms after stimulus appearance, there was an additional ERP component that was present over the central scalp areas, which the authors associated with the allocation of attention. In the time window of 400–600 ms there was also an additional positive component over the occipital cortex, which probably represented additional monitoring of the stimuli in that block.

15.8.3 PROSPECTIVE MEMORY IN EVERYDAY LIFE

Prospective memory is also crucially involved in many daily activities. In some occupations, forgetting an action can be life-threatening. Dismukes (2012) discusses various circumstances that can lead to prospective memory failure. He argues that the distinction between time-based and event-based prospective memory is too simplistic to explain all causes of prospective memory problems. For example, in aviation, four different situations can be distinguished that can result in prospective memory failures (Loukopoulos, Dismukes, & Barshi, 2009). These are interruptions, lack of cues that normally trigger habits, getting caught up in habitual responses, and multitasking.

15.8.3.1 Interruptions

Interruptions are often unavoidable and annoying in everyday life. In some occupations, however, they can result in fatal consequences. For example, a number of major air crashes have resulted from the crew having been interrupted while bringing their aircraft into a flight-ready configuration. After the interruption, they continued with the next task, not realising that the previous task was not yet completed. The reason these interruptions can be so catastrophic is often because they require immediate attention, leaving no opportunity to store the intention to complete the task at hand in working memory. A second reason is that the task immediately following the interruption also demands immediate attention, leaving the operator unable to check the status of the previous task. Finally, it is possible that there are no more cues present to remind the operator that there is still a task to be completed.

15.8.3.2 Breaking Habits

Many of the specialist tasks that are executed by pilots, surgeons, or other highly trained specialists consist of sequences of well-practiced routine actions. These actions are often performed in response to specific cues from the environment. Usually, the execution of these procedures is quite reliable, but there are specific situations that may result in the inability to execute the action in question. A good example of such a routine action is the deployment of the wing flaps on a commercial aircraft. Without these flaps, the aircraft's wings will not be able to generate enough lift to get off the ground during take-off. Various aircraft accidents have shown that external circumstances, such as icing, led to pilots deciding to postpone the completion of the checklist for this phase of the flight until just before take-off, after which the sequence of actions were no longer executed.

15.8.3.3 Formation of Habits

A third factor that plays an important role in prospective memory problems is that an atypical action that might be required for a specific situation is replaced by an inappropriate routine action. Such a situation can also occur during the take-off of a flight. For example, an aircraft may be instructed to take off via a specific route consisting of a sequence of turns and specific instructions to climb to a certain prescribed altitude. Such departure may partly consist of a standard route that is commonly used at the airport in question but may deviate from it at a later stage. Pilots, who are busy with a multitude of tasks during departure, may fall back on their routine and follow the standard route in the later part of the route. In daily life, we can make this kind of mistake when we do not pay attention on a weekend and unconsciously follow our daily route to work again.

15.8.3.4 Multitasking

The last factor that is involved in prospective memory errors is multitasking. As discussed in Chapter 5, there are several limiting factors when performing multiple tasks simultaneously. In most cases, practice allows us to switch flexibly between different tasks, but when problems arise during the performance of one of the two tasks, the phenomenon of cognitive tunnelling may occur (Ververs & Wickens, 2000). Cognitive tunnelling involves situations where one forgets to switch between different tasks. How serious the consequences of tunnelling can be is aptly illustrated by the Eastern Airlines Flight 401 plane crash into the Florida Everglades in 1972. During the descent, the crew had noticed that an indicator light, which was supposed to show that the nose wheel was down, did not turn green. While the plane was circling in a holding pattern, the pilots tried to solve the problem. Every member of the flight crew was so preoccupied with this that nobody realised that the autopilot had accidentally been disengaged and that the aircraft had therefore started a slow and imperceptible decent into the marsh lands surrounding Miami international airport.

15.8.4 THEORETICAL PERSPECTIVES

Finally, we will consider two theoretical perspectives on prospective memory. The previous section shows that many prospective memory failures appear to stem from our limitations in performing complex dual tasks. This limitation suggests that executive processes play an important role in prospective memory. Marsh and Hicks (1998) found evidence for this idea. Participants were required to perform an event-based prospective memory task. When they also had to generate random number sequences, a task that is known to make strong demands on executive processes, their performance on the prospective memory task was significantly impaired, compared to a control condition.

Dual tasks involving the visuospatial sketchpad and the phonological loop had no effect on prospective memory performance, however, implying that it is specifically the executive control processes that interfere with prospective memory. This interference probably occurs because, while performing a prospective memory task, we must continue to monitor the environment for cues that indicate whether we can or should perform the task in question.

The question now is whether prospective memory tasks always demand these active and attentional executive monitoring processes. The two main theoretical frameworks on prospective memory differ in the answer to this question. According to Smith and Bayen's (2005) preparatory attentional and memory processes (PAM) theory, it is 'yes', whereas according to the multiprocess theory developed by Einstein and McDaniel (2005) it is 'sometimes'.

15.8.4.1 PAM Theory

According to the PAM theory (Smith & Bayen, 2005), prospective memory requires two processes. The first is a capacity-demanding monitoring system that is started as soon as we formulate the intention to perform an action. This monitoring system remains active as long as we have not yet carried out the intention. The second is a retrospective memory process, which ensures that we remember which action we intend to perform.

PAM theory is generally well supported by empirical evidence. For example, performance on prospective memory tasks is generally best when participants are able to fully focus their attention on it (McDaniel, Robinson-Riegler, & Einstein, 1998). Moreover, prospective memory tasks may interfere with other tasks when there is no immediate need to perform the task (Smith, 2003). Despite this empirical support, it seems rather implausible that we always need attention when we need to remember a prospective task. Kvavilashvili and Fisher (2007) found evidence that this was indeed not always the case. For example, participants who had to practice a future task often did so on the basis of an external stimulus or on the basis of an internal thought.

Based on the latter results, Smith, Hunt, McVay, and McConnell (2007) modified the PAM theory somewhat so that it no longer assumes that we are continuously engaged in an attentional monitoring process over prolonged periods of time. For example, when we have to run an errand on the way home, we will only start thinking about it when we are actually on our way. Smith et al., however, remain convinced that retrieving the intention to perform a task always involves a cost and always requires attention.

15.8.4.2 Multiprocess Theory

According to the multiprocess theory (Einstein & McDaniel, 2005) the execution of planned actions takes place primarily on the basis of a variety of cognitive processes, including attention. However, in contrast to PAM theory, Einstein and McDaniel argue that much of the execution of these tasks takes place on the basis of cues from the environment that are associated with the task at hand. Einstein and McDaniel further hypothesise that these cues are salient. Attention is drawn to these cues because of the demands of the ongoing task.

An important difference with the PAM theory is that the multiprocess theory assumes that the retrieval of an intention can, in principle, take place automatically and without monitoring. Einstein et al. (2005) found evidence for this idea on the basis of a word verification task, in which participants had to judge whether a given word fit into a sentence. This task was combined with a prospective memory task, in which participants had to react to a specific target word from time to time. Slightly more than half of the participants were slower in the dual-task condition than in the single-task condition. The other participants showed no delay, which implies that these participants were able to perform the prospective memory task at no extra cost.

In a second study, Einstein et al. (2005) compared PAM theory more directly with multiprocess theory. Here, participants performed a complex task in which they were first presented with a specific target word to be used in the prospective memory task. Next, participants had to rate seven items on representability, after which they had to decide for another 18 trials whether letter sequences were words or **non-words** (a lexical decision task; see Chapter 17). Finally, they had to rate another seven items for predictability. While judging predictability, participants had to press a button as soon as they perceived the previously given target word. In the lexical decision task, however, they did not have to do so. According to the PAM theory, participants would not monitor during the lexical decision task, so the prospective memory task would not interfere with task performance on the lexical decision task. According to the multiprocess theory, the target word would activate automatic processes that would interfere with the lexical decisions. The results obtained by Einstein et al. were consistent with the latter view, suggesting that, indeed, we mainly use external cues.

Smith et al. (2007) were not convinced by this result, however, because of the relatively small effects reported by Einstein et al. and because none of their experimental manipulations met all the criteria for an automatic task. For this reason, Smith et al. conducted an experiment in which the prospective memory task consisted of simply pressing the 'p' key as soon as a pink stimulus appeared. Despite its simplicity, this task had a disruptive effect on the central task that participants had to perform. These results are consistent with Smith et al.'s assumption that prospective memory tasks do always require some processing capacity.

15.9 SUMMARY

Traditional memory studies often use relatively trivial items that have to be memorised. The main focus of these studies is how many items can be remembered, how long they can be remembered, and whether there is a distinction between the different types of items. In most cases, the items that are used have little personal relevance to the individual. Studies involving everyday memory, on the other hand, focus on memories that are personally relevant, how they are stored during our lifespans, and how they contribute to the generation of our self-image. An important consequence of this approach is that the accuracy of personal memories can be verified against external sources. Studies in which participants were instructed to retell stories have shown that these retellings often contain significant distortions, and that these distortions can eventually affect how these memories are retained.

Wagenaar introduced an influential method of studying everyday memory by noting his memories of several daily events in a diary, along with several cues. The number of cues he needed to retrieve a memory increased as a function of the time between the event and the memory test. Although diary studies have contributed to our knowledge of everyday memory, they are limited because many memories of major events are not restricted to daily activities but include larger episodes involving multiple days, months, or years. In time, several daily episodes merge into larger life themes that collectively form autobiographical memory. This autobiographical memory comprises our personal life story and plays an important role in the creation of our self-image.

Conway and colleagues have argued that autobiographical memory is a crucial part of a self-memory system, in which personal memories are linked to personal life goals. Autobiographical memories can be generated through generative or direct retrieval. Generative retrieval operates on the basis of an associative process, whereas direct retrieval is triggered in a more automatic way via a cue. The triggering of memories by specific odours is a good example of direct retrieval.

Flashbulb memories are generated by important dramatic and public events. According to some researchers, they are a special form of memory, because some of the initial studies appeared to show that they are particularly accurate and salient. Subsequent studies have shown, however, that flashbulb memories are susceptible to the same type of distortion as ordinary memories, but they are remembered as particularly vivid for a number of specific reasons.

When examining the distribution of memories in older adults, we notice that they are not evenly distributed across their lifespan but that they are, on the one hand, characterised by a complete lack of memories from before the age of three and, on the other hand, by a relatively concentrated number of memories from the period between the age of 10 and 30 years. Childhood amnesia might be explained, among other things, by the idea that very young children have no self-image yet, while the fact that the hippocampus is still developing may also play a role, because old memories can be overgrown by new neural connections and the formation of new neurons, which continues in the hippocampus for a number of years after birth.

For the reminiscence bump, a life script may be involved in the increase in the number of memories that are reported during adolescence and early adulthood. Precisely because many unique changes take place in an individual's personal life during this period, this period is also rich in unique and salient memories, which implies that they are also better consolidated. This is specifically the case for voluntary, spontaneously retrieved positive memories.

Cabeza and St Jacques have introduced an influential neurobiological model for autobiographical memory. This model describes six main processes involved in memory: search, self-reference, recollection, emotion, visual processing, and monitoring for accuracy.

An important practical application of everyday memory concerns eyewitness testimonies. Several studies have shown that these testimonies are often highly inaccurate. There are several possible reasons for these inaccuracies, such as false memories, confirmation bias, intrusions of cognitive schemas, influence by the interviewer or by the situation, or selective attention due to threat.

In addition to these issues, it has been found that many witnesses have difficulties with identifying a potential perpetrator. A common method for identifying perpetrators is by using line-ups. Identification is often complicated by the fact that we generally have many more difficulties with identifying unfamiliar faces than with familiar ones. In addition, the other-race effect, the phenomenon that we are generally better able to recognise people of our own ethnicity than those of another, may hamper our ability to identify perpetrators. Finally, the likelihood that incorrect information results in a false memory is much more pronounced among old adults than among young adults, while older adults often have more confidence in their memory.

One procedure to improve eyewitness testimony is to use a cognitive interview. This cognitive interview involves a number of structured steps that encourage the witness to view the crime scene from a number of different perspectives. In addition, improvements in the procedures used in line-ups can also result in a more reliable identification of offenders.

Because autobiographical memory is based on reconstructive processes, we can easily construct memories from false information. These false memories were initially described by Loftus and colleagues based on their Lost in the Mall experiment. Subsequent studies have shown that false memories can also occur during word-list learning. Some individuals are characterised by a particularly good autobiographical memory. These individuals are described as having a hyperthymic syndrome and they are often characterised by an obsession with their own past. In theory, this could make them less susceptible to false memories. However, this does not appear to be the case.

The problem of false memories is particularly important in our judicial system. Evidence has recently been found to show that it is relatively easy to convince people that they once committed a crime.

A final aspect of everyday memory concerns actions that must be performed in the future. Prospective memory is involved in remembering an action that has yet to be performed and monitoring the environment for the time when this action can or must be performed. Prospective memory can be either time-based or event-based.

Prospective memory is involved in many everyday tasks, and problems with it can sometimes lead to life-threatening situations. Analysis of accidents in the aviation industry suggests that many pilot errors often stem from problems with prospective memory. These errors often involve resuming an interrupted task, missing cues that prompt a person to perform routine actions or performing a routine action when an atypical action was required. In addition, forgetting to switch between multiple tasks can also cause problems.

Two theoretical approaches to prospective memory differ in the extent to which they call for attention. The preparatory attentional and memory processes (PAM) theory assumes that we need to continuously monitor the environment to perform a prospective task, whereas the multiprocess theory assumes we can infer this mainly on the basis of cues from the environment. There is no unequivocal evidence yet for one of the two perspectives. Some studies are better explained by the PAM theory, yet other processes are better explained by the multiprocess theory.

FURTHER READING

Loftus, E. F. (1996). *Eyewitness testimony*. Cambridge, MA: Harvard University Press.

Rubin, D. C. (1999). *Remembering our past: Studies in autobiographical memory*. Cambridge, UK: Cambridge University Press.

Thompson, C. P., Skowronski, J. J., Larsen, S. F., & Betz, A. L. (1996). *Autobiographical memory: Remembering what and remembering when*. Mahwah, NJ: Lawrence Erlbaum Associates.

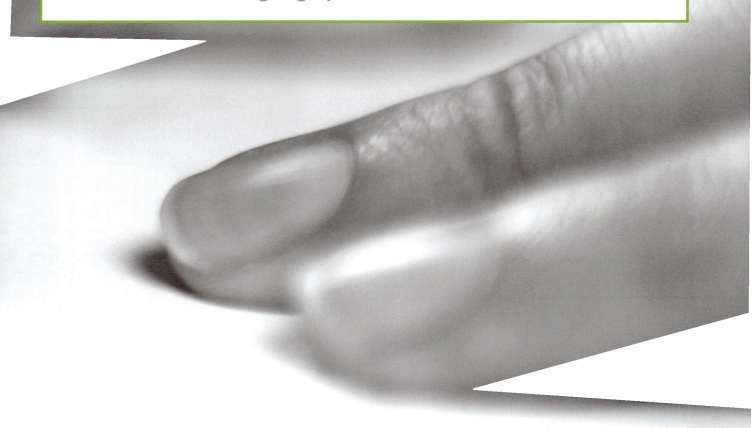

PART 7

The Psychology of Language

CHAPTER 16
Language functions

16.1 INTRODUCTION

Imagine a world without language. What would it be like? It is almost impossible to imagine. Almost all the knowledge you have would be gone. The representation that you have of others would be based entirely on the primary sensory impressions that you had acquired during your life. No one would have a name, and you would have to deduce other people's intentions from non-verbal signals. However, upon close consideration, we might also conclude that these non-verbal signals are a form of language and would thus also be non-existent in our imaginary world. We would not be able to form abstract concepts and our higher cognitive abilities would probably be completely absent.

We may thus conclude that language, and in particular its communicative aspect, is crucial for us. In this first chapter on language, we will focus on the social and intellectual functions of language, along with the cognitive processes that form the basis for communication. After this, we will deal with the processes of language perception and production in more detail in the next two chapters. The purpose of this first chapter is therefore twofold. First, we focus on the social aspect of language. The central question in this part is how interlocutors manage to understand each other. An important challenge in conducting a conversation is that we must consider our conversation partner's level of knowledge. How are we able to do so and what cues do we use to ensure a smooth conversation? A related problem is how we should decide when language is not to be taken literally.

The second major theme of this chapter is how we can use language to form mental representations or situation models and how we can manipulate these models. The processing of long texts results in situation models that are not just based on the text that is being read; they are supplemented with details from our existing background knowledge. We will thus consider how we build such situation models from language. Finally, we will discuss how we best communicate our own ideas to someone else. In other words, how do we develop an efficient writing style?

16.2 WHAT IS LANGUAGE?

Harley (2014) describes language as a system of symbols and rules that enables us to communicate. The symbols represent other things: words, spoken or written, are symbols. The rules describe how the symbols should be ordered to form sentences. This description contains a number of core properties of language, such as the fact that specific things can be represented by symbols and the fact that there are rules that impose restrictions on the possible combinations. Language is thus characterised by semantics and syntax. **Semantics** deals with the meaning of words, and **syntax** deals with the rules that govern the ordering of words.

A major problem, however, is that there is no formal definition of language. The absence of such a definition makes it difficult to determine which requirements an organism must meet before it qualifies as mastering language. More specifically, the absence of such a definition makes it difficult to address the questions of whether (1) language is innate, and (2) whether language is unique to humans. Communication is an important property of language, yet it is also involved in thinking, storing information, expressing emotions, pretending to be animals (e.g., imitating the barking of dogs), or identifying with a group (e.g., cheering or singing along at a rock concert).

16.2.1 IS LANGUAGE UNIQUE TO HUMANS?

In his influential book 'The knowledge of language: it's nature, origin, and use', the American linguist Noam Chomsky (1957) argued that language is innate. Moreover, Chomsky (1959) strongly argued against the then prevailing view among behaviourists that language is nothing more than a series of conditioned responses to a series of stimuli. According to Chomsky, the brain contains a language centre that enables us to generate an infinite number of sentences based on a limited set of rules, and that this ability is unique to humans. He reasoned that if animals had an aptitude for language, it would be very unlikely that they would not use it. Evolutionary biologists, however, argue that without a thorough study of each and every form of communication

DOI: 10.4324/9781003319344-23

Figure 16.1 Associations related to the symbol for 'gorilla' that are assumed to be present in a bonobo's semantic memory. Also shown on the right are the errors that were generated in connection to the symbol for 'gorilla'. (source: Lyn, 2007)

that might be possible in animals, Chomsky's claim cannot be justified (Corballis, 2017). The biologists therefore argue that the sudden emergence of a complex cognitive function such as language is highly improbable. They also point to the anatomical and physiological similarities between human brains and those of other species. Moreover, several studies have hinted at the presence of a rudimentary form of language comprehension in dolphins and primates (see fig 16.1). It should be noted, however, that these forms of language comprehension are typically not characterised by the use of syntax (Lyn, 2007).

16.2.2 IS LANGUAGE INNATE?

Although Chomsky argued that language is innate, there is also much controversy on this point. One reason for this is that Chomsky assumed the existence of an innate universal grammar. That is, a set of universal grammatical principles that can be found in any language. Although it is not clear what this universal grammar exactly consists of there are specific properties of a language that may be part of it. These include the different lexical categories (nouns, verbs, prefixes, etc.), word order, and recursion. Chomsky's ideas have been considerably revised in recent decades, and in particular the idea of a universal grammar has been narrowed down so that it actually only includes recursion, that

is, the phenomenon that an additional clause can always be inserted into an existing sentence.

Christiansen and Chater (2008) fundamentally disagree with Chomsky's notion of a universal grammar. First, they argue that there is an enormous amount of variability among languages. These differences are so extensive that they make a universal grammar highly unlikely. Secondly, it is also highly unlikely that natural selection has given us genes that can handle properties of languages that we have never experienced. Thirdly, languages change extremely quickly. For example, the entire collection of Indo-European languages emerged in less than 10,000 years (Baronchelli, Chater, Pastor-Satorras, & Christiansen, 2012). This diversity cannot be easily explained by natural selection. Fourthly, Christiansen and Chater argue that language is shaped by the brain: language reflects existing human learning and processing mechanisms.

Based on the latter argument, Christiansen and Chater have concluded that children can learn a language so easily because it has adapted to the limitations of our human cognitive abilities. The fact that we can learn a language is, in other words, not the result of a universal language organ, but because we can use existing cognitive processes in a flexible way to achieve this.

16.2.3 PIDGIN LANGUAGES

Bickerton (1984) introduced the bioprogram hypothesis. This hypothesis states that children, even without exposure to a language in early childhood, eventually develop a grammar. Evidence for this hypothesis has been found in studies of pidgin languages. These are new, primitive languages that emerge when two or more groups of people, each with a different native language, are brought together. For example, towards the beginning of the 20th century, workers from China, Japan, Korea, Puerto Rico, Portugal, and the Philippines were brought together in Hawaii as sugar plantation workers. These workers developed a pidgin language that was very simple and lacked grammatical structure. However, the descendants of these workers have developed a new language, which is complex and contains a full-fledged grammar.

Further evidence that we can spontaneously develop a new language was reported by Sanghas, Kita, and Özyürek (2004). They studied deaf children in Nicaragua. Attempts to teach these children Spanish were mostly unsuccessful. Sanghas et al. noticed, however, that these children had developed a new system of gestures that spontaneously developed into a new sign language. This sign language was later passed on to new children who took part in the programme. Since the new sign language showed no similarities to either Spanish or the official sign language of Nicaragua, we may conclude that the resulting language was a completely new one. Although these results show that people have a strong intrinsic, innate motivation to learn a language, they do not provide evidence for an innate universal grammar.

16.2.4 GENETIC RESEARCH

The notion that some aspects of language acquisition are innate is consistent with the results from studies investigating the genetic basis of language (Graham & Fisher, 2013; Grigorenko, 2009), since some individual differences can be traced back to genetic factors. For example, about half the members of a London-based family were characterised by severe language impairments. Genetic testing showed that the affected family members had an anomaly in a gene known as FOX2P (Lai, Gerrelli, Monaco, Fisher, & Copp, 2003). Presumably, this gene is involved in the expression of specific brain functions that are involved in language processing. In addition to this gene, other genes, such as the ATP2C2 and CMIP genes, have been found to play a role in language processing. FOX2P has also been found in other animal species. It is therefore incorrect to assume that FOX2P is a language gene. It probably does play a role in language processing because it affects generic brain functions that happen to be involved in language processing.

16.3 DOES LANGUAGE INFLUENCE OUR THINKING?

One of the best-known theories on the relationship between language and thought is Benjamin Lee Whorf's (1956) linguistic relativity theory. This theory states that language influences our thinking (see fig 16.2). There are various ways in which this could happen (Wolff & Holmes, 2011). According

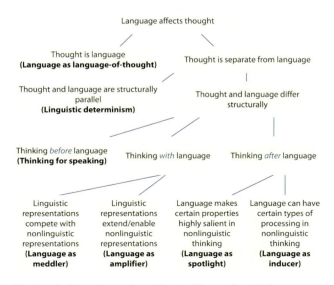

Figure 16.2 Schematic overview of the possible ways in which language can influence our thoughts. (source: Wolff & Holmes, 2011)

to the most extreme form of the Whorfian theory, differences in language will irrevocably lead to differences in thought. A more moderate position is that differences in language influence cognitive functions such as perception and memory.

Evidence for the idea that language can influence perception comes from categorisation research (see also Chapter 20). A general finding from these studies is that participants are generally more accurate in distinguishing stimuli that belong to different categories than in distinguishing stimuli that belong to the same category. Moreover, several studies have shown that participants can distinguish stimuli better when their language has different words for these stimuli. For example, the Russian language has different words for light blue and dark blue, and Russian participants were better able to discriminate stimuli that met the category of light blue (*siniy*) than English participants (Winawer et al., 2007).

A similar study was carried out by Robertson, Davies, and Davidoff (2000) based on colour perception among the Berinmo, a tribe living in Papua New Guinea. The Berinmo language is characterised by having only five colour terms. Tribe members do not distinguish between the colour categories green and blue, but they do distinguish the categories *nol* (roughly equivalent to green) and *wor* (roughly equivalent to yellow). Robertson et al. presented three colours and asked their participants to choose the two that were the most similar. If two stimuli were normally described as green and the third as blue, we would probably select the two green ones. However, we should not necessarily expect the Berinmo to do so, because their language does not distinguish between green and blue. Similarly, if the Berinmo were presented with two *nol*-stimuli and a *wor*-stimulus, we should expect them to select the two *nol*-stimuli. This is indeed what Robertson et al. found.

Lupyan, Abdel Rahman, Boroditsky, and Clark (2020) explain these effects on the basis of a predictive coding mechanism. According to their explanation, predictions that are generated by colour labels cause the colour representations in our minds to be warped, such that all colours that are described by the same colour label appear to be more similar, whereas colours that are described by different labels appear to be more distinct.

16.4 ADVANTAGES AND DISADVANTAGES OF MULTILINGUALISM

Many people nowadays master two or more languages. Although most of the studies that we discuss within the field of psycholinguistics deal with the processing of one specific language, it is interesting to consider the effects of multilingualism on our cognitive abilities. While mastering more than one language obviously offers various advantages from a social perspective, another intriguing benefit of bilingualism was suggested around the turn of the century. When we master more than one language, we have to select which language to use and inhibit potential intrusions from another language. For this reason, **bilingualism** was expected to have a positive effect on cognitive control processes.

A few studies initially provided some evidence for a **bilingual advantage effect**, ranging from phonological awareness (Bialystok, Majumder, & Martin, 2003) to task switching (Prior & Macwhinney, 2009). More recently, however, it has been argued that the theoretical basis for a bilingual advantage effect is very weak (Hartsuiker, 2015), and it has also been found that the original results are very difficult to replicate. In an extensive literature review, Paap and Greenberg (2013) argued, for example, that the empirical studies on the bilingual advantage effect yield highly contradictory and inconsistent results. For instance, Morton and Harper (2007) found that bilingual advantages disappeared after controlling for factors such as socio-economic status. Finally, based on a literature review, Blanco-Elorrieta and Pylkkanen (2018) have concluded that switching between two languages is in itself a process that requires little mental effort, so that multilinguals' reliance on cognitive control processes is also very limited.

16.5 PSYCHOLINGUISTICS AS A SCIENTIFIC DISCIPLINE

Psycholinguistics aims to explain which cognitive functions are involved in the understanding, comprehension, and production of language. Since we cannot observe these cognitive functions directly, we must try to understand language processes by manipulating every possible aspect of a language imaginable so that we can measure the effect of these manipulations on behaviour. For language perception, there are several standard methods that we can use for this purpose. For example, we can measure a participant's reading speed, record their eye movement patterns during a reading task, or identify the errors they make when reading.

For speech perception, we can also manipulate the properties of language, for example by masking specific parts of a sentence and by determining the effects of such manipulations on the intelligibility of speech. We can also manipulate sentences by, for example, placing words in a sentence that a listener will not expect.

16.5.1 LANGUAGE FEATURES INFLUENCING WORD RECOGNITION

Psycholinguistics frequently takes ingenious advantage of the complexities of language to uncover the underlying cognitive processes. An important factor here is **word frequency**; that is, the fact that some words occur much more frequently in a language than others. Another factor to consider is the use of **homophones**, that is, words (such as 'rows' and 'rose') that have the same pronunciation but have a different spelling and meaning. Homophones can be used, for example, to investigate whether the sound of words (i.e., **phonology**) affects their processing. We also have words with multiple meanings, such as 'bank' (riverside or financial institution) or 'rose' (flower or past tense of rise). These are examples of **homographs**. When processing these kinds of words, context will determine which of the alternative interpretations should be chosen.

A word is defined as a meaningful, pronounceable array of letters. In linguistics, a further distinction can be made between non-words and pseudo-words. **Pseudo-words** are meaningless units, which, according to the rules of the language in question, can be pronounced (and therefore, in principle, could have been 'real' words). **Non-words** consist of a random array of letters that cannot be pronounced. In psycholinguistics, however, the term 'non-word' is frequently used as a synonym for 'pseudo-word', and this convention will also be followed in the remainder of this book.

16.5.2 RESEARCH METHODS

A very important goal of psycholinguistics involves the development of tasks that take advantage of the aforementioned properties of language. Some of these tasks include the **lexical decision task**, the **word naming task**, and the **priming task**. The lexical decision task consists of presenting participants a series of letters, after which they must decide, as quickly as possible, whether the sequence in question is a word or a non-word. In the naming task, participants are presented with a printed word that has to be named as quickly as possible. In both tasks, reaction time can be influenced by properties such as word frequency, but also for example by phonology or the semantic meaning of a word. Finally, the priming task also requires participants to find a target word as quickly as possible, but in this case another word is presented immediately before the target word, which may or may not be related to it (Meyer & Schvaneveldt, 1971).

16.6 SPEECH AS A MEANS OF COMMUNICATION

Many studies approach the psychology of language from the rather narrow perspective of the monologue, whereas the most common forms of language take the form of a dialogue, in which speech perception and speech production are strongly intertwined (Pickering & Garrod, 2004, 2013). For this reason, it is not only insufficient to discuss speech production and speech perception separately, it is also essential to consider the communicative aspect of speech; that is, the interactions between speakers and listeners.

The study of language as a means of communication is complementary to the studies of language perception and production but extends them by discussing how speakers and listeners switch roles and to what extent they can take each other's position into account. Here, not only the content but also the form of communication is important. For this reason, the importance of partner-specific processing (i.e., the way in which your interlocutor processes language-specific information) and audience design (the study of the ways in which a speaker adapts his or her communication to the needs of the audience) has recently become increasingly important in theories of language processing.

16.6.1 GRICEAN MAXIMS

The British philosopher Herbert Paul Grice (fig 16.3) was one of the first to discuss the conditions that spoken language had to satisfy for it to serve as an efficient means of communication (Grice, 1967). Grice based his discussion on the **cooperative principle**, according to which speakers and listeners try to cooperate as much as possible while trying to understand each other. Based on this principle, Grice formulated nine maxims that any good form of communication must satisfy. These maxims can be divided into four groups, namely those of quantity, quality, relation, and manner. These maxims are, successively:

The maxims of quantity

1. Make your contribution as informative as necessary.
2. Do not make your contribution more informative than necessary.

Figure 16.3 Paul Herbert Grice (1913–1998).

The maxims of quality

3. Do not say something you think is wrong.
4. Do not say something for which you have no evidence.

The maxim of relation

5. Be relevant.

The maxims of manner

6. Avoid obscure expressions.
7. Avoid ambiguities.
8. Be brief (avoid unnecessary elaboration).
9. Be orderly.

In practice, speakers regularly violate these rules, however. For example, some speakers, such as politicians and used car salesmen, are guided by self-interest and will therefore often violate one or more of these maxims (Faulkner, 2008). Even when this is not the case, it often happens that speakers produce unnecessarily detailed sentences. Whether this is the case, however, depends on the complexity of the situation (Davies & Katsos, 2013).

16.6.2 COMMON GROUND

For optimal communication, speakers and listeners must strive to match each other's needs. Audience design relates to the way speakers tailor their speech to a specific audience. One of the ways in which this can be done is by having the speaker try to find a **common ground**. Because the speaker and listener often start from different perspectives, and occasionally possess different levels of background knowledge, the search for common ground implies that the speaker has to consider the perspective of the listener and vice versa.

16.6.2.1 Audience Design: the Speaker's Perspective

An essential aspect of language as a means of communication is that effective speakers adapt to the needs of their audience. In doing so, they can, for example, make use of reference material that is available to both the speaker and the listener. This reference material can be physical, that is, in the form of objects that can be perceived by both speaker and listener, but also linguistic, that is, in the form of information that was mentioned earlier in a conversation. The adjustments that speakers must make are known as **audience design** and can be made on the basics of various assumptions about the listener. Global assumptions include characteristics such as the listener's preferred language or general knowledge, but also shared personal experiences that the speaker can refer to. Local assumptions relate to what the listener knows or attends to at a specific moment. In general, speakers make more incorrect local assumptions than global ones, because the former are more volatile and change more often than the latter (Arnold, 2008).

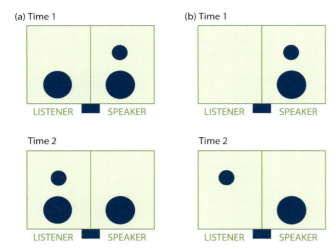

(a) Time 1   (b) Time 1

LISTENER   SPEAKER   LISTENER   SPEAKER

Time 2   Time 2

LISTENER   SPEAKER   LISTENER   SPEAKER

Figure 16.4 Examples of displays used to investigate the extent to which speakers take account of the common ground. (a) When there is a shared context, as represented here by a large circle at the bottom of the display, speakers can use this to describe a target object to a listener before the listener actually perceives the object. (b) A similar situation, but now the reference object is not visible to the listener, so the speaker should not refer to it either. (source: Horton and Keysar, 1996)

Horton and Keysar (1996) aimed to determine how speakers can establish a common ground. Participants were engaged in a communication game, in which they were required to describe an object to the experimenter's assistant (fig 16.4). These objects, which consisted of simple and relatively easy to recognise clip art items, were initially shown only to the speaker, who had to describe the items to the listener. Next, the items were shown to the listener, who then had to judge whether the speaker's description was adequate. To manipulate to presence of a common ground, some trials used a reference object that was visible to both the speaker and the listener. Here, the speaker could now use the properties of this reference object to describe the unknown object. For example, if a relatively large circle was used as a reference object and the object to be described was a smaller circle, the speaker could describe this object as a relatively small circle. However, in some trials the reference object was only available to the speaker and not to the listener, so the speaker could not use the properties of this reference object.

The question in which Horton and Keysar were particularly interested was whether speakers automatically consider the common ground, or whether they tend to act from their own egocentric perspective. It is a plausible assumption that speakers automatically take the common ground into account when this information is available, and that speakers therefore incorporate this information directly into the **initial design** of their communication. If the speakers automatically take the common ground into account, it should make no difference whether they formulate their descriptions under time pressure or not. If, however, they are more inclined to think from their own perspective, time pressure should reveal that participants initially show a stronger tendency to refer to the reference object, even if this object is not available to the listener. This is indeed what the participants did. When they formulated object descriptions under a time constraint, they initially stuck more to descriptions that referred to the reference object, without taking the listener's perspective into account. Subsequent, additional information was better adapted to the listener's perspective.

Thus, it appears that the speaker's ability to adapt to the listener's perspective is limited. Instead, it appears that speakers start from an **egocentric heuristic** that is adjusted to the needs of the listener on the basis of feedback. According to the **monitoring and adjustment model**, speakers do not directly consider the perspective of the listeners, implying that not all utterances contribute directly to effective communication. An important consequence of this idea is that speakers monitor and check their own utterances for effectiveness and may notice that they violate the common ground. According to Horton and Keysar, speakers do not use context because it is shared with the listener, but because this context is salient for themselves. It is only because this salient context is sometimes shared by the listener that it appears that speakers automatically take the listener into account.

Fukumura and van Gompel (2012) found that speakers tend to generate descriptions from their own perspectives when they have to describe simple scenes to a listener. Speakers are often relatively specific in the first sentence, for example, when referring to an object they use a description such as 'the red book', whereas in subsequent sentences they tend to fall back on a simple reference ('it'). This reference is only appropriate when the listener has fully understood the first sentence. In many cases, the speakers still used this reference even when the listener had not heard the first sentence, which implies that in such cases the speakers were acting mainly from their own perspectives.

Despite the difficulties that speakers have in maintaining a common ground, there are simple and effective strategies that can be, and often are, used to enhance the effectiveness of communication. Speakers often copy words, phrases, and ideas from their interlocutor. These expressions thus serve as a prime. An example of such use of priming is found in the case of **syntactic priming**. In syntactic priming, the syntactic structure used by one person is unconsciously adopted by the other. The use of the passive form, for example, increases the likelihood that this sentence will be followed up by another passive sentence by the interlocutor (Pickering & Ferreira, 2008).

16.6.2.2 Audience Design: The Listener's Perspective

The second question is to what extent listeners take a shared context into account. Keysar et al. (2000) investigated this by using an experimental set-up such as the one

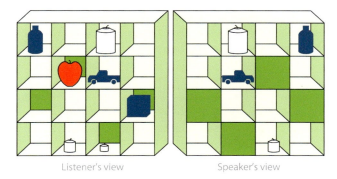

Figure 16.5 Illustration of an experiment to investigate the extent to which listeners take account of the common ground. According to the speakers' direction, they have to move objects that are positioned in the rack and had to consider the fact that the speakers cannot see some objects. (source: Keysar, Barr, Balin, and Brauner, 2000)

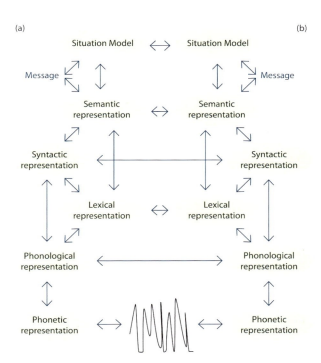

Figure 16.6 A schematic overview of various automatic processes involved in creating a common ground. (source: Pickering and Garrod, 2004)

shown in Figure 16.5. A speaker and a listener were each seated on opposite sides of a rack in which a number of different objects were placed. A few openings on the speaker's side were covered so that the speaker could only see two candles, while the listener could see three. The speaker, an accomplice of the experimenter, instructed the listener to move 'the smallest candle'. However, the smallest candle in the rack was in a compartment that was not visible to the speaker. If the listeners were to use the common ground, they would not move the smallest candle in the rack, but the smallest candle that was visible to the speaker.

In addition to the listener's behaviour (i.e., which candle they actually moved), their eye movements were also recorded. These recordings showed that the listeners initially fixated on the smallest candle in the rack and then made a corrective eye movement towards the candle that was the smallest from the speaker's perspective. The results thus also show that listeners sometimes use an egocentric heuristic when interpreting speech. According to Keysar et al. this egocentric heuristic may cause listeners to detect ambiguities with relatively little cognitive effort, taking advantage of corrections from the speaker's side, when it turns out that not considering the common ground results in an incorrect interpretation.

According to Ferreira (2008) speaking should serve language comprehension. It follows from this that speakers should also strive to produce speech that is easy to understand. In practice, however, they hardly avoid ambiguities at all, whereas for the listener it is often precisely these ambiguities that make spoken language difficult to understand. Despite these problems, however, speech is typically informative enough for the listener to decipher what the speaker means. This implies that a balance is reached where both the speaker and the listener have to invest a certain amount of effort to understand each other. If the speaker is very careful to avoid all ambiguities, it will make it easier for the listener to understand, but at the cost of the effort the speaker has to invest. Similarly, a sloppy speaker will require a lot of effort from the listener.

Because the interlocutors often lack the processing power to maximise the common ground, Pickering and Garrod (2004) argue that is rare for participants to explicitly adopt the other person's perspective.

According to Pickering and Garrod (2004), however, several automatic processes ensure a relatively effortless processing of the common ground (see fig 16.6). For instance, interlocutors frequently copy each other's phrasing, make use of each others' ideas, or take advantage of syntactic priming. Shintel and Keysar (2009) add that the interaction between interlocutors facilitates the automatic emergence of a shared context for mutual understanding.

16.6.3 NON-VERBAL ASPECTS OF COMMUNICATION

Although communication is primarily verbal, it is easy to imagine how quickly an endless string of words, read out in a machine-like fashion without intonation or pause, would quickly become extremely boring, causing the listener to lose focus. Therefore, many non-verbal cues are involved in enhancing communication and the understanding of spoken language.

16.6.3.1 Role Switching

During a conversation, it is very rare for interlocutors to speak simultaneously. They alternate with remarkable ease, with pauses between two speakers that generally do not exceed 500 ms. The smoothness of the alternation can be explained by the fact that individuals engaged in a conversation tend to follow certain implicit rules (Sacks, Schegloff, & Jefferson, 1974). For example, by looking at listeners, speakers can invite them to switch roles. In addition, other non-verbal signals, such as hand gestures or meaningless sounds, also have important signalling functions that facilitate the switching of roles. Moreover, the expectation that the roles are to be changed can also be given in a more explicit manner by using a so-called **adjacency pair**, that is, a conversational unit that implies a role change. Examples of adjacency pairs involve a greeting, which will be followed by a greeting from the interlocutor; or a question, which will be followed by an answer.

16.6.3.2 Gestures

Consider talking to someone on the phone. Depending on the conversation, it is not unlikely that we enliven it with a large number of gestures. Likewise, when observing people in the street who are engaged in a conversation, we can often guess the nature of the conversation based on the gestures they make. For example, gestures are clear giveaways as to whether people are arguing or joking with each other. We may therefore assume that gestures facilitate communication one way or another, because the speaker gives visual cues to the listener that enhance comprehension. However, even when we cannot see the listener, such as during a telephone conversation, we will still make these types of gestures quite frequently.

Bavelas, Gerwing, Sutton, and Prevost (2008) investigated the extent to which specific factors contribute to people making gestures. To this end, they asked participants to describe an 18th-century painting in (1) a face-to-face conversation, (2) a telephone conversation, and (3) a monologue that was recorded on a tape recorder. The gestures made by participants were larger and more expressive in the face-to-face conversation. In addition, the gestures were also more interwoven in the communication: they contained information that was sometimes referred to in the verbal communication. When communicating via telephone, the participants made more gestures than when they recorded their description via a monologue on tape, but these gestures were less meaningful. Thus, it appears that gestures are part of a dialogue, whereas during a monologue we are less strongly inclined to produce them.

16.6.3.3 Prosodic Cues

Prosodic cues are formed by rhythm, emphasis, and intonation; they make it easier for a listener to understand a message. The extent to which speakers make use of prosodic cues depends strongly on the situation. For example, prosody is more likely to be used in spontaneous communication than when people are reading ambiguous sentences out loud.

According to Snedeker and Trueswell (2003) the probability of using prosodic cues is much higher when the context fails to clarify the meaning of an ambiguous sentence. For example, the sentence 'The man beat the dog with the stick' may refer to a dog being beaten with a stick or to a dog having a stick and being beaten. Inserting a pause after 'dog' will disambiguate the meaning of the sentence in favour of the first interpretation, whereas inserting a pause after 'beat' will disambiguate the sentence in favour of the second interpretation instead. Although prosodic cues can resolve syntactic ambiguities, Kraljic and Brennan (2005) suggest that speakers do not adapt their style to meet the needs of a listener. When producing spontaneous speech, speakers produce prosodic cues in abundance, but this production is spontaneous rather than targeted towards meeting the specific needs of the listener.

16.6.3.4 Discourse Markers

An important difference between spontaneous utterances and a well-rehearsed speech is that the former is full of seemingly meaningless utterances, such as 'you know', 'well, 'and' or 'so…'. These so-called **discourse markers** do not directly contribute to the content of a conversation, but they nevertheless appear to have a function. For instance, Flowerdew and Tauroza (1995) found that participants understood a video recording of a lecture much better when the discourse markers were left in than when they were edited out.

Moreover, Bolden (2006) found that discourse markers that are specific to the English language also served specific purposes. For example, 'oh' was frequently uttered when the speaker wanted to start a new topic, while 'so' was mainly used when the utterance was directly relevant to the listener. The use of discourse markers also appears to depend on context. For example, markers such as 'oh' and 'well' are widely used in spontaneous speech, but much less so in interviews, whereas this difference was not the case for, for example, 'like', 'yeah', and 'I mean' (Fuller, 2003) (see fig 16.7).

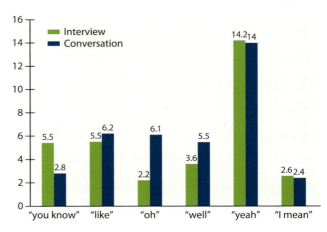

Figure 16.7 The relative frequency of discourse markers during spontaneous conversations and formal interviews. (source: Fuller, 2003)

16.7 SIGN LANGUAGE

Non-verbal forms of communication, such as prosody and gestures, already imply the possibility that language forms other than speech and writing exist. Of these forms, sign language is probably the best known. Although it was, until recently, only studied to a limited extent, interest in sign language has increased sharply in recent years. It is not only the output modality that is different to that of speaking or writing, sign language itself is also intrinsically different. There is, for instance, no universal sign language, and existing sign languages are not a manual form of the corresponding spoken languages. American and British sign languages, are, for example, not interchangeable (Hickok, Bellugi, & Klima, 1996).

Although sign languages are characterised by the same linguistic features as ordinary languages, it is in particular the output modality that is drastically different, and it also takes significantly longer to produce the basic units of language – hand gestures – compared to a spoken language. In addition, sign language relies intrinsically on spatial processes, which might also imply that the cognitive functions involved in processing sign language involve more right hemispheric processes, compared to regular languages. However, this does not appear to be the case: Hickok et al. (1996) found a strong left hemispheric lateralisation for both sign language processing and regular language processing.

The study of sign language may also be able to address how mental representations are formed in short-term linguistic memory. Some researchers argue that this representation takes the form of an abstract phonological code, while others argue that it takes a more general sensory form (Pa, Wilson, Pickell, Bellugi, & Hickok, 2008). An fMRI study involving participants that were fluent in both English and American Sign Language reported that linguistic representations that had to be retained in memory activated brain areas that were partly modality specific (including visual areas in the occipital cortex) and partly modality independent (Buchsbaum et al., 2005; Pa et al., 2008).

16.8 SELF-MONITORING

16.8.1 LANGUAGE AND MONITORING

The communicative aspect of language emphasises its social function: after all, our language is of crucial importance for the exchange of information. As such, language is most likely strongly related to social cognition. Social cognition focuses, among other things, on how two individuals interact (see Chapter 23). The impact of these interactions on language perception and production was, however, originally severely underestimated.

Pickering and Garrod (2013) argue, however, that the processes of language perception and production are highly integrated. For a conversation to run smoothly, we must simultaneously produce our own contribution and process the information from our interlocutor. This requires a high degree of flexibility, as we constantly have to monitor both ourselves and our interlocutor and adapt our own speech production to the new information we receive from our interlocutor. This self-monitoring process influences both our own speech production and our speech perception. Pickering and Garrod illustrate this dynamic interaction with the following simple examples:

1. A: I am afraid I burnt the kitchen ceiling.
2. B: But have you…
3. A: Burned myself? Fortunately not.

These three expressions illustrate that in many cases a conversation involves more than the simple exchange of a few messages. In the second step, the second interlocutor starts a question, which is interrupted by the first interlocutor. The first interlocutor not only finishes the question but answers it at the same time. This implies that interlocutor B does not simply formulate a message and translate it into sound, but rather that interlocutors A and B jointly decode the message during the course of the last two fragments.

The idea of a strong link between language perception and production is based on earlier work by Liberman et al. (1967), who hypothesised that speech perception can be influenced by the subvocal repetition of perceived speech. Liberman's motor theory mainly aimed to explain how limitations in our articulatory system could constrain the possible interpretations of an ambiguous speech signal (see Chapter 17). According to Pickering and Garrod, however, the language production system influences the interpretation of a speech signal at a higher level, because we are mainly concerned with monitoring the content of the conversation. More recently, an increasing amount of evidence for overlap in the neural systems involved in speech perception and production had been reported (Scott & Johnsrude, 2003). For example, it was found that brain regions associated with speech perception were activated when participants whispered, but could not hear themselves (Paus, Perry, Zatorre, Worsley, & Evans, 1996). Also, we often appear to activate our tongue and lip muscles when listening to speech (see fig 16.8), while this does not happen while listening to non-speech sounds (Watkins, Strafella, & Paus, 2003).

Pickering and Garrod's (2013) self-monitoring principle can explain how we actively form a representation of a conversation through imitation and prediction processes, involving both speech perception and speech production processes. As such, the involvement of speech production

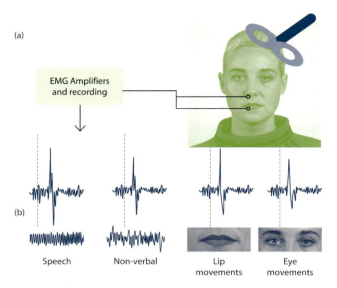

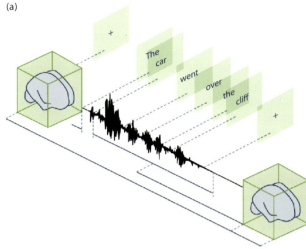

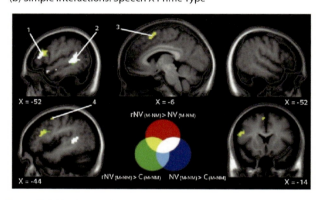

Figure 16.8 The activation of tongue and lip muscles while listening to speech. (a) Example of the experimental set-up used to produce the lip movements. A TMS pulse stimulated the part of the left motor cortex that represents the facial muscles, resulting in a clearly detectable pulse in the EMG signal that could be measured around the lips. (b) Examples of the EMG pulses evoked under four different conditions; from left to right: listening to a speech signal, listening to non-verbal sounds, visually observing speech-related lip movements, and visually observing movements around the eyes, such as frowning. When listening to speech, the TMS-evoked EMG pulse was larger than when listening to non-verbal sounds, suggesting that listening to speech activates our own speech production system. (source: Watkins et al., 2003)

Figure 16.9 The impact of visual information on auditory speech recognition. (a) Participants listened to speech signals that were either distorted or undistorted. During the presentation, the text that was spoken could also be primed by visual presentation. (b) fMRI results showing the interaction between distortion and priming. Areas highlighted in white represent a visual priming-induced increase in activation in the superior temporal sulcus. (source: Wild et al., 2012)

processes in language processing is not so much a reflection of a mechanism that is involved in making the speech signal more consistent, as Liberman et al. (1967) originally imagined (see Chapter 17). Rather, it would imply that speech production processes are part of a more extensive mechanism that is involved in representing language on a conceptual level.

16.8.2 LANGUAGE PERCEPTION AND PREDICTIVE CODING

From Pickering and Garrod's (2013) self-monitoring principle, it follows that language perception production processes cannot be separated from top-down predictive processes. The idea that top-down prediction processes play an important role in speech intelligibility has been demonstrated by several studies. For example, Wild, Davis, and Johnsrude (2012) used a special type of speech stimulus known as **noise-vocoded speech**. This is a distorted speech signal in which most of the temporal cues are still intact, while the finer details of the speech signal have been removed. To most listeners, this form of speech is largely unintelligible. When presented together with a verbal representation, however, its intelligibility improves significantly (Davis, Johnsrude, Hervais-Adelman, Taylor, & McGettigan, 2005). Wild et al. presented such a noise-vocoded speech signal while participants were shown written lines of text which either corresponded to the speech signal or which consisted of random series

of consonants (see fig 16.9). fMRI results showed that the activation of one of the most primary nuclei of the auditory cortex varied as a function of the text-induced intelligibility of the speech signal.

Evidence for the involvement of top-down prediction processes was presented in an fMRI study by von Kriegstein et al. (2008). Although earlier studies had already found that visual input can have a strong influence on speech intelligibility (McGurk & MacDonald, 1976), Von Kriegstein et al. wondered to what extent listeners need to actively perceive the speaker's voice movement, or whether previous experience of observing a speaker would be sufficient for improving speech intelligibility. To investigate this, participants observed a speaker for two minutes, after which they heard a speech fragment without seeing the speaker. The main finding was that participants were able to understand the speaker much better compared to a condition in which a similar speech fragment was presented, where participants did not have the opportunity to observe the speaker beforehand. The improvement in speech perception was related to an increase in activation in a brain region that is involved in the processing of facial movements. Interestingly, this improvement was found not only in neurotypical controls but also in a group of prosopagnosia patients.

The latter finding implies not only that the representation of facial movements is still intact in these patients, but also that they are still able to use this representation to influence their speech perception. This suggests that, while listening to speech, we can activate speaker-specific predictions that limit the possible interpretations of the speech signal. Speech perception therefore appears not to be just an audiovisual process but also a process that can make use of predictions arising from internal representations.

Lupyan and Clark (2015) assume that words, along with larger verbal units, such as phrases and sentences, constitute a special type of perceptual input. Our everyday visual experience will always result in the activation of the representation of specific objects. For instance, perceiving a vehicle will always result in the activation of a specific instance of a vehicle, such as a bicycle. Yet, the word 'vehicle' is categorical. Perception of this word can activate the category 'vehicle' in our semantic network. This activation can, in turn, cause the visual cortex to be more strongly primed for the perception of vehicles. Evidence for this idea was found by Lupyan and Ward (2013) in a study in which hearing a word had a facilitating effect on the perception of images that, under normal circumstances, were too noisy to be classified (see also Chapter 6).

From the perspective of a predictive coding mechanism, language is thus a powerful tool for manipulating thoughts and reasoning, both in ourselves and in others. Words, phrases, and sentences, when considered from this perspective, are not just simple ways of communicating our pre-existing thoughts, but they are also a flexible and effective way of creating an expectation and prioritising the processing of specific information. As such, language can serve as an artificial context which helps us to determine which representations are activated and what impact those representations have on reasoning processes (see Chapter 19).

Because words can thus prioritise information very efficiently (Lupyan & Bergen, 2016), language may be considered to be a very efficient mental programming language that has the potential to give our intelligence an enormous boost. Language is therefore linked to a wide variety of behaviours, and language proficiency correlates strongly with scores on non-verbal intelligence tests, such as the raven-progressive matrices (Cunningham & Stanovich, 1997), while limitations in our language skills are related to various cognitive deficits (Baldo, Bunge, Wilson, & Dronkers, 2010).

16.9 PRAGMATICS

Pragmatics deals with the practical aspects of language processing and understanding; those aspects of language understanding that go beyond the literal interpretation of language. In our daily lives, we often use metaphorical figures of speech that should not be interpreted literally. Consider, for example, the following example, based on a Dutch television documentary, in which a young adolescent's experiences were documented while serving as a Dutch Railway employee for a day:

Boy:	'Its so wonderful to experience this from the perspective of a train driver!'
Interviewer:	'How do you feel?'
Boy:	'I sit much higher than I expected!'

The final statement becomes a lot less surprising when we realise that the programme in question focused on a boy with an autism spectrum disorder (ASD) diagnosis. This diagnosis is characterised by, among other things, an excessive focus on the literal meaning of language. One of the obstacles that many individuals diagnosed with ASD face in everyday life is the fact that we use an overwhelming amount of language that is not to be taken literally. The fact that we often expect a non-literal meaning is also demonstrated by this example, in which we probably expected an answer that referred to the experience of driving a train, the tasks of a train driver, his responsibilities and so on.

Other examples of non-literal language are stylistic forms such as cynicism or irony. For example, a statement like: 'Oh, what a lovely day today!' may be assumed to be cynical if we had just traversed a thunderstorm. Other examples of non-literal language can be found in situations where we give an indirect and seemingly irrelevant answer to a question. Consider the following example given by Holtgraves (1998):

Bob:	'How did you like my presentation?'
Mike:	'It is difficult to give a good presentation'.

Many people interpret this answer in a negative way, namely that Bob gave a bad presentation. In some cases, these kinds of evasive answers are given to save face, as in another example from Holtgraves (1998):

Ken:	'So, did Paula want to go out with you?'
Bob:	'She's not my type'.

Most people interpret this answer as a way of disguising the fact that Paula did not want to go out with Bob, and that Bob gave an answer intended to save face. Holtgraves therefore found that when Bob gave an indirect answer that did not have the intention of saving face ('She's my type'), listeners needed about 50% more time to process this answer than when he did.

Box 16.1 Fries with dog: the role of the N400 in psycholinguistic research

The Dutch language has a well-known anachronism: patatje met, or 'fries with'. After all, in the Netherlands it is so common to order fries with mayonnaise that it has become customary to leave out the word 'mayonnaise' altogether. In the early 1990s, for many Dutch psychology students the phrase was not only linked to their regular dietary habits, it was also strongly associated with participating in psychophysiological experiments on sentence processing. In such an experiment, the words SHE … ATE … FRIES … WITH were presented one by one on a computer screen while the participating student's EEG was recorded. Then, the sentence could be concluded with the word 'mayonnaise', which – given the prevailing Dutch culinary culture – was so standard that our brains did not respond to it. Alternatively, however, it could be concluded with the word 'dog', which resulted in a violation of semantic expectation, which is detected approximately 400 ms after the presentation of the word in the form of a negative ERP component known as the N400.

Kutas and Hillyard (1980) reported the discovery of an ERP component that was sensitive to violations of semantics that was published in the prestigious journal Science (see fig 16.10). This component, known as the N400, is widely used in psycholinguistic research, but it is not considered to be a language-specific component anymore. Nowadays, the N400 is mainly interpreted as a component that can signal a multitude of violations that relate to the meaning of concepts (Kutas & Federmeier, 2011). For example, the N400 is used to investigate how information from a sentence can be integrated into an already existing representation and how violations in

the information that is already given can be resolved. In addition, the N400 can be used in studies of figurative language use, such as the processing of metaphors, or violations of predictions. Outside of psycholinguistics, effects on the N400 are found, for example, in arithmetic or in the recognition of information. Due in part to these properties, the N400 has become one of the most widely used physiological markers in cognitive psychological brain research since its discovery in the late 1970s. More recent work suggests that the N400 component is a neurophysiologic marker of an implicit learning process that drives adaptation (Hodapp & Rabovsky, 2021).

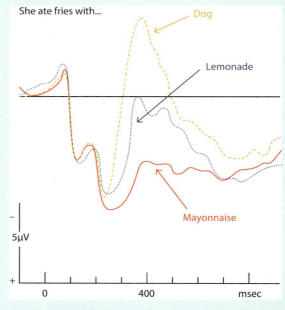

Figure 16.10 The N400 component.

Figurative language is a form of language that is not meant to be taken literally. In contrast to the preceding examples, which can also be taken literally, we frequently use metaphors and other figures of speech that do not have a literal meaning at all, as in the case of the statement: 'Our office is like a pigsty', or 'Feeling lost at sea'. Much research on non-literal language has focused on figurative language, and in particular on the use of metaphors. According to Grice's (1975) standard pragmatic model, the extraction of a non-literal meaning involves three stages. The first stage involves the activation of the literal meaning. Then the listener evaluates whether this literal meaning makes sense within the context in which the sentence was uttered. Only when the literal meaning does not make sense will the listener look for a non-literal meaning in the final stage. Thus, one of the predictions of this model is that the literal meaning is automatically and immediately activated, while the activation of the non-literal meaning is optional.

The standard pragmatic model, however, is incompatible with many empirical findings. In particular, the model assumes that the literal meaning is automatically activated, while the figurative meaning is not. Evidence for the exact opposite, however, was found by Glucksberg (2003). Participants were given sentences for which they had to decide whether the literal meaning was correct. For this task, it was therefore not necessary to process the figurative meaning. Three different types of sentences were used: sentences without a metaphorical meaning (of which the literal meaning could be true or false), metaphors (e.g., 'Some surgeons are like butchers') and scrambled metaphors, such as 'Some professions are like butchers'. In the case of metaphors, participants took longer to determine that the literal meaning of a sentence was false (fig 16.11). Moreover, it is often found that the non-literal meaning of a sentence is processed more quickly than the literal meaning. Blasko and Connine

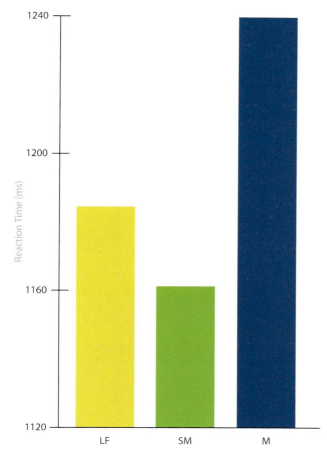

Figure 16.11 The time required to decide that the literal meaning of a sentence is false for literal false (LF) sentences, scrambled metaphors (SM), and actual metaphors (M). (source: Glucksberg, 2003)

(1993) found, for example, that the non-literal meaning of relatively unfamiliar metaphors (e.g., 'Loneliness is like a desert') was understood as rapidly as the literal meaning. For these reasons Glucksberg (2003), among others, argued that the non-literal meaning is more likely to be activated in parallel to that of the literal meaning and that the same processes are involved.

Arzouan, Goldstein, and Faust (2007) used ERPs and response times to determine how rapidly the meaning of sentences could be retrieved. They gave participants conventional metaphors such as 'a clear mind' or literal sentences, such as 'a burning fire'. Decisions as to whether these phrases were meaningful were roughly the same for both types of sentences. The amplitude of the N400 component (see Box 16.1) was larger for the metaphors than for the literal phrases, however. This result implies that the same mechanisms are involved in the interpretation of literal expressions and conventional metaphors, but that the interpretation of the metaphors is more difficult and therefore requires the deployment of more neural processing power.

Arzouan et al. (2007) found that response times for novel metaphors, such as 'a ripe dream' were prolonged.

Moreover, this type of metaphor elicited the largest N400 amplitude. In addition, for these novel metaphors the N400 ERP component was followed by an additional negative wave, which was not found for the other types of expressions.

These results are compatible with the graded salience hypothesis by the Israeli linguist Rachel Giora (1997, 2002). Giora argues that the initial meaning of a sentence is mainly determined by its salience rather than by the type of meaning. According to Giora, salience is here determined by previous experience with the material, the context in which it is presented, or with other comparable material. According to Giora's hypothesis, repeated exposure to metaphors would result in the non-literal meaning becoming represented in our lexicon. For non-literal expressions that are not represented in our lexicon, the intended meaning has to be inferred from the context.

Giora and Fein (1999) tested the graded salience hypothesis by using familiar metaphors, which have salient literal and metaphorical meanings, and less familiar metaphors, of which only the literal meaning is salient. These metaphors were presented in a context in which either the salience of the literal meaning or that of the metaphorical meaning was emphasised. For example, the sentence 'Only now did they wake up' was used as a target sentence and this sentence could be preceded by a paragraph about a group of friends who had partied all night (priming of literal meaning), or by a paragraph about the horrors of the Holocaust (priming of figurative meaning). Giora and Fein argued that if the salience of the metaphorical meaning is decisive for the interpretation, it should not be influenced by the context. They therefore expected that both literal and figurative meanings would be activated for familiar metaphors, regardless of the context, but that for unknown metaphors the context would play a role in the activation of figurative meaning. This is indeed exactly what Giora and Fein found (see fig 16.12).

Further support for the graded salience hypothesis was found in an ERP study from Laurent, Denhieres, Passerieux, Iakimova, and Hardy-Bayle (2006). Here, the N400 components evoked by target words that were associated with salient metaphorical meanings were smaller than the N400 evoked by non-salient metaphorical meanings or literal meanings. In addition, Laurent et al. found that participants understood both salient metaphorical meanings and literal meanings of non-salient metaphors relatively quickly; a finding that is consistent with the idea that salient metaphorical meanings are activated relatively quickly.

To explain the processing of metaphors, Kintsch (2000) has formulated a model that describes the underlying processes. According to this predcation model, finding the metaphorical meaning of a sentence involves a combination of two processes. The first process consists of a

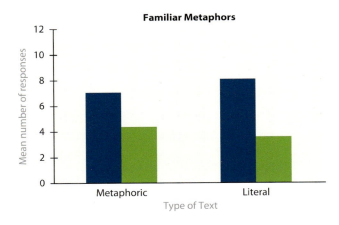

Familiar Metaphors

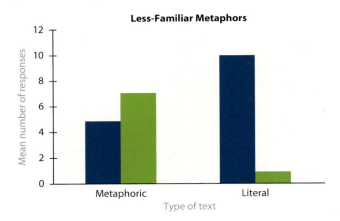

Less-Familiar Metaphors

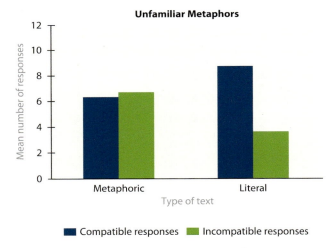

Unfamiliar Metaphors

■ Compatible responses ■ Incompatible responses

Figure 16.12 Results of a study in which participants had to decide whether a target sentence was compatible with a previously given context. This context could activate either the literal meaning of the target sentence or the figurative one. For familiar metaphors, it was found that both the literal and figurative meanings were activated, whereas for less familiar metaphors, participants mainly indicated that they were compatible with the literal meaning. (source: Giora and Fein, 1999)

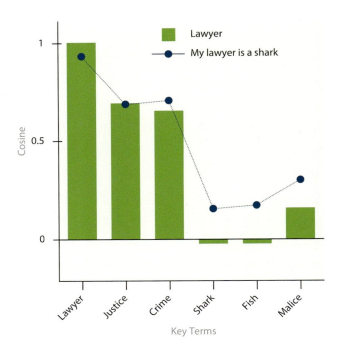

Figure 16.13 The semantic structure underlying a metaphor according to the construction-integration model, here detailed for the target word 'lawyer'. (source: Kintsch, 2000)

That is, the information obtained from the latent semantic analysis is used to create interpretations in the form of an 'ARGUMENT is like a PREDICATE' structure. In our earlier example, 'A surgeon is like a butcher', those aspects of the predicate that are relevant to the argument are activated, such as 'cutting', while those aspects that are irrelevant are inhibited, such as the killing of animals, or the processing of meat for consumption.

An important aspect of metaphors is that they are not reversible (Chiappe & Chiappe, 2007). The metaphor 'My surgeon is like a butcher' loses its meaning when we reverse the argument and the predicate. 'My butcher is like a surgeon' has a completely different meaning. This phenomenon can be explained well by Kintsch's (2000) predication model. According to this model, only those properties of the predicate that are relevant to the argument are selected, so that swapping the two results in the selection of completely different properties (try making a representation for both metaphors to illustrate this point!).

Kintsch's (2000) model is also able to explain an interesting finding from McGlone and Manfredi (2001). Suppose we use a metaphor such as 'My lawyer is a shark'. According to the predicate model, it should take longer to process this metaphor when we have activated the literal properties of a shark (has fins, can swim). McGlone and Manfredi investigated this question by preceding this type of metaphor with a context sentence that emphasised the literal properties of the predicate and found that it indeed took longer to process the metaphorical meaning afterwards.

latent semantic analysis. This analysis determines word meaning on the basis of the relationship that each word has with 300–400 other words and the mutual relationship between those words (see fig 16.13). The second process includes a **construction-integration** component.

This finding points to an important feature of metaphor processing, namely, that our ability to process metaphors depends largely on our ability to inhibit the literal properties of the predicate. If this is the case, we might expect that participants with a larger working memory capacity, who are after all better at inhibiting irrelevant information (see Chapter 14), would be more efficient at processing metaphors than participants with a lower working memory capacity. Indeed, Chiappe and Chiappe (2007) found that individuals with a larger working memory capacity were, on average, 23% faster at interpreting metaphors and that the quality of their interpretations was also higher.

16.10 STORY PROCESSING

One of the most important functions of language is that it enables us to form a mental representation of a wide variety of situations. The details of mental representations will be further elaborated in Chapter 19. For now, we can define a representation as a physical depiction of information, for example in the form of symbols on paper, magnetic tracks on a hard disk, or neural activation patterns in the brain. The question we will address in the next section is how the complexity of information that is represented in a story can be moulded into an internally consistent mental representation.

One key process involves converting the meaning of individual sentences either into a new mental representation or to use this information to adapt an existing mental representation on the basis of new information. In other words, we must form a **situation model** on the basis of the information that we are given. In Chapter 17 we will discuss the mechanisms involved in interpreting and understanding individual sentences. In reality, however, it is rare that we have to understand situations on the basis of just a single sentence. We often have to process longer pieces of text consisting of several sentences. The following sections will discuss how we can combine information from different sentences to build complex mental representations of stories.

In many cases, the processing of information is incomplete or ambiguous, as aptly illustrated by Rumelhart and Ortony (1977). Suppose we have the following three sentences:

1. Marie heard the ice cream van coming.
2. She remembered her pocket money.
3. She rushed into the house.

These three sentences form a short story that we can effortlessly interpret. You probably deduced that Marie wanted to buy an ice cream, that she wanted to use her pocket money for it, which was inside, and that she was short on time, so she had to run inside to get it. In processing this story, we

have drawn several conclusions that are not explicitly stated in the text. In other words, we have made an **inference**.

16.10.1 INFERENCES

Inferences allow us to deduce something that was not explicitly mentioned by the author. We draw these inferences every day when we listen to someone or when we read texts, and we generally do so completely unconsciously. Drawing inferences is therefore an essential part of language processing: if we were to read stories in which all inferences were worked out in detail, we would probably be bored to death! We generally encounter three types of inference: logical, bridging, and extensive inference.

16.10.1.1 Logical Inferences
Logical inferences are the simplest inferences and depend entirely on the meaning of words. For example, we infer that a stewardess is a woman because of the meaning of the word.

16.10.1.2 Bridging Inferences
Bridging inferences are made to establish coherence between the current part of a text and the previous part. These inferences are also known as **backward inferences**. The inference made earlier that Marie wanted to use her pocket money to buy an ice cream is an example of a bridging inference. A special form of bridging inference is formed by **anaphor resolution**, where a pronoun or a noun has to be linked to a previous noun, as in the sentence 'Fred sold John his lawnmower and then he sold him his garden hose'. We have to make a bridging inference here to realise that 'him' refers to John and not to Fred (Arnold, Eisenband, Brown-Schmidt, & Trueswell, 2000).

16.10.1.3 Elaborative Inferences
Finally, elaborative inferences aim to add details to the literal text. These details are added based on our background knowledge of the situation at hand. An example of this type of inference is forward inference, which we use to predict what will happen in the future.

16.10.1.4 Complex Inferences
The question now is how we are able to make these kinds of inferences. Suppose we present the following two sentences:

1. John drove to London yesterday.
2. The car overheated constantly.

You probably had no problem deducing that John drove to London in a car that overheated. According to Garrod and Terras (2000), there are two possible mechanisms that can explain how we make this inference. The first mechanism involves the verb 'drove' activating key concepts in long-term memory that are related to driving, so that

Figure 16.14 The two stages of bonding and resolution, as proposed by Garrod and Terras (2000).

the word 'car' from the second sentence is automatically associated with the first sentence. The second possibility is that we form an extended mental representation based on the first sentence and the information from the second sentence is interpreted in this context. Garrod and Terras used eye-tracking to determine how we make these types of inferences. Participants were given sentences to read, such as 'The teacher wrote a letter' or 'The teacher wrote on the blackboard'. These sentences created a context in which the following sentence was interpreted: 'However, she was disturbed by a loud scream at the back of the classroom and the pen fell to the floor'. When the word 'pen' was unexpected, participants returned to the earlier context more often. This suggests that there is initially an automatic process in which key words are activated (a process identified by Garrod and Terras as bonding; fig 16.14). Then, according to Garrod and Terras, there is a higher-order integration in which the sentence is interpreted to be as consistent as possible with the given context; a process identified by Garrod and Terrace as resolution.

16.10.2 INFERENCES: THEORETICAL APPROACHES

The essential step in the integration of an individual sentence is the construction of a mental representation. The question remains how extensive this mental representation

is and the different theoretical positions on this issue differ considerably. At one end of the spectrum Bransford, Barclay, and Franks (1972) suggest that we form a relatively complete representation, whereas at the other end McKoon and Ratcliff (1992) argue that we only form the most minimalist representation possible.

16.10.2.1 Constructionist Approach

Bransford et al. (1972) have argued that readers generally form a fairly extensive mental representation of the situation and actions described in a text. This implies that reading a text generally results in the formation of a large number of extensive inferences, even when these inferences are not directly necessary for understanding the text. Bransford et al. based this conclusion on the results of a sentence recognition experiment, in which participants were given a series of sentences to memorise. They presented participants sentences such as the following:

1. Three turtles rested beside a floating log and a fish swam beneath them.
2. Three turtles rested on a floating log and a fish swam beneath them.

The difference between these two sentences is that the second sentence implies that the fish also swim under the floating log, whereas the first sentence does not; an inference that we can make on the basis of our general knowledge about spatial relations. After the participants had heard these sentences, they were subjected to a memory test. This memory test also involved sentences such as the following:

3. Three turtles rested beside a floating log and a fish swam beneath it.
4. Three turtles rested on a floating log and a fish swam beneath it.

Bransford et al. found that when sentence number 2 was presented, participants indicated that they had also heard sentence 4. Although the participants had not seen this sentence literally, its content corresponded to the inference the participants had made on the basis of the information given in sentence number 2, which implies that the sentence had been recognised on the basis of the inference.

16.10.2.2 Minimalist Approach

McKoon and Ratcliff (1992) on the other hand, argued that inferences are formed to a much more limited extent. They distinguished two different types: automatic or strategic (goal-oriented) inferences. Automatic inferences achieve local coherence. Here, the information given in the sentence, which is readily available, is integrated with our general background knowledge. According to McKoon and Ratcliff, this is an attempt to find a coherent interpretation of the information contained in the sentences currently in working memory. In particular, the information that is explicitly given in the text is used for this.

16.10.2.3 Memory-based Approach

The main difference between the constructionist approach and the minimalist hypothesis involves the number of automatic inferences that are drawn, since this is much lower according to the minimalist hypothesis than according to the constructionist approach. The minimalist approach has subsequently been developed into a memory-based framework in which the underlying cognitive processes were more clearly specified. According to the latter framework, the incoming text has a signalling function that activates all relevant memory traces in long-term memory. This, in turn, activates the meaning of the text that is being read at that instant (Gerrig & O'Brien, 2005). The inferences that are then formed thus depend on the degree of attention that is directed to the representations that are being activated. Which aspects of these representations are activated is thus largely dependent on the readers' goals.

16.10.2.4 Search after Meaning

The memory-based framework thus implies that the reader's goals are critically involved in the formation of inferences, because they are formed as a result of focusing attention on specific aspects of the information that is being processed. The idea that the readers' goals are involved in the formation of inferences was previously put forward by Graesser, Singer, and Trabasso (1994), as it may explain why we form inferences in some situations and not in others. Situations in which we form relatively few inferences occur, for example, when we check a text for spelling and grammatical errors, when we speed-read, when we have to struggle our way through an incoherent text, or simply when we do not have enough background knowledge about the topic at hand. In these situations, the inferences that are being drawn are consistent with what is being predicted by the minimalist approach. In other situations, for example when we read for pleasure, or when we read to acquire knowledge at a leisurely pace, we will draw many more elaborate inferences; especially when the topic we are reading about matches our background knowledge and when the text is well-structured.

The hypothesis that the number of inferences we make depends on the goals of the reader is consistent with data from Calvo, Castillo, and Schmalhofer (2006). They instructed participants to read sentences and then to focus either on understanding the sentence or to anticipate what would follow. The participants who read anticipatively formed more inferences and did so faster than the participants who read comprehensively.

16.10.2.5 Individual Differences and Working Memory Capacity

The extent to which inferences are formed depends not only on the goal of the reader; there are also large individual differences in the extent to which inferences are being drawn. Calvo (2001), for instance, found a link between working memory capacity and the efficiency of the inference drawing process. In this study, participants had to read sentences that were preceded by a context sentence. This context sentence was either predictive of the information that was given in the subsequent sentence, or not. It was found that participants with a large working memory capacity were better able to integrate the information from the context sentence with the subsequent sentence when this was predictive of the content of the subsequent sentence.

16.10.2.6 Integration of Sentence Meaning and Context

More evidence for a simultaneous integration of different sources of information in story processing was obtained by Nieuwland and Van Berkum (2006). In their study, story fragments such as the following were used:

> A woman saw a dancing peanut who had a big smile on his face. The peanut was singing about a girl he had just met. And judging from the song, the peanut was totally crazy about her. The woman thought it was really cute to see the peanut singing and dancing like that. The peanut was [salted/in love], and by the sound of it, this was definitely mutual.

Some participants heard 'salted', which fit in terms of word meaning but not in the context of the story, while other participants heard 'in love', which did not fit in terms of word meaning but did fit in the context of the story. An **N400** component that was evoked by 'salted' was larger than one that was evoked by 'in love'. It thus appears that the former did not fit the context of the story (see fig 16.15). This result thus implies that contextual information can have a very rapid impact on story comprehension and sentence processing.

A final remarkable finding that implies that we use non-verbal background knowledge when making inferences comes from a study by van den Brink et al. (2012). These authors presented sentences such as 'I have a large

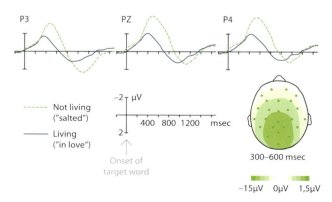

Figure 16.15 An N400 component as evoked by a previous context. (source: Nieuwland and Van Berkum, 2006)

tattoo on my back' in a British upper-class accent, 'I have trouble sleeping without my teddy bear' spoken by an adult, or 'Every night I go to sleep after drinking a glass of wine' spoken by a child. In these cases, for female participants, it was found that the target words ('tattoo', 'teddy bear', 'wine') were followed by an N400 when there was a mismatch between the word meaning and the context created by the speaker's voice. Remarkably, this effect was not found for male participants.

16.10.3 SCHEMA THEORIES

A large part of story processing involves the integration of new information with knowledge that is already present in our long-term memory. Already in 1932, the renowned British psychologist Sir Frederic Bartlett assumed that we make use of **schemas**, that is, structured units of background knowledge that we have previously acquired. Bartlett (1932) argued that schemas are crucial for story processing. He hypothesised that our memory is influenced not only by the new elements in a story but also by our previously stored schematic knowledge, so that our understanding of a story – and memory of it – is influenced by top-down processing, based on the background knowledge stored in these schemas.

Schemas can be subdivided into **scripts** and **frames** (Schank & Abelson, 1975). Frames describe the fixed knowledge structures of the world, whereas scripts contain information about sequences of actions that are performed in normal situations (see also Chapter 14). The classic example of a script, as described by Schank and Abelson, is the 'restaurant script'. Such scripts are not only valuable as guidelines for our own behaviour (it would make life unnecessarily complicated if we had to use our cognitive resources again each time we visited a restaurant to figure out what to do), they are also valuable for understanding stories, as was implied by Bartlett's research.

One of Bartlett's great innovations in the study of story processing is that he presented participants with stories that contained elements that conflicted with the participants' background knowledge. He tested this idea by using stories about Native American culture. The most famous story he used was 'The war of the ghosts'. Background knowledge or stereotypical views held by the participant could result in systematic distortions in the way they remembered these stories.

Bartlett identified three types of error. The first and most important type of error is **rationalisation**. Rationalisation errors are characterised by distortions that aim to make the memory more rational and consistent with one's own cultural beliefs. The second type of error was described by Bartlett as **levelling**, an error characterised by the omission of unknown details during the retrieval of the

story. Finally, the third type of error was **sharpening**. Sharpening involves some details of the story being highlighted and emphasised for embellishment.

Rationalisations can manifest themselves in two different ways: first, schematic knowledge can directly affect the understanding of the story and second, it can distort the memory during retrieval. Bartlett (1932) assumed that in particular the second process was important, because he was convinced that recalling stories is a constructive process. He therefore expected the influence of schemas to increase with the passage of time. The evidence for the latter hypothesis is not unequivocal, however. Indeed, many studies have failed to find this effect (Roediger, 2010). A clear exception is a study by Bergman and Roediger (1999). This study also used the 'War of the ghosts' story and tested participants' knowledge of the story for 15 minutes, one week, and six months after participants initially read the story. The proportion of distortions in memory increased progressively from 27% at the shortest interval to 59% at the longest.

Bartlett's original study has been sharply criticised, however (Roediger, 2010). For example, Bartlett gave his participants no specific instructions, in an attempt to influence their behaviour as little as possible. One consequence of this, however, is that it is possible that many of the errors reported by Bartlett's participants may have been the result of conscious guessing rather than a problem with remembering. Gauld and Stephenson (1967) tried to replicate Bartlett's study but emphasised accuracy in their instructions and found that participants made about half as many errors as when the same instructions as Bartlett's were used.

The impact of schemas is also reflected in the fact that inferences can depend on the reader's goal. The latter involves strategic inferences. According to McKoon and Ratcliff, these strategic inferences are formed not so much while reading, but rather during the retrieval of information. Evidence for the latter can be found in a study by American psychologist James Dooling and colleagues (see: Dooling & Christiaansen, 1977; Sulin & Dooling, 1974). Participants were given a story about a brutal dictator named Gerald Martin. Another group of participants was given exactly the same story to read, with the only difference being that the name Gerald Martin had been replaced by Adolf Hitler. After the participants had read the story, they were given a memory test either after five minutes or after a week. The crucial manipulation in the experiment consisted of embedding sentences in the memory test that were typical of Hitler's Nazi regime but that did not appear in the original story, such as: 'He hated the Jews in particular and therefore persecuted them'.

When participants were subjected to the memory test immediately, they mostly rejected these sentences

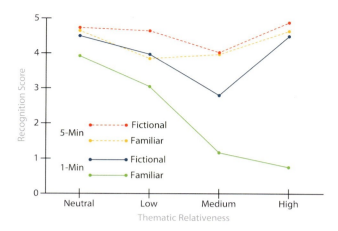

Figure 16.16 Distortions in story recall due to background knowledge. When participants were questioned one week later, it appeared that the recall of stories that related to public figures was strongly distorted. (source: Sulin and Dooling, 1974)

in both the fictional Gerald Martin and Adolf Hitler variants. However, when they were subjected to the memory test after a week, participants who had read the Hitler variant were much less successful in rejecting these sentences than those who had read the Martin variant (see fig 16.16). This result is consistent with Bartlett's hypothesis, and shows that inference was not made instantaneously, but rather that there is a gradual integration of new information with existing cognitive schemas, which helps us to structure information about our environment.

The fact that schemas are involved in the retrieval of information from memory was also aptly demonstrated by Anderson and Pichert (1978). These authors asked participants to read a story about the activities of two boys in a house while they were skipping school. The story contained a number of details that were of potential interest to burglars (such as the fact that the doors were unlocked) or homebuyers (such as the fact that the roof was leaking). Participants were asked to read the story from the perspective of a potential burglar or from the perspective of a potential buyer. Those who had read the story from the perspective of a burglar were able to recall more details about burglary-related issues than details of issues of interest to homebuyers. For the participants who had read the story from a homebuyer's perspective, the reverse was true. After the participants had retrieved the story, they were asked to retrieve the story again, but this time from the other perspective. It turned out that the participants now remembered more details that corresponded to the new perspective.

In other words, schemas and scripts help us to keep the world orderly. The fact that schemas are not only involved in remembering a story, but that they can also be essential in understanding it was aptly demonstrated by Bransford

and Johnson (1972). They presented participants with fragments such as the following:

> *If the balloons popped, the sound wouldn't be able to carry since everything would be too far away from the correct floor. A closed window would also prevent the sound from carrying, since most buildings tend to be well insulated. Since the whole operation depends on a steady flow of electricity, a break in the middle of the wire would also cause problems. Of course, the fellow could shout, but the human voice is not loud enough to carry that far. An additional problem is that a string could break on the instrument. Then there could be no accompaniment to the message. It is clear that the best situation would involve less distance. Then there would be fewer potential problems. With face to face contact, the least number of things could go wrong.*
>
> (Bransford & Johnson, 1972)

What is this passage about? Bransford and Johnson investigated this by asking participants, after they heard the cited fragment, to reproduce it as accurately as possible. The participants were divided into five groups. One group received no contextual information but heard the story twice. The other groups were shown a cartoon that either completely (fig 16.17a) or partially (fig 16.17b) provided the context. These cartoons were either shown before the story or afterwards. When the cartoons were shown afterwards, most participants indicated that they understood the story poorly, whereas understanding was much better in the group that had seen the cartoon beforehand. In addition, the participants who had been given the context beforehand were also able to reproduce many more sentences from the excerpt than participants who had only been given the context afterwards. These results thus underline that it is extremely important for story comprehension to be able to integrate new information with an existing context.

16.10.4 KINTSCH'S CONSTRUCTION-INTEGRATION MODEL

The American psychologist Walter Kintsch (1998) has developed an influential model for explaining human language comprehension. This **construction-integration model** is based on Philip Johnson-Laird's (2010b) mental model theory (see Chapter 19). More specifically, it is based on the idea that while reading a text we convert it into **propositions** which represent the meaning of the sentence. The propositions that follow from the text are stored in memory, together with several propositions that are associated with this text. These latter propositions form the inferences that are being drawn. At this stage, many propositions are stored. Then a spreading activation mechanism activates those propositions that represent the whole text. The propositions that represent the current sentence are integrated

Figure 16.17 Cartoons used by Bransford and Johnson to activate cognitive schemas. (a) Context completely provided; (b) context partially provided. (source: Bransford and Johnson, 1972)

with the already existing representation of the previous parts of the text, and the propositions that are activated the most form the representation of the text as a whole. Within this text representation, it is difficult to distinguish between the propositions that are the direct result of the actual text and those that are the result of inferences. The final result of this process is that, according to Kintsch, three different levels of textual representation are formed:

1. A surface representation.
2. Propositional representations.
3. A situation presentation.

The surface representation is formed by the text itself, while the propositional representations are derived directly from the text. Finally, the situation representation is formed by a mental model that describes the situation that is referred to in the text. More specifically, this is formed by the integration process.

The question is how the construction-integration model differs from the previously discussed schema theories. One important difference is that schema theories mainly emphasise the top-down processes involved in story comprehension and recollection, whereas construction-integration theory puts more emphasises on the bottom-up processes. According to Kaakinen and Hyönä (2007), the text itself initiates a bottom-up construction process in the reader's knowledge base, whereas top-down processes are mainly active during the integration phase.

Much empirical support has been found for the construction-integration model: for example, it predicts that readers and listeners have difficulty distinguishing between information that was explicitly stated in the text and inferences that were drawn from the text. This prediction has been confirmed by many studies, as we

have discussed earlier (Sulin & Dooling, 1974). Kintsch, Welsch, Schmalhofer, and Zimny (1990) have also found evidence for the prediction that propositions are formed at three different levels. More specifically, participants were instructed to read short descriptions of different situations and were then tested for recognition of the situations immediately, or at different times afterwards (up to four days after the initial reading). The forgetting curves (fig 16.18) for the surface, propositional, and situational representations were significantly different. Surface representations were quickly forgotten, whereas situation representations showed hardly any signs of decay. Mulder and Sanders (2012) investigated the recognition of causal relations within a story and found that they were part of the situation representation but not of the propositional or surface representations.

It is not necessarily the case, however, that situation representations are always remembered more accurately than surface representations. Dixon and Bortolussi (2013) predicted, for example, that the extent to which participants form a situation representation depends to a large extent on how interesting a text is, because they suspected that interest is strongly related to the integration phase in Kintsch's model. For this reason, they gave their participants an interesting text ('Interview with the vampire') and an uninteresting one ('The history of Pendennis') and asked them to indicate how interesting they had found these texts and to what extent they had paid attention to the text. The participants were then tested on the extent to which they could remember these texts. It was found that the amount of attention that was given to the text correlated with both the construction phase and the integration phase.

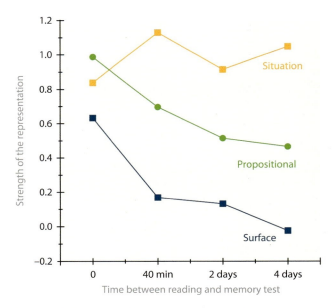

Figure 16.18 The theoretical forgetting curves for surface, propositional, and situation representations. (source: Kintsch et al., 1990)

The construction-integration model assumes that the reader's goal primarily influences the integration phase rather than the construction phase. It is unlikely, however, that this always happens in reality. Suppose you are reading a text that is directly relevant to a specific purpose, as might be the case when you read a text about a rare disease, because one of your close friends is affected by it. If your goal is to gather information about this disease to inform your other friends, you will probably spend a lot of time reading the relevant sentences and little time reading sentences that are irrelevant for this purpose. Kaakinen and Hyönä (2007) designed a study based on this idea and found indeed that their participants spent a considerable amount of time reading the relevant sentences and relatively little time reading the irrelevant ones (see fig 16.19). This result thus shows that the reader's goal can indeed influence the construction phase, a finding that is inconsistent with the model.

A final prediction of the model concerns the link between textual information and background knowledge. The construction-integration model predicts that textual information is linked to background knowledge before it is linked to contextual information provided by the rest of the text. Cook and Myers (2004) tested this hypothesis by using text fragments such as the following:

> The movie was being filmed on location in the Sahara Desert. It was a small and independent film with a low budget and small staff, so everyone involved had to take on extra jobs and responsibilities. On the first day of filming, 'Action!' was called by the actress so that shooting could begin…

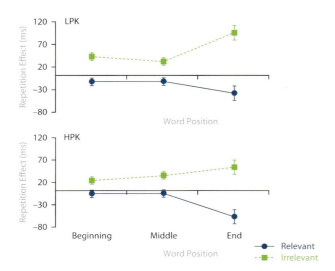

Figure 16.19 Changes in fixation time during the rereading of a text. Results are shown separately for relevant and irrelevant text passages and for texts about which the reader had little prior knowledge (top, LPK) or much prior knowledge (bottom, HPK). Negative values imply that participants fixated longer on these phrases during rereading than during first reading. (source: Kaakinen and Hyönä, 2007)

Cook and Myers were interested in the question of how long readers fixated on the word 'actress'. This word does not fit the sentence based on our background knowledge, which tells us that it is normally the director who calls 'Action!'. However, the additional context (the underlined phrase) gives a reason why there is no director. According to the construction-integration model, readers should, driven by their background knowledge, fixate longer on the unexpected word 'actress', because the model assumes that integration with the earlier text only takes place at a later stage. Cook and Myers found, however, that this is not the case. This result implies that readers can already make use of the context immediately. Cook and Myers' results are consistent with the previously discussed results from Nieuwland and Van Berkum (2006), which show that we are not limited in processing semantically incongruent information when a previously given context justifies it (e.g., peanuts falling in love).

Although the construct-integration model can explain a large number of empirical findings very well, the last of the studies discussed here shows that it also has some limitations. Thus, it is unlikely that the initial construction phase is characterised only by inefficient bottom-up processes. Indeed, selective attention to specific information can strongly influence this phase, as was shown by the Cook and Myers (2004) and Nieuwland and Van Berkum (2006) studies. In addition, the model also appears to ignore some key factors that are essential for comprehension, such as the reader's goal, the emotional response to the text, and the reader's visual imagination (McNamara & Magliano, 2009). Moreover, Graesser, Millis, and Zwaan (1997) argue that there are two more levels of representation that are not described by the construction-integration model: the text genre level and the communication level. The text genre level describes the style of a text (exposition, humour, storyline, etc.), whereas the communication level describes how the writer communicates with the reader (as an invisible storyteller in a more distant style, as a storyteller etc.).

16.10.5 SITUATION MODELS

While Kintsch's construction-integration model mainly describes how knowledge is integrated into an existing semantic network, situation models mainly describe the role of events in the processing of stories. The event-indexing model developed by Zwaan, Langston, and Graesser (1995) describes the processes involved in the processing of a narrative text, such as a novel. Although the event-indexing model differs from the construction-integration model in that respect, both models have in common that readers construct situation models when they read a text. A fundamental assumption of the event-indexing model is that our cognitive system is better equipped to detect dynamic events than to absorb static information (McNamara &

Magliano, 2009). According to the event-indexing model, readers monitor five different aspects of a story to decide whether a situation model needs to be adjusted. These are as follows:

1. The protagonist: that is, the central character in the current event, compared to the previous one.
2. The sequentiality: that is, the relationship between the time of the current event, compared to the previous one.
3. Causality: that is, the causal relationship between the current and the previous event.
4. Spatiality: that is, the spatial relationship between the location of the current and the previous event.
5. Intentionality: that is, the relationship between a character's goals and current events.

A discontinuity in any of these five aspects, such as a change of location or a flashback, will, according to Zwaan et al. (1995), result in an update of the situation model. Evidence for this assumption was found by Rinck and Weber (2003) and by Curiel and Radvansky (2014). These authors found that reading speeds decreased when one of the aforementioned aspects changed, compared to situations where there was no change.

When one or more discontinuities results in an adjustment of the situation model, we may wonder about the influence of outdated information. Zwaan and Madden (2004) discuss two alternative possibilities: the first of these can be described as the here-and-now view. According to this view, which is consistent with the event indexing model, only current information is considered. The second view is the resonance view, which assumes that all information, including obsolete information, can interfere with the description of the current situation.

The currently available evidence is not conclusive enough to distinguish between these two views, however: O'Brien, Rizzella, Albrecht, and Halleran (1998) found evidence for the resonance view, based on studies in which inconsistent elaborations in a story interfered with the situation model. Zwaan and Madden (2004) argue, however, that O'Brien et al.'s results are mainly the result of the specific stimuli that were used. Indeed, the O'Brien et al. study used short situation sketches and descriptions of persons. For example, one of these sketches consisted of a person taking a walk and running across the street to rescue a young boy. In one condition, this person, Bill, was portrayed as a fit young athletic man and in another condition as an old man with declining health who had to walk with a stick. Obviously, the description of Bill as an old man is inconsistent with the description of his act of running across the street. To undo the impact of this inconsistent description, an additional qualifying sentence was added in some conditions. This sentence described how Bill had not lost his athletic abilities in emergencies.

Zwaan and Madden (2004) argue that this stimulus material is inadequate because the qualifying sentence is implausible: it seriously conflicts with our background knowledge that makes it highly implausible that an 81-year-old man can still respond quickly in emergencies. For this reason, they attempted a replication in which the inconsistent description of Bill as an old man was presented as a lie. Under these circumstances, Zwaan and Madden found no interference from the outdated information. However, in a follow-up study by O'Brien, Cook, and Gueraud (2010), it was still found that outdated information interfered with the situation model.

Zacks, Speer, Swallow, Braver, and Reynolds (2007) present a more general description of how we form internal representations of situations and events. According to their event segmentation theory, we can update an internal situation model in two ways: either by updating individual aspects, as described by the event indexing model, or by constructing a completely new model. Kurby and Zacks (2012) found evidence for both forms of updating. According to Zacks et al. events are characterised by discrete boundaries. For example, the event of putting up a tent (or reading a description of this) be broken down into a number of discrete stages (unpacking, rolling out, putting up poles, laying down the tarpaulin, etc.). According to Zacks et al. a global update takes place at the boundary between one stage and the next.

Zacks, Kurby, Eisenberg, and Haroutunian (2011) found evidence for the hypothesis that a completely new model is constructed at a boundary between two stages. Participants were shown film clips and had to try to predict what was going to happen five seconds after the film was stopped. When this stop took place just before a boundary, this prediction was significantly worse than when the film was stopped in the middle of a stage.

Ezzyat and Davachi (2011) found evidence for the idea that also during reading, scenes are segmented into discrete episodes. In this study, participants read short stories in which boundaries between episodes had been drawn. These were indicated by the phrase 'a while later'. A later memory test showed that memories that crossed such a boundary took longer to retrieve than memories that referred to one specific episode.

16.10.6 IN CONCLUSION

Both the construction-integration model and the situation models are successful in explaining the processes involved in story processing. However, the models are complementary in the sense that they both explain other aspects of story processing. While the construction-integration model mainly aims to explain how new information is linked to existing knowledge in the processing of non-fiction, the situation models mainly try to describe how the dynamic properties of narrative stories are processed.

16.11 WRITING: KNOWLEDGE CREATION

While understanding a narrative relies on the ability to relate the information provided in a text to our background knowledge, the ability to produce stories or texts mainly relies on the skill of structuring the necessary information and relating it to the expected background knowledge of the reader or listener. Most research in this area has focused on the development of writing expertise: what factors make one writer better than another? Daane (1991) reported a link between writing and reading skills: students with better writing skills also scored higher on text comprehension tests. A lot of reading experience probably results in a better understanding of the structure of a text. In addition, reading experience also contributes to the writer's vocabulary and knowledge.

16.11.1 DEVELOPMENT OF WRITING SKILLS

Bereiter and Scardamalia (1987) identified two main strategies used by writers. The knowledge-telling strategy consists of writers simply writing down everything they know about a given topic, with a minimum of planning. The knowledge-transformation strategy, on the other hand, is more complex and considers not only the topic but also the rhetoric. Rhetoric refers to, for example, the question of how to make an argument stronger, while writing content mainly refers to the question of what content you select to support your argument. When the knowledge-transformation strategy is used properly, the rhetorical and content-related aspects influence each other mutually. The use of this strategy generally results in texts that are more consistent and that convey the main thrust of an argument in a more

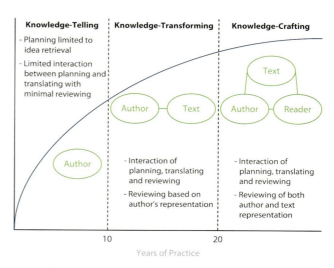

Figure 16.20 The three stages of writing expertise. (source: Kellogg, 2008)

consistent manner, compared to the knowledge-telling strategy (Bereiter, Burtis, & Scardamalia, 1988).

Bereiter and Scardamalia (1987) argue that experienced writers increasingly shift to using the knowledge-transformation strategy. Kellogg (2008) elaborated on this argument and identified a third strategy beyond knowledge transformation. According to Kellogg, highly experienced writers make use of the knowledge creation strategy (see fig 16.20). This strategy considers not only content and rhetoric, but also the perspective of the reader. The use of this strategy generally results in writing experts trying to anticipate all possible interpretations the reader may give to a text and that they are striving to remove all of these possible ambiguities from a text during revision.

The knowledge creation strategy thus focuses on the needs of the reader. One reason why this is important is that many writers implicitly assume that the readers already possess a great deal of the writer's knowledge. This assumption is known as the **knowledge effect**. Hayes and Bajzek (2008) found, for example, that people who are familiar with specific technical terms greatly overestimate how familiar others are with these terms.

16.12 SUMMARY

Language is a system of rules and symbols that enables us to communicate. This system is characterised by semantics and syntax. Partly due to the lack of a formal definition of the concept of language, it is still unclear, however, whether language is a uniquely human trait or whether language skills are also – partly – shared with other species. There is also much debate as to whether language skills are innate. Chomsky argues that language skills are innate in the form of a universal grammar, but this position is disputed by evolutionary biologists.

One influential hypothesis is that language influences our thinking. In its strongest form, this Whorfian hypothesis states that the constraints of language influence our thoughts. Although this hypothesis has long been unpopular, the idea that language can influence our perception has become more prominent again in recent decades. Categorisation processes can be influenced by the degree to which a concept appears to be represented in a specific language. The idea that multilingualism may have a positive effect on cognitive control processes was put forward at the turn of the century, but it has hardly been supported by empirical evidence.

Psycholinguistics uses specific properties of a language, such as word frequency, phonology, or the fact that words can have multiple meanings, to investigate the cognitive processes of language perception. It also makes use of pseudo-words and non-words. Well-known psycholinguistic tasks include the naming task, the lexical decision task, and the priming task.

An important aspect of language is communication. In a conversation, the interaction between speaker and listener is very important. In order to exchange information efficiently, speakers and listeners need to coordinate their actions. Grice argues that speakers and listeners do this on the basis of a cooperative principle, and he has formulated several maxims that interlocutors should ideally comply with. In practice, however, these rules are regularly broken.

Although interlocutors often strive to find a common ground, this is not an automatic process. Especially when there is time pressure, we often fall back on an egocentric perspective, which is corrected at a later stage. However, the use of relatively simple strategies, such as syntactic priming, can prevent interlocutors from losing common ground.

A large number of non-verbal processes are also involved in the switching of roles between speaker and listener. Switching occurs, for example, through the use of adjacency pairs, such as a question followed by an answer, or through non-verbal cues, such as hand gestures. Prosodic cues contribute to the intelligibility of speech. This is particularly the case when sentences are ambiguous. Seemingly meaningless remarks, discourse markers, play a role in increasing language comprehension because they mark specific structural aspects of a spoken text.

In recent years, there has been increasing interest in the study of sign language. Sign languages can develop independently of spoken or written languages. A comparison between the processing of sign language and regular language implies that the representation of linguistic information takes place partly in a modality-specific format and partly in a modality-independent format.

Language perception processes can be explained from the predictive coding framework. Self-monitoring plays an important role here. Self-monitoring takes place when speakers and listeners continuously monitor their own speech and that of the other person while anticipating what the other person is saying. Through this anticipation, listeners can increase the intelligibility of the conversation partner on the basis of a covert speech production process. A unique aspect of language is that it can directly activate abstract concepts. From the perspective of predictive coding framework, language might be considered to be a tool that can activate concepts, and thus form expectations that influence our perception.

Besides literal meanings, language is also characterised by a multitude of non-literal meanings. Pragmatics is concerned with the study of the practical aspects of language, in particular the interpretation of figurative language. Examples of non-literal language use are metaphors, and stylistic devices such as irony, cynicism, or giving evasive answers. A special characteristic of a metaphor is that the literal meaning is often incorrect. Precisely for this reason, metaphors are often used in pragmatics research.

According to the standard pragmatic model, the figurative meaning of a statement is only interpreted after an attempt has been made to interpret the literal meaning. However, studies in which participants were asked to interpret the literal meaning of sentences have shown that this assumption is incorrect. Empirical results are therefore more consistent with the graded salience model, which assumes that the relative salience of the literal and figurative meanings of a metaphor determine whether the literal or figurative meaning is activated first.

The predication model assumes that the interpretation of metaphors takes place in two stages. The first stage involves a semantic analysis and the second a construction and integration stage. In the latter stage, concepts related to the figurative meaning are activated and concepts related to the literal meaning are inhibited.

Story processing can take place as we integrate and relate information presented in individual sentences to a context provided by background knowledge. The formation of inferences plays an important role in this. Inferences form a bridge between different sentences and our background knowledge that fills in implicitly leftover information. We can distinguish between the following types of inferences: logical inferences are derived from the meaning of a word, whereas bridging inferences establish the connection between different parts of a text. A special form of this type of inference is anaphor resolution. Comprehensive inferences embellish the text on the basis of information that is left implicit and that we fill in from our background knowledge.

According to the constructionist approach, we automatically make many elaborate inferences when reading, while according to the minimalist approach, we only make those inferences that are strictly necessary for text comprehension. In addition, the memory-based approach and the search after meaning approach are distinguished. Which type of inference we form, however, depends partly on the purpose for which we read. In addition, the process of inference formation is also determined by the context in which information is presented.

Cognitive schemas play a key role in forming a representation of a text. Information that is inconsistent with a cognitive schema is less well remembered than information that is consistent. In addition, schema-consistent details that were not in the original story are sometimes reported. The process of inference formation not only occurs during reading but also during the retrieval of a story from memory. In addition to forming inferences, cognitive schemas also aid with the understanding of texts. Ambiguous texts can be interpreted better when they can be linked to a specific schema.

Two alternative theoretical approaches attempt to describe the processes involved in forming a mental representation of a written text. The construction-integration model aims to do so by describing how information is stored in a text in the form of a series of propositions that represent the text at different levels of description. Situation models, on the other hand, primarily describe the processes involved in encoding actions.

While in understanding a story we transform the information that is given into a mental representation, in writing a story we have to do exactly the opposite. Writing results in a transition from a knowledge-telling strategy, through a knowledge-transformation strategy, to a knowledge-creation strategy. The knowledge-telling strategy focuses mainly on content. The knowledge-transformation strategy adds a focus on rhetoric, while the knowledge-creation strategy also considers the knowledge and needs of the reader.

FURTHER READING

Caroll, D. W. (2007). *Psychology of language*. Belmont, CA: Thompson Higher Education.

Ellis, A., & Beattie, G. (1986). *The psychology of language and communication*. Hove, UK: Psychology Press.

Harley, T. A. (2014). *The psychology of language: From data to theory*. Hove, UK: Psychology Press.

Ludden, D. (2015). *The psychology of language: An integrated approach*. Singapore: Lawrence Erlbaum Associates.

Tomasello, M. (2003). *The new psychology of language: Cognitive and functional approaches to language structure*. Mahwah, NJ: Lawrence Erlbaum Associates.

Whitney, P. (1998). *The psychology of language*. Belmont, CA: Cengage Learning.

CHAPTER 17

Language perception and understanding

17.1 INTRODUCTION

A hilarious sketch from the American comedy show 'Saturday Night Live' depicts TV personality Kylie Jenner's private jet being in an emergency somewhere over Scotland. A panicking pilot tries to maintain contact with air traffic control in Glasgow. Although the initial contact is reasonable, the pilot is eventually instructed to contact another controller – the best specialist in assisting pilots in distress. Unfortunately, there is one problem: the good man's Scottish accent is so strong that it is impossible to understand him.

This skit powerfully illustrates the importance of understanding and comprehending language. In this chapter, we will take a closer look at the main cognitive processes involved in these aspects of language. The two most common forms of language perception are reading and listening to speech, and as such, they are based on visual and auditory perception, respectively. Thus, language perception is modality specific. Although there is no clear boundary between language perception and language comprehension, the cognitive processes involved in language perception are generally tied to a specific input modality, while those related to understanding are far less so.

17.2 READING AND LISTENING: DIFFERENCES AND SIMILARITIES

Although listening and reading each make use of a different sensory modality, there are some important similarities. For example, the processes involved in understanding a sentence are similar regardless of whether you are reading it or hearing it.

Nevertheless, we can also identify some important differences. Written words can be perceived instantaneously, whereas spoken words are spread out over time and are transitive. That is, once spoken, words fade and have to be

kept active in working memory, whereas written words, sentences, or even entire passages can be read again. Therefore, listening to speech is more memory demanding than reading. Not only is the auditory speech signal volatile, it is also ambiguous. The word boundaries are not clearly distinguishable, which implies that listening to speech places a heavy demand on the word **segmentation** process, that is, the process that identifies the individual words that are embedded in a continuous audio signal.

Despite these problems, spoken text is generally much less ambiguous than written text. An important feature of spoken text is **prosody**, that is, the rhythm, emphasis, and intonation that is produced by a speaker. Prosody is effective in resolving ambiguities in a sentence. In written texts, such ambiguities are often resolved by punctuation. Punctuation marks are, however, much less effective in resolving ambiguities, specifically when it comes to the representation of subtle stylistic forms, such as irony or cynicism.

17.3 READING SINGLE WORDS

According to Balota, Paul, and Spieler (1999) reading involves the use of several different properties of language, such as **orthography** (the spelling of words), **phonology** (the sound of words), **semantics** (the meaning of words), **syntax** (the rules that describe the structure of a language) and higher-order discourse integration. Obviously, word recognition lies at the heart of reading. Rayner and Sereno (1994) suggest that this process is generally quite automatic. This suggestion is plausible when we consider that by the time we are young adults, we have already read between 20 and 70 million words and that we can process an average of 300 words per minute. How do we do that? The next sections aim to address this question.

A naive, purely bottom-up driven explanation for word recognition could be the following. First, our visual system detects the individual elements that make up letters and generates object representations of the individual letters based on these elements. Then, the letters that are

DOI: 10.4324/9781003319344-24

identified this way are processed in sequence and compared to the entries stored in an internal **lexicon** until there is a match with the written word. This naive idea cannot be correct, however, as was aptly demonstrated by the very robust **word superiority effect**. After all, as early as 1885, James McKeen Cattell already reported that words could still be recognised when presentation times were so short that individual letters could not be recognised (Cattell, 1885).

More than 80 years later, Reicher (1969) reported a similar result: he instructed participants to identify letters which were presented for a very short time (35–85 ms). Immediately following the presentation, these letters were masked, and participants were shown two new letters from which they had to choose the one that matched the previously presented target letter. The key manipulation in the experiment was that the letters that had to be identified were either presented alone, were part of a word, or were part of a random sequence of four letters. When the letters were part of a word, participants turned out to be much more accurate in recognising the letter than when they were part of a random sequence of letters. This implies that the context that is formed by a word can positively influence letter recognition. Subsequently, it turned out that it is not even necessary to use real words to achieve this improvement in recognition. For instance, Carr, Davidson, and Hawkins (1978) showed that pseudo-words will also facilitate recognition. The latter is known as the **pseudo-word superiority effect**, which suggests that orthography is involved in letter recognition, without necessarily activating word meaning.

17.3.1 THE INTERACTIVE ACTIVATION MODEL

To explain these context effects, McClelland and Rumelhart (1981) developed a neural network model in which word recognition is assumed to involve three levels: the word level, the letter level, and the feature level. The model assumes that top-down and bottom-up processes interact with each other (see fig 17.1). More specifically, the interactive activation model consists of recognition units at all three levels. The lowest level consists of units involved in recognising the constituent features of letters, such as horizontal, vertical, or curved lines. The second, intermediate level contains units that are involved in recognising letters, and the highest level consists of units that recognise complete words. The model is interactive because activation at higher levels can influence activation levels at lower levels.

Suppose we see a four-letter word. When a feature of a letter has been detected, for example a central vertical line, all letter units containing this feature are activated, such as the 'E', the 'F', or the 'H', while all other letters are inhibited. The activated letters then activate all word representations containing the corresponding letter, while

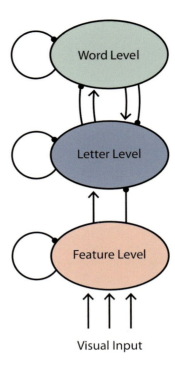

Figure 17.1 The interactive activation model. (source: McClelland and Rumelhart, 1981)

all words not containing this letter are inhibited. This process involves each feature and letter comprising a word, eventually activating all four-letter words that consist of the recognised letters and letter features.

Top-down influences manifest themselves because the activated candidate words subsequently also activate the candidate letters that are present in these words, while they inhibit the candidate letters that are not present in the candidate words. The strengthening of the candidate letters, in turn, results in a strengthening of the activation of the relevant features and the inhibition of the irrelevant ones. This top-down influence then strengthens the contrast between activated and inhibited units, which in turn influences activation at the letter and word level. The word superiority effect can thus be explained by the fact that word information can facilitate the recognition of individual letters by means of these recurrent feedback projections. Nevertheless, the question still remains how the pseudo-word effect can be explained, because they cannot activate the word level. When letters are embedded in pronounceable non-words, however, there will always be some overlap with existing words, which can also result in additional activation of the letters comprising the pseudo-word and thus facilitate the recognition of this word.

The latter finding also hints at an additional prediction of the model, namely that the time needed to recognise a word depends, at least in part, on its **orthographic neighbours**. The orthographic neighbours of a word are formed by all the words that can be formed by changing only one letter in the word. The orthographic neighbours of 'stop' are, for example, 'step', 'atop', and 'swop'. When a word is presented, the model predicts that all its orthographic neighbours are also activated, each inhibiting each other as well as the target word. The higher the number of neighbours, the stronger the combined inhibition will be, according to the model. In theory, this inhibitory effect should also depend on the neighbours' word frequency. The more frequent an orthographic neighbour occurs in a language, the more easily it should be activated. Although this effect has been found for some languages, including Dutch, French, and Spanish, it is difficult to establish it for the English language (Sears, Campbell, & Lupker, 2006). Moreover, the interactive activation model also assumes that the word superiority effect should be stronger as a function of word frequency. After all, words that are used frequently in the language will be activated more easily. However, no evidence was found for the latter prediction (Günther, Gfroerer, & Weiss, 1984).

17.3.2 POSITION CODING

A further prediction that is made by the interactive activation model is that letters should occupy a fixed position within a word (Gomez, Ratcliff, & Perea, 2008). Letter order is certainly important, because otherwise we would not be able to distinguish anagrams such as 'creative' versus 'reactive'. We are, however, much more flexible in processing the order of letters than the interactive activation model assumes. Gomez et al. note that non-words in which two letters are swapped from an existing word (e.g., 'jugde') are often recognised as an existing word. For the interactive activation model, the non-word 'jugde' is as similar to 'judge' as to 'jumpe' because only three of the five letters match. However, this does not correspond to our intuitive experience that 'judge' is more similar to 'jugde' than to 'jumpe'.

Alternative models have thus been formulated which can explain these effects of position coding. In Gomez et al.'s **overlap model** the letters of a word are not assigned to a fixed position. Instead, each letter is probabilistically assigned to a position (see fig 17.2). In the word 'detail', for example, the letter 't' is mainly associated with the third position, but also to some extent with the second and fourth positions, which enables the model to assign probabilities to several candidate words that only differ in letter positions. Although the letter positions are probabilistic, the overlap model is still essentially a variant of the interactive activation model. More recent models for word recognition are based on Bayesian inference (Norris, 2013). These models assume that information about the identity and position of letters accumulates with the passage of time.

Two important models that fall into this category are the Letters in Time and Retinotopic Space (LTRS) model and

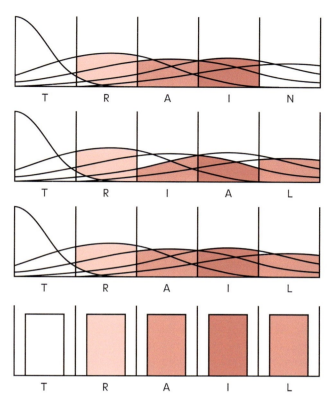

Figure 17.2 Graphic representation of the overlap model. This model assigns a stochastic probability to the position of each letter in a word. (source: Gomez et al., 2008)

the Bayesian Reader (BR). Both the LTRS and BR models are specified at a relatively abstract level and make no assumptions about their specific implementation. The essence of these models is that they aim to explain how statistical evidence for different candidate words accumulates during reading. For each word in the lexicon, the model calculates a probability that this is the word that has been read. This calculation considers not only the physical characteristics of the word but also word frequency, meaning, and expectation.

17.3.3 THE INFLUENCE OF WORD MEANING AND EXPECTATION

The fact that both word meaning and expectation are involved in word recognition has been established for a long time. In 1935, the American psychologist John Ridley Stroop demonstrated that word meaning is processed automatically. As discussed in detail in Chapter 5, using a now-famous experiment, Stroop presented a series of words consisting of the names of colours, and found that it took participants much longer to name the print colour of these words when the meaning of the word conflicted with this colour, compared to a condition in which the meaning of the word did not interfere with the print colour (Stroop, 1935).

17.3.4 PRIMING AND EXPECTATION

The individual words that appear in a sentence are usually related to each other, and this relationship also facilitates word recognition. In yet another classic study, Meyer and Schvaneveldt (1971) found that participants were able to decide more quickly whether 'doctor' was a word when it was preceded by a semantically related concept, such as 'nurse', than when it was preceded by an unrelated concept, such as 'library'.

Neely (1977) wondered to what extent this **priming** effect automatically activates word meaning. Is this activation fully automatic and bottom-up, or is it possible that controlled processes, based on expectation, activate word meaning? To address this question, he designed an ingenious experiment involving category names as a prime (e.g., 'bird') which could be followed 250, 400, or 700 ms later by a letter sequence (the target stimulus). Participants had to decide whether or not this letter sequence was a word. Moreover, they were instructed that the prime 'bird' would usually be followed by the name of a specific bird species, while the prime word 'body' would usually be followed by a part of a building. This combination of prime and target stimulus allowed for a total of four conditions, along with a fifth control condition:

1. Expected and semantically related   (e.g., bird – robin)
2. Expected and semantically unrelated   (e.g., body – door)
3. Unexpected and semantically related   (e.g., body – heart)
4. Unexpected and semantically unrelated (e.g., bird – arm)
5. Control condition   (e.g., xxxx – robin)

Neely (1977) found that there were two distinct priming effects (see fig 17.3). The first was a short-term facilitation effect that was purely driven by the semantic relation between the prime and target word. When the time between the presentation of the prime and the target stimulus was short, that is, 250 ms, the combinations 'bird – robin' and 'body – heart' were processed relatively fast. In addition, there was an effect of expectation, which arose later and lasted longer. At an interval of 700 ms between prime and target stimulus, expected combinations ('bird – robin' and 'body – door') were processed relatively fast, whereas unexpected combinations ('body – heart' and 'bird – arm') were processed more slowly. We can therefore conclude that both semantics and expectation are involved in word recognition, with the influence of semantics being fast and automatic, and the influence of expectation being slower and more task-dependent.

The question is when exactly do we make use of this context: do we use the context of a previous sentence to predict what the next word in a sentence will be, or are we passive and do we use the context only when we have already read the next word? There is currently much evidence for the first alternative, namely that we

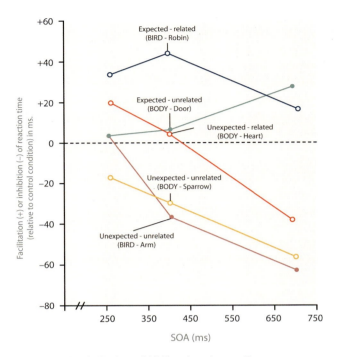

Figure 17.3 The facilitation or inhibition of word recognition processes as a function of the delay between prime and target words for four different experimental conditions, based on the combination of expectation and semantic relatedness. (source: Neely, 1977)

use the context as a predictor (Kutas, Delong, & Smith, 2011). Using ERPs, Penolazzi, Hauk, and Pulvermuller (2007) have shown that context can influence lexical access at a very early stage. More specifically, they used sentences such as: 'He was just around the corner' or 'He was just near the corner'. These sentences were presented one word at a time and the researchers were interested in the processing of one specific target word: here 'corner'. The word 'corner' is more likely to be expected when it is preceded by 'around' than when it is preceded by 'near', and this difference in expectation was also reflected in ERPs that were evoked by the target word 'corner'. When it was expected, the P200 component was larger, compared to when it was not expected. The latency of this effect is remarkable, because 200 ms marks the final stage of the initial visual processing of a word. Thus, this effect implies that expectation can influence the processing of a word at a relatively early stage.

17.3.5 THE ROLE OF PHONOLOGY

In addition to meaning and expectation, what impact does phonology have on word recognition during reading. Upon close consideration, phonology should not necessarily be involved in silent reading. It is nevertheless plausible that we activate a word's phonological code by pronouncing it sub-vocally during reading. According to Frost (1998), this is even essential for reading. Frost's strong phonological model postulates that phonological information is processed automatically and that it is crucial for word recognition.

Why should phonology be so crucial for reading? During reading, we do not, in principle, need to access the sounds of words for their recognition. During our childhood, however, we typically learn to speak and to understand speech many years before we learn to read. We often learn on the basis of a phonetic approach, in which we first learn to recognise the relationship between speech sounds and their corresponding letters or groups of letters (Share, 2008). Children's phonetic skills are therefore good predictors of their later reading skills (Melby-Lervag, Lyster, & Hulme, 2012).

Evidence for the idea that phonology is involved in word recognition was obtained in a study of Van Orden (1987). This study used **homophones**, that is, words that have the same pronunciation but a different spelling and meaning. Participants were given a target word to read, about which they had to answer a question, such as 'Is it a flower? ROWS'. When given this target word, they made more errors than when asked the question: 'Is it a flower? ROBS'. These errors resulted from the fact that participants were processing the phonological code of the word ROWS, which also activated the word meaning of the homophone ROSE.

The extent to which phonology can affect word recognition also depends on the **phonological neighbourhood** of a word. The phonological neighbourhood consists of all words that differ from the target word by only one phoneme. For example, the word 'cheap' has 'chap', 'weep', and 'cheat' as phonological neighbours. If phonology affects word recognition, we might expect that words with many phonological neighbours are more easily recognised, because the different phonological associations contribute to the recognition (Yates, 2005). A study by Yates, Friend, and Ploetz (2008) did indeed find that, during a reading task, participants processed words with many phonological neighbours faster than words with few phonological neighbours. This effect was only found, however, when the phonological neighbours were relatively distinct. When they were very similar in pronunciation, it was found that the phonological neighbourhood interfered, thus slowing down word recognition (Yates, 2013).

The influence of phonology on word recognition is also evident in various phonological priming studies. In these studies, a target word (e.g., 'clip') is immediately preceded by a phonologically identical non-word prime (e.g., 'klip'). The prime is presented so briefly that it is not consciously perceived. In control conditions, however, prime and target words are used that are less similar to each other. Rastle and Brysbaert (2006) conducted a meta-analysis involving many studies that used this paradigm and concluded that words were processed faster when they were preceded by phonologically identical non-word primes, rather than by the non-identical control primes. This result also shows that the phonology of a word can be activated quickly and automatically, as predicted by the strong phonological model of Frost (1998).

How do we make use of the phonological information of words? While reading, we frequently have the subjective experience of reading the text silently, using our 'inner voice'. Filik and Barber (2011) wondered to what extent this inner voice reflects our own speaking voice. To investigate this, they instructed residents of the North and South of England to read limericks. Differences in Northern and Southern English accents imply that words that rhyme for the Northerners do not for the Southerners and vice versa. Filik and Barber found that when, according to the local accent, the last word in the limerick did not rhyme, the participants kept looking at that word longer compared to when the words did rhyme according to the local accent. This result implies that when you read to yourself you activate the phonological code of your local dialect. Your inner voice is, in other words, equivalent to your speaking voice.

Despite the major influence of phonology, it also appears that phonological information is not strictly necessary for word recognition. In contrast to Frost, other researchers assume that the processing of phonological information is actually relatively slow and not essential for word processing during reading (Coltheart, Rastle, Perry, Langdon, & Ziegler, 2001). Results consistent with this view were found by Hanley and McDonnell (1997). They presented observations of a patient with a speech production disorder. This patient, PS, was able to understand the meaning of written homophones when they were both presented explicitly. PS was unable to produce the alternative meaning of a homophone, however, when only one of them was presented. In addition, PS was unable to correctly pronounce many words. This result suggests that while PS had full access to all word meanings when these words were explicitly presented, the phonological code itself was not sufficient to automatically activate these words.

These results are similar to those of Han and Bi (2009), who also studied a patient, YGA, whose phonological processing was impaired. However, YGA's ability to understand the meaning of visually presented words was also intact. What is interesting about Han and Bi's study is that YGA's native language is Chinese Mandarin, which implies that the results generalise across very strongly differing languages. These findings indicate that phonology can be processed quickly and can have a strong influence on word processing. However, they also imply that access to phonology is not necessary for word comprehension.

17.4 READING ALOUD

There is at least one situation in which phonology must play a significant role in reading, that is, when we are reading aloud. A common method in psycholinguistics takes advantage of this fact and investigates language perception processes by instructing participants to read words out loud. A problem with this method is, of course, that it addresses both language perception and language production processes, a fact that we should always take into consideration when interpreting results from these studies (Bock, 1996). Despite this limitation, the studies of reading out loud can be very fruitful in unravelling language perception processes, especially if we can relate the results to well-documented neuropsychological conditions. In addition, studies investigating how we pronounce irregular words, that is, words having a pronunciation that deviates from a regular rule, along with non-words, can also teach us a lot about language perception.

The fact that we can easily recognise irregularly pronounced words, combined with the fact that we can process these irregular words without much difficulty, implies that we have an internal **lexicon** in which specific information about the pronunciation of individual words is stored. The assumption that the pronunciation of words is entirely based on retrieving relevant information from a lexicon is inadequate, however. After all, it cannot explain how we are able to pronounce new words (existing words which we have never encountered before) and non-words. The pronunciation of these new words and non-words thus appears to be based on a generic pronunciation rule. More specifically, it appears that generating the pronunciation of a word relies on looking up the correct pronunciation in a lexicon on the one hand, and on applying a rule on the other. This observation is consistent with many of the difficulties found in patients with specific brain injuries. These patients have selective problems with either existing irregular words or with new/non-existing words.

17.4.1 DYSLEXIA

Many of the difficulties just discussed manifest themselves in **dyslexia**. Dyslexia is a general term for a class of reading problems. More specifically, we can distinguish between central and peripheral dyslexia. Central dyslexia affects higher-order reading processes, whereas peripheral dyslexia affects the processes that convert visual information into a linguistic code. Next we will focus on types of central dyslexia, because they are theoretically relevant to the reading and naming of irregular words and non-words, as discussed earlier.

17.4.1.1 Surface Dyslexia

Individuals diagnosed with **surface dyslexia** have specific difficulties with reading irregular words. McCarthy and Warrington (1984) discussed case studies of surface dyslexics and concluded that these patients' speech is often characterised by a high degree of over-regularisation when they read irregular words aloud. Their ability to read regular words and non-words remained intact, however. Consider

for example patient KT. KT was characterised by an intact ability to read regular words (81% correct) and non-words (100% correct pronunciation), but had many difficulties with reading irregular words (41% correct). Similar results were found in other patients. These results imply that surface dyslexics' processing of lexical information is impaired. Since the irregularities are believed to be stored in this lexicon, these patients' pronunciation is forced to follow the generic rule, resulting in regularisation.

17.4.1.2 Phonological Dyslexia

While surface dyslectics are mainly affected by the pronunciation of irregular words, patients with **phonological dyslexia**, on the other hand, have difficulties with pronouncing non-words, even though their ability to pronounce similarly sounding existing words remains intact. Phonological dyslexia was first described by Shallice and Warrington (1975), who described the case study of patient KF. A more systematic study of phonological dyslexia was carried out by Beauvois and Dérouesné (1979), with their study of patient RG. RG was able to successfully read existing words, but he could only pronounce 10% of the non-words. This limitation suggests that phonological dyslexics have a deficiency in their rule-based conversion of spelling to pronunciation and therefore rely exclusively on lexical information that is still intact.

It is questionable, however, whether phonological dyslexia only affects the rule-based system. For example, Coltheart (1996) discusses several phonological dyslexia patients who are all characterised by more general limitations in phonological processing, such as difficulties in finding rhyming words, or in deciding whether two words sound similar. A subset of phonological dyslexics, however, do not appear to conform to the pattern just described. For instance, Caccappolo-van Vliet, Miozzo, and Stern (2004b) describe two phonological dyslexics who had specific difficulties with reading non-words, while their performance on other phonological tasks was virtually intact, suggesting that these patients have a very specific limitation.

17.4.2 THEORETICAL APPROACHES

The relationship between a lexical and a rule-based system can be explained by two different theoretical perspectives. These are the **triangle model**, originally proposed by Seidenberg and McClelland (1989), and the **dual-route cascade model**, developed by Coltheart et al. (2001). These approaches differ quite drastically from each other, in the sense that the triangle model is based on a distributed connectionist approach, in which orthography, phonology, and also contextual and lexical information jointly determine the final pronunciation of a word, whereas in the case of the dual-route cascade model there is a stricter separation between the lexical and the rule-based systems.

17.4.2.1 Analogy Models

As a precursor to the current models, the first models emerged towards the end of the 1970s, when the influence of lexical effects on the reading of words and non-words first became apparent. These models assumed that we pronounce words and non-words by using analogies with other words. Moreover, these analogy models assumed that the pronunciation of words involved a single process that operates on the basis of the activation of similar words. A major issue with these models, however, was that they were unable to adequately account for the distinction between lexical and non-lexical effects (Caccappolo-van Vliet, Miozzo, & Stern, 2004a).

17.4.2.2 The Triangle Model

Despite the limitations of the original analogy models, the mechanisms underlying these models did form the basis for the later connectionist models, which were much more capable of explaining the pronunciation of both words and non-words. One of the most influential of these connectionist models is the triangle model, originally formulated by Seidenberg and McClelland (1989) and later considerably further elaborated by Plaut, McClelland, Seidenberg, and Patterson (1996). The original triangle model, also known as the Seidenberg-McClelland model, shares properties with the interactive activation model for letter and word recognition discussed earlier in this chapter (see fig 17.4).

In their original formulation, Seidenberg and McClelland proposed a model capable of describing how we recognise series of letters as words and then pronounce them.

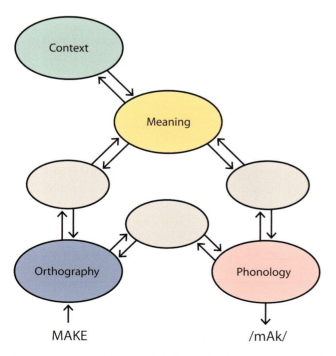

Figure 17.4 The triangle model for lexical processing. (source: Seidenberg and McClelland, 1989)

The conversion from orthography to phonology is, however, only one part of a more general model of lexical processing. Reading and speech involve three different types of information: in addition to the orthographic and phonological codes, it also involves a semantic system, as discussed earlier. These three types of information are connected via feedback loops; these triangular connections form the basis for the model's name.

Seidenberg and McClelland (1989) originally only simulated the direct conversion of orthography to phonology using a connectionist network. This simulation consisted of a network with an input layer, an intermediate layer, and an output layer representing phonological units. As is typically the case with a connectionist network, the weights of the connections between the nodes were obtained by training the network. After training, the network proved to be very capable of selecting the correct phonemes for regular words and for irregular words.

Despite this success, the original Seidenberg-McClelland model was strongly criticised by Coltheart, Curtis, Atkins, and Haller (1993). According to these authors, the model was unable to explain some fundamental aspects of reading aloud. In particular, the model was deemed to be deficient in determining how we can read non-words. Moreover, it was also believed to fail in explaining the development of surface and phonological dyslexia. For this reason, the model has been thoroughly revised by, among others, Plaut et al. (1996). This revised model, known as PMSP (after the authors' initials), used more realistic input and output representations, which made it much better at selecting the correct phonemes for non-words. However, this model still only simulated the relationship between orthography and phonology. The influence of semantics was later added by Harm and Seidenberg (2004).

The latter model thus implements the full triangle proposed by Seidenberg and McClelland in 1989. All parts of the final model contribute to the activation of word meaning. According to the model, meaning is activated via two separate routes: a direct route from orthography to semantics and an indirect route from orthography via phonology to semantics. When the model is fully trained, word meaning is generally activated slightly faster via the direct route than via the indirect route. Although the indirect route is slightly slower, it is nevertheless involved in the activation of word meaning. Because of the interactive connections, the meaning units also activate the phonological units, so semantics are also involved in the selection of the phonological output units.

17.4.2.3 Dual-route Cascade Model

The different types of dyslexia introduced earlier suggest that there are at least two different ways in which the conversion from a grapheme to a phonological code can proceed. More specifically, a **grapheme** is the basic unit of a written language. It can consist of individual letters or combinations of letters which correspond to a specific speech sound. A **phoneme** is the basic unit of spoken language. Coltheart et al. (2001) developed a computational model to explain the involvement of the different conversion routes, since the original triangle model was deficient in this respect. Coltheart et al.'s model has been given the somewhat misleading name **dual-route cascade model**. It is misleading because the model actually comprises three instead of two routes (see fig 17.5).

The basic assumption of the model, however, is that there are two main routes through which orthographic information can be converted to phonological codes: a rule-based route and a lexical route. The lexical route is divided into one that involves the semantic system and one that involves just the phonological and orthographic lexical systems. The model is based on a cascading principle, that is, it assumes that processing at the next stage of processing can already start while the processing at an earlier stage is still going on.

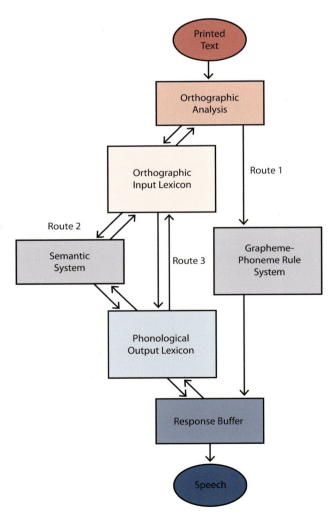

Figure 17.5 The dual-route cascade model. (source: Coltheart et al., 2001)

The model is able to adequately simulate the effects of lexical decision tasks and naming tasks, and it can adequately reproduce the effects of word frequency, the regularisation of pseudo-homophones, the effects of orthographic and phonological neighbours, along with various priming effects. Regularity is an important factor in the model: irregular words take longer to process, due to the fact that the lexical and non-lexical routes produce conflicting phonological codes. The model can explain surface dyslexia by making the lexicon less accessible, and phonological dyslexia by damaging the grapheme-phoneme conversion pathway.

17.4.2.4 Grapheme-Phoneme Conversion (Route 1)

Route 1 differs from the other two routes in that it can convert graphemes to phonemes on the basis of a rule-based system, without requiring lexical access. If brain damage forces a patient to fully rely on using route 1, we would find that each grapheme would be translated into the phoneme that is most closely associated with it. Thus, we would expect these patients to still be accurate in pronouncing words with a regular spelling-sound relationship. However, they should have problems pronouncing words that do not conform to these rules. In this case, they would be expected to **regularise** these words, that is, their pronunciation would conform to the general rule. In contrast, these patients should have no problems with the pronunciation of non-words, as these can be pronounced according to the conversion rules. These symptoms are indeed found in patients with surface dyslexia, such as the previously described patient KT, who showed a high degree of regularisation while pronouncing irregular words.

17.4.2.5 The Lexical Routes (Routes 2 and 3)

In contrast to rule-based route 1, routes 2 and 3 retrieve information from a lexicon to determine the correct pronunciation. The presence of such a lexicon facilitates the search for grapheme-phoneme relationships for existing words. In addition, exceptions are also assumed to be stored here. If brain damage forces patients to solely rely on the lexical pathways, we may expect that they will no longer be able to pronounce non-words correctly, since non-words are not encoded in the patient's lexicon. Moreover, these patients will also have more difficulties with words that they are unfamiliar with, since these words are not, or at most only very weakly, represented in their lexicon. Patients with phonological dyslexia fit this description well: they specifically have difficulties with reading unfamiliar words but perform generally well when pronouncing irregular words.

The main difference between routes 2 and 3 is that the latter route does not involve the semantic system. Difficulties with semantic processing are often found in patients with **deep dyslexia**. These patients typically have difficulties with pronouncing unfamiliar words and non-words. A particularly striking feature of deep dyslexia, however, is that these patient's semantic system also appears to be affected. Consequently, patients often replace words with a semantically related word, such as 'ship' being replaced by 'boat'. Although these symptoms indicate that these patients have damage to both routes 1 and 2, the symptoms of deep dyslexia are often too complex to be fully explained by the dual-route cascade model (Coltheart et al., 2001). Although deep dyslexia appears to be a severe form of phonological dyslexia, there is also evidence that the symptoms are due to the fact that the language functions in these patients have been taken over by the right hemisphere. Evidence for this hypothesis was found by Patterson, Vargha-Khadem, and Polkey (1989), who studied a girl (NI) whose left hemisphere had been surgically removed at the age of 15, as a result of extreme epileptic seizures. Two years after the operation, NI had all the symptoms of deep dyslexia, suggesting a link between her dyslectic symptoms and her still intact right hemisphere.

The dual-route cascade model is consistent with many neuropsychological studies, and much evidence supporting the model has been found in studies involving neurotypical participants. Yet, the model is also characterised by some important limitations. One of these is, of course, the fact that the model cannot properly explain the results of deep dyslexia. This implies that the model cannot adequately explain the involvement of semantics during word reading. This is a serious limitation, because there is much evidence that semantics are often very important in reading processes. Neuroimaging studies have found, for example, that brain areas involved in the processing of semantics are frequently activated during reading (Cattinelli, Borghese, Gallucci, & Paulesu, 2013).

A second limitation is that the model cannot learn, so it cannot explain how the grapheme-phoneme relationships can arise in the first place, nor can it explain how new information can be incorporated into the lexicon as we start to read during childhood or continue to expand our vocabulary later in life. A third limitation is that the model assumes that phonological processing is slow and has only a limited impact on word recognition and reading performance. This assumption is, however, far from consistent with many empirical studies that have shown that phonology can indeed have a very rapid impact on word recognition (Rastle & Brysbaert, 2006). A fourth limitation is that the model is by no means universal. It is only suitable for explaining the processing of monosyllabic words. Since it is not possible to write monosyllabic non-words in

Chinese or in Japanese Kanji script, there cannot even be a distinction between a lexical and a non-lexical route for these languages.

Finally, the model is rather complex. When two models can explain approximately the same data, the simplest of these models should always be preferred. The complexity of a model can be expressed in the number of free parameters it contains. The values of these parameters are typically chosen in such a way that the model closely matches the empirical findings. The lower the number of free parameters a model contains, the simpler (or more economical) the model is. With 30 free parameters, the dual-route cascade model is certainly not an economical model, so it is not really surprising that it fits well to a large amount of data.

17.4.2.6 Converging Ideas

The dual-route cascade model and the triangle model have evolved considerably in recent years to better describe existing data. One of the consequences of this development is that the two models are ever so increasingly converging, as concluded by Taylor, Rastle, and Davis (2013) based on a meta-analysis of 36 neuroimaging studies.

For example, both models predict that different processes are involved in the processing of words and non-words. Some brain areas should therefore be activated more strongly by words than by non-words, while for other brain areas the opposite should apply. Indeed, words activate the anterior fusiform gyrus more strongly than non-words. This brain area is often associated with the orthographic lexicon and/or the semantic system. In addition, words evoked more activation in the angular and mid-temporal gyri; areas that are mainly related to the phonological lexicon and/or the semantic system.

Non-words, on the other hand, have been found to activate the posterior fusiform and occipitotemporal cortex more strongly. These areas are mainly involved in the processing of orthographic information. In addition, non-words also activated the inferior parietal cortex and the inferior frontal gyrus; areas that are mainly involved in converting orthographic information to a phonological code. The inferior frontal gyrus was also activated more by irregular words than by regular words. The latter effect was interpreted as being due to the extra effort that is required to pronounce irregular words, as a result of the conflict between the output of the rule-based system and the lexical system.

Taylor et al. (2013) used the results of their meta-analysis to identify the main brain regions involved in reading aloud (see fig 17.6) and related these brain processes to both the dual-route cascade model and the triangle model.

483

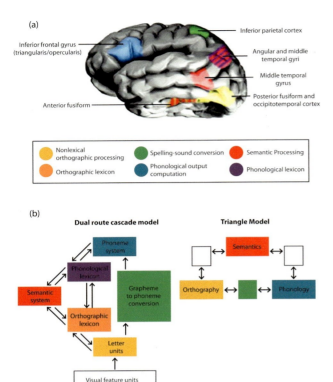

Figure 17.6 Overlapping functionality of the triangle and dual-route cascade models. (a) Overview of the processes involved and their most likely neural implementation. (b) The relationship between these processes and their role in the dual-route cascade model and the triangle model, respectively. (source: Taylor et al., 2013)

17.5 READING SENTENCES

In the previous sections, we considered some of the complexities of language perception. Yet, we have still only focused on the processing of single words on the basis of some fundamental properties of these words. In everyday life, however, it is relatively rare to just read single words. After all, the vast majority of the text we read consists of one or more sentences. To read a sentence, we have to move our eyes along the text, and the patterns of our eye movements can provide new insights into how we process texts.

17.5.1 EYE MOVEMENTS

Each day we make thousands of eye movements, usually even without being aware of them. In most cases, our eyes rapidly jump from one location to another. These jumps are known as **saccades** (see also Chapter 6) and they are ballistic, that is, once initiated their trajectory cannot be changed anymore. A saccade takes about 20–30 ms. While reading, we make saccades of about eight letters or spaces. Each saccade is followed by a fixation that takes about 200–250 ms.

During a saccade, our eyes cannot process information; that only happens during **fixations**. How much information we can take in during a fixation can be determined by using a moving window technique (Rayner, 2014). This technique involves masking the text to be read, except for a small window around the point of fixation (see fig 17.7.a). By manipulating the size of this window, we can determine when reading performance is affected. Based on this technique, it has been established that each fixation allows us to process approximately three to four letters to the left of the fixation point and up to a maximum of 15 letters to the right. At least, this applies to languages written from left to right. For languages written from right to left, the exact opposite has been found.

The words on which we fixate are not random: in 80% of all cases, we fixate on content words, such as nouns, verbs, or adjectives; the remaining 20% of fixations are on function words, such as articles, conjunctions, or pronouns. A remarkable, and at first glance counterintuitive, effect is that the fixation time on a word depends not only on the word itself but also on the frequency of the previously fixated word. The lower the frequency of that word, the longer we remain fixated on the current word. This effect is known as the **spillover effect**.

17.5.2 E-Z READER

If we were to set up a naive model for eye movements during reading, we would start from the idea that we would fixate on each word separately and that we only execute a saccade to the next word when we have fully processed the current one. There are some significant problems with naive idea, however, forcing us to reconsider the involvement of eye movements in reading. First, it takes about 85–200 ms for each eye movement to be planned and executed. This could imply that a considerable amount of time would be lost between the processing of two words if we could only initiate each eye movement after having fully processed a word. Second, we have already noted that we sometimes skip words when fixing. This too would be difficult to explain using a model that assumes we can only process a word after we have already fixated on it.

It thus appears that we already plan an eye movement to the next word, while still processing the one currently fixated. An influential model for explaining this type of eye movement planning is the E-Z Reader[1] model, which was developed by the American psycholinguists Erik Reichle, Keith Rayner, and Alexander Pollatsek (Pollatsek, Reichle, & Rayner, 2006; Reichle, Pollatsek, Fisher, & Rayner, 1998; Reichle, Rayner, & Pollatsek, 2003). According to this model, we program an eye movement to the next part of a sentence after we have already partially processed the information we are going to fixate on during a previous fixation, thus allowing much faster reading (see fig 17.7b). According to the model, readers can focus their attention on two words during a fixation: the word that is currently

(a)

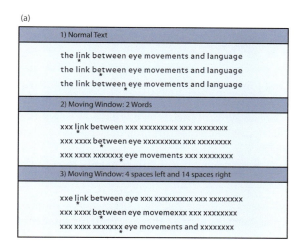

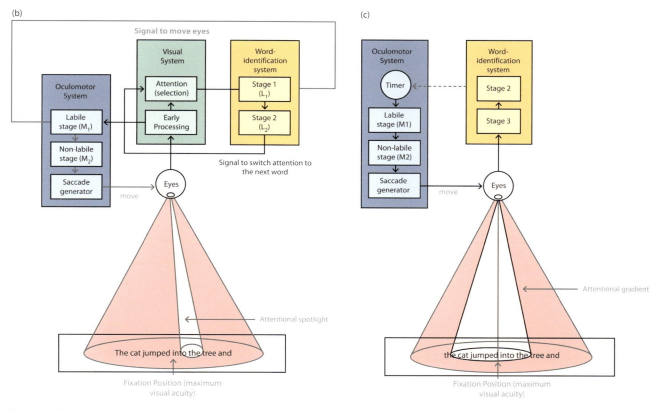

Figure 17.7 The E-Z Reader and SWIFT models for saccadic eye movement patterns during reading. (a) Example of using the moving window technique to determine how much information is processed during a single fixation. (b) Schematic representation of the E-Z Reader model. (c) The SWIFT model. (source: Reichle et al., 2003)

fixated and the next word. According to the model, however, only one word can be processed at a time. The E-Z Reader model assumes that this is done on the basis of the following processes.

1. Checking the familiarity of the word being fixated.
2. Assessing word frequency. This is the first step in gaining lexical access. Completion of this check also initiates the programming of the next saccade.
3. Establishing lexical access and activating the semantic and phonological codes.
4. Initiating a switch of attention to the next (unfixated) word.

An important assumption of the model is that frequency checks and lexical access are faster for high-frequency words than for low-frequency words. This is specifically the case for lexical access. In addition, the model assumes that these processes are faster for words that are expected in the context of a sentence than for words that are not expected. One implication of this is that there is time available for the processing of the adjacent, non-fixated word. The time allowed for this is the period between the completion of processing the fixated word and the actual execution of the saccade to the next word. Since the processing of highly-frequent and expected words can be relatively fast, there is more time left for processing the next word. Thus, the fixation of a word not only depends on the frequency of the currently fixated word but also on the frequency of the previously fixated word. That is, when the latter is relatively infrequent or unexpected, there was little time available during the previous fixation to process the current word and we would therefore have to fixate longer to process this word completely.

The E-Z Reader model can also explain why we often skip short function words. These words are often so frequent, short, and expected that we have already fully processed them during the previous fixation, so there is no longer any need to fixate them.

The part of the sentence that we fixate on is projected onto the **fovea**, that is, the part of the retina that allows us to perceive fine details (see Chapter 6). According to the E-Z Reader model, we can also process information that is projected outside of the fovea, the so-called parafoveal information. The assumption that readers use parafoveal information during a previous fixation to process the current word was tested by Reingold, Reichle, Glaholt, and Sheridan (2012). They used sentences such as: 'I was told that the table was made out of expensive wood'. While participants were reading this sentence, In some trials the word 'table' was replaced by the word 'banjo', at the moment they started to make a saccade to 'table'. When this happened, fixation times turned out to be much longer than when the word had not been changed. This prolonged fixation time can be explained by the fact that the processing of 'banjo' could not benefit from the parafoveal processing during the preceding fixations.

17.5.2.1 Parallel versus Serial Processes

An assumption of the E-Z Reader model is that words are processed serially, and this feature of the model seems to be incompatible with a specific phenomenon known as the **parafoveal-to-foveal effect**. This phenomenon implies that not only the properties of the previous word but also those of the next word influence the fixation time on the current word. This effect implies, however, that the current word and the next word are processed in parallel. Models that assume parallel processing, such as the **saccade generation with inhibition by foveal targets (SWIFT)** model (Engbert, Longtin, & Kleigl, 2002; Engbert, Nuthmann, Richter, & Kliegl, 2005) can better explain these effects.

The main difference with the E-Z Reader model is that the SWIFT model does not assume that attention switches sequentially between the two words, but that a certain amount of attention is allocated to all the words that are perceived during fixation (see fig 17.7c). Thus, the words in question would all, to a certain degree, be

processed in parallel. The degree to which each word is processed can be described by a gradient. That is, the closer words are to the fixation point, the more attention they receive, and thus the higher priority they get during processing. High-frequency, short words can still be processed quickly, however, even when they are further away from the fixation point. As such, they can directly influence the initiation of the next saccade: when these words are fully processed, while the processing of the current word is still going on, they can be skipped safely.

Although some evidence for the existence of parafoveal effects has been provided, there is still much debate about the role they play during reading (Schotter, Angele, & Rayner, 2012). The most important effects have been found for orthographic information. For example, Pynte, Kennedy, and Ducrot (2004) found that spelling errors in a parafoveal word resulted in a shorter fixation time on the foveal word. Also, word frequencies of parafoveal words appear to have an influence on current fixation. However, the effects are generally relatively small, so the contribution of parallel processes to the reading process seems to be relatively limited.

17.6 LISTENING TO SPEECH

Listening to speech is the second major way in which we perceive language, and, at the same time, speech recognition is one of the core functions of our auditory system (see Chapter 7). Speech recognition is a particularly complex process, not only because we must be able to deal with a substantial variation in speech sounds, but also because we must be able to identify the speech signal amidst an enormous variety of background noises. For this reason, we should start the discussion of speech perception by introducing all the problems listeners have to overcome before we can understand speech.

17.6.1 SPEECH RECOGNITION PROCESSES: AN OVERVIEW

Speech perception is, in a way, an extension of the auditory scene analysis process that is crucial for auditory perception (see Chapter 7). Here, these processes are specifically involved in extracting a meaningful message from the mix of auditory signals that reach our ears. Cutler and Clifton (1999) have identified the main processes involved in speech perception (see fig 17.8). The first set of processes jointly form the decoding stage. The first step of decoding involves distinguishing the speech signal from any background noise, including environmental noise, along with other possible voices in the background. After this stage, the relevant speech units (phonemes or syllables) must be

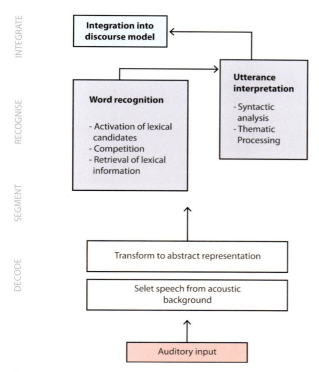

INTEGRATE

RECOGNISE

SEGMENT

DECODE

Figure 17.8 An overview of the main processes involved in speech recognition. (source: Cutler and Clifton, 1999)

extracted from the speech signal. In the third stage, the individual words that are embedded in the speech signal must then be identified. This stage, known as the segmentation of the speech signal, is particularly complex and error prone, for reasons that we will discuss in more detail later.

The fourth and fifth stages mainly concern speech comprehension. More specifically, the fourth stage involves the interpretation of an utterance. Here, interpretation implies generating a coherent meaning of each sentence based on the individual words and their position in the sentence. Finally, in the fifth stage, the meaning of the current sentence is integrated with those of the previous sentences to construct a coherent mental representation of the speaker's message.

17.6.2 IMPORTANT PERCEPTUAL PHENOMENA

From the preceding, it is clear that listening to speech is much more complex than we might initially have assumed. In addition, we need to be capable of recognising speech under various adverse conditions. According to Mattys, Davis, Bradlow, and Scott (2012), an 'adverse condition' is any factor that results in a reduction of speech intelligibility compared to the level of intelligibility under optimal conditions.

Mattys, Brooks, and Cooke (2009) have identified two different types of common adverse conditions, which they describe using the terms energetic masking and

informational masking. **Energetic masking** involves distracting sounds interfering with the speech signal and consequently reducing its intelligibility. This form of masking is mainly bottom-up driven and is often problematic in everyday life. Examples are traffic noise or the fact that other people in the background are also talking to each other. In contrast, **informational masking** is mainly a consequence of performing a second, attention-demanding task. This form of masking is therefore mainly top-down driven.

Despite these problems, we are able to process speech very rapidly and efficiently. On average we speak at a rate of about ten phonemes per second and we can easily analyse speech at the same speed. Based on this division into top-down and bottom-up driven adverse conditions, we can identify several specific problems that we as listeners regularly encounter in everyday life, as elaborated next.

17.6.2.1 The Segmentation Problem
The first problem our speech recognition system has to overcome is that of speech segmentation or extracting the relevant phonemes and words from a continuous speech signal. Although words are discrete units, a speech signal is more or less continuous. In spontaneous speech, there are often no significant pauses between individual words, while some phonemes consist of relatively silent **formants**. Added to this is the problem that most words in our language are composed of a very limited set of about 35 phonemes. Consequently, many spoken words are relatively similar to each other, which increases the likelihood of misinterpreting a sequence of sounds, especially when the speech signal is ambiguous. For this reason, Hickok (2012) has suggested that predictive coding processes contribute to word recognition. This would be done by expectations that are created by the motor system, as we sub-vocally articulate the speech signals we perceive and use these articulations to generate an expectation. It is also possible that predictions are formed on the basis of an external expectation, which is, for example, driven by the context in which we hear somebody speak (Mattys et al., 2012).

17.6.2.2 Context Effects
One of the contextual cues that we can use to disambiguate a speech signal involves the speaker's lip movements. As we have already discussed in Chapter 9, lip movements can strongly influence our perception of a speech signal (McGurk & MacDonald, 1976). However, other visual information can also strongly influence our interpretation of a speech signal.

For example, Brock and Nation (2014) showed how contextual cues that participants could derive from visual information had an impact on the interpretation of a spoken word. Here, participants were shown four objects on

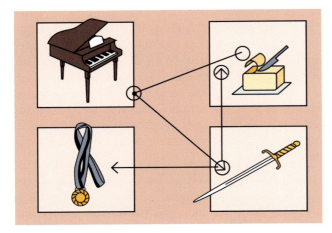

Figure 17.9 Example of the stimuli used in an eye-movement study that investigated the use of contextual information in word recognition. (source: Brock and Nation, 2014)

a computer display (see fig 17.9). They listened to a spoken sentence and had to respond by clicking, as rapidly as possible, on the object that was mentioned in the sentence. The critical manipulation in this experiment was that sometimes sentences were presented that referred to an object that was not shown, but which had a strong phonetical resemblance with an object that was shown. This was the case, for example, when the sentence referred to the word 'button', while the display showed an image of butter. During the experiment, participants' eye movements were recorded, and Brock and Nation found that, in this case, participants made eye movements towards the picture of the butter when processing the word 'button', because the phonological similarity between 'button' and 'butter' facilitated this expectation. It is important to note, however, that they only did so when the previous context provided by the sentence did not exclude the possibility that it would contain the word 'butter'. For example, when the sentence: 'Alex chose the button' was presented, participants did briefly look at the butter. However, when the sentence: 'Alex fastened the button' was presented, they did not look at it, because the word 'fastened' makes it very unlikely that the word 'butter' will follow.

17.6.2.3 Coarticulation

Coarticulation is the phenomenon that phonemes are pronounced in a context-dependent manner. The sound of a specific phoneme depends not only on the phoneme itself but also on the ones preceding and following it. For example, a /b/ sounds slightly differently in the phrases 'butter', 'pale blue', 'abacus', or 'dark brown'. The reason for this is that our motor system cannot keep up with the speed at which we are speaking – that is, if it had to generate separate motor commands for all the individual phonemes separately. To overcome this problem, some of these motor commands are programmed in parallel, with the consequence that the sounds of the individual phonemes become context-dependent. Coarticulation can be problematic because it increases the variability of the speech signal. This disadvantage

can also be considered as an advantage, however, because the differences in pronunciation between these phonemes can also be used as a cue to predict the next phoneme.

17.6.2.4 Accents and Individual Differences

Although there are enormous differences in the speed of speaking, accent, and intonation, we typically manage to understand each other without any significant problems. How are we able to understand each other so easily despite these enormous differences? According to Kraljic, Brennan, and Samuel (2008), there are two possible answers to this question. The first is that we recognise speech by identifying acoustic invariants, that is, features that remain constant in every speech signal despite all the variations. The second possible answer involves **perceptual learning** processes. Perceptual learning is the process by which we learn through experience to recognise ambiguities in perceptual input. For instance, Magnuson and Nusbaum (2007) found that expectation is an important factor in the understanding of speech. This can be observed when listeners expected to hear two speakers, when in reality there was only one. In this case they tend to perform less accurately than when they expected only one speaker.

17.6.3 PROCESSES INVOLVED IN IMPROVING SPEECH RECOGNITION

17.6.3.1 Segmentation

The segmentation of words from the speech signal is, according to Mattys, White, and Melhorn (2005), controlled by a combination of different cues. According to Mattys et al.'s hierarchical model, we can classify the cues that influence the segmentation process into three different categories (see fig 17.10): lexical cues (syntax, words, or

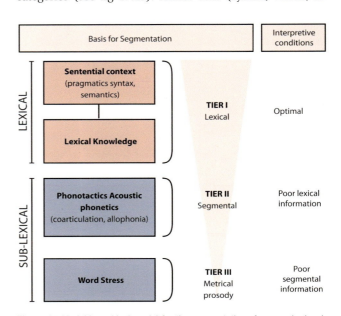

Figure 17.10 A hierarchical model for the segmentation of a speech signal. (source: Mattys et al., 2005)

knowledge), segmental cues (e.g., coarticulation) and metric cues (emphasis, intonation). Cues situated at the first, lexical, level are preferred, but when these cues are not available, cues at the segmental or metric level can be used for the segmentation process.

17.6.3.2 Phonemic Restoration Effect

In 1970, the American psychologist Richard Warren reported a remarkable finding: when he replaced a phoneme in a sentence with a meaningless sound, namely a cough, participants reported that the sentence was perfectly understandable, while they reported not perceiving the disrupting sound (Warren, 1970). When he replaced the same phoneme with a silence, however, participants did report the interference. In a follow-up experiment, Warren presented the following sentences:

- It was found that the *eel was on the axle.
- It was found that the *eel was on the shoe.
- It was found that the *eel was on the table.
- It was found that the *eel was on the orange.

Note that the first part of the sentence was always exactly the same; it was only the last word in the sentence that differed. The asterisk marks the phoneme that was replaced by a cough. Interestingly, depending on which sentence was presented, participants heard 'wheel' (sentence 1), 'heel' (sentence 2), 'meal' (sentence 3), or 'peel' (sentence 4), respectively. One possible explanation for this phenomenon is that participants use lexical information to automatically fill in the missing information on the basis of expectations (Samuel, 2011). Alternatively, the filling in could already take place at a lower level. For instance, Shahin, Kerlin, Bhat, and Miller (2012) found that successful phonemic restoration was associated with a reduction in activation of the auditory cortex, which coincided with the disrupting sound. Moreover, Shahin et al. found that listeners strongly relied on their top-down expectations, which also contributed to the automatic filling in of the missing phoneme.

17.6.3.3 Categorical Perception and the Lexical Identification Shift (The Ganong Effect)

The final phenomenon that significantly contributes to the intelligibility of speech involves categorical perception. Suppose we present a series of speech sounds that vary systematically between /ba/ and /da/. How do we perceive these intermediate forms? Do we perceive a gradual transition from one phoneme to another, or is the transition abrupt? Historically, it has been argued that it is the latter: we hear either /ba/ or /da/ and the intermediate forms are classified as one of these two phonemes. This phenomenon is known as **categorical perception**. Note, however, that McMurray (2022) has recently argued that more refined methods suggest that phoneme perception is much more

continuous than the original studies suggested, and that the notion of categorical perception should be re-evaluated.

Ganong (1980) wondered about the influence of lexical information on categorical perception. To investigate this, he used a speech synthesiser to generate a series of speech sounds that systematically varied between a word, such as 'dash', and a non-word, such as 'tash'. When the initial phoneme was ambiguous, the sound was preferably classified as a word rather than a non-word. This phenomenon is known as the **lexical identification shift**, but in honour of its discoverer it is also known as the **Ganong effect**.

17.7 SPOKEN-WORD RECOGNITION: THEORIES

Several theories explaining the recognition of spoken words have been developed over the years. One of the oldest theories in this field, the motor theory, suggests that speech production processes are crucially involved in speech perception. Although this idea has long been unpopular in favour of more cognitively oriented models, such as the cohort model and the trace model (both of which will be discussed here), the idea of a link between speech production and speech perception mechanisms has gained more attention in recent years, partly due to the discovery that motor processes are involved in the prediction of speech signals (Hickok, 2012).

17.7.1 THE MOTOR THEORY

Liberman et al. (1967) stated that one of the great challenges for a listener is formed by the accurate recognition of words amidst a huge variety of speech signals. According to Liberman et al. listeners can mitigate this problem by imitating the speaker's articulatory movements. Liberman et al. suggest that the resulting motor signal is much more consistent, and therefore capable of facilitating speech comprehension.

Evidence for the involvement of the articulatory system in speech recognition was provided by Dorman, Raphael, and Liberman (1979). These authors were interested in the effects of inserting artificial silences on the perception of words. They found, for example, that the fragment 'sa' was interpreted as 'sta' when a short silence was fitted before its onset. Dorman et al. argued that this effect is caused by a speaker's inability to produce a '/t/' sound without closing the vocal cords and that it is equally impossible to close the vocal cords without producing a '/t/' sound. In other words, a silence is predictive of a '/t/' because it represents a limit to the speech production system. In the same study, Dorman et al. presented sentences such as 'Please say shop'. When a 50 ms pause between 'say' and 'shop' was inserted into these sentences, participants were found to perceive 'Please say chop'. Our facial muscles force us to insert a pause between 'say' and 'chop', while this is not the case for 'say' and 'shop'. So, the limitations of our speech system influence our interpretation of a sentence.

More direct evidence for the involvement of the motor system in speech perception has also been reported. For instance, Fadiga et al. (2002) used TMS to stimulate the area in the motor cortex that controls our tongue muscles, lowering the tongue's activation threshold. This allowed Fadiga et al. to determine the extent to which listening to speech resulted in a vocalisation of the perceived sounds. The Italian participants were presented with words that required strong tongue movements during pronunciation (e.g., 'terra') and other words that did not (e.g., 'baffo'). The perpection of words from the former category did indeed result in stronger tongue movements compared to words from the latter category, suggesting that the speech production system was involved in the perception of these words. In a similar vein Wilson, Saygin, Sereno, and Iacoboni (2004) required participants to pronounce a series of syllables and subsequently asked them to listen to the same series of syllables. Consistent with the motor theory, their fMRI results showed that the motor cortex not only became active during the pronunciation of these syllables but also when participants were listening to them.

A major criticism of the motor theory has always been that it is not clear how the motor cortex can contribute to decoding the speech signal. What processes are involved? Because these questions have remained unanswered for a long time, the motor theory has long been ignored in favour of other, more cognitively inclined theories. Since the discovery of a special type of neurons in monkeys (Rizzolatti & Fabbri-Destro, 2010), which are active both when performing one's own action and when observing the action of another (the mirror neuron system; see Chapter 23), a possible explanatory mechanism has been uncovered, which has caused a resurgence of interest in interactions between perception and motor processes.

In later versions of the motor theory, the motor cortex is, however, not so much regarded as an interpreter, as it is considered to be part of a predictive coding mechanism. This mechanism is supposed to actively monitor a conversation and to dynamically predict what the interlocutor is about to utter. Both the auditory cortex and the motor cortex are believed to play an active role in this predictive mechanism (Hickok, 2012; Okada, Matchin, & Hickok, 2017; Pickering & Garrod, 2013). Since the dynamics between speaker and listener are essential for this predictive mechanism, details on this predictive framework have already been discussed in Chapter 16.

17.7.2 THE COHORT MODEL

Marslen-Wilson and Tyler (1980) aimed to explain word recognition by proposing a selection mechanism. According to their **cohort theory**, the selection of candidate words is progressive and based on the available auditory input. As more auditory information becomes available, a progressive number of words will be eliminated from the cohort. Words are eliminated when their phonological code is no longer consistent with the available auditory information or when they no longer fit the context. For example, 'captain' and 'capital' can be part of the initial cohort, but 'capital' will be eliminated as soon as the /t/ sound is heard. The elimination on the basis of new information continues until only one candidate word remains. This stage is reached at the point of uniqueness. Not only the sound but also the context in which a word is used contributes to reaching the point of uniqueness. According to the model, all possible sources of information are processed in parallel and jointly contribute to reaching the point of uniqueness.

O'Rourke and Holcomb (2002) investigated the importance of the point of uniqueness by using ERPs. Participants were presented with words and pseudo-words and had to decide as quickly as possible whether the stimulus was a word or not. The words that were used in this study varied according to their point of uniqueness (early: 427 ms after the words' onset vs. late: 533 ms after the onset). The investigators were interested in the N400, a component that signals the semantic processing of a word. Interestingly, this N400 peaked about 100 ms earlier for words with an early point of uniqueness than for words with a late point of uniqueness (see fig 17.11), suggesting that the identification of a word does indeed depend on this point of uniqueness.

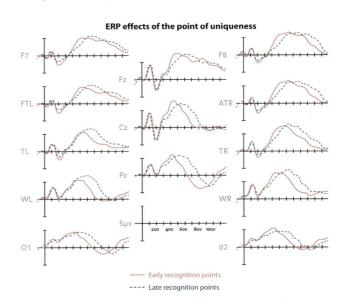

Figure 17.11 Results of an ERP study investigating the impact of the point of uniqueness on word recognition. The N400 component reached its peak amplitude about 100 ms earlier for words with an early point of uniqueness than for words with a late point of uniqueness. (source: O'Rourke and Holcomb, 2002)

A second important aspect of the cohort model is that different candidate words in a cohort are competing with each other. Interestingly, Weber and Cutler (2004) found that this competition can even extend across languages. Dutch participants with a good command of the English language were instructed to select pictures that corresponded to an English word (see fig 17.12). For example, they were given the English target word 'panda' and had to select this picture on the board. To the Dutch participants the initial phoneme of 'panda' sounds very similar to that of 'pencil', whereas for English participants this was not the case. When the Dutch students heard the target word, they initially made a significant amount of eye movements towards the competing object 'pencil', which was also on the board. Likewise, Dutch language distractors (e.g., Deksel [lid]) with initial phonemes that were strongly related to English target words (e.g., desk) resulted in a relatively high proportion of fixations on the distractor object. Together, these effects suggest that (a) phonological competition is stronger in one's non-native language than in one's native language, and (b) that it extends across languages.

During the early 1990s, the cohort model received a major update (Marslen-Wilson & Warren, 1994). One of the most significant changes involved the way words were selected. In the original model, words were either part of a cohort or not, whereas in the revised model, words could vary in terms of their level of activation, making cohort membership stochastic instead of binary. This modification allowed words with small variations in the initial phoneme to remain members of the cohort. In the original model,

these would have been rejected immediately; an aspect of the model that was clearly inconsistent with many empirical findings (Frauenfelder, Scholten, & Content, 2001).

A second important change concerns the role of context. In the original model, context was crucially involved in the initial selection of words, whereas in the revised model it is mainly involved in the integration of a word into a sentence. Indications that context may exert an influence only after the point of uniqueness were found by Zwitserlood (1989), based on a cross-modal priming paradigm. While hearing a word, participants had to decide whether a string of visually presented letters formed a word or not. The auditory material consisted of fragments such as the following.

1. The next word is cap___.
2. They mourned the loss of their cap___.
3. The men stood around the grave in a subdued mood. They mourned the loss of their cap___.

The first two fragments are neutral in the sense that they do not give a context that is predictive of 'captain' or a related word, such as 'capital'. The third fragment does provide a contextual prior. In each of these sentences, the word 'captain' was only partially pronounced ('cap___') and the visual target stimulus followed, of which the participant had to decide whether it was a word or not. The target stimulus could either be a word that was strongly associated with the final word of the sentence that had been played (such as 'ship') or a word associated with a competitive word (such as 'money', which is associated with 'capital'). When 'captain' was only partially pronounced, lexical decisions involving the words 'money' and 'ship' were both faster than decisions involving unrelated words, implying that both the words 'captain' and 'capital' were still activated in the cohort. The question now is what happened in the third sentence, where a context is created prior to the sentence containing the relevant word. For these sentences, too, it was found that the competitive words in the cohort ('capital' in our example) were still activated, which implies that the given context was not strong enough to inhibit the competing word.

This effect was only found, however, when both interpretations of the word were still possible. When a larger part of the final word was pronounced, allowing participants to guess the word, it was found that context did have an effect: in this case, for the context sentences, priming effects were only found for the target word that was compatible with 'captain'.

Results that are consistent with the conclusion that context effects only occur after the point of uniqueness were reported by Friederich and Kotz (2007). They used a method that was similar to that of Zwitserlood (1989) and combined it with ERP recordings. More specifically,

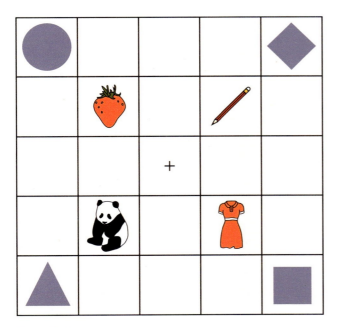

Figure 17.12 Displays used to investigate the multi-language competition among phonological representations. For Dutch participants, the initial phoneme of the word 'pencil' interfered with that of the English word 'panda', whereas for English participants no such interference was found. (source: Weber and Cutler, 2004)

they presented spoken sentences that ended with an incomplete word, for example: 'To light up the dark, she needed her can___'. Immediately following this sentence, a written word was presented that was either appropriate in both form and meaning ('candle'), appropriate in form but not in meaning ('candy'), appropriate in meaning but not in form ('lantern') or a totally unrelated word (e.g., 'number'). Two ERP effects were found: an effect of word meaning manifested itself around 220 ms and an effect of word form appeared around 250 ms after the presentation of the visual word. The occurrence of this word form effect implies that form-compatible words are still part of the initial cohort, although they could have been rejected on the basis of the context.

Although the studies just described have shown that context effects typically occur after the point of uniqueness, there are also results that show that this is not necessarily the case. For instance, Van Petten, Coulson, Rubin, Plante, and Parks (1999) presented sentences such as 'Sir Lancelot spared the man's life when he begged for ___'. This was later followed by a word that was congruent ('mercy') or incongruent ('mermaid'). Also in this study, ERPs were used to investigate the processing of these words. Significant N400 effects were found, which occurred 200 ms prior to the point of uniqueness. Thus, this result suggests that context effects can be found before the point of uniqueness is reached if the context is strong enough.

17.7.3 THE TRACE MODEL

McClelland and Elman (1986) have developed a speech recognition model that is based on connectionist principles. Their **trace model** was designed as the auditory counterpart of the interactive activation model that has been developed for written word recognition (McClelland & Rumelhart, 1981). The trace model describes how top-down and bottom-up processes interact in a flexible way during word recognition. This implies that all sources of information are used during the word recognition process. The trace model is based on the assumption that processing units ('nodes') are processing spoken words at three different levels, namely the feature level, the phonemic level, and the word level. The feature level is connected to the phonemic level, and the phonemic level to the word level. The connections between these levels are bidirectional and facilitatory. Moreover, the model assumes the existence of connections between the nodes within a given level and these are inhibitory. All nodes influence each other according to their activation level and the strength of their connections.

When activation and inhibition spread across the nodes, a pattern of activation, also known as a trace, emerges. The word that is eventually perceived by the listener is the word that has the highest activation at the word level. An important difference with the cohort model is that the trace model assumes that the top-down and bottom-up processes continue to interact as the word is perceived. Evidence for such interactions was found in an auditory variant of the word superiority effect. Mirman, McClelland, Holt, and Magnuson (2008) instructed listeners to detect specific phonemes (/t/ or /k/) that were presented in words and non-words. In one condition, 80% of all trials consisted of words and the other 20% of non-words. In another condition, the ratio was exactly the reverse. Mirman et al. expected that processing at the word level would be the most effective when the majority of the stimuli were words, and that this would strengthen the word superiority effect. This was indeed what was found: the target phonemes were detected faster in words than in non-words, and this reaction time effect was larger when most of the stimuli were words.

The trace model is also very well capable of explaining the lexical identification shift effect (Ganong, 1980). According to the model, activation at the word level biases the interpretation of a phoneme such that our subjective experience results in hearing the word in question. Likewise, we can explain categorical speech perception: according to the trace model, the multiple inhibitory connections cause the boundaries between two phonemes to become sharper, so that eventually one phoneme will reach the highest activation level while the others will be inhibited. Norris, McQueen, and Cutler (2003) found evidence for the idea that phoneme identification can be influenced by top-down processes. In their study, listeners were presented with words ending in an /f/ or an /s/. One group was then presented with words in which the /s/ had been replaced with an ambiguous phoneme that held the middle between an /s/ and an /f/. A second group was given words in which the /f/ had been replaced with this ambiguous phoneme. The listeners had to classify this ambiguous phoneme. The group that heard the phoneme mainly in the context where it replaced /s/, classified it as an /s/, while the group that heard it as a substitute for the /f/ classified it as an /f/.

17.8 NEUROPSYCHOLOGY: SPOKEN WORD REPETITION

Evidence for a strong interaction between the auditory cortex and the speech production system has also been found in neuropsychology, specifically in the context of repeating spoken words. Despite the apparent simplicity of the task of repeating a spoken word, it appears that many neuropsychological patients have severe difficulties with this task. These patients have typically no hearing problems, as shown by audiometric tests. Brain damage in these patients apparently leaves their primary auditory processing unaffected, but instead has affected the already discussed areas involved in the higher-order analysis of word information.

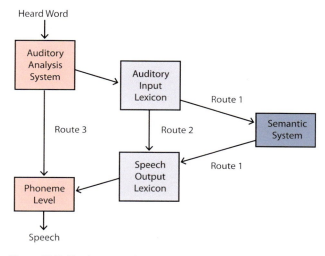

Figure 17.13 The three-route framework for the processing and repetition of spoken words. (source: Ellis and Young, 1988)

17.8.1 THE THREE-ROUTE FRAMEWORK

Ellis and Young (1988) introduced an influential theoretical framework to explain the various difficulties that patients may encounter while repeating spoken words (see fig 17.13). Depending on the nature of their condition, patients may have selective difficulties with the processing of phonology, word meaning, word regularity, or non-words. Ellis and Young's **three-route framework** involves three different ways in which acoustic information might be transferred to phonological speech codes. One of these comprises a rule-based acoustic to phonological conversion while the other two involve a lexical system. The distinction between the two latter routes is that one of them involves the semantics of words in the conversion from heard to spoken words, whereas the other route bypasses the semantic system. The routes in the model bear some similarity to the dual-route cascade model for reading aloud (Coltheart et al., 2001).

17.8.1.1 The Auditory Analysis System

The **auditory analysis system** extracts phonemes and other sounds from the speech signal. Although Ellis and Young did not specify how this is done, this system bears some similarities to the theoretical speech recognition models described in the previous section of this chapter. If a patient were to have a specific impairment in their auditory processing system, we would expect this to result in specific difficulties with phoneme processing. The perception of words and non-words would be impaired, especially when they contain phonemes that are difficult to distinguish. The patient should have no difficulties, however, in perceiving other non-speech related background sounds and speech production should also be intact. Patients meeting these criteria have been diagnosed as having **pure word deafness**.

A crucial assumption for pure word deafness is that the auditory impairments are explicitly limited to speech perception and do not affect the processing of any other type of sound. Evidence for this was found by Peretz et al. (1994). They reported case studies concerning two patients who had functional impairments in perceiving music and prosody, but whose ability to process phonological information remained intact. Although most patients appear to meet the criterion for such a dissociation, it should be noted that this is not always the case. For instance, Pinard, Chertkow, Black, and Peretz (2002) noted that of the 63 patients with pure word deafness that had been reported in the literature up to then, 57 still also showed some mild impairments in processing non-speech related stimuli. In most cases, these involved problems with discriminating between musical stimuli or environmental sounds.

17.8.1.2 Lexical and Semantic Systems

The auditory input lexicon contains information about spoken words that the listener is familiar with. As such, it is believed to contain a memory trace of the sound of words. The auditory input lexicon may be considered to be one of the spokes of the spoke-and-hub model of semantic memory that was discussed in Chapter 13. In contrast, word meaning is believed to be stored in the semantic system. This semantic system may be considered to be the hub in semantic memory, as discussed in Chapter 13. Finally, the speech output lexicon is a memory system that stores information about the spoken form of a word.

17.8.1.3 Phonemic Response Buffer

The phonemic response buffer is believed to contain information related to the pronunciation of words along with instructions on how to convert this information to motor commands.

17.8.1.4 Three Routes

According to the three-route framework, there are three different ways in which listeners can recognise and convert spoken words into their own speech. Route 1 uses three complementary parts of the language processing system, namely the auditory input lexicon, the semantic system, and the speech output lexicon. Route 2 is similar to route 1, but bypasses the semantic system, while route 3 uses a rule-based system exclusively.

Routes 1 and 2 are assumed to be used for the pronunciation of familiar words, while route 3 is mainly believed to be involved in processing unfamiliar words and non-words. The main difference between routes 1 and 2 is that the latter does not involve the semantic system. A consequence of this is that if someone uses route 2 exclusively, it will result in a correct pronunciation, while the patient will not know the meaning of the word.

17.8.2 DIFFICULTIES WITH WORD REPETITION

17.8.2.1 Word Meaning Deafness

When patients only have route 2 at their disposal, they should be able to recognise familiar words without knowing what they mean. In addition, they should have difficulties reproducing non-words and unknown words, since these are not stored in the input lexicon. They should, however, be able to distinguish words from non-words. Patients with **word meaning deafness** appear to fit this description. Although only a handful of patients have been found who meet all the criteria, resulting in a diagnosis that is therefore still somewhat controversial, there are some relatively clear cases, such as patient GCM, described by Jacquemot, Dupoux, and Bachoud-Levi (2007).

Another case of word meaning deafness concerns Dr O, described by Franklin, Turner, Lambon Ralph, Morris, and Bailey (1996). Dr O had an impairment in comprehending spoken language, while his understanding of written language and his ability to repeat words was significantly better than his ability to repeat non-words. In contrast, he scored very well on discriminating between words and non-words. Despite these clear results, it cannot be firmly established that Dr O had only damage to routes 1 and 3. Tyler and Moss (1997), for instance, reported that Dr O might also have impairments at an earlier stage of auditory processing. When asked to repeat words as quickly as possible, he made a significant number of errors, suggesting that he had difficulty extracting precise phonological features from the speech signal under time pressure.

17.8.2.2 Transcortical Sensory Aphasia

Patients who can only use route 3 should have a relatively good ability to repeat both words and non-words, however, their understanding of these words should be extremely limited. This pattern of results is exhibited in some patients with **transcortical sensory aphasia** (Coslett, Roeltgen, Gonzalez Rothi, & Heilman, 1987; Raymer, 2001). These patients are typically characterised by severely impaired reading skills on top of a marked reduction in their ability to understand spoken language, implying that they have an impaired semantic system.

17.8.2.3 Deep Dysphasia

Finally, patients with **deep dysphasia** have serious difficulties with speech perception and production. For example, they produce many semantic errors when instructed to repeat a word, often producing a semantically related word (e.g., they say 'air' when they have to repeat 'cloud'). In addition, they have specific difficulties with abstract words compared to concrete words and they are strongly limited in their ability to repeat non-words.

The three-route framework allows several possibilities to explain deep dysphasia. For example, we could assume that all three pathways are damaged. Another possibility is that it is specifically route 3 that is severely damaged, in combination with some damage in the semantic system. Some researchers have argued that deep dysphasia is crucially related to a general deficit in processing phonological information (Jefferies, Sage, & Ralph Lambon, 2007). This deficit could result in semantic errors, since the patient must rely more strongly on word meaning to convert an utterance on the basis of the limited phonological information available. Indeed, many deep dysphasia patients performed relatively poorly on tasks involving the manipulation of phonemes, such as the phoneme subtraction task (a task in which patients must omit the initial phoneme of a word) or a task in which they had to decide whether two words matched (Jefferies et al., 2007).

17.9 PARSING

After perception, the next stage of language processing consists of integrating the individual words into phrases, sentences, paragraphs, and eventually complete stories or discourses. These stages are much less dependent on the modality of perception (reading or listening), compared to the low-level language perception processes. Nevertheless, prosody of spoken language is to some extent involved in sentence parsing. Parsing involves linking the individual words comprising a sentence together, on the basis of syntax and semantics.

17.9.1 THE INFLUENCE OF SYNTAX AND SEMANTICS

A major problem in sentence parsing is that many sentences are syntactically ambiguous. Consider for example a sentence such as 'They are cooking apples'. This sentence is grammatically correct, yet it can be interpreted in two different ways. (Are people cooking apples or is it a description of a specific type of apples?) Another example is 'I met the daughter of the general on the balcony'. (Did the meeting take place on the balcony, or did it specifically concern a general that was standing on the balcony?) These sentences are globally ambiguous, because even after sentence parsing is completed, the ambiguity still remains. In addition, a sentence can also be locally ambiguous, that is, it is ambiguous at some point during the parsing process, while the ambiguity is resolved as the parsing process continues. Because these ambiguities can provide many insights into the parsing process, psycholinguistics frequently employs ambiguous sentences as stimulus material.

17.9.2 PROSODY AND PUNCTUATION

There are typically far fewer ambiguities in spoken language than in written language. Why is that? As a listener, we can typically rely on the prosodic cues given by the speaker. That is, the emphasis, intonation, and duration of words contain a wealth of clues that we can use to ascertain the intended syntactic structure. For example, when pronouncing the sentence 'I met the daughter of the general on the balcony', it can be disambiguated by placing a short pause before 'on the balcony' (the meeting took place on the balcony) or before 'of the general' (it concerns the general on the balcony). Another example: consider the sentence 'The old men and women sat on the bench'. Are the women old too, or does 'old' only refer to the men? If the women are not old, the word 'men' will be emphasised and there will be a longer pause between 'men' and 'and'. When the speaker implies that the women are also old, these cues will simply be omitted. The importance of prosody was demonstrated by constructing sentences in which each word was equally weighted and pronounced in a monotone manner. Under these conditions, people appear to have many difficulties with interpreting spoken language (Duffy & Pisoni, 1992).

In written texts, prosodic cues are implied by using punctuation. Steinhauer and Friederici (2001) required participants to listen to or to read sentences in which the boundaries between a phrase were marked by prosody or by punctuation. ERPs evoked by the processing of these phrase boundaries were similar for both the punctuation marks and the prosodic cues.

It is too simplistic, however, to assume that a single prosodic cue can be effective. Instead, it is more likely that it is the pattern of cues that are important for resolving syntactic ambiguities in a sentence (Frazier, Carlson, & Clifton, 2006). Consider, for example, again the sentence 'I met the daughter (#1) of the general (#2) on the balcony'. For this sentence, we can conclude the following. When a phrase boundary, that is, a short pause, is inserted at both marked positions, it is the relative duration of these boundaries that is important. More specifically, Frazier et al. introduced a fixed pause at position (#2), whereas the pause at position (#1) could be shorter, as long, or longer than the one at (#2). The interpretation of the sentence was mainly determined by the relative length of these pauses: when the pause at position (#1) was relatively long, most listeners thought that the general was on the balcony, while they considered this interpretation much less likely when the first pause was relatively short.

Prosodic cues are presumably effective because they focus the listener's attention on relevant details (Snedeker & Trueswell, 2003). Participants in Snedeker and Trueswell's study were given a number of toy items, which they were allowed to arrange themselves (see fig 17.14) after which they had to perform a task involving these items. Specific instructions for this task were read aloud by another participant who had access to the same items. This set-up ensured that the speaker became aware of the potential

Figure 17.14 Example of the objects used to study how prosody is used to disambiguate ambiguous sentences. (source: Snedeker and Trueswell, 2003)

ambiguities in the instructions. For example, one instruction read 'Tap the frog with the flower'. The speaker knew which action had to be performed (touch the frog that has the flower or use the flower to touch the frog) but had to communicate the task literally as instructed. The results showed that the prosodic cues given by the speaker were effective in disambiguating the sentences, although the listeners still made about 30% errors because the listener's attention was focused on the relevant objects at an early stage of sentence processing.

17.9.3 THEORIES OF SENTENCE PARSING

Over the years, many theories on sentence parsing have been developed, so a complete discussion involving all theoretical developments is impracticable. Therefore, the following discussion represents a rather coarse overview that will mainly focus on the question of when semantic information affects the processing of grammatical information. There are different theoretical views on the role of semantics: according to some theoretical models, semantics are only processed after syntactic analysis has been completed, whereas other theoretical models assume that semantics can already exert its influence early on during sentence parsing. This distinction is reflected in two of the most influential theoretical models found in the literature, the garden path model and the constraint-based models. The garden path model assumes that syntactic analysis fully precedes semantic analysis, whereas constraint-based models assume that all sources of information are processed in parallel.

17.9.3.1 The Garden Path Model
According to Frazier and Rayner (1982) sentence parsing involves two stages. Their garden path model is named after the expression 'to lead someone up the garden path', that is, to confuse someone. More specifically, the garden path model is based on the following assumptions.

First, only one grammatical structure is considered at a time, and semantics are not involved in the selection of the initial grammatical structure. Moreover, the choice of the syntactic structure is based on simplicity. From there on, parsing is believed to be based on two general principles: minimal attachment and late closure. The principle of minimal attachment states that the syntactic structure containing the fewest nodes is preferred, and the principle of late closure states that new words being processed are added to the existing syntactic structure, as long as this does not result in a conflict. If there is a conflict between these two principles, it will be resolved in favour of the principle of minimal attachment. When the final syntactic structure resulting from this analysis conflicts with the semantics of the sentence, a second analysis step will take place, in which the grammatical structure will be reinterpreted and revised.

17.9.3.2 Minimal Attachment

The principle of minimal attachment can be illustrated by the following two sentences: 'The girl knew the answer by heart' and 'The girl knew the answer was wrong'. According to the minimal attachment principle, 'the answer' should be the direct object of 'knew'; a principle that applies only to the first sentence, but not to the second, which in the case of the second sentence requires a reinterpretation of the grammatical structure after reading 'was wrong'.

17.9.3.3 Late Closure

The principle of late closure can be illustrated by the following sentence: 'Since Jay always jogs a mile this seems like a short distance to him'. This sentence can be easily parsed according to the late closure principle since each successive word fits within the initial grammatical structure. This becomes problematic, however, when we have to process the following sentence: 'Since Jay always jogs a mile seems like a short distance to him'. According to the late closure principle, 'a mile' will be linked to the preceding phrase, whereas it actually marks the start of a new phrase. The example also illustrates the effectiveness of punctuation in disambiguating garden path sentences (Hill & Murray, 2000), since a comma between 'jogs' and 'a mile' can resolve the ambiguity.

Although many studies have shown that readers use the principles of minimal attachment and late closure when interpreting sentences, a crucial assumption of the garden path model is that semantics are not involved in the initial processing of the sentence. Ferreira and Clifton (1986) found evidence consistent with this assumption. Participants' eye movements were recorded while they read sentences such as: 'The defendant examined by the lawyer turned out to be unreliable' or 'The evidence examined by the lawyer turned out to be unreliable'. According

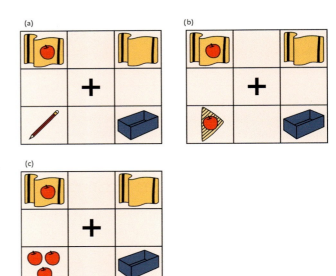

Figure 17.15 Example of displays that were shown to participants while they were hearing the sentence 'Put the apple on the towel in the box'. Panel (a) contains only one relevant object (the apple) along with the correct goal (the box) and the incorrect goal (towel); panel (b) contains the relevant object (apple on the towel) and an irrelevant object (apple on a napkin) and both the correct and incorrect goals; panel (c) contains the relevant object (apple on the towel) and an irrelevant object (three apples), and both the correct and incorrect goals. (source: Spivey et al., 2002)

to the minimal attachment principle, readers should initially associate the verb 'examined' with the phrase that immediately preceded it and therefore experience an ambiguity. However, if participants were able to take advantage of the semantic content of the sentence, this ambiguity should be greater in the first sentence, because in principle a defendant can examine something, whereas evidence cannot. Reading times and eye movement patterns did not differ between the two types of sentences, however, which implies that participants do not consider the semantic information.

Spivey, Tanenhaus, Eberhard, and Sedivy (2002) did find, however, that participants use semantic information to disambiguate sentences at an early stage. Participants were presented displays such as those shown in Figure 17.15. They were then given instructions such as: 'Put the apple on the towel in the box'. When this type of instruction is presented, participants will initially be misled causing them to interpret it as an instruction to put the apple on the towel. It is only when the whole sentence is spoken that it becomes clear that the instruction is to place the apple that is already on the towel in the box. Spivey et al. were interested in participants' viewing behaviour when this sentence was presented while one of the three displays from Figure 17.15 was shown. When panel (a) was shown, paricipants immediately directed their gaze at the correct object, and subsequently fixated almost exclusively on the incorrect goal (the towel). When panel (b) was shown, both the object and the goal were ambiguous, so participants fixated relatively frequently on both the irrelevant object (apple on the napkin) and the incorrect goal (the towel). When panel (c) was shown, however, the goal was immediately disambiguated, causing a strong reduction in fixations on the irrelevant object(s) (the three apples) and an immediate disambiguation of the phrase structure ('apple on the towel'), which also resulted in a near absence of fixations on the incorrect goal (towel). The latter result implies that syntactic ambiguities in this type of sentence can be rapidly disambigued on the basis of semantics.

17.9.3.4 Constraint-based Theories

An alternative theoretical framework, which differs fundamentally from the garden path model, does assume that semantic information is processed immediately. Within this framework, several different theories have been formulated, which, although they differ in detail, are all based on putting constraints on the possible interpretations of a sentence. According to these **constraint-based theories**, all possible sources of information contribute to the final interpretation. An influential theory that is part of this framework has been formulated by MacDonald, Pearlmutter, and Seidenberg (1994).

MacDonald et al.'s (1994) model is based on a connectionist network architecture and assumes that all information is immediately available to the sentence parsing process. According to the model, multiple competing sentence parsing processes are initiated simultaneously and ranked in order of activation strength. The stronger a specific interpretation is supported by the data, the higher the activation value of this interpretation. Confusion can arise when the correct syntactic structure is not the one that receives the highest activation value. According to this theory, there are four linguistic properties that can be used to resolve ambiguities:

1. Grammatical knowledge limits the possible interpretations of a sentence.
2. The different forms of information that are associated with a particular word are often interdependent.
3. Words may be ambiguous, but this may vary for the different types of information that are associated with that word: for example, a word may be ambiguous in terms of time but not in terms of grammatical category.
4. The different interpretations that are possible often vary enormously in frequency and probability, based on previous experience with the processing of similar sentences.

Semantics can influence the interpretation of a syntactic structure in multiple ways. Specific verbs are, for example, more often associated with one syntactic structure than another. Consider the word 'read', which is often associated with a direct object, as in 'The ghost read the book

during the plane journey' but can sometimes be associated with a sentence complement, as in 'The ghost read the book had been burned'. The preference for the former association, known as **verb bias**, causes us to initially try to interpret phrases following the word 'read' as a direct object. When the sentence structure is consistent with verb bias, readers are able to resolve syntactic ambiguities much faster than when it is not (Garnsey, Pearlmutter, Myers, & Lotocky, 1997). This finding is inconsistent with the garden path model because it assumes no influence of semantics.

Boland and Blodgett (2001) exploited the fact that some homonyms, such as 'duck' or 'train', can be either a verb or a noun. They presented sentences that started with 'She saw her duck and...'. At this point, it is not clear whether 'duck' is a verb or a noun, and this ambiguity is only resolved when the sentence continues with '...stumble near the barn' (verb) or '...and chickens near the barn' (noun). According to constraint-based theories, readers should first create a grammatical structure in which the homophone is consistent with the most commonly used form (in the case of 'duck', the verb). Indeed, participants had more difficulties processing sentences in which the homophone was used in the least frequent form, as evidenced by eye-movement patterns that indicated that in such cases they reread the sentence more often.

Pickering and Traxler (1998) found evidence for an early influence of semantics using eye movements, in which participants were given sentences such as the following: 'As the women edited the magazine amused all the reporters' and 'As the women sailed the magazine amused all the reporters'. Both sentences are syntactically identical and contain a local ambiguity that initially makes readers choose the wrong syntactic structure. However, the semantic constraints are stronger in the second sentence than in the first, so that participants took longer to interpret the first sentence. The fact that they had more difficulties interpreting the first sentence was also evident from longer fixations on the verb ('edited') and the parts of the sentence that followed it.

Cognitive neuroscience has made a significant contribution to our understanding of sentence parsing in recent decades. In particular, ERPs have contributed significantly to our understanding of sentence parsing, since they can determine the timing of cognitive processes with very high accuracy. One specific ERP component, the N400 (see Box 16.1), has contributed significantly to this.

Traditional sentence parsing models assumed that word meaning was processed before the meaning of the sentence as a whole was evaluated. ERP studies that have used the N400 component have largely refuted this

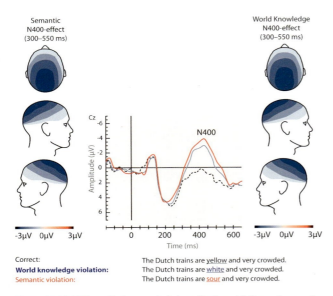

Correct: The Dutch trains are <u>yellow</u> and very crowded.
World knowledge violation: The Dutch trains are <u>white</u> and very crowded.
Semantic violation: The Dutch trains are <u>sour</u> and very crowded.

Figure 17.16 ERP results from a study investigating violations of semantics and of background knowledge during sentence parsing processes. Both types of violations evoked an N400 component that was comparable in amplitude and latency. (source: Hagoort et al., 2004)

assumption. For instance, Hagoort, Hald, Bastiaansen, and Petersson (2004), used sentences such as the following (see fig 17.16).

1. Dutch trains are yellow and overcrowded.
2. Dutch trains are sour and overcrowded.
3. Dutch trains are white and overcrowded.

Sentences of type 1 are correct. Sentences of type 2 are incorrect because the word 'sour' does not semantically fit into this sentence, while sentences of type 3 are incorrect because they conflict with the participants' background knowledge; Dutch trains are yellow. According to the traditional hypothesis, the conflicting background knowledge in sentence type 3 would require more processing time than the semantic conflict in sentence type 2. Hagoort et al. found that this is not the case, however. Both sentence types 2 and 3 resulted in an N400 component that is comparable in amplitude and latency. This result implies that we process word meaning and real-world knowledge in parallel during reading. It thus suggests that we indeed make use of all available sources of information, as suggested by the constraint-based model of MacDonald et al. (1994).

17.9.3.5 Unrestricted Race Model

Although much of the evidence is consistent with the predictions of the constraint-based models, they have also been criticised. Supporters of the garden path model argue that the initial syntactic analysis is very fast and that the effects of semantics described in the previous sections actually relate to the second stage of parsing. In addition, MacDonald et al. (1994) assume that multiple competitive interpretations are considered in parallel, while in reality there is little direct evidence for the existence of such parallel interpretations.

To address these issues, some alternative models have been developed that attempt to reconcile aspects of both the garden path model and constraint-based theories. One such model is the unrestricted race model developed by van Gompel, Pickering, and Traxler (2000). Similar to the constraint-based models, this model assumes that all sources of information are used simultaneously to build up a syntactic structure. According to the unrestricted race model, however, only one structure is considered, and this structure is maintained as long as it is consistent with the information that is being read. When the chosen structure is no longer maintainable, an extensive analysis will have to be done to choose a new structure. The assumption that only one structure is considered at a time and the assumption that a second stage of processing is required are aspects of the garden path model.

The unrestricted race model can explain some seemingly counterintuitive results. For instance, van Gompel, Pickering, and Traxler (2001) presented participants sentences such as the following:

1. Ambiguous. The burglar stabbed only the guy with the dagger during the night.
2. Verb phrase. The burglar stabbed only the dog with the dagger during the night.
3. Noun phrase. The burglar stabbed only the dog with the collar during the night.

The first sentence is ambiguous because it can be either the 'burglar' or the 'guy' who has the dagger. In sentence 2, there is verb-phrase coupling, because 'dog' is coupled with the verb 'stabbed', while in sentence 3 there is noun-phrase coupling, because 'dog' is coupled with the noun 'collar'. The garden path model would predict that sentence 2 is easier to process than sentence 3, because sentence 3 requires a more complex syntactic structure. In contrast, the constraint-based theories predict that sentences 2 and 3 should be processed faster than sentence 1 because they are not ambiguous.

Van Gompel et al. (2001) found, however, that in this case the ambiguous sentence was actually processed faster than the non-ambiguous sentences, while there was no difference in processing time between the two non-ambiguous sentences. How is this possible? The sentences used in the van Gompel et al. (2000) study were designed in such a way that there was no preference for either verb-phrase coupling or noun-phrase coupling. This implies that participants started to read and interpret the non-ambiguous sentences based on an initial syntactic structure, which would only have a 50% change of being the correct one of the unambiguous sentence, forcing them to reinterpret the sentence when it was no longer consistent with the initially chosen structure. This was not necessary for the ambiguous sentences, however, because both syntactic structures were consistent with the initially chosen structure so that no reinterpretation was ever necessary for these ambiguous sentences.

17.9.4 GOOD-ENOUGH REPRESENTATIONS

The sentence parsing theory just discussed is characterised by one major limitation, which is the assumption that the language parsing processes generate a detailed and accurate representation of the linguistic input (Ferreira, Bailey, & Ferraro, 2002). Upon consideration, such a detailed representation should result in a particularly inefficient type of processing, because in many cases it would form an overly detailed representation that might place an unnecessarily strong burden on our working memory. For this reason, Ferreira and colleagues propose an alternative model, which is based on the assumption that listeners and readers form mental representations that are just good enough for the goals that they want to achieve (Swets, Desmet, Clifton, & Ferreira, 2008). A good example of such a limited representation is given by the Moses illusion. When asked how many of each animal Moses carried in the ark, many people answered 'two',[2] suggesting that we fail to process crucially important information. Moreover, Ferreira (2003) found that the representation of spoken sentences was often incomplete. A sentence such as 'The mouse was eaten by the cheese' was sometimes misinterpreted as 'The mouse ate the cheese'.

According to Ferreira (2003), these errors are an indication that we often use heuristics, or rules of thumb, when processing sentences. A common heuristic, known as the noun-verb-noun (NVN) strategy, is that a sentence's subject is considered to be the agent that performs an action, while the direct object is considered to be the recipient of the action. Christianson, Luke, and Ferreira (2010) argued that the type of interpretation errors encountered in the Ferreira (2003) example can be easily explained by a conflict between the syntactic structure of the passive sentence and our background knowledge about mice and cheese. When such a conflict occurs, it can be resolved by letting our background knowledge prevail over the syntactic structure of the sentence. Christianson et al. tested this hypothesis by presenting participants passive sentences, such as 'The fish was caught by the angler', after which participants were given an unrelated line drawing which they had to describe (fig 17.17).

It was found that participants often used the passive form in these descriptions. Another group of participants were given implausible passive sentences, such as 'The angler was caught by the fish', after which they also had to describe an unrelated drawing. Interestingly, these

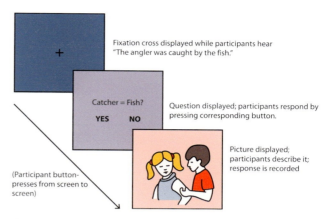

Figure 17.17 Schematic representation of a study into the conflicting roles of grammar and background knowledge in sentence comprehension. Participants listened to a passive sentence, after which they had to answer a question testing their comprehension of the sentence. Finally, they had to describe an unrelated line drawing. The investigators were particularly interested in the question to which extent participants would also use the passive form here. When the original sentence conflicted with the participants' background knowledge, they relatively often switched to the active form when describing this picture, which implies that they had interpreted the original sentence as an active sentence. (source: Christianson et al., 2010)

participants made little use of the passive form, implying that they had paid little attention to the passive form of the original sentence, interpreting it as an active sentence ('The angler caught the fish').

Does that mean that we always interpret sentences very superficially? According to Swets et al. (2008) this is not necessarily the case. When we are forced into a deeper understanding, for example when we expect detailed questions about the sentences in question, this can lead to a much deeper processing. According to Swets et al. the extent to which we process a sentence is therefore strongly dependent on our reading goals. They also found that participants read syntactically ambiguous sentences more slowly when they expected deep comprehension questions than when they expected superficial questions. On the other hand, when superficial questions were expected, participants read the ambiguous sentences faster.

Other studies, however, suggest that participants can be forced to fully process sentences only with difficulty. Dwivedi (2013), for example, gave participants the following sentences:

1. Every kid climbed that tree.
2. The tree was in the park.

Although every participant knew that they would be asked detailed questions about each sentence, about one-third of the participants incorrectly reported the kids climbing several trees, implying that readers and listeners often form only a flawed and heuristic representation, which can lead to misinterpretation of the sentences.

17.10 SUMMARY

Language processing is one of our most complex cognitive abilities. Language perception involves both reading and speech processing. Both written texts and spoken forms of language share some important properties. In both cases, there is a message to be communicated, but the way in which this is done differs considerably. Psycholinguistics take advantage of several basic linguistic features to investigate language perception. Not only word frequency but also the phonology and orthography of words are involved in word processing.

Several standard methods can be used to investigate language processes, such as the lexical decision task, the naming task, or the priming task. In addition, much electrophysiological research involves studying violations in semantics. Ambiguities in spoken language can be avoided by the use of prosody. In written language, these ambiguities are less efficiently avoided by the use of punctuation.

Orthography, phonology, and semantics are involved in the reading of words. Furthermore, top-down processes are involved in word recognition, as evidenced by the word superiority effect. The interactive activation model is an influential model capable of explaining this effect, however, it cannot properly explain the flexibility in the positional coding of individual letters. More recent models, such as the overlap model, are better at this. Meaning and expectation are also involved in word recognition, as evidenced by the classical priming effects reported by Neely (1977). Phonology is also involved in the recognition of written words, even when it is not relevant.

Reading words aloud is characterised by several specific deficiencies that can be found in dyslexia patients. These include a selective deficiency to pronounce either unknown words or irregular words, which points to two different ways in which orthographic information can be converted into a phonological code: via a lexical system or via a rule-based system. Two models are proposed to explain these effects. The triangle model is based on a neural network architecture and the dual-route cascade model is assumed to employ two different routes to process the irregular and unknown words. Recent developments show that both models may be compatible with each other. Eye movements are crucial for the reading of sentences. We can already prepare a saccade to the next word while we are still processing the currently fixated word. The E-Z Reader model was proposed to explain fixation times.

Listening to speech is the second important way of perceiving language. The speech signal is ambiguous, and a major challenge for speech recognition theories involves adequately explaining how we are able to unambiguously interpret the large variety of speech signals. The segmentation process consists of extracting individual words from a continuous acoustic signal. A number of perceptual phenomena, such as the phonemic restoration effect and the Ganong effect, imply that top-down processes are involved in the segmentation of the speech signal.

The motor theory of speech recognition assumed that we disambiguate the speech signal by repeating it subvocally. Although this theory had been long abandoned, there is currently new interest in this idea from the perspective of predictive coding and the mirror neuron system. The cohort model attempts to describe speech recognition based on a selection and elimination process, while the trace model is based on connectionist principles.

Neuropsychological studies in the field of speech recognition have also identified specific deficiencies, such as pure word deafness, word meaning deafness, transcortical sensory aphasia, or deep dysphasia. These conditions also imply the existence of independent systems involved in converting auditory signals into articulatory movements.

Language comprehension starts with sentence parsing processes. The scientific study of these processes often employs ambiguous sentences. An influential sentence parsing theory is named after this type of sentence: the garden path model. This model assumes that we parse sentences on the basis of the simplest grammatical structure possible. New information that becomes available during reading or listening will be added to this grammatical structure if possible. A reanalysis takes place when the chosen grammatical structure no longer fits. The garden path model also assumes that semantic information is only processed after the syntactic analysis is complete. Constraint-based theories, on the other hand, assume that semantic and syntactic analyses are performed in parallel. An extension to these models is the unrestricted race model. In recent years, however, it has become increasingly clear that we do not form a fully comprehensive representation of a sentence, but that our interpretation is strongly dependent on its purpose. As a result, we often form a representation that is 'good enough'.

NOTES

1 Contrary to popular belief, the name of the model (pronounced 'easy reader') was not inspired by the film classic *Easy Rider*, but by a character from a cartoon series that researcher Erik Reichle enjoyed watching as a child. This character, called Easy Reader and portrayed by Morgan Freeman, tried to inspire young children to start reading. It was only after the model had been published that Reichle was informed, by his co-author Alexander Pollatsek, that the name of Freeman's character was again inspired by the film.

2 The correct answer should of course be zero: the Biblical story of the Flood is associated with Noah and not with Moses.

FURTHER READING

Lieberman, P., & Blumstein, S. E. (1988). *Speech physiology, speech perception, and acoustic phonetics*. Cambridge, UK: Cambridge University Press.

Pisoni, D., & Remez, R. (2008). *The handbook of speech perception*. Oxford, UK: Blackwell Publishing.

Rayner, K., & Pollatsek, A. (2013). *The psychology of reading*. London, UK: Routledge.

CHAPTER 18
Language production

18.1 INTRODUCTION

Suppose you have to give a presentation. How do you go about it? Most likely, you will start by writing down the main ideas that you want to get across. Then you arrange these ideas in a logical order and think about the amount of information that you want to present. How detailed should your presentation be? What should you say and what not? Once you have made these decisions, you can start working on the presentation itself.

The next question is how to go about this. You can choose to write out the entire presentation and learn it by heart. Alternatively, you can write down only a few key words and fill in the details on the spot, preparing and producing the individual sentences as you speak. The advantage of the first approach is that your talk can come across as very structured, but you run the risk of losing engagement with your audience. The advantage of a more spontaneous form of narration is that your story will be livelier, but here you run the risk of forgetting important details and wasting too much time with unimportant sidetracks, which will also reduce the clarity of your story. In addition, you run the risk that your nerves will prevent you from finding the right words, causing you to stutter. As a novice speaker, you will probably choose to follow a precise, preconceived plan, whereas as a more experienced speaker, you will probably adopt a much looser style.

This example highlights the importance of our ability to produce language. Without language production, no efficient communication is possible. Although language production is as important as language perception, we know much less about it. Why is this? One of the main reasons is that we are considerably more limited in systematically investigating language production, compared to language perception. While language perception studies can manipulate many aspects of the stimulus material, studies of language production are much more limited in our ability to manipulate the spontaneous production processes. For these reasons, we are in many cases limited to just observing these spontaneous processes.

There are essentially two different ways in which we can produce language: speaking and writing. We currently know more about speech production processes than we do about writing. In general, we also spend more time speaking than writing. Yet both forms of language production are important. Both speaking and writing aim at communication, and both tap into the same knowledge database. While growing up, we typically found writing much more difficult than speaking, which also implies that there are also major differences between speaking and writing.

18.2 SPEAKING AND WRITING: SIMILARITIES AND DIFFERENCES

18.2.1 SIMILARITIES

An important similarity between speaking and writing is that both forms of language production start with the selection of the information that we want to communicate (Dell, Burger, & Svec, 1997; Hayes & Flower, 1986). This planning phase takes place at a relatively abstract level and precedes the actual selection of words to be spoken or written down. Sentence production only starts after this general planning phase and individual sentences are then planned clause by clause.

Evidence for similarities between speaking and writing comes from a study of the planning behaviour of Eric Sotto, an experienced writer and lecturer, while he was writing or dictating academic letters (Hartley, Sotto, & Pennebaker, 2003). Despite his relative lack of experience with dictation software, the letters produced while dictating hardly differed from written ones in terms of readability and grammatical errors. This result is consistent with earlier findings that show that even individuals who are very experienced at dictating letters dictate only about 35% faster than they write (Gould, 1978). This fact is in itself remarkable, since we can speak five to six

DOI: 10.4324/9781003319344-25

times faster than we can write. In the case of dictation, however, a considerable amount of time is spent on planning, which minimises the differences between writing and dictating.

18.2.2 DIFFERENCES

Note, however, that there are also many differences between speaking and writing. Written texts generally consist of longer and more complex sentences, and they often contain a more complex and richer vocabulary. Compared to speakers, writers also tend to more strongly emphasize the structure of a text through the use of specific words or expressions. More specifically, we can summarise the main differences between speaking and writing as follows. (1) Speakers are generally well aware of who their audience is. As a result, they can adapt their message to the needs of the listener or audience. (2) Speakers also receive instant feedback. This feedback may be verbal, for example, in the form of a question for clarification, or non-verbal, for example, in the form of frowning or nodding in agreement. (3) Speakers can also adjust their communication on the basis of this feedback.

In general, speakers have much less time than writers to plan their utterances. Consequently, spoken language tends to be simpler and sentences tend to be shorter than written language. Writers, on the other hand, have direct access to what they produced and, unlike speakers, can revise it before it is actually used for communication. An important consequence of these differences is that spoken language is often much more informal than written text. The sentences are typically shorter, and spoken information is conveyed rapidly. Writers, on the other hand, have to be very precise as they cannot benefit from the immediate feedback that speakers receive.

Neuropsychological studies have also reported differences between speaking and writing. Some patients can still write more or less normally despite having severe deficiencies in their speech producing system (Levine, Cavanio, & Popovich, 1992), and other patients can speak fluently while their writing skills are severely impaired.

18.3 SPEECH PRODUCTION

The first main theme of this chapter covers speech production. Studies involving speech production deal with all aspects related to the transformation of an idea into a string of speech sounds. Speech production appears to be deceivingly simple. While talking to a friend, acquaintance, or colleague, we can easily produce two to three words per second, or about 150 words per minute. The fact that we can speak so quickly suggests that speech production requires almost no cognitive processing.

18.3.1 BASIC PROPERTIES OF SPOKEN LANGUAGE

In reality, however, speech production differs considerably from the simplistic view just depicted. Producing coherent speech does demand a great deal of cognitive processing power. To speak fluently, we often use many different strategies to reduce the demands on our cognitive processing capacity. An example of such a strategy is **preformulation**. Preformulation involves the reuse of word combinations that we have used before, thus reducing the cognitive resources we need to devote to the planning process.

18.3.2 SPEECH PLANNING

It is clear that planning an utterance is extremely important, and that this planning must take place within a very limited time frame. But how far ahead do we plan? Some studies suggest that planning occurs at the subordinate clause level (a phrase that includes a verb and a noun), while other studies suggest that planning occurs at the phrase level. A phrase is a group of words that encompasses a single idea, which is often a smaller unit than a subordinate clause.

Evidence suggesting that planning occurs at the subordinate clause level has been provided by studies investigating speech production errors. Sometimes words are exchanged during speech production (see Section 18.3.3), and these exchanges can often be found within a subordinate clause, yet they can also extend beyond a phrase boundary. Moreover, it has been found that, during spontaneous speech, speakers often pause before starting a new subordinate clause, as if they need to plan that clause first (Holmes, 1988). Martin, Miller, and Vu (2004) found evidence for planning at the phrase level. In their study, participants had to name pictures. These pictures were chosen in such a way that the speakers had to utter a simple initial phrase, or a complex one, in order to adequately describe the pictures (see fig 18.1). When they uttered a complex initial phrase, they paused longer than when they uttered a simple phrase, suggesting that they planned the phrase in question during that pause.

It is important to note that the degree of forward planning depends on what exactly is being planned. For example, phonemes are typically swapped over shorter distances than words, suggesting that word selection takes place within a larger structure than phoneme selection. From this we can deduce that the planning of speech is very flexible and strongly dependent on the goals of the speakers and the current situation. Ferreira and Swets (2002), for example, required participants to solve mathematical problems and instructed them to pronounce the answers as they solved them. When there was no time pressure, the difficulty of the solution did have an effect on

Figure 18.1 Examples of a display used to instruct participants to pronounce the phrase 'The tie and the candle move above the foot'. Variants of this type of sentence, which were instructed by similar displays, required more or less preparation time, depending on the complexity of the initial phrase. (source: Martin et al., 2004)

participants' planning. In this case, the harder the problem, the longer they waited before speaking. When there was time pressure, however, participants took less time to plan. They started speaking earlier and planned the rest of their answer as they spoke.

Wagner, Jescheniak, and Schriefers (2010) identified several additional factors that influenced the degree of planning. More specifically, they found that slow speakers plan their utterances more than fast speakers. Speakers also planned more when they produced simple sentences than complex ones. Finally, they found that there was more planning when cognitive load was low than when it was high. These results suggest that planning is a trade-off between error avoidance and cognitive load: when speakers strive to avoid errors, cognitive load is high. On the other hand, when they strive to minimise their cognitive load, this will come at the cost of speech errors.

On a somewhat similar note, Goldberg and Ferreira (2022) argue that, similar to our speech perception processes, speech production is often characterised by speech that is just 'good enough' to be comprehensible. Good enough speech may, according to Goldberg and Ferreira, result in the avoidance of newly learned low-frequency words, over-regularisation, word substitutions, and many of the following speech errors.

18.3.3 SPEECH ERRORS

Although our speech is generally fluent and coherent, we do occasionally make errors in our everyday speaking life; it is estimated that we make about one slip in every 500 sentences (Vigliocco & Hartsuiker, 2002). So, speech errors are relatively rare, but they are diverse because they can be triggered at different levels of the speech production system.

Although speech errors are relatively rare, they are an essential tool for psycholinguists to understand the language production process: we can gain insights into the workings of the complex language production system when we find out what can go wrong and why it can go wrong. One of the key findings in the study of speech production errors is that they are not random but follow systematic patterns; as we will discuss next.

18.3.3.1 Word-exchange Errors
The word-exchange error consists of reversing two words in a sentence, as in: 'I still have to put the drawer in the towel'. This type of error suggests that we are planning parts of a sentence ahead and that we may make an occasional mistake during the planning process.

18.3.3.2 Spoonerisms
A **spoonerism** is also an example of a mix error, named after the well-known British lecturer William Archibald Spooner, who was known for his numerous and striking speech errors, such as 'You have hissed my mystery lectures' or 'Our queer old dean'. Although there is still much debate as to whether Spooner's errors were spontaneous or the result of some deliberate linguistic virtuosity on Spooner's part (see Box 18.1), they do illustrate a specific type of error, namely the systematic swapping of the initial phoneme of two words.

18.3.3.3 Morpheme-exchange Errors
The third type of error that is common is the morpheme-exchange error, in which the inflections of two words remain in the correct place in the sentence, while the roots of these words are swapped, as in 'He trunked two packs'. This suggests that the word stem is positioned before the inflections are generated, and that the process that generates these inflections is independent of the positioning of the word stem. Although the inflections typically remain in their correct place, this is not always the case, as in 'sing in the gardening' where the words are in their correct place, while the inflections are swapped.

18.3.3.4 Number-agreement Errors
Number-agreement errors occur when a singular verb is related to a plural noun, or the other way around. For example, a sentence such as: 'The city council has made poor call of judgement', may sometimes be pronounced as: 'The city council have made a poor call of judgement'. This type

Box 18.1 The Life and work of William Archibald Spooner

William Archibald Spooner was born on July 22, 1844, and worked for much of his life as a lecturer at Oxford University, teaching ancient history, religion, and philosophy. Spooner was a kind man with a gentle nature. He was well-liked in Oxford and a person whose opinion was highly valued. On several occasions, he took the fate of his students to heart. As such, he insisted, for example, on providing an Egyptian student with extra blankets and clothes in the cold British climate. On another occasion, he paid for all the medical expenses of a student who had suffered an injury during a hockey match, as the student's parents could not afford the expenses.

To Spooner's own great annoyance, however, he became mostly known for his characteristic speech errors, which consisted of swapping two morphemes, often resulting in humorous statements. Over the years, many of these mistakes have been attributed to Spooner. Well-known examples are: 'Is the bean dizzy?' or 'It is kisstomary to cuss the bride?' The question is whether Spooner produced these errors himself. It is likely that the answer to this question is mostly 'yes', but never as perfectly as they were later reported. As a general rule, the more perfect and the

funnier the statement, the more likely it is that it was made up by someone else and later attributed to Spooner. Many spoonerisms were probably made up by Spooner's students, inspired by mistakes made by Spooner himself.

It is not clear why Spooner produced these characteristic slips. One possible explanation is that they were the result of a nervous trait that resulted in frequent morpheme-exchange errors. Another possible explanation is that Spooner, being an albino, suffered from a visual impairment and consequently also suffered from dysgraphia (Potter, 1976). Potter also argues that Spooner's frequent confusion errors were not limited to oral expressions but could also manifest themselves in conceptual confusion or incorrect actions. It is rumoured that Spooner once accidentally spilled salt on the tablecloth and then poured several drops of red wine on it. Another anecdote is that Spooner once invited a new Oxford lecturer to a tea party, with the words: 'To welcome Stanley Casson, our new archaeology lecturer', to which the new lecturer replied: 'But I am Stanley Casson'. According to folklore, Spooner replied: 'Never mind, come anyway'.

of error is mainly related to an overload in working memory (McDonald, 2008). Moreover, it may be triggered when a sentence contains conflicting information. This may be the case when a sentence contains phrases such as 'a number' or 'a family'. In these cases, we tend to use constructions such as 'a number of people have'. Here, the confusion arises because of the immediately preceding plural 'people'.

18.3.3.5 Semantic Substitution Errors

A final exchange error that we frequently encounter involves semantic substitution. Semantic substitution occurs when a word is replaced by another, but semantically related word, as in 'Where is my table tennis racket', where 'bat' is substituted with 'racket'. In this case, the substituted word always belongs to the same category as the intended word. So, a noun is always replaced by a related noun, or a verb is always replaced by a related verb. This type of slip suggests that we always plan the grammatical structure of a sentence first, before filling it in with the exact words.

18.3.3.6 Freudian Slips

The final category of speech errors that we discuss here is perhaps not only the most infamous but also the most controversial one (see also Box 18.2). According to the well-known Austrian psychiatrist Sigmund Freud (1901), speech errors could serve as a window onto the otherwise inaccessible unconscious desires of a person. The errors

that were cited by Freud himself are too anecdotal to serve as evidence, and it has already been argued that these slips can be explained just as well, if not better, by assuming that they are scheduling errors. Nevertheless, we can consider the possibility that sexually related speech errors are produced more frequently than other types.

Motley, Baars, and Camden (1983) argue that there is indeed some evidence for the Freudian slip. In their study, participants were put in situations where they were triggered to produce sexually oriented spoonerisms. More specifically, male participants were required to pronounce items such as 'goxi furl', 'tool kits', 'fast luck' or 'bine foddy', while a provocatively dressed female accomplice of the experimenter tried to seduce them. Under these conditions, participants were indeed found to produce more sexually related spoonerisms than non-sexually related ones. It should be noted, however, that these conditions are extreme and that in normal situations the vast majority of slips are not Freudian.

Substantial evidence against the Freudian slip was also obtained by examining how we deal with taboo words (Dhooge & Hartsuiker, 2011; Severens, Janssens, Kuhn, Brass, & Hartsuiker, 2011; Severens, Kuhn, Hartsuiker, & Brass, 2012). These studies used a task in which participants had to name an object that was presented in a photograph. While performing this task, they were

Box 18.2 The slip wars

Around 1889, the Austrian professor Rudolf Meringer, along with his colleague, neurologist Carl Mayer, began to keep records of speech errors they overheard in the Viennese restaurants where the academics of the university of Vienna used to go for lunch. As a linguist, Meringer was particularly interested in the genesis of words, and he started his project with the idea that speech errors might be the key to explaining why the pronunciation of words change over time. The famous linguist Jacob Grimm (who, together with his brother Wilhelm, also compiled an extensive catalogue of classic fairy tales), noted several consistent changes in the pronunciation of words over time. Grimm's work describes, among other things, how in the classical Western European languages the 'p' has slowly changed into an 'f' and the 'b' into a 'p'. This is how, for example, the Latin word *labium* evolved into 'lip'. The problem was that Grimm merely described that these changes occurred, but not why.

Meringer had the idea that speech errors could provide insights into the mechanisms behind these changes. His hypothesis was that speech production is a dynamic process that aims to adapt to the current pronunciation rules but occasionally makes a mistake in doing so. Although a single error would not lead to a change in the pronunciation rule, Meringer believed it should be possible for them to have a snowball effect. If several people made the same mistake at the same time, it could lead others to believe that the new pronunciation is the norm, and as such our languages would adapt systematically as a result of these mistakes.

To test this hypothesis, Meringer and Meyer started to monitor the conversations they had with their fellow professors during their extensive lunches. Meringer and Meyer did this very carefully. They only noted an error if it had been heard by at least two people, and Meringer also tried to classify the nature of the error. This way Meringer and Mayer collected an impressive number of 8800 speech errors, which were published a few years later in their book 'Versprechen und Verlesen' (Meringer & Mayer, 1895). Despite the very careful classification and the meticulous recording, Meringer could not find any evidence for his hypothesis. What Meringer did find, however, were a number of other regularities that could be linked to properties of language. Meringer concluded for example that a speech error had no mysterious background but that it was simply the result of the systematics by which we produce language. One of Meringer's discoveries involved the distinction between anticipation and perseveration errors; a distinction that is still made today.

Meringer's careful collection and analysis of speech errors would, however, put him on a collision course with a Viennese celebrity of the time. This was of course Sigmund Freud, who had published his most popular work, 'Zur Psychopathologie des Alltagslebens' in 1901, in which he cited a fairly random series of mundane speech errors, that he used to promote the idea that speech errors formed a window into an individual's true, and normally hidden, unconscious desires. Freud had also cited some examples from Meringer and Mayer. Although Meringer was praised for his work in the first edition of 'Zur Psychopathologie', Freud's tone changed drastically when it turned out that Meringer fundamentally disagreed with Freud's interpretation.

Meringer was particularly concerned by the fact that, in the examples cited, Freud argued that each error reflected a speaker's hidden desire, while it could be easily explained in a much simpler way. Meringer therefore reacted strongly against Freud's work, which he described as scientific bluff and a hoax. He also strongly opposed Freud's classification of 'Versprechen und Verlesen' as a preliminary work. Meringer started a fierce polemic against Freud's ideas in the form of scientific articles, letters, newspaper articles, and finally in 1908 another book: 'Aus dem Leben der Sprache', in which he lashed out at Freud. At first Freud ignored the attacks: his celebrity status allowed him to ignore Meringer's criticism. In 1908, however, Freud expressed his annoyance with Meringer in a letter to his then follower Carl Jung, using the words: 'Professor Mehringer in Graz surpasses himself in his malicious polemics'. The spelling error in Freud's letter is likely an inside-joke, since in German, 'Mehr-inger' implies being an over-doer.

In 1910, Freud completely removed his expression of gratitude to Meringer from the third edition of 'Zur Psychopathologie', stating that it had been a mistake to have ever given him any credit. Around 1912, the clash reached a climax when Meringer declared that he was not only a scientific opponent of Freud, but that he also hated every supporter of Freud's work.

The end of the clash started to emerge when, in 1923, Meringer launched a final attack on Freud. In that year, Meringer published an article in which he carefully debunked all the explanations for the errors that Freud had given in the sixth edition of 'Zur Psychopathologie'. In his article, Meringer argued that most speech errors can be explained simply on the basis of phonological effects, and he criticised Freud for not having a method to explain each and every speech error, but instead only

(Continued)

Box 18.2 (Continued)

selectively considered those that fit his theory. When a slip resulted in an obscenity, Meringer argued, it was according to Freud, a sign that the speaker was expressing a hidden desire. But, Meringer continued, what would give Freud the right to justify this conclusion when we make countless errors that are relatively insignificant? Meringer drew his conclusions from Freud's adherence to the idea that speech errors provide insights into hidden desires and denounced psychoanalysis as a caricature of a science and an invented fad.

After this final assault, the battle was, beyond Meringer's influence, provisionally ended in Freud's favour. 'Zur Psychopathologie' had made Freud an international superstar. The book was now in its ninth edition and had been published in several languages. Meringer, on the other hand, remained a local academic who continued to publish only in German and spent the rest of his life in relative obscurity.

Nowadays, however, Meringer's work is beginning to gain appreciation again, while Freud's ideas no longer carry any scientific weight (Crews, 2017). Motley and Baars (1976) argue that despite the intuitive popularity of the Freudian slip, there is still no empirical basis for this phenomenon and that there is no known mechanism to explain how central semantic encoding stages can affect speech production systems. These authors also argue that in the absence of a semantic theory of speech error production, all evidence suggesting the existence of Freudian slips is anecdotal, weak, and ad hoc. Finally, the British psycholinguist Andrew Ellis (1980) has analysed each speech error that was discussed by Freud in terms of a modern process approach. He also concluded that the evidence for Freud's theory is very weak and that the cited slips can be explained perfectly well by slips of the language production system.

distracted by a word. In this type of task, it is generally found that the naming time of a picture is prolonged when a semantically related word is presented (e.g., the word 'cat' when the picture of a dog is presented), whereas the naming time of the word is shortened by the presentation of a phonologically related word (e.g., the word 'dog'). But what happens when a taboo word is presented? Will this type of word result in more Freudian slips or not?

Dhooge and Hartsuiker (2011) actually found that taboo words had the opposite effect. Naming times were longer and there were fewer speech errors, suggesting that an internal error-monitoring system is particularly alert to these types of situations. fMRI results (see fig 18.2) showed that the inhibition of taboo evoking Spoonerisms was associated with activation in the right inferior frontal gyrus (Severens et al., 2012). This result is consistent with previous ERP findings that showed that taboo word presentation resulted in a negative ERP component approximately 600 ms after taboo word presentation (Severens et al., 2011). This component is similar to one found in an earlier study involving spoonerisms (Moller, Jansma, Rodriguez-Fornells, & Munte, 2007) and probably reflects the conflict between two alternative speech plans that are generated in parallel. These results suggest that internally, during the speech planning process, we frequently make blunders, but that our speech production system corrects the vast majority of these blunders already before we utter them. Interestingly, this happens even more frequently in taboo situations than in normal situations, which of course seriously questions the idea of a slip as a window into the unconscious.

18.4 SPEECH PRODUCTION THEORIES

Over the years, various speech production theories have been developed. These models emphasise either the processes involved in producing speech errors, such as Dell's (1986) spreading activation theory, or the processing stages that convert a global concept into a phonetic code, such Levelt et al. (1999)'s WEAVER++ model.

An important assumption in speech production theories is that the transformation of ideas into expressions involves several distinct processing stages. For example, Dell (1986) argues that speech production involves four different levels. The first of these is the semantic level. At this level the meaning of what is to be said is processed, and processes here are mainly involved in the planning of an utterance. One level below, we find the syntactic level. Here, the syntactic structure of the utterance is planned. That is, the word order is determined and put into the right grammatical structure. Another level down, we find the morphological level, where specific **morphemes** (words and word forms) are selected. Finally, at the phonological level the selected morphemes are converted into a phonological code.

18.4.1 SPREADING ACTIVATION THEORY

As the name of the model suggests, the concept of spreading activation is a crucial concept in Dell's (1986) theory. Dell assumes that the words and concepts that are stored in

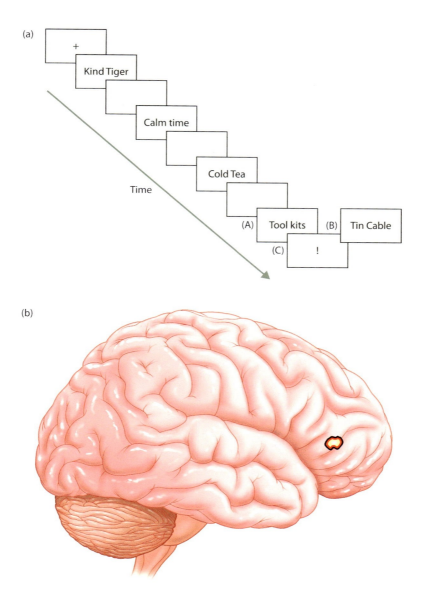

Figure 18.2 An experiment to induce the pronunciation of taboo words. (a) Three pairs of words were presented in quick succession, and participants had to pronounce the third pair of words aloud as quickly as possible. This could be a taboo-inducing word pair or a neutral word pair. (b) Inhibition of taboo words corresponded to activation in the right inferior frontal gyrus. (source: Adapted from Severens et al., 2012)

long-term memory are represented as nodes in a network (see also Chapter 13). When a concept is activated, its activation will subsequently spread to all associated concepts (see fig 18.3). Dell also assumes that phonemic information is part of this network, so that when concepts are activated, the corresponding speech sounds are automatically activated as well. Collectively, this network of words, concepts, and speech sounds a lexicon.

In addition, Dell assumes the existence of categorical rules that impose restrictions on which items, or categories of items, can be combined. These syntactic rules specify, for example, that within a sentence, two verbs will not be placed next to each other or that an adjective will be inserted before a noun.

Finally, Dell assumes the presence of **insertion rules** that ensure that the correct items are selected and inserted at the right place while a sentence is constructed. According to Dell, the spreading activation principle will ensure that all concepts within the lexicon that are relevant will have a high activation value at the start of the construction of a sentence. Then, the item with the highest activation level that is eligible according to the relevant categorical rule will be selected. If, for example, the syntactic categorical rule determines that the next word must be a verb, then the insertion rule will determine that the next word to be added to the sentence will be the verb with the highest activation value. Once this item has been chosen, its activation level will immediately be reduced to zero, to prevent it from being chosen again.

SYNTACTIC FRAMES **LEXICAL NETWORK**

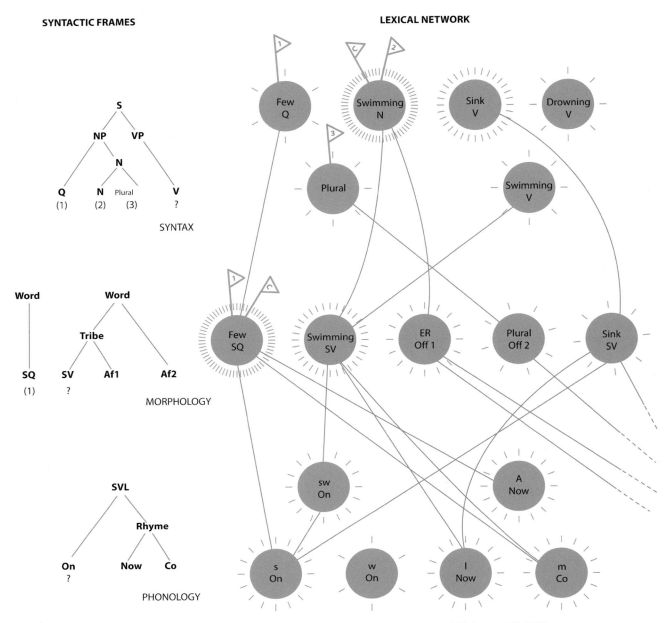

Figure 18.3 The spreading activation model in action during the production of the sentence 'Some swimmers sink'. (source: Dell, 1986)

According to the spreading activation model, we can occasionally make speech errors because noise may occasionally cause an incorrect item to have a higher activation value than the correct item, causing this item to be selected incorrectly, or at least prematurely. Due to the way the activation levels are distributed across the lexicon, several items are active at once, which increases the chance of a mix-up. How is it then that these mix-ups are not random but remain limited to a specific category? Obviously, the categorical rules are of crucial importance here, but Dell, Oppenheim, and Kittredge (2008) also suggest that we learn to reduce these errors. Dell et al. focused specifically on the question of why we sometimes confuse a verb with another verb or a noun with another

noun. They concluded that, based on learning processes, we develop an inhibition mechanism that prevents these types of syntactic violations from occurring.

18.4.1.1 Evidence

The spreading activation model is consistent with many of the types of speech errors just discussed. Moreover, the model also predicts the presence of more specific types of speech errors, such as the **mixed error effect**. This effect involves the selection of an incorrect word that is both semantically and phonemically related to the intended word. The existence of this type of error implies that the different processing levels interact in a flexible way and suggests that the semantic and

		Speaker reads concealment phrase	Speaker naming photo:	Correct response	Phonemes
Semantic competition	Related	The woman went to the convent to become a ...		"priest"	/nʌn/
	Check	He lit the candle with just one ...		"priest"	/mætʃ/
phonological competition	Related	I thought that there would still be some cookies left, but there were...		"priest"	/nʌn/
	Check	Debbie returned the blouse to the store because the colors just didn't...		"priest"	/mætʃ/

Figure 18.4 Examples of sentences used in a study of the mixed error effect. (source: Ferreira and Griffin, 2003)

phonological levels both influence the word selection process simultaneously.

Ferreira and Griffin (2003) found evidence for the idea that semantics and phonology can simultaneously affect the word selection process. In their study, participants had to name pictures, for example of a priest, while they had just read incomplete sentences that could prime a competing word. They used three different types of sentences (fig 18.4). The first could prime a semantically related concept, for example the sentence 'The woman went to the convent to become a . . . (nun)'. The second type of sentence could prime a homophone, such as 'I thought there were still cookies on the table, but there were . . . (none)'. Finally, the third sentence primed unrelated concepts. Both the first and second sentence types induced more naming errors, with the participant naming the picture with 'nun' instead of 'priest'.

The fact that speech errors rarely involve non-words is indicative of a **lexical bias effect** (Baars, Motley, & MacKay, 1975; Dell, 1986; Hartsuiker, Corley, & Martensen, 2005). Corley, Brocklehurst, and Moat (2011) studied this lexical bias effect by using tongue twisters: complex sentences, such as 'Give papa a cup of proper coffee in a copper coffee cup' (Try saying that ten times in quick succession) that elicit phoneme exchanges. Corley et al. found that when real words were used in these sentences, a significant number of speech errors were produced, but when the words were replaced by pronounceable non-words, far fewer phoneme exchanges were produced.

The spreading activation model can explain this effect because our lexicon only contains words, so non-words cannot be activated. It is also possible, however, that we monitor and edit our speech internally (see also the Freudian slip discussion). Nooteboom and Quené (2008) found evidence for such an editing process: when

speakers were about to make a speech error, they often corrected themselves, as in the case of a situation in which they had to repeat 'barn door' and uttered the following: 'd... barn door'.

The spreading activation model also predicts that speakers will make many anticipation errors. An anticipation error is when a speech sound is inserted too early into a sentence. This type of error can occur because all words in a sentence are activated during the planning phase, allowing the possibility that a word that should be inserted later in the sentence is selected too early. Nooteboom and Quené (2013) have found that this is indeed the case.

A final prediction of the spreading activation model is that many slips consist of exchange errors. According to Dell, the reason for these exchange errors is that the activation of a word is immediately reduced to zero after selection, which makes the likelihood that the word in question can be selected again in the right place extremely small. As a result, an inappropriate but highly activated word may be selected instead. Nooteboom and Quené (2013) found evidence for this too. It is important to note, however, that the spreading activation model predicts that exchanges will generally only cover relatively short distances. The words that are about to be selected are generally also those that have the highest activity. When we start to prepare a sentence, these are the words at the beginning of the sentence and the words that should come at the end of the sentence will still have low activation. This makes it unlikely that words will be interchanged across long distances.

18.4.1.2 Error Detection Mechanisms

Although we do occasionally make a speech error, their numbers nevertheless remain relatively small. Our previous discussion involving the Freudian slip has also shown that we appear to monitor our speech internally and correct it where necessary. How are we able to do that? Levelt (1983) argued that speakers detect their own errors by listening to themselves and by discovering what they say is sometimes different from what they mean. According to Levelt's perceptual loop theory, speakers thus use their understanding of speech to detect their own errors, in a way that is similar to how we detect errors in others' speech.

Nozari, Dell, and Schwartz (2011) have argued, on the other hand, that comprehension is hardly involved at all in detecting speech errors. They argue that error detection is based on an internal monitoring of the speech production system. Their speech error detection model is based on the idea that there is an internal conflict monitoring process active in our speech production system when different candidate words are in competition with each other for inclusion in a sentence. Nozari et al. have based their idea

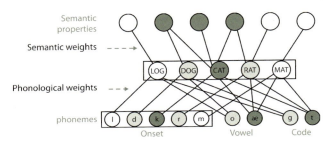

Figure 18.5 The interactive two-step model of word production. (source: Nozari et al., 2011)

on a two-stage word production model that was originally developed by Kempen and Huijbers (1983). According to this model (see fig 18.5), semantic units are connected to **lemmas**. Lemmas are abstract word forms consisting of syntactic and semantic properties but lacking a phonological code. The latter can be accessed because lemmas are connected to phonemes.

If speech comprehension mechanisms were involved in the detection of speech errors, a weakened connection (represented by the semantic weight (s-weight); fig 18.5) between the semantic level and the lemma level should lead to a reduction in our ability to detect these errors. If, on the other hand, it is primarily the speech production system that is involved in detecting speech errors, a weakening of the connections between the lemma level and the phonemic level (represented by the phonological weight (p-weight); fig 18.5) should lead to a weakening of our ability to detect speech errors. Nozari et al. (2011) tested a large group of **aphasia** patients to determine whether their speech errors were due to their speech comprehension or to their speech production ability. A computational modelling procedure was used to estimate each patient's s- and p-weights. Nozari et al. found no significant correlation between estimated s-weight and the ability to detect their speech errors, however, they did find a significant correlation between p-weight and the patient's ability to detect their speech errors, implying that the detection of speech errors mainly takes place during phoneme selection.

Nozari et al.'s (2011) conflict theory also predicts that error correction can take place rapidly, that is, already while the utterance is produced. Data from Blackmer and Mitton (1991) suggest that this is indeed the case. Transcripts of individuals dialling in to a radio show showed that many speech errors were corrected immediately. These findings are more consistent with the conflict theory than with Levelt's perceptual loop theory.

18.4.2 WEAVER++

Levelt et al. (1999) have developed a computational model for speech production that is known as WEAVER++.[1] This model is conceptually similar to the already discussed two-stage model that was developed by Kempen and Huijbers

(1983), however, it is more elaborate. WEAVER++ is a network model based on the principles of **spreading activation** and consists of three main levels. The highest level consists of nodes representing lexical concepts; one level below we find nodes representing lemmas and finally, the third and lowest level consists of nodes representing morphemes and their phonological aspects.

According to the WEAVER++ model, word selection involves a competitive process that is based on the number of lexical units that are activated. The actual word production then involves several distinct processing stages (see fig 18.6). In essence, the WEAVER++ model aims to describe how word production proceeds from the global conceptual level to the production of specific phonemes. On the basis of a literature review, Indefrey (2011) discusses

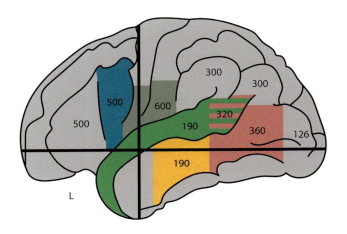

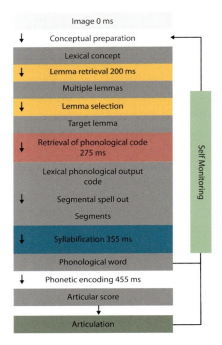

Figure 18.6 A schematic overview of the WEAVER++ model. The top panel gives an overview of the brain areas involved. Each colour corresponds to a process in the lower panel. The lower panel gives an overview of the sequence of processes involved in the conversion from semantics to articulation. (source: Indefrey, 2011)

the timing of all the sub-processes that, according to Levelt et al. (1999), are involved in speech production. Moreover, Indefrey discusses the brain areas that might be related to these processes (see fig 18.6).

18.4.2.1 Access to Grammatical and Phonological Information

One prediction that the WEAVER++ model makes is that speakers should have access to semantic and syntactic word information before they have access to phono-logical codes. Evidence for this was found using ERPs. Van Turennout, Hagoort, and Brown (1998) made use of the fact that Dutch nouns have a gender (see fig 18.7). Participants were shown pictures of objects, including a bear, a book, a shoe, and a sheep. Note that these target words differ with respect to their initial phoneme ('s' or 'b'). In Dutch, two of the words (Shoe [Schoen] and Bear [Beer]) have the common gender, which implies that they are preceded by the article 'De' (e.g., 'De Schoen' and 'De Beer'). The other two words (Book [Boek] and Sheep [Schaap]) have the neuter gender, which is preceded by the article "Het' (e.g., 'Het Boek' and 'Het Schaap'). Van Turennout's experiment thus comprises two factors: gender ('De' or 'Het') and initial phoneme ('S' or 'B'). In one condition, participants were required to respond on the basis of a target word's initial phoneme (e.g., respond with the left hand when the depicted object begins with a 'b' and with the right hand when it begins with an 's'). They only had to do that for one of the two genders; they were instructed not to respond to the other gender (e.g., respond to bear and shoe, but not to book or sheep). Thus, the task also involves a go/no-go decision.

In the second condition, these instructions were reversed: now participants had to make a gender-dependent choice, but they had to make the go/no-go decision on the basis of the initial phoneme (e.g., respond to bear and book, but not to shoe and sheep). While performing this task, EEGs were recorded, and Van Turennout et al. were inter-ested in one specific component, the **lateralised readiness potential (LRP)**. The LRP represents the electrical potential difference that we obtain by comparing the ERPs measured above the left and right motor cortex. For example, pre-paring a response with our left hand will result in greater activation over the right motor cortex than over the left.

Van Turennout et al. (1998) were mainly interested in whether LRP activity could be found when stimuli were involved to which the participants were not supposed to respond. This was indeed the case when the initial letter determined whether the participant had to respond or not. In this case, a residual LRP activation was found, which indicated that the participant was already prepar-ing a response on the basis of the gender information, which had to be interrupted on the basis of the pho-nological information that only became subsequently available.

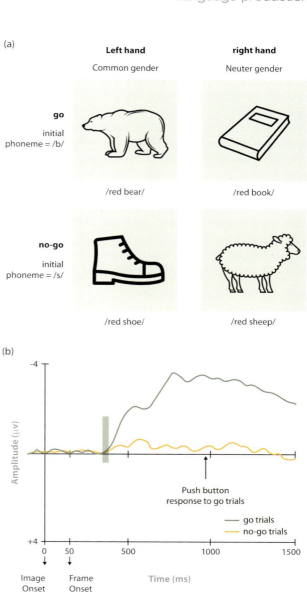

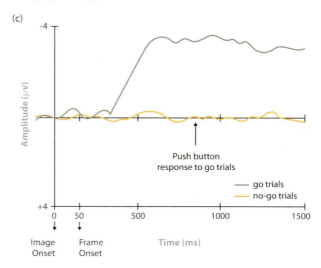

Figure 18.7 Experimental design and results of an ERP study on the effects of syntax and phonology on a go/no-go decision task. (a) Examples of stimuli used in the experiment. (b) LRP results when the go/no-go decision had to be made on the basis of the initial letter of the word. (c) Similar results when the decision was based on the word's gender. Here, a small LRP effect was also found in the no-go condition. (source: Van Turennout et al., 1998)

18.4.2.2 Evidence: Tip of the Tongue

Somewhat anecdotal evidence for the existence of the lemma stage is provided by the well-known 'tip of the tongue' phenomenon, which involves our inability to pronounce a word, despite the fact that we know its meaning perfectly well. This phenomenon implies that the semantic processing of the word in question was successful, whereas its phonological processing was not. Evidence for the idea that limited phonological access underlies the 'tip of the tongue' phenomenon was reported by Harley and Bown (1998). They found that relatively unique sounding words (i.e., words with a small phonological neighbourhood) were much more susceptible to this phenomenon than words with a large phonological neighbourhood. The unusual phonological form probably makes these words more difficult to retrieve.

According to Levelt, participants who experience the 'tip of the tongue' phenomenon should still be able to access words' gender. Vigliocco, Antonini, and Garrett (1997) found that this was indeed the case among Italian participants. Participants who were unable to pronounce a word could still accurately guess the gender of the word in 85% of all cases.

Biedermann, Ruh, Nickels, and Coltheart (2008), however, found results that were inconsistent with the aforementioned Van Turennout et al. (1998) study. In the former study, German participants had to guess the gender and initial phoneme of nouns when they were in a 'tip of the tongue' state. This was done by using low frequency words. Participants were, for example, shown a picture of an abacus and asked to name the picture. If they could not name the correct word, they were asked whether it was on the tip of their tongue or whether they really did not know the words. The WEAVER++ model would predict that the grammatical gender of German words (masculine 'der', feminine 'die' or neutral 'das') is accessible in a 'tip of the tongue' condition, while their initial phoneme would not be accessible.

Moreover, Biedermann et al.'s (2008) participants were given a number of definitions and had to name a word based on these definitions. If they failed to do so, they were asked whether it was on the tip of their tongue and then they had to try to guess (1) the gender of the word and (2) the initial phoneme. Based on the WEAVER++ model, it would be expected that participants would score above chance level when guessing the gender of the word, while they would remain at chance level when guessing the initial phoneme. Interestingly, however, Biedermann et al. (2008) found that this was not the case: both the gender and the initial phoneme were guessed correctly significantly more often than we would expect by chance (fig 18.8), implying that participants had some degree of access to the phonological code even though they could not reproduce the full word.

18.4.2.3 Competition

Levelt et al.'s (1999) prediction that word selection is based on a competitive process suggests that the presence of distractor words should interfere with the naming of objects

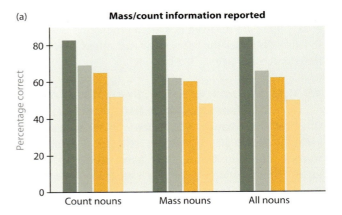

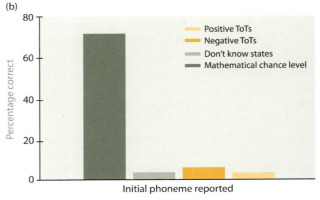

Figure 18.8 Results of a study investigating to which extent the gender and initial phoneme of words that are in a tip of the tongue state can be guessed. (a) Participants had to try to find a concept on the basis of a verbal description. When they failed to do so, they had to indicate whether the concept was on the tip of their tongue or whether they did not know it at all. Then they had to report whether the concept was comprised of countable units or whether it was a continuous mass. Participants were considered to be in a positive tip of the tongue (ToT) state when they retrospectively recognised the concept they had to find. Similarly, they were in a negative ToT state when they had a different concept in mind. In all cases, participants were able to judge the countability of the requested concept well above chance level. (b) The degree to which participants in a positive ToT state succeeded in guessing the initial phoneme of the requested concept. This was also far above chance level. (source: Biedermann et al., 2008)

that are shown in pictures. There is indeed some evidence for this prediction: when distractors were used from the same category as the object to be named, it was found that the naming of the target object was delayed (Melinger & Abdel Rahman, 2013). Piai, Roelofs, and Schriefers (2014) studied this interference effect in more detail. For example, they presented pictures of a dog together with a semantically related distractor word (e.g., 'cat'), a semantically unrelated word (e.g., 'pin'), or an identical word ('dog'). According to Levelt et al. (1999) possible candidate words are initially selected, followed by a competitive word selection process involving the frontal cortex.

Piai et al. found that activity in the frontal lobe was highest when semantically related words were presented and lowest when identical words were presented. This finding is consistent with the hypothesis that the processing of related words results in strong competition between candidate words. In addition, Piai et al. also found activation of the temporal cortex to be greater when unrelated and related words were presented than when identical words were presented. This finding is consistent with the idea that only one candidate word is activated during the presentation of an identical word, whereas several words are activated in the other conditions.

18.4.2.4 Lemma Selection

A final prediction that follows from the WEAVER++ model is that lemma selection should precede the selection of the corresponding phonological codes. Most empirical results are inconsistent with this prediction, however. For instance, Meyer and Damian (2007) instructed participants to name images while they simultaneously presented distracting images. These images were either phonologically related or unrelated to the one that had to be named. Phonologically related pictures involved, for example, the combination of a dog and a doll or a wall and a ball. According to the WEAVER++ model, the phonological code should only be activated after the word selection process has been completed. We should therefore expect no interference from phonologically related pictures, yet that is not what was found: the phonologically related pictures were named faster than the unrelated ones. Similar results have been reported by Oppermann, Jescheniak, and Gorges (2014).

Along similar lines, Madebach, Oppermann, Hantsch, Curda, and Jescheniak (2011) found that the time needed to name pictures was longer when phonologically similar words were used as distractors. They found this effect only, however, when the demand for cognitive control was low. More specifically, in one set of experiments, participants had to name pictures while words were presented that served as distractors. In a second set of experiments, participants had to regularly switch between naming the pictures and naming the words. In the latter set of experiments, no interference effects were found, suggesting that a high demand for cognitive control reduces interference from phonologically similar distractors.

18.4.2.5 Limitations

The results just discussed imply that word production processes operate much more in parallel than the WEAVER++ model implies (see also: Rapp & Goldrick, 2004). Moreover, the existence of speech errors, such as the word-exchange errors and the mixed error effect imply a much higher degree of parallel processing than the WEAVER++ model assumes. In addition, we may question the need to introduce the concept of the lemma (Harley, 2014). Most empirical evidence is consistent with a distinction between a semantic and a phonological level (for example Kempen & Huijbers, 1983). Finally, it should be noted that WEAVER++ has a relatively narrow scope. The model focuses mainly on describing the processes involved in the production of individual words. As such, the processes involved in the planning and production of complete sentences are beyond the scope of the model.

18.5 SPEECH PRODUCTION: NEUROPSYCHOLOGY

The first neuropsychological studies involving speech production were published in the 19th century and identified specific speech production difficulties that have subsequently become known as aphasias. Initially, it was suspected that there was a dissociation between aphasias characterised by difficulties with syntactic processing and aphasias characterised by difficulties with semantic processing. This resulted in the now classic distinction between Broca's and Wernicke's aphasias. Although this distinction is now believed to be incorrect it is nevertheless still useful to discuss the original findings of Paul Broca and Carl Wernicke, since they are still clinically relevant (Harley, 2014).

18.5.1 BROCA'S APHASIA

Patients with **Broca's aphasia** are characterised by non-fluent speech. More specifically, their speech is characterised by a slow, troublesome articulation, which contains many pauses and lack of prosody. These patients have difficulties articulating and also with producing the correct word order. Putting the relevant linguistic units in the right order appears to be one of the most prominent features of Broca's aphasia. Broca's aphasia is often associated with lesions in the left inferior frontal gyrus, a brain area that is also known as Broca's area.

18.5.2 WERNICKE'S APHASIA

Wernicke's aphasia is often associated with a lesion in the left superior temporal gyrus. This aphasia typically results in the production of fluent but meaningless speech. The sentences that are formulated by a patient diagnosed with Wernicke's aphasia appear eloquent, as they are characterised by complex grammatical structures and normal intonation. However, they are typically meaningless and Wernicke patients have many difficulties with finding the right words, resulting in several words being made up on the spot. Moreover, comprehension of words appears to be impaired as well. Wernicke patients typically have difficulties with selecting the most familiar word when triads of words are presented to them (Zurif, Caramazza, Myerson, & Galvin, 1974). Carl Wernicke originally argued that this type of aphasia resulted from the disruption of the 'sensory representation' of the words. For this reason, it is sometimes also identified as 'sensory aphasia'.

18.5.3 BROCA'S VERSUS WERNICKE'S APHASIA

Although at first glance, Broca's and Wernicke's aphasics appear to mirror each other, this characterisation is not entirely correct. After all, there is not just one distinguishing feature, but two. First, we have the distinction between intact and impaired understanding, and second, we have the distinction between the availability or unavailability of grammatical information. Moreover, the distinction between Broca's and Wernicke's aphasia appears to be based on damage of the underlying brain areas. This might not be a correct characterisation, because for at least Broca's area it has been established that this brain area is heterogeneous, that is, it is characterised by many different functions (Fedorenko & Blank, 2020). Thus, it would be more accurate to focus on functional distinctions, which are based on the underlying psycholinguistic models.

For this reason, it is currently much more common to distinguish between fluent and non-fluent aphasia. In addition, it is also possible to distinguish between aphasias that are characterised by comprehension problems and aphasias that are not (Harley, 2014). Traditional Broca patients are not fluent, but have no difficulties with comprehension, whereas classical Wernicke patients are fluent, but have difficulties with comprehension. Of course, we must consider the fact that no classification scheme is perfect when it comes to categorising neuropsychological patients. The nature, extension, and complexity of a neuropsychological disorder can always result in a pattern of symptoms that does not fit into this scheme.

18.5.4 AGRAMMATISM

One of the major limitations of patients with non-fluent aphasia is that they are unable to generate grammatically correct sentences, or at least have many difficulties doing so. Traditionally, these difficulties have been identified as **agrammatism**. Agrammatism consists of three components (Harley, 2014). The first involves a limitation in sentence production, which makes it difficult for patients to place words in the correct order. Their speech production appears to be limited to producing short sentences. Second, some aspects of their speech production appear to be selectively preserved. More specifically, the sentences that are produced consist mainly of content words (verbs and nouns), while function words ('the', 'a', 'in', 'and') and word endings are missing. The latter is an important feature, because function words and word endings play an important role in defining the grammatical structure of a sentence. Third, agrammatism is also often characterised by the fact that some patients have difficulties with understanding grammatically complex sentences.

The term 'agrammatism' implies that the aforementioned aspects form a syndrome, which also implies that there is a common cause for these deficiencies. There is indirect evidence that agrammatism is related to damage to Broca's area (Cappa, 2012). Note, however, that agrammatism cannot be considered a syndrome, because it is characterised by too many individual differences. Moreover, we can question whether agrammatism is specific to language production or whether it is a manifestation of a more general deficiency in the use of procedural knowledge. Evidence for the latter comes from a study by Christiansen, Kelly, Shillcock, and Greenfield (2010), who found that agrammatism patients also scored lower on a sequence learning task, which implies that at least in some patients agrammatism is related to an impaired ability to produce sequences (see fig 18.9).

Grodzinsky and Friederici's (2006) model of syntactic processing can possibly explain the great diversity in symptoms that can be observed in agrammatism. The model identifies three stages of syntactic processing, each of which is assumed to be located in a specific brain area.

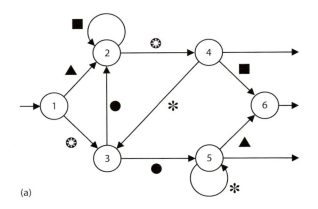

(a)

Test Stimulus

| Grammatical | Ungrammatical |

(b) ᵃThis item was repeated due to a programming error.

Figure 18.9 Outline of a sequence production task using an artificial grammar. (a) A flowchart depicting the rule that defined the artificial grammar. (b) Examples of stimuli that either conformed to the rule or violated it. (source: Christiansen et al., 2010)

The first stage involves the formation of local phrase structures from information about word categories. This function is associated with activation in the frontal operculum and the anterior superior temporal sulcus. The second stage involves the establishment of dependencies among various elements of the sentence (what is the subject?; what is the direct object?, etc). Broca's area is involved in this stage; activation in this area is greater for grammatically complex sentences than for simple sentences (Friederici, Fiebach, Schlesewsky, Bornkessel, & von Cramon, 2006). Finally, the third stage involves the integration of lexical and syntactic information. This is assumed to involve the posterior superior temporal gyrus and sulcus; areas that encompass Wernicke area.

In addition to Wernicke's and Broca's areas themselves, the connections between these areas also appear to be involved in syntactic processing. More specifically, two pathways have been found to connect Wernicke's and Broca's areas: a dorsal and a ventral one (see fig 18.10). Griffiths, Marslen-Wilson, Stamatakis, and Tyler (2013) concluded that damage to both the dorsal and ventral routes resulted in an increase in syntactic errors. This conclusion is based on a study involving patients with damage to either the dorsal or ventral pathway. These patients had to listen to sentences such as 'The woman is being hugged by the man', after which they had to choose an image that corresponded to this sentence. There were three different images to choose from: 1) a correct one; 2) a syntactic distractor (an image of a woman hugging a man); and 3) a semantic distractor (an image of a man painting a woman). Patients with damage to either the dorsal of ventral pathway chose the syntactic distractor relatively often instead of the correct image. These results imply that syntactic processing for comprehension, and possibly also for sentence production, depends on both the dorsal and ventral pathways.

Although these results imply that patients with agrammatism are impaired at producing grammatically correct sentences, it is also possible that they still possess this skill, but that they have difficulties in applying it. Evidence for the latter hypothesis was reported by Burkhardt,

Avrutin, Piñango, and Ruigendijk (2008), who found that patients were still reasonably successful in processing syntactically complex information, but that they needed more time to do so, compared to neurotypical controls. It is also possible that the somewhat artificial nature of the tasks that are often used by neuropsychologists (such as picture naming) may actually accentuate the problems. For example, Beeke, Wilkinson, and Maxim (2007), studied an agrammatic patient in both laboratory and natural environments and found that this patient had fewer difficulties expressing himself in a natural environment than in a laboratory environment.

18.5.5 FLUID APHASIA: ANOMIA

Anomia is characterised by a limitation in the ability to name objects. According to the WEAVER++ model (Levelt et al., 1999) anomia is related to the process of lexicalisation, that is, the translation of word meaning into sound. This process can be impaired because word selection is disrupted, either at the semantic or at the phonological level. If the process is disrupted at the semantic level, patients may have difficulties finding the correct lemma. When this is the case, patients should name words incorrectly, in the sense that they choose words that correspond in meaning to the requested word, but which do not necessarily identify the object correctly. In case of a disruption at the phonological level, a naming error should result in an incorrect pronunciation, even though the correct word was intended.

Howard and Orchard-Lisle (2007) reported the case study of JCU, a 47-year-old woman who had developed severe aphasia as a result of a haematoma in the left fronto-temporal region of her brain. Her speech was limited to simple utterances, and she was no longer able to speak spontaneously without being given any cues. When she had to name objects, she often gave an incorrect answer when she was given the initial sound of the object as a cue. These observations imply an impairment at the semantic level. Note, however, that when she had produced an incorrect word, she rejected her own answer in many cases, implying that her understanding of words was at least partially intact. In contrast, Kay and Ellis (1987) have reported a case study of a patient who was characterised with difficulties at the phonological level. This patient, EST, was able to select the correct lemma but not the phonological word form. In particular, EST had difficulties in finding words, except for the most common ones, a situation that Kay and Ellis described as a permanent 'tip of the tongue' condition.

Is it possible to find direct evidence for a distinction between semantic and phonological impairments? Laganaro, Morand, and Schnider (2008) aimed to address this question by using ERPs. To this end, they divided a group of aphasic patients into two subgroups according to the specific difficulties they experienced. Both subgroups

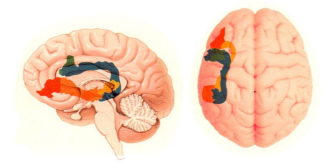

Figure 18.10 Reconstruction of the dorsal and ventral pathways between Wernicke's and Broca's areas. (source: Griffiths et al., 2013)

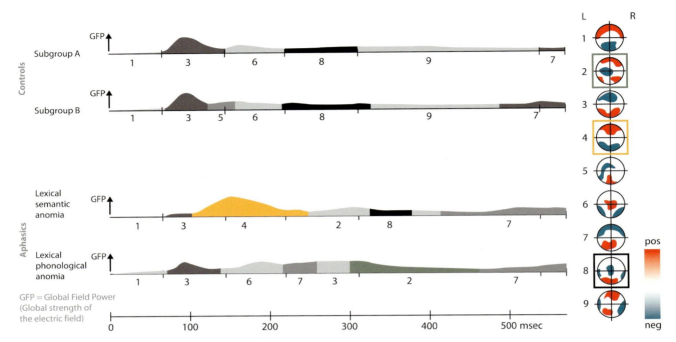

Figure 18.11 ERP results implying a functional distinction between semantic and phonological problems in aphasic patients. ERPs were evoked by a picture that the participants had to describe. The time course of the electric field power is shown for two groups of control participants and for the phonological and semantic aphasia patients. The latter groups each show a unique set of deviations in their electric field power. The numbers placed along for these field power graphs correspond to the electrical potential scalp distribution plots shown on the far right. The highlighted potential distributions correspond to the abnormal activities in the aphasia patients. (source: Laganaro et al., 2008)

had to name pictures. The group with semantic difficulties showed an unusual ERP pattern that occurred relatively early (100–250 ms) after the presentation of the target picture (see fig 18.11). In contrast, the group with phonological difficulties showed a relatively late deviation in the ERP pattern (300–450 ms). These results are consistent with the idea that anomia can be caused by both an early semantic deficiency and a late phonological deficiency.

There may be more interactions between processing at the semantic and phonological level than the WEAVER++ model would suggest, however. Evidence for this comes from several studies by the British psycholinguist Maya Soni and her colleagues. One study involved a naming task, showing for example a picture of a lion (Soni et al., 2009). In one condition, a correct cue was given, in the form of the letter 'l'. In a second condition, however, an incorrect cue was given, such as the 't', which implies the incorrect name 'tiger'. According to the WEAVER++ model, the object's name should be available before the phonological code is being processed. Thus, an incorrect cue should have no effect. According to interactive models, on the other hand, phonology might have an impact on semantic processing. Soni et al. found that the latter is indeed the case: the incorrect cues resulted in an increase in the number of incorrect namings.

In a follow-up study, anomia patients also had to name images and here they were given auditory cues. The experiment included a total of four different conditions. For example, when shown a picture of a bathtub, the following auditory cues could be given: (1) /b/ (correct); (2) /s/ (for 'shower'; a related category); (3) /w/ (for 'water'; an associated word); or (4) any other non-associated letter. The incorrect cues were effective in inducing pronunciation errors, again implying that phonology is crucially involved in semantic processing.

Thus, while much research is consistent with the WEAVER++ model, there are also many results that are inconsistent with the assumption of seriality. More specifically, the effects of phonology on semantic selection suggest that there is a stronger interaction between these two levels than Levelt et al. (1999) originally assumed.

18.5.6 FLUID APHASIA: JARGON APHASIA

Jargon aphasia is characterised by patients' failure to produce the correct content words, while grammatically their sentences are still relatively correct. These patients tend to substitute one specific word for another, and they also typically produce **neologisms**. They are also frequently unaware of their errors and may become annoyed when others indicate that they have difficulties understanding them (Marshall, 2006). Ellis, Miller, and Sin (1983) discuss the case of patient RD, who developed a speech disorder at the age of 69 following a stroke. RD produced many neologisms, especially when the word he was looking for was relatively infrequent.

The fact that jargon aphasic patients produce many neologisms limits our ability to determine to what extent their speech is still grammatically correct. The neologisms that are produced, however, are often embedded in the correct phrase structures. Furthermore, if these patients can indeed produce a correct grammatical structure, we would expect their neologisms to be correctly embedded into the sentence.

Why do jargon aphasic patients often produce neologisms? An investigation of the types of neologisms that are produced allows us to conclude that some of them are phonologically related to the word that the patient is searching for, while others are not. This raises the question of whether the same mechanisms are involved in generating these different types of neologisms. The results obtained from a study involving VS, an 84-year-old woman with jargon aphasia, suggest that this may indeed be the case (Olson, Romani, & Halloran, 2007). Her neologisms were affected by factors such as word frequency and word length, as well as the degree of concreteness of the word, regardless of phonological similarity to the word that she was looking for. This suggests that there is one underlying disability that produces both phonologically similar and non-similar words.

Notice, however, that several factors may contribute to the production of neologisms. First, when neologisms are produced, they frequently contain phonemes that are also part of the intended word. Second, one particular amnesia patient, LT, tended to produce consonants that are common in the English language (see fig 18.12), regardless of whether they fit the context of the word being sought (Robson, Pring, Marshall, & Chiat, 2003). Third, it was found that jargon aphasic patients tended to incorporate recently used phonemes into their neologisms, probably because they were still activated in their lexicon (Goldmann, Schwartz, & Wilshire, 2001).

Finally, why are jargon aphasic patients impaired with respect to monitoring and correcting their own speech? This question allows multiple answers (Marshall, 2006). One possibility is that they have difficulties with simultaneously speaking and monitoring their speech. Shuren,

Hammond, Maher, Rothi, and Heilman (1995) asked one patient to indicate whether his own speech was correct. When he heard his own speech through a recording, he was correct in identifying his errors in 90% of all cases. When he had to make a similar assessment immediately after pronunciation, he was correct in only 6.7% of all cases, however, which implies a limitation in simultaneous processing.

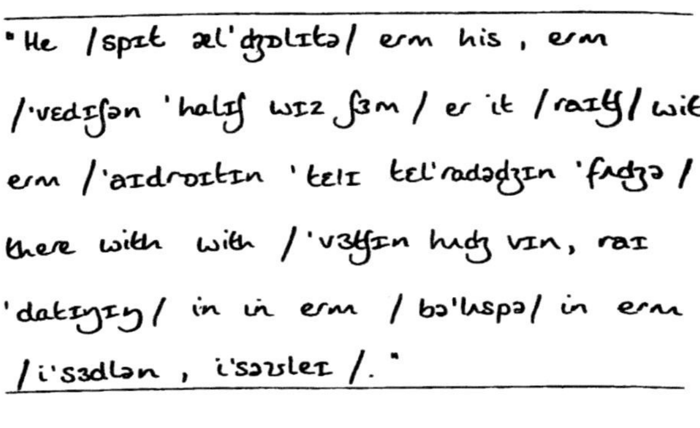

Another possibility is that difficulties with speech monitoring arise when phonological information has to be derived from semantic information. Marshall, Robson, Pring, and Chiat (1998) studied a patient, CM, while he had to describe pictures. Subsequently he had to repeat the words he had produced in these descriptions. While repeating, he was much better at recognising neologisms than while describing. Since CM was mainly processing semantic word information while describing the pictures, this may have impaired his ability to recognise pronunciation errors.

18.6 WRITING

Next to speech, writing is the second-most important way of producing language. Our modern society places a greater demand on our ability to write than ever before. Moreover, writing is one of the most complex cognitive skills imaginable. It draws on almost every cognitive process available to us, ranging from the elementary motor control processes that are involved in the complex sequences of finger movements required for typing and for handwriting, through the more complex language production processes for transforming a thought into grammatically correct sentences, to the social empathy processes that enable writers to adopt the perspective of their readers. Breaking down complex ideas into a logically ordered series of sub-steps, each simple enough to be understood, incurs strong demands on both planning and working memory.

Due to this complexity, much less is known about the psychology of writing than about speech production. Nevertheless, there have been a limited number of studies that have uncovered some of the mechanisms involved in writing.

18.6.1 PROCESSES INVOLVED IN WRITING

Hayes and Flower (1986) have developed an influential model that characterises the main processes involved in writing. Although the details of this model are still subject to debate, there is a high degree of consensus on the hypothesis that writing mainly consists of planning, sentence formation, and revision. The original Hayes and Flower model has been further developed by Chenoweth and Hayes (2003). In this revised model, the sentence formation

Figure 18.12 Example of a speech fragment of patient LT. (source: Robson et al., 2003)

process is split into a translation and a transcription process. In this context, translation involves the conversion of ideas into word sequences, or concrete sentences, while transcription consists of converting these word sequences into the actual text fragments. The main reason for this split was that Hayes originally believed that transcribing a text required no cognitive resources, however this assumption turned out to be incorrect. Hayes and Chenoweth (2006) found that transcribing an existing text was slower, resulting in more errors when participants were required to simultaneously perform a secondary working memory demanding task, suggesting that the transcription processes were impaired by concurrent cognitive activities.

In the latest revision of Hayes's writing model (fig 18.13), the four writing processes that Chenoweth and Hayes (2003) have identified have been integrated with the generic cognitive processes that are involved in writing (Hayes, 2012). In addition to the process level, where the four original processes of Chenoweth and Hayes are situated, the model has been expanded to include a control level and a resource level. The control level is involved in setting specific goals. This level is related to motivation and setting the end goal of the writing process. It also contains general writing schemes that can be accessed during the writing process. The resource level includes basic cognitive processes such as attention, memory, and reading comprehension, which can also be accessed during the writing process.

Much of our knowledge about these writing processes has been acquired using a method known as **controlled retrospection**. Using this method, participants are given the task of writing an essay, during which they are interrupted at predetermined intervals, requiring them to indicate what they were doing at that moment. Kellogg (1988) found that participants who were asked to write an

outline first produced manuscripts that received higher ratings than participants who did not. Generating an outline also resulted in participants being able to focus more on sentence generation and production and less on planning. An interesting fact here was that it did not matter whether participants produced a physical outline or merely a mental one.

Writing is highly dependent on the writer's knowledge. As such, Alexander, Schallert, and Hare (1991) have identified three relevant types of knowledge that are relevant here. The first of these is conceptual knowledge, that is, information about concepts and schemes stored in long-term memory. This type of knowledge is strongly related of the contents that the writer intents to communicate. The second type is sociocultural knowledge, that is, knowledge about the social background or context of a problem. Finally, the third type is metacognitive knowledge, that is, knowledge about what someone knows. In addition to these types of knowledge, Hayes and Flower (1986) also identified strategic knowledge. The latter form of knowledge relates to the way goals and subgoals can be organised in a text, and this knowledge can be used specifically when a writing plan needs to be adjusted.

The final version of an essay is typically much longer than the original outline. It is therefore not surprising that writers spend a considerable amount of their time on the sentence generation process. Kaufer, Hayes, and Flower (1986) found that experienced and average writers accepted about 75% of the sentence fragments they verbalised. Moreover, experienced writers (experts) produced on average slightly longer sentences than average writers. Beauvais, Olive, and Passerault (2011) found that writers frequently switch between the different processes. The writers involved in their study switched about six to eight times per minute. Translation took about 16 to 17 seconds each time, planning about 8 to 12 seconds, and revision 4 seconds. Thus, planning and revision generally took slightly less time than the sentence formation process. An interesting finding, however, is that experts spent much more time on text revision than non-experts (Hayes & Flower, 1986). It was found that experts spend more time refining the coherence and structure of an argument than non-experts. Faigly and Witte (1981) also found that revisions made by experts involved a much greater degree of change in meaning compared to revisions made by student writers.

A final question involves the situations that give rise to switching from one process to another. According to Flower and Hayes (1980) we have an internal monitor that checks all activities. This monitor appears to be somewhat related to our working memory's central executive (Baddeley & Hitch, 1974), which regulates the switching of attention and the inhibition of irrelevant information. Quinlan, Loncke, Leijten, and Van Waes (2012) investigated whether this monitor does actually involve working

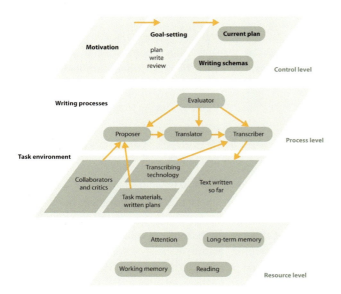

Figure 18.13 Hayes' (2012) writing model.

memory. They hypothesised that if it did, the monitor would be less likely to trigger a task switch under high mental load conditions. This hypothesis was investigated by evaluating how participants dealt with correcting errors. More specifically, participants could choose whether to continue finishing a sentence before correcting an error, or to correct it immediately. Most participants chose to finish the sentence first before correcting the error, and this tendency became stronger as the demands on processing capacity increased.

18.6.2 WRITING VERSUS TYPING

Ironically, the most basic aspect of the writing process, that is, the actual word production process, received initially very little attention in the psycholinguistic research community. The introduction of the transcription process in the revised Chenoweth and Hayes (2003) model has brought this aspect of the writing process more to the forefront of psycholinguistic research. Indeed, producing written words involves more than the simple concatenation of individual letters. In handwriting, we tend to group letters together to form chunks. The way letters are grouped affects the motor commands that control writing movements.

For Spanish and French, it has been found that writers group these letters in units that roughly correspond to syllables. In addition, the writing process can also be influenced by bigram frequencies (Kandel, Peereman, Grosjacques, & Fayol, 2001). A **bigram** is formed by two adjacent units in a sequence of letters. These units can be letters, syllables, or words. A good example of a common bigram is the letter combination 'th'. Participants in Kandel et al.'s study were instructed to use a digitisation tablet to write words that varied in the frequency of the bigrams that formed the boundary between the first and second syllables. For example, in the word 'syllable', the bigram 'll' overlaps the syllables 'syl' and 'la'. It was expected that the frequency of these bigrams would affect writing time. If our handwritten output is only grouped by syllables, we should not expect any effects of bigram frequency. In contrast, when grouping involves both bigrams and syllables, we should expect longer transition times from one bigram to another when the bigram frequency in question is low. Kandel et al. found that both syllables and bigrams influence the writing process, but that the effects of bigrams are mainly present in adults (see fig 18.14).

18.6.2.1 Handwriting and Motor Commands

Producing a handwritten text requires a high degree of control over the finer motor systems. Handwriting is characterised by many individual differences. An interesting finding, however, is that the letters produced by one individual contain remarkably characteristic features, regardless of whether they are produced by the

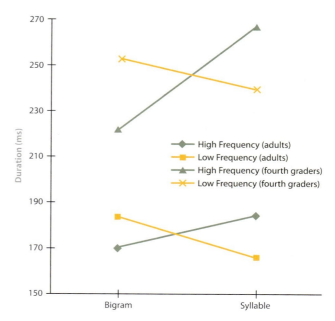

Figure 18.14 The effects of bigram frequency on writing time, as a function of the position of the bigram in the word. HF = high frequency bigrams; LF = low frequency bigrams. (source: Kandel et al., 2001)

muscles of the hand, by muscles of the arm, or by other parts of the body. Indeed, letters written with chalk on a blackboard are often very similar in shape to those written on paper. These findings imply, as already discussed in Chapter 3, a high degree of motor equivalence. This implies that the instructions to produce letters are generated at a relatively high level in the neural hierarchy of the motor system.

Wing (2000) has provided an overview of all the processes involved in the production of handwritten texts (see fig 18.15). According to Wing, handwriting consists of discrete stages, starting with the selection of graphemes. This selection depends either on lexical information or on a phonological to graphemic conversion rule. After this the model assumes that effector-independent **allographs** are selected. Allographs define the basic shapes of letters, possibly in terms of a specific sequence of strokes. According to Wing, these allographs generate effector-specific motor commands that, depending on the specific context, result in the production of a handwritten text.

18.6.2.2 Typing

If you have any experience with typing, you are probably familiar with the experience that while you are focusing on your computer screen, your fingers race effortlessly across the keyboard, finding the right location automatically, seemingly bypassing any visual input. However, when asked where, for example, the letter 'b' is located on the board, you may have to think long and hard to find it. The complex skill that typing actually is, apparently involves many low-level motor skills and the locations

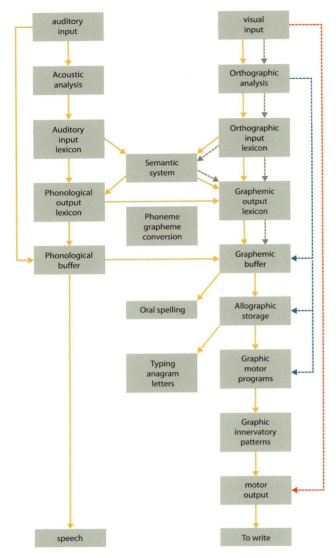

Figure 18.15 Wing's model for handwriting. (source: Wing, 2000)

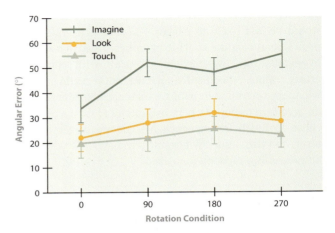

Figure 18.16 The average estimation error for determining where a key was located on a keyboard when participants had to imagine it, and when they could look at it, or touch it. (source: Liu et al., 2010)

of the individual keys appear to be largely represented in our procedural memory. The American cognitive psychologists Gordon Logan and Matthew Crump wondered to what extent we have control over our typing skill and which factors are involved in it. In doing so, they made a number of remarkable observations.

For instance, Liu, Crump, and Logan (2010) wondered to what extent we actually have explicit knowledge about the layout of a keyboard. To investigate this, they instructed participants to indicate the relative positions of two letters. Participants either had to imagine a keyboard, look at an existing keyboard, or type the two letters. The group that had to imagine the keyboard made more errors: they overestimated the difference between the two positions and took longer to respond, compared to the other two groups (fig 18.16). This result does indeed suggest that we have very weak explicit knowledge about the layout of a keyboard. Moreover, it

is consistent with the idea that typing itself is primarily a motor skill. Because typing is so highly automated and executed at the level of the motor system, we might suspect that peripheral features of a keyboard have a very limited influence on our typing ability.

As experienced typists, we should be able to plan each subsequent keystroke on the basis of a **forward model**, suggesting that factors such as changes in keystroke sensitivity should only have a minimal impact on our typing speed. One practical consequence of this is that we can generally switch to a new computer with relatively little effort, as long as the layout of the keyboard does not vary too much. On the other hand, we can also intuitively guess that a drastic change in tactile feedback from the keyboard requires a serious adjustment of our motor system, which in turn my have a huge impact on our typing skills.

Crump and Logan (2010b) investigated this issue by having participants type on a regular keyboard, on two keyboards that had been partially disassembled (one board from which the keys had been removed and a second board from which not only the keys but also the rubber layer providing the tactile feedback had been removed) and on a virtual keyboard that was projected onto a table by means of a laser light. Compared to the regular keyboard, the typing speed on all other boards was significantly lower and the error rate was also significantly higher. This result implies that keystrokes are not programmed in a strict feedforward manner during typing, but that we also make use of the tactile feedback generated by the keystrokes.

The fact that typing is a motor skill is also consistent with the idea that attention to detail can have a negative impact on motor skills: if you try to figure out exactly what you are doing, you often fail. Logan and Crump (2009) found evidence for this by focusing attention specifically on the typing process. Experienced typists were given a number of words to type and they were instructed to type only those letters that they would normally type with one hand. Responses from the other hand had to be ignored. This instruction had a dramatic effect on typing speed and the number of errors that were made. Interestingly, this deterioration only occurred when participants were directly asked to inhibit the responses of one hand. When the same instruction was given indirectly, it had no effect. That is, when all letters of the word that had to be typed were coloured either red (corresponding to one hand) or green (corresponding to the other hand) and the participants were asked to type only the letters of one given colour, no slowing was observed. Based on these results, Logan and Crump conclude that the typing process is controlled by two nested control processes: an outer loop that controls what should be typed, and an inner loop that controls which hand should act.

18.6.2.3 Typing and Language

In the preceding, we were introduced to some general motor aspects of the typing process. The final question we focus on here is how these processes relate to the processing of language. How do we plan a series of keystrokes when we need to type out words, sentences, or even whole paragraphs? Crump and Logan (2010a) investigated to what extent the activation of words can affect our typing speed by using a priming technique. Participants were given a prime word and then had to type, as quickly as possible, either a whole word or a single letter. When participants had to type one letter, this letter could either be one of the letters from the prime or a randomly selected different letter. Participants were faster when this letter was part of the prime, regardless of whether it was presented visually or aurally, and also regardless of the position of the target letter in the prime word. This result suggests a form of hierarchical processing, whereby a representation at the word level activates all the individual letters of this word in parallel and facilitates the corresponding motor responses.

In a follow-up study, Logan and Crump (2010) found a dissociation between typing errors that we detect and typing errors that we make. While participants were typing, errors were automatically corrected, and correctly written words were automatically mutilated. Participants attributed the automatically corrected errors to their own typing skills and took responsibility for errors they did not actually make. Interestingly, however, their behaviour showed a different pattern: after an actual error they slowed down, while an error that was artificially added had no effect on typing speed. Logan and Crump conclude from this that there are two error detection systems: one that is based on the visual information on the screen and one that is based on a motor loop.

18.7 SPELLING

18.7.1 A NEUROPSYCHOLOGICAL SPELLING MODEL

Of course, spelling is as important for handwriting as it is for typing. Rapp and Dufor (2011) have presented an overview of the main processes that are involved in spelling (see fig 18.17). Their overview is based on an earlier model that was originally developed by Goldberg and Rapp (2008). According to this model, there are two main routes converting a word that has been heard to its spelling, namely a lexical route and a non-lexical route.

The lexical route contains information that is required to relate phonological, semantic, and orthographic information to each other. Detailed information about these aspects of the to-be-written word can be used to look up the spelling of a word in an internal orthographic lexicon and this information can be used to convert the aural information into a written representation. This route is mainly used to produce the correct spelling of familiar words.

The non-lexical route is based on a rule-based system that can be used when we do not have access to our lexicon. This route converts phonological information into orthographic information, using a rule-based system. In this process, sounds or phonemes are converted into letters. We use this route mainly for the spelling of non-words or unknown words. This route produces correct spellings for words with regular phoneme to grapheme

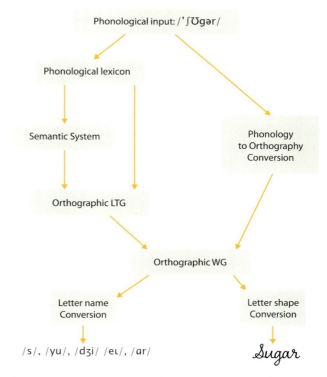

Figure 18.17 A model for spelling. (LTM = long-term memory; WM = working memory). (source: Rapp and Dufor, 2011)

relations, while it produces incorrect spellings for irregular or unusual words.

Both routes make use of orthographic working memory, a system that was originally identified by Goldberg and Rapp (2008) as the graphemic buffer. This memory system stores the graphical representation of the letters until they are written or typed.

18.7.1.1 Phonological Dysgraphia

Damage to the non-lexical pathway results in a condition that is characterised by difficulties with the spelling of unknown words and non-words, while the spelling of known words is still largely intact. These patients are characterised by **phonological dysgraphia**.

The neuropsychological literature has identified several patients with such a condition. For example, Shelton and Weinrich (1997) studied patient EA, who was unable to spell non-words correctly, but spelled 50% of regular and 45% of irregular words correctly. Cholewa, Mantey, Heber, and Hollweg (2010), found that children with phonological dysgraphia were also much less accurate in spelling non-words and irregular words.

The difficulties that phonological dysgraphia patients experience can possibly be explained by the hypothesis that their phonological processing is impaired. According to this hypothesis, these patients should therefore experience many difficulties with tasks involving phonology, even when it does not relate to spelling. A study by Cholewa et al. (2010) found evidence for this. They gave the children a battery of phonological tasks, such as judging whether two words sounded the same, or requiring them to repeat a non-word in which a consonant was removed. Children with phonological dysgraphia performed more poorly on these tasks than children in a control group.

18.7.1.2 Surface Dysgraphia

Patients with an impairment of their lexical pathways are characterised by the fact that they produce many spelling errors while writing existing words, while they are still able to spell non-words and unknown words to some extent. Moreover, their ability to spell regular words is better than their ability to spell irregular ones. These patients are characterised by a condition known as surface dysgraphia. Macoir and Bernier (2002) reported a case study of a patient, MK, who spelled 92% of all regular words correctly, but only 52% of all irregular words. Cholewa et al. (2010) also investigated children with surface dysgraphia. These children misspelled 56% of the irregular words, while they only misspelled 19% of the non-words.

According to Rapp and Dufor's (2011) model, surface dysgraphia patients have particular difficulties with obtaining information about words. We might therefore expect these individuals to be better at spelling words for which they have access to the semantics. Macoir and Bernier (2002)

found that this is indeed the case. Moreover, Bormann, Wallesch, Seyboth, and Blanken (2009) reported a case study of a patient with surface dysgraphia, who had an impairment in accessing word-related information. When he heard two words in a row, he sometimes wrote them down as one meaningless word. For example, he wrote the German phrase 'Lass Dass' (let it) as 'lasdas'.

We might expect that, unlike individuals with phonological dysgraphia, patients with surface dysgraphia would not experience any difficulties with the phonological processing of words. The Cholewa et al. (2010) study, discussed above, found evidence for this as well: children with surface dysgraphia performed much more accurately on the phonological tasks than the children with phonological dysgraphia. However, their performance was still more impaired compared to that of children in the control group.

18.7.1.3 Independent Pathways?

Finally, we can ask whether the lexical and non-lexical pathways are independent or not. Rapp, Epstein, and Tainturier (2002) reported the case study of patient LAT, a 78-year-old male diagnosed with Alzheimer's disease. LAT made many spelling errors, but his non-lexical pathway still functioned reasonably well, as evidenced by the fact that he still spelled non-words reasonably accurately. Some of his incorrect spellings suggested that he was integrating information from the lexical and non-lexical pathways, however. For example, he wrote 'bouquet' as 'bouket' and 'knowledge' as 'knolige'. These spellings suggest some influence from the non-lexical route because part of the spelling appears to be driven by a rule (see fig 18.18).

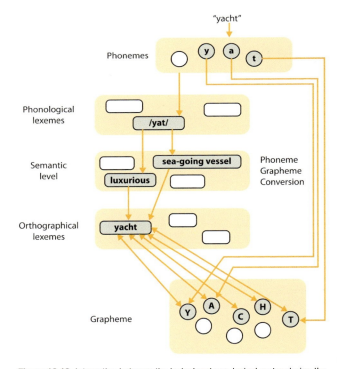

Figure 18.18 Interaction between the lexical and non-lexical routes during the spelling of words. (source: Rapp et al., 2002)

He could only have known that 'bouquet' ends with a 't' or that 'knowledge' begins with a 'k' by accessing his lexical system, however.

Influences from the lexical route on non-lexical processing have also been reported in neurotypical individuals. For instance, one could write the non-word /vi:m/ either as 'veam' or as 'veme'. Which version would you choose? Martin and Barry (2012) found that participants who had just heard the word 'dream' were more likely to choose 'veam', whereas participants who had heard 'theme' were more likely to choose 'veme'. This result corroborates the finding that the lexical route has some influence on the non-lexical route. Finally, it was found that writing irregular words takes longer than writing regular ones (Delattre, Bonin, & Barry, 2006). This effect can be explained by assuming that for irregular words there is a conflict between the output of the lexical and the non-lexical routes.

18.7.2 ONE OR TWO ORTHOGRAPHIC LEXICONS?

Knowledge about spelling is crucial for both reading and writing. We can therefore ask whether we have one orthographic lexicon that is shared by reading and writing processes, or whether each process has its own lexicon.

The idea that we have two lexicons, one for reading and one for writing, is suggested by some studies involving neuropsychological patients (see fig 18.18). For example, Tainturier, Schiemenz, and Leek (2006) reported the case study of a 58-year-old patient, CWS, who had suffered a stroke. His ability to spell words was severely impaired, although his reading ability was barely affected. Many studies report similar cases of patients who have significantly more difficulties with spelling than with reading, while other patients have much more difficulties with reading than with spelling.

Despite these differences, patient studies do not provide convincing evidence for the existence of two orthographic lexicons (Rapp & Lipka, 2011). After all, patients with reading impairments are also frequently characterised by damage to brain areas associated with visual perception, whereas patients who mainly have spelling impairments are frequently characterised by damage to the premotor areas. We can therefore conclude from patient studies that perception is important for reading and motor skills for spelling. These results are, however, not very informative about whether we have one or two lexicons.

Evidence for the idea that we have one orthographic lexicon has also been provided by patient studies. After all, many patients with a reading disorder have impairments in their writing and spelling abilities. This suggests a strong link between dyslexia and dysgraphia. Dyslexia and dysgraphia patients are often characterised by damage to the fusiform temporal cortex and the inferior frontal gyrus. These are areas associated with the orthographic lexicon, as shown in neuroimaging studies by Rapp and Lipka (2011) and Rapp and Dufor (2011), as well as from a patient study by Tsapkini and Rapp (2010). Moreover, many of these patients have difficulties with specific words, both in reading and writing, again suggesting the presence of a shared lexicon.

Studies involving neurotypical participants have also provided evidence in favour of a single orthographic memory. For example, Holmes and Carruthers (1998) presented participants with five different versions of words that they could not spell correctly. These included the correct spelling and the (incorrect) spelling that they had generated themself. The participants' task was to point out the correctly spelled version of the word, yet they often failed to do so and preferred their own spelling.

Although the question of whether there are one or two orthographic lexicons has not yet been conclusively answered, most evidence indicates that there is one lexicon, shared by reading and writing processes. Neuroimaging and patient studies suggest that this lexicon is strongly associated with the fusiform temporal gyrus.

18.8 SUMMARY

The two major forms of language production are speaking and writing. Most research in this area focuses on speech production processes. Speech and writing both serve a similar purpose, namely communication, and both make use of the same source of knowledge. They are therefore similar in many ways, especially in the planning phase. However, there are also important differences between speech and writing processes. Written texts generally consist of longer and more complex sentences than spoken utterances. Speech, on the other hand, is more spontaneous, less complete, and more attuned to the audience, with whom the speaker usually has direct contact and feedback.

A fluent speaker can produce about 150 words per minute. Producing coherent speech at this rate requires a great deal of cognitive processing power, and speakers can maintain this speed by using preformulation and planning ahead at strategic moments. Much of the knowledge about speech planning has been gained by studying speech errors, and by determining when speakers pause. Planning is flexible and can be adapted to changing task requirements.

Speech errors are an important source of information and as such they have contributed significantly to our understanding of speech production. Most of these errors involve one of the following categories: word exchange errors, spoonerisms, morpheme exchange errors, number agreement errors, or semantic substitutions. A final category is formed by the Freudian slip. Several researchers have disputed whether this type of error exists in its own right. Many apparent Freudian slips can be easily explained by simpler principles. Initially, researchers found that participants could be pressured by a sexual context to produce Freudian slips. However, more recent research suggests that people internally monitor their speech for taboo words and actually produce these words less often than non-taboo words.

The spreading activation theory aims to explain speech production processes by analysing speech production errors. The model is based on the idea that concepts are represented in an associative semantic network and that the concepts with the highest activation value are selected for inclusion in the sentence. Errors in the activation values result in an incorrect insertion in the sentence, resulting in speech errors.

Many speech errors are detected and corrected by an internal monitoring system before they are uttered. Two alternative theoretical approaches aim to explain how this is done. According to the perceptual loop theory, we listen to our own speech and detect errors by interpreting it. Speech comprehension is therefore assumed to play a central role in this process. According to the conflict monitoring theory, however, speech errors are detected at a much earlier stage and lower level of processing. Evidence showing that speech errors are detected at an early stage is more compatible with the conflict monitoring theory than with the perceptual loop theory.

The WEAVER++ model aims to explain speech production processes on the basis of speech production times. Several empirical results are consistent with the model, such as the fact that grammatical information is available before phonological information, the 'tip of the tongue' phenomenon, and the effects of competition on word selection. The WEAVER++ model also assumes strictly serial processing of words, however, while much evidence now suggests that there is a high degree of parallelism in word production processes. Moreover, the model is only aimed at describing the production of single words and little informative about sentence production.

In neuropsychology, two main speech disorders have traditionally been distinguished: Broca's aphasia and Wernicke's aphasia. Although this distinction is no longer tenable on theoretical grounds, it is still widely used in practice because the original findings of Broca and Wernicke are still clinically relevant. Broca's aphasia is characterised by a non-fluent form of speech, in which language comprehension is still largely intact, whereas Wernicke's aphasia is characterised by a very fluent form of speech, which is, however, largely meaningless.

Nowadays, however, distinctions between fluent and non-fluent forms of aphasia on the one hand and between comprehension problems on the other are much more common. Based on these distinctions, aphasia patients are classified into one of the categories of agrammatism, anomia, or jargon aphasia. In addition to lesions in Broca's and Wernicke's areas, specific forms of aphasia can also occur because one or both of the pathways connecting these areas are damaged. Damage to either the dorsal or to the ventral route can result in agrammatism. Anomia is characterised by a patient's inability to name objects. Finally, jargon aphasia is characterised by the fact that, although patients are still able to produce sentences that are grammatically relatively correct, they are no longer able to find the correct content words. They often replace them either with other existing words or with self-generated neologisms. Jargon aphasic patients are likely to have particular difficulty in the simultaneous planning and monitoring of their speech.

Writing is the second most important way of producing language. It involves almost every cognitive process available, from the production of complex finger or hand movements to complex language production processes, to planning and control processes that structure and shape complex ideas. Partly because of this complexity, relatively little is known about writing processes.

The writing process consists of planning, sentence formation, and revision, where sentence formation can be divided into a translation and a transcription process. Much of our knowledge about writing processes has been gained by using the method of guided retrospection. Using this method, writers are interrupted at regular intervals and required to report what aspect of the writing process they were engaged in at that moment. Participants who were explicitly asked to make an outline first tend to produce more consistent texts that receive higher ratings.

Different forms of knowledge are relevant for a writer. Conceptual knowledge refers to the content the writer wants to communicate. Sociocultural knowledge includes the social background or context of a problem and metacognitive knowledge relates to knowledge about what someone knows about a participant. In addition, there is strategic knowledge. This type of knowledge refers to the way goals and subgoals are organised in a text, and it plays an important role in developing a writing plan.

Most time is spent on sentence production, yet writers regularly switch between the different processes. Experts spend a relatively large amount of time on revision, compared to non-experts. The time spent on revision is mainly directed at improving the coherence and structure of an argument. Switching between the different processes involves an internal monitor, which is comparable to the central executive of working memory.

The most basic part of the writing process involves the production of letters and words. This can be done in two ways: handwriting or typing. For both forms of writing, it has been found that a series of motor commands spanning several letters is generated. In handwriting, these commands are found to be grouped together by bigrams and by syllables. The phenomenon of motor equivalence implies that the motor commands are not formed at effector level, but at a higher, more abstract level. For typing, it has been found that the programming of keystrokes is largely an implicit process, but that it does not take place solely on the basis of feedforward processes. Various aspects, such as the tactile feedback of a keyboard, play an important role in the efficiency of the typing process.

Much research on spelling has been based on studies related to the conversion of spoken to written words. Based on studies involving neuropsychological patients, it has been established that this conversion can involve two routes: a lexical route and a non-lexical one. Patients with an impairment of their lexical route have difficulties with the spelling of familiar words, especially irregular words, whereas participants with an impairment of their non-lexical route have difficulties with spelling unknown words and non-words. These routes are probably not independent: studies in patients as well as in neurotypical participants have shown that information from the lexical route can influence processing in the non-lexical route. In addition, it has been found that conflicts between the lexical and the non-lexical route can have a negative impact on the speed of the spelling process.

There has been a long-standing debate about whether we have one or two orthographic lexicons. Patient studies initially led us to suspect that we have two lexicons, but more recent results argue rather in favour of the existence of one single orthographic lexicon that is shared by reading and writing processes.

NOTE

1 WEAVER stands for *word-form encoding by activation and verification*; the model we are discussing here is an extended version of the original model, indicated by the symbol ++.

FURTHER READING

Baars, B. J. (1992). *Experimental slips and human error: Exploring the architecture of volition*. New York: Plenum Press.

Erard, M. (2007). *Um ...slips, stumbles, and verbal blunders, and what they mean*. New York, NY: Pantheon Books.

Goldrick, M., Ferreira, V., & Miozzo, M. (2014). *The Oxford handbook of language production*. Oxford, UK: Oxford University Press.

Hartsuiker, R. J., Bastiaanse, R., Postma, A., & Wijnen, F. (2005). *Phonological encoding and monitoring in normal speech*. Hove, UK: Psychology Press.

Kellogg, R. T. (1994). *The psychology of writing*. Oxford, UK: Oxford University Press.

Poulisse, N. (1999). *Slips of the tongue: Speech errors in first and second language production*. Amsterdam: John Benjamins Publishing Company.

PART 8

Higher Cognition

CHAPTER 19

Mental representations and reasoning skills

19.1 INTRODUCTION

The movie adaptation of 'Lord of the Rings' trilogy was one of the first to make extensive use of artificial intelligence while animating the thousands of extras that are taking part in the massive battle scenes depicted in the movie. On the DVD's commentary track, the movie's director, Peter Jackson, explains how an initial test revealed quite remarkable behaviour by some of the artificially intelligent agents. They were programmed to approach an enemy and engage in combat. However, the test showed that some of the agents appeared to be fleeing the battlefield. A closer look revealed that the computer programme controlling the agents' behaviour had been set up in such a way that it had been assumed that the artificially intelligent agents would always encounter an enemy. When this was not the case, they simply ran off in a random direction, which made it appear that they were fleeing. The programmers' mistake made here can be traced back to the fact that they focused on what needed to be done when the 'enemy in sight' condition was true while they did not consider the actions to be carried out when it was false. This example illustrates a typical human trait that can play a prominent role in human reasoning. We apparently make a **mental representation** of the situation we are considering, but we are very selective in evaluating each and every possible condition.

19.2 THE NATURE OF A REPRESENTATION

One of the great evolutionary advantages that our mental abilities have given us is that they enable us to not only construct an internal mental representation of our environment but also to manipulate it. Manipulating mental representations allows us to work out hypothetical future scenarios and to evaluate the validity of abstract problems. A representation is the physical denotation of information, for example in the form of symbols on paper, magnetic tracks on a hard disk, or neural activation patterns in the brain. Representations consist of a specific form on the one hand and content on the other.

This chapter aims to address the question of how mental representations are formed, how these representations can explain how we deal with reasoning problems and how they can contribute to reasoning errors. The form of a representation refers not only to the elements used to represent information and to the arrangement of these elements, but also to the properties of the processes that can operate on the basis of these elements. Mental representations can be described in four different ways. More specifically, they can be modality-specific or amodal. Modality-specific representations involve the perceptual and motor systems, whereas amodal representations involve a more abstract type of code.

19.2.1 MODALITY-SPECIFIC REPRESENTATIONS: IMAGES

In many cases, it makes sense to represent information in terms of mental images. We may wonder, however, whether our brain actually represents information in terms of images. The idea that we use images is intuitive. Consider, for example, situations in which you imagine 'seeing' a solution to a problem. As we have already discussed in Chapter 6, the idea that we generate visual representations corresponds well with the notion that mental imagery is related to the activation of visual brain areas (Kosslyn, 1999). We also learned in Chapter 14 that memorising visual information corresponds to an increase in these brain areas (Klaver et al., 1999; Vogel & Machizawa, 2004).

The question now is what happens when we try to imagine something. Is a mental image the same as a photograph? To address this question, let us first consider what a photograph is. Try to imagine a scene of a penguin standing on a beach. Does the mental image you generated resemble fig 19.1? A photograph like this is defined, among other things, by the framing and the time the picture is taken. Where we point the camera and when we take the picture determines to a large degree what will appear in the picture. Moreover, a photograph is made up of individual pixels, which represent the brightness of a specific colour in a particular part of the grid that makes up the photo. The combination of all these pixels, that is, the

DOI: 10.4324/9781003319344-27

Figure 19.1 Photo of a penguin on the beach in South Georgia. (source: The Goldilock Project)

pattern of these light intensities, determines the content of the photo; what is represented in it. This content can consist of various objects. Some of these objects partially overlap, like the two penguins in Figure 19.1.

Research into the retinotopic organisation of the primary visual cortex suggests that information at the earliest stages of visual processing may take the form of images (Hubel & Wiesel, 1962). The neurons in area V1 not only receive bottom-up input from the visual system but also top-down input from higher areas (Rao & Ballard, 1999). At these higher levels, Reddy et al. (2010) found activation patterns in the ventral temporal cortex that corresponded to category-specific information when participants viewed images of different categories, such as food, tools, faces, or buildings. Interestingly, these activation patterns were not only found when participants were shown pictures of these objects but also when they had to imagine pictures of these categories.

Vetter et al. (2014) found a similar result in the visual cortex. As already discussed in more detail in Chapter 9, their study reported category-specific information patterns in the visual cortex. Interestingly, these patterns were found not only when participants were instructed to listen to specific categories of sounds, but also when they had to image specific visual scenes. Vetter et al. explain these results by assuming that a predictive coding mechanism feeds back an abstract representation to the lower visual areas, resulting in a representation from a higher-order conceptual representation that gradually becomes more concrete at the lower levels of the visual hierarchy.

19.2.2 MODALITY-SPECIFIC REPRESENTATIONS: FEATURES

Although this description already paints a fairly complete picture of how we generate a mental image, it is little informative about what we can do with such images. An important

aspect of what is still missing is the **meaningful unit**. In this context, a meaningful unit is an object or an event that is crucial for the pursuit of the organism's goals. For example, a pixel, the basic unit of a photograph, is not a meaningful unit, whereas a fluffy penguin is. Therefore, in everyday life, we are not so much interested in analysing individual pixels as we are in extracting these meaningful units. As already discussed in Chapter 6, neurons in the higher levels of the visual systems respond to increasingly abstract and meaningful units. These higher areas no longer represent a concrete image but the scene in terms of the presence or absence of meaningful units instead.

19.2.3 AMODAL SYMBOLS

The modality-specific representations just described exist mainly in the perceptual systems of the brain and thus correspond to a large extent to the way we perceive these objects. The next question is whether information is represented in an amodal manner that is entirely composed of arbitrary abstract symbols. Although many cognitive scientists have argued that this is the case, and while it has even been the dominant position in the early days of cognitive psychology, this position has increasingly been challenged in recent times.

Amodal symbols are assumed to be part of our semantic knowledge system. For example, an amodal description of Figure 19.1 could consist of the following:

sea(behind(rocks(in-front-of(penguin(right-of(penguin))))))

Although this symbolic representation does not constitute an image, you can already form some idea of the picture on the basis of the given symbolic representation. Since the relations are described with words such as sea, back, rock, front, and penguin, we might conclude that amodal representations are linguistic. This is not the case, however; words are merely considered references to the amodal symbols that represent the units of knowledge. To illustrate this, we could replace the preceding description with the following:

$$@(\#(\$(\%(\^\wedge(\&(\^\wedge))))))$$

Amodal symbols comprise three different types of amodal representation: frames, semantic networks, and property lists. A **frame** is a structure that defines a set of relationships that place an object in its environment. In the example, frames are formed by front, back, and right-of. A **semantic network** represents basically the same information in the form of a diagram. Finally, a **property list** describes the properties of an object and/or the category to which it belongs. For example, the properties 'yellow bill', 'upright', and 'feathers' are part of the property list of a king penguin.

19.2.4 STATISTICAL PATTERNS IN NEURAL NETWORKS

Although amodal symbols are useful in computer programmes, it is not yet clear how they would be implemented in biological systems. A final form of representation that we should therefore consider is that of the neural network. As already discussed in Chapter 1, a neural network can be used to represent knowledge. The different properties of an object are represented as a distributed statistical pattern in this network. According to Smolensky (1988) this representation has two advantages over the classical amodal approach.

First, the elements that shape the statistical pattern can be equated to neurons or populations of neurons. For this reason, the statistical approach can serve as a possible candidate for providing a biological implementation of an amodal representation. Secondly, in a classical amodal representation, there is a single symbol that represents a category, whereas in a neural network there are several patterns that can each represent the same category. This corresponds better to reality, in which different copies of one specific category are also characterised by variations, which can thus be encoded in a realistic manner.

19.3 MENTAL REPRESENTATIONS AS PREDICTORS FOR FUTURE OUTCOMES

As discussed in Chapter 13, our episodic memory is constructive, that is, it does not store episodes from our past as fully integrated elements, but rather it reconstructs these memories on the basis of separate elements that are stored (Schacter & Addis, 2007). An important consequence is that the reconstructive process also allows us to generate possible future scenarios that can be used for, for example, planning purposes or evaluating future outcomes.

According to Johnson-Laird, we use **mental models** to solve reasoning problems. Such mental models are assumed to represent the possible outcomes of a given scenario. Suppose we throw a dice: with each throw there are six possible outcomes. Each of these future outcomes corresponds to a different mental representation of the dice (one is up; two is up, etc.). As we already discussed in Chapter 6, it is plausible that these kinds of mental representations are evoked by activation of the visual cortex based via an internal generative process (Kosslyn, 1999) which causes them to take the form of a visual representation (fig 19.2), suggesting that there are strong ties between mental models and mental imagery.

However, it is questionable whether this is always necessarily the case. Suppose we are presented with the

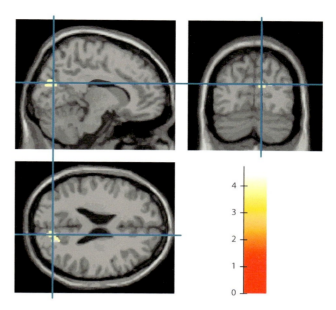

Figure 19.2 Activation in the secondary visual cortex during reasoning about problems that lend themselves for easy visualisation. (source: Johnson-Laird, 2010b)

following problem: Rob is taller than Dirk and Nico is taller than Rob. Is Nico taller than Dirk? To solve this problem, we can create a visual representation that immediately allows us to give the solution. Suppose, however, that you have to evaluate a variant of this problem: John is smarter than Martin and Eric is smarter than John. Is Eric smarter than Martin? Although this problem can be solved in a similar way, it is now a lot harder to create a simple visual representation of the problem. The first is a type of problem we can simply visualise, whereas the second is considerably more difficult to visualise. Nevertheless, we can make a mental representation of the problem. To differentiate between these two types of problems, Knauff and Johnson-Laird (2002) distinguish between visualising and envisaging. The extent to which a mental model is modal, that is, involves visualising, thus appears to depend on the nature of the problem that is presented (Johnson-Laird, 2010b).

19.4 MENTAL MODELS

The mental model theory, as developed by the American cognitive psychologist Philip Johnson-Laird and his colleagues, is still very influential in the field of mental representations. The theory plays a key role in explaining human reasoning skills. What exactly is the role of mental models in this process? According to Johnson-Laird, a mental model is initially constructed from information that is available in a problem description and conclusions are generated that are consistent with this model. Next, the theory assumes that we search for counterexamples that could possibly reject this conclusion. In other words, are there other, alternative models possible that invalidate our conclusion? We can illustrate this process with a simple example. Suppose we have the following information:

1. The lamp is on the left side of the block.
2. The book is to the right of the block.
3. The clock is in front of the book.
4. The vase is in front of the lamp.

What is the relationship between the vase and the lamp?

It will be clear that on the basis of the information given, only one spatial organisation is possible:

lamp	block	book
vase	clock	

We can therefore conclude that the vase is on the left with respect to the clock. However, it becomes more complicated with the next problem:

1. The Porsche is to the right of the Ferrari.
2. The Volkswagen is to the left of the Porsche.
3. The Vauxhall is in front of the Volkswagen.
4. The Tesla is in front of the Porsche.

What is the relationship between the Volkswagen and the Ferrari?

The problem is that there are two possible mental models:

Ferrari	Volkswagen	Porsche
	Vauxhall	Tesla

or:

Volkswagen	Ferrari	Porsche
Vauxhall	Tesla	

Thus, we have to create two different mental models to arrive at the conclusion that the Volkswagen can be either to the left or to the right of the Ferrari. Each mental model will require the use of some of our limited working memory capacity. The more mental models a problem requires, the more difficult it will become to (in)validate the conclusion.

Bell and Johnson-Laird (1998) found evidence for the assumption that we sometimes create multiple mental models to represent a situation. They made a distinction between possibility and necessity questions. A possibility question is, for example: 'Is it possible to pass a library while walking from the bank to the church?', while a necessity question can read: 'Do you necessarily have to pass a library while walking from the bank to the church?' Bell and Johnson-Laird hypothesised that the first type of question can be answered more quickly when the answer is 'yes' than when it is 'no'. After all, to answer this question we have to make mental models of a number

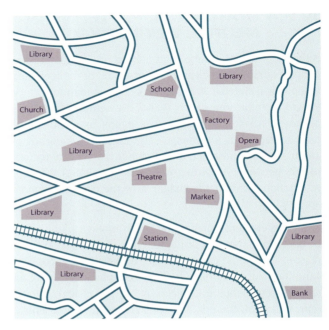

Figure 19.3 Example of road maps used in a study of how people deal with possibility and necessity questions. (source: Bell and Johnson-Laird, 1998)

of different routes, and we can stop this process as soon as a route with a library along it is found (see fig 19.3). If the answer is no, it follows that we had to consider all possible routes. For the second type, they assumed that the reaction times for 'no' answers are actually faster than 'yes' answers. After all, we can give the answer 'no' as soon as we have constructed a mental model of a route that does not lead us past a library. However, we can only answer 'yes' once we have considered all the routes and concluded that every possible route will take you past a library. The results reported by Bell and Johnson-Laird matched this prediction exactly.

19.5 PROBABILISTIC APPROACHES

Although the mental model theory provides an adequate description of how we can solve problems, it is unlikely that we will always use it in many everyday situations. In particular, there are many situations in which we are unlikely to explicitly look for counterexamples, which implies that attempts to falsify our mental representation are often non-existent. In addition, we often include background knowledge and previous experiences in solving a reasoning problem, even when such knowledge is irrelevant for the given problem. For this reason, Chater and Oaksford (2001) have argued that human reasoning is based on the application of everyday experiences and intuitions rather than on the basis of a fundamental logical analysis of the problem itself. According to Chater and Oaksford, our everyday rationality is therefore strongly based on dealing with uncertainties and on assigning probabilities to possible outcomes. According to this idea, probabilistic approaches are therefore better suited to describe human reasoning than the formal logic that forms the basis for the mental model theory.

19.6 DUAL SYSTEM THEORIES: SYSTEM 1 VERSUS SYSTEM 2

In recent decades, an increasing number of researchers have developed dual systems theories. Although these theories differ in detail, they all have in common that they assume a distinction between unconscious, intuitive processing on the one hand and conscious, deliberate reasoning on the other. For instance, Evans (2003, 2006) has proposed a heuristic-analytic theory (see fig 19.4) based on the distinction between System 1 and System 2 processes originally proposed by Stanovich and West (2000) and popularised by Kahneman (see Chapter 1).

According to Evans, System 1 arose early on in the evolution of our species. Moreover, it is assumed to be highly unconscious, characterised by a high degree of parallel processing, and operate independently of general intelligence. System 2, on the other hand, is assumed to consist of conscious deliberation. These System 2 processes are assumed to operate slowly and serially, to be an evolutionarily recent addition to our cognitive arsenal, and to be based on explicit rules, limited in capacity, and linked to intelligence.

When we need to solve a reasoning problem, the heuristic processes that are part of System 1 will evaluate the task, the goal of the problem, and apply background knowledge to create one mental model of the possible solution. This mental model can be influenced by irrelevant information, resulting in a relatively high probability of finding an incorrect solution.

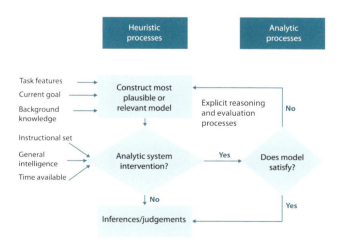

Figure 19.4 Schematic representation of the revised heuristic-analytic theory. (source: Evans, 2006)

The solution proposed by System 1 can then be evaluated by a time-consuming and strenuous verification process carried out by System 2 processes. This evaluation may result in the rejection of the original mental model and its corresponding solution. According to Evans, this intervention by System 2 is most likely when (1) the task instructions explicitly state that abstract or logical reasoning skills must be employed; (2) the problem-solver is highly intelligent; and (3) there is sufficient time available to carry out a strenuous analytical process. Because System 2 can employ many cognitive processes to verify the problem, we should not assume that abstract logic will automatically be used to evaluate mental models. For this reason, we cannot consider applying System 2 processes to be equivalent to employing formal logic. Although the involvement of System 2 processes often results in an improvement of a solution, it does not guarantee that the proposed solution is actually correct.

According to Evans, human reasoning and hypothetical thinking is therefore based on the use of three general principles.

1. The singularity principle: we only consider one mental model at a time.
2. The relevance principle: the most relevant, that is, the most plausible or probable mental model based on our background knowledge and the current context, is considered.
3. The satisficing principle: The current mental model is evaluated by System 2, and it is accepted when it is adequate. The use of this principle often results in the acceptance of conclusions that, although they may be true, do not necessarily have to be true.

A key difference between Evans' heuristic-analytic theory and Johnson-Laird et al.'s mental model theory is that the latter assumes that we use reasoning processes that are based on formal logic to create the initial mental model, in which we can be distracted by background knowledge. Formal reasoning processes therefore occupy a much less prominent place in heuristic-analytic theory than in mental model theory.

Our reasoning skills are strongly influenced by both our ability to form complex mental representations and our ability to evaluate these models by applying formal logic. Historically, reasoning studies have strongly focused on formal logic. In this tradition, we can distinguish between **inductive reasoning** and **deductive reasoning**, as we will discuss next.

19.7 INDUCTIVE REASONING

Inductive reasoning refers to the process of finding generalisations based on individual observations. As we make more observations that fit our generalisation, we will be increasingly inclined to assume that there is an underlying connection between these observations. We will never be able to conclusively generalise across these observations, however. After all, a single discrepant observation can drastically undermine our generalisation, as was dramatically illustrated by the fate of Russell's turkey.

19.7.1 RUSSELL'S TURKEY

Once upon a time – at least according to the influential British philosopher and logician Bertrand Russell (1872–1970) – there was a turkey who discovered that he was fed at nine o'clock every morning. Because our good turkey was an inductivist, he did not want to jump to conclusions, and he set out to make a long series of observations under a wide range of conditions to confirm his discovery. Whether it was Wednesday or Saturday, hot or cold, wet or dry, each day he was fed punctually at nine o'clock. Each day he added a new data point to his list, and at some point, his inductive conscience was so appeased that he concluded, 'I am always fed at nine o'clock'. Unfortunately, his conclusion was rather brutally invalidated when, one morning before Christmas, he was not fed, but had his throat cut.

19.7.2 HYPOTHESIS TESTING

What Russell's unfortunate turkey discovered is that we can never confirm a hypothesis based on observation and induction: as long as we obtain hypothesis-consistent results, our confidence in it may increase. However, only one discrepant observation will suffice to reject it. The latter has an important consequence: our progress in solving inductive reasoning problems is higher when we explicitly look for discrepancies, that is, when we actively aim to falsify our hypothesis.

Given the problem just outlined, the British-Austrian philosopher of science Karl Popper (1935) rejected the inductivist approach to scientific research that had been prevailing up to that point. This inductivist approach is based on the principle of confirmation, that is, finding evidence that confirms the correctness of one's hypothesis. The human tendency to seek for confirmation, known as the **confirmation bias**, was already noted more than 300 years ago by Sir Francis Bacon, who wrote: 'The human mind, when it has once adopted an opinion draws all else to support and agree with it' (cited in Reason, 1995).

Falsification, on the other hand, is an attempt to actively reject a hypothesis by searching for counterevidence. According to Popper, and following the unfortunate ending of Bertrand Russell's turkey, it is impossible to confirm a hypothesis by finding supporting evidence. Even when all the evidence that has been gathered up to a certain point supports a hypothesis, it only needs one discrepant finding to disconfirm it. An additional problem is that if

we only search for confirmation, we cannot differentiate between different hypotheses. Let us illustrate the latter using a simple example: suppose that we suspect that a deficiency for a certain nutrient (x) is uniquely related to a skin rash (y). In logical terms, we could state that a deficiency of x is a necessary and a sufficient condition for y. Suppose we were to test this hypothesis empirically by putting participants on a diet. As long as we observe that a deficiency of x results in y, we can conclude that the deficiency of x is indeed a sufficient condition for y; in other words, a deficiency of x does indeed always result in y.

We might mistakenly assume that the rash is a measure of a deficiency of x, but that is not necessarily true. After all, there may be other causes for the same rash. In other words, we have not yet addressed the question of whether a deficiency of x is also a necessary condition for y. Thus, we can still falsify our hypothesis by finding a single case of rash in a patient who does not have a deficiency of x. It also follows, according to Popper, that falsifiability is an important characteristic that distinguishes science from non-scientific activities, such as religion or pseudoscience (for example, psychoanalysis).

19.7.3 THE 2-4-6 TASK

From the aforementioned discussion, it would appear to be obvious that scientists should focus on the falsification of hypotheses. Yet, in practice, much more activity is directed towards finding confirmatory results than towards finding disconfirmatory results. This is a fact that has also been found in many laboratory studies on hypothesis testing processes.

The British psychologist Peter Wason (1960) developed a bizarrely simple task to investigate the hypothesis testing process. The task was as follows: participants were presented with the following sequence of numbers, 2-4-6, and they were informed that this sequence complied with a hidden rule. The participant's task was to uncover the rule in question. They had to do this by generating new triplets, writing them down, and noting the reason why they had chosen this sequence. Then they had to ask the experimenter whether or not these numbers complied with the rule. When participants believed they had found the rule, they had to report this to the experimenter, who then indicated whether they were right or not. If the rule was incorrect, participants had to continue until they either found the rule, gave up, or when the allotted time (45 minutes) had passed. The rule that had to be found, by the way, was very simple: 'Three numbers in increasing order'.

Although at first glance, this task appears to be deceptively simple, the results were quite dramatic: only 21% of the participants found the rule at their first attempt and

28% never found it. The main reason why participants had so much trouble finding the rule was because they did not formulate hypotheses that tested the necessity principle. Participants gave in to their confirmation bias when formulating hypotheses and additional numbers, so they continued to generate hypotheses that were unnecessarily complex.

19.7.4 SIMULATED RESEARCH ENVIRONMENTS

Mynatt, Doherty, and Tweney (1977) found evidence for confirmation bias in a simulated research environment. Here, participants were instructed to fire a virtual electron beam at geometric figures (circles and triangles) presented on a screen. These figures were presented at two levels of brightness: dim and bright. At the beginning of the study, the participants had to fire at the objects to determine which objects reflected the electron beam (see fig 19.5). The participants did not know that the dim objects reflected the beam. Moreover, they were initially given the impression that it was the triangles that reflected the beam, rather than the dim objects. Thus, participants' initial hypothesis was incorrect.

After participants had formulated their initial hypothesis, they were assigned to one of three groups: one group was given the explicit task of confirming their initial hypothesis, another group was given the task of disconfirming it, and a third group was given no specific task. After being assigned to a group, participants could choose new displays and fire the beam at the geometric figures again. They could choose between two different types of displays. The first was configured in such a way that participants were able to confirm their original hypothesis. More specifically, these displays consisted of triangles that did reflect the beam (i.e., dim triangles) and/or other shapes that did not (i.e., bright shapes). The second type of display, on the other hand, allowed alternative hypotheses to be tested. These displays consisted of triangles that did not reflect the beam (i.e., bright triangles) and/or other shapes that did (i.e., dim shapes).

Mynatt et al. were particularly interested in which screens participants chose. They found that 71% of all participants chose screens of the first type, which is a strong indication that most participants were influenced by their confirmation bias. Interestingly, the instruction to use a disconfirmation strategy did not affect this: participants in this group did not use a different strategy than participants in the other groups.

Dunbar (1993) examined the role of confirmation bias in an experimental situation where participants had to discover how the expression of genes is controlled by other genes, using a simulated research environment (see fig 19.6). The study that was simulated was based on a series of experiments that had earned French molecular biologists François Jacob and Jacques Monod the Nobel Prize in Physiology and Medicine in 1965. Jacob and Monod's discovery was revolutionary because it was the first time that they found that some genes inhibit other genes, whereas the prevailing hypothesis at the time had been that genes had an activating effect. They made this discovery by studying *E. coli* bacteria that was being attacked by a virus.

Dunbar's participants had to try to discover the mechanism behind this interaction between genes by making simulated mutations in their genetic material. Most of these mutations were consistent with the activation hypothesis. The participants who actively tried to analyse data that were consistent with this activation hypothesis therefore failed to find the right answer. Only a small percentage of participants found the correct hypothesis and they did so by focusing on the discrepant findings. In most cases, they tested each potential gene, and when the activation hypothesis failed for each individual gene, it resulted in some participants turning to an attempt to explain the data that was inconsistent with the activation hypothesis.

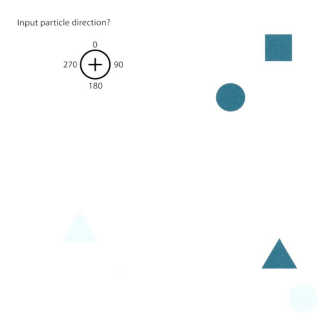

Figure 19.5 Example of a display that was used in a study where participants had to try to determine what type of objects reflected particles that were fired at them. (source: Mynatt et al., 1977)

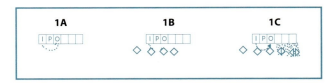

Figure 19.6 Examples of the problems that were used to study how people handle discrepant findings. The study is based on an actual biology study that was eventually awarded a Nobel Prize. (source: Dunbar, 1993)

19.8 DEDUCTIVE REASONING: CONDITIONAL LOGIC

Johnson-Laird (2010a) has defined deductive reasoning as the mental process of forming logical inferences. Although deductive reasoning is only one form of reasoning, it is a crucial element of intelligence and therefore deductive reasoning problems are often part of standard intelligence tests. In cognitive-psychological research, two of the most prominent forms of logical problems involve conditional and syllogistic reasoning.

19.8.1 A BRIEF INTRODUCTION TO CLASSICAL PROPOSITIONAL LOGIC

19.8.1.1 Conditional Reasoning

To properly interpret how humans process reasoning problems, we need to briefly introduce some of the basic principles of classic logical problem-solving. **Conditional reasoning** is based on propositional logic, in which logical operators such as 'and', 'or', 'if', 'then', and 'only if' are used in sentences or **propositions**. In this system, sentences are represented by symbols, and logical operators are applied to these symbols to draw conclusions. For example, in the sentence: 'If it rains then Mary gets wet', we can replace the proposition 'it rains' with the symbol P and 'Mary gets wet' with Q, thus writing the relations between the two propositions in abbreviated form as 'If P then Q'. It is important to realise that the meaning of words and propositions in classic logic differs from their natural linguistic meaning. First, propositions can only have two states: they are either true or false. For example, if P stands for 'it rains' then P is true if it is indeed raining and untrue if it is not. Propositional logic does not allow for uncertainty about the state of P (as in: 'it is drizzling', or 'it rains so little, it is almost dry').[1]

19.8.1.2 Conditional Reasoning Problems

Conditional reasoning problems are generally presented in the form of two premises and a conclusion, such as the following:

> If it rains, then Mary gets wet.
> It rains.
> Conclusion: Mary gets wet.

This conclusion is valid because Q must necessarily be true if P is true. In the second premise, we see that P is true, from which it follows that Q must also be true. Most individuals who have to evaluate this problem rightly accept that the conclusion is true. The classic name for this problem is **modus ponens**.

Now suppose we have the following problem:

> If it rains, then Mary gets wet.
> Mary does not get wet.
> Conclusion: It does not rain.

This conclusion is also valid, because the second premise states that Q is not true, so it follows from the first premise that must necessarily not be true P (for, if P was true, Q must also be true). Most people have more difficulties with evaluating this problem, known as **modus tollens**, and are therefore inclined to argue that the conclusion does not necessarily follow from the premises.

In addition to these two forms of reasoning, there are two more possibilities. Suppose you have the following problem:

> If it rains, then Mary gets wet.
> It does not rain.
> Conclusion: Mary does not get wet.

Does this conclusion necessarily follow from the premises? Many will accept the conclusion of this problem, known as **denial of the antecedent**. Yet the conclusion is not valid! Why not? The first premise is only informative about the truth of Q if P is true. Therefore, if P is not true (it is not raining), Q can either be true or false, so the conclusion is not valid.

Finally, we have:

> If it rains, then Mary gets wet.
> Mary gets wet.
> Conclusion: It is raining.

Many will accept this conclusion, but you might already have realised that the conclusion of this problem, known as **affirmation of the consequent**, is not correct either. Why not? In this case, the truth of Q is not informative about the truth of P. It is only if P is true that Q must be true, but it does not necessarily follow that if Q is true, P must also be true. So, the inference is invalid.

19.8.2 INFLUENCE BY IRRELEVANT CONTEXT

A major issue that already emerges here is that research on conditional reasoning has traditionally focused on **disinterested reasoning** (Bonnefon, Girotto, & Legrenzi, 2012). Here 'disinterested' implies that one's goals or preferences should not affect the reasoning process. This approach contrasts sharply with our everyday experience, where our goals and preferences do interfere. Moreover, in our everyday lives, we tend to interpret a conditional premise such as 'If P then Q', often to mean 'If and only if P then Q'. For example, the sentence 'If you run an errand,

I will give you five euros' is also interpreted as 'If you don't run an errand, I won't give you five euros'.

Similarly, we often involve already existing semantic background knowledge in reasoning processes and strictly speaking this knowledge should not affect our judgement validity of the conclusion. The latter is nicely illustrated by a finding from Byrne (1989). She presented conditional reasoning problems to which contextual information was added, shown here in brackets, such as:

> Premise: If she has to write an essay, then she will stay up late studying in the library.
> Context: [If the library is open, then she will study in the library until late.]
> Premise: She has to write an essay.

The conclusion 'She will study in the library until late' follows from the premises, yet Byrne (1989) found that the presentation of additional, contextual information strongly influenced participants' willingness to accept the conclusions. More specifically, their willingness to accept the modus ponens was much lower, compared to a standard condition in which no additional contextual information had been added. De Neys, Schaeken, and d'Ydewalle (2005) conducted a similar study but manipulated the context by providing counterexamples that appeared to negate a valid conclusion. They gave participants examples such as the following:

> Rule: If Jenny turns on the air conditioner, she feels cold.
> Fact: Jenny turns on the air conditioner.
> Conclusion: Jenny feels cold.

Counterexamples that could be given included: 'If it is particularly warm in the room, Jenny does not feel cold', or 'If the air conditioner is not working properly, Jenny does not feel cold'. De Neys et al. (2005) found results that were similar to Byrne (1989): counterexamples resulted in a decrease in participants' willingness to accept the modus ponens and modus tollens and an increase in their willingness to accept the denial of the antecedent and the affirmation of the consequent. Moreover, De Neys et al. found that participants scoring high on working memory capacity were less affected by these counterexamples than participants scoring low on working memory capacity (see fig 19.7).

Bonnefon et al. (2012) argue that our normal everyday reasoning processes are often inconsistent with the principle of disinterested reasoning. Our inferences are typically based on underlying background knowledge, which we also attribute to another individual. For example, when we encounter the premise 'If she eats oysters, she will get sick', we will tend to conclude that 'She is not going to eat oysters' because we are including our own desire not to get sick in the reasoning process. Such inferences often result in accepting invalid conclusions: the inferences

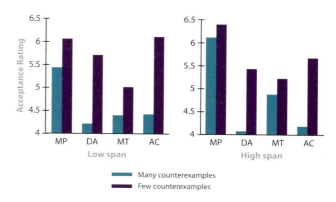

Figure 19.7 The extent to which participants are willing to accept the conclusion of a conditional reasoning problem depends on the type of problem, the number of counterexamples provided, and the participant's working memory capacity. MP = modus ponens; MT = modus tollens; DA = denial of the antecedent; AC = affirmation of the consequent. (source: De Neys et al., 2005)

made are inconsistent with the rules of classic logic, do not consider our individual background knowledge and desires (i.e., that being sick is undesirable).

Even when affirming the consequent, we often allow ourselves to be influenced by irrelevant contextual information that is not actually part of the problem description. For example, Markovits, Brunet, Thompson, and Brisson (2013) found that the number of possible causes of an action that we can think of affects our tendency to affirm the consequent. Suppose we have the following two problems:

> Premise: If a stone is thrown against a window, then the window will break.
> Premise: The window is broken.
> Conclusion: A stone was thrown against the window.

> Premise: If a finger is cut, then it will bleed.
> Premise: The finger is bleeding.
> Conclusion: The finger was cut.

In both cases, the conclusion is invalid, but we are much more inclined to accept the conclusion for the second problem than that for the first problem. According to Markovits et al. (2013) we can use two different strategies for this type of reasoning problem.

1. The first strategy is based on statistical intuitions where the truth of the conclusion is based on making an estimate of its likelihood. This estimate is based on the background knowledge we have of a particular problem. The probability that a finger bleeds because of a cut is much larger than the probability that a window is broken due to a stone being thrown at it. In other words, this is a System 1 approach.
2. The second strategy is based on generating counterexamples, and this strategy is cognitively more demanding. The essence of this strategy is to think of situations that would make the conclusion invalid. In the case of the broken window, this is also an easier strategy than in the case of the bleeding finger: the window may have been broken by the wind, by a football, by wear and tear, and so on, whereas for the bleeding finger it is less straightforward to find alternative causes.

19.8.3 CONDITIONAL REASONING: STRATEGIES

De Neys et al.'s (2005) results suggest that there are strong individual differences in reasoning strategies. Bonnefon, Eid, Vautier, and Jmel (2008) focused specifically on these differences and found four different strategies that individuals use, which are based on the distinction between System 1 and System 2 processing.

- The pragmatic strategy is based on System 1 and consists of informally processing a problem as it would be presented during a conversation. This strategy results in making numerous errors.
- The semantic strategy is also based on System 1 and makes use of background knowledge, but not in the form of a formal analysis of the problem, so this strategy still yields a reasonable number of errors.
- The inhibitory strategy is based on System 2 and consists of inhibiting the impact of the pragmatic strategy and the impact of background knowledge. This strategy proved to work well for some problems, but not for others.
- Finally, the generative strategy is also based on System 2 and consists of combining the inhibitory strategy with the use of abstract analytical processes. This strategy resulted in consistently good task performance.

19.8.4 WASON'S SELECTION TASK

Earlier in this chapter, we already introduced Peter Wason's 2-4-6 task for the study of inductive reasoning processes. Wason's other major contribution to the field involved the development of a simple card selection task for studying deductive reasoning processes (Wason, 1966). More specifically, this is a task that is used to study hypothesis testing processes based on a conditional rule. In the standard version of the task, four cards are placed on a table, showing the symbols R, G, 2, 7 (see fig 19.8a). Participants are informed that there is a rule describing the relation between the symbols, for example: 'If there is an R on one side of the card, there must be a 2 on the other side of the card'. Participants' task was then to select those cards that must be turned over to decide whether the rule has been met. Which cards would you choose?

If you decide to choose the R and the 2, you have, like most people, chosen the wrong solution. After all, you have to check which cards may violate the rule, and the 2 is therefore irrelevant. If there were an R, it would only imply that the rule might be correct, and if there were any other letter, it would also not be violating the rule. The correct answer is that the R and the 7 must be selected: if there were an R on the back of the 7, the rule would be violated. Of course, you have to select the R, because if there is no 2 there, the rule is definitely invalid. Only 5–10% of the university students who were presented with this problem chose the correct solution.

A possible reason why many people choose the R and the 2 is that we exhibit a **matching bias** (Evans, 1998). That is, we tend to simply choose those items that are mentioned in the problem description. Stenning and van Lambalgen (2004) found that participants tend to not realise that they need to indicate all their choices before receiving feedback. When participants were explicitly instructed that they had to make all choices before receiving feedback, the percentage of participants finding the correct answer increased from 3.7% to 18%.

Oaksford (1997) has argued that the way we should solve the card selection problem conflicts with the way we deal with this type of problem in everyday life situations. We can illustrate this with the example of how people tend to verify the statement 'All swans are white'. Formally, we can rewrite this rule as 'If swan then white', or 'If P then Q'. According to formal logic, this would require us to find all swans and all non-white birds. In reality, however, only a small minority of all birds are swans, and the overwhelming majority of all birds are non-white, making it an extremely suboptimal strategy to determine that all of these birds are not swans. It is therefore much more efficient to just look for white birds and determine whether they are swans. In other words, we tend to choose a probabilistic strategy.

The rule to be tested with the card selection task is also in the form of 'If P then Q'. When we have to evaluate multiple cards, the probabilistic approach predicts that we would choose Q cards when they are relatively rare, but non-Q cards when Q cards are highly frequent. Oaksford, Chater, Graingers, and Larkin (1997) conducted a study in which the likelihood of encountering Q cards was manipulated. They used a variant of Wason's selection task, known as the reduced array selection task. Here, two packs of 25 cards each were used. One pack contained cards with red circles on one side (the red pack),

Figure 19.8 Examples of cards used in Wason's card selection task. (a) Standard version; (b) socially relevant version.

while the other pack contained cards with blue trian-gles (the blue pack). The other side, the one that the participants initially perceived, was blank. Participants were given the rule 'All triangles are blue' after which they were given two piles of cards, one of which was drawn from the red pack and the other from the blue pack. Although the participant could not see the cards initially, the stacks were labelled as 'red shapes' (non-Q cards) and 'blue cards' (Q cards). The percentage of Q cards handed out to the participants varied: 17%, 50%, or 83%. Participants then had to select cards from the piles they had been given to evaluate the rule. The cru-cial finding was that when the percentage of Q cards that participants had been given was low, indeed far fewer were selected, while they were evaluating the rule.

19.8.5 SOCIAL CONTRACT THEORY

In its traditional formulation, Wason's selection task uses an indicative rule. **Indicative rules** describe at a relatively abstract level what conditions must be met for the rule to be valid. In some cases, however, deontic rules are used. **Deontic rules** are concerned with the detection of viola-tions, which often occur in a social context (Crockett, 2013). When deontic rules are involved, task performance is gen-erally significantly better (Evans, 2007). Cosmides (1989) argues that the improvement in task performance evoked by the use of deontic rules can be explained by assuming that participants have a highly developed ability to achieve goals in social situations and in doing so form social con-tracts with others. To form these social contracts, we must agree to share costs and benefits and, consequently, accord-ing to Cosmides's **social contract theory**, we would have built up a highly developed mechanism to detect violations of this type of situation.

According to the social contract theory, we should therefore be specifically well adapted to finding the right rule when Wason's card selection task is formu-lated in a way that reflects violations of social situations (fig 19.8b). Sperber and Girotto (2002) found some evi-dence for this. They administered a Wason card selection task with the following cover story: Paolo buys articles on the Internet, but he is afraid that he will be cheated. Therefore, he keeps a card for each item on which he states on one side whether he has already paid for the item and on the other side whether he has received the item. He has ordered four items and has the following cards: 'Item paid', 'Item not paid', 'Item received', 'Item not received'. Which cards should Paolo check to deter-mine whether he has been cheated? Most participants chose the correct cards.

Although these results are consistent with social contract theory, Sperber and Girotto (2002) argue that there may be a much simpler explanation for their results. According

Figure 19.9 Examples of cards that were used in a study examining the effects of social violations on Wason's selection task. (a) Cards that represent a social contract; (b) cards that do not. (source: Sperber and Girotto, 2002)

to their relevance theory, most individuals use a relatively simple strategy in the selection process where they sim-ply evaluate the relevance of each card to the conditional rule. In fact, they also found much better performance on items that did not represent a social contract, as was the case with the cover story: Paolo collects cards that describe gliders. Which cards should Paolo set aside for this purpose (see fig 19.9b)? Again, in this experiment, most participants choose the right cards, suggesting that the evaluation is merely based on relevance.

19.9 DEDUCTIVE REASONING: SYLLOGISMS

The second form of reasoning that is often used in the study of deductive reasoning processes is **syllogistic** rea-soning. A syllogism is a reasoning problem that consists of two statements, namely a major premise and a minor premise, and a conclusion that may or may not logically follow from the premises. One of the best-known exam-ples of a syllogism is:

All human beings are mortal.	(major)
Socrates is a human being.	(minor)
Socrates is mortal.	(conclusion)

An important task in evaluating a syllogism is whether the conclusion necessarily follows from the premises, assuming that the premises are true. The task, then, is to verify that the form of the syllogism is correct. The possibility that the premises are incorrect is irrelevant for the evaluation.

In practice, however, the content of the premises will often interfere with the evaluation of the form, as the following, somewhat absurd-sounding example shows.

All children are obedient.	(major)
All wolves are children.	(minor)
All wolves are obedient.	(conclusion)

This conclusion is valid, assuming that the premises are correct. We can easily verify this solution by replacing 'children', 'obedient entities', and 'wolves' with the symbols 'A', 'B', and 'C' respectively. When we now rewrite the syllogism, we get the following:

All A are B.	(major)
All C are A.	(minor)
All C are B.	(conclusion)

Now we can easily see that A is a subset of B, and that C is a subset of A, so it logically follows that C must be a subset of B. The relations between the sets can often be illustrated in the form of a Venn diagram. Figure 19.10 illustrates a variety of examples.

It follows from the previous example that many syllogistic reasoning errors are made when the premises are not credible. For example, Klauer, Musch, and Naumer (2000) identified a **belief bias**. In their study, half of the conclusions were either credible, such as 'Some fish are not bass', or implausible, such as 'Some bass are not fish'. In addition, half of the syllogisms were valid and the other half invalid. Some participants were informed, however, that only one-sixth of the syllogisms were valid, while other participants were informed that five-sixths of the syllogisms were valid.

Using this set-up, Klauer et al. (2000) found three important effects. First, they found a base rate effect: participants who had been informed that five-sixths of the syllogisms were correct were willing to accept many more conclusions than participants who had been informed that only one-sixth of the syllogisms were correct. Second, they found a clear belief bias effect. Conclusions that appeared plausible were accepted more frequently than conclusions that appeared implausible. Third, an interaction was found between belief bias and logic. That is, participants' ability to judge syllogisms with valid conclusions was better when conclusions were credible, whereas their ability

to detect invalid conclusions was impaired when their conclusions appeared to be credible.

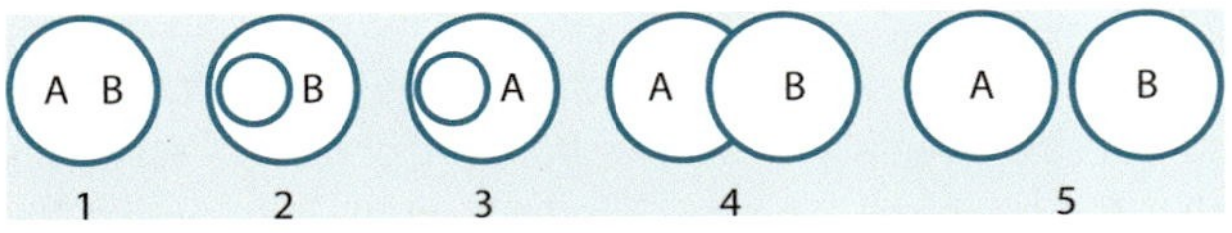

These results imply that participants are often guided by factors other than logic. Stupple and Ball (2008) found results consistent with this conclusion. More specifically, they found that participants took longer to process syllogisms containing implausible premises than syllogisms containing credible premises. This result implies that participants experience a conflict between their background knowledge and the information that is given in the premises.

Some forms of syllogisms consist of premises whose superficial properties correspond to those of the conclusion (e.g., No A are not B; no B are not C; therefore: no C are not A), while this is not the case with other syllogisms (e.g.: All A are B; all B are C; therefore: no A are not C). According to the rules of formal logic, these superficial correspondences between premises and conclusions are irrelevant. Stupple, Ball, and Ellis (2013), however, found that participants were more willing to accept the validity of a syllogism when the superficial properties of the premises match those of the conclusion. This matching bias shows that syllogistic reasoning can also be influenced by the form of the syllogism.

A final factor that can affect our syllogistic reasoning skills is that there is often confusion about how a premise should be interpreted. For example, in our everyday lives, we often assume that the premise 'All A are B' also implies 'All B are A', or that 'Some A are not B' also implies 'Some B are not A'. Ceraso and Provitera (1971) aimed to remove this source of confusion by explicitly disambiguating the premises, for example, by writing them in the following form: 'All A are B, but some B are not A'. This approach resulted in a substantial improvement in reasoning performance. A related issue here is that the term 'some' in formal logic has a different meaning than in everyday language: in formal logic it means 'at least one and possibly all', whereas in everyday language it is typically interpreted to mean 'at least one, but not all' (Schmidt & Thompson, 2008). When this ambiguity is made explicit, syllogistic reasoning performance also improves considerably.

19.10 DEDUCTIVE REASONING: RELATIONAL PROBLEMS

Earlier in this chapter we introduced the mental model theory developed by Johnson-Laird and colleagues (Bell & Johnson-Laird, 1998; Johnson-Laird, 1994; Legrenzi, Giriotto, & Johnson-Laird, 2003; Platt & Johnson, 1971). This theory assumes that mental representations of a problem are iconic, in the sense that the structure of the model

Figure 19.10 Examples of possible relations between sets A and B. (source: Ceraso and Provitera, 1971)

corresponds to what it represents. Mental models therefore preserve the spatial relations of the represented objects. This presents the question of whether mental imagery processes are involved in deductive reasoning. The answer to this question is that it depends on the type of problem that is being investigated. For example, Knauff, Fangmeier, Ruff, and Johnson-Laird (2003) found that deductive reasoning processes were slower when mental imagery processes were involved, because participants generated irrelevant details that negatively affected the reasoning process.

Knauff et al. (2003) focused on the distinction between imagining and envisaging introduced earlier. In their study, participants were presented with a number of reasoning problems that varied in difficulty on the dimensions of imaginability and envisagibility. More specifically, they were presented with problems such as the following:

If the monkey is smarter than the cat, then the cat is smarter than the dog.
The monkey is smarter than the cat.
Does it follow that the monkey is smarter than the dog?

The problems were formulated to contain either clear visual relations (e.g., X is cleaner than Y), clear spatial relations (e.g., X is a descendant of Y), clear visuospatial relations (e.g., X is superior to Y), or control relations that were neither well imagined nor well envisaged (e.g., X is better than Y). Knauff et al. found that participants were significantly slower at the visual inferences, compared to the control or visuospatial inferences. They argued that this could be due to the fact that in the visual condition, participants generated visual images that contained many irrelevant details that negatively affected the effectiveness of their inferences.

19.11 DEDUCTIVE REASONING: LIMITING FACTORS

19.11.1 WORKING MEMORY CAPACITY

An important assumption of mental model theory is that the number of mental models that can be constructed is limited by working memory capacity. Copeland and Radvansky (2004) found evidence for this assumption. In their study, participants had to decide which conclusions followed from a set of premises. Working memory load was manipulated by varying the number of mental models that were consistent with the premises. When the premises allowed only one mental model, 86% of the participants drew the correct conclusion, while only 31% of them drew the correct conclusion when the premises allowed three mental models. In addition, the investigators also found that participants' task performance correlated with their working memory capacity.

19.11.2 THE PRINCIPLE OF TRUTH

A final important assumption of mental model theory is that people adhere to the principle of truth, that is, people's tendency to minimise working memory load by generating only mental models that represent what is true and omitting this for situations that represent what is false, as described in the introductory example to this chapter. Legrenzi et al. (2003) tested the principle of truth by using illusory problems. Participants had to decide whether descriptions of everyday objects contained inconsistencies. Some of these descriptions were formulated in such a way that participants made a mistake when sticking to the truth principle. An example of such a description that participants often consider consistent, but which is actually inconsistent, is the following:

Only one of the following statements is true (1):
The tray is heavy or elegant or both (1a)
The tray is elegant and movable (1b)
The following statement is definitely true (2):
The tray is elegant and movable (2a)
Please describe the tray: _____

The correct description should be: elegant and movable. Since heavy is not part of premises (1b) and (2a), many people tend to describe the object with the opposite: light, elegant, and movable. Moreover, many people erroneously report that this description is consistent, based on the following reasoning: from premise (2) we deduce that premise (2a) is also true. It follows that premise (1b) must also be true, so we can deduce from premise (1) that (1a) must not be true. What most people fail to do, however, is to build a mental model for premises (1a) and (1b). After all, if premise (1b) is true, it follows that premise (1a) must also be true. (Do you see why that is?) But, according to premise (1), it cannot be true, which makes the description inconsistent.

19.11.3 BELIEF BIAS

Earlier, we introduced the phenomenon of belief bias in syllogistic reasoning processes. Here, we will specifically focus on to what extent this belief bias is a general limitation of our reasoning ability. According to Evans' heuristic-analytic theory (Evans, 2003, 2006), we will initially try to solve a logical problem primarily by employing an intuitive System 1 process and only involve a more analytic System 2 strategy when there is reason to reject the intuitive solution. We may therefore expect the belief bias to be greater when reasoning is primarily based on System 1 processes and smaller when it is primarily based on System 2 processes. Evans and Curtis-Holmes (2005) investigated the influence of time pressure on participants' sensitivity to the belief bias. They presented conditional reasoning problems with valid and believable conclusions, valid but unbelievable

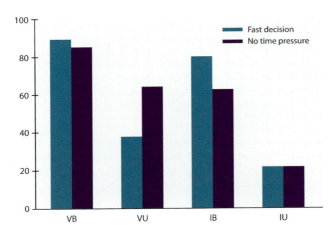

Figure 19.11 The effects of time pressure and credibility of the premises of a conditional reasoning problem on participants' willingness to accept the conclusion. VB = valid and believable; VU = valid and unbelievable; IB = invalid and believable; IU = invalid and unbelievable. (source: Evans and Curtis-Holmes, 2005)

conclusions, invalid but believably conclusions, and invalid and unbelievable conclusions. Under time pressure, the willingness to accept valid but unbelievable conclusions decreased, whereas the willingness to accept invalid but believable conclusions increased (fig 19.11).

19.11.3.1 Feeling of Rightness

What are the conditions that allow us to reject an intuitive System 1 answer? This question represents a major problem for most dual systems theories, because it introduces an unsolvable paradox: To know that the intuitive answer is incorrect, we need the answer from System 2, but how do we get that answer without activating System 2? Thompson, Prowse Turner, and Pennycook (2011) investigated this question by presenting participants with syllogistic and conditional reasoning problems. Participants had to give an intuitive answer as soon as they read the problem. Then they had to indicate whether they felt that the initial answer was correct or not. The latter was done by giving a feeling or rightness rating to the answer. Finally, participants were given an unlimited amount of time to give a final (reasoned) answer. Thompson et al. argue that we have an internal monitoring system that evaluates the output of the heuristic System 1 answer. Low feeling-of-rightness scores would then result in more extensive deliberation, while high scores should result in a quick acceptance of the initial answer. This was indeed what Thompson et al. found. However, the use of analytical processes did not guarantee a correct outcome: indeed, the analytical answers produced by the participants in Thompson et al.'s study were correct in only 65% of all cases.

19.11.3.2 Intuitive Logic

Another possible answer to the question of how we can reject an intuitive answer is that we detect a conflict, without exactly knowing what the nature of this conflict is. De Neys (2013) states that this is done by applying intuitive logic.

The high percentage of errors that Thompson, Prowse Turner, et al. (2011) reported could be indicative of the fact that we often fail to identify the logical structure of a problem and therefore also fail to notice the conflict between the logical validity of the problem and its believability. De Neys, Moyens, and Vansteenwegen (2010), however, found results that imply that we do notice this conflict, albeit not consciously. In their study, syllogisms were presented that did or did not include a conflict between the logically valid conclusion and their believability. Chance level task performance for conflicting syllogisms implied that participants had a particularly strong belief bias. Their low performance also implies that participants failed to identify the logical structure of the problem. De Neys et al. also recorded skin conductance to estimate physiological arousal. Interestingly, they found that participants' arousal levels were higher in conflicting trials than in non-conflicting trials. This implies that the conflict was registered, but more in the form of gut feeling than in the form of a strong conviction that the premises did contain a conflict.

According to De Neys (2012, 2013) a conflict can be detected by assuming that we initially try to solve logical problems using two intuitive processes operating in parallel: an intuitive heuristic process and an intuitive logical process. It is only when a conflict is detected between the heuristic and the logical process that an analytical deliberation process follows (fig 19.12). The idea that logical processes can operate intuitively may appear to be rather counterintuitive and it is inconsistent with classical analytic-heuristic theories. De Neys (2012, 2013) argues, however, that traditional logical principles can be activated relatively easily. According to de Neys, this happens in the form of a feeling that the heuristic answer conflicts with logic, but without this

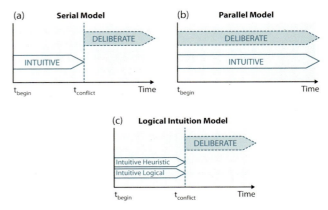

Figure 19.12 Three possible models describing the relationship between intuitive and deliberate reasoning processes. (a) According to the classical serial model, the detection of a conflict results in the intuitive System 1 solution being verified by a deliberate System 2 reasoning process. (b) According to the parallel model, the intuitive and deliberate reasoning processes proceed in parallel. c) According to the logical intuition model, there are initially two intuitive reasoning processes, of which one is based on heuristics and the other on logical intuitions. According to this model, in case of a conflict, these two processes are followed by a deliberate reasoning process. (source: De Neys, 2012)

automatically leading to a solution. As such, it is considered to be a feeling of rightness. The conflict then results in a switch to actual System 2 processing.

19.12 THE NEURAL BASIS OF FORMAL REASONING

Prado, Chadha, and Booth (2011) have reported a meta-analysis of 28 neuroimaging studies that examined deductive reasoning processes. Based on this analysis, they concluded that brain areas in the left frontal and parietal regions are involved in solving deductive reasoning problems. In particular, they found that the middle frontal gyrus, the median frontal gyrus, the precentral gyrus, and the basal ganglia were activated. The specific involvement of the left hemisphere, as reported by Prado et al., is consistent with neuropsychological data. For instance, Goel et al. (2007) studied patients with damage to the left or right hemisphere and found that left hemisphere damage resulted in impaired performance, compared to right hemisphere damage. The finding of a left hemispheric dominance in reasoning tasks is consistent with Gazzaniga's idea of a unitary consciousness (see Chapter 4). According to Gazzaniga (2013) the left hemisphere performs the role of interpreter that strives to make a coherent representation of the information it receives. The left hemispheric dominance just described can possibly be explained by the idea that reasoning processes are at least in part dependent on this interpreter.

Prado, Chadha, et al. (2011) found that the specific activation patterns were partly dependent on the specific task requirements (see fig 19.13). Some tasks involved relational encoding ('X is to the left of Y'...), while others involved categorical arguments ('All A are B') and still others propositional arguments ('If P then Q'). Prado et al.'s meta-analysis showed that relational reasoning was more strongly associated with activation in the parietal cortex, compared to the other two forms of reasoning.

These results are consistent with a patient study by Waechter, Goel, Raymont, Kruger, and Grafman (2013). These authors found that patients with parietal damage performed relatively poorly on a relational reasoning task compared to neurotypical controls. For patients with damage to the anterior prefrontal cortex, however, no performance differences were found in these tasks. The link between relational reasoning tasks and parietal damage can be well explained by the idea that the parietal cortex is involved in the encoding of spatial relations (Sack et al., 2002). Relational problems often lend themselves well to generating spatial representation, making it likely that the parietal cortex is involved in solving such reasoning problems. The left inferior frontal gyrus has been found to be more strongly involved in categorical problems compared

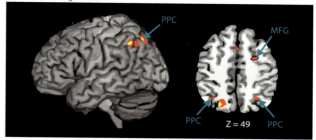

(a) Relational arguments

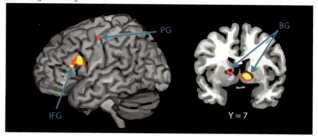

(b) Categorical arguments

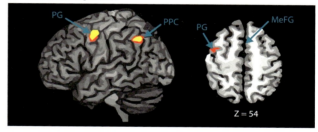

(c) Propositional arguments

Figure 19.13 The relationship between brain activation and the type of argument that is processed. (a) Relational arguments are associated with activation in the posterior parietal cortex (PPC) and the medial frontal gyrus (MFG). (b) Categorical arguments are associated with activation in the basal ganglia (BG), inferior frontal gyrus (IFG), and precentral gyrus (PG). (c) Propositional arguments are associated with activation in the precentral gyrus (PG), posterior parietal cortex (PPC), and medial frontal gyrus (MeFG). (source: Prado, Chadha et al., 2011)

to relational or propositional problems, whereas the left precentral gyrus was mainly activated by propositional reasoning problems (Prado, Chadha, et al., 2011).

Because reasoning problems require the formation of a mental representation that is based on a linguistic description, language is also crucially involved in reasoning processes. In a literature review, Monti and Osherson (2012) discuss how language is primarily involved in the initial processing of the problem and in the encoding of the verbal instructions. After these initial steps, however, language no longer appears to play a significant role.

19.12.1 PROCESSING STAGES

The preceding results describe the global neural activation patterns in brain areas that are involved in reasoning problems, but they are not very informative about the sequence of steps that have to be taken in a reasoning process.

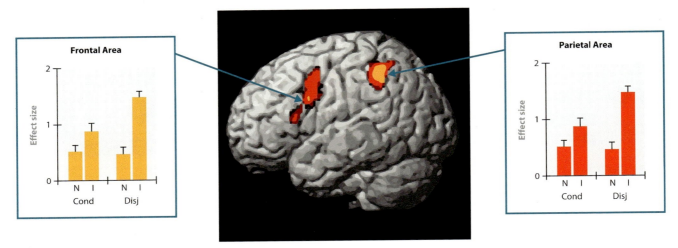

Figure 19.14 Activation of the frontal and parietal brain areas involved in generating a deductive inference for conditional (cond) and disjunctive (disj) reasoning problems. N = non-integrable problems, that is, problems where no new conclusion can be derived from the premises; I = integrable problems, that is, problems where a new conclusion can be derived from the premises. (source: Reverberi et al., 2007)

Based on the mental model theory, Fangmeier, Knauff, Ruff, and Sloutsky (2006) formulated the hypothesis that reasoning processes involve three processing stages. These are, successively, the processing of the premises, the integration of the premises, and the validation of the conclusion. Using fMRI, Fangmeier et al. found evidence suggesting that each of these stages was associated with the activation of specific brain areas. More specifically, the processing of the premises was associated with activation of the temporo-occipital regions. This activation presumably reflects visuospatial processing. The integration of the premises was mainly associated with activation of the anterior prefrontal cortex, which presumably reflects the involvement of executive processes (see Chapter 5). Finally, the validation stage was associated with activation in the parietal and frontal areas. This activation implies that modality-independent representations in the parietal cortex are validated by a cognitive control process.

Bonnefond et al. (2013) used MEG to investigate the processing of modus ponens problems. They found that participants expected the second premise to match the first. When this was not the case, a sharp increase in brain activity followed, approximately 300 ms after the presentation of this premise. In addition, Bonnefond et al. found that participants formed inferences based on the second premise approximately 400 ms after presentation. This was reflected in the activation of the frontoparietal network and occurred before the conclusion was presented. These results imply that participants strongly anticipated the presentation of this conclusion.

19.12.2 INDIVIDUAL DIFFERENCES

De Neys and colleagues (De Neys, 2012, 2013; De Neys et al., 2010; De Neys et al., 2005) had already reported that there can be considerable individual differences in our reasoning skills. These differences can be partly explained by the idea that there are different strategies for solving reasoning

problems. These strategies are influenced by, among other things, sensitivity to the logical form of a problem, sensitivity to the validity of conclusions, and the use of heuristics (Reverberi et al., 2012). Individuals who were mainly driven by the logical form of the problem showed increased activation in the left inferior lateral frontal and superior medial frontal areas. These brain areas appear to be involved in extracting and representing the structure of the problem. In contrast, individuals who were mainly driven by the validity of the conclusions showed a stronger activation in the left ventrolateral frontal area. The latter area is mainly involved in the selection and application of the correct inferential rules (Reverberi et al., 2007) (see fig 19.14). No specific pattern of brain activity was found for the use of heuristics, however.

In addition to these differences, large individual differences have been reported for belief bias; the tendency to accept credible but incorrect conclusions. According to Tsujii and Watanabe (2009) the right inferior frontal cortex is involved in inhibiting incorrect responses induced by the heuristic System 1. Tsujii and Watanabe therefore hypothesised that the degree of activation in this area would be a predictor for the strength of belief bias. While solving reasoning problems, participants had to perform an N-back task, which could vary in terms of its cognitive demands. A stronger belief bias was found in the high-demand condition, compared to the low-demand condition. In both conditions, however, there was a correlation between the accuracy of the answers and the degree of right frontal cortex activation.

19.13 INFORMAL REASONING

Research on formal deductive reasoning processes, in which background knowledge is largely irrelevant, has a very limited scope, as it appears to have little relevance to our everyday informal reasoning processes. Informal reasoning is a form of reasoning in which knowledge and experience does play a crucial role, and in which we usually strive to make a convincing argument in favour of a specific position. This form of reasoning has therefore very little to do with formal logic.

One of the main differences between formal and informal reasoning is that in informal reasoning the content of the argument is important, whereas in a formal argument only its form is important. A second difference is that in informal reasoning, the context is relevant. For example, we are much more convinced when an informal argument is formulated by an expert than when the same argument is formulated by a non-expert (Walton, 2010).

Perhaps the most important difference between formal and informal reasoning is that research on formal reasoning focuses primarily on binary logic, that is, every proposition is assumed to be true or false, while informal logic is primarily based on probabilities (Evans, 2012). For this reason, informal logic is also more closely adhering to Bayesian inference rules than to strict binary true/false assertions (Hahn & Oaksford, 2007). According to the logic of Bayesian inference rules, the likelihood of an argument being true may be assigned a probability, and this probability may change on the basis of new arguments.

To what extent are there similarities between informal and deductive reasoning? The first part of this chapter already shows that many people are guided by background knowledge even in formal reasoning, resulting in a belief bias (Klauer et al., 2000). Ricco (2007) examined the extent to which there are similarities between formal and informal reasoning ability, based on the analysis of frequently used fallacies. Examples of this type of fallacy include the argument from irrelevance (trying to support an argument based on an irrelevant reason) or the slippery slope argument (claiming that an innocent first step will result in very bad consequences, without giving a reason). Ricco found that the ability to recognise these fallacies strongly correlated with deductive reasoning skills.

19.13.1 MOTIVATED REASONING

A final difference between formal and informal reasoning is that in informal reasoning motivation is different from formal reasoning. In formal reasoning we should be motivated to use inferential logic as much as possible to solve the issues as accurately as possible. In contrast, in informal reasoning we are often driven by other motives. According to Mercier and Sperber (2011) the most important function of informal reasoning involves finding arguments that can convince someone else. Like skilled politicians, people who want to convince someone else are not looking to find the truth, but rather to find arguments that will strengthen their own position as much as possible. This position has been criticised by Evans (2011), however, arguing that informal

reasoning is not just used for argumentation, but that it also plays an important role in all kinds of thought processes, including anticipating and planning for the future.

There is currently much evidence showing that many individuals' informal reasoning and thinking is deeply flawed. Consider, for example the fact that millions of people refuse to accept the theory of evolution, are convinced that vaccinations cause autism, that the moon landings never happened, that the Earth is flat, or that climate change is a hoax. Why do many otherwise reasonably intelligent people hold on to such absurd ideas? Thagard (2011) explains this phenomenon on the basis of the concept of **motivated inference**, which is a form of biased reasoning that allows people to distort their judgement due to underlying personal goals (see fig 19.15). Motivated inference is, according to Thagard, based on wishes and desires rather than on facts.

The concept of motivated inference is similar to that of **my-side bias**. My-side bias is the tendency to evaluate arguments on the basis of our own preconceived notions, rather than on their own merit. Evidence for my side bias was reported by Stanovich and West (2007), based on a study involving the following suggestive, but incorrect, arguments:

1. Students who drink alcohol are more likely to become alcoholics later.
2. The difference in salary between men and women generally disappears when they are employed in a similar position.

Students who regularly drank alcohol rated the probability that argument 1 was true lower than students who did not. Similarly, women rated the probability that argument 2 was true lower than men. Interestingly, these results were unrelated to intelligence or other cognitive skills, implying that this my-side bias is not dependent on the ability to use System 2 processes.

A notable finding is that the motivation to find evidence for one's own position can sometimes actually influence reasoning skills in a positive way. For example, Dawson,

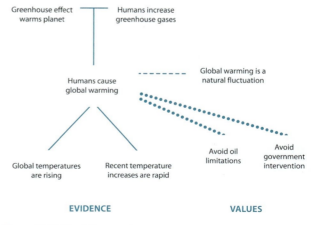

Figure 19.15 The influence of emotional and explanatory factors on the acceptance of arguments in informal reasoning. (source: Thagard, 2011)

Gilovich, and Regan (2002) found that performance on Wason's card selection task (see fig 19.8) improved when participants were strongly motivated to disprove the rule. This was done by using a variant of the task where the rule implied that the participant would die young.

19.13.2 PROBABILITIES

As discussed earlier, probabilities are much more prominent in informal reasoning than in formal reasoning. More specifically, Hahn and Oaksford (2007) found evidence that informal reasoning follows the principles of Bayesian inference. That is, they found that the following factors could influence the perceived strength of a conclusion: (1) the strength of the original belief; (2) the nature of the argument: positive arguments had a stronger impact than negative ones; and (3) the strength of the evidence (see fig 19.16).

According to the classical view of human reasoning, we can classify various types of arguments as fallacies, such as the slippery-slope argument described earlier. According to the Bayesian approach, however, there is no unambiguous distinction between valid arguments and invalid arguments. Instead, it considers the persuasiveness of an argument as proxy to its strength. More specifically, we can classify each argument in terms of its persuasiveness and the extent to which an argument implies a negative outcome.

Corner, Hahn, and Oaksford (2011) investigated the extent to which these factors influence the persuasiveness of a slippery-slope argument. To this end, they presented participants various arguments on topics such as the legalisation of euthanasia or the compulsory introduction of identity cards. The estimated persuasive power of each argument was consistent with the prediction based on Bayesian inference.

Although the Bayesian approach has been very successful in explaining informal reasoning processes, there are still some important limitations related to this approach. Bowers and Davis (2012) argue, for example, that the Bayesian approach is too flexible, making it difficult to falsify specific assumptions. Griffiths, Chater, Norris, and Pouget (2012), however, counter this argument by stating that the Bayesian approach is a theoretical framework, which is by definition not falsifiable. From this framework, however, various specific models have been formulated that are falsifiable. For example, Harris, Hsu, and Madsen (2012) studied the ad hominem argument (ignoring a proposition due to perceived negative traits of the person making the argument). Harris et al. identified all factors that are relevant according to Bayesian theorists and found very strong evidence in favour of a Bayesian model.

19.14 IN CLOSING

The fact that we commit many fallacies illustrates an intriguing question that we will address here at the end of this chapter: are we, human beings, rational? In this chapter, we have discussed various studies that jointly point to the fact that we frequently violate the principles of formal logic, that we allow ourselves to be influenced by irrelevant information, that we have very limited statistical intuitions, and that we find it difficult to look beyond the superficial features of a problem representation. Collectively, these studies imply a strong limitation of our rationality.

The fact that our rationality is apparently limited has led to countless debates (Tetlock & Mellers, 2002). After all, most of us do reasonably well in everyday life, while we appear to fail immediately when even the most basic properties of our rationality are tested under laboratory conditions. How can we explain this apparent paradox? First, we must realise that our everyday life functioning is much less rational than we usually assume. On the other hand, our performance in the laboratory is often not as poor as the studies discussed in this chapter so far suggest. To start with the latter point, there are several reasons to believe that our apparent shortcomings on laboratory tasks are not as extreme as the literature suggests.

It is, for example, a misconception to dismiss the use of heuristics as irrational (see also Box 21.1). Heuristics enable us to find solutions quickly and with relatively little cognitive effort, and often they turn out to yield practical and workable solutions. In addition, performance on a laboratory task is often relatively poor because it is not always immediately clear which information is important. For example, in probability judgements (see Chapter 21), important information is often ignored because its relevance to the problem is not always immediately clear. A simple reformulation of the problem, in which its importance is stressed, can already result in a significant increase in task performance (Krynski & Tenenbaum, 2007).

In addition, in many cases, the errors that are made on reasoning problems also highlight the artificiality of the problem. In syllogistic reasoning problems, for example, the validity of a conclusion does not depend on the credibility of the premises. In everyday life, however, we rarely encounter comparable conditions. Similarly, we typically encounter very few situations where conclusions are absolutely true or false, or where additional information should not affect

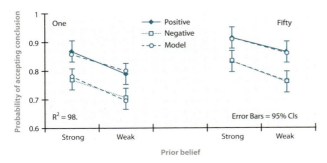

Figure 19.16 The impact of a priori beliefs, the number of arguments, and the positive or negative persuasiveness of an argument on participants' willingness to accept a conclusion. The empirical results are compared with the predictions of a computational model based on Bayesian inference principles. (CIs = Confidence intervals) (source: Hahn and Oaksford, 2007)

the validity of a conclusion. Taking all these factors into account, we can conclude that laboratory research into decision-making, judgement, and problem-solving behaviour drastically underestimates human rationality.

Despite these problems, however, we must conclude that human rationality is limited. For example, Camerer and Hogarth (1999) reviewed 74 studies that examined the effects of motivation on decision-making processes and concluded that giving incentives hardly results in a better solution. Likewise, Brase, Fiddick, and Harries (2006) found that participants who were recruited at top-ranking American universities scored better on base rate problems than students who came from a lower-ranking university. But even when researchers took very explicit steps to make sure that participants understood the problems, they still made many errors. A good example of this is the conjunction fallacy discussed by Tversky and Kahneman (1983), which we will discuss in more detail in Chapter 21. Finally, many studies also find that not only novices but also experts are susceptible to cognitive biases (Redelmeier, Koehler, Liberman, & Tversky, 1995; Schwartz, Chapman, & Brewer, 2004).

19.14.1 THE DUNNING-KRUGER EFFECT

An important reason why many individuals perform poorly on complex tasks is that it appears to be specifically those individuals who perform poorly that have limited insights into the fact that they are performing poorly! This phenomenon, named after the original discoverers, Justin Kruger and David Dunning (1999), is now known as the Dunning-Kruger effect. It describes 'how those who are incompetent lack insight into their incompetence' (Dunning, 2011, page 260). The Dunning-Kruger effect occurs because the skill of being able to verify the correctness of an answer often requires the very same knowledge that is needed to solve the problem. Dunning (2011) examined the Dunning-Kruger effect using Wason's selection task (see fig 19.17). Some participants solved the problem using the correct rule across several variants of the task and thus scored 100% correct. Other participants tried to solve the problem but consistently used the wrong rule, scoring 0% correct. Both groups, however, were convinced that they had solved 80–90% of the problems correctly.

19.14.2 WHAT IS RATIONALITY?

To address the question whether humans are rational, we must also address what rationality is. Traditionally, cognitive psychology assumed that rational thought is guided by the principles of classic inferential logic. It followed that deductive reasoning processes were particularly relevant for determining human rationality. Unfortunately, as we have already discussed, many individuals tend to perform very poorly on these kinds of tasks, suggesting that they are indeed not rational when we equate rationality with being able to apply the rules of classic logic in a limited laboratory environment.

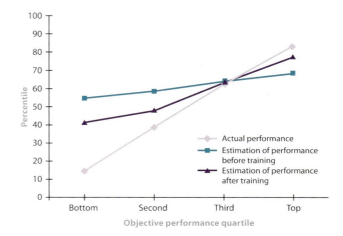

Figure 19.17 The relationship between participants' self-assessed performance on Wason's card selection task and their actual performance, before and after training. Participants who performed the worst overestimated their own performance the most. (source: Dunning, 2011)

This reasoning may be flawed, however, in that it assumes that participants are always aware of what is expected of them (Szollosi & Newell, 2020). Moreover, the idea of equating rationality to classic inferential logic can be conceived as a form of normativism, that is, the idea that human thought reflects a normative system. According to this view, human thinking is correct when it conforms to classical logic and incorrect when it does not. This view is highly debatable, however. After all, there are few problems in everyday life that conform to the rules of classical logic. An alternative and preferable approach, on the other hand, assumes that human rationality is founded on determining the likelihood of a multitude of possible outcomes. This approach makes sense when we consider that we live in a world characterised by uncertainty and imprecise information. Tsetsos et al. (2016) report that indeed people often make better decisions when faced with this kind of uncertainty. Oaksford and Chater (2009) present an influential probabilistic approach to human rationality, based on Bayesian principles, which corresponds much better to human choices than classic inferential logic predicts (see fig 19.18). The core of Oaksford

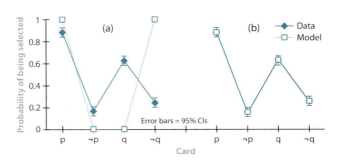

Figure 19.18 Comparison between two computational models predicting the likelihood that individuals will select the P, Q, non-P, and non-Q cards in Wason's card selection task, compared to observed rates of human participants actually selecting these cards. (a) The predictions made by a model that was based on classical logic. (b) The predictions made by a Bayesian model; these predictions correspond much better to human selection behaviour than those made by the classical model. (source: Oaksford and Chater, 2009)

and Chater's approach is that a priori beliefs can change on the basis of new information.

Although the debate about whether humans are rational is still ongoing (Tetlock & Mellers, 2002), a few conclusions already begin to emerge: first, we can conclude that the normative approach, which equates rationality to classic deductive reasoning, is a poor model of how we function in everyday life. This normative approach is thus also a poor model for human rationality. Although approaches based on probabilities are better suited to do so, we still have to conclude that there are limitations to human rationality. These limitations are more closely tied to the limitations of our cognitive processing capacity than that they represent a fundamental lack of rationality, however. To compensate for these limitations, we often fall back to using heuristics. In practice, these heuristics not only provide useful solutions in many cases, in some exceptional cases they are more efficient and may even result in better quality solutions (Gigerenzer & Gray, 2017).

Given all these limitations, we can also wonder whether human cognition is unique. Laland and Seed (2021) recently addressed this question in a literature review and concluded that human cognition does not contain any unique features, but that instead each of our cognitive abilities is shared by other species. What is unique about human cognition, however, is that according to Laland and Seed, we are unique cognitive all-rounders and that our proficiency arises from flexible interaction and reinforcement across multiple cognitive domains.

19.15 SUMMARY

Internal mental representations are essential for almost all forms of higher cognition. This chapter discusses four possible forms that these representations can take. These forms can be divided into modal and amodal systems. Modal representations can take the form of mental images or features. Amodal representations can take the form of symbols or statistical patterns in neural networks. These mental representations are assumed to play an important role in generating predictions about the future, and in evaluating possible alternative scenarios, in the form of mental simulations.

An influential way of describing reasoning can be found in the mental models theory. Mental models describe possible alternative outcomes based on a problem description, assuming that a different model is generated for each possible outcome. These models can either be imagined or envisaged. Johnson-Laird and colleagues hypothesise that a mental model is constructed from the information that is available in a problem description, after which individuals start searching for counterexamples to refute a tentative conclusion obtained from the model. Problems that require multiple mental models tend to be solved less accurately than problems that require only one model.

Chater and Oakford argue that there are many situations in which individuals fail to generate mental models and therefore assume that many reasoning problems are tackled using a probabilistic approach, in which an estimate is made of the probability that a proposition is true, based on the combination of the problem description and our background knowledge.

Dual systems theories are a hybrid combination of the principles of mental model theory and the probabilistic approach. According to these theories, we initially formulate an intuitive answer to a problem, based on a System 1 process. It is only when there are reasons to doubt the correctness of this answer that it will be verified by a more analytical, formal, System 2 process. System 1 is here assumed to be automatic, to operate on the basis of associations formed in long-term memory, and to have arisen early in evolution. System 2 is assumed to have arisen relatively late in evolution, to operate on the basis of conscious processes, and to be analytical and limited in capacity.

Theories of mental representation are frequently tested by presenting participants with formal reasoning problems. Within formal logic, a distinction can be made between inductive and deductive reasoning processes. Induction occurs when we attempt to derive a general principle from incomplete data, whereas deduction occurs when we want to draw a conclusion that follows with certainty from the data.

In inductive logic, it is never possible to find evidence for the general validity of a principle, whereas discrepant findings can prove the invalidity of a principle. This principle is also an important cornerstone of scientific research. Yet many people have a strong confirmation bias. This confirmation bias can be examined by using simple tasks, such as Wason's 2-4-6 task. In addition, much research is conducted on the basis of simulated research environments.

Research into deductive reasoning takes place on the basis of three different logical problems: conditional logic, relational logic, and syllogistic logic. Within conditional logic, two forms of reasoning can be distinguished that lead to a valid conclusion, namely the modus ponens and the modus tollens. In addition, there are two other forms of reasoning that do not necessarily lead to a valid conclusion, namely the denial of the antecedent and the affirmation of the consequent. Violations of the inference rules often occur because individuals allow themselves to be influenced by irrelevant context, additional arguments, or background knowledge.

A common way of investigating deductive reasoning processes involves Wason's card selection task. Here, many individuals are misguided by irrelevant aspects of the task. Possible explanations for this are given by the matching bias, or the idea that we are not good at handling indicative rules. A reformulation of the task based on deontic rules generally results in a strong increase in reasoning performance.

Syllogisms consist of two basic statements, namely a major premise and a minor premise, and a conclusion whose correctness must be assessed, under the assumption that the premises are correct. Because of this property, syllogisms are interesting tools for investigating deductive reasoning processes. Humans often appear to be influenced by the believability of the premises. In addition to this belief bias, a matching bias can be found. Moreover, we also tend to make many mistakes because there can be confusion about the exact meaning of the premises, since the definitions of logical operators in logic often have a different meaning than what is implied by everyday language usage.

Relational reasoning is assumed to be based on the construction of mental images in which the underlying relationships play a central role. In this context, a distinction can be made between imaging and envisaging. Although mental images can be advantageous in relational reasoning, in some cases they can be disadvantageous because of irrelevant details that are generated.

A number of factors limit the human capacity for reasoning. Our limited working memory capacity plays an important role in this. This limitation often results in the application of the principle of truth, which states that we predominantly generate mental models for conditions that are true but fail to do so for conditions that are not true. In addition, the aforementioned belief bias also plays an important role in this, as believable premises are associated with a strong feeling of rightness, causing logical problems to be solved through an intuitive System 1 process and avoiding an analytical check by System 2.

Over the past two decades, there has been much progress in identifying the neural basis of formal reasoning processes. In particular, the left frontal and parietal cortical areas are crucial here. These brain areas each appear to play a specific role in relational, categorical, and conditional operations. In addition, evidence has been found for a differentiation between the various stages of reasoning. Furthermore, considerable individual differences in reasoning skills have been identified, which may be related to differences in the strategies people use and which are also reflected in various neural activation patterns.

Research on deductive reasoning processes implies that there are few similarities between the way we reason in everyday life and the way deductive reasoning processes take place. For this reason, a more recent approach is formed by studies investigating informal reasoning processes. Informal reasoning is driven by a motivation to persuade rather than a motivation to arrive at the truth, and it is better described by the principles of Bayesian inference than by the binary logic underlying classical reasoning theories.

Given the many violations of logic that we often make, we can ask ourselves whether we humans are rational. At first glance, there seems to be a strong discrepancy between rationality in experimental settings and rationality in everyday life. We must conclude, however, that the classical normative definition of rationality, as derived from classical formal inferential logic, is not a good model for human rationality, which is much more strongly based on probabilities and uncertainties. Yet human rationality is certainly limited. The Dunning-Kruger effect describes how people who perform poorly on a given task often do not have the insight and knowledge to realise that they are performing poorly.

NOTE

1 The validity of classic inferential logic is still undisputed and forms the basis for the operation of computers. All modern programming languages are based on classic inferential logic. Nevertheless, the restriction that propositions can only be true or false is a major limitation in describing many everyday phenomena. To circumvent this limitation, an alternative form of logic has been developed towards the end of the 20th century, in which the truth of P is described as a stochastic probability. This type of fuzzy logic is often much more capable of describing natural phenomena.

FURTHER READING

Evans, J. S. B. T., Newstead, S. E., & Byrne, R. M. J. (1993). *Human reasoning: The psychology of deduction*. Hove, UK: Taylor & Francis.

Feeney, A., & Heit, E. (2007). *Inductive reasoning: Experimental, developmental, and computational approaches*. Cambridge, UK: Cambridge University Press.

Gabbay, D. M., Hartmann, S., & Woods, J. (2011). *Inductive logic*. Handbook of the History of Logic. Volume 10. Amsterdam: North Holland Publishing.

Hitchcock, D. (2017). *On reasoning and argument: Essays in informal logic and on critical thinking*. Heidelberg: Springer Verlag.

Marbach, E. (1994). *Mental representations and consciousness: Towards a theory of representation and reference*. Heidelberg: Springer Verlag.

CHAPTER 20
Numbers and categories

20.1 INTRODUCTION

One of the higher cognitive skills that is uniquely human is the ability to represent the external world in discrete and abstract units. To minimise memory load, we do not remember all the information that we process every day. Instead, we generate abstractions from everyday observations by retaining the core features of objects and by generating categories based on their most important distinguishing features. Abstract geometric shapes, for example, can be subdivided into squares, circles, cubes, or spheres. In this example, the boundaries between categories are quite clearly defined, but there are many situations where this is not the case. Consider colours, for example. Colours can be generated by mixing three different wavelengths of light (see Chapter 6), allowing for an infinite number of combinations. Yet we perceive colours as discrete units, such as red, yellow, orange, or purple. A colour is red or green, but never an intermediate form, such as reddish green or greenish red. The fact that we also perceive these kinds of continuous units and divide them into discrete categories indicates that we can somehow make abstract and discrete representations of our environment.

Although at first glance the categorisation process is fairly easy to understand – extract the most characteristic property of an object as the basis for a category – we can only gain an appreciation of the complexity of this process when we investigate how classification systems have been applied in, for example, biology. Animals are classified into mammals, fish, insects, amphibians, reptiles, and birds. Some animal species, such as dolphins or whales, resemble the superficial characteristics of fish, yet belong to the class of mammals. Penguins belong to the class of birds, but they are not representative of this class because their external characteristics are very different from those of birds.

Even in other situations, we tend to accept the classification of one species more readily than that of another. Domestic animals such as cats and dogs are much more prevalent in our immediate environment than, for example, lynxes or guanacos. Consequently, for the latter two species we are much slower in deciding which class they belong to. All these factors, such as typicality, availability, but also the distribution of different individual species across a category, determine the efficiency and accuracy with which we can classify an object (Dale, Kehoe, & Spivey, 2007).

In addition to classifying, we are also able to count the objects in our environment, or, in the case of large quantities, to estimate numbers or quantities. In other words, we have a sense of size or numerosity. Moreover, we have developed a unique ability to manipulate this representation of size: we can perform mental arithmetic. How are numeric units represented and how can we use these units in mental arithmetic? In summary, the question of how we can make abstractions from sets of elements is the central theme of this chapter.

20.2 NUMERICAL COGNITION

The fact that we have developed the ability to count objects implies that we have somehow managed to convert our sense of numerocity into a mental representation, to connect symbols to this representation, and to manipulate these symbols in a systematic way (Dehaene, 1992). To what extent are our arithmetic skills and our intuitions for size innate? Do they, for instance, depend on acquired skills, such as language? To address these questions, Gordon (2004) studied how members of the Pirahã tribe in the Amazon rainforest were able to make numeric judgements. This tribe's language contains a very rudimentary system of counting, consisting of just the words 'one', 'two', and 'many'. When asked to indicate how many objects they saw, members of the tribe were significantly inaccurate for sets of three or more elements, even when asked to report these numbers with their fingers, implying that language and our sense of numerosity are linked (see fig 20.1).

Although Kahneman and Tversky (1972) found that even trained statisticians can make gross errors of judgement when making statistical inferences, it does appear that a certain sense of magnitude, number, and proportion

DOI: 10.4324/9781003319344-28

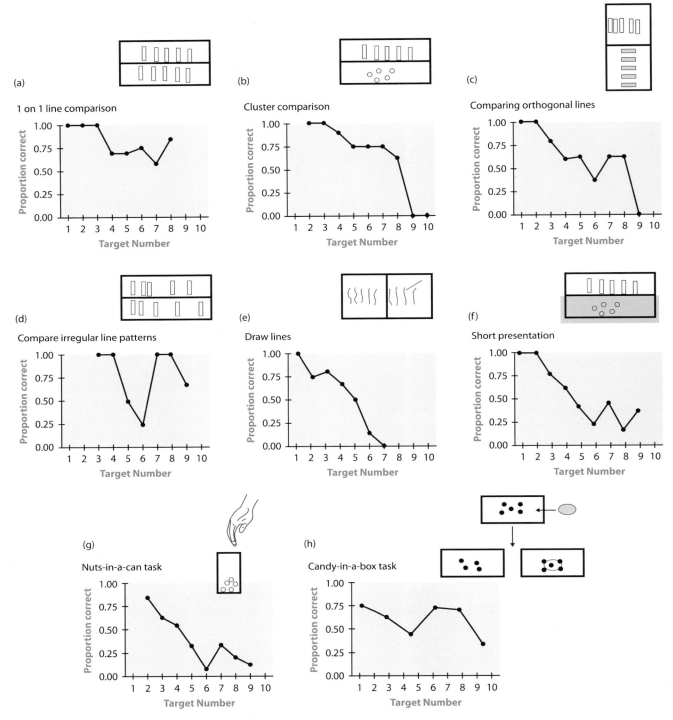

Figure 20.1 Results of a study on number awareness among the Pirahã tribe in the Amazon rainforest. For each different situation (a–h), members of the tribe either had to report the number of objects they were shown or they had to compare two different quantities. For most tasks, accuracy dropped very rapidly when the task involved sets of three objects or more. (source: Gordon, 2004)

is already present in eight-month-old children (Xu & Garcia, 2008). In a study involving these children, Xu and Garcia took five ping-pong balls out of a closed box. This set consisted of either one white and four red balls, or of one red and four white balls. Then, the remaining contents of the box were shown to the children. These could either consist of mainly white balls combined with only a few red ones, or of mainly red balls combined with only a few white ones. The experimenters found that the children looked longer at the box when the proporotion of red to white balls in the box did not match the sample. Since viewing time is considered to be a measure of interest or surprise in young children, Xu and Garcia concluded that the children were surprised when the contents of the boxes did not correspond to the sample.

Fontanari, Gonzalez, Vallortigara, and Girotto (2014) also found evidence for an intuitive sense of probability among Mayan tribes in Guatemala. Here, participants were given two sets of red and black coins. Both the absolute numbers of coins and the ratio between red and black coins varied from set to set. The participants' task was to obtain a red coin. To do so, they had to choose one of the two sets, from which a coin was then drawn at random. Task performance was measured as the proportion of trials in which a coin was won. Although the Mayan participants scored overall slightly lower than an Italian control group, their results were similar and significantly above chance.

These results allow us to conclude that a basic awareness of size and proportion is probably innate and does not depend on learned linguistic and cultural factors. Moreover, it appears to be shared by many other species (Nieder, 2021). As we will discuss in the next chapter, however, our intuition for probabilities is limited to relatively simple situations and may even be counterproductive when estimating complex statistical probabilities.

Before discussing counting and mental arithmetic, we first need to understand how magnitude is represented in the mind. Gallistel and Gelman (2000) and also Gallistel and Gibbon (2000) argue that magnitude can be represented both verbally and non-verbally. The verbal representation takes the form of discrete numbers and the non-verbal form that of a mental image. According to Gallistel and Gelman, we are thus able to count in a non-verbal way by constantly adding units of a specific size to this mental image. To illustrate, consider creating a mental representation of pouring cups of water into a measuring cup (see fig 20.2). The amount of water we pour into the cup represents a unit. Counting then involves adjusting the representation of the amount of water in the cup according to the number of units that are poured in. This representation is essentially continuous, is already available in young children (Feigenson, Dehaene, & Spelke, 2004), and, according to Gallistel and Gelman, is shared with other species.

Feigenson et al. (2004) identify two core systems for the representation of magnitude: core system I is available from an early age and is comparable to the continuous representation proposed by Gallistel and Gelman (2000). Six-month-old children appear to be able to detect relatively coarse differences in size. The extent to which these differences can be detected is expressed in a ratio. For children of six months of age, this ratio is 1:2, that is, when they have to make choices between sets of, for example, one versus two dots, or two versus four dots, they can accurately indicate which of the two sets is the larger. For smaller proportions, however, the decision as to which set is largest becomes much less accurate. Children's accuracy increases with age, however: at the age of ten months, babies can already distinguish ratios of 2:3.

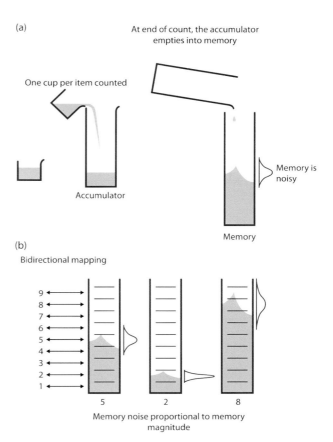

Figure 20.2 A schematic representation of the non-verbal counting system. (a) The way a representation of size and numbers is constructed non-verbally. (b) The bidirectional relationship between numbers, size, and inaccuracy. (source: Gallistel and Gelman, 2000)

Feigenson et al. argue that in addition to this global core system I, we have a more precise number representation, known as core system II, which also develops in early infancy. When babies had to choose between one or two crackers, or between two and three crackers, they always chose the larger quantity. However, when they had to choose between three or four, two or four, or even one or four crackers, their choices were much more random, suggesting that young babies have a limit of three individual discrete items they can represent. The major difference with the babies' behaviour when discriminating between the dots is that it was now predominantly determined by the absolute number. From these results, Feigenson et al. concluded that core system II is initially limited to representing a maximum of three discrete units.

20.3 NUMBER REPRESENTATION

In addition to our ability to represent magnitude, we are able to relate this representation to a symbolic code. This is a uniquely human skill: we have words to express numbers or sizes. Apart from words, we can also express these numbers in abbreviated form, using numerical symbols.

The human species have developed many different ways of representing numbers, ranging from the Babylonian cuneiform system from around 5000 years ago, through the Roman number system developed 3000 years ago, to the Arabic number system developed in the 9th century. In Western society, we are mainly familiar with the Arabic system, although the Roman system is still used on occasion.

Most of these are decimal, or base 10, systems, that is, they consist of ten different symbols to represent the numbers 0–9, while representing larger numbers using a combination of two or more symbols. Note that it is not strictly necessary to use a decimal system. Some cultures have developed number systems with a base of 20 or even 60. Finally, in our modern society, we also frequently employ binary (base 2), octal (base 8), or hexadecimal (base 16) systems, as they are naturally suited for digital computers.

20.3.1 BASIC PROPERTIES OF NUMBERS

20.3.1.1 Number Processing

The investigation of processing times of numbers has revealed some interesting effects. Obviously, it takes longer to name large numbers than small numbers, simply because it takes longer to name the longer sequence of digits. In addition, however, a number of other, less obvious effects, can be observed (Brysbaert, 1995). For example, the processing time of a number also depends on the frequency with which we encounter it: frequently occurring numbers are processed faster than less frequently occurring ones. In addition, number size also influences the processing speed of a subsequent number. When we have to process sequences of numbers, the next number in the sequence is processed faster when it has the same size as the previous number in the sequence (see fig 20.3).

20.3.1.2 The Symbolic Distance Effect

Another remarkable finding is the symbolic distance effect. This effect describes how our assessment of the relative size of two numbers depends on the absolute size of these numbers. For example, when we need to judge which of

two numbers is larger, we are faster to do this for the numbers 2 and 4 than for 3 and 5.

20.3.1.3 The Apprehension Span

From the previous discussion, it is clear that our ability to represent magnitude is limited. The question of how many items we can represent at once was posed in the 19th century by the British economist and logician William Stanley Jevons (1871) (fig 20.4). In a remarkable study published in the leading scientific journal *Nature*, Jevons subjected himself to an experiment in which he took an unknown number of beans (between 3 and 15) and dropped them into a bowl. Jevons then tried to estimate as quickly as possible how many beans had been dropped and then wrote down this number. He then proceeded to count the exact number of beans he had dropped. For three and four beans, his estimates were always correct, but for larger numbers of beans his accuracy gradually declined. Based on these results, Jevons concluded that the **apprehension span**, that is, the maximum number of elements that we can consciously process simultaneously, is about four to five items.

Logan and Zbrodoff (2003) replicated Jevons' study, but under better controlled conditions using modern technology. They showed participants displays that were filled with a random number of one to ten dots. Participants then had to verbally report the number of dots as quickly as

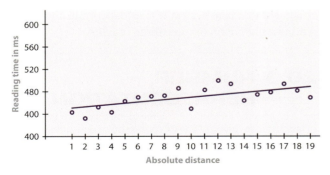

Figure 20.3 Reading times of numbers as a function of numerical size of the previous number. (source: Brysbaert, 1995)

Figure 20.4 The British economist and logician William Stanley Jevons (1835–1882).

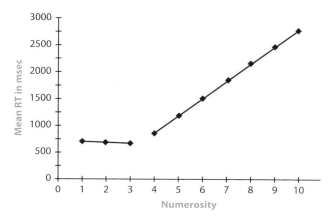

Figure 20.5 Reaction times as a function of the number of dots presented on a computer screen. (source: Logan and Zbrodoff, 2003)

possible. A remarkable finding was that for displays containing only one, two, or three dots, participants were able to report this number within 700 ms, and these response times were similar for these numbers of dots (see fig 20.5). From four dots onwards, however, the response time increased linearly with the number of dots present in the display.

The fact that beyond four items it takes us progressively more time to assess the size of increasingly large sets indicates that we do this by counting them. The fact that this increase in reaction time only starts from sets of size four onwards indicates the existence of a special case for small sets: apparently, we can determine the size of those sets at a glance. This is a process known as **subitizing**.

20.3.2 SUBITISING

Why do we subitize small set sizes while we need to count larger ones? In the following sections, we will discuss some alternative – not necessarily exclusive – explanations for this phenomenon.

20.3.2.1 Working Memory Capacity

One of the first explanations for the subitizing phenomenon was formulated by Klahr (1973). The prevailing theoretical framework at the time was that information in working memory was represented in an abstract form (see Chapter 13). According to Klahr et al., we could form such an abstract representation by counting the elements in a set. For this we would determine the size of a set by serially comparing each element with their rank number (1, 2,. . . etc.), and Klahr assumed that each of these rank numbers would have to be activated in working memory. Since working memory capacity is limited, Klahr argued that we can only activate the first four rank numbers. For higher rank numbers, we would have to update the contents of our working memory to make room for new rank numbers. This explanation thus implies that we are still counting even in the case of small numbers, but that this counting is extremely fast, so that it is manifested in the reaction time pattern.

This explanation is highly implausible, however, for several reasons. First of all, if rank number updating in working memory is involved, we would expect task performance to decrease when working memory is overloaded with irrelevant information. A study using irrelevant distracting stimuli reported, however, that these stimuli did affected counting but not subitizing (Tuholski, Engle, & Beylis, 2001). This result implies that subitizing is not influenced by attention and thus not by working memory load.

20.3.2.2 Weber's Law

A potentially better explanation for subitizing is that for higher numbers of items we become less capable of detecting the small differences in the patterns they form. Intuitively, this is plausible: the relative difference between displays with one and two dots is considerable; whereas the relative difference between displays with two and three dots is already slightly less, and the relative difference between three and four dots is even less. This phenomenon could be the basis for the fact that from four to five dots we can no longer instantaneously determine how many items had to be presented. The question now is why this limits the subitizing process to a maximum of four items. A possible answer can be found by applying Weber's law. This law states that the smallest difference between two stimuli that we can still reliably observe is linearly related to the absolute size of the stimuli themselves. In other words, if a stimulus is twice as large, the difference with another stimulus must also become twice as large for us to perceive it. The relationship between the relative and the absolute sizes of stimuli is known as the **Weber fraction**, or the **just noticeable difference**. The just noticeable difference is defined as the smallest difference that we can still perceive in 50% of all trials.

We can also apply this law to the observation of numbers of dots. Van Oeffelen and Vos (1982) did so by briefly presenting displays filled with dot patterns. For each dot pattern, participants were given a reference value and then had to decide whether the displayed pattern did ('yes') or did not ('no') contain the number of dots given in the reference value. For each reference value, either a pattern containing the corresponding number of dots could be shown, or a pattern that deviated from this to a greater or lesser extent. For example, for the reference value 8, deviating patterns with 9 to 12 dots could be shown.

Then, for each dot pattern, the Weber fraction could be computed from the answers that participants had given. The smaller the difference between the reference value and the number of dots that were actually shown, the smaller the proportion of 'no' answers the participants gave, implying that participants had increasing difficulties assessing that there was a difference between the reference value and the actual number of dots, the smaller the difference was. Based on this, Van Oeffelen and Vos determined how big the difference between the reference value and the number of dots in the displays had to be for participants to give a reliable answer. It turned out that this difference had to be 0.16 times the reference value, that is, a deviant pattern had to contain at least 0.16 times larger than the reference value to be reliably identifiable as being different. Differences between six and seven dots should, according to this calculation, still be just perceptible, since seven is 1/6 (~ 0.17) times larger than six. For sets of items smaller than six, we should therefore be able to instantly observe whether their size deviates from a reference value, and thus instantly assess their size. For sets of items larger than six, this is no longer possible since the smallest possible difference with another set is clearly smaller than the Weber fraction.

This explanation is problematic, however, for two main reasons. The first is that it overestimates the transition point between counting and subitizing. The second reason is that van Oeffelen and Vos (1982) suggest that subitizing is a continuous process that is slowly diminishing as we observe larger numbers of elements. This conclusion is inconsistent, however, with the reaction time studies discussed earlier, which show a discrete transition from subitizing to counting for sets of four elements or more.

20.3.2.3 Pattern Recognition

An explanation that is more in line with the observed reaction time data assumes that we are limited in our ability to recognise patterns. In principle, small sets of items can always be visually represented as a geometrical pattern: one item equals a point, two items a line, three an imaginary triangle, four a **quadrilateral**, and so on. The larger the set of items, the more degrees of freedom there are in these patterns. From four points onwards, the number of variations in the possible patterns increases sharply with the result that the assessment of set size becomes increasingly less efficient if we were to rely on pattern recognition. Wender and Rothkegel (2000) found evidence for this hypothesis by establishing that canonical patterns, that is, highly recognisable geometric patterns, can be recognised more rapidly than random patterns. Moreover, Wender and Rothkegel found that when it is possible to decompose a complex geometric pattern into several individual canonical patterns, we can easily access the number of items in each individual canonical pattern by subitizing (see fig 20.6).

Although Wender and Rothkegel's data, just like those of Van Oeffelen and Vos, suggest that the ability for subitizing gradually decreases with increasing set sizes, Piazza, Fumarola, Chinello, and Melcher (2011) argue that subitizing is a discrete process that is closely related to the process of **object individuation**. In this context, individuation refers to the process by which individual objects in a scene are isolated, identified, and stored in working memory. As we discussed in Chapter 14, visual working memory capacity is estimated at about four objects (Cowan, 2000). Both the results from Piazza et al. (2011) and those of Wender and Rothkegel (2000) point to limitations in our visual perception as an underlying explanation for the subtraction process.

20.3.2.4 The Biological Basis of Subitizing

Possible neurophysiological correlates of this limitation in object individuation have been reported by both Ester, Drew, Klee, Vogel, and Awh (2012) and Nieder and Miller (2004). Ester et al. instructed participants to report the number of dots that were presented in one visual half-field while their EEGs were recorded. The investigators found that for one to four dots, the amplitude of the **N2pc** ERP component increased with the number of dots that were presented, however, this amplitude did not increase any further for larger numbers of dots (fig 20.7).

Nieder and Miller found similar results based on single-cell recordings in primates. Neuronal activity was recorded in parietal and frontal areas of rhesus monkeys that were trained to memorise sets of dots. Neurons in the intraparietal sulcus responded selectively to the number of dots that had been presented. One neuron was found to be selective for the number of dots that were actually presented: the more dots presented, the less it fired, up to a number of four dots; from that number the firing frequency did not decrease any further. A second neuron in the intraparietal sulcus was selectively sensitive to numeric information when the monkey had to

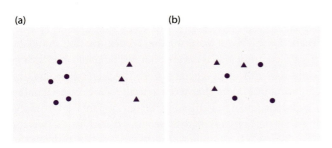

Figure 20.6 Examples of decomposable (a) and non-decomposable (b) patterns as used in a study on subitizing. (source: Wender and Rothkegel, 2000)

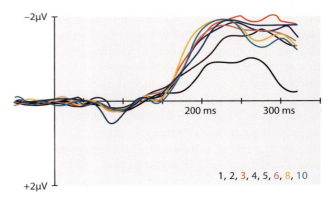

Figure 20.7 The relationship between numbers of dots presented in one visual half-field and the amplitude of the N2pc component that was evoked by these dots. After four elements, the amplitude of this component did not increase any further. (source: Ester et al., 2012)

retain the dots. Here it was found that the activity of this neuron actually increased as a function of the number of dots, but again a ceiling was reached at the presentation of four dots: from five dots onwards the firing frequency of this neuron did not increase any further.

These results suggest that there is a strong relationship between our visual working memory capacity and our ability to subitize. Indeed, Piazza et al. (2011) found a relationship between the ability to subitize and working memory capacity. In addition, it was also found that the ability to subitize was constrained by competing visual attention tasks that limit effective use of working memory (Anobile, Turi, Cicchini, & Burr, 2012).

20.3.3 COUNTING

Counting is an essential basic cognitive function that we learn at a very early age. The essence of counting is that we determine the number of item present in a set. Mathematically, this is known as determining the **cardinality** of the set. The essence of counting is that we run through all the items and give each subsequent item a higher rank number. However, if we consider the counting process in more detail, we encounter several specific adverse conditions that limit our ability to successfully carry out a counting task. The first is that we must keep track of which elements we have already counted and which ones we still have to. In the case of counting a collection of fixed elements, this is generally not a problem, but when the elements are randomly distributed, such as the stars in the night sky, it is much more difficult to keep track of which elements we have already seen and which we have not yet seen. It is even more problematic when the elements themselves move, as in the case of counting a herd of sheep or cows. In the latter case, the counting process places a greater demand on visual working memory than in the former.

Apart from keeping track of which elements have already been processed, we also have to keep track of the rank number: every time we have processed one element, we have to increase the rank number by one unit. This implies that we have to keep a representation of this rank number activated in working memory and that this representation has to be incremented by one unit after each element. Distraction can cause this representation to be lost from working memory, resulting in the fact that we 'lost count'.

20.3.3.1 Strategies

Depending on the nature of the set, we can use different strategies to assess how many items it contains. For example, if the elements are arranged in groups of smaller elements, we can count much faster by counting the groups and after each group increasing the rank-order counter with the number of elements in each group. This strategy is particularly useful when the number of

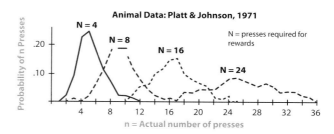

Figure 20.8 The relationship between the required number of times animals had to press a button to earn a reward and the actual number of responses they gave. The results suggest a probabilistic awareness of numbers in animals. (source: Whalen et al., 1999)

elements in each group can be subdivided. When the elements are arranged in a regular grid, we can simply count the number of rows and the number of columns in the grid and multiply them.

20.3.3.2 Counting Out Loud

It has long been assumed that counting involves either vocal or subvocal articulation. Landauer (1962) has shown, however, that the speed of counting does not depend on the way in which it is done; that is, counting out loud is as fast as counting subvocally. Whalen, Gallistel, and Gelman (1999) argue that counting can proceed not only in the aforementioned vocal and subvocal ways, but also in non-verbal ways. They tested this assumption by requiring participants to rapidly press a button a predetermined number of times. Due to time constraints, participants were unable to verbally count the exact number of button presses.

Earlier studies had already shown that under such conditions animals are able to produce the approximate number of button presses (Platt & Johnson, 1971) (see fig 20.8). Whalen et al. (1999) found that when humans had to count in this way, they were oftentimes reasonably accurate, and that the deviations shown by human participants corresponded with those shown by animals. When human participants had to count flashes, which were presented at speeds too high to allow an explicit verbal counting strategy, their answer was probabilistic rather than exact. From these results we can deduce that when we have to count at speeds that are too high to use a verbal counting strategy, we can fall back on a mental size representation that is approximately proportional to the correct quantities. Recently, Anobile, Arrighi, Castaldi, and Burr (2021) have argued that this type of approximate number representation involves sensory and motor processes.

20.3.4 APPROXIMATION

There are many situations in which we are hardly able to count. For example, if we want to know how many people attended a free music festival, or how many penguins make

Figure 20.9 How many penguins are there in this picture? (source: The Goldilock Project)

up a colony in Antarctica (see fig 20.9), we will have to try to approximate this number. In other words, we need to estimate the number of elements in the collection. To make estimates, we can use different strategies, depending on the situation. Important here is whether the units whose number we want to determine are structured or unstructured. For example, if we want to estimate how many students attend a lecture, we can count for one row in the auditorium how many people are sitting there and multiply this number by the number of rows. The problem with this approach, of course, is that the row we chose may not be representative of the auditorium's occupancy rate, which can lead to a significant estimation error.

Another estimation method involved the use of a known reference object. For example, if we want to determine how long a standard sheet of A4 writing paper is, we can compare its length with an object of which we know the length, for example a ruler, and give a reasonable estimate based on this (Siegel, Goldsmith, & Madson, 1982).

20.3.5 THE SNARC EFFECT

A particularly remarkable side effect of numerosity was first reported by Dehaene, Bossini, and Giraux (1993). These authors instructed participants to decide whether a given number was even or odd. More specifically, participants had to decide as quickly as possible by pressing a button with their left or right hand (e.g., even is left and odd is right). What Dehaene et al. noticed was that for the smallest numbers used in the experiment, participants were relatively fast with their left hand, whereas for the largest numbers used, they were relatively fast with their right hand. This effect, labelled by Dehaene et al. as the **spatial-numerical association of response codes (SNARC)**, implies that we associate relatively small numbers with the left and relatively large numbers with the right. What is remarkable about this effect is that it is relative: for example, when using numbers from the sequence 1–12, the number 12 was associated with the right hand, whereas when using the sequence 12–23, 12 was more likely to be associated with the left.

20.3.6 NUMBER REPRESENTATION IN WORKING MEMORY: THE MENTAL NUMBER LINE

How can we explain this effect? A plausible hypothesis is that we represent numbers on an imaginary line from left to right (Schwarz & Keus, 2004). There is indeed some evidence for this idea. For example, based on a symbolic cueing experiment, Ranzini, Dehaene, Piazza, and Hubbard (2009) reported that attention can be directed to the left by relatively small numbers and to the right by relatively large numbers.

A similar result was obtained by Cattaneo, Silvanto, Battelli, and Pascual-Leone (2009). They investigated to what extent numbers were able to prime activation in visual cortex. For this purpose, the authors took advantage of the phenomenon of **phosphene perception**. Phosphene perception is the sensation of perceiving a visual flash of light that results from pressure on the eyeball or from direct stimulation of the visual system. In Cattaneo et al.'s study, phosphenes were evoked using TMS. The intensity of the TMS pulse was set such that phosphenes were on average perceived on 50% of all the trials. Prior to the presentation of the TMS pulse, participants were primed with a number. When the left visual cortex was stimulated with the TMS pulse, the following results were found. Priming with a relatively small number resulted in a decrease of the proportion of phosphenes reported by the participants, while priming with a relatively large number resulted in an increase of the proportion of phosphenes reported (see fig 20.10). When the right visual cortex was stimulated, exactly the opposite result was found: an increase in the proportion of phosphenes due to priming with a small number and a decrease in the proportion of phosphenes due to priming with a large number. Note that the left visual cortex processes information from our right visual field and vice versa. These results are therefore also consistent with the **mental number line hypothesis**. Small numbers stimulate the sensitivity of the visual cortex to information in our left visual field and large numbers to information presented in the right.

Not all results can be explained by assuming the existence of a simple mental number line, however. For example, Santens and Gevers (2008) instructed participants to judge whether a given number deviated to a greater or lesser extent from the target number 5. The numbers 1, 4, 6, and 9 were used for this purpose, where 1 and 9 represent the numbers with a large deviation and 4 and 6 represent those with a small deviation from the target number.

The main result of this study was that the small deviation was processed more quickly by the left hand (regardless of whether a 4 or a 6 was presented) while the large deviation was processed more quickly by the right hand (also, regardless of whether it involved a 1 or a 9). These results suggest that it is the task instructions ('large' or 'small' deviation) that are associated with the specific location rather than the relative size of the digit itself.

This idea is consistent with the **mental white board hypothesis** of Abrahamse, van Dijck, and Fias (2017). This hypothesis states that we order mental representations in working memory in a serial manner. The way this ordering takes place can be compared to the way we write information on a blackboard: the first items are placed on the left and the last items on the right. According to this hypothesis, it is therefore not so much the numerical size that determines whether we make a left or right association, but rather the order in which we remember task-relevant stimuli.

20.3.7 ARITHMETIC

20.3.7.1 Simple Mental Arithmetic

Research concerning the mental processes involved in arithmetic skills dates back to the early 1970s (Groen & Parkman, 1972). Groen and Parkman were interested in the involvement of memory processes in simple addition tasks in children. They reported that, based on the time required to complete a simple addition of two single digit numbers, children start by taking the larger of the two digits and then adding the smaller digit step by step. For example, when adding the digits 3 and 5, Groen and Parkman argued that children started at 5 and added 3 step by step, each time updating the result of the addition (4, 5, 6) in memory. Green and Parkman came to this conclusion because the average time taken to find the solution depended on the smaller of the two operands to be processed (see fig 20.11).

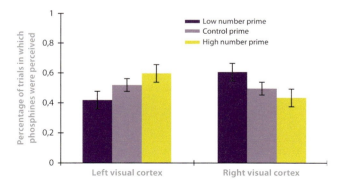

Figure 20.10 TMS-evidence for the mental number line. Priming with a relatively small number made the right primary cortex relatively sensitive to phosphene perception, whereas priming with a relatively large number had a similar effect on the left visual cortex. (source: Cattaneo et al., 2009)

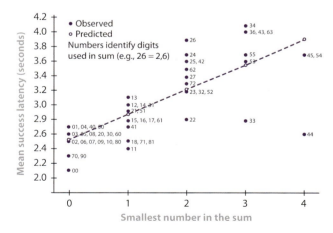

Figure 20.11 The average time needed by children needed to solve simple addition problems as a function of the value of the smaller of the two operands used in the addition. The predicted times are represented by an open circle. The processing times for tie problems deviate significantly from the predicted result. (source: Groen and Parkman, 1972)

Although the conclusion that children solve simple addition problems this way appears plausible, we should be careful about generalising these results. As such, Siegler (1987) points out that the use of average solution times entails the risk of hiding individual differences in solution strategies. When he interviewed children about the strategy they had used, it turned out that they reported using as many as five different strategies.

An additional problem is that it is very difficult to extrapolate the data obtained in children to adults. Although Groen and Parkman (1972) found similar results among adults, they were much faster at solving arithmetic problems than one might expect on the basis of a counting strategy. For this reason, we might safely assume that, as adults, we no longer use counting strategies to solve arithmetic problems, but instead rely on long-term memory to retrieve arithmetic facts. Groen and Parkman thus hypothesised that the time taken by adults to solve arithmetic problems does not so much reflect a counting process but more so the time taken to retrieve arithmetic facts from memory.

20.3.7.2 The Problem Size Effect

The **problem size effect** is a fundamental finding in many mental arithmetic studies. This effect relates to the fact that the time required to solve a single-digit addition or multiplication problem increases with the size of the operands (Butterworth, Zorzi, Girelli, & Jonckheere, 2001; Stoianov, Zorzi, & Umiltà, 2003). For example, solving 8×9 may take 200 ms longer than solving 2×3. A notable exception to this rule involves the so-called tie problems, such as 4×4 or $8 + 8$. For these types of tasks, there is hardly any problem size effect. Models that attempt to explain the results for tie problems are all based on the idea that, as adults, we have stored arithmetic facts such as $2 \times 2 = 4$ in an internal lexicon. The problem size effects – and their absence in tie problems – may thus reflect the efficiency with which such facts can be retrieved from the lexicon. As such, the problem size effect may be similar to the word frequency effects in lexical access (see Chapter 17).

20.3.7.3 The Role of Working Memory

Ashcraft and Battaglia (1978) aimed to explain the problem size effect in adults by suggesting that it reflects search processes in working memory. According to these authors, arithmetic facts are stored in tabular form in memory. The solution time would then be obtained by looking up the corresponding row in the table for the first operand and then the corresponding column for the second operand. Since the search for the correct row and column would be done incrementally, the total time to find a solution to additions would increase with the size of the operands.

Although this explanation is in good agreement with data from Ashcraft and Battaglia (1978), it is very ad hoc and, moreover, biologically implausible. A more plausible explanation is that arithmetic tasks are represented in

memory in the form of an associative network. Specifically for simple mental arithmetic, it is a reasonable assumtion that as we gain experience in arithmetic, we form various associations with different arithmetic tasks. Correct solutions are remembered, but the mistakes we make can also be retained in memory and become a cause of interference. When we have to solve a math problem, it is thus possible that the task will not only activate the correct solution in memory but also any incorrect solutions, and it will be the competition between these solutions that determines how quickly a solution can be found. Now the final assumption is that larger numbers are associated with more arithmetic problems, and thus also with a relatively higher percentage of incorrect solutions. For larger numbers, therefore, the interference that can be expected from these incorrect solutions is also considerably larger than that which we expect for small numbers, making it plausible that for larger outcomes it takes longer to activate the correct representation in working memory.

20.3.7.4 The COMP Model

Butterworth, Zorzi, Girelli, and Jonckheere (2001) present a cognitive model for simple additions. Their COMP model is based on the hypothesis that children continuously store new arithmetic facts in memory while learning; facts that are based on the max + min strategy originally described by Groen and Parkman (1972). According to this model, solving arithmetic problems should involve a distinct number of stages (see fig 20.12). The first stage involves

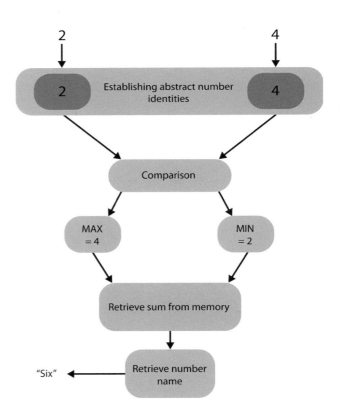

Figure 20.12 Schematic overview of the COMP model for simple addition. (source: Butterworth et al., 2001)

identifying the numbers; then these numbers are compared to determine which one is the larger (max) and the smaller (min) number respectively. Based on this information, the result is then extracted from memory as an arithmetic fact, which is converted into a verbal code that can be reported.

Butterworth et al. (2001) used reaction times to test some specific aspects of this model. They were particularly interested in the problem size effect. Groen and Parkman (1972) had tried to explain this effect as a consequence of increasing the smaller of the two operands. After all, adding 8 + 4 requires four counting steps, whereas adding 8 + 5 requires one additional counting step. An important assumption of the COMP model, however, is that each stage in the model contributes to the total reaction time.

Butterworth et al. used three different tasks to find evidence for this hypothesis. The first task consisted of simply naming all numbers from 0 to 18; that is, all the possible outcomes of single-digit sums. Thus, using this task, an estimate of the naming time of each number could be obtained. In the second task, participants were shown all possible combinations of the one-digit number pairs and they had to report the larger of the two. Thus, by comparing the naming times on this task with the naming times on the first task, it was possible to estimate the duration of the comparison process, following the logic of the subtraction method (see Box 1.2, Chapter 1). Finally, in the third task, participants were also given pairs of digits, but now they had to add them up and produce the answer. By comparing the reaction time to this task with that to the comparison task, an estimate could be obtained for the duration of the addition process.

Butterworth et al. (2001) found that naming time did not depend on number size; it was mainly influenced by the sound of the initial phoneme. Reaction times in the comparison task were mainly determined by the numeric difference between the two digits, that is, the split. Only for the digit 0 a different result was found. Here the reaction time was almost equal to that in the first task, which implied that participants did not consider the zero. The same applied to tie problems. The data were fitted to the COMP model using a linear regression analysis. This resulted in a good fit, with 71% of the total variance in the data explained. These results were significantly better than the model-fits performed using the models of Groen and Parkman (1972) and of Ashcraft and Battaglia (1978).

20.3.7.5 Complex Mental Arithmetic
The results we have discussed so far mainly concern simple tasks limited to single-digit operands. This type of task, however, constitutes by far the minority of all mental arithmetic tasks that we would typically encounter. In most cases, we are dealing with tasks where at least one of the operands consists of two or more digits. In many cases, such problems can only be solved by breaking the problem down into subproblems. In case of addition, we can find the answer by first adding the units, then the tens, then the hundreds, and so on. Each digit in this sequence is known as a position. If the sum in one of these positions is greater than 10, we only need to denote the unit for this position and add 1 to the next position, a process that is known as carry over. Therefore, arithmetic problems that require carrying over a digit are always solved more slowly than problems that do not require it (DeStefano & LeFevre, 2004). In addition to carrying over, we must also retain the intermediate results of the individual positions in memory. For this reason, working memory is crucially involved in multi-digit mental arithmetic (Hitch, 1978).

Logie, GilHooly, and Wynn (1994) conducted a study in which participants were required to add a series of two-digit numbers and found that the errors rate increased when they were required to perform additional tasks that influenced working memory performance. Performance on the arithmetic task was influenced mainly by a random-letter generation task and to a slightly lesser extent by an articulatory-suppression task. These results were found mainly when the arithmetic problems were presented auditorily; with visual presentation, the effects were still present, but less pronounced.

20.3.8 MENTAL ARITHMETIC: THEORETICAL APPROACHES

In recent decades, several theoretical frameworks have been developed to explain how numerical information can be represented mentally. These models, which will be briefly introduced next, differ mainly in terms of the internal code that is assumed to represent the numerical information and its meaning.

20.3.8.1 The Abstract Code Model
McCloskey (1992) assumes that numeric input is translated into a single abstract code. This code is assumed to represent the semantic aspects of the input, in terms of size information, and it is used in calculations. When, according to McCloskey, the calculation is complete, the abstract code is converted back into an appropriate output code, which depends on the output modality used (written or verbal reporting). One implication of this model is that the different processing stages (encoding, computation, and response generation) are independent of each other, in the sense that code used in one of these stages does not affect code used in a subsequent stage.

20.3.8.2 The Triple Code Model
Dehaene (1992) proposed a triple-code model in which the code used to process the numerical information depends on the nature of the task. According to Dehaene, access to the arithmetic facts involves accessing an auditory-verbal code. Other operations, such as comparing numbers, would

involve a size code or visual code. The latter code would be used, for example, when determining whether a number is even or odd. In other words, specific tasks each have their own specific code.

20.3.8.3 The Encoding Complex Model

Campbell and Clark (1992) suggest that different internal codes may all become active up to a certain level, depending on the format in which the information is presented and what is to be done with it. A number word, for example, 'four', would strongly activate verbal codes, whereas actual numbers, such as '6', would rather activate the visual codes and the arithmetic processes. Presenting arithmetic problems in word form would results in a stronger activation of the verbal codes compared to representing the problem as numbers. This interaction between input format, tasks, and internal processes suggests that computational processes use a variety of different codes and that their activation depends on the specific context and task requirements (DeStefano & LeFevre, 2004).

Several empirical studies have provided evidence for the idea that we use different codes to solve arithmetic problems (Campbell, 1994; LeFevre, Lei, Smith-Chanti, & Mullins, 2001; Noël, Fias, & Brysbaert, 1997). These results render it unlikely that there is a single type of code: it is more likely that the specific code that is activated depends on task requirement. Evidence for this idea was found by Lee and Kang (2002). They had participants solve simple subtraction and multiplication problems under dual-task conditions. Performance on the multiplication task was mainly affected by a secondary task that invoked phonological codes, whereas performance on the subtraction problems was mainly affected by a visuospatial task (see fig 20.13).

Fürst and Hitch (2000) found that short presentation times influenced the activation of a phonological representation. When arithmetic problems were presented briefly, this resulted in the problem being phonologically encoded. In other words, participants maintained a mental representation by repeating the task subvocally. Consequently, performance on the arithmetic task was strongly influenced by a secondary working memory task that involved phonological processes. When the task remained visible during the entire trial, the interference was much smaller. These latter results are clearly inconsistent with arithmetic models that assume a single code that remains active during the mental arithmetic task.

20.3.8.4 Neural Basis for Numeracy

Dehaene and Cohen (1995) have proposed that our arithmetic skills are the result of recycling mental functions that evolved from a rudimentary ability to estimate numbers and quantities (see also: Dehaene, Molko, Cohen, & Wilson, 2004). If this hypothesis is correct, then there should be some degree of overlap between the original estimation skills and the more recently developed mental arithmetic skills.

To test this hypothesis Prado, Mutreja, et al. (2011) used fMRI while participants solved a wide range of arithmetic problems (see fig 20.14). They wondered whether an area in the intraparietal sulcus, which is known to be involved in comparison, would also be activated in a numerical task. In particular, they were interested in whether this area would be activated more strongly by an arithmetic task than by a task that required the retrieval of numerical facts from memory (in this particular case, the retrieval of the product of two one-digit number multiplications).

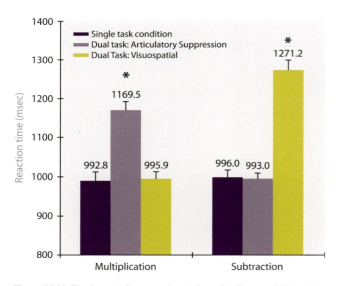

Figure 20.13 The impact of a secondary task on the time needed to solve multiplication and subtraction problems. Compared to a single-task condition, multiplications were mainly negatively affected by an articulatory-suppression task, while subtractions were mainly negatively affected by a visuospatial task. (source: Lee and Kang, 2002)

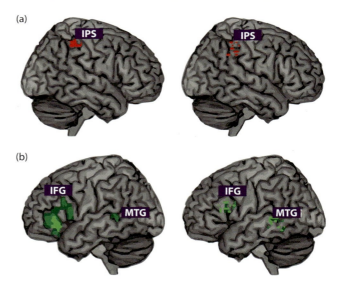

Figure 20.14 Results of an fMRI study on mental arithmetic. (a) Activation in the intraparietal sulcus (IPS) was mainly associated with performing subtracting. (b) Activation in two brain regions, the inferior frontal gyrus (IFG) and the middle temporal gyrus (MTG) was mainly associated with multiplication. (source: Prado, Mutreja et al., 2011)

Indeed, the intraparietal sulcus was more strongly activated by a subtraction task (a task that essentially consists of comparing the size of numbers). The multiplication task, on the other hand, activated areas involved in verbal processing.

The conclusion that the neural mechanisms used in computational processes are shared with other cognitive processes is also supported by a study of Gruber, Indefrey, Steinmetz, and Kleinschmidt (2001). These authors found a strong overlap between the brain areas activated by a mental arithmetic task on the one hand and by a variety of other cognitive tasks on the other. The bilateral prefrontal, premotor and parietal areas were activated by these tasks. In addition to this overlap, however, differences were found in subregions of the parietal areas. Within these areas, it was found that the left dorsal angular gyrus and the medial parietal cortices were activated more strongly by the subtraction task than by a fact retrieval task. Moreover, complex arithmetic tasks were associated with an increase in activation in the left inferior frontal areas. The latter areas are also known to be involved in working memory functions, which implies that activation in these areas is related to the working memory functions described earlier.

As already mentioned, it is currently still subject to debate how numerical information is represented. Some researchers assume that this information is mainly represented in a linguistic code, while others assume that this representation is visuospatial. Zago et al. (2001) found a network of brain areas that were involved in arithmetic activities. They used a method similar to that of Gruber et al. (2001) in that they also compared brain activity evoked by a fact retrieval task and an arithmetic task. In this study, however, both tasks involved multiplications. In the fact retrieval task, participants had to recall the answers to simple multiplications, such as 2×4, while in the arithmetic task, they had to find the answer to multiplications such as 32×24. This study found that a network of frontal and parietal brain regions was involved in this calculation. Again, this study suggested that this activity reflects working memory involvement. In addition, activation of the bilateral inferior temporal gyri was found, which was associated with a visuospatial solution strategy.

In contrast, Baldo and Dronkers (2007) found evidence for the hypothesis that numerical information is represented in a linguistic code, based on a patient study. A group of 68 patients with a lesion in their left hemisphere was tested for language and numeracy skills and these scores were correlated with the extent of the lesion. The results showed some similarity between language and numeracy skills, although a subset of patients showed a dissociation between these tasks. This showed that arithmetic skills were primarily associated with an area in the left inferior

parietal lobule. Brain areas that were involved in both language comprehension and arithmetic skills were found mainly in the inferior frontal gyrus.

20.3.9 DYSCALCULIA

What can we learn about our numeracy skills from brain-damaged patients? McCloskey (1992) discusses neuropsychological research related to acquired **dyscalculia**, that is, an impairment of our arithmetic ability. Acquired dyscalculia refers to an impairment of our numeracy skills following brain injury (Lewandowsky & Stadelmann, 1908). In addition to acquired dyscalculia, we can also identify developmental dyscalculia, that is, an impaired development of the skills needed to process numerical information (Butterworth, 2008).

Warrington (1982) discusses the case of DRC, a doctor who had difficulties performing simple mental arithmetic tasks after a brain haemorrhage in his left parietal-occipital region. DRC was able to read and write numbers without any difficulties, and he also had no difficulties judging which of two numbers was the larger one. Moreover, he was capable of making estimates and relating numerical information to these estimates. When DRC was asked about his condition, he mentioned that he often knew the approximate answer to arithmetic problems but that he had difficulties finding the exact solution (see fig 20.15). By counting explicitly, however, he could find the correct solution to a given problem. His understanding of arithmetic operations was therefore not impaired and, when asked, he could give reasonable definitions of basic arithmetic operations, such as addition, subtraction, multiplication, and division.

Warrington (1982) interpreted these results as evidence for a dissociation between numeric and arithmetic knowledge. According to Warrington, DRC's difficulties could be explained by the idea that his arithmetic knowledge was impaired, while his numerical knowledge was still intact. In addition, Warrington suggested that there was a distinction between knowledge of arithmetic facts and arithmetic operations, and that it was DRC's knowledge of arithmetic facts that was particularly affected. His difficulties with arithmetic tasks could be explained by the fact that his memory for arithmetic facts, such as the answer to $8 + 4 = 12$, was impaired. As these arithmetic facts were not available to DRC, he had to work out the answer using an elaborate counting process.

Impairments in producing answers to an arithmetic task have also been reported by Benson and Denckla (1969). They reported the case of a 58-year-old man with left hemispheric damage following a cardiovascular accident (CVA). This patient consistently chose the correct answer to simple arithmetic tasks when presented in multiple

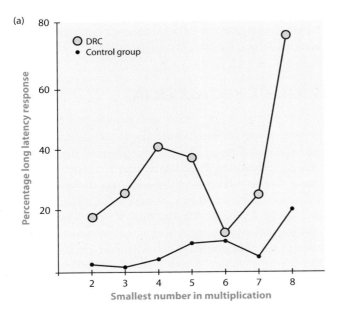

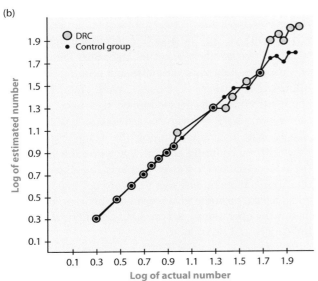

Figure 20.15 Results of a patient with acquired dyscalculia. (a) Patient DRC's percentage of 'late' responses on a multiplication task, compared to those from a control group. (b) The relationship between the estimated number of dots and the actual number for DRC and for a control group. (source: Warrington, 1982)

choice format, implying that both number sense and understanding of arithmetic facts and operations were intact. He was also able to point to the correct number in a list when this number was read to him. However, when asked to name numbers himself, his ability to do so was significantly impaired. For example, in solving the problem '4 + 5' for example, he verbally reported '8', wrote down '5', but chose the correct answer '9' on a multiple-choice test. Also, when was asked to write down numbers that were dictated to him, he made many numerical errors. For example, when asked to write down the number 'two hundred and twenty-one', he wrote down 215. These results imply a strong dissociation between understanding and producing numbers.

Limitations in the syntactic processing of numbers have been reported by Singer and Low (1933). They examined a 44-year-old man with brain damage due to carbon monoxide poisoning. This patient's lexical skills were intact; however, his syntactic processing of numbers was impaired. For one- and two-digit numbers, he was generally correct. For larger numbers, it appeared that his processing of all digits that were unequal to 0 was generally correct, but that he wrote down numbers in a way that was often incorrect by an order of magnitude. For example, he wrote 'two hundred forty-two' as 20042 and 'two thousand five hundred' as 2000500. That this deficiency was specifically related to number production was demonstrated by the fact that the patient was perfectly capable of deciding which of two given numbers was larger.

A final case study that we will discuss concerns two Portuguese patients with a selective deficiency to process the symbols representing operators (e.g., +, -, ×, /) (Ferro & Silveira Botelho, 1980). When these patients were asked to complete written arithmetic tasks, they often used the wrong operation correctly. For example, when presented with the task 721 + 36, they answered with the (correct) multiplication, that is, 25,956. The fact that the incorrect operation was performed correctly suggests that these patients had an intact number sense, could produce these numbers correctly, understood the arithmetic procedures, and could perform them correctly. Interestingly, this deficiency was limited to the written representation of the operators. When the arithmetic tasks were presented verbally, the patients had no difficulties applying the correct operators.

Landerl, Bevan, and Butterworth (2004) discuss developmental dyscalculia. In contrast to the specific impairments found in acquired dyscalculia, developmental dyscalculia is more likely to be a general impairment in a child's numeracy. Traditional definitions, such as those found in the Diagnostic and Statistical Manual of Mental Disorders (DSM), state that a child should show a substantially lower performance on a standardised test, relative to the level that would be expected at the age of the child in question. Despite this global definition, there are some specific characteristics of dyscalculia in children. For example, most children with dyscalculia have difficulties with learning and remembering arithmetic facts. In addition, they are often characterised by difficulties in carrying out arithmetic procedures, insufficiently developed problem-solving strategies, long execution times, and high error rates (Geary, 1993). In contrast to acquired dyscalculia, developmental dyscalculia does not appear to involve a clear dissociation between factual and procedural knowledge (Russell & Ginsburg, 1984).

Geary and Hoard (2001) have suggested that difficulties with semantic memory may underlie development-related dyscalculia and possibly also the comorbid reading problems that are often found in dyscalculic children. This suggestion is based on the finding that children with dyscalculia often have difficulties learning and remembering arithmetic facts. In such cases, however, we would also expect all dyslexic children to have arithmetic problems and vice versa. There is little evidence for this though. Also working memory impairments are associated with developmental dyscalculia (Geary, 1993). These impairments would limit not only the ability to learn arithmetic facts but also the ability to execute complex arithmetic procedures. More specifically, this limitation is assumed to be related to the phonological loop component of working memory (see Chapter 14). Although the evidence for this theory is not yet unequivocal, it has been found that dyscalculic children's performance is generally impaired on tasks that involve phonological working memory and that their capacity for numeric information is smaller than that of control children.

These explanations assume deficits in general cognitive mechanisms. Another explanation is that dyscalculia arises from a specific deficit in those neural mechanisms that are specialised in numeric processing. Indeed, more recent evidence suggests that our proficiency with numbers is dissociable from other cognitive functions, such as language proficiency (Cohen, Dehaene, Chochon, Lehericy, & Naccache, 2000), non-numerical semantic memory (Cappelletti, Butterworth, & Kopelman, 2001), or working memory (Butterworth, Cipolotti, & Warrington, 1996). According to this idea, our arithmetic ability arises from an innate ability to process numerical information and it is precisely these functions that are impaired in dyscalculia. If this hypothesis is correct, we would expect children with dyscalculia to be characterised by impairments on a range of skills, all of which involve our basic ability to deal with quantitative information. Children should not only have difficulties with complex numeric skills but also with basic tasks such as subitizing, naming numbers, and comparing relative sizes.

There is some evidence for this hypothesis: Koontz and Berch (1996) found, for example, that children with dyscalculia determined the cardinality of a set by counting instead of subitizing, even for very small sets. Kirby and Becker (1988) found that children with dyscalculia were slower in naming numbers, compared to neurotypical controls. Geary, Hoard, and Hamson (1999) found small differences between dyscalculia and controls in naming and writing numbers and making numerical comparisons. Finally, Geary, Bow-Thomas, and Yao (1992) found that children with dyscalculia were less capable of detecting counting errors compared to control children. They also appear to have a developmental delay in their ability to learn the principle of counting.

Russell and Ginsburg (1984) found, however, that the difficulties that children with dyscalculia experience

are specifically related to working memory. They tested children on informal numerical concepts, for example, by requiring them to indicate which of two numbers is greater or which of two numbers is closest to a reference value. Using this approach, they found that, despite a deficit in mathematical numerical skills, children with dyscalculia scored relatively normally on these informal skill tests.

Finally, Landerl et al. (2004) found that children with dyscalculia had specific difficulties with numerical skills. In this study, eight- and nine-year-old children with dyscalculia were tested on a range of numerical skills as well as a number of different intelligence and working memory abilities. It was only on the numerical ability tests that these children scored lower than those in a control group (fig 20.16).

20.4 CATEGORICAL REPRESENTATION

In a sense, the numerical skills just discussed represent our capacity to generalise information. For example, counting enables us to summarise the characteristics of large sets of items into one generalising unit: a number. This ability to abstract and summarise individual items is a cognitive skill that makes it possible to organise our environment in an orderly fashion. In addition to summarising our environment in quantitative units, we are also able to summarise qualitative properties of individual objects. The latter process is known as categorisation or **conceptualisation**.

When we have to find our bicycle in a crowded city, we will notice that we can recognise it without any effort, while all other bicycles appear to be highly similar. This example illustrates the interaction between our ability to detect unique features of an object while also being able to generalise very easily. In their classic work 'A study of

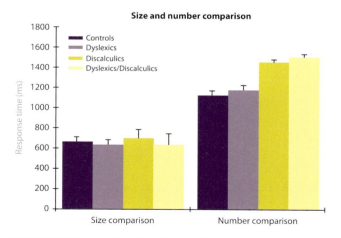

Figure 20.16 Reaction times found in four different groups of eight- and nine-year-old children engaged in a size and number comparison task. Children with dyscalculia are specifically slower on the latter task. (source: Landerl et al., 2004)

thinking', Bruner et al. (1956) already marvelled at this capacity for object **individuation**. At the same time, they also emphasised the importance of **categorisation**, that is, the process by which we can regard copies of a set of stimuli as equivalent.

In a way, the processes of individuation and categorisation appear to be completely opposite, as the former is concerned with the specific and the latter with the generic. Yet there is a high degree of coherence between these processes (Knowlton & Squire, 1993). This is also apparent, for example, when listening to music. Here we are capable of determining to which genre (e.g., heavy metal, hip-hop, classical, jazz, techno, or K-pop) a song belongs, while we are also capable of picking out the unique features, such as an incredible guitar solo or a beautiful vocal line, and even possibly to anticipate them. The central question that will be addressed in the second part of this chapter is how we can form more complex concepts based on the perception of individual stimuli and how we can use concepts in our thought processes.

20.4.1 THE NATURE OF CONCEPTS

In Chapter 13, we introduced to the idea that concepts are involved in the organisation of knowledge in semantic long-term memory. Most theories of semantic memory assume that knowledge is somehow represented as a network of concepts. Collins and Quillian (1969) have argued that semantic memory is organised in hierarchical semantic networks in which the main concepts, such as 'animal', 'bird', and 'canary' are presented as nodes (see fig 20.17). Each of these nodes represents specific properties associated with a concept. A property such as 'can fly' is associated with the concept 'bird'. The reason that this characteristic is linked to the concept bird follows from the fact that being able to fly is a typical characteristic of birds, whereas the exceptions

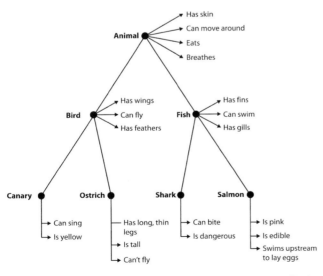

Figure 20.17 The organisation of concepts in semantic memory according to Collins and Quillian (1969).

are rather stored in representations of the specific birds that cannot fly, such as penguins.

According to Collins and Quillian (1969) we should be able to very quickly decide whether a canary is yellow, because the information about the specific type of the concept ('canary') and the property ('is yellow') are stored at the same level. Deciding whether the sentence 'A canary can fly' is correct should take longer, according to Collins and Quillian, because the concept and the property are stored at different levels in the hierarchy. Indeed, it was found that when we have to answer this type of questions, it takes longer as the distance between the concept and the properties in the hierarchy increases (see also Chapter 13).

The Collins and Quillian (1969) model is also capable of explaining how we can answer questions about topics that we have no explicit knowledge about, but where we can deduce the answer from our common knowledge stored in semantic memory. For example, we can deduce an answer to the question of whether Albert Einstein had an elbow from the fact that we know that Einstein was a human being and that humans normally have elbows. Collins and Quillian's model is also characterised, however, by features that cannot be easily explained. For example, the model would predict that verifying the sentence 'A canary has skin' will take longer than verifying the sentence 'A canary can fly', because the property 'has skin' is represented at a higher level in the hierarchy than the property 'can fly'. The problem, however, is that not only the hierarchical distance increases but also the familiarity of the question. The likelihood that you have ever had to decide whether a canary has a skin is very small. Probably much smaller than the chance that you have had to decide whether a canary can fly. When controlling for these familiarity effects, the hierarchical organisation does not appear to have any effect on reaction times (Conrad, 1972).

Another problem is the following: suppose you have to judge the following two statements: 'A canary is a bird' and 'A penguin is a bird'. According to Collins and Quillian, both judgements should take the same amount of time, because in both cases the concepts that are to be compared are represented at the same levels in the hierarchy. In reality, however, it takes us much longer to verify whether a penguin is a bird than to do so for a canary (fig 20.18). Why is this? One important reason is that individual members of a category vary enormously in the degree to which they are typical of the category, and this typicality affects decision times: we are much faster at processing representative members of a category (in our example, 'canaries') than non-representative members ('penguins'). This type of typicality effect is found for many natural categories (Rips, Shoben, & Smith, 1973). Rosch and Mervis (1975), for example, found that oranges, apples, bananas, and peaches were considered more typical of the concept 'fruit' than, say, olives, tomatoes, coconuts, or dates.

(a)

(b)

Figure 20.18 Examples of a typical (a) and an atypical (b) bird.

Dale et al. (2007) found that competition is also involved in the classification of atypical exemplars. They recorded the trajectory of their participants' response hand to a target button while they were classifying typical and atypical exemplars of the categories 'mammal' and 'fish'. Participants had to do so by moving their hand to one of the two buttons that were associated with the respective

category. Dale et al. found that this trajectory is relatively straight while classifying typical exemplars, but in cases of the classification of atypical exemplars it is characterised by a deviation towards the button that represented the competing category.

Typical members of a category tend to contain more of the characteristics that are associated with a category than less typical members of the category. Rosch (1973) investigated this phenomenon by producing a number of sentences containing the word 'bird', such as 'Birds eat worms', 'I heard a bird sing', 'I saw a bird fly over the house', and 'The bird perched on a twig'. Now try to replace the word bird in each of these sentences with 'robin', 'eagle', 'ostrich', and 'penguin'. 'Robin' fits each of the sample sentences, but the other bird species do not fit as well. This implies that penguins and ostriches are less typical birds than eagles, while an eagle in itself is less typical than a robin (fig 20.18).

The implication of these findings is that the concepts that we use are not rigidly defined, but that the definition of a category is relatively vague. Convincing evidence for this was provided by McCloskey and Glucksberg (1978). They gave participants cunning questions, such as 'Is a brain haemorrhage a disease?' or 'Is a pumpkin a type of fruit?' Sixteen of the 30 participants answered that a cerebral haemorrhage is indeed a disease, while the remaining participants answered that it was not. Another 16 participants believed that a pumpkin is a fruit, while the remaining participants believed it was not. This result implies that there are considerable individual differences in the representation of concepts. The result was even more surprising when McCloskey and Glucksberg tested the same participants again a month later. It turned out that 11 participants had changed their opinion of the status of cerebral haemorrhage as a disease and that eight participants had changed their opinion of the status of a pumpkin as a member of the fruit category!

Because of this vagueness in the boundaries between categories, Barsalou (1987) has argued that the variations in representativeness of the individual members of a category can be best described as a graded structure, that is, a structure in which individual members can be ordered on a continuum from highly representative members to highly unrepresentative non-members. Just as members of a category can vary in representativeness, so can non-members of a category: For example, a chair is a clearer example of a non-member of the category 'birds' than a butterfly is!

Most of the categories we encounter in everyday life are characterised by such a graded structure. In case of the Rosch and Mervis's (1975) study, we have already identified that the typicality varied for members of the concept 'fruit', but we can also find such a gradient for the category furniture, for example. Even for concepts where we would not expect such a gradient, for example for formal categories such as 'even numbers' or 'squares', it has been found that some members are considered more representative than others (Armstrong, Gleitman, & Gleitman, 1983). Barsalou (1983) found these kinds of gradients even in categories that we are barely aware of, such as 'ways to escape being killed by the mafia' or 'things that can fall on our heads'. This latter type, known as an **ad hoc category**, is one that is not really clearly represented in semantic memory, but that we can generate on the spot to represent a newly determined goal.

Barsalou (1987) has stated that the gradient is an important concept that can explain a wide range of category-related effects. Not only are typical members of a category generally identified more quickly than non-typical members (McCloskey & Glucksberg, 1979), the gradient can also predict which members of a category we are more likely to mention. When we are requested to spontaneously name members of a given category, the typical members will be named significantly more often than the atypical members. Typicality is also very important for learning categories: we generally learn to identify a category much more quickly on the basis of typical than on the basis of atypical members (Mervis & Pani, 1980). We will discuss why this is the case later on in the chapter.

20.4.2 CONCEPTS AND CATEGORIES

In general, concepts and categories can be classified in different ways. A common distinction is that of natural and artefact categories. Natural categories are those that occur in nature, such as birds or trees. Artefact categories, on the other hand, are categories designed by humans for specific purposes or functions. Examples are bicycles, tools, or kitchen utensils. These categories are generally fairly stable in the sense that we typically agree on which members belong to these categories and in the sense that this classification remains fairly stable over time. Concepts, however, are not always stable. Sometimes we generate categories on the spot (Barsalou, 1983; Little, Lewandowsky, & Heit, 2006): we generate these ad hoc categories for a specific purpose, such as the category 'things to write down'. This category is obviously not stable, because its content will differ from person to person and from situation to situation (fig 20.19). After all, when we have to write a speech, the content of this category will be completely different from when we have to make a shopping list(!).

A special type of category is the **nominal type**. This type of category consists of a random assignment of a label to a member that meets one or more specific criteria (Kloos & Sloutsky, 2004). In some cases, the criteria are clear: for example, a 'widow' is a woman whose husband has died, and a quadrilateral is any geometric figure with four

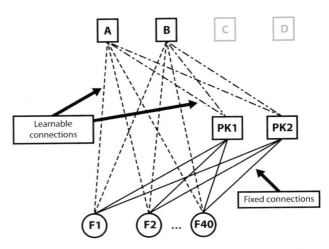

Figure 20.19 A neural network model for the spontaneous generation of categories. (source: Little et al., 2006)

sides. In other cases, however, the properties are much less clear, as in the case of 'lover' or 'irritation'. In the latter cases, it is therefore difficult to determine how meaning can be given to such concepts.

20.4.3 CONCEPT IDENTIFICATION

Now that we have become acquainted with some basic properties of concepts, how concepts may be represented, and how we may subdivide them into categories, we can turn to the next question, namely, how we identify new concepts. To do so, we will first discuss the processes involved in concept identification for well-defined concepts and then for ill-defined concepts.

A well-defined concept can be classified on the basis of unambiguous rules and here the task is to discover the classification rule. In the case of ill-defined concepts, we are faced with situations where a concept can only be partially described by these rules, making the classification much more ambiguous. For ill-defined concepts, the question is therefore how we can combine specific sources of information to classify these concepts. Although in daily life we can classify a wide variety of concepts, from physical stimuli to abstract thoughts, the remainder of this chapter will discuss concept identification mainly in the context of visual stimuli that need to be classified. For this reason, we will often use the word 'stimulus' as a synonym for the term 'concept' in the remainder of this chapter.

20.4.3.1 Associative Learning versus Hypothesis Testing

How do we learn to distinguish between different categories of stimuli? We could do this using an associative process, whereby through repeated exposure to different stimuli we gradually learn to distinguish the essence of the differences between the categories. Pattern recognition could play an important role in this process. On the other hand, we can also assume that we learn to distinguish different categories of stimuli in a more active way by formulating hypotheses about the classification rule and by subsequently testing these hypotheses in practice.

Studies on concept identification typically employ a task involving a stimulus that consists of multiple features that can vary on different dimensions. For example, the stimulus may consist of a number of different geometric shapes (triangles, squares, etc.) in different colours. This stimulus belongs to one of two possible categories and the participants' task is to determine what the classification rule is. For example, the stimulus can be classified according to the number of objects shown, the colour of the objects, or their shape. After a stimulus has been presented, participants have to indicate whether it belongs to category 1 or 2. Then, feedback is presented to indicate whether the classification was correct or not.

20.4.3.2 The Effect of Feedback

During the classification process, feedback on participants performance is important. After all, it is only through feedback that they can determine whether they have classified a stimulus correctly or not. Depending on the exact learning mechanism, however, we may expect different effects from feedback. If classification is based on associative learning, we would expect feedback to be effective only when it is presented immediately after the response. In this case, feedback would act as a reinforcer in a conditioning process. It has been found, however, that delaying the feedback has no effect on the efficiency of the learning process (Bourne, Guy, Dodd, & Justesen, 1965), which implies that concept identification is based on an active hypothesis testing process rather than on an associative learning process.

Further evidence for the idea that concept identification may involve an active hypothesis testing process was obtained by manipulating the nature of the feedback. In case of a **partial feedback** condition, feedback is given only on a subset of the trials. In this case, we should expect that we need more trials to learn a classification rule, regardless of the underlying mechanism. Here, we can distinguish between associative learning and learning based on hypothesis-testing, however, when we focus specifically on the effects of negative feedback. After all, negative feedback implies that we have made an incorrect classification and thus have not yet found the right rule. When we learn associatively, we would expect both positive feedback and negative feedback to be important. The positive feedback would reinforce the associations being formed; the negative feedback would weaken them. In case of hypothesis-based learning, however, we would expect participants to discard positive feedback, since it merely confirms our belief that our hypothesis is correct. Negative feedback, on the other hand, would indicate

that the hypothesis is incorrect and force the formulation of a new one. The process underlying the latter process conforms to the **win-stay, lose-shift principle**, which suggests that we only shift to a different classification rule after negative feedback.

Aiken, Santa, and Ruskin (1972) found that participants who received feedback on only half of all trials took longer to find the correct classification rule compared to participants who received feedback on all trials. More interestingly, however, the number of trials on which negative feedback was given was the same for both groups of participants, implying that it is indeed these trials that are crucial for concept identification (see also: Kalish, Lewandowsky, & Davies, 2005).

A further finding in favour of hypothesis-based learning is that increasing the time interval between two successive trials has a positive effect on learning performance. Wells (1972) reported that extending the interval between two trials from 1 to 7 seconds resulted in a significant increase in the consistency of participant's responses (fig 20.20). This is probably due to the fact that the extra time gained by lengthening the interval allows the participant to process the feedback more efficiently and allows them more time to generate a new hypothesis.

A final finding that argues for a hypothesis-testing process is that finding the right rule is an all-or-nothing process. If we were to learn associatively, we would expect to respond more and more accurately over the course of the experiment. In the case of hypothesis-based learning our error-rates should be roughly constant until we find the right rule. Moreover, we should show near-perfect scores as soon as we do find the rule. Indeed, Bower and Trabasso (1964) found no learning effects until the correct classification rule was found, and near perfect performance after finding the rule.

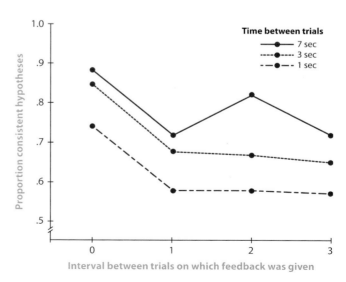

Figure 20.20 The consistency of participants' responses as a function of the time they were given to process feedback. (source: Wells, 1972)

20.4.3.3 The Hypotheses File

The next question is how we formulate hypotheses and test them: do we generate one hypothesis, or do we try to test several hypotheses simultaneously? In case of the latter, which hypotheses are formulated and how do we group our hypotheses together? Gumer and Levine (1971) found that hypotheses related to the same stimulus dimension are often tested together (e.g., category 1 is 'red' or category 1 is 'blue'). More specifically, this implies that participants initially focus on this dimension, without paying specific attention to the question of which attributed corresponds to a specific category. Participants initially put together a limited set of hypotheses, which they then test. If the classification rule that they are looking for is not part of this set of hypotheses, they cannot find the solution, unless they build a new set of hypotheses at some point.

Fink (1972) found evidence suggesting that participants indeed tend to consider several hypotheses simultaneously. He used stimulus material that consisted of four dimensions, which could be manipulated independently of each other. More concretely, each stimulus consisted of a grid of four columns and two rows. The four columns represented four independent stimulus dimensions and the value of each of these dimensions was indicated by a light in either the top or bottom cell of the corresponding column. This arrangement allowed Fink to vary from trial to trial which dimensions were shown. For the dimensions on which no information was shown, no light was lit in the corresponding column.

Participants were divided into three groups. Two groups could request information on specific stimulus dimensions, while the third group received information on all four dimensions at once. One of the two self-selecting groups could request information on as many dimensions as they wanted, while the other group could only request information for a single dimension per trial. When testing multiple hypotheses simultaneously, we would expect the latter group to be at a disadvantage because the limited selection possibilities would force the participants in this group to test only one hypothesis per trial. Indeed, this group needed more trials to find the correct rule than the other two groups, which implies that we are indeed testing multiple hypotheses simultaneously.

We might also expect that if we test several hypotheses at the same time, our reaction times would gradually decrease during the experiment, up to the point where we believe to have found the right rule. From that moment on, reaction time should not decrease any further. Why do we expect this? The idea is that reaction time reflects the number of hypotheses we are considering, so the more hypotheses we have already eliminated, the less we have to consider and the faster the response can be. Once we have found the right rule, there is no more room for a further speed-up. Indeed, it has been found that after the final error, participants generally showed no further decrease in their reaction times, suggesting that at that point the last hypothesis had been considered.

Although the idea of hypothesis testing is consistent with a large body of empirical results collected in the second half of the 20th century, it is still possible that in our everyday lives categorisation is based on other principles. One of the reasons for this is that the concept identification studies that were carried out in the 1960s and 1970s mainly involved **bivariate concepts**, that is, concepts that were characterised by either the presence or absence of a certain feature. From these simple concepts, more complex concepts were derived that consisted of multiple bivariate properties, and the categories that could be formed on the basis of this property were either conjunctive or disjunctive. Conjunctive categories were defined by the fact that objects belonged to a particular category only if they had both properties (e.g., blue circles), whereas disjunctive categories were formed by the fact that objects were allowed to have only one of the two properties (e.g., blue non-circular objects, or non-blue circles). A major problem with this approach is that the categories are highly artificial and, consequently, the underlying categorisation processes studied in these studies had only very limited relevance to categorisation processes that take place in everyday life.

20.5 REPRESENTATION OF ILL-DEFINED CATEGORIES

A further limitation of the studies just discussed is that they always involved **well-defined categories**. In our daily lives, however, such well-defined categories are typically quite rare. Even when certain categories are perfectly defined, we still tend to perceive some exemplars as more representative than others (Armstrong et al., 1983). In other situations, however, we can identify members of a category effortlessly, even when no single criterion is available that can be used unambiguously to do so.

For example, in our daily lives we effortlessly classify humans as 'male' or 'female', but if we think about it, none of the criteria we use for this purpose is perfectly reliable. We will, of course, carry out this classification on the basis of recognising facial features, hair style, clothing style, facial hair, voice, name, and a number of other characteristics. None of these characteristics is all-decisive, however; clothing styles for men and women can be very similar. The same applies to hair length. The other characteristics can also be ambiguous (e.g., androgynous faces) or, in exceptional cases, give false information, such as a woman with a very hairy face or a man with a typical female voice.

Figure 20.21 Example of the ill-defined category 'the Smith Brothers'. Note that there is no single feature that is defining the category. (source: Armstrong et al., 1983)

When there is no single defining feature that we can use for categorisation, we have encountered an **ill-defined category**. As the previous example will show, in such cases, we typically do not categorise on the basis of one criterion, but we will somehow have to weigh several criteria together before deciding to which category a specific stimulus belongs (see fig 20.21). The hypothesis testing mechanism is therefore not well suited to describing the psychological processes involved in precisely this form of categorisation.

20.5.1 TYPICALITY

One of the first studies on the processing of ill-defined categories was conducted by Posner, Goldsmith, and Welton (1967). This study used dot patterns which represented geometric shapes, such as triangles, diamonds, or the letters M and F. Then Posner et al. made variations of each of these basic patterns by randomly displacing each dot. The larger and more random the displacement, the less the resulting stimulus resembled the original basic pattern, or prototype, or in other words, the more distorted the prototype was.

Posner et al. asked participants to rate the extent to which each deformed stimulus differed from the prototype, on the one hand, and from another deformed stimulus, on the other. The main finding reported by Posner et al. was that the participants' subjective ratings showed a linear relationship that depended on the largest distortion. In other words, the more severely the reference object was deformed, the less the participants believed that the object they had to evaluate resembled it and the more they

believed it resembled the original prototype. These results imply that the degree to which an individual stimulus can be assigned to a category depends on the overall match between the prototype of a category and its individual members.

20.5.2 MULTIDIMENSIONAL STIMULI

The stimuli that Posner et al. (1967) used are in fact still one-dimensional: the match between a prototype and the individual members is namely only determined by the degree of distortion of this prototype. However, the underlying principle can also be applied to stimuli with multiple dimensions. In the example of classification based on gender, for example, we will also use a combination of several features, whereby each feature will contribute to our classification judgement to a greater or lesser extent.

When we have to consider information from multiple dimensions, we need to integrate the information that is provided by each of these features (Ashby & Maddox, 2005). This integration process is crucial in a wide range of categorisation tasks. A relatively simple example of multidimensional stimuli that can be used in classification studies is shown in Figure 20.22. Panel (a) displays three examples of stimuli; grid patterns that vary both in spatial frequency and orientation. Panels (b) and (c) then illustrate two different rules that determine to which category a stimulus belongs. The rule in panel (b) is the most straightforward because only spatial frequency determines the distinction between the categories, whereas in panel (c), the categories are determined by a combination of spatial frequency and orientation. The rule shown in panel (b) can be simply translated as: category 1 = 'thick bars' and category 2 = 'thin bars'. Although the rule corresponding to panel (b) is still relatively simple, we can already identify a potential problem here. How should we categorise stimuli that fall exactly on the category boundary? After all, the spatial frequencies and orientations can vary continuously. For panel (c), it is much more difficult to give a clear verbal rule.

Ashby and Maddox (2005) argue that for a categorisation rule to be verbalised it must meet several specific conditions. First, it must be possible to give a semantic label to the relevant properties, such as 'width' in the example in panel (b). Second, we must be able to focus attention on each individual property. In the given example, this is possible because width and orientation are independent properties, but in categorising colours based on saturation, for example, this is much more problematic. After all, saturation can hardly be perceived independently of a colour's hue and/or brightness. Third, we must also be able to verbalise the rule that combines the individual properties of a stimulus. In the case of the previous

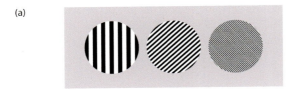

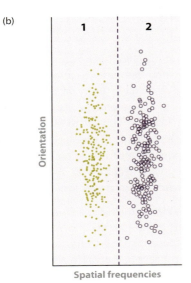

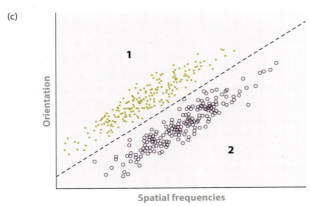

Figure 20.22 Example of multidimensional stimuli. (a) Three grid patterns defined by both the spatial frequency and the orientation of the pattern. (b) These grids can be classified into two categories based on spatial frequency: thick versus thin bars. (c) A category classification based on both spatial frequency and orientation. (source: Ashby and Maddox, 2005)

examples, this is only possible to a limited extent. A somewhat complex rule could be 'Category 1 consists of thick bars with a steep orientation; the rest is category 2'.

Although categorisation processes have been studied in a multitude of patients with a wide range of brain injuries, the data obtained from these studies are rather inconsistent, even within populations of patients with similar conditions. Patient groups that have been studied are characterised by frontal lesions, diseases related to basal ganglia functions (such as Parkinson's or Huntington's disease), or amnesia. The most consistent finding concerns the perseveration behaviour on the **Wisconsin card sorting test** in patients with damage to their prefrontal cortex. In this test, participants are given a stack of cards that they

must sort according to a specific, but unknown, criterion. They have to discover the correct sorting rule based on the feedback provided by the experimenter. When the participant has found the correct rule, the feedback changes and the participant must try again to find the new sorting rule. Many patients persevere in sorting cards according to an old rule that is no longer valid, and the degree to which they do is indicative of damage to the frontal lobes. This finding is consistent with results showing that frontal lobe patients are characterised by category learning impairments (Robinson, Heaton, Lehman, & Stilson, 1980).

Patients diagnosed with Parkinson's disease are also to some extend characterised by difficulties with the processing of categorisation rules (Brown & Marsden, 1988; Downes et al., 1989). Most damage in Parkinson's disease is found in the caudate nucleus, an area that is part of the striatum and characterised by many reciprocal connections with the prefrontal cortex. This finding is consistent with the hypothesis that categorisation is mediated by frontal-striatal circuits (Ashby, Alfonso-Reese, Turken, & Waldron, 1998) as well as with results from neuroimaging studies that have shown that performance of the Wisconsin card sorting test results in activation of the prefrontal cortex and the caudate nucleus (Konishi et al., 1999; Lombardi et al., 1999; Rao et al., 1997; Rogers, Andrews, Grasby, Brooks, & Robbins, 2000; Volz et al., 1997).

20.5.3 THEORETICAL APPROACHES

Most theoretical approaches that attempt to explain categorisation processes are either **exemplar-based** or **prototype-based**. The first theory that aimed to describe rule-based classification processes is known as the classic categorisation theory (Bruner et al., 1956). This theory assumes that each category is represented by a set of sufficient and necessary properties. According to the classic theory, participants are assumed to retrieve a list of relevant properties from memory and to check whether the given stimulus matches these properties.

This theory is able to explain some properties of rule-based categorisation, such as the fact that the stimuli from the preceding bar example can be compared with the property: 'thick bars' or the conjunction of the properties 'thick bars' and 'steep orientation'. There are also some obvious problems with the classic theory, however, such as the fact that it has difficulties explaining the classification of disjunctive categories. To circumvent this problem, there have been several adaptations over the years that have resulted in a more general model capable of rule-based classifications. The latter theories are based on the idea that while performing complex classification processes we activate multiple rules in working memory and then combine these rules in a conjunctive or disjunctive manner.

20.5.3.1 Integration of Information

Although we have already become acquainted with more complex forms of categorisation, note that the categorisation processes described here are still rule-based in the sense that the correct classification can be obtained by combining the right rules in the right way. There is only a real integration of information when a simple (linear) combination of classification rules is no longer possible, as is for example the case while classifying colours based on saturation. Theories that aim to explain the classification of stimuli with these types of non-separable dimensions can be divided into parametric and non-parametric models. **Parametric classification models** assume that the categories have a specific underlying structure or that the category boundaries are characterised by a specific structure. An example of such a structure can be found in Figure 20.22, where in panels (b) and (c) the boundary between the two categories is distinguished by a clear line. **Non-parametric classification models** make no assumptions about the underlying structure.

In this respect, Kloos and Sloutsky (2008) emphasise the importance of statistical density (see fig 20.23). Categories are characterised by a high statistical density when several related properties are all indicative of category membership. A good example of this is the concept of 'dog'. Dogs are characterised by a specific set of shapes, sizes, and colours, have four legs, a tail, and they bark. These characteristics are all indicative of the category. In contrast, low statistical density is examplified by a scientific concept such as 'acceleration'. Both the orbit of a planet around the sun and a cat chasing a mouse are examples of this concept, but the only thing these examples share is the fact that they involve a motion vector.

20.5.3.2 Prototype Models

Prototype models are based on the assumption that we form a mental representation of a prototype of a stimulus on the basis of our experience with individual samples of a specific category (Reed, 1972). These models are generally parametric because they assume a linear boundary

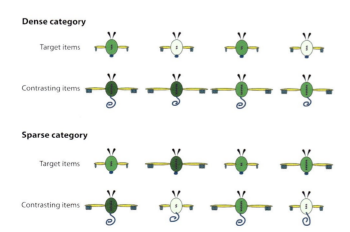

Figure 20.23 Examples of categories with high and low statistical density. (source: Kloos and Sloutsky, 2008)

between categories. According to these models, individual exemplars are compared with the prototypes of different categories and the category that most closely matches the exemplar that is to be classified is the category to which it is assigned. Although the idea of a prototype is intuitively appealing, the theory cannot explain how we are able to identify non-linear category boundaries.

The idea that we store prototypical information about categories was initially supported by the finding that when judging a collection of stimuli that bear some resemblance to each other, we are sensitive to the central tendency in the collection. When participants are required to classify stimuli developed by distorting prototypical patterns as was done in Posner et al.'s (1967) study, it is often found that the prototypes are perceived as very typical, even when participants have never encountered prototypes during a previous training phase (Nosofsky, 1988). Although this **prototype effect** implies that we form category prototypes during the categorisation process, Nosofsky also notes that, despite high typicality ratings, the prototypical stimuli themselves scored relatively low on a subsequent recognition test. According to Nosofsky, the latter finding implies that we do not represent category information in the form of a prototype, but rather in the form of a representative collection of individual exemplars.

20.5.3.3 Exemplar Models

In contrast to prototype models, exemplar models do not assume that we represent a prototype of a stimulus, but that categories are represented as a collection of representative exemplars (Nosofsky, 1986). These models are non-parametric because the individual samples that represent the category are stored in memory, together with a category label. Because a category is represented on the basis of a large number of exemplars, which can individually differ greatly in terms of the representativeness of the category, exemplar models are much more capable of explaining why participants are ultimately able to identify category boundaries, even when they are non-linear.

20.5.3.4 Decision-based Categorisation Models

Ashby and Maddox (1993) assume that categorisation processes are primarily related to decision processes. According to their **decision-based categorisation model**, participants learn to assign specific responses to parts of the multidimensional perceptual space that describes an object (see fig 20.22). According to these decision-based models, categorisation is strongly linked to visual recognition processes and relies to a much lesser extent on prototype retention or the matching of a stimulus with exemplars stored in memory. Maddox and Asby (1993) compared their decision model with exemplar models, and found that their decision-based models can explain Nosofsky's

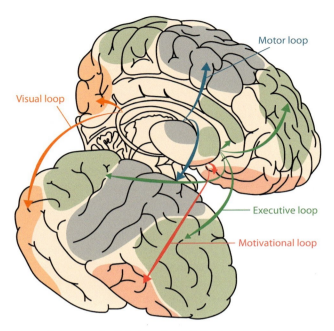

Figure 20.24 Overview of the neural processes involved in categorisation processes, according to Seger and Miller (2010).

empirical categorisation data significantly better than the exemplar-based models.

20.5.3.5 The Neural Basis of Categorisation

In a literature review, Seger and Miller (2010) provided an extensive overview of neural processes involved in categorisation. They concluded that a particularly extensive network of brain areas is involved in categorisation processes, including sensory areas, the prefrontal cortex, the parietal and temporal cortices, and the motor cortex (fig 20.24). In addition, several subcortical areas were also found to be involved in categorisation processes, such as the basal ganglia and the dopaminergic systems of the midbrain. According to Seger and Miller, both the perceptual properties of an object and the decision processes that determine whether a stimulus belongs to a category are involved in categorisation. Ashby and Ell (2001) have reached a similar conclusion and emphasise that the specific interaction between the brain areas involved in categorisation depends on the specific nature of the category. For instance, when a category can be learned on the basis of explicit rules, other systems are involved than when it comes to detecting distorted prototypes or integrating information.

20.5.4 THE SIMPLICITY PRINCIPLE

Although the prototype-, exemplar-, and decision-based models just discussed are reasonably well capable of explaining a wide range of empirical results, they fall short in explaining many everyday life categorisation processes. Here we define categories much more on the basis of the generalisation of properties of individual exemplars than exemplar theory

predicts. To reconcile the ideas behind the prototype and exemplar theories, Feldman (2003) argues that a **simplicity principle** forms the basis of the categorisation process. The basic idea behind this simplicity principle is that we always try to use the simplest category that is consistent with a given set of objects that we aim to categorise. When defining a category, we thus aim to generate a representation that is consistent with the basic properties of a set of examples. Feldman argues that sometimes this can be done quite easily on the basis of a relatively small number of examples.

For example, for the concept chair it is possible to form a representation of the underlying concept based on a relatively small number of exemplars, so that we can also easily generate a prototype for it. For another collection of objects, such as a hat, a piano, the sun, and the King of Sweden (to use Feldman's example), this is much more difficult, because the underlying collection is extremely inconsistent, so that no regularities can be discovered, with the result that the collection cannot be compressed into a single category. We are therefore forced to categorise the latter collection in the form of a number of individually labelled exemplars.

Thus, although we can define categories as collections of single objects, this is often inefficient. This inefficiency of the exemplar models is, according to Feldman (2003), not compatible with the simplicity principle. While models that conform to the simplicity principle attempt to extract a minimal set of regularities, exemplar models simply store all instances of a category without attempting to extract the commonalities, making the representation unnecessarily complex. In summary, the simplicity principle states that we seek to categorise on the basis of the least complex representation that is possible.

20.5.4.1 Complexity and Compressibility

Although the aforementioned descriptions might already have given us an intuitive idea of what **complexity** entails, mathematics can provide a more formal definition of the concepts of complexity and simplicity. One of the reasons why the original prototype and exemplar models from the 1960s and 1970s fall short in their explanatory power is that a fundamental mathematical description of complexity was not yet available at that time. Indeed, a formal definition of complexity was only developed later, more or less independently by three mathematicians, notably the American Argentine Gregory Chaitin, the Russian Andrey Kolmogorov, and the American Ray Solomonoff. In essence, their definition of complexity is related to compressibility.

What do we mean by this? Suppose we have the following sequence of symbols: *ababababababababababab*. We can simply represent this sequence as: *13 × ab*. In the latter notation, only five symbols are needed, instead of 26. Compare that with the following sequence: *nqadigxojbmltcepzrwkysvhufr*. The latter sequence cannot easily be represented in a shorter way. In other words, the first sequence is highly compressible, whereas the second sequence is not (see also Box 1.3).[1] Complexity is in this case formally defined as the length of the shortest computer programme that can be written to reproduce the original sequence of symbols.

In the context of categorisation, we can apply this principle to the number of properties that we should consider when categorising. For example, when we have two apples, a big one and a small one, we can define the formal rule 'big apple vs. small apple', which is equivalent to (big or small) apple, which we can further compress to 'size'. This maximally compressed criterion consists of only one variable. Now consider the concept 'large apples or small oranges'. We cannot compress this concept in a similar vein, so this concept is more complex. It consists of four independent variables (apples, oranges, large, and small). Feldman (2000) found that the accuracy with which we can classify stimuli decreases more or less linearly as a function of the formal complexity of the category to which it belongs (fig 20.25). He therefore argues that when we study individual exemplars, we aim to encode them in the most compact way possible and that in doing so we try to establish the minimum set of features that we can identify as being indicative of category membership. The more the relevant dimensions can be compressed, the more we succeed in doing so.

20.5.4.2 Rules and Exceptions

The simplicity principle can also offer a good explanation for the way we deal with exceptions. As illustrated in the previous examples, we can classify some objects based on very simple rules (e.g., based on the criterion of size, or based on the colour red), whereas other concepts cannot be reduced to simple rules (e.g., the example of the hat, the piano, the sun, and the king of Sweden). Since the items in the latter example cannot be reduced to a simple criterion, we are necessarily forced to represent this concept on the basis of all the individual items, that is, as a list of exceptions. Between these two extremes, however, we can think of plenty of examples of concepts in which a

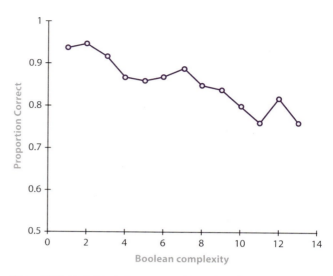

Figure 20.25 Limitations in our accuracy of classifying objects as determined by a categories' mathematical complexity. (source: Feldman, 2003)

relatively simple variable describes most of the items, plus an additional variable that describes the exceptions.

For example, if we see a collection of 27 red objects plus a banana, the formula describing the concept may consist of the variables 'red' and 'banana', where a disjunctive formula ('red or banana') describes the concept. Here, 'red' describes the rule, while 'banana' describes the exception to the rule. Yet, 'banana' is formally part of the formula in the sense that it is part of the minimal description of the concept. The more complex a concept becomes, the more the formal description of the concept is dominated by a description of the list of exceptions.

The implication of the latter is that particularly complex concepts should be presented as a list of individual exemplars. The formula describing the concept then consists merely of a list of exceptions. According to Feldman (2003), the exemplar models discussed earlier succeed particularly well in explaining how we represent complex non-compressible concepts, but they fall short in explaining how we represent simple concepts. The representation of the latter concepts is better explained by the prototype models.

20.6 SUMMARY

The ability to represent our environment in numbers and categories enables us to drastically reduce the load on our memory and gives us the ability to form abstractions from concrete examples. The complexity of the categorisation process is mainly characterised by the fact that in the formation of categories we often have to deal with exceptions. Factors such as representativeness, typicality, and diversity play important roles in the effectiveness with which we can classify a stimulus. The ability to represent numbers is based on a rudimentary innate sense of magnitude. Although this sense of magnitude appears to be

innate, its finesse is influenced by linguistic and cultural factors. Young infants have a rudimentary sense of magnitude and statistical regularities; a sense of proportion and intuitive probability is also present in cultures with a limited numerical vocabulary.

Based on developmental studies, it has been established that our understanding of numbers probably consists of a verbal (numeric) and a non-verbal (mental imagery) representation. The verbal representation is discrete and the non-verbal one continuous. The non-verbal representation is available from an early age and evolves strongly in the first months of life after birth. Discrete number representation develops later and is initially limited to three units. Various number systems have been developed throughout human history to represent quantities. The processing of numbers is characterised by specific effects, including the symbolic distance effect and the apprehension span.

When we observe a set containing a maximum of four items, we can immediately determine its cardinality without having to count; a process that is known as subitizing. Various explanations for subitizing have been formulated, of which the explanation of object individuation is the most plausible. This explanation is supported by neurobiological correlates: in humans in the form of a flattening of the increase in N2pc components as a function of the increase in the number of objects and in non-human primates in the form of neurons showing a similar pattern in firing frequency. When subitizing is no longer sufficient, we must count all the elements of a set. Counting is done by mentally traversing all objects and updating a rank number in working memory. When the objects to be counted are arranged in a specific order, it is possible to increase the efficiency of the counting process. Counting is not necessarily subvocal. When we are no longer able to count subvocally, we can still approximate the actual number of items presented. When counting is not possible, the number can be determined by means of estimation.

Relative number size is associated with a specific location. The SNARC effect describes how relatively small numbers are associated with the left and large numbers with the right. Several studies have shown that this effect is flexible and can be influenced by task instructions. These results have led to the mental white board hypothesis, which states that we tend to order information from left to right in an imaginary space in our working memory.

Many studies in the field of arithmetic are based on the idea that arithmetic ability starts with counting. Eventually, arithmetic results are stored as facts in memory and the time it takes to solve an arithmetic problem depends, among other things, on the time it takes to retrieve the result from memory. The problem size effect describes how the time needed to solve a problem depends on the size of the operands. The challenge of cognitive computational models is to explain this effect. In complex mental arithmetic with transference, working memory is involved. An important, still partly unanswered question is related to the way numerical information is represented. Some theoretical models assume that specific stages of the process each have their own code, while other models postulate that the

way numerical information is represented depends on the nature of the task.

Some theorists assume that arithmetic skills developed from other cognitive functions; especially functions used in estimating numbers and quantities and functions involved in evaluating differences. Indeed, neuroscientific evidence suggests that there is overlap between brain areas involved in subtraction and difference estimation as well as between brain areas involved in addition and number estimation.

Concepts were initially assumed to be represented hierarchically in long-term memory, but this idea has proven to be problematic, since the underlying model cannot explain some of the important effects of atypical and infrequent exemplars of a category. For this reason, it can be concluded that concepts are characterised by a graded structure, which describes how some exemplars are considered more representative of a category than others. This gradation can even be found for well-defined categories, where exemplar do or do not belong to the category according to an unambiguous rule.

A central question in the study of concept formation is whether it is done on the basis of association or on the basis of a more concrete hypothesis testing process. Initially, it was assumed that the classification of concepts was primarily based on a hypothesis testing process. However, classic studies in this area were limited in the sense that they mainly used well-defined concepts characterised by bivariate properties. In everyday life, however, we usually deal with concepts that are ill-defined. For these concepts in particular, typicality effects play an important role. Specifically multidimensional categories, that is, categories with more than one defining characteristic, are poorly defined and the way in which information about these different dimensions can be integrated determines the classification.

Originally, three different models describing the classification processes were proposed. Prototype models assume that we compare individual exemplars with a prototype of a stimulus. Exemplar models, on the other hand, assume that we compare individual exemplars to a representative set of members of the category in our memory, while decision-based models are mainly based on the idea that we attribute specific responses to a stimulus, based on its visual properties.

More recent models for stimulus classification are based on the simplicity principle and combine properties of the prototype and exemplar models. According to this simplicity principle, the exact representation of the category will be a weighted balance between a general rule and the exceptions to this rule. The minimum number of necessary rules determines how exactly a concept will be represented.

NOTE

1 This principle also underlies the compression of data files on your computer. Note that the actual mathematics of data compression are a bit more complicated than the simple example given here; however, a detailed discussion would be beyond the scope of this chapter.

FURTHER READING

Bellos, A. (2010). *Alex's adventures in numberland*. London, UK: Bloomsbury.

Cohen, H., & Lefebre, C. (2005). *Handbook of categorization in cognitive science*. Amsterdam: Elsevier.

Cohen Kadosh, R., & Dowker, A. (2015). *The Oxford handbook of numerical cognition*. Oxford, UK: Oxford University Press.

Henik, A., & Fias, W. (2018). *Heterogeneity of function in numerical cognition*. Amsterdam: Elsevier.

CHAPTER 21
Judgement and decision-making

21.1 INTRODUCTION

Each day we encounter numerous situations in which we have to judge the likelihood of a possible event or make a decision that will have consequences for our future. Consider, for example, judging whether a nagging sore throat is a sign of a cold, tonsillitis, or perhaps something worse. This judgement will affect your decision to remain inside, to go and see a doctor, or to just go to class or work. An important theme that will emerge in this chapter is the distinction between intuitive System 1 and deliberate System 2 judgements, as proposed by Kahneman. In many cases, judgements and decisions are made on the basis of distorted mental representations. A good example of this is the way in which we judge probabilities. Why, for example, do we participate in lotteries when the expected utility of a lottery is negative? The short answer to this question is that our mental representation is often distorted by a large number of peripheral factors that are actually irrelevant, but it strongly influences our perception of reality.

Although judgement and decision-making processes are closely related, there are also some clear differences. The main difference is that judgements are about determining the likelihood of an event taking place on the basis of incomplete data, whereas decision-making is primarily about selecting one option from various available options.

21.2 JUDGEMENT AND INTUITIVE STATISTICS

Judgement research is mainly concerned with how we estimate the likelihood of a given outcome. Although the previous chapter already discussed some evidence suggesting that we have a primitive innate ability to make these kinds of estimates (Fontanari et al., 2014; Téglás, Girotto, Gonzalez, & Bonatti, 2007), several studies show that many of our statistical intuitions conflict with reality (Kahneman & Tversky, 1972, 1982a, 1982b). For example, we tend to overestimate the probability of being involved in a plane crash because the few crashes that do occur are widely reported in the media. Likewise, we are often convinced that, after a series of coin tosses that have resulted in the outcome 'heads', the next toss must result in a 'tail'; a belief that is known as the **gambler's fallacy** (Ayton & Fischer, 2004) (see fig 21.1). The fact that this belief is false can be easily verified by considering that any outcome is completely independent of the previous ones. The fact that the first throws all resulted in 'heads' is extremely unlikely (but no more or less unlikely than, e.g., a series of 'heads-tails-tails-heads-tails'!), yet these previous results have no influence at all on the current toss.

This example shows that our judgement of probabilities can be influenced by our limited realisation that independent events do not influence each other's outcome. In addition, there are many other factors that influence these judgements, such as the over- or under-representation of certain events in our memory or the distortion that can occur when the a priori probability of a given event is extremely low or high.

21.3 BAYES' THEOREM

The British theologian and logician Thomas Bayes (1701–1761) developed an elaborate mathematical theorem that describes how one should adjust one's beliefs when new evidence becomes available. Appendix provides an elaborate example to illustrate this theorem in action. In the example, a new disease is introduced that affects 0.5% of the population and a test with a very high reliability (99% sensitive and 99% selective) that is going to be administered to a randomly selected person.

As described in Appendix, the likelihood that a randomly selected individual who tests positive is actually ill is less than one in three, *despite the high reliability of the test* (if the explanation in Appendix is not yet completely clear: don't worry, there will be an explanation later which will hopefully make the problem more understandable). The reason for this low probability is the low **base rate** of the disease in the population, which greatly increases the risk of a false alarm.

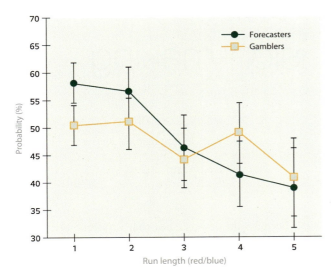

Figure 21.1 The accuracy of predicting whether a ball in a simulated game of roulette will end on the same colour as in a previous game, as a function of the number of consecutive outcomes that fell on the same colour. Predictors were asked to directly predict the outcome of the gamble, while gamblers were asked to place a bet on the outcome. (source: Ayton and Fischer, 2004)

21.4 THE TAXI PROBLEM

A similar logic can be applied to Kahneman and Tversky's (1972) famous taxi problem. According to Kahneman and Tversky, there are two different taxi companies operating in a city. The 'green' company encompasses 85% of all taxis, while the remaining 15% are from the competing 'blue' company. At one point, one of these taxis is involved in an accident and a witness has stated that it was from the blue company. When this witness was tested on her ability to judge the colour of a taxi, she was found to be wrong in 20% of the cases. What is the likelihood that the taxi involved in the accident was from the blue company? When we apply Bayes' formula to the taxi problem, we get the answer:

$$P\left(blue \mid BLUE\right) = \frac{0.80 \times 0.15}{0.80 \times 0.15 + 0.20 \times 0.85} \approx 0.41$$

where P(blue|BLUE) reflects the probability that the witness reports blue under the condition that the taxi in question is indeed blue. This probability is about 41%; however, this is not the answer given by most of the participants, who reported mostly that they believed this probability to be about 80%.

21.4.1 IGNORING BASE RATES

The study by Kahneman and Tversky (1972) showed that most individuals completely ignored the base rate and only considered the reliability of the witness. The scenario, however, is just one of many in which participants ignored the base rate, and in the years to follow, Kahneman and

Tversky reported numerous other examples of incorrect statistical intuitions.

For instance, a follow-up study (Kahneman & Tversky, 1973) investigated the reasons why the base rate was ignored in a more systematic manner. In this study, a group of participants was presented with a series of study programmes and had to rank these programmes according to the probability that a random student named Tom W. followed each programme. In this case, the ranking that was given by the participants was entirely determined by the relative size of the discipline. For example, the probability that Tom W. would be a psychology student was estimated to be much higher than the probability that he would be a computer science student.

A second group of participants was given a slightly different assignment. They were given a description of Tom W., which read:

> Tom W. is of high intelligence, although lacking in true creativity. He has a need for order and clarity, and for neat and tidy systems in which every detail finds its appropriate place. His writing is rather dull and mechanical, occasionally enlivened by somewhat corny puns and by flashes of imagination of the sci-fi type. He has a strong drive for competence. He seems to have little feel and little sympathy for other people and does not enjoy interacting with others. Self-centered, he nonetheless has a deep moral sense.

The participants now had to decide again to what extent they believed that each discipline on the list was a good match for Tom. The results showed that the technical subjects, such as computer science and theoretical physics, were judged to be a much better match for Tom than, for instance, psychology, humanities, or law. A third group of participants was given additional information:

> The preceding personality sketch of Tom W. was written during Tom's senior year in high school by a psychologist, on the basis of projective tests. Tom W. is currently a graduate student. Please rank the following nine fields of graduate specialization in order of the likelihood that Tom W. is now a graduate student in each of these fields.

The problem presented to the third group of participants is different from the problem presented to the second group, because we now have to assume that Tom W. is a randomly selected student, which makes the a priori probability that Tom W. is obtaining a doctorate from a large discipline, such as psychology or humanities, much larger than the probability that he obtains it from a small discipline such as computer science. Most of the participants' judgements showed that they were completely guided by the stereotypes, however, so that they estimated the likelihood of Tom W. obtaining a doctorate in computer science to be much higher than we might expect if we do consider the base rate.

21.5 JUDGEMENTS BASED ON HEURISTICS

21.5.1 JACK AND THE REPRESENTATIVENESS HEURISTIC

A second example from a study by Kahneman and Tversky (1973) shows that we base our probability judgements almost entirely on the representativeness of individual examples. In this study, participants were informed that psychologists had collected the personality profiles of 30 engineers and 70 lawyers. They were given five descriptions, which they were told were drawn randomly from the 100 available profiles. Participants then had to estimate for each of these profiles whether it belonged to an engineer. For example, one of these descriptions read:

Jack is a 45-year-old man. He is married and has four children. He is generally quite conservative, careful, and ambitious. He has no interest in political or social affairs and spends most of his free time pursuing one of his many hobbies, including home improvement, sailing, and solving mathematical puzzles.

The probability that Jack is one of 30 engineers in the sample of 100 is ____.

After the participants had rated five of these personal descriptions, they were asked a final question:

Now suppose you have not got any information about an individual drawn at random from this sample. What is then the probability that this person is one of the 30 engineers in the sample of 100?

In the latter case, the participants answered that this probability was 30%. However, when this description was replaced by a non-informative person description, such as the following, the participants indicated that there was a 50% probability that Dick was an engineer:

Dick is a man of 30. He is married but has no children. He is a man of many skills, highly motivated, and it seems that he is going to be very successful in his profession. He is well appreciated among his colleagues.

Kahneman and Tversky concluded that in these situations participants were entirely guided by an intuitive judgement that is based on a rule of thumb, or **heuristic**. This particular study highlighted the use of the **representativeness**

heuristic, that is, it showed that the representativeness of the individual descriptions is a strong determinant in this type of likelihood judgement.

As the examples of Tom W. and Jack show, the representativeness heuristic can lead to a systematic distortion of our likelihood judgements. Other examples show that these biases can manifest themselves in many different ways. The representativeness heuristics can even lead to remarkable logical fallacies, as is aptly illustrated by the **conjunction fallacy**.

21.5.2 LINDA AND THE CONJUNCTION FALLACY

Kahneman and Tversky (1982a) presented personality descriptions such as the following:

Linda is 31 years old, single, outspoken, and very bright. She majored in philosophy. As a student, she was deeply concerned with issues of discrimination and social justice, and also participated in anti-nuclear demonstrations.

Participants then had to decide which of the following two statements was more likely: (1) Linda is a bank teller; or (2) Linda is a bank teller who is also active in the feminist movement. Since this description does not fit the stereotype of a bank teller, but does fit the stereotype of a feminist, most participants considered statement (2) more likely than statement (1). This result conflicts with formal logic, however, because the more general category of 'bank tellers' completely envelops the narrower category of 'bank tellers who are also active in the feminist movement'. Indeed, statement (2) consists of the conjunction of the categories 'bank employee' and 'feminist activist'.

Also, when participants had to judge several scenarios on their likelihood, again on the basis of this personality description, a similar result was found (Tversky & Kahneman, 1983). In the latter study, participants were again given the description of Linda and now they had to judge the following statements for their likelihood:

- Linda is a teacher at elementary school.
- Linda works in a bookstore and takes yoga classes.
- Linda is active in the feminist movement.
- Linda is a psychiatric social worker.
- Linda is a member of the League of Women Voters.
- Linda is a bank teller.
- Linda is an insurance salesperson.
- Linda is a bank teller and is active in the feminist movement.

As in the case of Tom W.'s personality description, participants had to judge the likelihood of each of these statements. Because the statements 'bank teller' and 'bank teller who is active in the feminist movement' were intentionally placed close together in this list, Tversky and Kahneman were convinced that participants would notice that the former category completely envelopes the latter, and that they would therefore rank the probability that Linda is a feminist bank teller lower than the probability that Linda is a bank teller. This, however, turned out not to be the case: almost all participants gave the opposite answer. That is, the category 'bank teller active in the feminist movement' was almost always considered more likely than the categories 'bank teller' or 'active in the feminist movement'.

One of the reasons why we consider these more specific categories to be more likely than the more general ones is that the more specific description makes it easier for us to retrieve relevant information from memory. The latter is also reflected in the **availability heuristic**, which describes how our likelihood judgement of events is influenced by the ease with which we can retrieve relevant information.

21.5.3 JAWS AND THE AVAILABILITY HEURISTIC

How great is the risk that you will be injured or even killed by a shark? On average, each year about 83 people are injured by sharks, about five of them being fatal. Most casualties occur among surfers, who spend a relatively large amount of time in sharks' natural habitats. It is estimated that there are a grand total about 23 million surfers worldwide, which makes the likelihood of a surfer experiencing a shark incident less than 1 in 3.6 million and the likelihood of a fatal accident even less than 1 in 20 million. By comparison, the likelihood of dying from smoking is as high as one in three (Mattson, Pollack, & Cullen, 1987). Due to extensive media coverage and the stigma that has been attached to sharks in movies such as 'Jaws', many of us fear sharks much more than cigarettes!

Lichtenstein, Slovic, Fischhoff, Layman, and Combs (1978) found evidence that many of us use the availability heuristic. They did so by asking participants to estimate the likelihood of different causes of death. Here, they found that causes that receive a lot of publicity, such as murder, were estimated as being more likely than causes that receive little publicity, such as suicide, even when in reality suicide is more prevalent than murder (see fig 21.2). According to Hertwig, Pachur, and Kurzenhauser (2005), there are two ways to explain this result. First, we can use a direct memory mechanism, which involves thinking of examples of different causes of death in our own environment. Hertwig et al. describe this mechanism as availability by recall. The second form, known as regressed frequency, is more abstract and consists of trying to imagine how easy it would be to come up with examples of each of the different causes, without retrieving these examples directly from memory. Again, murders are more often in the news than suicides, so information about murders is more readily available than information about suicides.

Tversky and Kahneman (1973) found that participants used the availability heuristic when they had to judge what was more common: words beginning with an R or

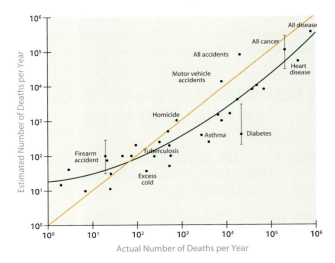

Figure 21.2 The relation between estimates of the frequencies of various causes of death in the United States versus their actual frequencies. Deviations from the diagonal straight line imply a bias. (source: Hertwig et al., 2005)

words where the letter R is in third position. Because it is generally easier to recall words that begin with an R than words where the R is in third position, most participants reported that the former was more common, while in reality the latter is much more common.

Mamede, van Gog, Rikers, van Guldener, and Schmidt (2010) found that diagnoses made by medical students were also influenced by the availability heuristic. When these students had to formulate a diagnosis, they were influenced by information that had been given for a previous case, resulting in the fact that this information was still easily accessible from memory.

Yet, we do not always let ourselves be guided by the availability heuristic. Specifically in situations where it is known that easily available examples involve relatively rare cases, we will often not use this heuristic, or at least use it to give an opposite answer. For example, Oppenheimer (2004) found that when (American) participants had to judge pairs of names, such as Bush versus Stevenson, or Nixon versus Winters on their relative frequency, they were more likely to choose the unknown name. By doing so, they not only ignored the availability heuristic but also the actual statistics, because the familiar names were in fact slightly more frequent.

21.6 SUPPORT THEORY

In part based on the availability heuristic, Tversky and Koehler (1994) have described which cognitive processes underlie judgements. Their **support theory** states that the way an event is described strongly influences its likelihood judgements: the more explicit a description of a possible event is, the more plausible people believe it is that this event will actually occur.

For example, Mandel (2005) asked participants how likely they believed it to be that a terrorist attack would take place in the six months following the survey. This survey was carried out immediately after the September 11, 2001, attacks on the U.S. World Trade Center. This was a time when the organisation responsible for the attacks, al-Qaeda, received a great deal of attention in the media. Other participants had to answer a similar question, but it was phrased somewhat more specifically. They had to judge how likely they believed it to be that a terrorist attack would be carried out by al-Qaeda or by another organisation in the next six months. The explicit addition of 'al-Qaeda or by another organisation' meant that participants not only took an attack by al-Qaeda into account, but also assigned a small probability to the possibility that other organisations could carry out an attack, so that the total likelihood of an attack was estimated to be higher in the latter group than in the former.

There are two principles that might contribute to this effect. First, a more explicit description will focus our attention on details that are less obvious in the more general description. Second, the limited accessibility of our memory may cause us not to remember all the relevant information in the more general description. This explanation would predict that experts are to a lesser degree influenced by the nature of the description because it is likely that experts can fill in the gaps in their knowledge more easily than non-experts.

Yet, experts can also be strongly influenced by the explicitness of the description, as was shown by Redelmeier et al. (1995). These investigators asked doctors to judge the likelihood of a series of medical diagnoses, given the description of a specific patient. One group of doctors was presented with two possible diagnoses and an additional 'other' category, while the other group was presented with an additional three possible diagnoses. The essential manipulation in this experiment was that these additional diagnoses were in fact a further specification of the 'other' category that was given to the first group, thus describing this category more explicitly for the second group than for the first group. The effect of this manipulation was that the 'other' category was deemed to be more likely in the second group than in the first group; that is, collectively the three additional diagnoses were judged to be more likely than the one 'other' category in the first group.

Weisberg, Keil, Goodstein, Rawson, and Gray (2008) found, however, that experts are not always as sensitive to the form of a description as beginners (see fig 21.3). These authors were interested in the question of why neuroscientific explanations for psychological phenomena are not only used very frequently but also often inappropriately. To address this question, they had participants read explanations for psychological phenomena, which had to be judged for correctness. Irrelevant neuroscientific information was added to half of these statements, while the other half was

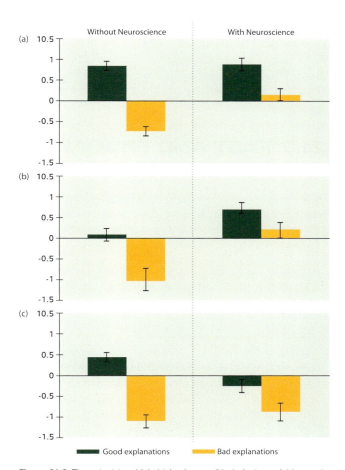

Figure 21.3 The extent to which (a) beginners, (b) students, and (c) experts are prepared to accept explanations of psychological phenomena. (source: Weisberg et al., 2008)

limited to giving explanation in terms of pure psychological mechanisms. Three groups of participants had to judge these explanations for their plausibility: a group of lay people, a group of students who had just completed an introductory course in neuroscience, and a group of experienced neuroscientists. Both the lay people and the students rated the explanations to which neuroscientific terminology had been added as more plausible than the purely psychological explanations. Only the experienced neuroscientists, however, were not misled by this information.

Incidentally, some findings have been reported that are completely inconsistent with the support theory. Sloman, Rottenstreich, Wisniewski, Hadjichristidis, and Fox (2004), for example, instructed participants to rate the likelihood that a randomly chosen American citizen would eventually die from a disease. The question was formulated along the lines of: 'How likely do you believe it is that Mr. X will die from a heart attack, cancer or any other disease'. Obviously the addition of 'from any other disease' meant that participants should just judge the likelihood that this person would die from a disease, as opposed to any other cause of death. This study found that the examples that were given were ineffective when they involved diseases that were typical causes of death (such as heart attack, cancer, or cerebral haemorrhage). When atypical diseases were used as examples, the likelihood of disease being the cause of death was judged to be lower than when no examples were given. These results show that a more explicit description can also reduce subjective likelihood estimates when the description focuses on low probabilities.

21.7 FAST AND FRUGAL HEURISTICS

In the previous sections, we introduced the idea that the framing of a problem can systematically bias our likelihood judgements. Although a more explicit problem description

typically results in an increase of the likelihood judgement, the previous section introduced an experiment in which participants' likelihood judgements actually decreased from a more explicit description. How can we explain these results?

One of the main conclusions is that our judgements are often guided by heuristics. While the use of simple heuristics may appear to be inefficient and inaccurate, Gigerenzer and Gray (2017) argue that in practice it is often the case that simple rules of thumb give surprisingly accurate results (see Box 21.1). According to Gigerenzer and Gray, it requires great effort to match or surpass the outcome of these heuristics through more complex, deliberate processes. For this reason, simple heuristics may be

---

Box 21.1 Frisbees, air forces, and financial risk: the power of simple heuristics

In everyday practice, simple heuristics can often provide much better solutions than complex algorithms. Gigerenzer and Gray (2017) illustrate this point using the interception heuristic, which was discovered by Royal Air Force pilots just before the start of the Second World War. To better understand the idea of this interception heuristic, we can first start with a simpler example from Gigerenzer and Brighton (2009). How will an experienced baseball player catch a ball? Is this done by solving a complex series of differential equations or is there a simpler mechanism involved? Gigerenzer and Brighton (2009) assume the latter. According to them, it is the effective use of the gaze heuristic, which can be successfully applied when the ball is already in the air. The gaze heuristic boils down to the following: 'fixate on the ball and start running, while keeping the angle of your gaze constant'. Based on this heuristic, players do not need to solve any complex equation: the heuristic will lead them to the right place to catch the ball.

The gaze heuristic is a simplified version of an elegant heuristic that has been successfully applied by a large number of mammals, birds and insects that fly, along with some non-flying animals (rats). This interception heuristic is capable of successfully intercepting targets that can intentionally change course to escape their interceptor, such as prey – or German Luftwaffe pilots. The heuristics is based on the idea of using the best input available at any given time to adjust course in order to intercept a target. The interception heuristic proved ultimately to be far more successful than the German strategy of intercepting British fighters using radar.

The interception heuristic illustrates how a simple rule of thumb can result in task performance that is much more efficient than what would be possible with a complex series of analytical processes. The heuristic is one of the numerous examples we will cover in the current theme. Gigerenzer and Gray (2017) argue that commonly used

heuristics are actually used so much, exactly because they are successful. For example, the recognition heuristic can be applied because there is often a correlation between familiarity and scores on another variable: for example, athletes that we are highly familiar with also tend to be the better athletes. In other words, heuristics are strongly adapted to the domain to which they are applied, and for different domains we have different heuristics. From this perspective, cognitive reasoning processes might be considered as a toolbox full of heuristics, from which we can select a heuristic that applies to the problem at hand.

The fact that simple heuristics often give equally good, if not better, results in practice is aptly illustrated by decision models used in economics. These models, which perform risk analyses for banks, often include thousands of variables and millions of covariates that need to be calculated, and yet these models are often of very little use when predicting financial crises. In other words, the results of these calculations are often as ineffective as the methods used by the Royal Air Force before they discovered simple interception heuristics.

To underline the importance of simple and robust procedures, the former chief economist at the Bank of England, Andrew G. Haldane, entitled his speech at the annual Jackson Hole conference 'The dog and the frisbee' (Haldane, 2012). To the amazement of the attending bank directors and financial analysts, Haldane argued that averting a financial crisis is as complex as catching a Frisbee. Yet, a dog is far more capable of catching a Frisbee than humans are of averting a financial crisis. The difference is that dogs rely on heuristics, whereas financial analysts make complex analyses. Haldane's call for simple reliable methods resulted in his lecture being recognised as speech of the year by the Wall Street Journal.

particularly effective. Gigerenzer and Gaissmaier (2011) argue that we make judgements on the basis of a multitude of simple heuristics; rules that they describe with the term 'fast and frugal'. These **fast and frugal heuristics** are so effective because they produce surprisingly adequate judgements on the basis of little amounts of information (see fig 21.4).

21.7.1 TAKE THE BEST

A good example of such a fast and frugal heuristic is the **take the best strategy**. Suppose we have to choose which of two American cities – Shreveport, Louisiana, or Atlanta, Georgia – is the larger in terms of population. If we have no other information about these cities, we might decide that recognising or not recognising the name of the city is a good indicator of a city's size. But if we recognise both

names, we can look for another criterion. For example, we can assume that an international airport is an indicator of the size of a city. For Atlanta, we happen to know that the city has an international airport and for Shreveport we are not sure. For this reason, we choose Atlanta.[1]

The 'take the best' heuristic consists of three components: (1) a search rule that considers the most important cues (recognition of name; airport) in the order of their validity; (2) a stop rule that determines whether the found rule discriminates between the two alternatives; and (3) a decision rule that formulates the outcome of the judgement.

21.7.2 RECOGNITION HEURISTICS

A more specific example of the 'take the best' strategy is the **recognition heuristic**. This heuristic consists of simply choosing the one option that we recognise out of the two alternatives presented to us. Goldstein and Gigerenzer (2002) have concluded that recognition is often the only cue we use while making a judgement. This conclusion was based on a study in which participants were informed that German cities with a soccer team were generally larger than cities without a soccer team. Participants were asked to judge which of the two given cities was larger and were given additional information on whether or not the cities in question had a soccer team. In most cases, they chose the city they recognised, even if it did not have a soccer team. Thus, participants apparently ignored the conflicting information about the soccer teams.

21.7.3 THE HIATUS HEURISTIC

A third example of a very simple heuristic involves managers of fashion stores using a very simple and efficient way to judge which customers are active and which ones are passive. The heuristic states that customers who have recently bought something are active customers and are likely to buy something again in the future. Wübben and Wangenheim (2008) found that this heuristic, known as the hiatus heuristic, classified customers better than a considerably more complex model.

21.7.4 REDUNDANCY OF INFORMATION

Finally, we can ask when simple heuristics are most effective and when we need to adopt more elaborate strategies. Dieckmann and Rieskamp (2007) argued that redundancy of information is a crucial determinant here. In their study, participants were to imagine that they were geologists hired by an oil company (see fig 21.5). Their task was to judge which of two possible test sites would yield more oil, and they could commission a large number of tests (chemical analyses etc.) to make an informed judgement. More specifically, participants had six possible tests at their disposal.

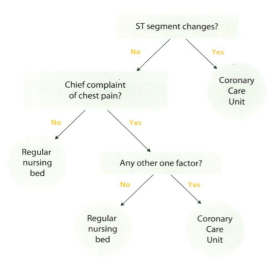

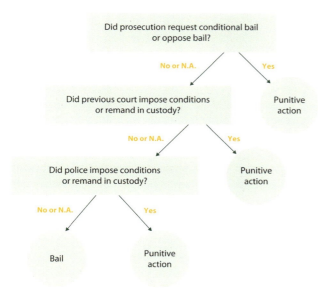

Figure 21.4 Examples of fast and frugal heuristics, as used in medical (top) and legal decisions (bottom). (source: Gigerenzer and Gaissmaier, 2011)

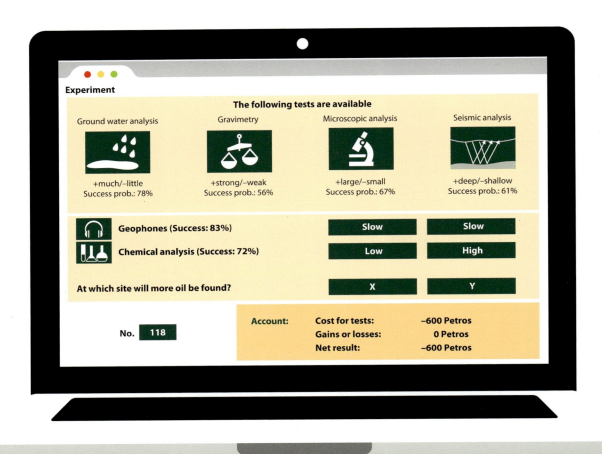

Figure 21.5 Overview of a computerised task that was used in a study on the processing of redundant information. Participants had to perform various geophysical tests to determine whether a specific area contained oil. When the different tests were highly redundant and costing money, participants often chose a 'take the best' strategy. (source: Dieckmann and Rieskamp, 2007)

Each of these tests had a specific validity. For half of the participants, the test results were highly redundant, whereas for the other participants, the test results had to be combined to reach an informed judgement. Participants were first given the opportunity to learn how to use the system during a practice phase. During this phase, the commissioning of a test was free of charge. This learning phase was followed by a decision phase, in which performing a test would cost money. When the test results were highly redundant, participants were significantly more likely to use the 'take the best' heuristic than when the tests were less redundant. In other words, when redundant, participants tended to rely on using just a single test; the one they considered to be the best.

21.8 WORKING WITH CONCRETE UNITS: NATURAL FREQUENCY HYPOTHESIS

A possible reason for our limited ability to deal with base rate information is that on many occasions we have difficulties dealing with proportions and probabilities (Gigerenzer

& Hoffrage, 1995, 1999). This conclusion was based on a study by Fiedler (1988), in which a group of participants was given the Linda problem discussed earlier. In this study, however, participants' judgements were compared to an alternative version of the problem, in which participants had to judge how many out of a hundred possible candidates matching Linda's description were either bank tellers or feminist bank tellers (see also: Mellers, Hertwig, & Kahneman, 2001). When given this version of the problem, the label 'feminist bank teller' was assigned significantly less frequently than the label 'bank teller'. For this reason, Gigerenzer and Hoffrage argue that judgements should become more accurate when problems are represented in natural units. As such, they argue that everyday judgements are often based on the process of considering real-world examples in the population, a process that Gigerenzer and Hoffrage describe with the term **natural sampling**.

Let's illustrate the process of natural sampling with the disease example discussed in the beginning of this chapter, which also forms the basis for the more formal elaboration in Appendix. Suppose you are a physician in a village with a population of exactly 1000 inhabitants. A population screening has identified that five out of every 1000 inhabitants are affected by a new, unknown disease.

You have just received the test described in Appendix and you administer it to one random villager who happens to be visiting your practice at that moment. The test is positive. What is the likelihood that this person is affected by the disease?

To continue this thought experiment, suppose that we were able to test all inhabitants. The test itself has a sensitivity of 99%, so in a population of a thousand inhabitants, this would most likely result in 0.99×5, or about five positive results that were actually caused by the disease. The test, however, also has a 1% probability of yielding a false alarm. Since 995 people are not ill, we have 995 times a 1% probability (or 995×0.01) of a false alarm. So, we may expect about ten false alarms. Consequently, we can expect a total of fifteen positive test results, of which only five are actually caused by the disease. It follows, then, that there is only about a one in three chance that the random person yielding a positive test result is actually ill. Many people find this explanation much easier to follow than the version given in Appendix, because we are now working with natural units.

21.8.1 NATURAL FREQUENCIES

What is meant by **natural frequency** in this context? We can equate natural frequency to the absolute number of members in a population that satisfy a given characteristic, such as 995 healthy residents or five sick residents. If we know both the frequency and the total size of the population, we can easily convert these frequencies to proportions. Note that this definition deviates somewhat from the popular way in which frequency is sometimes reported in the media where it actually represents a proportion (e.g., '1/50 respondents agree with the statement. . . ' while the actual numbers might have been 20 out of a population of 1000).

21.8.2 EVIDENCE: NATURAL SAMPLING

Hoffrage, Krauss, Martignon, and Gigerenzer (2015) investigated the effectiveness of natural sampling by having advanced medical students judge the probability that a woman had breast cancer. This question was presented to the students in two different variants. In the probabilistic version, the description was as follows:

The probability of breast cancer is 1% for a woman at age 40 who participates in routine screening. If a woman has breast cancer, the probability is 80% that she will have a positive mammogram. If a woman does not have breast cancer, the probability is 9.6% that she will also have a positive mammogram. If a woman has breast cancer, the probability is 95% that she will have a positive ultrasound test. If a woman does not have breast cancer, the probability is 4% that she will also have a positive ultrasound test.

What is the probability that a 40-year-old woman who participates in routine screening has breast cancer, given that she as a positive mammogram and a positive ultrasound test?

In the natural frequency version, the description was as follows:

One hundred out of every 10,000 women at age 40 who participate in routine screening have breast cancer. Eighty out of every 100 women with breast cancer will receive a positive mammogram. Nine hundred and fifty out of every 9900 women without breast cancer will also receive a positive mammogram. Seventy-six out of 80 women who had a positive mammogram and have cancer also have a positive ultrasound test. Thirty-eight out of 950 women who had a positive mammogram, although they do not have cancer, also have a positive ultrasound test.

How many of the women who receive a positive mammogram and a positive ultrasound test do you expect to actually have breast cancer?

Correct result is of course 0.667 for the probabilistic version and 76 (out of 114) for the natural frequency version (see fig 21.6). Hoffrage et al. found that participants generally performed much better when presented with the problem in the frequency version, compared to the probabilistic version.

21.8.3 BIASED SAMPLING

Although a representation in natural frequencies is generally helpful in reducing our biases, it still does not completely eliminate them. Fiedler, Brinkmann, Betsch, and Wild (2000) were interested in how participants solved a

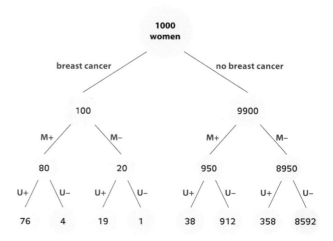

Figure 21.6 Representation of the mammogram problem in natural frequencies M(+/−) = positive/negative mammogram; U(+/−) = positive/negative ultrasound. (source: Hoffrage et al., 2015)

slightly simpler variant of the breast cancer problem. Here, participants had to assess the probability that a woman had breast cancer, given a positive mammogram. The correct solution to this problem is 0.078 (i.e., 80/(80 + 950)). Fiedler et al. did not present the problem in the standard way just described. Instead, they were interested in what would happen when participants could gather information about the problem themselves. For this reason, they gave their participants descriptions of individual test results, which were printed on separate index cards. These cards were grouped separately for women with and without breast cancer. Participants then had to select cards that indicated whether the test result was positive or negative. When participants were given this choice, their sampling behaviour appeared to be highly biased towards the cases with breast cancer, with the result that participants greatly overestimated the risk of breast cancer (63% instead of 7.8%).

21.9 CAUSAL MODELS

The results discussed so far suggest that we are generally highly inaccurate in making judgements and that, although representations in terms of natural frequencies can help us, we may remain susceptible to biases. How is it possible that we human beings are generally so efficient and successful in daily life, given these structural biases? Krynski and Tenenbaum (2007) argue that biases in likelihood judgements are in part due to the fact that in normal, everyday situations we can depend on a considerable amount of **causal knowledge**, that is, on background knowledge that is relevant for problem-solving. In most laboratory situations, however, this knowledge is of very limited use, resulting in many of the biases already discussed.

Krynski and Tenenbaum (2007) used scenarios similar to those used by Fiedler et al. (2000), Hoffrage et al. (2015), and Kahneman and Tversky (1972). When these scenarios were presented in the standard way, Krynski and Tenenbaum found that participants often ignored the base rate. According to these authors, one of the major reasons for this is that the problem description does not encourage us to find alternative causes. For example, when we have to evaluate problems involving mammograms, breast cancer is typically the only cause for a positive mammogram that is emphasised in the problem description. If, however, we reformulate the problem so that alternative causes are explicitly mentioned, we will be able to find a very different result. Krynski and Tenenbaum did this by formulating the problem as follows:

There is a 6% chance that a woman without breast cancer will have a dense, but harmless cyst, which looks like a cancerous tumour and causes a positive result on a mammogram.

When the problem was formulated in this way, participants suddenly considered the base rate much more and their estimates were much closer to the actual likelihood. A similar result was found for the classic taxi problem, when the following information was added to the problem description.

When testing a sample of cabs, only 80% of the Blue Co. cabs appeared blue in colour, and only 80% of the Green Co. cabs appeared green in colour. Due to faded paint, 20% of the Blue Co. cabs appeared to be green in colour and 20% of the Green Co. cabs appeared to be blue in colour.

Again, it was found that when participants had to evaluate this version of the problem, the estimates became much more accurate.

21.10 DECISION-MAKING

Our daily lives are filled with decisions. From relatively trivial matters, such as what to eat next, what book to read next, or when to do our household chores, to life-changing matters, such as what study programme to enrol in, where to live, and whether or not to see a doctor for a medical check-up, all these situations require us to make a choice from several possible alternatives. Based on the currently available evidence, decision processes can be found in almost every cognitive processes, from the relatively low-level processes involved in selecting where to move our eyes next to the potential life-changing decisions affecting careers, family life, economic status, happiness, and so on. Further on in this chapter, we will discuss the latter type of decisions, but let's start with the role of accumulating evidence in basic decision-making processes.

One of the most important processes involved in deciding involves the accumulation of evidence. Suppose we are driving towards a busy intersection and suddenly the brakes fail. Now, within a split second, we have to decide where to steer. Although this appears to be a fairly easy task, it is actually a very complex one, involving three stages. First, we need to gather evidence; in this case, consisting of observing the other cars and pedestrians approaching the intersection. Second, we must determine when to stop collecting this evidence; waiting too long can have disastrous consequences. Third and finally, we must select an appropriate action. This is a difficult task because the sensory evidence is constantly changing and its reliability is not guaranteed; for example, it is more reliable on a sunny day than on a foggy one, and its reliability may improve as we approach the intersection, because visibility increases, affecting the moment when to stop accumulating evidence.

How can we optimally accumulate this information so that it can result in an optimal decision? Beck et al. (2008) have

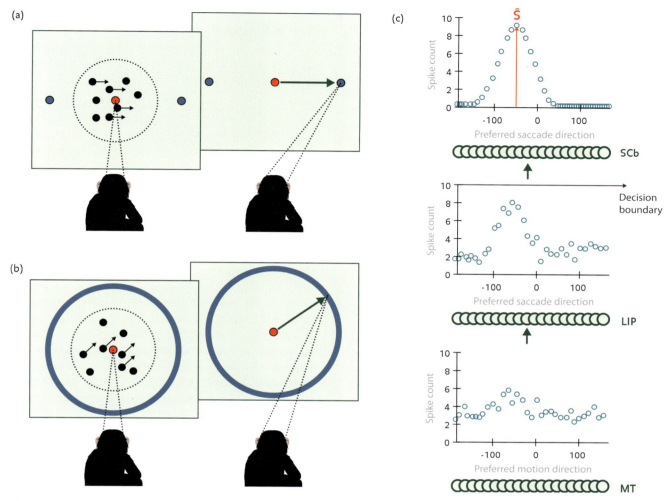

Figure 21.7 Simulations for a decision model based on the detection of coherent motion in monkeys. (a–b) When monkeys detect that a part of the dots is moving in a coherent direction, they make an eye movement in that direction. (c) A three-layer neural network represents activation in the middle temporal gyrus (MT), the lateral inferior parietal cortex (LIP), and the superior colliculus (SCb). By accumulating evidence, the network calculates the directional vector for the eye movement. (source: Beck et al., 2008)

presented a neural network model, based on the principles of Bayesian inference, that is capable of simulating this accumulation process. The model assumes that the accumulation of evidence involves the integration of neural activity. Beck et al. hypothesised that the interparietal cortex is involved in this process. They tested this by comparing model simulations with the firing patterns of neurons in this brain region, while monkeys had to decide on the direction of movement of a random dot pattern (see fig 21.7). More specifically, a random number of moving dots were shown, most of which moved in a random direction. A small proportion of the dots moved consistently to the left or to the right. The amount of evidence about the overall motion of the pattern was manipulated by varying the proportion of consistently moving dots: the higher this proportion, the higher the coherence of the motion and the stronger the evidence. In this case, the monkeys had to respond by making a saccade in the direction of the global movement.

In their simulation studies, Beck et al. found that the firing rate of simulated neurons in the intraparietal cortex increased as a function of accumulated evidence. This simulation result implies that accumulation does indeed take place based on the integration of neural activation. Moreover, the accumulation is faster the greater the coherence of the movement. The simulated results are consistent with measurements of the firing frequency of neurons in the lateral intraparietal sulcus (see fig 21.7).

21.11 UTILITY THEORY

For a long time, it was assumed that human beings act like fully rational decision-makers who always select the best option, or at least strive to do so. This idea was derived from normative theories in behavioural economics. One of the best-known examples of such a normative theory is the subjective expected **utility theory**. This theory is based on the pioneering work of the Hungarian-born American mathematician and computer-science pioneer John Von Neumann and the German-born American economist Oskar Morgenstern (1947) on **game theory**. Formally, game theory comprises a set of mathmetical models that describe how cooperation and competition affect intelligent rational decision makers. More generally, according to the utility theory, a decision is considered to be a bet on a possible outcome. According to this idea, individuals should make decisions in such a way that their expected return, or utility, is maximised. Here, utility is the subjective value of an expected outcome. According to utility theory, when choosing between two simple options, we determine the expected outcome of each of the options by multiplying the likelihood of a given outcome by the expected utility of that outcome.

For decisions that are more complex, we would calculate the utility of each variable of a given option to estimate its outcome. For example, if we had to choose between two different holiday destinations, say a trip through Namibia or a week in a local holiday resort, we would have to take several factors into account. Namibia is probably a more exotic location than the local resort, but it probably has better weather, more interesting wildlife, and a different culture. On the other hand, Namibia is also considerably more expensive, and you spend a lot more time travelling to get there, compared to a local resort. In such a situation, we would have to calculate the utility or cost (that is, negative utility) for each variable to obtain the total expected utility for both options. In reality, however, we very frequently base our decisions on factors other than the pure maximisation of utility, as we will illustrate next.

21.12 PROSPECT THEORY

Suppose someone wants to persuade you into accepting the following bet. You flip a coin and if the outcome is 'heads' you will receive 200 euros, but if the outcome is 'tails' you owe her 100 euros. Of course, you will take the bet. After all, its' expected utility is 50 euros. Or would you not take it?

Another example: what would you prefer, a certain win of 800 euros or an 85% chance of winning 1000 euros and a 15% chance of winning nothing? Since the expected outcome of the second option is greater than that of the first, it makes sense to prefer the second option (or not?).

Finally, what would you rather have: a certain loss of 800 euros or an 85% chance of losing 1000 euros and a 15% chance of losing nothing. Even in the latter case, the expected negative utility is greater with the second option, so you go for the optimal choice: in this case, the first option (or not?).

These three examples are variants of problems that were developed by Tversky and Shafir (1992) and Kahneman and Tversky (1984). Using several versions of this type of problem, they found that in many cases, participants were often unwilling to gamble on a greater potential

gain, but typically did so when the bet would incur a larger potential loss!

Kahneman and Tversky (1979, 1984) developed their **prospect theory** to explain these seemingly paradoxical findings. Prospect theory is based on the assumption that individuals take their current situation as a reference and evaluate the possible outcome of a choice either as a potential loss or as a potential gain, compared to the current situation. Moreover, Kahneman and Tversky argued that humans are more sensitive to potential losses than to potential gains, a phenomenon they described as **loss aversion**. Loss aversion may explain, for example, why we are reluctant to take bets with a 50% chance of losing unless the potential gain is about twice as high as the potential loss (Kahneman, 2003).

The basic principles of the prospect theory are illustrated in Figure 21.8. The reference value is located at the intersection of the two axes (loss-profit vs. subjective value). The positive subjective value that is associated with profits levels off as the objective profits increase. For this reason, for many people, the subjective value associated with winning 2000 euros is far less than twice the subjective value associated with winning 1000 euros. The negative value associated with losses, however, rises much more rapidly as the objective losses increase.

Prospect theory allows us to much better explain why we make seemingly irrational choices when dealing with the problems that we have just discussed: the objectively higher utility in the first problem does not outweigh the uncertainty of actually receiving it, so we play it safe. Similarly, in the last example, the certainty of incurring a loss weighs heavily in the decision, so that in this case we often choose the option that offers a chance to limit it.

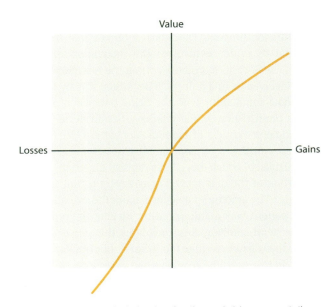

Figure 21.8 The hypothetical value function underlying prospect theory. (source: Kahneman and Tversky, 1984)

Prospect theory makes two additional predictions. First, when we make decisions, we attach more weight to low-probability events than their actual probability justifies. This effect may explain why many of us frequently participate in national lotteries, despite the extremely small chance of winning the grand prize and the objectively negative utility that is associated with lotteries. Second, most people give much lower weight to high-frequency events than they deserve on the basis of their frequency, as illustrated by the fact that many people continue to smoke tobacco, despite the obvious health risk.

21.12.1 THE DOMINANCE PRINCIPLE

According to the **dominance principle**, when all other factors are equal, we should preferably choose the outcome with the highest utility. We have already encountered some examples of choice behaviour that violate this principle. Suppose we are presented with the following choices (Kahneman & Tversky, 1984):

1. You can get 240 euros.

Vs.

2. You have a 25% chance of winning 1000 euros and a 75% chance of winning nothing.

Or

3. You will lose 750 euros anyway.

Vs.

4. You have a 76% chance of losing 1000 euros and a 24% chance of losing nothing.

Based on the dominance principle, we would expect people to choose options (2) and (3). Due to loss aversion, however, most people prefer to choose options (1) and (4).

Although prospect theory does, in itself, not make any predictions about individual differences, it has been shown that some individuals are more loss-averse than others. For example, in a study on the risk of losing, Josephs, Larrick, Steele, and Nisbett (1992) asked participants who scored high and low on self-esteem to choose between two options that differed in terms of risk associated with them. These participants were offered the possibility of gaining $8 versus a two in three chance of winning $12 (note that the expected utility of both options is equal). Participants scoring low on self-esteem were more likely to choose the first option than the participants scoring high on self-esteem.

In the same study, Josephs et al. (1992) let participants choose a possible bet. More specifically, they could choose from five different bets, ranging from not risky at all to highly risky. The least risky bet had a 95% chance of

winning $2.10 and the riskiest bet had a 25% chance of winning $8. Note again that the expected utility was the same for bets. High self-esteem participants were significantly more likely to choose the riskiest bet than low self-esteem participants (see also Box 21.2).

21.12.2 THE FRAMING EFFECT

In addition to loss aversion, prospect theory also predicts that decisions can be strongly influenced by the way a problem is formulated, a phenomenon that is known as the **framing effect**. Tversky and Kahneman (1981) used their **Asian disease problem** to study this effect. The problem consisted of the following description that was given to participants:

> *Imagine that the United States is preparing for the outbreak of an unusual Asian disease that is expected to kill 600 people. Two alternative programmes have been proposed to combat the disease. Imagine that the consequences of the programmes are as follows.*

Half of the participants (those in the gain frame condition) were then given the following description:

- If programme A is chosen, 200 people will be saved.
- If programme B is chosen, there is a chance of 1 in 3 of 600 people being saved and a chance of 2 in 3 of no one being saved.

The other half of the participants (those in the loss frame condition) received a slightly different description:

- If programme A is chosen, 400 people will die.
- If programme B is chosen, there is a chance of 1 in 3 that nobody will die and a chance of 2 in 3 that 600 people will die.

A remarkable result of this study was that in the gain frame condition, 72% of the participants chose programme A, while in the loss frame condition as many as 78% of the participants chose programme B. This result is remarkable because the expected utility of both programmes is the same. Thus, the strong preference for one of the two programmes appears to be purely driven by the framing of the problem.

Although these results initially appeared to provide strong evidence for the prospect theory, it should be noted that the results might be affected by the fact that the deterministic option (programme A) was formulated in a more ambiguous way than the probabilistic option (programme B). Consequently, it is possible that at least some participants interpreted the gain frame condition as implying that *at least* 200 people would be saved. Similarly, participants in the loss frame condition may have interpreted the wording as meaning that *at least* 400 people will die. According to this interpretation, programme A becomes

Box 21.2 Decision-making and multiple-choice exams

A multiple-choice exam is a good example of a decision-making process that you are undoubtedly familiar with. It is typical that for each question there are a number of possible answers (often three, four, or five), of which only one is correct, and your task is to decide which one it is. Consider a four-choice multiple-choice exam. Each alternative answer is associated with an expected utility. If you are fully confident, you can assign the answer you believe to be correct a 1-point score and the other answers a score of 0. When you are in doubt, you may assign a lower value to the answer you believe to be correct, while the competing alternatives each get a residual low score. The problem is what you would do best when you really do not know what the right answer is. In case of a pure guess, the expected utility of each alternative would be ¼ point.

Because guessing is often considered a problem in multiple choice exams, the possible effects of guessing are taken into consideration when designing the exam, so that the final score reflects your actual academic performance and not the possible outcome of a lucky guess. In many exams, for example in the Netherlands, the effect of guessing is taken into consideration when determining the pass/fail cut-off point. If we assume four choice alternatives, the expected utility from guessing would be that you would get 25% of all the questions right. Thus, it would only be the case that when you get more than this proportion of questions right that you start earning points for your exam. In other situations, a guess-correction system can be employed. Using this system, one would earn 1 point for every correct answer, but also lose one-third of a point for every incorrect answer. Thus, to prevent the loss of points, this system requires you not only to be able to recognise the correct answer but also to decide whether or not to actually answer the question.

If we take a purely utilitarian view of the guess-correction system, the expected return for pure guesses would be exactly zero. After all, for every four questions you would be expected to win one point once and lose one-third of a point three times. If we now consider that our guessing process is typically not random, because we can usually eliminate one or two alternatives, or deem them at least highly unlikely, we find that in practice the expected utility of a guess is still considerably larger than zero. The bottom line is that even under a system that attempts to penalise guessing, it is still beneficial to do so. At least from a utilitarian perspective!

In practice, however, it frequently happens that students score much lower on exams with a guess-correction system in place than on an exam where the likelihood of guessing is incorporated into the cut-off point. For many students, the chance of losing one-third of a point outweighs the potential gains of winning a point, so many students tend to leave questions open when they are not absolutely sure what the correct answer is; a problem that particularly affects students with low self-esteem. In extreme cases, students scoring low on self-esteem may answer even fewer questions than the minimum number required to pass the exam! A systematic investigation into this type of behaviour has been the direct reason for some universities to abolish the guess-correction system from multiple-choice exams in favour of a system that factors in guessing while scoring the exam.

a more attractive programme in the win-frame condition and a less attractive programme in the win-loss condition. Indeed, when this ambiguity was removed from the formulation, the framing effect disappeared (Mandel & Vartanian, 2011).

Wang (1996b) argued that in addition to framing, there are other social and moral factors that can influence choice behaviour on the Asian disease problem. In Wang's study, participants had to make a choice between a deterministic version in which one-third of all affected people survive the disease with certainty and a probabilistic version in which there is a one in three chance that all affected people survive and a two in three chance that no one survives. Note that this is similar to Tversky and Kahneman's (1981) experiment. Wang, however, manipulated the number of individuals who were affected and found that participants had a strong preference for the deterministic option in positively formulated problems, and a preference for the probabilistic option in negatively formulated problems, but only when the scenarios involved relatively large populations (fig 21.9).

In a follow-up study, Wang (1996a) manipulated the proportions in the choice options, in the sense that in the deterministic option two-thirds of those affected survived the disease, while in the probabilistic version there was a one in three chance that everyone survived the disease and two in three that everyone died. In addition, Wang varied the size of the group that was affected: group size was either 600, 6, or 3 unknown patients. In addition, he included six patients who were introduced as being close relatives of the participant. An important consequence of the preceding formulation is that the deterministic option

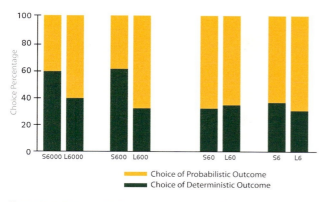

Figure 21.9 The percentage of choices in favour of a deterministic versus probabilistic treatment programme for a hypothetical disease, as a function of the framing of the problem and the total number of individuals involved in the problem description (S = life-saving framing; L = life-losing framing. 6000, 600, 60, and 6 = size of the population that is affected by the life-or-death decision. (source: Wang, 1996b)

has a utility that is twice that of the probabilistic option. However, the probabilistic option appears to be fairer, because all patients would suffer the same fate. When the problem involved unknown patients, most participants preferred the deterministic option. When the problem involved six close relatives, however, most participants preferred the probabilistic option because participants' choices were more strongly driven by fairness.

To avoid framing problems, it is thus important to mention both the positive and the negative consequence of each option. Almashat, Ayotte, Edelstein, and Margrett (2008) presented their participants with medical scenarios about treating cancer and found that the framing effect disappeared when the participants named both the pros and cons of all available options and when they had to defend their decision.

21.12.3 THE SUNK COST EFFECT

A phenomenon that is strongly related to the framing effect is the **sunk cost effect** (see also Box 21.3). This effect describes our tendency to continue with a specific action, even when it is suboptimal, because costly resources have already been devoted to it (Braverman & Blumenthal-Barby, 2012).

Suppose you are on your way to a hotel for which you have already made a non-refundable 100 euro reservation.

Box 21.3 Failed megaprojects: the sunk cost effect in practice

The sunk cost effect has a counterpart that is less familiar to psychologists, which has been studied almost exclusively in lower species of animals, known as the Concorde fallacy (Arkes & Ayton, 1999). This fallacy describes the tendency of lower species to exhibit the sunk cost effect. Interestingly, the term is derived from one of the most striking forms of sunk cost effects in existence. In the 1960s, the British and French governments decided to collaborate on the development of a supersonic airliner that would eventually become known as the Concorde.

Even before the first test flight, the expected commercial possibilities of the aircraft turned out to be very disappointing: rising fuel prices, increasing unrest about the expected noise pollution, and the mass transport realised by the American Boeing 747 jumbo jet meant that there was hardly a commercial market for the Concorde. Nevertheless, the British and French governments continued to invest in the project, arguing that too much had already been invested to discontinue it. In the end, only 14 Concorde aircraft were built for commercial use, and because they were impossible to sell for their market price, the French and British governments sold them to their national airlines for a symbolic price. Until the year 2000, these airlines operated the Concorde on a limited service between Paris and New York and London and New York respectively. This era came to a dramatic end on July 25,

2000, following the spectacular crash of an Air France Concorde in Paris.

A similar story can be found in the United States with the development of the Space Shuttle. Its development was motivated by a desire to reduce the operational cost of space launches. Before the shuttle era, disposable rockets were used, and the idea of being able to reuse a spacecraft sounded attractive on paper. Unfortunately, the shuttle fell victim to numerous compromises during its design stages, resulting not only in an operational cost that ended up being far above what was originally estimated but also considerable compromises in the vehicles' safety, resulting in the loss of two of the five flight-worthy shuttles that were eventually built. Consequently, the project not only failed to deliver on its original promise but also put a disproportionate strain on the budget of the U.S. space agency, NASA, making it impossible for several other promising projects to be carried out. Despite this economically troublesome situation, the project continued until 2012, when the last shuttle made its final flight.

Finally, an interesting footnote is that although Concorde is the namesake for a phenomenon studied in lower species, there is very little evidence that lower species actually exhibit this Concorde effect. So, it seems that lower animals behave more rationally than humans in some ways.

Suddenly, you become seriously ill and would prefer to go home. What is the best thing to do? Many people would answer that the best thing to do is to go on, because otherwise you would lose the money you had already invested, even though you would incur an even greater cost to get to the hotel and you would probably not enjoy your weekend.

Simonson and Staw (1992) found that the extent to which we can be held responsible for our actions can contribute significantly to the sunk cost effect. In their study, participants were given information about a company that produced two different types of beer. They then had to decide to which of these two products an additional 3 million dollars of marketing budget should be allocated. After choosing, they were informed that the president of the company had made the same decision but that the marketing campaign had been disappointing. Finally, they were informed that the company still had $10 million available for marketing purposes, an amount that could be split between the two products.

Participants were assigned to a high-responsibility and a low-responsibility condition. In the high-responsibility condition, they were informed that their decision about the distribution of these marketing funds would be shared with other students and with their lecturers. Moreover, they were asked for their permission to publicly discuss their decision afterwards. In the low-responsibility condition, participants were informed that their decisions would be kept confidential and that there was no relationship between their decisions on this task and their management skills. There was also an intermediate group, in which participants were simply told that the information they received should be sufficient to make an adequate decision. Simonson and Staw's (1992) main finding was that the sunk cost effect was larger the more responsible participants could be held for their decisions. That is, participants in the high-responsibility group probably felt a strong inclination to justify their earlier ineffective decision by continuing to invest in a previously unsuccessful product.

The question is how to avoid this sunk cost effect. An important factor is the availability of all relevant information. Indeed, economics students solving an investment problem, who had all relevant information available, focused less on the investments already made and were less susceptible to the sunk cost effect (Bagila & Ely, 2011).

21.12.4 NEURAL CORRELATES OF GAINS, LOSSES, AND EXPECTATIONS

Breiter, Aharon, Kahneman, Dale, and Shizgal (2001) used fMRI to investigate the neural responses related to expectation and the experience of winning or losing money. To do so, participants were shown a spinner that depicted three amounts of money (comparable to a wheel in a slot machine; fig 21.10). The spinner in question was selected from a set of three.

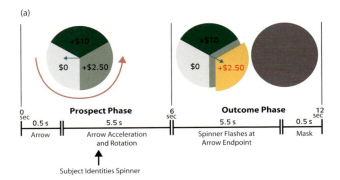

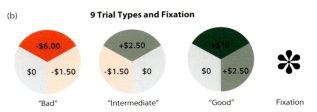

Figure 21.10 Example of stimuli used in a study of the neural basis for the processing of gains and losses. (a) During the first phase of the experiment a spinner was shown with predominantly favourable, neutral, or negative outcomes. After the spinner came to a stop, one of the possible outcomes was revealed. (b) Overview of the nine possible outcomes of each trial. (source: Breiter et al., 2001)

The first of these was a 'good' spinner, as it contained two positive amounts (10 dollars or 2.50 dollars) and one neutral amount (0 dollars). The second was a neutral spinner and contained the amounts 2.50, −1.50, and 0 dollars. Finally, the third one was a 'bad' spinner, which contained the amounts −6.00, −1.50, and 0 dollars. After the wheel was shown and the spinning stopped, the final outcome was revealed. This was the amount of money that the participant had won or lost.

Using this design, Breiter et al. (2001) were able to investigate two different aspects of processing gains and loss. First, the prospect phase, that is, the expectation of gains or losses corresponded to the presentation of the spinner. Second, the actual processing of the outcome corresponded to the moment when the exact amount the participant had won or lost was revealed. The prospect phase corresponded to activation in the sublenticular amygdala and the orbital gyrus, while the outcome corresponded to activation in the nucleus accumbens, the sublenticular amygdala, and the hypothalamus.

21.12.5 LOSS AVERSION IN EVERYDAY LIFE

That idea that loss aversion influences many everyday decision-making processes has now been convincingly demonstrated. For example, Pope and Schweitzer (2011) found that many professional golfers, including Tiger Woods, show signs of loss aversion while playing. Smith, Levere, and Kurtzman (2009) found similar results among experienced poker players. These players sometimes won or lost more than $200,000 – and played more aggressively,

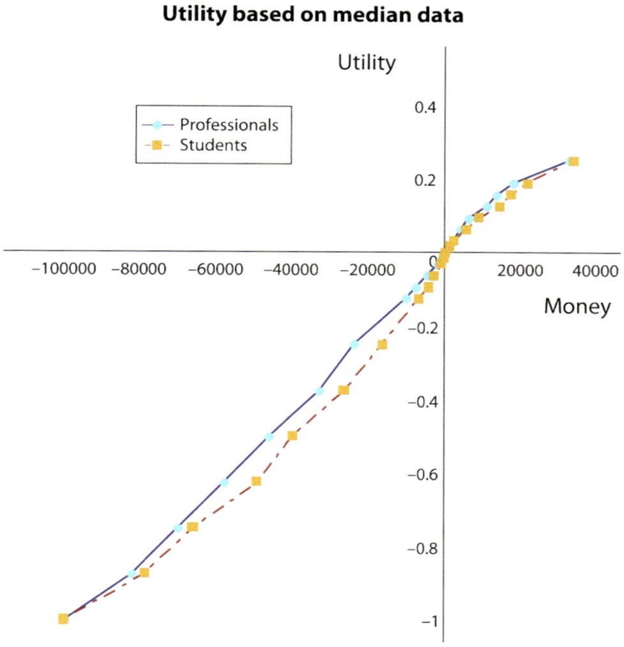

Utility based on median data

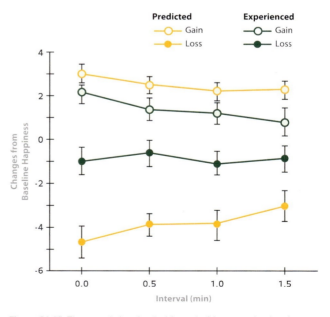

Figure 21.11 The utility function found by Abdellaoui et al. among financial professionals and students. (source: Abdellaoui et al., 2011)

for example by betting more and increasing their stakes after a loss, behaviour that was driven by loss aversion. Finally, Abdellaoui, Bleichrodt, and Kammoun (2011) studied the behaviour of professionals in the financial sector, who had on average 240 million euros under their management. Consistent with prospect theory, these professionals showed risk aversion for potential losses and risk-seeking behaviour for potential gains, during a task in which decisions about financial transactions had to be made. Their risk behaviour for profits was similar to that of a control group, but it was smaller for losses (fig 21.11).

21.12.6 LIMITATIONS

Although prospect theory has successfully explained several important, seemingly irrational aspects of our decision-making behaviour in recent decades, there still remain some phenomena that cannot be adequately explained by the theory, such as the occurrence of loss neutrality.

Imagine that you are given a choice between the following two alternatives: (1) a 50% chance of winning 1 euro and a 50% chance of losing 1 euro; or (2) a 50% chance of winning 6 euro and a 50% chance of losing 6 euro. According to prospect theory, we would have a strong aversion to losses. Thus, prospect theory would predict that we would rather choose option 1 than option 2. Many studies, however, have found that, as long as the stakes are not extremely high, most participants have no specific preference for either option 1 or option 2 (Yechiam & Hochman, 2013). Why would there be no loss aversion in this particular case? According to Yechiam and Hochman, this may be related to the involvement of attention. These authors suggest that the prospect of

a possible loss would cause a temporary increase in arousal, making us more sensitive to both potential reinforcers (i.e., the potential losses and the potential gains). When both occur simultaneously, according to Yechiam and Hochman, loss neutrality would occur because we pay equal attention to the potential gains and the potential losses.

Apart from the problem of loss neutrality, there are other limitations in the implementation of the theory, such as the fact that the theory does not take into account the specific circumstances under which gains or losses can occur. For example, not winning is much worse when you had a 90% chance of winning a million than when your chance of winning this amount was only one in a million. Moreover, the theory does not take many of the social and emotional factors into account that can play an important role in decision-making processes (Wang, 1996a).

21.13 EMOTIONAL FACTORS

21.13.1 IMPACT BIAS

As we discussed in Chapter 12, emotions can exert an important influence on our cognitive processes. For example, emotion is involved in the processing of losses, although it appears that we often overestimate the expected impact of such emotions. Kermer, Driver-Linn, Wilson, and Gilbert (2006) found, for example, that participants predicted that a possible loss of 3 dollars would have a greater impact on their emotions than a possible gain of 5 dollars. Then, the outcome of a game was determined by the tossing of a coin. Participants who lost the game actually felt much better than they had previously predicted (fig 21.12). This overestimation of the impact of a loss on our emotional state is known as **impact bias**. Impact bias is not only found in coin toss

Figure 21.12 The expected and actual impact of losses and gains. (source: Kermer et al. 2006)

gamble situations but also in all kinds of everyday experiences, such as losing a job or breaking up with a partner.

The actual emotions that are experienced prior to making a decision are also indicative of the risks that are associated with the decision. In this respect, we can distinguish between anticipatory emotion, that is, the emotion we expect to experience as a result of our decision, and experienced emotion, that is, the actual emotion that occurs after the decision. Schlösser, Dunning, and Fetchenhauer (2013) found that both types of emotion are indicative of the risks associated with a decision.

The type of emotion that is experienced is highly dependent on the situation, making the relationship between emotion and decisions particularly complex. For example, Giorgetta et al. (2013) used a gambling task in which the choices were made by either the participant or by a computer. When the participant lost because of their own choice, regret was experienced, but when the loss was due to a choice made by the computer, disappointment was experienced. Regret was followed by riskier behaviour, whereas this was not the case for disappointment. When the participant won, this was experienced as joy when the choice was made by the participant, and as elation when the choice was made by the computer.

Now that we have discussed how emotion can have an impact on decision processes, we can turn to whether emotions can have a negative or a positive impact on our decision processes. As discussed in Chapter 12, the amygdala and the ventromedial frontal cortex are particularly involved in the processing of emotions such as fear. Weller, Levin, Shiv, and Bechara (2007) found that patients with damage to the ventromedial frontal cortex were characterised by increased levels of risky behaviour, both in terms of potential gains and potential losses. Patients with damage to the amygdala are characterised by limited loss aversion. De Martino, Camerer, and Adolphs (2010) reported, for example, two case studies (patients SP and AP) of severe brain damage to the amygdala. These two patients showed no loss aversion. A normally functioning amygdala can therefore be regarded as a brake on behaviour, prompting us to be cautious.

Wong, Yik, and Kwong (2006) also found that strong negative emotions can have a positive influence on decision processes. They examined the sunk cost effect and hypothesised that an initially unfavourable outcome of an investment would result in negative affect. When this negative affect is sufficiently strong, it should result in actions aimed at reducing this feeling. For these reasons, one might expect that individuals who score high on neuroticism, a personality trait characterised by high levels of negative affect, would be more likely to withdraw from situations that cause negative affect. In other words, individuals who score high on neuroticism should be characterised by a less pronounced sunk cost effect. Wong et al. found that this was indeed the case.

These results suggest that emotions can have a positive effect on decision-making because they reduce excessive risk-taking behaviour or prevent people from continuing to make poor decisions. Shiv, Loewenstein, Bechara, Damasio, and Damasio (2005), however, report data that suggest that emotions can also have a negative effect on decision-making behaviour. Patients with brain damage to areas associated with emotional processing performed better on a gambling task than a control group. The main reason for this difference could be explained by the fact that the control group was less inclined to invest again after a loss, thus missing out on potential gains in the next round, whereas the patients continued to invest.

21.13.2 OMISSION BIAS

Emotions can also strongly influence our willingness to act. When a given action involves a certain risk, this may result in a preference to not perform this action, even if the consequence of remaining passive has a larger negative utility than performing the action. This tendency to omit an action is known as **omission bias**. Ritov and Baron (1990) found omission bias in a study on participants' willingness to have their children vaccinated. These participants had to imagine that their children had a ten in 10,000 likelihood of dying from a flu epidemic if they were not vaccinated. They were then informed that there was a vaccine that could reliably save them from the flu, but that it had a number of side effects that were potentially lethal. Ritov and Baron found that five deaths per 10,000 was the limit at which participants were willing to have their child vaccinated. This implies that many participants were unwilling to have their child vaccinated in situations where the risk of death from side effects was less than the risk of death from the disease. This is interesting, because a fully utilitarian decision would imply that the willingness to participate in the vaccination programme should only disappear at a maximum risk of ten deaths due to side effects per 10,000 cases.

Participants in Ritov and Baron's study argued that they would feel much more responsible for their child's death if it resulted from acting rather than not acting. Similar results were found by Brown et al. (2010). Although this sense of responsibility can be extended to many other moral dilemmas, it might be possible to explain the omission bias using on a simpler mechanism. Crockett (2013) proposes a Pavlovian classical conditioning mechanism that automatically stimulates actions linked to attractive stimuli and inhibits actions linked to unattractive stimuli.

21.13.3 STATUS QUO BIAS

A second example of the impact that emotions may have on decision-making processes is the **status quo bias**. This bias describes how individuals sometimes prefer the current state (the status quo) to an alternative, potentially better state. In daily life we can observe this bias among people

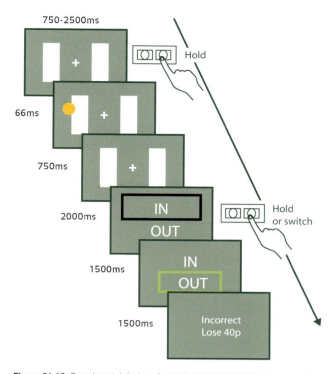

Figure 21.13 Experimental design of a study investigating the status quo bias. Participants had to decide, using a simulated tennis game, whether the ball was in or out. In doing so, they either had to stick to their previous decisions or to switch to the other option. (source: Nicolle et al., 2011)

who stay with the same energy provider for years, or among those who leave their telephone subscription plan unchanged, despite the fact that better options have become available. In the United States, much research focuses on the way people manage their pension funds. Here, it also appears that many people continue to invest in the same fund, even though it is no longer the best performing fund by a long shot (Samuelson & Zeckhauser, 1988).

Nicolle, Fleming, Bach, Driver, and Dolan (2011) found a status quo bias in a difficult perceptual decision task. In their study, participants had to decide whether a ball fell inside (in) or outside (out) the lines of a simulated tennis court (see fig 21.13). Participants were informed of their previous decision and, at each trial, were given the choice of keeping it (i.e., maintaining the status quo) or switching to the other decision. The experiment was designed so that in 50% of all trials, the participants would have to maintain the status quo. That is, the position of the ball was the same as the position of the ball in the previous trial. In the other 50% of the trials, they should abandon the status quo. In these trials, the ball changed position; where it was in on the previous trial, it was now out, or vice versa. When participants made mistakes, it was due to maintaining the status quo in 62.7% of all trials while in only 37.3% of all cases was it due to leaving the status quo. Participants reported regret as the most important reason for maintaining the status quo. The latter was also found in the brain activation patterns. Incorrect rejection of the status quo was associated with an increase in activation

in the prefrontal cortex and the insula, two brain areas associated with the processing of regret.

21.13.4 RATIONAL-EMOTIONAL MODEL

Anderson (2003) proposed a rational-emotional model to explain the effects of avoiding a decision (including the already discussed omission bias and status quo bias). According to this model, decisions are determined by rational factors such as inferences and expected outcomes, and by the expected and experienced emotions. The model attempts to explain the effects of decision avoidance based on fear and regret. As we have already illustrated, regret is an important factor. Fear may also be involved, because this emotion can be reduced by temporarily refraining from making decisions. Although it is a plausible premise that both emotions play an important role, there are a number of important findings that cannot be adequately explained by this model. The most important is that the effects mentioned only apply to the short term. In the long term, it is often found that regret is more often associated with inactivity than with performing an action (Leach & Plaks, 2009). A second problem is that we can also find status quo bias in many trivial everyday situations, for example, in the decision whether or not to switch television channels (Esteves-Sorensen & Perretti, 2012). It is indeed difficult to imagine that this choice is influenced by fear or regret.

21.13.5 SOCIAL-FUNCTIONALIST APPROACH

The American psychologist Philip Tetlock (2002) has explained decision-making processes in terms of social factors. According to his **social functionalist approach**, the social consequences of a decision play a very important role in behaviour. According to Tetlock, our decision-making processes arose from the need to recognise social deception. As we discussed in Chapter 19, we are generally much better at solving the Wason (1968) card selection task when the contents of the cards involve social deception. Similarly, social consequences can have a strong influence on decisions. The previously discussed study by Simonson and Staw (1992), discussing the sunk cost effect, for example, showed that being held responsible for a decision can have a strong influence on a decision to continue with an investment that has already been made.

The pressure of being accountable can also influence the decision of experts. For example, Schwartz et al. (2004) asked general practitioners to choose between two possible treatments for osteoarthritis. Half of the participating doctors were informed that a patient advocacy group could ask for a justification of the prescribed treatment after they had made their decision, so they had to write a short report explaining their choice. The doctors in the other group did not have to do this. In each group, half the doctors were given a choice of two alternative treatments: (1) medication using Diclofenac and referral to a specialist, or (2) referral to a specialist only. The other half of the doctors were also presented a third option: treatment with the drug Piroxicam. In the latter group, there is a higher degree of conflict because the doctors were given the choice between two different types of medication that they could prescribe. In this condition, the participating doctors more often avoided making this choice, opting to only refer their patients to a specialist. Interestingly, doctors were much more likely to do so when they were held accountable for their decisions (fig 21.14).

21.14 COMPLEX DECISIONS

The decision processes that we discussed so far have been relatively simple, as they have involved choices consisting of a limited number of options, each of which contain only a limited number of properties to consider. Many of the decisions that we make in our daily lives require us to consider many different options, however, making these decisions much more complex (see also Box 21.4).

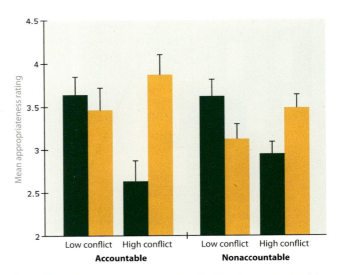

Figure 21.14 The extent to which doctors referred patients to a specialist as a function of the extent to which they were held responsible for their decisions and the number of choices they have. (source: Schwarz and Keus, 2004)

Box 21.4 Fact or fiction: do you make better decisions unconsciously?

The best decisions are made by consciously considering our options for a while and carefully weighing the alternatives; at least that is what most people believe. Dijksterhuis, Bos, Nordgren, and van Baaren (2006), however, argue that this is not the case. According to their unconscious thought advantage theory (Dijksterhuis & Nordgren, 2006; Dijksterhuis et al., 2006), conscious thoughts are specifically advantageous for simple decisions, whereas unconscious thoughts are beneficial for complex decisions. According to Dijksterhuis and colleagues, conscious thoughts are too much limited by the limited capacity of attention and consciousness. For this reason, they argue that unconscious thoughts are better suited for the integration of large amounts of information than conscious thoughts. The idea of an unconscious influence also fits with the concept of a gut decision, a gut feeling, or an intuition. Although these ideas are appealing, the question is whether it is actually true that these intuitive processes can positively influence our decision-making processes. Although the study by Dijksterhuis et al. did not go unnoticed, the idea that unconscious thoughts would be more effective than conscious thoughts has not been beyond criticism, in particular because the results have been proven to be very difficult to replicate (Nieuwenstein & van Rijn, 2012; Nieuwenstein et al., 2015).

In a very comprehensive literature review in the journal Behavioural & Brain Sciences, Newell and Shanks (2014) discuss the possible influences that unconscious processes might have on decision strategies. They conclude that the idea that unconscious processes can affect decision processes stems from one or more of the following factors: (1) the use of inadequate research methods, (2) a failure to consider the fact that some explanations are artificial and contrived, and (3) an uncritical acceptance of conclusions that fit within the original authors' frame of mind.

With regard to the unconscious thought advantage theory, Newell and Shanks note that two conditions must be met, before it can be concluded that there are benefits from unconscious thoughts. First, decisions that are made when a participant is distracted must be better than decisions in a condition in which the participant can deliberate consciously. Second, these decisions must also be better than those obtained when participants are required to answer immediately (i.e., when they cannot deliberate at all). Most of the studies investigating the unconscious thought advantage effect used only a conscious deliberation condition, in which the participants were asked to carefully weigh all aspects of the decision, and an unconscious deliberation condition, in which participants were distracted for a while by solving puzzles. Studies that tested decision processes involving all three conditions typically found no unconscious thought advantage. In other words, the unconscious decision was no better than the immediate decision, which may lead us to suspect that the design of the experiment was such that the conscious deliberation actually led to a reduced performance. How can this be?

Many studies on the unconscious thought advantage effect use an experimental context in which participants

(Continued)

Box 21.4 (Continued)

have to choose between a number of alternative options, for example cars. For each car, a number of relevant attributes are presented, such as the fuel consumption, the number of cup holders, and the purchase price. These attributes are presented serially, and participants have to remember the value of each of these attributes, for each product. Of course, this results in an enormous strain working memory, because each attribute has to be tied to the right context (see Chapter 14).

In addition, in these studies, the 'optimal choice' is often determined by the researchers in a rather arbitrary way see e.g., (Nordgren, Bos, & Dijksterhuis, 2011). In the original study by Dijksterhuis et al. (2006) for example, the number of cup holders was given equal weight to fuel consumption (while of course we all know, as Newell and Shanks (2014) point out with a great sense of irony, that *cup holders are far more important*!). This, of course, makes it extremely difficult to determine what the optimal choice would have been if the actual weighting of the participants were considered. Finding the 'optimal choice' in these studies is therefore not so much a deliberation process, as it appears to be a guessing game aimed at determining what the experimenters believed would be the optimal choice. When these factors are considered, the possible advantage of unconscious thought disappears.

Mamede, Schmidt, et al. (2010) tested the effects of conscious and unconscious deliberation among medical students and medical experts. Among medical experts, they found that, specifically for complex cases, the quality of their diagnoses was significantly better when they were able to deliberate consciously than when they had to make a choice unconsciously. These results directly contradict one of the predictions of unconscious thought theory, namely that unconscious deliberation would be more beneficial as a function of the complexity of the problem.

Although Dijksterhuis and Nordgren (2006) claim that unconscious processes have a greater capacity for integrating multiple attributes of each option, compared to the capacity-limited, conscious processes, this claim is theoretically very implausible. After all, one of the most important functions attributed to consciousness is the integration of information (Baars, 2005; Dehaene & Naccache, 2001; Tononi, 2004). Moreover, an overwhelming number of cognitive psychological studies have shown that tasks that can be automated and bypass conscious awareness are often the simple repetitive ones, while complex tasks cannot be automated to the same degree (Schneider & Shiffrin, 1977; Shiffrin & Schneider, 1977). So, do we make our best decisions unconsciously? The answer is: no, probably not!

Medical experts, for example, have to consider many different factors in their diagnosis (see Chapter 22) and much may depend on whether it is correct or not. A more mundane decision, such as whether or not to move apartments and – if so – on the basis of which criteria to choose a new home, is also an example of a complex, non-trivial decision. In addition, in everyday life, the decisions we make are often not isolated events, but rather comprise a series of decisions that can have a lasting impact on the rest of our lives. For example, will you continue your studies? What will you choose to study? Where will you do your internship? Which vacancies will you apply for? These are all examples of decisions that, in a certain sense, are interdependent, while you are pursuing a certain goal. We will see that there is quite a strong discrepancy between the way you should ideally make these decisions and the way they are made in practice.

21.14.1 THE MULTIPLE-ATTRIBUTE UTILITY THEORY

Let us start with the ideal way we should make complex decisions. According to the multiple-attribute utility theory (Wright, 1984), a complex decision should involve five stages: (1) identify all the attributes that are relevant to our

decision; (2) decide how these attributes will factor into the decision; (3) make a list of all the options that we consider; (4) for each option, rate all the attributes; and (5) for each option; determine the total utility and choose the option with the highest utility.

To illustrate how the choice process works, we can consider someone in the process of buying a new car. There are several attributes that can be important: design, fuel consumption, purchase price, expected maintenance costs, quality of the audio system, the number of cup holders, the load capacity, the size, the presence of spoilers and/or decorative rims, the tone of the horn, and so on. The first thing to do involves identifying all the relevant attributes and determining how much weight these attributes should carry. For example, depending on the budget, the purchase price and fuel consumption may weigh more heavily. On the other hand, a plumber will attach greater importance to a larger cargo space, and a music lover to the quality of the audio system. Next, for each model under consideration, the utility for each of these options must be determined, and the total utility must then be calculated.

If we follow this strategy, we will generally make the best decision, assuming that all relevant options are considered and that all criteria are independent of each other. In reality, however, we rarely ever make a decision this way. There are several reasons for this. First, the decision process becomes very complex if we are to consider all options, and, second, it is often not possible to determine all attributes that are relevant to a decision. Third, it is often not possible to determine whether all relevant attributes are completely independent of each other. In the case of cars, for example, the purchase price is strongly related to the number of additional options, fuel consumption, and size.

21.14.2 BOUNDED RATIONALITY

For these reasons, Herbert Simon (1957) proposed an alternative decision model. According to this model, we can distinguish between unbounded and **bounded rationality**. According to Simon, our rationality is bounded, that is, constrained, by the environment. In the context of decision-making processes, we can identify two different kinds of constraints: constraints from the environment, for example in the form of costs associated with gathering information, and constraints in our cognitive skills. The latter constraints are, for example, formed by limitations in working memory capacity or limitations in attention span.

In essence, Simon's bounded-rationality concept implies that we are only as rational as our internal and external environment allows. In practice, bounded rationality often results in **satisficing** (a contraction of satisfactory and sufficing). Satisficing does not always result in the best decision, but it often results in a decision that is good enough, specifically in situations where not all options are available at the same time.

According to Schwartz et al. (2002) decision-makers can also be divided into satisficers, that is, people who are satisfied with a reasonable decision, and maximisers (perfectionists). Satisficers are generally happier and more optimistic about their lives than maximisers, according to Schwartz et al. The study by Schwartz et al. involved American participants. A study by Roets, Schwartz, and Guan (2012), however, found that Chinese participants showed no such differences, implying that the effects of choice strategies on psychosocial well-being may be culturally determined.

21.14.3 ELIMINATION-BY-ASPECT THEORY

Tversky (1972) developed a decision theory that is based on Simon's (1957) bounded-rationality principle. This **elimination-by-aspect theory** describes how decision-makers try to optimise complex decisions by eliminating options. They do this by sequentially traversing the relevant attributes or aspects and eliminating those options that do not meet a specific criterion. To illustrate this principle using

our previous example, a potential car buyer might first consider the purchase price. All options outside the budget are eliminated from the list of potential candidates. Then, for example, the fuel type can be evaluated. For example, if the buyer wants to purchase an electric car, all diesel and petrol vehicles are eliminated from the list. Next, when there are still multiple candidates remaining, a third aspect (the number of cup holders) can be evaluated until only one candidate remains. Although this strategy is efficient, it is problematic in the sense that the outcome of the decision depends on the first attribute that was evaluated (suppose that if we were to start with an elimination based on the number of cup holders, we could quickly end up with an extremely suboptimal choice). Indeed, human decision-makers often try to reduce the complexity of decisions by eliminating options, but the way Tversky describes this process is probably too rigid.

Indeed, evidence suggests that we might use multiple strategies. Payne (1976) found, for example, that when students were looking for accommodation, they initially followed an eliminative strategy which corresponded to the elimination-by-attribute theory when they had many options. When there were only a few flats left, however, they would perform a more elaborate comparison, which was more in line with the multiple-attribute utility theory discussed earlier. For this reason, Kaplan, Bekhor, and Shiftan (2011) developed a modified version of the elimination-by-aspect theory, which consists of two stages. The first stage involves the elimination of all options that do not satisfy a criterion. The second stage involves a more detailed evaluation of the remaining options (see fig 21.15). Kaplan et al. found results similar to those of Payne. Students selected a flat after having access to information about 600 different

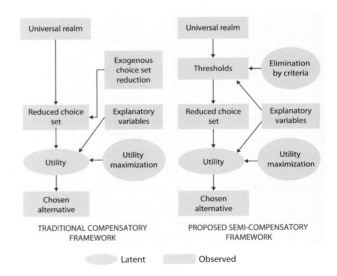

Figure 21.15 Outline of Kaplan et al.'s compensatory choice model that is based on Tversky's elimination-by-aspects theory. The left panel shows Kaplan's original model that most strongly resembles Tversky's original approach. The right panel shows a modified version involving two stages. (source: Kaplan et al. 2011)

flats. Initially, they selected on the basis of the criteria of 'location', 'walking distance to university', and 'rent'. This was followed by a more extensive evaluation of the remaining candidate flats.

Lenton and Stewart (2008) found similar results in the dating behaviour of single women, based on their choice behaviour on real-life dating sites. The more options they had, the simpler their choice strategy became. Women who had a choice of four potential partners used a strategy that corresponded to the multiple-attribute utility theory in 81% of cases. In contrast, women who had a choice of 64 potential partners only used this strategy in 41% of the cases. For the elimination-by-aspect theory, these percentages were 39% and 69% respectively, and for the satisficing strategy, 6% and 16%. Most women used multiple strategies, so the total percentages do not add up to 100.

21.14.4 DECISION-MAKING STRATEGIES

In this final section, we can reflect on some of the factors that may influence a decision. For example, do we stick to a particular decision, or can we change it on the basis of new evidence? And what do we do with evidence that does not match our biases?

21.14.4.1 Changed Preferences and Facts

Most of the theories discussed in this chapter are based on the assumption that the subjective utility of a specific attribute remains constant. Simon, Krawezyk, and Holyoak (2004), however, found that this was not the case. Participants had to choose between two different jobs in a department store, based on four different attributes, such as salary, travel time, location, and holidays. After making their choice, they were informed that one of the two jobs was at a much better location, and this information often caused participants to change their decision. Then the participants had to re-evaluate their preferences. Here, it turned out that the favourable attributes of the job that was eventually chosen were valued more, and the unfavourable attributes less.

The fact that individuals cannot only change their preferences but also have a selective memory for facts was demonstrated in a study by Svenson, Salo, and Lindholm (2009). Nursing students had to decide which of two patients should be prioritised for surgery. After the participants had made the decision, it turned out that memories of objective facts, such as life expectancy and the chance of surviving the operation, were strongly distorted, so that they appeared to be consistent with the decision they had made.

Stone, Mattingley, and Rangelov (2022) consider decision-making as a continuous process of evidence accumulation. According to these authors, a decision is made once

this accumulation process reaches a threshold. A chance of mind can occur when evidence for another option overtakes that of the initial preference.

21.14.4.2 Selective Exposure

In addition to selective memory, selective exposure is an important feature of poor decision-making. This phenomenon describes the fact that most people prefer information that is consistent with their beliefs over information that is not. Fischer and Greitemeyer (2010) assume that there is an increase in selective exposure when people feel the need to defend their own positions. In addition, according to Fischer and Greitemeyer, selective exposure can also occur when decision-makers are motivated to make the most accurate decision possible, but when they only have access to a limited amount of information. When decision-makers are strongly motivated, however, and instructed to make the best possible decision, selective exposure is often relatively limited (Hart et al., 2009).

21.15.4.3 Flexibility in Decision-Making Strategies

The theories on complex decisions discussed so far assume that decisions are made according to a relatively specific fixed pattern. It is questionable, however, whether natural decision-making processes are actually made this way. For instance, Galotti (2007) assumes that there is a considerable degree of flexibility in the way we make decisions. Her theory of natural decision processes assumes that a complex decision consists of five phases: (1) goal setting, (2) information gathering, (3) structuring the decision, (4) choosing, and (5) evaluating the decision.

Galotti assumes that there is considerable flexibility in the order in which these phases are applied (see fig 21.16). For example, decision-makers can return to an earlier stage if they encounter problems in a later stage. She also found

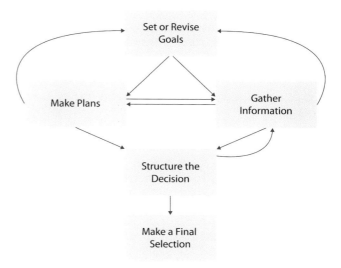

Figure 21.16 Different stages of a decision process. (source: Galotti and Tinkelenberg, 2009)

that decision-makers generally limit the amount of information they gathered to about four options, and the number of options slowly decreases over time. For each option, the decision-makers considered approximately three to six attributes. This number did not decrease, however, but either remained constant or even increased slightly over time. In addition, the number of attributes considered by the decision-makers depended on their skill or level of education.

Similar results have been reported by Galotti and Tinkelenberg (2009). This study followed parents who had to choose a primary school for their child. These parents also considered a limited number of options, and evaluated them based on a limited set of about five attributes. An important observation in this study, however, was that the decision process was dynamic. Over a six-month period, about one-third of the options and more than half of the criteria changed.

21.15 SUMMARY

Judgement and decision-making processes are strongly related to each other, but also differ in one important aspect. Judgement involves determining the likelihood of a particular event taking place, based on incomplete data, whereas decision-making involves selecting from several options. Judgement is related to our intuitive notion of statistical probabilities. In many cases, these statistical intuitions conflict with objectively calculated probabilities. For example, the gambler's fallacy describes the intuitive fallacy that probabilities related to independent events appear to be dependent on each other.

The likelihood of a given event, given a specific a priori probability, is described by Bayes' theorem. The taxi problem is a classic problem that is used in many studies to investigate the extent to which people take the base rate into account. Often people do not take this into account, so that the probability of a relatively rare event is greatly overestimated. They tend to let themselves be guided by relatively simple heuristics when making their probability judgements. The representativeness heuristic describes how the extent to which individual examples are representative of a certain category can strongly influence judgements. The use of this heuristic may result in the conjunction fallacy, that is, the misconception that a description consisting of a conjunction of two features applies more to a person than a description that includes only one of the two features.

The conjunction fallacy can possibly be explained on the basis of the availability heuristic. This heuristic describes how the estimation of the probability of a certain event is influenced by the ease with which we can retrieve relevant information from memory. The availability heuristic may also explain why many people have an unrealistic fear of particularly infrequent events, such as shark attacks or terrorist attacks.

Support theory assumes that the way events are described can have a strong influence on their estimated probability. A possible reason for this is that the details in the description focus our attention on these details,

thus activating the corresponding memory traces. Some studies show that experts are also influenced by this more explicit description, but the results are not always consistent. In very specific cases, however, the more explicit description can also have a negative effect on the probability judgement. This is especially the case when the description involves particularly rare events.

In general, most results show that judgements are strongly influenced by heuristics. Although heuristics can often lead to inaccurate judgements, they are also often useful in practice, because they produce very effective results requiring little cognitive effort. A special class of heuristics, which is particularly efficient, is formed by the collection of fast and frugal heuristics. Examples of this class of heuristics are the 'take the best' strategy, the recognition heuristic, and the hiatus heuristic. Which of these heuristics is most efficient depends on the degree of redundancy in the information presented and the nature of the problem.

According to Gigerenzer and Hoffrage, biases in judgements often occur because of our inability to deal with proportions. When problems are represented in more natural, concrete units, many judgement errors are significantly reduced. When problems are represented this way, we can make use of the process of natural sampling. Although natural sampling can result in better judgements, it can also result in a bias when we have the choice of which cases to consider. This phenomenon is known as biased sampling. A second factor that can reduce judgement errors is the extent to which the assessor has access to causal information, that is, has background knowledge relevant to the judgement.

Decisions range from the relatively trivial to the life-changing ones. All decision processes involve the accumulation of evidence and the execution of an action based on this information. A major problem is that the reliability of the information can vary considerably, so every decision can be considered as solving a statistical problem.

Decision processes were originally predominantly studied from the perspective of normative behavioural economic theories. These theories describe decision processes from the perspective of game theory and consider a decision as a bet on a possible outcome. The utility theory assumed that most people strive to maximise this outcome. Various psychological studies have shown, however, that people often make decisions that conflict with this principle. In contrast, Kahneman and Tversky's prospect theory assumes that people consider both potential gains and potential losses in their decisions and that losses are often given greater weight than gains. The latter effect is known as loss aversion. Subsequent studies have shown that there are large individual differences in the degree of loss aversion. In particular, people with low self-esteem are characterised by high levels of loss aversion.

In addition to loss aversion, decisions are strongly influenced by the way information is presented. The framing effect describes how, when the positive aspects of an option are mentioned, but not the negative ones, people are more inclined to choose this option, while a description of the exact same option in which only the negative aspects are mentioned results in a tendency to not choose that option.

The sunk cost effect describes the tendency of individuals to stand behind decisions already made, even when these decisions are suboptimal, because valuable resources have already been invested in the decision. The sunk cost effect occurs particularly when decision-makers are held accountable for their choices. Although prospect theory can explain a very large number of aspects of human choice behaviour well, there are also a number of limitations to the theory. One of these limitations is the fact that loss aversion does not always occur. In addition,

the theory does not consider the specific circumstances under which profit, or loss, can be expected.

Emotional factors play a significant role in decision-making processes. These processes also form the basis for loss aversion. Most people, however, overestimate the potential impact of a loss on their emotions. In other words, they show an impact bias. Regret is often related to losses that result from one's own decision, whereas disappointment is often related to losses that result from the choices of others. Although prefrontal damage often results in an increase in risk-taking behaviour that usually has negative effects on choice behaviour, for a limited number of cases it was found that patients who did not experience negative emotions for a risky choice actually presented better, because they did not show loss aversion.

In the case of choices involving risks, most people tend not to change the current situation, or only change it when the benefits clearly outweigh the costs; a phenomenon known as omission bias or a status quo bias. The social-functionalist approach assumes that the cognitive functions that form the basis for decision-making processes originate from the need to recognise social deception.

Complex decisions are often made by considering multiple attributes of different options. Since we are unable to consider all relevant attributes of all options, we must necessarily constrain ourselves. To describe these processes, Herbert Simon introduced the notion of bounded rationality. Elimination-by-aspect theory describes how decision-makers try to optimise complex decisions by eliminating options that do not meet a specific criterion. Complex decision processes, however, are flexible and can adapt to changed circumstances.

NOTE

1   With 498,715 inhabitants, Atlanta is indeed larger than Shreveport (393,406 inhabitants) (data Wikipedia: retrieved October 3, 2022).

FURTHER READING

Hastie, R., & Dawes, R. (2010). *Rational choice in an uncertain world: The psychology of judgment and decision making*. Los Angeles, CA: SAGE Publishing.

Kim, N. S. (2017). *Judgment and decision making: In the lab and in the world*. London, UK: McMillan Education.

Mankelow, K. (2012). *Thinking and reasoning: An introduction to the psychology of reason, judgment, and decision making*. Hove, UK: Taylor and Francis.

Wilhelms, E. A., & Reyna, V. F. (2015). *Neuroeconomics, judgment, and decision making*. Hove, UK: Taylor and Francis.

CHAPTER 22

Problem-solving and development of expertise

22.1 INTRODUCTION

The city of Königsberg, in the former Prussian Empire (currently known as Kaliningrad, a Russian enclave on the Baltic Sea sandwiched between Lithuania and Poland), lies on both banks of the river Pregel, including two islands in the middle of the river. All parts of the city are connected by seven bridges (see fig 22.1). The question is whether it is possible to map out a walking route along all the parts of the city, crossing each bridge only once. You don't have to end up at the same point as where you started. Solutions that involve crossing the river other than by bridge or that involve going onto a bridge without fully crossing it are not allowed. Before reading on, try to see if it is possible to find such a solution. How would you tackle this problem?

If you have not managed to find a route, or to prove that such a route does not exist, you are not alone! It took until 1736 for none other than the Swiss mathematician, physicist, logician, astronomer, and engineer Leonhard Euler to prove that the problem has no solution. Euler's proof also laid the foundations for a new form of mathematics that is currently known as **graph theory**.

Euler's approach was as follows: represent each landmass that you want to visit as a point in a graph. Now represent each bridge between two land masses as a line between the two corresponding points. Euler noted that, apart from the starting and ending points, every time you arrive at a landmass, you have to leave it by a different route. This implies that every point on the graph that does not represent the start or end of your route must have an even number of connections (i.e., for each landmass you visit you have to use one route to reach it and another to leave). If we inspect the graph representing the connections between the land masses, we notice immediately that all land masses have an odd number of connections to the other land masses, which leads us to conclude that it is impossible to find a route. This example shows how a change in the representation of a problem is sometimes necessary to find a solution.

22.2 PROBLEM SOLVING

The main theme of this chapter is **problem-solving**. We are engaged in problem-solving when we meet the following four conditions (Goel, 2010): (1) two different states are involved; (2) we are in one state and want to be in the other; (3) it is not immediately clear how to bridge the difference between these two states; and (4) bridging the two states has to be done in several steps, using a consciously controlled process.

22.2.1 CHARACTERISTICS OF PROBLEM-SOLVING

22.2.1.1 Well-Defined versus Ill-Defined Problems

Although the four conditions just mentioned form the core of almost every problem, there is a great variation in the types of problems that we can identify. First, we can distinguish between **well-defined problems** and **ill-defined problems**. In well-defined problems, all aspects of the problem, such as the initial state, the possible steps and strategies, and the final state, are fully defined. Various puzzles, such as mazes or strategy games, are examples of well-defined problems. In particular, the game of chess is a special example of a well-defined problem, and it is one of the most studied problems. There is a specific initial state, a goal (to defeat the opponent's king), and all allowed moves are defined according to specific rules. The game of chess is interesting for cognitive psychologists because, despite the strict rules, the number of possible moves is so large that it is impossible to plan a chess game completely in advance. This implies that even for grandmasters the outcome of a game is not fixed in advance and a wide range of cognitive strategies must be used to win a game.

Unlike well-defined problems, ill-defined problems are under-specified. Suppose you are confronted with the fact that the battery of your cell phone is dead, and you need to send a message urgently. Although the end-state is known, there are an unknown number of options: you

DOI: 10.4324/9781003319344-30

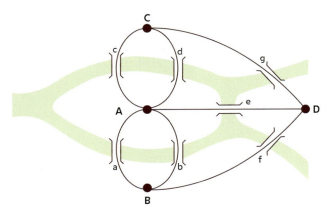

Figure 22.1 Schematic representation of the classic seven bridges of Königsberg problem.

could use a friend's or neighbour's phone, for example; you could find a charger; or you could even buy a new battery. How you should solve the problem is not immediately clear, and it depends entirely on the situation which options you have available. Moreover, each option also has its own unknown advantages and disadvantages. For example, using your neighbour's mobile phone will enable you to send a message quickly, but it will arrive in someone else's name. Depending on the nature of the message, this might be less desirable, so there is no single solution available in this case.

Although most problems we encounter in everyday life are ill-defined, as just illustrated, research on problem-solving behaviour is mainly conducted on the basis of well-defined problems (Goel, 2010). The main reason for this is that well-defined problems have an optimal solution strategy and a defined solution. This enables researchers to compare the solution provided by a participant with the ideal solution. Based on these errors, it is possible to determine which solution strategies were used.

22.2.1.2 Knowledge-Poor versus Knowledge-Rich Problems

A second important distinction involves the difference between **knowledge-poor problems** and **knowledge-rich problems**. A problem is known to be knowledge-poor when the solution strategy does not require any specific background knowledge or when all relevant knowledge is part of the problem description. A good example of this is the **nine-dot problem**, which involves connecting nine dots on a sheet of paper using four lines. In contrast, knowledge-rich problems can only be solved if the solver has the relevant knowledge to solve the problem. Most of the problems we encounter in everyday life are knowledge-rich problems. Yet, here too we find that most research into problem-solving behaviour focuses on knowledge-poor problems. One of the main reasons for this is that knowledge-poor problems are less sensitive to individual differences in solution strategies as a result of differences in background knowledge.

22.2.1.3 Goal Directedness

Despite the differences just discussed, there are several recurring features in problem-solving processes. The first feature is that problem-solving is always goal-directed. As a problem solver, you always have a specific goal in mind, and the solution strategies will always be aimed at getting you to that goal.

22.2.1.4 Involvement of System 2 Processes

The second common feature of problem-solving behaviour is the involvement of controlled System 2 processes. These processes ensure that automatic solutions which turn out to be inadequate can be rejected in favour of a new strategy. Solutions that are retrieved via automatic processes are not considered part of a problem-solving process.

22.2.1.5 Solution Not Immediately Available

It follows then that the solution to a problem cannot be found immediately. The latter also implies that a problem is only a problem as long as the solver is not familiar with the strategy that has to be followed. Examples are the well-known puzzles in which three travellers have to cross a river in a specific order, or the already discussed classic nine-dot problem, which seize to be problems once the strategy is known. It follows, then, that something that is a problem for one person is not necessarily so for someone else.

22.2.2 PRODUCTIVE VERSUS REPRODUCTIVE THINKING

One of the first studies in the field of problem-solving was published by the American psychologist Edward Thorndike (1898). Thorndike (see fig 22.2) studied cats and other small animals' problem-solving skills. These animals were placed in a device known as a puzzle box, from which they could only escape by pulling a series of handles in a specific order. Thorndike observed that the animals locked up in the puzzle box initially made little progress and only got closer to the solution by trial and error. From these results, Thorndike formulated his now famous **law of effect**, which states that behaviour that has a favourable outcome is more likely to be repeated, while behaviour that has an unfavourable outcome is less likely to be repeated (see also Chapter 3).

We must, however, consider whether Thorndike really studied problem-solving behaviour, since the relationship between the observed behaviour and the desired goal was rather arbitrary, and the animals in Thorndike's studies appeared to be involved in **reproductive thinking** rather than in **productive thinking**. Reproductive thinking implies the reuse of previous experiences, without actively seeking the solution to a problem. Productive thinking, on

Figure 22.2 Edward Thorndike (1874–1949).

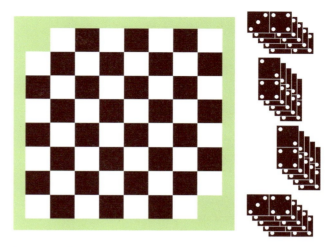

Figure 22.3 An illustration of a mutilated checkerboard. Can you cover it completely with dominoes?

the other hand, involves the innovative restructuring of the problem in such a way that the nature of the problem can be understood. Further studies that have been conducted since Thorndike suggest that animals often solve problems on the basis of reproductive problem-solving behaviour (Köhler, 1925), and that they show little or no sign of understanding (Birch, 1945).

22.3 INSIGHT

The distinction between reproductive and productive thinking was first made between about 1920 and 1940 by German gestalt psychologists. These psychologists objected to the arbitrary nature of Thorndike's tasks and argued that problems requiring productive thinking could be solved on the basis of **insight**. Insight often results from a sudden restructuring of a problem; it is a process that is sometimes accompanied by the subjective 'aha experience'.

More formally, we can define insight as any sudden understanding, realisation, or problem-solving process in which a reorganisation of the elements of the mental representation of a stimulus, situation, or event results in an unusual or non-dominating interpretation (Kounios & Beeman, 2014). Consider the **mutilated checkerboard problem** as a good example of an insight problem. Here, a checkerboard is initially covered with dominoes, in such a way that each domino covers exactly two squares.

Then two black squares are removed from the edges of the board (see fig 22.3). The question now is whether you can still completely cover the checkerboard with dominoes. When trying to solve this problem, many of us will probably try to mentally cover the board with dominoes, only to find out that this strategy is not very successful. Thus, a different approach is needed. We can solve the problem when our attention is drawn to an underlying property of the dominoes. That is, each domino covers exactly one black square and one white square. Thus, to cover the board completely, it must contain as many white squares as it contains black squares. Yet our mutilated checkerboard is missing two black squares. In other words, the board has more white squares than black squares, so it is impossible to fill the board completely with dominoes.

Another widely used method to investigate understanding is the **remote associates task (RAT)**. Here, three words are presented, such as 'fame', 'firmament', and 'asterisk'. The goal of the task is to find a word that is associated with all three words.[1]

22.3.1 INSIGHT: ALL OR NOTHING?

Finding the solution to an insight problem is often accompanied by the subjective experience of having found the solution, even before the details of the solution are fully available. Metcalfe and Wiebe (1987) instructed participants to regularly indicate how strongly they experienced a feeling of warmth, that is, how close they believed to be to finding a solution. They had to do this both when solving insight problems and when solving non-insight problems. With insight problems, participants often reported a strong, sudden increase in this feeling of warmth just before they found the solution, whereas with non-insight problems, they reported a much more gradual increase in warmth.

How is it possible that we subjectively experience having found a solution before actually finding it. According to

Smith and Kounios (1996), this is due to the fact that no information is available to consciousness before the solution is found. Then, according to Smith and Kounios, the transition from a state of no solution to a state of realising how the solution can be found involves one discrete transition.

22.3.2 THE NEURAL BASIS OF INSIGHT

An important, yet still partly unanswered, question is which neural mechanisms are involved in gaining insight (Kounios & Beeman, 2014). Bowden, Jung-Beeman, Fleck, and Kounios (2005) used the already discussed remote associates test to address this question. More specifically, participants reported that some solutions required insight, whereas others did not. Differences in brain activation were linked to these self-reports. Insight problems activated the anterior superior temporal gyrus of the right hemisphere more strongly than non-insight problems (see fig 22.4). According to Bowden and Jung-Beeman (2007) it is specifically the right hemisphere that is involved in solving insight problems, because weak and remote associations – which are essential for insight – are mainly formed in the right hemisphere, whereas strong and more close associations are preferentially processed by the left hemisphere.

In addition to the right temporal cortex, the anterior cingulate gyrus and prefrontal cortex were also found to be involved in solving insight problems. The anterior cingulate gyrus is involved in the detection of conflict situations (see Chapter 5) and in breaking out of a specific mindset. These two processes are essential for gaining insight, because it requires replacing a specific way of thinking by another, more efficient, form of thinking. Finally, several studies have found activation in the prefrontal cortex.

22.3.3 INSIGHT AND EXPERIENCE

Previous experience with a problem can usually help us to solve a new, similar problem, but this is not always the case. In many situations, this experience can even prevent us from finding the correct solution. Next, we turn to the main reasons why.

22.3.3.1 Functional Fixation

A clear example of the negative impact of previous experience is the phenomenon of **functional fixation**. This is the phenomenon that causes us to believe that certain tools

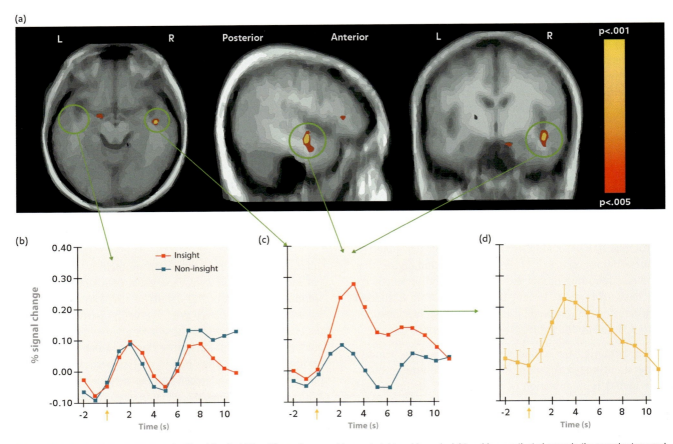

Figure 22.4 Brain activation associated with solving insight problems. Compared to non-insight problems, insight problems activated areas in the superior temporal gyrus of the right hemisphere more strongly. (a) Three-dimensional impression of the nuclei more strongly activated by insight problems. (b) For the left hemisphere, fMRI signals were similar for insight and non-insight problems. (c) In the right hemisphere there was a clear increase in the fMRI signal during the solving of insight problems. (d) The difference in right hemisphere fMRI signal responses between insight and non-insight problems. (source: Bowden et al., 2005)

Figure 22.5 Duncker's candle problem.

can only be used for one specific purpose, causing us to miss out on other, creative uses. In a now classic work, the German psychologist Karl Duncker (1945) published a series of inventive problems for studying this phenomenon. For example, participants were given a candle, a box of push pins, a box of matches, and some other objects lying on a table. Their task was to attach the candle to a wall next to the table in such a way that the burning candle would not drip onto the table (see fig 22.5).

Most participants tried to attach the candle directly to the wall using the push pins, or the melting candle wax for this purpose. There were only a few participants who came up with the correct solution, namely, to use the inside of the pin box as a candle holder and to attach it to the wall with the push pins. According to Duncker (1945), the most important reason why most participants failed to find this solution was the fact that they considered the pin box to be mainly a container for the push pins, which did not give them the idea that it could also be used as a candlestick. When Duncker had already removed the pins from the box before the start of the experiment, many more participants were able to find the solution, because

they probably now conceived the box as an object that they could possibly use to fix the candle.

More direct evidence for functional fixation was found by Ye, Cardwell, and Mark (2009). Here, participants were given several objects and then they had to decide which of them were suitable for use in a specific task, such as packing eggs in a box. Immediately after this task, participants had to decide whether the given objects were suitable for a second task, for example a game of catch ball. Some objects, such as a ski cap or a pillow, could be used for both tasks, yet Ye et al. found that when participants considered an object suitable for the first task, they were less inclined to find a second use for this object.

The question is how to overcome our functional fixation. McCaffrey (2012) argued that we ignore the often crucial but obscure properties of objects because we focus on the more typical uses based on the shape, size, and materials from which the object is made, along with the classical uses we know from experience and description. According to McCaffrey, functional fixation can, on the one hand, be reduced by providing a function-free description of an object, and, on the other, by letting people judge whether these descriptions imply a certain use.

When McCaffrey (2012) used this technique to introduce the objects available in the candle problem, he found a significant increase in correct solutions. Eighty-three per cent of the participants who were given a description according to McCaffrey's method succeeded in finding the correct solution, compared to 49% who were given the classical problem description.

Another factor that may play a role in functional fixation is a high degree of cognitive control. Chrysikou et al. (2013) found evidence for this using a technique known as **transcranial direct current stimulation (tDCS)**, while participants had to think of possible uses for objects. tDCS is a technique in which a small electric current is delivered to the brain which – in the case of the study described here – has an inhibitory function. When this current was applied to the left prefrontal cortex, participants thought of more unusual possibilities than in a control condition where no current was applied. This result implies that inhibiting cognitive control processes from the prefrontal cortical areas has a positive effect on finding creative solutions.

22.3.3.2 Einstellung

A second way in which our previous experience can have a negative influence on our ability to solve a problem is because it depends on a **mental set**. Mental sets are formed by persisting in a solution strategy which worked before, but which is no longer adequate for the current problem. A classic study of mental sets was conducted by the American psychologist Abraham Luchins (1942), based on the **water jug problem**. The classic version of the problem is as follows: suppose you have two jugs. One can hold 3 litres of water and the other can hold 5 litres. Your task is to measure out exactly 4 litres of water. How do you do that?[2] Luchins used variations on this problem where the number of jugs needed to get the right amount of water would vary. Participants who had practised with similar problems generally had little difficulties solving the problem. In contrast, participants who had been trained on more difficult problems, had much more trouble finding the right solution to easy problems, due to a phenomenon that Luchins described with the term **Einstellung**.

22.4 REPRESENTATIONAL CHANGE

Ohlsson (1992) has formulated an explanation for insight that is based on an information processing approach. The core of Ohlsson's representational change theory is that we often reach an impasse while solving a problem due to an incorrect representation of the problem (see fig 22.6). We have already encountered examples of such impasses in the seven bridges of Königsberg and mutilated checkerboard problems. The key to the solution is thus to break out of the impasse by changing the problem representation. According to Ohlsson, this involves three successive stages: (1) reducing the constraints that we impose on the problem – a process that Ohlsson identifies as constraint relaxation; (2) recoding, that is, reinterpreting part of the problem representation; and (3) elaboration, that is, adding new information to the newly formed problem representation.

22.4.1 PROGRESS MONITORING

MacGregor, Ormerod, and Chronicle (2001) argue that we tend to use the rate of progress as a signal to indicate whether we have reached an impasse or not. These authors developed a model that describes how people solve the classic nine-dot problem introduced earlier. One of the reasons why many people are unable to find the solution to this problem is that they assume that the lines must remain

within the boundaries of the grid pattern. The most important constraint relaxation, therefore, consists of the realisation that it is allowed to draw beyond these boundaries. Even after this realisation, however, many people still fail to find the right solution. According to MacGregor and colleagues, this depends in part on the search strategy. Many individuals tend to look for solutions where each subsequent line connects as many dots as possible. This strategy fails, however, because the correct solution contains a line that connects only two dots and, moreover, this is a line that can never be drawn last.

MacGregor et al. (2001) tested their hypothesis by giving participants examples of possible moves (see fig 22.7). Figure 22.7(c) shows an example of a line that falls outside the grid, while Figure 22.7(d) shows an example of a line where this is not the case. Although example (c) may help in understanding that the lines may extend beyond the grid, MacGregor et al. found that example (d) was more effective in finding the solution. The reason is that from example (c) it is always possible to connect more than two dots with the next two lines (without going outside the grid), whereas this is not the case in example (d). Example (c), in other words, stimulates participants much less to draw lines outside the box than example (d) does. The lack of progress provided by example (d) thus stimulates participants to relax their constraints.

22.4.2 PROCESSES INVOLVED IN REPRESENTATIONAL CHANGE

Öllinger, Jones, and Knoblich (2014) have further developed Ohlsson's theory into a model that describes how the various processes involved in a representational change are

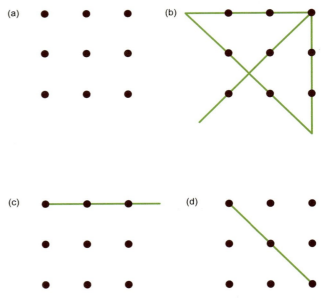

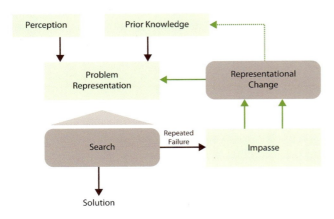

Figure 22.6 Overview of the main processes involved in problem-solving, according to the representational change theory. (source: Öllinger et al., 2014)

Figure 22.7 (a) The nine-dot problem with (b) the correct solution and (c–d) two examples of possible moves as given by MacGregor et al. (2001).

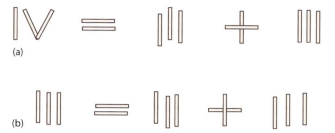

Figure 22.8 Examples of matchstick problems as used by Knoblich et al. (source: Knoblich et al., 1999)

one of the digits (e.g., by moving one stick in IV so that it becomes VI), while the second problem (b) has a less obvious solution.[3] Because we typically only manipulate numeric information during arithmetic tasks, it is therefore also much more difficult to find the correct solution for problems such as (b). Consequently, participants found far fewer solutions to the second type of problem than to the first. A follow-up study also recorded eye movements (Knoblich, Ohlsson, & Raney, 2001). These results showed that the participants mainly fixated on the numbers, which implies that the initial problem representation was based on the idea that the numbers had to be modified instead of the operators.

interrelated. The processing of the problem description, combined with our existing background knowledge, will result in a problem representation. Within this problem representation we will then search for a solution. If this search is repeatedly unsuccessful, however, we will reach an impasse that can only be broken by the aforementioned constraint relaxation processes, which can result in a representational change. Then, within the new representation, the search for a solution will resume.

22.4.3 CONSTRAINT RELAXATION

The importance of constraint relaxation was demonstrated by Knoblich, Ohlsson, Haider, and Rhenius (1999). In this study, participants were given arithmetic problems that were represented by matchsticks (see fig 22.8). They were allowed to displace only one match to change the original incorrect statement to a correct one. The first type of problem – (a) – requires changing the value of

22.4.4 SEARCH AFTER INSIGHT

One of Öllinger et al.'s (2014) fundamental contributions to the problem-solving literature involves the notion that insight problems are still not immediately solved after a representation change, but we must actively search for a solution within the changed representation. This conclusion is also based on results obtained using the nine-dot problem. If insight led to an immediate solution, this would imply that the correct solution would follow immediately after this realisation. Even after this change in the problem representation, there are still an extremely large number of patterns possible, and only a few will lead to the correct solution (see fig 22.9). In other words, we still need to search within the new problem representation.

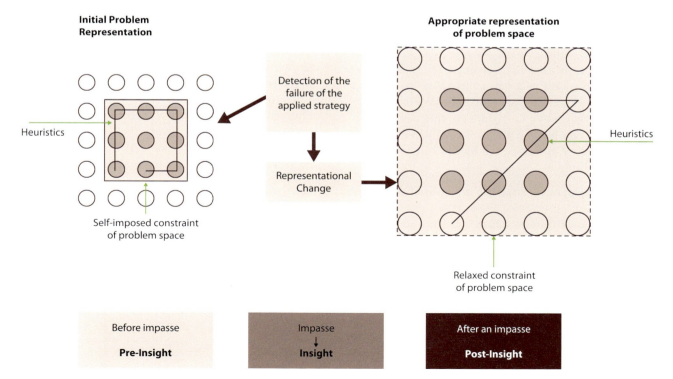

Figure 22.9 Search after a change in problem representation. (source: Öllinger et al., 2014)

22.5 INCUBATION

Wallas (1926) has already argued that **incubation**, that is, the temporary letting go of a problem, is an important aspect of problem-solving. He hypothesised that unconscious mental processes continue to operate in the background to find a solution while we are actively engaged in something else. Contemporary incubation research focuses on the solution strategies that are being employed by participants who had a break in their search for a solution. These strategies are then compared to those of individuals who did have not have a break. In a meta-analysis of the incubation literature, Sio and Ormerod (2009) found a small but highly significant effect of incubation in 73% of all studies. These incubation effects were found mainly when creative problems with multiple solutions were involved. The main effect was that incubation stimulates the search for knowledge and information; a process that is especially effective for problems with multiple solutions. In addition, Sio and Ormerod found that the effects of incubation were stronger the longer participants had been working on the problem. It is possible that this effect can be explained by the fact that the long solution time resulted in a very strong impasse, which was sustained by the continuous search, but interrupted by a break in the search process.

The incubation effect is similar to the intuitive notion of 'sleeping on it'. We may wonder whether sleep is indeed an effective form of incubation. Wagner, Gais, Haider, Verleger, and Born (2004) tested this hypothesis by using a task that involved solving mathematical problems. Participants were given a series of numbers, on the basis of which they had to generate a new series of numbers. This could be done by applying two simple rules to each number in the original series. What the participants did not know, however, was that each new series could also be found on the basis of a very simple rule. Participants were trained to perform this task and were required to do it again eight hours later. Interestingly, participants who had been able to sleep in the intervening time proved to be much better at finding the hidden rule than those who had not slept.

Although incubation is effective, we still do not know exactly why this is the case. Simon (1966) assumed that incubation allows tried-but-failed strategies to be more easily forgotten. Because information about these strategies disappears, the problem solver is less inclined to stick to them, creating an opportunity to choose a different approach. Evidence for this idea was found by Penaloza and Calvillo (2012), by using the remote associates task. Half of the participants were given a misleading target word next to each word, such as 'water [faucet], cube [root], and skate [board]' (solution: ice), while the other half were given the standard version of the task. The distracting target words were chosen so that they formed a strong association with each individual word and thus prevented finding the solution. After participants tried to solve the problems once, they had to try again. On this second attempt, no distractors were presented. Half of each group was given a two-minute break during which they read an article, while the other half tried again immediately. Of the participants who had been presented with distractors, those who had been given a break performed better, as this allowed them to forget the misleading information.

22.6 PROBLEM-SOLVING STRATEGIES

22.6.1 THE GENERAL PROBLEM SOLVER

By the end of the 1950s, the American computer scientist Allen Newell joined the economist and political scientist Herbert A. Simon to develop a computer programme to solve problems (Newell & Simon, 1972; Newell et al., 1958). This programme, which had been given the somewhat misleading name of **general problem solver**, was developed for the purpose of solving various well-defined problems. The programme assumed that information processing is serial, that is, that one step is considered at a time. Moreover, Newell and Simon assumed that humans have a limited working memory capacity, and that they can retrieve relevant knowledge from long-term memory.

Newell and Simon (1972) initially aimed to determine how we solve problems by asking participants to think aloud while working out a solution. These verbal reports were then used as a basis for determining which strategy had been used. These strategies were then dissected in detail so that they could be implemented in the **problem space** of the general problem solver. The problem space consists of the initial state of the problem, the target state, and the allowed mental operations (moves) that can be applied to a given state to transform the problem space from one state to another.

22.6.2 TYPES OF PROBLEMS

Problems that can be solved with the general problem solver typically consist of puzzles in which elements must be moved in a specific order to a specific position. There are always restrictions on the moves that are allowed. Next, we will discuss two of these types of problems in more detail.

22.6.2.1 The Tower of Hanoi

One of the best-known well-defined problems, which is also widely used in neuropsychology to identify frontal cortical

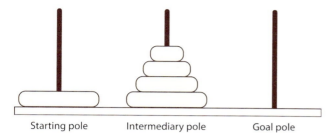

Figure 22.10 The Tower of Hanoi problem.

damage, is the **Tower of Hanoi** (see Figure 22.10). Its initial state consists of five discs stacked in order of decreasing size around one of three pins. The participants' task is to move the entire stack from this pin to a second pin. In doing so, they may only move one disc at a time while a larger disc may never be placed on top of a smaller one. To solve the puzzle successfully, participants have to make temporary stacks and sometimes return part of the stack back to the original pile.

22.6.2.2 River Crossing Puzzles

We can also find variants of the same type of problem in games such as the well-known river crossing puzzles. Examples include the well-known missionaries-and-cannibals[4] problem or the problem of the farmer with the wolf, the goat, and the cabbage.[5] In both cases, the solution to the problem is to sail back and forth several times, sometimes taking a person or an object back to its origin. In both the Tower of Hanoi problem and the river crossing puzzles, the goal state cannot be reached without making moves that temporarily move the current state of the problem further away from the goal state. The main difference between these types of problems lies in the **framing**. For example, the cover story can prevent us from even realising that we are capable of taking a step back. Thus, these problems do not only appeal to our analytical faculties but also to our insight. In the case of the Tower of Hanoi, the nature of the problem makes it clearer that we can take steps backwards, whereas the framing in the river crossing puzzles may prevent this.

22.6.3 HEURISTICS AND ALGORITHMS

Once we have determined what the target position should be, we need to determine what steps we need to carry out and according to which rules. According to Newell and Simon (1972) the complexity of most problems implies that we often use rules of thumb, that is, **heuristics**. In the context of problem-solving, we can contrast heuristics with **algorithms**. An algorithm is a complex procedure or method that is guaranteed to lead to a solution (if one exists). Algorithms are cognitively demanding, however, so most problem solvers fall back on cognitively less demanding strategies. Newell and Simon (1972) applied the general

problem solver to 11 completely different problems, including the river crossing puzzles and the Tower of Hanoi. They found that the general problem solver was able to solve all of these problems, but the solution strategy often differed significantly from the way human participants solved these types of problems. The deviations between the human solution and the solutions proposed by the general problem solver imply that human problem solvers used one of the following heuristics.

22.6.3.1 Means-Ends Analysis

One of the simplest heuristics to use is the **means-ends analysis**. This analysis consists of starting with observing the difference between the current problem state and the target state. Based on this difference, we formulate a sub-goal that aims to reduce the difference between the current state and the target state. Next, we specify the moves that are required to achieve the sub-goal. This process is then repeated as long as there is a discrepancy between the current state and the target state. Means-ends analysis is a heuristic, not an algorithm, because it is not guaranteed to lead to a solution. For example, it is possible that there are no more moves possible from a given sub-goal that will lead to the solution.

The means-ends analysis is one of the most widely used heuristics. Convincing evidence that we sometimes stick to this heuristic, even when it does not result in a solution, was presented by Sweller and Levine (1982). In their study, participants had to find their way through a maze. Most of the maze was invisible since participants only saw the part that represented the current problem state (see fig 22.11). Some participants could also see the goal,

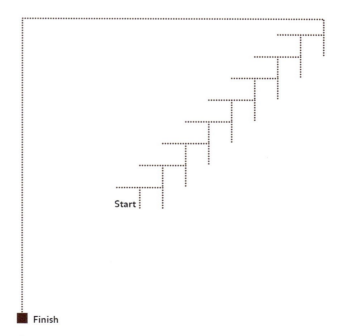

Figure 22.11 An example of a maze where knowledge of the final state had a negative impact on task performance. (source: Sweller and Levine, 1982)

while others could not. Therefore, only those participants who could see the goal were able to employ a means-ends analysis. Notice, however, that the study was designed in such a way that each step that had to be performed was a step away from the goal state (see fig 22.11), which made a means-ends analysis meaningless. The results of the study therefore showed that the participants who could see the goal performed very poorly. Only 10% of them found the solution and they needed at least 298 moves to do so. The participants who could not see the goal found the solution in about 38 moves.

22.6.3.2 Hill Climbing

Another commonly used heuristic is **hill climbing**. Here, the current state of the problem is always changed in such a way that the next move brings us one step closer to the goal state. Hill climbing is similar to mountain climbing in the dark: all you know is that you have to go up, so every next step you take is in the direction in which you are climbing the most. Hill climbing becomes problematic, however, when there is no direct step available that brings us closer to the goal state. Just as in mountain climbing in the dark, we can get stuck on a local hilltop without finding a way to cross a valley to reach the real mountain top. Hill climbing is thus a simple but also often very inefficient heuristic.

Thomas (1974) argued that individuals should be particularly troubled when they have to take a step back; that is, when they have to make a move that temporarily increases the distance between the current state and the target state. In such cases, as already discussed, heuristics are often particularly inadequate. Thomas used a variant of the missionaries-and-cannibals problem, in which hobbits and orcs had to cross a river together in a boat and found that human participants experienced difficulties when they had to take a step back. The general problem solver, however, had no problem with this step. Besides the fact that human problem solvers had trouble taking a step back, Thomas also found that they often generate sub-goals. Participants often performed a series of steps in quick succession, only to take a longer pause during which the next series of actions was planned. In general, Thomas reported that participants were found to solve the problem in three to four sub-goals.

22.6.3.3 Progress Monitoring

Newell and Simon (1972) assumed that human problem solvers would switch strategies or heuristics when the then employed strategy turned out to be inefficient. Progress monitoring is thus an additional heuristic that is used in combination with other heuristics, such as the ones described here. Newell and Simon's assumption is consistent with the previously presented findings of MacGregor et al. (2001) who used the already discussed

nine dots problem to show that the initial choice of a relatively inefficient strategy results in a more rapid switch to a new strategy.

Similarly, Payne and Duggan (2011) found that being under the illusion of making progress can lead to a resistance in giving up the current strategy. These investigators gave participants unsolvable variants of the water jug problem. Some of these variants involved a large number of possible moves, while other problems only had a few. In the latter case, participants were quickly forced to repeat moves, so that they soon experienced no progress towards the goal and gave up on these problems much sooner than on those with many possible moves.

22.6.4 PLANNING

The study by Sweller and Levine (1982) also illustrates that we generally do very little forward planning when looking for a solution. Why is that? Newell and Simon (1972) assumed that it is mainly due to the limited capacity of short-term memory. There might be another possibility, however, namely that planning is costly in terms of time and effort and that it is often unnecessary because simple heuristics suffice in many everyday situations. According to the latter view, we are therefore able to plan ahead, but we often choose not to do so in order not to overburden our mental processes.

22.6.4.1 How Far Ahead Do We Plan?

Delaney, Ericsson, and Knowles (2004) found evidence for the idea that we often plan much less ahead than we can, based on a study involving the water jug problem. One group of participants was instructed to work out the entire solution before actually carrying out the steps, while another group received no specific instructions and was allowed to decide on their own strategy. Delaney et al. reported that the participants in the latter group hardly planned at all. The participants in the first group, on the other hand, showed clear planning behaviour and found the correct solution in far fewer steps than the other participants. Moreover, these participants' performance remained higher when they were subsequently given the same task without an explicit requirement to plan ahead (fig 22.12). We can deduce from these results that we can plan much more than Newell and Simon (1972) originally assumed, but that we often choose not to do so.

22.6.4.2 Cognitive Miserliness

Many theorists assume that the distinction between intuitive and analytical processes may offer a possible explanation for the relative lack of planning in problem-solving (see Evans, 2008, for a review). Also in this context, Kahneman (2003) makes a distinction between System 1 thinking (fast, effortless, and intuitive) and System 2 thinking (slow and laborious).

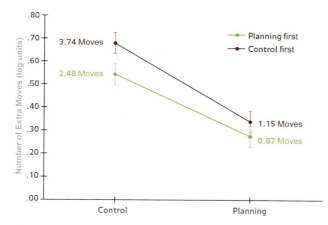

Figure 22.12 Results of a study of the effects of planning on the number of steps that participants needed to solve the water jug problem. Note that participants who were instructed to explicitly plan their steps ahead from the start of the experiment were significantly more efficient in solving the problem, even when they were subsequently on longer required to plan their solution in advance. (source: Delaney et al., 2004)

Most proponents of this dual process approach assume that we humans are cognitive misers. **Cognitive miserliness** implies that we are economical with our time and with the effort that we put into tasks that require elaborative thought. Kahneman (2003), for example, assumes that System 2 monitors the functions of System 1, checking its answers in the process. It is assumed, however, that this process frequently fails, even when System 1's answer is incorrect. The cognitive reflection test (Frederick, 2005) gives a nice indication of the extent to which we are cognitive misers. A few examples from this test follow:

1. A racket and a ball together cost 1.10 euros. The racket costs 1 euro more than the ball. How much does the ball cost?
2. If it takes five machines five minutes to make five appliances, how long does it take 100 machines to make 100 appliances?
3. A pack of lilies floats in a lake. Each day the pack doubles in size. If it takes 48 days for the whole lake to be covered, how long will it take for half the lake to be covered?

If you got one or more answers wrong, you also experienced cognitive miserliness, but do not worry. When this test was administered at two of the most prestigious universities in the United States – Princeton and Harvard – 75% of the students got at least one answer wrong and 20% got all of the questions wrong! The most frequently given answers to these questions are 10 cents, 100 minutes, and 24 days[6]; answers that suggest we are cognitive misers. Consider question 1; you may have immediately thought of 10 cents. But, if that were the answer, the racket would have to cost 1.10 euros, making the total price 1.20 euros.

People who score low on the cognitive reflection test generally typically score low on a wide range of judgement and reasoning tasks as well (Toplak, West, & Stanovich, 2011). This correlation can be partially explained by the idea that those individuals who score low are cognitive

misers, but also partially by the fact that performance on the cognitive reflection test correlates positively with intelligence (Toplak et al., 2011). Toplak, West, and Stanovich (2013) investigated this relationship further by using an extended version of the cognitive reflection test and found that scores on this test were highly indicative of performance on other thinking tasks, even when corrected for the effects of intelligence.

There is a high degree of similarity between the idea of cognitive miserliness and the idea from Newell and Simon (1972) that problem solvers make frequent use of heuristics or rules of thumb. Both involve reverting to simple and sometimes inaccurate strategies. There is also an important difference, however: according to Newell and Simon, we use heuristics because we are forced to do so by our limited processing capacity. The existence of cognitive miserliness, on the other hand, implies that we use heuristics because we are just reluctant to engage in laborious cognitive processes, instead of not being capable of doing so.

22.7 PROBLEM-SOLVING BASED ON ANALOGIES

Suppose you had to solve a problem once in the past. When, at a later time, you have to solve a similar problem, you may expect to benefit from your past experience. In such cases, we might observe a **positive transfer**. In other cases, however, an earlier problem can hinder you in finding the right solution, which is an example of a **negative transfer**. Many analogy reasoning exercises are based on such past experiences and on discovering similarities between the current problem and a previous one.

One of the best-known examples of the use of analogies in scientific reasoning is provided by the development of the Rutherford model of the atom. In the early 20th century, the New Zealand-based physicist Ernest Rutherford succeeded in explaining some properties of atoms by assuming that electrons orbit a nucleus in a way similar to how planets orbit the sun. Although the Rutherford model has since been disproven and replaced by a model that is based on quantum physics, it did represent an important step forward in nuclear physics.

In physics and biology, we can find numerous examples of analogical reasoning. Consider for example the billiard ball model of ideal gases or the hydraulic model of blood pressure regulation (see also Chapter 8, or Chapter 11 for an application of this analogy to motivational processes). In our own field, we can recognise the well-known computer metaphor for human cognition as an analogy. Finally, in case law, we often find that jurisprudence is based on cases that show a given similarity to the case being investigated.

A famous example is a case in which a British manufacturer of ginger beer was found to be liable for the death of a customer who had died because a snail had crept into a bottle and died there. The court ruled that the producer had a 'reasonable' responsibility to ensure the safety of the product and that the customer's death was caused by the manufacturer's negligence. The principle formulated in this case was later used in a case where a maintenance company was held liable for negligence while repairing an elevator that had subsequently crashed. The principle was not applied, however, in a case where a worker was injured by a defective crane, since the worker had been given the opportunity to inspect the crane, in addition to being aware of the defect.

22.7.1 DUNCKER'S RADIATION PROBLEM

In addition to the candle problem already discussed, the German psychologist Karl Duncker introduced another series of innovative problems to study problem-solving skills (Duncker, 1945). Among these, his famous radiation problem (fig 22.13) describes a patient with a malignant tumour, which can only be treated by exposing it to a lethal dose of X-rays. These rays will kill the malignant tumour tissue, but the problem is that the healthy tissue lying in the path of the beam will also be destroyed. A weaker beam, which leaves the healthy tissue intact, is also unable to destroy the tumour.[7] So the question is how we can safely, yet effectively apply the doses required to kill the malignant tissue while keeping the surrounding tissues healthy.

Gick and Holyoak (1980) found that only 10% of all participants were able to find the solution to this radiation problem without any further hints. Other participants were instructed to study and remember three stories, one of which showed a structural similarity to the radiation problem. The story in question concerned a general who attacked a heavily defended fort by distributing his troops along various roads that all lead to the fort. When it was pointed out that the story had a similarity with the radiation problem, 80% of the participants were able to find the solution.

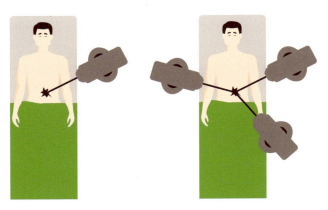

Figure 22.13 Example of Duncker's radiation problem.

Without a specific hint, however, this was only 40%, which implies that many participants failed to use the analogy of the story.

22.7.2 SIMILARITIES

The preceding examples illustrate that we can use analogies in many situations, but that we do not automatically employ them. Then what exactly does enable us to use analogies? One of the crucial factors here is that we need to recognise the similarities between the current problem and a previously encountered problem. As such, Chen (2002) identified three different types of similarities.

1. Superficial similarities: these are details, often irrelevant to the solution, that can be found in both problems.
2. Structural similarities: these are the solution principles that are shared by both problems.
3. Procedural similarities: these are procedures used in the analogue, which correspond to those needed to solve the current problem.

Chen (2002) illustrates these three types of similarity using the weigh the elephant problem, which is based on a traditional Chinese folk tale. According to the story, a little boy has to weigh an elephant, but there are no scales available that are large enough. There is, however, a small scale. The solution to the problem is to collect smaller objects that collectively weigh as much as the elephant and then weigh each of those separately. This reduces the problem to finding a method of equalising the weight of the elephant and the smaller objects.

Two solutions were available in Chen's study: the boat solution (determining how deep a boat sinks into the water when the elephant stands in it) and the tree solution (hanging a large balance from a tree, on which the elephant and the objects must be balanced). A superficial analogy consisted of a story that also involved a curious little boy and an elephant, but otherwise there were no similarities. The structural analogy, on the other hand, consisted of the introduction of similar goals, obstacles, and available resources. Chen also introduced the procedural similarity by instructing participants to solve the 'weigh the elephant' problem and presenting them with a number of solution procedures in the form of pictograms (see fig 22.14).

Although Chen's results imply that the superficial features of an analogy are not involved in finding a solution to a problem, it has been found that the absence of these superficial similarities prevents participants from understanding the relevance of an analogy and, consequently, that they are also less likely to use an analogy (Keane, 1987). Dunbar and Blanchette (2001) studied the use of analogies among molecular biologists and immunologists and found that the extent to which these experts used analogies varied depending on the nature of the task.

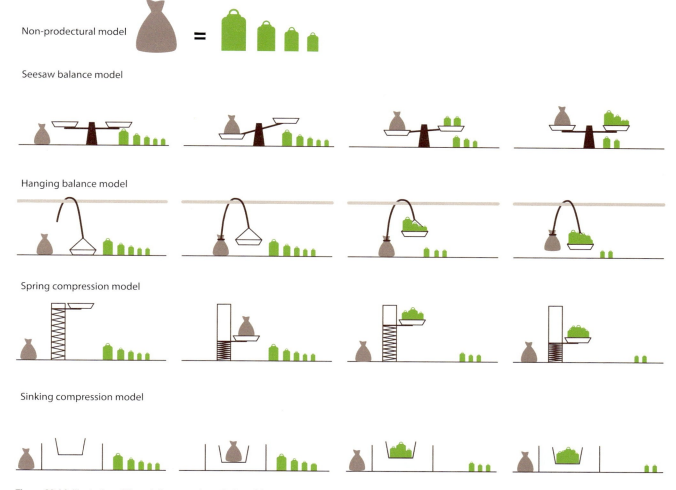

Non-prodectural model

Seesaw balance model

Hanging balance model

Spring compression model

Sinking compression model

Figure 22.14 Illustration of the solution procedures that participants were presented to solve the 'weigh the elephant' problem. (source: Chen, 2002)

When they had to solve problems with experiments, they often generated analogies that had many superficial similarities to the problem. However, when they had to generate hypotheses, they generated many more analogies with structural similarities to the problem.

These results possibly explain the fact that in the Gick and Holyoak (1980) study, very few participants found a solution spontaneously. Gick and Holyoak used a paradigm in which participants were merely presented with an analogy, and it was only after it was presented that they had to solve the radiation problem. In everyday life, however, we tend to actively search for analogies when we have to solve a problem. Thus, when we actively generate analogies ourselves, this will typically result in more elaborate processing of a problem, which also makes us better able to identify the structural similarities between the analogy and the problem. Active search also allows this to happen when the superficial similarities are virtually absent (Day & Goldstone, 2011). Blanchette and Dunbar (2000) reported results consistent with this idea: when participants were passively presented an analogy, they were much less able to find a solution to a problem than when they had to actively search for an analogy themselves.

Loewenstein (2010) argued that the efficiency with which we can retrieve an analogy from memory is essential for effective problem-solving, and that this efficiency is largely determined by the extent to which we can discover the underlying structure of a problem. Kurtz and Loewenstein (2007) found evidence for this by instructing participants to examine the underlying structure of two problems (including Duncker's radiation problem). One group was instructed to study two problems simultaneously, while another group was instructed to study the problems separately. The group that had studied the problems simultaneously was, on average, better at solving them than the group that had studied them separately. This advantage could be attributed to a more efficient retrieval of the fort problem in the simultaneous group. Gentner, Loewenstein, Thompson, and Forbus (2009) found similar results with a group of management consultants who had to study the structure of management contracts.

Which cognitive processes are involved in analogical problem-solving or reasoning? Much research related to this question is based on the use of **four-term analogy problems**. These problems typically take the form of an a:b::c:d structure. Consider the following example from

Schmidt et al. (2012): flame:candle::steeple:church. Here, participants have to indicate whether a:b have the same relationship to each other as c:d, in other words, is a flame to a candle what a steeple is to a church? An advantage of using such problems is that they can be well-controlled. All relevant information is given in the problem statement and there is, in principle, only one correct answer.

Knowlton, Morrison, Hummel, and Holyoak (2012) discuss computational models that are based on the assumption that analogical problem-solving consists of several stages. They conclude that the processes involved in analogical problem-solving must be strictly serial, due to the amount of processing that is required. Knowlton et al. identify the stages of collection, mapping, inference, and induction.

Over the past decade, an increasingly clear picture has emerged of how these stages relate to neural activity (Krawczyk, 2012; Maguire, McClelland, Donovan, Tillman, & Krawczyk, 2012; Volle, Gilbert, Benoit, & Burgess, 2010). The main processes are illustrated in Figure 22.15. Encoding a problem is strongly related to the activation of several frontal brain regions, including the inferior frontal gyrus, the dorsolateral prefrontal cortex, and the rostrolateral prefrontal cortex. Similar brain regions are associated with the mapping stage.

Morrison, Holyoak, and Bao (2001) found that working memory is involved in analogical problem-solving. Here, participants had to verify verbal analogies such as black:white::noisy:quiet. In addition, analogies were presented in pictorial form. Performance on both the verbal and pictorial tasks decreased when participants were simultaneously engaged in tasks involving executive processes, implying that analogy verification relies on the limited capacity of working memory. In addition, performance on the verbal task was found to interfere with a secondary task involving the phonological loop, whereas performance on the visual task interfered with a secondary task involving the visuospatial sketchpad. Finally, according to Knowlton et al., induction results in an abstract schema, in which the structural similarity between problem and analogy is represented.

22.8 EXPERTISE

The problems discussed so far typically had to be solved in a relatively short amount of time, leaving little time for learning. In everyday life, however, we encounter numerous situations in which we build up considerable efficiency in certain cognitive processes through repeated experience throughout our lives. A skill is defined by the ability to perform a task within a certain domain with a high degree of efficiency. The ability to achieve goals in this domain grows with the amount of practice.

The development of expertise bears some similarities to problem-solving processes in the sense that experts are extremely efficient in solving a problem. Problem-solving strategies are often studied on the basis of knowledge-poor problems, however, whereas expertise is often characterised by the efficient application of knowledge that has been acquired across the life span (see Box 22.1). Because knowledge is so important, studies investigating the development of expertise often use knowledge-rich problems. Consider, for example, the following physics problem introduced by Larkin, McDermott, Simon, and Simon (1980), which they presented to both a layperson and to a physicist with expertise in the field of kinematics.

> *Suppose a rifle bullet has a velocity of 400 metres per second when it leaves the barrel. The length of the barrel is 0.5 metres. Assuming that the bullet was uniformly accelerated, what is the average speed of the bullet while it was in the barrel?*

The most striking difference between the layperson and the expert was that the latter solved the problem in less than a quarter of the time, and that the solution was more accurate than that of the layperson. The second major difference emerged from the analysis of the worksheets and the transcripts of the thought processes. The layperson often solved the problem by working backwards from the unknown quantities to the ones given. In doing so, the layperson made explicit use of all equations that were related to constant accelerations: these equations were mentioned explicitly in the transcripts. The expert, on the other hand, gained insight into the structure of the problem much earlier and made much less explicit use of the formulas. More specifically, the

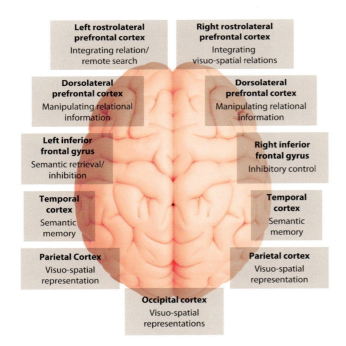

Figure 22.15 Overview of brain areas involved in analogical problem-solving. (source: Krawczyk, 2012)

Box 22.1 Expertise and 'the knowledge' among London cab drivers

The question of how our brains are affected by acquiring extremely detailed knowledge was investigated among London taxi drivers. Before these drivers can obtain a licence, they must demonstrate that they have *the knowledge*. For unknown reasons, drivers of the classic black London cabs are not allowed to use satellite navigation systems and are expected to know the exact location of more than 25,000 streets, thousands of hospitals, tube stations, and so on, by heart, a process that takes them about three years.

One brain structure that appears to play an important role in the acquisition of this knowledge is the hippocampus, as shown in a number of studies by British neuroscientist Eleanor A. Maguire and her colleagues. The posterior part of the hippocampus was found to be enlarged among London cab drivers (Maguire et al., 2000). Moreover, this part of the brain is active during the retrieval of navigation data (Maguire, Frackowiak, & Frith, 1997). An older driver who had suffered extensive hippocampal brain damage still had a very good spatial knowledge of the city of London and knew most landmarks and their underlying spatial relationships. However, his navigational skills had deteriorated

dramatically, and he regularly got lost on the secondary roads (Maguire, Nannery, & Spiers, 2006).

The question is, however, whether acquiring the knowledge results in a change in the hippocampus. The data just discussed are correlational and cannot exclude the alternative explanation that people with a larger anterior hippocampus are in a better position to become taxi drivers. Some evidence for a causal relationship was, however, provided by Woollett and Maguire (2011). They followed a group of individuals during their training to become taxi drivers. Those who qualified to become taxi drivers showed a greater increase in the size of the hippocampus than those who did not.

Learning this vast amount of knowledge, however, does appear to come at the expense of other skills. Licenced taxi drivers had more trouble learning new word-word associations and object-place associations compared to a control group (Woollett & Maguire, 2009). These drivers had a smaller amount of grey matter in the anterior part of the hippocampus; the part that is involved in processing new stimuli and encoding them.

expert's reasoning was something along the following lines: 'If the speed at the beginning of the run is 0, at the end 400 m/s, and the acceleration is constant, then the average speed is exactly the difference between these two values'.

Another classic study on expertise in physics reported that experts tend to classify problems on the basis of their underlying structure, whereas beginners tend to classify problems on the basis of their superficial features (Chi, Feltovich, & Glaser, 1981). Novice and advanced physics students were presented with problems, such as those shown in Figure 22.16. Novice students grouped the problems according to their superficial features, such as 'blocks on an inclined plane' or 'something with rotation'. Experts, on the other hand, made a classification based on the underlying physics and grouped the problems, for example, on the characteristic 'conservation of energy'.

22.8.1 TYPES OF EXPERTISE

In the remainder of this chapter, we will elaborate on two forms of expertise, namely chess expertise and medical expertise. For several reasons, the game of chess is ideally suited for studying expertise. First, chess is an abstract and well-defined problem, which makes it possible to study chess performance under well-controlled conditions. Moreover,

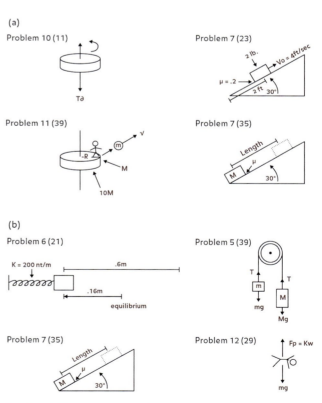

Figure 22.16 The classification of physics problems by (a) beginners and (b) experts. (source: Chi et al., 1981)

what makes chess unique, compared to many other well-defined problems, is that the number of possible moves is so large that it is never possible to win a chess game on the basis of a specific pre-conceived strategy, or planning ahead for all possible moves. For this reason, most chess computers are also still unable to win against a grandmaster chess player.

The most sensational chess match of a grandmaster against a computer was that of the then world champion Garry Kasparov against the IBM supercomputer Deep Blue in May 1997. Deep Blue defeated Kasparov by processing about 200 million positions per second and planning up to six moves ahead. In addition, chess is interesting to study because there is an international ranking system for chess masters, which makes it possible to relate individual differences in performance to the players' level of expertise. Finally, chess players develop specific cognitive skills that can be applied to other domains.

Medical expertise is interesting to investigate for a series of other reasons. Unlike a chess game, a medical problem is often ill-defined, and a diagnosis must be made on the basis of a large number of indicators, redundant or otherwise. Medical expertise therefore requires a considerable amount of substantive professional knowledge. In addition, medical expertise is of considerable social importance.

22.8.2 CHESS EXPERTISE

The Dutch experimental psychologist Adriaan Dingeman de Groot (1914–2006) was one of the first to study the cognitive psychological aspects of chess. De Groot (1946) compared, for instance, memory performance between grandmaster chess players and novice players. He showed his participants chess positions, which they then had to reconstruct on a board. Then, he did the same for pieces that were randomly placed on a board. De Groot's remarkable finding was that while chess experts had as much trouble reconstructing the random positions as beginners, they were much better at reconstructing real positions. So, it is specifically this information that is used to relate the position of the current game to that of previous games.

22.8.2.1 Chunking Theory

Chase and Simon (1973) reported that chess players who memorise board positions do so by grouping these positions into about seven chunks. Importantly, Chase and Simon assumed that the chunks formed by chess experts contain more information than those formed by novice players. They reached this conclusion by instructing chess players to study a position and then reconstruct it on another board. While they were doing this, the original position remained visible. Chase and Simon used the number of pieces placed on the board after each viewing of the original as a measure of the amount of information stored in a chunk. For experts, this number averaged about 2.5, whereas for beginners it was about 1.9. Subsequent studies, however, have shown

that this is probably a huge underestimation (Gobet & Simon, 1998), as it was found that an expert may hold up to about 14 to 17 positions per chunk, when the duration of the viewing process was also considered (see fig 22.17).

Chase and Simon hypothesised that experts are so good at the game because they have a huge number of chunks stored in their long-term memories. Simon and Gilmartin (1973) have estimated this number to be 10,000 to 30,000, whereas later computer simulations have suggested it to be as high 100,000 (Gobet & Simon, 2000). While these numbers are impressive, we should not forget that a larger and more detailed memory of chess positions is not the only advantage grandmaster chess players have. They also employ substantially different strategies that could not be accurately described by Simon and Chase's chunking theory. Therefore, to better understand these strategies, their theory needs to be extended.

22.8.2.2 Template Theory

Gobet and Waters' (2003) template theory represents a significant extension of the chunking theory. These authors argued that chunking theory cannot explain two important aspects of chess playing. First, it has a problem explaining how individual chunks are integrated into the higher-order representations that are used by chess experts. Second, according to chunking theory, the encoding of board positions should take much more time than it actually does.

The template theory largely removes these limitations. It is implemented as a computer programme that aims to simulate a chess player's thought processes. More specifically, the template theory assumes that a chess player will determine the next move by traversing an associative

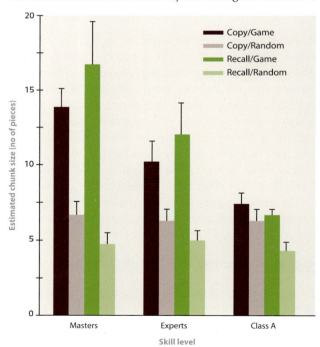

Figure 22.17 Estimated number of chess positions that can be stored in a chunk. (source: Gobet and Simon, 1998)

network. This network consists of a set of nodes (consisting of chunks) which are linked together in the form of a tree structure. Each node consists of a number of tests that can be used to check several properties of the external stimuli. The result of this test will determine which link will be followed to the next level in the decision tree. When the end of the decision tree is reached, the chunk that is located at this position will be compared to the actual position on the board, using a pattern recognition mechanism. The associative network grows on the basis of two learning mechanisms: familiarisation and discrimination.

Chunks that are commonly used will evolve into templates. These templates consist of a core, which is in fact formed by the original chunks, and slots, in which additional information can be stored. In particular, slots are created for positions where there is a large variation in moves, pieces, and relative positions at the next level in the decision tree. Templates contain, according to Gobet and Waters (2003), information on about 10 to 20 chess pieces.

Template theory is capable of generating several testable predictions. First, it predicts that chess positions are stored in up to three templates, some of which are relatively large. Evidence for this prediction was found by Gobet and Clarkson (2004). In this study, too, participants had to copy board positions, as was done in Chase and Simon's (1973) study, but now the positions were presented either physically or on a computer screen. Gobet and Clarkson found that reconstructing the board always involved three or fewer steps, and that chess masters could in some cases place as many as 15 pieces at a time. For beginning chess players, this number was much lower – about six.

Second, template theory predicts that the best chess players owe their outstanding performance mainly to their superior template-based knowledge rather than to their ability to think strategically. Here, the assumption is that the template-based knowledge can be retrieved rapidly, which implies that expert players can reduce the number of possible moves very rapidly. If this assumption is correct, we should expect chess experts to continue to deliver high-quality performance even under time pressure. Evidence for this prediction is rather inconsistent, however. If chess expertise is related to the rapid retrieval of relevant knowledge, eye movement data should also demonstrate this. Charness, Reingold, Pomplun, and Stampe (2001) found eye movement results that were consistent with this hypothesis. Chess experts and intermediate-level players were instructed to determine the best move for a number of positions, while their first five fixations were recorded. These fixations took place within one second. Even within this short time span the experts fixed more often on the tactically relevant positions than the intermediate-level chess players (fig 22.18).

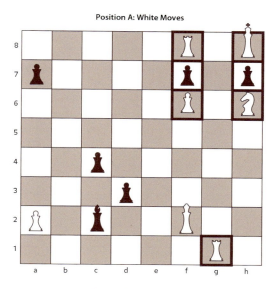

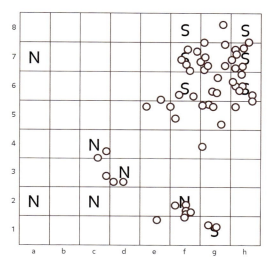

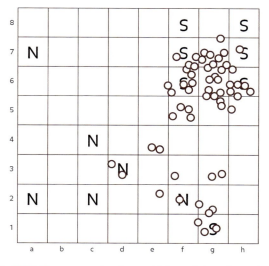

Figure 22.18 Eye movement patterns of intermediate and expert chess players. Compared to intermediate-level players, experts fixated more frequently on salient pieces and empty positions. S = Salient piece, N = non-salient piece. (source: Charness et al., 2001)

Further evidence for the prediction that experts continue to perform relatively well under time pressure was found by Burns (2004), who studied chess performance during rapid chess games. In these games, which must be played within five minutes, it may be assumed that chess players must rely entirely on their template knowledge, as there is too little time for slow strategic deliberation. Burns indeed found a high correlation between normal chess performance and performance during a rapid chess game. Van Harreveld, Wagenmakers, and van der Maas (2007) found, however, that players' ratings were increasingly less predictive of game results as the time available for a game decreased. This result therefore suggests that slow strategic processes do play a role during a normal game. Moxley, Ericsson, Charness, and Krampe (2012) gave chess players five minutes to choose the best move given a specific position. The players thought aloud while performing this task, allowing the researchers to compare the participants' initial thoughts with the move that was eventually chosen. The final move was much stronger than the one mentioned in the initial thought. This result was found for both experts and regular players participating in tournaments and generalised across different levels of difficulty. These findings also emphasise the importance of slow strategic processes in chess performance.

22.8.3 MEDICAL EXPERTISE

For several reasons, the study of medical expertise is complementary to the study of chess. In contrast to chess, medical diagnoses are ill-defined problems that, moreover, require a considerable amount of professional knowledge. In other words, medical diagnoses are also knowledge-rich problems. In addition, correctly formulating a medical diagnosis serves a significantly important medical and social purpose. After all, an incorrect medical diagnosis can have a significantly negative impact on a patient's well-being, or in the most extreme case, even be life-threatening.

Inspired by De Groot's research on chess expertise, research on medical expertise initially started with an extensive research programme that was set up by Arthur Elstein in the United States (Ericsson, 2007). Elstein designed tasks that were representative of situations that a medical specialist might encounter in everyday life. The participating experts were placed in a room that simulated a medical practice and actors were hired to play patients. Elstein was particularly interested in how the best specialists made diagnoses and he took extreme care to find medical specialists who excelled in their diagnostic skills and compared their performance with a representative group of regular doctors. Because Elstein was specifically interested in how experts form their diagnoses, all sessions were filmed for later analysis. Based on these analyses, however, Elstein had to conclude that the best experts did not outperform the average doctors.

One of the problems that Elstein subsequently identified was that his method of identifying top experts was ineffective. He had recruited these experts based on nominations from fellow specialists, and Elstein had to conclude that most doctors knew too little about their colleagues to formulate effective nominations. Therefore, the number of years of experience, certification by relevant government agencies, and responsibilities appeared to be more effective indicators for the development of expertise than excellence alone (Elstein, Shulman, & Sprafka, 1990).

The conclusion that medical expertise develops gradually implies that it is not necessary to actively select the best expert, but that it is sufficient to study medical decision-making processes as a function of the number of years of experience that a medical specialist has. In addition, the expensive simulations of a medical practice also turned out to be ineffective, opening the way to other, more cost-effective studies, in which researchers regularly took advantage of methods used in cognitive psychology to investigate medical expertise. For example, experimental designs developed to study concept formation (Bordage, 2007) or exemplar-based categorisation strategies (Norman, Young, & Brooks, 2007).

22.8.3.1 Implicit versus Explicit Reasoning

The Bordage (2007) and Norman et al. (2007) studies imply that much medical expertise is implicit; a conclusion that was also drawn by Engel (2008). The main difference between medical experts and beginners would be that experts make much more use of fast, intuitive System 1 processes, while beginners use the more explicit deliberate reasoning strategies associated with System 2. Engel has noted that these implicit strategies are mainly used in medical specialities that rely heavily on visual pattern recognition, such as pathology, radiology, and dermatology, and to a lesser extent in specialities that involve technical specialities, such as surgery or anaesthesiology.

Moreover, it has been found that even when medical specialists use an implicit strategy, they still check their results using an explicit reasoning strategy. For example, among medical students, these checks positively affected the quality of medical diagnoses (Coderre, Wright, & McLaughlin, 2010; McLaughlin, Rikers, & Schmidt, 2007). In these studies, students were instructed to make a medical diagnosis. When this diagnosis had to be verified on the basis of additional discrepant findings, the accuracy of the final diagnosis turned out to be much better than when non-discrepant additional findings were used.

Patel and Groen (1986) already assumed that pattern recognition is an important determinant of expertise. They reached this conclusion using an experimental method that was derived from Chase and Simon's (1973) chess expertise studies. Patel and Groen had medical students and specialists read a description of a patient, after which they had to try to formulate a diagnosis. In doing so, they had to try to give a description of the underlying pathology that was as complete as possible. Afterwards, the students had to report their diagnosis. This allowed Patel and Groen to determine how information had been structured after the students had finished formulating a diagnosis. A similar approach was followed by Schmidt and Rikers (2007).

Norman et al. (2007) have argued that medical problem-solving strategies are, at least in part, based on discovering similarities with a previously encountered case that the diagnostician is familiar with. This applies, according to Norman, to both beginners and experts, and the comparison involves non-analytical reasoning processes. Since these processes are not accessible to introspection, Norman believes that it is not necessary to collect verbal reports, but that it makes more sense to use cognitive psychological experiments.

The studies conducted by Norman and colleagues show that the specific characteristics of diagnostic examples (e.g., photographs of skin conditions or an electrocardiogram) that are initially presented to participants can introduce a strong bias among the diagnostician. Young, Brooks, and Norman (2007), for example, studied the influence of examples on the fomulation of a diagnosis. To this end, they taught psychology students to recognise four different diagnoses of pseudo-psychiatric symptoms. They found that a strong bias was introduced by the examples the students had been studying when they learned to recognise these symptoms. Norman et al. (2007) found these biases not only among psychology students but also among medical students and practising physicians who had not yet achieved specialist status. Specialists were less susceptible to these biases because they were more likely to use analytical reasoning for difficult cases.

Eva, Hatala, Leblanc, and Brooks (2007) reported that these biases could be reduced among psychology students when they were explicitly instructed to use both non-analytical and analytical reasoning skills. Mamede, Schmidt, et al. (2010) found a similar result, namely that specifically for complex diagnoses, medical experts benefited from the use of explicit conscious analysis (see fig 22.19). However, non-experts did not benefit from this. The results reported by Mamede, Schmidt et al. are clearly inconsistent with the idea that unconscious decisions are better than conscious ones (see Box 21.4).

How can we determine whether medical experts are indeed using implicit strategies? For visual specialisations, we can do so by analysing eye movements. Krupinski, Graham, and Weinstein (2013) conducted a longitudinal study among pathologists who detected breast biopsies at respectively the beginning of their first, second, third, and fourth year of practice. A key finding of this study was

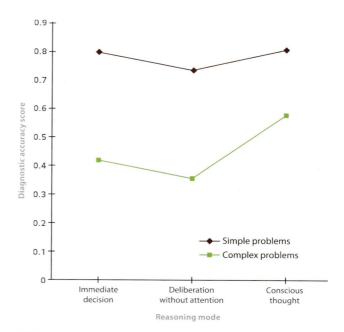

Figure 22.19 The relationship between the accuracy of a diagnosis and the type of reasoning involved. (source: Mamede, Schmidt et al., 2010)

that as these specialists became more experienced, they spent less and less time inspecting the non-diagnostic parts of an image (see fig 22.20).

Kundel et al. (2007) used eye movement recordings to determine how experienced doctors inspected mammograms. The average search time per mammogram showing a tumour was about 27 seconds. The median fixation time on the tumour was only 1.13 seconds and it was often less than a second for many doctors. In addition, a strong negative correlation of -0.9 was found between the time of the first fixation on the tumour and the accuracy with which the diagnosis was made. This implies that rapid detection was a very good predictor of diagnostic accuracy.

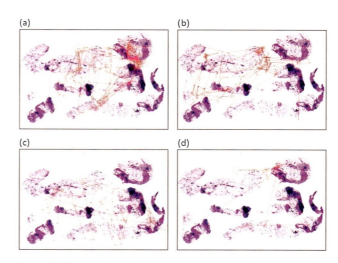

Figure 22.20 The relationship between eye movement patterns and expertise in scanning for pathologies in tissue samples. Results from individuals with (a) one year, (b) two years, (c) three years, and (d) four years of experience. (source: Krupinski et al., 2013)

The doctors with the greatest expertise focused almost directly on the tumour, which implies that they used a holistic or global strategy. In contrast, doctors with the least expertise relied on a slower and more deliberate strategy. This conclusion is consistent with the results of an older study by Kundel and Nodine (1975). Here they reported that medical experts could detect abnormalities in chest radiographs. To avoid deliberate visual search, these pictures were shown for only 200 ms. Nevertheless, the experts were able to classify these pictures correctly in 70% of the cases.

22.8.3.2 Efficiency of Recognition Processes

How is it possible that medical experts focus almost immediately on a tumour or cyst in a medical image? In Chapter 6, we discussed how our visual system is able to recognise objects extremely rapidly, within 150 ms. We can, therefore, wonder whether medical experts have developed a particularly efficient prediction system for the recognition of tumours, cysts, and other medical conditions. If so, we might expect similar effects to emerge in other areas of expertise. A meta-analysis from Gegenfurtner, Lehtinen, and Säljö (2011) found evidence suggesting that this is indeed the case. Consistent differences were found between experts and non-experts in various domains of expertise, including medicine, sport, and transportation. Compared to non-experts, experts were found to (1) fixate for a shorter time, (2) fixate earlier on task-relevant information, (3) fixate more frequently on task-relevant information, (4) fixate less frequently on task-irrelevant information, and (5) make longer saccades.

Melo et al. (2011) investigated whether medical experts used the same strategies to detect pathologies that we normally use to detect objects in visual scenes in more detail. They found that it took about the same amount of time to detect lesions on X-rays as it did to name animals. Moreover, both tasks were found to activate a similar set of brain regions, although activation in the frontal sulcus and the posterior cingulate cortex was higher in the diagnostic task than in the animal naming task. The latter result suggests that making a medical diagnosis requires more cognitive processes than naming an animal. Melo et al. suggest that medical experts use a rapid pattern recognition process, comparing each image with an internal representation of the abnormality to be detected. According to Melo et al. experts thus rely to a large degree on a visual strategy.

Additional evidence for this conclusion was found in a study by Kulatunga-Moruzi, Brooks, and Norman (2004). In this study, participants were given photographs of skin diseases they needed to evaluate. One group of participants had to make the diagnosis purely on the basis of these photos, while another group was also given an extensive verbal description of the pathology. The remarkable result of this study was that the experts did not only not benefit from this additional description but actually performed worse, compared to the experts who were only shown the photos. This result implies that these experts use a very efficient visual strategy, and that the verbal description interferes with this strategy.

22.8.3.3 Pattern Recognition and Decision Processes

Most of the forms of expertise that we have discussed so far involve complex problems that can, in principle, be solved after careful deliberation. But what if such a complex decision has to be made quickly. Many professionals, such as firefighters, pilots, or air traffic controllers, may occasionally need to make complex decisions under high time pressure. According to Klein (2008), pattern recognition processes play a very important role in this type of decision-making. According to his **recognition-primed decision model** (see fig 22.21), experts will try to compare a given situation with a previous one. When there is a match, they will use a previously chosen solution. This process results in the retrieval of one solution, based on pattern recognition. According to Klein, this solution is then first applied in the form of a mental simulation, and if the result of this simulation is satisfactory, the solution is applied to the actual problem. It is only when the situation is unknown, or when the selected solution is not expected to have the intended effect, that a follow-up step will be necessary. This may take the form of an additional diagnosis of the problem or the consideration of additional data.

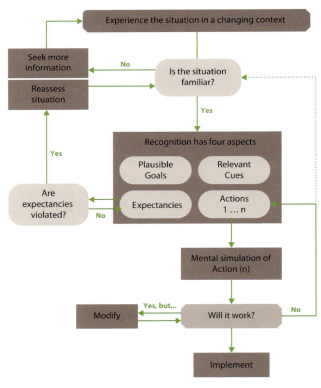

Figure 22.21 The recognition-primed decision model. (source: Klein, 2008)

There is generally good empirical support for this idea. Experts are typically quick to interpret new situations as variations of a known type of problem. When they succeed, they simply retrieve an appropriate decision from their long-term memories. Although some decision-makers use this strategy, it also appears to be the case that not everyone does (Turpin & Marais, 2004). Moreover, the recognition-primed decision model contrasts quite sharply with the heuristic System 1 approach (Kahneman & Klein, 2009). Note, however, that Klein's recognition-primed decision model focuses mainly on the decision-making behaviour of experts, while Kahneman's System 1 approach mainly aims to explain human errors.

22.8.3.4 Experience versus Expertise

The increase in efficiency in pattern recognition is an example of expertise that develops as a function of experience. Mylopoulos and Regehr (2007a) argue, however, that medical expertise research has put too much emphasis on experience. For this reason, they argue that the idea that the development of expertise is a consequence of accumulating experience is incorrect. Although this is true for some forms of expertise (known as **routine expertise**), it is not necessarily true for other forms of expertise (known as **adaptive expertise**). Routine expertise is related to someone becoming particularly efficient at performing routine procedures, such as inspecting mammograms or X-rays. Adaptive expertise, on the other hand, is related to individuals who continue to grow in their field because of their intentional commitment to solving problems in new and innovative ways. In these adaptive experts, there is a continuous engagement of cognitive processes, with the goal of not only achieving better performance, but also of achieving a better understanding of the problems in their field. Mylopoulos and Regehr (2007a) conclude that many medical educations are focused on the training of routine expertise and that new forms of education are desirable to stimulate adaptive expertise.

The past decade has indeed witnessed a shift in the idea that there is a correlation between expertise and experience; a conclusion that applies not only to medical expertise but also to a large number of other areas of expertise (Ericsson, 2007). Ericsson states that recent studies have found that the correlations between expertise and the number of years of experience are often very small or non-existent. In some cases, even a small negative correlation can be found (Choudhry, Fletcher, & Soumerai, 2006; Ericsson, 2004; Ericsson, Whyte, & Ward, 2007), which implies that some individuals actually lose some of their original skills.

For this reason, Ericsson (2007) proposes to approach the study of medical expertise differently. His expert performance approach is based on the identification of individuals who have a proven better than average performance on specific medical tasks in a specific domain, such as

more effective treatments or more accurate diagnoses. According to this approach, expert performance begins with an analysis of natural behaviour, such as making rapid diagnoses in the operating theatre. Here, critical situations are identified in which a critical action is required. Subsequently, the effectiveness of these actions can be evaluated and used in subsequent training material for other participants with a different level of expertise. These participants would then be exposed to the critical situation and be asked what action they would perform.

By using this method, an inventory can be made of which types of behaviour are associated with expertise. The major difference between this expert performance approach and the classic Elstein approach is that the expert performance approach focuses on which skills result in superior performance in exceptional cases, whereas Elstein initially focused on typicall routine cases. It is, however, precisely in these unusually challenging cases where the superior performance of experts, and in particular adaptive experts, becomes crucially important (Mylopoulos & Regehr, 2007a).

22.8.3.5 Deliberate Practice

Ericsson (2007) argues that deliberate practice can contribute to the acquisition of a skill, provided that a number of specific conditions are met. More specifically, Ericsson and Towne (2010) identify deliberate practice as being characterised by the following aspects: (1) the task is sufficiently difficult; (2) while practising, informative feedback is available; (3) there is a sufficient opportunity to repeat the task; and (4) there is ample opportunity for correcting any mistakes that might have been made.

The condition of immediate feedback is often difficult to achieve in medical activities since the result of a treatment or diagnosis may often take weeks or even years to arrive. Medical students, for example, who have to interpret the result of a mammogram or an X-ray, must do so on the basis of feedback from their instructors, whose interpretation of the results is often only correct in 70% of all cases (Ericsson, 2004; Nodine et al., 1999). In other situations, such as surgery or first aid, immediate feedback might be available, but these situations are often not representative for the entire medical field.

In this respect, medical expertise occupies a special position compared to other disciplines where immediate feedback is available. Within the medical sciences, the most remarkable results are currently achieved with the help of simulator training, particularly in the operation of laboratory equipment. The best results of this simulator training are therefore obtained when the procedures meet the criterion of deliberate practice, such as goal-orientation or possibilities for immediate feedback. Under these conditions, practice resulted in an improvement of the skill in question (McGaghie, Issenberg, Petrusa, & Scalese, 2006).

According to Ericsson and Kintsch (1995), deliberate practice has the consequence that we can bypass the limitations of working memory. To this end, they introduced the concept of **long-term working memory**. This long-term working memory concept is similar to the working memory models proposed by Oberauer (2002), Cowan (1988), and Jonides et al. (2008), in the sense that it postulates that we can remember information by activating representations in long-term memory (see Chapter 14 for a discussion of these models). According to Guida, Gobet, Tardieu, and Nicolas (2012), expertise can facilitate the rapid transfer of information to long-term memory, allowing it to take over some of the functionality of working memory. It is important that new information can be directly associated with existing knowledge in long-term memory. For example, chess experts can remember board positions much easier because they can be related to their knowledge of existing positions. Novice chess players, who do not yet have this knowledge, will have to remember the positions purely on the basis of working memory.

An impressive demonstration of the effectiveness of deliberate practice was provided by Ericsson and Chase (1982). They trained a student, SF, for 230 hours, over a period of 20 months, in memorising number sequences. During this time, SF's digit span improved from seven to eighty. SF succeeded by using his knowledge of running races. If the first four digits were, for example, 3, 5, 9, and 4, he associated them with Bannister's record time on the mile and stored them as a chunk. He then organised all the chunks in a hierarchical way, allowing him to retrieve all the digits by simply going through this structure (see fig 22.22).

Guida et al. (2012) and Guida, Gobet, and Nicolas (2013) also concluded that experts use working memory more efficiently. For tasks that depended on working memory, they found reduced activation of the prefrontal cortex in experts compared to non-experts. In addition, for experts, they found increased activation in brain areas that are typically associated with long-term memory, namely the medial temporal regions.

Within some domains, a strong correlation between the level of expertise and the amount of deliberate practice has been found. Among chess players, for example, the correlation between the level of performance and the number of hours of practice was greater than 0.50 (Campitelli & Gobet, 2011). World renowned chess players, for example, had all spent more than 25,000 hours of practising!

Campitelli and Gobet (2011) also note, however, that deliberate practice is a necessary but not a sufficient condition for developing expertise. According to these authors, the following three predictions follow from Ericsson and Towne's (2010) deliberate practice theory: (1) everyone who exercises frequently and deliberately should eventually reach a very high level of performance; (2) for each individual, the total amount of exercise time should be about the same to reach a certain level; and (3) everyone's skill should benefit roughly equally from exercise.

For chess expertise, Campitelli and Gobet found no support for any of these predictions. For example, there are chess players who have spent more than 20,000 hours practising without reaching the master level. In addition, Campitelli and Gobet found considerable individual differences: the number of hours needed to reach the master level varied between 3000 and 23,600 hours. Evidence against the third prediction was reported by Howard (2009). Here, candidates (international players who competed for the chance to challenge the world champion) benefited much more from practice than grandmasters, who in turn benefited more from practice than regular players. Here, the effectiveness of practice was strongly determined by the player's initial level. The higher their initial level, the greater the effectiveness of deliberate practice became. Moreover, the effectiveness of practice also levelled off over time (see fig 22.23).

These results imply that although exercise has a positive effect, the effectiveness of deliberate practice is limited. Thus, in principle, it should be possible to determine who will benefit the most from deliberate practice, on the basis of the talent that is displayed early on. The question now is, which indicators show whether someone is talented? It turns out that for generic skills, general intelligence is an important indicator. A literature review by Gottfredson

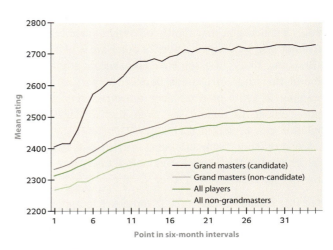

Figure 22.23 The relationship between performance level and number of months of practice in chess players. (source: Howard, 2009)

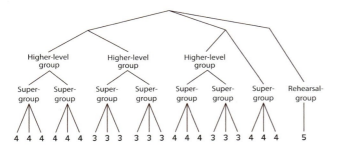

Figure 22.22 The hierarchical organisation of chunks of numbers that student SF used to achieve a digit span of 80. (source: Ericsson and Chase, 1982)

(1997) discusses the relationship between intelligence and subsequent career success. For complex occupations, the correlation between intelligence and job performance was approximately +0.58. The average IQ in these professions was about 120–130, that is, significantly higher than the population average of 100. It was also found that chess experts generally had a high IQ of at least 110–115 (Grabner, Stern, & Neubauer, 2007).

For specific skills, however, intelligence is a less important factor. Ceci and Liker (1986) studied experts who calculated the odds of winning in horse racing. Calculating these odds requires various factors to be considered, such as the length of the track, the average speed of a horse, and so on. The experts studied varied in IQ between 81 and 128, but no correlation was found between task performance and IQ.

22.9 SUMMARY

In cognitive psychology, problem-solving is typically studied using situations in which the problem solver is in one state and needs to get into another state. Although the steps allowed are often defined, problem-solving only occurs when it is not immediately clear how the difference between the two states can be bridged.

Although problem-solving can be defined by the difference in states, there is a considerable amount of variation in the nature of problems. On the one hand, problems can be well-defined or ill-defined; on the other hand, problems can be knowledge-rich or knowledge-poor. In problem-solving research, well-defined knowledge-poor problems are generally used because they are the best controlled. In the study of expertise, however, knowledge-rich and ill-defined problems are often used.

Problem-solving relies heavily on productive thinking, that is, on the thought processes involved in finding innovative new solutions. Historically, however, the study of problem-solving behaviour has emerged from the study of reproductive thought processes. Reproductive thinking refers to the application of previously found solutions and the memorisation of solutions found by chance.

Gestalt psychology focused on the processes involved in insight. Insight is any form of understanding, realisation, or problem-solving where the solution is suddenly found through a reorganisation of the problem representation. Examples of tasks to study insight include the mutilated checkerboard problem or the remote associates task. Insight often involves a sudden realisation of the problem.

Experience with previous solutions can help us to discover the underlying structure of a problem, so experience is generally beneficial for solving insight problems. Sometimes, however, experience can also have negative effects on our problem-solving skills. This is exemplified by functional fixation or Einstellung. Functional fixation implies that we focus too strongly on the traditional use cases of objects, so that alternative uses are not recognised. Einstellung refers to the expected difficulty of

a problem. When problems are easier than expected, we are often less capable of finding a solution. A high degree of cognitive control can also be unfavourable for gaining insight.

The representational change theory aims to explain insight on the basis of cognitive processes. When we have tried to solve a problem unsuccessfully for several times, this lack of progress results in a need to adapt the representation of the problem. Progress monitoring is also of crucial importance here. As long as we are under the impression that we are getting closer to a solution, we do not experience the need to represent the problem differently. As a result, problems for which we appear to be making progress are often more difficult to solve than problems where no progress can be made at first. One of the processes that is important in finding a new representation of the problem is constraint relaxation, that is, the letting go of self-imposed limitations. An example of this is the matchstick problem. Although insight can contribute greatly to finding a solution, after changing the problem representation, a solution is often not immediately available. Even within the new representation, many times we still need to search for the correct solution.

Incubation refers to the fact that letting a problem rest for a while often results in finding the solution more efficiently. The effectiveness of incubation may be related to forgetting irrelevant aspects of the problem or letting go of ineffective solution strategies.

In the 1950s, a successful line of research into solving well-defined problems started with the development of the computer programme General Problem Solver. This programme was capable of solving problems in which the problem state was brought to the goal state via a number of well-defined steps. The steps taken by the general problem solver were compared to the steps performed by humans. Examples of these problems involve the Tower of Hanoi or various river crossing puzzles. Since a complete elaboration of the problem is often not possible, the solution often involves a number of simplified heuristics. Examples of such heuristics are the means-end analysis and the hill-climbing strategy. When humans make little progress, this should result in a change of strategy.

These problems require us to plan ahead to some extent. However, for many problems it has been found that humans often only plan ahead to a very limited extent. It was originally believed that this lack of planning was the result of a lack of capacity. More recent studies, however, attribute it to cognitive economy: we can plan more ahead, but we often do not do so for cognitive-economic reasons.

The availability of an analogy can be very important for solving problems. In analogical problem-solving, we can distinguish between analogies with superficial similarities, analogies with structural similarities, and analogies with procedural similarities. Although superficial similarities are, in principle, irrelevant to the solution, the absence of these similarities can sometimes prevent us from being able to recognise the structural and procedural similarity between the problem and the analogy. The active search for an analogy is often more effective than being presented with one. Empirical research into analogies often takes place on the basis of the four-term analogy problem.

Research on expertise focuses on the cognitive psychological factors that contribute to the lifelong development of cognitive skills. This often involves the use of knowledge-rich problems. Studies investigating how people classify physics problems suggest that beginners often classify them on the basis of superficial features, while experts do so mainly on the basis of the underlying structure.

Research on chess expertise has focused on how experienced chess players represent board positions. Simon and Chase hypothesised that chess players represent board positions in chunks and that these chunks are larger for experts than for beginners. They further hypothesised that experienced chess players are so good because they have stored a very large amount of such chunks in their long-term memory. However, experienced chess players also use other strategies described by the template theories.

In addition to chess expertise, many studies focus on the development of medical expertise. Part of this line of research is inspired by the original studies on chess expertise. Elstein aimed to identify top medical practitioners and tried to determine how their diagnoses differed from those of regular doctors. Later studies focused more on the development of expertise as a function of years of experience. Among experienced doctors, a large part of their diagnostic skills is implicit and based on pattern recognition; skills that are primarily driven by a System 1 process. These implicit findings are, however, often verified on the basis of a System 2 process. Eye movement studies have shown that medical experts can very rapidly identify pathologies on X-rays or photos of skin conditions.

This increase in efficiency in recognising pathologies is a typical example of expertise that develops with age. We must, however, also distinguish between routine expertise and adaptive expertise. Routine expertise develops with experience, whereas adaptive expertise is primarily associated with an intrinsic intentional motivation to continuously develop and be innovative.

An important but also somewhat controversial factor in the development of expertise is deliberate practice. Practice is effective when there is sufficient opportunity to practice, when adequate feedback is provided, and when the exercises are of the right level of difficulty to remain challenging. One reason why practice can be effective is that it can circumvent the limitations of our working memory. Exercise is a necessary but not sufficient condition, however, to excel in a specific domain. For chess players it was found, for example, that not only the number of hours of practice but also their initial skill level determined the rating they could eventually achieve. These results imply that initial talent also plays a very significant role in determining subsequent task performance.

NOTES

1 The correct answer: star.
2 There are two solutions to the problem. The first is as follows: fill the 5 litre jar completely and transfer 3 litres of this to the 3 litre jar. Empty that and pour the remaining 2 litres into the 3 litre pot as well. Fill the 5 litre jar again and use this to fill the 3 litre water jar. Try to find the second solution.
3 Here you must turn one stick of the + so that it forms an = .
4 Three cannibals and three missionaries are standing on the bank of a wide river and want to get to the other side. There is a boat, but it can only take two people at a time. As soon as there are more cannibals than missionaries together, the cannibals eat the missionaries. How can they reach the other side without being eaten?

5 Similar to the previous problem: the farmer can only take one object. If the goat and the cabbage are left alone, the goat eats the cabbage; if the wolf and the goat are left alone, the wolf eats the goat.

6 The answers are: 5 cents, 5 minutes, and 47 days respectively.

7 The correct solution is to fire several weaker beams from different positions, which converge on the location of the tumour.

FURTHER READING

Ericsson, K. A., & Smith, J. (1991). *Towards a general theory of expertise: Prospects and limits*. Cambridge, UK: Cambridge University Press.

Gilhooly, K. J. (2012). *Human and machine problem solving*. London, UK: Plenum Press.

Hofmann, R. R. (1992). *The psychology of expertise: Cognitive research and empirical AI*. Hove, UK: Psychology Press.

Newell, A., & Simon, H. A. (1972). *Human problem solving*. Englewood Cliffs, NJ: Prentice-Hall.

PART 9

A Broader Perspective

CHAPTER 23
Social cognition

23.1 INTRODUCTION

Suppose you wake up one morning to find a message on your cell phone. It is from a close friend saying: 'Thanks man!' What does it mean? Depending on the situation, you can interpret it in different ways. If you helped her the other night by carrying a heavy cupboard two floors up, it will probably be a sincere thank you. If, on the other hand, you have done something to disadvantage her, accidentally or otherwise, then the message will probably have a cynical undertone. Here we see some essential aspects of social cognition. In order to correctly evaluate the message, we must be able to put ourselves in the position of someone else, so that we can interpret their perception of the situation. Similarly, helping another person is in itself a good example of social cognition. Consider the simple task of moving a cupboard together. You have to be able to coordinate your actions with those of another person if you are to successfully complete the task.

A justified criticism of cognitive psychology is that research into human cognitive functions has always focused on the individual. This is somewhat surprising, given that we humans are social animals. We not only pursue our own goals, but we often also act on behalf of others. We carry out tasks for the benefit of others, we take each other's positions into account (to a certain degree), we try to empathise with the thoughts and needs of others, and we cooperate with other human beings. The study of human behaviour in a social context is the domain of social psychology and therefore also largely beyond the scope of this book. There are, however, many cognitive and neural processes that underlie these social interactions, and recently the study of social cognition has expanded considerably. In particular, perceptual and action processes have increasingly been studied in a social context (Sebanz, Bekkering, & Knoblich, 2006). For this reason, it is appropriate that the final theme of this handbook approaches cognitive psychology from a broader, social perspective.

23.2 IMPLICIT SOCIAL COGNITION

One major problem that is intrinsic to social cognition research is that many social-cognitive processes remain implicit. We are often unaware of why we perform certain social actions (Nosek, Hawkins, & Frazier, 2011). For this reason, Greenwald and Banaji (1995) introduced the term **implicit social cognition** to describe those processes that are beyond our conscious awareness and related to social psychological constructs such as attitudes, stereotypes, and self-concepts. To investigate these social cognitive processes, Greenwald and Banaji suggested using implicit measures. These implicit measures are used to identify the processes that form the basis of social perceptions, judgements, and actions that cannot be described introspectively, or otherwise measured through self-report. These kinds of implicit measures are obtained, for example, by applying priming procedures or implicit association tests.

The **affect misattribution procedure** is an example of such a priming procedure (Payne, Cheng, Govorun, & Stewart, 2005). In this task, participants are shown faces of different ethnicities, which serve as a prime stimulus. These primes are presented shortly before the appearance of an unknown Chinese character (see fig 23.1). Participants are instructed to ignore the faces and to judge whether the Chinese character is more or less attractive than an average character. Although the faces are irrelevant to the task, they do appear to influence the ratings of the characters, according to Payne et al.

Implicit association tests are used to investigate racial attitudes (Greenwald, McGhee, & Schwartz, 1998). These tests involve a somewhat more complicated procedure in which participants are initially shown a series of names that are representative of two population groups (e.g., African Americans and Caucasians). Participants are then instructed to rapidly respond with their left hand to an African American name and with their right hand to a Caucasian name. They are then shown a series of

DOI: 10.4324/9781003319344-32

Figure 23.1 An example of the affect misattribution procedure. Participants are first presented with a picture of a face, after which they have to judge the attractiveness of a Chinese character. (source: Payne et al., 2005)

emotionally laden words to which they have to rapidly respond. More specifically, for these words they have to use their left hand for positive words and their right hand for negative words. This is then followed by a block of trials in which the two categories are intermixed. Thus, participants have to use their left hand to respond to the African American names and the positive words and their right hand to respond to the Caucasian names and the negative words.

Next, participants are instructed to reverse their response to the names. First, they are given a series of names-only trials where they have to use their right hand to respond to an African American name and their left hand to respond to a Caucasian name. Finally, after completing this block, they are given another combined block in which they must respond to both the names and the emotion words. Here, the task is to respond to Caucasian names and positive emotion words with the left hand and to African American and negative emotion words with the right hand. The essence of the task consists of the reversal of the response mapping on the latter task. The reasoning is that if the participant already has an implicit association with an emotional valence and a certain population group (such as a negative association with African Americans, for example, due to negative stereotyping), it should be evident from the fact that the participant can perform this mapping more efficiently than the other mapping, so they are less affected by the reversal than participants who do not have this implicit association.

23.3 SOCIAL PRIMING

Based on the idea that social perception is largely unconscious, we can ask to what extent social situations unconsciously influence behaviour. In recent decades, the question of how subtle exposure to a social situation can be, while still

influencing behaviour, has been a core theme of social psychology, with sometimes surprising results as a consequence (Molden, 2014). One consequence of this is that a considerable amount of research in social psychology is guided by the idea that mere unconscious exposure to socially relevant stimuli can lead to the facilitation, or priming, of a variety of behaviours, such as judgements, decisions, or actions.

The term **priming** refers to a wide range of changes in perceptions, judgements, and behaviours that are triggered by a minimal exposure to words, pictures, or other stimuli. Some forms of priming are very robust, such as the perceptual (Lupyan & Ward, 2013) or semantic priming effects (Meyer & Schvaneveldt, 1971; Neely, 1977) discussed in earlier chapters. The mechanisms underlying this form of priming are also relatively simple: the increased accuracy on a word-naming task can be explained by activation spreading through an associative semantic network in long-term memory.

When considering the effects of social priming, however, we face a much more complex situation, since the relationship between prime and target behaviour is considerably more complex and also far more indirect than is the case for a simple word recognition task. To cite a few examples: some studies have reported that participants walked slower after unconscious exposure to concepts related to age (Bargh, Chen, & Burrows, 1996; see Box 23.1), that they were less willing to do voluntary work after being exposed to money-related words (Vohs, Mead, & Goode, 2006), or that they performed better at answering Trivial Pursuit questions when they thought of the stereotype of a professor (Dijksterhuis & van Knippenberg, 1998). Yet other studies have suggested that American participants reported having more conservative political views 11 months after exposure to an American flag (Carter, Ferguson, & Hassin, 2011).

The wide variety of cause-and-effect relationships in these social-priming studies presupposes a much more complex mechanism of indirect associations; a mechanism that is so complex that it is highly unlikely that simple exposure to the primes can bring about the reported robust behavioural changes. There is also a notable difference between perceptual and social-priming effects: the former effects have been replicated numerous times, whereas the latter effects have been difficult or even impossible to replicate (Doyen, Klein, Pichon, & Cleeremans, 2012; Harris, Coburn, Rohrer, & Pashler, 2013; Newell & Shanks, 2014; Pashler & Wagenmakers, 2012; Shanks et al., 2013). As a result, the unconscious influence of these types of primes on our behaviour can be questioned. Without a clear theoretical framework, there is the danger of overreaching conclusions that are not actually supported by the data. For this reason, the future will have to show whether the reported effects of social priming will be proven to be robust enough (see Box 23.1).

Box 23.1 Fact or fiction: social priming

In Chapter 1, we introduced the phenomenon of priming, that is, the fact that the presentation of a prime word (such as 'nurse') can activate semantically related concepts in long-term memory, thereby facilitating the processing of target words (such as 'doctor'). Moreover, in Chapter 13, we discussed the underlying memory processes. Priming is a primarily unconscious process that can robustly activate concepts that are associated with the prime.

One question that was addressed in social psychology is whether priming can not only influence our memory but also our behaviour. In 1996, the American social psychologist John Bargh and his colleagues reported the results of a remarkable study. Without being aware of it, participants were primed with several stereotypes of a concept (Bargh et al., 1996). The second experiment in this study dealt with the stereotype of ageing. Participants were required to produce a grammatically correct sentence based on a set of words that was given to them. Half of the participants were given a set that was linked to the concept of ageing, such as 'grey', 'wrinkles', 'Florida', 'dentures', or 'walker', while the other half were given a neutral set of words.

Although the participants were informed that they were participating in an experiment about language skills, the real aim of the experiment was to determine what the participants did after the experiment. As they left the experiment room, an assistant to the experimenter used a stopwatch to measure how long it took them to walk to the elevator at the end of the hallway. It turned out that participants who had been primed with stereotypical concepts about ageing took about one second longer to walk the 10 metres to the elevator than those who had not.

The study described here is considered one of the first studies in the field of **social priming**; the field that studies the unconscious influence of various stereotypes and unconscious judgements on our social behaviour. Another example of social priming is the finding that people are more willing to contribute to the communal coffee pot at work when there is a poster in the kitchen with probing eyes than when there is a scene with flowers (Bateson, Nettle, & Roberts, 2006). Likewise, the finding that forcing a smile on one's face would result in a more positive evaluation of cartoons (Strack, Martin, & Stepper, 1988) may be considered to be an example of social priming.

These priming studies may provide a somewhat pessimistic conclusion, as they suggest that our behaviour is mainly determined by all sorts of unconscious influences and environmental factors that are beyond our control. This conclusion, however, needs serious reconsideration. First, priming is only one of many factors that affect behaviour, and it is certainly not an all-determining factor. For example, if you really believe that a cartoon is not funny, a pencil clamped between your teeth (the method used by Strack et al. to force a smile on participants' mouths) will not make you burst into a spontaneous laughing fit. All else being equal, however, behaviour could in theory be influenced ever so slightly. If a subtle change in behaviour occurs in only a few people, it could be just enough to measure these effects experimentally.

Although numerous studies have since been published that report effects of social priming, there are three important caveats to this phenomenon. The first is that the effects are difficult to explain theoretically. What mechanism could possibly explain that an unconscious influence has such a far-reaching effect that it can affect our behaviour? According to Schroder and Thagard (2013), the primed concepts evoke internal mental representations that are associated with the prime. These internal representations have psychological, biological, and cultural components which could impose constraints on each other and ultimately influence our behaviour. More importantly, the action codes that are associated with specific concepts could play a role here. We must, however, continue to question why the mere thought of specific concepts, for example those related to ageing, initiates action patterns that are associated with ageing (such as walking more slowly), while we ourselves are still young.

Also note that the relationship between prime and outcome measure is typically so indirect that the expected effect is often difficult, if not impossible, to predict. Why would thinking of older people actually make us walk slower and not (as any driver who is stuck behind a slow elderly driver on a busy country road can attest) feel like stepping on the gas a bit more. We might also expect the latter outcome, according to Kahneman (2011), but only if you have a dislike for older individuals.

Finally, the effects of social priming are extremely difficult to replicate (see, for example, also: Doyen et al., 2012; Wagenmakers, Beek, et al., 2016). This lack of replication is all the more remarkable given that the effects reported in the original studies were typically very large and should therefore be easy to replicate. In recent years, this has inadvertently forced social priming research to become the epicentre of the replication crisis in psychology. One contributing factor has been

(Continued)

Box 23.1 (Continued)

the controversy that arose after Bargh incited an outrage among experimental psychologists by subjecting a Belgian replication attempt (Doyen et al., 2012) of his original 1996 study to an ad hominem attack on his personal blog that was hosted by the website of the American journal Psychology Today.

Although the outrage over this blog post has now largely subsided, partly due to the fact that the post in question was carefully removed from the Internet, the question remains as to how plausible the idea of social priming is. Whether, and if so, how strong, unconscious influence is exerted on behaviour is a question that has become highly topical again, partly due to the replication crisis. Time will have to tell which of the reported findings can be replicated, and based on these studies, the question of whether social priming exists will be better answered. In any case, the field has indirectly – and largely unwillingly – contributed to an awareness in psychology as a whole that a tightening of experimental procedures is needed.

23.4 THEORY OF MIND

Our ability to consider someone else's perspective is known as **theory of mind**. The term describes how we are able to form a theory about another individual's mental representations. A simple test of theory of mind is illustrated by the following example (Wimmer & Perner, 1983). Imagine that little Max has just picked up a chocolate bar. He eats half the bar, puts the rest in a green kitchen cupboard, and then goes outside to play. While Max is playing outside, his mother comes into the kitchen and finds the chocolate in the cupboard. She takes it away and puts it in a blue cupboard. Max then enters the kitchen again and wants to take the remaining piece of chocolate. Where would Max look first? If you answered this question with 'in the kitchen green cupboard, you have just shown that you have theory of mind. You have put yourself in Max's position and realised that Max could not know that his mother put the chocolate in a different location (fig 23.2).

Fletcher et al. (1995) used PET scans to investigate which brain areas are involved in theory of mind processes. To this end, participants were given stories like the preceding and had to answer a question related to the intentions of one of the main characters in the story. An increase in activation was found in the medial frontal gyrus, compared to a control condition in which participants did not have to guess the intentions of a protagonist. Bull, Phillips, and Conway (2008) found that theory of mind is sensitive to interference from executive dual tasks. This included the use of stories as well as a task that measured participants' ability to infer emotion from pictures of eyes (Baron-Cohen, Wheelwright, Hill, Raste, & Plumb, 2001). Performance on both the story task and the eye task was impaired when participants were required to perform executive tasks simultaneously. These results suggest that theory of mind is not an automatic but a controlled process that makes use of attention-demanding cognitive resources.

A concept strongly related to theory of mind is **mind reading** (also known as mentalising), that is, the ability

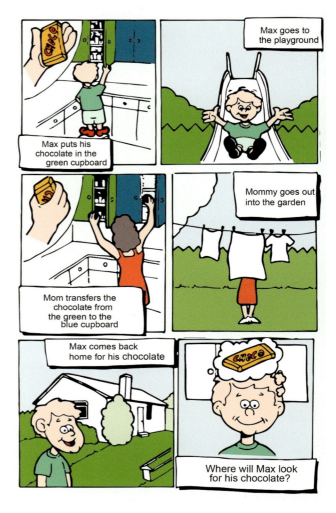

Figure 23.2 The principle of theory of mind. (source: Perner and Lang, 1999)

to represent the mental state of another. We often attribute perspectives, feelings, goals, intentions, knowledge, and beliefs to others, and form expectations on the basis of these (Carruthers, 2009). Our mind reading skills can also be used to interpret our own emotional states. A central question is to what extent this skill is innate or acquired.

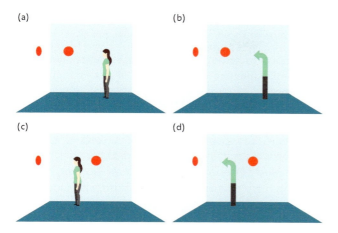

Figure 23.3 Example of an experiment used to study mind reading. Participants were asked to report how many dots they saw. They were quicker to determine this when all the dots were in front of a virtual avatar (a versus c). Similar results were found when the avatar was replaced by an arrow (b versus d), which implies that the results can be explained by a general attention mechanism. (source: Heyes and Frith, 2014)

According to Heyes and Frith (2014) it is partly innate and partly refined through training. Just like the normal reading process involves developing the ability to decode and interpret letters and words, mind reading skills can, according to Heyes and Frith, also be developed by learning to interpret facial expressions, body language, and utterances, and by translating these into the mental state of the person we are reading. It cannot be ruled out completely, however, that these mechanisms operate specifically in a social context (see fig 23.3). Neuroimaging studies have found that, in addition to the already described medial prefrontal cortex, the temporoparietal junction and precuneus become active when we think about the mental state of others (Van Overwalle, 2009).

23.5 THE NEURAL BASIS OF SOCIAL COGNITION

Initially, important insights into the neural basis for social cognition were gained by studying social impairments in patients with frontal cortex lesions (Adolphs, 1999). Another significant contribution to the field of social cognition involves studies investigating autism spectrum disorder (ASD). ASD is characterised by a disproportionate impairment in one specific aspect of social cognition, namely the ability to recognise the mental states of others (Leslie, 1987). Evidence for the possible modularity of social cognition can be obtained by comparing the results obtained from individuals diagnosed with autism with those obtained in individuals characterised by another syndrome, known as Williams syndrome. This syndrome is characterised by features that are almost the complete opposite of autism. Individuals with Williams syndrome are hypersocial. These social skills are remarkable in light of the fact that Williams syndrome patients often score low

on other non-social skills (Karmiloff-Smith, Klima, Bellugi, Grant, & Baron-Cohen, 1995). Comparisons between individuals with ASD, Williams syndrome, and individuals with focal brain lesions may provide further insight into the mechanisms underlying social cognition.

One of the results that has emerged from such a comparison is that Williams syndrome patients have an intact ability to read people's mental states from pictures of their eyes, an ability that many patients with autism lack. In neurotypical controls, this ability has been related to activation of the amygdala, and it appears that this function is impaired in individuals with autism (Baron-Cohen et al., 1999). It should be noted, however, that patients with Williams syndrome judge the approachability of strangers unusually favourably, based on photographs of their faces (see fig 23.4). This type of behaviour is consistent

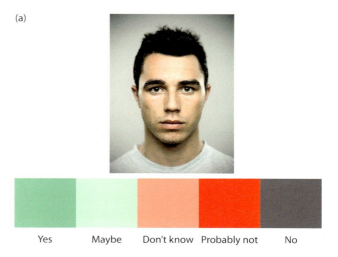

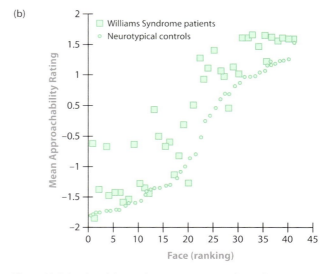

Figure 23.4 Results of face rating scores among patients diagnosed with Williams syndrome. (a) Participants were shown faces and had to indicate to what extent they believed the person was approachable. (b) The mean ratings Williams syndrome patients compared to healthy controls, as a function of the overall rating of each face. Williams syndrome patients consistently gave higher ratings than controls. (source: Bellugi et al., 1999)

with abnormalities in social behaviour in patients with bilateral amygdala damage (Bellugi, Aldolphs, Cassady, & Chiles, 1999).

23.5.1 THE AMYGDALA AND THE SOCIAL JUDGEMENT OF FACES

As we noted in Chapter 6, face recognition is a function of the temporal cortex, particularly the fusiform face area. The visual areas in the temporal cortex project, among others, to the amygdala, an area involved in the processing of emotions (see Chapter 12). A small proportion of neurons in the amygdala are characterised by the property that their activation is specifically modulated by the presence of faces. Both neuroimaging studies and the study of patients with damage to the amygdala have shown that this brain region is crucial for the recogntion of emotions in facial expressions. This is specifically the case for negative emotions, such as fear or anger. These results are consistent with those from animal studies, which have shown that lesions in the amygdala result in a reduced ability to recognise emotions.

Although most studies have focused on the role of the amygdala in the recognition of negative emotions, additional research indicates that the amygdala is also involved in the recognition of positive emotions. These results indicate that the amygdala is probably involved in allocating cognitive processes to biologically salient, but ambiguous, stimuli. These stimuli require additional processing, regardless of the emotional valence of these stimuli. In this respect, the role of the amygdala is probably not a strictly social one. Indeed, it was also found that patients with damage to the amygdala gave deviant ratings to affective stimuli that were not specifically social, such as pictures of landscapes or abstract block patterns. Patients gave these stimuli consistently higher affective ratings as compared to neurotypical controls. Thus, although the function of the amygdala is probably not a strictly social one, these affective judgements do probably affect social functioning.

The next question is what the consequences of damage to the amygdala are for social functioning. Although it is extremely difficult to evaluate the full impact in a real-life setting, one aspect often recurs in a variety of patients and social situations, which is the fact that patients with amygdala damage are often extremely friendly to others. This observation is consistent with the idea that they lack a basic mechanism that warns them that it is better to avoid some people. Compared to other animals, however, humans with amygdala damage show less socially aberrant behaviour. This can possibly be explained by the fact that, apart from the primary social detection system just described, humans are still able to show socially adept behaviour on the basis of other processes. Higher-order cognitive processes, information retained in long-term memory, and social linguistic

cues may partially compensate for a lack of immediate recognition of social situations.

In addition to recognising emotion in faces, the amygdala is also likely to be involved in detecting social cues from motion patterns. Healthy participants have a specific ability to recognise biological motion patterns (see Chapter 10). One of the reasons we are so good at this is because these patterns are probably socially relevant: based on these motion patterns, we recognise whether we are meeting a peer or a possible threat. Not only are we generally very efficient at distinguishing biological from non-biological motion, we are generally also very efficient at deriving psychological attributes from motion patterns.

Consider for example a remarkable study (Heider & Simmel, 1944) in which participants were shown short film fragments of three geometric figures moving across a pure white background. In addition to these, there was one large square on the screen, part of which could be opened as if it were a door (see fig 23.5). Although motion was the only cue in this study, most participants had no trouble assigning the movements they perceived to social categories. Mental properties, such as goals, beliefs, desires, and motivations, were attributed to the figures on the basis of the movements they made. However, one participant with bilateral damage to the amygdala did not display this behaviour. Her descriptions were limited to pure geometric terms, implying that she lacked automatic interpretation in social terms.

All the findings just discussed indicate that the amygdala plays an important role in the neural processing of emotions and in determining the salience of these emotions. The amygdala is most likely involved in the relatively fast and automatic evaluation of biologically relevant stimuli. This is done in cooperation with other brain areas, however. In particular, it appears that the amygdala and the prefrontal cortex cooperate to process the rewarding aspects of emotionally salient stimuli (Gaffan, Murray, &

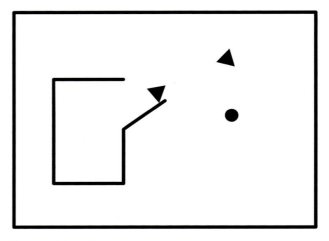

Figure 23.5 Example of a display used in the study by Heider and Simmel (1944).

Fabre-Thorpe, 1993). It is therefore likely that these two brain areas also function as a unit in a social context, as we will discuss next.

23.5.2 THE VENTROMEDIAL PREFRONTAL CORTEX: SOCIAL REASONING AND DECISION-MAKING

The ventromedial prefrontal cortex is involved in linking perceptual representations of stimuli with representations of their emotional and social significance (Damasio, 1994). In this capacity, this part of the cortex shows some similarities with the amygdala, although there are also some important differences. First, the ventromedial prefrontal cortex is involved in the processing of both rewarding and aversive stimuli, whereas the amygdala responds primarily to aversive stimuli. Second, reward-related representations in the ventromedial prefrontal cortex are less stimulus-driven compared to the amygdala; they may also result from a more complex emotional appraisal process (see Chapter 12). As such, the ventromedial prefrontal cortex is primarily involved in mediating outcomes that may result from both rewarding and punishing conditions.

The limited range of social behaviours of individuals with damage to the ventromedial prefrontal cortex is particularly evident in an inability to organise or to plan future activities, a reduced ability to respond to punishment, stereotypical and sometimes inadequate social manners, and an apparent lack of care and interest in others. Particularly striking is the frequently observed complete lack of interest in somebody else's well-being and a remarkable lack of empathy. The details of this impaired emotional and social functioning, due to damage to the ventromedial prefrontal cortex, are complex and can vary greatly from individual to individual. In essence, however, it amounts to a dysfunctional mechanism that prevents cognitive mechanisms from making effective use of essential emotional knowledge (see also Chapters 5 and 12).

A second domain of social cognition in which the ventromedial prefrontal cortex plays an important role is social reasoning. One of the simplest and at the same time one of the most widely used tasks to study reasoning processes is Wason's (1968) card selection task. As we have already discussed in Chapter 19, people generally perform much better on this seemingly simple task when the rules are somehow socially relevant: when participants have to verify whether a **deontic rule** has been violated, they are much better at this task than when they have to verify whether an **indicative rule** has been met. According to Cosmides (1989) this skill arose evolutionarily, from the perspective of social interaction. In particular, this reasoning skill would have arisen to detect social deception. Patients with damage to the ventromedial prefrontal cortex are therefore characterised by an impaired performance on these tasks, even though they showed hardly any impairment on normal abstract reasoning tasks.

23.5.3 THE SOMATOSENSORY CORTEX: EMPATHY AND SIMULATION

The mechanisms just discussed are all still relatively specific, as they range from mechanisms for interpreting the emotions of faces to mechanisms involved in social reasoning. Each of these mechanisms makes an important contribution to the phenomenon of social cognition. To qualify social cognition as a higher-order cognitive process, however, we still need to be able to explain how we can represent another person. As social beings, we must not only be able to represent our own body and our own thoughts, but we must also be able to do so for those of another. That is, we need to be capable of empathising with others. In other words, our social cognitive skills must enable us to create a mental model of another human being. In doing so, we must be able to identify what is important to know about the other person and realise that, as a social being, they can potentially interact with us.

To address the question of how we represent others, we must first know how we represent ourselves. According to some researchers, one of the most important functions of consciousness is that it enables us to put ourselves in someone else's position (see also Chapter 4). Taking this line of reasoning one step further, we could argue that this would imply that we simulate the other individual in our own brains. That is, we can feel empathy for another because we generate a mental model of their thoughts and feelings in our own mind.

From this perspective, it is a logical assumption that emotion processing and social cognition are closely related. After all, the processes that are relevant for our own emotion processing would then be relevant for the processing of social situations. The common factor that both processes share could be paraphrased as 'feeling'. That is, these processes would represent the emotional state of the body, regardless of whether this would be one's own emotional response or an empathic response to that of another individual.

As already discussed, both the amygdala and the ventromedial prefrontal cortex are involved in detecting emotions. There is a third neural structure that is probably involved in generating a mental representation of another person. This structure is located in parts of the right somatosensory cortex, and damage to this structure results in an impaired ability to infer emotions from faces. It is possible that under normal conditions, the emotional state is inferred because the somatosensory cortex generates an impression of the facial expression that is being observed. In other words, the somatosensory cortex is believed to simulate, as it were, the facial expression that is displayed by the other person.

Note that this idea is consistent with the hypothesis that the somatosensory cortex contains a body model, as discussed in Chapter 8. In this case, however, it is not just a simulation of one's own body but also that of another individual.

23.5.4 THE MIRROR NEURON SYSTEM

The idea that we can simulate another person's actions and emotional states is consistent with an important insight into the neural basis of social cognition that was accidentally discovered in 1991 (Bonini, Rotunno, Arcuri, & Gallese, 2022). In that year, members of the Italian neuroscientist Giacomo Rizzolatti's research team, at the University of Parma, found that some neurons in the ventral premotor cortex of monkeys became active both when the monkey was required to perform a certain action itself and when it observed the experimenter performing the action (di Pellegrino, Fadiga, Fogassi, Gallese, & Rizzolatti, 1992). These neurons have been described as **mirror neurons** because they mirror the actions that someone else performs in order to be able to perform the action themselves later (see fig 23.6). In humans, it is much more difficult to

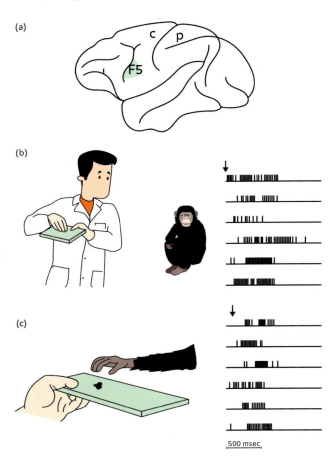

Figure 23.6 Example of a neuron from area F5 that responds both when a monkey is observing an action and when it is performing the action itself. (a) The location of area F5 in the monkey brain. (b) The neural firing patterns of neurons in area F5 in monkeys observing an action performed by the experimenter. (c) A similar firing pattern when the monkey performs the action itself. (source: Rizzolatti and Fabbri-Destro, 2010)

conduct single cell recordings than in monkeys. Therefore, it is also much more difficult to establish a human equivalent of the mirror neuron system. However, much indirect evidence for a human equivalent of the mirror neuron system has since been found (Grafton, Arbib, Fadiga, & Rizzolatti, 1996; Iacoboni, 1999; Rizzolatti, Fadiga, Gallese, & Fogassi, 1996; Tremblay et al., 2004).

Rizzolatti and Fabbri-Destro (2010) have highlighted the implications of the discovery of the mirror neuron system. Although the discovery was initially received with scepticism, the existence of the mirror neuron system now appears to be playing an increasingly important role in theories of motor learning, imitation, and social perception. According to some theorists, the mirror neuron system would therefore play a particularly important role in the understanding of actions and intentions.

Although it was originally believed that learning by imitation was one of the most important functions of the mirror neuron system, this explanation has not been sufficiently substantiated, because there is little evidence that animals can learn by imitation. For this reason, Rizzolatti and Fabbri-Destro hypothesised that the understanding of another person's actions was the basic function of the mirror neuron system. According to these authors, the ability to learn by imitation was developed later during the evolution of our species from the function of understanding actions.

Although there is little evidence for learning by imitation in animals, neuroscientific studies in humans have found evidence for the involvement of the mirror neuron system in imitation. For example, Buccino et al. (2004) carried out an fMRI study in which participants, who did not play a musical instrument themselves, had to observe how guitarists formed chords (fig 23.7). In one condition, they only had to observe, while in a second condition, they had to try to imitate moving their fingers into the observed positions. When they had to imitate the movement, they were given a few seconds after the observation to practice these movements themselves. During this period, a strong overlap was found with the network of brain areas that became active while observing the actions, indeed suggesting overlap between the neural structures responsible for observation and execution.

23.5.4.1 Mirror Neurons and Actions Understanding: Evidence

Gallese et al. (2004) argue that the mirror neuron system is a fundamental mechanism underlying our ability to understand the intentions and actions of others. According to Gallese and colleagues, this happens because we internally replicate (or simulate) these actions and intentions. Although we are, in principle, capable of reasoning explicitly about others, Gallese et al. assume that simulation processes are implicit. An important difference between interpreting

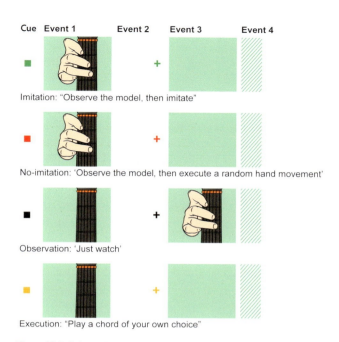

Figure 23.7 Schematic overview of the experimental design of a study investigating the relationship between observation and imitation. Participants had to observe how a guitarist formed chords, after which they either had to passively observe this action, imitate it, or perform another movement. (source: Buccino et al., 2004)

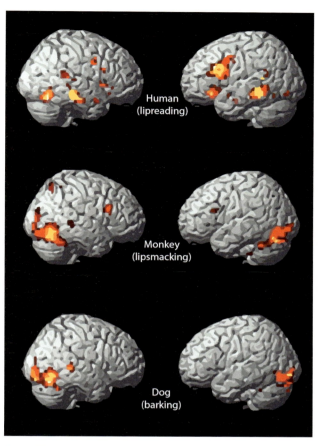

Figure 23.8 The cortical activation that can be observed when humans observe different forms of oral communication performed by humans, monkeys, and dogs. (source: Gallese et al., 2004)

the non-living outside world and interpreting other persons is that we are not only able to interpret the actions of others but also to perform similar actions ourselves. In this particular case, we share a body and brain with the person we are observing, and an important explanatory mechanism for social cognition, according to Gallese et al., would be our ability to make direct connections between our own perspective and the perspective of the other.

Evidence for the involvement of the mirror neuron system in action understanding was provided by studies investigating the properties of neurons in the F5 brain region of macaques (Kohler et al., 2002; Umilta et al., 2001). Umilta et al. (2001) recorded the activity of mirror neurons under two different conditions. In the first condition, a sequence of actions was shown in which a hand grasped an object. In the second condition, the sequence was identical, except that the object in question was hidden behind a screen, so that the hand-object interaction could only be inferred. Umilta et al. found that more than half of the mirror neurons under investigation also responded in the hidden condition. In the Kohler et al. (2002) study, the actions that were presented were accompanied by sounds, such as the cracking of peanuts or the tearing up of a piece of paper. The mirror neurons in this study fired not only when the monkeys were performing these actions but also when they were observing them. A proportion of these neurons (approximately 15%) fired not only when performing or observing but also when only the sound of the action was represented, which according to Gallese et al. (2004) implies that these neurons are involved in

the understanding of the actions because they activate the motor representation of the observed actions.

Evidence has also been found in humans that the mirror neuron system can be involved in understanding the intentions and actions of others (see fig 23.8). Gallese et al. (2004) suggest that the human mirror neuron system responds in a more subtle way and to a wider range of actions than the equivalent system in monkeys. In monkeys, it appears that the mirror neuron system is only activated when the goal of the action, the object being manipulated, is actually present (even though it may be hidden from view; as just described). In humans, on the other hand, it is sufficient that an action is merely represented (Iacoboni, 1999). Moreover, it has been found that in humans, the administration of TMS pulses results in an increase of the motor potentials generated by muscles when a person observes an action (Fadiga, Fogassi, Pavesi, & Rizzolatti, 1995).

23.5.4.2 Mirror Neurons and Action Understanding: Limitations

Although these results imply that the mirror neuron system is involved in action understanding, it should be noted that there is no consensus yet with respect to this conclusion.

For example, Newman-Norlund, van Schie, van Hoek, Cuijpers, and Bekkering (2010) conducted an fMRI study involving action understanding. Participants had to distinguish between meaningful and meaningless actions (e.g., grasping a pen with the hands or with the feet). This study found that the brain areas traditionally associated with the mirror neuron system could not differentiate between these two types of actions, suggesting a very limited role of action understanding.

On similar grounds, Hickok (2009) has identified eight problems related to the idea that mirror neurons are involved in action understanding. The essence of these problems is formed by the findings that (1) it is very likely that other neural mechanisms are also involved in the understanding of actions and intentions; (2) the classical mirror neuron system is not able to differentiate between meaningful and meaningless actions; (3) there is also evidence for a dissociation between the execution of an action and the understanding of actions; and (4) the evidence for similarities between the human mirror neuron system and that of other primates is very weak. Note that similar arguments were formulated by Csibra (2005). Although it is clear from the currently available evidence that the mirror neuron system is involved in representing an action, the conclusion that this system is also involved in understanding these actions is therefore perhaps still somewhat premature.

23.5.4.3 Mirror Neurons and Emotions

Although the literature just discussed shows that there is not yet an unambiguous answer to the question of whether mirror neurons are related to the understanding of actions, some researchers assume that this system is not only involved in the understanding of actions but also in the understanding of emotions. In monkeys, the insula has been found to be involved in the understanding of emotions, in particular disgust. This brain area receives connections from the olfactory and gustatory system as well as from the superior temporal sulcus, an area containing neurons that have been found to respond to the perception of faces.

Moreover, it has been found that the insula receives connections from interoceptive projections. **Interoception** is the perception of the physiological state of the body; in particular, the internal organs (Craig, 2002). For this reason, the insula is an important candidate for representing the internal state of the body. In monkeys, electrical stimulation of the insula has been found to result in specific actions. Unlike the stimulation of the classic motor areas, however, stimulation of the insula also results in a variety of specific autonomic visceromotor responses, such as changes in breathing or heart rate (Kaada, Pribram, & Epstein, 1949). For this reason, the insula not only appears to represent the state of the body, but it also appears to play an important role in visceromotor integration.

In humans, the insula also appears to be involved in the processing of disgust. Olfactory stimuli that are perceived as disgusting evoke strong activation of the insula; particularly in the left insula (Small et al., 2003). In the context of understanding the emotions of others, however, it is interesting to note that the insula is also activated by the facial expressions of another individual (Phillips et al., 1998; Phillips et al., 1997; Sprengelmeyer, Rausch, Eysel, & Przuntek, 1998). For example, Phillips et al. (1997) manipulated the degree of disgust in a facial expression and found an increase in activation in the amygdala as a function of this degree of disgust. These results were confirmed by Krolak-Salmon et al. (2003) using depth electrode recordings in epilepsy patients. As in monkeys, electrical stimulation of the insula resulted in visceromotor responses (Penfield & Faulk, 1955). In two of the four patients studied by Krolak-Salmon et al. (2003) this stimulation resulted in an unpleasant sensation in the mouth, lips, and nose.

Clinical studies have also shown that the insula appears to be involved in the recognition of facial expressions that are associated with disgust. For example, Calder, Keane, Manes, Antoun, and Young (2000) describe patient NK, who had a selective impairment in recognising disgust in facial expressions due to a lesion in the left insula (fig 23.9), while his ability to recognise other emotions was not impaired. Interestingly, NK's impairment in recognising disgust was not limited to facial expressions but also included an impairment in his ability to recognise auditory cues associated with disgust (such as gagging), whereas he had no difficulties recognising sounds associated with other emotions, such as laughter. NK also had a limited ability to experience feelings of disgust himself. Taken together, these results support the idea that the insula plays an important role in experiencing negative emotions (particularly disgust) and processing motor responses related to that emotion.

Similar results were found by Adolphs, Tranel, and Damasio (2003). These authors reported the case of patient B, who, due to bilateral insula damage, showed a

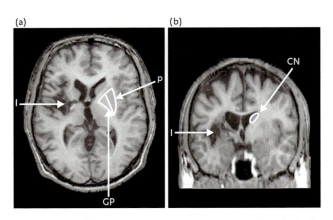

Figure 23.9 An MRI scan of the lesion in patient NK's the left insula (I). The intact right hemisphere putamen (P), globus pallidus (GP), and the intact apex of the right hemisphere caudate nucleus (CN) are also shown. (a) Transverse view. (b) Coronal view. (source: Calder et al., 2000)

substantial impairment in recognising facial expressions associated with disgust, but had no problem recognising other facial expressions. To demonstrate that this limitation in recognising disgust was multimodal, the investigators staged an ingenious pantomime play expressing different aspects of disgust. This play included eating, re-chewing, and spitting out food, followed by gagging and facial expressions of disgust. B's inability to recognise disgust was also expressed by the fact that he took in food in a random manner, including inedible items. In addition, he did not show signs of disgust when confronted with items that most people would find disgusting, such as pictures of food being overflooded with cockroaches.

These results already suggest that the insula plays an important role in experiencing one's own emotions along with recognising these emotions in others, however direct evidence has been provided by an fMRI study of Wicker et al. (2003). In this study, participants were exposed to odours that evoked disgust. In addition, they were shown films of others smelling from a glass of liquid and then expressing signs of disgust. These results were compared to conditions where participants were exposed to pleasant odours and observed pleasant facial expressions from others. The insula was activated both by the participants' own experience of disgust and by observing someone else expressing disgust.

In summary, it appears that observing an action, an intention, or an emotion in another individual is recognised by activating the same neural circuits that are involved in experiencing the same actions, intentions, or emotions in ourselves. As such, a bridge is formed between another person and ourselves (Gallese et al., 2004). Based on this mechanism, we can conclude that we do not just perceive such actions, intentions, or emotions, but that in addition to the visual representation of these actions, we also activate a mental representation similar to the way in which we ourselves would experience the emotion, intention, or action.

Although this description has focused on disgust, there is evidence that similar systems exist for other aspects of processing information about another person. For example, similar results have been found for empathy for pain (Hutchison, Davis, Lozano, Tasker, & Dostrovsky, 1999; Singer et al., 2004). For example, using fMRI Singer et al. (2004) showed that the same structures that are involved in processing one's own pain are also involved in recognising pain in others. These results imply that recognising emotions in others can involve at least in part a simulation mechanism that contributes to experiencing these emotions oneself (de Vignemont & Singer, 2006).

23.5.4.4 Mirror Neurons and Sign Language

Although the aforementioned results imply that the mirror neuron system is involved in understanding the actions of others, results have also been reported that imply that this skill does have limitations. For example, Rogalsky et al. (2013) investigated the possible involvement of the mirror neuron system in the processing of sign language. Deaf sign language users with focal cortical lesions were asked to perform two tasks: in one task they had to try to interpret single gestures and in the second task complete sentences. In a study involving 21 patients, it was investigated how the location of the lesion affected the patient's ability to perform the task. Rogalsky et al. found that lesions in the left hemisphere had no significant effect on the interpretation of single gestures, while their ability to interpret complete sentences was impaired by lesions in the left temporal-parietal regions. However, lesions in areas associated with the mirror neuron system, in the left frontal lobe, did not affect language comprehension, making it unlikely that these parts of the mirror neuron system were involved in the comprehension of the associated actions.

23.5.4.5 Mirror Neurons and Predictive Coding

In Chapter 3, we introduced the idea of forward models of action control (Davidson & Wolpert, 2005; Wolpert et al., 2003). These models assume the presence of an internal 'efferent' copy of the motor commands that we generate in order to predict the sensory consequences of our actions (for example, how high and how fast will we lift a bucket of water from the ground, given a certain amount of muscle force). According to some theorists, the mirror neuron system can be explained by making exactly the opposite prediction: based on sensory impressions, we could generate specific motor commands (Keysers & Perrett, 2004; Wolpert et al., 2003). This is an example of an inverse model.

According to Kilner et al. (2007), the relationship between forward models and inverse models can be well explained using the predictive coding framework. Indeed, this framework is based on the idea that predictions are generated at different levels in the cortical hierarchy, which are corrected on the basis of sensory input. The essence of the predictive coding framework is that at each level in the hierarchy, the prediction error is minimised by a continuous interaction between prediction and error correction at each level in the hierarchy (see fig 23.10). As already discussed in Chapter 2, at each level, this prediction is compared with the actual representation at the lower level and the difference between the predicted representation and the actual representation is fed back as a prediction error via the feedforward links to the higher level.

For the mirror neuron system, this would imply that the brain regions that are involved in the observation of motion are part of this hierarchy and that the anatomical connections between the different levels are also reciprocal. In addition, this hierarchical organisation involves both the visual system and the motor system, so that the representations at the highest levels of the hierarchy will

(a) The mirror neuron system as a forward recognition model

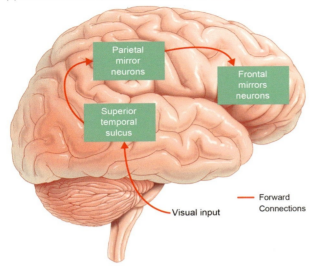

(b) The mirror neuron system as a predictive coding model

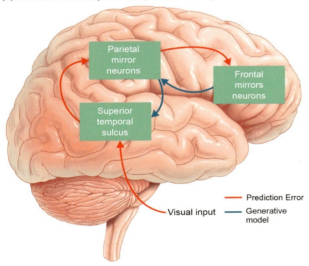

Figure 23.10 Two different interpretations of the mirror neuron system: (a) as a forward recognition model; (b) as a predictive coding model. (source: Kilner et al., 2007)

result in predictions that inform both of these systems. These predictions are then fed back to the lower levels via recurrent connections, and this happens for both the visual system and the motor system.

Kilner et al. (2007) assume that forward models are used to generate motor commands that are based on the actions observed in others. Note that Chater and Manning (2006) suggest a similar idea for language production (see Chapter 16). Kilner et al. (2007) argue that while performing an action, the motor commands are optimised to minimise the difference between the predicted and actual movement, assuming that the intended movements (and on a related note, the goals of the movement) are known. In case of observing an action in others, these goals and, hence, the corresponding movements are not yet known, and these must therefore be inferred from the observed actions.

In both cases, however, a forward model of the action is required.

This may still sound somewhat abstract, but we illustrate it using a thought experiment discussed by Jacob and Jeannerod (2005). Suppose you are asked to observe a movement that was made either by Dr Jekyll or by Mr Hyde. Dr Jekyll is a respected neurosurgeon while Mr Hyde is a dangerous sadist who takes pleasure in hurting people.[1] In both cases, you observe an individual taking a scalpel and making an incision in a human body. In one case, however, we have Dr Jekyll using the scalpel to heal a patient, while in the other we have Mr Hyde using the same scalpel, using exactly the same movement, to inflict pain on someone.

Jacob and Jeannerod (2005) argue that the mirror neuron system cannot possibly differentiate between these two situations because the observed motion is identical in both situations. This is indeed the case when we try to explain the mirror neuron system using an inverse model, but not when we try to explain it using the predictive coding mechanism. In the latter case, the observed motion pattern will have to be explained at many levels in the processing hierarchy, such as its visual representation, its underlying motor signals, its immediate goal (e.g., grasping the scalpel), and its long-term intention ('cure' or 'hurt'). These levels are schematically represented in Figure 23.11.

At the intentional level, the predictive coding mechanism aims to predict the goal of the action. This goal then predicts a kinematic representation of the motor actions. More generally, at each level in the hierarchy, this prediction is compared with the actual situation and the difference is fed back to the higher level in the form of a prediction error. In cases where multiple intentions may

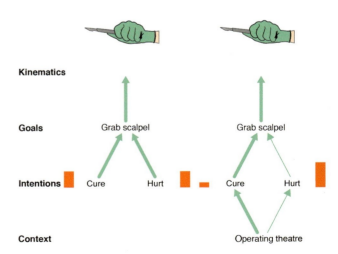

Figure 23.11 Inferring intentions from a given context based on the prediction errors created by different contexts. Left: when there is no context, the system cannot differentiate between two different intentions. Right: when there is a context, i.e., the fact that the action takes place in an operating theatre allows the system to disambiguate the situation and assess the intention of the action. (source: Kilner et al., 2007)

be associated with identical movements, identical prediction errors will be generated, so the predictive coding mechanism cannot differentiate between the two intentions either. In contrast to the simpler inverse models, the predictive coding mechanism also needs to explain the sensory information related to the context in which the motion took place. This context is strongly informative with respect to the intention of the action: if it took place in an operating theatre, it is very likely that the intention causing the action was to heal someone, whereas if it took place 'at night' in an obscure back room, it is more likely that the intention was to hurt someone. In other words, if the action took place in an operating theatre, there would be a small prediction error for the intention to cure, but a large error for the intention to hurt. For the back room, the exact opposite would be expected.

Even when the prediction error would be the same for all other levels, the overall minimisation of the prediction error would still allow the mirror neuron system to infer the intention of the action from the context. Note that there is also empirical evidence for this idea: mirror neurons in brain area PF (part of the parietal lobule) respond differently to nearly identical movements that differ in intention. Moreover, Kilner et al. (2007) argue that the fact that the context is involved in inferring the intention of an action does not imply that this context is also encoded in the mirror neuron system, but rather that the mirror neuron system is part of a larger hierarchical network that does involve this context in determining intention.

23.5.4.6 Mirror Touch Synaesthesia

Ishida, Suzuki, and Grandi (2015) consider the predictive coding framework in explaining a social-cognitive illusion,

namely the phenomenon of mirror touch synaesthesia (see Seth, 2014, for a comparable approach). This form of synaesthesia is characterised by the fact that individuals who observe someone else being touched experience this touch themselves (Banissy & Ward, 2007; Holle, Banissy, & Ward, 2013). According to Ishida et al., synaesthetic effects can be explained in part by the idea that neuronal networks in the parietal cortex and insula are shared for the representation of one's own body and that of another (see fig 23.12). The synaesthetic experience would occur here because the boundary between the representation of one's own body and that of another is blurred.

23.6 SOCIAL PERCEPTION

Social perception is the study of how we draw conclusions from someone else's non-verbal behaviour. Following the example of the mirror neuron system, more and more evidence has recently become available to suggest that neural processes that are involved in the regulation of one's own cognitive and bodily functions can also be used to interpret the actions and intentions of others. For example, we have already discussed studies that found that the insula and cingulate cortex are not only involved in interpreting our own emotions but also in interpreting those of others (Wicker et al., 2003). We have also already been introduced to the idea that the motor areas and the emotional circuits, along with the somatosensory cortices (Keysers, Kaas, & Gazzola, 2010) and the superior temporal sulcus, are involved in social perception (Deen, Koldewyn, Kanwisher, & Saxe, 2015). In this section, we will elaborate on those results by discussing how these mechanisms play a role in the evaluation of another person's behaviour.

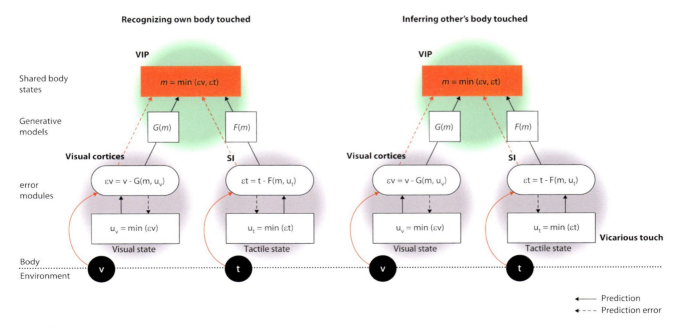

Figure 23.12 Shared predictive coding mechanisms involved in identifying a touch to one's own body or someone else's body. (source: Ishida et al., 2015)

23.6.1 SOCIAL EXCLUSION

Eisenberger, Lieberman, and Williams (2003) published remarkable results of a study investigating the relation between social perception and emotion. These authors had a group of participants play a virtual ball game during an fMRI recording session to investigate the neural basis for social exclusion. Although the participants were informed that the game involved two other participants being involved in the game from outside the scanner, the actions of these other players were actually controlled by a computer. The game consisted of throwing a virtual ball to one of the other players. The task was designed in such a way that at a certain point, the computerised players changed strategy, by only passing the ball to each other, thus excluding the participant from the game. This exclusion resulted in an increase in activation in the anterior cingulate cortex. This increase in activation corresponded strongly with the participants' self-reported level of social distress that resulted from this exclusion (see fig 23.13). Eisenberger and Lieberman (2004) suggest that this form of exclusion represents a form of social pain that is processed by the same neural mechanisms that are involved in the processing of the affective component of physical pain.

23.6.2 VICARIOUS PAIN

One of the clearest examples of a social situation that evokes a palpable sensation in most individuals is that of seeing someone else in pain. This experience is known as **vicarious pain** and also results in an increase in activation of the anterior cingulate gyrus (Morrison, Lloyd, di Pellegrino, & Roberts, 2004). Despite these similarities, it is, however, unlikely that somatic pain and vicarious pain are identical, as there are also several difference between these two forms of pain.

Krishnan et al. (2016) investigated these differences by either administering a painful stimulus to the participants themselves or by requiring them to observe another person being subjected to this stimulus. Both types of stimuli

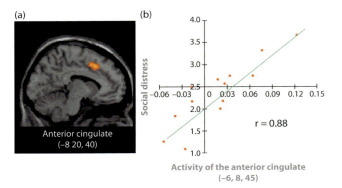

Figure 23.13 The correlation between subjectively experienced social distress and activation of the anterior cingulate cortex. (a) The location of the anterior cingulate cortex. (b) The correlation between social distress and the degree of activation in this area. (source: Eisenberger et al., 2003)

resulted in a significant difference in the pattern of brain areas that were activated. Whereas somatic pain mainly resulted in the activation of the anterior insula, the dorsal anterior cingulate cortex, the dorsoposterior insula, and the secondary somatosensory cortex, vicarious pain resulted mainly in activation of the dorsomedial prefrontal cortex, the amygdala, the posterior cingulate cortex, and the temporoparietal junction. The latter areas are primarily associated with **mentalisation** processes, that is, processes involved in thinking about others (Frith & Frith, 2006).

23.6.3 TOUCHING ANOTHER PERSON

In addition to the motor cortex and the emotion- and pain-related centres, another brain area that plays an important role in social perception is the somatosensory cortex (Keysers et al., 2010). For example, fMRI studies have shown that the secondary somatosensory cortex is involved in perceiving the somatosensory perception of another person. More specifically, during a scanning session, participants were touched on their legs and then shown pictures of others being touched on their legs. The touch activated the primary and secondary somatosensory cortices, while the pictures activated the secondary somatosensory cortex in particular (Keysers et al., 2004). Keysers et al. (2010) argue that this photo-induced activation may be due to the simulation of the qualitative experience of touch as felt by another person.

23.7 JOINT ACTION

Our ability to coordinate our motor actions with those of others is crucial to our success – both as a species and as individuals (Sebanz et al., 2006). Examples of this are plentiful: from musicians performing a complicated improvisation together, to top players of a premier league football team, to more mundane situations such as the one described in the introduction in which you help carry a cupboard up two flights of stairs. Sebanz et al. (2006) define **joint action** as any form of social interaction in which two or more individuals must coordinate their actions in time and space to bring about a change in the environment (see fig 23.14).

Initially, we learned a lot about joint action processes through the study of language skills (Garrod & Pickering, 2004). After all, language is an important skill for exchanging information. There are many situations, however, where the actions of individuals need to be coordinated while verbal communication is impossible. According to Sebanz et al. (2006), successful joint action will therefore depend on three conditions. First, individuals need to be able to share representations. Second, they need to be able

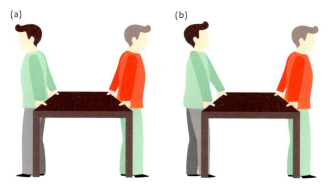

Figure 23.14 In joint action, individuals not only (a) imitate each other, sometimes they also have to (b) complement each other. (source: Sebanz et al., 2006)

to predict the actions of others. Third, they need to be able to integrate the consequences of their own and others' predicted actions.

23.7.1 JOINT ATTENTION: SHARED REPRESENTATIONS

One of the conditions for a successful joint action is that the same intentions are shared by the collaborating partners (Moll & Tomasello, 2007). A second condition for carrying out a joint action is that there must be shared knowledge. A key success factor in obtaining shared knowledge is the ability to coordinate your own and your partner's attention processes in such a way that you both attend to the same aspects of the task (Frischen & Tipper, 2004). It has been suggested that the eyes (Friessen & Kingstone, 1998), but also other cues, such as the position of the head and the gestures made (Langton, Watt, & Bruce, 2000), have an important function in directing attention in this context.

This common focus of attention would be the basis for creating a perceptual common ground that could serve two purposes. An example of such common ground is when you both keep your eyes on the same obstacle when you are moving an object together. The first of the two possible goals is formed by initiating the coordinated action, while the second goal is formed by continuing to coordinate once the action has been initiated.

23.7.2 ACTION OBSERVATIONS

Although shared attention is the basis for common ground, there is a second, more direct way to achieve it, namely through action observation. Several studies have shown that while observing an action, the corresponding response is activated in the observer (Blakemore & Decety, 2001; Gallese et al., 2004). It is assumed that the mirror neuron system plays an important role in sharing action presentations and the underlying task goals. This way,

the performance of one's own motor representation and the actions of the other could be locked together. The effectiveness of this motor representation depends, among other things, on one's own expertise in performing the observed actions.

Being able to observe the actions of another individual is not sufficient for successful cooperation, however. It is also crucial that we are able to predict the other's actions. The motor interlocking described here would also play a crucial role in predicting the actions of another. This is shown, for example, in studies in which individuals observed another person stacking blocks (fig 23.15). The eye movement patterns of these observers anticipated the actions observed, in a way that was very similar to the eye movement of the builders themselves. This result suggests that the observers were predicting the next phase of the action (Flanagan & Johansson, 2003).

It is possible that the mirror neuron system is involved in the prediction of these actions. For example, using fMRI, Newman-Norlund, van Schie, van Zuijlen, and Bekkering (2007) found that brain areas that are part of the mirror neuron system were activated more strongly when performing an action that was complementary to an actor's action than when imitating the actor.

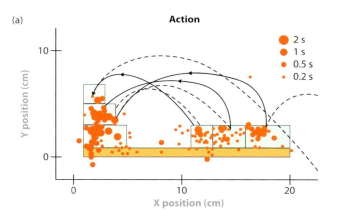

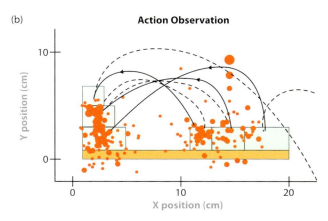

Figure 23.15 Eye movement patterns of an individual stacking blocks (a) and those of an observer (b). (source: Flanagan and Johansson, 2003)

23.7.3 SHARING TASKS

The third way of sharing actions does not so much involve observing actions, but knowing what the other person's task is. Examples of such situations can be found in traffic. When driving on a road where you have the right of way, you predict that a driver on an oncoming road will most likely stop, or when you see that another road user has a green traffic light, you may also assume that he will probably drive on.

Several studies have found evidence for the idea that individuals form shared task representations in these kinds of situations. In a study by van Schie, Mars, Coles, and Bekkering (2004), participants had to observe actions that the actor was only allowed to perform under specific conditions. EEG measurements showed that activation in the motor cortex of the observers occurred before the action was actually performed by the actor, suggesting that the participants activated a representation of the action as soon as the actor was instructed to perform it. Moreover, the activation pattern of the observer changed as a function of the accuracy of the actor's action. When the actor made a mistake, the neural response elicited by the observer strongly resembled that of the **error-related negativity** (ERN; see Chapter 5). The latter suggests that similar mechanisms are active when monitoring someone else's mistakes as when monitoring mistakes that one makes oneself (see fig 23.16).

Ramnani and Miall (2004) found that observers are able to anticipate someone else's actions on the basis of task instructions, even when these actions are not directly observable. In this study, participants were taught a specific stimulus-response mapping. During the experiment, one of three things could happen, depending on the colour of the stimuli. That is, participants had to respond to a stimulus themselves, another participant had to respond, or the response had to be left to the computer. Although the participants could not observe their partner's actions, they anticipated them. That anticipation was associated with an increase in motor cortex activation. These results suggest that a predictive coding mechanism is active to predict the mental state of another participant (Sebanz & Frith, 2004).

23.7.4 ACTION COORDINATION

Probably the greatest challenge in understanding shared action involves adapting one's actions to those of another. Although the assumption of shared representations is essential here, this assumption alone is not sufficient for explaining how we can exchange information with another. We still do not know how we can move from predicting the action of someone else to choosing an appropriate action ourselves.

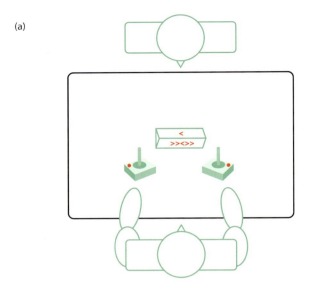

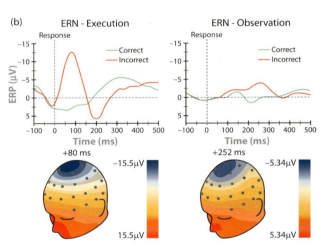

Figure 23.16 Design and results of a study on error-monitoring processes among performers and observers of an action. (a) Experimental design. Participants either had to perform an action themselves or observe how another person performed that action. (b) When participants made an error, this resulted in an ERN. A similar ERN-like component was found when participants observed how another person made an error. (source: Van Schie et al., 2004)

Richardson, Marsh, and Baron (2007) have attempted to address this question by having participants move planks together, which were transported on a conveyor belt (see fig 23.17). These planks could only be grasped at their ends, and they varied in length, so that either one person alone could pick them up or two persons were needed to do so. The planks came off the conveyor belt in either an ascending order of length or in a descending order. The authors hypothesised that, in the case of ascending order, participants would initially pick up planks individually and then switch to collaborating at some point. The moment at which this happens is interesting, because both participants had to take each other's capacities into consideration. This capacity depended on each participants' arm length, which varied considerably among the

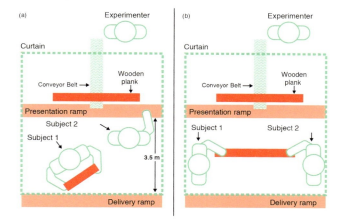

Figure 23.17 Experimental design of a study that examined how individuals cooperated in moving planks that exceeded their own or their partner's arm length. (a) When moving relatively short planks, both participants worked independently. (b) When the planks' length exceeds the average length of the two participants' arms they started collaborating and moved planks jointly. (source: Richardson, Marsh and Baron, 2007)

participants. Interestingly, the point at which the switch was made varied as a function of the average arm length of the two individuals cooperating: the longer the average arm length, the later they switched to cooperating. This implies that the perceived **affordance** (see Chapter 10) of objects not only depends on one's own abilities but also on those of another.

23.7.5 AGENCY

The strong link between one's own actions and those of another can sometimes lead to confusion about who exactly performed an action (Wegner & Wheatley, 1999). When a change occurs shortly after our own action, we tend to attribute this consequence to our own actions; we have the impression that we ourselves are the agent of our actions (see also Chapter 4). Stoit et al. (2011) investigated this possible blurring between self and others in a group of participants with autism spectrum disorder (ASD). Participants with a diagnosis of ASD had to perform a task together, using a joystick to balance a virtual ball on a moveable beam. Compared to neurotypical controls, couples diagnosed with ASD were found to separate their actions to a much greater extent in order to avoid problems with agency.

23.8 SOCIAL DECISIONS

Social factors are involved in many of our everyday decisions. As already discussed in earlier sections of this chapter, our reasoning skills may even have developed because they allow us to detect violations of social conventions (Cosmides, 1989). Social decision-making involves more than simply being able to detect such

violations, however, as it also requires us to imagine the thoughts and emotional reactions of another individual. How another individual will perceive the consequences of our decision will also determine to a large extent the outcome of our decision.

Interestingly, human beings share this form of social behaviour with other primates (Tremblay, Sharika, & Platt, 2017), which makes it possible to study the neural basis of social decision-making processes directly. Ballesta and Duhamel (2015) found, for example, that when rhesus macaques had to perform a task together, they tried to avoid situations where one of their peers had an aversive puff of air being blown into their eye. Instead, they encouraged their peers to receive a reward. In a similar study, rhesus monkeys were trained to play a variant of the **dictator game**. In this game, one participant is given a number of goods and instructed to divide them among each other. Chang et al. (2015) recorded activity in the basolateral amygdala and found neurons in this region that responded to the value of these goods, including both the goods assigned to themselves and those assigned to the other. These neurons were active when the dictator decided whether or not to allocate goods to the other, but not when this decision was made by a computer. The latter finding suggests that these neurons are involved in social decision-making processes.

In humans, the neurobiological basis of social decision processes has been investigated using fMRI (see fig 23.18). For example, Rilling, King-Casas, and Sanfey (2008) argue that, despite the complexity of many social decisions, the processes involved are strongly similar to how we make decisions in a non-social context. According to Rilling et al., decisions are mainly made to reach a state that corresponds to a higher valued reward, regardless of whether this reward consists of a chunk of food, passing an exam, or a promotion at work.

According to Rilling et al., however, there is one important difference between a social and a non-social decision. That is, a social decision depends not only on one's own intentions and actions but also on the actions and mental state of another. Neuroimaging methods are often used to investigate these processes while participants perform tasks that are based on **game theory**. Game theory is the study of mathematical models that describe conflict and cooperation between intelligent rational decision-makers. The dictator game is a relatively simple form of such a task.

Another task that is often used is the **trust game**. In this game, one of the participants assumes the role of an investor who can give the other participant a part of his/her assets. The other participant then receives a multitude of these assets and has the choice to return all, nothing, or part of it. If the original receiver honours the investor's trust, both players may yield a return that is higher than

(a)

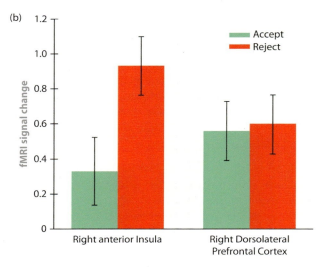

Dorsolateral prefrontal cortex

Anterior Insula

Anterior cingulate gyrus

(b)

Figure 23.18 Neural responses in the right insula and dorsolateral prefrontal cortex due to an unfair offer being accepted or rejected. (a) An anatomical MRI scan with the activated areas superimposed. (b) Responses of the anterior insula and dorsolateral prefrontal cortex in response to unfair offers as a function of whether the offer was accepted or rejected. (source: Rilling et al., 2008)

the original stake, but if the trust is broken, the giver may suffer a substantial loss.

23.8.1 NEUROECONOMICS

The previously discussed studies on trust form the basis for the relatively new field of **neuroeconomics** (Loewenstein, Rick, & Cohen, 2008). A central problem with classical economic studies is that important concepts, such as preferences and beliefs, cannot easily be operationalised (Fehr & Camerer, 2007). Neuroeconomics seeks to identify the neural correlates of these concepts and to measure the neural responses associated with them during economic decision-making tasks. It does so by not only using social dilemmas but also by involving the somatic markers associated with risk behaviour, or

choice behaviour under uncertainty, as it is related to the Iowa gambling task.

23.8.2 SOCIAL DILEMMAS

The aforementioned trust game is a good example of a **social dilemma**. Social dilemmas are formed by situations in which decisions that are favourable for an individual ultimately have an unfavourable outcome for the population or group. A classic example of this can be found in the well-known **commons dilemma**. The term was introduced in 1833 by British economist William Forster Lloyd (Hardin, 1968). The dilemma refers to a tradition among British farmers who were free to use the common grounds to graze their animals. For each individual farmer, grazing animals on common grounds was advantageous because they could maximise their farm's milk or meat production at no additional cost. As long as each farmer limited this use to the common grounds to just a few animals, all would remain well. When one farmer would then decide to let a few more cows onto the common grounds, this would be beneficial for the individual farmer, as his yields would increase. This would then trigger the other farmers to also allow more cows onto the common grounds, eventually leading to overgrazing of the common grounds and diminished yields for everyone. In modern society, this problem applies to many situations, from vandalism of public spaces to spam mail, to overfishing of the oceans, to excessive forestry. For this reason, Hardin (1968) argues that there is no technical solution to the common's dilemma, but that it requires a higher morality.

It can be argued that decisions involving social dilemmas require knowledge about three different aspects of the problem. The first involves the expected outcome of the decision for ourselves, the second the intentions of the other person(s) involved, and the third the expected outcome of the other. Mentalisation is required for reading the other person's intention. Haroush and Williams (2015) studied mentalisation in rhesus monkeys by training them using a variant of another well-known social dilemma, known as the **prisoners' dilemma game**. This game is based on an interrogation technique in which a suspect can receive a reduced sentence in exchange for giving incriminating evidence about another suspect. The person who betrays the other will be released, while the one who is betrayed will end up with a heavy prison sentence. If both suspects betray each other, they will each receive a lighter sentence, and if they do not betray each other, they will both receive a very light sentence for lack of evidence. All in all, it is advantageous not to betray the other, but only if the other does not also betray you either.

In the Haroush and Williams (2015) study, rhesus monkeys were trained to play a variant of this game (see fig 23.19). They could collaborate to obtain a large but unknown reward, or they could go for a smaller immediate reward.

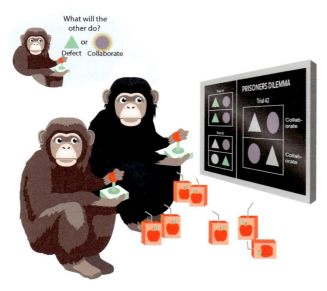

Figure 23.19 Rhesus monkeys performing a variant of the prisoners' dilemma game experiment. (source: Haroush and Williams, 2015)

During the performance of this task, activity in the monkey's anterior cingulate cortex was recorded. Based on these recordings, Haroush and Williams identified three types of neurons, namely those that responded mainly to their own choice, those that responded to the partner's choice, and a third group of neurons that responded mainly to the partner's predicted choice. The latter group of neurons is probably involved in making socially strategic decisions. When the researchers electrically stimulated the anterior cortex, this had a negative impact on strategic choice behaviour.

Both the trust game and the prisoners' dilemma are examples of social dilemmas in which there is reciprocal exchange. In other words, the outcome of an action depends not only on one's own decision but also on that of the other. Various neuroimaging studies have found evidence that the human caudate nucleus is involved in this (Delgado, Frank, & Phelps, 2005; King-Casas et al., 2005; Rilling et al., 2002). In particular, it has been found that the caudate nucleus is activated when the partner performs a reciprocal action. This activation intensifies as successive actions are followed by an increasing degree of cooperation. Based on this, it has been hypothesised that caudate activity is linked to the processing of social prediction errors (Rilling et al., 2008). Interestingly, increased caudate activity is not found when players do not base their decisions on direct feedback about the other's actual behaviour, but from external factors, such as the other's reputation (King-Casas et al., 2005). Reputations, in other words, result in the rejection of feedback. From this we can conclude that both top-down and bottom-up processes play a role in making social decisions.

For the prisoners' dilemma game, it has also been found that cooperative actions that are not reciprocated result in an increase in anterior insula activation. Individuals who do not cooperate, or receive benefits without paying a fair price, are known as free-riders. Many studies have found that people generally dislike free-riders, as evidenced by the fact that many people are willing to punish them at the cost of personal inconvenience (Fehr & Fischbacher, 2003; Fehr & Gächter, 2002). Insula activation may be a neural correlate of this aversive response, as this area responds not only to physical pain but also to a multitude of negative social interactions, such as social exclusion, unfair treatment, or observing the pain of a loved one.

23.8.3 TRUST

Rilling et al. (2008) argue that trusting someone else is essential for the reciprocal exchange of goods, as occurs in the trust game. So how do we initiate and sustain trust in someone? How can we suppress our fear of being betrayed and our aversion to risk and uncertainty? One way to investigate this is by adding **intranasal** oxytocin while playing a trust game. Oxytocin is a neuropeptide that is easily absorbed by the blood after nasal administration and readily crosses the blood-brain barrier. It is known to reduce stress and anxiety (Heinrichs, Baumgartner, Kirschbaum, & Ehlert, 2003; McCarthy, McDonald, Brooks, & Goldman, 1996). The administration of oxytocin also had the effect of making participants more willing to transfer larger initial sums of money in a trust game (Kosfeld, Heinrichs, Zak, Fischbacher, & Fehr, 2005). When oxytocin administration was combined with fMRI, it was found to decrease amygdala activation and to increase behavioural actions involving trust (Domes et al., 2007; Kirsch et al., 2005). Thus, these results imply that oxytocin can induce trust by reducing anxiety about the possible absence of reciprocal action.

23.9 MORAL DILEMMAS

Moral dilemmas are problems in which a participant must choose between two different scenarios that each have a negative outcome associated with them. Traditionally, reasoning and other higher cognitive functions were assumed to play important roles in making a moral decision (Greene, Nystrom, Engell, Darley, & Cohen, 2004). This tradition stands in stark contrast to more recent developments that have emphasised the role of intuitive and emotional processes (Damasio, 1994), along with social aspects (Devine, 1989), in dealing with moral questions. Greene et al. (2004) argue that moral judgements are likely to involve both forms of processing: some moral problems predominantly involve rational cognitive processes, while other forms of moral problems predominantly involve intuitive and emotional processes.

This interaction between rational cognitive and intuitive emotional processing is probably the most explicit in cases of violations of personal moral values. A moral violation can be considered 'personal' when three criteria are met. First, the violation must result in serious bodily harm. Second, this injury must apply to a specific person, or group of persons, and third, this injury must not be the result of shifting an existing threat onto someone else. In other words, there is a moral dilemma when one's own actions cause direct suffering to someone else. These criteria can be summarised with the expression 'ME HURT YOU'. Here, the HURT criterion represents the negative consequence of the action; YOU, in this case, stands for the fact that the victim is clearly represented as an individual. Finally, ME represents the criterion of **agency** – the fact that the action that is carried out is intentional. Dilemmas that do not meet this criterion are considered to be 'impersonal' (Greene et al., 2004).

A classic example of an impersonal dilemma is the **trolley dilemma** (Thomson, 1976). In this dilemma, a runaway trolley is heading towards five people, who will surely die if it is not stopped (fig 23.20a). The only way you can prevent this accident is to pull a handle that will cause the trolley to switch tracks, where it will kill only one person instead of five. Would you pull the handle or not? Most people will answer 'yes' to this question (Green, Sommervill, Nystrom, Darley, & Cohen, 2001).

The **footbridge dilemma**, on the other hand, is an example of a personal moral dilemma (fig 23.20b). Again, there

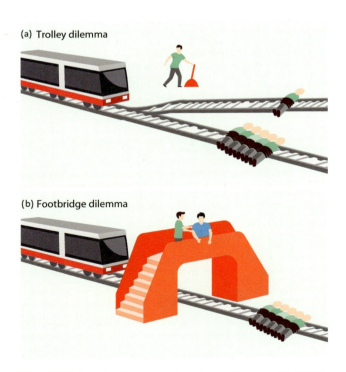

(a) Trolley dilemma

(b) Footbridge dilemma

Figure 23.20 Example of two commonly used moral dilemmas. (a) In the trolley problem, participants have to decide whether they can prevent five innocent bystanders from being run over by a runaway trolley, by pulling a handle. This will come at the cost of one other innocent bystander. (b) The footbridge problem presents a similar dilemma, but now the participants must decide whether or not to throw an innocent bystander in front of the trolley.

is a runaway trolley that threatens to kill five people. This time, however, you are standing next to a heavy-weight stranger on a footbridge above tracks between the oncoming trolley and its potential victims. The only way to stop the trolley is to push the person next to you off the bridge, causing him to crash onto the rails. He will die, but his body will derail the trolley and the other five strangers will be saved. Would you throw this stranger off the bridge? Most people here say 'no' (Green et al., 2001). The trolley dilemma is impersonal because it merely consists of shrugging off an existing threat, while the footbridge dilemma is personal, because it involves the act of intentionally killing an individual.

According to Greene, Morelli, Lowenberg, Nystrom, and Cohen (2008), personal moral dilemmas evoke a strong emotional response. On the one hand, we have a strong emotional incentive to not kill the heavy-weight stranger, while on the other hand, we have a strong cognitive argument for doing so. If you throw this person off the footbridge, more people will be saved than if you do not. Greene et al. propose a dual-process model consisting of a fast, automatic, and affective System 1-like system and a slower, reasoned System 2-like 'cognitive' system. Individuals who make **deontic judgements** based on moral rules react primarily from this System 1 process, whereas individuals who make practical or **utilitarian judgements** act primarily on the basis of the System 2 process.

Different brain areas are associated with these two types of decisions. The dorsolateral prefrontal cortex and the anterior cingulate cortex are mainly involved in cognitive control (see Chapter 5) and play an important role in making utilitarian decisions. The ventromedial prefrontal cortex, on the other hand, is mainly involved in generating emotions.

Incidentally, Duke and Begue (2015) recently reported a remarkable finding: participants' propensity to answer 'yes' to the footbridge problem appears to depend on the amount of alcohol they had consumed. In a field study conducted in two cafes in Grenoble, the investigators asked the visitors to what extent they were willing to throw the person off the bridge and found that the willingness to do so was positively correlated with the participants' blood-alcohol levels.

Although the use of moral dilemmas has become particularly popular in recent decades in research on utilitarian versus deontological decisions, its use has been increasingly criticised in recent years. For example, Bauman, McGraw, Bartels, and Warren (2014) argue that particularly the footbridge problem is extremely unrealistic, and that it is more likely to incite laughter than it is to produce serious results about ethical judgements.

A major reason for this is that the moral dilemmas just introduced were originally developed as a philosophical thought experiment to illustrate the unexpected moral consequences of an action (Foot, 1967). The examples provided by Foot were intentionally witty, to lighten up the heaviness of the participant matter. Although the proposed moral dilemmas work well in this form, the resulting absurdity of the dilemmas is very likely to have a negative effect when used in empirical studies. As a result, the validity of the problems is very low. The humorous effect, combined with the extremely low probability that the scenario is even plausible in reality, results in a situation where morality is disconnected from the decision that is being made. Such a situation can be disastrous for the plausibility of the studies in question.

An additional problem with the use of unrealistic scenarios is that the disconnection from reality results in a lack of disgust or anger being experienced that realistic social dilemmas could provoke (Haidt, Rozin, McCauley, & Imada, 1997; Tetlock, Kristel, Elson, Green, & Lerner, 2000), which may be an additional reason why participants' responses bear little resemblance to their actual moral values. For this reason, Bauman et al. (2014) have recommended using more realistic moral scenarios (see also Box 23.2).

Box 23.2 Social insight, moral dilemmas, and self-driving traffic

In the past decade, rapid technological developments have made autonomous self-driving cars possible. Since the first autonomous cars hit public roads on an experimental basis in 2007, test models from Google and others have already covered several thousand kilometres, and at the time of writing, full self-driving capabilities are 'just around the corner', according to entrepreneurs such as Tesla CEO Elon Musk. These autonomous vehicles can, in principle, use public roads much more efficiently than human drivers and, in addition, are capable of drastically reducing the number of traffic accidents. Still, their introduction creates an interesting new set of social problems for which appropriate answers must be found.

Despite the potential for autonomous vehicles to improve road safety, in recent years we have witnessed some high-profile incidents involving autonomous vehicles. One notable incident involved a hop-on-hop-off bus in the United States. As a pilot project, the bus was scheduled to run a predetermined route through the centre of Las Vegas. Following its inauguration in the fall of 2017, it would serve to investigate, among other things, how people would respond to the idea of an autonomously operating shuttle bus. Within an hour of becoming operational, however, it was involved in an accident! While approaching a reversing truck, it followed its preprogrammed instructions and stopped. The truck driver, who could not see the bus because it was in his blind spot, continued backing up, causing the bus to skid. Although the bus was following its preprogrammed instructions, a situation like this was not foreseen, and the possibility to take an evasive action in such a case was missing from its repertoire of possible actions.

Another high-profile case involved the autopilot system developed by electric car maker Tesla. In 2016, a driver in the United States crashed because the Tesla autopilot system was unable to detect a truck that was swerving into his lane. The consternation that resulted from the ensuing crash was mainly due to the fact that it could

most likely have been avoided if the driver had been in control himself. Yet, in many other situations, intervention by the very same autopilot system had actively contributed to avoiding accidents and to saving lives. An interesting moral dilemma that arises here is whether the number of fatal accidents that autopilot systems can prevent outweighs the limited number of deaths that they may cause. Can we blindly trust these systems, or should we, human drivers, remain in control? In the case of the situation just outlined, this question appears to be fairly easy to answer, especially when we consider the fact that the driver involved in the accident had, in hindsight, ignored several warnings and thus would have had ample opportunities to avoid the accident.

There are various other situations related to the development of autonomous vehicles, however, in which social insight and moral dilemmas do play an important role. For an autonomous vehicle to function independently, it must have insights into the social behaviour of others. Although autonomous vehicles should, in principle, behave on the basis of traffic rules, there are numerous situations in which the logic of these rules fails to support an actual decision. To give a very simple example: one of the most basic traffic rules is that at a roundabout, you must yield to approaching traffic or cars already on the roundabout. In daily life, this rule is usually generic enough that it does not cause any problems. Imagine, however, what happens when four cars approach a small roundabout, each from a different entrance, exactly at the same time. Who has the right of way? After all, each car must give way to another. In artificial intelligence, such a situation is known as a deadlock, and special rules are needed to resolve it.

Simple rules no longer suffice to break a deadlock when human drivers and autonomous vehicles share the road. A number of potentially conflicting situations are described by Chater, Misyak, Watson, Griffiths, and Mouzakitis (2017). Suppose that one of the lanes

(Continued)

Box 23.2 (Continued)

is partially blocked by a barrier, so that a car trying to pass it has to swerve into the left lane. An interesting social problem arises when there is an oncoming vehicle. What should be done to avoid the obstruction? Normally, the car in the free lane has the right of way, so we will have to wait until the oncoming car has passed. But what should we do when it drives very slowly or when it starts flashing its lights? What if this car slows down to take a side road, so that it does not have to pass the obstruction?

In all of these situations, it is necessary to interpret the intentions of the other road user and adapt our behaviour accordingly. A good autonomous system must somehow be able to interpret these intentions. For example, what is the intention of a driver who flashes his headlights? Does it mean 'Go ahead, I'll wait' or 'Watch out, I'll drive on!'? The correct distinction between these two signals can mean the difference between life and death. In such a situation, an autonomous vehicle has to be able to 'negotiate' with human drivers, and some sort of artificial joint action system is needed for this, according to Chater et al. (2017). Insights from social cognitive neuroscience may help to solve these problems; both in the area of self-driving vehicles as well as in other areas, such as human-robot interactions (Henschel, Hortensius, & Cross, 2020).

Another remarkable result relates to the choices that an artificial system should make when an autonomous vehicle enters a situation where an accident is no longer avoidable, as in the case of a group of pedestrians suddenly crossing a busy road. Bonnefon, Shariff, and Rahwan (2016) asked a large number of American respondents to evaluate moral dilemmas such as the following. 'Suppose an autonomous vehicle is about to collide with a group of pedestrians that unexpectedly crosses the road. The only possible action the car can take to avoid a fatal collision is to swerve, causing an innocent passer-by to be run over. Should the car swerve or not?'

Another dilemma asked what the car should do if it had to choose between running over one innocent pedestrian or sacrificing itself and its passenger. Or what to do when it had to choose between running over a group of pedestrians and sacrificing itself and its passenger. Most respondents indicated that they preferred the utilitarian decision, that is, that they preferred the decision in which the car caused the least number of casualties. The same participants also indicated that they considered self-sacrificing behaviour by human drivers to be a highly moral act, and most respondents therefore indicated that they would recommend others to buy cars with such a utilitarian control system. Remarkably, the same respondents also indicated that they themselves would rather buy a car that would protect its occupants at all costs!

No matter what technological developments will take place, the introduction of new technologies always provokes a certain amount of resistance and introduces new, sometimes temporary, social problems. Around the year 2000, with the introduction of the first hybrid vehicles, there were discussions about the lack of engine noise that characterised these vehicles when driven electrically. Pedestrians would not be sufficiently alerted to this, and it was suggested that an artificial engine sound should be produced through speakers. When the first steam cars were introduced in 1801, it was made compulsory by law in Great Britain for every automobile to be preceded by a man holding a red flag. In a similar way, the introduction of autonomous vehicles will probably also involve a period of familiarisation.

23.10 SUMMARY

The field of social cognition is involved in studying the cognitive processes that are related to interaction with others. Because many social cognitive processes are implicit, much of the research effort in social cognition focuses on the development of implicit measures. For this purpose, the affect misattribution procedure and the implicit-association tests are used. A still relatively controversial question within the study of implicit social cognition is to what extent implicit social stereotypes can influence human behaviour. Social priming studies claim to have found evidence for this, but these results prove mostly difficult to replicate.

A crucial part of social functioning involves the ability to empathise with another individual. This skill is described by the term 'theory of mind' and includes the ability to reason about what another may or may not know. A closely related concept is mind reading, that is, the ability to represent the mental state of another. This skill is probably partly innate but can be further refined through practice.

Many social-cognitive functions are related to the activation of the frontal cortex. The ventromedial prefrontal cortex is assumed to play an important role in linking emotional experiences with complex social decisions. Much of our knowledge about social cognition has been gathered from comparing the results of studies on autism spectrum disorders with those of studies on Williams syndrome. Patients with Williams syndrome are often particularly good at reading someone's emotional state from photographs of their face. This ability to read emotional expressions from faces is probably associated with amygdala functions. This is particularly true for negative emotions, although a small number of studies show that the amygdala is also involved in recognising positive emotions. In addition to recognising emotions, the amygdala may also play a role in recognising social cues in movement patterns.

In social reasoning and decision-making, the ventromedial prefrontal cortex plays an important role in relating a perceptual representation of a stimulus to its emotional and social relevance. Patients with brain damage to this area are often characterised by a limitation in the range of social behaviours they exhibit, along with a decreased response to punishment, inadequate social manners, and a lack of empathy and interest in the well-being of others. This area also plays an important role in social reasoning.

The somatosensory cortex also plays an important role in social-cognitive processes; this area appears to play a particularly important role in empathy and in simulating the formation of a representation of another. Representing another individual also takes place on the basis of the mirror neuron system. The existence of this system was first demonstrated in monkeys and consists of neurons that respond both when the monkey must perform an action and when it observes this action in another person. An equivalent of this system has also been found in humans and forms the basis of learning by imitation and understanding the intentions of another. The emotional state of another may also be encoded by the mirror neuron system. Recognising disgust in others is highly related to being able to recognise disgust in oneself, and processing of these emotional signals is related to activation of the insula. The functioning of the mirror neuron system can be explained on the basis of the predictive coding framework. Internal generative models that try to minimise prediction error at all levels of the hierarchy play an important role here.

Social perception describes the phenomenon that we can draw conclusions from the non-verbal behaviour of another person. This skill also appears to be based on the reuse of cognitive skills that we use to interpret our own behaviour. Evidence for this conclusion has been found in studies of social exclusion and vicarious pain. The latter is the sensation that we ourselves feel pain when observing another in pain.

One of the most important aspects of our social behaviour consists of the ability to cooperate with another individual. This skill is described as joint action. Joint action plays a role in, for example, a conversation, but also in many situations where verbal communication is impossible. In such cases, actions must be coordinated non-verbally. This happens by participants sharing a common representation, by predicting the actions of another, and by being able to integrate their own actions and the actions of another.

Social factors are also involved in decision-making processes, and it is possible that our reasoning ability arose from a need to detect violations of social conventions. Many studies of social decision-making processes are based on tasks that are grounded in game theory. Well-known examples of commonly used tasks are the dictator game and the trust game. Many social decision-making processes are studied in neuroeconomics. A specific case of this type of game is formed by social dilemmas. In social dilemmas, the outcome depends not only on one's own decision but also on that of another. Here, the general rule is that the decision that is favourable to the individual is not so for the group, implying that in the end, the individual will also suffer.

Moral dilemmas are studied by using artificial situations that evoke a conflict between a rational choice and an intuitive emotional choice. Examples are the trolley dilemma and the footbridge dilemma. Although the results obtained on the basis of these dilemmas imply that decisions are made either on the basis of utilitarian rules or on the basis of deontological rules, these results should be interpreted with caution because the dilemmas used often evoke little real moral resistance.

NOTE

1 The characters in Jacob and Jeanerrod's example are loosely based on the story 'The strange case of Dr. Jekyll and Mr. Hyde' by Scottish author Robert Louis Stevenson.

FURTHER READING

Augostinous, M., Walker, I., & Donaghue, N. (2014). *Social cognition: An integrated introduction*. Los Angeles, CA: SAGE Publishing.

Carlston, D. E. (2013). *The Oxford handbook of social cognition*. Oxford, UK: Oxford University Press.

Hickok, G. (2014). *The myth of mirror neurons: The real neuroscience of communication and cognition*. New York, NJ: W.W. Norton and Company.

Metcalfe, J., & Terrace, H. S. (2013). *Agency and joint attention*. Oxford, UK: Oxford University Press.

Rizzolatti, G., & Sinigaglia, C. (2008). *Mirrors in the brain: How our minds share actions and emotions*. Oxford, UK: Oxford University Press.

CHAPTER 24

To err is human: the role of errors in human cognition

24.1 INTRODUCTION

Although far from complete, the previous chapters have discussed a representative cross-section of the current state of scientific research into human cognition. Of course, much of this research is still ongoing, and new insights are reported on an almost daily basis. A central theme that has emerged from this research is that errors and error processing is a crucial ingredient of human cognition. In almost all areas of cognitive psychology, it is observed that we make errors, that these errors are processed in a very systematic way, and that they play an increasingly important role in explaining human behaviour. The scope of error processing ranges from perceptual illusions to the generation of incorrect responses, to the occurrence of distortions in mental representations, to errors of judgement, slips of the tongue, and the emergence of psychopathologies.

Error detection and correction mechanisms are therefore also rapidly becoming a crucial ingredient in theories of human cognition. In the first part of this chapter, we will therefore also briefly review a selection of topics that we covered previously, which we will specifically discuss from the perspective of error detection and correction mechanisms, as formulated in the predictive coding framework.

Moreover, errors are also involved in our everyday functioning. For this reason, a substantial part of psychological research focuses on the question of how we deal with errors. The question is not so much how we can prevent ourselves from making errors, but how we can reduce the consequences they may have. The latter is essential for making risk assessments. As such, it forms an important part of human factors studies. The effect of human error on the work floor and the question of how we can prevent the consequences of these errors will comprise the second part of this chapter.

The original view that human cognition could be compared to a computer has changed significantly in recent years. This is in part due to the realisation that it is precisely these error correction mechanisms that are crucial to human cognition. Although cognitive psychology still aims to uncover the laws guiding our behaviour, the underlying cognitive models are increasingly inspired by biology and neuroscience, at the expense of the computer metaphor.

This change in perspective is also evident from a 2018 survey organised by the Universities of Chicago, Wisconsin, and Royal Holloway College in London. Among other things, the survey questioned scientists who have published in scientific journals covering psychological topics about their perspective on the study of cognitive processes. One striking result was that the vast majority of respondents strongly disagreed with the statement that a modern digital computer is a good metaphor for human cognition. Other striking results were that the majority of respondents believed that human behaviour depends on a social context and that studying individual cognitive processes (such as attention, working memory, or object recognition) in isolation from other processes is not the optimal way to make scientific progress.

The developments outlined here fit within existing developments in cognitive psychology. These include developments that intrinsically link human cognition to the need to control our bodies (Clark, 1999; Wolpert et al., 2003), or developments suggesting that the interpretation of bodily sensations is crucial for cognition (Damasio, 1996). It follows from this perspective that perception and action integration is another crucial ingredient of human cognition. In everyday life, making a decision often requires us to perform an action. In many cases, we have to select from several alternative actions. The choices that we make are implicitly stored as associations, and as similar decisions are made more and more often, the decision-making process can become increasingly automated.

The developments outlined in the previous paragraphs are part of a continuous development that characterises the field of cognitive psychology and its related fields. What will the future bring in this field? Although it is almost impossible to answer this question, the final part of this chapter will attempt to extrapolate some existing developments, as it will briefly look ahead towards possible future developments.

DOI: 10.4324/9781003319344-33

24.2 LOOKING BACK: ERROR CORRECTION AS A CORE PRINCIPLE OF HUMAN COGNITION

The idea that the living brain is continuously generating predictions – which are informed by internal generative models of the environment and updated by the processing of prediction errors – has been one of the central themes in the preceding chapters. The growing influence of this predictive coding framework is evidenced by an enormous increase in scientific papers that have recently been published on this topic, and by the increasing diversity of areas in which the predictive coding framework is being proposed as an explanatory mechanism. For this reason, we will start with a brief review of the predictive coding framework and highlight some of these recent developments.

24.2.1 PREDICTIONS

The predictive coding framework can be regarded as one of the most influential theoretical developments of the past two decades. Although some researchers consider this framework to be (an initial step towards) a **grand unifying theory** of the cognitive neurosciences, this characterisation is still premature (see: Clark, 2013). Although the framework can offer a plausible explanation for many cognitive phenomena, there are still several phenomena and effects that cannot yet be readily explained by the predictive coding framework, such as, for example, the emergence of beliefs and desires (Yon, Heyes, & Press, 2020). The following sections will provide an overview of some recent successful developments, along with some challenges in this area.

24.2.2 PREDICTION AND RATIONALITY

24.2.2.1 Predictive Coding and Bounded Rationality

It is likely that predictive processes are involved in reasoning and decision-making processes. For example, Friston et al. (2014) explain the idea of bounded rationality (Simon, 1957), that is, the apparent limitation in our rational decision-making behaviour, by assuming that generative models form a representation that fits optimally with the available data. When, according to Friston et al. (2014), these data are processed according to the principles of Bayesian inference, the decisions that are made correspond to those that we make in everyday life.

A similar idea has been formulated by Ortega and Braun (2013), who describe a model that can explain decision-making processes on the basis of thermodynamic principles of information processing (see Box 1.3; Chapter 1).

According to Friston et al. (2014) and Ortega and Braun (2013) models, the expected utility of a complex choice is determined by generating an internal model for each option, while the decision eventually relates to selecting the optimal model (FitzGerald, Dolan, & Friston, 2014). According to these principles, the generation of the internal models involves combining the attributes for each option in a Bayesian fashion, after which the model with the best fit is chosen on the basis of a model comparison process. In other words, given the available data, the model yielding the smallest prediction error is the one that is selected.

24.2.2.2 Predictive Coding, Fear, and Irrationality

Pezzulo (2013) describes an intriguing idea to explain a well-known phenomenon that affects many people: why can we sometimes be overcome by an irrational fear of a bogeyman, why does this typically happen at night, and specifically so after watching a horror movie? Pezzulo's idea assumes that interoceptive and other bodily perceptions are involved in the formation of perceptual inferences. The predictive coding framework allows us to compare sensory input with multiple alternative hypotheses. For example, was the sound you just heard generated by the wind or by an intruder? The embodied predictive coding theory proposed by Pezzulo extends this idea by including both sensory and interoceptive information into the inference process.

When we have just watched a horror movie, we are more inclined to accept an unlikely hypothesis, such as the one stating that the sound is caused by a burglar or by the bogeyman. The reason for this is that this hypothesis explains both what we hear (a squeaking or creaking window) and what we feel (e.g., an increased heart rate). According to Pezzulo, normal circumstances would allow us to find sufficient evidence for the hypothesis that the squeaking window is caused by the wind, based on our a priori knowledge. Specifically, when the weather forecast predicts a storm and when there are few news reports about burglaries in our neighbourhood, this information should in principle be enough to formulate a strong a priori hypothesis that the squeaking window is caused by the wind. Watching a horror movie could possibly result in priming the concepts of 'burglar' or 'bogeyman', giving these concepts a strong a priori bias. Thus, these kinds of seemingly irrational fears can quite easily manifest themselves, even when there are apparently no events that can directly prime the concept of 'burglar' or 'bogeyman'.

If we also consider interoceptive signals as sensory evidence, the subjective likelihood of the burglar hypothesis becomes even larger. After watching a horror movie or having been involved in a car accident, our physiological arousal level is typically much higher than normal. The physiological signals corresponding to this increased arousal can now be much better explained by the burglar hypothesis than by the wind hypothesis, whereas the

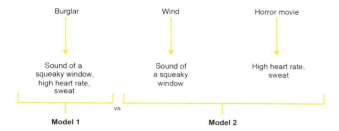

Figure 24.1 Two alternative generative models that are involved in generating predictions. The increased heart rate and perspiration resulting from a previously watched horror film are more consistent with the burglar hypothesis than with the wind hypothesis. (source: Pezzulo, 2013)

sound of the squeaking windows is equally well explained by both hypotheses.

Moreover, the Bayesian inference method also considers the uncertainty of the data. At night, our ability to make causal inferences about the sounds we hear is limited, and in the dark, our ability to do so for visual information is even more restricted. Therefore, the impact that our visual and auditory modalities may exert on the inference process is extremely limited. The interoceptive signals, on the other hand, are relatively clear, which implies that they also play a relatively large role in the inference process (see fig 24.1). For this reason, it is plausible that the relatively strong precision weighting of interoceptive signals occurs mainly at night.

An additional phenomenon that comes into play here is that the bogeyman is an imaginary concept that can actually only be experienced on the basis of interoceptive signals. That is, the concept is often used by parents to frighten children when they are about to misbehave. For this reason, the bogeyman has no clear visual form, and the concept can only be recognised on the basis of the interoceptive signals associated with the threat. Since it is these interoceptive signals that weigh relatively heavily at night, Pezzulo (2013) suspects that it is for this reason that the bogeyman also only 'visits' us at night. Interpreted from the perspective of an embodied predictive coding framework, the seemingly irrational fear of burglars, bogeymen, and other threats is not irrational, but the result of the interpretation of interoceptive signals, which have a relatively strong weight – too strong perhaps – in the inference process.

24.3 THE ROLE OF ERROR CORRECTION MECHANISMS IN COGNITIVE DYSFUNCTIONS

The bogeyman example illustrates how a relatively normal everyday situation can result in a seemingly irrational experience, due to the relative weight that is assigned to our sensory inputs. It is therefore relatively easy to extrapolate

this example. When the correction by sensory feedback is further weakened, for example, during sleep, we can experience even more extreme perceptual experiences, which then manifest themselves in the form of dreams (Llewellyn, 2016). Recent evidence suggests that anomalies in the balance between prediction and prediction error processing may also occur during our waking hours and manifest themselves in the form of hallucinations. (Horga et al., 2014; Powers, Kelley, & Corlett, 2016b; Schmack et al., 2017). These anomalies could form the neural basis for psychoses and thus manifest themselves in, for example, schizophrenia patients.

Schizophrenia is a mental condition that is characterised by abnormal behaviour, aberrant speech, and a distorted perception of reality. The condition is characterised by negative symptoms, that is, the absence of patterns of behaviour that are normally present in healthy individuals, and by positive symptoms, that is, patterns of behaviour that are present in schizophrenia patients but not in healthy individuals. Negative symptoms include flat affect, slurred speech, an inability to experience pleasure, and a lack of motivation. Positive symptoms include delusions, disturbed thoughts, and hallucinations.

A second syndrome that may, in part, be explained by anomalies in the predictive coding mechanism is autism spectrum disorder (ASD). ASD is a developmental condition that is characterised by difficulties in social interactions, communication, and repetitive and restrictive behaviours. In addition, ASD is often associated with dysfunctions in sensory integration. Individuals diagnosed with ASD often have difficulties coping with unexpected changes in their environment. ASD symptoms typically manifest themselves during the first years after birth. One of the great challenges of neuroscience will be to identify a mechanism that underlies the wide variety of symptoms that occur in schizophrenia and ASD.

24.3.1 SCHIZOPHRENIA

Ebisch and Gallese (2015) hypothesise that in schizophrenia patients, the distinction between a mental representation of the individual and a representation of others has become blurred. As discussed in Chapter 23, it is hypothesised that for representing the intentions, thoughts, and actions of others we use the same neural mechanisms that we use to represent our own intentions, thoughts, and actions. This would be done through a predictive coding mechanism that forms the basis of the mirror neuron system. Although this mechanism assumes the use of shared neural mechanisms, there would still be a clear distinction between the self-representation and the representation of the other in neurotypical individuals. Ebisch et al. (2013) found evidence for the assumption that this distinction is blurred in schizophrenic patients by using fMRI. Patients in whom the first manifestations of schizophrenia had been observed were asked to perform a social recognition task. They had to observe video fragments in which others touched inanimate objects or bodies, or in which they had to touch these objects themselves. For neurotypical controls, activation was found in the ventral premotor cortex for the observation of touching bodies. In schizophrenia patients, this activity was reduced and, moreover, the activity that was measured correlated negatively with the severity of the symptoms.

Seth, Suzuki, and Critchley (2011) hypothesise that the subjective experience of **presence** can be explained by a predictive coding mechanism that is involved in the processing of interoceptive signals. Here, the term 'presence' describes the subjective experience of our environment, and in particular our own position in this environment (Metzinger, 2017). According to Seth et al., the successful suppression of interoceptive signals plays an important role in the emergence of presence. This idea is similar to the predictive coding mechanism that is believed to be important in the generation of unrealistic fears discussed earlier (Pezzulo, 2013). These mechanisms are also believed to be disrupted in schizophrenia.

Horga et al. (2014) also argue that deficits in the predictive coding mechanism form the neural basis for hallucinations. They focused predominantly on the auditory modality, however. Schizophrenia patients who experienced auditory hallucinations participated in an fMRI study (see fig 24.2). Here, they had to indicate whether they had heard a voice or not. The patient's expectation of whether or not a speech signal would be present was systematically manipulated. Trials in which the patients indicated that they had heard a voice, while it was not present, were classified as auditory verbal hallucinations. These hallucinations corresponded to an increase in activation in the auditory cortex.

Moreover, the patients were characterised by a deficient prediction error, with respect to the presence of the speech signal. The degree to which this prediction error was deficient correlated strongly with the hallucination-induced auditory cortex activation. Evidence that the predictive processes are disrupted in schizophrenia patients was found in an EEG study by Fogelson, Litvak, Peled, Fernandez-del-Olmo, and Friston (2014). These investigators found that in schizophrenia patients, the backward projections from higher-order representational brain areas to the lower perceptual areas were disturbed. Corlett et al. (2019) argue that extremely strong priors, that is, predictions created by the generative models, are the basis for these hallucinations.

Schmack, Schnack, Priller, and Sterzer (2015) have reported a correlation between the degree to which schizophrenia patients report delusions and their ability to perceive bistable images consistently. A key finding of this study was that in schizophrenia patients, the subjective experience between the two possible interpretations of a bistable image changed much more rapidly and irregularly than it did in neurotypical controls, and the extent to which these changes occurred strongly depended on the extent to which these patients reported delusions.

24.3.2 AUTISM SPECTRUM DISORDER

Although at first glance ASD appears to be a clinical syndrome that bears almost no similarities to schizophrenia, we can nevertheless identify some similar principles. For example, Ebisch and Gallese (2015) found that both ASD and schizophrenia are characterised by a deficiency to distinguish between self and others. This deficiency, described by Ebisch and Gallese as one of the core mechanisms of schizophrenia, was originally identified by the Swiss psychiatrist Eugen Bleuler (1911) as a 'disconnection from the outside world and a predominant focus on the inner life'. Bleuler introduced the term 'autism' to describe this condition.

For this and other reasons, it is not surprising that deficiencies in the predictive coding mechanism are also assumed to form the basis for the symptoms that are associated with ASD. For example, Pellicano and Burr (2012) have argued that an underdeveloped ability to generate top-down predictions might be an important explanatory mechanism for ASD. As top-down predictions diminish, the higher-order networks of the brain are less capable of forming clear generalisations, resulting in a much greater emphasis on the literal meaning and the detailed processing of information. Moreover, the raw sensory inputs result in prediction errors that

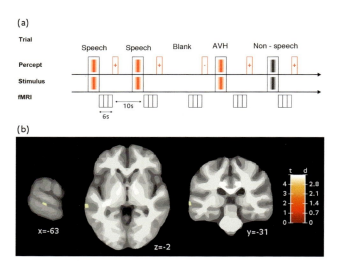

Figure 24.2 Schizophrenia patients and neurotypical controls participated in an fMRI study in which the expectation that they would hear speech fragments was manipulated. (a) Auditory verbal hallucinations (AVHs) occurred when no speech stimulus was presented, while participants reported perceiving one. MRI scanning took place during the silent periods following each stimulus to avoid contamination with scanner noise. (b) The occurrence of AVHs corresponded to an increase in activity in the auditory cortex, compared to trials in which no AVHs occurred. (source: Horga et al., 2014)

are much larger than those in neurotypical controls. One of the possible consequences of this is that sensory inputs result in extremely intense experiences. Partly for this reason, it is possible that individuals diagnosed with ASD often exhibit strongly stressful responses to unexpected and intense sensory stimuli (see also: van Boxtel & Lu, 2013).

An alternative, but not necessarily incompatible, view of the relationship between ASD and the predictive coding framework is proposed by Van de Cruys et al. (2014). They hypothesise that individuals with ASD assign too much weight to prediction errors, causing the internal representations that are being formed to be characterised by excessive regularities and large degrees of inflexibility in behaviour. This over-weighting of prediction errors can result in a wide range of behaviours that are consistent with clinical symptoms. Because the biasing capacity of attention is linked to the weights assigned to the prediction errors (see Chapter 4), assigning too much weight to these errors may also result in an attentional focus that is too narrow.

Moreover, rigorously assigning a strong weight to prediction errors may prevent individuals with ASD from learning through exploration. This mechanism may therefore also explain why ASD is a developmental disorder. Initially, ASD manifests itself in young children as an extremely limited form of attention. In normal development, the growing child will learn which prediction errors are the most informative. In doing so, the child will learn to distinguish between trivial prediction errors, essential prediction errors, and prediction errors with which the child, given the current stage of development, is not yet able to do anything. A crucial condition for this mechanism, however, is that the weight assigned to prediction errors is flexible. When this weight is rigid and too strong, the mechanism will prevent the child from moving on to the next stage of development.

A second consequence of assigning too much weight to a prediction error is that information that has been learned is recorded in an extremely precise manner. This can be advantageous when an exact reproduction of this information is requested, but disadvantageous when part of the details must be sacrificed for a generalisation. An additional consequence is that it is extremely difficult to deal with exceptions to a rule. The latter can obviously be a problem when processing social information.

Finally, it is interesting to compare the hypotheses that have been formulated for schizophrenia and ASD. While the symptoms of ASD can possibly be explained from the perspective of weak predictions (Pellicano & Burr, 2012) or extremely strong prediction errors (Van de Cruys et al., 2014), the opposite may be true for schizophrenia. Although research in this area is not yet complete, it appears that extremely strong predictions (see fig 24.3) (Corlett et al., 2019) or maladaptive prediction errors (Fletcher & Frith, 2009b) are the basis for schizophrenia.

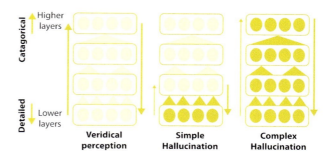

Figure 24.3 The neural basis of a hallucination according to Corlett et al. (2019). Left: veridical perception involves a delicately balanced interaction between predictions and prediction error correction. Middle: simple hallucinations would result from perturbations at the lowest levels of the predictive coding network. Right: complex hallucinations would result from perturbations at multiple levels in the predictive coding hierarchy. According to the model, both types of perturbations are the result of overweighted predictions. (source: Corlett et al., 2019)

24.4 HUMAN FACTORS: COGNITIVE PSYCHOLOGY IN THE WORKPLACE

There are several professions in which human error can have dramatic consequences. Examples which we have already discussed in previous chapters involve medical specialists or pilots, but human errors can also have dramatic consequences in other cases, such as the case discussed in Chapter 15 of a man who forgot to drop off his child at the childcare centre. The latter example illustrates an important aspect of human errors: they are often not intentional. Moreover, many errors are also made with the intention of solving a problem. In such cases, errors are made as a result of an error of judgement or inadequate training.

The latter type of error is illustrated by the fatal actions of the crew of Air France flight 447, which resulted in a fatal crash on the night of 1 June 1, 2009. The aircraft, an Airbus A330, was on its way from Rio de Janeiro in Brazil to Paris, crossing the Atlantic Ocean amidst a heavy storm. Probably due to icing conditions, the airspeed indicator stopped functioning, which resulted in the disengagement of the autopilot, and the flight computers switching to an alternate law mode, which disabled several built-in safety measures. This alternate law mode is designed for emergency situations to give the pilot more authority over the aircraft. One of the consequences of this was that the aircraft responded much more sensitively to control commands than it normally would have done. The pilot, who was not aware that the flight computers had been switched to this emergency mode, made corrections that were too strong, with the ultimate result that the nose of the aircraft was pulled up way too far, causing the wings to lose their lift and the aircraft ending up in a dive that the pilots could not recover from.

This accident illustrates a condition in which the mental representation of the pilot no longer corresponds with reality: that is, the responses of the aircraft no longer matched the pilot's expectations. In other words, there was a disruption of the pilot's **situation awareness** (Endsley, 1995). According to Endsley, situation awareness depends on more than just being aware of the situation in which an operator (pilot, surgeon, etc.) has to work. Other cognitive factors, such as the limited capacity of working memory or a far-reaching understanding of the situation, are also of crucial importance.

24.4.1 MEDICAL BLUNDERS DUE TO SOFTWARE PROBLEMS

The environment in which an operator works must also allow situation awareness to develop. If you have ever bought a cheap electronic device, you probably know how problematic its operation can be. The reason for this lack of transparency is that the operation of the device does not provide enough insight into its internal workings. Although this lack of control is limited to mere annoyance for simple digital watches, there are cases where a faulty design can have fatal consequences. The latter is well illustrated by a software problem with the Therac-25 radio therapy machine, which was first brought onto the market in the early 1980s. This device could either be used to emit X-rays at high power or to emit an electron beam at low power. In X-ray mode, the electron gun was switched into full power mode, while a metal plate was placed between it and the patient which converted the intense electron beam into a safe dose of therapeutic X-rays.

On March 22, 1986, then 33-year-old Isaac Dahl was to receive radio therapy following the removal of a tumour from his left shoulder, which required a low dose of electron radiation. While preparing the session, the Therac-25's operator accidentally punched the 'X' key while entering a value for the 'BEAM TYPE' input field (see fig 24.4), causing the machine to switch to X-ray mode. She soon discovered her mistake, however, and immediately corrected it by rapidly moving the cursor back to the 'BEAM TYPE' field and hitting the 'E' key, which caused the machine to reconfigure into electron mode. She then continued to rapidly finish the configuration, by moving the cursor through all the subsequent input fields, without changing any data. This took her only a few seconds to complete and the display confirmed that the device was now in electron beam mode. After the technician had checked that the device was operational and correctly configured, she then proceeded to enter the 'B' command into the COMMAND input field, which triggered the actual firing. What she did not know – and could not have known – was that due to a software bug, switching beam types within 8 seconds of each other resulted in a fatal configuration error. Although the metal plate was removed, the machine failed to reduce the power of the electron gun.

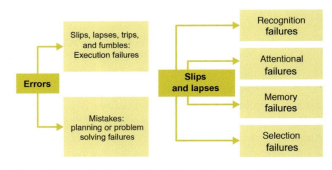

Figure 24.4 The interface of the Therac-25 radio therapy machine. The poor design of this interface, combined with the fact that information on the display did not adequately represent the machine's internal state, led to a number of fatal accidents in the 1980s.

Consequently, 16,000–25,000 rads of electromagnetic radiation were unleashed onto the patient's unprotected shoulder. Dahl felt an excruciating pain, saw a flash of blue Cherenkov radiation light, and heard the flesh of his shoulder being scorched. Because the intercom was switched off, the technician, in the adjacent room, did not notice any of this. Her display only showed a 'malfunction 54' error code. Unaware of the code's meaning and based on previous frequent encounters of this code, she interpreted it as a sign that the electron beam had not fired and reset the machine to fire again. Since this was Dahl's ninth session, he immediately knew that something was wrong and tried to get up from the table. As he was getting up, the technician fired again, this time hitting Dahl in his neck and shoulder. Dahl died five months later due to complications from radiation poisoning.

24.4.2 CLASSIFICATION OF ERROR TYPES

The two preceding examples illustrate errors that can occur as a result of a limitation in situation awareness. The British cognitive psychologist and human factors expert James Reason (1995) has made a distinction between various types of errors that may occur, based on the possible underlying causes (see fig 24.5). Reason defined an error as the failure of a planned action to achieve the intended goal.

Figure 24.5 Classification of different types of errors, as distinguished by James Reason (1995).

On the one hand, the action plan may be adequate in itself, yet problems may occur with its implementation. According to Reason, this results in a slip or a lapse. Slips are related to observable actions that are not correctly carried out as a result of attention problems, whereas lapses are mainly associated with internal events and the incorrect recall of crucial information. On the other hand, the action plan itself can also be inadequate, which, according to Reason, results in a mistake. Reason states that mistakes can be divided into knowledge-based and rule-based mistakes.

Because Reason (1995) associates slips and lapses with the failure of an action plan that is itself adequate, these types of errors typically occur during the execution of highly automated, routine tasks (see Chapter 5). The occurrence of this type of error may be facilitated by unexpected changes, which may occur either in the action plan itself or in the external conditions related to the action. The slips and lapses can themselves be subdivided into more specific issues, such as problems with recognition, attention, memory, or the selection of relevant aspects of a task.

Mistakes typically occur after a problem has been detected. Here a problem is defined as any circumstance that requires a change or modification of the current action plan. More specifically, we can distinguish two different types of mistakes, namely rule-based or knowledge-based mistakes (see also Rasmussen, 1983; Chapter 3).

Rule-based mistakes occur when operators are faced with problems that they can in principle solve through training or experience. Under these circumstances, mistakes can manifest themselves in several different forms. For instance, an otherwise applicable rule may be applied under the wrong circumstances. Consider, for example, an operator failing to notice certain contraindications. This type of mistake may have played a crucial role in the Air France flight 447 crash. The corrective actions that the pilot carried out were adequate under normal circumstances, yet they were no longer adequate when the on-board systems were operating under alternate law conditions while adequate airspeed indications were no longer present. Not noticing the indications of these conditions can be considered a rule-based error. In addition, an error can also be the result of applying an inadequate rule or failing to apply the correct rule. A very mundane example of this is when you decide not to bring rainwear, even though the weather forecast indicates that it is most likely going to rain.

Knowledge-based errors, on the other hand, are most likely to happen when an operator is confronted with a new situation for which a novel solution must be found on the spot. This often involves the use of slow controlled forms of task processing that put a strain on the limited capacity of our attentional and cognitive control processes. To solve a problem, we must often make a decision on the basis of an incomplete internal mental representation of the problem. Consequently, various cognitive biases, such as those described in Chapters 19–22, can interfere with finding the correct solution. One of the most important biases that can play a role is the **confirmation bias**. This confirmation bias manifests itself especially when we try to diagnose a problem.

24.4.3 ERRORS VERSUS VIOLATIONS

In addition to the aforementioned errors, Reason (1995) identifies violations as an important cause of major disasters. Violations consist of deviations from standard procedures and can be classified into three different groups.

1. Routine violations, which aim to save work or time, for example, by skipping security procedures.
2. Violations that arise from a desire to pursue personal rather than task-related goals, for example, actions performed for a personal thrill or to relieve boredom.
3. Violations that are carried out because, given the current situation, they appear to be the only option to complete the task successfully. These violations occur mainly when the existing rules appear to be inadequate in a specific situation.

Violations differ from errors in several important ways. Errors mainly result from capacity problems in information processing or the unavailability of information. The latter was already illustrated by the radiologist who could not have known that rapidly changing an 'X' to an 'E' in an input field would result in a fatal reconfiguration of an electron beam. Violations, on the other hand, are mainly related to motivational aspects, such as low morale, poor supervision, a lack of dedication, or a lack of opportunities to reward compliance. The latter is illustrated, for example, by the fact that the developers of the Therac-25 radio therapy machine had reused parts of the software that was developed for an older model, while ignoring some crucial differences between the Therac-25 and these older models.

Moreover, errors often occur as a result of the actions of an individual, whereas violations are more often linked to problems in the organisation and a social context. Consequently, we can often prevent errors by providing better information and developing better training programmes, while violations should be prevented by improving the organisational culture.

24.4.4 ACUTE VERSUS LATENT FAILURES

A third distinction involves acute and latent failures. The major difference between these two types of failures is the time lag between the error and its consequences. Acute failure implies immediate consequences, whereas latent failures only manifest themselves after a prolonged period of time.

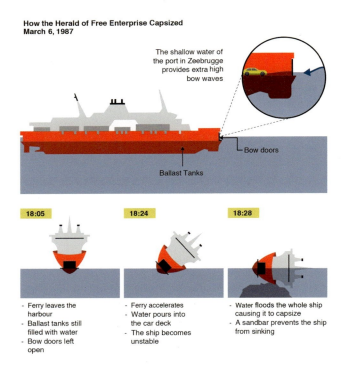

How the Herald of Free Enterprise Capsized
March 6, 1987

The shallow water of the port in Zeebrugge provides extra high bow waves

Bow doors

Ballast Tanks

18:05
- Ferry leaves the harbour
- Ballast tanks still filled with water
- Bow doors left open

18:24
- Ferry accelerates
- Water pours into the car deck
- The ship becomes unstable

18:28
- Water floods the whole ship causing it to capsize
- A sandbar prevents the ship from sinking

Figure 24.6 Schematic representation of the main factors that contributed to the capsizing and sinking of the British ferry Herald of Free Enterprise off the coast of Zeebrugge in 1987.

A prime example of such a latent failure is the accident involving the British ferry Herald of Free Enterprise, which capsized off the coast of the Belgian town of Zeebrugge on March 6, 1987, due to an unfortunate series of mistakes and violations (see fig 24.6). On that fatal day, the Herald of Free Enterprise had to replace another ferry, forcing it to dock in a port it was not designed for. This meant that the ship's two car decks could not be loaded simultaneously, as the port of Zeebrugge only had one ramp. Moreover, this ramp could only reach the Herald's upper deck when its ballast tanks were fully loaded. Finally, the Herald was also fully booked as a result of a special offer. Nevertheless, the crew was heavily pressured by the operator's management to leave on time. Consequently, the crew decided to leave immediately once the ship was loaded, and it was not noticed that the bow doors were not yet closed. According to standard procedures, these doors should have been closed before the mooring lines were released, but due to an error by the boatswain, it was not noticed that they were still open. The ship's captain did not notice either, because he could not see the bow doors from the bridge; nor were there any indicators to signal that they were still open.

An investigation into the disaster revealed that it had happened before that Enterprise class ferries had departed, or even crossed the entire British channel, while their bow doors were still open. It had not been noticed because the person responsible had been asleep during those incidents and, moreover, the open doors had not had any negative consequences. So why did it go wrong in 1987 in Zeebrugge? The reason was an unfortunate concurrence of circumstances, including the fact that the Herald of Free Enterprise was positioned deeply in the water due to the extra ballast and extremely heavy loading. Moreover, the shallow waters in the port of Zeebrugge also caused extra-large bow waves, which could flow freely into the car deck. Finally, it was also found that the organisational culture of the shipping company Townsend Thoresen, the owner of the Herald, had contributed to the disaster by putting the crew under severe pressure to leave on time.

The Herald of Free Enterprise accident not only illustrates a latent failure, it also illustrates a model of risk analysis known as the Swiss cheese model. This model compares operational procedures with layers of stacked slices of Swiss cheese, where each slice is considered to be a protective mechanism that reduces the likelihood of an accident. Operational procedures that are designed according to this principle should prevent an individual slip or lapse, represented as a hole in the slice of cheese, from resulting in an accident.

Although the accidents just described had enormous consequences, it is precisely because the Swiss cheese model is applied to many complex risk analyses that medical equipment, ferries, and aircraft have reached unprecedented levels of safety in everyday life. It is only in extreme circumstances, when all the slices of cheese are stacked in such a way that the holes line up, that a fatal accident occurs.

According to Reason, the cause of an accident can often be traced back to problems in one or more of the following four areas: organisation, supervision, preconditions, and specific actions. Problems at the organisational level involve, for example, putting crews under pressure to leave on time, cutting back on maintenance, not installing safety systems, or cutting back on training. These types of problems were crucial in the Herald of Free Enterprise accident, where the crew was put under intense pressure to leave on time, which led to the captain being willing to violate standard operating procedures. In addition, this type of organisational culture contributed to the fact that the crew was fatigued, so that the boatswain responsible for closing the bow doors was asleep at a crucial moment.

Factors such as fatigue or unclear communication protocols are preconditions for an accident. In the case of the Herald of Free Enterprise accident, not only the sleeping boatswain contributed to this, but also the fact that there was no possibility of communicating the condition of the doors directly to the captain. Another good example of a supervision problem is when a relatively inexperienced pilot is given control of an aircraft during a night flight and under extreme weather conditions. This was, for example, one of the contributing factors to the crash of Air France flight 447, where the captain had retreated to his bunk to get some sleep after a relatively inexperienced relief pilot had taken over the main flying duties.

24.4.5 RELYING ON AUTOMATIC SYSTEMS

In the last 50 years, many tasks have become computerised, which has changed the role of workers from an executive function to a supervisory one. Although this is often designated as automation, in practice this automation is limited because the computer systems still operate under human supervision. As a result, the human role in this labour process has changed in the last 50 years from that of a performer to that of a monitor. Although the automation of many tasks in critical situations has resulted in an increase in safety, it has also led to an increased risk of blind faith in automatic systems, so that errors made by these systems go unnoticed. The automatic systems in question are often designed to take over complex routine tasks. In many cases, however, these still involve relatively basic procedures that must be used by a human operator to control the higher-order aspects of a process.

A good example of this is the autopilot installed in modern commercial aircraft. This system consists of a number of basic functions, which can ensure that the aircraft maintains a pre-set altitude – or climbs or descends to this altitude at a predetermined vertical speed. Other functions ensure that the aircraft maintains a fixed heading or flies at a specific speed. These automatic systems relieve the pilot's workload, in the sense that they do not have to continuously be involved in a basic steering task: a task that places heavy demands on sustained attention and vigilance systems. It is, however, the pilot's task to use these systems in such a way that the aircraft remains within operational parameters, for example, by preventing an abrupt climb from causing the aircraft's airspeed to drop too much.

Endsley (1996) discusses several examples where blind faith in automatic safety systems resulted in accidents. In 1987, for example, an aircraft crashed during take-off in Detroit because the automatic system that controls the configuration of the wing flaps (large flaps on the back of the wing that give an aircraft more lift during take-off and landing) had not indicated that they were not deployed. Similarly, two years later, a plane crashed at New York's LaGuardia Airport because the pilots had inadvertently disabled the engine's automatic thrust controller during take-off. This problem went unnoticed because neither the captain nor the co-pilot was monitoring critical flight parameters during that critical phase. Both examples illustrate the role of a limited situational awareness that resulted from extensive automation.

Why does automation result in reduced situational awareness? Endsley (1996) identifies three possible reasons for this: (1) changes in vigilance and sufficiency that result from the monitoring of the automatic systems; (2) the assumption of a passive rather than an active role; and

(3) changes in the quality or form of feedback that is fed back to the human operator.

Changes in vigilance often occur when the role of the human operator is passive. Although this type of vigilance is particularly common in simple routine automatic tasks, problems can also be found in complex tasks. For example, Billings (1991) reported that problems with this kind of routine vigilance are more likely to occur when the systems report seemingly reasonable but incorrect values. An additional problem is that the high degree of trust in automatic systems leads to the operator paying less attention to the automatic process in favour of other tasks, resulting in a decrease in situational awareness. This reduction in monitoring can also occur, however, when using systems that are characterised by a high ratio of false alarms. In this case, however, there is a reduction in confidence in the automatic systems, so that important warning signals may be missed.

24.4.6 LUGGAGE SCREENING AND VISUAL SEARCH

Since the September 11, 2001, attacks on the World Trade Center in New York and the Pentagon in Washington DC, airport security measures have drastically increased. One of the standard procedures involves screening the baggage of passengers by security personnel. This involves the use of an X-ray machine to scan hand luggage, thereby detecting dangerous and/or illegal items. The effective detection of these types of items obviously relies heavily on visual search processes (see Chapter 6). A crucial question is what factors are involved in the successful detection of these items. Based on cognitive psychological research, two factors have been identified that may hamper the effectiveness of security staff.

First, luggage inspectors are confronted with a huge variety of items that they have to check on a daily basis (see fig 24.7). Moreover, the suspicious items are not always easy to identify (McCarley, Kramer, Wickens, Vidoni, & Boot, 2004). Unlike a standard laboratory task, which involves searching for one specific item, airport security officers must look for a multitude of objects, such as knives, guns, or improvised explosive devices. This type of search is characterised by a host of unique problems. For example, Menneer, Cave, and Donnelly (2009) found that observers who had to search for more than one type of object (i.e., metal threats and improvised explosive devices) were less accurate than observers who only had to search for one type of object. This result was found for stimuli that did not share physical properties, such as colour or shape. When these stimuli did share some physical properties, task performance was similar in both conditions. In that case, observers could use one search template (see Chapter 14) which allows them to detect both types of objects (Bravo & Farid, 2012).

Figure 24.7 Example of a display as used in the study on airport security staff's efficiency at detecting a multitude of different suspicious objects in passengers' hand luggage. (source: McCarley et al., 2004)

A second limiting factor is that the relevant items are only present in an extremely small proportion of the number of objects to be scanned. This rarity makes it extremely difficult for security staff to actually detect the items (Mitroff & Biggs, 2014; Wolfe et al., 2005). Wolfe et al. (2007) instructed participants to inspect X-ray photographs of packed luggage for the presence of weapons (knives and handguns). When these target items were present in 50% of all trials, they detected them in 80% of all cases. When these items were present in only 2% of all trials, however, they were only detected in 54% of all cases. Wolfe et al. explain this finding by assuming that participants are extremely careful in reporting suspicious items when they are rare, because the a priori expectation of finding these items is extremely low. How can we improve search performance under these circumstances?

Schwark, Sandry, Macdonald, and Dolgov (2012) used a procedure in which false negative feedback was given, implying that participants had missed a target stimulus. The result was improved performance. In practice, security guards are often confronted with artificial items added to the baggage flow in order to artificially increase the base ratio of suspicious items. This measure also increases task performance. In addition, modern scanning equipment can generate multiple images of each baggage item, using different viewpoints. In addition, different false colour images are generated, which make specific properties of suspicious items more salient. Although these types of images have a positive effect on the identification of suspicious items, it has a disadvantage in that

the total inspection time per item increases (von Bastian, Schwaninger, & Michel, 2008).

The results reported by Wolfe et al. (2007) have been somewhat nuanced in a later study by Fleck and Mitroff (2007). The latter authors argue that although rare target stimuli can be easily missed, this is mainly due to incorrect response selection. When target stimuli are rare, participants often switch to a strategy in which they respond more quickly and generate a 'no' response in a more automatic manner. According to Fleck and Mitroff, the relatively frequent missing of these target stimuli is therefore also a reflection of this response strategy, which manifests itself mainly when participants are unable to correct their response. When they can, performance often turns out to be much improved.

24.5 ACTION CONTROL AND MENTAL FATIGUE

We have already been introduced to the idea that fatigue, as a major source of latent failure, can contribute to the occurrence of an accident. During the 20th century, fundamental changes in our society resulted in major changes in our working environment. More specifically, our society shifted from a strong emphasis on physical labour to a far greater emphasis on mental labour. One of the consequences is that many individuals now suffer more from mental fatigue than from physical fatigue (Ricci, Chee, Lorandeau, & Berger, 2007). It is therefore not surprising that mental fatigue has become a major source of errors on the work floor. Although studies on mental fatigue already date back to the early 20th century (Bills, 1931), a renewed interest in this phenomenon has emerged towards the late 20th century.

For instance, Boksem and Tops (2008) have provided a literature review of more recent studies in the area of mental fatigue. As such, they relate the effects of fatigue to changes in cognitive control. For example, mental fatigue has been characterised by problems with focusing attention, reduced planning skills, and the flexible updating of strategies following negative outcomes (Van der Linden, Frese, & Sonntag, 2003). Moreover, Boksem, Meijman, and Lorist (2006) found that fatigued participants reported difficulties in adequately preparing a response and that they also had difficulties in staying focused on a task, resulting in more frequent distractions.

It is an intuitively appealing idea that mental fatigue results from long continuous working hours, with the fatigue slowly increasing over time. This is not the case, however, as several studies have shown that in some cases fatigue can already be experienced after a short burst of mental effort, whereas in other cases long working hours do not necessarily result in mental fatigue

(Park, Kim, Chung, & Hisanaga, 2001; Sparks & Cooper, 1997). This is particularly the case when the reward that is associated with long working hours is high, both in terms of a financial reward and in terms of appreciation from colleagues and superiors (Siegirst, 1996; Van Der Hulst & Geurts, 2001).

The latter result implies a strong link between mental fatigue and reward. According to Boksem and Tops (2008), these results can be explained by assuming that mental fatigue is related to two complementary and interacting motivational mechanisms, both of which are involved in producing goal-directed behaviour. These are the motivation to receive rewards and to avoid punishment and harm (see fig 24.8). The assumption here is that although punishment and reward can both motivate us to engage in specific forms of behaviour, they are also associated with energetic costs. Boksem and colleagues hypothesise that the feeling of fatigue is the result of a process that determines whether it would be better to spend or to save energy (Boksem et al., 2006). Consequently, individuals will only want to spend energy on tasks where the costs are relatively low and the benefits relatively high. When tasks are performed over extensive periods of time, the amount of effort invested in task performance will gradually accumulate, and, at some point, the costs will no longer outweigh the benefits. The result is a decrease in motivation to perform the specific task when it no longer results in obtaining the intended rewards.

Boksem et al. (2006) found evidence for the idea that mental fatigue is related to the degree to which participants

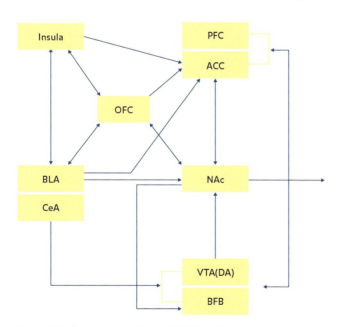

Figure 24.8 A neural model for mental fatigue. A network of brain regions is involved in evaluating whether a reward obtained outweighs the cost of obtaining it. ACC = anterior cingulate cortex; BLA = basolateral amygdala; CeA = central nucleus of the amygdala; OFC = orbitofrontal cortex; PFC = prefrontal cortex; NAc = nucleus accumbens; VTA = ventral tegmental area; BFB = basal forebrain; DA = dopamine. (source: Boksem and Tops, 2008)

are prepared to persevere with a task. In their study, participants were engaged in a letter discrimination task that lasted for two hours and 20 minutes while their EEG was recorded. The purpose of the first two hours of this task was to induce mental fatigue, while the brain activity that was recorded in the last 20 minutes was used to determine the effects of this fatigue. The letter discrimination task consisted of a relatively complex instruction that induced a relatively large number of errors, allowing the researchers to study how mental fatigue affected the processing of these errors. This was done by extracting the **error-related negativity** (ERN) component from the EEG signals (see Chapter 5). Some of the participants were extra motivated when, after the first two hours, they were informed that they would receive an extra sum of money if they belonged to the 50% best performing participants. Boksem et al. found that the amplitude of the ERN was clearly reduced in fatigued participants, while the extra motivation resulted in an increase of its amplitude.

Such an explanation of mental fatigue is consistent with Holroyd and Coles' (2002) interpretation of the ERN, which they assumed to be reflecting the processing of a prediction error that relates to an expected reward and that this ERN is related to motivation (Gehring et al., 1993).

Neurophysiological studies have suggested that mental fatigue is related to impaired functioning of the dopaminergic systems in neural systems that are part of a circuit that includes the striatum, the thalamus, and the cortex (Chaudhuri & Behan, 2000; Lorist & Tops, 2003). Chaudhuri and Behan (2000) suggest, in this context, that mental fatigue is related to a disease of these systems. Although it is probably too far-fetched to associate mental fatigue in everyday life with damage to these neural systems, a down-regulation of the dopaminergic systems has been observed for these areas. Since the nucleus accumbens, one of the nuclei of the striatum involved in dopamine regulation, is an important source of input for the anterior cingulate cortex, it may be assumed that mental fatigue directly affects cognitive control processes.

The idea that mental fatigue affects cognitive control processes in particular is consistent with not only the aforementioned findings that mental fatigue results in a decreased attentional focus or that it has a negative impact on participants' flexibility (Boksem et al., 2006; Van der Linden et al., 2003) but also with findings indicating that mentally fatigued participants are less adequate in correcting errors or in processing feedback after an error (Boksem et al., 2006; Lorist, Boksem, & Ridderinkhof, 2005).

Since mental fatigue appears to have predominantly negative consequences, we may wonder why it occurs in the first place. Boksem and Tops (2008) argue that, despite its apparently negative consequences, mental fatigue may have a crucial function in the regulation of long-term goals. According to this view, mental fatigue signals that current task goals are no longer adequate, since they do not appear to be achieved despite the investment of considerable effort in the past. In particular, mental fatigue signals the need to reduce the pursuit of existing long-term goals in favour of short-term goals, which are ultimately a necessary part of the pursuit of long-term goals.

In light of the idea that mental fatigue has a signalling function indicating that long-term goals are not being sufficiently achieved, it is interesting to take a closer look at the effects of mental fatigue in our modern-day labour process – particularly in those situations where employees have little control over their situations. It is therefore mainly in these situations that employees begin to feel mentally fatigued. The lack of control then forces them to ignore the signs of fatigue, leaving the imbalance between mental effort and the achievement of goals intact. While the ability to ignore this balance is in itself an adaptive process that can be sustained over long periods of time in emergency situations, prolonged disregard of this imbalance can result in sustained levels of stress (McEwen & Wingfield, 2003). Ultimately, this can result in chronic fatigue or burnout.

24.6 MENTAL LOAD, SOFTWARE, AND USER-FRIENDLINESS

The previously described shift from physical to mental labour is closely related to a strong emergence of computer use in the workplace. Although computer systems are often introduced to simplify the labour process, it is a well-known fact that this goal is far from being achieved. One of the main reasons for this is that inadequately developed software often results in additional mental strain, because the programme's interface does not take sufficient account of the human user. It is important that developers take both physical and cognitive factors into account. Of course, the nature of the software largely determines the requirements it must meet. A flight simulator requires a different user interface than a word processor or an accounting programme. Nevertheless, there are some general principles that well-designed software should adhere to.

24.6.1 FEEDBACK AND SITUATION AWARENESS

A guiding principle is that the user of a software programme must always be able to form a mental representation of the internal state of a programme. As illustrated earlier in this chapter with the example of the Therac-25 radiotherapy machine's inadequate interface, failure to do so can have catastrophic consequences (see fig 24.4). Even in more trivial situations, inadequate information can result in impaired task performance. A good example of this is the

automatic formatting that is enabled by default in some word processors, which may result in the incorrect layout of bullet points or numbered lists.

Well-designed software should also always inform the user about the tasks it is performing. A common complaint from users concerns programmes that do not respond to input for a long time, because a long, computationally intensive process is running in the background, blocking the interface. In principle, an interface should always remain responsive, and when this is not possible, the user should be informed of this. For shorter times, it is often sufficient to change the cursor into a waiting symbol, such as a spinning wheel or an hourglass. For waiting times longer than ten seconds, ideally a progress indicator should appear that gives the user adequate feedback on the progress of the task in the background. Although current applications display this type of indicator, they are often inadequate because the underlying calculation process contains non-linear operations, making the progress of the indicator erratic. In particular, prolonged periods in which the progress meter shows no change can be interpreted by the user as an indication that the background process has stalled. The absence of such feedback often leads the user to believe that an operation has not been performed, resulting in frequent random button clicks in the hope of making the programme responsive again.

24.6.2 VISUAL INTERFACE DESIGN

Well-designed software should not only provide the user with continuous feedback on its internal operation; the way in which information is presented should also be clear. Designers can make use of a number of cognitive psychological principles for this. For example, interface elements that have similar functions should be grouped according to the gestalt principles discussed in Chapter 6, with specific functions being clustered according to the laws of proximity and similarity. It is also important that computer users are given as much freedom as possible on the one hand, while the software guides them through the process as adequately as possible on the other hand. Users must be given the opportunity to correct errors and make informed choices. Finally, a well-designed interface will make as much use of recognition as possible to minimise dependence on the user's working memory.

A good example of a problematic design element in a graphical interface are the pull-down menus that many programmes have. These menus usually give direct access to all functions of a programme. A problem here is that not all functions always perform sensible actions. In a word processor, for example, the function to execute the spelling checker only makes sense after a document has been loaded, whereas functions relating to editing figures only make sense when a figure has been selected. To minimise these problems, visual feedback can be used, whereby menu items that are not accessible are displayed in grey and are not clickable. Although this graphical feedback is an improvement in itself, it often still results in an interface that can become cluttered because all the irrelevant functions still remain visible. This can greatly increase the load on visual search processes.

A second problem is that a flat menu structure often gives users too little feedback about the status of the process that is being performed. This is often the case with processes where operations have to be executed as a series of discrete steps. A good example of this is an installer, which must gather information about the computer system before it can perform the final installation of a software package. This often requires the user to make a number of choices, each of which may influence another. For example, the decision of where to install a programme may determine how many additional components can be installed. Another example is software used for analysing research data. The processing of EEG or fMRI data, for example, consists of a processing pipeline. This implies that some steps can only be carried out when specific conditions have been met. For example, an ERP can only be calculated when recording artefacts have been removed from the raw data, and the calculation of the potential distribution of these ERPs across the scalp can only be carried out after the ERPs themselves have been calculated.

For this kind of process, a flat menu structure is typically inadequate, and it is better to consider using an interface that guides the user through the process. A good example of such an interface is provided by the installation wizards, which ask the user for input at each step, and present this input in the form of multiple-choice options. The advantage of using multiple choice options is that the user can rely on recognition, which relieves the burden placed on the user's working memory. It is also important that the user has the option to step back to an earlier stage in order to adjust previous choices.

24.6.3 ROUTINE OPERATIONS

Some tasks require many routine actions. The graphical elements of the user interface should aid the user through these steps, but that is often not enough. A well-designed interface must also consider how people perform routine actions. Here it is important that the design of the software protects the user from errors that may result from the automation of routine actions. For example, the repetitive execution of a simple motor action can be automated relatively quickly, but there is a risk that the action will be performed too often. For example, when we need to select a series of items from a list, if we can only select one item at a time, the risk is that routine clicking will result in selecting too many items. Our response criterion has shifted, reducing our ability to suppress a response.

A better option is therefore to design interfaces in such a way that routine actions are avoided as much as possible. This can be applied to the example by expanding the interface in such a way that items can be filtered according to specific criteria, after which the remaining items can be selected with one click. If it is not possible to completely exclude routine actions, then at least the option to undo each action must be provided. It is also very important that routine actions cannot result in crucial errors. For this reason, buttons with completely different functions should preferably not be placed next to each other, so that an action slip does not result in a crucial error. A good example of this is formed by the 'yes', 'no', and 'cancel' buttons that are often presented in a dialogue box when a user wants to close a programme.

24.6.4 CONSISTENT PROTOCOLS

One of the most frequently used questions, which has resulted in a high degree of automation on the part of the user, concerns the already described question of whether the user wants to save the last changes before closing the programme in question. Because of the high degree of automation in our response to this question, it is very important that this question is asked consistently. It is nowadays almost always posed in the positive form, 'Do you want to save changes before you exit?' In the past, some programmes have posed the question in the negative form, 'Do you want to exit without saving your changes?' This form is, of course, particularly prone to errors with potentially catastrophic consequences.

24.7 BRAIN-COMPUTER INTERFACES AND LIE DETECTION

If you have watched the television series Breaking Bad, you are undoubtedly familiar with the character of Hector Salamanca. Salamanca, a former drug runner and right hand to a Mexican drug lord, has been paralysed by a stroke and can only communicate via a little bell mounted on his wheelchair. This way, he can answer simple questions: the ringing of the bell means 'yes'. When he wants to pass on a more complex message, his nurse takes a card on which all the letters of the alphabet are tabulated. She goes through each row of letters step by step and stops when Salamanca rings his bell. She then goes through each letter in the row until Salamanca rings his bell again. The nurse then writes down the corresponding letter. Although the neurological details of Salamanca's condition are not given in the series,[1] it appears that the stroke affected the efferent neural tracts connecting the brain to the spinal cord, causing Salamanca to lose almost all voluntary motor control over his body.

A similar method of communication is used in the French movie *Le scaphandre et le papillon* (*The Diving Bell and the Butterfly*), based on the true story of protagonist Jean-Dominique Bauby, who is only capable of moving his eyes. Bauby's condition is known as the locked-in syndrome, which is often characterised by patients having control over their eye muscles only. Despite this de-efferentation, a locked-in patient's somatosensory nervous system is typically still intact, allowing all bodily perceptual signals to be perceived without the patient being able to react to them (in The Diving Bell and the Butterfly, this is rather strikingly illustrated when a fly lands on Bauby's nose.) Locked-in syndrome results from damage to specific parts of the brainstem as a result of a stroke, poisoning, or other types of injury. In more extreme cases, patients may also lose control over their eye muscles, resulting in complete paralysis.

24.7.1 BRAIN-COMPUTER INTERFACES

In recent decades, several methods have been developed to enable locked-in patients to communicate by using brain-computer interfaces. As illustrated in Figure 24.9, a method similar to Salamanca's bell, or Bauby's eye movement, is used here, but instead of a bell or eye movement, neurophysiological markers from the EEG are used to determine which letter the patient wants to select (Curran & Stokes, 2003; Silvoni et al., 2011; Vaughan, 2003; Wolpaw et al., 2000). Traditionally, the P300 component is used for this purpose. The P300 is a positive ERP component which is elicited mainly when a stimulus is relevant. Participants think of a specific letter, after which a series of letters is presented. When the letter that the participant had in mind is shown, this results in a measurable P300 component. The EEG data are analysed online and when the computer detects an enlarged P300 component, the letter that evoked this component is selected.

Although methods based on the P300 component have been shown to be reasonably effective, the high noise levels of single-trial ERP components can be a problem. In Chapter 2, Box 2.3, we indicated that the amplitude of ERPs is considerably smaller than that of the background EEG, so ERPs are typically calculated by averaging a large number of repetitions of the evoking stimulus. For brain-computer interfaces this method is not useful, as this repetition would be required for each letter the patient wants to communicate, which would make communication extremely slow. For this reason, advanced signal analysis techniques are used to estimate for each letter whether it evokes a P300 component. Of course, this method is sensitive to noise, and there are also considerable individual differences in the decodability of neural signals (Ahn & Jun, 2015). Finally, methods based on the detection of the P300 component can often only detect one letter at a time, which drastically limits the speed of communication. For these reasons, the use of these traditional brain-computer interface methods remains relatively limited (Amiri, Fazel-Rezai, & Asadpour, 2013).

Newer and more reliable systems often use a hybrid approach, combining multiple physiological markers to increase reliability and detection rates. One way of doing this is to make use of the fact that the brain produces different EEG rhythms, combined with the fact that these activation patterns are characterised by different scalp distributions. Brain-computer interface systems that are based on the detection of these rhythms can often be used to control complex robotic systems that respond to neural input generated by, for example, the motor cortex or the speech centres of the brain (Ramadan & Vasilakos, 2017). Another method that is commonly used is based on classification algorithms. Here, different neurophysiological markers are taken together and analysed by a pattern recognition algorithm (Lotte, Congedo, Lécuyer, Lamarche, & Arnaldi, 2007). Thus, the software can be trained to relate specific patterns to specific thought patterns, such as words or intentions formulated by the patient.

24.7.2 LIE DETECTION AND THE CONCEALED-KNOWLEDGE TEST

The P300 method could, in principle, also be used to determine whether someone is trying to withhold information. Objects or situations that are relevant to a participant evoke a P300 component, whereas neutral objects do not. Based on this fact, it is in principle possible to determine whether a crime suspect is withholding crucial information. As such, suspects are presented a series of pictures for passive viewing. Some of these pictures are related to a crime, such as pictures of the murder weapon, the victim, or the crime scene. When the suspect's brain recognises these objects, it will produce a P300, whereas the neutral photos will not. A difference in P300 amplitude between crime-related and crime-neutral photos can therefore be an indication that a suspect is withholding information (Farwell & Donchin, 1991).

Although there is evidence that the P300 component can be used as a marker for concealed information, there is debate about how reliable this method is. Farwell and

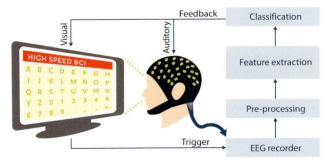

Figure 24.9 Schematic representation of an EEG-based computer system to allow locked-in patients to communicate.

Smith (1998) argue that the P300 method is significantly more reliable than the classic concealed-knowledge tests that are based on skin conductance methods (i.e., the classic polygraph or lie detection tests). Farwell and Smith also argue that the P300-based tests are not susceptible to cognitive strategies to fool the method. Rosenfeld et al. (2004), however, report counter-evidence to this claim. According to these investigators, simple but effective cognitive strategies can prevent offence-related stimuli from evoking a larger P300 component than offence-neutral stimuli. In this study, participants were involved in a fictitious crime and were presented with a series of stimuli a few weeks later, some of which were crime related. For participants who had received no specific instructions, it was found that the items associated with the crime evoked a larger P300 component than the stimuli that were not. A second group of participants, however, received a specific instruction to generate a covert response after each stimulus. Because this instruction resulted in each stimulus becoming relevant, the difference in P300 amplitude between the relevant and irrelevant stimuli disappeared.

An interesting recent development is that it may not even be necessary at all to use physiological measures to reveal hidden information. Seymour, Seifert, Shafto, and Mosmann (2000) have reported that participants generally respond more slowly to stimuli about which they want to hide their knowledge. Verschuere and Kleinberg (2016) have reported that this method can, in principle, also be implemented in an online system. In their study, participants were first asked to provide a number of personal details via a web application, after which they were instructed to assume a false identity for the duration of the experiment. After they had practised sufficiently to reproduce the false information, they were given several questions. More specifically, they were presented with words that were followed by the question: 'Is this you?' Of the 600 questions that were asked, 100 were related to the participants' false identity and 100 to their true identity. The remaining 400 questions were irrelevant items intended to distract the participant's attention from the research question. In particular, reaction times to the questions relating to true identity were significantly larger than those to the irrelevant questions and the questions relating to false identity.

24.8 ERRORS IN SPATIAL NAVIGATION: DO LOST PEOPLE REALLY WALK IN CIRCLES?

Many people believe that we walk in circles when we get lost in unknown territory and this idea is popular in literature (e.g., Mark Twain's Roughing It, Leo Tolstoy's Master and Men, J.R.R. Tolkien's Lord of the Rings: The Two Towers), movies (Laurel & Hardy: Beau Hunks, The Flight of the Phoenix, The Blair Witch Project), and comic books (e.g., Tintin: Land of Black Gold, Explorers on the Moon). Souman, Frissen, Sreenivasa, and Ernst (2009) investigated, in response to a request from a German television programme to what extent we are capable of walking in a straight line in unfamiliar terrain. In a first study, this was tested in two different environments, namely in a large forest area in Germany and in the Sahara Desert.

Six participants volunteered for a walk in the forest. They walked for several consecutive hours through a dense forest area, where they were instructed to walk in as much of a straight line as possible, traversing through various degrees of vegetation. During these walks, their position was tracked by a global positioning system (GPS). Four of the six participants completed the walk on a cloudy day, which meant that the sun was hidden by the clouds, and all four walked around in circles, with three of these four participants repeatedly crossing their own tracks without being aware of it. During the walk of the other two participants, the sun was shining and these two walked in an almost straight line, except during the first few minutes when the sun had not yet broken through the clouds. These results suggest that the availability of a reliable external source of information about the direction of travel is a critical factor in maintaining a course in unfamiliar terrain. Three other participants walked for several hours in the Sahara Desert of southern Tunisia. Two participants who walked during the day deviated from their course but did not walk around in circles. The third participant walked at night, during a full moon. When the moon disappeared behind the clouds, this participant made a number of sharp turns, which eventually brought him back to his starting point.

Although these observations are relatively anecdotal, various attempts have been made to explain this supposed behaviour based on the popular belief that we walk in circles. These explanations are partly based on the idea that people have an implicit tendency to deviate in one direction. Various underlying biological mechanisms for this bias have been hypothesised, ranging from an asymmetry in the dopaminergic system to differences in leg length or muscle strength. These deviations should result in a specific one-way bias. Souman et al. (2009) tested this hypothesis by requiring participants to walk blindfolded through an open area for 50 minutes and found no evidence for a specific bias. Participants generally failed to hold a straight line, but the deviations from the straight line were not systematic. Three of the 15 participants who did show a systematic deviation walked around in circles with a sometimes surprisingly small diameter of

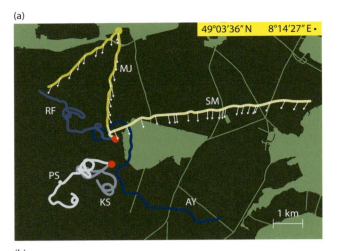

(a)

49°03'36" N   8°14'27" E •

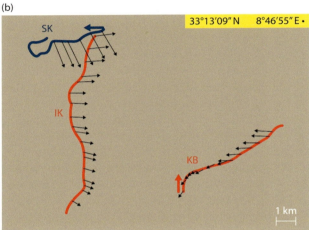

(b)

33°13'09" N   8°46'55" E •

Figure 24.10 Results of a study in which participants had to walk blindfolded in an unknown environment: (a) in a forest in Germany, (b) in the Sahara. (source: Souman et al., 2009)

approximately 20 metres (see fig 24.10). The deviations that were found could not be attributed to biomechanical differences and an experimental manipulation of the participants' leg length (by giving them shoes with different sole thicknesses) did not result in a systematic deviation of their walking direction.

An interesting result from the study of Souman et al. (2009) is that when we have no external reference source, we indeed tend to walk around in circles, but when we can orient ourselves to an external reference point, we continue to walk in a relatively straight line. This was the case when the participants could keep their bearings on the sun. Remarkable in this respect was the fact that, when participants were able to keep their orientation on the sun for several hours, they continued to walk in a relatively straight line, whereas the position of the sun changed significantly during the time of the walk. This result therefore implies that we are able to correct for this change in position.

A second remarkable finding was that during both the forest walk and the blindfolded walk there were periods of random deviations, which alternated with periods of circular movements. These deviations could not be explained by the idea that participants had to avoid obstacles, since the blindfolded walks took place on a flat terrain. Souman et al. (2009) have explained this phenomenon by assuming that random errors in the sense of direction occur, which strongly influence the participants' sense of 'straight ahead'. This explanation is based on the idea that with every step, a random component is added to the feeling of straight ahead, causing this feeling to deviate from the actual direction to a greater or lesser degree.

As long as the deviation remains close to the actual direction, participants will show small deviations randomly to the left or right. When the deviation becomes large, however, it can result in walking around in a circle. Souman et al. (2009) assume that this deviation may be the result of the accumulation of noise in all components of the sensorimotor system. Evidence for the idea that multiple senses are involved in location determination comes from Campos, Butler, and Bulthoff (2012), who found that the determination of the distance walked can be based on the integration of proprioceptive and vestibular cues.

24.9 LOOKING AHEAD: WHAT WILL THE FUTURE BRING?

We are now at the beginning of the third decade of the 21st century. In the approximately 65 years since cognitive psychology has existed as an official scientific discipline, our understanding of human cognition has changed dramatically. Although we are beginning to grasp the essentials of human functioning, we still have a long way to go before all the missing details are clarified. Moreover, with the advancement of insight, new possibilities to apply the knowledge we have gathered will arise. Moreover, the possibility remains that new research methods will be developed. Such new methods may fundamentally change our understanding of brain functions, as well as our understanding of the relationship between brain and behaviour. For this reason, it is interesting to take a brief look at the future and speculate about some of the possible developments that lie ahead.

24.9.1 NEW ETHICS AND RESEARCH METHODS

The developments, as outlined in Chapter 1, that marked the beginning of the replication crisis at the start of the previous decade, have ultimately contributed to the reali- sation that the use of existing research methods can some- times be problematic. In particular, the established methods of hypothesis testing allow individual researchers too much freedom, which can bias the results to align with the pre-ex- isting views and assumptions of the researcher in question. With the introduction of new protocols that require the research question, hypotheses, and research methods to be published before the start of data collection, this bias can be avoided. This is possible because pre-registration of the research question and the proposed methods prevent any methods from being adjusted a posteriori, so as to cover up discrepant results.

In the past decade, several important steps have already been taken in this area, such as the creation of the **Center for Open Science** (COS; https://cos.io) and its associated **open science framework** (OSF). The COS is a website where researchers can register research projects and store the raw research data, together with the exact protocols that were used for the data analysis. The latter is typically done in the form of scripts that are used by the analysis software to process the raw data. When both the raw data and the scripts are made available via such an online platform, other researchers can always verify whether the analyses were carried out correctly and whether they cor- respond to the way the original research group described them. It is important here that the methods that are used are disclosed before the data are collected, as this pre- vents discrepant results from leading to choices that were not originally planned.

Although the first steps have been taken to introduce these methods, it is still relatively common to collect data first and only then publish the methods that were used to analyse them. The transition to pre-registration protocols is relatively slow, partly because the policy of many scientific journals needs to be adapted to this method. It is highly likely, however, that this trend will continue in the coming decades, leading to a much greater degree of openness. The possibility of storing raw data and data analysis scripts will probably also contribute to a higher degree of transparency in the future. Online publications will also allow accessing the results of a study directly from the publication, allowing for much better integration between a scientific article and the underlying data. Moreover, online data storage also offers unprecedented new opportunities for inter- national cooperation. Once a research protocol has been agreed upon, researchers in different parts of the world can each collect parts of the data and compare their findings directly with each other.

In a somewhat analogous fashion, Griffiths (2015) has called for a new cognitive revolution that is based on the analysis of the data trail that we now naturally leave behind while surfing the Internet. These data, which are nowadays of particular interest to Internet businesses because of their advertising potential, are in principle also of interest to cognitive psychologists because they can offer insights into judgement and deci- sion-making processes that cannot be studied in any other way, or only with great difficulty. Until recently, cognitive psychology studies were mainly carried out in the form of computer tasks that were administered in the laboratory.

Since the outbreak of the Covid-19 pandemic in early 2020, focus has shifted to conducting online experiments. Here, experiments are brought to the participants homes via a web browser. This procedure has the obvious advantage that researchers can collect a large amount of data in a short amount of time, and several online platforms, such as Amazon's Mechanical Turk (https:// www.mturk.com), have specialised in presenting online experiments or questionnaires. Note, however, that this procedure also comes with several disadvantages, one of them being a loss of control: experimenters of online experiments are no longer able to precisely monitor the extent to which participants follow instructions, which increases the risk of biases in the results. Participants may also be less motivated to complete an experiment, and response time measurements may become less meaningful.

Response time measurements can be a problem in online experiments anyway, since the Internet is based on data transmission protocols that are not intrinsically real- time. The use of these protocols may induce time delays. Although most online platforms dedicated to online experiments aim to limit these delays by handing off the timing control to the web browser, caution is still needed in these cases.

As such, the period from about 1985 to the present may, in a sense, be considered a golden age of cognitive psy- chology research. In earlier times, accurate reaction times could only be measured using specialist devices that were developed by instrument makers for one specific purpose. In the 1980s, these instruments were gradually replaced by personal computers (PCs). Although these computers were extremely slow by today's standards, they could operate in real-time, making highly accurate reaction time measurements possible.

Modern computers may be much faster, but they typi- cally no longer operate in real-time, so there is a danger of disruptions in reaction time measurements. This can be a particular problem when the computer in question is performing many tasks in the background. Although there is still a large market for fast PCs these days, par- ticularly for running performance-demanding games or performing large computational tasks, the market for these is declining, in favour of mobile phones, tablets, and laptops. A consequence of this may be that in the future experimental psychologists may again have to acquire specialised equipment that is specifically developed to carry out experiments. In contrast to the traditional instruments, these newly developed devices will most likely be computer-controlled, however, albeit based on specialised devices such as Arduino microcontrollers.

24.9.2 PERCEPTION, MOTOR SKILLS, AND INTEGRATION

In terms of content, there have also been several past developments that hold much promise for the future. As already widely discussed in earlier chapters, there have been many studies in the field of perceptual and motor processes that have attempted to explain how these processes are related. This has forced us to reinterpret some classic conclusions from neuroscience. For example, in Chapter 3 we were introduced to the observation that the role of the primary motor cortex has not yet been firmly established. For example, Kao and Hennequin (2018) report results suggesting that the motor cortex is not the primary controller of motor functions, but that this brain region is a dynamic system, itself under the control of other neural structures. This idea is consistent with other observations suggesting that sensory brain areas also play an important role in the initiation of actions, for example in the form of a simulation model of our body (Brecht, 2017).

Brecht's (2017) body model fits nicely into recent theoretical frameworks that argue that control of one's own body plays a crucial role in cognitive processes. Although this idea of embodied cognition has been around since the late 1990s, recent developments have given this realisation a central place, for example by emphasising the role of emotions in cognitive control processes (Inzlicht, Bartholow, & Hirsh, 2015) or by studying the role of factors such as stress and emotion on learning processes (Trapp, O'Doherty, & Schwabe, 2018). In the past decade, much research has focused on how these processes relate to each other and how the interactions between perception, motor control, attention, cognitive control, emotion, motivation, and learning processes take place (see fig 24.11).

Due to the increased interest in our body's role in cognitive functions, much research currently focuses on how we signal threats to our bodies. Partly for this reason, there is increasing academic interest in the peripersonal space, or the immediate space surrounding our bodies

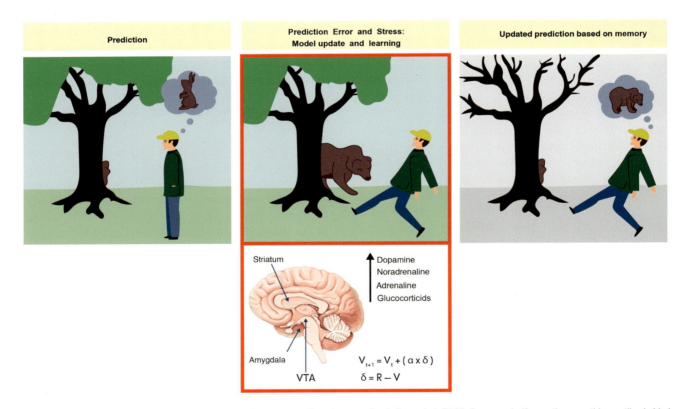

Figure 24.11 The relationship between perception, prediction, stress, and learning according to Trapp et al. (2018). For example, if we notice something rustling behind a tree, we may suspect it to be a harmless rabbit, but are then confronted with an aggressive bear. This will result in a strong prediction error and a strong stress response. The combined stress response and prediction error results in the experience being strongly anchored in memory. Moreover, our prediction will be updated (here formally represented as a delta function).

(see Chapters 8 and 9). For example, Bufacchi and Iannetti (2018) argue that peripersonal space is not a clearly defined area with an unambiguous boundary, but the transition between peripersonal space and extrapersonal space is gradual. In addition, Bufacchi and Iannetti describe that the shape of peripersonal space can be influenced by a multitude of factors, including walking, the use of tools, the valence of stimuli, and also by social cues. This also makes the peripersonal space unmistakably related to action selection.

24.9.3 MEMORY

Memory research is also currently undergoing a clear evolution, in which the classic distinction between procedural and declarative memories is being questioned in favour of models that identify memory processes on the basis of the underlying neural processes (Cabeza & Moscovitch, 2013; Henke, 2010). This also appears to blur the classic distinction between short- and long-term memory, so that many new studies have focused on the role of the hippocampus in consolidating memories. For example, Barry and Maguire (2019) reject the classical interpretation of consolidation processes and replace it with a theoretical model in which the hippocampus is actively involved in reconstructing recent memories on the basis of fragmented memory traces stored in the neocortex.

In addition to the hippocampus, the striatum has also attracted a strong interest from cognitive neuroscientists in the past decade. Although it has been known since the 1950s that the nucleus accumbens, a part of the ventral striatum, is crucially involved in motivational processes, it was originally assumed that the striatum, and in particular the dorsal striatum (as part of the basal ganglia), is involved in automating motor processes, sequence learning, and procedural memory. Recent cognitive control theories suggest, however, that both the dorsal and ventral striatum are crucially involved in the regulation of adaptive behaviour (Cools, 2016; Holroyd & Yeung, 2012). Moreover, activation of the ventral striatum appears to be strongly associated with adolescents' risk-taking behaviour (van Duijvenvoorde, Peters, Braams, & Crone, 2016). Given these developments, it is highly likely that further research into the role of the striatum will occupy a very prominent place in cognitive neuroscience in the coming decades.

24.9.4 HIGHER COGNITION AND SOCIAL COGNITION

Studies of higher cognition have traditionally distinguished between intuitive and deliberate processing, or in other words between a System 1 and a System 2 process (Stanovich & West, 2000). This distinction is typically well capable of explaining how cognitive biases arise, and the studies involved have identified several clear sources of these biases. Still, a key challenge for the future will be to identify the neural mechanisms underlying these cognitive processes. For example, how do we extract information from a problem description and how do we use this information to generate a mental representation? Which neural processes contribute to updating this representation? In addition, most importantly, to what extent can cultural factors influence mental representations (Verguts & Chen, 2017)?

Culture also plays an important role in the creation of social norms and conventions. For cognitive psychologists, this is still relatively unexplored territory. In a literature review, Hawkins, Goodman, and Goldstone (2019) discuss the results of several studies that have investigated which cognitive processes are involved in the formation of social norms and how these norms can, in turn, influence our cognitive processes. Now, at the beginning of the 21st century, we are more connected than ever before, and social media is beginning to connect individuals on a global scale for the first time in human history. Yet, at the same time, society appears to be more divided than ever, with many groups accusing each other of spreading 'fake news' (Pennycook & Rand, 2021). Why do some individuals blatantly reject established facts? What are the consequences of global connectedness on our development? How does it affect the formation of our opinions, analytic capabilities, and our ability to perceive social deception? The first 20 years since the introduction of social media were characterised by a high degree of anarchy and a lack of social conventions. Do children who grow up with social media spontaneously develop social norms for this? What cognitive processes underlie this? Questions like these will certainly play an important role in the decades to come.

24.9.5 IN CONCLUSION

Questions about the nature of the human soul are, as stated in Chapter 1, probably as old as humanity itself, yet they are still relevant today. For this reason, cognitive psychology is a dynamic science, which, after centuries of a relatively dormant existence within philosophy, blossomed towards the end of the 20th century and has undergone a gigantic development in the second half of its existence up to now. The end of this development is not yet in sight. The last two decades have seen the introduction of theoretical frameworks that have the potential to be of great explanatory power and have inspired countless scholars to undertake new studies in order to test specific theories formulated on the basis of these frameworks. New developments in society ensure that new scientific questions become topical and new developments in the discipline ensure that new research methods become available. In this respect, cognitive psychology is more exciting than ever!

24.10 SUMMARY

The central theme of this chapter involved error processing and the consequences of making errors in everyday life. Errors and error processing play an important role in recent theoretical models of human cognition. Although theoretical models based on prediction and the correction of prediction errors originally arose from visual perception, these predictive models are now also applied to a variety of domains within cognitive psychology, and the interpretation of signals from the body plays an important role in this. Recent theoretical models aim to find explanations for concepts such as bounded rationality or irrational fears.

Mental conditions that are characterised by a great diversity of symptoms can possibly also be (partly) explained from the perspective of a predictive coding mechanism, whereby too much weight can be assigned to either the predictions or the prediction errors. This erroneous weighting, possibly in combination with aberrant processing of the prediction errors, can result in a range of cognitive dysfunctions that can form the basis for schizophrenia or autism, respectively.

In our everyday lives, we often make mistakes, and, under critical circumstances, human errors can have fatal consequences and lead to major disasters. Examples include plane crashes, maritime disasters, or major medical blunders. James Reason identified several different types of errors. Slips and lapses are non-intentional and the result of incorrectly applying an action plan that is in itself correct. A mistake, on the other hand, is the result of applying an incorrect action plan. Mistakes are often the result of an error of judgement in uncertain situations. In addition, Reason makes a distinction between mistakes and violations. Violations are formed by deliberate deviations from an action plan, for example to save work or to gain time.

Errors or violations of procedures may have immediate or latent consequences. A latent consequence occurs when the consequences of incorrect procedures only manifest themselves under very specific circumstances. These procedures are often situated at the level of the organisation, the supervision, or in preconditions. Acute failure is often the direct result of specific actions.

In recent decades, there has been a far-reaching automation of many complex tasks. This development is particularly evident in aviation. Although automation has had a positive effect on safety in most cases, it has also resulted in the fact that crews sometimes rely too much on automated systems, thereby failing to notice critical problems. In order to function optimally, flight crews must have situational awareness at all times.

Even in basic visual search tasks, people can make mistakes when what they are looking for is extremely rare. Airport security officers must screen luggage for the presence of weapons, and when these target stimuli are extremely rare, they are often missed when they are present. A possible reason why target stimuli are missed is that security guards often have to search for multiple targets, which implies that they have to keep multiple search templates active in working memory. Because reporting the presence of a weapon is a relatively automatic process, this may result in a strong response bias, making participants inclined to quickly report 'no'. In studies where participants cannot correct their responses, this can result in a strong underestimation.

The far-reaching automation of the labour process in the 20th century has also resulted in many more people performing cognitive work than physical work. Mental fatigue is associated with prolonged mental labour, but probably cannot be explained by this. Instead, evidence for a relationship between mental fatigue, cognitive control, and motivation has been found. According to this view, mental fatigue is the result of an imbalance between the effort invested and the degree to which intended goals are achieved. Particularly in situations where people fail to achieve their goals but are forced to continue working, this can result in chronic mental fatigue and possible burn-out.

Another consequence of the extensive automation is that we now work with computers almost every day. The software we have to deal with on a daily basis must be attuned to human cognition, whereby a number of properties are of crucial importance. Automatic actions must not result in fatal errors, the user must be given feedback about the operation of the programme at all times and must have freedom of choice but at the same time irrelevant options must be hidden from the user as much as possible. If possible, the software must guide the user through the workflow, and the visual presentation of information must remain clear, so that visual search processes are optimised.

At present, locked-in patients today can communicate via brain-computer interfaces. These systems register various neurophysiological signals and attempt to deduce the patient's intentions based on these signals. These intentions can be converted to written text or used to control equipment. EEG measurements can also be used for lie detection. Here, neural responses are recorded while objects are shown that the suspect denies knowing. When the suspect does recognise these objects, this may be reflected in an EEG P300 component or other physiological markers. Cognitive strategies can be used, however, to circumvent EEG-based lie detection tests. Recent developments imply that lie detection is also possible on the basis of reaction times.

The scientific study of human cognition is an ongoing process. New developments in the coming decades will possibly focus on the implementation of new research protocols, ways of exchanging data, and the way in which the results of these studies will be published. Substantive developments will mainly focus on the question of how the various research areas within cognitive psychology are related to each other.

NOTE

1 This description was originally written while the author had not yet started watching the prequel 'Better call Saul', which does provide some additional details about both Salamanca's background and the nature of his condition.

FURTHER READING

Dekker, S. (2013). *The field guide to understanding human error*. Aldershot, UK: Ashgate Publishing.

Dismukes, R. K. (2009). *Human error in aviation*. London, UK: Routledge.

Hohwy, J. (2013). *The predictive mind*. Oxford, UK: Oxford University Press.

Reason, J. (1990). *Human error*. Cambridge, UK: Cambridge University Press.

Rosenfield, J. P. (2018). *Detecting concealed information and deception: Recent developments*. Amsterdam, NL: Elsevier.

Appendix: Bayesian inference

The past decade has been characterised by a renewed interest in an age-old theorem that was formulated by the British Presbyterian minister and logician Thomas Bayes (1701–1761). This theorem describes how one should adjust one's beliefs in light of new evidence. The classic formulation of this theorem is as follows:

$$P(A \mid B) = \frac{P(B \mid A) P(A)}{P(B)} \qquad (A.1)$$

In this equation P(A|B) is a conditional probability, that is, the probability that event A occurs, given that B is true. P(B|A) is also a conditional probability, that is, the probability that event B occurs, given that A is true. P(A) and P(B) are here the probabilities of A or B without any conditions. These are also known as the unconditional probabilities or prior probabilities.

The following example makes the equation more concrete. Suppose a new disease has broken out and, based on previous research, we know that it affects 0.5% of the population. A new test has recently been developed that can easily determine whether someone is affected by the disease. It takes a sample of saliva from the patient, and, if the patient is affected by the disease, the sample causes the test to turn black. The test is 99% sensitive and 99% selective. In other words, the test has a 99% chance of being positive for someone who has been affected by the disease and a 99% chance of being negative for someone who has not been affected by the disease. A doctor tests a random person, and the test turns black. What is the probability that this person is affected by the disease? Try to formulate an answer to this question before continuing to read.

When we put these data into the Bayesian equation, we get the following result:

$$P(Sick \mid +) = \frac{P(+ \mid Sick) P(Sick)}{P(+)}$$

$$= \frac{P(+ \mid Sick) P(Sick)}{P(+ \mid Sick) P(Sick) + P(+ \mid Healthy) P(Healthy)}$$

In the equation, P(Sick|+) represents the probability that someone is sick, given a positive result. This probability is represented by the sensitivity of the test multiplied by the prior probability that someone is actually sick [P(+|Sick)P(Sick)], divided by the prior probability of obtaining a positive test result: [P(+)]. Further elaboration of this example yields:

$$P(Sick \mid +) = \frac{0.99 \times 0,005}{0.99 \times 0.005 + 0,01 \times 0.995} \approx 0.33$$

Thus, the probability that a randomly selected patient who tests positive is actually ill is less than one in three, despite the high reliability of the test. In everyday life, we often do not consider the low prior probability that someone is actually sick, so we often wrongly overestimate the chances of this kind of rare event. The prior probability is also known as the incidence or the base rate.

How can we now use this equation to determine the extent to which we should adapt our views in light of new evidence? Wagenmakers, Morey, and Lee (2016) describe how this can be done by simply rewriting equation (A.1) as:

$$P(A \mid B) = P(A) \times \frac{P(B \mid A)}{P(B)} \qquad (A.2)$$

This rewrite makes it clear that the conditional probability P(A|B) is the product of two factors, namely the prior probability of A on the one hand and the quotient of the conditional and prior probabilities of B on the other.

Here, the prior probability P(A) is an assumption about the probability of A that we make before we actually have access to data. We can use this prior to make a more accurate estimate of the probability of A by collecting data. We do that by multiplying the prior with a predictive updating factor (Wagenmakers, Morey, et al., 2016), which is formed by the third term in the equation, P(B|A)/P(B). The result is an a posteriori estimate of the probability of A after the data have been collected. In Bayesian terms, a posteriori estimate is also known as the posterior.

Intuitively, we can understand the prior as the background knowledge we have about a given situation, without having specific data at our disposal. In the example of the new disease that has broken out, this background information can be formed by scientific articles that we have read about the disease. Based on this information, we can determine that a random person we meet has an a priori chance of 0.005 of being affected by the disease. Now we start collecting data: we test this person. The test's reliability data informs us that $P(B|A) = 0.99$, while we determine that $P(B) = 0.0149$. The quotient of these two numbers constitutes the updating factor, which we must apply to revise our a priori hypothesis about our randomly selected patient being affected by the disease. After taking the test, and finding a positive test result, it has become about 66.4 times more likely that this person is affected by the disease than before we took the test. However, given the low base rate of 0.005, this shift still results in a probability of only about one in three that the person we tested is actually affected by the disease.

These examples illustrate two important aspects of the Bayesian inference method. First, they illustrate the importance of the base rate (or in Bayesian terms, the prior). The extremely low base rate of the hypothetical disease in our example illustrates that even an extremely reliable test method can only have a relatively limited diagnostic value when the base rate is very low. The second aspect illustrated, however, is the power of data collection, especially when these data are reliable: after taking the test, the person is more than 66 times more likely to be affected by the disease than before the test.

But what is the impact of reliability on the Bayesian inference method? Let's illustrate that by using the previous example, but now using a different test. The new test uses a completely different method to determine the disease, which is less reliable. The sensitivity and selectivity are both 90%. We apply this new test again to a random person; the test is again positive. What is the probability that this person is affected by the disease? We now use $P(B|A) = 0.90$ and we determine that $P(B) = 0.104$. We therefore find a predictive updating factor of 8.66. Thus, after taking the test it has become more likely by a factor of 8.66 that the person subjected to the test is ill, so that after testing the probability is now 0.043.

These examples imply that we need extremely reliable tests to get a reliable diagnosis when base rates are extremely low. How can we improve the reliability of our diagnostic test? A naive thought might be that we need to improve the reliability of the test even further, but on closer inspection this turns out not to be a good idea. If we were to develop a test based on our given example that increases the posterior probability of being affected by the disease to at least 0.9, we would need to achieve a sensitivity and selectivity of about 0.99944.

However, the beauty of the Bayesian inference method is that we can continue to use the a posteriori probability as

a prior in a new evaluation. If we monetarily return to the result of our first test, we have found that the probability of this person actually being affected by the disease is about 0.33. We can now use this as a prior and administer the second test, which also gives a positive result. With 0.33 as the prior and a reliability of 90%, this test now results in an updating factor of 2.47, which raises the probability of the chosen person being ill to 0.82. We have a third test available, but this one has a very limited reliability (sensitivity and selectivity of 70%). This test is also positive, which, using 0.82 as a prior, results in a new updating factor of 1.11, raising the probability that the person being tested is affected by the disease to 0.91.

The general idea will be clear: every additional positive test increases the probability that the person who is tested is affected by the disease, whereby the extent to which we have to adjust our assessment depends on both the reliability of the test and our prior. The more reliable the test, the more impactful this information gets. Although it is not illustrated in the example, there could also be a negative test result, and this test would actually reduce the estimated probability somewhat. Ultimately, the combination of different tests will give an ever better estimate of the probability that the person in question is actually affected by the disease.

These examples are relatively simple. We are trying to estimate the probability that a person is affected by a disease or not based on the available evidence. In mathematical terms, we are using a discrete variable, disease, which can take on two values (affected or not affected). Mathematically, this can be represented using the values of 1 (affected) or 0 (not affected). In other words, we are trying to estimate the probability that disease has the value 1. We can also extend the Bayesian model, however, and use it to estimate the relative probability that a continuous variable falls within a given range. A nice example of this is provided by Wagenmakers, Morey, et al. (2016) and it involves estimating the IQ of a randomly selected prisoner, named Bob, based on a number of IQ tests. The background story is that Bill's lawyers want to prove that Bob's IQ is less then 70, so he can be acquitted from killing his wife. For the normal population, the average IQ is defined as 100, with a standard deviation of 15. IQ is a continuous variable, which means that in principle it can take on any value between 0 and infinity. In practice, however, it is most likely that the IQ of a random person will be somewhere between 70 and 130. We can express the distribution of IQ scores as a **probability density function**.

For prisoners, it has been established that their average IQ is 75, with a standard deviation of 20. The relatively large standard deviation found here implies that there is a relatively large spread among the IQs of prisoners. When we use these data as an a priori estimate of Bob's IQ, we

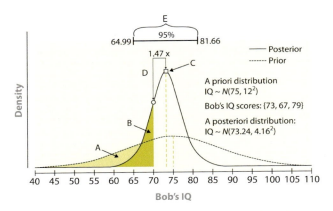

Figure A.1 An example of two probability density functions. These functions describe the uncertainty of Bob's IQ, before (prior) and after (posterior) taking a series of IQ tests. The shaded part of the curve marked with (A) represents the a priori probability that Bob's IQ is less than 70; the area under the curve marked (B) represents this probability after obtaining the results of the IQ tests. The probability that Bob's IQ is 73.24 (point C on the curve), is 1.47 times greater than the probability that it is 70 (point D on the curve). Finally, the confidence interval (marked E) shows that we can determine with 95% certainty that Bob's true IQ will be somewhere between 64.99 and 81.66). (source: Wagenmakers, Morey, et al., 2016)

have to take this uncertainty into account. This is shown in Figure A.1 by the dotted curve, which represents the a priori probability density function of Bob's IQ. The total area under this curve is 1, and this area represents the total probability that Bob's IQ is somewhere between 0 and infinity. If we now want to know the probability that Bob's IQ is less than 70, we only consider the left part of the curve (marked A in the figure). The area of this part of the curve (approximately 1/3) represents the probability, based on the a priori available data, that Bob's IQ is less than 70.

After the administration of a number of additional tests, which were completed by Bob himself, we find an a posteriori estimate which is much more accurate. This estimate is represented by the solid curve. Based on new tests, we find a new estimate of Bob's IQ, namely 73.24. Although this estimate is lower than that of the population average of 75, we also notice that, based on these new measurements, the probability of Bob's IQ being lower than 70 has decreased significantly. Why is that? The reason is that the probability density function representing the posterior estimate of Bob's IQ also has a total area that is equal to 1. What is striking, however, is that this curve is much more strongly centred around the average. This steepness is an indication that the probability that Bob's actual IQ matches the test's scores is significantly larger than that his IQ matches the a priori estimates. The probability that Bob's IQ is less than 70 is, in this case, represented by the shaded area B, and this area covers about 1/5 of the total curve. Thus, the a posteriori probability that Bob's IQ is smaller than 70 is also reduced to about 1/5.

Although these examples concern relatively simple probability calculations, more and more evidence has become available in the last two decades which suggests that the brain also gathers evidence in a way that resembles Bayesian principles. The brain forms priors on the basis of background knowledge and previous experience. These priors take the form of generative models that generate predictions about our environment. The evidence we gather from the environment, for example through our senses, is then used as a predictive updating factor to adjust these representations.

Glossary

Access awareness	A fully conscious experience that is accompanied by attending the evoking stimulus.
Accommodation reflex	The automatic response of the eye lens to the changes in distance of the object that the eye fixates on.
Achromatopsia	A neuropsychological condition that is characterised by the inability to perceive colours.
Action potential	A relatively large electrical voltage spike that is generated on the soma of a neuron, resulting from the sudden depolarisation of the neuron's resting potential.
Adaptive expertise	A form of expertise involving individuals who continue to grow in their field because of their intentional commitment to solving problems in new and innovative ways.
Ad hoc category	A class of categories that an individual can spontaneously generate for specific purposes.
Additional flash illusion	An audiovisual illusion in which two auditory stimuli that are presented in rapid succession have the effect of causing one visual flash to be perceived as two flashes.
Additive factors method	An experimental method that can estimate the duration of the individual stages of a psychological process by recording reaction times.
Adjacency pair	A conversational unit, such as a greeting or a question, that implies a reversal of roles between interlocutors.
Affect	The nature (positive or negative) of an emotional state of mind.
Affect misattribution procedure	A procedure that requires participants to evaluate the affective value of a neutral stimulus while these evaluations can potentially be influenced by a prime stimulus involving racial stereotypes.
Affective significance	The positive or negative motivational value that specific items might have for the organism.
Afferent	Incoming.
Afferent neurons	Neurons that project information from internal organs and sensory systems to the brain.
Affirmation of the consequent	An invalid inference rule from propositional logic that is drawn by inferring the inverse of the original statement.
Affordance	The description of the potential actions that we could perform with a visual object, which according to James Gibson, would be automatically activated upon perceiving the object.
Agency	An action or intervention that results in a specific effect.
Agrammatism	A neuropsychological condition resulting in speech production that is characterised by a lack of grammatical structure.
Akinetic mutism	A neuropsychological condition that is characterised by a marked reduction in, or complete absence of, spontaneous behaviour, while all motor skills are still intact.

Akinetopsia	A neuropsychological condition that is characterised by the inability to perceive motion; usually due to a lesion in area V5/MT.
Algorithm	A process or set of rules that are used in a calculation or problem-solving strategy.
Alliesthesia	The change in the hedonic value that a sensation evokes.
Allographs	The basic shapes of letters described as a specific sequence of pen strokes.
Allostasis	A self-regulating process that leads to changes in the organism, resulting in its growth and development.
Amacrine cells	Inhibitory interneurons in the retina, which are involved in transmitting the output of the photoreceptors to the retinal ganglion cells.
Amnesia	Memory loss. See also Anterograde amnesia and Retrograde amnesia.
Amusia	Tone deafness.
Amygdala	A brain structure in the forebrain. It is part of the limbic system and involved in the processing of emotions.
Amyloid plaques	Protein fragments that can form between the cortical neurons. Their presence is indicative of Alzheimer's disease.
Anaphor resolution	The linking of a pronoun or noun to a previous noun.
Anatomical modularity	An assumption from cognitive neuropsychology suggesting that cognitive modules are localised in specific brain areas.
Anaxonic neurons	A type of neuron where the axon is indistinguishable from the dendrites.
Anomia	A neuropsychological condition, a subclass of aphasia, that is characterised by impairment in the ability to name objects.
Anterior	An anatomical term indicating that a structure is in front of a reference object.
Anterior cingulate	The frontal part of the cingulate cortex; a brain area that is, among others, involved in many cognitive control functions.
Anterograde amnesia	A form of amnesia that is characterised by the patient's inability to retain new memories that date after the event that caused the amnesia.
Anticipatory goal reactions	A mechanism describing how a response to a specific goal can be triggered by a stimulus.
Anti-saccade task	A commonly applied cognitive task that is used to measure response inhibition, involving participants making a saccade in the direction opposite to the direction in which a fixation cross moves.
Aphasia	A neuropsychological condition characterised by a reduced ability to understand or produce language.
Appraisal theories	A collection of theories that describe how emotional responses are the result of determining the subjective value of an emotional event or its expectation.
Apprehension span	An estimate of the number of elements that our conscious awareness can perceive simultaneously.
Ascending reticular activating system	A nucleus of neurons in the reticular formation of the brainstem whose axons project to the rest of the brain. It is involved in the regulation of arousal.
Asian disease problem	A problem that is commonly used in decision-making research, in which participants must choose between a deterministic option and a probabilistic option.
Association	The formation of new thoughts or cognitive content on the basis of combining two or more simultaneous observations or combining observations with pre-existing thoughts or memories.
Association areas	Cortical brain areas that are not directly involved in the processing of sensory or motor signals. Signals from different sensory and motor modalities were originally believed to converge in these areas. The term is mainly of historical value.
Associativist theories of thought	Ideas that originate from an ancient Greek philosophical movement, which state that the mind is composed of elements, especially sensations and ideas that are organised through associations.

Attention	An essential cognitive function that allows humans and other animals to dynamically select continuously from all the information that is available externally in the outside world or internally in the organism itself, such that more neural processing capacity can be allocated to it.
Attentional blink	The phenomenon of not being able to process a second stimulus shortly after processing the first one.
Attentional capture	The phenomenon whereby salient stimuli attract attention in an automatic, bottom-up fashion.
Attractor dynamics	A mechanism that causes a dynamic system to converge to a stable state.
Audience design	The process by which speakers adapt what they say to the needs of their audience.
Auditory analysis system	A part of the three-route model for spoken word recognition and reproduction. The system is involved in extracting phonemes or other sounds from the speech signal.
Auditory brainstem response	A series of five specific peaks in the EEG evoked by the presentation of a short tone.
Auditory scene analysis	The set of neural and cognitive processes that groups perceived acoustic signals into auditory sources. See also Segmentation.
Autobiographical memory	A memory system consisting of a collection of episodes from our personal lives.
Autonomic nervous system	Part of the nervous system that regulates the functioning of our internal organs. The autonomic nervous system consists of the sympathetic and parasympathetic nervous system.
Availability heuristic	A rule of thumb that is characterised by the fact that we consider events that are readily accessible from memory to be more likely than events that are not directly accessible.
Axon	Extension of a neuron across which a signal is passed on to an adjacent neuron by means of an action potential.
Backpropagation	A technique for improving the performance of neural networks by adjusting the weights of the connections between the nodes in the network.
Backward conditioning	A form of classical conditioning in which the conditioned stimulus is presented after the unconditioned stimulus, resulting in the extinction of a conditioned response.
Backward inferences	See Bridging inference.
Basal ganglia	A group of subcortical brain areas that are involved in the planning of sequences of actions.
Base rate	The relative occurrence of a given characteristic in the population.
Basilar membrane	Part of the cochlea, in the inner ear, where the cilia that register sound waves are located.
Basis functions	Linear combinations of non-linear functions that can describe complex mathematical transformations.
Belief bias	The tendency to accept conclusions of reasoning problems more readily when the premises are believable than when the premises are unbelievable.
Bias	A systematic deviation from a norm or rationality in a judgement.
Biased competition theory	A theory describing attention as a competition between multiple inputs and representations; this competition can take place at any processing stage and be affected by top-down processes.
Bigram	A unit of adjacent letters.
Bilingual advantage effect	The conjecture that bilingualism is advantageous for cognitive control.
Bilingualism	The ability to master two languages.
Binding of item and context model	A theoretical model aimed at explaining the difference between familiarity and recollection.
Binding problem	A theoretical problem that arises from the idea that specialised brain areas contribute to the processing of individual stimulus properties, while subjectively we experience our environment as a unity.

Binocular disparity	A consequence of both eyes registering a slightly different image of our environment, allowing depth to be perceived.
Binocular rivalry	The phenomenon that, upon presenting a different image to each eye, conscious perception constantly switches between these two images.
Biological motion	A special form of motion that is characteristic of biological organisms.
Bipolar neuron	A type of neuron that connects the photoreceptors in the retina to the retinal ganglion cells that transmit the optical signal to the brain.
Bistable images	An image that can be interpreted in two different ways. Only one of the two interpretations can be active at any given time, but conscious experience can switch between them.
Bit	Binary digit; a basic unit of information introduced by Claude Shannon that forms the basis for digital information processing.
Bivariate concepts	Concepts that are defined by the presence or absence of a specific property.
Blindsight	A neuropsychological condition, usually due to damage to visual area V1, characterised by the inability to consciously perceive objects, while the ability to respond to these objects is still partly intact.
Block design	An experimental design, where all trials belonging to one condition are grouped in blocks.
Bottom-up processing	A form of information processing that is driven by the properties of a stimulus.
Bounded rationality	The idea, formulated by Herbert Simon, that our rationality is constrained by both environmental factors and limitations in processing capacity.
Bridging inference	An inference that is made to establish the coherence between the present part of a text and the previous part. Also known as backward inference.
Broad focus	Part of the single storage model of working memory. More specifically, a part of long-term memory that has a higher state of activation, allowing information in this part of memory to influence task goals.
Broaden and build theory	A theory, developed by Barbara Frederickson, proposing that positive emotions result in a broader focus of attention.
Broca's aphasia	A neuropsychological condition, characterised by non-fluent speech, and associated with damage to the left inferior frontal gyrus.
Brown-Peterson paradigm	An experimental method developed in the late 1950s to measure trace decay in memory.
Cardinality	The number of elements in a set.
Categorical perception	The phenomenon that intermediate forms of two phonemes are always perceived as either one or the other phoneme, but never as an intermediary.
Categorisation	The cognitive process of determining to which category a stimulus or concept belongs.
Caudate nucleus	A subcortical brain region that is part of the basal ganglia. It is involved in motor control and several other functions, such as procedural and associative learning and the inhibitory control of actions.
Causal knowledge	Knowledge about the underlying causal structure of a problem.
Cell assembly	Groups of neurons involved in performing a specific action or representing a specific concept.
Center for Open Science	A non-profit organisation that promotes openness and transparency in scientific research.
Central bottleneck	The idea that central decision processes can only perform one task at a time.
Central executive	A part of working memory that is assumed to be regulating access to, and the manipulation of, information stored in working memory.
Central nervous system	The brain and spinal cord.
Cerebellum	A part of the hindbrain that is involved in motor control.
Cerebral cortex	The outer shell surrounding the forebrain.
Cerebrum	Part of the forebrain, consisting of the cerebral cortex and several subcortical nuclei.
Change blindness	A manifestation of the limited capacity of attention, resulting in the failure to notice changes in visual displays.

Childhood amnesia	The fact that most adults have no memories from the first two or three years of their lives.
Chunk (memory)	The grouping of related items that can be stored as a unit in short-term memory.
Chunk (motor process)	A group of motor commands that are combined into one unit to be executed.
Classical conditioning	A learning method that was developed by the Russian physiologist Ivan Pavlov, in which a conditioned stimulus is paired with an unconditioned stimulus by association.
Coarticulation	The phenomenon of preparing several phonemes simultaneously by our speech production process, causing the specific sounds of each phoneme to be influenced by both the preceding and the following phoneme.
Cochlea	Part of the inner ear that converts sound vibrations into a neuronal signal.
Cocktail party problem	The problem of separating several overlapping auditory sources in complex environments, such that we are only aware of one source.
Cognitive architectures	A set of computer models that aim to simulate major cognitive functions.
Cognitive bias modification	An experimental technique for teaching people to acquire or remove cognitive biases.
Cognitive control	The ability to coordinate one's thoughts and actions according to one's internal goals.
Cognitive interview	A structured way of interviewing witnesses that aims to obtain the most complete and reliable eyewitness testimony possible.
Cognitive map	A mental representation of the spatial organisation of our environment.
Cognitive miserliness	The idea that humans are economical with their time and with the effort that they put into tasks that require elaboration.
Cognitive neuropsychology	A scientific discipline that aims to explain cognitive functions from behavioural changes that occur as a result of brain damage.
Cognitive neuroscience	A scientific discipline that aims to unravel the relationship between brain functions and behaviour by studying activity in the living brain during the performance of cognitive tasks.
Cognitive schema	A cognitive structure used to organise knowledge.
Cognitive self	Part of our self-image; more specifically, the aspects of the self-image that play a role in generating autobiographical memories.
Cohort theory	A cognitive theory aimed at describing how spoken words are recognised. It assumes that words are selected and eliminated via the accumulation of information.
Cold cognition	An approach within cognitive psychology that attempts to disregard emotions as much as possible.
Colour constancy	The phenomenon whereby we perceive the colour of objects in our environment as constant under a particularly wide range of lighting conditions.
Common ground	The knowledge and views shared by a speaker and a listener that can help promote understanding.
Commons dilemma	A classic example of a social dilemma which describes how actions that are good for the individual can have a negative impact on society.
Comorbidity	The co-occurrence of two or more mental conditions.
Complexity	Mathematically expressed as the degree to which a set of instructions can be compressed.
Computational model	A computer model that aims to approximate the cognitive processes employed by humans as closely as possible.
Computer metaphor	An approach, adopted in cognitive psychology, in which the operation of a computer is considered as a model for human information processing.
Conceptualisation	The ability to synthesise and represent the qualitative properties of individual objects or ideas.
Conditional reasoning	A form of reasoning based on classic inferential logic, in which IF. . . THEN relationships play a central role.

687

Conditioned response	A response to a conditioned stimulus.
Conditioned stimulus	A stimulus that is associated with an unconditioned stimulus through classical conditioning.
Cone-excitability ratio	The ratio of excitability of a specific colour receptor, which is mainly determined by the properties of the surface reflecting the light and not by the light source.
Confirmation bias	A cognitive bias that is characterised by the search for information that intends to confirm one's pre-existing beliefs.
Conflict monitoring	A process attributed to the anterior cingulate gyrus that is involved in regulating cognitive control processes.
Conjunction fallacy	The erroneous assumption that the conjunction of two properties is more likely than that of either of the individual properties.
Conjunction search	A form of visual search in which a unique object is to be found that is defined by a unique combination of features that are each on their own not unique.
Consistent mapping	An experimental procedure in which a given class of stimuli is used either as a target stimulus or a distractor, but never both at the same time.
Consolidation theory	A theory that assumes that there is a long-term process of consolidating episodic memories in the hippocampus before these memories are transferred to long-term memory.
Constraint-based theories	A model of sentence interpretation based on the idea that both syntax and semantics increasingly constrain the possible interpretations of a sentence as more information becomes available.
Constructed emotion theory	A theory inspired by the predictive coding framework that states that emotions are the result of awareness of the expected bodily response to an emotional situation.
Construction integration	The process that describes how new information given in a sentence is integrated with an already existing mental representation.
Construction-integration model	A model, developed by the American psychologist Walter Kintsch, that describes how linguistic information is processed into a series of propositions that are integrated with existing background knowledge.
Continuous flash suppression	The phenomenon that, when a static image is presented to one eye and a continuously flashing image is presented to the other eye, the static image is hardly perceived at all.
Control experiments	A set of experiments necessary to rule out alternative explanations.
Converging operations	An approach in which different methods and approaches, each with their own strengths and weaknesses, all converge towards the same result or conclusion.
Cooperative principle	The principle that speakers and listeners try to collaborate to understand each other.
Corollary discharge signal	A neuronal copy of the motor signal sent to muscles. Its purpose is to allow predicting the consequences of an initiated action, for example, to maintain balance or to neutralise the effects of eye movements. See also Efferent signal and Efferent copy.
Coronal plane	A vertical plane used to divide the body into a ventral part and a dorsal part.
Corpus callosum	A bundle of nerve fibres connecting the left and right cerebral cortex.
Covert attention	The focusing of attention on a particular location without moving the eyes to that location.
Cranial nerves	A group of 12 nerves that provide communication between senses and muscles in the head and the brain.
Cross-modal correspondence	The phenomenon that specific visual and auditory percepts (e.g., low tones and large objects) are more strongly associated with each other than others.
Data compression	The process of encoding, restructuring, or otherwise modifying data in order to reduce the size of a data file.
Deafferentation	A condition that is characterised by the afferent nerves of (parts of) the body no longer being connected to the brain.

Decision-based categorisation model	A theoretical cognitive psychological model of categorisation that is based on the idea that the distinction between categories is learned on the basis of decisions that have been made about them.
Declarative knowledge	Factual knowledge.
Declarative memory	Part of long-term memory in which our consciously accessible memories are stored.
Deductive reasoning	A form of reasoning that involves determining whether a conclusion must follow from a given set of premises.
Deep brain stimulation	A form of psychosurgery in which a depth electrode inserted into the brain regulates specific brain functions through electrical stimulation.
Deep dyslexia	A form of dyslexia that is characterised not only by the pronunciation of unknown words and non-words but also by problems with the processing of word meaning.
Deep dysphasia	A neurological condition characterised by severe impairments in speech perception and production.
Default mode network	A network of brain areas that is mainly active during rest, and is associated with self-reference, autobiographical memories, and self-other perspective taking.
Dendrites	Branched extensions of a neuron that transmit signals received from other neurons to the soma.
Denial of the antecedent	An invalid type of inference in propositional logic which consists of incorrectly assuming that the inverse of a statement is also automatically valid.
Deontic judgements	A form of judgement that is based on the application of moral rules or obligations. See also Utilitarian judgements.
Deontic rule	A rule relating to social and ethical conventions and the violation thereof.
Dermatome	The part of the body to which a nerve is connected.
Dichotic listening task	A commonly used experimental procedure applied to studying the effects of auditory attention.
Dichromacy	A form of colour blindness characterised by the absence of one type of colour receptor.
Dictator game	A game used to investigate social interactions, where one participant is given a number of goods and instructed to divide them between him/herself and another participant.
Diencephalon	A part of the forebrain that sprouts from the prosencephalon during embryonic development and develops into the thalamus and hypothalamus.
Diffusion tensor imaging (DTI)	An MRI scanning technique that can measure the diffusion of water molecules in the brain. A specific application of this technique makes it possible to identify the white matter tracts.
Direct perception theory	A theory that was developed soon after the end of World War II by James Gibson which describes how the perception of movement can directly result in motor actions.
Direct retrieval	The involuntary retrieval of information from memory that is triggered by an external stimulus.
Directed forgetting	An experimental procedure involving the learning of multiple lists of items, followed by an instruction to forget the contents of one or more of these lists.
Directed retrospection	A method in which participants are given the task of writing an essay, during which they are interrupted at predetermined intervals, to indicate what they are then doing.
Discourse markers	Seemingly meaningless verbal utterances, such as 'but', 'so', and 'you know', which nevertheless play a role in facilitating the comprehension of spoken text.
Discrete sequence production task	A cognitive task that is widely used to study motor processes, especially the formation of motor chunks.
Disinterested reasoning	A form of reasoning in which one's goals or preferences are irrelevant and therefore not expected to influence the reasoning process.

Dissociation	In cognitive neuropsychology, an indication that a lesion affects one specific function.
Distractor positivity (Pd)	A positive ERP component that is associated with the suppression of salient but irrelevant stimuli.
Dominance principle	In decision-making research, the principle that the best of several comparable options will always be preferred.
Dorsal	An anatomical term indicating that a structure is located on the back side of the organism.
Dorsal root ganglia	Nodes of cell bodies of the neurons forming the sensory nerves of the body, which are located on the dorsal side just outside the spinal column.
Dorsal route	A pathway through the brain, from the primary visual cortex to the parietal areas, which is mainly involved in the processing of locations and the integration of visual input and motor actions.
Double dissociation	A stronger form of a dissociation, indicating that two experimental manipulations each have a different effect on two dependent variables.
Drive	A hypothetical process that underlies our internal state regulation. It is considered to be an important factor in motivational processes.
Dual-route cascade model	A neuropsychological model aimed at describing the conversion of written to spoken language.
Dyscalculia	A neuropsychological condition that is characterised by an impaired ability to process numerical information.
Dysexecutive syndrome	A cognitive syndrome characterised by a wide variety of problems related to inhibitory control, focus, task switching, and so on.
Dyslexia	A neuropsychological condition characterised by reading problems.
Eardrum	A thin membrane in the middle ear that vibrates with the frequencies of sound, amplifying these vibrations.
Easy problems of consciousness	A collection of phenomena and questions about consciousness that are accessible through empirical research.
Echoic memory	A buffer where auditory information is stored temporarily (< 500 ms) before it is fully attended.
Effector systems	The muscles and muscle groups that are actually used to perform a certain action.
Efferent	Outgoing.
Efference copy	A copy of a neural signal, usually a motor programme, that is used by the brain to regulate or evaluate the consequences of this programme.
Efferent neurons	Neurons that project signals from the brain to muscles or internal organs.
Egocentric heuristic	A strategy whereby listeners interpret a message on the basis of their own knowledge instead of using knowledge that is shared with the speaker.
Einstellung	The phenomenon that we are relatively bad at solving simple problems when we are focused on solving complex ones.
Elaborative rehearsal	A type of rehearsal of memorised stimuli that involves deep processing, forming associations, et cetera.
Electroconvulsive therapy	A method of treating the acute symptoms of depression by administering electric shocks that induce artificial epileptic seizures.
Electroencephalography (EEG)	A technique that is used to measure the spontaneous electrical activity of the brain by attaching electrodes to the scalp.
Electromagnetic spectrum	The full range of electromagnetic radiation frequencies.
Electromyogram (EMG)	A recording of electrical muscle activity. It is often used in psychology to determine the earliest onset of a motor response, or to investigate the excitability of the motor cortex.
Elimination-by-aspects theory	A cognitive theory that aims to describe how complex choices, based on multiple attributes, can be simplified by eliminating irrelevant aspects.

Embodied cognition	A movement within cognitive psychology that is based on the idea that human cognition is inextricably linked to the functioning of our bodies, and that bodily functions and the interpretation of signals from the body play an intrinsic role in human cognition.
Emergent property	A property of a complex system that results from the interaction of its constituent parts.
Emission theory	A theory of visual perception, formulated by the Greek philosopher Empedocles around the year 400 BCE, which is based on the idea that the eyes emit (radiate) light through an inner fire that illuminates objects in our environment.
Emotion regulation	The process of regulating the intensity and duration of an emotional response through a host of cognitive strategies.
Emotions	A usually short-lived affective state, resulting from an external stimulus or situation.
Encoding specificity principle	A principle that describes how the probability of successfully retrieving a memory will increase as a function of the overlap between the memory and the information available during retrieval.
Endogenous attention	The voluntary focusing of attention that is driven by our internal goals.
Endogenous cue	A cue that can be used to make participants voluntarily focus their attention on something in an endogenous, top-down controlled manner. Also referred to as symbolic cue.
Energetic masking	An impaired recognition of a speech signal due to interference from background noise.
Engram	The hypothetical physical representation of a memory in the brain.
Episodic buffer	A part of working memory, where auditory-phonological information and visuo-spatial information are integrated with long-term representations.
Episodic memory	The part of our memory in which personal memories are stored.
Episodic-to-semantic shift theory	A theory that assumes that episodic memories are gradually transformed into semantic memories.
Equipotentiality	The idea that one part of the cortex can take over the functionality of another part.
Equivalent exposure model	A model that aims to explain the phenomenon of colour constancy on the basis of Bayesian statistical principles.
Eriksen flanker task	A cognitive psychological task that is commonly used to measure conflict or interference between multiple stimuli.
Error-related negativity	A negative brain potential, visible in the ERP, that is elicited by an erroneous response.
Ethology	The scientific study of animal behaviour.
Event file	A hypothetical file that contains a description of the properties of an object, the context in which the object was observed, and the actions associated with it.
Event-related design	An experimental design in which trials from all conditions are intermixed.
Event-related potentials	A set of changes in brain electrical activity that are evoked by an external or internal event, such as a stimulus or response. These changes can be made visible by repeating the evoking event and averaging the corresponding segments of EEG.
Excitatory	In neurophysiology, the lowering of the resting potential, making the neuron more likely to generate an action potential.
Excitatory postsynaptic potential	A depolarisation of the postsynaptic membrane of a neuron, which increases the excitability of the cell.
Executive functions	A set of cognitive functions that are involved in achieving task goals and in allowing our behaviour to adapt flexibly to changing circumstances. Inhibition, task switching, and working memory updating are considered core aspects.
Exemplar-based	A theoretical approach that assumes that categories are defined on the basis of a collection of representative exemplars.
Exogenous attention	The involuntary focusing of attention because it is captured by a salient stimulus.

691

Exogenous cue	A cue that involuntarily captures one's attention due to its salience.
Expansion point	A static point in a moving visual scene, from which all other points appear to drift away.
Experimental method	A method of studying behaviour under controlled conditions. By manipulating specific variables, it can be determined whether these variables are the cause of the observed changes in behaviour.
Experimental psychology	A scientific discipline within psychology that studies behaviour using the experimental method.
Extinction	The diminishing of a conditioned response by the systematic removal of the unconditioned stimulus.
Face inversion effect	The effect that faces which are presented upside down are much harder to recognise than normally presented faces.
False memory	An autobiographical memory of an event that never actually happened, but which is formed by suggestion, for example by a researcher or therapist.
Falsification	The process of trying to disprove an idea, theory, or hypothesis by trying to find results that do not conform to the theory.
Fast and frugal heuristics	A set of heuristics describing how we can make a probability judgement by using just a few elementary properties.
Feature integration theory	A theory that describes visual search processes by assuming that attention binds together the different features of a stimulus.
Feature search	A type of visual search that can be used when the target object is characterised by a single distinguishing feature.
Feedback-related negativity	A negative ERP component evoked by a feedback signal.
Figurative language	A form of language in which the literal meaning is not important, as in a metaphor.
File drawer effect	A bias in the scientific literature that can arise because positive results are published but negative results are not.
Fitts' law	A psychophysical law that describes how the time required to perform a rapid movement to a target location is a function of the ratio between the distance to the location and the diameter of the target.
Fixation	The locking of the eye onto a specific location or object.
Flashbulb memory	A particularly vivid autobiographical memory that is formed at the moment of a surprising, intense, and emotional event.
Focal hand dystonia	A phenomenon often found in trained musicians, characterised by a dyscoordination of the hand, due to the fact that representations of different parts of the body overlap and interfere with each other.
Footbridge dilemma	A social dilemma in which participants must decide whether saving the lives of five individuals justifies actively killing other individuals.
Formant	The broad spectral maximum that results from an acoustic resonance of the human vocal tract.
Forward conditioning	A form of classical conditioning in which the conditioned stimulus is presented before the unconditioned stimulus.
Forward model	An internal model of our motor actions which is used to internally track the consequences of the action.
Four-term analogy problem	A structured method for investigating analogy reasoning. These are written in the form a:b::c:d.
Fovea	The centre of the retina that has the highest density of colour receptors and the location that allows us to perceive detail.
Frame (cognitive schema)	Part of a cognitive schema that describes the fixed knowledge structures of the world.
Frame (representation)	A structure that defines a set of relations that positions an object in its environment.
Framing	The influence that the form in which a problem is represented may have on our ability to solve it.

Framing effect	An effect that describes how the nature of a problem representation, for example by selectively emphasising positive or negative consequences, can influence our choices.
Frontal lobe	The most anterior part of the cerebral cortex,, which is involved in a wide range of higher cognitive control functions, such as planning, inhibition, goal maintenance, and the focusing of attention.
Frontal lobotomy	A surgical procedure that severs all connections between the prefrontal cortex and the rest of the brain in an attempt to cure psychiatric patients from their most dramatic psychotic problems.
Frontotemporal dementia	A relatively rare form of dementia that is mainly characterised by impairments in the sequencing of cognitive actions.
Functional connectivity	A measure of synchronicity across brain areas.
Functional fixation	A limitation in our ability to solve problems due to a restriction in our ability to use objects for purposes other than those they were originally designed for.
Functional modularity	The assumption, within cognitive neuropsychology, that cognitive functions are modular.
Functional MRI	A technique based on magnetic resonance imaging (MRI) that allows changes in blood flow in the brain to be tracked over time. This technique allows us to determine very precisely which brain areas are involved in a particular process.
Functional specialisation	The theory that the higher-order visual areas are characterised by the selective specialised processing of colour, shape, and motion aspects of a stimulus.
Fusiform face area	A brain area located in the temporal lobe and part of the ventral pathway, involved in the processing of facial information.
Gambler's fallacy	The logical fallacy that the outcome of a gamble is affected by previous outcomes.
Game theory	A collection of mathematical models that describe how conflict and cooperation affect intelligent rational decision-makers.
Ganglion	A cluster of neurons generally located outside the brain or spinal cord. This includes the soma of the sensory and autonomic nervous system.
Ganong effect	The phenomenon that an ambiguous phoneme that is embedded in a speech sound will be preferentially interpreted as a word rather than as a non-word.
Garden path model	A model for sentence analysis that is based on the idea that syntactic analysis precedes semantic analysis, and which attempts to form the simplest possible syntactic representation of a sentence.
General Problem Solver	A computer programme developed in the 1950s by Newell and Simon for solving well-defined problems.
Generative model	A mental representation of our environment that is actively created by the brain.
Generative retrieval	A form of retrieval of information from autobiographical memory based on an active search process.
Genetic algorithm	A dynamically adaptive algorithm used in computer sciences that is based on random variations and non-random selection.
Geons	Contraction of 'geometric icons'. Proposed by Irving Biederman, they are the building blocks of internal representations of objects.
Glia cells	A type of brain cell that fulfils various functions. Although it was initially believed that they mainly gave structure to brain tissue, they also appear to influence or modulate communication between neurons in various ways.
Global workspace theory	A theory of consciousness, originally developed by Bernard Baars and colleagues, which states that awareness is related to the integrated activity of a large network of neural and cognitive processes.
Globs	Clusters of neurons in area V4 of the visual cortex that are sensitive to colour and to some extent also to shape, but not to luminance.
Globus pallidus	A subcortical structure that is part of the basal ganglia. It is involved in the regulation of voluntary movements.

Go/no-go task	A commonly used experimental paradigm which requires participants to selectively respond or not respond to a stimulus according to a predetermined property.
Goal neglect	An extreme failure to follow task rules, due to the complexity of remembering these rules rather than to the complexity of executing them.
Grand unifying theory	A generally accepted theory that can explain all aspects of a particular phenomenon.
Graph theory	A mathematical theory that describes how logical problems can be presented as points and lines in a diagram.
Grapheme	The smallest unit of a written language, such as letters, typographic symbols, numbers, oriental characters, or punctuation marks.
Grey matter	The outer layers of the cerebral cortex, which mainly contains the soma and dendrites of cortical neurons.
Guided search	A theoretical model for visual search processes that assumes that different saliency maps are combined with each other.
Gyrus	A ridge in the cortex that results from the folding of the cortical surface.
Habituation	The alteration of a reflex by the repeated presentation of the stimulus that evokes the reflex, typically when the intensity of the evoking stimulus is low.
Hard problem of consciousness	A collection of questions about consciousness that are, by definition, inaccessible to empirical research.
Hardware	In computer terms, the electronic circuits that form the basis for computational operations. In terms of the computer metaphor, the neural circuits that shape cognitive operations.
Hebbian learning	A general learning neural learning principle that describes how the joint activity of two neurons can affect the synaptic strength between them.
Hemineglect	An attention deficit that is characterised by the inability to report information presented to a specific hemifield (usually the left side).
Herschl's gyrus	The primary auditory cortex; also known as A1.
Heuristic	Rule of thumb.
Hill climbing	A simple heuristic that describes how the next step in solving a problem will always be one that takes you one step closer to the goal.
Hippocampus	A seahorse-like structure in the forebrain and part of the limbic system that plays an important role in the formation of new memories.
Hit rate	The proportion of correct responses to a target stimulus.
Homeostasis	A self-regulating process which aims to maintain a stable internal state by means of a negative feedback loop.
Homeostatic motivation	A group of motivational processes, especially those related to the internal state regulation, which are based on homeostatic principles.
Homograph	A group of words with the same spelling, but with different meanings.
Homophone	A group of words characterised by the same pronunciation, while having a different spelling and meaning.
Horizontal cell	A type of neuron that regulates the output of multiple photoreceptors in the retina.
Hormone	An organic molecule with a signalling function. They are released by glands and can globally change the internal regulation of bodily functions.
Hub-and-spoke model	A hypothetical model for the representation of concepts in semantic memory, consisting of both abstract and sensory and motor representations of the concept.
Huntington's disease	A progressive neurological condition characterised by uncontrolled movements and emotional and cognitive impairments.
Hydraulic-drive model	A theory of internal state regulation developed by the ethologist Konrad Lorenz. The model assumes that internal motivation forces function in a manner similar to the way in which pressure builds up in a water tank.
Hyperthymic syndrome	A condition that causes some individuals to have an extremely detailed autobiographical memory.

Hypothalamic-Pituitary-Adrenal Axis (HPA)	A complex set of direct and indirect (feedback regulated) interactions between the hypothalamus, pituitary, and adrenal cortex, which jointly contribute to stress responses.
Hypothalamus	A brain structure composed of several small nuclei with various functions. One of its most important functions involves controlling the pituitary gland and thus controlling the release of hormones.
Iconic memory	The temporary retention of information in a visual buffer before attention can transfer it to long-term memory.
Ideomotor theories	A class of theories that conjectures that thinking about the consequences of an action leads to the automatic execution of this action.
Ill-defined categories	A type of category that is characterised by the fact that its members cannot be classified by an unambiguous criterion.
Ill-defined problems	A type of problem where (parts of) the initial or final state, or possible strategies are not fully specified.
Illusory figure	A visual illusion based on the perception of edges, in the absence of any contrast or colour change along these edges.
Immision theory	A theory of visual perception developed around the year AD 1011 by the Arab mathematician, physicist, and astronomer Ibn al-Haytham (Alhazen), which describes how light reflected by objects is absorbed by the eye.
Impact bias	A cognitive bias that describes how we often greatly overestimate the expected emotional impact of potential gains or losses.
Implicit association test	A widely used test for identifying implicit negative associations, for example caused by racial stereotypes.
Implicit learning process	A learning process that is characterised by the gradual accumulation of knowledge. The knowledge itself, and the associated learning process, is not accessible to consciousness. See also Procedural learning.
Implicit memory	The part of our memory in which implicitly learned skills are stored. Information in this part of memory is inaccessible to consciousness.
Implicit social cognition	Social cognitive processes that operate unconsciously.
Inattentional blindness	The failure of noticing unexpected changes in a visual scene when attention is focused on other aspects of the scene.
Incentive	A condition that can lead to a reward.
Incidental emotions	Emotions evoked by past events that are unrelated to a decision.
Incubation	A stage in a problem-solving process in which the problem solver is not actively engaged in searching for a solution.
Indicative rule	A relatively abstract formal rule in a reasoning problem.
Individuation	The recognition of individual exemplars of a given category.
Inductive reasoning	A form of reasoning in which generalisations must be formed on the basis of a limited set of data.
Inference	The process of drawing a conclusion.
Inferior	Anatomical term indicating that a structure is relatively at the bottom compared to a reference object.
Inferior colliculus	Structure in the midbrain that is involved in the transmission of auditory signals from the ear to the cortex.
Information	The amount of uncertainty that is removed by a transmission.
Informational masking	The process that reduces the quality of speech perception due to an attention-demanding secondary task.
Inhibition	Suppression.
Inhibition of return	The phenomenon whereby attention, after being directed exogenously to a salient stimulus, temporarily fails to return to the location of that stimulus.
Inhibitory	A property of a neurotransmitter that makes the postsynaptic cell less excitable.

Inhibitory postsynaptic potential	The polarisation of the postsynaptic membrane of a neuron, which reduces the excitability of the cell.
Initial design	A strategy where speakers immediately incorporate the shared knowledge with the listener into their communication.
Inner scribe	Part of visual working memory, involved in the storage of spatial information and motion and in the repetition of visual information.
Insertion rules	Rule-based processes that select and insert the correct items in a sentence that is under construction.
Insight	The experience of suddenly realising how a problem can be solved.
Instance theory	A theory describing how a task can be automatised by accumulating experience through repetition.
Integral emotions	Emotions that are triggered by the evaluation of the consequences of a decision.
Inter key interval	The amount of time between two successive key presses in a discrete-sequence production task.
Interaural intensity difference	The intensity difference between the auditory signals being registered by the left and right ear.
Interaural time difference	The time difference between a sound reaching the left and right ear.
Intercranial EEG	A form of EEG that is measured by means of depth electrodes in the brain.
Interneurons	Neurons that form the connection between afferent sensory neurons and efferent motor neurons.
Interoception	The perception of the physiological state of the body; specifically the internal organs.
Interpretation bias	A bias that describes how, in particular, individuals with an anxiety disorder preferentially choose a threatening interpretation when faced with a possible ambiguity in a sentence.
Intervening variable	A non-directly observable variable that is capable of describing the complex relationship between a set of independent variables and a set of dependent variables in a relatively straightforward manner.
Intranasal	A method of administrating a stimulus through the nose.
Introspection	A scientific method that was developed towards the end of the 19th century to study the basic structure of consciousness. It consists of standardised protocols for describing subjective experiences.
Inverse model	An internal model that calculates and adjusts the consequences of a motor action on the basis of sensory feedback.
Ionotropic	An immediate and short-lasting change in a cells likelihood to depolarise, resulting from neurotransmitter release.
Iowa gambling task	A task in which participants can earn a reward by choosing cards from a deck. Each deck of cards is characterised by a specific risk of losing.
Joint action	The execution and coordinating of an action involving two or more individuals.
Just noticeable difference	The smallest perceivable difference. It is defined as the smallest difference between two stimuli that are still perceptible in 50% of all trials.
Knowledge effect	The implicit assumption of many writers that their audience has access to the same knowledge as they do.
Knowledge-poor problems	A type of problem where all the knowledge required to solve it is contained in the problem description.
Knowledge-rich problems	A type of problem that can only be solved when the solver has relevant background knowledge.
Korsakoff's syndrome	A neurological condition that is characterised by anterograde and retrograde amnesia, typically caused by a vitamin B_1 (thiamine) deficiency resulting from chronic alcohol abuse.
Latency	The time delay between the input and the response of a system.

Lateral	An anatomical term indicating that a structure is located to the side of the body.
Lateral inhibition	The phenomenon whereby neighbouring photoreceptors inhibit each other's activation.
Lateralised readiness potential (LRP)	An ERP component obtained by calculating the difference between left and right motor cortex activity. It is considered a measure of the relative activation of the motor cortex.
Law of effect	A classic law, formulated by Edward Thorndike, which states that behaviour that has a favourable outcome is more likely to be repeated, whereas behaviour that has an unfavourable outcome is less likely to be repeated.
Law of inverse effectiveness	A general multisensory integration principle which describes how weaker stimuli integrate more strongly with each other than strong stimuli.
Law of Prägnanz	A principle developed by gestalt psychologists which states that of all possible interpretations of a configuration of elements in a display, the simplest is the most likely to be perceived.
Lemma	An abstract word form that contains syntactic and semantic properties, but no phonological ones.
Leucotomy	A surgical procedure aimed at selectively removing portions of the prefrontal lobe for the purpose of relieving the symptoms of psychiatric disorders. Precursor of the lobotomy.
Levelling	A type of error made while interpreting a story, characterised by the omission of schema inconsistent details during the retrieval of this story.
Lexical bias effect	The fact that non-words are hardly ever produced while making a speech error.
Lexical decision task	A task in which participants have to indicate as quickly as possible whether a series of letters forms a word or not.
Lexical identification shift	See Ganong effect.
Lexicon	An internal dictionary that stores meaning, spelling (orthography), and pronunciation (phonology).
Life script	A description of the essential stages we expect to pass through in life, given the culture in which we live.
Limbic system	A collection of brain structures, including the cerebrum, hippocampus, hypothalamus, amygdala, and anterior cingulate cortex. These areas form the border between the cerebrum and the brainstem.
Lobe	A major subdivision of the cortex.
Logical inferences	The simplest type of inference we can make that is entirely dependent on the meaning of words.
Long-term memory	Part of our memory where information is stored in a more or less fixed form.
Loss aversion	The phenomenon that, for most people, potential losses often outweigh potential gains.
Machine learning algorithms	Computer programmes that aim to recognise complex patterns based on neural network technologies.
Magnocellular pathway	Part of the visual pathway which is mainly involved in the detection of movement, and consists of relatively large neurons.
Maintenance rehearsal	The automatic repetition of a stimulus resulting from previous processing of a stimulus when memorising stimuli.
Mass action	A theory developed by Karl Lashley that states that the time required to learn a skill depends on the amount of cortex available.
Matching bias	A tendency of many individuals, when faced with reasoning problems, to choose those items that are mentioned in the problem description.
McGurk effect	The effect that our perception of a phoneme can change due to the mismatch between the phoneme that is heard and the lip movement that is seen.
Meaningful unit	As part of a mental representation; an object or event that is involved in pursuing an organism's goals.

697

Means-ends analysis	A heuristic that is often used in problem-solving, consisting of specifying sub-goals and the steps to reach those sub-goals.
Medial	An anatomical term indicating that a structure is relatively close to the central body axis.
Medulla oblongata	Part of the brainstem that controls important autonomic functions.
Meissner's corpuscles	Somatosensory receptors sensitive to low-frequency vibrations and sudden skin movement.
Memory architecture	A description of all the subsystems that comprise our memory system.
Memory processes	The set of cognitive processes, such as retention, retrieval, and encoding, that are related to the basic functions of our memory.
Memory set	A collection of items that has to be retained in memory for a short period of time in a memory task.
Memory span	The capacity of our short-term memory, expressed in terms of the number of units of information that can be retained.
Mental imagery	The internal activation of a visual representation of the environment for mental simulation purposes.
Mental models	An influential theory of mental representations and reasoning skills developed by Philip Johnson-Laird.
Mental number line hypothesis	A hypothetical line on which we organise numbers internally in working memory.
Mental representation	A hypothetical internal cognitive symbol that represents the external world or a mental process that uses this symbol.
Mental rotation	The phenomenon that we can rotate mental representations of objects as if they were real objects.
Mental set	Persisting in a strategy that worked before but is no longer adequate for the current problem.
Mental white board hypothesis	An extension of the mental number line, which assumes that we order objects in specific sequences in working memory.
Mentalisation	The process of thinking about another and understanding another's actions and intentions.
Meta-analysis	A statistical analysis technique that combines data from multiple studies.
Metabotropic	A sustained change in a cell's likelihood to depolarise, resulting from neurotransmitter release.
Microstimulation	A technique in which a small population of neurons is electrically stimulated by means of a micro-electrode to bring about a change in brain activation and/or behaviour.
Mind reading	The ability to represent the mental state of another.
Mirror neurons	A class of neurons that fire both when an animal performs an action itself and when it observes how an actor performs this action.
Mirror trace task	A neuropsychological test in which a patient has to draw a pre-printed pattern, where the task is to stay within the lines and visual feedback is given via a mirror.
Misery-is-not-miserly effect	An effect describing the observation that when we are sad we are generally willing to pay much more for goods than when we are in a neutral state of mind.
Mismatch negativity	A negative ERP component evoked by an auditory stimulus that differs from what is expected.
Mixed error effect	A type of speech error that is characterised by the incorrect word being semantically and phonemically related to the intended word.
Modality appropriateness hypothesis	The hypothesis that the sensory modality best suited to process a particular form of information will exert the most influence when integrating it with signals from another modality.
Modus ponens	An inference rule in propositional logic that consists of confirming the antecedent.
Modus tollens	An inference rule in propositional logic which is based on the rule that if a statement is true, then the statement's contrapositive must also be true.

Monitoring and adjustment model	A strategy whereby a speaker adapts his or her wording to the listener's shared knowledge.
Monocular cues	Visual depth cues that can be processed by one eye.
Mood	The affective state of mind that is mainly determined by internal processes that can last for a relatively long time.
Mood congruence	The phenomenon whereby subjects tend to recall memories that are congruent with their mood at the time.
Mood-state dependent memory	The phenomenon that memory performance is generally better when the mood-state of the participant during testing is the same as it was during learning.
Morphemes	Words and word forms.
Motivated inference	The phenomenon whereby individuals distort their judgement because of underlying personal goals.
Motivational intensity	The degree to which a positive or negative emotion has motivational relevance.
Motor anticipation	The set of processes that must be carried out to prepare a motor programme.
Motor chunk	See Chunk (motor process).
Motor cognition	The idea that cognition is embedded in motor processes.
Motor cortex	The part of the cortex that is involved in planning motor responses.
Motor equivalence	The fact that specific actions can be achieved in different ways by different muscle groups or even by different effectors.
Motor imagery	A form of mental imagery in which motor actions are covertly executed.
Motor unit	The unit of one motor neuron and the muscle fibres that it controls.
Multiple comparison problem	A problem in statistics related to the fact that the more inferences are made, the more likely erroneous inferences become.
Multiple trace theory	A theory that assumes the hippocampus is always involved in declarative memory; both in consolidating memories and in retrieving/reactivating them.
Multipolar neurons	A type of neuron that is characterised by one axon and several dendrites.
Multisensory integration	The process whereby the interaction of input from multiple senses results in the formation of a new representation.
Multisensory interaction	The process by which the inputs from multiple senses influence each other's action.
Mutilated checkerboard problem	A logic problem that questions whether dominoes can completely cover a mutilated checkerboard.
Myoelectric prosthesis	A motorised prosthesis which can be controlled via myoelectric signals that are generated at the stump of the amputated limb.
My-side bias	Our tendency to evaluate statements on the basis of our own preconceived notions, rather than on their own merit.
N2pc	An event-related potential component that is elicited approximately 200 ms after presentation of a visual stimulus that captures attention.
N400	A negative ERP component that manifests itself approximately 400 ms after the presentation of a stimulus and that is sensitive to semantic violations.
Natural frequency	In judgement tasks, a representation that is based on natural numbers of individuals, objects, or cases that occur in a given population.
Natural sampling	The formation of a mental representation of statistical proportions in a population by considering individual concrete cases.
Navon task	A cognitive task in which one global letter is composed of a series of smaller local letters. Participants must either indicate what the global or the local letter is.
N-back task	A task that measures the effects of working memory load by requiring participants to compare the current item with the item that was presented N positions back.
Negative afterimage	An optical illusion that is created when, after staring at a picture for a few seconds, one suddenly looks at a white surface.

Negative transfer	The phenomenon that having experience with solving a given problem has a negative impact on solving slightly different problems.
Neologisms	Words invented by jargon aphasic patients that are used as substitutes for the word they cannot produce.
Nervus vagus	The tenth cranial nerve, which influences the parasympathetic activation of many internal organs, including the heart, lungs, and digestive system.
Neural networks	A type of computational model based on neuronal principles. They consist of nodes, which represent artificial neurons, and connections between these nodes.
Neuroeconomics	A field of scientific enquiry that seeks to identify the neural correlates of preferences and beliefs and to measure the neural responses associated with them during economic decision-making tasks.
Neurogenesis	The formation of new neurons from stem cells.
Neuroma	A tangled mass of axons that cannot reconnect to the original tissue after amputation of a body part.
Neuromuscular junction	A special type of synapse between the axons of a motor neuron and the muscle fibres that it controls.
Neuron	A type of brain cell that is characterised by one or more extensions, typically consisting of several branched dendrites and one unbranched axon.
Neurotransmitters	Chemicals released at the terminal of an axon that can cause a biochemical change in the dendrites of the recipient neuron.
Nine-dot problem	A classic logic puzzle, where nine dots must be connected by four lines.
Nociception	The afferent component of pain signals.
Noise-vocoded speech	A form of degraded speech, in which most of the temporal cues are still intact, while the finer details of the speech signal have been removed.
Nominal type (category)	A category type that consists of the random assignment of a label to an instance that meets one or more specific criteria.
Non-declarative memory	The part of memory where our implicit knowledge is stored. This includes motor skills and detecting regularities along with priming, conditioning, and habituation/sensitisation.
Non-invasive technique	A neuroscientific recording technique that does not invade the body.
Non-parametric classification models	A class of categorisation models that makes no assumptions about the underlying category structure.
Non-word	According to the strict definition, a random series of letters that do not form an existing word and cannot form a word according to the rules of the language in question. In practice, often used as a synonym for pseudo-word.
Nucleus accumbens	A subcortical brain area, part of the striatum, that is involved in the processing of rewards.
Null hypothesis	The assumption that results do not differ between conditions. It is part of a commonly used statistical technique to test whether or not any observed difference are due to chance or not.
Null result	A finding that provides inconclusive evidence of a relationship between two variables.
Object file	A hypothetical file that represents both an object itself and the context in which it is observed.
Object individuation	The process by which individual objects in a scene are isolated, identified, and stored in working memory.
Objective perception threshold	In visual perception, the limit at which we are just able to detect meaningful information in a visual stimulus during a forced choice procedure.
Occasion setting	The phenomenon whereby an association is linked to specific circumstances and is primarily activated under those circumstances.
Occipital lobes	The most posterior part of the cerebral cortex. It is involved in the processing of visual information.

Oddball paradigm	An experimental paradigm often used in auditory or visual attention and in perception research. This involves the use of a sequence of standard stimuli, occasionally interrupted by a deviant stimulus.
Olfactory bulb	A brain region in the inferior anterior part of the cerebrum, also known as the bulbus olfactorius. This area is part of the limbic system and receives input directly from the chemical receptors located in the nasal cavity.
Omission bias	The preference of not to act when there are potential negative consequences associated with the act, even when the benefits of the act outweigh the costs of the inactivity.
Open science framework	An Internet platform that allows researchers to preregister experiments and make raw data and analysis scripts available.
Operant conditioning	A form of conditioning in which certain spontaneous behaviours are reinforced and others are not.
Operation span	A technique for measuring working memory capacity.
Opponent-process model of motivation	A model describing how an immediate hedonic response to a stimulus is followed by a longer-lasting, internally generated anti-hedonic response (and vice versa).
Optic ataxia	A neuropsychological syndrome characterised by patients' difficulties with pointing to or grasping objects. It is characterised by damage to the parietal cortex.
Optical array	The information contained in the continuously changing patterns of light falling on our eyes. See also Direct perception theory.
Optimal-feedback control	A regulatory model that describes how the motor system is controlled.
Organs of Ruffini	Somatosensory receptors sensitive to skin stretching.
Orthographic neighbours	The set of all words that can be formed by changing only one letter of a target word.
Orthography	The spelling of words.
Oscillation	Periodic fluctuation in a signal. In electrophysiology, it is used to describe the spontaneous rhythms of electrical brain activity.
Other-race effect	The phenomenon that we are less capable of recognising the faces of people of a different ethnicity than our own.
Overlap model	A word recognition model that does not assign a fixed position to individual letters, but a probabilistic one.
Overt attention	The focusing of attention on a specific location, with one's eyes on this location.
Pacinian corpuscles	Somatosensory receptors sensitive to high frequency vibrations of the skin.
Pain matrix	A network of brain regions initially believed to be involved in pain perception, but now believed to be a multimodal mechanism involved in signalling threats to the body.
Paradigm specificity	The fact that some results do not readily generalise but are only valid in the context of an experiment that has been conducted.
Parafoveal-to-foveal effects	The effect that fixation time during reading depends not only on the current word but also on subsequent words in the sentence.
Parahippocampal place area	A brain area that is selectively sensitive to location-related stimuli, such as images of houses.
Parametric classification models	A class of categorisation models that assumes that categories have a specific underlying structure or that the category boundaries are characterised by a specific structure.
Parietal lobe	The superior posterior part of the cerebral cortex. It is involved in encoding spatial locations and directing attention.
Parkinson's disease	A neurodegenerative condition that is characterised by tremors, rigidity, slow movements, and/or blocking. It is frequently associated with damage to the basal ganglia.
Part-whole effect	The fact that it is easier to recognise a facial feature when it is presented in the context of a face than when it is presented in its own right.
Partial feedback	Feedback that is not given on every trial in an experiment, but only on a subset of them.

Parvocellular pathway	Part of the visual system that is mainly involved in the processing of detailed object and colour information.
Perception	The ability to become aware of our surroundings by processing information through our senses.
Perception threshold	The threshold at which an individual can still report a stimulus in 50% of cases.
Perception-action cycle	A cycle that describes how perceptual input can be used to plan actions, with the action then influencing the visual environment.
Perception-for-action system	A visual system that is primarily involved in detecting the spatial layout of our environment and integrating it into our motor actions.
Perceptual learning	The process by which we learn through experience to recognise ambiguities in perceptual input.
Peripersonal space	The space immediately surrounding the body.
Peripheral nervous system	The part of the nervous system that is located outside of the brain and spinal cord. It consists of the autonomic and the somatic nervous systems.
Permastore	A term introduced by Bahrick to describe the robustness of some episodic memories.
Phantom limb	The sensation that an amputated limb is still part of the body.
Phantom pain	The phenomenon that patients can still experience pain in an amputated body part.
Phenomenal awareness	A short-lived and fleeting conscious experience due to the absence of attending the evoking stimulus.
Philosophical zombies	A concept introduced in the philosophy of consciousness, consisting of imaginary individuals whose actions are in all respects equal to those of regular people, but who lack consciousness.
Phoneme	The basic unit of a spoken word.
Phonological dysgraphia	A neuropsychological condition that is characterised by difficulties with the spelling of unknown words and non-words, while the spelling of known words is still largely intact.
Phonological dyslexia	A form of dyslexia that is characterised by specific problems with the pronunciation of non-words and unknown words.
Phonological neighbourhood	A set of all words that differ from a target word by only one phoneme.
Phonological similarity effect	The effect whereby phonologically similar words are less well remembered than phonologically more distinctive words.
Phonology	The sound of words.
Phosphene perception	The perception of a flash of light resulting from direct mechanical stimulation of the eyeball or from direct stimulation of the visual system.
Pituitary gland	Brain structure that releases hormones which, among other things, regulate growth and reproductive mechanisms.
Planum temporale	The human equivalent of the belt and parabelt areas of the auditory cortex.
Pons	Part of the brainstem that is involved in the regulation of various autonomous functions.
Pop-out effect	The phenomenon that a single deviant object can be immediately detected in a crowded visual display.
Positive feedback loop	A process whereby an initial response to a change contributes to even larger subsequent responses to that change.
Positive transfer	The phenomenon whereby one can benefit from the earlier successful solution of a problem.
Positron emission tomography (PET)	A neuroimaging technique that uses radioactive markers to determine the localisation of brain activity.
Post-error slowing	The phenomenon that after making an error, participants are generally slower on the next trial.

Posterior	Anatomical term indicating that a structure is behind to a reference object.
Prediction	An informed extrapolation based on known data.
Predictive coding	A theory that is based on the assumption that the brain continually generates models of the world that are used to predict sensory input, while these predictions are corrected by the processing of a prediction error that is based on actual sensory input.
Preformulation	A strategy that is used to achieve fluency through the reuse of many well-practised phrases.
Premise	In syllogistic reasoning, a statement that is assumed to be true.
Premotor theory	A theory that states that attention plays an important role in selecting new locations for fixations.
Prepared reflex	The idea that participants prepare themselves for a task by putting themselves in a state that allows the task to be performed efficiently.
Presence	Our awareness of our environment and our position in it.
Primacy effect	The phenomenon that, after memorising a list of words, a relatively large proportion of the words that are successfully reproduced are words from the beginning of the list.
Priming	The influencing of behaviour by a prior stimulus that is somehow associated with the behaviour in question.
Prisoners' dilemma game	A type a social dilemma in which the interaction between one's own decision and the decision of the other determines the outcome.
Probability density function	A mathematical function that describes the relative probability of an event y occurring as a function of an independent variable x.
Problem size effect	The fact that the time required to solve a one-digit addition or multiplication problem increases with the size of the operands.
Problem-solving	A cognitive process that seeks to bridge the discrepancy between the current state and a target state.
Problem space	The initial state, the final state, and all permitted steps to change a problem from one state to another.
Procedural learning	Learning how to do something.
Process dissociation procedure	A method to determine to what extent a learning process is procedural and to what extent the acquired knowledge is declarative.
Production system	A computational model that aims to simulate cognitive processes based on long sequences of IF ... THEN ... rules.
Productive thinking	A complex form of thinking that aims to restructure a problem in an innovative way to find a solution to it.
Property list	As part of a mental representation, a description of the properties of an object and/or the category to which it belongs.
Feature search	A form of visual search in which an object must be found that is defined by one unique feature.
Proposition	In classical inferential logic, a statement that may be true or false.
Prosencephalon	One of three structures that arise during embryonic development of the brain. It develops into parts of the forebrain.
Prosodic cues	Features of spoken language, such as rhythm, emphasis, and intonation, that help to disambiguate it.
Prosody	The patterns of stress and intonation in a language.
Prosopagnosia	A neuropsychological condition characterised by a problem in recognising faces.
Prospect theory	A decision theory, developed by Kahneman and Tversky, that considers seemingly irrational aspects of a decision.
Prospective memory	The memory process involved in memorising actions that are to be performed in the near future.
Prototype-based	A theoretical approach that assumes that categories are defined by constructing a category prototype.

Prototype effect	The phenomenon that category prototypes receive high familiarity ratings, even when these prototypes have never been shown during an earlier training phase.
Proust phenomenon	The subjective experience that intense olfactory cues can activate memories from early childhood.
Pseudo-unipolar neurons	A type of neuron that is characterised by the fact that one extension can function either as a dendrite or as an axon.
Pseudo-word	A series of letters which do not form an existing word, but which could have been a word according to the rules of the language concerned.
Pseudo-word superiority effect	The phenomenon that letters which are part of a pseudo-word are recognised faster than letters which are part of a non-word.
Psychological refractory period	The phenomenon that, when two stimuli, each requiring a decision and a response, are presented shortly after each other, the response to the second stimulus is delayed.
Psychonomics	A term emphasising the quantitative nature of the study of human functioning: the measurement and precise mapping of the laws of human behaviour, as opposed to the traditionally more descriptive, qualitative nature of psychology.
Psychophysics	An approach that aims to establish precise laws governing human behaviour. This approach has been particularly successful in describing perceptual processes.
Psychophysiology	A discipline concerned with the study of the relationship between the physiology of the brain (or body) and psychological processes.
Psychosurgery	A surgical procedure that removes brain tissue in order to treat psychiatric problems. Not to be confused with neurosurgery. See also Leucotomy, Frontal lobotomy, and Transorbital lobotomy.
Pupillary light reflex	The automatic dilation or narrowing of the pupil as a result of a change in the intensity of light shining into the eyes.
Pure word deafness	The inability of some neurological patients to recognise words in a speech signal, while their other audiological functions appear to be unimpaired.
Pursuit rotor task	A task in which subjects must try to keep a stylus positioned on a small plate, about 2 cm in diameter, mounted on the edge of a turntable.
Putamen	One of the nuclei of the basal ganglia.
Pyramidal	A type of neuron that is characterised by a large, pyramid-shaped soma.
Quadrilateral	A polygon with four edges and four corners.
Qualia	A quality or characteristic that is subjectively experienced.
Questionable research practices	A collection of research practices that may result in biased or inaccurate outcomes or flawed interpretation of research data.
Race model	A theoretical model that aims to explain reaction times from the idea that two independently operating processes are simultaneously active, with the reaction time being determined by the process that completes the process fastest.
Rationalisation	Distortions in the interpretation and/or recollection of a story that are characterised by making it more rational and consistent with one's own cultural beliefs.
Readiness potential	A slow negative EEG component that is recorded over the motor cortex, which signals the preparation of a motor action.
Reading span	A measure of working memory capacity.
Recency effect	The phenomenon that, after memorizing a list of words, a relatively large proportion of the words that are successfully recalled are from the end of the list.
Receptive field	The property of a stimulus to which a neuron is sensitive.
Recognition heuristic	A specific implementation of the take the best strategy that is based on the recognition of options.
Recognition-primed decision model	A decision model that is based on the assumption that experts will first try to find a solution based on a similar problem they have solved previously.

Reflex arc	A relatively simple neural circuit consisting of a sensory neuron, an interneuron, and a motor neuron.
Refractory period	A brief amount time during which a neuron is unable to generate a new action potential, due to hyperpolarisation.
Region of direct access	See Broad focus.
Regularisation	The phenomenon whereby some dyslexics pronounce words that have an irregular spelling-sound relationship as if they were regular.
Reinforcement learning	The selective reinforcement of behaviour that has a positive outcome.
Relational learning	The formation of new relationships between items and their context.
Remapping	The recoding of a neuron's receptive fields in response to an action, such as an eye movement or a body movement.
Reminiscence bump	The observation that the spontaneous personal memories of most older individuals are not evenly distributed across their life span, but show a strong peak in the period between the ages of 10 and 30.
Remote associates task (RAT)	A cognitive task in which a participant must find a target word that matches three given words. It is widely used in research on insight and creativity.
Replication	The process of rerunning a study to check whether the results obtained are not based on chance, to demonstrate the robustness of a particular effect.
Representation	A mental model of our environment.
Representativeness heuristic	The assumption that an object or individual is a member of a specific category because it is representative of that category.
Reproductive thinking	A form of thinking that primarily involves the reuse of previous experiences.
Resource theories	A class of cognitive theories that attempts to explain dual-task effects based on the idea that cognitive processes are limited in capacity and that the use of these limited resources determines when interference occurs between tasks.
Response	The internal or external result of a cognitive process.
Resting potential	The default electrical potential difference of -70 mV between the inner and outer parts of a neuron's cell membrane.
Reticular formation	A complex bundle of neural fibres that runs from the spinal cord through the central parts of the hindbrain to the midbrain. Extensions from of this bundle project to large parts of the forebrain, where they are crucial to the regulation of arousal and awareness. See Ascending reticular activating system.
Retinal ganglion cells	Neurons that project the output of the eye to the lateral geniculate nucleus of the thalamus.
Retinotopic map	The relationship between a location on the retina and the representation of this location in the visual cortex.
Retrograde amnesia	A form of amnesia that is characterised by the fact that memories prior to the accident are affected. See also Anterograde amnesia.
Reuptake	The recycling of neurotransmitters by the releasing axon terminal.
Reward	In the study of motivation, behaviour is strongly related to the neural representation of the expected outcome or proceeds of an action. This outcome or result takes the form of a reward.
Reward priming	The extent to which participants are influenced by the prospect of a reward, even when better choices are available.
Routine expertise	A form of expertise that involves someone becoming particularly efficient at performing routine procedures, such as inspecting mammograms or X-rays.
Rumination	The systematic retrieval of memories from negative life events, not intended to improve the current state of mind.
Saccade	A rapid eye movement, between two moments of fixation.

Saccade generation with inhibition by foveal targets (SWIFT)	A model aimed at explaining eye movement patterns during the reading process.
Sagittal plane	One of the two vertical anatomical planes. It divides the body into a left half and a right half.
Salience	The relative property of an object to stand out from its environment.
Satisficing	To be satisfied with the outcome of a decision that is good enough.
Savings method	A method developed by Hermann Ebbinghaus to quantify the degree of forgetting in long-term memory.
Schema	A structured unit of background knowledge that we have previously learned.
Script	A form of cognitive schema that contains information about sequences of actions that are to be performed in normal situations.
Segmentation	The process of splitting the continuous auditory speech signal into discrete words.
Selective attention	The process by which one stimulus, or stimulus feature, is given a higher priority in perceptual processing than other stimuli or features.
Self-memory system	A theory of autobiographical memory that links autobiographical memories with self-image.
Semantic congruence	Multisensory inputs are semantically congruent when they convey the same meaning, as is the case for the image and sound of a barking dog.
Semantic dementia	A neurological condition that is characterised by a severe loss of conceptual knowledge, while episodic memories and most cognitive functions are still reasonably intact.
Semantic memory	A memory system in which abstract, factual knowledge is stored.
Semantic network	A network of long-term memory representations that are associated with each other.
Semanticisation	The phenomenon whereby episodic memories change into semantic memories over time.
Semantics	The meaning of words.
Sensitisation	The strengthening of a reflex as a result of repeated presentation of an intense evoking stimulus. It occurs when this response becomes more intense with repetition.
Sensory gain	The attention-related amplitude increase of early sensory ERP components.
Sensory gating	The finding that the auditory P1 ERP amplitude to a second click is smaller in amplitude than that to the first click.
Serial position curve	A curve describing the probability of successfully remembering a word as a function of the original order of presentation.
Settling point	A natural equilibrium resulting from the balance between several opposing forces.
Shadowing	An experimental procedure in which, during a dichotic listening task, a participant must repeat aloud a message presented to one ear.
Shadowing task	An experimental paradigm often used in research on auditory attention processes, consisting of requiring the participant to actively repeat one of two auditory messages.
Shaping	The process of gradual behavioural change as a result of rewarding desired behaviour and/or punishing undesired behaviour.
Sharpening	An error in the processing of a story that consists of highlighting and emphasising certain details of the story for the purpose of embellishment.
Signal detection theory	A theoretical model that can be used to describe the sensitivity of detecting a signal in a noisy background.
Significant	A statistical term indicating that the results of a scientific study are highly unlikely to be coincidental.
Simon task	A task where stimuli can differ on two dimensions and where the action to be performed is associated with the irrelevant stimulus dimension.
Simplicity principle	A theoretical approach to categorisation that is based on the idea that we always try to use the simplest category that is consistent with a given set of objects that we aim to categorise.

Simultaneity judgement task	A task that requires participants to decide whether two stimuli were presented simultaneously or not.
Simultaneous conditioning	A form of classical conditioning in which the conditioned and unconditioned stimulus are presented simultaneously.
Sine wave speech	A synthetic form of speech that is typically not recognised as speech at first.
Single cell recording	A technique whereby a microelectrode that is inserted into the brain records the activity of a single neuron.
Situation awareness	The correspondence between the mental representation of our environment and reality.
Situation model	An internal mental representation that is formed on the basis of linguistic information.
Social contract theory	A theory that states that we often gain insights in reasoning problems more easily when they are formulated in a way that implies social deception.
Social dilemma	A set of situations where the outcome of a decision depends not only on one's own decision but also on the decision of someone else.
Social functionalist approach	An approach that attempts to explain decision-making processes in terms of social factors. It suggests that the ability to recognise social deception would underlie our decision-making ability.
Social perception	The study of how we draw conclusions from someone else's non-verbal behaviour.
Social priming	The study of the possible ways in which unconscious exposure to specific concepts may affect our social behaviour.
Software	A set of pre-programmed instructions that define the tasks of a computer.
Soma	Cell body.
Somatic markers	Changes in bodily responses, such as an increase in the heart rate, tremors, or sweating, due to an emotional situation. According to some theories, these bodily signals underlie emotions.
Somatic nervous system	Part of the peripheral nervous system that projects sensory information from the body to the brain, and motor commands from the brain to the body.
Somatosensory cortex	A part of the cortex where sensory stimuli are processed. It is currently also believed to be involved in the simulation of bodily functions.
Somatosensory receptor	A type of receptor located in the skin that registers specific sensations such as stretching, pressure, pain, cold, or heat.
Spatial attention	Attention's capacity to focus on specific locations in our environment.
Spatial frequency	A characteristic of any structure that is periodic across position in space. In images, it is typically expressed as the number of cycles per degree of visual angle.
Spatial proximity principle	The principle that the degree to which two stimuli in different sensory modalities interact or integrate depends on the correspondence of their locations.
Spatial resolution	In cognitive neuroscience, the accuracy with which a technique is able to determine where in the brain activity can be localised.
Spatial-numerical association of response codes (SNARC)	The phenomenon that relatively small numbers are associated with a left-hand response and relatively large numbers with a right-hand response.
Spillover effect	The effect that our eyes' fixation time is not only determined by the currently fixated word but also by the frequency of the previous word.
Spinal cord	An extension of the central nervous system in the spinal column, where the nerves that connect the body and the brain are located.
Split-brain patient	A patient whose corpus callosum has been surgically dissected, resulting in limited communication between the two hemispheres.
Spoonerism	A speech error that is characterised by the exchange of the initial phonemes of two words.
Spreading activation theory	A general principle that describes how semantic knowledge is stored in an associative network.

Stapedius reflex	An automatic reflex that is caused by the contraction of a muscle in the middle ear in response to a sound.
Status quo bias	A tendency to leave the current situation as it is, by taking no action, even when the expected utility of a change is positive.
Steady-state visual evoked potential	A rhythmic electrophysiological response to a stimulus that is presented at a specific frequency.
Stereopsis	The phenomenon that each of our eyes perceives a slightly different image. See Binocular disparity.
Stimulus	A signal perceived by a biological organism.
Stimulus onset asynchrony (SOA)	The time between the onset of two stimuli.
Stop-signal paradigm	An experimental paradigm used to investigate response inhibition processes.
Stop-signal reaction time (SSRT)	An estimate of the time required to inhibit a planned manual response.
Striatum	A subcortical brain area, consisting of a ventral and a dorsal part, involved in automating routine actions and in processing rewards and maintaining motivated behaviour.
Stroop task	A classic experimental paradigm for inducing conflict by presenting colour words.
Subitizing	Our ability to immediately determine the cardinality of small sets of objects.
Subjective perceptual threshold	The threshold at which participants report becoming unaware of the presence of a stimulus.
Subjective simultaneity	The moment when a participant subjectively experiences two stimuli being presented simultaneously.
Subliminal	A form of stimulus presentation that causes participants to be unaware of them. This is typically done using a very short presentation time.
Substantia nigra	A midbrain structure that is linked to Parkinson's disease.
Subtractability	An assumption in neuropsychology stating that brain damage only affects one or more specific modules, or connections between modules, and that patients are unable to develop new modules to compensate for the damaged ones.
Subtraction method	A method, developed by Franciscus Cornelius Donders, to measure the duration of mental processes by comparing reaction times to complex tasks with those to simpler tasks.
Sulcus	A groove in the cortical surface.
Sunk cost effect	The phenomenon that we tend to keep throwing good money after bad money.
Super-additive responses	A type of response made by neurons in the superior colliculus as a result of the presentation of multisensory stimuli, characterised by the fact that it is greater than the sum of the responses that this neuron makes when only the unisensory stimuli are presented.
Superconducting quantum interference device (SQUID)	A superconducting magnetometer at the heart of a MEG scanner.
Superior	An anatomical term indicating that a structure is relatively at the top of a reference object.
Superior colliculus	A midbrain structure that is involved in programming eye movements and integrating auditory and visual information.
Support theory	A theory that assumes that more elaborate descriptions are assigned a higher likelihood of being true.
Surface dyslexia	A reading disorder characterised by problems with reading irregular words.
Sustained attention	A form of attention that requires you to perform one specific task over a long period of time.
Syllogism	A form of reasoning that consists of a major premise, a minor premise, and a conclusion that may or may not logically follow from the premises.
Symbolic cue	See Endogenous cue.

Synaesthesia	The phenomenon whereby some people associate two unrelated percepts, such as colours and graphs, with each other.
Synchronisation hypothesis	The hypothesis that a congruent visual experience can arise from the specialised visual modules through synchronisation of neural activity.
Syntactic priming	The phenomenon that two interlocutors often adopt each other's syntactic structure.
Syntax	The set of rules describing the structure of a language.
System 1	A fast, intuitive, and automatic mode of thinking.
System 2	A slow, deliberate, and consciously controlled mode of thinking.
Take the best strategy	A specific form of a fast and frugal heuristic, which is based on considering the most important cues.
Tangential point	The point along a curve where the apparent direction of the road changes direction.
Directed forgetting	The phenomenon that information in long-term memory can be forgotten in a targeted manner, by means of instructions.
Task model	An internal representation in working memory that details all relevant facts, rules, and requirements of a task.
Task set	A specific configuration of mental processes that are associated with a particular stimulus.
Task switching costs	The phenomenon that responses are delayed on the first trial after switching to a new task.
Tau	One of the first psychophysical parameters that was proposed as a determinant for the time until contact.
Tau over time	A measure derived from Tau that is important in determining the remaining braking time.
Tectum	The upper part of the midbrain.
Tegmentatum	The lower part of the midbrain.
Telencephalon	One of three structures that arise during embryonic brain development. It develops into parts of the forebrain.
Telescoping	The phenomenon that a phantom limb is perceived as being closer to the body than the intact limb.
Temporal lobe	The inferior lateral part of the cortex. It is involved, among other things, in processing auditory information, visual form recognition, and – in the left hemisphere – language processing.
Temporal order judgement task	A cognitive task in which participants must decide which of two stimuli is presented first.
Temporal proximity principle	The principle that two stimuli presented in different sensory modalities interact or integrate better when they are presented closer in time.
Temporal resolution	In cognitive neuroscience, it represents the accuracy with which a technique is able to determine how brain activity develops over time.
Terminal	The end of an axon.
Test stimulus	A stimulus used in a cognitive task that has to be compared with a previously presented stimulus, or with an internal mental representation.
Testing effect	The phenomenon that information is better remembered when you test yourself regularly.
Thalamo-cortical connections	A network of neural connections between the thalamus and the neocortex, linking the thalamus to almost all parts of the neocortex.
Thalamus	A subcortical structure located centrally in the forebrain. It is connected to the whole cortex and plays an important role in regulating information flows to and from the cortex.
Theory of mind	The ability to attribute mental states to ourselves and others and to understand that others have mental states different from our own.

709

Thought congruence	The idea that the content of our thoughts often matches the valence of our emotional state.
Threaded cognition theory	A theoretical computational model that can explain dual-task performance by assuming that multiple cognitive processes can operate autonomously, but that interference occurs when two cognitive processes want to use the same processing unit.
Three-route framework	A neuropsychological framework aimed at explaining the problems that can occur when repeating spoken text aloud.
Tinnitus	An auditory hallucination that usually takes the form of a continuous ringing in the ears, typically resulting from permanent tissue damage, deafferentation, and/or plasticity of the auditory cortex.
Tonotopical organisation	The organisation of both the auditory receptors in the inner ear and the primary auditory cortex in ascending pitch order.
Top-down processing	A form of processing that is primarily driven by our internal goals.
Tower of Hanoi	Example of a well-defined problem consisting of a number of discs that must be moved from one pin to another.
Trace model	A neural network model for the recognition of spoken words.
Transcortical sensory aphasia	A neuropsychological condition generally characterised by a severely impaired ability to read in addition to a marked reduction in the ability to understand spoken language.
Transcranial direct current stimulation (tDCS)	A form of brain stimulation using a continuous direct current through electrodes applied to the scalp.
Transcranial magnetic stimulation (TMS)	A technique whereby a brief electromagnetic pulse is directed to a part of the cortex, with the aim of influencing its activation.
Transfer-appropriate processing theory	A theory that describes why the specific aspects of a stimulus that are stored in memory depend on the nature of the learning task.
Transference	A memory error that occurs when an eyewitness to a crime misidentifies a familiar but innocent person from a police line-up.
Transorbital lobotomy	A psychosurgical procedure developed in the 1950s by Walter Freeman that involved destroying the connections between the prefrontal cortex and the rest of the brain by wiggling an ice pick through an eye socket.
Transversal plane	The horizontal anatomical plane which divides the body into a lower and an upper part.
Trial	A coherent series of stimuli or events in a psychological experiment that aims to trigger a specific process.
Triangle model	A connectionist network model that aims to describe the relationship between phonology, orthography, and semantics.
Trolley dilemma	A social dilemma in which a participant indirectly decides whether one or five people will be killed.
Trust game	A social game, where one player can increase the return on assets by giving part of those assets to another.
Tuning curve	The relationship between the sound frequency that is presented and the activity of a neuron in the auditory cortex.
Unconditioned response	The response to an unconditioned stimulus.
Unconditioned stimulus	A stimulus that will typically evoke a specific response.
Uniform connectedness	A principle of visual organisation that describes how each region with uniform visual properties (such as colour, texture, or brightness) is perceived as a single perceptual unit.
Unipolar neurons	A type of neuron that has only one extension – either a dendrite or an axon.
Unity assumption	The cognitive top-down expectation that multisensory inputs have a common cause.

Utilitarian judgements	Judgements based on the application of utilitarian rules which encourage actions that cause happiness and discourage actions that cause unhappiness.
Utility	The expected return of a decision.
Utility theory	An economic theory of rational decision-making that describes how individuals would always make choices that result in maximum return or utility.
Vacuum behaviour	The phenomenon of spontaneous outbursts of motivated behaviour even in the absence of a stimulus.
Valence	A continuous dimension that can vary from extremely negative to extremely positive affect.
Varied mapping	An experimental manipulation in which distractors are chosen from the same set of stimuli that are used as target stimuli.
Ventral	An anatomical term indicating that a structure is located towards the underside organism.
Ventral route	A visual pathway through the brain, through which object properties are processed.
Ventriloquist illusion	The illusion that sound, due to synchronisation with a visual stimulus, appears to originate from a different location than where it actually originates.
Verb bias	The phenomenon that specific verbs are more often associated with one syntactic structure than another.
Vicarious pain	A pain experience that is evoked by seeing others in pain.
Visceroceptive input	Perceptual signals that originate from the internal organs.
Vision-for-action system	A visual system that allows us to interact with the outside world by encoding the positions of objects in real time and integrating this information into our motor programmes.
Vision-for-perception system	A visual system that enables us to make detailed mental representations of objects and to imagine them under different hypothetical situations.
Visual agnosia	A neuropsychological syndrome that is characterised by the inability to recognise visual objects.
Visual cache	A part of visual working memory where information about visual form and colour is stored.
Voice leading	The progression of the individual voices or instruments in a piece of music over time.
Water jug problem	A classic logic problem, where the aim is to measure a precise amount of water using two or more jugs of different sizes.
Weapon focus	The tendency of eyewitnesses to focus their attention on a weapon when it is present, thus weakening the memory of other relevant details.
Weber fraction	A constant describing how large a change in a stimulus must be for it to be perceived, as a function of the absolute size of this stimulus.
Well-defined categories	Categories that can be distinguished from each other on the basis of unambiguous rules.
Well-defined problems	A type of problem, of which the initial state, the final state, and all allowed steps to bridge the difference between these two states are fully defined.
Wernicke's aphasia	A speech production impairment that is often associated with a lesion in the left superior temporal gyrus and is marked by fluent but meaningless speech.
White matter	Neural tissue that mainly consists of myelinated axons.
Win-stay, lose-shift principle	A strategy that is often used when processing feedback during category learning.
Wisconsin card sorting task	A widely used neuropsychological test to determine damage to the frontal cortex. While participants sort a pile of cards, the sorting rule periodically changes.

Word frequency	The relative frequency with which a word occurs in a language.
Word length effect	The phenomenon that the number of words you can remember is also determined by the length of these words. The longer the words, the fewer you can remember.
Word meaning deafness	A neurological condition that is characterised by an inability to pronounce unknown words and non-words, although the patient can distinguish words from non-words.
Word Naming task	A task in which a participant must name a visually presented word as quickly as possible.
Word superiority effect	The phenomenon that letter recognition is much more accurate when a letter is part of a word than when it is part of a random sequence of letters.
Working memory	A short-term memory system that can not only retain information for a short period of time, but is also capable of manipulating this information.

References

Abdellaoui, M., Bleichrodt, H., & Kammoun, H. (2011). Do financial professionals behave according to prospect theory? An experimental study. *Theory and Decision*, *74*(3), 411–429. doi:10.1007/s11238-011-9282-3

Abrahamse, E., Majerus, S., Fias, W., & van Dijck, J. P. (2015). Editorial: Turning the mind's eye inward: The interplay between selective attention and working memory. *Frontiers in Human Neuroscience*, *9*, 616. doi:10.3389/fnhum.2015.00616

Abrahamse, E. L., Ruitenberg, M. F., de Kleine, E., & Verwey, W. B. (2013). Control of automated behavior: Insights from the discrete sequence production task. *Frontiers in Human Neuroscience*, *7*, 82. doi:10.3389/fnhum.2013.00082

Abrahamse, E. L., van Dijck, J. P., & Fias, W. (2017). Grounding verbal working memory: The case of serial order. *Current Directions in Psychological Science*, *26*(5), 429–433.

Abramov, I., & Gordon, J. (1994). Color appearance: On seeing red – or yellow, or green, or blue. *Annual Review of Psychology*, *45*, 451–485.

Adams, R. A., Shipp, S., & Friston, K. J. (2013). Predictions not commands: Active inference in the motor system. *Brain Structure and Function*, *218*(3), 611–643.

Adcock, R. A., Thangavel, A., Whitfield-Gabrieli, S., Knutson, B., & Gabrieli, J. D. (2006). Reward-motivated learning: Mesolimbic activation precedes memory formation. *Neuron*, *50*(3), 507–517. doi:10.1016/j.neuron.2006.03.036

Addante, R. J., Ranganath, C., Olichney, J., & Yonelinas, A. P. (2012). Neurophysiological evidence for a recollection impairment in amnesia patients that leaves familiarity intact. *Neuropsychologia*, *50*(13), 3004–3014. doi:10.1016/j.neuropsychologia.2012.07.038

Addis, D. R., & Schacter, D. L. (2012). The hippocampus and imagining the future: Where do we stand? *Frontiers in Human Neuroscience*, *5*, 173. doi:10.3389/fnhum.2011.00173

Addis, D. R., Wong, A. T., & Schacter, D. L. (2007). Remembering the past and imagining the future: Common and distinct neural substrates during event construction and elaboration. *Neuropsychologia*, *45*(7), 1363–1377. doi:10.1016/j.neuropsychologia.2006.10.016

Adlam, A. L., Patterson, K., & Hodges, J. R. (2009). 'I remember it as if it were yesterday': Memory for recent events in patients with semantic dementia. *Neuropsychologia*, *47*(5), 1344–1351. doi:10.1016/j.neuropsychologia.2009.01.029

Adler, J., Giabbiconi, C. M., & Muller, M. M. (2009). Shift of attention to the body location of distracters is mediated by perceptual load in sustained somatosensory attention. *Biological Psychology*, *81*(2), 77–85. doi:10.1016/j.biopsycho.2009.02.001

Adolphs, R. (1999). Social cognition and the human brain. *Trends in Cognitive Sciences*, *3*(12), 469–479.

Adolphs, R., Tranel, D., & Damasio, A. R. (2003). Dissociable neural systems for recognizing emotions. *Brain and Cognition*, *52*(1), 61–69. doi:10.1016/s0278-2626(03)00009-5

Aggleton, J. P., Vann, S. D., Denby, C., Dix, S., Mayes, A. R., Roberts, N., & Yonelinas, A. P. (2005). Sparing of the familiarity component of recognition memory in a patient with hippocampal pathology. *Neuropsychologia*, *43*(12), 1810–1823. doi:10.1016/j.neuropsychologia.2005.01.019

Agus, T. R., Thorpe, S. J., & Pressnitzer, D. (2010). Rapid formation of robust auditory memories: Insights from noise. *Neuron*, *66*(4), 610–618. doi:10.1016/j.neuron.2010.04.014

Ahn, M., & Jun, S. C. (2015). Performance variation in motor imagery brain-computer interface: A brief review. *Journal of Neuroscience Methods*, *243*, 103–110. doi:10.1016/j.jneumeth.2015.01.033

Ahveninen, J., Huang, S., Nummenmaa, A., Belliveau, J. W., Hung, A. Y., Jääskeläinen, I. P. … Raij, T. (2013). Evidence for distinct human auditory cortex regions for sound location versus identity processing. *Nature Communications*, *4*, 2585. doi:10.1038/ncomms3585

Ahveninen, J., Jääskeläinen, I. P., Raij, T., Bonmassar, G., Devore, S., Hämäläinen, M. … Belliveau, J. W. (2006). Task-modulated 'What' and 'Where' pathways in human auditory cortex. *Proceedings of the National Academy of Sciences of the United States of America*, *103*(39), 14608–14613. doi:10.1073/pnas.0510480103

Aiken, L. S., Santa, J. L., & Ruskin, A. B. (1972). Nonreinforced trials in concept identification: Presolution statistics and local consistency. *Journal of Experimental Psychology*, *93*(1), 100–104.

References

Akers, K. G., Martinez-Canabal, A., Restivo, L., Yiu, A. P., De Cristofaro, A., Hsiang, H. L. ... Frankland, P. W. (2014). Hippocampal neurogenesis regulates forgetting during adulthood and infancy. *Science, 344*(6184), 598–602. doi:10.1126/science.1248903

Alais, D., & Burr, D. (2004). The ventriloquist effect results from near-optimal bimodal integration. *Current Biology, 14*(3), 257–262. doi:10.1016/j.cub.2004.01.029

Alais, D., Newell, F. N., & Mamassian, P. (2010). Multisensory processing in review: From physiology to behaviour. *Seeing and Perceiving, 23*(1), 3–38. doi:10.1163/187847510X488603

Albe-Fessard, D., Berkley, K. J., Kruger, L., Ralston, H. J., & Willis, W. D. (1985). Diencephalic mechanisms of pain sensation. *Brain Research Reviews, 9*, 217–296.

Albouy, G., King, B. R., Maquet, P., & Doyon, J. (2013). Hippocampus and striatum: Dynamics and interaction during acquisition and sleep-related motor sequence memory consolidation. *Hippocampus, 23*(11), 985–1004. doi:10.1002/hipo.22183

Albright, T. D. (1984). Direction and orientation selectivity of neurons in visual area MT of the macaque. *Journal of Neurophysiology, 52*(6), 1106–1130.

Albright, T. D., Desimone, R., & Gross, C. G. (1984). Columnar organization of directionally selective cells in visual area MT of the macaque. *Journal of Neurophysiology, 51*(1), 16–31.

Alexander, P. A., Schallert, D. L., & Hare, V. C. (1991). Coming to terms: How researchers in learning and literacy talk about knowledge. *Review of Educational Research, 61*(3), 315–343.

Alkire, M. T., Haier, R. J., & Fallon, J. H. (2000). Toward a unified theory of narcosis: Brain imaging evidence for a thalamocortical switch as the neurophysiologic basis of anesthetic-induced unconsciousness. *Consciousness and Cognition, 9*(3), 370–386.

Allen, E. A., Pasley, B. N., Duong, T., & Freeman, R. D. (2007). Transcranial magnetic stimulation elicits coupled neural and hemodynamic consequences. *Science, 317*, 1918–1921.

Allen, P., Laroi, F., McGuire, P. K., & Aleman, A. (2008). The hallucinating brain: A review of structural and functional neuroimaging studies of hallucinations. *Neuroscience and Biobehavioral Reviews, 32*(1), 175–191. doi:10.1016/j.neubiorev.2007.07.012

Allport, D. A., Antonis, B., & Reynolds, P. (1972). On the division of attention: A disproof of the single channel hypothesis. *The Quarterly Journal of Experimental Psychology, 24*, 225–235.

Almashat, S., Ayotte, B., Edelstein, B., & Margrett, J. (2008). Framing effect debiasing in medical decision making. *Patient Education and Counseling, 71*(1), 102–107. doi:10.1016/j.pec.2007.11.004

Alsius, A., Navarra, J., & Soto-Faraco, S. (2007). Attention to touch weakens audiovisual speech integration. *Experimental Brain Research, 183*(3), 399–404.

Alsius, A., Navarra, J., Campbell, R., & Soto-Faraco, S. (2005). Audiovisual integration of speech falters under high attention demands. *Current Biology, 15*(9), 839–843.

Amer, T., Campbell, K. L., & Hasher, L. (2016). Cognitive control as a double-edged sword. *Trends in Cognitive Sciences, 20*(12), 905–915. doi:10.1016/j.tics.2016.10.002

Amir, N., Bomyea, J., & Beard, C. (2010). The effect of single-session interpretation modification on attention bias in socially anxious individuals. *Journal of Anxiety Disorders, 24*(2), 178–182. doi:10.1016/j.janxdis.2009.10.005

Amiri, S., Fazel-Rezai, R., & Asadpour, V. (2013). A review of hybrid brain-computer interface systems. *Advances in Human-Computer Interaction, 2013*, 1–8. doi:10.1155/2013/187024

Anaki, D., & Bentin, S. (2009). Familiarity effects on categorization levels of faces and objects. *Cognition, 111*(1), 144–149. doi:10.1016/j.cognition.2009.01.002

Anderson, B. (2011). There is no such thing as attention. *Frontiers in Psychology, 2*, 246. doi:10.3389/fpsyg.2011.00246

Anderson, C. J. (2003). The psychology of doing nothing: Forms of decision avoidance result from reason and emotion. *Psychological Bulletin, 129*(1), 193–167.

Andersen, R. A., & Buneo, C. A. (2002). Intentional maps in posterior parietal cortex. *Annual Review of Neuroscience, 25*, 189–220. doi:10.1146/annurev.neuro.25.112701.142922

Andersen, S. K., Fuchs, S., & Müller, M. M. (2010). Effects of feature-selective and spatial attention at different stages of visual processing. *Journal of Cognitive Neuroscience, 23*(1), 238–246.

Anderson, J. R., Fincham, J. M., Qin, Y., & Stocco, A. (2008). A central circuit of the mind. *Trends in Cognitive Sciences, 12*(4), 136–143. doi:10.1016/j.tics.2008.01.006

Anderson, M. C., & Green, C. (2001). Suppressing unwanted memories by executive control. *Nature, 410*, 366–369.

Anderson, S. J., Holliday, I. E., Singh, K. D., & Harding, G. F. A. (1996). Localisation and functional analysis of human cortical area V5 using magneto-encephalography. *Proceedings of The Royal Society B-Biological Sciences, 263*, 423–431.

Anderson, M. C., Ochsner, K. N., Kuhl, B., Cooper, J., Robertson, E., Gabrieli, S. W. ... Gabrieli, J. D. E. (2004). Neural systems underlying the suppression of unwanted memories. *Science, 303*, 232–235.

Anderson, R. C., & Pichert, J. W. (1978). Recall of previously unrecallable information following a shift in perspective. *Journal of Verbal Learning and Verbal Behavior, 17*, 1–12.

Anderson, S. W., Rizzo, M., Skaar, N., Stierman, L., Cavaco, S., Dawson, J., & Damasio, H. (2007). Amnesia and driving. *Journal of Clinical and Experimental Neuropsychology, 29*(1), 1–12. doi:10.1080/13803390590954182

Andersen, R. A., Snyder, L. H., Bradley, D. C., & Xing, J. (1997). Multimodal representation of space in the posterior parietal cortex and its use in planning movements. *Annual Review of Neuroscience, 20*, 303–330.

Andrews-Hanna, J. R., Smallwood, J., & Spreng, R. N. (2014). The default network and self-generated thought: Component processes, dynamic control, and clinical relevance. *Annals of the New York Academy of Sciences, 1316*, 29–52. doi:10.1111/nyas.12360

Angelaki, D. E., Gu, Y., & DeAngelis, G. C. (2009). Multisensory integration: Psychophysics, neurophysiology, and computation. *Current Opinion in Neurobiology, 19*(4), 452–458. doi:10.1016/j.conb.2009.06.008

Angie, A. D., Connelly, S., Waples, E. P., & Kligyte, V. (2011). The influence of discrete emotions on judgement and decision-making: A meta-analytic review. *Cognition & Emotion, 25*(8), 1393–1422. doi:10.1080/02699931.2010.550751

Anllo-Vento, L., & Hillyard, S. A. (1996). Selective attention to the color and direction of moving stimuli: Electrophysiological correlates of hierarchical feature selection. *Perception & Psychophysics, 58*(2), 191–206.

Anobile, G., Arrighi, R., Castaldi, E., & Burr, D. C. (2021). A sensorimotor numerosity system. *Trends in Cognitive Sciences, 25*(1), 24–36. doi:10.1016/j.tics.2020.10.009

Anobile, G., Turi, M., Cicchini, G. M., & Burr, D. C. (2012). The effects of cross-sensory attentional demand on subitizing and on mapping number onto space. *Vision Research, 74*, 102–109. doi:10.1016/j.visres.2012.06.005

Apkarian, A. V., Bushnell, M. C., Treede, R. D., & Zubieta, J. K. (2005). Human brain mechanisms of pain perception and regulation in health and disease. *European Journal of Pain, 9*(4), 463–484. doi:10.1016/j.ejpain.2004.11.001

Apkarian, A. V., Sosa, Y., Krauss, B. R., Thomas, P. S., Fredrickson, B. E., Levy, R. E. … Chialvo, D. R. (2004). Chronic pain patients are impaired on an emotional decision-making task. *Pain, 108*(1–2), 129–136. doi:10.1016/j.pain.2003.12.015

Ardila, A., & Surloff, C. (2006). Dysexecutive agraphia: A major executive dysfunction sign. *International Journal of Neuroscience, 116*(5), 653–663. doi:10.1080/00207450600592206

Arkes, H. R., & Ayton, P. (1999). The sunk cost and Concorde effects: Are humans less rational than lower animals? *Psychological Bulletin, 125*(5), 591–600.

Armel, K. C., & Ramachandran, V. S. (2003). Projecting sensations to external objects: Evidence from skin conductance response. *Proceedings of the Royal Society B-Biological Sciences, 270*(1523), 1499–1506. doi:10.1098/rspb.2003.2364

Armstrong, S. L., Gleitman, L. R., & Gleitman, H. (1983). What some concepts might not be. *Cognition, 13*(3), 263–308.

Arnold, J. E. (2008). Reference production: production-internal and addressee-oriented processes. *Language and Cognitive Processes, 23*(4), 495–527. doi:10.1080/01690960801920099

Arnold, J. E., Eisenband, J. G., Brown-Schmidt, S., & Trueswell, J. C. (2000). The rapid use of gender information: Evidence of the time course of pronoun Resolution from eyetracking. *Cognition, 76*, B13–B26.

Aron, A. R. (2007). The neural basis of inhibition in cognitive control. *Neuroscientist, 13*(3), 214–228. doi:10.1177/1073858407299288

Aron, A. R., & Poldrack, R. A. (2006). Cortical and subcortical contributions to stop signal response inhibition: Role of the subthalamic nucleus. *The Journal of Neuroscience, 26*(9), 2424–2433. doi:10.1523/JNEUROSCI.4682-05.2006

Arzouan, Y., Goldstein, A., & Faust, M. (2007). Brainwaves are stethoscopes: ERP correlates of novel metaphor comprehension. *Brain Research, 1160*, 69–81. doi:10.1016/j.brainres.2007.05.034

Ashby, F. G., & Ell, S. W. (2001). The neurobiology of human category learning. *Trends in Cognitive Sciences, 5*(5), 204–210.

Ashby, F. G., & Maddox, W. T. (1993). Relations between prototype, exempla, and decision bound models of categorization. *Journal of Mathematical Psychology, 37*, 372–400.

Ashby, F. G., & Maddox, W. T. (2005). Human category learning. *Annual Review of Psychology, 56*, 149–178. doi:10.1146/annurev.psych.56.091103.070217

Ashby, F. G., Alfonso-Reese, L. A., Turken, A. U., & Waldron, E. M. (1998). A neuropsychological theory of multiple systems in category learning. *Psychological Review, 105*(3), 442–481.

Ashcraft, M. H., & Battaglia, J. (1978). Cognitive arithmetic: Evidence for retrieval and decision processes in mental addition. *Journal of Experimental Psychology: Human Learning and Memory, 1978*(4), 5.

Atkinson, A. P., & Adolphs, R. (2011). The neuropsychology of face perception: Beyond simple dissociations and functional selectivity. *Philosophical Transactions of the Royal Society B: Biological Sciences, 366*(1571), 1726–1738. doi:10.1098/rstb.2010.0349

Atkinson, A. P., Dittrich, W. H., Gemmell, A. J., & Young, A. W. (2004). Emotion perception from dynamic and static body expressions in point-light and full-light displays. *Perception, 33*(6), 717–746. doi:10.1068/p5096

Atkinson, R. C., & Shiffrin, R. M. (1968). Human memory: A proposed system and its control processes. In K. W. Spence & J. T. Spence (Eds.), *The psychology of learning and motivation* (Vol. 2). London: Academic Press.

Augustine, A. A., & Hemenover, S. H. (2009). On the relative effectiveness of affect regulation strategies: A meta-analysis. *Cognition and Emotion, 23*(6), 1181–1220. doi:10.1080/02699930802396556

Awh, E., & Jonides, J. (2001). Overlapping mechanisms of attention and spatial working memory. *Trends in Cognitive Sciences, 5*(3), 119–126.

Awh, E., & Pashler, H. (2000). Evidence for split attentional foci. *Journal of Experimental Psychology: Human Perception and Performance, 26*(2), 834–846.

Ayton, P., & Fischer, I. (2004). The hot hand fallacy and the Gambler's fallacy: Two faces of subjective randomness? *Memory & Cognition, 32*(8), 1369–1378.

Aziz-Zadeh, L., Cattaneo, L., Rochat, M., & Rizzolatti, G. (2005). Covert speech arrest induced by rTMS over both motor and nonmotor left hemisphere frontal sites. *Journal of Cognitive Neuroscience, 17*(6), 928–938.

Baars, B. J. (1997). Some essential differences between consciousness and attention, perception, and working memory. *Consciousness and Cognition, 6,* 363–371.

Baars, B. J. (2005). Global workspace theory of consciousness: Toward a cognitive neuroscience of human experience. *Progress in Brain Research, 150,* 45–53.

Baars, B. J., & Franklin, S. (2003). How conscious experience and working memory interact. *Trends in Cognitive Sciences, 7*(4), 166–172. doi:10.1016/s1364-6613(03)00056-1

Baars, B. J., & Franklin, S. (2007). An architectural model of conscious and unconscious brain functions: Global workspace theory and IDA. *Neural Networks, 20*(9), 955–961. doi:10.1016/j.neunet.2007.09.013

Baars, B. J., Motley, M. T., & MacKay, D. G. (1975). Output editing for lexical status in artificially elicited slips of the tongue. *Journal of Verbal Learning and Verbal Behavior, 14,* 382–391.

Bachorowski, J.-A., & Owren, M. J. (2006). Sounds of emotion. *Annals of the New York Academy of Sciences, 1000*(1), 244–265. doi:10.1196/annals.1280.012

Backer, K. C., & Alain, C. (2014). Attention to memory: Orienting attention to sound object representations. *Psychological Research, 78*(3), 439–452. doi:10.1007/s00426-013-0531-7

Baddeley, A. (1996). Exploring the central executive. *The Quarterly Journal of Experimental Psychology, 49A*(1), 5–28.

Baddeley, A. D. (1992). Working memory. *Science, 255,* 556–559.

Baddeley, A. D. (2000). The episodic buffer: A new component of working memory? *Trends in Cognitive Sciences, 4*(11), 417–423.

Baddeley, A. D. (2003). Working memory: Looking back and looking forward. *Nature Reviews Neuroscience, 4*(10), 829–839. doi:10.1038/nrn1201

Baddeley, A. D., & Hitch, G. J. (1974). Working memory. In G. A. Bower (Ed.), *Recent advances in learning and memory* (Vol. 8, pp. 47–89). New York, NY: Academic Press.

Baddeley, A., Thomson, N., & Buchanan, M. (1975). Word length and the structure of short-term memory. *Journal of Learning and Verbal Behavior, 14,* 575–589.

Baddeley, A. D., & Wilson, B. (2002). Prose recall and amnesia implications for the structure of working memory. *Neuropsychologia, 40,* 1737–1743.

Bagila, S., & Ely, J. C. (2011). Mnemonomics: The sunk cost fallacy as a memory kludge. *American Economic Journal: Microeconomics, 3*(4), 35–67.

Bahrick, H. P. (1984). Semantic content in permastore: Fifty years of memory for Spanish learned in school. *Journal of Experimental Psychology: General, 113*(1), 1–29.

Bahrick, H. P., Bahrick, O., & Wittlinger, R. P. (1975). Fifty years of memory for names and faces: A cross-sectional approach. *Journal of Experimental Psychology: General, 104*(1), 54–75.

Bahrick, H. P., Hall, L. K., & Da Costa, L. A. (2008). Fifty years of memory of college grades: Accuracy and distortions. *Emotion, 8*(1), 13–22. doi:10.1037/1528-3542.8.1.13

Bain, A. (1868). *The senses and the intellect.* New York, NY: D. Appleton and Company.

Baldo, J. V., Bunge, S. A., Wilson, S. M., & Dronkers, N. F. (2010). Is relational reasoning dependent on language? A voxel-based lesion symptom mapping study. *Brain & Language, 113*(2), 59–64. doi:10.1016/j.bandl.2010.01.004

Baldo, J. V., & Dronkers, N. F. (2007). Neural correlates of arithmetic and language comprehension: A common substrate? *Neuropsychologia, 45*(2), 229–235. doi:10.1016/j.neuropsychologia.2006.07.014

Baliki, M. N., Chialvo, D. R., Geha, P. Y., Levy, R. M., Harden, R. N., Parrish, T. B., & Apkarian, A. V. (2006). Chronic pain and the emotional brain: Specific brain activity associated with spontaneous fluctuations of intensity of chronic back pain. *The Journal of Neuroscience, 26*(47), 12165–12173. doi:10.1523/JNEUROSCI.3576-06.2006

Bálint, R. (1909). Seelenlähmung des 'Schauens', optische ataxie, räumliche störung der aufmerksamkeit. *Monatschrift Für Psychiatrische Neurolologie, 25*(1), 51–66.

Ballesta, S., & Duhamel, J.-R. (2015). Rudimentary empathy in Macaques' social decision-making. *Proceedings of the National Academy of Sciences of the United States of America, 112*(50), 15516–15521. doi:10.1073/pnas.1504454112

Balota, D. A., Paul, S. T., & Spieler, D. H. (1999). Attentional control of lexical processing pathways during word recognition and reading. In S. Garrod, & M. J. Pickering (Eds.), *Language processing.* Hove: Psychology Press

Banissy, M. J., & Ward, J. (2007). Mirror-touch synesthesia is linked with empathy. *Nature Neuroscience, 10*(7), 815–816. doi:10.1038/nn1926

Banks, W. P., & Isham, E. A. (2009). We infer rather than perceive the moment we decided to act. *Psychological Science, 20*(1), 17–21.

Bantick, S. J., Wise, R. G., Ploghaus, A., Clare, S., Smith, S. M., & Tracey, I. (2002). Imaging how attention modulates pain in humans using functional MRI. *Brain, 125,* 310–319.

Bar, M., Kassam, K. S., Ghuman, A. S., Boshan, J., Schmid, A. M., Dale, A. M. ... Halgren, E. (2006). Top-down facilitation of visual recognition. *Proceedings of the National Academy of Sciences of the United States of America, 103*(2), 449–454.

Barbas, H. (1995). Anatomic basis of cognitive-emotional interaction in the primate prefrontal cortex. *Neuroscience and Biobehavioral Reviews, 19*(3), 499–510.

Barense, M. D., Ngo, J. K., Hung, L. H., & Peterson, M. A. (2012). Interactions of memory and perception in amnesia: The figure-ground perspective. *Cerebral Cortex*, *22*(11), 2680–2691. doi:10.1093/cercor/bhr347

Bargh, J. A., Chen, M., & Burrows, L. (1996). Automaticity of social behavior: Direct effects of trait construct and stereotype activation on action. *Journal of Personality and Social Psychology*, *71*(2), 230–244.

Barlow, J. S. (1997). The early history of EEG data-processing at the Massachusetts General Hospital. *International Journal of Psychophysiology*, *26*, 443–454.

Baronchelli, A., Chater, N., Pastor-Satorras, R., & Christiansen, M. H. (2012). The biological origin of linguistic diversity. *PLoS One*, *7*(10), e48029. doi:10.1371/journal.pone.0048029

Baron-Cohen, S., Ring, H. A., Wheelwright, S., Bullmore, E. T., Brammer, M. J., Simmons, A., & Williams, S. C. R. (1999). Social intelligence in the normal and autistic brain: An fMRI study. *European Journal of Neuroscience*, *11*, 1891–1898.

Baron-Cohen, S., Wheelwright, S., Hill, J., Raste, Y., & Plumb, I. (2001). The 'Reading the mind in the eyes' test revised version: A study with normal adults, and adults with Asperger syndrome or high-functioning autism. *Journal of Child Psychology and Psychiatry*, *42*(2), 241–251. doi:10.1111/1469-7610.00715

Barraclough, N. E., Xiao, D., Baker, C. I., Oram, M. W., & Perrett, D. I. (2005). Integration of visual and auditory information by superior temporal sulcus neurons responsive to the sight of actions. *Journal of Cognitive Neuroscience*, *17*, 377–391.

Barrett, L. F. (2017). The theory of constructed emotion: An active inference account of interoception and categorization. *Social Cognitive and Affective Neuroscience*, *12*(1), 1–23. doi:10.1093/scan/nsw154

Barrett, L. F., & Russel, J. P. (1999). The structure of current affect: Controversies and emerging consensus. *Current Directions in Psychological Science*, *8*(1), 10–14.

Barry, R. J. (1975). Low intensity auditory stimulation and the GSR orienting response. *Physiological Psychology*, *3*(1), 98–100.

Barry, D. N., & Maguire, E. A. (2019). Remote memory and the hippocampus: A constructive critique. *Trends in Cognitive Sciences*, *23*(2), 128–142. doi:10.1016/j.tics.2018.11.005

Barsalou, L. W. (1983). Ad hoc categories. *Memory & Cognition*, *11*(3), 211–227.

Barsalou, L. W. (1987). The instability of graded structure: Implications for the nature of concepts. In U. Neisser (Ed.), *Concepts and conceptual development: Ecological and intellectual factors in categorization*. London: Cambridge University Press.

Barsalou, L. W. (2008). Grounded cognition. *Annual Review of Psychology*, *59*, 617–645. doi:10.1146/annurev.psych.59.103006.093639

Barsalou, L. W. (2009). Simulation, situated conceptualization, and prediction. *Philosophical Transactions of the Royal Society B-Biological Sciences*, *364*(1521), 1281–1289. doi:10.1098/rstb.2008.0319

Bartlett, F. C. (1932). *Remembering: A study in experimental and social psychology*. Cambridge, MA: Cambridge University Press.

Bartolomeo, P., Thiebaut de Schotten, M., & Chica, A. B. (2012). Brain networks of visuospatial attention and their disruption in visual neglect. *Frontiers in Human Neuroscience*, *6*, 110. doi:10.3389/fnhum.2012.00110

Bastuji, H., Frot, M., Perchet, C., Magnin, M., & Garcia-Larrea, L. (2016). Pain networks from the inside: Spatiotemporal analysis of brain responses leading from nociception to conscious perception. *Human Brain Mapping*, *37*(12), 4301–4315. doi:10.1002/hbm.23310

Basu Mallick, D., Magnotti, J., & Beauchamp, F. (2015). Variability and stability in the McGurk effect: Contributions of participants, stimuli, time, and response type. *Psychonomic Bulletin & Review*, *22*(5), 1299–1307. doi:10.3758/s13423-015-0817-4

Bateson, M., Nettle, D., & Roberts, G. (2006). Cues of being watched enhance cooperation in a real-world setting. *Biology Letters*, *2*(3), 412–414. doi:10.1098/rsbl.2006.0509

Battaglia-Mayer, A., Ferraina, S., Mitsuda, T., Marconi, B., Genovesio, A., Onorati, P. … Caminiti, R. (2000). Early coding of reaching in the parietooccipital cortex. *Journal of Neurophysiology*, *83*, 2374–2391.

Battelli, L., Walsh, V., Pascual-Leone, A., & Cavanagh, P. (2008). The 'When' parietal pathway explored by lesion studies. *Current Opinion in Neurobiology*, *18*(2), 120–126. doi:10.1016/j.conb.2008.08.004

Baucom, L. B., Wedell, D. H., Wang, J., Blitzer, D. N., & Shinkareva, S. V. (2012). Decoding the neural representation of affective States. *Neuroimage*, *59*(1), 718–727. doi:10.1016/j.neuroimage.2011.07.037

Bauman, C. W., McGraw, A. P., Bartels, D. M., & Warren, C. (2014). Revisiting external validity: Concerns about trolley problems and other sacrificial dilemmas in moral psychology. *Social and Personality Psychology Compass*, *8/9*, 536–554.

Baumeister, R. F. (1984). Choking under pressure: Self-consciousness and paradoxical effects of incentives on skillful performance. *Journal of Personality and Social Psychology*, *46*(3), 610–620.

Bäuml, K.-H. T., & Kliegl, O. (2013). The critical role of retrieval processes in release from proactive interference. *Journal of Memory and Language*, *68*(1), 39–53. doi:10.1016/j.jml.2012.07.006

Bavelas, J., Gerwing, J., Sutton, C., & Prevost, D. (2008). Gesturing on the telephone: Independent effects of dialogue and visibility. *Journal of Memory and Language*, *58*(2), 495–520. doi:10.1016/j.jml.2007.02.004

Baxendale, S. (2004). Memories aren't made of this: Amnesia at the movies. *British Medical Journal*, *329*, 1480–1483.

Bayley, P. J., Frascino, J. C., & Squire, L. R. (2005). Robust habit learning in the absence of awareness and independent of the medial temporal lobe. *Nature*, *436*(7050), 550–553. doi:10.1038/nature03857

Bayley, P. J., Hopkins, R. O., & Squire, L. R. (2006). The fate of old memories after medial temporal lobe damage. *The Journal of Neuroscience*, *26*(51), 13311–13317. doi:10.1523/JNEUROSCI.4262-06.2006

Bayne, T., Hohwy, J., & Owen, A. M. (2016). Are there levels of consciousness? *Trends in Cognitive Sciences*, *20*(6), 405–413. doi:10.1016/j.tics.2016.03.009

Beauvais, C., Olive, T., & Passerault, J.-M. (2011). Why are some texts good and others not? Relationship between text quality and management of the writing processes. *Journal of Educational Psychology*, *103*(2), 415–428. doi:10.1037/a0022545

Beauvois, M. F., & Dérouesné, J. (1979). Phonological alexia: Three dissociations. *Journal of Neurology, Neurosurgery, and Psychiatry*, *42*, 1115–1124.

Bechara, A., Damasio, H., Tranel, D., & Damasio, A. R. (2005). The Iowa gambling task and the somatic marker hypothesis: Some questions and answers. *Trends in Cognitive Sciences*, *9*(4), 159–162; discussion 162–154. doi:10.1016/j.tics.2005.02.002

Beck, A. T. (1976). *Cognitive therapy and the emotional disorders*. New York, NY: International Universities Press.

Beck, A. T., & Clark, D. A. (1988). Anxiety and depression: An information processing perspective. *Anxiety Research*, *1*(1), 23–36. doi:10.1080/10615808808248218

Beck, A. T., & Clark, D. A. (1997). An information processing model of anxiety: Automatic and strategic processes. *Behavioral Research Therapy*, *35*(1), 49–58.

Beck, J. M., Ma, W. J., Kiani, R., Hanks, T., Churchland, A. K., Roitman, J. ... Pouget, A. (2008). Probabilistic population codes for Bayesian decision making. *Neuron*, *60*(6), 1142–1152. doi:10.1016/j.neuron.2008.09.021

Beckers, G., & Zeki, S. (1995). The consequences of inactivating areas V1 and V5 on visual motion perception. *Brain*, *118*, 49–60.

Beeke, S., Wilkinson, R., & Maxim, J. (2007). Grammar without sentence structure: A conversation analytic investigation of agrammatism. *Aphasiology*, *21*(3–4), 256–282. doi:10.1080/02687030600911344.

Bekker, E. M., Kenemans, J. L., Hoeksma, M. R., Talsma, D., & Verbaten, M. N. (2005). The pure electrophysiology of stopping. *International Journal of Psychophysiology*, *55*(2), 191–198. doi:10.1016/j.ijpsycho.2004.07.005

Bell, V. A., & Johnson-Laird, P. N. (1998). A model theory of modal reasoning. *Cognitive Science*, *22*(1), 25–51.

Bellugi, U., Aldolphs, R., Cassady, C., & Chiles, M. (1999). Towards the neural basis for hypersociability in a genetic syndrome. *Neuroreport*, *10*, 1653–1657.

Bennett, C. M., Baird, A. A., Miller, M. B., & Wolford, G. L. (2009). *Neural correlates of interspecies perspective taking in the post-mortem atlantic salmon: An argument for multiple comparisons correction*. Paper presented at the Human Brain Mapping.

Bennett, P., & Lowe, R. (2008). Emotions and their cognitive precursors: Responses to spontaneously identified stressful events among Hospital nurses. *Journal of Health Psychology*, *13*(4), 537–546.

Benson, D. F., & Denckla, M. B. (1969). Verbal paraphasia as a source of calculation disturbance. *Archives of Neurology*, *21*(1), 96–102.

Benton, T. R., Ross, D. F., Bradshaw, E., Thomas, W. N., & Bradshaw, G. S. (2006). Eyewitness memory is still not common sense: Comparing jurors, judges and law enforcement to eyewitness experts. *Applied Cognitive Psychology*, *20*(1), 115–129. doi:10.1002/acp.1171

Bereiter, C., Burtis, P. J., & Scardamalia, M. (1988). Cognitive operations in constructing main points in written composition. *Journal of Memory and Language*, *27*, 261–278.

Bereiter, C., & Scardamalia, M. (1987). *The psychology of written composition*. Hillsdale, NJ: Lawrence Erlbaum Associates, Inc.

Berger, H. (1929). Uber das elekrenkephalogramm das menschen. *Archif Für Psychiatrie*, *87*, 527–570.

Berger, C. C., & Ehrsson, H. H. (2013). Mental imagery changes multisensory perception. *Current Biology*, *23*(14), 1367–1372. doi:10.1016/j.cub.2013.06.012

Berger, C. C., & Ehrsson, H. H. (2014). The fusion of mental imagery and sensation in the temporal association cortex. *The Journal of Neuroscience*, *34*(41), 13684–13692. doi:10.1523/JNEUROSCI.0943-14.2014

Bergman, E. T., & Roediger, H. L. (1999). Can Bartlett's repeated reproduction experiments be replicated? *Memory & Cognition*, *27*(6), 937–947.

Bergstrom, Z. M., O'Connor, R. J., Li, M. K., & Simons, J. S. (2012). Event-related potential evidence for separable automatic and controlled retrieval processes in proactive interference. *Brain Research*, *1455*, 90–102. doi:10.1016/j.brainres.2012.03.043

Bernier, P. M., & Grafton, S. T. (2010). Human posterior parietal cortex flexibly determines reference frames for reaching based on sensory context. *Neuron*, *68*(4), 776–788. doi:10.1016/j.neuron.2010.11.002

Berntsen, D., Rubin, D. C., & Siegler, I. C. (2011). Two versions of life: Emotionally negative and positive life events have different roles in the organization of life story and identity. *Emotion*, *11*(5), 1190–1201. doi:10.1037/a0024940

Berridge, K. C. (2004). Motivation concepts in behavioral neuroscience. *Physiology and Behavior*, *81*(2), 179–209. doi:10.1016/j.physbeh.2004.02.004

Berridge, K. C. (2007). The debate over Dopamine's role in reward: The case for incentive salience. *Psychopharmacology (Berl)*, *191*(3), 391–431. doi:10.1007/s00213-006-0578-x

Berridge, K. C., & Valenstein, E. S. (1991). What psychological process mediates feeding evoked by electrical stimulation of the lateral hypothalamus? *Behavioral Neuroscience*, *105*(1), 3–14.

Bertelson, P. (1998). Starting from the ventriloquist: The perception of multimodal events. In M. Sabourin, & C. Fergus (Eds.), *Advances in psychological science, volume 2: Biological and cognitive aspects*. Hove, England: Psychology Press.

Bertelson, P., Vroomen, J., & De Gelder, B. (2003). Recalibration of auditory speech identification: A McGurk after effect. *Psychological Science, 14*(6), 592–597.

Bertelson, P., Vroomen, J., De Gelder, B., & Driver, J. (2000). The ventriloquist effect does not depend on the direction of deliberate visual attention. *Perception & Psychophysics, 62*(2), 321–332.

Berthoud, H.-R. (2002). Multiple neural systems controlling food intake and body weight. *Neuroscience and Biobehavioral Reviews, 26*, 393–428.

Besson, M., & Friederici, A. D. (2005). Part II: Language and music–a comparison. Introduction. *Annals of the New York Academy of Sciences, 1060*(1), 57–58. doi:10.1196/annals.1360.061

Betz, V. (1874). Anatomischer Nachweis zweier Gehirncentra. *Centralblatt für die medizinische Wissenschaften, 12*, 578–580.

Bhandari, A., & Duncan, J. (2014). Goal neglect and knowledge chunking in the construction of novel behaviour. *Cognition, 130*(1), 11–30. doi:10.1016/j.cognition.2013.08.013

Bialystok, E., Majumder, S., & Martin, M. M. (2003). Developing phonological awareness: Is there a bilingual advantage? *Applied Psycholinguistics, 24*, 27–44.

Bickerton, D. (1984). The language bioprogram hypothesis. *Behavioral and Brain Sciences, 7*, 173–221.

Biderman, N., Bakkour, A., & Shohamy, D. (2020). What are memories for? The hippocampus bridges past experience with future decisions. *Trends in Cognitive Sciences, 24*(7), 542–556. doi:10.1016/j.tics.2020.04.004

Biederman, I. (1987). Recognition by components: A theory of human image understanding. *Psychological Review, 94*(2), 115–147.

Biederman, I., & Gerhardstein, P. C. (1993). Recognizing depth-rotated objects: Evidence and conditions for three-dimensional viewpoint invariance. *Journal of Experimental Psychology: Human Perception and Performance, 19*(6), 1162–1182.

Biedermann, B., Ruh, N., Nickels, L., & Coltheart, M. (2008). Information retrieval in tip of the Tongue States: New data and methodological advances. *Journal of Psycholinguistic Research, 37*(3), 171–198. doi:10.1007/s10936-007-9065-8

Bier, N., Bottari, C., Hudon, C., Joubert, S., Paquette, G., & Macoir, J. (2013). The impact of semantic dementia on everyday actions: Evidence from an ecological study. *Journal of the International Neuropsychological Society, 19*(2), 162–172. doi:10.1017/S1355617712001105

Bilalic, M., Langner, R., Erb, M., & Grodd, W. (2010). Supplemental material for mechanisms and neural basis of object and pattern recognition: A study with chess experts. *Journal of Experimental Psychology: General, 139*(4), 728–742. doi:10.1037/a0020756.supp

Billings, C. E. (1991). *Human-centered aircraft automation: A concept and guidelines (NASA Technical Memorandum 103885)*. Moffet Field, CA: NASA Ames Research Center.

Bills, A. G. (1931). Blocking: A new principle of mental fatigue. *The American Journal of Psychology, 43*(2), 230–245.

Binder, J. R., & Desai, R. H. (2011). The neurobiology of semantic memory. *Trends in Cognitive Sciences, 15*(11), 527–536. doi:10.1016/j.tics.2011.10.001

Binder, J. R., Desai, R. H., Graves, W. W., & Conant, L. L. (2009). Where is the semantic system? A critical review and meta-analysis of 120 functional neuroimaging studies. *Cerebral Cortex, 19*(12), 2767–2796. doi:10.1093/cercor/bhp055

Bindra, D. (1974). A motivational view of learning, performance, and behavior modification. *Psychologiscal Review, 81*(3), 199–213.

Bindra, D. (1978). How adaptive behavior is produced: A perceptual-motivational alternative to response-reinforcement. *Behavioral and Brain Sciences, 1*, 41–91.

Bindschaedler, C., Peter-Favre, C., Maeder, P., Hirsbrunner, T., & Clarke, S. (2011). Growing up with bilateral hippocampal atrophy: From childhood to teenage. *Cortex, 47*(8), 931–944. doi:10.1016/j.cortex.2010.09.005

Birch, H. G. (1945). The relation of previous experience to insightful problem-solving. *Journal of Comparative Psychology, 38*(6), 367–383.

Bishop, S. J. (2007). Neurocognitive mechanisms of anxiety: An integrative account. *Trends in Cognitive Sciences, 11*(7), 307–316. doi:10.1016/j.tics.2007.05.008

Bisiach, E., & Luzzatti, C. (1978). Unilateral neglect of representational space. *Cortex, 14*(1), 129–133. doi:10.1016/S0010-9452(78)80016-1

Blackmer, E. R., & Mitton, J. L. (1991). Theories of monitoring and the timing of repairs in spontaneous speech. *Cognition, 39*, 173–194.

Blakemore, S. J., & Decety, J. (2001). From the perception of action to the understanding of intention. *Nature Reviews Neuroscience, 2*(8), 562–567.

Blakemore, S. J., Frith, C., & Wolpert, D. M. (1999). Spatio-temporal prediction modulates the perception of self-produced stimuli. *Journal of Cognitive Neuroscience, 11*(5), 551–559.

Blakemore, S.-J., Wolpert, D. M., & Frith, C. (2000). Why can't you tickle yourself? *Neuroreport, 11*(11), R11–R16.

Blanchette, I., & Dunbar, K. (2000). How analogies are generated: The roles of structural and superficial similarity. *Memory & Cognition, 28*(1), 108–124.

Blanco-Elorrieta, E., & Pylkkanen, L. (2018). Ecological validity in bilingualism research and the bilingual advantage. *Trends in Cognitive Sciences, 22*(12), 1117–1126. doi:10.1016/j.tics.2018.10.001

Blanke, O., Ortigue, S., Landis, T., & Seeck, M. (2002). Simulating illusory own-body perceptions. *Nature, 419*, 269–270.

References

Blasco, M. A., & Redleaf, M. I. (2014). Cochlear implantation in unilateral sudden deafness improves tinnitus and speech comprehension: Meta-analysis and systematic review. *Otology & Neurology, 35*, 1426–1432.

Blasko, D. G., & Connine, C. M. (1993). Effects of familiarity and aptness on metaphor processing. *Journal of Experimental Psychology: Learning, Memory, and Cognition, 19*(2), 295–308.

Bleuler. (1911). Dementia praecox order gruppe der schizophrenien. In G. Aschaffenburg (Ed.), *Handbuch der psychiatrie*. Leipzig: Franz Deuticke.

Block, N. (2005). Two neural correlates of consciousness. *Trends in Cognitive Sciences, 9*(2), 46–52. doi:10.1016/j.tics.2004.12.006

Bloom, F. E., & Lazeron, A. (1988). *Brain, mind, and behavior.* New York, NY: W. H. Freeman and Company.

Bob, P. (2008). Pain, dissociation and subliminal self-representations. *Conscious and Cognition, 17*(1), 355–369. doi:10.1016/j.concog.2007.12.001

Bock, K. (1996). Language production: Methods and methodologies. *Psychonomic Bulletin & Review, 3*(4), 395–421.

Boehler, C. N., Münte, T. F., Krebs, R. M., Heinze, H. J., Schoenfeld, M. A., & Hopf, J. M. (2009). Sensory meg responses predict successful and failed inhibition in a stop-signal task. *Cerebral Cortex, 19*(1), 134–145.

Bohannon, J. N. I. (1988). Flashbulb memories for the space shuttle disaster: A tale of two theories. *Cognition, 29*, 179–196.

Boksem, M. A., Meijman, T. F., & Lorist, M. M. (2006). Mental fatigue, motivation and action monitoring. *Biological Psychology, 72*(2), 123–132. doi:10.1016/j.biopsycho.2005.08.007

Boksem, M. A., & Tops, M. (2008). Mental fatigue: Costs and benefits. *Brain Research Reviews, 59*(1), 125–139. doi:10.1016/j.brainresrev.2008.07.001

Boland, J. E., & Blodgett, A. (2001). Understanding the constraints on syntactic generation: Lexical bias and discourse congruency effects on eye movements. *Journal of Memory and Language, 45*(3), 391–411. doi:10.1006/jmla.2000.2778

Bolden, G. B. (2006). Little words that matter: Discourse markers 'So' and 'Oh' and the doing of other-attentiveness in social interaction. *Journal of Communication, 56*(4), 661–688. doi:10.1111/j.1460-2466.2006.00314.x

Bolles, R. C. (1972). Reinforcement, expectancy, and learning. *Psychological Review, 79*(5), 394–409.

Bolton, T. A. W., Morgenroth, E., Preti, M. G., & Van De Ville, D. (2020). Tapping into multi-faceted human behavior and psychopathology using fMRI brain dynamics. *Trends in Neurosciences, 43*(9), 667–680. doi:10.1016/j.tins.2020.06.005

Bonath, B., Noesselt, T., Martinez, A., Mishra, J., Schwiecker, K., Heinze, H. J., & Hillyard, S. A. (2007). Neural basis of the ventriloquist illusion. *Current Biology, 17*(19), 1697–1703. doi:10.1016/j.cub.2007.08.050

Bonini, L., Rotunno, C., Arcuri, E., & Gallese, V. (2022). Mirror neurons 30 years later: Implications and applications. *Trends in Cognitive Sciences, 26*(9), 767–781. doi:10.1016/j.tics.2022.06.003

Bonnefon, J. F., Eid, M., Vautier, S., & Jmel, S. (2008). A mixed Rasch model of dual-process conditional reasoning. *The Quarterly Journal of Experimental Psychology, 61*(5), 809–824. doi:10.1080/17470210701434573

Bonnefon, J.-F., Girotto, V., & Legrenzi, P. (2012). The psychology of reasoning about preferences and unconsequential decisions. *Synthese, 185*(S1), 27–41. doi:10.1007/s11229-011-9957-x

Bonnefon, J. F., Shariff, A., & Rahwan, L. (2016). The social dilemma of autonomous vehicles. *Science, 352*(6293), 1573–1576.

Bonnefond, M., Noveck, I., Baillet, S., Cheylus, A., Delpuech, C., Bertrand, O. ... Van der Henst, J.-B. (2013). What meg can reveal about inference making: The case of if...then sentences. *Human Brain Mapping, 34*, 684–697. doi:10.1002/hbm.21465

Boot, W. R., & Kramer, A. F. (2014). The brain-games conundrum: Does cognitive training really sharpen the mind? *Cerebrum, 15.* https://www.ncbi.nlm.nih.gov/pmc/articles/PMC4445580/

Booth, M. C. A., & Rolls, E. T. (1998). View-invariant representations of familiar objects by neurons in the inferior temporal visual cortex. *Cerebral Cortex, 8*, 510–523.

Bor, D., & Seth, A. K. (2012). Consciousness and the prefrontal parietal network: Insights from attention, working memory, and chunking. *Frontiers in Psychology, 3*, 63. doi:10.3389/fpsyg.2012.00063

Bordage, G. (2007). Prototypes and semantic qualifiers: From past to present. *Medical Education, 41*(12), 1117–1121. doi:10.1111/j.1365-2923.2007.02919.x

Borghi, A. M., & Cimatti, F. (2010). Embodied cognition and beyond: Acting and sensing the body. *Neuropsychologia, 48*(3), 763–773. doi:10.1016/j.neuropsychologia.2009.10.029

Bormann, T., Wallesch, C.-W., Seyboth, M., & Blanken, G. (2009). Writing two words as one: Word boundary errors in a German case of acquired surface dysgraphia. *Journal of Neurolinguistics, 22*(1), 74–82. doi:10.1016/j.jneuroling.2008.06.002

Borst, J. P., Buwalda, T. A., van Rijn, H., & Taatgen, N. A. (2013). Avoiding the problem state bottleneck by strategic use of the environment. *Acta Psychologica, 144*(2), 373–379. doi:10.1016/j.actpsy.2013.07.016

Borst, J. P., Taatgen, N. A., & van Rijn, H. (2010). The problem state: A cognitive bottleneck in multitasking. *Journal of Experimental Psychology. Learning, Memory, and Cognition, 36*(2), 363–382. doi:10.1037/a0018106

Both, S., Everaerd, W., & Laan, E. (2007). Desire emerges from excitement: A psychophysiological perspective on sexual motivation. In E. Janssen (Ed.), *The psychophysiology of sex* (pp. 327–339). Bloomington: Indiana University Press.

Botvinick, M. M., Braver, T. S., Barch, D. M., Carter, S. C., & Cohen, J. D. (2001). Conflict monitoring and cognitive control. *Psychological Review, 108*(3), 624–692.

Botvinick, M. M., & Cohen, J. D. (1998). Rubber hands 'Feel' touch that eyes see. *Nature, 391*, 756.

Botvinick, M. M., Niv, Y., & Barto, A. C. (2009). Hierarchically organized behavior and its neural foundations: A reinforcement learning perspective. *Cognition, 113*(3), 262–280. doi:10.1016/j.cognition.2008.08.011

Bourke, P. A., Duncan, J., & Nimmo-Smith, I. (1996). A general factor involved in dual-task performance decrement. *The Quarterly Journal of Experimental Psychology Section A, 49*(3), 525–545. doi:10.1080/713755635

Bourne, L. E., Guy, D. E., Dodd, D. H., & Justesen, D. R. (1965). Concept identification: The effects of varying length and informational components of the intertrial interval. *Journal of Experimental Psychology, 69*(6), 624–629.

Bouvier, S. E., & Engel, S. A. (2006). Behavioral deficits and cortical damage loci in cerebral achromatopsia. *Cerebral Cortex, 16*(2), 183–191. doi:10.1093/cercor/bhi096

Bowden, E. M., & Jung-Beeman, M. (2007). Methods for investigating the neural components of insight. *Methods, 42*(1), 87–99. doi:10.1016/j.ymeth.2006.11.007

Bowden, E. M., Jung-Beeman, M., Fleck, J., & Kounios, J. (2005). New approaches to demystifying insight. *Trends in Cognitive Sciences, 9*(7), 322–328. doi:10.1016/j.tics.2005.05.012

Bower, G. H. (1981). Mood and memory. *American Psychologist, 36*(2), 129–148.

Bower, G. H., & Trabasso, T. R. (1964). Concept identification. In R. C. Atkinson (Ed.), *Studies in mathematical psychology*. Stanford: Stanford University Press.

Bower, G. H., Black, J. B., & Turner, T. J. (1979). Scripts in memory for text. *Cognitive Psychology, 11*, 177–220.

Bowers, J. S., & Davis, C. J. (2012). Bayesian just-so stories in psychology and neuroscience. *Psychological Bulletin, 138*(3), 389–414. doi:10.1037/a0026450

Bowles, B., Crupi, C., Mirsattari, S. M., Pigott, S. E., Parrent, A. G., Pruessner, J. C. … Kohler, S. (2007). Impaired familiarity with preserved recollection after anterior temporal-lobe resection that spares the hippocampus. *Proceedings of the National Academy of Sciences of the United States of America, 104*(41), 16382–16387. doi:10.1073/pnas.0705273104

Bowles, B., Crupi, C., Pigott, S., Parrent, A., Wiebe, S., Janzen, L., & Kohler, S. (2010). Double dissociation of selective recollection and familiarity impairments following two different surgical treatments for temporal-lobe epilepsy. *Neuropsychologia, 48*(9), 2640–2647. doi:10.1016/j.neuropsychologia.2010.05.010

Bowles, B., O'Neil, E. B., Mirsattari, S. M., Poppenk, J., & Kohler, S. (2011). Preserved hippocampal novelty responses following anterior temporal-lobe resection that impairs familiarity but spares recollection. *Hippocampus, 21*(8), 847–854. doi:10.1002/hipo.20800

Boyer, J. L., Harrison, S., & Ro, T. (2005). Unconscious processing of orientation and color without primary visual cortex. *Proceedings of the National Academy of Sciences of the United States of America, 102*(46), 16875–16879. doi:10.1073/pnas.0505332102

Bradley, L. A., Mckendree-Smith, N. L., Alarcon, G. S., & Cianfrini, L. (2002). Is fibromyalgia a neurologic disease? *Current Pain and Headache Report, 6*, 106–114.

Braem, S., Verguts, T., Roggeman, C., & Notebaert, W. (2012). Reward modulates adaptations to conflict. *Cognition, 125*(2), 324–332. doi:10.1016/j.cognition.2012.07.015

Brainard, D. H., & Maloney, L. T. (2011). Surface color perception and equivalent illumination models. *Journal of Vision, 11*(5), 1–18.

Brainard, D. H., Longere, P., Delahunt, P. B., Freeman, W. T., Kraft, J. M., & Xiao, B. (2006). Bayesian model of human color constancy. *Journal of Vision, 6*(11), 1267–1281. doi:10.1167/6.11.10

Brainerd, C. J., & Mojardin, A. H. (1998). Children's and adult' spontaneous false memories: Long-term persistence and mere-testing effects. *Child Development, 69*(5), 1361–1377.

Brainerd, C. J., Reyna, V. F., & Ceci, S. J. (2008). Developmental reversals in false memory: A review of data and theory. *Psychological Bulletin, 134*(3), 343–382. doi:10.1037/0033-2909.134.3.343

Brandwein, A. B., Foxe, J. J., Butler, J. S., Russo, N. N., Altschuler, T. S., Gomes, H., & Molholm, S. (2013). The development of multisensory integration in high-functioning autism: High-density electrical mapping and psychophysical measures reveal impairments in the processing of audiovisual inputs. *Cerebral Cortex, 23*(6), 1329–1341. doi:10.1093/cercor/bhs109

Bransford, J. D., Barclay, J. R., & Franks, J. J. (1972). Sentence memory: A constructive versus interpretive approach. *Cognitive Psychology, 3*, 193–209.

Bransford, J. D., & Johnson, M. K. (1972). Contextual prerequisites for understanding: Some investigations of comprehension and recall. *Journal of Verbal Learning and Verbal Behavior, 11*, 717–726.

Brase, G. L., Fiddick, L., & Harries, C. (2006). Participant recruitment methods and statistical reasoning performance. *The Quarterly Journal of Experimental Psychology, 59*(5), 965–976. doi:10.1080/02724980543000132

Brass, M., Liefooghe, B., Braem, S., & De Houwer, J. (2017). Following new task instructions: Evidence for a dissociation between knowing and doing. *Neuroscience and Biobehavioral Reviews, 81*, 16–28.

Brass, M., Wenke, D., Spengler, S., & Waszak, F. (2009). Neural correlates of overcoming interference from instructed and implemented stimulus-response associations. *The Journal of Neuroscience, 29*(6), 1766–1772. doi:10.1523/jneurosci.5259-08.2009

Brauer, L. H., Goudie, A. J., & de Wit, H. (1997). Dopamine ligands and the stimulus effects of amphetamine: Animal models versus human laboratory data. *Psychopharmacology, 130*, 2–13.

References

Braver, T. S. (2012). The variable nature of cognitive control: A dual mechanisms framework. *Trends in Cognitive Sciences, 16*(2), 106–113. doi:10.1016/j.tics.2011.12.010

Braver, T. S., & Barch, D. M. (2002). A theory of cognitive control, aging cognition, and neuromodulation. *Neuroscience and Biobehavioral Reviews, 26*, 806–817.

Braver, T. S., Krug, M. K., Chiew, K. S., Kool, W., Westbrook, J. A., Clement, N. J. ... group, M. (2014). Mechanisms of motivation-cognition interaction: Challenges and opportunities. *Cognitive, Affective & Behavioral Neuroscience, 14*(2), 443–472. doi:10.3758/s13415-014-0300-0

Braver, T. S., Reynolds, J. R., & Donaldson, D. I. (2003). Neural mechanisms of transient and sustained cognitive control during task switching. *Neuron, 39*(4), 713–726. doi:10.1016/s0896-6273(03)00466-5

Braverman, J. A., & Blumenthal-Barby, J. S. (2012). Assessment of the sunk-cost effect in clinical decision-making. *Social Science & Medicine, 75*(1), 186–192. doi:10.1016/j.socscimed.2012.03.006

Bravo, M. J., & Farid, H. (2012). Task demands determine the specificity of the search template. *Attention, Perception, & Psychophysics, 74*(1), 124–131. doi:10.3758/s13414-011-0224-5

Brecht, M. (2017). The body model theory of somatosensory cortex. *Neuron, 94*(5), 985–992. doi:10.1016/j.neuron.2017.05.018

Bregman, A. (1990). *Auditory scene analysis.* Cambridge, MA: MIT Press.

Breiter, H. C., Aharon, I., Kahneman, D., Dale, A., & Shizgal, P. (2001). Functional imaging of neural responses to expectancy and experience of monetary gains and losses. *Neuron, 30*, 619–639.

Breivik, H., Collett, B., Ventafridda, V., Cohen, R., & Gallacher, D. (2006). Survey of chronic pain in Europe: Prevalence, impact on daily life, and treatment. *European Journal of Pain, 10*(4), 287–333. doi:10.1016/j.ejpain.2005.06.009

Bremner, A. J., Mareschal, D., Lloyd-Fox, S., & Spence, C. (2008). Spatial localization of touch in the first year of life: Early influence of a visual spatial code and the development of remapping across changes in limb position. *Journal of Experimental Psychology: General, 137*(1), 149–162. doi:10.1037/0096-3445.137.1.149

Bresciani, J. P., Dammeier, F., & Ernst, M. O. (2006). Vision and touch are automatically integrated for the perception of sequences of events. *Journal of Vision, 6*(5), 554–564. doi:10.1167/6.5.2

Brewer, N., & Wells, G. L. (2011). Eyewitness identification. *Current Directions in Psychological Science, 20*(1), 24–27. doi:10.1177/0963721410389169

Britten, K. H., & van Wezel, R. J. A. (1998). Electrical microstimulation of cortical area MST biases heading perception in monkeys. *Nature Neuroscience, 1*(1), 59–63.

Britz, J., Pitts, M. A., & Michel, C. M. (2011). Right parietal brain activity precedes perceptual alternation during binocular rivalry. *Human Brain Mapping, 32*(9):1432–1442. doi:10.1002/hbm.21117

Broadbent, D. E. (1954). The role of auditory localization in attention and memory span. *Journal of Experimental Psychology, 47*(3), 191–196.

Brock, J., & Nation, K. (2014). The hardest butter to button: Immediate context effects in spoken word identification. *The Quarterly Journal of Experimental Psychology, 67*(1), 114–123. doi:10.1080/17470218.2013.791331

Brosch, T. (2013). Comment: On the role of appraisal processes in the construction of emotion. *Emotion Review, 5*(4), 369–373.

Brosch, T., Sander, D., Pourtois, G., & Scherer, K. R. (2008). Beyond fear: Rapid spatial orienting toward positive emotional stimuli. *Psychological Science, 19*(4), 362–370.

Brown, J. (1958). Some tests of the decay theory of immediate memory. *The Quarterly Journal of Experimental Psychology, 10*(1), 12–21.

Brown, C. A., Seymour, B., Boyle, Y., El-Deredy, W., & Jones, A. K. (2008). Modulation of pain ratings by expectation and uncertainty: Behavioral characteristics and anticipatory neural correlates. *Pain, 135*(3), 240–250. doi:10.1016/j.pain.2007.05.022

Brown, K. F., Kroll, J. S., Hudson, M. J., Ramsay, M., Green, J., Vincent, C. A. ... Sevdalis, N. (2010). Omission bias and vaccine rejection by parents of healthy children: Implications for the influenza A/H1n1 vaccination programme. *Vaccine, 28*(25), 4181–4185. doi:10.1016/j.vaccine.2010.04.012

Brown, R., & Kulik, J. (1977). Flashbulb memories. *Cognition, 5*, 73–99.

Brown, R. G., & Marsden, C. D. (1988). Internal versus external cues and the control of attention in Parkinson's disease. *Brain, 111*, 323–345.

Brown, R. M., & Robertson, E. M. (2007). Off-line processing: Reciprocal interactions between declarative and procedural memories. *The Journal of Neuroscience, 27*(39), 10468–10475. doi:10.1523/JNEUROSCI.2799-07.2007

Bruce, V., & Young, A. (1986). Understanding face recognition. *British Journal of Psychology, 77*, 305–327.

Bruner, J. S., Goodnow, J. J., & Austin, G. A. (1956). *A study of thinking.* New York, NY: Wiley.

Brunia, C. H. M. (1999). Neural aspects of anticipatory behavior. *Acta Psychologica, 101*, 213–242.

Bruyer, R. (2011). Configural face processing: A meta-analytic survey. *Perception, 40*(12), 1478–1490. doi:10.1068/p6928

Brysbaert, M. (1995). Arabic number reading: On the nature of the numerical scale and the origin of phonological recoding. *Journal of Experimental Psychology: General, 124*(4), 434–452.

Buccino, G., Vogt, S., Ritzi, A., Fink, G. R., Zilles, K., Fruend, H.-J., & Rizzolatti, G. (2004). Neural circuits underlying imitation learning of hand actions: An event-related fMRI study. *Neuron, 42*, 323–334.

Buchanan, T. W., Tranel, D., & Adolphs, R. (2006). Impaired memory retrieval correlates with individual differences in cortisol response but not autonomic response. *Learning & Memory, 13,* 382–386.

Büchel, C., Geuter, S., Sprenger, C., & Eippert, F. (2014). Placebo analgesia: A predictive coding perspective. *Neuron, 81*(6), 1223–1239. doi:10.1016/j.neuron.2014.02.042

Buchsbaum, B., Pickell, B., Love, T., Hatrak, M., Bellugi, U., & Hickok, G. (2005). Neural substrates for verbal working memory in deaf signers: fMRI study and lesion case report. *Brain and Language, 95*(2), 265–272. doi:10.1016/j.bandl.2005.01.009

Bucker, B., Belopolsky, A. V., & Theeuwes, J. (2014). Distractors that signal reward attract the eyes. *Visual Cognition, 23*(1–2), 1–24. doi:10.1080/13506285.2014.9 80483

Budinger, E., Heil, P., Hess, A., & Scheich, H. (2006). Multisensory processing via early cortical stages: Connections of the primary auditory cortical field with other sensory systems. *Neuroscience, 143*(4), 1065–1083. doi:10.1016/j.neuroscience.2006.08.035

Bueno, C. A., Jarvis, M. R., Batista, A. P., & Andersen, R. A. (2002). Direct visuomotor transformations for reaching. *Nature, 416,* 632–636.

Bufacchi, R. J., & Iannetti, G. D. (2018). An action field theory of peripersonal space. *Trends in Cognitive Sciences, 22*(12), 1076–1090. doi:10.1016/j.tics.2018.09.004

Bull, R., Phillips, L. H., & Conway, C. A. (2008). The role of control functions in mentalizing: Dual-task studies of theory of mind and executive function. *Cognition, 107*(2), 663–672. doi:10.1016/j.cognition.2007.07.015

Bullard, P. (2016). *Eighteenth-century minds: From associationism to cognitive psychology* (Vol. 1). Oxford, MS: Oxford University Press.

Bullmore, E., & Sporns, O. (2012). The economy of brain network organization. *Nature Reviews Neuroscience, 13*(5), 336–349. doi:10.1038/nrn3214

Burgess, P. W., Simons, J. S., Dumontheil, I., & Gilbert, S. J. (2007). The gateway hypothesis of rostral prefrontal cortex (Area 10) function. In J. Duncan, L. Philips, & P. McLeod (Eds.), *Measuring the speed of mind: Speed, control, and age* (pp. 217–248). Oxford: Oxford University Press.

Burkhardt, P., Avrutin, S., Piñango, M. M., & Ruigendijk, E. (2008). Slower-than-normal syntactic processing in agrammatic Broca's aphasia: Evidence from Dutch. *Journal of Neurolinguistics, 21*(2), 120–137. doi:10.1016/j.jneuroling.2006.10.004

Burns, B. D. (2004). The effects of speed on skilled chess performance. *Psychological Science, 15*(7), 442–447.

Burr, D., & Thompson, P. (2011). Motion psychophysics: 1985–2010. *Vision Research, 51*(13), 1431–1456. doi:10.1016/j.visres.2011.02.008

Burt, C. D. B., Kemp, S., & Conway, M. A. (2003). Themes, events, and episodes in autographical memory. *Memory & Cognition, 31*(2), 317–325.

Burton, H., Abend, N. S., MacLeod, A.-M. K., Sinclair, R. J., Snyder, A. Z., & Raichle, M. E. (1999). Tactile attention tasks enhance activation in somatosensory regions of parietal cortex: A positron emission tomography study. *Cerebral Cortex, 9,* 662–674.

Burton, H., Snyder, A. Z., Diamond, J. B., & Raichle, M. E. (2002). Adaptive changes in early and late blind: A fMRI study of verb generation to heard nouns. *Journal of Neurophysiology, 88,* 3359–3371.

Bush, G., Luu, P., & Posner, M. I. (2000). Cognitive and emotional influences in anterior cingulate cortex. *Trends in Cognitive Sciences, 4*(6), 215–222.

Bushman, B. J. (2002). Does venting anger feed or extinguish the flame? Catharsis, rumination, distraction, anger, and aggressive responding. *Personality and Social Psychology Bulletin, 28*(6), 724–731.

Busigny, T., Joubert, S., Felician, O., Ceccaldi, M., & Rossion, B. (2010). Holistic perception of the individual face is specific and necessary: Evidence from an extensive case study of acquired prosopagnosia. *Neuropsychologia, 48*(14), 4057–4092. doi:10.1016/j.neuropsychologia.2010.09.017

Busse, L., Roberts, K. C., Crist, R. E., Weissman, D. H., & Woldorff, M. G. (2005). The spread of attention across modalities and space in a multisensory object. *Proceedings of the National Academy of Sciences of the United States of America, 102*(51), 18751–18756.

Butterworth, B. (2008). Developmental dyscalculia. In J. Reed, & J. Warner-Rogers (Eds.), *Child neuropsychology*. Chichester: Wiley-Blackwell.

Butterworth, B., Cipolotti, L., & Warrington, E. K. (1996). Short-term memory impairment and arithmetical ability. *The Quarterly Journal of Experimental Psychology, 49A*(1), 251–262.

Butterworth, B., Zorzi, M., Girelli, L., & Jonckheere, A. R. (2001). Storage and retrieval of addition facts: The role of number comparison. *The Quarterly Journal of Experimental Psychology, 54*(4), 1005–1029. doi:10.1080/713756007

Buys, E. J., Lemon, R. N., Mantel, G. W. H., & Muir, R. B. (1986). Selective facilitation of different hand muscles by single corticospinal neurons in the conscious monkey. *Journal of Physiology, 381,* 529–549.

Byrne, R. M. J. (1989). Suppressing valid inferences with conditionals. *Cognition, 31,* 61–83.

Cabanac, M. (1979). Sensory pleasure. *The Quarterly Review of Biology, 54*(1), 1–29.

Cabeza, R., & Moscovitch, M. (2013). Memory systems, processing modes, and components: Functional neuroimaging evidence. *Perspectives on Psychological Science, 8*(1), 49–55. doi:10.1177/1745691612469033

Cabeza, R., Prince, S. E., Daselaar, S. M., Greenberg, D. L., Budde, M., Dolcos, F. … Rubin, D. C. (2004). Brain activity during episodic retrieval of autobiographical and laboratory events: An fMRI study using a novel photo paradigm. *Journal of Cognitive Neuroscience, 16*(9), 1583–1594.

Cabeza, R., & St Jacques, P. (2007). Functional neuroimaging of autobiographical memory. *Trends in Cognitive Sciences, 11*(5), 219–227. doi:10.1016/j.tics.2007.02.005

References

Caccappolo-van Vliet, E., Miozzo, M., & Stern, Y. (2004a). Phonological dyslexia without phonological impairment? *Cognitive Neuropsychology, 21*(8), 820–839. doi:10.1080/02643290342000465

Caccappolo-van Vliet, E., Miozzo, M., & Stern, Y. (2004b). Phonological dyslexia: A test case for reading models. *Psychological Science, 15*(9), 583–590.

Cain, M. S., & Mitroff, S. R. (2011). Distractor filtering in media multitaskers. *Perception, 40*(10), 1183–1192. doi:10.1068/p7017

Calder, A. J., Keane, J., Manes, F., Antoun, N., & Young, A. W. (2000). Impaired recognition and experience of disgust following brain injury. *Nature Neuroscience, 3*(11), 1077–1078.

Calvert, G. A., Campbell, R., & Brammer, M. J. (2000). Evidence from functional magnetic resonance imaging of crossmodal binding in the human heteromodal cortex. *Current Biology, 10*, 649–657.

Calvo, M. G. (2001). Working memory and inferences: Evidence from eye fixations during Reading. *Memory, 9*(4–6), 365–381. doi:10.1080/09658210143000083

Calvo, M. G., Castillo, M. D., & Schmalhofer, F. (2006). Strategic influence on the time course of predictive inferences in reading. *Memory & Cognition, 34*(1), 68–77.

Camerer, C. F., & Hogarth, R. M. (1999). The effects of financial incentives in experiments: A review and capital-labor-production framework. *Journal of Risk and Uncertainty, 19*(1–3), 7–42.

Cameron, B. D., Enns, J. T., Franks, I. M., & Chua, R. (2009). The hand's automatic pilot can update visual information while the eye is in motion. *Experimental Brain Research, 195*(3), 445–454. doi:10.1007/s00221-009-1812-7

Campbell, J. I. D. (1994). Architectures for numerical cognition. *Cognition, 53*, 1–44.

Campbell, J. I. D., & Clark, J. M. (1992). Chapter 12 Cognitive number processing: An encoding-complex perspective. In J. I. D. Campbell (Ed.), *The nature and origins of mathematical skills* (pp. 457–491). Amsterdam: Elsevier.

Campitelli, G., & Gobet, F. (2011). Deliberate practice: Necessary but not sufficient. *Current Directions in Psychological Science, 20*(5), 280–285. doi:10.1177/0963721411421922

Campos, J. L., Butler, J. S., & Bulthoff, H. H. (2012). Multisensory integration in the estimation of walked distances. *Experimental Brain Research, 218*(4), 551–565. doi:10.1007/s00221-012-3048-1

Campos, B., Shiota, M. N., Keltner, D., Gonzaga, G. C., & Goetz, J. L. (2013). What is shared, what is different? Core relational themes and expressive displays of eight positive emotions. *Cognition & Emotion, 27*(1), 37–52. doi:10.1080/02699931.2012.683852

Candia, V., Elbert, T., Altenmüller, E., Rau, H., Schäfer, T., & Taub, E. (1999). Constraint-induced movement therapy for focal hand dystonia in musicians. *The Lancet, 353*(9146). doi:10.1016/s0140-6736(05)74865-0

Cannon, W. B. (1927). The James-Lange theory of emotions: A critical examination and an alternative theory. *The American Journal of Psychology, 39*(1), 106–124.

Cannon, W. B. (1932). *The wisdom of the body.* New York, NY: W. W. Norton and Company.

Cannon, J. J., & Patel, A. D. (2021). How beat perception co-opts motor neurophysiology. *Trends in Cognitive Sciences, 25*(2), 137–150. doi:10.1016/j.tics.2020.11.002

Cappa, S. F. (2012). Imaging semantics and syntax. *Neuroimage, 61*(2), 427–431. doi:10.1016/j.neuroimage.2011.10.006

Cappelletti, M., Butterworth, B., & Kopelman, M. (2001). Spared numerical abilities in a case of semantic dementia. *Neuropsychologia, 39*(11), 1224–1239.

Carlsson, K., Petrovic, P., Skare, S., Petersson, K. M., & Ingvar, M. (2000). Tickling expectations: Neural processing in anticipation of a sensory stimulus. *The Journal of Neuroscience, 12*(4), 691–703.

Carpenter, W. B. (1852). On the influence of suggestion in modifying and directing muscular movement, independently of volition. *Proceedings of the Royal Institution*, 147–154.

Carr, T. H., Davidson, B. J., & Hawkins, H. L. (1978). Perceptual flexibility in word recognition: Strategies affect orthographic computation but not lexical access. *Journal of Experimental Psychology: Human Perception and Performance, 4*(4), 674–690.

Carrasco, M., Ling, S., & Read, S. (2004). Attention alters appearance. *Nature Neuroscience, 7*(3), 308–313. doi:10.1038/nn1194

Carruthers, P. (2009). How we know our own minds: The relationship between mindreading and metacognition. *Behavioral and Brain Sciences, 32*(2), 121–138; discussion 138–182. doi:10.1017/S0140525X09000545

Carter, T. J., Ferguson, M. J., & Hassin, R. R. (2011). A single exposure to the American flag shifts support toward republicanism up to 8 months later. *Psychological Science, 22*(8), 1011–1018. doi:10.1177/0956797611414726

Caruso, J. P., & Sheehan, J. P. (2017). Psychosurgery, ethics, and media: A history of Walter Freeman and the lobotomy. *Neurosurgical Focus, 43*(3), E6. doi:10.3171/2017.6.FOCUS17257

Cattaneo, Z., Silvanto, J., Battelli, L., & Pascual-Leone, A. (2009). The mental number line modulates visual cortical excitability. *Neuroscience Letters, 462*(3), 253–256.

Cattell, J. M. (1885). Ueber die zeit der erkennung und benennung von schriftzeichten, bildern, und farben. *Philosophische Studien, 2*, 635–650.

Cattinelli, I., Borghese, N. A., Gallucci, M., & Paulesu, E. (2013). Reading the reading brain: A new meta-analysis of functional imaging data on Reading. *Journal of Neurolinguistics, 26*(1), 214–238. doi:10.1016/j.jneuroling.2012.08.001

Cavaco, S., Anderson, S. W., Allen, J. S., Castro-Caldas, A., & Damasio, H. (2004). The scope of preserved procedural memory in amnesia. *Brain, 127*(Pt 8), 1853–1867. doi:10.1093/brain/awh208

Ceci, S. J., & Liker, J. K. (1986). A day at the races: A study of IQ, expertise, and cognitive complexity. *Journal of Experimental Psychology: General, 115*(3), 255–266.

Ceraso, J., & Provitera, A. (1971). Sources of error in syllogistic reasoning. *Cognitive Psychology, 2*, 400–410.

Challis, B. H., Velichkovsky, B. M., & Craik, F. I. M. (1996). Levels-of-processing effects on a variety of memory tasks: New findings and theoretical implications. *Consciousness and Cognition, 5*, 142–164.

Chalmers, D. J. (1995). Facing up to the problem of consciousness. *Journal of Consciousness Studies, 2*(3), 200–219.

Chalmers, D. J. (1999). Materialism and the metaphysics of modality. *Philosophy and Phenomenological Research, 59*(2), 473–496.

Chanda, M. L., & Levitin, D. J. (2013). The neurochemistry of music. *Trends in Cognitive Sciences, 17*(4), 179–193. doi:10.1016/j.tics.2013.02.007

Chang, S. W., Fagan, N. A., Toda, K., Utevsky, A. V., Pearson, J. M., & Platt, M. L. (2015). Neural mechanisms of social decision-making in the primate amygdala. *Proceedings of the National Academy of Sciences of the United States of America, 112*(52), 16012–16017. doi:10.1073/pnas.1514761112

Charness, N., Reingold, E. M., Pomplun, M., & Stampe, D. M. (2001). The perceptual aspect of skilled performance in chess: Evidence from eye movements. *Memory & Cognition, 29*(8), 1146–1152.

Chase, W. G., & Simon, H. A. (1973). Perception in chess. *Cognitive Psychology, 4*, 55–81.

Chater, N. (2003). How much can we learn from double dissociations? *Cortex, 39*(1), 167–169. doi:10.1016/s0010-9452(08)70093-5

Chater, N., & Manning, C. D. (2006). Probabilistic models of language processing and acquisition. *Trends in Cognitive Sciences, 10*(7), 335–344. doi:10.1016/j.tics.2006.05.006

Chater, N., Misyak, J., Watson, D., Griffiths, N., & Mouzakitis, A. (2017). Negotiating the traffic: Can cognitive science help make autonomous vehicles a reality? *Trends in Cognitive Sciences, 22*(2), 93–95. doi:10.1016/j.tics.2017.11.008

Chater, N., & Oaksford, M. (2001). Human rationality and the psychology of reasoning: Where do we go from here? *British Journal of Psychology, 92*, 193–216.

Chaudhuri, A., & Behan, P. O. (2000). Fatigue and basal ganglia. *Journal of the Neurological Sciences, 179*, 34–42.

Chen, Z. (2002). Analogical problem solving: A hierarchical analysis of procedural similarity. *Journal of Experimental Psychology: Learning, Memory, and Cognition, 28*(1), 81–98. doi:10.1037/0278-7393.28.1.81

Chen, L. M., Friedman, R. M., & Roe, A. W. (2003). Optical imaging of a tactile illusion in area 3b of the primary somatosensory cortex. *Science, 302*, 881–885.

Chen, Y. C., & Spence, C. (2017). Assessing the role of the 'Unity Assumption' on multisensory integration: A review. *Frontiers in Psychology, 8*, 445. doi:10.3389/fpsyg.2017.00445

Chen, L., & Vroomen, J. (2013). Intersensory binding across space and time: A tutorial review. *Attention, Perception, & Psychophysics, 75*(5), 790–811. doi:10.3758/s13414-013-0475-4

Chenoweth, N. A., & Hayes, J. R. (2003). The inner voice in writing. *Written Communication, 20*(1), 99–118. doi:10.1177/0741088303253572

Cherry, E. C. (1953). Some experiments on the recognition of speech, with one and with two ears. *The Journal of the Acoustical Society of America, 25*(5), 975–979.

Chesney, M. A., & Shelton, J. L. (1976). A comparison of muscle relaxation and electromyogram biofeedback treatments for muscle contraction headache. *Journal of Behavioral Therapy and Experimental Psychiatry, 7*, 221–225.

Chevallier, C., Hacquin, A. S., & Mercier, H. (2021). Covid-19 vaccine hesitancy: Shortening the last Mile. *Trends in Cognitive Sciences, 25*(5), 331–333. doi:10.1016/j.tics.2021.02.002

Chevallier, C., Kohls, G., Troiani, V., Brodkin, E. S., & Schultz, R. T. (2012). The social motivation theory of autism. *Trends in Cognitive Sciences, 16*(4), 231–239. doi:10.1016/j.tics.2012.02.007

Chi, M. T. H., Feltovich, P. J., & Glaser, R. (1981). Categorisation and representation of physics problems by experts and novices. *Cognitive Science, 5*, 121–152.

Chiappe, D. L., & Chiappe, P. (2007). The role of working memory in metaphor production and comprehension. *Journal of Memory and Language, 56*(2), 172–188. doi:10.1016/j.jml.2006.11.006

Cholewa, J., Mantey, S., Heber, S., & Hollweg, W. (2010). Developmental surface and phonological dysgraphia in German 3rd graders. *Reading and Writing, 23*, 97–127.

Chomsky, N. (1957). *Knowledge of language: Its nature, origin, and use.* New York, NY: Praeger.

Chomsky, N. (1959). Review of verbal behavior by B. F. Skinner. *Language, 35*(1), 26–58.

Choudhry, N. K., Fletcher, R. H., & Soumerai, S. B. (2006). Systematic review: The relationship between clinical experience and quality of health care. *Yearbook of Diagnostic Radiology, 2006*, 224–225. doi:10.1016/s0098-1672(08)70399-0

Christiansen, M. H., & Chater, N. (2008). Language as shaped by the brain. *Behavioral and Brain Sciences, 31*(5), 489–508; discussion 509–458. doi:10.1017/S0140525X08004998

Christiansen, M. H., Kelly, M. L., Shillcock, R. C., & Greenfield, K. (2010). Impaired artificial grammar learning in agrammatism. *Cognition, 116*(3), 382–393. doi:10.1016/j.cognition.2010.05.015

Christianson, K., Luke, S. G., & Ferreira, F. (2010). Effects of plausibility on structural priming. *Journal of Experimental Psychology: Learning, Memory, and Cognition, 36*(2), 538–544. doi:10.1037/a0018027

References

Chrysikou, E. G., Hamilton, R. H., Coslett, H. B., Datta, A., Bikson, M., & Thompson-Schill, S. L. (2013). Noninvasive transcranial direct current stimulation over the left prefrontal cortex facilitates cognitive flexibility in tool use. *Cognitive Neuropsychology, 4*(2), 81–89. doi:10.1080/17588928.2013.768221

Chu, S., & Downes, J. J. (2004). Proust reinterpreted: Can Proust's account of odour-cued autobiographical recall really be investigated? A reply to Jellinek. *Chemical Senses, 29*, 459–461.

Chukoskie, L., Snider, J., Mozer, M. C., Krauzlis, R. J., & Sejnowski, T. J. (2013). Learning where to look for a hidden target. *Proceedings of the National Academy of Sciences of the United States of America, 110*(Suppl 2), 10438–10445. doi:10.1073/pnas.1301216110

Chun, M. M., Golomb, J. D., & Turk-Browne, N. B. (2011). A taxonomy of external and internal attention. *Annual Review of Psychology, 62*, 73–101. doi:10.1146/annurev.psych.093008.100427

Churchland, P. S., & Sejnowski, T. J. (1994). *The computational brain.* Cambridge, MA: MIT Press.

Clark, A. (1999). An embodied cognitive science. *Trends in Cognitive Sciences, 3*(9), 345–351.

Clark, A. (2013). Whatever next? Predictive brains, situated agents, and the future of cognitive science. *Behavioral and Brain Sciences, 36*(3), 1–73. doi:10.1017/S0140525X12000477

Cleeremans, A., & Jiménez, L. (2002). Implicit learning and consciousness: A graded, dynamic perspective. In R. M. French, & A. Cleeremans (Eds.), *Implicit learning and consciousness: An empirical, philosophical, and computational consensus in the making.* Hove: Psychology Press.

Close, J., & Pothos, E. M. (2012). 'Object categorization: Reversals and explanations of the basic-level advantage' (Rogers & Patterson, 2007): A simplicity account. *The Quarterly Journal of Experimental Psychology, 65*(8), 1615–1632. doi:10.1080/17470218.2012.660963

Coderre, S., Wright, B., & McLaughlin, K. (2010). To think is good: Querying an initial hypothesis reduces diagnostic error in medical students. *Academic Medicine, 85*(7), 1125–1129.

Cohen, G. (2008). The study of everyday memory. In G. Cohen, & A. R. Conway (Eds.), *Memory in the real world* (3 ed., pp. 1–19). Hove: Psychology Press.

Cohen, M. A., Alvarez, G. A., & Nakayama, K. (2011). Natural-scene perception requires attention. *Psychological Science, 22*(9), 1165–1172. doi:10.1177/0956797611419168

Cohen, L. G., Celnik, P., Pascual-Leone, A., Corwell, B., Faiz, L., Dambrosia, J. … Hallett, M. (1997). Functional relevance of cross-modal plasticity in blind humans. *Nature, 389*, 180–183.

Cohen, J. D., Dunbar, K. N., & McClelland, J. L. (1990). On the control of automatic processes: A parallel distributed processing account of the Stroop effect. *Psychological Review, 3*, 332–361.

Cohen, L., Dehaene, S., Chochon, F., Lehericy, S., & Naccache, L. (2000). Language and calculation within the parietal lobe: A combined cognitive, anatomical and fMRI study. *Neuropsychologia, 38*, 1426–1440.

Cohen, N. J., & Squire, L. R. (1980). Preserved learning and retention of pattern-analyzing skill in amnesia: Dissociation of knowing how and knowing that. *Science, 210*, 207–210.

Cohen, J. R., Young, J. F., & Abela, J. R. Z. (2011). Cognitive vulnerability to depression in children: An idiographic, longitudinal examination of inferential styles. *Cognitive Therapy and Research, 36*(6), 643–654. doi:10.1007/s10608-011-9431-6

Cohen-Kdoshay, O., & Meiran, N. (2007). The representation of instructions in working memory leads to autonomous response activation: Evidence from the first trials in the flanker paradigm. *The Quarterly Journal of Experimental Psychology, 60*(8), 1140–1154. doi:10.1080/17470210600896674

Colby, C. L., & Goldberg, M. E. (1999). Space and attention in parietal cortex. *Annual Review of Neuroscience, 22*, 319–349.

Cole, M. W., Bagic, A., Kass, R., & Schneider, W. (2010). Prefrontal dynamics underlying rapid instructed task learning reverse with practice. *The Journal of Neuroscience, 30*(42), 14245–14254. doi:10.1523/JNEUROSCI.1662-10.2010

Collette, F., Van der Linden, M., Laureys, S., Delfiore, G., Degueldre, C., Luxen, A., & Salmon, E. (2005). Exploring the unity and diversity of the neural substrates of executive functioning. *Human Brain Mapping, 25*(4), 409–423. doi:10.1002/hbm.20118

Collins, A. M., & Loftus, E. F. (1975). A spreading-activation theory of semantic processing. *Psychological Review, 82*(6), 407–428.

Collins, A. M., & Quillian, M. R. (1969). Retrieval time from semantic memory. *Journal of Verbal Learning and Verbal Behavior, 8*, 240–247.

Coltheart, M. (1996). Phonological dyslexia: Past and future issues. *Cognitive Neuropsychology, 13*(6), 749–762. doi:10.1080/026432996381791

Coltheart, M. (2010). Lessons from cognitive neuropsychology for cognitive science: A reply to Patterson and Plaut. *Topics in Cognitive Science, 2*, 3–11.

Coltheart, M., Curtis, B., Atkins, P., & Haller, M. (1993). Models of reading aloud: Dual-route and parallel-distributed-processing approaches. *Psychological Review, 100*(4), 589–608.

Coltheart, M., Rastle, K., Perry, C., Langdon, R., & Ziegler, J. (2001). DRC: A dual route cascaded model of visual word recognition and reading aloud. *Psychological Review, 108*(1), 204–256.

Combs, L. A., & Polich, J. (2006). P3a from auditory white noise stimuli. *Clinical Neurophysiology, 117*(5), 1106–1112. doi:10.1016/j.clinph.2006.01.023

Cona, G., Arcara, G., Tarantino, V., & Bisiacchi, P. S. (2012). Electrophysiological correlates of strategic monitoring in event-based and time-based prospective memory. *PLoS One*, *7*(2), e31659. doi:10.1371/journal.pone.0031659

Connor, S. (2000). *Dumbstruck: A cultural history of ventriloquism*. Oxford: Oxford University Press.

Conrad, C. (1972). Cognitive economy in semantic memory. *Journal of Experimental Psychology*, *92*(2), 149–154.

Conway, B. R., Moeller, S., & Tsao, D. Y. (2007). Specialized color modules in macaque extrastriate cortex. *Neuron*, *56*(3), 560–573. doi:10.1016/j.neuron.2007.10.008

Conway, M. A. (2005). Memory and the self. *Journal of Memory and Language*, *53*(4), 594–628. doi:10.1016/j.jml.2005.08.005

Conway, M. A., & Pleydell-Pearce, C. W. (2000). The construction of autobiographical memories in the self-memory system. *Psychological Review*, *107*(2), 261–288. doi:10.1037/0033-295x.107.2.261

Conway, M. A., Anderson, S. J., Larsen, S. F., Donnely, C. M., McDaniel, M. A., McClelland, A. G. R. … Logie, R. H. (1994). The formation of flashbulb memories. *Memory & Cognition*, *22*(3), 326–343.

Conway, N., Conway, A. R. A., & Bunting, M. E. (2001). The cocktail party phenomenon revisited: The importance of working memory capacity. *Psychonomic Bulletin & Review*, *8*(2), 331–335.

Conway, M. A., Pleydell-Pearce, C. W., & Whitecross, S. E. (2001). The neuroanatomy of autobiographical memory: A slow cortical potential study of autobiographical memory retrieval. *Journal of Memory and Language*, *45*(3), 493–524. doi:10.1006/jmla.2001.2781

Conway, M. A., Wang, Q., Hanyu, K., & Haque, S. (2005). A cross-cultural investigation of autobiographical memory. *Journal of Cross-Cultural Psychology*, *36*(6), 739–749. doi:10.1177/0022022105280512

Cook, A. E., & Myers, J. L. (2004). Processing discourse roles in scripted narratives: The influences of context and world knowledge. *Journal of Memory and Language*, *50*, 268–288. doi:10.1016/j.jml.2003.11.003

Cools, R. (2016). The costs and benefits of brain dopamine for cognitive control. *Wiley Interdisciplinary Review in Cognitive Science*, *7*(5), 317–329. doi:10.1002/wcs.1401

Copeland, D., & Radvansky, G. (2004). Working memory and syllogistic reasoning. *The Quarterly Journal of Experimental Psychology*, *57*(8), 1437–1457. doi:10.1080/02724980343000846

Corballis, M. C. (2017). Language evolution: A changing perspective. *Trends in Cognitive Sciences*, *21*(4), 229–236. doi:10.1016/j.tics.2017.01.013

Corbetta, M., & Shulman, G. L. (2002). Control of goal-directed and stimulus-driven attention in the brain. *Nature Reviews Neuroscience*, *3*(3), 201–215. doi:10.1038/nrn755

Corbetta, M., Miezin, F. M., Dobmeyer, S., Shulman, G. L., & Petersen, S. E. (1991). Selective and divided attention during visual discriminations of shape, color, and speed: Functional anatomy by positron emission tomography. *The Journal of Neuroscience*, *11*(8), 2383–2402.

Corbetta, M., Patel, G., & Shulman, G. L. (2008). The reorienting system of the human brain: From environment to theory of mind. *Neuron*, *58*(3), 306–324. doi:10.1016/j.neuron.2008.04.017

Corlett, P. R., Horga, G., Fletcher, P. C., Alderson-Day, B., Schmack, K., & Powers, A. R. 3rd. (2019). Hallucinations and strong priors. *Trends in Cognitive Sciences*, *23*(2), 114–127. doi:10.1016/j.tics.2018.12.001

Corlett, P. R., Krystal, J. H., Taylor, J. R., & Fletcher, P. C. (2009). Why do delusions persist? *Frontiers in Human Neuroscience*, *3*, 12. doi:10.3389/neuro.09.012.2009

Corley, M., Brocklehurst, P. H., & Moat, H. S. (2011). Error biases in inner and overt speech: Evidence from Tongue twisters. *Journal of Experimental Psychology: Learning, Memory, and Cognition*, *37*(1), 162–175. doi:10.1037/a0021321

Corner, A., Hahn, U., & Oaksford, M. (2011). The psychological mechanism of the slippery slope argument. *Journal of Memory and Language*, *64*(2), 133–152. doi:10.1016/j.jml.2010.10.002

Cosentino, S., Chute, D., Libon, D., Moore, P., & Grossman, M. (2006). How does the brain support script comprehension? A study of executive processes and semantic knowledge in dementia. *Neuropsychology*, *20*(3), 307–318. doi:10.1037/0894-4105.20.3.307

Coslett, H. B., Roeltgen, D. P., Gonzalez Rothi, L., & Heilman, K. M. (1987). Transcortical sensory aphasia: Evidence for subtypes. *Brain and Language*, *32*, 362–378.

Cosmides, L. (1989). The logic of social exchange: Has natural selection shaped how humans reason? Studies with the Wason selection task. *Cognition*, *31*, 187–276.

Coull, J. T., & Nobre, A. C. (1998). Where and when to pay attention: The neural systems for directing attention to spatial locations and to time intervals as revealed by both PET and fMRI. *The Journal of Neuroscience*, *18*(18), 7426–7435.

Cowan, N. (1988). Evolving conceptions of memory storage, selective attention, and their mutual constraints within the human information-processing system. *Psychological Bulletin*, §*04*(2), 163–191.

Cowan, N. (2000). The magical number 4 in short-term memory: A reconsideration of mental storage capacity. *Behavioral and Brain Sciences*, *24*(1), 87.

Cowie, D., Sterling, S., & Bremner, A. J. (2016). The development of multisensory body representation and awareness continues to 10 years of age: Evidence from the rubber hand illusion. *Journal of Experimental Child Psychology*, *142*, 230–238. doi:10.1016/j.jecp.2015.10.003

Cracco, R. Q., Cracco, J. B., Maccabee, P. J., & Amassian, V. E. (1999). Cerebral function revealed by transcranial magnetic stimulation. *Journal of Neuroscience Methods*, *86*, 209–219.

Craig, A. D. (2002). How do you feel? Interoception: The sense of the physiological condition of the body. *Nature Reviews Neuroscience*, *3*, 655–666.

References

Craig, A. D. (2003). Interoception: The sense of the physiological condition of the body. *Current Opinion in Neurobiology, 13*(4), 500–505. doi:10.1016/s0959-4388(03)00090-4

Craig, A. D. (2004). Human feelings: Why are some more aware than others? *Trends in Cognitive Sciences, 8*(6), 239–241. doi:10.1016/j.tics.2004.04.004

Craig, A. D., Krout, K., & Andrew, D. (2001). Quantitative response characteristics of thermoreceptive and nociceptive lamina I spinonthalamic neuron in the cat. *Journal of Neurophysiology, 86*(3), 1459–1480.

Craighero, L., Carta, A., & Fadiga, L. (2001). Peripheral oculomotor palsy affects orienting of visuospatial attention. *Neuroreport, 12*(15), 3283–3286.

Craighero, L., Nascimben, M., & Fadiga, L. (2004). Eye position affects orienting of visuospatial attention. *Current Biology, 14*(4), 331–333. doi:10.1016/j.cub.2004.01.054

Craik, F. I. M., & Lockhart, R. S. (1972). Levels of processing: A framework for memory research. *Journal of Verbal Learning and Verbal Behavior, 11*, 671–684.

Craik, F. I. M., & Tulving, E. (1975). Depth of processing and the retention of words in episodic memory. *Journal of Experimental Psychology: General, 104*(3), 268–294.

Crawford, J. D., Henriques, D. Y., & Medendorp, W. P. (2011). Three-dimensional transformations for goal-directed action. *Annual Review of Neuroscience, 34*, 309–331. doi:10.1146/annurev-neuro-061010-113749

Crawford, J. D., Medendorp, W. P., & Marotta, J. J. (2004). Spatial transformations for eye-hand coordination. *Journal of Neuophysiology, 92*, 10–19.

Cree, G. S., & McRae, K. (2003). Analyzing the factors underlying the structure and computation of the meaning of chipmunk, cherry, chisel, cheese, and cello (and many other such concrete nouns). *Journal of Experimental Psychology: General, 132*(2), 163–201. doi:10.1037/0096-3445.132.2.163

Crespi, L. P. (1942). Quantitative variations of incentive and performance in the white rat. *The American Journal of Psychology, 55*(4), 467–517.

Crevecoeur, F., Munoz, D. P., & Scott, S. H. (2016). Dynamic multisensory integration: Somatosensory speed trumps visual accuracy during feedback control. *The Journal of Neuroscience, 36*(33), 8598–8611. doi:10.1523/JNEUROSCI.0184-16.2016

Crews, F. (2017). *Freud: The making of an illusion.* New York, NY: Metropolitan Books.

Critchley, H. D., Wiens, S., Rotshtein, P., Ohman, A., & Dolan, R. J. (2004). Neural systems supporting interoceptive awareness. *Nature Neuroscience, 7*(2), 189–195. doi:10.1038/nn1176

Crivellato, E., & Ribatti, D. (2007). Soul, mind, brain: Greek Philosophy and the birth of neuroscience. *Brain Research Bulletin, 71*(4), 327–336. doi:10.1016/j.brainresbull.2006.09.020

Crockett, M. J. (2013). Models of morality. *Trends in Cognitive Sciences, 17*(8), 363–366. doi:10.1016/j.tics.2013.06.005

Crombez, G., Eccleston, C., Van den Broek, A., Goubert, L., & Van Houdenhove, B. (2004). Hypervigilance to pain in fibromyalgia: The mediating role of pain intensity and catastrophic thinking about pain. *Clinical Journal of Pain, 20*, 98–102.

Crone, E. A., & Dahl, R. E. (2012). Understanding adolescence as a period of social-affective engagement and goal flexibility. *Nature Reviews Neuroscience, 13*(9), 636–650. doi:10.1038/nrn3313

Cross, E. S., Hamilton, A. F., & Grafton, S. T. (2006). Building a motor simulation de novo: Observation of dance by dancers. *Neuroimage, 31*(3), 1257–1267. doi:10.1016/j.neuroimage.2006.01.033

Crowley, K. E., & Colrain, I. M. (2004). A review of the evidence for P2 being an independent component process: Age, sleep and modality. *Clinical Neurophysiology, 115*(4), 732–744. doi:10.1016/j.clinph.2003.11.021

Crump, M. J., & Logan, G. D. (2010a). Hierarchical control and skilled typing: Evidence for word-level control over the execution of individual keystrokes. *Journal of Experimental Psychology: Learning, Memory, and Cognition, 36*(6), 1369–1380. doi:10.1037/a0020696

Crump, M. J., & Logan, G. D. (2010b). Warning: This keyboard will deconstruct–the role of the keyboard in skilled typewriting. *Psychonomic Bulletin & Review, 17*(3), 394–399. doi:10.3758/PBR.17.3.394

Cryder, C. E., Lerner, J. S., Gross, J. J., & Dahl, R. E. (2008). Misery is not miserly: Sad and self-focused individuals spend more. *Psychological Science, 19*(6), 525–530.

Csibra, G. (2005). Mirror neurons and action observation: Is simulation involved? ESF Interdisciplines. http://www.interdisciplines.org/mirror/papers/4.

Cunningham, A. E., & Stanovich, K. E. (1997). Early reading acquisition and its relation to reading experience and ability 10 years later. *Developmental Psychology, 33*, 6934–6945.

Curiel, J. M., & Radvansky, G. A. (2014). Spatial and character situation model updating. *Journal of Cognitive Psychology, 26*(2), 205–212. doi:10.1080/20445911.2013.879590

Curran, E., & Stokes, M. J. (2003). Learning to control brain activity: A review of the production and control of EEG components for driving brain–computer interface (BCI) systems. *Brain and Cognition, 51*(3), 326–336. doi:10.1016/s0278-2626(03)00036-8

Cusack, R. (2005). The intraparietal sulcus and perceptual organization. *Journal of Cognitive Neuroscience, 17*(4), 641–651.

Custers, R., & Aarts, H. (2005). Positive affect as implicit motivator: On the nonconscious operation of behavioral goals. *Journal of Personality and Social Psychology*, *89*(2), 129–142.

Cutler, A., & Clifton, C. E. (1999). Comprehending spoken language: A blueprint of the listener. In C. Brown, & P. Hagoort (Eds.), *Neurocognition of language* (pp. 123–166). Oxford: Oxford University Press.

Daane, M. C. (1991). Good readers make good writers: A description of four college students. *Journal of Reading*, *35*(3), 184–188.

D'Esposito, M., Detre, J. A., Alsop, D. C., Shin, R. K., Atlas, S., & Grossman, M. (1995). The neural basis of the central executive system of working memory. *Nature*, *378*(6554), 279–281. doi:10.1038/378279a0

Dale, R., Kehoe, C., & Spivey, M. J. (2007). Graded motor responses in the time course of categorizing atypical exemplars. *Memory & Cognition*, *35*(1), 15–28.

Dalton, A. L., & Daneman, M. (2006). Social suggestibility to central and peripheral misinformation. *Memory*, *14*(4), 486–501. doi:10.1080/09658210500495073

Dalton, P., & Fraenkel, N. (2012). Gorillas we have missed: Sustained inattentional deafness for dynamic events. *Cognition*, *124*(3), 367–372. doi:10.1016/j.cognition.2012.05.012

Damasio, A. R. (1994). *Descartes' error: Emotion, reason, and the human brain*. New York, NY: Avon Books.

Damasio, A. R. (1996). The somatic marker hypothesis and the possible functions of the prefrontal cortex. *Philosophical Transactions of the Royal Society B-Biological Sciences*, *351*, 1413–1420.

Damasio, A., & Carvalho, G. B. (2013). The nature of feelings: Evolutionary and neurobiological origins. *Nature Reviews Neuroscience*, *14*(2), 143–152. doi:10.1038/nrn3403

Damasio, H., Grabowski, T., Frank, R., Galaburda, A. M., & Damasio, A. R. (1994). The return of Phineas Gage: Clues about the brain from the skull of a famous patient. *Science*, *264*(5162), 1102–1105.

Daneman, M., & Carpenter, P. A. (1980). Individual differences in working memory and Reading. *Journal of Verbal Learning and Verbal Behavior*, *19*, 450–466.

Darwin, C. J. (2008). Listening to speech in the presence of other sounds. *Philosophical Transactions of the Royal Society B-Biological Sciences*, *363*(1493), 1011–1021. doi:10.1098/rstb.2007.2156

Daselaar, S. M., Rice, H. J., Greenberg, D. L., Cabeza, R., LaBar, K. S., & Rubin, D. C. (2008). The spatiotemporal dynamics of autobiographical memory: Neural correlates of recall, emotional intensity, and reliving. *Cerebral Cortex*, *18*(1), 217–229. doi:10.1093/cercor/bhm048

Davidson, P. R., & Wolpert, D. M. (2005). Widespread access to predictive models in the motor system: A short review. *Journal of Neural Engineering*, *2*(3), S313–S319. doi:10.1088/1741-2560/2/3/S11

Davidson, R. J. (2000). Cognitive neuroscience needs affective neuroscience (and vice versa). *Brain and Cognition*, *42*(1), 89–92. doi:10.1006/brcg.1999.1170

Davies, C., & Katsos, N. (2013). Are speakers and listeners 'Only moderately Gricean'? An empirical response to Engelhardt et al. (2006). *Journal of Pragmatics*, *49*(1), 78–106. doi:10.1016/j.pragma.2013.01.004

Davis, M. H., Johnsrude, I. S., Hervais-Adelman, A., Taylor, K., & McGettigan, C. (2005). Lexical information drives perpetual learning of distorted speech: Evidence from the comprehension of noise-vocoded sentences. *Journal of Experimental Psychology: General*, *134*(2), 222–241.

Daw, N. D., & Shohamy, D. (2008). The cognitive neuroscience of motivation and learning. *Social Cognition*, *26*(5), 593–620.

Dawson, E., Gilovich, T., & Regan, D. T. (2002). Motivated reasoning and performance on the Wason selection task. *Personality and Social Psychology Bulletin*, *28*(10), 1379–1387.

Day, S. B., & Goldstone, R. L. (2011). Analogical transfer from a simulated physical system. *Journal of Experimental Psychology: Learning, Memory, and Cognition*, *37*(3), 551–567.

De Felipe, C., Herrero, J. F., O'Brian, J. A., Palmer, J. A., Doyle, C. A., Smith, A. J. H. … Hunt, S. P. (1998). Altered nociception, analgesia and aggression in mice lacking the receptor for substance P. *Nature*, *392*, 394–397.

de Gelder, B., Tamietto, M., van Boxtel, G., Goebel, R., Sahraie, A., van den Stock, J. … Pegna, A. (2008). Intact navigation skills after bilateral loss of striate cortex. *Current Biology*, *18*(24), R1128–1129. doi:10.1016/j.cub.2008.11.002

De Groot, A. D. (1946). *Het Denken Van Den Schaker: Een Experimenteel-Psychologische Studie*. Amsterdam: Noord-Hollandse Uitgeversmaatschappij.

de Haan, B., Karnath, H. O., & Driver, J. (2012). Mechanisms and anatomy of unilateral extinction after brain injury. *Neuropsychologia*, *50*(6), 1045–1053. doi:10.1016/j.neuropsychologia.2012.02.015

de Haan, E. H., & Cowey, A. (2011). On the usefulness of 'What' and 'Where' pathways in vision. *Trends in Cognitive Sciences*, *15*(10), 460–466. doi:10.1016/j.tics.2011.08.005

De Houwer, J., Beckers, T., Vandorpe, S., & Custers, R. (2005). Further evidence for the role of mode-independent short-term associations in spatial simon effects. *Perception & Psychophysics*, *67*(4), 659–666.

De Jong, R. (2000). An intention-activation account of residual switch costs. In S. Monsell, & J. Driver (Eds.), *Control of cognitive processes: Attention and performance Xviii*. Cambridge, MA: MIT Press.

De Jong, R., Berendsen, E., & Cools, R. (1999). Goal neglect and inhibitory limitations: Dissociable causes of interference effects in conflict situations. *Acta Psychologica*, *101*, 379–394.

De Jong, R., Coles, M. G. H., Logan, G. D., & Gratton, G. (1990). In search of the point of no return: The control of response processes. *Journal of Experimental Psychology: Human Perception and Performance*, *16*(1), 164–182.

References

De Loof, E., Ergo, K., Naert, L., Janssens, C., Talsma, D., Van Opstal, F., & Verguts, T. (2018). Signed reward prediction errors drive declarative learning. *PLoS One, 13*(1), e0189212. doi:10.1371/journal.pone.0189212

De Martino, B., Camerer, C. F., & Adolphs, R. (2010). Amygdala damage eliminates monetary loss aversion. *Proceedings of the National Academy of Sciences of the United States of America, 107*(8), 3788–3792. doi:10.1073/pnas.0910230107

De Neys, W. (2012). Bias and conflict: A case for logical intuitions. *Perspectives On Psychological Science, 7*(1), 28–38. doi:10.1177/1745691611429354

De Neys, W. (2013). Conflict detection, dual processes, and logical intuitions: Some clarifications. *Thinking & Reasoning, 20*(2), 169–187. doi:10.1080/13546783.2013.854725

De Neys, W., Moyens, E., & Vansteenwegen, D. (2010). Feeling we're biased: Autonomic arousal and reasoning conflict. *Cognitive, Affective, & Behavioral Neuroscience, 10*(2), 208–216. doi:10.3758/CABN.10.2.208

De Neys, W., Schaeken, W., & d'Ydewalle, G. (2005). Working memory and everyday conditional reasoning: Retrieval and inhibition of stored counterexamples. *Thinking & Reasoning, 11*(4), 349–381. doi:10.1080/13546780442000222

De Paepe, A. L., Crombez, G., Spence, C., & Legrain, V. (2014). Mapping nociceptive stimuli in a peripersonal frame of reference: Evidence from a temporal order judgment task. *Neuropsychologia, 56*, 219–228. doi:10.1016/j.neuropsychologia.2014.01.016

De Raedt, R., & Koster, E. H. (2010). Understanding vulnerability for depression from a cognitive neuroscience perspective: A reappraisal of attentional factors and a new conceptual framework. *Cognitive, Affective & Behavioral Neuroscience, 10*(1), 50–70. doi:10.3758/CABN.10.1.50

de Vanssay-Maigne, A., Noulhiane, M., Devauchelle, A. D., Rodrigo, S., Baudoin-Chial, S., Meder, J. F. … Chassoux, F. (2011). Modulation of encoding and retrieval by recollection and familiarity: Mapping the medial temporal lobe networks. *Neuroimage, 58*(4), 1131–1138. doi:10.1016/j.neuroimage.2011.06.086

de Vignemont, F., & Singer, T. (2006). The empathic brain: How, when and why? *Trends in Cognitive Sciences, 10*(10), 435–441. doi:10.1016/j.tics.2006.08.008

de Vignemont, F., Ehrsson, H. H., & Haggard, P. (2005). Bodily illusions modulate tactile perception. *Current Biology, 15*(14), 1286–1290. doi:10.1016/j.cub.2005.06.067

de Vries, M., Holland, R. W., & Witteman, C. L. M. (2008). Fitting decisions: Mood and intuitive versus deliberative decision strategies. *Cognition & Emotion, 22*(5), 931–943. doi:10.1080/02699930701552580

de Vries, M., Holland, R. W., Corneille, O., Rondeel, E., & Witteman, C. L. M. (2012). Mood effects on dominated choices: Positive mood induces departures from logical rules. *Journal of Behavioral Decision Making, 25*(1), 74–81. doi:10.1002/bdm.716

Decety, J., Jeannerod, M., & Prablanc, C. (1989). The timing of mentally represented actions. *Behavioural Brain Research, 34*, 35–42.

Decety, J., Kawashima, R., Gulyás, B., & Roland, P. E. (1992). Preparation for reaching: A PET study of the participating structures in the human brain. *Neuroreport, 3*, 761–764.

Deen, B., Koldewyn, K., Kanwisher, N., & Saxe, R. (2015). Functional organization of social perception and cognition in the superior temporal sulcus. *Cerebral Cortex, 25*(11), 4596–4609. doi:10.1093/cercor/bhv111

Deffenbacher, K. A., Bornstein, B. H., Penrod, S. D., & McGorty, E. K. (2004). A meta-analytic review of the effects of high stress on eyewitness memory. *Law and Human Behavior, 28*(6), 687–706. doi:10.1007/s10979-004-0565-x

Degerman, A., Rinne, T., Salmi, J., Salonen, O., & Alho, K. (2006). Selective attention to sound location or pitch studied with fMRI. *Brain Research, 1077*(1), 123–134. doi:10.1016/j.brainres.2006.01.025

Dehaene, S. (1992). Varieties of numerical abilities. *Cognition, 44*, 1–42.

Dehaene, S., & Changeux, J. P. (2011). Experimental and theoretical approaches to conscious processing. *Neuron, 70*(2), 200–227. doi:10.1016/j.neuron.2011.03.018

Dehaene, S., & Cohen, L. (1995). Towards an anatomical and functional model of number processing. In B. Butterworth (Ed.), *Mathematical cognition*. Hove: Psychology Press.

Dehaene, S., & Naccache, L. (2001). Towards a cognitive neuroscience of consciousness: Basic evidence and a workspace framework. *Cognition, 79*, 1–37.

Dehaene, S., Bossini, S., & Giraux, P. (1993). The mental representation of parity and number magnitude. *Journal of Experimental Psychology: General, 122*(3), 371–396.

Dehaene, S., Changeux, J.-P., Naccache, L., Sackur, J., & Sergent, C. (2006). Conscious, preconscious, and subliminal processing: A testable taxonomy. *Trends in Cognitive Sciences, 10*(5), 204–211. doi:10.1016/j.tics.2006.03.007

Dehaene, S., Molko, N., Cohen, L., & Wilson, A. J. (2004). Arithmetic and the brain. *Current Opinion in Neurobiology, 14*(2), 218–224. doi:10.1016/j.conb.2004.03.008

Dehais, F., Causse, M., Vachon, F., Regis, N., Menant, E., & Tremblay, S. (2014). Failure to detect critical auditory alerts in the cockpit: Evidence for inattentional deafness. *Human Factors, 56*(4), 631–644. doi:10.1177/0018720813510735

Deiber, M.-P., Ibanez, V., Honda, M., Sadato, N., Raman, R., & HAllett, M. (1998). Cerebral processes related to visuomotor imagery and generation of simple finger movements studied with positron emission tomography. *Neuroimage, 7*, 73–85.

Dekker, S. W. A., & Woods, D. D. (2010). The high reliability organization principle. In E. Salas, & D. Maurino (Eds.), *Human factors in aviation* (pp. 123–143). Amsterdam: Elsevier.

Delaney, P. F., Ericsson, K. A., & Knowles, M. E. (2004). Immediate and sustained effects of planning in a problem-solving task. *Journal of Experimental Psychology: Learning, Memory, and Cognition, 30*(6), 1219–1234. doi:10.1037/0278-7393.30.6.1219

Delattre, M., Bonin, P., & Barry, C. (2006). Written spelling to dictation: Sound-to-spelling regularity affects both writing latencies and durations. *Journal of Experimental Psychology: Learning, Memory, and Cognition, 32*(6), 1330–1340. doi:10.1037/0278-7393.32.6.1330

Delgado, M. R., Frank, R. H., & Phelps, E. A. (2005). Perceptions of moral character modulate the neural systems of reward during the trust game. *Nature Neuroscience, 8*(11), 1611–1618. doi:10.1038/nn1575

Dell, G. S. (1986). A spreading-activation theory of retrieval in sentence production. *Psychological Review, 93*(3), 283–321.

Dell, G. S., Burger, L. K., & Svec, W. R. (1997). Language production and serial order: A functional analysis and a model. *Psychological Review, 104*(1), 123–147.

Dell, G. S., Oppenheim, G. M., & Kittredge, A. K. (2008). Saying the right word at the right time: Syntagmatic and paradigmatic interference in sentence production. *Language and Cognitive Processes, 23*(4), 583–608. doi:10.1080/01690960801920735

Della Sala, S., Gray, C., Baddeley, A. D., Allamano, N., & Wilson, L. (1999). Pattern span: A tool for unwelding visuo-spatial memory. *Neuropsychologia, 37*, 1189–1199.

Dennett, D. C. (1991). *Consciousness explained*. Boston: Back Bay Books.

Denny-Brown, D. (1949). Interpretation of the electromyogram. *Archives of Neurology and Psychiatry, 61*(2), 99–128.

Desimone, R., & Duncan, J. (1995). Neural mechanisms of selective visual attention. *Annual Review of Neuroscience, 18*, 193–222.

DeStefano, D., & LeFevre, J. A. (2004). The role of working memory in mental arithmetic. *European Journal of Cognitive Psychology, 16*(3), 353–386. doi:10.1080/09541440244000328

Deutsch, J. A., & Deutsch, D. (1963). Attention: Some theoretical considerations. *Psychological Review, 70*(1), 80–90.

DeValois, R. L., & Devalois, K. K. (1975). Neural coding of color. In E. C. Carterette, & M. P. Friedman (Eds.), *Handbook of perception* (Vol. 5): Seeing. New York, NY: Academic Press.

Devine, P. G. (1989). Stereotypes and prejudice their automatic and controlled components. *Journal of Personality and Social Psychology, 56*(1), 5–18.

Devinsky, O., Morrell, M. J., & Vogt, B. A. (1995). Contributions of anterior cingulate cortex to behaviour. *Brain, 118*, 279–306.

Dew, I. T. Z., & Cabeza, R. (2011). The porous boundaries between explicit and implicit memory: Behavioral and neural evidence. *Annals of the New York Academy of Sciences, 1224*, 174–190. doi:10.1111/j.1749-6632.2010.05946.x

Dewar, M. T., Cowan, N., & Sala, S. D. (2007). Forgetting due to retroactive interference: A fusion of Müller and Pilzecker's (1900) early insights into everyday forgetting and recent research on anterograde amnesia. *Cortex, 43*(5), 616–634. doi:10.1016/s0010-9452(08)70492-1

Dhooge, E., & Hartsuiker, R. J. (2011). How do speakers resist distraction? Evidence from a taboo picture-word interference task. *Psychological Science, 22*(7), 855–859. doi:10.1177/0956797611410984

Di Liberto, G. M., Lalor, E. C., & Millman, R. E. (2018). Causal cortical dynamics of a predictive enhancement of speech intelligibility. *Neuroimage, 166*, 247–258. doi:10.1016/j.neuroimage.2017.10.066

di Pellegrino, G., Fadiga, L., Fogassi, L., Gallese, V., & Rizzolatti, G. (1992). Understanding motor events: A neurophysiological study. *Experimental Brain Research, 91*, 176–180.

di Pellegrino, G., Làdavas, E., & Farne, A. (1997). Seeing where your hands are. *Nature, 388*, 730.

Di Piero, V., Jones, A. K. P., Iannotti, F., Powell, M., Perani, D., Lenzi, G. L., & Frackowiak, R. S. J. (1991). Chronic pain: A PET study of the central effects of percutaneous high cervical cordotomy. *Pain, 46*, 9–12.

Di Russo, F., Aprile, T., Spitoni, G., & Spinelli, D. (2008). Impaired visual processing of contralesional stimuli in neglect patients: A visual-evoked potential study. *Brain, 131*(Pt 3), 842–854. doi:10.1093/brain/awm281

Diaconescu, A. O., Alain, C., & McIntosh, A. R. (2001). Modality-dependent 'What' and 'Where' preparatory processes in auditory and visual systems. *Journal of Cognitive Neuroscience, 23*(7), 1609–1623.

Diamantopoulou, S., Poom, L., Klaver, P., & Talsma, D. (2011). Visual working memory capacity and stimulus categories: A behavioral and electrophysiological investigation. *Experimental Brain Research, 209*(4), 501–513. doi:10.1007/s00221-011-2536-z

Diamond, R., & Carey, S. (1986). Why faces are not special: An effect of expertise. *Journal of Experimental Psychology: General, 115*(2), 107–117.

Diana, R. A., Yonelinas, A. P., & Ranganath, C. (2007). Imaging recollection and familiarity in the medial temporal lobe: A three-component model. *Trends in Cognitive Sciences, 11*(9), 379–386. doi:10.1016/j.tics.2007.08.001

Dieckmann, A., & Rieskamp, J. (2007). The influence of information redundancy on probabilistic inferences. *Memory & Cognition, 35*(7), 1801–1813.

Dieterich, M., Bense, S., Lutz, S., Drzezga, A., Stephan, T., Bartenstein, P., & Brandt, T. (2003). Dominance for vestibular cortical function in the non-dominant hemisphere. *Cerebral Cortex, 13*, 994–1007.

References

Dijksterhuis, A., & Nordgren, F. W. (2006). A theory of unconscious thought. *Perspectives on Psychological Science, 1*(2), 95–109.

Dijksterhuis, A., & van Knippenberg, A. (1998). The relation between perception and behavior, or how to win a game of trivial pursuit. *Journal of Personality and Social Psychology, 1998*(74), 4.

Dijksterhuis, A., Bos, M. W., Nordgren, F. W., & van Baaren, R. W. (2006). On making the right choice: The deliberation-without-attention effect. *Science, 311*, 1005–1007.

Dimberg, U. (1990). Facial electromyographic reactions and autonomic activity to auditory stimuli. *Biological Psychology, 31*, 137–147.

Dismukes, R. K. (2012). Prospective memory in workplace and everyday situations. *Current Directions in Psychological Science, 21*(4), 215–220. doi:10.1177/0963721412447621

Dixon, P., & Bortolussi, M. (2013). Construction, integration, and mind wandering in reading. *Canadian Journal of Experimental Psychology, 67*(1), 1–10. doi:10.1037/a0031234

Dodson, C. S., & Krueger, L. E. (2006). I misremember it well: Why older adults are unreliable eyewitnesses. *Psychonomic Bulletin & Review, 13*(5), 770–775.

Domes, G., Heinrichs, M., Glascher, J., Buchel, C., Braus, D. F., & Herpertz, S. C. (2007). Oxytocin attenuates amygdala responses to emotional faces regardless of Valence. *Biological Psychiatry, 62*(10), 1187–1190. doi:10.1016/j.biopsych.2007.03.025

Donders, F. C. (1868). Over de snelheid van psychische processen. *Onderzoekingen Gedaan in Het Physiologisch Laboratorium Der Utrechtse Hoogeschool, Tweede Reeks II,* 92–120.

Dooling, D. J., & Christiaansen, R. E. (1977). Episodic and semantic aspects of memory for prose. *Journal of Experimental Psychology: Human Learning and Memory, 3*(4), 428–436.

Dorman, M. F., Raphael, L. J., & Liberman, A. M. (1979). Some experiments on the sound of silence in phonetic perception. *Journal of the Acoustical Society of America, 65*(6), 1518–1532.

Downes, J. J., Roberts, A. C., Sahakian, B. J., Evenden, J. L., Morris, R. G., & Robbins, T. W. (1989). Impaired extra-dimensional shift performance in medicated and unmedicated Parkinson's disease: Evidence for a specific attentional dysfunction. *Neuropsychologia, 27*(11/12), 1329–1343.

Downing, P. E. (2000). Interactions between visual working memory and selective attention. *Psychological Science, 11*(6), 467–473. doi:10.1111/1467-9280.00290

Downing, P. E., Chan, A. W. Y., Peelen, M. V., Dodds, C. M., & Kanwisher, N. (2006). Domain specificity in visual cortex. *Cerebral Cortex, 16*(10), 1453–1461. doi:10.1093/cercor/bhj086

Doyen, S., Klein, O., Pichon, C.-L., & Cleeremans, A. (2012). Behavioral priming: It's all in the mind, but whose mind? *PLoS One, 7*(1), e29081.

Draaisma, D. (2002). *Age of Precision.* Nijmegen University.

Draganski, B., & May, A. (2008). Training-induced structural changes in the adult human brain. *Behavioral and Brain Sciences, 192*(1), 137–142. doi:10.1016/j.bbr.2008.02.015

Driskell, J. E., Copper, C., & Moran, A. (1994). Does mental practice enhance performance? *Journal of Applied Psychology, 79*(4), 481–492.

Driver, J., & Spence, C. (1998). Cross-modal links in spatial attention. *Philosophical Transactions of the Royal Society B: Biological Sciences, 353*(1373), 1319–1331.

Drost, U. C., Rieger, M., Brass, M., Gunter, T. C., & Prinz, W. (2005a). Action-effect coupling in pianists. *Psychological Research, 69*(4), 233–241. doi:10.1007/s00426-004-0175-8

Drost, U. C., Rieger, M., Brass, M., Gunter, T. C., & Prinz, W. (2005b). When hearing turns into playing: Movement induction by auditory stimuli in pianists. *The Quarterly Journal of Experimental Psychology Section A, 58*(8), 1376–1389. doi:10.1080/02724980443000610

Duchaine, B., Cosmides, L., & Tooby, J. (2001). Evolutionary psychology and the brain. *Current Opinion in Neurobiology, 11,* 225–230.

Dudai, Y. (2012). The restless engram: Consolidations never end. *Annual Review of Neuroscience, 35,* 227–247. doi:10.1146/annurev-neuro-062111-150500

Dudai, Y., & Morris, R. G. (2013). Memorable trends. *Neuron, 80*(3), 742–750. doi:10.1016/j.neuron.2013.09.039

Dudukovic, N. M., Marsh, E. J., & Tversky, B. (2004). Telling a story or telling it straight: The effects of entertaining versus accurate retellings on memory. *Applied Cognitive Psychology, 18*(2), 125–143. doi:10.1002/acp.953

Duffy, S. A., & Pisoni, D. B. (1992). Comprehension of synthetic speech produced by rule: A review and theoretical interpretation. *Language and Speech, 35*(4), 351–389.

Duhamel, J. R., Colby, C. L., & Goldberg, M. E. (1998). Ventral intraparietal area of the macaque: Congruent visual and somatic response properties. *Journal of Neurophysiology, 79*(1), 126–136.

Duhamel, J.-R., Colby, C. L., & Goldberg, M. E. (1992). The updating of the representation of visual space in parietal cortex by intended eye movements. *Science, 255,* 90–92.

Duke, A. A., & Begue, L. (2015). The drunk utilitarian: Blood alcohol concentration predicts utilitarian responses in moral dilemmas. *Cognition, 134,* 121–127. doi:10.1016/j.cognition.2014.09.006

Dumontheil, I., Thompson, R., & Duncan, J. (2010). Assembly and use of new task rules in fronto-parietal cortex. *Journal of Cognitive Neuroscience, 23*(1), 168–182.

Dunbar, K. N. (1993). Concept discovery in a scientific domain. *Cognitive Science, 17,* 397–434.

Dunbar, K., & Blanchette, I. (2001). The in Vivo/in vitro approach to cognition: The case of analogy. *Trends in Cognitive Sciences, 5*(8), 334–339.

Duncan, J. (1996). Cooperating brain systems in selective perception and action. In T. Inui & J. J. McClelland (Eds.), *Attention and performance* (Vol. XVI, pp. 549–578). Cambridge, MA: The MIT Press.

Duncan, J., Burgess, P., & Emslie, H. (1995). Fluid intelligence after frontal lobe lesions. *Neuropsychologia*, *33*(3), 261–268.

Duncan, J., Emslie, H., Williams, P., Johnson, R., & Freer, C. (1996). Intelligence and the frontal lobe: The organization of goal-directed behavior. *Cognitive Psychology*, *30*(3), 257–303.

Duncan, J., & Humphreys, G. (1989). Visual search and stimulus similarity. *Psychological Review*, *96*(3), 433–458.

Duncan, J., Humphreys, G., & Ward, R. (1997). Competitive brain activity in visual attention. *Current Opinion in Neurobiology*, *7*, 255–261.

Duncan, J., Parr, A., Woolgar, A., Thompson, R. A., Bright, P., Cox, S. … Nimmo-Smith, I. (2008). Goal neglect and Spearman's g: Competing parts of a complex task. *Journal of Experimental Psychology: General*, *137*(1), 131–148. doi:10.1037/0096-3445.137.1.131

Duncker, K. (1945). On problem-solving. *Psychological Monographs*, *58*(5), I–113.

Dunn, B. D., Galton, H. C., Morgan, R., Evans, D., Oliver, C., Meyer, M. … Dalgleish, T. (2010). Listening to your heart. How interoception shapes emotion experience and intuitive decision making. *Psychological Science*, *21*(12), 1835–1844. doi:10.1177/0956797610389191

Dunn, J. C. (2008). The dimensionality of the remember-know task: A state-trace analysis. *Psychological Review*, *115*(2), 426–446. doi:10.1037/0033-295X.115.2.426

Dunning, D. (2011). The Dunning–Kruger effect. *Advances in Experimental Social Psychology*, *44*, 247–296. doi:10.1016/b978-0-12-385522-0.00005-6

Duss, S. B., Oggier, S., Reber, T. P., & Henke, K. (2011). Formation of semantic associations between subliminally presented face-word pairs. *Consciousness and Cognition*, *20*(3), 928–935. doi:10.1016/j.concog.2011.03.018

Dustman, R. E., & Beck, E. C. (1965). Phase of alpha brain waves, reaction time and visually evoked potentials. *Electroencephalography and Clinical Neurophysiology*, *18*, 433–440.

Dwivedi, V. D. (2013). Interpreting quantifier scope ambiguity: Evidence of heuristic first, algorithmic second processing. *PLoS One*, *8*(11), e81461. doi:10.1371/journal.pone.0081461

Eakin, D. K., & Smith, R. (2012). Retroactive interference effects in implicit memory. *Journal of Experimental Psychology: Learning, Memory, and Cognition*, *38*(5), 1419–1424. doi:10.1037/a0027208

Eardley, A. F., & van Velzen, J. (2011). Event-related potential evidence for the use of external coordinates in the preparation of tactile attention by the early blind. *European Journal of Neuroscience*, *33*(10), 1897–1907. doi:10.1111/j.1460-9568.2011.07672.x

Eason, R. G. (1981). Visual evoked potential correlates of early neural filtering during selective attention. *Bulletin of the Psychonomic Society*, *18*(4), 203–206.

Eason, R. G., Harter, M. R., & White, C. T. (1969). Effects of attention and arousal on visually evoked cortical potentials and reaction time in man. *Physiology and Behavior*, *4*(3), 283–289.

Easterbrook, J. A. (1959). The effect of emotion on cue utilization and the organizing of behavior. *Psychological Review*, *66*(3), 183–201.

Ebbinghaus, H. (1885). *Über Das Gedächtnis: Untersuchungen zur experimentellen psychologie*. Leipzig: Duncker & Humblot.

Ebisch, S. J. H., & Gallese, V. (2015). A neuroscientific perspective on the nature of altered self-other relationships in schizophrenia. *Journal of Consciousness Studies*, *22*(1–2), 220–240.

Ebisch, S. J. H., Salone, A., Ferri, F., De Berardis, D., Romani, G. L., Ferro, F. M. … Gallese, V. (2013). Out of touch with reality? Social perception in first-episode schizophrenia. *Social, Cognitive, and Affective Neuroscience*, *8*(4), 394–403. doi:10.1093/scan/nss012

Eccles, J. C. (1992). Evolution of consciousness. *Proceedings of the National Academy of Sciences of the United States of America*, *89*(16), 7320–7324.

Edwards, R. R., Bingham, C. O., 3rd, Bathon, J., & Haythornthwaite, J. A. (2006). Catastrophizing and pain in arthritis, fibromyalgia, and other rheumatic diseases. *Arthritis & Rheumatism*, *55*(2), 325–332. doi:10.1002/art.21865

Egly, R., Driver, J., & Rafal, R. D. (1994). Shifting visual attention between objects and locations: Evidence from normal and parietal lesion subjects. *Journal of Experimental Psychology: General*, *123*(2), 161–177.

Egner, T., & Hirsch, J. (2005). Cognitive control mechanisms resolve conflict through cortical amplification of task-relevant information. *Nature Neuroscience*, *8*(12), 1784–1790. doi:10.1038/nn1594

Ehinger, K. A., Hidalgo-Sotelo, B., Torralba, A., & Oliva, A. (2009). Modeling search for people in 900 scenes: A combined source model of eye guidance. *Visual Cognition*, *17*(6–7), 945–978. doi:10.1080/13506280902834720

Ehrsson, H. H., Spence, C., & Passingham, R. E. (2004). That's my hand! Activity in premotor cortex reflects feeling of ownership of a limb. *Science*, *305*(5685), 875–877.

Eich, E. (1995). Searching for mood dependent memory. *Psychological Science*, *6*(2), 67–75.

Eich, E., & Metcalfe, J. (1989). Mood dependent memory for internal versus external events. *Journal of Experimental Psychology: Learning, Memory, and Cognition*, *15*(3), 443–455.

Eimer, M. (1995). Stimulus-response compatibility and automatic response activation: Evidence from psychophysiological studies. *Journal of Experimental Psychology: Human Perception and Performance*, *21*(4), 837–854.

References

Eimer, M. (1996). The N2pc component as an indicator of attentional selectivity. *Electroencephalography and Clinical Neurophysiology, 99*, 225–234.

Eimer, M., Cockburn, D., Smedley, B., & Driver, J. (2001). Cross-modal links in endogenous spatial attention are mediated by common external locations: Evidence from event-related brain potentials. *Experimental Brain Research, 139*(4), 398–411. doi:10.1007/s002210100773

Eimer, M., Forster, B., & Van Velzen, J. (2003). Anterior and posterior attentional control systems use different spatial reference frames: ERP evidence from covert tactile-spatial orienting. *Psychophysiology, 40*(6), 924–933.

Eimer, M., & Schöger, E. (1998). ERP effects of intermodal attention and cross-modal attention in spatial attention. *Psychophysiology, 35*, 313–327.

Eimer, M., & Van Velzen, J. (2002). Crossmodal links in spatial attention are mediated by supramodal control processes: Evidence from event-related potentials. *Psychophysiology, 39*(4), 437–449.

Eimer, M., Van Velzen, J., & Driver, J. (2002). Cross-modal interactions between audition, touch, and vision in endogenous spatial attention: ERP evidence on preparatory states and sensory modulations. *Journal of Cognitive Neuroscience, 14*(2), 254–271.

Einstein, G. O., & McDaniel, M. A. (2005). Prospective memory. *Current Directions in Psychological Science, 14*(6), 286–290.

Einstein, G. O., McDaniel, M. A., Thomas, R., Mayfield, S., Shank, H., Morrisette, N., & Breneiser, J. (2005). Multiple processes in prospective memory retrieval: Factors determining monitoring versus spontaneous retrieval. *Journal of Experimental Psychology: General, 134*(3), 327–342. doi:10.1037/0096-3445.134.3.327

Eisenberger, N. I., & Lieberman, M. D. (2004). Why rejection hurts: A common neural alarm system for physical and social pain. *Trends in Cognitive Sciences, 8*(7), 294–300. doi:10.1016/j.tics.2004.05.010

Eisenberger, N. I., Lieberman, M. D., & Williams, K. D. (2003). Does rejection hurt? An fMRI study of social exclusion. *Science, 302*(5643), 290–292. doi:10.1126/science.1089134

Elbert, T., Candia, V., Altenmüller, E., Rau, H., Sterr, A., Rockstroh, B. ... Taub, E. (1998). Alterations of digital representations in somatosensory cortex in focal hand dystonia. *Neuroreport, 9*, 3571–3575.

Elbert, T., Pantev, C., Wienbruch, C., Rockstroh, B., & Taub, E. (1995). Increased cortical prepresentation of the fingers of the left hand in string players. *Science, 270*(5234), 305–307.

Elgoyhen, A. B., Langguth, B., De Ridder, D., & Vanneste, S. (2015). Tinnitus: Perspectives from human neuroimaging. *Nature Reviews Neuroscience, 16*(10), 632–642. doi:10.1038/nrn4003

Elhilali, M., Ma, L., Micheyl, C., Oxenham, A. J., & Shamma, S. A. (2009). Temporal coherence in the perceptual organization and cortical representation of auditory scenes. *Neuron, 61*(2), 317–329. doi:10.1016/j.neuron.2008.12.005

Ellis, A. W. (1980). On the Freudian theory of speech errors. In V. A. Fromkin (Ed.), *Errors in linguistic performance*. Hove: Lawrence Erlbaum Associates.

Ellis, A. W., Miller, D., & Sin, G. (1983). Wernicke's aphasia and normal language processing: A case study in cognitive neuropsychology. *Cognition, 15*, 111–144.

Ellis, A. W., & Young, A. W. (1988). *Human cognitive neuropsychology*. Hove: Psychology Press.

Elstein, A. S., Shulman, L. S., & Sprafka, S. A. (1990). Medical problem solving: A ten-year retrospective. *Evaluation & the Health Professions, 13*(1), 5–36.

Endsley, M. R. (1995). Toward a theory of situation awareness in dynamic systems. *Human Factors, 37*(1), 32–64.

Endsley, M. R. (1996). Automation and situation awareness. In R. Parasuraman & M. Mououa (Eds.), *Automation and human performance: Theory and applications* (pp. 163–181). Mahwah, NJ: Lawrence Erlbaum Associates.

Engbert, R., Longtin, A., & Kleigl, R. (2002). A dynamic model of saccade generation in reading based on spatially distributed lexical processing. *Vision Research, 42*, 621–636.

Engbert, R., Nuthmann, A., Richter, E. M., & Kliegl, R. (2005). Swift: A dynamical model of saccade generation during reading. *Psychological Review, 112*(4), 777–813. doi:10.1037/0033-295X.112.4.777

Engel, P. J. H. (2008). Tacit knowledge and visual expertise in medical diagnostic reasoning: Implications for medical education. *Medical Teacher, 30*(7), e184–e188. doi:10.1080/01421590802144260

Engelmann, J. B., Damaraju, E., Padmala, S., & Pessoa, L. (2009). Combined effects of attention and motivation on visual task performance: Transient and sustained motivational effects. *Frontiers in Human Neuroscience, 3*, 4. doi:10.3389/neuro.09.004.2009

Engelmann, J. B., & Pessoa, L. (2007). Motivation sharpens exogenous spatial attention. *Emotion, 7*(3), 668–674. doi:10.1037/1528-3542.7.3.668

Epstein, R., & Joker, V. R. (2007). A threshold theory of the humor response. *The Behavior Analyst, 30*(1), 49–58.

Ericsson, K. A. (2004). Deliberate practice and the acquisition and maintenance of expert performance in medicine and related domains. *Academic Medicine, 79*(10), S70–S81.

Ericsson, K. A. (2007). An expert-performance perspective of research on medical expertise: The study of clinical performance. *Medical Education, 41*(12), 1124–1130. doi:10.1111/j.1365-2923.2007.02946.x

Ericsson, K. A., & Chase, W. G. (1982). Exceptional memory. *American Scientist, 70*(6), 607–615.

Eriksen, B. A., & Eriksen, C. W. (1974). Effects of noise letters upon identification of a target letter in a non-search task. *Perception & Psychophysics, 16*, 143–149.

Ericsson, K. A., & Kintsch, W. (1995). Long-term working memory. *Psychological Review, 102*(2), 211–245.

Ericsson, A. K., & Towne, T. J. (2010). Expertise. *Wiley Interdisciplinary Review in Cognitive Science, 1*(3), 404–416. doi:10.1002/wcs.47

Ericsson, K. A., Whyte, J., & Ward, P. (2007). Expert performance in nursing: Reviewing research on expertise in nursing within the framework of the expert-performance approach. *Advances in Nursing Science, 30*(1), E58–E71.

Eriksen, C. W., & St. James, J. D. (1986). Visual attention within and around the field of focal attention: A zoom Lens model. *Perception & Psychophysics, 40*(4), 225–240.

Eriksson, P. D., Perfilieva, E., Björk-Eriksson, T., Alborn, A. -M., Nordborg, C., Peterson, D. A. ... Gage, F. H. (1998). Neurogenesis in the adult hippocampus. *Nature Medicine, 4*(11), 1313–1317.

Erkelens, C. J., & van Ee, R. (2002). The role of the cyclopean eye in vision: Sometimes inappropriate, always irrelevant. *Vision Research, 42,* 1157–1163.

Ernst, M. O. (2007). Learning to integrate arbitrary signals from vision and touch. *Journal of Visualized, 7*(5), 1–14. doi:10.1167/7.5.7

Ernst, A., Alkass, K., Bernard, S., Salehpour, M., Perl, S., Tisdale, J. ... Frisen, J. (2014). Neurogenesis in the striatum of the adult human brain. *Cell, 156*(5), 1072–1083. doi:10.1016/j.cell.2014.01.044

Ernst, M. O., & Banks, M. S. (2002). Humans integrate visual and haptic information in a statistically optimal fashion. *Nature, 415*(6870), 429–433.

Ernst, M. O., & Bülthoff, H. H. (2004). Merging the senses into a robust percept. *Trends in Cognitive Sciences, 8*(4), 162–169. doi:10.1016/j.tics.2004.02.002

Escera, C., & Corral, M. J. (2007). Role of mismatch negativity and novelty-P3 in involuntary auditory attention. *Journal of Psychophysiology, 21*(3–4), 251–264. doi:10.1027/0269-8803.21.34.251

Ester, E. F., Drew, T., Klee, D., Vogel, E. K., & Awh, E. (2012). Neural measures reveal a fixed item limit in subitizing. *The Journal of Neuroscience, 32*(21), 7169–7177. doi:10.1523/JNEUROSCI.1218-12.2012

Esteves-Sorensen, C., & Perretti, F. (2012). Micro-costs: Inertia in television viewing. *The Economic Journal, 122*(563), 867–902.

Eva, K. W., Hatala, R. M., Leblanc, V. R., & Brooks, L. R. (2007). Teaching from the clinical reasoning literature: Combined reasoning strategies help novice diagnosticians overcome misleading information. *Medical Education, 41*(12), 1152–1158. doi:10.1111/j.1365-2923.2007.02923.x

Evans, J. S. (2008). Dual-processing accounts of reasoning, judgment, and social cognition. *Annual Review of Psychology, 59,* 255–278. doi:10.1146/annurev.psych.59.103006.093629

Evans, P. M. (1991). Tactile attention and the perception of moving tactile stimuli. *Perception & Psychophysics, 49*(4), 355–364.

Evans, J. S. B. T. (1998). Matching bias in conditional reasoning: Do we understand it after 25 years? *Thinking & Reasoning, 4*(1), 45–110. doi:10.1080/135467898394247

Evans, J. S. B. T. (2003). In two minds: Dual-process accounts of reasoning. *Trends in Cognitive Sciences, 7*(10), 454–459. doi:10.1016/j.tics.2003.08.012

Evans, J. S. B. T. (2006). The heuristic-analytic theory of reasoning: Extension and evaluation. *Psychonomic Bulletin & Review, 13*(3), 378–395

Evans, J. S. B. T. (2007). On the resolution of conflict in dual process theories of reasoning. *Thinking & Reasoning, 13*(4), 321–339. doi:10.1080/13546780601008825

Evans, J. S. B. T. (2011). Reasoning is for thinking, not just for arguing. *Behavioral and Brain Sciences, 34*(2), 77–78. doi:10.1017/S0140525X10002773

Evans, J. S. B. T. (2012). Questions and challenges for the new psychology of reasoning. *Thinking & Reasoning, 18*(1), 5–31. doi:10.1080/13546783.2011.637674

Evans, J. S. B. T., & Curtis-Holmes, J. (2005). Rapid responding increases belief bias: Evidence for the dual-process theory of reasoning. *Thinking & Reasoning, 11*(4), 382–389. doi:10.1080/13546780542000005

Everaert, J., Koster, E. H., & Derakshan, N. (2012). The combined cognitive bias hypothesis in depression. *Clinical Psychology Review, 32*(5), 413–424. doi:10.1016/j.cpr.2012.04.003

Everaert, T., Theeuwes, M., Liefooghe, B., & De Houwer, J. (2014). Automatic motor activation by Mere instruction. *Cognitive, Affective, & Behavioral Neuroscience, 14*(4), 1300–1309. doi:10.3758/s13415-014-0294-7

Eysenck, M. W., & Calvo, M. G. (1992). Anxiety and performance: The processing efficiency theory. *Cognition & Emotion, 6*(6), 409–434. doi:10.1080/02699939208409696

Eysenck, M. W., Derakshan, N., Santos, R., & Calvo, M. G. (2007). Anxiety and cognitive performance: Attentional control theory. *Emotion, 7*(2), 336–353. doi:10.1037/1528-3542.7.2.336

Eysenck, M. W., & Eysenck, M. C. (1980). Effects of processing depth, distinctiveness, and word frequency on retention. *British Journal of Psychology, 71,* 263–274.

Eysenck, M. W., MacLeod, C., & Mathews, A. (1987). Cognitive functioning and anxiety. *Psychological Research, 49,* 189–195.

Eysenck, M., Payne, S., & Santos, R. (2006). Anxiety and depression: Past, present, and future events. *Cognition & Emotion, 20*(2), 274–294. doi:10.1080/02699930500220066

Ezzyat, Y., & Davachi, L. (2011). What constitutes an episode in episodic memory? *Psychological Science, 22*(2), 243–252. doi:10.1177/0956797610393742

Fadiga, L., Craighero, L., Buccino, G., & Rizzolatti, G. (2002). Speech listening specifically modulates the excitability of tongue muscles: A TMS study. *European Journal of Neuroscience, 15,* 399–402.

Fadiga, L., Fogassi, L., Pavesi, G., & Rizzolatti, G. (1995). Motor facilitation during action observation: A magnetic stimulation study. *Journal of Neurophysiology, 73*(6), 2608–2611.

Fahrenfort, J. J., Scholte, H. S., & Lamme, V. A. F. (2007). Masking disrupts reentrant processing in human visual cortex. *Journal of Cognitive Neuroscience, 19*(9), 1488–1497.

Faigly, L., & Witte, S. (1981). Analyzing revision. *College Composition and Communication, 32*(4), 400–414.

Failing, M., Nissens, T., Pearson, D., Le Pelley, M., & Theeuwes, J. (2015). Oculomotor capture by stimuli that signal the availability of reward. *Journal of Neurophysiology, 114*(4), 2316–2327. doi:10.1152/jn.00441.2015

Failing, M. F., & Theeuwes, J. (2014). Exogenous visual orienting by reward. *Journal of Vision, 14*(5), 6. doi:10.1167/14.5.6

Fairhall, S. L., & Macaluso, E. (2009). Spatial attention can modulate audiovisual integration at multiple cortical and subcortical sites. *European Journal of Neuroscience, 29*(6), 1247–1257. doi:10.1111/j.1460-9568.2009.06688.x

Fairhurst, M., Wiech, K., Dunckley, P., & Tracey, I. (2007). Anticipatory brainstem activity predicts neural processing of pain in humans. *Pain, 128*(1–2), 101–110. doi:10.1016/j.pain.2006.09.001

Falchier, A., Clavagnier, S., Barone, P., & Kennedy, H. (2002). Anatomical evidence of multimodal integration in primate striate cortex. *The Journal of Neuroscience, 22*(13), 5749–5759.

Falkenstein, M., Hohnsbein, J., Hoormann, J., & Blanke, O. (1991). Effects of crossmodal divided attention on late ERP components II. Error processing in choice reaction tasks. *Electroencephalography and Clinical Neurophysiology, 78*, 447–455.

Fallon, J. B., & Macefield, V. G. (2007). Vibration sensitivity of human muscle spindles and Golgi tendon organs. *Muscle and Nerve, 36*, 21–29.

Fama, R., Pitel, A. L., & Sullivan, E. V. (2012). Anterograde episodic memory in Korsakoff syndrome. *Neuropsychology Review, 22*(2), 93–104. doi:10.1007/s11065-012-9207-0

Fangmeier, T., Knauff, M., Ruff, C. C., & Sloutsky, V. (2006). fMRI evidence for a three-stage model of deductive reasoning. *Journal of Cognitive Neuroscience, 18*(3), 320–334.

Farag, C., Troiani, V., Bonner, M., Powers, C., Avants, B., Gee, J., & Grossman, M. (2010). Hierarchical organization of scripts: Converging evidence from fMRI and frontotemporal degeneration. *Cerebral Cortex, 20*(10), 2453–2463. doi:10.1093/cercor/bhp313

Farah, M. J. (1988). Is visual imagery really visual? Overlooked evidence from neuropsychology. *Psychological Review, 95*(3), 307–317.

Farwell, L. A., & Donchin, E. (1991). The truth will out: Interrogative polygraphy ('Lie detection') with event-related brain potentials. *Psychophysiology, 28*(5), 531–547.

Farwell, L. A., & Smith, S. S. (1998). Using brain mermer testing to detect knowledge despite efforts to conceal. *Journal of Forensic Sciences, 46*, 135–143.

Faulkner, P. (2008). Cooperation and trust in conversational exchanges. *Theoria, 61*, 23–34.

Fedorenko, E., & Blank, I. A. (2020). Broca's area is not a natural kind. *Trends in Cognitive Sciences, 24*(4), 270–284. doi:10.1016/j.tics.2020.01.001

Fehr, E., & Camerer, C. F. (2007). Social neuroeconomics: The neural circuitry of social preferences. *Trends in Cognitive Sciences, 11*(10), 419–427. doi:10.1016/j.tics.2007.09.002

Fehr, E., & Fischbacher, U. (2003). The nature of human altruism. *Nature, 425*, 785–791.

Fehr, E., & Gächter, S. (2002). Altruistic punishment in humans. *Nature, 415*, 137–140.

Feigenson, L., Dehaene, S., & Spelke, E. (2004). Core systems of number. *Trends in Cognitive Sciences, 8*(7), 307–314. doi:10.1016/j.tics.2004.05.002

Feldman, J. (2000). Minimization of Boolean complexity in human concept learning. *Nature, 407*, 630–633.

Feldman, J. (2003). The simplicity principle in human concept learning. *Current Directions in Psychological Science, 12*(6), 227–232.

Feldman, D. E., & Brecht, M. (2005). Map plasticity in somatosensory cortex. *Science, 310*, 810–815.

Feldmeyer, D. (2010). Signals far and away. *Nature, 464*, 1134–1136.

Ferman, L., Collewijn, H., Jansen, T. C., & Van Den Berg, A. V. (1987). Human gaze stability in the horizontal, vertical, and torsional direction during voluntary head movements, evaluated with a three-dimensional scleral induction coil technique. *Vision Research, 27*(5), 811–828.

Fermuller, C., Ji, H., & Kitaoka, A. (2010). Illusory motion due to causal time filtering. *Vision Research, 50*(3), 315–329. doi:10.1016/j.visres.2009.11.021

Ferrarelli, F., Massimini, M., Sarasso, S., Casali, A., Riedner, B. A., Angelini, G. … Pearce, R. A. (2010). Breakdown in cortical effective connectivity during midazolam-induced loss of consciousness. *Proceedings of the National Academy of Sciences of the United States of America, 107*(6), 2681–2686. doi:10.1073/pnas.0913008107

Ferreira, F. (2003). The misinterpretation of noncanonical sentences. *Cognitive Psychology, 47*, 164–203. doi:10.1016/S0010-0285(03)00005-7

Ferreira, V. S. (2008). Ambiguity, accessibility, and a division of labor for communicative success. *Psychology of Learning and Motivation, 49*, 209–246. doi:10.1016/s0079-7421(08)00006-6

Ferreira, F., Bailey, K. G. D., & Ferraro, V. (2002). Good-enough representations in language comprehension. *Current Directions in Psychological Science, 11*(1), 11–15.

Ferreira, V. S., & Griffin, Z. M. (2003). Phonological influences on lexical (Mis) selection. *Psychological Science, 14*(1), 86–90.

Ferreira, F., & Swets, B. (2002). How incremental is language production? Evidence from the production of utterances requiring the computation of arithmetic sums. *Journal of Memory and Language, 46*(1), 57–84. doi:10.1006/jmla.2001.2797

Ferreira, F., & Clifton, C. (1986). The independence of syntactic processing. *Journal of Memory and Language, 25,* 348–368.

Ferro, J. M., & Silveira Botelho, M. A. (1980). Alexia for arithmetical signs a cause of disturbed calculation. *Cortex, 16*(1), 175–180. doi:10.1016/s0010-9452(80)80032-3

Fiedler, K. (1988). The dependence of the conjunction fallacy on subtle linguistic factors. *Psychological Research, 50,* 123–129.

Fiedler, K., Brinkmann, B., Betsch, T., & Wild, B. (2000). A sampling approach to biases in conditional probability judgments: Beyond base rate neglect and statistical format. *Journal of Experimental Psychology: General, 129*(3), 399–418. https://doi.org/10.1037/0096-3445.129.3.399

Filik, R., & Barber, E. (2011). Inner speech during silent reading reflects the Reader's regional accent. *PLoS One, 6*(10), e25782. doi:10.1371/journal.pone.0025782.g001

Fink, R. T. (1972). Response latency as a function of hypothesis testing strategies in concept identification. *Journal of Experimental Psychology, 95*(2), 337–342.

Finkenauer, C., Luminet, O., Gisle, L., El-Ahmadi, A., van der Linden, M., & Philippot, P. (1998). Flashbulb memories and the underlying mechanisms of their formation: Toward an emotional-integrative model. *Memory & Cognition, 26*(3), 516–531.

Fischer, P., & Greitemeyer, T. (2010). A new look at selective-exposure effects. *Current Directions in Psychological Science, 19*(6), 384–389. doi:10.1177/0963721410391246

Fisher, R. P., Geiselman, R. E., & Amador, M. (1989). Field test of the cognitive interview: Enhancing the recollection of actual victims and witnesses of crime. *Journal of Applied Psychology, 74*(5), 722–727.

Fitousi, D., & Wenger, M. J. (2013). Variants of independence in the perception of facial identity and expression. *Journal of Experimental Psychology: Human Perception and Performance, 39*(1), 133–155. doi:10.1037/a0028001

Fitts, P. M. (1954). The information capacity of the human motor system in controlling the amplitude of movement. *Journal of Experimental Psychology, 47*(6), 381–391.

FitzGerald, T. H., Dolan, R. J., & Friston, K. J. (2014). Model averaging, optimal inference, and habit formation. *Frontiers in Human Neuroscience, 8,* 457. doi:10.3389/fnhum.2014.00457

Fiveash, A., Thompson, W. F., Badcock, N. A., & McArthur, G. (2018). Syntactic processing in music and language: Effects of interrupting auditory streams with alternating timbres. *International Journal of Psychophysiology, 129,* 31–40. doi:10.1016/j.ijpsycho.2018.05.003

Fivush, R. (2010). Speaking silence: The social construction of silence in autobiographical and cultural narratives. *Memory, 18*(2), 88–98. doi:10.1080/09658210903029404

Fivush, R., Gray, J. T., & Fromhoff, F. A. (1987). Two-year olds talk about the past. *Cognitive Development, 2,* 393–409.

Flanagan, J. R., & Johansson, R. S. (2003). action plans used in action observation. *Nature, 424,* 769–771.

Flanagan, J. R., & Wing, A. M. (1997). The role of internal models in motion planning and control: Evidence from grip force adjustments during movements of hand-held loads. *The Journal of Neuroscience, 17*(4), 1519–1528.

Flanders, M., Tillery, S. I. H., & Soechting, J. F. (1992). Early stages in a sensorimotor transformation. *Behavioral and Brain Sciences, 15,* 309–362.

Fleck, M. S., & Mitroff, S. R. (2007). Rare targets are rarely missed in correctable search. *Psychological Science, 18*(11), 943–947.

Fletcher, P. C., & Frith, C. D. (2009). Perceiving is believing: A Bayesian approach to explaining the positive symptoms of schizophrenia. *Nature Reviews Neuroscience, 10*(1), 48–58. doi:10.1038/nrn2536

Fletcher, P. C., Happé, F., Frith, U., Baker, S. C., Dolan, R. J., Frackowiak, R. S. J., Frith, C. D. (1995). Other minds in the brain: A functional imaging study of 'Theory of mind' in story comprehension. *Cognition, 57,* 109–128.

Flevaris, A. V., Martinez, A., & Hillyard, S. A. (2014). Attending to global versus local stimulus features modulates neural processing of low versus high spatial frequencies: An analysis with event-related brain potentials. *Frontiers in Psychology, 5,* 277. doi:10.3389/fpsyg.2014.00277

Flor, H., Denke, C., Schaefer, M., & Grüsser, S. (2001). Effect of sensory discrimination training on cortical reorganisation and phantom limb pain. *The Lancet, 357*(9270), 1763–1764. doi:10.1016/s0140-6736(00)04890-x

Flor, H., Nikolajsen, L., & Staehelin Jensen, T. (2006). Phantom limb pain: A case of maladaptive CNS plasticity? *Nature Reviews Neuroscience, 7*(11), 873–881. doi:10.1038/nrn1991

Flower, L. S., & Hayes, J. R. (1980). The cognition of discovery: Defining a rhetorical problem. *College Composition and Communication, 31*(1), 21–32.

Flowerdew, J., & Tauroza, S. (1995). The effect of discourse markers on second language lecture comprehension. *Studies in Second Language Acquisition, 17,* 435–458.

Fodor, J. A. (1983). The modularity of mind: An essay on faculty psychology. In J. E. Adles & L. J. Rips (Eds.), *Reasoning: Studies of human inference and its foundations.* Cambridge, MA: Cambridge University Press.

Foerde, K., Knowlton, B. J., & Poldrack, R. A. (2006). Modulation of competing memory systems by distraction. *Proceedings of the National Academy of Sciences of the United States of America, 103*(31), 11778–11783. doi:10.1073/pnas.0602659103

Fogelson, N., Litvak, V., Peled, A., Fernandez-del-Olmo, M., & Friston, K. (2014). The functional anatomy of schizophrenia: A dynamic causal modeling study of predictive coding. *Schizophrenia Research, 158*(1–3), 204–212. doi:10.1016/j.schres.2014.06.011

Folk, C. L., Remington, R. W., & Johnston, J. C. (1992). Involuntary covert orienting is contingent on attentional control settings. *Journal of Experimental Psychology: Human Perception and Performance, 18*(4), 1030–1044.

References

Fonoaryova Key, A. P., Dove, G. O., & Maguire, M. J. (2005). Linking brainwaves to the brain: An ERP primer. *Developmental Neuropsychology, 27*(2), 183–215.

Fontaine, J. J. R., Scherer, K. R., & Soranio Salinas, C. (2013). *Components of emotional meaning: A sourcebook.* New York, NY: Oxford University Press.

Fontanari, L., Gonzalez, M., Vallortigara, G., & Girotto, V. (2014). Probabilistic cognition in two indigenous Mayan groups. *Proceedings of the National Academy of Sciences of the United States of America, 111*(48), 17075–17080. doi:10.1073/pnas.1410583111

Foot, P. (1967). The problem of abortion and the doctrine of the double effect. *Oxford Review, 5*, 5–15.

Ford, J. M., & Mathalon, D. H. (2012). Anticipating the future: Automatic prediction failures in schizophrenia. *International Journal of Psychophysiology, 83*(2), 232–239. doi:10.1016/j.ijpsycho.2011.09.004

Ford, J. M., Palzes, V. A., Roach, B. J., & Mathalon, D. H. (2014). Did I do that? Abnormal predictive processes in schizophrenia when button pressing to deliver a tone. *Schizophr Bull, 40*(4), 804–812. doi:10.1093/schbul/sbt072

Foss-Feig, J. H., Kwakye, L. D., Cascio, C. J., Burnette, C. P., Kadivar, H., Stone, W. L., Wallace, M. T. (2010). An extended multisensory temporal binding window in autism spectrum disorders. *Experimental Brain Research, 203*(2), 381–389. doi:10.1007/s00221-010-2240-4

Foster, D. H., & Nascimento, S. M. C. (1994). Relational colour constancy from invariant cone-excitation ratios. *Proceedings of the Royal Society B-Biological Sciences, 257*(1349), 115–121.

Fox, C. J., Hanif, H. M., Iaria, G., Duchaine, B. C., & Barton, J. J. (2011). Perceptual and anatomic patterns of selective deficits in facial identity and expression processing. *Neuropsychologia, 49*(12), 3188–3200. doi:10.1016/j.neuropsychologia.2011.07.018

Fox, E., Russo, R., Bowles, R., & Dutton, K. (2001). Do threatening stimuli draw or hold visual attention in subclinical anxiety? *Journal of Experimental Psychology: General, 130*(4), 681–700. doi:10.1037/0096-3445.130.4.681

Foxe, J. J., Wylie, G. R., Martinez, A., Schroeder, C. E., Javitt, D. C., Guilfoyle, D. … Murray, M. M. (2002). auditory-somatosensory multisensory processing in auditory association cortex: An fMRI study. *Journal of Neurophysiology, 88*, 540–543.

Franklin, S., Turner, J., Lambon Ralph, M. A., Morris, J., & Bailey, P. J. (1996). A distinctive case of word meaning deafness? *Cognitive Neuropsychology, 13*(8), 1139–1162.

Frauenfelder, U. H., Scholten, M., & Content, A. (2001). Bottom-up inhibition in lexical selection: Phonological mismatch effects in spoken word recognition. *Language and Cognitive Processes, 16*(5–6), 583–607. doi:10.1080/01690960143000146

Frazier, L., & Rayner, K. (1982). Making and correcting errors during sentence comprehension: Eye movements in the analysis of structurally ambiguous sentences. *Cognitive Psychology, 14*(2), 178–210.

Frazier, L., Carlson, K., & Clifton, C. Jr. (2006). Prosodic phrasing is central to language comprehension. *Trends in Cognitive Sciences, 10*(6), 244–249. doi:10.1016/j.tics.2006.04.002

Frederick, S. (2005). Cognitive reflection and decision making. *Journal of Economic Perspectives, 19*(4), 25–42.

Frederickson, B. (2001). The role of positive emotions in positive psychology: The broaden-and-build theory of positive emotions. *The American Journal of Psychology, 56*(3), 218–226.

Freud, S. (1901). *Zur psychopathologie des alltagslebens.* Frankfurt am Main: Fischer Taschenbuch Verlag.

Friederich, C. K., & Kotz, S. A. (2007). Event-related potential evidence of form and meaning coding during online speech recognition. *Journal of Cognitive Neuroscience, 19*(4), 594–604.

Friederici, A. D., Fiebach, C. J., Schlesewsky, M., Bornkessel, I. D., & von Cramon, D. Y. (2006). Processing linguistic complexity and grammaticality in the left frontal cortex. *Cerebral Cortex, 16*(12), 1709–1717. doi:10.1093/cercor/bhj106

Friedman, M. I. (1997). An energy sensor for control of energy intake. *Proceedings of the Nutrition Society, 56*, 41–50.

Friedman, N. P., Miyake, A., Young, S. E., DeFries, J. C., Corley, R. P., & Hewitt, J. K. (2008). Individual differences in executive functions are almost entirely genetic in origin. *Journal of Experimental Psychology: General, 137*(2), 201–225. doi:10.1037/0096-3445.137.2.201

Friessen, C. K., & Kingstone, A. (1998). The eyes have it! Reflexive orienting is triggered by nonpredictive gaze. *Psychonomic Bulletin & Review, 5*(3), 490–495.

Frischen, A., & Tipper, S. P. (2004). Orienting attention via observed gaze shift evokes longer term inhibitory effects: Implications for social interactions, attention, and memory. *Journal of Experimental Psychology: General, 133*(4), 516–533.

Friston, K. (2010). The free-energy principle: A unified brain theory? *Nature Reviews Neuroscience, 11*(2), 127–138. doi:10.1038/nrn2787

Friston, K. (2011). What is optimal about motor control? *Neuron, 72*(3), 488–498. doi:10.1016/j.neuron.2011.10.018

Friston, K., Adams, R. A., Perrinet, L., & Breakspear, M. (2012). Perceptions as hypotheses: Saccades as experiments. *Frontiers in Psychology, 3*, 151. doi:10.3389/fpsyg.2012.00151

Friston, K. J., & Feldman, H. (2010). Attention, uncertainty, and free-energy. *Frontiers in Human Neuroscience, 4.* doi:10.3389/fnhum.2010.00215

Friston, K., Schwartenbeck, P., FitzGerald, T., Moutoussis, M., Behrens, T., & Dolan, R. J. (2014). The anatomy of choice: Dopamine and decision-making. *Philosophical Transactions of the Royal Society B-Biological Sciences, 369*(1655). doi:10.1098/rstb.2013.0481

Frith, C. D., & Frith, U. (2006). The neural basis of mentalizing. *Neuron*, *50*(4), 531–534. doi:10.1016/j.neuron.2006.05.001

Frith, C. D., Blakemore, S. J., & Wolpert, D. M. (2000). Abnormalities in the awareness and control of action. *Philosophical Transactions of the Royal Society B-Biological Sciences*, *355*(1404), 1771–1788. doi:10.1098/rstb.2000.0734

Fritz, J. B., Elhilali, M., David, S. V., & Shamma, S. A. (2007). Auditory attention–focusing the searchlight on sound. *Current Opinion in Neurobiology*, *17*(4), 437–455. doi:10.1016/j.conb.2007.07.011

Frost, R. (1998). Toward a strong phonological theory of visual word recognition: True issues and false trails. *Psychological Bulletin*, *123*(1), 71–99.

Fujisaki, W., Shimojo, S., Kashino, M., & Nishida, S. (2004). Recalibration of audiovisual simultaneity. *Nature Neuroscience*, *7*(7), 773–778. doi:10.1038/nn1268

Fukumura, K., & van Gompel, R. P. (2012). Producing pronouns and definite noun phrases: Do speakers use the Addressee's discourse model? *Cognitive Science*, *36*(7), 1289–1311. doi:10.1111/j.1551-6709.2012.01255.x

Fuller, J. M. (2003). The influence of speaker roles on discourse marker use. *Journal of Pragmatics*, *35*, 23–45.

Fürst, A. J., & Hitch, G. J. (2000). Separate roles for executive and phonological components of working memory in mental arithmetic. *Memory & Cognition*, *28*(5), 774–782.

Fuster, J. M. (2007). Jackson and the frontal executive hierarchy. *International Journal of Psychophysiology*, *64*(1), 106–107. doi:10.1016/j.ijpsycho.2006.07.014

Fuster, J. M., Bodner, M., & Kroger, J. K. (2000). Cross-modal and cross-temporal association in neurons of frontal cortex. *Nature*, *405*, 347–351.

Fuster, J. M. (2004). Upper processing stages of the perception–action cycle. *Trends in Cognitive Sciences*, *8*(4), 143–145. doi:10.1016/j.tics.2004.02.004

Gabay, S., Henik, A., & Gradstein, L. (2010). Ocular motor ability and covert attention in patients with duane retraction syndrome. *Neuropsychologia*, *48*(10), 3102–3109. doi:10.1016/j.neuropsychologia.2010.06.022

Gable, P., & Harmon-Jones, E. (2010). The blues broaden, but the nasty narrows: Attentional consequences of negative affects low and high in motivational intensity. *Psychological Science*, *21*(2), 211–215. doi:10.1177/0956797609359622

Gable, P. A., & Harmon-Jones, E. (2011). Attentional consequences of pregoal and postgoal positive affects. *Emotion*, *11*(6), 1358–1367. doi:10.1037/a0025611

Gabrieli, J. D. E., Corkin, S., Mickel, S. F., & Growdown, J. H. (1993). Intact acquisition and long-term retention of mirror-tracing skill in Alzheimer's disease and in global amnesia. *Behavioral Neuroscience*, *107*(6), 899–910.

Gaesser, B., Spreng, R. N., McLelland, V. C., Addis, D. R., & Schacter, D. L. (2013). Imagining the future: Evidence for a hippocampal contribution to constructive processing. *Hippocampus*, *23*(12), 1150–1161. doi:10.1002/hipo.22152

Gaffan, D., Murray, E. A., & Fabre-Thorpe, M. (1993). Interaction of the amygdala with the frontal lobe in reward memory. *European Journal of Neuroscience*, *5*, 968–975.

Gaillard, R., Dehaene, S., Adam, C., Clémenceau, S., Hasboun, D., Baulac, M. … Naccache, L. (2009). Converging intracranial markers of conscious access. *PLoS Biology*, *7*(3), e1000061.

Gainotti, G., & Marra, C. (2011). Differential contribution of right and left temporo-occipital and anterior temporal lesions to face recognition disorders. *Frontiers in Human Neuroscience*, *5*, 55. doi:10.3389/fnhum.2011.00055

Gallese, V., Keysers, C., & Rizzolatti, G. (2004). A unifying view of the basis of social cognition. *Trends in Cognitive Sciences*, *8*(9), 396–403. doi:10.1016/j.tics.2004.07.002

Gallese, V., & Lakoff, G. (2005). The brain's concepts: The role of the sensory-motor system in conceptual knowledge. *Cognitive Neuropsychology*, *22*(3), 455–479. doi:10.1080/02643290442000310

Gallese, V., & Sinigaglia, C. (2011). What is so special about embodied simulation? *Trends in Cognitive Sciences*, *15*(11), 512–519. doi:10.1016/j.tics.2011.09.003

Gallese, V., Murata, A., Kaseda, M., Niki, N., & Sakata, H. (1994). Deficit of hand preshaping after muscimol injection in monkey parietal cortex. *Neuroreport*, *5*, 1525–1529.

Gallistel, C. R., & Gelman, R. (2000). Non-verbal numerical cognition: From reals to integers. *Trends in Cognitive Sciences*, *4*(2), 59–65.

Gallistel, C. R., & Gibbon, J. (2000). Time, rate, and conditioning. *Psychological Review*, *107*(2), 289–344.

Galotti, K. M. (2007). Decision structuring in important real-life choices. *Psychological Science*, *18*(4), 320–325.

Galotti, K. M., & Tinkelenberg, C. E. (2009). Real-life decision making: Parents choosing a first-grade placement. *The American Journal of Psychology*, *122*(4), 455–468.

Gambetti, E., & Giusberty, F. (2012). The effect of anger and anxiety traits on investment decisions. *Journal of Economic Psychology*, *33*, 1059–1069. doi:10.1016/j.joep.2012.07.001

Gamble, M. L., & Luck, S. J. (2011). N2ac: An ERP component associated with the focusing of attention within an auditory scene. *Psychophysiology*, *48*(8), 1057–1068. doi:10.1111/j.1469-8986.2010.01172.x

Gamble, M. L., & Woldorff, M. G. (2015). The temporal cascade of neural processes underlying target detection and attentional processing during auditory search. *Cereb Cortex*, *25*(9), 2456–2465. doi:10.1093/cercor/bhu047

Ganong, W. F. I. (1980). Phonetic categorization in auditory word perception. *Journal of Experimental Psychology: Human Perception and Performance*, *6*(1), 110–125.

Gao, Z., Li, J., Liang, J., Chen, H., Yin, J., & Shen, M. (2009). Storing fine detailed information in visual working memory–evidence from event-related potentials.

Journal of the International Neuropsychological Society, *9*(7), 17. doi:10.1167/9.7.17

Garavan, H. (1998). Serial attention within working memory. *Memory & Cognition*, *26*(2), 263–276.

Gardiner, J. M. (1983). On recency and echoic memory. *Philosophical Transactions of the Royal Society B-Biological Sciences*, *302*, 267–282.

Gardiner, J. M., Brandt, K. R., Baddeley, A. D., Vargha-Khadem, F., & Mishkin, M. (2008). Charting the acquisition of semantic knowledge in a case of developmental amnesia. *Neuropsychologia*, *46*(11), 2865–2868. doi:10.1016/j.neuropsychologia.2008.05.021

Garnsey, S. M., Pearlmutter, N. J., Myers, E., & Lotocky, M. A. (1997). The contributions of verb bias plausibility to the comprehension of temporarily ambiguous sentences. *Journal of Memory and Language*, *37*, 58–93.

Garrido, M. I., Kilner, J. M., Stephan, K. E., & Friston, K. J. (2009). The mismatch negativity: A review of underlying mechanisms. *Clin Neurophysiol*, *120*(3), 453–463. doi:10.1016/j.clinph.2008.11.029

Garrod, S., & Pickering, M. J. (2004). Why is conversation so easy? *Trends in Cognitive Sciences*, *8*(1), 8–11. doi:10.1016/j.tics.2003.10.016

Garrod, S., & Terras, M. (2000). The contribution of lexical and situational knowledge to resolving discourse roles: Bonding and resolution. *Journal of Memory and Language*, *42*(4), 526–544. doi:10.1006/jmla.1999.2694

Gaspar, J. M., Christie, G. J., Prime, D. J., Jolicoeur, P., & McDonald, J. J. (2016). Inability to suppress salient distractors predicts low visual working memory capacity. *Proceedings of the National Academy of Sciences of the United States of America*, *113*(13), 3693–3698. doi:10.1073/pnas.1523471113

Gauld, A., & Stephenson, G. M. (1967). Some experiments relating to Bartlett's theory of remembering. *British Journal of Psychology*, *58*(1–2), 39–49.

Gauthier, I., & Tarr, M. J. (2002). Unraveling mechanisms for expert object recognition: Bridging brain activity and behavior. *Journal of Experimental Psychology: Human Perception and Performance*, *28*(2), 431–446. doi:10.1037/0096-1523.28.2.431

Gazzaniga, M. S. (2013). Shifting gears: Seeking new approaches for mind/brain mechanisms. *Annual Review of Psychology*, *64*, 1–20. doi:10.1146/annurev-psych-113011-143817

Geary, D. C. (1993). Mathematical disabilities: Cognitive, neuropsychological, and genetic components. *Psychological Bulletin*, *114*(2), 345–362.

Geary, D. C., Bow-Thomas, C., & Yao, Y. (1992). Counting knowledge and skill in cognitive addition: A comparison of normal and mathematically disabled children. *Journal of Experimental Child Psychology*, *54*, 372–391.

Geary, D. C., & Hoard, M. K. (2001). Numerical and arithmetical deficits in learning-disabled children: Relation to dyscalculia and dyslexia. *Aphasiology*, *15*(7), 635–647. doi:10.1080/02687040143000113

Geary, D. C., Hoard, M. K., & Hamson, C. O. (1999). Numerical and arithmetical cognition: Patterns of functions and deficits in children at risk for a mathematical disability. *Journal of Experimental Child Psychology*, *74*, 213–239.

Gegenfurtner, A., Lehtinen, E., & Säljö, R. (2011). Expertise differences in the comprehension of visualizations: A meta-analysis of eye-tracking research in professional domains. *Educational Psychology Review*, *23*(4), 523–552. doi:10.1007/s10648-011-9174-7

Gehring, W. J., Goss, B., Coles, M. G. H., Meyer, D. E., & Donchin, E. (1993). A neural system for error detection and compensation. *Psychological Science*, *4*, 385–390.

Gehring, W. J., Goss, B., Coles, M. G. H., Meyer, D. E., & Donchin, E. (2018). The error-related negativity. *Perspectives on Psychological Science*, *13*(2), 200–204.

Geiselman, R. E., Fisher, R. P., MacKinnon, D. P., & Holland, H. L. (1985). Eyewitness memory enhancement in the police interview: Cognitive retrieval mnemonics versus hypnosis. *Journal of Applied Psychology*, *70*(2), 401–412.

Geisler, W. S., Perry, J. S., Super, B. J., & Gallogly, D. P. (2001). Edge co-occurrence in natural images predicts contour grouping performance. *Vision Research*, *41*, 711–724.

Geldard, F. A., & Sherrick, C. E. (1972). The cutaneous 'Rabbit': A perceptual illusion. *Science*, *178*(4057), 178–179.

Gentner, D., Loewenstein, J., Thompson, L., & Forbus, K. D. (2009). Reviving inert knowledge: Analogical abstraction supports relational retrieval of past events. *Cognitive Science*, *33*(8), 1343–1382. doi:10.1111/j.1551-6709.2009.01070.x

Geraerts, E., & McNally, R. J. (2008). Forgetting unwanted memories: Directed forgetting and thought suppression methods. *Acta Psychologica*, *127*(3), 614–622. doi:10.1016/j.actpsy.2007.11.003

Gerrig, R. J., & O'Brien, E. J. (2005). The scope of memory-based processing. *Discourse Processes*, *39*(2&3), 225–242.

Ghazanfar, A. A., & Schroeder, C. E. (2006). Is neocortex essentially multisensory? *Trends in Cognitive Sciences*, *10*(6), 278–285. doi:10.1016/j.tics.2006.04.008

Ghazanfar, A. A., Maier, J. X., Hoffman, K. L., & Logothetis, N. K. (2005). Multisensory integration of dynamic faces and voices in rhesus monkey auditory cortex. *The Journal of Neuroscience*, *25*(20), 5004–5012.

Ghitza, O. (2011). Linking speech perception and neurophysiology: Speech decoding guided by cascaded oscillators locked to the input rhythm. *Frontiers in Psychology*, *2*, 130. doi:10.3389/fpsyg.2011.00130

Ghitza, O., & Greenberg, S. (2009). On the possible role of brain rhythms in speech perception: Intelligibility of time-compressed speech with periodic and aperiodic insertions of silence. *Phonetica*, *66*(1–2), 113–126. doi:10.1159/000208934

Giard, M.-H., & Peronnet, F. (1999). Auditory-visual integration during multimodal object recognition in humans: A behavioral and electrophysiological study. *Journal of Cognitive Neuroscience*, *11*(5), 473–490.

Gibson, J. J. (1950). *The perception of the visual world.* Cambridge, MA: The Riverside Press.

Gibson, J. J. (1979). *The ecological approach to visual perception.* London: Psychology Press.

Gick, M. L., & Holyoak, K. J. (1980). Analogical problem solving. *Cognitive Psychology, 12,* 306–355.

Giesecke, T., Gracely, R. H., Williams, D. A., Geisser, M. E., Petzke, F. W., & Clauw, D. J. (2005). The relationship between depression, clinical pain, and experimental pain in a chronic pain cohort. *Arthritis & Rheumatism, 52*(5), 1577–1584. doi:10.1002/art.21008

Gigerenzer, G., & Brighton, H. (2009). Homo heuristicus: Why biased minds make better inferences. *Topics in Cognitive Science, 1*(1), 107–143. doi:10.1111/j.1756-8765.2008.01006.x

Gigerenzer, G., & Gaissmaier, W. (2011). Heuristic decision making. *Annual Review of Psychology, 62,* 451–482. doi:10.1146/annurev-psych-120709-145346

Gigerenzer, G., & Gray, W. D. (2017). A simple heuristic successfully used by humans, animals, and machines: The story of the RAF and Luftwaffe, hawks and ducks, dogs and frisbees, baseball outfielders and sidewinder missiles—Oh my! *Topics in Cognitive Science, 9,* 260–263. https://doi.org/10.1111/tops.12269

Gigerenzer, G., & Hoffrage, U. (1995). How to improve Bayesian reasoning without instruction: Frequency formats. *Psychological Review, 102*(4), 684–704.

Gigerenzer, G., & Hoffrage, U. (1999). Overcoming difficulties in Bayesian reasoning: A reply to Lewis and Keren (1999) and Mellers and Mcgraw (1999). *Psychologiscal Review, 106*(2), 425–430.

Gilbert, C. D., & Li, W. (2013). Top-down influences on visual processing. *Nature Reviews Neuroscience, 14*(5), 350–363. doi:10.1038/nrn3476

Gilboa, A. (2004). Autobiographical and episodic memory–one and the same? Evidence from prefrontal activation in neuroimaging studies. *Neuropsychologia, 42*(10), 1336–1349. doi:10.1016/j.neuropsychologia.2004.02.014

Gilboa, A., Ramirez, J., Köhler, S., Westmacott, R., Black, S. E., & Moscovitch, M. (2005). Retrieval of autobiographical memory in Alzheimer's disease: Relation to volumes of medial temporal lobe and other structures. *Hippocampus, 15,* 535–550.

Gilboa, A., Winocur, G., Rosenbaum, R. S., Poreh, A., Gao, F., Black, S. E. … Moscovitch, M. (2006). Hippocampal contributions to recollection in retrograde and anterograde amnesia. *Hippocampus, 16*(11), 966–980. doi:10.1002/hipo.20226

Gilchrist, A. L., & Cowan, N. (2011). Can the focus of attention accommodate multiple, separate items? *Journal of Experimental Psychology: Learning, Memory, and Cognition, 37*(6), 1484–1502. doi:10.1037/a0024352

Gioanni, Y., & Lamarche, M. (1985). A reappraisal of rat motor cortex organization by intracortical microstimulation. *Brain Research, 344,* 49–61.

Giora, R. (1997). Understanding figurative and literal language: The graded salience hypothesis. *Cognitive Linguistics, 8*(3), 183–206.

Giora, R. (2002). Literal vs. Figurative language: Different or equal? *Journal of Pragmatics, 34,* 487–506.

Giora, R., & Fein, O. (1999). On understanding familiar and less-familiar figurative language. *Journal of Pragmatics, 31,* 1601–1618.

Giorgetta, C., Grecucci, A., Bonini, N., Coricelli, G., Demarchi, G., Braun, C., & Sanfey, A. G. (2013). Waves of regret: A meg study of emotion and decision-making. *Neuropsychologia, 51*(1), 38–51. doi:10.1016/j.neuropsychologia.2012.10.015

Giraud, A. L., & Poeppel, D. (2012). Cortical oscillations and speech processing: Emerging computational principles and operations. *Nature Neuroscience, 15*(4), 511–517. doi:10.1038/nn.3063

Gitelman, D., Nobre, A. C., Parrish, T., LaBar, K. S., Kim, Y.-H., Meyer, J. R., & Mesulam, M. M. (1999). A large-scale distributed network for covert spatial attention: Further anatomical delineation based on stringent behavioural and cognitive controls. *Brain, 122,* 1093–1106.

Glanzer, M., & Cunitz, A. R. (1966). Two storage mechanisms in free recall. *Journal of Verbal Learning and Verbal Behavior, 5,* 351–360.

Gläscher, J., Adolphs, R., Damasio, H., Bechara, A., Rudrauf, D., Calamia, M. … Tranel, D. (2012). Lesion mapping of cognitive control and value-based decision making in the prefrontal cortex. *Proceedings of the National Academy of Sciences of the United States of America, 109*(36), 14681–14686. doi:10.1073/pnas.1206608109

Glass, J. M. (2008). Fibromyalgia and cognition. *Journal of Clinical Psychiatry, 69,* 20–24.

Glover, J. A. (1989). The 'Testing' phenomenon: Not gone but nearly forgotten. *Journal of Educational Psychology, 81*(3), 392–399.

Glover, S. (2004). Separate visual representations in the planning and control of action. *Behavioral and Brain Sciences, 27,* 3–78.

Glover, S., & Dixon, P. (2004). A step and a hop on the muller-lyer: Illusion effects on lower-limb movements. *Experimental Brain Research, 154*(4), 504–512. doi:10.1007/s00221-003-1687-y

Glück, J., & Bluck, S. (2007). Looking back across the life span: A life story account of the reminiscence bump. *Memory & Cognition, 35*(8), 1928–1939.

Glucksberg, S. (2003). The psycholinguistics of metaphor. *Trends in Cognitive Sciences, 7*(2), 92–96. doi:10.1016/s1364-6613(02)00040-2

Gobet, F., & Clarkson, G. (2004). Chunks in expert memory: Evidence for the magical number four … or is it two? *Memory, 12*(6), 732–747. doi:10.1080/09658210344000530

Gobet, F., & Simon, H. A. (1998). Expert chess memory: Revisiting the chunking hypothesis. *Memory, 6*(3), 225–255. doi:10.1080/741942359

Gobet, F., & Simon, H. A. (2000). Five seconds or sixty? Presentation time in expert memory. *Cognitive Science*, *24*(2), 651–682.

Gobet, F., & Waters, A. J. (2003). The role of constraints in expert memory. *Journal of Experimental Psychology: Learning, Memory, and Cognition*, *29*(6), 1082–1094. doi:10.1037/0278-7393.29.6.1082

Goddard, E., Mannion, D. J., McDonald, J. S., Solomon, S. G., & Clifford, C. W. (2011). Color responsiveness argues against a dorsal component of human V4. *Journal of Vision*, *11*(4). doi:10.1167/11.4.3

Godden, D. R., & Baddeley, A. D. (1975). Context-dependent memory in two natural environments: On land and underwater. *British Journal of Psychology*, *66*(3), 325–331.

Godefroy, O., Azouvi, P., Robert, P., Roussel, M., LeGall, D., & Meulemans, T., & Groupe de Reflexion sur l'Evaluation des Fonctions Executives Study Group (2010). Dysexecutive syndrome: Diagnostic criteria and validation study. *Annals of Neurology*, *68*(6), 855–864. doi:10.1002/ana.22117

Goel, V. (2010). Neural basis of thinking: Laboratory problems versus real-world problems. *Wiley Interdisciplinary Review in Cognitive Science*, *1*(4), 613–621. doi:10.1002/wcs.71

Goel, V., Tierney, M., Sheesley, L., Bartolo, A., Vartanian, O., & Grafman, J. (2007). Hemispheric specialization in human prefrontal cortex for resolving certain and uncertain inferences. *Cerebral Cortex*, *17*(10), 2245–2250. doi:10.1093/cercor/bhl132

Goldberg, A. E., & Ferreira, F. (2022). Good-enough language production. *Trends in Cognitive Sciences*, *26*(4), 300–311. doi:10.1016/j.tics.2022.01.005

Goldberg, A. M., & Rapp, B. (2008). Is compound chaining the serial-order mechanism of spelling? A simple recurrent network investigation. *Cognitive Neuropsychology*, *25*(2), 218–255. doi:10.1080/02643290701862332

Goldenberg, D. L., Burckhart, C., & Croffert, L. (2004). Management of fibromyalgia syndrome. *Journal of the American Medical Association*, *292*(19), 2388–2395.

Goldman, A., & de Vignemont, F. (2009). Is social cognition embodied? *Trends in Cognitive Sciences*, *13*(4), 154–159. doi:10.1016/j.tics.2009.01.007

Goldmann, R. E., Schwartz, M. F., & Wilshire, C. E. (2001). The influence of phonological context on the sound errors of a speaker with Wernicke's aphasia. *Brain and Language*, *78*(3), 279–307. doi:10.1006/brln.2001.2468

Goldstein, D. G., & Gigerenzer, G. (2002). Models of ecological rationality: The recognition heuristic. *Psychological Review*, *109*(1), 75–90. doi:10.1037/0033-295x.109.1.75

Goldstein, R. Z., Craig, A. D., Bechara, A., Garavan, H., Childress, A. R., Paulus, M. P., & Volkow, N. D. (2009). The neurocircuitry of impaired insight in drug addiction. *Trends in Cognitive Sciences*, *13*(9), 372–380. doi:10.1016/j.tics.2009.06.004

Gollwitzer, P. M. (1999). Implementation intentions: Strong effects of simple plans. *American Psychologist*, *54*, 493–503.

Gomes, H., Duff, M., Ramos, M., Molholm, S., Foxe, J. J., & Halperin, J. (2012). Auditory selective attention and processing in children with attention-deficit/hyperactivity disorder. *Clinical Neurophysiology*, *123*(2), 293–302. doi:10.1016/j.clinph.2011.07.030

Gomez, P., Ratcliff, R., & Perea, M. (2008). The overlap model: A model of letter position coding. *Psychological Review*, *115*(3), 577–600. doi:10.1037/a0012667

Goodale, M. A., & Haffenden, A. (1998). Frames of reference for perception and action in the human visual system. *Neuroscience and Biobehavioral Reviews*, *22*(2), 161–172.

Goodale, M. A., & Milner, A. D. (1992). Separate visual pathways of perception and action. *Trends in Neurosciences*, *15*(1), 20–25.

Goodale, M. A., & Milner, A. D. (2006). One brain - two visual systems. *The Psychologist*, *19*(11), 660–663.

Goolkasian, P., & Woodberry, C. (2010). Priming effects with ambiguous figures. *Attention, Perception, & Psychophysics*, *72*(1), 168–178. doi:10.3758/APP.72.1.168

Gordon, P. (2004). Numerical cognition without words: Evidence from amazonia. *Science*, *306*, 496–499.

Gotlib, I. H., & Joormann, J. (2010). Cognition and depression: Current status and future directions. *Annual Review of Clinical Psychology*, *6*, 285–312. doi:10.1146/annurev.clinpsy.121208.131305

Gott, J. A., Liley, D. T., & Hobson, J. A. (2017). Towards a functional understanding of PGO waves. *Frontiers in Human Neuroscience*, *11*, 89. doi:10.3389/fnhum.2017.00089

Gottfredson, L. S. (1997). Why g matters: The complexity of everyday life. *Intelligence*, *24*(1), 79–132.

Gould, J. D. (1978). How experts dictate. *Journal of Experimental Psychology: Human Perception and Performance*, *4*(4), 648–661.

Goyal, M. S., Hansen, P. J., & Blakemore, C. B. (2006). Tactile perception recruits functionally related visual areas in the late-blind. *Neuroreport*, *17*(13), 1381–1384.

Grabner, R. H., Stern, E., & Neubauer, A. C. (2007). Individual differences in chess expertise: A psychometric investigation. *Acta Psychologica*, *124*(3), 398–420. doi:10.1016/j.actpsy.2006.07.008

Gracely, R. H., Geisser, M. E., Giesecke, T., Grant, M. A., Petzke, F., Williams, D. A., & Clauw, D. J. (2004). pain catastrophizing and neural responses to pain among persons with fibromyalgia. *Brain*, *127*(Pt 4), 835–843. doi:10.1093/brain/awh098

Graesser, A. C., Millis, K. K., & Zwaan, R. A. (1997). Discourse comprehension. *Annual Review of Psychology*, *48*, 163–189.

Graesser, A. C., Singer, M., & Trabasso, T. (1994). Constructing inferences during narrative text comprehension. *Psychological Review*, *101*(3), 371–395.

Graf, P. (2012). Prospective memory: Faulty brain, flaky person. *Canadian Psychology*, *53*(1), 7–13.

Grafton, S. T., Arbib, M. A., Fadiga, L., & Rizzolatti, G. (1996). Localization of grasp representations in humans by positron emission tomography. *Experimental Brain Research*, *112*, 103–111.

Graham, S. A., & Fisher, S. E. (2013). Decoding the genetics of speech and language. *Current Opinion in Neurobiology*, *23*(1), 43–51. doi:10.1016/j.conb.2012.11.006

Granzier, J. J., Brenner, E., & Smeets, J. B. (2009). Reliable identification by color under natural conditions. *Journal of Visualized*, *9*(1), 39. doi:10.1167/9.1.39

Graziano, M. S., & Kastner, S. (2011). Human consciousness and its relationship to social neuroscience: A novel hypothesis. *Cognitive Neuropsychology*, *2*(2), 98–113. doi:10.1080/17588928.2011.565121

Green, J. D., Sommervill, R. B., Nystrom, L. E., Darley, J. M., & Cohen, J. D. (2001). An fMRI investigation of emotional engagement in moral judgment. *Science*, *293*, 2105–2108.

Greenberg, D. L., & Verfaellie, M. (2010). Interdependence of episodic and semantic memory: Evidence from neuropsychology. *Journal of the International Neuropsychological Society*, *16*(5), 748–753. doi:10.1017/S1355617710000676

Greene, J. D., Morelli, S. A., Lowenberg, K., Nystrom, L. E., & Cohen, J. D. (2008). Cognitive load selectively interferes with utilitarian moral judgment. *Cognition*, *107*(3), 1144–1154. doi:10.1016/j.cognition.2007.11.004

Greene, J. D., Nystrom, L. E., Engell, A. D., Darley, J. M., & Cohen, J. D. (2004). The neural bases of cognitive conflict and control in moral judgment. *Neuron*, *44*(2), 389–400. doi:10.1016/j.neuron.2004.09.027

Greenwald, A. G. (1970). Sensory feedback mechanisms in performance control: With special reference to the ideo-motor mechanism. *Psychological Review*, *77*(2), 73–99.

Greenwald, A. G., & Banaji, M. R. (1995). Implicit social cognition: Attitudes, self-esteem, and stereotypes. *Psychological Review*, *102*(1), 4–27.

Greenwald, A. G., McGhee, D. E., & Schwartz, J. L. K. (1998). Measuring individual differences in implicit cognition: The implicit association test. *Journal of Personality and Social Psychology*, *74*(6), 1464–1480.

Grice, H. P. (1967). Logic and conversation. In P. Cole & J. L. Morgan (Eds.), *Studies in syntax* (Vol. III). New York, NY: Seminar Press.

Grice, H. P. (1975). Logic and conversation. In R. J. Stainton (Ed.), *Perspectives in the philosophy of language: A concise anthology*. Petersborough, CA: Broadview Press.

Griffiths, T. L. (2015). Manifesto for a new (Computational) cognitive revolution. *Cognition*, *135*, 21–23. doi:10.1016/j.cognition.2014.11.026

Griffiths, T. L., Chater, N., Norris, D., & Pouget, A. (2012). How the Bayesians got their beliefs (and what those beliefs actually are): Comment on Bowers and Davis (2012). *Psychological Bulletin*, *138*(3), 415–422. doi:10.1037/a0026884.

Griffiths, J. D., Marslen-Wilson, W. D., Stamatakis, E. A., & Tyler, L. K. (2013). Functional organization of the neural language system: Dorsal and ventral pathways are critical for syntax. *Cerebral Cortex*, *23*(1), 139–147. doi:10.1093/cercor/bhr386

Griffiths, T. D., & Warren, J. D. (2002). The planum temporale as a computational hub. *Trends in Neurosciences*, *25*(7), 348–353.

Grigorenko, E. L. (2009). At the height of fashion: What genetics can teach us about neurodevelopmental disabilities. *Current Opinion in Neurology*, *22*(2), 126–130. doi:10.1097/WCO.0b013e3283292414

Griskevicius, V., Shiota, M. N., & Neufeld, S. L. (2010). Influence of different positive emotions on persuasion processing: A functional evolutionary approach. *Emotion*, *10*(2), 190–206. doi:10.1037/a0018421

Grodzinsky, Y., & Friederici, A. D. (2006). Neuroimaging of syntax and syntactic processing. *Current Opinion in Neurobiology*, *16*(2), 240–246. doi:10.1016/j.conb.2006.03.007

Groen, G. J., & Parkman, J. M. (1972). A chronometric analysis of simple addition. *Psychological Review*, *79*(4), 329–343.

Grol, M. J., Majdandzic, J., Stephan, K. E., Verhagen, L., Dijkerman, H. C., Bekkering, H. … Toni, I. (2007). Parieto-frontal connectivity during visually guided grasping. *The Journal of Neuroscience*, *27*(44), 11877–11887. doi:10.1523/JNEUROSCI.3923-07.2007

Gross, J. J. (1998). The emerging field of emotion regulation: An integrative review. *Review of General Psychology*, *2*(3), 271–299.

Gross, J. J. (2013). Emotion regulation: Taking stock and moving forward. *Emotion*, *13*(3), 359–365. doi:10.1037/a0032135

Gross, J. J., & Barrett, L. F. (2011). Emotion generation and emotion regulation: One or two depends on your point of view. *Emotion Review*, *3*(1), 8–16. doi:10.1177/1754073910380974

Gross, J. J., Sheppes, G., & Urry, H. L. (2011). Cognition and emotion lecture at the 2010 SPSP emotion preconference. *Cognition & Emotion*, *25*(5), 765–781. doi:10.1080/02699931.2011.555753

Gross, J. J., & Thompson, R. A. (2007). Emotion regulation: Conceptual foundations. In J. J. Gross (Ed.), *Handbook of emotion regulation*. New York, NY: Guilford Press.

Grossenbacher, P. G., & Lovelace, C. T. (2001). Mechanisms of synesthesia: Cognitive and physiological constraints. *Trends in Cognitive Sciences*, *5*(1), 36–41.

Gruber, O., Indefrey, P., Steinmetz, H., & Kleinschmidt, A. (2001). Dissociating neural correlates of cognitive components in mental calculation. *Cerebral Cortex*, *11*, 350–359.

Guida, A., Gobet, F., & Nicolas, S. (2013). Functional cerebral reorganization: A signature of expertise? Reexamining Guida, Gobet, Tardieu, and Nicolas' (2012) two-stage framework. *Frontiers in Human Neuroscience*, *7*. doi:10.3389/fnhum.2013.00590

Guida, A., Gobet, F., Tardieu, H., & Nicolas, S. (2012). How chunks, long-term working memory and templates offer a cognitive explanation for neuroimaging data on expertise acquisition: A two-stage framework. *Brain and Cognition, 79*(3), 221–244. doi:10.1016/j.bandc.2012.01.010

Guldin, W. O., & Grüsser, O.-J. (1998). Is there a vestibular cortex? *Trends in Neurosciences, 21*, 254–259.

Gumer, E., & Levine, M. (1971). The missing dimension in concept learning: Dimensionality or local consistency. *Journal of Experimental Psychology, 90*(1), 39–44.

Günther, H., Gfroerer, S., & Weiss, L. (1984). Inflection, frequency, and the word superiority effect. *Psychological Research, 46*, 261–281.

Gutschalk, A., Micheyl, C., Melcher, J. R., Rupp, A., Scherg, M., & Oxenham, A. J. (2005). Neuromagnetic correlates of streaming in human auditory cortex. *The Journal of Neuroscience, 25*(22), 5382–5388. doi:10.1523/jneurosci.0347-05.2005

Guttman, S. E., Gilroy, L. A., & Blake, R. (2007). Spatial grouping in human vision: Temporal structure trumps temporal synchrony. *Vision Research, 47*(2), 219–230. doi:10.1016/j.visres.2006.09.012

Gyurak, A., Gross, J. J., & Etkin, A. (2011). Explicit and implicit emotion regulation: A dual-process framework. *Cognition & Emotion, 25*(3), 400–412. doi:10.1080/02699931.2010.544160

Hackett, T. A., & Kaas, J. H. (2004). Auditory cortex in primates: Functional subdivisions and processing streams. In *Cognitive neurosciences III* (3rd ed., pp. 215–232). https://psycnet.apa.org/record/2005-01373-019

Hagbarth, K.-E., & Kerr, D. I. B. (1954). Central influences on spinal afferent conduction. *Journal of Neurophysiology, 17*, 295–307.

Haggard, P. (2008). Human volition: Towards a neuroscience of will. *Nature Reviews Neuroscience, 9*(12), 934–946. doi:10.1038/nrn2497

Hagoort, P., Hald, L., Bastiaansen, M., & Petersson, K. M. (2004). Integration of word meaning and world knowledge in language comprehension. *Science, 304*(5669), 438–441.

Hahn, S., Andersen, J. A., & Saidpour, A. (2003). Static scene analysis for the perception of heading. *Psychological Science, 14*(6), 543–548.

Hahn, U., & Oaksford, M. (2007). The rationality of informal argumentation: A Bayesian approach to reasoning fallacies. *Psychological Review, 114*(3), 704–732. doi:10.1037/0033-295X.114.3.704

Haidt, J., Rozin, P., McCauley, C., & Imada, S. (1997). Body, psyche, and culture: The relationship between disgust and morality. *Psychology and Developing Societies, 9*(1), 107–131.

Haldane, A. G. (2012). *The Dog and the Frisbee.* Paper presented at the Proceedings of The Economic Policy Symposium, Jackson Hole, WY.

Hall, G. S. (1897). The psychology of tickling, laughing, and the comic. *The American Journal of Psychology, 9*(1), 1–41.

Halligan, P. W., Marshall, J. C., Wade, D. T., Davey, J., & Morrison, D. (1993). Thumb in cheek? Sensory reorganization and perceptual plasticity after limb amputation. *Neuroreport, 4*, 233–236.

Hallion, L. S., & Ruscio, A. M. (2011). A meta-analysis of the effect of cognitive bias modification on anxiety and depression. *Psychol Bull, 137*(6), 940–958. doi:10.1037/a0024355

Hameroff, S. R. (1998). 'Funda-Mentality': Is the conscious mind subtly linked to a basic level of the universe? *Trends in Cognitive Sciences, 2*(4), 119–124.

Han, Z., & Bi, Y. (2009). Reading Comprehension without phonological mediation: Further evidence from a Chinese aphasic individual. *Science in China Series C Life Sciences, 52*(5), 492–499. doi:10.1007/s11427-009-0048-x

Hanley, J. R., & McDonnell, V. (1997). Are Reading and spelling phonologically mediated? Evidence from a patient with a speech production impairment. *Cognitive Neuropsychology, 14*(1), 3–33.

Hannula, D. E., & Greene, A. J. (2012). The hippocampus reevaluated in unconscious learning and memory: At a tipping point? *Frontiers in Human Neuroscience, 6*, 80. doi:10.3389/fnhum.2012.00080

Hannula, D. E., Tranel, D., & Cohen, N. J. (2006). The long and the short of it: Relational memory impairments in amnesia, even at short lags. *The Journal of Neuroscience, 26*(32), 8352–8359. doi:10.1523/JNEUROSCI.5222-05.2006

Hansen, T., Olkkonen, M., Walter, S., & Gegenfurtner, K. R. (2006). Memory modulates color appearance. *Nature Neuroscience, 9*(11), 1367–1368. doi:10.1038/nn1794

Harand, C., Bertran, F., La Joie, R., Landeau, B., Mezenge, F., Desgranges, B. … Rauchs, G. (2012). The hippocampus remains activated over the long term for the retrieval of truly episodic memories. *PLoS One, 7*(8), e43495. doi:10.1371/journal.pone.0043495

Harbart, J. F. (1825). *Psychologie als wissenschaft neu gegründet auf erfahrung, metaphysik und mathematik. Zweiter, analytischer teil.* Königsberg, Germany: Unzer.

Hardin, G. (1968). The tragedy of the commons. *Science, 162*(3859), 1243–1248.

Hardt, O., Einarsson, E. O., & Nader, K. (2010). A bridge over troubled water: Reconsolidation as a link between cognitive and neuroscientific memory research traditions. *Annual Review of Psychology, 61*, 141–167. doi:10.1146/annurev.psych.093008.100455

Hardt, O., Nader, K., & Nadel, L. (2013). Decay happens: The role of active forgetting in memory. *Trends in Cognitive Sciences, 17*(3), 111–120. doi:10.1016/j.tics.2013.01.001

Hari, R., Aittoniemi, K., Jävinen, M.-L., Katila, T., & Varpula, T. (1980). Auditory evoked transient and sustained magnetic fields of the human brain. *Experimental Brain Research, 40*, 237–240.

Harley, T. A. (2014). *The psychology of language.* Howe: Psychology Press.

Harley, T. A., & Bown, H. E. (1998). What causes a top-of-the-Tongue state? Evidence for lexical neighbourhood effects in speech production. *British Journal of Psychology, 89,* 151–174.

Harm, M. W., & Seidenberg, M. S. (2004). Computing the meanings of words in reading: Cooperative division of labor between visual and phonological processes. *Psychological Review, 111*(3), 662–720. doi:10.1037/0033-295X.111.3.662

Harmon-Jones, E., Gable, P. A., & Price, T. F. (2011). Toward an understanding of the influence of affective States on attentional tuning: Comment on Friedman and Förster (2010). *Psychological Bulletin, 137*(3), 508–512.

Haroush, K., & Williams, Z. M. (2015). Neuronal prediction of opponent's behavior during cooperative social interchange in primates. *Cell, 160*(6), 1233–1245. doi:10.1016/j.cell.2015.01.045

Harrington, D. L., Haaland, K. Y., Yeo, R. A., & Marder, E. (1990). Procedural memory in Parkinson's disease: Impaired motor but not visuoperceptual learning. *Journal of Clinical and Experimental Neuropsycholog, 12*(2), 323–339. doi:10.1080/01688639008400978

Harris, A. J. L., Hsu, A. S., & Madsen, J. K. (2012). Because Hitler did it! Quantitative tests of Bayesian argumentation using ad hominem. *Thinking & Reasoning, 18*(3), 311–343. doi:10.1080/13546783.2012.670753

Harris, C. M., & Wolpert, D. M. (1998). Signal-dependent noise determines motor planning. *Nature, 394,* 780–784.

Harris, C. R. (1999). The mystery of ticklish laughter. *American Scientist, 87*(4), 344–351.

Harris, C. R., & Christenfeld, N. (1997). Humour, tickle, and the Darwin-hecker hypothesis. *Cognition & Emotion, 11*(1), 103–110. doi:10.1080/026999397380050

Harris, C. R., Coburn, N., Rohrer, D., & Pashler, H. (2013). Two failures to replicate high-performance-goal priming effects. *PLoS One, 8*(8). doi:10.1371/journal.pone.0072467

Harrison, S. A., & Tong, F. (2009). Decoding reveals the contents of visual working memory in early visual areas. *Nature, 458*(7238), 632–635. doi:10.1038/nature07832

Hart, W., Albarracin, D., Eagly, A. H., Brechan, I., Lindberg, M. J., & Merrill, L. (2009). Feeling validated versus being correct: A meta-analysis of selective exposure to information. *Psychological Bulletin, 135*(4), 555–588. doi:10.1037/a0015701

Harter, M. R., Miller, S. L., Price, N. J., LaLonde, M. E., & Keyes, A. L. (1989). Neural processes involved in directing attention. *Journal of Cognitive Neuroscience, 1*(3), 223–237.

Hartley, J., Sotto, E., & Pennebaker, J. (2003). Speaking versus typing: A case-study of the effects of using voice-recognition software on academic correspondence. *British Journal of Educational Technology, 34*(1), 5–16.

Hartstra, E., Kühn, S., Verguts, T., & Brass, M. (2011). The implementation of verbal instructions: An fMRI study. *Human Brain Mapping, 32*(11), 1811–1824.

Hartsuiker, R. J. (2015). Why it is pointless to ask under which specific circumstances the bilingual advantage occurs. *Cortex, 73,* 336–337. doi:10.1016/j.cortex.2015.07.018

Hartsuiker, R. J., Corley, M., & Martensen, H. (2005). The lexical bias effect is modulated by context, but the standard monitoring account doesn't fly: Related reply to Baars et al. (1975). *Journal of Memory and Language, 52*(1), 58–70. doi:10.1016/j.jml.2004.07.006

Hassabis, D., Kumaran, D., Vann, S. D., & Maguire, E. A. (2007). Patients with hippocampal amnesia cannot imagine new experiences. *Proceedings of the National Academy of Sciences of the United States of America, 104*(5), 1726–1731. doi:10.1073/pnas.0610561104

Hassin, R. R. (2013). Yes it can: On the functional abilities of the human unconscious. *Perspectives on Psychological Science, 8*(2), 195–207. doi:10.1177/1745691612460684

Haubrich, J., Bernabo, M., Baker, A. G., & Nader, K. (2020). Impairments to consolidation, reconsolidation, and long-term memory maintenance lead to memory erasure. *Annual Review of Neuroscience, 43,* 297–314. doi:10.1146/annurev-neuro-091319-024636

Haueisen, J., & Knösche, T. R. (2001). Involuntary motor activity in pianists evoked by music perception. *Journal of Cognitive Neuroscience, 13,* 786–792.

Hauk, O., Johnsrude, I., & Pulvermüller, F. (2004). Somatotopic representation of action words in human motor and premotor cortex. *Neuron, 41,* 301–307.

Hawkins, R. X. D., Goodman, N. D., & Goldstone, R. L. (2019). The emergence of social norms and conventions. *Trends in Cognitive Sciences, 23*(2), 158–169. doi:10.1016/j.tics.2018.11.003

Haxby, J. V., Hoffman, E. A., & Gobbini, M. I. (2000). The distributed human neural system for face perception. *Trends in Cognitive Sciences, 4*(6), 223–233.

Hayes, J. R. (2012). Modeling and remodeling writing. *Written Communication, 29*(3), 369–388. doi:10.1177/0741088312451260

Hayes, J. R., & Bajzek, D. (2008). Understanding and reducing the knowledge effect: Implications for writers. *Written Communication, 25*(1), 104–118.

Hayes, J. R., & Chenoweth, N. A. (2006). Is working memory involved in the transcribing and editing of texts? *Written Communication, 23*(2), 135–149. doi:10.1177/0741088306286283

Hayes, J. R., & Flower, L. S. (1986). Writing research and the writer. *American Psychologist, 41*(10), 1106–1113.

Hayes, S. M., Fortier, C. B., Levine, A., Milberg, W. P., & McGlinchey, R. (2012). Implicit memory in Korsakoff's syndrome: A review of procedural learning and priming studies. *Neuropsychology Review, 22*(2), 132–153. doi:10.1007/s11065-012-9204-3

Hayhhoe, M. M., Shrivastava, A., Mruczek, R., & Pelz, J. B. (2003). Visual memory and motor planning in a natural task. *Journal of Vision, 3,* 49–63.

References

Hayward, W. G. (2012). Whatever happened to object-centered representations? *Perception, 41*(9), 1153–1162. doi:10.1068/p7338

Hebb, D. E. (1949). *The organization of behavior*. New York, NY: Wiley.

Hedden, T., & Gabrieli, J. D. E. (2010). Shared and selective neural correlates of inhibition, facilitation, and shifting processes during executive control. *Neuroimage, 51*(1), 421–431. doi:10.1016/j.neuroimage.2010.01.089

Hegarty, M., Shah, P., & Miyake, A. (2000). Constraints on using the dual-task methodology to specify the degree of Central executive involvement in cognitive tasks. *Memory & Cognition, 2000*(28), 3.

Hegdé, J. (2008). Time course of visual perception: Coarse-to-fine processing and beyond. *Progress in Neurobiology, 84*(4), 405–439. doi:10.1016/j.pneurobio.2007.09.001

Heider, F., & Simmel, M. (1944). An experimental study of apparent bahavior. *The American Journal of Psychology, 57*(2), 243–259.

Heimer, L., & Van Hoesen, G. W. (2006). The limbic lobe and its output channels: Implications for emotional functions and adaptive behavior. *Neuroscience and Biobehavioral Reviews, 30*(2), 126–147. doi:10.1016/j.neubiorev.2005.06.006

Heindel, W. C., Butters, N., & Salmon, D. P. (1988). Impaired learning of a motor skill in patients with Huntington's disease. *Behavioral Neuroscience, 102*(1), 141–147.

Heinrichs, M., Baumgartner, T., Kirschbaum, C., & Ehlert, U. (2003). Social support and oxytocin interact to suppress cortisol and subjective responses to psychosocial stress. *Biological Psychiatry, 54*(12), 1389–1398. doi:10.1016/s0006-3223(03)00465-7

Held, R. T., Cooper, E. A., & Banks, M. S. (2012). Blur and disparity are complementary cues to depth. *Current Biology, 22*(5), 426–431. doi:10.1016/j.cub.2012.01.033

Helmholtz, H. (1858). Über integrale der hydrodynamischen gleihungen, welche den wirbelbewegungen entsprechen. *Journal Für Die Reine Und Angewandte Mathmatik Crelles Journal, 55*, 25–55.

Helmholtz, H. (1860). *Handbucht der physiologischen optik*. Leipzig: Leopold Voss.

Helmholtz, H. (1862). *Die Lehre Von Den Tonempfindungen Als Physiologische Grundlage Für Die Theorie Der Musik*. Braunsweig: Friedr. Vieweg & Sohn.

Henik, A., Rafal, R., & Rhodes, D. (1994). Endogenously generated and visually guided saccades after lesions of the human frontal eye fields. *Journal of Cognitive Neuroscience, 6*(4), 400–411.

Henke, K. (2010). A model for memory systems based on processing modes rather than consciousness. *Nature Reviews Neuroscience, 11*, 523–531.

Henke, K., Mondadori, C. R. A., Treyer, V., Nitsch, R. M., Buck, A., & Hock, C. (2003). Nonconscious formation and reactivation of semantic associations by way of the medial temporal lobe. *Neuropsychologia, 41*(8), 863–876. doi:10.1016/s0028-3932(03)00035-6

Henriques, D. Y., Klier, E. M., Smith, M. A., Lowy, D., & Crawford, J. D. (1998). Gaze-centered remapping of remembered visual space in an open-loop pointing task. *The Journal of Neuroscience, 18*(4), 1583–1594.

Henriques, D. Y., Medendorp, W. P., Gielen, C. C., & Crawford, J. D. (2003). Geometric computations underlying eye-hand coordination: Orientations of the two eyes and the head. *Experimental Brain Research, 152*(1), 70–78. doi:10.1007/s00221-003-1523-4

Henschel, A., Hortensius, R., & Cross, E. S. (2020). Social cognition in the age of human-robot interaction. *Trends in Neurosciences, 43*(6), 373–384. doi:10.1016/j.tins.2020.03.013

Herculano-Houzel, S. (2009). The human brain in numbers: A linearly scaled-up primate brain. *Frontiers in Human Neuroscience, 3*, 31. doi:10.3389/neuro.09.031.2009

Hering, E. (1878). *Zur Lehre Von Lichtsinne*. Wien: Carl Gerold's Sohn.

Hertwig, R., Pachur, T., & Kurzenhauser, S. (2005). Judgments of risk frequencies: Tests of possible cognitive mechanisms. *Journal of Experimental Psychology: Learning, Memory, and Cognition, 31*(4), 621–642. doi:10.1037/0278-7393.31.4.621

Heslenfeld, D. J., Kenemans, J. L., Kok, A., & Molenaar, P. C. M. (1997). Feature processing and attention in the human visual system: An overview. *Biological Psychology, 45*, 183–215.

Hesselmann, G., Flandin, G., & Dehaene, S. (2011). Probing the cortical network underlying the psychological refractory period: A combined EEG-fMRI study. *Neuroimage, 56*(3), 1608–1621. doi:10.1016/j.neuroimage.2011.03.017

Hesslow, G. (2002). Conscious thought as simulation of behaviour and perception. *Trends in Cognitive Sciences, 6*(6), 242–247.

Heyes, C. M., & Frith, C. D. (2014). The cultural evolution of mind Reading. *Science, 344*(6190), 1243091. doi:10.1126/science.1243091

Heywood, C. A., & Kentridge, R. W. (2000). Affective blindsight? *Trends in Cognitive Sciences, 4*(4), 125–126.

Hickey, C., Chelazzi, L., & Theeuwes, J. (2010a). Reward changes salience in human vision via the anterior cingulate. *The Journal of Neuroscience, 30*(33), 11096–11103. doi:10.1523/JNEUROSCI.1026-10.2010

Hickey, C., Chelazzi, L., & Theeuwes, J. (2010b). Reward guides vision when it's your thing: Trait reward-seeking in reward-mediated visual priming. *PLoS One, 5*(11), e14087. doi:10.1371/journal.pone.0014087

Hickey, C., Chelazzi, L., & Theeuwes, J. (2011). Reward has a residual impact on target selection in visual search, but not on the suppression of distractors. *Visual Cognition, 19*(1), 117–128. doi:10.1080/13506285.2010.503946

Hickok, G. (2009). Eight problems for the mirror neuron theory of action understanding in monkeys and humans. *Journal of Cognitive Neuroscience, 21*(7), 1229–1243.

Hickok, G. (2012). The cortical organization of speech processing: Feedback control and predictive coding the context of a dual-stream model. *Journal of Communication Disorders, 45*(6), 393–402. doi:10.1016/j.jcomdis.2012.06.004

Hickok, G., Bellugi, U., & Klima, E. S. (1996). The neurobiology of sign language and its implications for the neural basis of language. *Nature, 381*, 699–702.

Hill, R. L., & Murray, W. S. (2000). Commas and spaces: Effects of punctuation on eye movements and sentence parsing. In A. Kennedy, R. Radach, D. Heller, & J. Pynte (Eds.), *Reading as a perceptual process* (pp. 565–589). Amsterdam: Elsevier Science Ltd.

Hillier, S., Immink, M., & Thewlis, D. (2015). Assessing proprioception: A systematic review of possibilities. *Neurorehabilitation and Neural Repair, 29*(10), 933–949. doi:10.1177/1545968315573055

Hills, P. J., Werno, M. A., & Lewis, M. B. (2011). Sad people are more accurate at face recognition than happy people. *Consciousness and Cognition, 20*(4), 1502–1517. doi:10.1016/j.concog.2011.07.002

Hillyard, S. A., & Anllo-Vento, L. (1998). Event-related brain potentials in the study of visual selective attention. *Proceedings of the National Academy of Sciences of the United States of America, 95*(3), 781–787.

Hillyard, S. A., & Galambos, R. (1967). Effects of stimulus and response contingencies on a surface negative slow potential shift in man. *Electroencephalography and Clinical Neurophysiology, 22*(4), 297–304.

Hillyard, S. A., Hink, R. F., Schwent, V. L., & Picton, T. W. (1973). Electrical signs of selective attention in the human brain. *Science, 182*(4108), 177–180.

Hillyard, S. A., Vogel, E. K., & Luck, S. J. (1998). Sensory gain control (amplification) as a mechanism of selective attention: Electrophysiological and neuroimaging evidence. *Philosophical Transactions of the Royal Society B: Biological Sciences, 353*(1373), 1257–1270.

Hirsch, C. R., Clark, D. M., & Matthews, A. (2006). Imagery and interpretations in social phobia: Support for the combined cognitive biases hypothesis. *Behavior Therapy, 37*, 223–236.

Hirsch, C. R., & Mathews, A. (2012). A cognitive model of pathological worry. *Behaviour Research and Therapy, 50*(10), 636–646. doi:10.1016/j.brat.2012.06.007

Hitch, G. J. (1978). The role of short-term working memory in mental arithmetic. *Cognitive Psychology, 10*, 302–323.

Hobson, J. A., & Friston, K. J. (2012). Waking and dreaming consciousness: Neurobiological and functional considerations. *Progress in Neurobiology, 98*(1), 82–98. doi:10.1016/j.pneurobio.2012.05.003

Hobson, J. A., & Friston, K. J. (2014). Consciousness, dreams, and interference. *Journal of Consciousness Studies, 21*(1–2), 6–32.

Hodapp, A., & Rabovsky, M. (2021). The N400 ERP component reflects an error-based implicit learning signal during language comprehension. *European Journal of Neuroscience, 54*(9), 7125–7140. doi:10.1111/ejn.15462

Hoffrage, U., Krauss, S., Martignon, L., & Gigerenzer, G. (2015). Natural frequencies improve Bayesian reasoning in simple and complex inference tasks. *Frontiers in Psychology, 6*, 1473. doi:10.3389/fpsyg.2015.01473

Hohwy, J. (2007). Functional integration and the mind. *Synthese, 159*(3), 315–328. doi:10.1007/s11229-007-9240-3

Holland, A. C., & Kensinger, E. A. (2010). Emotion and autobiographical memory. *Physics of Life Reviews, 7*(1), 88–131. doi:10.1016/j.plrev.2010.01.006

Holle, H., Banissy, M. J., & Ward, J. (2013). Functional and structural brain differences associated with mirror-touch synaesthesia. *Neuroimage, 83*, 1041–1050. doi:10.1016/j.neuroimage.2013.07.073

Hollingworth, A., & Henderson, J. M. (2002). Accurate visual memory for previously attended objects in natural scenes. *Journal of Experimental Psychology: Human Perception and Performance, 28*(1), 113–136. doi:10.1037//0096-1523.28.1.113

Holmes, V. M. (1988). Hesitations and sentence planning. *Language and Cognitive Processes, 3*(4), 323–361. doi:10.1080/01690968808402093

Holmes, V. M., & Carruthers, J. (1998). The relation between reading and spelling in skilled adult readers. *Journal of Memory and Language, 39*, 264–289.

Holroyd, C. B., & Coles, M. G. H. (2002). The neural basis of human error processing: Reinforcement learning, dopamine, and the error-related negativity. *Psychological Review, 109*(4), 679–709. doi:10.1037/0033-295X.109.4.679

Holroyd, C. B., & Yeung, N. (2012). Motivation of extended behaviors by anterior cingulate cortex. *Trends in Cognitive Sciences, 16*(2), 122–128. doi:10.1016/j.tics.2011.12.008

Holtgraves, T. (1998). Interpreting indirect replies. *Cognitive Psychology, 37*, 1–27.

Hommel, B. (2000). The prepared reflex: Automaticity and control in stimulus-response translation. In S. Monsell & J. Driver (Eds.), *Control of cognitive processes: Attention and performance Xviii*. Cambridge, MA: MIT Press.

Hommel, B. (2009). Action control according to TEC (theory of event coding). *Psychological Research Psychologische Forschung, 73*(4), 512–526. doi:10.1007/s00426-009-0234-2

Hommel, B., Müsseler, J., Aschersleben, G., & Prinz, W. (2002). Codes and their vicissitudes. *Behavioral and Brain Sciences, 24*(05), 910–926. doi:10.1017/s0140525x01520105

Horga, G., Schatz, K. C., Abi-Dargham, A., & Peterson, B. S. (2014). Deficits in predictive coding underlie hallucinations in schizophrenia. *The Journal of Neuroscience, 34*(24), 8072–8082. doi:10.1523/JNEUROSCI.0200-14.2014

Horton, W. S., & Keysar, B. (1996). When do speakers take into account common ground? *Cognition, 59*, 91–117.

Horvath, J. (2015). Action-related auditory ERP attenuation: Paradigms and hypotheses. *Brain Research, 1626*, 54–65. doi:10.1016/j.brainres.2015.03.038

References

Hosking, S. G., & Crassini, B. (2010). The effects of familiar size and object trajectories on time-to-contact judgements. *Experimental Brain Research, 203*(3), 541–552. doi:10.1007/s00221-010-2258-7

Houtkamp, R., & Roelfsema, P. R. (2009). Matching of visual input to only one item at any one time. *Psychological Research, 73*(3), 317–326. doi:10.1007/s00426-008-0157-3

Houtsma, A. J. M., & Goldstein, J. L. (1971). The central origin of the pitch of complex tones: Evidence from musical interval recognition. *The Journal of The Acoustical Society of America, 51*(2), 520–529.

Howard, R. W. (2009). Individual differences in expertise development over decades in a complex intellectual domain. *Memory & Cognition, 37*(2), 194–209. doi:10.3758/MC.37.2.194

Howard, D., & Orchard-lisle, V. (2007). On the origin of semantic errors in naming: Evidence from the case of a global aphasic. *Cognitive Neuropsychology, 1*(2), 163–190. doi:10.1080/02643298408252021

Howe, M. L., & Courage, M. L. (1997). The emergence and early development of autobiographical memory. *Psychological Review, 104*(3), 499–523.

Hu, Y., & Goodale, M. A. (2000). Grasping after a delay shifts size-scaling from absolute to relative metrics. *Journal of Cognitive Neuroscience, 12*(5), 856–868.

Hubel, D. H., & Wiesel, T. N. (1962). Receptive fields, binocular interaction and functional architecture in the cat's visual cortex. *Journal of Physiology, 160*, 106–154.

Hubel, D. H., & Wiesel, T. N. (1979). Brain mechanisms of vision. *Scientific American, 249*, 150–162.

Hukin, R. W., & Darwin, C. J. (1995). Comparison of the effect of onset asynchrony on auditory grouping in pitch matching and vowel identification. *Perception & Psychophysics, 57*(2), 191–196.

Hull, C. L. (1931). Goal attraction and directing ideas conceived as habit phenomena. *Psychological Review, 38*, 487–506.

Hull, C. L. (1943). *Principles of behavior: An introduction to behavior theory.* New York, NY: Appleton-Century-Crofts, Inc.

Hullfish, J., Sedley, W., & Vanneste, S. (2019). Prediction and perception: Insights for (and from) tinnitus. *Neuroscience and Biobehavioral Reviews, 102*, 1–12. doi:10.1016/j.neubiorev.2019.04.008

Hume, D. (1739). *A treatise of human nature.* Oxford: Clarendon Press.

Humphrey, N. (2002). *The mind made flesh: Frontiers of psychology and evolution.* Oxford: Oxford University Press.

Humphries, C., Love, T., Swinney, D., & Hickok, G. (2005). Response of anterior temporal cortex to syntactic and prosodic manipulations during sentence processing. *Human Brain Mapping, 26*(2), 128–138. doi:10.1002/hbm.20148

Hunt, T. (2011). Kicking the psychophysical laws into gear. *Journal of Consciousness Studies, 18*(11–12), 96–134.

Hunt, A. R., & Cavanagh, P. (2011). Remapped visual masking. *Journal of Vision, 11*(1), 13. doi:10.1167/11.1.13

Hunter, J. P., Katz, J., & Davis, K. D. (2003). The effect of tactile and visual sensory inputs on phantom limb awareness. *Brain, 126*(3), 579–589. doi:10.1093/brain/awg054

Huron, D. (2001). A derivation of the rules of voice-leading from perceptual principles. *Music Perception: An Interdisciplinary Journal, 19*(1), 1–64.

Hurvich, L. M., & Jameson, D. (1957). An opponent-process theory of color vision. *Psychological Review, 64*(6), 384–404.

Huse, E., Preissl, H., Larbig, W., & Birbaumer, N. (2001). Phantom limb pain. *The Lancet, 358*(9286), 1015. doi:10.1016/s0140-6736(01)06144-x

Hutchison, W. D., Davis, K. D., Lozano, A. M., Tasker, R. R., & Dostrovsky, J. O. (1999). Pain-related neurons in the human cingulate cortex. *Nature Neuroscience, 2*(5), 403–405.

Hyde, K. L., & Peretz, I. (2004). Brains that are out of tune but in time. *Psychological Science, 15*(5), 356–360.

Iacoboni, M. (1999). Cortical mechanisms of human imitation. *Science, 286*(5449), 2526–2528. doi:10.1126/science.286.5449.2526

Iggo, A., & Andres, K. H. (1982). Morphology of cutaneous receptors. *Annual Review of Neuroscience, 5*, 1–31.

Indefrey, P. (2011). The spatial and temporal signatures of word production components: A critical update. *Frontiers in Psychology, 2*, 255. doi:10.3389/fpsyg.2011.00255

Indovina, I., Maffei, V., Bosco, G., Zago, M., Macaluso, E., & Lacquaniti, F. (2005). Representation of visual gravitational motion in the human vestibular cortex. *Science, 308*(5720), 416–419.

Ingvar, D. H., & Philipson, L. (1977). Distribution of cerebral blood flow in the dominant hemisphere during motor ideation and motor performance. *Annals of Neurology, 2*(3), 230–237.

Inzlicht, M., Bartholow, B. D., & Hirsh, J. B. (2015). Emotional foundations of cognitive control. *Trends in Cognitive Sciences, 19*(3), 126–132. doi:10.1016/j.tics.2015.01.004

Iriki, A., Tanaka, M., & Iwamura, Y. (1996). Coding of modified body schema during tool use by macaque postcentral neurones. *Neuroreport, 7*, 2325–2330.

Ishida, H., Suzuki, K., & Grandi, L. C. (2015). Predictive coding accounts of shared representations in parieto-insular networks. *Neuropsychologia, 70*, 442–454. doi:10.1016/j.neuropsychologia.2014.10.020

Ison, M. J., & Quiroga, R. Q. (2008). Selectivity and invariance for visual object perception. *Frontiers in Bioscience, 13*, 4880–4903.

Ittelson, W. H. (1951). Size as a cue to distance: Static localization. *The American Journal of Psychology, 61*(1), 54–67.

Itti, L., & Koch, C. (2001). Computational modelling of visual attention. *Nature Reviews Neuroscience, 2*, 194–203.

Izard, C. E. (2007). Basic emotions, natural kinds, emotion schemas, and a new paradigm. *Perspectives on Psychological Science*, 2(3), 260–280.

Jack, F., & Hayne, H. (2010). Childhood amnesia: Empirical evidence for a two-stage phenomenon. *Memory*, 18(8), 831–844. doi:10.1080/09658211.2010.510476

Jack, F., MacDonald, S., Rees, E., & Hayne, H. (2009). Maternal reminiscing during early childhood predicts the age of adolescents' earliest memories. *Child Development*, 80(2), 496–505.

Jackson, G. M., Jackson, S. R., Harrison, J., Henderson, L., & Kennard, C. (1995). Serial reaction time learning and Parkinson's disease: Evidence for a procedural learning deficit. *Neuropsychologia*, 33(5), 577–593.

Jackson, P. L., Lafleur, M. F., Malouin, F., Richards, C., & Doyon, J. (2001). Potential role of mental practice using motor imagery in neurologic rehabilitation. *Archives of Physical and Medical Rehabilitation*, 82(8), 1133–1141. doi:10.1053/apmr.2001.24286

Jackson, S. R., Newport, R., Husain, M., Fowlie, J. E., O'Donoghue, M., & Bajaj, N. (2009). There may be more to reaching than meets the eye: Re-thinking optic ataxia. *Neuropsychologia*, 47(6), 1397–1408. doi:10.1016/j.neuropsychologia.2009.01.035

Jacob, P., & Jeannerod, M. (2005). The motor theory of social cognition: A critique. *Trends in Cognitive Sciences*, 9(1), 21–25. doi:10.1016/j.tics.2004.11.003

Jacoby, L. L. (1991). A process dissociation framework: Separating automatic from intentional uses of memory. *Journal of Memory and Language*, 30, 513–541.

Jacoby, L. L., Debner, J. A., & Hay, J. F. (2001). Proactive interference, accessibility bias, and process dissociation: Valid subjective reports of memory. *Journal of Experimental Psychology: Learning, Memory, and Cognition*, 27(3), 686–700.

Jacquemot, C., Dupoux, E., & Bachoud-Levi, A. C. (2007). Breaking the mirror: Asymmetrical disconnection between the phonological input and output codes. *Cognitive Neuropsychology*, 24(1), 3–22. doi:10.1080/02643290600683342

James, W. (1884). What is an emotion? *Mind*, 9, 188–205.

James, W. (1890). *Principles of psychology*. New York, NY: Holt.

Janelle, C. M., Singer, R. N., & Williams, A. M. (1999). External distraction and attentional narrowing: Visual search evidence. *Journal of Sport & Exercise Psychology*, 21, 70–91.

Jansma, J. M., Ramsey, N. F., Slagter, H. A., & Kahn, R. S. (2001). Functional anatomical correlates of controlled and automatic processing. *Journal of Cognitive Neuroscience*, 13(6), 730–743.

Janssen, C. P., & Brumby, D. P. (2010). Strategic adaptation to performance objectives in a dual-task setting. *Cognitive Science*, 34(8), 1548–1560. doi:10.1111/j.1551-6709.2010.01124.x

Janssen, T. W. P., Heslenfeld, D. J., van Mourik, R., Geladé, K., Maras, A., & Oosterlaan, J. (2018). Alterations in the ventral attention network during the stop-signal task in children with ADHD: An event-related potential source imaging study. *Journal of Attention Disorders*, 22(7), 639–650.

Jeannerod, M. (1994). The representing brain: Neural correlates of motor intention and imagery. *Behavioral and Brain Sciences*, 17, 187–245.

Jeannerod, M. (1995). Mental imagery in the motor context. *Neuropsychologia*, 33(11), 1419–1432.

Jeannerod, M. (2001). Neural simulation of action: A unifying mechanism for motor cognition. *Neuroimage*, 14(1 Pt 2), S103–S109. doi:10.1006/nimg.2001.0832

Jeannerod, M., & Frak, V. (1999). Mental imaging of motor activity in humans. *Current Opinion in Neurobiology*, 9, 735–739.

Jefferies, E., Sage, K., & Ralph Lambon, M. A. (2007). Do deep dyslexia, dysphasia and dysgraphia share a common phonological impairment? *Neuropsychologia*, 45(7), 1553–1570. doi:10.1016/j.neuropsychologia.2006.12.002

Jeneson, A., Mauldin, K. N., Hopkins, R. O., & Squire, L. R. (2011). The role of the hippocampus in retaining relational information across short delays: The importance of memory load. *Learning & Memory*, 18(5), 301–305. doi:10.1101/lm.2010711

Jenkins, R., & Burton, A. M. (2011). Stable face representations. *Philosophical Transactions of the Royal Society B: Biological Sciences*, 366(1571), 1671–1683. doi:10.1098/rstb.2010.0379

Jenkins, R., White, D., Van Montfort, X., & Burton, M. A. (2011). Variability in photos of the same face. *Cognition*, 121(3), 313–323. doi:10.1016/j.cognition.2011.08.001

Jensen, G. B., & Pakkenberg, B. (1993). Do alcoholics drink their neurons away? *The Lancet*, 342, 1201–1204.

Jensen, M. S., Yao, R., Street, W. N., & Simons, D. J. (2011). Change blindness and inattentional blindness. *Wiley Interdisciplinary Reviews: Cognitive Science*, 2(5), 529–546. doi:10.1002/wcs.130

Jersild, A. T. (1927). Mental set and shift. *Archives of Psychology*, 14(89), 81.

Jestreboff, P. J. (1990). Phantom auditory perception (Tinnitus): Mechanisms of generation and perception. *Neuroscience Research*, 8, 221–254.

Jevons, W. S. (1871). The power of numerical discrimination. *Nature*, 3, 281–282.

Ji, R. R., Kohno, T., Moore, K. A., & Woolf, C. J. (2003). Central Sensitization and LTP: Do pain and memory share similar mechanisms? *Trends in Neurosciences*, 26(12), 696–705. doi:10.1016/j.tins.2003.09.017

Jiang, Y., Costello, P., Fang, F., Huang, M., & He, S. (2006). A gender- and sexual orientation-dependent spatial attentional effect of invisible images. *Proceedings of the National Academy of Sciences of the United States of America*, 103(45), 17048–17052. doi:10.1073/pnas.0605678103

Jimenez, L., Mendez, A., Pasquali, A., Abrahamse, E., & Verwey, W. (2011). Chunking by colors: Assessing

References

discrete learning in a continuous serial reaction-time task. *Acta Psychologica, 137*(3), 318–329. doi:10.1016/j.actpsy.2011.03.013

Johansen, J. P., Tarpley, J. W., LeDoux, J. E., & Blair, H. T. (2010). Neural substrates for expectation-modulated fear learning in the amygdala and periaqueductal gray. *Nature Neuroscience, 13*(8), 979–986. doi:10.1038/nn.2594

Johansson, G. (1973). Visual perception of biological motion and a model for its analysis. *Perception & Psychophysics, 14*(2), 201–211.

Johansson, R. S., & Cole, K. J. (1992). Sensory-motor coordination during grasping and manipulative actions. *Current Opinion in Neurobiology, 2*, 815–823.

Johansson, G., von Hofsten, C., & Jansson, G. (1980). Event-perception. *Annual Review of Neuroscience, 31*, 27–63.

Johnson, M. K., Hashtroudi, S., & Lindsay, D. (1993). Source monitoring. *Psychological Bulletin, 114*, 3–28.

Johnson-Laird, P. (1994). Mental models and probabilistic thinking. *Cognition, 50*, 189–209.

Johnson-Laird, P. N. (2010a). Deductive reasoning. *Wiley Interdisciplinary Review in Cognitive Science, 1*(1), 8–17. doi:10.1002/wcs.20

Johnson-Laird, P. N. (2010b). Mental models and human reasoning. *Proceedings of the National Academy of Sciences of the United States of America, 107*(43), 18243–18250. doi:10.1073/pnas.1012933107

Johnson-Laird, P. N., & Shafir, E. (1993). The interaction between reasoning and decision making: An introduction. *Cognition, 49*, 1–9.

Johnson-Laird, P. N., Kang, O. E., & Leong, Y. C. (2012). On musical dissonance. *Music Perception: An Interdisciplinary Journal, 30*(1), 19–35. doi:10.1525/mp.2012.30.1.19

Jolij, J., & Lamme, V. A. F. (2005). Repression of unconscious information by conscious processing: Evidence from affective blindsight induced by transcranial magnetic stimulation. *Proceedings of the National Academy of Sciences of the United States of America, 102*(30), 10747–10751.

Jonides, J., Lewis, R. L., Nee, D. E., Lustig, C. A., Berman, M. G., & Moore, K. S. (2008). The mind and brain of short-term memory. *Annual Review of Psychology, 59*, 193–224. doi:10.1146/annurev.psych.59.103006.093615

Joormann, J., Yoon, K. L., & Zetsche, U. (2007). Cognitive inhibition in depression. *Applied and Preventive Psychology, 12*(3), 128–139. doi:10.1016/j.appsy.2007.09.002

Josephs, R. A., Larrick, R. P., Steele, C. M., & Nisbett, R. E. (1992). Protecting the self from the negative consequences of risky decisions. *Journal of Personality and Social Psychology, 62*(1), 26–37.

Jusczyk, P. W. (1999). How infants begin to extract words from speech. *Trends in Cognitive Sciences, 3*(9), 323–328.

Justus, T. C., & Bharucha, J. J. (2001). Modularity in musical processing: The automaticity of harmonic priming. *Journal of Experimental Psychology: Human Perception and Performance, 27*(4), 1000–1011.

Kaada, B. R., Pribram, K. H., & Epstein, J. A. (1949). Respitory and vascular responses in monkeys from temporal pole, insula, orbital surface and cingulate gyrus: A preliminary report. *Journal of Neurophysiology, 12*, 347–356.

Kaakinen, J. K., & Hyönä, J. (2007). Perspective effects in repeated reading: An eye movement study. *Memory & Cognition, 35*(6), 1323–1336.

Kaas, J. H., & Hackett, T. A. (1999). 'What' and 'Where' processing in auditory cortex. *Nature Neuroscience, 2*(12), 1045–1047.

Kaas, J. H., & Hackett, T. A. (2000). Subdivisions of auditory cortex and processing streams in primates. *Proceedings of the National Academy of Sciences of the United States of America, 97*(22), 11793–11799.

Kaas, J. H., Hackett, T. A., & Tramo, M. J. (1999). Auditory processing in primate cerebral cortex. *Current Opinion in Neurobiology, 9*, 164–170.

Kaas, J. H., Qi, H. X., Burish, M. J., Gharbawie, O. A., Onifer, S. M., & Massey, J. M. (2008). Cortical and subcortical plasticity in the brains of humans, primates, and rats after damage to sensory afferents in the dorsal columns of the spinal cord. *Experimental Neurology, 209*(2), 407–416. doi:10.1016/j.expneurol.2007.06.014

Kahneman, D. (1973). *Attention and effort.* Englewood Cliffs, NJ: Prentice-Hall, Inc.

Kahneman, D. (2003). A perspective on judgment and choice: Mapping bounded rationality. *American Psychologist, 58*(9), 697–720. doi:10.1037/0003-066X.58.9.697

Kahneman, D. (2011). *Thinking, fast and slow.* New York, NY: Farrar, Straus and Giroux

Kahneman, D., & Chajczyk, D. (1983). Tests of the automaticity of reading: Dilution of Stroop effects by color-irrelevant stimuli. *Journal of Experimental Psychology: Human Perception and Performance, 9*(4), 497–509.

Kahneman, D., & Klein, G. (2009). Conditions for intuitive expertise: A failure to disagree. *American Psychologist, 64*(6), 515–526. doi:10.1037/a0016755

Kahneman, D., & Tversky, A. (1972). Subjective probability: A judgement of representativeness. *Cognitive Psychology, 3*, 430–454.

Kahneman, D., & Tversky, A. (1973). On the psychology of prediction. *Psychological Review, 80*(4), 237–251.

Kahneman, D., & Tversky, A. (1979). Prospect Theory: An analysis of decision under risk. *Econometrica, 47*(2), 263–291.

Kahneman, D., & Tversky, A. (1982a). On the study of statistical intuitions. *Cognition, 11*, 123–141.

Kahneman, D., & Tversky, A. (1982b). Variants of uncertainty. *Cognition, 11*, 143–157.

Kahneman, D., & Tversky, A. (1984). Choices, values, and frames. *American Psychologist, 39*(4), 341–350.

Kahneman, D., Onuska, L., & Wolman, R. E. (1968). Effects of grouping on the pupillary response in a short-term memory task. *The Quarterly Journal of Experimental Psychology, 20*(3), 309–311. doi:10.1080/14640746808400168

Kahneman, D., Treisman, A., & Gibbs, B. J. (1992). The reviewing of object files: Object-specific integration of information. *Cognitive Psychology, 24*, 175–219.

Kalish, M. L., Lewandowsky, S., & Davies, M. (2005). Error-driven knowledge restructuring in categorization. *Journal of Experimental Psychology: Learning, Memory, and Cognition, 31*(5), 846–861.

Kandel, S., Peereman, R., Grosjacques, G., & Fayol, M. (2001). For a psycholinguistic model of handwriting production: Testing the syllable-bigram controversy. *Journal of Experimental Psychology: Human Perception and Performance, 37*(4), 1310–1322.

Kandil, F. I., Rotter, A., & Lappe, M. (2009). Driving is smoother and more stable when using the tangent point. *Journal of Visualization, 9*(1), 11. doi:10.1167/9.1.11

Kanwisher, N., McDermott, J., & Chun, M. M. (1997). The fusiform face area: A module in human extrastriate cortex specialized for face perception. *The Journal of Neuroscience, 17*(11), 4302–4311.

Kao, T. C., & Hennequin, G. (2018). Null ain't dull: New perspectives on motor cortex. *Trends in Cognitive Sciences, 22*(12), 1069–1071. doi:10.1016/j.tics.2018.09.005

Kaplan, S., Bekhor, S., & Shiftan, Y. (2011). Development and estimation of a semi-compensatory residential choice model based on explicit choice protocols. *The Annals of Regional Science, 47*(1), 51–80. doi:10.1007/s00168-009-0350-3

Kappas, A. (2011). Emotion and regulation are one! *Emotion Review, 3*(1), 17–25. doi:10.1177/1754073910380971

Karmiloff-Smith, A., Klima, E., Bellugi, U., Grant, J., & Baron-Cohen, S. (1995). Is there a social module? Language, face processing and theory of mind in individuals with Williams syndrome. *Journal of Cognitive Neuroscience, 7*(2), 196–208.

Kaufer, D. S., Hayes, J. R., & Flower, L. S. (1986). Composing written sentences. *Research in The Teaching of English, 20*(2), 121–141.

Kawato, M. (1999). Internal models for motor control and trajectory planning. *Current Opinion in Neurobiology, 9*, 718–727.

Kawato, M., Kuroda, T., Imamizu, H., Nakano, E., Miyauchi, S., & Yoshioka, T. (2003). Internal forward models in the cerebellum: fMRI study on grip force and load force coupling. *Progress in Brain Research, 142*, 171–188.

Kay, J., & Ellis, A. W. (1987). A cognitive neuropsychological case study of anomia. *Brain, 110*, 613–629.

Keane, M. (1987). On retrieving analogues when solving problems. *The Quarterly Journal of Experimental Psychology Section A, 39*(1), 29–41. doi:10.1080/02724988743000015

Kellogg, R. T. (1988). Attentional overload and writing performance: Effects of rough draft and outline strategies. *Journal of Experimental Psychology: Learning, Memory, and Cognition, 14*(2), 355–365.

Kellogg, R. T. (2008). Training writing skills: A cognitive developmental perspective. *Journal of Writing Research, 1*, 1–26.

Kelly, S. P., Gomez-Ramirez, M., & Foxe, J. J. (2008). Spatial attention modulates initial afferent activity in human primary visual cortex. *Cerebral Cortex, 18*(11), 2629–2636.

Kelso, J. A. S., Fuchs, A., Lancaster, R., Holroyd, T., Cheyne, D., & Weinberg, H. (1998). Dynamic cortical activity in the human brain reveals motor equivalence. *Nature, 392*, 814–818.

Kempen, G., & Huijbers, P. (1983). The lexicalization process in sentence production and naming: Indirect election of words. *Cognition, 14*, 185–209.

Kenealy, P. M. (1997). Mood-state-dependent retrieval: The effects of induced mood on memory reconsidered. *The Quarterly Journal of Experimental Psychology, 50A*(2), 290–317.

Kenemans, J. L., Smulders, F. T. Y., & Kok, A. (1995). Selective processing of two-dimensional visual stimuli in young and old subjects: Electrophysiological analysis. *Psychophysiology, 32*, 108–120.

Kermer, D. A., Driver-Linn, E., Wilson, T. D., & Gilbert, D. T. (2006). Loss aversion is an affective forecasting error. *Psychological Science, 17*(8), 649–653.

Kerr, C. E., Shaw, J. R., Wasserman, R. H., Chen, V. W., Kanojia, A., Bayer, T., & Kelley, J. M. (2008). Tactile acuity in experienced tai chi practitioners: Evidence for use dependent plasticity as an effect of sensory-attentional training. *Experimental Brain Research, 188*(2), 317–322. doi:10.1007/s00221-008-1409-6

Keysar, B., Barr, D. J., Balin, J. A., & Brauner, J. S. (2000). Taking perspective in conversation: The role of mutual knowledge in comprehension. *Psychological Science, 11*(1), 32–38.

Keysers, C., Kaas, J. H., & Gazzola, V. (2010). Somatosensation in social perception. *Nature Reviews Neuroscience, 11*(6), 417–428. doi:10.1038/nrn2833

Keysers, C., & Perrett, D. I. (2004). Demystifying social cognition: A Hebbian perspective. *Trends in Cognitive Sciences, 8*(11), 501–507. doi:10.1016/j.tics.2004.09.005

Keysers, C., Wicker, B., Gazzola, V., Anton, J.-L., Fogassi, L., & Gallese, V. (2004). A touching sight: SII/PV activation during the observation and experience of touch. *Neuron, 42*, 335–346.

Kilner, J. M., Friston, K. J., & Frith, C. D. (2007). Predictive coding: An account of the mirror neuron system. *Cognitive Processes, 8*(3), 159–166. doi:10.1007/s10339-007-0170-2

Kimberg, D. Y., & Farah, M. J. (1993). A unified account of cognitive impairments following frontal lobe damage: The role of working memory in complex, organized behavior. *Journal of Experimental Psychology: General, 122*(4), 411–428

Kimchi, R., & Peterson, M. A. (2008). Figure-ground segmentation can occur without attention. *Psychological Science, 19*(7), 660–668.

King-Casas, B., Tomlin, D., Anen, C., Camerer, C. F., Quartz, S. R., & Montague, P. R. (2005). Getting to know you: Reputation and trust in a two-person economic exchange. *Science, 308,* 78–83.

Kintsch, W. (1998). The role of knowledge in discourse comprehension: A construction - integration model. *Psychological Review, 95*(2), 163–182.

Kintsch, W. (2000). Metaphor comprehension: A computational theory. *Psychonomic Bulletin & Review, 7*(2), 257–266.

Kintsch, W., Welsch, D., Schmalhofer, F., & Zimny, S. (1990). Sentence memory: A theoretical analysis. *Journal of Memory and Language, 29,* 133–159.

Kirby, J. R., & Becker, L. D. (1988). Cognitive components of learning problems in arithmetic. *Remedial and Special Education, 9*(5), 7–15.

Kirchner, W. K. (1958). Age differences in short-term retention of rapidly changing information. *Journal of Experimental Psychology, 55*(4), 352–358.

Kirsch, P., Esslinger, C., Chen, Q., Mier, D., Lis, S., Siddhanti, S. ... Meyer-Lindenberg, A. (2005). Oxytocin modulates neural circuitry for social cognition and fear in humans. *The Journal of Neuroscience, 25*(49), 11489–11493. doi:10.1523/JNEUROSCI.3984-05.2005

Klahr, D. (1973). A production system for counting, subitizing, and adding. In W. G. Chase (Ed.), *Visual information processing* (pp. 527–546). New York: Academic Press.

Klauer, K. C., Musch, J., & Naumer, B. (2000). On belief bias in syllogistic reasoning. *Psychological Review, 107*(4), 852–884. doi:10.1037//0033-295x.107.4.852

Klauer, K. C., & Zhao, Z. (2004). Double dissociations in visual and spatial short-term memory. *Journal of Experimental Psychology: General, 133*(3), 355–381. doi:10.1037/0096-3445.133.3.355

Klaver, P., Talsma, D., Wijers, A. A., Heinze, H. J., & Mulder, G. (1999). An event-related brain potential correlate of visual short-term memory. *Neuroreport, 10*(10), 2001–2005.

Klein, G. (2008). Naturalistic decision making. *Human Factors, 50*(3), 456–460. doi:10.1518/001872008X288385

Klein, I., Dubois, J., Mangin, J. F., Kherif, F., Flandin, G., Poline, J. B. ... Le Bihan, D. (2004). Retinotopic organization of visual mental images as revealed by functional magnetic resonance imaging. *Brain Research Cognitive Brain Research, 22*(1), 26–31. doi:10.1016/j.cogbrainres.2004.07.006

Klein, R. M. (1980). Does oculomotor readiness mediate cognitive control of visual attention? In R. Nickerson (Ed.), *Attention and performance* (Vol. IX, pp. 259–276). Hillsdale, NJ: Lawrence Erlbaum.

Kloos, H., & Sloutsky, V. M. (2004). *Are natural kinds psychologically distinct from nominal kinds? Evidence from learning and development.* Paper presented at the Proceedings of The Annual Meeting of The Cognitive Science Society, Chicago, Il.

Kloos, H., & Sloutsky, V. M. (2008). What's behind different kinds of kinds: Effects of statistical density on learning and representation of categories. *Journal of Experimental Psychology: General, 137*(1), 52–72. doi:10.1037/0096-3445.137.1.52

Knauff, M., Fangmeier, T., Ruff, C. C., & Johnson-Laird, P. (2003). Reasoning, models, and images: Behavioral measures and cortical activity. *Journal of Cognitive Neuroscience, 15*(4), 559–573.

Knauff, M., & Johnson-Laird, P. N. (2002). Visual imagery can impede reasoning. *Memory & Cognition, 30*(3), 363–371.

Knoblich, G., Ohlsson, S., & Raney, G. E. (2001). An eye movement study of insight problem solving. *Memory & Cognition, 29*(7), 1000–1009.

Knoblich, G., Ohlsson, S., Haider, H., & Rhenius, D. (1999). Constraint relaxation and chunk decomposition in insight problem solving. *Journal of Experimental Psychology: Learning, Memory, and Cognition, 25*(6), 1534–1555.

Knopman, D., & Nissen, M. J. (1991). Procedural learning is impaired in Huntington's disease: Evidence from the serial reaction time task. *Neuropsychologia, 29*(3), 245–254.

Knowlton, B. J., & Squire, L. R. (1993). The learning of categories: Parallel brain systems for item memory and category knowledge. *Science, 262,* 1747–1749.

Knowlton, B. J., Morrison, R. G., Hummel, J. E., & Holyoak, K. J. (2012). A neurocomputational system for relational reasoning. *Trends in Cognitive Sciences, 16*(7), 373–381. doi:10.1016/j.tics.2012.06.002

Knowlton, B. J., Siegel, A. L. M., & Moody, T. D. (2017). Procedural learning in humans. learning and memory: A comprehensive reference. In H. Eigenbaum (Ed.), *Memory Systems* (pp. 295–312). Oxford: Academic Press.

Knutson, B., Fong, G. W., Adams, C. M., Varner, J. L., & Hommer, D. (2001). Dissociation of reward anticipation and outcome with event-related fMRI. *Neuroreport, 12*(17), 3683–3687.

Knyazev, G. G., Levin, E. A., & Savostyanov, A. N. (2008). A failure to stop and attention fluctuations: An evoked oscillations study of the stop-signal paradigm. *Clinical Neurophysiology, 119*(3), 556–567. doi:10.1016/j.clinph.2007.11.041

Koch, C., & Tsuchiya, N. (2007). Attention and consciousness: Two distinct brain processes. *Trends in Cognitive Sciences, 11*(1), 16–22. doi:10.1016/j.tics.2006.10.012

Koch, C., & Tsuchiya, N. (2012). Attention and consciousness: Related yet different. *Trends in Cognitive Sciences, 16*(2), 103–105. doi:10.1016/j.tics.2011.11.012

Koechlin, E., Ody, C., & Kouneiher, F. (2003). The architecture of cognitive control in the human prefrontal cortex. *Science, 302,* 1181–1185.

Koelsch, S. (2005). Neural substrates of processing syntax and semantics in music. *Current Opinion in Neurobiology, 15*(2), 207–212. doi:10.1016/j.conb.2005.03.005

Koelsch, S., Kasper, E., Sammler, D., Schulze, K., Gunter, T., & Friederici, A. D. (2004). Music, language and meaning: Brain signatures of semantic processing. *Nature Neuroscience*, 7(3), 302–307. doi:10.1038/nn1197

Koelsch, S., & Siebel, W. A. (2005). Towards a neural basis of music perception. *Trends in Cognitive Sciences*, 9(12), 578–584. doi:10.1016/j.tics.2005.10.001

Koelsch, S., Vuust, P., & Friston, K. (2019). Predictive processes and the peculiar case of music. *Trends in Cognitive Sciences*, 23(1), 63–77. doi:10.1016/j.tics.2018.10.006

Koenderink, J. (1986). Optic flow. *Vision Research*, 26(1), 161–180.

Kohler, E., Keysers, C., Umilta, M. A., Fogassi, L., Gallese, V., & Rizzolatti, G. (2002). Hearing sounds, understanding actions: Action representations in mirror neurons. *Science*, 297, 846–848.

Köhler, W. (1925). *The mentality of apes*. New York, NY: Hartourc, Brace and Company.

Kohn, N., Eickhoff, S. B., Scheller, M., Laird, A. R., Fox, P. T., & Habel, U. (2014). Neural network of cognitive emotion regulation–An Ale meta-analysis and Macm analysis. *Neuroimage*, 87, 345–355. doi:10.1016/j.neuroimage.2013.11.001

Koivisto, M., Railo, H., Revonsuo, A., Vanni, S., & Salminen-Vaparanta, N. (2011). Recurrent processing in V1/V2 contributes to categorization of natural scenes. *The Journal of Neuroscience*, 31(7), 2488–2492. doi:10.1523/JNEUROSCI.3074-10.2011

Kok, P., & de Lange, F. P. (2015). Predictive coding in sensory cortex. In B. U. Forstmann & E. J. Wagenmakers (Eds.), *An introduction to model-based cognitive neuroscience* (pp. 221–244). New York, NY: Springer Verlag.

Kok, P., Jehee, J. F., & de Lange, F. P. (2012). Less is more: Expectation sharpens representations in the primary visual cortex. *Neuron*, 75(2), 265–270. doi:10.1016/j.neuron.2012.04.034

Komatsu, H. (2006). The neural mechanisms of perceptual filling-in. *Nature Reviews Neuroscience*, 7(3), 220–231. doi:10.1038/nrn1869

Kondo, H. M., & Kashino, M. (2007). Neural mechanisms of auditory awareness underlying verbal transformations. *Neuroimage*, 36(1), 123–130. doi:10.1016/j.neuroimage.2007.02.024

Kondo, H. M., & Kashino, M. (2009). Involvement of the thalamocortical loop in the spontaneous switching of percepts in auditory streaming. *The Journal of Neuroscience*, 29(40), 12695–12701. doi:10.1523/JNEUROSCI.1549-09.2009

Konishi, M. (2003). Coding of auditory space. *Annual Review of Neuroscience*, 26, 31–55. doi:10.1146/annurev.neuro.26.041002.131123

Konishi, M., Kawazu, M., Uchida, I., Kikyo, H., Asakura, I., & Miyashita, Y. (1999). Contribution of working memory to transient activation in human inferior prefrontal cortex during performance of the Wisconsin card sorting test. *Cerebral Cortex*, 9, 745–753.

Koob, G. F., & Le Moal, M. (2001). Drug addiction, dysregulation of reward, and allostasis. *Neuropsychopharmacology*, 24(2), 97–129.

Koontz, K. L., & Berch, D. B. (1996). Identifying simple numerical stimuli: Processing inefficiencies exhibited by arithmetic learning disabled children. *Mathematical Cognition*, 2(1), 1–24. doi:10.1080/135467996387525

Kopelman, M. D., & Bright, P. (2012). On remembering and forgetting our autobiographical pasts: Retrograde amnesia and Andrew Mayes's contribution to neuropsychological method. *Neuropsychologia*, 50(13), 2961–2972. doi:10.1016/j.neuropsychologia.2012.07.028

Körding, K. P., & Wolpert, D. M. (2004). Bayesian integration in sensorimotor learning. *Nature*, 427, 244–247.

Kording, K. P., & Wolpert, D. M. (2006). Bayesian decision theory in sensorimotor control. *Trends in Cognitive Sciences*, 10(7), 319–326. doi:10.1016/j.tics.2006.05.003

Kornhuber, H. R., & Deecke, L. (1965). Hirnpotentialänderungen bei willkürbewegungen und passiven bewegungen des menschen: Bereitschaftspotential und reafferente potentiale. *Pflügers Archiv*, 284, 1–17.

Korzyukov, O., Pflieger, M. E., Wagner, M., Bowyer, S. M., Rosburg, T., Sundaresan, K. … Boutros, N. N. (2007). Generators of the intracranial P50 response in auditory sensory gating. *Neuroimage*, 35(2), 814–826. doi:10.1016/j.neuroimage.2006.12.011

Kosfeld, M., Heinrichs, M., Zak, P. J., Fischbacher, U., & Fehr, E. (2005). Oxytocin increases trust in humans. *Nature*, 435(7042), 673–676. doi:10.1038/nature03701

Koshev, N., Butorina, A., Skidchenko, E., Kuzmichev, A., Ossadtchi, A., Ostras, M. … Vetoshko, P. (2021). Evolution of meg: A first meg-feasible fluxgate magnetometer. *Human Brain Mapping*, 42(15), 4844–4856. doi:10.1002/hbm.25582

Kosslyn, S. M. (1999). The role of area 17 in visual imagery: Convergent evidence from pet and RTMS. *Science*, 284(5411), 167–170. doi:10.1126/science.284.5411.167

Kosslyn, S. M., Ganis, G., & Thompson, W. L. (2001). Neural foundations of imagery. *Nature Reviews Neuroscience*, 2, 635–642.

Kounios, J., & Beeman, M. (2014). The cognitive neuroscience of insight. *Annual Review of Psychology*, 65, 71–93. doi:10.1146/annurev-psych-010213-115154

Kourtzi, Z., & Connor, C. E. (2011). Neural representations for object perception: Structure. Category, and Adaptive Coding. *Annual Review of Neuroscience*, 34, 45–67. doi:10.1146/annurev-neuro-060909-153218

Kourtzi, Z., Krekelberg, B., & van Wezel, R. J. (2008). Linking form and motion in the primate brain. *Trends in Cognitive Sciences*, 12(6), 230–236. doi:10.1016/j.tics.2008.02.013

Kraljic, T., & Brennan, S. E. (2005). Prosodic disambiguation of syntactic structure: For the speaker or for the addressee? *Cognitive Psychology*, 50(2), 194–231. doi:10.1016/j.cogpsych.2004.08.002

References

Kraljic, T., Brennan, S. E., & Samuel, A. G. (2008). Accommodating variation: Dialects, idiolects, and speech processing. *Cognition*, *107*(1), 54–81. doi:10.1016/j.cognition.2007.07.013

Kravitz, D. J., Saleem, K. S., Baker, C. I., & Mishkin, M. (2011). A new neural framework for visuospatial processing. *Nature Reviews Neuroscience*, *12*(4), 217–230. doi:10.1038/nrn3008

Krawczyk, D. C. (2012). The cognition and neuroscience of relational reasoning. *Brain Research*, *1428*, 13–23. doi:10.1016/j.brainres.2010.11.080

Krebs, R. M., Boehler, C. N., Roberts, K. C., Song, A. W., & Woldorff, M. G. (2012). The involvement of the dopaminergic midbrain and cortico-striatal-thalamic circuits in the integration of reward prospect and attentional task demands. *Cereb Cortex*, *22*(3), 607–615. doi:10.1093/cercor/bhr134

Krebs, R. M., Boehler, C. N., & Woldorff, M. G. (2010). The influence of reward associations on conflict processing in the Stroop task. *Cognition*, *117*(3), 341–347. doi:10.1016/j.cognition.2010.08.018

Krishnan, A., Woo, C. W., Chang, L. J., Ruzic, L., Gu, X., Lopez-Sola, M. ... Wager, T. D. (2016). Somatic and vicarious pain are represented by dissociable multivariate brain patterns. *Elife*, *5*. doi:10.7554/eLife.15166

Krolak-Salmon, P., Hénaf, M.-A., Isnard, J., Tallon-Baudry, C., Guénot, M., Vighetto, A. ... Mauguiere, F. (2003). A attention modulated response to disgust in human ventral insula. *Annals of Neurology*, *5*(3), 446–453.

Kruger, J., & Dunning, D. (1999). Unskilled and unaware of it: How difficulties in recognizing one's own incompetence lead to inflated self-assessments. *Journal of Personality and Social Psychology*, *77*(6), 1121–1134.

Krupa, D. J., Wiest, M. C., Shuler, M. G., Laubach, M., & Nicolelis, M. A. L. (2004). Layer-specific somatosensory cortical activation during active tactile discrimination. *Science*, *304*, 1989–1992.

Krupinski, E. A., Graham, A. R., & Weinstein, R. S. (2013). Characterizing the development of visual search expertise in pathology residents viewing whole slide images. *Human Pathology*, *44*(3), 357–364. doi:10.1016/j.humpath.2012.05.024

Krynski, T. R., & Tenenbaum, J. B. (2007). The role of causality in judgment under uncertainty. *Journal of Experimental Psychology: General*, *136*(3), 430–450. doi:10.1037/0096-3445.136.3.430

Kugler, R., Connolly, T., & Ordonez, L. D. (2012). Emotion, decision, and risk: Betting on gambles versus betting on people. *Journal of Behavioral Decision Making*, *25*, 123–134.

Kuhn, S., Vanderhasselt, M. A., De Raedt, R., & Gallinat, J. (2012). Why ruminators Won't stop: The structural and resting state correlates of rumination and its relation to depression. *Journal of Affective Disorders*, *141*(2–3), 352–360. doi:10.1016/j.jad.2012.03.024

Kujala, T., Huotilainen, M., Sinkkonen, J., Ahonen, A. I., Alho, K., Hämäläinen, M. ... Näätänen, R. (1995). Visual cortex activation in blind humans during sound discrimination. *Neuroscience Letters*, *183*, 143–146.

Kulatunga-Moruzi, C., Brooks, L. R., & Norman, G. R. (2004). Using comprehensive feature lists to bias medical diagnosis. *Journal of Experimental Psychology: Learning, Memory, and Cognition*, *30*(3), 563–572. doi:10.1037/0278-7393.30.3.563

Kundel, H. L., & Nodine, C. F. (1975). Interpreting chest radiographs without visual search. *Radiology*, *116*, 527–523.

Kundel, H. L., Nodine, C. F., Conant, E. F., & Weinstein, S. P. (2007). Holistic component of image perception in mammogram interpretation. *Radiology*, *242*, 396–402.

Kuppens, P., Van Mechelen, I., Smits, D. J., & De Boeck, P. (2003). The appraisal basis of anger: Specificity, necessity and sufficiency of components. *Emotion*, *3*(3), 254–269. doi:10.1037/1528-3542.3.3.254

Kurby, C. A., & Zacks, J. M. (2012). Starting from scratch and building brick by brick in comprehension. *Memory & Cognition*, *40*, 812–826.

Kurtz, K. J., & Loewenstein, J. (2007). Converging on a new role for analogy in problem solving and retrieval: When two problems are better than one. *Memory & Cognition*, *35*(2), 334–341.

Kutas, M., & Federmeier, K. D. (2011). Thirty years and counting: Finding meaning in the N400 component of the event-related brain potential (ERP). *Annual Review of Psychology*, *62*, 621–647. doi:10.1146/annurev.psych.093008.131123

Kutas, M., & Hillyard, S. A. (1980). Reading senseless sentences: Brain potentials reflect semantic incongruity. *Science*, *207*, 203–205.

Kutas, M., Delong, K. A., & Smith, N. J. (2011). A look around at what lies ahead: Prediction and predictability in language processing. In M. Bar (Ed.), *Predictions in the brain: Using our past to generate a future*. Oxford: Oxford University Press.

Kvavilashvili, L., & Fisher, L. (2007). Is time-based prospective remembering mediated by self-initiated rehearsals? Role of incidental cues, ongoing activity, age, and motivation. *Journal of Experimental Psychology: General*, *136*(1), 112–132. doi:10.1037/0096-3445.136.1.112

Kwakye, L. D., Foss-Feig, J. H., Cascio, C. J., Stone, W. L., & Wallace, M. T. (2011). Altered auditory and multisensory temporal processing in autism spectrum disorders. *Frontiers in Integrative Neuroscience*, *4*, 129. doi:10.3389/fnint.2010.00129

Laberge, D. (1983). Spatial extent of attention to letters and words. *Journal of Experimental Psychology: Human Perception and Performance*, *9*(3), 371–379.

LaBerge, D. (1990). Thalamic and cortical mechanism of attention suggested by recent positron emission tomography. *Journal of Cognitive Neuroscience*, *2*(4), 358–372.

Làdavas, E. (2002). Functional and dynamic properties of visual peripersonal space. *Trends in Cognitive Sciences*, *6*(1), 17–22.

Làdavas, E., di Pellegrino, G., Farne, A., & Zeloni, G. (1998). Neuropsychological evidence of an integrated visuotactile representation of peripersonal space in humans. *Journal of Cognitive Neuroscience*, *10*(5), 581–589.

Laganaro, M., Morand, S., & Schnider, A. (2008). Time course of evoked-potential changes in different form of anomia in aphasia. *Journal of Cognitive Neuroscience*, *21*(8), 1499–1510.

Lagrain, V., Guérit, J.-M., Bruyer, R., & Plaghki, L. (2002). Attentional modulation of the nociceptive processing into the human brain: Selective spatial attention, probability of stimulus occurrence, and target detection effects on laser evoked potentials. *Pain*, *99*, 21–39.

Lagrois, M. E., Peretz, I., & Zendel, B. R. (2018). Neurophysiological and behavioral differences between older and younger adults when processing violations of tonal structure in music. *Frontiers in Neuroscience*, *12*, 54. doi:10.3389/fnins.2018.00054

Lai, C. S., Gerrelli, D., Monaco, A. P., Fisher, S. E., & Copp, A. J. (2003). Foxp2 expression during brain development coincides with adult sites of pathology in a severe speech and language disorder. *Brain*, *126*(Pt 11), 2455–2462. doi:10.1093/brain/awg247

Laland, K., & Seed, A. (2021). Understanding human cognitive uniqueness. *Annual Review of Psychology*, *72*, 689–716. doi:10.1146/annurev-psych-062220-051256

Lamme, V. A. F. (2003). Why visual attention and awareness are different. *Trends in Cognitive Sciences*, *7*(1), 12–18.

Lamme, V. A. F. (2004). Separate neural definitions of visual consciousness and visual attention; A case for phenomenal awareness. *Neural Networks*, *17*(5–6), 861–872. doi:10.1016/j.neunet.2004.02.005

Lamme, V. A. F. (2006a). Towards a true neural stance on consciousness. *Trends in Cognitive Sciences*, *10*(11), 494–501. doi:10.1016/j.tics.2006.09.001

Lamme, V. A. F. (2006b). Zap! Magnetic tricks on conscious and unconscious vision. *Trends in Cognitive Sciences*, *10*(5), 193–195. doi:10.1016/j.tics.2006.03.002

Lamme, V. A. F. (2010). How neuroscience will change our view on consciousness. *Journal of Cognitive Neuroscience*, *1*(3), 204–220. doi:10.1080/17588921003731586

Lamme, V. A. F., & Roelfsema, P. R. (2000). The distinct modes of vision offered by feedforward and recurrent processing. *Trends in Neurosciences*, *23*, 571–579.

Lamy, D., Salti, M., & Bar-Haim, Y. (2009). Neural correlates of subjective awareness and unconscious processing: An ERP study. *Journal of Cognitive Neuroscience*, *21*(7), 1435–1446.

Land, E. H. (1986). An alternative technique for the computation of the designator in the retinex theory of color vision. *Proceedings of the National Academy of Sciences*, *83*, 3078–3080.

Land, M. F., & Lee, D. N. (1994). Where we look when we steer. *Nature*, *369*, 742–744.

Land, E. H., & McCann, J. J. (1971). Lightness and retinex theory. *Journal of the Optical Society of America*, *61*(1), 1–11.

Landauer, T. K. (1962). Rate of implicit speech. *Perceptual and Motor Skills*, *15*, 646.

Landerl, K., Bevan, A., & Butterworth, B. (2004). Developmental dyscalculia and basic numerical capacities: A study of 8-9-year-old students. *Cognition*, *93*(2), 99–125. doi:10.1016/j.cognition.2003.11.004

Landman, R., Spekreijse, H., & Lamme, V. A. F. (2003). Large capacity storage of integrated objects before change blindness. *Vision Research*, *43*(2), 149–164.

Lang, P. J., Davis, M., & Öhman, A. (2000). Fear and anxiety: Animal models and human cognitive psychophysiology. *Journal of Affective Disorders*, *61*, 137–159.

Lange, C. G. (1885). *Om sindsbevaegelser*. Whitefish, MT: Kessinger Publishing.

Lange, J. J., Wijers, A. A., Mulder, L. J. M., & Mulder, G. (1998). Color selection and location selection in ERPS: Differences, similarities and 'neural specificity'. *Biological Psychology*, *48*, 153–182.

Langford, Z. D., Krebs, R. M., Talsma, D., Woldorff, M. G., & Boehler, C. N. (2016). Strategic down-regulation of attentional resources as a mechanism of proactive response inhibition. *European Journal of Neuroscience*, *44*(4), 2095–2103. doi:10.1111/ejn.13303

Langner, R., Kellermann, T., Boers, F., Sturm, W., Willmes, K., & Eickhoff, S. B. (2011). Modality-specific perceptual expectations selectively modulate baseline activity in auditory, somatosensory, and visual cortices. *Cerebral Cortex*, *21*(12), 2850–2862. doi:10.1093/cercor/bhr083

Langton, S. R. H., Watt, R. J., & Bruce, V. (2000). Do the eyes have it? Cues to the direction of social attention. *Trends in Cognitive Sciences*, *4*(2), 50–59.

Lappi, O., Pekkanen, J., & Itkonen, T. H. (2013). Pursuit eye-movements in curve driving differentiate between future path and tangent point models. *PLoS One*, *8*(7), e68326. doi:10.1371/journal.pone.0068326

Larkin, J., McDermott, J., Simon, D. P., & Simon, H. A. (1980). Expert and novice performance in solving physics problems. *Science*, *208*, 1335–1342.

Larsen, J. D., Baddeley, A. D., & Andrade, J. (2000). Phonological similarity and the irrelevant speech effect: Implications for models of short-term verbal memory. *Memory*, *8*(3), 145–157.

Lashley, K. S. (1930). Basic neural mechanisms in behavior. *Psychological Review*, *37*, 1–24.

Lashley, K. S. (1944). Studies of cerebral function in learning. XIII. Apparent absence of transcortical association in maze learning. *Journal of Comparative Neurology (and Psychology)*, *80*, 257–281. https://doi.org/10.1002/cne.900800207

Lashley, K. S. (1950). In search of the engram. *Symposia. Society of Experimental Biology*, *4*, 454–482.

References

Lashley, K. S., and Wiley, L. E. (1935). Studies of cerebral function in learning IX. Mass action in relation to the number of elements in the problem to be learned. *Journal of Comparative Neurology, 57,* 3–55. https://doi.org/10.1002/cne.900570102

Laurent, J. P., Denhieres, G., Passerieux, C., Iakimova, G., & Hardy-Bayle, M. C. (2006). On understanding idiomatic language: The salience hypothesis assessed by ERPS. *Brain Research, 1068*(1), 151–160. doi:10.1016/j.brainres.2005.10.076

Laureys, S. (2005). The neural correlate of (Un)Awareness: Lessons from the vegetative state. *Trends in Cognitive Sciences, 9*(12), 556–559. doi:10.1016/j.tics.2005.10.010

Lavie, N. (1995). Perceptual load as a necessary condition for selective attention. *Journal of Experimental Psychology: Human Perception and Performance, 21*(3), 451–468.

Lavie, N. (2005). Distracted and confused? Selective attention under load. *Trends in Cognitive Sciences, 9*(2), 75–82. doi:10.1016/j.tics.2004.12.004

Lavie, N. (2010). Attention, distraction, and cognitive control under load. *Current Directions in Psychological Science, 19*(3), 143–148. doi:10.1177/0963721410370295

Laylock, T. (1878). Reflex function of the brain. *Reprinted from No. XXXVII of the British and Foreign Medical Review.* London: Adlard.

Lazarus, R. S., & Alfert, E. (1964). Short-circuiting of threat by experimentally altering cognitive appraisal. *Journal of Abnormal and Social Psychology, 69*(2), 195–205.

Leach, F. R., & Plaks, J. E. (2009). Regret for errors of commission and omission in the distant term versus near term: The role of level of abstraction. *Personality and Social Psychology Bulletin, 35*(2), 221–229. doi:10.1177/0146167208327001

Lederman, R. J. (1988). Occupational cramp in instrumental musicians. *Medical Problems of Performing Artists, 3*(2), 45–51.

LeDoux, J. E. (1995). Emotion: Clues from the brain. *Annual Review of Psychology, 46,* 209–235.

Lee, D. N. (1976). A theory of visual control of braking based on information about time-to-collision. *Perception, 5,* 437–459.

Lee, H., Heller, A. S., van Reekum, C. M., Nelson, B., & Davidson, R. J. (2012). Amygdala-prefrontal coupling underlies individual differences in emotion regulation. *Neuroimage, 62*(3), 1575–1581. doi:10.1016/j.neuroimage.2012.05.044

Lee, D. Y., Kim, E., & Choi, M. H. (2015). Technical and clinical aspects of cortisol as a biochemical marker of chronic stress. *BMB Reports, 48*(4), 209–216. doi:10.5483/bmbrep.2015.48.4.275

Lee, K.-M., & Kang, S.-Y. (2002). Arithmetic operation and working memory: Differential suppression in dual tasks. *Cognition, 83*(3), B63–B68.

Lee, A. K., Larson, E., Maddox, R. K., & Shinn-Cunningham, B. G. (2014). Using neuroimaging to understand the cortical mechanisms of auditory selective attention. *Hearing Research, 307,* 111–120. doi:10.1016/j.heares.2013.06.010

Lee, D. H., Mirza, R., Flanagan, J. G., & Anderson, A. K. (2014). Optical origins of opposing facial expression actions. *Psychological Science, 25*(3), 745–752. doi:10.1177/0956797613514451

Lee, A. K., & Wilson, M. A. (2002). Memory of sequential experience in the hippocampus during slow wave sleep. *Neuron, 36,* 1183–1194.

LeFevre, J. A., Lei, Q., Smith-Chanti, B. L., & Mullins, D. B. (2001). Multiplication by eye and by ear for Chinese speaking and English-speaking adults. *Canadian Journal of Experimental Psychology, 55*(5), 277–284.

Leggio, M., & Molinari, M. (2015). Cerebellar sequencing: A trick for predicting the future. *Cerebellum, 14*(1), 35–38. doi:10.1007/s12311-014-0616-x

Legrain, V., Crombez, G., & Mouraux, A. (2011). Controlling attention to nociceptive stimuli with working memory. *PLoS One, 6*(6), e20926. doi:10.1371/journal.pone.0020926

Legrain, V., Iannetti, G. D., Plaghki, L., & Mouraux, A. (2011). The pain matrix reloaded: A salience detection system for the body. *Progress in Neurobiology, 93*(1), 111–124. doi:10.1016/j.pneurobio.2010.10.005

Legrenzi, P., Giriotto, V., & Johnson-Laird, P. N. (2003). Models of consistency. *Psychological Science, 14*(2), 131–137.

Lehle, C., Steinhauser, M., & Hübner, R. (2009). Serial or parallel processing in dual tasks: What is more effortful? *Psychophysiology, 46*(3), 502–509. doi:10.1111/j.1469-8986.2009.00806.x

Leinonen, L., Hyvärinen, J., & Sovijärvi, A. R. A. (1980). Functional properties of neurons in the temporo-parietal association cortex of the awake monkey. *Experimental Brain Research, 39,* 203–215.

Leman, M., & Maes, P. -J. (2014). The role of embodiment in the perception of music. *Empirical Musicology Review, 9*(3–4), 236–246.

Lench, H. C., Flores, S. A., & Bench, S. W. (2011). Discrete emotions predict changes in cognition, judgment, experience, behavior, and physiology: A meta-analysis of experimental emotion elicitations. *Psychological Bulletin, 137*(5), 834–855. doi:10.1037/a0024244.supp

Lenton, A. P., & Stewart, A. (2008). Changing her ways: The number of options and mate-standard strength impact mate choice strategy and satisfaction. *Judgement and Decision Making, 3*(7), 501–511.

Leopold, D. A., & Logothetis, N. K. (1999). Multistable phenomena: Changing views in perception. *Trends in Cognitive Sciences, 3*(7), 254–264.

LePort, A. K., Mattfeld, A. T., Dickinson-Anson, H., Fallon, J. H., Stark, C. E., Kruggel, F. ... McGaugh, J. L. (2012). Behavioral and neuroanatomical investigation of highly superior autobiographical memory (Hsam). *Neurobiology of Learning and Memory, 98*(1), 78–92. doi:10.1016/j.nlm.2012.05.002

LePort, A. K., Stark, S. M., McGaugh, J. L., & Stark, C. E. (2015). Highly superior autobiographical memory: Quality and quantity of retention over time. *Frontiers in Psychology, 6*, 2017. doi:10.3389/fpsyg.2015.02017

Lerner, J. S., & Keltner, D. (2001). Fear, anger, and risk. *Journal of Personality and Social Psychology, 81*(1), 146–159.

Leslie, A. M. (1987). Pretense and representation: The origins of 'Theory of mind'. *Psychological Review, 94*(4), 412–426.

Levelt, W. J. M. (1983). Monitoring and self-repair in speech. *Cognition, 14*, 41–104.

Levelt, W. J. M., Roelofs, A., & Meyer, A. S. (1999). A theory of lexical access in speech production. *Behavioral and Brain Sciences, 22*, 1–75.

Levine, D. N., Cavanio, R., & Popovich, A. (1992). Language in the absence of inner speech. *Neuropsychologia, 20*(4), 391–409.

Levine, J. D., Gordon, N. C., Smith, R., & Fields, H. L. (1982). Post-operative pain: Effect of extent of injury and attention. *Brain Research, 234*, 500–504.

Lewald, J., & Guski, R. (2003). Cross-modal perceptual integration of spatially and temporally disparate auditory and visual stimuli. *Cognitive Brain Research, 16*(3), 468–478. doi:10.1016/s0926-6410(03)00074-0

Lewandowsky, M., & Stadelmann, E. (1908). Über einen bemerkenswerten fall von hirnblutung und Über rechenstörungen bei herderkrankung des gehirns. *Journal Für Psychologie Und Neurologie, 11*, 249–265.

Lewinsohn, P. M., Joiner, T. E. Jr., & Rohde, P. (2001). Evaluation of cognitive diathesis-stress models in predicting major depressive disorder in adolescents. *Journal of Abnormal Psychology, 110*(2), 203–215. doi:10.1037/0021-843x.110.2.203

Lewis, C. I. (1929). *Mind and the world*. New York, NY: C. Scribners Sons.

Liberman, A. M., Cooper, F. S., Shankweiler, D. P., & Studdert-Kennedy, M. (1967). Perception of the speech code. *Psychological Review, 74*(6), 431–461.

Libet, B., Gleason, C. A., Wright, E. W., & Pearl, D. K. (1983). Time of conscious intention to act in relation to onset of cerebral activity (Readiness potential). The unconscious initiation of a freely voluntary act. *Brain, 106*(3), 623–642.

Lichtenstein, S., Slovic, P., Fischhoff, B., Layman, M., & Combs, B. (1978). Judged frequency of lethal events. *Journal of Experimental Psychology: Human Learning and Memory, 4*(6), 551–578.

Licklider, J. C. R. (1956). Audio frequency analysis. In C. Cherry (Ed.), *Information theory* (pp. 253–268). London: Butterworth.

Liefooghe, B., Wenke, D., & De Houwer, J. (2012). Instruction-based task-rule congruency effects. *Journal of Experimental Psychology: Learning, Memory, and Cognition, 38*(5), 1325–1335. https://doi.org/10.1037/a0028148

Lien, M.-C., Ruthruff, E., & Johnston, J. C. (2006). Attentional limitations in doing two tasks at once. *Current Directions in Psychological Science, 15*(2), 89–93.

Lim, S. L., Padmala, S., & Pessoa, L. (2008). Affective learning modulates spatial competition during low-load attentional conditions. *Neuropsychologia, 46*(5), 1267–1278. doi:10.1016/j.neuropsychologia.2007.12.003

Lin, A.-L., Gao, J.-H., & Fox, P. T. (2012). Neurovascular and neurometabolic uncoupling in the visual cortex. In S. Molotchnikoff & J. Rouat (Eds.), *Visual cortex: Current status and perspectives*. InTechOpen. https://www.intechopen.com/about-intechopen

Lindholm, T., & Christianson, S. A. (1998). Intergroup biases and eyewitness testimony. *The Journal of Social Psychology, 138*(6), 710–723. doi:10.1080/00224549809603256

Lindsay, S. D., Allen, B. P., Chan, J. C. K., & Dahl, L. C. (2004). Eyewitness suggestibility and source similarity: Intrusions of details from one event into memory reports of another event. *Journal of Memory and Language, 50*(1), 96–111. doi:10.1016/j.jml.2003.08.007

Lipp, O. V., & Purkis, H. M. (2005). No support for dual process accounts of human affective learning in simple Pavlovian conditioning. *Cognition & Emotion, 19*(2), 269–282. doi:10.1080/02699930441000319

Little, D. R., Lewandowsky, M., & Heit, E. (2006). Ad hoc category restructuring. *Memory & Cognition, 34*(7), 1398–1413.

Liu, X., Crump, M. J., & Logan, G. D. (2010). Do you know where your fingers have been? Explicit knowledge of the spatial layout of the keyboard in skilled typists. *Memory & Cognition, 38*(4), 474–484. doi:10.3758/MC.38.4.474

Llewellyn, S. (2016). Dream to predict? Rem dreaming as prospective coding. *Frontiers in Psychology, 6*, 1961. doi:10.3389/fpsyg.2015.01961

Llinás, R. (2003). Consciousness and the thalamocortical loop. *International Congress Series, 1250*, 409–416. doi:10.1016/s0531-5131(03)01067-7

Llinás, R., & Paré, D. (1991). Of dreaming and wakefulness. *Neuroscience, 44*(3), 521–535.

Llinas, R., Ribary, U., Contreras, D., & Pedroarena, C. (1998). The neuronal basis for consciousness. *Philosophical Transactions of the Royal Society B-Biological Sciences, 353*(1377), 1841–1849. doi:10.1098/rstb.1998.0336

Locke, H. S., & Braver, T. S. (2008). Motivational influences on cognitive control: Behavior, brain activation, and individual differences. *Cognitive, Affective, & Behavioral Neuroscience, 8*(1), 99–112. doi:10.3758/cabn.8.1.99.

Lockhart, R. S., & Craik, F. I. M. (1990). Levels of processing: A retrospective commentary on a framework for memory research. *Canadian Journal of Psychology, 44*(1), 87–112.

Loewenstein, G., Rick, S., & Cohen, J. D. (2008). Neuroeconomics. *Annual Review of Psychology, 59*, 647–672. doi:10.1146/annurev.psych.59.103006.093710

Loewenstein, J. (2010). How One's Hook is baited matters for catching an analogy. In B. H. Ross (Ed.), *The psychology of learning and motivation: Advances in research and theory* (pp. 149–182). Amsterdam: Elsevier.

Loftus, E. F., & Palmer, J. C. (1974). Reconstruction of automobile destruction: An example of the interaction between language and memory. *Journal of Verbal Learning and Verbal Behavior, 13,* 585–589.

Loftus, E. F., & Pickrell, J. E. (1995). The formation of false memories. *Psychiatric Annals, 25,* 720–725.

Loftus, E. F., Coan, J. A., & Pickrell, J. E. (1996). Manufacturing false memories using bits of reality. In L. Reder (Ed.), *Implicit memory and metacognition.* Hillsdale, JN: Lawrence Erlbaum Associates.

Loftus, E. F., Loftus, G. R., & Messo, J. (1987). Some facts about 'Weapon focus'. *Law and Human Behavior, 11*(1), 55–62.

Logan, G. D. (1988). Toward an instance theory of automatization. *Psychological Review, 95*(4), 492–527.

Logan, G. D., & Cowan, W. B. (1984). On the ability to inhibit thought and action: A theory of an act of control. *Psychological Review, 91*(3), 295–327.

Logan, G. D., & Crump, J. C. (2010). Cognitive illusions of authorship reveal hierarchical error detection in skilled typists. *Science, 330,* 683–686.

Logan, G. D., & Crump, M. J. C. (2009). The left hand doesn't know what the right hand is doing: The disruptive effects of attention to the hands in skilled typewriting. *Psychological Science, 20*(10), 1296–1300.

Logan, G. D., & Zbrodoff, N. J. (2003). Subitizing and similarity: Toward a pattern-matching theory of enumeration. *Psychonomic Bulletin & Review, 10*(3), 676–682.

Logan, G. D., Taylor, S. E., & Etherton, J. L. (1999). Attention and automaticity: Toward a theoretical integration. *Psychological Research, 62,* 165–181.

Logie, R. H. (1995). *Visuo-spatial working memory.* Hove: Lawrence Erlbaum Associates.

Logie, R. H., GilHooly, K. J., & Wynn, V. (1994). Counting on working memory in arithmetic problem solving. *Memory & Cognition, 22*(4), 395–410.

Logothetis, N. K., & Schall, J. D. (1989). Neuronal correlates of subjective visual perception. *Science, 245*(4919), 761–763.

Logothetis, N. K., Pauls, J., & Poggio, T. (1995). Shape representation in the inferior temporal cortex of monkeys. *Current Biology, 5,* 552–562.

Lombardi, W. J., Andreason, P. J., Sirocco, K. Y., Rio, D. E., Gross, R. E., Umhau, J. C., & Hommer, D. W. (1999). Wisconsin Card sorting test performance following head injury: Dorsolateral fronto-striatal circuit activity predicts perseveration. *Journal of Clinical and Experimental Neuropsychology, 21*(1), 2–16. doi:10.1076/jcen.21.1.2.940

Longo, M. R. (2022). Distortion of mental body representations. *Trends in Cognitive Sciences, 26*(3), 241–254. doi:10.1016/j.tics.2021.11.005

Longo, M. R., & Haggard, P. (2010). An implicit body representation underlying human position sense. *Proceedings of the National Academy of Sciences of the United States of America, 107*(26), 11727–11732. doi:10.1073/pnas.1003483107

Lorenz, J., Hauck, M., Paur, R. C., Nakamura, Y., Zimmermann, R., Bromm, B. ... Engel, A. K. (2005). Cortical correlates of false expectations during pain intensity judgments–A possible manifestation of Placebo/Nocebo cognitions. *Brain, Behavior, and Immunity, 19*(4), 283–295. doi:10.1016/j.bbi.2005.03.010

Lorist, M. M., Boksem, M. A., & Ridderinkhof, K. R. (2005). Impaired cognitive control and reduced cingulate activity during mental fatigue. *Cognitive Brain Research, 24*(2), 199–205. doi:10.1016/j.cogbrainres.2005.01.018

Lorian, C. N., & Grisham, J. R. (2011). Clinical implications of risk aversion: An online study of risk-avoidance and treatment utilization in pathological anxiety. *Journal of Anxiety Disorders, 25*(6), 840–848. doi:10.1016/j.janxdis.2011.04.008

Lorist, M. M., & Tops, M. (2003). Caffeine, fatigue, and cognition. *Brain and Cognition, 53*(1), 82–94. doi:10.1016/s0278-2626(03)00206-9

Lotte, F., Congedo, M., Lécuyer, A., Lamarche, F., & Arnaldi, B. (2007). A review of classification algorithms for EEG-base brain-computer interfaces. *Journal of Neural Engineering, 4,* 24.

Lotze, M., & Halsband, U. (2006). Motor imagery. *Journal of Physiology: Paris, 99*(4–6), 386–395. doi:10.1016/j.jphysparis.2006.03.012

Lotze, M., Montoya, P., Erb, M., Hülsmann, E., Flor, H., Klose, U. ... Grodd, W. (1999). Activation of cortical and cerebellar motor areas during executed and imagined hand movements: An fMRI study. *Journal of Cognitive Neuroscience, 11*(5), 491–501.

Loukopoulos, L. D., Dismukes, R. K., & Barshi, I. (2009). The perils of multitasking. *Aerosafety World, 4*(8), 18–23.

Luchins, A. S. (1942). Mechanization in problem solving. *Psychological Monographs, 54*(6), 1–95.

Luck, S. J., & Hillyard, S. A. (1994). Electrophysiological correlates of feature analysis during visual search. *Psychophysiology, 31,* 291–308.

Luck, S. J., & Vogel, E. K. (1997). The capacity of visual working memory for features and conjunctions. *Nature, 390*(6657), 279–284.

Luck, S. J., Hillyard, S. A., Mouloua, M., Woldorff, M. G., Clark, V. P., & Hawkins, H. L. (1994). Effects of spatial cuing on luminance detectability: Psychophysical and electrophysiological evidence for early selection. *Journal of Experimental Psychology: Human Perception and Performance, 20*(4), 887–904.

Luck, S. J., Vogel, E. K., & Shapiro, K. L. (1996). Word meanings can be accessed but not reported during the attentional blink. *Nature, 383*(6601), 616–618.

Luna, B., Padmanabhan, A., & O'Hearn, K. (2010). What has fMRI told us about the development of cognitive control through adolescence? *Brain and Cognition, 72*(1), 101–113. doi:10.1016/j.bandc.2009.08.005

Lupyan, G., & Bergen, B. (2016). How language programs the mind. *Topics in Cognitive Science, 8*(2), 408–424. doi:10.1111/tops.12155

Lupyan, G., & Clark, A. (2015). Words and the world. *Current Directions in Psychological Science*, *24*(4), 279–284. doi:10.1177/0963721415570732

Lupyan, G., & Ward, E. J. (2013). Language can boost otherwise unseen objects into visual awareness. *Proceedings of the National Academy of Sciences of the United States of America*, *110*(35), 14196–14201.

Lupyan, G., Abdel Rahman, R., Boroditsky, L., & Clark, A. (2020). Effects of language on visual perception. *Trends in Cognitive Sciences*, *24*(11), 930–944. doi:10.1016/j.tics.2020.08.005

Luria, A. R. (1965). *The mind of a mnemonist: A little book about a vast memory*. New York, NY: Basic Books Inc. Publishers.

Luria, R., Sessa, P., Gotler, A., Jolicœur, P., & Dell'Acqua, R. (2009). Visual short-term memory capacity for simple and complex objects. *Journal of Cognitive Neuroscience*, *22*(3), 496–512.

Lyn, H. (2007). Mental representation of symbols as revealed by vocabulary errors in two bonobos (Pan paniscus). *Animal Cognition*, *10*(4), 461–475. doi:10.1007/s10071-007-0086-3

MacDonald, M. C., Pearlmutter, N. J., & Seidenberg, M. S. (1994). Lexical nature of syntactic ambiguity resolution. *Psychological Review*, *101*(4), 676–703.

Mace, J. H. (2003). Study-test awareness can enhance priming on an implicit memory task: Evidence from a word completion task. *The American Journal of Psychology*, *116*(2), 257–279.

MacGregor, J. N., Ormerod, T. C., & Chronicle, E. P. (2001). Information processing and insight: A process model of performance on the nine-dot and related problems. *Journal of Experimental Psychology: Learning, Memory, and Cognition*, *27*(1), 176–201.

Macmillan, M. (2000). Restoring Phineas Gage: A 150th retrospective. *Journal of the History of the Neurosciences*, *9*(1), 46–66. doi:10.1076/0964-704x(200004)9:1;1-2;ft046

Macoir, J., & Bernier, J. (2002). Is surface dysgraphia tied to semantic impairment? Evidence from a case of semantic dementia. *Brain and Cognition*, *48*(2–3), 452–457.

Maddox, W. T., & Asby, F. G. (1993). Comparing decision bound and exemplar models of categorization. *Perception & Psychophysics*, *53*(1), 49–70.

Maddox, W. T., & Markman, A. B. (2010). The motivation-cognition interface in learning and decision-making. *Current Directions in Psychological Science*, *19*(2), 106–110. doi:10.1177/0963721410364008

Madebach, A., Oppermann, F., Hantsch, A., Curda, C., & Jescheniak, J. D. (2011). Is there semantic interference in delayed naming? *Journal of Experimental Psychology: Learning, Memory, and Cognition*, *37*(2), 522–538. doi:10.1037/a0021970

Magnuson, J. S., & Nusbaum, H. C. (2007). Acoustic differences, listener expectations, and the perceptual accommodation of talker variability. *Journal of Experimental Psychology: Human Perception and Performance*, *33*(2), 391–409. doi:10.1037/0096-1523.33.2.391

Maguire, E. A., Frackowiak, R. S., & Frith, C. (1997). Recalling routes around London: Activation of the right hippocampus in taxi drivers. *The Journal of Neuroscience*, *17*(18), 7103–7110.

Maguire, E. A., Gadian, D. G., Johnsrude, I. S., Good, C. D., Ashburner, J., Frackowiak, R. S., & Frith, C. D. (2000). Navigation-related structural change in the hippocampi of taxi drivers. *Proceedings of the National Academy of Sciences of the United States of America*, *97*(8), 4398–4403. doi:10.1073/pnas.070039597

Maguire, E. A., Nannery, R., & Spiers, H. J. (2006). Navigation around London by a taxi driver with bilateral hippocampal lesions. *Brain*, *129*(Pt 11), 2894–2907. doi:10.1093/brain/awl286

Maguire, M. J., McClelland, M. M., Donovan, C. M., Tillman, G. D., & Krawczyk, D. C. (2012). Tracking cognitive phases in analogical reasoning with event-related potentials. *Journal of Experimental Psychology: Learning, Memory, and Cognition*, *38*(2), 273–281.

Makeig, S., Westerfield, M., Jung, T. P., Enghoff, S., Townsend, J., Courchesne, E., & Sejnowski, T. J. (2002). Dynamic brain sources of visual evoked responses. *Science*, *295*(5555), 690–694. doi:10.1126/science.1066168

Mamassian, P. (1997). Prehension of objects oriented in three-dimensional space. *Experimental Brain Research*, *114*, 235–245.

Mamede, S., Schmidt, H. G., Rikers, R. M. J. P., Custers, E. J. F. M., Splinter, T. A. W., & van Saase, J. L. C. M. (2010). Conscious thought beats deliberation without attention in diagnostic decision-making: At least when you are an expert. *Psychological Research*, *74*, 586–592.

Mamede, S., van Gog, T., Rikers, R. M. J. P., van Guldener, C., & Schmidt, H. G. (2010). Effect of availability bias and reflective reasoning on diagnostic accuracy among internal medicine residents. *Journal of the American Medical Association*, *304*(11), 1198–1203.

Mandel, D. R. (2005). Are risk assessments of a terrorist attack coherent? *Journal of Experimental Psychology: Applied*, *11*(4), 277–288. doi:10.1037/1076-898X.11.4.277

Mandel, D. R., & Vartanian, O. (2011). Frames, brains, and content domains: Neural and behavioral effects of descriptive context on preferential choice. In O. Vartanian & D. R. Mandel (Eds.), *Neuroscience of decision making*. Hove: Psychology Press.

Mandler, G. (1975). Consciousness: Respectable, useful, and probably necessary. In R. Solso (Ed.), *Information processing and consciousness*. New Jersey: Lawrence Erlbaum Associates.

Manns, J. R., Hopkins, R. O., & Squire, L. R. (2003). Semantic memory and the human hippocampus. *Neuron*, *38*, 127–133.

Marcum, J. I. (1960). A statistical theory of target detection by Pulsed Radar. *IRE Transactions on Information Theory*, vol. 6, no. 2, pp. 59-267. doi: 10.1109/TIT.1960.1057560.

Markov, N. T., Ercsey-Ravasz, M., Van Essen, D. C., Knoblauch, K., Toroczkai, Z., & Kennedy, H.

(2013). Cortical high-density counterstream architectures. *Science, 342*(6158), 1238406. doi:10.1126/science.1238406

Markovits, H., Brunet, M. L., Thompson, V., & Brisson, J. (2013). Direct evidence for a dual process model of deductive inference. *Journal of Experimental Psychology: Learning, Memory, and Cognition, 39*(4), 1213–1222. doi:10.1037/a0030906

Markowitsch, H. J., Kalbe, E., Kessler, J., von Stockhausen, H. M., Ghaemi, M., & Heiss, W. D. (1999). Short-term memory deficit after focal parietal damage. *Journal of Clinical and Experimental Neuropsychology, 21*(6), 784–797. doi:10.1076/jcen.21.6.784.853

Marois, R., Yi, D. J., & Chun, M. M. (2004). The neural fate of consciously perceived and missed events in the attentional blink. *Neuron, 41*(3), 465–472.

Marotta, J. J., Medendorp, W. P., & Crawford, J. D. (2003). Kinematic rules for upper and lower arm contributions to grasp orientation. *Journal of Neuophysiology, 90*, 3816–3827.

Marques, J. F., Raposo, A., & Almeida, J. (2013). Structural processing and category-specific deficits. *Cortex, 49*(1), 266–275. doi:10.1016/j.cortex.2011.10.006

Marr, D. (1982). *Vision: A computational investigation into the human representation and processing of visual information*. San Francisco: W. H. Freeman & Co.

Marsh, R. L., & Hicks, J. L. (1998). Event-based prospective memory and executive control of working memory. *Journal of Experimental Psychology: Learning, Memory, and Cognition, 24*(2), 336–349.

Marsh, E. J., & Tversky, B. (2004). Spinning the stories of our lives. *Applied Cognitive Psychology, 18*(5), 491–503. doi:10.1002/acp.1001

Marsh, E. J., Tversky, B., & Hutson, M. (2005). How eyewitnesses talk about events: Implications for memory. *Applied Cognitive Psychology, 19*(5), 531–544. doi:10.1002/acp.1095

Marshall, J. (2006). Jargon aphasia: What have we learned? *Aphasiology, 20*(5), 387–410. doi:10.1080/02687030500489946

Marshall, J. C., & Halligan, P. W. (1994). The Yin and the Yang of visuo-spatial neglect: A case study. *Neuropsychologia, 32*(9), 1037–1057.

Marshall, J. C., Robson, J., Pring, T., & Chiat, S. (1998). Why does monitoring fail in jargon aphasia? Comprehension, judgment, and therapy evidence. *Brain and Language, 63*, 79–107.

Marslen-Wilson, W., & Tyler, L. K. (1980). The temporal structure of spoken language understanding. *Cognition, 8*, 1–71.

Marslen-Wilson, W., & Warren, P. (1994). Levels of perceptual representation and process in lexical access: Words, phonemes, and features. *Psychological Review, 101*(4), 653–675.

Martin, D. H., & Barry, C. (2012). Writing nonsense: The interaction between lexical and sublexical knowledge in the priming of nonword spelling. *Psychonomic Bulletin & Review, 19*(4), 691–698. doi:10.3758/s13423-012-0261-7

Martin, R. C., Miller, M., & Vu, H. (2004). Lexical-semantic retention and speech production: Further evidence from normal and brain-damaged participants for a phrasal scope of planning. *Cognitive Neuropsychology, 21*(6), 625–644. doi:10.1080/02643290342000302

Martin, L. L., & Tesser, A. (1996). Some ruminative thoughts. In R. S. J. Wyer (Ed.), *Ruminative thoughts* (Vol. IX, pp. 1–49). Mahway, NJ: Lawrence Erlbaum Associates.

Massimini, M., Ferrarelli, F., Huber, R., Esser, S. K., Singh, H., & Tononi, G. (2005). Breakdown of cortical effective connectivity during sleep. *Science, 309*, 2228–2232.

Mathews, A. (2012). Effects of modifying the interpretation of emotional ambiguity. *Journal of Cognitive Psychology, 24*(1), 92–105. doi:10.1080/20445911.2011.584527

Mathews, A., & Mackintosh, B. (1998). A cognitive model of selective processing in anxiety. *Cognitive Therapy and Research, 22*(6), 539–560.

Mathôt, S., & Theeuwes, J. (2010). Evidence for the predictive remapping of visual attention. *Experimental Brain Research, 200*(1), 117–122. doi:10.1007/s00221-009-2055-3

Mathôt, S., & Theeuwes, J. (2011). Visual attention and stability. *Philosophical Transactions of the Royal Society B: Biological Sciences, 366*(1564), 516–527. doi:10.1098/rstb.2010.0187

Mathy, F., & Feldman, J. (2012). What's magic about magic numbers? Chunking and data compression in short-term memory. *Cognition, 122*(3), 346–362. doi:10.1016/j.cognition.2011.11.003

Mattson, M. E., Pollack, E. S., & Cullen, J. W. (1987). What are the odds the smoking will kill you? *American Journal of Public Health, 77*(4), 425–431.

Mattys, S. L., Brooks, J., & Cooke, M. (2009). Recognizing speech under a processing load: Dissociating energetic from informational factors. *Cognitive Psychology, 59*(3), 203–243. doi:10.1016/j.cogpsych.2009.04.001

Mattys, S. L., Davis, M. H., Bradlow, A. R., & Scott, S. K. (2012). Speech recognition in adverse conditions: A review. *Language and Cognitive Processes, 27*(7–8), 953–978. doi:10.1080/01690965.2012.705006

Mattys, S. L., White, L., & Melhorn, J. F. (2005). Integration of multiple speech segmentation cues: A hierarchical framework. *Journal of Experimental Psychology: General, 134*(4), 477–500. doi:10.1037/0096-3445.134.4.477

Matyas, F., Sreenivasan, V., Marbach, F., Wacongne, C., Barsy, B., Mateo, C. … Petersen, C. C. H. (2010). Motor control by sensory cortex. *Science, 330*, 1240–1243.

Mayberry, E. J., Sage, K., & Lambon Ralph, M. A. (2011). At the Edge of semantic space: The breakdown of coherent concepts in semantic dementia is constrained by typicality and severity, but not modality. *Journal of Cognitive Neuroscience, 23*(9), 2240–2251.

Mayer, A. R., Harrington, D., Adair, J. C., & Lee, R. (2006). The neural networks underlying endogenous auditory covert orienting and reorienting. *Neuroimage*, *30*(3), 938–949. doi:10.1016/j.neuroimage.2005.10.050

Maylor, E. A., Carter, S. M., & Hallett, E. L. (2002). Preserved olfactory cuing of autobiographical memories in old age. *Journal of Gerontology*, *57B*(1), 41–46.

Mayr, U., & Kliegl, R. (2000). Task-set switching and long-term memory retrieval. *Journal of Experimental Psychology: Learning, Memory, and Cognition*, *26*(5), 1124–1140.

Mazzone, M., & Lalumera, E. (2010). Concepts: Stored or created? *Minds and Machines*, *20*(1), 47–68. doi:10.1007/s11023-010-9184-0

McCabe, C. S., Haigh, R. C., Halligan, P. W., & Blake, D. R. (2005). Simulating sensory-motor incongruence in healthy volunteers: Implications for a cortical model of pain. *Rheumatology*, *44*(4), 509–516. doi:10.1093/rheumatology/keh529

McCaffrey, T. (2012). Innovation relies on the obscure: A key to overcoming the classic problem of functional fixedness. *Psychological Science*, *23*(3), 215–218. doi:10.1177/0956797611429580

McCarley, J. S., Kramer, A. F., Wickens, C. D., Vidoni, E. D., & Boot, W. R. (2004). Visual skills in airport-security screening. *Psychological Science*, *15*(5), 302–306.

McCarthy, M. M., McDonald, C. H., Brooks, P. J., & Goldman, D. (1996). An anxiolytic action of oxytocin is enhanced by estrogen in the mouse. *Physiology and Behavior*, *60*(5), 1209–1215.

McCarthy, R., & Warrington, E. K. (1984). A two-route model of speech production. *Brain*, *107*, 463–485.

McClelland, J. J., & Elman, J. L. (1986). The trace model of speech perception. *Cognitive Psychology*, *18*, 1–86.

McClelland, J. L., & Rumelhart, D. E. (1981). An interactive activation model of context effects in letter perception: Part 1. An account of basic findings. *Psychological Review*, *88*(5), 375–407.

McCloskey, D. I. (1978). Kinesthetic sensibility. *Phyiological Reviews*, *58*, 763–820.

McCloskey, M. (1992). Cognitive mechanisms in numerical processing: Evidence from acquired dyscalculia. *Cognition*, *44*, 107–157.

McCloskey, M., & Glucksberg, S. (1978). Natural categories: Well defined or fuzzy sets? *Memory & Cognition*, *6*(4), 462–472.

McCloskey, M., & Glucksberg, S. (1979). Decision processes in verifying category membership statements: Implications for models of semantic memory. *Cognitive Psychology*, *11*, 1–37.

McClure, S. M., Daw, N. D., & Read Montague, P. (2003). A computational substrate for incentive salience. *Trends in Neurosciences*, *26*(8), 423–428. doi:10.1016/s0166-2236(03)00177-2

McDaniel, M. A., Robinson-Riegler, B., & Einstein, G. O. (1998). Prospective remembering: Perceptually driven or conceptually driven processes? *Memory & Cognition*, *26*(1), 121–134.

McDermott, J. H. (2009). The cocktail party problem. *Current Biology*, *19*(22), R1024–R1027. doi:10.1016/j.cub.2009.09.005

McDermott, J. H., Wrobleski, D., & Oxenham, A. J. (2011). Recovering sound sources from embedded repetition. *Proceedings of the National Academy of Sciences of the United States of America*, *108*(3), 1188–1193. doi:10.1073/pnas.1004765108

McDonald, J. L. (2008). Differences in the cognitive demands of word order, plural, and subject-verb agreement constructions. *Psychonomic Bulletin & Review*, *15*(5), 980–984. doi:10.3758/PBR.15.5.980

McEachrane, M. (2009). Emotion, meaning, and appraisal theory. *Theory & Psychology*, *19*(1), 33–53. doi:10.1177/0959354308101418

McElree, B., & Dosher, B. A. (1989). Serial position and set size in short-term memory: The time course of recognition. *Journal of Experimental Psychology: General*, *118*(4), 346–373.

McEwen, B. S., & Wingfield, J. C. (2003). The concept of allostasis in biology and biomedicine. *Hormones and Behavior*, *43*(1), 2–15. doi:10.1016/s0018-506x(02)00024-7

McFadyen, J., Dolan, R. J., & Garrido, M. I. (2020). The influence of subcortical shortcuts on disordered sensory and cognitive processing. *Nature Reviews Neuroscience*, *21*(5), 264–276. doi:10.1038/s41583-020-0287-1

McGaghie, W. C., Issenberg, S. B., Petrusa, E. R., & Scalese, R. J. (2006). Effect of practice on standardised learning outcomes in simulation-based medical education. *Medical Education*, *40*(8), 792–797. doi:10.1111/j.1365-2929.2006.02528.x

McGlone, M., & Manfredi, D. A. (2001). Topic-vehicle interaction in metaphor comprehension. *Memory & Cognition*, *29*(8), 1209–1219.

McGuire, L. M., & Sabes, P. N. (2009). Sensory transformations and the use of multiple reference frames for reach planning. *Nature Neuroscience*, *12*(8), 1056–1061. doi:10.1038/nn.2357

McGurk, H., & MacDonald, J. (1976). Hearing lips and seeing voices. *Nature*, *264*(5588), 746–748.

McIntyre, J., Stratta, F., & Lacquaniti, F. (1997). Viewer-centered frame of reference for pointing to memorized targets in three-dimensional space. *Journal of Neuophysiology*, *78*, 1601–1618.

McKeefry, D. J., Burton, M. P., Vakrou, C., Barrett, B. T., & Morland, A. B. (2008). Induced deficits in speed perception by transcranial magnetic stimulation of human cortical areas V5/Mt+ and V3a. *The Journal of Neuroscience*, *28*(27), 6848–6857. doi:10.1523/JNEUROSCI.1287-08.2008

McKeefry, D. J., Watson, J. D. G., Frackowiak, R. S. J., Fong, K., & Zeki, S. (1997). The activity in human areas V1/V2, V3, and V5 during the perception of coherent and incoherent motion. *Neuroimage*, *5*, 1–12.

McKemy, D. D., Neuhausser, W. M., & Julius, D. (2002). Identification of a cold receptor reveals a general role for TRP channels in thermosensation. *Nature*, *416*, 52–58.

References

McKone, E., Kanwisher, N., & Duchaine, B. C. (2007). Can generic expertise explain special processing for faces? *Trends in Cognitive Sciences, 11*(1), 8–15. doi:10.1016/j.tics.2006.11.002

McKoon, G., & Ratcliff, R. (1992). Inference during reading. *Psychological Review, 99*(3), 440–466.

McLaughlin, K., Rikers, R. M., & Schmidt, H. G. (2007). Is analytic information processing a feature of expertise in medicine? *Advances in Health Sciences Education, 13*(1), 123–128. doi:10.1007/s10459-007-9080-4

McLeod, P. (1977). A dual task response modality effect: Support for multiprocessor models of attention. *The Quarterly Journal of Experimental Psychology, 29,* 651–667.

McMurray, B. (2022). The myth of categorical perception, *Journal of the Acoustical Society of America, 152,* 3819. https://doi.org/10.1121/10.0016614

McNamara, D. S., & Magliano, J. (2009). Toward a comprehensive model of comprehension. *Psychology of Learning and Motivation, 51,* 297–384. doi:10.1016/S0079-7421(09)51009-2

McVay, J. C., & Kane, M. J. (2009). Conducting the train of thought: Working memory capacity, goal neglect, and mind wandering in an executive-control task. *Journal of Experimental Psychology: Learning, Memory, and Cognition, 35*(1), 196–204. doi:10.1037/a0014104

Medendorp, W. P., & Heed, T. (2019). State estimation in posterior parietal cortex: Distinct poles of environmental and bodily States. *Progress in Neurobiology, 183.*

Medendorp, W. P., Goltz, H. C., Crawford, J. D., & Vilis, T. (2005). Integration of target and effector information in human posterior parietal cortex for the planning of action. *Journal of Neurophysiology, 93*(2), 954–962. doi:10.1152/jn.00725.2004

Megreya, A. M., Sandford, A., & Burton, A. M. (2013). Matching face images taken on the same day or months apart: The limitations of photo id. *Applied Cognitive Psychology, 27*(6), 700–706. doi:10.1002/acp.2965

Megreya, A. M., White, D., & Burton, A. M. (2011). The other-race effect does not rely on memory: Evidence from a matching task. *The Quarterly Journal of Experimental Psychology, 64*(8), 1473–1483. doi:10.1080/17470218.2011.575228

Meiran, N., Pereg, M., Kessler, Y., Cole, M. W., & Braver, T. S. (2015a). The power of instructions: Proactive configuration of stimulus–response translation. *Journal of Experimental Psychology: Learning, Memory, and Cognition, 41*(3), 768–786. doi:10.1037/xlm0000063

Meiran, N., Pereg, M., Kessler, Y., Cole, M. W., & Braver, T. S. (2015b). Reflexive activation of newly instructed stimulus-response rules: Evidence from lateralized readiness potentials in no-go trials. *Cognitive, Affective, & Behavioral Neuroscience, 15*(2), 365–373. doi:10.3758/s13415-014-0321-8

Melby-Lervag, M., Lyster, S. A., & Hulme, C. (2012). Phonological skills and their role in learning to read: A meta-analytic review. *Psychological Bulletin, 138*(2), 322–352. doi:10.1037/a0026744.supp

Melcher, D. (2009). Selective attention and the active remapping of object features in trans-saccadic perception. *Vision Research, 49*(10), 1249–1255. doi:10.1016/j.visres.2008.03.014

Melcher, D. (2011). Visual stability. *Philosophical Transactions of the Royal Society B-Biological Sciences, 366*(1564), 468–475. doi:10.1098/rstb.2010.0277

Melinger, A., & Abdel Rahman, R. (2013). Lexical selection is competitive: Evidence from indirectly activated semantic associates during picture naming. *Journal of Experimental Psychology: Learning, Memory, and Cognition, 39*(2), 348–364. doi:10.1037/a0028941

Mellers, B., Hertwig, R., & Kahneman, D. (2001). Do frequency representations eliminate conjunction effects? *Psychological Science, 12*(4), 2001.

Melloni, L., Molina, C., Pena, M., Torres, D., Singer, W., & Rodriguez, E. (2007). Synchronization of neural activity across cortical areas correlates with conscious perception. *The Journal of Neuroscience, 27*(11), 2858–2865. doi:10.1523/JNEUROSCI.4623-06.2007

Melloni, L., Schwiedrzik, C. M., Muller, N., Rodriguez, E., & Singer, W. (2011). Expectations change the signatures and timing of electrophysiological correlates of perceptual awareness. *The Journal of Neuroscience, 31*(4), 1386–1396. doi:10.1523/JNEUROSCI.4570-10.2011

Melo, M., Scarpin, D. J., Amaro, E. Jr., Passos, R. B., Sato, J. R., Friston, K. J., & Price, C. J. (2011). How doctors generate diagnostic hypotheses: A study of radiological diagnosis with functional magnetic resonance imaging. *PLoS One, 6*(12), e28752. doi:10.1371/journal.pone.0028752

Melzack, R. (1999). From the gate to the neuromatrix. *Pain, 82,* S121–S126.

Memon, A., Meissner, C. A., & Fraser, J. (2010). The cognitive interview: A meta-analytic review and study space analysis of the past 25 years. *Psychology, Public Policy, and Law, 16*(4), 340–372. doi:10.1037/a0020518

Menneer, T., Cave, K. R., & Donnelly, N. (2009). The cost of search for multiple targets: Effects of practice and target similarity. *Journal of Experimental Psychology: Applied, 15*(2), 125–139. doi:10.1037/a0015331

Mercier, H., & Sperber, D. (2011). Why do humans reason? Arguments for an argumentative theory. *Behavioral and Brain Sciences, 34*(2), 57–74; discussion 74–111. doi:10.1017/S0140525X10000968

Mercier, M. R., Foxe, J. J., Fiebelkorn, I. C., Butler, J. S., Schwartz, T. H., & Molholm, S. (2013). Auditory-driven phase reset in visual cortex: Human electrocorticography reveals mechanisms of early multisensory integration. *Neuroimage, 79,* 19–29. doi:10.1016/j.neuroimage.2013.04.060

Merikle, P. M., Smilek, D., & Eastwood, J. D. (2001). Perception without awareness: Perspectives from cognitive psychology. *Cognition, 79,* 115–134.

Meringer, R., & Mayer, K. M. (1895). *Versprechen Und Verlesen. Eine psychologisch-linguistische studie.* Stuttgart: Goschense.

Mervis, C. B., & Pani, J. R. (1980). Acquisition of basic object categories. *Cognitive Psychology, 12*, 496–522.

Metcalfe, J., & Wiebe, D. (1987). Intuition in insight and noninsight problem solving. *Memory & Cognition, 15*(3), 238–246.

Metzinger, T. (2017). The problem of mental action: Predictive control without sensory sheets. In T. Metzinger & W. Wiese (Eds.), *Philosophy and predictive processing* (Vol. 19). Frankfurt am Main: MIND Group.

Meyer, A. S., & Damian, M. F. (2007). Activation of distractor names in the picture-picture interference paradigm. *Memory & Cognition, 35*(3), 494–503.

Meyer, D. E., & Schvaneveldt, R. W. (1971). Facilitation in recognizing pairs of words: Evidence of a dependence between retrieval operations. *Journal of Experimental Psychology, 90*(2), 227–234.

Micheyl, C., Tian, B., Carlyon, R. P., & Rauschecker, J. P. (2005). Perceptual organization of tone sequences in the auditory cortex of awake macaques. *Neuron, 48*(1), 139–148. doi:10.1016/j.neuron.2005.08.039

Mickes, L., Seale-Carlisle, T. M., & Wixted, J. T. (2013). Rethinking familiarity: Remember/Know judgments in free recall. *Journal of Memory and Language, 68*(4), 333–349. doi:10.1016/j.jml.2013.01.001

Mifsud, N. G., Beesley, T., Watson, T. L., & Whitford, T. J. (2016). Attenuation of auditory evoked potentials for hand and eye-initiated sounds. *Biological Psychology, 120*, 61–68. doi:10.1016/j.biopsycho.2016.08.011

Migo, E. M., Mayes, A. R., & Montaldi, D. (2012). Measuring recollection and familiarity: Improving the Remember/Know procedure. *Consciousness and Cognition, 21*(3), 1435–1455. doi:10.1016/j.concog.2012.04.014

Millan, M. J. (2002). Descending control of pain. *Progress in Neurobiology, 66*, 355–474.

Miller, G. A. (1956). The magical number seven, plus or minus two: Some limits on our capacity for processing information. *Psychological Review, 63*(2), 81–97.

Miller, E. K., & Cohen, J. D. (2001). An integrative theory of prefrontal cortex function. *Annual Review of Neuroscience, 24*, 167–202. doi:10.1146/annurev.neuro.24.1.167

Miller, B. T., & D'Esposito, M. (2005). Searching for 'the top' in top-down control. *Neuron, 48*(4), 535–538. doi:10.1016/j.neuron.2005.11.002

Miller, N. E., & Kessen, M. L. (1952). Reward effects of food via stomach fistula compared with those of food via mouth. *Journal of Comparative Physiological Psychology, 45*(6), 555–564.

Mills, C. B. (1999). Digit synaesthesia: A case study using a Stroop-type test. *Cognitive Neuropsychology, 16*(2), 181–191. doi:10.1080/026432999380951

Milner, A. D., & Goodale, M. A. (2008). Two visual systems re-viewed. *Neuropsychologia, 46*(3), 774–785. doi:10.1016/j.neuropsychologia.2007.10.005

Milner, A. D., Perrett, D. I., Johnston, R. S., Benson, P. J., Jordan, T. R., Heeley, D. W. … Davidson, D. L. W. (1991). Perception and action in 'Visual form Agnosia'. *Brain, 114*, 405–428.

Milner, B. (1962). Les troubles de la memoire accompagnant des lesions hippocampiques bilaterales. In P. Passouant (Ed.), *Physiologie de L'hippocampe* (pp. 257–272). Paris: Éditions Recherche Scientifique.

Milner, B. (1963). Effects of different brain lesions on card sorting. *Archives of Neurology, 9*(1), 100–110.

Miranda, R., & Kihlstrom, J. (2005). Mood congruence in childhood and recent autobiographical memory. *Cognition & Emotion, 19*(7), 981–998. doi:10.1080/02699930500202967

Mirman, D., McClelland, J. L., Holt, L. L., & Magnuson, J. S. (2008). Effects of attention on the strength of lexical influences on speech perception: Behavioral experiments and computational mechanisms. *Cognitive Science, 32*(2), 398–417. doi:10.1080/03640210701864063

Miron, D., Duncan, G. H., & Bushnell, M. C. (1989). Effects of attention on the intensity and unpleasantness of thermal pain. *Pain, 39*, 345–352.

Mishkin, M., Ungerleider, L. G., & Macko, K. A. (1983). Object vision and spatial vision: Two cortical pathways. *Trends in Neurosciences, 6*, 414–417.

Misra, M., Guo, T., Bobb, S. C., & Kroll, J. F. (2012). When bilinguals choose a single word to speak: Electrophysiological evidence for inhibition of the native language. *Journal of Memory and Language, 67*(1). doi:10.1016/j.jml.2012.05.001

Mitchell, D. B. (2006). Nonconscious priming after 17 years: Invulnerable implicit memory? *Psychological Science, 17*(11), 925–929.

Mitroff, S. R., & Biggs, A. T. (2014). The ultra-rare-item effect: Visual search for exceedingly rare items is highly susceptible to error. *Psychological Science, 25*(1), 284–289. doi:10.1177/0956797613504221

Mitte, K. (2008). Memory bias for threatening information in anxiety and anxiety disorders: A meta-analytic review. *Psychol Bull, 134*(6), 886–911. doi:10.1037/a0013343

Miyake, A., & Friedman, N. P. (2012). The nature and organization of individual differences in executive functions: Four general conclusions. *Current Directions in Psychological Science, 21*(1), 8–14.

Miyake, A., Friedman, N. P., Emerson, M. J., Witzki, A. H., Howerter, A., & Wager, T. D. (2000). The unity and diversity of executive functions and their contributions to complex 'Frontal Lobe' tasks: A latent variable analysis. *Cognitive Psychology, 41*(1), 49–100. doi:10.1006/cogp.1999.0734

Molden, D. C. (2014). Understanding priming effects in social psychology: What is 'Social priming' and how does it occur? *Social Cognition, 32*, 1–11.

Moll, H., & Tomasello, M. (2007). Cooperation and human cognition: The Vygotskian intelligence hypothesis. *Philosophical Transactions of the Royal Society*

References

B-Biological Sciences, 362(1480), 639–648. doi:10.1098/rstb.2006.2000

Moller, J., Jansma, B. M., Rodriguez-Fornells, A., & Munte, T. F. (2007). What the brain does before the tongue slips. *Cerebral Cortex*, 17(5), 1173–1178. doi:10.1093/cercor/bhl028

Monsell, S. (2003). Task switching. *Trends in Cognitive Sciences*, 7(3), 134–140. doi:10.1016/s1364-6613(03)00028-7

Monti, M. M., & Osherson, D. N. (2012). Logic, language and the brain. *Brain Research*, 1428, 33–42. doi:10.1016/j.brainres.2011.05.061

Moors, A., & De Houwer, J. (2006). Automaticity: A theoretical and conceptual analysis. *Psychological Bulletin*, 132(2), 297–326. doi:10.1037/0033-2909.132.2.297

Moran, J., & Desimone, R. (1985). Selective attention gates visual processing in the extrastriate cortex. *Science*, 229, 782–784.

Moray, N. (1959). Attention in dichotic listening: Affective cues and the influence of instructions. *The Quarterly Journal of Experimental Psychology*, 11(1), 56–60.

Morris, C. D., Bransford, J. D., & Franks, J. J. (1977). Levels of processing versus transfer appropriate processing. *Journal of Verbal Learning and Verbal Behavior*, 16, 519–533.

Morrison, I., Lloyd, D., di Pellegrino, G., & Roberts, N. (2004). Vicarious responses to pain in anterior cingulate cortex: Is empathy a multisensory issue? *Cognitive, Affective, & Behavioral Neuroscience*, 4(2), 270–278.

Morrison, R. G., Holyoak, K. J., & Bao, T. (2001). *Working-memory modularity in analogical reasoning*. Paper presented at the Proceedings of the Annual Meeting of the Cognitive Science Society.

Morton, J. B., & Harper, S. N. (2007). What did Simon say? Revisiting the bilingual advantage. *Developmental Science*, 10(6), 719–726. doi:10.1111/j.1467-7687.2007.00623.x

Motley, M. T., & Baars, B. J. (1976). Semantic bias effects on the outcomes of verbal slips. *Cognition*, 4, 177–187.

Motley, M. T., Baars, B. J., & Camden, C. T. (1983). Experimental verbal slip studies: A review and an editing model of language encoding. *Communication Monographs*, 50(2), 79–101. doi:10.1080/03637758309390156

Mountcastle, V. B. (1997). The columnar organization of the neocortex. *Brain*, 120, 701–722.

Mountcastle, V. B., Lynch, J. C., Georgopoulos, A., Sakata, H., & Acuna, C. (1975). Posterior parietal association cortex of the monkey: Command functions for operations within extrapersonal space. *Journal of Neurophysiology*, 38(4), 871–908.

Moxley, J. H., Ericsson, K. A., Charness, N., & Krampe, R. T. (2012). The role of intuition and deliberative thinking in experts' superior tactical decision-making. *Cognition*, 124(1), 72–78. doi:10.1016/j.cognition.2012.03.005

Mueller, S. T., Seymour, T. L., Kieras, D. E., & Meyer, D. E. (2003). Theoretical implications of articulatory duration, phonological similarity, and phonological complexity in verbal working memory. *Journal of Experimental Psychology: Learning, Memory, and Cognition*, 29(6), 1353–1380. doi:10.1037/0278-7393.29.6.1353

Mulckhuyse, M., Talsma, D., & Theeuwes, J. (2007). Grabbing attention without knowing: Automatic capture of attention by subliminal spatial cues. *Visual Cognition*, 15(7), 779–788. doi:10.1080/13506280701307001

Mulder, G., & Sanders, T. J. M. (2012). Causal coherence relations and levels of discourse representation. *Discourse Processes*, 49, 501–522. doi:10.1080/0163853X.2012.692655

Munoz, D. P., & Everling, S. (2004). Look away: The anti-saccade task and the voluntary control of eye movement. *Nature Reviews Neuroscience*, 5(3), 218–228. doi:10.1038/nrn1345

Murphy, B. J. (1978). Pattern thresholds for moving and stationary gratings during smooth eye movement. *Vision Research*, 18, 521–530.

Murray, M. M., Lewkowicz, D. J., Amedi, A., & Wallace, M. T. (2016). Multisensory processes: A balancing act across the lifespan. *Trends in Neurosciences*, 39(8), 567–579. doi:10.1016/j.tins.2016.05.003

Murre, J. M. J. (1996). Tracelink: A model of amnesia and consolidation of memory. *Hippocampus*, 6, 675–684.

Musacchia, G., Arum, L., Nicol, R., Garstecki, D., & Kraus, N. (2009). Audiovisual deficits in older adults with hearing loss: Biological evidence. *Ear & Hearing*, 30(5), 505–514.

Musel, B., Kauffmann, L., Ramanoel, S., Giavarini, C., Guyader, N., Chauvin, A., & Peyrin, C. (2014). Coarse-to-fine categorization of visual scenes in scene-selective cortex. *Journal of Cognitive Neuroscience*, 26(10), 2287–2297. doi:10.1162/jocn_a_00643

Muthukrishna, M., & Henrich, J. (2019). A problem in theory. *Nature Human Behaviour*. doi:10.1038/s41562-018-0522-1

Mylopoulos, M., & Regehr, G. (2007). Cognitive metaphors of expertise and knowledge: Prospects and limitations for medical education. *Medical Education*, 41(12), 1159–1165. doi:10.1111/j.1365-2923.2007.02912.x

Mynatt, C. R., Doherty, M. E., & Tweney, R. D. (1977). Confirmation bias in a simulated research environment: An experimental study of scientific inference. *The Quarterly Journal of Experimental Psychology*, 29, 85095.

Näätänen, R. (1970). Evoked potential, EEG, and slow potential correlates of selective attention. *Acta Psychologica*, 33(C), 178–192.

Näätänen, R. (2007). The mismatch negativity: Where is the big fish? *Journal of Psychophysiology*, 21(3–4), 133–137.

Näätänen, R. (2008). Mismatch negativity (MMN) as an index of Central auditory system plasticity. *International Journal of Audiology*, 47(SUPPL. 2), S16–20.

Näätänen, R., Gaillard, A. W. G., & Mäntysalo, S. (1978). Early selective-attention effect on evoked potential reinterpreted. *Acta Psychologica*, 42, 313–329.

Näätänen, R., Paavilainen, P., Rinne, T., & Alho, K. (2007). The mismatch negativity (Mmn) in basic research of central auditory processing: A review. *Clinical Neurophysiology, 118*(12), 2544–2590. doi:10.1016/j.clinph.2007.04.026.

Naccache, L., Blandin, E., & Dehaene, S. (2002). Unconscious masked priming depends on temporal attention. *Psychological Science, 13*(5), 416–424.

Nadel, L., Hupbach, A., Gomez, R., & Newman-Smith, K. (2012). Memory formation, consolidation and transformation. *Neuroscience and Biobehavioral Reviews, 36*(7), 1640–1645. doi:10.1016/j.neubiorev.2012.03.001

Nadel, L., & Moscovitch, M. (1997). Memory consolidation, retrograde amnesia and the hippocampal complex. *Current Opinion in Neurobiology, 7,* 217–227.

Nagy, A., Eordegh, G., Paroczy, Z., Markus, Z., & Benedek, G. (2006). Multisensory integration in the basal ganglia. *European Journal of Neuroscience, 24*(3), 917–924. doi:10.1111/j.1460-9568.2006.04942.x

Nairne, J. S. (2002). Remembering over the short-term: The case against the standard model. *Annual Review of Psychology, 53,* 53–81.

Nairne, J. S., Whiteman, H. L., & Kelley, M. R. (1999). Short-term forgetting of order under conditions of reduced interference. *The Quarterly Journal of Experimental Psychology, 52A*(1), 241–251.

Nakahara, K., Hayashi, T., Konishi, S., & Miyashita, Y. (2002). Functional MRI of macaque monkeys performing a cognitive set-shifting task. *Science, 295,* 1532–1536.

Nakayama, K. (1985). Biological image motion processing: A review. *Vision Research, 25*(5), 625–660.

Nath, A. R., & Beauchamp, M. S. (2012). A neural basis for interindividual differences in the McGurk effect, a multisensory speech illusion. *Neuroimage, 59,* 781–787. doi:10.1016/j.neuroimage.2011.07.024

Navon, D. (1977). Forest before trees: The precedence of global features in visual perception. *Cognitive Psychology, 9,* 353–383.

Navon, D. (1984). Resources: A theoretical soup stone? *Psychological Review, 91*(2), 216–234.

Nee, D. E., Jonides, J., & Berman, M. G. (2007). Neural mechanisms of proactive interference-Resolution. *Neuroimage, 38*(4), 740–751.

Neely, J. H. (1977). Semantic priming and retrieval from lexical memory: Roles of inhibitionless spreading activation and limited-capacity attention. *Journal of Experimental Psychology: General, 106*(3), 226–254.

Neisser, U. (1984). Interpreting Harry Bahrick's discovery: What confers immunity against forgetting? *Journal of Experimental Psychology: General, 113*(1), 32–35.

Németh, G., Hegedüs, K., & Molnár, L. (1988). Akinetic mutism associated with bicingular lesions: Clinicopathological and functional anatomical correlates. *European Archives of Psychiatry and Neurological Sciences, 237,* 218–222.

Neugebauer, V., Li, W., Bird, G. C., & Han, J. S. (2004). The amygdala and persistent pain. *Neuroscientist, 10*(3), 221–234. doi:10.1177/1073858403261077

Newell, A., Shaw, J. C., & Simon, H. (1958). *Report on a general problem solving program.* Paper presented at the International Conference On Information Processing.

Newell, B. R., & Shanks, D. R. (2014). Unconscious influences on decision making: A critical review. *Behavioral and Brain Sciences, 37*(1), 1–19. doi:10.1017/S0140525X12003214

Newell, A., & Simon, H. A. (1972). *Human problem solving.* Englewood Cliffs, NJ: Prentice-Hall.

Newman-Norlund, R. D., van Schie, H. T., van Zuijlen, A. M., & Bekkering, H. (2007). The mirror neuron system is more active during complementary compared with imitative action. *Nature Neuroscience, 10*(7), 817–818. doi:10.1038/nn1911

Newman-Norlund, R., van Schie, H. T., van Hoek, M. E., Cuijpers, R. H., & Bekkering, H. (2010). The role of inferior frontal and parietal areas in differentiating meaningful and meaningless object-directed actions. *Brain Research, 1315,* 63–74. doi:10.1016/j.brainres.2009.11.065

Nicolas, S., & Ferrand, L. (1999). Wundt's laboratory at Leipzig in 1981. *History of Psychology, 2*(3), 194–203.

Nicolle, A., Fleming, S. M., Bach, D. R., Driver, J., & Dolan, R. J. (2011). A regret-induced status quo bias. *The Journal of Neuroscience, 31*(9), 3320–3327. doi:10.1523/JNEUROSCI.5615-10.2011

Nieder, A. (2021). The evolutionary history of brains for numbers. *Trends in Cognitive Sciences, 25*(7), 608–621. doi:10.1016/j.tics.2021.03.012

Nieder, A., & Miller, E. K. (2004). A parieto-frontal network for visual numerical information in the monkey. *Proceedings of the National Academy of Sciences of the United States of America, 101*(19), 7457–7462.

Nieuwenhuis, S., Aston-Jones, G., & Cohen, J. D. (2005). Decision making, the P3, and the locus coeruleus-norepinephrine system. *Psychological Bulletin, 131*(4), 510–532. doi:10.1037/0033-2909.131.4.510

Nieuwenhuis, S., & Monsell, S. (2002). Residual costs in task switching: Testing the failure-to-engage hypothesis. *Psychonomic Bulletin & Review, 9*(1), 86–92.

Nieuwenhuis, S., & Yeung, N. (2005). Neural mechanisms of attention and control: Losing our inhibitions? *Nature Neuroscience, 8*(12), 1631–1633.

Nieuwenstein, M. R., & van Rijn, H. (2012). The unconscious thought advantage: Further replication failures from a search for confirmatory evidence. *Judgement and Decision Making, 7*(6), 779–798.

Nieuwenstein, M. R., Wieringa, T., Morey, R. D., Wicherts, J. M., Blom, T. N., Wagenmakers, E. J., & van Rijn, H. (2015). On making the right choice: A meta-analysis and large-scale replication attempt of the unconscious thought advantage. *Judgement and Decision Making, 10*(1), 1–17.

Nieuwland, M. S., & Van Berkum, J. J. A. (2006). When peanuts fall in love: N400 evidence for the power of discourse. *Journal of Cognitive Neuroscience, 18*(7), 1098–1111.

References

Nijboer, M., Taatgen, N. A., Brands, A., Borst, J. P., & van Rijn, H. (2013). Decision making in concurrent multitasking: Do people adapt to task interference? *PLoS One*, *8*(11), e79583. doi:10.1371/journal.pone.0079583

Nikolajsen, L., Ilkær, S., Krøner, K., Christensen, J. H., & Jensen, T. S. (1997). The influence of preamputation pain on postamputation stump and phantom pain. *Pain*, *72*, 393–405.

Nir, Y., & Tononi, G. (2010). Dreaming and the brain: From phenomenology to neurophysiology. *Trends in Cognitive Sciences*, *14*(2), 88–100. doi:10.1016/j.tics.2009.12.001

Nissen, M. J., & Bullemer, P. (1987). Attentional requirements of learning: Evidence from performance measures. *Cognitive Psychology*, *19*, 1–32.

Niv, Y. (2009). Reinforcement learning in the brain. *Journal of Mathematical Psychology*, *53*(3), 139–154. doi:10.1016/j.jmp.2008.12.005

Niv, Y., Daw, N. D., Joel, D., & Dayan, P. (2007). Tonic dopamine: Opportunity costs and the control of response vigor. *Psychopharmacology*, *191*, 507–520.

Nodine, C. F., Kundel, H. L., Mello-Thoms, C., Weinstein, S. P., Orel, S. G., Sullivan, D. C., & Conant, E. F. (1999). How experience and training influence mammography expertise. *Academic Radiology*, *6*, 575–585.

Noël, M.-P., Fias, W., & Brysbaert, M. (1997). About the influence of the presentation format on arithmetical-face retrieval processes. *Cognition*, *63*, 335–374.

Nooteboom, S. G., & Quené, H. (2013). Heft hemisphere: Exchanges predominate in segmental speech errors. *Journal of Memory and Language*, *68*(1), 26–38. doi:10.1016/j.jml.2012.08.004

Nooteboom, S., & Quené, H. (2008). Self-monitoring and feedback: A new attempt to find the main cause of lexical bias in phonological speech errors. *Journal of Memory and Language*, *58*(3), 837–861. doi:10.1016/j.jml.2007.05.003

Nordgren, L. F., Bos, M. W., & Dijksterhuis, A. (2011). The best of both worlds: Integrating conscious and unconscious thought Best solves complex decisions. *Journal of Experimental Social Psychology*, *47*(2), 509–511. doi:10.1016/j.jesp.2010.12.007

Norman, G., Young, M., & Brooks, L. (2007). Non-analytical models of clinical reasoning: The role of experience. *Medical Education*, *41*(12), 1140–1145. doi:10.1111/j.1365-2923.2007.02914.x

Norris, D. (2013). Models of visual word recognition. *Trends in Cognitive Sciences*, *17*(10), 517–524. doi:10.1016/j.tics.2013.08.003

Norris, D., McQueen, J. M., & Cutler, A. (2003). Perceptual learning in speech. *Cognitive Psychology*, *47*(2), 204–238. doi:10.1016/s0010-0285(03)00006-9

Nosek, B. A., Hawkins, C. B., & Frazier, R. S. (2011). Implicit social cognition: From measures to mechanisms. *Trends in Cognitive Sciences*, *15*(4), 152–159. doi:10.1016/j.tics.2011.01.005

Nosofsky, R. M. (1986). Attention, similarity, and the identification-categorization relationship. *Journal of Experimental Psychology: General*, *115*(1), 39–57.

Nosofsky, R. M. (1988). Exemplar-based accounts of relations between classification, recognition, and typicality. *Journal of Experimental Psychology: Learning, Memory, and Cognition*, *14*(4), 700–708.

Notebaert, W., Houtman, F., Opstal, F. V., Gevers, W., Fias, W., & Verguts, T. (2009). Post-error slowing: An orienting account. *Cognition*, *111*(2), 275–279. doi:10.1016/j.cognition.2009.02.002

Nowak, D. A., & Hermsdörfer, J. (2003). Sensorimotor memory and grip force control: Does grip force anticipate a self-produced weight change when drinking with a straw from a cup? *European Journal of Neuroscience*, *18*, 2883–2892. https://doi.org/10.1111/j.1460-9568.2003.03011.x

Nowak, D. A., Glasauer, S., & Hermsdorfer, J. (2004). How predictive is grip force control in the complete absence of somatosensory feedback? *Brain*, *127*(Pt 1), 182–192. doi:10.1093/brain/awh016

Nozari, N., Dell, G. S., & Schwartz, M. F. (2011). Is comprehension necessary for error detection? A conflict-based account of monitoring in speech production. *Cognitive Psychology*, *63*(1), 1–33. doi:10.1016/j.cogpsych.2011.05.001

Oaksford, M. (1997). Thinking and the rational analysis of human reasoning. *The Psychologist*, *10*, 257–260.

Oaksford, M., & Chater, N. (2009). Precis of Bayesian rationality: The probabilistic approach to human reasoning. *Behavioral and Brain Sciences*, *32*(1), 69–84; discussion 85–120. doi:10.1017/S0140525X09000284

Oaksford, M., Chater, N., Graingers, B., & Larkin, J. (1997). Optimal data selection in the reduced array selection task (Rast). *Journal of Experimental Psychology: Learning, Memory, and Cognition*, *23*(2), 441–458.

Oberauer, K. (2002). Access to information in working memory: Exploring the focus of attention. *Journal of Experimental Psychology: Learning, Memory, and Cognition*, *28*(3), 411–421. doi:10.1037//0278-7393.28.3.411

Oberauer, K. (2005). Control of the contents of working memory–a comparison of two paradigms and two age groups. *Journal of Experimental Psychology: Learning, Memory, and Cognition*, *31*(4), 714–728. doi:10.1037/0278-7393.31.4.714

Oberauer, K., & Bialkova, S. (2009). Accessing information in working memory: Can the focus of attention grasp two elements at the Same time? *Journal of Experimental Psychology: General*, *138*(1), 64–87. doi:10.1037/a0014738

Oberauer, K., & Bialkova, S. (2011). Serial and parallel processes in working memory after practice. *Journal of Experimental Psychology: Human Perception and Performance*, *37*(2), 606–614. doi:10.1037/a0020986

Oberauer, K., & Hein, L. (2012). Attention to information in working memory. *Current Directions in Psychological Science*, *21*(3), 164–169. doi:10.1177/0963721412444727

Obhi, S. S., & Goodale, M. A. (2005). The effects of landmarks on the performance of delayed and real-time pointing movements. *Experimental Brain Research*, *167*(3), 335–344. doi:10.1007/s00221-005-0055-5

O'Brien, E. J., Cook, A. E., & Gueraud, S. (2010). Accessibility of outdated information. *Journal of Experimental Psychology: Learning, Memory, and Cognition*, *36*(4), 979–991. doi:10.1037/a0019763

O'Brien, E. J., Rizzella, M. L., Albrecht, J. E., & Halleran, J. G. (1998). Updating a situation model: A memory-based text processing view. *Journal of Experimental Psychology: Learning, Memory, and Cognition*, *24*(5), 1200–1210.

Ochsner, K. N., & Gross, J. J. (2005). The cognitive control of emotion. *Trends in Cognitive Sciences*, *9*(5), 242–249. doi:10.1016/j.tics.2005.03.010

Ochsner, K. N., & Gross, J. J. (2008). Cognitive emotion regulation. *Current Directions in Psychological Science*, *17*(2), 153–158.

Ochsner, K. N., Ray, R. R., Hughes, B., McRae, K., Cooper, J. C., Weber, J. ... Gross, J. J. (2009). Bottom-Up and top-down processing in emotion generation: Common and distinct neural mechanisms. *Psychological Science*, *20*(11), 1322–1331.

Ochsner, K. N., Silvers, J. A., & Buhle, J. T. (2012). Functional imaging studies of emotion regulation: A synthetic review and evolving model of the cognitive control of emotion. *Annals of the New York Academy of Sciences*, *1251*, E1–E24. doi:10.1111/j.1749-6632.2012.06751.x

O'Craven, K. M., Downing, P. E., & Kanwisher, N. (1999). fMRI evidence for objects as the units of attentional selection. *Nature*, *401*, 584–587.

Odinot, G., Wolters, G., & van Koppen, P. J. (2009). Eyewitness memory of a supermarket robbery: A case study of accuracy and confidence after 3 months. *Law and Human Behavior*, *33*, 506–514.

Ofshe, R. J. (1992). Inadvertent hypnosis during interrogation: False confession due to dissociative state; Mis-identified multiple personality and the satanic cult hypothesis. *International Journal of Clinical and Experimental Hypnosis*, *40*(3), 125–156. doi:10.1080/00207149208409653

Ohlsson, S. (1992). Information-processing explanations of insight and relate phenomena. In M. T. Keane & K. J. GilHooly (Eds.), *Advances in the psychology of thinking* (Vol. 1). New York, NY: Harvester Wheatsheaf.

Öhman, A., & Soares, J. J. F. (1994). 'Unconscious anxiety': Phobic responses to masked stimuli. *Journal of Abnormal Psychology*, *103*(2), 231–240.

Öhman, A., Flykt, A., & Esteves, F. (2001). Emotion drives attention: Detecting the snake in the grass. *Journal of Experimental Psychology: General*, *130*(2), 466–478. https://doi.org/10.1037/0096-3445.130.3.466

Okada, K., Matchin, W., & Hickok, G. (2017). Neural evidence for predictive coding in auditory cortex during speech production. *Psychonomic Bulletin & Review*, *25*, 423–430. doi:10.3758/s13423-017-1284-x

Okada, K., Rong, F., Venezia, J., Matchin, W., Hsieh, I. H., Saberi, K. ... Hickok, G. (2010). Hierarchical organization of human auditory cortex: Evidence from acoustic invariance in the response to intelligible speech. *Cerebral Cortex*, *20*(10), 2486–2495. doi:10.1093/cercor/bhp318

Olds, J. (1973). The discovery of reward systems in the brain. In E. S. Valenstein (Ed.), *Brain stimulation and motivation: Research and commentary* (pp. 81–99). Glenville, Il: Scott, Foresman and Company.

Olds, J., & Milner, P. (1954). Positive reinforcement produced by electrical stimulation of septal area and other regions of rat brain. *Journal of Comparative Physiological Psychology*, *47*(6), 419–427.

Olio, K. A., & Cornell, W. F. (1998). The facade of scientific documentation: A case study of Richard Ofsche's analysis of the Paul Ingram case. *Psychology, Public Policy, and Law*, *4*(4), 1182–1197.

Olivers, C. N. L., Peters, J., Houtkamp, R., & Roelfsema, P. R. (2011). Different States in visual working memory: When it guides attention and when it does not. *Trends in Cognitive Sciences*, *15*(7), 327–334. doi:10.1016/j.tics.2011.05.004

Öllinger, M., Jones, G., & Knoblich, G. (2014). The dynamics of search, impasse, and representational change provide a coherent explanation of difficulty in the nine-dot problem. *Psychological Research*, *78*(2), 266–275. doi:10.1007/s00426-013-0494-8

Olson, A. C., Romani, C., & Halloran, L. (2007). Localizing the deficit in a case of jargonaphasia. *Cognitive Neuropsychology*, *24*(2), 211–238. doi:10.1080/02643290601137017

Olsson, H., & Poom, L. (2005). Visual memory needs categories. *Proceedings of the National Academy of Sciences of the United States of America*, *102*(24), 8776–8780.

Ono, H., & Barbeito, R. (1982). The cyclopean eye vs. the sighting-dominant eye as the center of visual direction. *Perception & Psychophysics*, *32*(3), 201–210.

Ono, H., Mapp, A. P., & Howard, I. P. (2002). The cyclopean eye in vision: The new and old data continue to hit you right between the yes. *Vision Research*, *42*, 1307–1324.

Ophir, E., Nass, C., & Wagner, A. D. (2009). Cognitive control in media multitaskers. *Proceedings of the National Academy of Sciences of the United States of America*, *106*(37), 15583–15587. doi:10.1073/pnas.0903620106

Oppenheimer, D. M. (2004). Spontaneous discounting of availability in frequency judgement tasks. *Psychological Science*, *15*(2), 100–105.

Oppermann, F., Jescheniak, J. D., & Gorges, F. (2014). Resolving competition when naming an object in a multiple-object display. *Psychonomic Bulletin & Review*, *21*(1), 78–84. doi:10.3758/s13423-013-0465-5

Orban, G. A., Fize, D., Peuskens, H., Denys, K., Nelissen, K., Sunaert, S. ... Vanduffel, W. (2003). Similarities and differences in motion processing between the human and macaque brain: Evidence from fMRI. *Neuropsychologia*, *41*(13), 1757–1768. doi:10.1016/s0028-3932(03)00177-5

References

O'Regan, J. K., & Noë, A. (2001). A sensorimotor account of vision and visual consciousness. *Behavioral and Brain Sciences, 24*, 939–1031.

O'Rourke, T. B., & Holcomb, P. J. (2002). Electrophysiological evidence for the efficiency of spoken word processing. *Biological Psychology, 60*, 121–150.

Ortega, P. A., & Braun, D. A. (2013). Thermodynamics as a theory of decision-making with information-processing costs. *Proceedings of the Royal Society A: Mathematical, Physical and Engineering Sciences, 469*(2153), 20120683. doi:10.1098/rspa.2012.0683

Ortu, D., & Vaidya, M. (2013). A neurobiology of learning beyond the declarative non-declarative distinction. *Frontiers in Behavioral Neuroscience, 7*, 161. doi:10.3389/fnbeh.2013.00161

Ost, J., Vrij, A., Costall, A., & Bull, R. (2002). Crashing memories and reality monitoring: Distinguishing between perceptions, imaginations and 'False memories'. *Applied Cognitive Psychology, 16*(2), 125–134.

Otten, L. J., Henson, R. N. A., & Rugg, M. D. (2002). State-related and item-related neural correlates of successful memory encoding. *Nature Neuroscience, 5*(12), 1339–1344.

Owen, A. M., Coleman, M. R., Boly, M., Davis, M. H., Laureys, S., & Pickard, J. D. (2006). Detecting awareness in the vegetative state. *Science, 313*, 1402.

Pa, J., Wilson, S. M., Pickell, H., Bellugi, U., & Hickok, G. (2008). Neural organization of linguistic short-term memory is sensory modality-dependent: Evidence from signed and spoken language. *Journal of Cognitive Neuroscience, 20*(12), 2198–2210.

Paap, K. R., & Greenberg, Z. I. (2013). There is no coherent evidence for a bilingual advantage in executive processing. *Cognitive Psychology, 66*(2), 232–258. doi:10.1016/j.cogpsych.2012.12.002

Packard, M. G., & Knowlton, B. J. (2002). Learning and memory functions of the basal ganglia. *Annual Review of Neuroscience, 25*, 563–593. doi:10.1146/annurev.neuro.25.112701.142937

Padmala, S., & Pessoa, L. (2010). Interactions between cognition and motivation during response inhibition. *Neuropsychologia, 48*(2), 558–565. doi:10.1016/j.neuropsychologia.2009.10.017

Padmala, S., & Pessoa, L. (2011). Reward reduces conflict by enhancing attentional control and biasing visual cortical processing. *Journal of Cognitive Neuroscience, 23*(11), 3419–3432.

Pagel, B., Heed, T., & Roder, B. (2009). Change of reference frame for tactile localization during child development. *Developmental Science, 12*(6), 929–937. doi:10.1111/j.1467-7687.2009.00845.x

Palmer, C., & Krumhansl, C. L. (1990). Mental representation for musical meter. *Journal of Experimental Psychology: Human Perception and Performance, 16*(4), 728–741.

Palmer, S., & Rock, I. (1994). Rethinking perceptual organization: The role of uniform connectedness. *Psychonomic Bulletin & Review, 1*(1), 29–55.

Palva, S., & Palva, J. M. (2007). New vistas for A-frequency band oscillations. *Trends in Neurosciences, 30*(4), 150–158. doi:10.1016/j.tins.2007.02.001

Palva, S., Linkenkaer-Hansen, K., Naatanen, R., & Palva, J. M. (2005). Early neural correlates of conscious somatosensory perception. *The Journal of Neuroscience, 25*(21), 5248–5258. doi:10.1523/JNEUROSCI.0141-05.2005

Panksepp, J., & Bernatzky, G. (2002). Emotional sounds and the brain: The neuro-affective foundations of musical appreciation. *Behavioral Processes, 60*, 133–155.

Pantev, C., Engelien, A., Candia, V., & Elbert, T. (2001). Representational cortex in musicians: Plastic alterations in response to musical practice. *Annals of the New York Academy of Sciences, 930*(1), 300–314.

Pantev, C., Hoke, M., Lütkenhöner, B., & Lehnertz, K. (1989). Tonotopic organization of the auditory cortex: Pitch versus frequency representation. *Science, 246*(4929), 486–488.

Pantev, C., Oostenveld, R., Engelien, A., Roberts, L. E., & Hoke, M. (1998). Increased auditory cortical representation in musicians. *Nature, 392*, 811–814.

Pappas, Z., & Mack, A. (2008). Potentiation of action by undetected affordant objects. *Visual Cognition, 16*(7), 892–915. doi:10.1080/13506280701542185

Paré, M., Smith, A. M., & Rice, F. L. (2002). Distribution and terminal arborizations of cutaneous mechanoreceptors in the glabrous finger pads of the monkey. *Journal of Comparative Neurology, 445*(4), 347–359.

Parise, C. V., & Spence, C. (2009). 'When birds of a feather flock together': Synesthetic correspondences modulate audiovisual integration in non-synesthetes. *PLoS One, 4*(5), e5664. doi:10.1371/journal.pone.0005664

Park, H., & Rugg, M. D. (2008). Neural correlates of successful encoding of semantically and phonologically mediated inter-item associations. *Neuroimage, 43*(1), 165–172. doi:10.1016/j.neuroimage.2008.06.044

Park, J., Kim, Y., Chung, H., & Hisanaga, K. (2001). Long working hours and subjective fatigue symptoms. *Industrial Health, 39*, 250–254.

Parker, A. J. (2007). Binocular depth perception and the cerebral cortex. *Nature Reviews Neuroscience, 8*(5), 379–391. doi:10.1038/nrn2131

Parker, E. S., Cahill, L., & McGaugh, J. L. (2006). A case of unusual autobiographical remembering. *Neurocase, 12*, 35–39.

Parkinson, B. (2011). How social is the social psychology of emotion? *British Journal of Social Psychology, 50*(3), 405–413. doi:10.1111/j.2044-8309.2011.02034.x

Parks, N. A., & Corballis, P. M. (2008). Electrophysiological correlates of presaccadic remapping in humans. *Psychophysiology, 45*(5), 776–783. doi:10.1111/j.1469-8986.2008.00669.x

Parks, N. A., & Corballis, P. M. (2010). Human transsaccadic visual processing: Presaccadic remapping and postsaccadic updating. *Neuropsychologia, 48*(12), 3451–3458. doi:10.1016/j.neuropsychologia.2010.07.028

Parncutt, R. (1989). *Harmony: A psychoacoustical approach.* Berlin: Springer Verlag.

Parsons, L. M., Denton, D., Egan, G., McKinley, M., Shade, R., Lancaster, J., & Fox, P. T. (2000). Neuroimaging evidence implicating cerebellum in support of sensory/cognitive processes associated with thirst. *Proceedings of the National Academy of Sciences of the United States of America, 97*(5), 2332–2336. doi:10.1073/pnas.040555497

Pascual-Leone, A., Dang, N., Cohen, L. G., Brasil-Neto, J. P., Cammarota, A., & Hallett, M. (1995). Modulation of muscle responses evoked by transcranial magnetic stimulation during the acquisition of new fine motor skills. *Journal of Neurophysiology, 74*(3), 1037–1045.

Pashler, H. (1984). Processing stages in overlapping tasks: Evidence for a central bottleneck. *Journal of Experimental Psychology: Human Perception and Performance, 10*(3), 358–377.

Pashler, H., & Wagenmakers, E. J. (2012). Editors' introduction to the special section on replicability in psychological science: A crisis of confidence? *Perspectives on Psychological Science, 7*(6), 528–530. doi:10.1177/1745691612465253

Pashler, H., Harris, C. R., & Nuechterlein, K. H. (2008). Does the central bottleneck encompass voluntary selection of hedonically based choices? *Experimental Psychology, 55*(5), 313–321. doi:10.1027/1618-3169.55.5.313

Patel, V. L., & Groen, G. J. (1986). Knowledge based solution strategies in medical reasoning. *Cognitive Science, 10*, 91–116.

Patihis, L., Frenda, S. J., LePort, A. K., Petersen, N., Nichols, R. M., Stark, C. E. … Loftus, E. F. (2013). False memories in highly superior autobiographical memory individuals. *Proceedings of the National Academy of Sciences of the United States of America, 110*(52), 20947–20952. doi:10.1073/pnas.1314373110

Patterson, K., Nestor, P. J., & Rogers, T. T. (2007). Where do you know what you know? The representation of semantic knowledge in the human brain. *Nature Reviews Neuroscience, 8*(12), 976–987. doi:10.1038/nrn2277

Patterson, K., Vargha-Khadem, F., & Polkey, C. E. (1989). Reading with one hemisphere. *Brain, 112*, 39–63.

Paulesu, E., Harrison, J., Baron-Cohen, S., Watson, J. D. G., Goldstein, L., Heather, J. … Frith, C. D. (1995). The physiology of coloured hearing: A pet activation study of colour-word synaesthesia. *Brain, 118*, 661–676.

Paus, T., Perry, D. W., Zatorre, R. J., Worsley, K. J., & Evans, A. C. (1996). Modulation of cerebral blood flow in the human auditory cortex during speech: Role of motor-to-sensory discharges. *European Journal of Neuroscience, 8*, 2236–2246.

Payne, B. K., Cheng, C. M., Govorun, O., & Stewart, B. D. (2005). An inkblot for attitudes: Affect misattribution as implicit measurement. *Journal of Personality and Social Psychology, 89*(3), 277–293. doi:10.1037/0022-3514.89.3.277

Payne, J. W. (1976). Task complexity and contingent processing in decision making: An information search and protocol analysis. *Organizational Behavior and Human Performance, 16*, 366–387.

Payne, S. J., & Duggan, G. B. (2011). Giving up problem solving. *Memory & Cognition, 39*(5), 902–913. doi:10.3758/s13421-010-0068-6

Pea, R. D., & Kurland, D. M. (1984). On the cognitive effects of learning computer programming. *New Ideas in Psychology, 2*(2), 137–168.

Pearce, M., & Rohrmeier, M. (2012). Music cognition and the cognitive sciences. *Topics in Cognitive Science, 4*(4), 468–484. doi:10.1111/j.1756-8765.2012.01226.x

Pearce, M. T., & Wiggins, G. A. (2012). Auditory expectation: The information dynamics of music perception and cognition. *Topics in Cognitive Science, 4*(4), 625–652. doi:10.1111/j.1756-8765.2012.01214.x

Peelle, J. E., & Sommers, M. S. (2015). Prediction and constraint in audiovisual speech perception. *Cortex, 68*, 169–181. doi:10.1016/j.cortex.2015.03.006

Pellicano, E., & Burr, D. (2012). When the world becomes 'too real': A Bayesian explanation of autistic perception. *Trends in Cognitive Sciences, 16*(10), 504–510. doi:10.1016/j.tics.2012.08.009

Penaloza, A. A., & Calvillo, D. P. (2012). Incubation provides relief from artificial fixation in problem solving. *Creativity Research Journal, 24*(4), 338–344. doi:10.1080/10400419.2012.730329

Penfield, W., & Boldrey, E. (1937). Somatic motor and sensory prepresentation in the cerebral cortex of man as studied by electrical stimulation. *Brain, 60*(4), 389–443.

Penfield, W., & Faulk, M. E. (1955). The insula: Further observations on its function. *Brain, 78*(4), 445–470.

Penfield, W., & Jasper, H. H. (1954). *Epilepsy and the functional anatomy of the human brain.* Boston, MA: Little Brown.

Penfield, W., & Rasmussen, T. (1950). *The cerebral cortex of man: A clinical study of localization of function.* Oxford, England: Macmillan.

Pennycook, G., & Rand, D. G. (2021). The psychology of fake news. *Trends in Cognitive Sciences, 25*(5), 388–402. doi:10.1016/j.tics.2021.02.007

Penolazzi, B., Hauk, O., & Pulvermuller, F. (2007). Early semantic context integration and lexical access as revealed by event-related brain potentials. *Biological Psychology, 74*(3), 374–388. doi:10.1016/j.biopsycho.2006.09.008

Peretz, I., Kolinsky, R., Tramo, M., Labrecque, R., Hublet, C., Demeurisse, G., & Belleville, S. (1994). Functional dissociations following bilateral lesions of auditory cortex. *Brain, 177*, 1283–1301.

Perner, J., & Lang, B. (1999). Development of theory of mind and executive control. *Trends in Cognitive Sciences, 3*(9), 337–344.

Pessoa, L. (2009). How do emotion and motivation direct executive control? *Trends in Cognitive Sciences, 13*(4), 160–166. doi:10.1016/j.tics.2009.01.006

Pessoa, L., & Engelmann, J. B. (2010). Embedding reward signals into perception and cognition. *Frontiers in Neuroscience, 4.* doi:10.3389/fnins.2010.00017

References

Peters, D. P. (1988). Eyewitness memory and arousal in a natural setting. In M. m. Gruneberg, P. E. Morris, & R. M. Sykes (Eds.), *Memory in everyday life* (Vol. 1). Oxford: Wiley & Sons.

Petersen, S. E., & Posner, M. I. (2012). The attention system of the human brain: 20 years after. *Annual Review of Neuroscience, 35*, 73–89. doi:10.1146/annurev-neuro-062111-150525

Peterson, L. R., & Peterson, M. J. (1959). Short-term retention of individual verbal items. *Journal of Experimental Psychology, 58*(3), 193–198.

Petkov, C. I., Kayser, C., Steudel, T., Whittingstall, K., Augath, M., & Logothetis, N. K. (2008). A voice region in the monkey brain. *Neuroforum, 14*(2), 211–212.

Petrovic, P., Kalso, E., Petersson, K. M., & Ingvar, M. (2002). Placebo and opioid analgesia-imaging a shared neuronal network. *Science, 295*, 1737–1740.

Pew, R. W. (1966). Acquisition of hierarchical control over the temporal organisation of a skill. *Journal of Experimental Psychology, 71*(5), 764–771.

Pezdek, K. (2003). Event memory and autobiographical memory for the events of September 11, 2001. *Applied Cognitive Psychology, 17*(9), 1033–1045. doi:10.1002/acp.984

Pezzulo, G. (2013). Why do you fear the bogeyman? An embodied predictive coding model of perceptual inference. *Cognitive, Affective, & Behavioral Neuroscience, 14*(3), 902–911. doi:10.3758/s13415-013-0227-x

Pezzulo, G., Rigoli, F., & Friston, K. (2015). Active inference, homeostatic regulation and adaptive behavioural control. *Progress in Neurobiology, 134*, 17–35. doi:10.1016/j.pneurobio.2015.09.001

Pezzulo, G., Zorzi, M., & Corbetta, M. (2021). The secret life of predictive brains: What's spontaneous activity for? *Trends in Cognitive Sciences, 25*(9), 730–743. doi:10.1016/j.tics.2021.05.007

Pfaffman, C. (1960). The pleasure of sensation. *Psychological Review, 67*(4), 253–268.

Phelps, E. A., Ling, S., & Carrasco, M. (2006). Emotion facilitates perception and potentiates the perceptual benefits of attention. *Psychological Science, 17*(4), 292–299.

Phillips, W. J., Hine, D. W., & Thorsteinsson, E. B. (2010). Implicit cognition and depression: A meta-analysis. *Clinical Psychology Review, 30*(6), 691–709. doi:10.1016/j.cpr.2010.05.002

Phillips, M. L., Young, A. W., Scott, S. K., Calder, A. J., Andrew, C., Giampietro, V. … Gray, J. A. (1998). Neural responses to facial and vocal expressions of fear and disgust. *Proceedings of the Royal Society B-Biological Sciences, 265*, 1809–1817.

Phillips, M. L., Young, A. W., Senior, C., Brammer, M., Andrew, C., Calder, A. J. … David, A. S. (1997). A specific substrate for perceiving facial expressions of disgust. *Nature, 389*, 495–498.

Piai, V., Roelofs, A., & Schriefers, H. (2014). Locus of semantic interference in picture naming: Evidence from dual-task performance. *Journal of Experimental Psychology: Learning, Memory, and Cognition, 40*(1), 147–165. doi:10.1037/a0033745

Piazza, M., Fumarola, A., Chinello, A., & Melcher, D. (2011). Subitizing reflects visuo-spatial object individuation capacity. *Cognition, 121*(1), 147–153. doi:10.1016/j.cognition.2011.05.007

Pickel, K. L. (1999). The influence of context on the 'Weapon focus' effect. *Law and Human Behavior, 23*(3), 299–311.

Pickering, M. J., & Ferreira, V. S. (2008). Structural priming: A critical review. *Psychological Bulletin, 134*(3), 427–459. doi:10.1037/0033-2909.134.3.427

Pickering, M. J., & Garrod, S. (2004). Toward a mechanistic psychology of dialogue. *Behavioral and Brain Sciences, 27*(02). doi:10.1017/s0140525x04000056

Pickering, M. J., & Garrod, S. (2013). An integrated theory of language production and comprehension. *Behavioral and Brain Sciences, 36*(4), 329–347. doi:10.1017/S0140525X12001495

Pickering, M. J., & Traxler, M. J. (1998). Plausibility and recovery from garden paths: An eye-tracking study. *Journal of Experimental Psychology: Learning, Memory, and Cognition, 24*(4), 940–961.

Picton, T. W., Hillyard, S. A., Krausz, H. I., & Galambos, R. (1974). Human auditory evoked potentials. I: Evaluation of components. *Electroencephalography and Clinical Neurophysiology, 36*, 179–190.

Picton, T. W., Lins, O. G., & Scherg, M. (1995). The recording and analysis of event-related potentials. In F. Boller & J. Grafman (Eds.), *Handbook of neuropsychology* (Vol. 10). Amsterdam: Elsevier.

Pillai, J. A., Hall, C. B., Dickson, D. W., Buschke, H., Lipton, R. B., & Verghese, J. (2011). Association of crossword puzzle participation with memory decline in persons who develop dementia. *Journal of the International Neuropsychological Society, 17*(6), 1006–1013. doi:10.1017/S1355617711001111

Pinard, M., Chertkow, H., Black, S., & Peretz, I. (2002). A case study of pure word deafness: Modularity in auditory processing? *Neurocase, 8*, 40–55.

Pinto, Y., de Haan, E. H. F., & Lamme, V. A. F. (2017). The split-brain phenomenon revisited: A single conscious agent with Split perception. *Trends in Cognitive Sciences, 21*(11), 835–851. doi:10.1016/j.tics.2017.09.003.

Platt, J. R., & Johnson, D. M. (1971). Localisation of position within a homogeneous behavior: Effects of error contingencies. *Learning and Motivation, 2*, 386–414.

Plaut, D. C., McClelland, J. L., Seidenberg, M. S., & Patterson, K. (1996). Understanding normal and impaired word reading: Computational principles in quasi-regular domains. *Psychological Review, 103*(1), 56–115.

Ploghaus, A., Becerra, L., Borras, C., & Borsook, D. (2003). Neural circuitry underlying pain modulation: Expectation, hypnosis, placebo. *Trends in Cognitive Sciences, 7*(5), 197–200. doi:10.1016/s1364-6613(03)00061-5.

Pobric, G., Jefferies, E., & Lambon Ralph, M. A. (2010a). Amodal semantic representations depend on both anterior temporal lobes: Evidence from repetitive transcranial magnetic stimulation. *Neuropsychologia*, *48*(5), 1336–1342. doi:10.1016/j.neuropsychologia.2009.12.036

Pobric, G., Jefferies, E., & Lambon Ralph, M. A. (2010b). Category-specific versus category-general semantic impairment induced by transcranial magnetic stimulation. *Current Biology*, *20*(10), 964–968. doi:10.1016/j.cub.2010.03.070

Poldrack, R. A., Sabb, F. W., Foerde, K., Tom, S. M., Asarnow, R. F., Bookheimer, S. Y., & Knowlton, B. J. (2005). The neural correlates of motor skill automaticity. *The Journal of Neuroscience*, *25*(22), 5356–5364. doi:10.1523/JNEUROSCI.3880-04.2005

Pollatsek, A., Reichle, E. D., & Rayner, K. (2006). Tests of the E-Z reader model: Exploring the interface between cognition and eye-movement control. *Cognitive Psychology*, *52*(1), 1–56. doi:10.1016/j.cogpsych.2005.06.001

Pope, D. G., & Schweitzer, M. E. (2011). Is tiger woods loss averse? Persistent bias in the face of experience, competition, and high stakes. *The American Economic Review*, *101*(1), 129–157.

Popper, K. (1935). *Logik Der forschung*. Wien: Springer Verlag.

Porreca, F., Ossipov, M. H., & Gebhart, G. F. (2002). Chronic pain and medullary descending facilitation. *Trends in Neurosciences*, *25*(6), 319–325.

Posner, M. I. (1980). Orienting of attention. *The Quarterly Journal of Experimental Psychology*, *32*(1), 3–25.

Posner, M. I., & Cohen, Y. (1984). Components of visual orienting. *Attention and Performance*, *10*, 531–556.

Posner, M. I., & Dehaene, S. (1994). Attentional networks. *Trends in Neurosciences*, *17*(2), 75–79.

Posner, M. I., & Gilbert, C. D. (1999). Attention and primary visual cortex. *Proceedings of the National Academy of Sciences of the United States of America*, *96*(6), 2585–2587.

Posner, M. I., & Petersen, S. E. (1990). The attention system of the human brain. *Annual Review of Neuroscience*, *13*, 25–42.

Posner, M. I., Goldsmith, R., & Welton, K. E. (1967). Perceived distance and the classification of distorted patterns. *Journal of Experimental Psychology*, *73*(1), 28–38.

Postle, B. R. (2006). Working memory as an emergent property of the mind and brain. *Neuroscience*, *139*(1), 23–38. doi:10.1016/j.neuroscience.2005.06.005

Potter, J. M. (1976). Dr. Spooner and his dysgraphia. *Proceedings of the Royal Society of Medicine*, *69*, 639–648.

Potts, G. F., & Tucker, D. M. (2001). Frontal evaluation and posterior representation in target detection. *Cognitive Brain Research*, *11*(1), 147–156.

Pouget, A., Deneve, s, & Duhamel, J. R. (2002). A computational perspective on the neural basis of multisensory spatial representations. *Nature Reviews Neuroscience*, *3*, 741–747.

Power, M., & Dalgeish, T. (2008). *Cognition and emotion: From order to disorder*. Hove: Psychology Press

Powers, A. R., Kelley, III, & Corlett, M. (2016). Hallucinations as top-down effects on perception. *Biological Psychiatry: Cognitive Neuroscience & Neuroimaging*, *1*(5), 393–400. doi:10.1016/j.bpsc.2016.04.003.

Prado, J., Chadha, A., & Booth, J. R. (2011). The brain network for deductive reasoning: A quantitative meta-analysis of 28 neuroimaging studies. *Journal of Cognitive Neuroscience*, *23*(11), 3483–3497.

Prado, J., Mutreja, R., Zhang, H., Mehta, R., Desroches, A. S., Minas, J. E., & Booth, J. R. (2011). Distinct representations of subtraction and multiplication in the neural systems for numerosity and language. *Human Brain Mapping*, *32*, 1932–1947. doi:10.1002/hbm.21159

Prass, M., Grimsen, C., Konig, M., & Fahle, M. (2013). Ultra rapid object categorization: Effects of level, animacy and context. *PLoS One*, *8*(6), e68051. doi:10.1371/journal.pone.0068051

Pressnitzer, D., Suied, C., & Shamma, S. A. (2011). Auditory scene analysis: The sweet music of ambiguity. *Frontiers in Human Neuroscience*, *5*, 158. doi:10.3389/fnhum.2011.00158

Pribram, K. H. (1960). The orienting reaction: Key to brain re-presentational mechanisms. In M. A. B. Brazier (Ed.), *The central nervous system and behavior*. New York, NY: Josiah Macy Jr., Foundation.

Price, D. D. (2000). Psychological and neural mechanisms of the affective dimension of pain. *Science*, *288*, 1769–1772.

Price, M. P., Lewin, G. R., McIlwrath, S. L., Cheng, C., Xie, J., Heppenstall, P. A. … Welsh, M. J. (2000). The mammalian sodium channel BNC1 is required for normal touch sensation. *Nature*, *407*, 1007–1011.

Price, K. J., Shiffrar, M., & Kerns, K. A. (2012). movement perception and movement production in Asperger's syndrome. *Research in Autism Spectrum Disorders*, *6*(1), 391–398. doi:10.1016/j.rasd.2011.06.013.

Prior, A., & Macwhinney, B. (2009). A bilingual advantage in task switching. *Bilingualism: Language and Cognition*, *13*(02). doi:10.1017/s1366728909990526

Proske, U., & Gandevia, S. C. (2012). The proprioceptive senses: Their roles in signaling body shape, body position and movement, and muscle force. *Physiological Reviews*, *92*(4), 1651–1697. doi:10.1152/physrev.00048.2011

Prull, M. W., & Yockelson, M. B. (2013). Adult age-related differences in the misinformation effect for context-consistent and context-inconsistent objects. *Applied Cognitive Psychology*, *27*(3), 384–395. doi:10.1002/acp.2916

Pulvermüller, F. (2005). Brain mechanism linking language and action. *Nature Reviews Neuroscience*, *6*, 576–582.

Pulvermuller, F. (2013). How neurons make meaning: Brain mechanisms for embodied and abstract-symbolic semantics. *Trends in Cognitive Sciences*, *17*(9), 458–470. doi:10.1016/j.tics.2013.06.004

Pulvermüller, F., Hauk, O., Nikulin, V. V., & Ilmoniemi, R. J. (2005). Functional links between motor and language systems. *European Journal of Neuroscience*, *21*(3), 793–797. doi:10.1111/j.1460-9568.2005.03900.x

Pulvermüller, F., Lutzenberger, W., & Preissl, H. (1999). Nouns and verbs in the intact brain: Evidence from event-related potentials and high-frequency cortical responses. *Cerebral Cortex*, *9*, 497–506.

Purwins, H., Herrera, P., Grachten, M., Hazan, A., Marxer, R., & Serra, X. (2008). Computational models of music perception and cognition i: The perceptual and cognitive processing chain. *Physics of Life Reviews*, *5*(3), 151–168. doi:10.1016/j.plrev.2008.03.004

Pyc, M. A., & Rawson, K. A. (2009). Testing the retrieval effort hypothesis: Does greater difficulty correctly recalling information lead to higher levels of memory? *Journal of Memory and Language*, *60*(4), 437–447. doi:10.1016/j.jml.2009.01.004

Pyc, M. A., & Rawson, K. A. (2010). Why testing improves memory: Mediator effectiveness hypothesis. *Science*, *330*, 335.

Pynte, J., Kennedy, A., & Ducrot, S. (2004). The influence of parafoveal typographical errors on eye movements in Reading. *European Journal of Cognitive Psychology*, *16*(1–2), 178–202. doi:10.1080/09541440340000169.

Quak, M. (2017). *The influence of auditory and contextual representations on visual working memory*. Ghent, Belgium: Ghent University.

Quak, M., Langford, Z. D., London, R. E., & Talsma, D. (2018). Contralateral delay activity does not reflect behavioral feature load in visual working memory. *Biological Psychology*, *137*, 107–115. doi:10.1016/j.biopsycho.2018.07.006

Quak, M., London, R. E., & Talsma, D. (2015). A multisensory perspective of working memory. *Frontiers in Neuroscience*, *9*, 197. doi:10.3389/fnhum.2015.00197

Quigley, K. S., Kanoski, S., Grill, W. M., Barrett, L. F., & Tsakiris, M. (2021). Functions of interoception: From energy regulation to experience of the self. *Trends in Neuroscience*, *44*(1), 29–38. doi:10.1016/j.tins.2020.09.008

Quinlan, T., Loncke, M., Leijten, M., & Van Waes, L. (2012). Coordinating the cognitive processes of writing. *Written Communication*, *29*(3), 345–368. doi:10.1177/0741088312451112

Quiroga, R. Q., Reddy, L., Kreiman, G., Koch, C., & Fried, I. (2005). Invariant visual representation by single neurons in the human brain. *Nature*, *435*(7045), 1102–1107. doi:10.1038/nature03687

Race, E., Keane, M. M., & Verfaellie, M. (2011). Medial temporal lobe damage causes deficits in episodic memory and episodic future thinking not attributable to deficits in narrative construction. *The Journal of Neuroscience*, *31*(28), 10262–10269.

Radeau, M., & Bertelson, P. (1974). The after-effects of ventriloquism. *Quarterly Journal of Experimental Psychology*, *26*(1), 63–71. doi:10.1080/14640747408400388

Rafal, P. D., Posner, M. I., Friedman, J. H., Inhoff, A. W., & Bernstein, E. (1988). Orienting of visual attention in progressive supranuclear palsy. *Brain*, *111*, 267–280.

Ragert, P., Schmidt, A., Altenmüller, E., & Dinse, H. R. (2004). Superior tactile performance and learning in professional pianists: Evidence for meta-plasticity in musicians. *European Journal of Neuroscience*, *19*, 473–478. https://doi.org/10.1111/j.0953-816X.2003.03142.x

Raghunathan, R., & Pham, M. T. (1999). All negative moods are not equal: Motivational influences of anxiety and sadness on decision making. *Organizational Behavior and Human Decision Processes*, *79*(1), 56–77.

Raichle, M. E., MacLeod, A. M., Snyder, A. Z., Powers, W. J., Gusnard, D. A., & Shulman, G. L. (2001). A default mode of brain function. *Proceedings of the National Academy of Sciences of the United States of America*, *98*(2), 676–682.

Ramachandran, V. S., & Rogers-Ramachandran, D. (1996). Synaesthesia in phantom limbs induced with mirrors. *Proceedings of the Royal Society B-Biological Sciences*, *263*(1369), 377–386.

Ramachandran, V. S., Rogers-Ramachandran, D., & Stewart, M. (1992). Perceptual correlates of massive cortical reorganization. *Science*, *258*(5085), 1159–1160.

Ramadan, R. A., & Vasilakos, A. V. (2017). Brain computer interface: Control signals review. *Neurocomputing*, *223*, 36–44.

Ramnani, N., & Miall, R. C. (2004). A system in the human brain for predicting the actions of others. *Nature Neuroscience*, *7*(1), 85–90. doi:10.1038/nn1168

Ranzini, M., Dehaene, S., Piazza, M., & Hubbard, E. (2009). Neural mechanisms of attentional shifts due to irrelevant spatial and numerical cues. *Neuropsychologia*, *47*(12), 2615–2624. doi:10.1016/j.neuropsychologia.2009.05.011

Rao, R. P. N., & Ballard, D. H. (1999). Predictive coding in the visual cortex: A functional interpretation of some extra-classical receptive-field effects. *Nature Neuroscience*, *2*(1), 79–87.

Rao, S. M., Binder, J. R., Bandettini, P. A., Hammeke, T. A., Yetin, F. Z., Jesmanowicz, A. ... Hyde, J. S. (1993). Functional magnetic resonance imaging of complex human movements. *Neurology*, *43*, 2311–2318.

Rao, S., Bobholz, J. A., Hammeke, T. A., Rosen, A. C., Woodley, S. J., Cunningham, J. M. ... Binder, J. R. (1997). Functional MRI evidence for subcortical participation in conceptual reasoning skills. *Neuroreport*, *8*, 1987–1993.

Rapp, B., & Dufor, O. (2011). The neurotopography of written word production: An fMRI investigation of the distribution of sensitivity to length and frequency. *Journal of Cognitive Neuroscience*, *23*(12), 4067–4081.

Rapp, B., & Goldrick, M. (2004). Feedback by any other name is still interactivity: A reply to roelofs (2004). *Psychological Review*, *111*(2), 573–578. doi:10.1037/0033-295x.111.2.573

Rapp, B., Epstein, C., & Tainturier, M. J. (2002). The integration of information across lexical and sublexical processes in spelling. *Cognitive Neuropsychology*, *19*(1), 1–29. doi:10.1080/0264329014300060

Rapp, B., & Lipka, K. (2011). The literate brain: The relationship between spelling and Reading. *Journal of Cognitive Neuroscience, 23*(5), 1180–1197.

Rasmussen, J. (1983). Skills, rules, and knowledge; Signals, signs, and symbols, and other distinctions in human performance models. *IEEE Transactions, Man and Cybernetics, SMC-13*(3), 257–266.

Rastle, K., & Brysbaert, M. (2006). Masked phonological priming effects in English: Are they real? Do they matter? *Cognitive Psychology, 53*(2), 97–145. doi:10.1016/j.cogpsych.2006.01.002

Ratcliff, R., & McKoon, G. (2008). The diffusion decision model: Theory and data for two-choice decision tasks. *Neural Computation, 20*, 873–922.

Rau, H., Elbert, T., Geiger, B., & Lutzenberger, W. (1992). Pres: The controlled noninvasive stimulation of the carotid baroreceptors in humans. *Psychophysiology, 29*(2), 164–172.

Rauschecker, J. P. (2015). Auditory and visual cortex of primates: A comparison of two sensory systems. *European Journal of Neuroscience, 41*(5), 579–585. doi:10.1111/ejn.12844

Rauschecker, J. P., & Scott, S. K. (2009). Maps and streams in the auditory cortex: Nonhuman primates illuminate human speech processing. *Nature Neuroscience, 12*(6), 718–724. doi:10.1038/nn.2331

Rauss, K., Pourtois, G., Vuilleumier, P., & Schwartz, S. (2011). Effects of attentional load on early visual processing depend on stimulus timing. *Human Brain Mapping, 33*, 63–74. doi:10.1002/hbm.21193

Raveh, D., & Lavie, N. (2015). Load-induced inattentional deafness. *Attention, Perception & Psychophysics, 77*(2), 483–492. doi:10.3758/s13414-014-0776-2

Raymer, A. M. (2001). Acquired language disorders. *Topics in Language Disorders, 21*(3), 42–59.

Rayner, K. (2014). The gaze-contingent moving window in reading: Development and review. *Visual Cognition, 22*(3–4), 242–258. doi:10.1080/13506285.2013.879084

Rayner, K., & Sereno, S. C. (1994). Regressive eye movements and sentence parsing: On the use of regression-contingent analyses. *Memory & Cognition, 22*(3), 281–285.

Reason, J. (1995). Understanding adverse events: Human factors. *Quality in Health Care, 4*, 80–89.

Reber, A. S. (1993). *Implicit learning and tacit knowledge: An essay on the cognitive unconscious.* Oxford: Oxford University Press.

Reber, P. J., Knowlton, B. J., & Squire, L. R. (1996). Dissociable properties of memory systems: Differences in the flexibility of declarative and nondeclarative knowledge. *Behavioral Neuroscience, 110*, 861–871.

Recanzone, G. H., & Sutter, M. L. (2008). The biological basis of audition. *Annual Review of Psychology, 59*, 119–142. doi:10.1146/annurev.psych.59.103006.093544

Reddy, L., Tsuchiya, N., & Serre, T. (2010). Reading the mind's eye: Decoding category information during mental imagery. *Neuroimage, 50*(2), 818–825. doi:10.1016/j.neuroimage.2009.11.084

Redelmeier, D. A., Koehler, D. J., Liberman, V., & Tversky, A. (1995). Probability judgment in medicine: Discounting unspecified possibilities. *Medical Decision Making, 15*, 227–230.

Reed, S. K. (1972). Pattern recognition and categorization. *Cognitive Psychology, 3*, 382–407.

Reicher, G. M. (1969). Perceptual recognition as a function of meaningfulness of stimulus material. *Journal of Experimental Psychology, 81*(2), 275–280.

Reichle, E. D., Pollatsek, A., Fisher, D. L., & Rayner, K. (1998). Toward a model of eye movement control in Reading. *Psychological Review, 105*(1), 125–157.

Reichle, E. D., Rayner, K., & Pollatsek, A. (2003). The E-Z reader model of eye-movement control in Reading: Comparisons to other models. *Behavioral and Brain Sciences, 26*(04). doi:10.1017/s0140525x03000104

Reingold, E. M., Reichle, E. D., Glaholt, M. G., & Sheridan, H. (2012). Direct lexical control of eye movements in Reading: Evidence from a survival analysis of fixation durations. *Cognitive Psychology, 65*(2), 177–206. doi:10.1016/j.cogpsych.2012.03.001

Remez, R. E., Rubin, P. E., Pisoni, D. B., & Carrell, T. D. (1981). Speech perception without traditional speech cues. *Science, 212*, 947–950.

Rensink, R. A., O'Regan, J. K., & Clark, J. J. (1997). To see or not to see: The need for attention to perceive changes in scenes. *Psychological Science, 8*(5), 368–373.

Reuter-Lorenz, P. A., & Park, D. C. (2014). How does it STAC up? Revisiting the scaffolding theory of aging and cognition. *Neuropsychology Review, 24*(3), 355–370. doi:10.1007/s11065-014-9270-9

Reverberi, C., Bonatti, L. L., Frackowiak, R. S., Paulesu, E., Cherubini, P., & Macaluso, E. (2012). Large scale brain activations predict reasoning profiles. *Neuroimage, 59*(2), 1752–1764. doi:10.1016/j.neuroimage.2011.08.027

Reverberi, C., Cherubini, P., Rapisarda, A., Rigamonti, E., Caltagirone, C., Frackowiak, R. S. J. … Paulesu, E. (2007). Neural basis of generation of conclusions in elementary deduction. *Neuroimage, 38*(4), 752–762.

Ricci, J. A., Chee, E., Lorandeau, A. L., & Berger, J. (2007). Fatigue in the U.S. workforce: Prevalence and implications for lost productive work time. *Journal of Occupational and Environmental Medicine, 49*(1), 1–10.

Ricco, R. B. (2007). Individual differences in the analysis of informal reasoning fallacies. *Contemporary Educational Psychology, 32*(3), 459–484. doi:10.1016/j.cedpsych.2007.01.001

Richardson, M. J., Marsh, K. L., & Baron, R. M. (2007). Judging and actualizing intrapersonal and interpersonal affordances. *Journal of Experimental Psychology: Human Perception and Performance, 33*(4), 845–859.

Richler, J. J., Cheung, O. S., & Gauthier, I. (2011). Holistic processing predicts face recognition. *Psychological Science, 22*(4), 464–471. doi:10.1177/0956797611401753

References

Riddoch, G. (1917). Dissociation of visual perceptions due to occipital injuries with especial reference to appreciation of movement. *Brain, 40*, 15–57.

Rilling, J. K., Gutman, D. A., Zeh, T. R., Pagnoni, G., Berns, G. S., & Kilts, C. D. (2002). A neural basis for social cooperation. *Neuron, 35*, 395–405.

Rilling, J. K., King-Casas, B., & Sanfey, A. G. (2008). The neurobiology of social decision-making. *Current Opinion in Neurobiology, 18*(2), 159–165. doi:10.1016/j.conb.2008.06.003

Rinck, M., & Becker, E. S. (2005). A comparison of attentional biases and memory biases in women with social phobia and major depression. *Journal of Abnormal Psychology, 114*(1), 62–74. doi:10.1037/0021-843X.114.1.62

Rinck, M., & Weber, U. (2003). Who when where: An experimental test of the event-indexing model. *Memory & Cognition, 31*(8), 1284–1292.

Rips, L. J., Shoben, E. J., & Smith, E. E. (1973). Semantic distance and the verification of semantic relations. *Journal of Verbal Learning and Verbal Behavior, 12*, 1–20.

Ritov, I., & Baron, J. (1990). Reluctance to vaccinate: Omission bias and ambiguity. *Journal of Decision Making, 3*, 263–277.

Ritter, A., Franz, M., Dietrich, C., Miltner, W. H., & Weiss, T. (2013). Human brain stem structures respond differentially to noxious heat. *Frontiers in Human Neuroscience, 7*, 530. doi:10.3389/fnhum.2013.00530

Rizzolatti, G., & Fabbri-Destro, M. (2010). Mirror neurons: From discovery to autism. *Experimental Brain Research, 200*(3-4), 223–237. doi:10.1007/s00221-009-2002-3

Rizzolatti, G., Fadiga, L., Gallese, V., & Fogassi, L. (1996). Premotor cortex and the recognition of motor actions. *Cognitive Brain Research, 3*, 131–141.

Rizzolatti, G., Riggio, L., Dascola, I., & Umilta, C. (1987). Reorienting attention across the horizontal and vertical meridians: Evidence in favor of a premotor theory of attention. *Neuropsychologia, 25*(1a), 31–40.

Rizzolatti, G., Scandolara, C., Matelli, M., & Gentilucci, M. (1981). Afferent properties of periarcuate neurons in macaque monkeys. II. Visual responses. *Behavioral Brain Research, 2*, 147–163.

Roach, N. W., Heron, J., & McGraw, P. V. (2006). Resolving multisensory conflict: A strategy for balancing the costs and benefits of audio-visual integration. *Proceedings of the Royal Society B-Biological Sciences, 273*(1598), 2159–2168. doi:10.1098/rspb.2006.3578

Robbins, T. W., Anderson, E. J., Barker, D. R., Bradley, A. C., Fearnyhough, C., Henson, R. … Baddeley, A. D. (1996). Working memory in chess. *Memory & Cognition, 24*(1), 83–93.

Roberts, B., & Bailey, P. J. (1996). Regularity of spectral pattern and its effect on the perceptual fusion of harmonics. *Perception & Psychophysics, 58*(2), 289–299.

Robertson, D., Davies, I., & Davidoff, J. (2000). Color categories are not universal: Replication and new evidence from a Stone-age culture. *Journal of Experimental Psychology: General, 129*(3), 369–398.

Robertson, E. M. (2012). New insights in human memory interference and consolidation. *Current Biology, 22*(2), R66–71. doi:10.1016/j.cub.2011.11.051

Robertson, E. M., Tormos, J. M., Maeda, F., & Pascual-Leone, A. (2001). The role of the dorsolateral prefrontal cortex during sequence learning is specific for spatial information. *Cerebral Cortex, 11*(7), 628–635.

Robinson, A. L., Heaton, R. K., Lehman, R. A. W., & Stilson, D. W. (1980). The utility of the Wisconsin card sorting test in detecting and localizing frontal lobe lesions. *Journal of Consulting and Clinical Psychology, 48*(5), 605–614.

Robson, J., Pring, T., Marshall, J., & Chiat, S. (2003). Phoneme frequency effects in jargon aphasia: A phonological investigation of nonword errors. *Brain and Language, 85*(1), 109–124. doi:10.1016/s0093-934x(02)00503-5

Rodriguez, E., George, N., Lachaux, J. -P., Martinerie, J., Renault, B., & Varela, F. J. (1999). Perception's shadow: Long-distance synchronization of human brain activity. *Nature, 397*, 430–433.

Roe, A. W., Chelazzi, L., Connor, C. E., Conway, B. R., Fujita, I., Gallant, J. L. … Vanduffel, W. (2012). Toward a unified theory of visual area V4. *Neuron, 74*(1), 12–29. doi:10.1016/j.neuron.2012.03.011

Roediger, H. L. (2010). Reflections on intersections between cognitive and social psychology: A personal exploration. *European Journal of Social Psychology. 40*(2), 189–205. doi:10.1002/ejsp.736

Roediger, H. L. I., & Karpicke, J. D. (2006). Test-enhanced learning: Taking memory tests improves long-term retention. *Psychological Science, 17*(3), 249–255.

Roediger, H. L., & McDermott, K. B. (1995). Creating false memories: Remembering words not presented in lists. *Journal of Experimental Psychology: Learning, Memory, and Cognition, 21*(4), 803–814.

Roelfsema, P. R., Lamme, V. A. F., & Spekreijse, H. (1998). Object-based attention in the primary visual cortex of the macaque monkey. *Nature, 395*(6700), 376–381.

Roepstorff, A., & Frith, C. (2004). What's at the top in the top-down control of action? Script-sharing and? top-top? control of action in cognitive experiments. *Psychological Research, 68*(2-3), 189–198. doi:10.1007/s00426-003-0155-4

Roets, A., Schwartz, B., & Guan, Y. (2012). The tyranny of choice: A cross-cultural investigation of maximizing-satisficing effects on well-being. *Judgement and Decision Making, 7*(6), 689–704.

Rogalsky, C., Raphel, K., Tomkovicz, V., O'Grady, L., Damasio, H., Bellugi, U., & Hickok, G. (2013). Neural basis of action understanding: Evidence from sign language aphasia. *Aphasiology, 27*(9), 1147–1158. doi:10.1080/02687038.2013.812779

Rogalsky, C., Rong, F., Saberi, K., & Hickok, G. (2011). Functional anatomy of language and music perception: Temporal and structural factors investigated using functional magnetic resonance imaging. *The Journal of Neuroscience, 31*(10), 3843–3852. doi:10.1523/JNEUROSCI.4515-10.2011

Rogers, B., & Graham, M. (1979). Motion parallax as an independent cue for depth perception. *Perception, 8,* 125–134.

Rogers, R. D., & Monsell, S. (1995). Costs of a predictable switch between simple cognitive tasks. *Journal of Experimental Psychology: General, 124*(2), 207–231.

Rogers, R. D., Andrews, T. C., Grasby, P. M., Brooks, D. J., & Robbins, T. W. (2000). Contrasting cortical and subcortical activations produced by attentional-set shifting and reversal learning in humans. *Journal of Cognitive Neuroscience, 12*(1), 142–162.

Rogers, T. T., & Patterson, K. (2007). Object categorization: Reversals and explanations of the basic-level advantage. *Journal of Experimental Psychology: General, 136*(3), 451–469. doi:10.1037/0096-3445.136.3.451

Roggeman, C., Klingberg, T., Feenstra, H. E., Compte, A., & Almeida, R. (2014). Trade-off between capacity and precision in visuospatial working memory. *Journal of Cognitive Neuroscience, 26*(2), 211–222. doi:10.1162/jocn_a_00485

Rohrmeier, M. A., & Koelsch, S. (2012). Predictive information processing in music cognition. A critical review. *International Journal of Psychophysiology, 83*(2), 164–175. doi:10.1016/j.ijpsycho.2011.12.010

Rolfs, M., Jonikaitis, D., Deubel, H., & Cavanagh, P. (2011). Predictive remapping of attention across eye movements. *Nature Neuroscience, 14*(2), 252–256. doi:10.1038/nn.2711

Romanski, L. M., & Averbeck, B. B. (2009). The primate cortical auditory system and neural representation of conspecific vocalizations. *Annual Review of Neuroscience, 32,* 315–346. doi:10.1146/annurev.neuro.051508.135431

Roorda, A., & Williams, D. R. (1999). The arrangement of the three cone classes in the living human eye. *Nature, 397,* 520–522.

Rosch, E. (1973). Natural categories. *Cognitive Psychology, 4,* 328–350.

Rosch, E., & Mervis, C. B. (1975). Family resemblances: Studies in the internal structure of categories. *Cognitive Psychology, 7,* 573–605.

Rosch, E., Mervis, C. B., Gray, W. D., Johnson, D. M., & Boyes-Braem, P. (1976). Basic object in natural categories. *Cognitive Psychology, 8,* 382–439.

Rose, J. E., Brugge, J. F., Anderson, D. J., & Hind, J. E. (1967). Phase-locked response to low-frequency tones in single auditory nerve fibers of the squirrel monkey. *Journal of Neurophysiology, 30*(4), 769–793.

Rosenbaum, D. A., Carlson, R. A., & Gilmore, R. O. (2001). Acquisition of intellectual and perceptual-motor skills. *Annual Review of Psychology, 52,* 453–470.

Rosenbaum, D. A., Inhoff, A. W., & Gordon, A. M. (1984). Choosing between movement sequences: A hierarchical editor model. *Journal of Experimental Psychology: General, 113*(3), 372–393.

Rosenfeld, J. P., Soskins, M., Bosh, G., & Ryan, A. (2004). Simple, effective countermeasures to P300-based tests of detection of concealed information. *Psychophysiology, 41*(2), 205–219. doi:10.1111/j.1469-8986.2004.00158.x

Rosenholtz, R., Huang, J., & Ehinger, K. A. (2012). Rethinking the role of top-down attention in vision: Effects attributable to a lossy representation in peripheral vision. *Frontiers in Psychology, 3,* 13. doi:10.3389/fpsyg.2012.00013

Ross, D. F., Ceci, S. J., Dunning, D., & Toglia, M. P. (1994). Unconscious transference and mistaken identity: When a witness misidentifies a familiar but innocent person. *Journal of Applied Psychology, 79*(6), 918–930.

Ross, L. A., Molholm, S., Blanco, D., Gomez-Ramirez, M., Saint-Amour, D., & Foxe, J. J. (2011). The development of multisensory speech perception continues into the late childhood years. *European Journal of Neuroscience, 33*(12), 2329–2337. doi:10.1111/j.1460-9568.2011.07685.x

Ross, L. A., Saint-Amour, D., Leavitt, V. M., Molholm, S., Javitt, D. C., & Foxe, J. J. (2007). Impaired multisensory processing in schizophrenia: Deficits in the visual enhancement of speech comprehension under noisy environmental conditions. *Schizophrenia Research, 97*(1–3), 173–183. doi:10.1016/j.schres.2007.08.008

Rossetti, Y., Pisella, L., & McIntosh, R. D. (2017). Rise and fall of the two visual systems theory. *Annals of Physical and Rehabilitation Medicine, 60*(3), 130–140. doi:10.1016/j.rehab.2017.02.002

Rossion, B., & Curran, T. (2010). Visual expertise with pictures of cars correlates with RT magnitude of the car inversion effect. *Perception, 39*(2), 173–183. doi:10.1068/p6270

Rouw, R., & Scholte, H. S. (2007). Increased structural connectivity in grapheme-color synesthesia. *Nature Neuroscience, 10,* 792–297.

Rowland, B., Stanford, T., & Stein, B. (2007). A Bayesian model unifies multisensory spatial localization with the physiological properties of the superior colliculus. *Experimental Brain Research, 180*(1), 153–161. doi:10.1007/s00221-006-0847-2

Roy, J. E., & Cullen, K. E. (2001). Selective processing of vestibular reafference during self-generate head motion. *The Journal of Neuroscience, 21*(6), 2131–2141.

Roy, C. S., & Sherrington, C. S. (1890). On the regulation of the blood-supply of the brain. *The Journal of Physiology, 11*(1–2), 85–158.

Rubia, K., Smith, A. B., Woolley, J., Nosarti, C., Heyman, I., Taylor, E., & Brammer, M. (2006). Progressive increase of frontostriatal brain activation from childhood to adulthood during event-related tasks of cognitive control. *Human Brain Mapping, 27*(12), 973–993. doi:10.1002/hbm.20237

Rubin, D. C., & Berntsen, D. (2003). Life scripts help to maintain autobiographical memories of highly positive, but not highly negative, events. *Memory & Cognition, 31*(1), 1–14.

References

Rubin, D. C., Rahhal, T. A., & Poon, L. W. (1998). Things learned in early adulthood are remembered best. *Memory & Cognition, 26*(1), 3–19.

Rubin, D. C., & Wenzel, A. E. (1996). One hundred years of forgetting: A quantitative description of retention. *Psychological Review, 103*(4), 734–760.

Ruge, H., & Wolfensteller, U. (2010). Rapid formation of pragmatic rule representations in the human brain during instruction-based learning. *Cerebral Cortex, 20*(7), 1656–1667. doi:10.1093/cercor/bhp228.

Ruitenberg, M. F., Verwey, W. B., Schutter, D. J., & Abrahamse, E. L. (2014). Cognitive and neural foundations of discrete sequence skill: A TMS study. *Neuropsychologia, 56,* 229–238. doi:10.1016/j.neuropsychologia.2014.01.014

Rumelhart, D. E., & Ortony, A. (1977). The representation of knowledge in memory. In R. C. Anderson, R. J. Spiro, & W. E. Montague (Eds.), *Schooling and the acquisition of knowledge.* Hillsdale, NJ: Lawrence Erlbaum Associates.

Rushton, S. K., & Wann, J. P. (1999). Weighted combination of size and disparity: A computational model for timing a ball catch. *Nature Neuroscience, 2*(2), 186–190.

Rushworth, M. F., Walton, M. E., Kennerley, S. W., & Bannerman, D. M. (2004). Action sets and decisions in the medial frontal cortex. *Trends in Cognitive Sciences, 8*(9), 410–417. doi:10.1016/j.tics.2004.07.009.

Russell, J. A. (1980). A circumplex model of affect. *Journal of Personality and Social Psychology, 39*(6), 1161–1178.

Russell, R. L., & Ginsburg, H. P. (1984). Cognitive analysis of children's mathematics difficulties. *Cognition and Instruction, 1*(2), 217–244. doi:10.1207/s1532690xci0102_3

Russo, N., Foxe, J. J., Brandwein, A. B., Altschuler, T., Gomes, H., & Molholm, S. (2010). Multisensory processing in children with autism: High-density electrical mapping of auditory-somatosensory integration. *Autism Research, 3*(5), 253–267. doi:10.1002/aur.152

Rusting, C. L., & DeHart, T. (2000). Retrieving positive memories to regulate negative mood: Consequences for mood-congruent memory. *Journal of Personality and Social Psychology, 78*(4), 737–752.

Ryan, J. D., Althoff, R. R., Whitlow, S., & Cohen, N. J. (2000). Amnesia is a deficit in relational memory. *Psychological Science, 11*(6), 454–461.

Sack, A. T., Hubl, D., Prvulovic, D., Formisano, E., Jandl, M., Zanella, F. E. … Linden, D. E. J. (2002). The experimental combination of RTMS and fMRI reveals the functional relevance of parietal cortex for visuospatial functions. *Cognitive Brain Research, 13,* 85–93.

Sacks, H., Schegloff, E. A., & Jefferson, G. (1974). A simplest systematics for the organization of turn-taking for conversation. *Language, 50*(4), 696–735.

Sadato, N., Pascual-Leone, A., Grafman, J., Ibanez, V., Deiber, M.-P., Dold, G., & Hallett, M. (1996). Activation of the primary visual cortex by braille reading in blind subjects. *Nature, 380,* 526–528.

Sadeh, T., Shohamy, D., Levy, D. R., Reggev, N., & Maril, A. (2011). Cooperation between the hippocampus and the striatum during episodic encoding. *Journal of Cognitive Neuroscience, 23*(7).

Sakai, K. (2008). Task set and prefrontal cortex. *Annual Review of Neuroscience, 31,* 219–245. doi:10.1146/annurev.neuro.31.060407.125642

Salamone, J. D. (2006). Will the last person who uses the term 'Reward' please turn out the lights? Comments on processes related to reinforcement, learning, motivation and effort. *Addiction Biology, 11,* 43–44. https://doi.org/10.1111/j.1369-1600.2006.00011.x

Salamone, J. D., & Correa, M. (2012). The mysterious motivational functions of mesolimbic dopamine. *Neuron, 76*(3), 470–485. doi:10.1016/j.neuron.2012.10.021

Salemink, E., Hertel, P., & Mackintosh, B. (2010). Interpretation training influences memory for prior interpretations. *Emotion, 10*(6), 903–907. doi:10.1037/a0020232

Saling, L. L., & Phillips, J. G. (2007). Automatic behaviour: Efficient not mindless. *Brain Research Bulletin, 73*(1–3), 1–20. doi:10.1016/j.brainresbull.2007.02.009

Salvucci, D. D., & Taatgen, N. A. (2008). Threaded cognition: An integrated theory of concurrent multitasking. *Psychological Review, 115*(1), 101–130. doi:10.1037/0033-295X.115.1.101

Salzman, C. D., Britten, K. H., & Newsome, W. T. (1990). Cortical microstimulation influences perceptual judgements of motion direction. *Nature, 346,* 174–177.

Samuel, A. G. (2011). Speech perception. *Annual Review of Psychology, 62,* 49–72. doi:10.1146/annurev.psych.121208.131643

Samuelson, W., & Zeckhauser, R. (1988). Status quo bias in decision making. *Journal of Risk and Uncertainty, 1,* 7–59.

Sanes, J. N., & Donoghue, J. P. (2000). Plasticity and primary motor cortex. *Annual Review of Neuroscience, 2*(3), 393–415.

Sanghas, A., Kita, S., & Özyürek, A. (2004). Children creating core properties of language: Evidence from an emerging sign language in Nicaragua. *Science, 305,* 1779–1782.

Santens, S., & Gevers, W. (2008). The SNARC effect does not imply a mental number line. *Cognition, 108*(1), 263–270. doi:10.1016/j.cognition.2008.01.002

Sarter, M., & Bruno, J. P. (1999). Cortical cholinergic inputs mediating arousal, attentional processing and dreaming: Differential afferent regulation of the basal forebrain by telencephalic and brainstem afferents. *Neuroscience, 95*(4), 933–952.

Sasai, S., Boly, M., Mensen, A., & Tononi, G. (2016). Functional split brain in a driving/listening paradigm. *Proceedings of the National Academy of Sciences of the United States of America, 113*(50), 14444–14449. doi:10.1073/pnas.1613200113

Sato, Y., Toyoizumi, T., & Aihara, K. (2007). Bayesian inference explains perception of unity and ventriloquism aftereffect: Identification of common sources of audio-visual stimuli. *Neural Computation*, *19*, 3335–3355.

Satterthwaite, T. D., Wolf, D. H., Erus, G., Ruparel, K., Elliott, M. A., Gennatas, E. D. … Gur, R. E. (2013). Functional maturation of the executive system during adolescence. *The Journal of Neuroscience*, *33*(41), 16249–16261. doi:10.1523/JNEUROSCI.2345-13.2013

Saunders, J. A., & Knill, D. C. (2003). Humans use continuous visual feedback from the hand to control fast reaching movements. *Experimental Brain Research*, *152*(3), 341–352. doi:10.1007/s00221-003-1525-2

Saunders, J. A., & Knill, D. C. (2004). Visual feedback control of hand movements. *Journal of Neuroscience*, *24*(13), 3223–3234. doi:10.1523/JNEUROSCI.4319-03.2004

Savelsbergh, G. J. P., Whiting, H. T. A., Pijpers, J. R., & van Santvoord, A. A. M. (1993). The visual guidance of catching. *Experimental Brain Research*, *93*, 148–156.

Schacter, D. L., & Addis, D. R. (2007). The cognitive neuroscience of constructive memory: Remembering the past and imagining the future. *Philosophical Transactions of the Royal Society B-Biological Sciences*, *362*(1481), 773–786. doi:10.1098/rstb.2007.2087

Schacter, D. L., Guerin, S. A., & St. Jacques, P. L. (2011). Memory distortion: An adaptive perspective. *Trends in Cognitive Sciences*. doi:10.1016/j.tics.2011.08.004

Schacter, S., & Singer, J. E. (1962). Cognitive, social, and physiological determinants of emotional state. *Psychological Review*, *69*(5), 379–399.

Schall, J. D., & Thompson, K. G. (1999). Neural selection and control of visually guided eye movements. *Annual Review of Neuroscience*, *22*, 241–259.

Schank, R. C., & Abelson, R. P. (1975). *Script, plans, and knowledge*. Paper presented at the Proceedings of the 4th International Joint Conference on Artificial Intelligence. Tblisi, USSR.

Schartau, P. E., Dalgleish, T., & Dunn, B. D. (2009). Seeing the bigger picture: Training in perspective broadening reduces self-reported affect and psychophysiological response to distressing films and autobiographical memories. *Journal of Abnormal Psychology*, *118*(1), 15–27. doi:10.1037/a0012906

Schlösser, T., Dunning, D., & Fetchenhauer, D. (2013). What a feeling: The role of immediate and anticipated emotions in risky decisions. *Journal of Behavioral Decision Making*, *26*, 13–30. https://doi.org/10.1002/bdm.757

Schmack, K., Rothkirch, M., Priller, J., & Sterzer, P. (2017). Enhanced predictive signalling in schizophrenia. *Human Brain Mapping*, *38*(4), 1767–1779. doi:10.1002/hbm.23480

Schmack, K., Schnack, A., Priller, J., & Sterzer, P. (2015). Perceptual instability in schizophrenia: Probing predictive coding accounts of delusions with ambiguous stimuli. *Schizophrenia Research: Cognition*, *2*(2), 72–77. doi:10.1016/j.scog.2015.03.005

Schmeiz, M., Schmidt, R., Bickel, A., Handwerker, H. O., & Torebjörk, H. E. (1997). Specific C-receptors for itch in human skin. *The Journal of Neuroscience*, *17*(20), 8003–8008.

Schmidhuber, J. (2015). Deep learning in neural networks: An overview. *Neural Networks*, *61*, 85–117. doi:10.1016/j.neunet.2014.09.003

Schmidt, G. L., Cardillo, E. R., Kranjec, A., Lehet, M., Widick, P., & Chatterjee, A. (2012). Not all analogies are created equal: Associative and categorical analogy processing following brain damage. *Neuropsychologia*, *50*(7), 1372–1379. doi:10.1016/j.neuropsychologia.2012.02.022

Schmidt, H. G., & Rikers, R. M. J. P. (2007). How expertise develops in medicine: Knowledge encapsulation and illness script formation. *Medical Education*, *41*(12), 1133–1139. doi:10.1111/j.1365-2923.2007.02915.x

Schmidt, J. R., & Thompson, V. A. (2008). 'At least one' problem with 'Some' formal reasoning paradigms. *Memory & Cognition*, *36*(1), 217–229. doi:10.3758/mc.36.1.217

Schneider, G. E. (1967). Contrasting visuomotor functions of tectum and cortex in the golden hamster. *Psychologische Forschung*, *31*, 52–62.

Schneider, W., & Shiffrin, R. M. (1977). Controlled and automatic human information processing I. Detection, search, and attention. *Psychological Review*, *84*(1), 1–66.

Schnitzler, A., & Gross, J. (2005). Normal and pathological oscillatory communication in the brain. *Nature Reviews Neuroscience*, *6*(4), 285–296. doi:10.1038/nrn1650

Schotter, E. R., Angele, B., & Rayner, K. (2012). Parafoveal processing in reading. *Attention, Perception, & Psychophysics*, *74*(1), 5–35. doi:10.3758/s13414-011-0219-2

Schroder, T., & Thagard, P. (2013). The affective meanings of automatic social behaviors: Three mechanisms that explain priming. *Psychological Review*, *120*(1), 255–280. doi:10.1037/a0030972

Schröger, E., & Wolff, C. (1998). Attentional orienting and reorienting is indicated by human event-related brain potentials. *Neuroreport*, *9*, 3355–3358.

Schurger, A., Hu, P., Pak, J., & Roskies, A. L. (2021). What is the readiness potential? *Trends in Cognitive Sciences*, *25*(7), 558–570. doi:10.1016/j.tics.2021.04.001

Schwabe, L., & Wolf, O. T. (2012). Stress modulates the engagement of multiple memory systems in classification learning. *The Journal of Neuroscience*, *32*(32), 11042–11049. doi:10.1523/JNEUROSCI.1484-12.2012

Schwark, J., Sandry, J., Macdonald, J., & Dolgov, I. (2012). False feedback increases detection of low-prevalence targets in visual search. *Attention, Perception, & Psychophysics*, *74*(8), 1583–1589. doi:10.3758/s13414-012-0354-4

Schwartz, S. (2003). Are life episodes replayed during dreaming? *Trends in Cognitive Sciences*, *7*(8), 325–327. doi:10.1016/s1364-6613(03)00162-1

Schwartz, J. L. K., Chapman, G., & Brewer, N. (2004). The effects of accountability on bias in physician decision making: Going from bad to worse. *Psychonomic Bulletin & Review*, *11*(1), 173–178.

Schwartz, B., Ward, A., Monterosso, J., Lyubomirsky, S., White, K., & Lehman, D. R. (2002). Maximizing versus satisficing: Happiness is a matter of choice. *Journal of Personality and Social Psychology, 83*(5), 1178–1197. doi:10.1037/0022-3514.83.5.1178

Schwarz, W., & Keus, I. M. (2004). Moving the eyes along the mental number line: Comparing SNARC effects with saccadic and manual responses. *Perception & Psychophysics, 66*(4), 651–664.

Scott, S. H. (2000). Role of motor-cortex in coordinating multi-joint movement: It is time for a new paradigm? *Canadian Journal of Physiology and Pharmacology, 78*, 923–933.

Scott, S. H. (2004). Optimal feedback control and the neural basis of volitional motor control. *Nature Reviews Neuroscience, 5*(7), 532–546. doi:10.1038/nrn1427

Scott, S. K., & Johnsrude, I. S. (2003). The neuroanatomical and functional organization of speech perception. *Trends in Neurosciences, 26*(2), 100–107.

Sears, C. R., Campbell, C. R., & Lupker, S. J. (2006). Is there a neighborhood frequency effect in English? Evidence from reading and lexical decision. *Journal of Experimental Psychology: Human Perception and Performance, 32*(4), 1040–1062. doi:10.1037/0096-1523.32.4.1040

Sebanz, N., Bekkering, H., & Knoblich, G. (2006). Joint action: Bodies and minds moving together. *Trends in Cognitive Sciences, 10*(2), 70–76. doi:10.1016/j.tics.2005.12.009

Sebanz, N., & Frith, C. (2004). Beyond simulation? Neural mechanisms for predicting the actions of others. *Nature Neuroscience, 7*(1), 5–6.

Segal, S. J., & Fusella, V. (1970). Influence of imaged pictures and sounds on the detection of visual and auditory signals. *Journal of Experimental Psychology, 83*(3), 458–464.

Seger, C. A., & Miller, E. K. (2010). Category learning in the brain. *Annual Review of Neuroscience, 33*, 203–219. doi:10.1146/annurev.neuro.051508.135546

Seidenberg, M. S., & McClelland, J. L. (1989). A distributed, developmental model of word recognition and naming. *Psychological Review, 96*(4), 523–568.

Sekuler, R., Sekuler, A. B., & Lau, R. (1997). Sound alters visual motion perception. *Nature, 385*, 308.

Sellen, A. J., Louie, G., Harris, J. E., & Wilkins, A. J. (1997). What brings intentions to mind? An in situ study of prospective memory. *Memory, 5*(4), 483–507. doi:10.1080/741941433

Senkowski, D., Röttger, S., Grimm, S., Foxe, J. J., & Herrmann, C. S. (2005). Kanizsa subjective figures capture visual spatial attention: Evidence from electrophysiological and behavioral data. *Neuropsychologia, 43*(6), 872–886.

Senkowski, D., Talsma, D., Herrmann, C. S., & Woldorff, M. G. (2005). Multisensory processing and oscillatory gamma responses: Effects of spatial selective attention. *Experimental Brain Research, 166*(3–4), 411–426. doi:10.1007/s00221-005-2381-z

Serences, J. T., & Yantis, S. (2006). Selective visual attention and perceptual coherence. *Trends in Cognitive Sciences, 10*, 38–45.

Sereno, A. B., Briand, K. A., Amador, S. C., & Szapiel, S. V. (2006). Disruption of reflexive attention and eye movements in an individual with a collicular lesion. *Journal of Clinical and Experimental Neuropsychology, 28*(1), 145–166. doi:10.1080/13803390590929298

Seth, A. K. (2013). Interoceptive inference, emotion, and the embodied self. *Trends in Cognitive Sciences, 17*(11), 565–573. doi:10.1016/j.tics.2013.09.007

Seth, A. K. (2014). A predictive processing theory of sensorimotor contingencies: Explaining the puzzle of perceptual presence and its absence in synesthesia. *Cognitive Neuroscience, 5*(2), 97–118. doi:10.1080/17588928.2013.877880

Seth, A. K., Suzuki, K., & Critchley, H. D. (2011). An interoceptive predictive coding model of conscious presence. *Frontiers in Psychology, 2*, 395. doi:10.3389/fpsyg.2011.00395

Severens, E., Janssens, I., Kuhn, S., Brass, M., & Hartsuiker, R. J. (2011). When the brain tames the tongue: Covert editing of inappropriate language. *Psychophysiology, 48*(9), 1252–1257. doi:10.1111/j.1469-8986.2011.01190.x

Severens, E., Kuhn, S., Hartsuiker, R. J., & Brass, M. (2012). Functional mechanisms involved in the internal inhibition of taboo words. *Social, Cognitive, and Affective Neuroscience, 7*(4), 431–435. doi:10.1093/scan/nsr030

Seymour, T. L., Seifert, C. M., Shafto, M. G., & Mosmann, A. L. (2000). Using response time measures to assess 'Guilty knowledge'. *Journal of Applied Psychology, 85*(1), 30–37. https://doi.org/10.1037/0021-9010.85.1.30

Shaham, Y., Shalev, U., Lu, L., de Wit, H., & Stewart, J. (2003). The reinstatement model of drug relapse: History, methodology and major findings. *Psychopharmacology (Berl), 168*(1–2), 3–20. doi:10.1007/s00213-002-1224-x

Shahin, A. J., Kerlin, J. R., Bhat, J., & Miller, L. M. (2012). Neural restoration of degraded audiovisual speech. *Neuroimage, 60*(1), 530–538. doi:10.1016/j.neuroimage.2011.11.097

Shallice, T., & Warrington, E. K. (1975). Word recognition in a phonemic dyslexic patient. *The Quarterly Journal of Experimental Psychology, 27*, 187–199.

Shamma, S. A., Elhilali, M., & Micheyl, C. (2011). Temporal coherence and attention in auditory scene analysis. *Trends Neurosci, 34*(3), 114–123. doi:10.1016/j.tins.2010.11.002

Shams, L., & Beierholm, U. R. (2010). Causal inference in perception. *Trends in Cognitive Sciences, 14*(9), 425–432. doi:10.1016/j.tics.2010.07.001

Shams, L., Iwaki, S., Chawla, A., & Bhattacharya, J. (2005). Early modulation of visual cortex by sound: An meg study. *Neuroscience Letters, 378*(2), 76–81. doi:10.1016/j.neulet.2004.12.035

Shams, L., Kamitani, Y., & Shimojo, S. (2000). Illusions: What you see is what you hear. *Nature, 408*(6814), 788.

Shanks, D. R. (2010). Learning: From association to cognition. *Annual Review of Psychology, 61*, 273–301. doi:10.1146/annurev.psych.093008.100519

Shanks, D. R., Newell, B. R., Lee, E. H., Balakrishnan, D., Ekelund, L., Cenac, Z. … Moore, C. (2013). Priming intelligent behavior: An elusive phenomenon. *PLoS One*, *8*(4), e56515. doi:10.1371/journal.pone.0056515

Shannon, C. E. (1948). A mathematical theory of communication. *The Bell Systems Technical Journal*, *27*, 623–656.

Shapiro, K. L., Arnell, K. M., & Raymond, J. E. (1997). The attentional blink. *Trends in Cognitive Sciences*, *1*(8), 291–296.

Shapiro, K., Driver, J., Ward, R., & Sorensen, R. E. (1997). Priming from the attentional blink: A failure to extract visual tokens but not visual types. *Psychological Science*, *8*(2), 95–100.

Share, D. L. (2008). On the anglocentricities of current reading research and practice: The perils of overreliance on an 'Outlier' orthography. *Psychological Bulletin*, *134*(4), 584–615. doi:10.1037/0033-2909.134.4.584

Shaw, J., & Porter, S. (2015). Constructing rich false memories of committing crime. *Psychological Science*, *26*(3), 291–301. doi:10.1177/0956797614562862

Shebani, Z., & Pulvermüller, F. (2013). Moving the hands and feet specifically impairs working memory for arm- and leg-related action words. *Cortex*, *49*(1), 222–231. doi:10.1016/j.cortex.2011.10.005

Sheffield, F. D. (1966). New evidence on the drive induction theory of reinforcement. In R. N. Haber (Ed.), *Current research in motivation* (pp. 111–122). New York, NY: Holt, Rinehart, and Winston.

Shelton, J. R., & Weinrich, M. (1997). Further evidence of a dissociation between output phonological and orthographic lexicons: A case study. *Cognitive Neuropsychology*, *14*(1), 105–129. doi:10.1080/026432997381637

Shepard, R. N. (1964). Circularity in judgements of relative pitch. *The Journal of the Acoustical Society of America*, *36*(12), 2346–2353.

Shepard, R. N., & Metzler, J. (1971). Mental rotation of three-dimensional objects. *Science*, *171*(3972), 701–703.

Sheppes, G., & Gross, J. J. (2011). Is timing everything? Temporal considerations in emotion regulation. *Personality and Social Psychology Review*, *15*(4), 319–331. doi:10.1177/1088868310395778

Sheppes, G., Scheibe, S., Suri, G., Radu, P., Blechert, J., & Gross, J. J. (2014). Emotion regulation choice: A conceptual framework and supporting evidence. *Journal of Experimental Psychology: General*, *143*(1), 163–181. doi:10.1037/a0030831

Sherman, R. A., Arena, J. G., Sherman, C. J., & Ernst, J. L. (1989). The mystery of phantom pain: Growing evidence for psychophysiological mechanisms. *Biofeedback and Self-Regulations*, *14*(4), 267–280.

Shiffrar, M., & Thomas, J. P. (2013). Beyond the scientific objectification of the human body: Differentiated analyses of human motion and object motion. In M. Rutherford & V. LKuhlmeier (Eds.), *Social perception: Detection and interpretation of animacy, agency, and intention*. Cambridge, MA: MIT Press.

Shiffrin, R. M., & Schneider, W. (1977). Controlled and automatic human information processing: II. Perceptual learning, automatic attending, and a general theory. *Psychological Review*, *84*(2), 127–190.

Shin, Y. K., Proctor, R. W., & Capaldi, E. J. (2010). A review of contemporary ideomotor theory. *Psychological Bulletin*, *136*(6), 943–974. doi:10.1037/a0020541

Shinn-Cunningham, B. G. (2008). Object-based auditory and visual attention. *Trends in Cognitive Sciences*, *12*(5), 182–186. doi:10.1016/j.tics.2008.02.003

Shintel, H., & Keysar, B. (2009). Less is more: A minimalist account of joint action in communication. *Topics in Cognitive Science*, *1*(2), 260–273. doi:10.1111/j.1756-8765.2009.01018.x

Shipp, S., Adams, R. A., & Friston, K. J. (2013). Reflections on agranular architecture: Predictive coding in the motor cortex. *Trends in Neuroscience*, *36*(12), 706–716. doi:10.1016/j.tins.2013.09.004

Shiv, B., Loewenstein, G., Bechara, A., Damasio, H., & Damasio, A. R. (2005). Investment behavior and the negative side of emotion. *Psychological Science*, *16*(6), 435–439. doi:10.1111/j.0956-7976.2005.01553.x

Shizgal, P. (2001). Brain stimulation reward. In N. J. Smelser, & P. B. Baltes (Eds.), *International encyclopedia of the social & behavioral sciences* (pp. 1358–1362). Amsterdam: Elsevier.

Shohamy, D. (2011). Learning and motivation in the human striatum. *Current Opinion in Neurobiology*, *21*(3), 408–414. doi:10.1016/j.conb.2011.05.009

Shohamy, D., & Adcock, R. A. (2010). Dopamine and adaptive memory. *Trends in Cognitive Sciences*, *14*(10), 464–472. doi:10.1016/j.tics.2010.08.002

Shohamy, D., & Turk-Browne, N. B. (2013). Mechanisms for widespread hippocampal involvement in cognition. *Journal of Experimental Psychology: General*, *142*(4), 1159–1170.

Shomstein, S., & Yantis, S. (2006). Parietal cortex mediates voluntary control of spatial and nonspatial auditory attention. *Journal of Neuroscience*, *26*(2), 435–439. doi:10.1523/JNEUROSCI.4408-05.2006

Shore, D. I., Spry, E., & Spence, C. (2002). Confusing the mind by crossing the hands. *Cognitive Brain Research*, *14*, 153–163.

Shore, S. E., Roberts, L. E., & Langguth, B. (2016). Maladaptive plasticity in Tinnitus–Triggers, mechanisms and treatment. *Nature Reviews Neurology*, *12*(3), 150–160. doi:10.1038/nrneurol.2016.12

Shriver, E. R., Young, S. G., Hugenberg, K., Bernstein, M. J., & Lanter, J. R. (2007). Class, race, and the face: Social context modulates the cross-race effect in face recognition. *Personality and Social Psychology Bulletin*, *34*(2), 260–274. doi:10.1177/0146167207310455

Shuren, J. E., Hammond, C. S., Maher, L. M., Rothi, L. J. G., & Heilman, K. M. (1995). Attention and anosognosia: The case of a jargonaphasic patient with unawareness of language deficit. *Neurology*, *45*, 376–378.

References

Siegel, A. W., Goldsmith, L. T., & Madson, C. R. (1982). Skill in estimation problems of extent and numerosity. *Journal For Research in Mathematics Education, 13*(3), 211–232.

Siegel, R. E. (1959). Theories of vision and color perception of Empedocles and Democritus: Some similarities to the modern approach. *Bulletin of the History of Medicine, 33*(2), 145–159.

Siegrist, J. (1996). Adverse health effects of high-effort/low-reward conditions. *Journal of Occupational Health Psychology, 1*(1), 27–41.

Siegler, R. S. (1987). The perils of averaging data over strategies: An example from children's additions. *Journal of Experimental Psychology: General, 16*(3), 250–264.

Siemer, M., & Reisenzein, R. (2007). The process of emotion inference. *Emotion, 7*(1), 1–20. doi:10.1037/1528-3542.7.1.1.

Siemer, M., Mauss, I., & Gross, J. J. (2007). Same situation–different emotions: How appraisals shape our emotions. *Emotion, 7*(3), 592–600. doi:10.1037/1528-3542.7.3.592

Silvoni, S., Ramos-Murguialday, A., Cavinato, M., Volpato, C., Cisotto, G., Turolla, A. … Birbaumer, N. (2011). Brain-computer interface in stroke: A review of progress. *Clinical EEG and Neuroscience, 42*(4), 245–252. doi:10.1177/155005941104200410

Simon, H. A. (1957). *Models of man: Social and rational.* New York, NY: John Wiley and Sons.

Simon, H. A. (1966). Scientific discovery and the psychology of problem solving. In H. A. Simon (Ed.), *Models of discovery.* Dordrecht: D. Reidel Publishing Company.

Simon, J. R. (1990). The effects of an irrelevant directional cue on human information processing. In R. W. Proctor, & T. G. Reeve (Eds.), *Stimulus-response compatibility* (pp. 31–86). Amsterdam: Elsevier Science Publishers.

Simon, H. A., & Gilmartin, K. (1973). A simulation of memory for chess positions. *Cognitive Psychology, 5*, 29–46.

Simon, D., Krawezyk, D., & Holyoak, K. J. (2004). Construction of preferences by constraint satisfaction. *Psychological Science, 15*(5), 331–336.

Simon, S. R., Khateb, A., Darque, A., Lazeyras, F., Mayer, E., & Pegna, A. J. (2011). When the brain remembers, but the patient doesn't: Converging fMRI and EEG evidence for covert recognition in a case of prosopagnosia. *Cortex, 47*(7), 825–838. doi:10.1016/j.cortex.2010.07.009

Simons, D. J., & Chabris, C. F. (1999). Gorillas in our midst: Sustained inattentional blindness for dynamic events. *Perception, 28*, 1059–1074.

Simons, D. J., & Levin, D. T. (1997). Change blindness. *Trends in Cognitive Sciences, 1*(7), 261–267.

Simons, D. J., & Rensink, R. A. (2005). Change blindness: Past, present, and future. *Trends in Cognitive Sciences, 9*(1), 16–20. doi:10.1016/j.tics.2004.11.006

Simonson, I., & Staw, B. M. (1992). Deescalation strategies: A comparison of techniques for reducing commitment to losing courses of actions. *Journal of Applied Psychology, 77*(4), 419–426.

Sinai, M. J., Ooi, R. L., & He, Z. J. (1998). Terrain influences the accurate judgement of distance. *Nature, 395*(1), 497–500.

Sincich, L. C., Park, K. F., Wohlgemuth, M. J., & Horton, J. C. (2004). Bypassing VI: A direct geniculate input to area MT. *Nature Neuroscience, 7*(10), 1123–1128. doi:10.1038/nn1318

Singer, T., Critchley, H. D., & Preuschoff, K. (2009). A common role of insula in feelings, empathy and uncertainty. *Trends in Cognitive Sciences, 13*(8), 334–340. doi:10.1016/j.tics.2009.05.001

Singer, H. D., & Low, A. A. (1933). Acalculia (Henschen): A clinical study. *Archives of Neurology & Psychiatry, 29*(3), 467–498.

Singer, T., Seymour, B., O'Doherty, J., Kaube, H., Dolan, R. J., & Frith, C. D. (2004). Empathy for pain involves the affective but not sensory components of pain. *Science, 303*(5661), 1157–1162.

Singer, W., & Gray, C. M. (1995). Visual feature integration and the temporal correlation hypothesis. *Annual Review of Neuroscience, 18*, 555–586.

Singh, J., & Knight, R. T. (1990). Frontal lobe contribution to voluntary movements in humans. *Brain Research, 531*, 45–54.

Sio, U. N., & Ormerod, T. C. (2009). Does incubation enhance problem solving? A meta-analytic review. *Psychological Bulletin, 135*(1), 94–120. doi:10.1037/a0014212

Sirigu, A., Grafman, J., Bressler, K., & Sunderland, T. (1991). Multiple representations contribute to body knowledge processing. *Brain, 114*, 629–642.

Sirigu, A., Zalla, T., Pillon, B., Grafman, J., Agid, Y., & Dubois, B. (1995). Selective impairments in managerial knowledge following pre-frontal cortex damage. *Cortex, 31*(2), 301–316. doi:10.1016/s0010-9452(13)80364-4

Skavenski, A. A., Hansen, R. M., Steinman, R. M., & Winterson, B. J. (1979). Quality of retinal image stabilization during small natural and artificial body rotations in man. *Vision Research, 19*, 675–683.

Skinner, E. I., & Fernandes, M. A. (2007). Neural correlates of recollection and familiarity: A review of neuroimaging and patient data. *Neuropsychologia, 45*(10), 2163–2179. doi:10.1016/j.neuropsychologia.2007.03.007

Slagter, H. A., Kok, A., Mol, N., & Kenemans, J. L. (2005). Spatio-temporal dynamics of top-down control: Directing attention to location and/or color as revealed by ERPS and source modeling. *Cognitive Brain Research, 22*(3), 333–348.

Slagter, H. A., Kok, A., Mol, N., Talsma, D., & Kenemans, J. L. (2005). Generating spatial and nonspatial attentional control: An ERP study. *Psychophysiology, 42*(4), 428–439. doi:10.1111/j.1469-8986.2005.00304.x

Sloman, S., Rottenstreich, Y., Wisniewski, E., Hadjichristidis, C., & Fox, C. R. (2004). Typical versus atypical unpacking and superadditive probability judgment. *Journal of Experimental Psychology: Learning, Memory, and Cognition, 30*(3), 573–582. doi:10.1037/0278-7393.30.3.573

Small, D. M., Gregory, M. D., Mak, Y. E., Gitelman, D., Mesulam, M. M., & Parrish, T. (2003). Dissociation of neural representation of intensity and affective valuation in human gustation. *Neuron*, *39*(4), 701–711. doi:10.1016/s0896-6273(03)00467-7

Smith, A. (1998). Ptolemy, Alhazen, and Kepler and the problem of optical images. *Arabic Sciences and Philosophy*, *8*(1), 9–44.

Smith, R. E. (2003). The cost of remembering to remember in event-based prospective memory: Investigating the capacity demands of delayed intention performance. *Journal of Experimental Psychology: Learning, Memory, and Cognition*, *29*(3), 347–361. doi:10.1037/0278-7393.29.3.347

Smith, R. E., & Bayen, U. J. (2005). The effects of working memory resource availability on prospective memory: A formal modeling approach. *Experimental Psychology*, *52*(4), 243–256. doi:10.1027/1618-3169.52.4.243

Smith, D. V., Davis, B., Niu, K., Haealy, E. W., Bonilha, L., Fridrikson, J. … Rorden, C. (2009). Spatial attention evokes similar activation patterns for visual and auditory stimuli. *Journal of Cognitive Neuroscience*, *22*(2), 347–361.

Smith, C. N., Frascino, J. C., Hopkins, R. O., & Squire, L. R. (2013). The nature of anterograde and retrograde memory impairment after damage to the medial temporal lobe. *Neuropsychologia*, *51*(13), 2709–2714. doi:10.1016/j.neuropsychologia.2013.09.015

Smith, R. E., Hunt, R. R., McVay, J. C., & McConnell, M. D. (2007). The cost of event-based prospective memory: Salient target events. *Journal of Experimental Psychology: Learning, Memory, and Cognition*, *33*(4), 734–746. doi:10.1037/0278-7393.33.4.734

Smith, D. T., Jackson, S. R., & Rorden, C. (2009). Repetitive transcranial magnetic stimulation over frontal eye fields disrupts visually cued auditory attention. *Brain Stimulation*, *2*(2), 81–87. doi:10.1016/j.brs.2008.07.005

Smith, E. E., & Jonides, J. (1999). Storage and executive processes in the frontal lobes. *Science*, *283*(5408), 1657–1661.

Smith, C. A., & Kirby, L. D. (2009). Putting appraisal in context: Toward a relational model of appraisal and emotion. *Cognition & Emotion*, *23*(7), 1352–1372. doi:10.1080/02699930902860386

Smith, G., Levere, M., & Kurtzman, R. (2009). Poker player behavior after big wins and big losses. *Management Science*, *55*(9), 1547–1555. doi:10.1287/mnsc.1090.1044

Smith, C. A., & Lazarus, R. S. (1993). Appraisal components, core relational themes, and emotions. *Cognition and Emotion*, *7*(3/4), 233–269.

Smith, D. T., Rorden, C., & Jackson, S. R. (2004). Exogenous orienting of attention depends upon the ability to execute eye movements. *Current Biology*, *14*(9), 792–795. doi:10.1016/j.cub.2004.04.035

Smith, D. T., & Schenk, T. (2012). The premotor theory of attention: Time to move on? *Neuropsychologia*, *50*(6), 1104–1114. doi:10.1016/j.neuropsychologia.2012.01.025

Smith, R. W., & Kounios, J. (1996). Sudden insight: All-or-none processing revealed by speed-accuracy decomposition. *Journal of Experimental Psychology: Learning, Memory, and Cognition*, *22*(6), 1443–1462.

Smith, S. M., Brown, H. O., Toman, J. E. P., & Goodman, L. S. (1947). The lack of cerebral effects of D-tubocurarine. *Anesthesiology*, *8*(1), 1–14.

Smolensky, P. (1988). On the proper treatment of connectionism. *Behavioral and Brain Sciences*, *11*(01), 1. doi:10.1017/s0140525x00052432.

Snedeker, J., & Trueswell, J. (2003). Using prosody to avoid ambiguity: Effects of speaker awareness and referential context. *Journal of Memory and Language*, *48*, 103–130.

Snyder, J. J., & Bischof, W. F. (2010). Knowing where we're heading–When nothing moves. *Brain Research*, *1323*, 127–138. doi:10.1016/j.brainres.2010.01.061

Sober, S. J., & Sabes, P. N. (2003). Multisensory integration during motor planning. *The Journal of Neuroscience*, *23*(18), 6982–6992.

Sobierajewicz, J., Jaskowski, W., & Van der Lubbe, R. H. J. (2019). Does transcranial direct current stimulation affect the learning of a fine sequential hand motor skill with motor imagery? *Journal of Motor Behavior*, *51*(4), 451–465. doi:10.1080/00222895.2018.1513395

Sohn, M.-H., & Anderson, J. R. (2001). Task preparation and task repetition: Two-component model of task switching. *Journal of Experimental Psychology: General*, *130*(4), 764–778. doi:10.1037/0096-3445.130.4.764

Sohoglu, E., Peelle, J. E., Carlyon, R. P., & Davis, M. H. (2012). Predictive top-down integration of prior knowledge during speech perception. *The Journal of Neuroscience*, *32*(25), 8443–8453. doi:10.1523/JNEUROSCI.5069-11.2012

Solomon, R. L., & Corbit, J. D. (1974). An opponent-process theory of motivation. *Psychological Review*, *81*(2), 119–145.

Solomon, S. G., & Lennie, P. (2007). The machinery of colour vision. *Nature Reviews Neuroscience*, *8*(4), 276–286. doi:10.1038/nrn2094

Somers, D. C., Dale, A., Seiffert, A. E., & Tootell, R. B. H. (1999). Functional MRI reveals spatially specific attentional modulation in human primary visual cortex. *Proceedings of the National Academy of Sciences of the United States of America*, *96*, 1663–1668.

Sommer, M. A., & Wurtz, R. H. (2002). A pathway in primate brain for internal monitoring of movements. *Science*, *296*, 1480–1482.

Soni, M., Lambon Ralph, M. A., Noonan, K., Ehsan, S., Hodgson, C., & Woollams, A. M. (2009). 'L' is for tiger: Effects of phonological (Mis)Cueing on picture naming in semantic aphasia. *Journal of Neurolinguistics*, *22*(6), 538–547. doi:10.1016/j.jneuroling.2009.06.002

Soon, C. S., Brass, M., Heinze, H. J., & Haynes, J. D. (2008). Unconscious determinants of free decisions in the human brain. *Nature Neuroscience*, *11*(5), 543–545. doi:10.1038/nn.2112

References

Souman, J. L., Frissen, I., Sreenivasa, M. N., & Ernst, M. O. (2009). Walking straight into circles. *Current Biology*, *19*(18), 1538–1542. doi:10.1016/j.cub.2009.07.053

Sowden, S., & Catmur, C. (2015). The role of the right temporoparietal junction in the control of imitation. *Cerebral Cortex*, *25*(4), 1107–1113. doi:10.1093/cercor/bht306

Sparks, K., & Cooper, C. (1997). The effects of hours of work on health: A meta-analytic review. *Journal of Occupational and Organisational Psychology*, *70*, 391–408.

Speisman, J. C., Lazarus, R. S., Mordkoff, A., & Davison, A. (1964). Experimental reduction of stress based on ego-defense theory. *Journal of Abnormal and Social Psychology*, *68*(4), 367–380.

Spelke, E., Hirst, W., & Neisser, U. (1976). Skills of divided attention. *Cognition*, *4*, 215–230.

Spence, C., & Driver, J. (1996). Audiovisual links in endogenous covert spatial attention. *Journal of Experimental Psychology: Human Perception and Performance*, *22*(4), 1005–1030.

Spence, C., & Driver, J. (1997). Audiovisual links in exogenous covert spatial orienting. *Perception & Psychophysics*, *59*, 1–22.

Spence, C., & McGlone, F. P. (2001). Reflexive spatial orienting of tactile attention. *Experimental Brain Research*, *141*(3), 324–330. doi:10.1007/s002210100883

Spencer, S. J., Steele, C. M., & Quinn, D. M. (1999). Stereotype threat and Woman's math performance. *Journal of Experimental Social Psychology*, *35*, 4–28.

Sperber, D., & Girotto, V. (2002). Use or misuse of the selection task? Rejoinder to Fiddick, Cosmides, and Tooby. *Cognition*, *85*, 277–290.

Sperling, G. (1960). The information available in brief visual presentations. *Psychological Monographs: General and Applied*, *74*(11), 1–29.

Sperry, R. W. (1968). Hemisphere deconnection and unity in conscious awareness. *American Psychologist*, *23*, 723–733.

Spiers, H. J., Maguire, E. A., & Burgess, N. (2011). Hippocampal amnesia. *Neurocase*, *7*, 357–382.

Spivey, M. J., Tanenhaus, M. K., Eberhard, K. M., & Sedivy, J. C. (2002). Eye movements and spoken language comprehension: Effects of visual context on syntactic ambiguity resolution. *Cognitive Psychology*, *45*, 447–481.

Spratling, M. W. (2008). Predictive coding as a model of biased competition in visual attention. *Vision Research*, *48*(12), 1391–1408. doi:10.1016/j.visres.2008.03.009

Spratling, M. W. (2017). A hierarchical predictive coding model of object recognition in natural images. *Cognition and Computation*, *9*(2), 151–167. doi:10.1007/s12559-016-9445-1

Sprengelmeyer, R., Rausch, M., Eysel, U. T., & Przuntek, H. (1998). Neural structures associated with recognition of facial expressions of basic emotions. *Proceedings of the Royal Society B-Biological Sciences*, *265*(1409), 1927–1931. doi:10.1098/rspb.1998.0522

Squire, L. R. (2009). The legacy of patient H.M. For neuroscience. *Neuron*, *61*(1), 6–9. doi:10.1016/j.neuron.2008.12.023

Squires, T. M. (2004). Optimizing the vertebrate vestibular semicircular canal: Could we balance any better? *Physical Review Letters*, *93*(19), 198106.

Srinivasan, R., Winter, W. R., & Nunez, P. L. (2006). Source analysis of EEG oscillations using high-resolution EEG and MEG. *Progress in Brain Research*, *159*, 29–42.

St. Jacques, P. L., Kragel, P. A., & Rubin, D. C. (2011). Dynamic neural networks supporting memory retrieval. *Neuroimage*, *57*(2), 608–616. doi:10.1016/j.neuroimage.2011.04.039

Stanovich, K. E., & West, R. F. (2000). Individual differences in reasoning: Implications for the rationality debate? *Behavioral and Brain Sciences*, *23*, 645–726.

Stanovich, K. E., & West, R. F. (2007). Natural myside bias is independent of cognitive ability. *Thinking & Reasoning*, *13*(3), 225–247. doi:10.1080/13546780600780796

Staresina, B. P., & Davachi, L. (2006). Differential encoding mechanisms for subsequent associative recognition and free recall. *The Journal of Neuroscience*, *26*(36), 9162–9172. doi:10.1523/JNEUROSCI.2877-06.2006

Staufenbiel, S. M., van der Lubbe, R. H., & Talsma, D. (2011). Spatially uninformative sounds increase sensitivity for visual motion change. *Experimental Brain Research*, *213*(4), 457–464. doi:10.1007/s00221-011-2797-6

Steblay, N. K. (1997). Social influence in eyewitness recall: A meta-analytic review of lineup instruction effects. *Law and Human Behavior*, *21*(3), 283–297.

Steblay, N. K., & Phillips, J. D. (2011). The not-sure response option in sequential lineup practice. *Applied Cognitive Psychology*, *25*(5), 768–774. doi:10.1002/acp.1755

Steblay, N. K., Dysart, J. E., & Wells, G. L. (2011). Seventy-two tests of the sequential lineup superiority effect: A meta-analysis and policy discussion. *Psychology, Public Policy, and Law*, *17*(1), 99–139. doi:10.1037/a0021650

Stefanics, G., Kremlacek, J., & Czigler, I. (2014). Visual mismatch negativity: A predictive coding view. *Frontiers in Human Neuroscience*, *8*, 666. doi:10.3389/fnhum.2014.00666

Stein, B. E., & Arigbede, M. O. (1972). Unimodal and multimodal response properties of neurons in the cat's superior colliculus. *Experimental Neurology*, *36*(1), 179–196.

Stein, B. E., & Stanford, T. R. (2008). Multisensory integration: Current issues from the perspective of the single neuron. *Nature Reviews Neuroscience*, *9*(4), 255–266. doi:10.1038/nrn2331

Stein, B. E., Burr, D., Constantinidis, C., Laurienti, P. J., Meredith, A. M., Perrault, T. J. … Lewkowicz, D. J. (2010). Semantic confusion regarding the development of multisensory integration: A practical solution. *European Journal of Neuroscience*, *31*(10), 1713–1720. doi:10.1111/j.1460-9568.2010.07206.x

Steinberg, L. (2007). Risk taking in adolescence: New perspectives from brain and behavioral science. *Current*

Directions in Psychological Science, *16*(2), 55–59. doi:10.1111/j.1467-8721.2007.00475.x

Steinhauer, K., & Friederici, A. D. (2001). Prosodic boundaries, comma rules, and brain responses: The closure positive shift in ERPS as a universal marker for prosodic phrasing in listeners and readers. *Journal of Psycholinguistic Research*, *30*(3), 267–295.

Steinvorth, S., Corkin, S., & Halgren, E. (2006). Ecphory of autobiographical memories: An fMRI study of recent and remote memory retrieval. *Neuroimage*, *30*(1), 285–298. doi:10.1016/j.neuroimage.2005.09.025

Stekelenburg, J. J., & Vroomen, J. (2012). Electrophysiological evidence for a multisensory speech-specific mode of perception. *Neuropsychologia*, *50*(7), 1425–1431. doi:10.1016/j.neuropsychologia.2012.02.027

Stenning, K., & van Lambalgen, M. (2004). A little logic Goes a long way: Basing experiment on semantic theory in the cognitive science of conditional reasoning. *Cognitive Science*, *28*(4), 481–529. doi:10.1207/s15516709cog2804_1

Stephens, A. N., & Groeger, J. A. (2011). Anger-congruent behaviour transfers across driving situations. *Cognition & Emotion*, *25*(8), 1423–1438. doi:10.1080/02699931.2010.551184

Sternberg, S. (1969). The discovery of processing stages: Extensions of Donders' methods. *Acta Psychologica*, *30*, 276–315.

Stoianov, I. P., Zorzi, M., & Umiltà, C. (2003). *A connectionist model of simple mental arithmetic*. Paper presented at the European Cognitive Science Conference.

Stoit, A. M. B., van Schie, H. T., Riem, M., Meulenbroek, R. G. J., Newman-Norlund, R. D., Slaats-Willemse, D. I. E. … Buitelaar, J. K. (2011). Internal model deficits impair joint action in children and adolescents with autism spectrum disorders. *Research in Autism Spectrum Disorders*, *5*(4), 1526–1537. doi:10.1016/j.rasd.2011.02.016

Stone, C., Mattingley, J. B., & Rangelov, D. (2022). On second thoughts: Changes of mind in decision-making. *Trends in Cognitive Sciences*, *26*(5), 419–431. doi:10.1016/j.tics.2022.02.004

Stone, D. B., Urrea, L. J., Aine, C. J., Bustillo, J. R., Clark, V. P., & Stephen, J. M. (2011). Unisensory processing and multisensory integration in schizophrenia: A high-density electrical mapping study. *Neuropsychologia*, *49*(12), 3178–3187. doi:10.1016/j.neuropsychologia.2011.07.017

Stoney, S. D., Thompson, W. D., & Asanuma, H. (1968). Excitation of pyramidal track cells by intracortical microstimulation: Effective extent of stimulating current. *Journal of Neurophysiology*, *31*(5), 659–669.

Strack, F., Martin, L. L., & Stepper, S. (1988). Inhibiting and facilitating conditions of the human smile: A nonobtrusive test of the facial feedback hypothesis. *Journal of Personality and Social Psychology*, *54*(5), 768–777.

Strick, P. L., Dum, R. P., & Rathelot, J. A. (2021). The cortical motor areas and the emergence of motor skills: A neuroanatomical perspective. *Annual Review of Neuroscience*, *44*, 425–447. doi:10.1146/annurev-neuro-070918-050216

Strobach, T., Liepelt, R., Pashler, H., Frensch, P. A., & Schubert, T. (2013). Effects of extensive dual-task practice on processing stages in simultaneous choice tasks. *Attention, Perception, & Psychophysics*, *75*(5), 900–920. doi:10.3758/s13414-013-0451-z

Stroop, J. R. (1935). Studies of interference in serial verbal reactions. *Journal of Experimental Psychology*, *18*(6), 643–662.

Stupple, E. J. N., & Ball, L. J. (2008). Belief–logic conflict resolution in syllogistic reasoning: Inspection-time evidence for a parallel-process model. *Thinking & Reasoning*, *14*(2), 168–181. doi:10.1080/13546780701739782

Stupple, E. J. N., Ball, L. J., & Ellis, D. (2013). Matching bias in syllogistic reasoning: Evidence for a dual-process account from response times and confidence ratings. *Thinking & Reasoning*, *19*(1), 54–77. doi:10.1080/13546783.2012.735622

Stuss, D. T. (2011). functions of the frontal lobes: Relation to executive functions. *Journal of the International Neuropsychological Society*, *17*(5), 759–765. doi:10.1017/S1355617711000695

Stuss, D. T., & Alexander, M. P. (2007). Is there a dysexecutive syndrome? *Philosophical Transactions of the Royal Society B-Biological Sciences*, *362*(1481), 901–915. doi:10.1098/rstb.2007.2096

Suied, C., Bonneel, N., & Viaud-Delmon, I. (2008). Integration of auditory and visual information in the recognition of realistic objects. *Experimental Brain Research*, *194*(1), 91–102. doi:10.1007/s00221-008-1672-6

Sulin, R. A., & Dooling, D. J. (1974). Intrusion of a thematic idea in retention of prose. *Journal of Experimental Psychology*, *103*(2), 255–262.

Sullivan, L. (1976). selective attention and secondary message analysis: A reconsideration of Broadbent's filter model of selective attention. *The Quarterly Journal of Experimental Psychology*, *28*, 167–178.

Summerfield, C., Egner, T., Greene, M., Koechlin, E., Mangels, J., & Hirsch, J. (2006). Predictive codes for forthcoming perception in the frontal cortex. *Science*, *314*, 1311–1314.

Summerfield, J. J., Hassabis, D., & Maguire, E. A. (2009). Cortical midline involvement in autobiographical memory. *Neuroimage*, *44*(3), 1188–1200. doi:10.1016/j.neuroimage.2008.09.033

Sun, L., Liu, F., Zhou, L., & Jiang, C. (2018). Musical training modulates the early but not the late stage of rhythmic syntactic processing. *Psychophysiology*, *55*(2). doi:10.1111/psyp.12983

Svenson, O., Salo, I., & Lindholm, T. (2009). Post-decision consolidation and distortion of facts. *Judgement and Decision Making*, *4*(5), 397–407.

Svoboda, E., McKinnon, M. C., & Levine, B. (2006). The functional neuroanatomy of autobiographical memory:

References

A meta-analysis. *Neuropsychologia*, *44*(12), 2189–2208. doi:10.1016/j.neuropsychologia.2006.05.023

Sweeney, J. A., Rosano, C., Berman, R. A., & Luna, B. (2001). Inhibitory control of attention declines more than working memory during normal aging. *Neurobiology of Aging*, *22*, 39–47.

Sweller, J., & Levine, M. (1982). Effects of goal specificity on means-ends analysis and learning. *Journal of Experimental Psychology: Learning, Memory, and Cognition*, *8*(5), 463–474.

Swets, B., Desmet, T., Clifton, C. J., & Ferreira, F. (2008). Underspecification of syntactic ambiguities: Evidence from self-paced reading. *Memory & Cognition*, *36*(1), 201–216. doi:10.3758/MC.36.1.201

Swindale, N. V. (1998). Cortical organisation: Modules, polymaps and mosaics. *Current Biology*, *8*, 270–273.

Szameitat, D. P., Darwin, C. J., Wildgruber, D., Alter, K., & Szameitat, A. J. (2011). Acoustic correlates of emotional dimensions in laughter: Arousal, dominance, and Valence. *Cognition & Emotion*, *25*(4), 599–611. doi:10.1080/02699931.2010.508624

Szollosi, A., & Newell, B. R. (2020). People as intuitive scientists: Reconsidering statistical explanations of decision making. *Trends in Cognitive Sciences*, *24*(12), 1008–1018. doi:10.1016/j.tics.2020.09.005

Tainturier, M.-J., Schiemenz, S., & Leek, E. C. (2006). Separate orthographic representations for reading and spelling? Evidence from a case of preserved lexical reading and impaired lexical spelling. *Brain and Language*, *99*(1–2), 40–41. doi:10.1016/j.bandl.2006.06.030

Taira, M., Mine, S., Georgopoulos, A. P., Murata, A., & Sakata, H. (1990). Parietal cortex neurons of the monkey related to the visual guidance of hand movement. *Experimental Brain Research*, 8329–36.

Talarico, J. M., & Rubin, D. C. (2003). Confidence, not consistency, characterizes flashbulb memories. *Psychological Science*, *14*(5), 455–461.

Tallon-Baudry, C., & Bertrand, O. (1999). Oscillatory gamma activity in humans and its role in object representation. *Trends in Cognitive Sciences*, *3*(4), 151–162.

Talsma, D. (2015). Predictive coding and multisensory integration: An attentional account of the multisensory mind. *Frontiers in Integrative Neuroscience*. doi:10.3389/fnint.2015.00019

Talsma, D., & Kok, A. (2001). Nonspatial intermodal selective attention is mediated by sensory brain areas: Evidence from event-related potentials. *Psychophysiology*, *38*(5), 736–751.

Talsma, D., & Kok, A. (2002). Intermodal spatial attention differs between vision and audition: An event-related potential analysis. *Psychophysiology*, *39*(6), 689–706.

Talsma, D., & Woldorff, M. G. (2005). Selective attention and multisensory integration: Multiple phases of effects on the evoked brain activity. *Journal of Cognitive Neuroscience*, *17*(7), 1098–1114.

Talsma, D., Coe, B., Munoz, D. P., & Theeuwes, J. (2010). Brain structures involved in visual search in the presence and absence of color singletons. *Journal of Cognitive Neuroscience*, *22*(4), 761–774.

Talsma, D., Doty, T. J., & Woldorff, M. G. (2007). Selective attention and audiovisual integration: Is attending to both modalities a prerequisite for early integration? *Cerebral Cortex*, *17*(3), 679–690. doi:10.1093/cercor/bhk016

Talsma, D., Mulckhuyse, M., Slagter, H. A., & Theeuwes, J. (2007). Faster, more intense! The relation between electrophysiological reflections of attentional orienting, sensory gain control, and speed of responding. *Brain Research*, *1178*(1), 92–105.

Talsma, D., Senkowski, D., Soto-Faraco, S., & Woldorff, M. G. (2010). The multifaceted interplay between attention and multisensory integration. *Trends in Cognitive Sciences*, *14*(9), 400–410. doi:10.1016/j.tics.2010.06.008

Talsma, D., Slagter, H. A., Nieuwenhuis, S., Hage, J., & Kok, A. (2005). The orienting of visuospatial attention: An event-related brain potential study. *Cognitive Brain Research*, *25*(1), 117–129.

Talsma, D., White, B. J., Mathôt, S., Munoz, D. P., & Theeuwes, J. (2013). A retinotopic attentional trace after saccadic eye movements: Evidence from event-related potentials. *Journal of Cognitive Neuroscience*, *25*(9), 1563–1577. doi:10.1162/jocn_a_00390

Talsma, D., Wijers, A. A., Klaver, P., & Mulder, G. (2001). Working memory processes show different degrees of lateralization: Evidence from event-related potentials. *Psychophysiology*, *38*(3), 425–439.

Tamietto, M., & de Gelder, B. (2010). Neural bases of the non-conscious perception of emotional signals. *Nature Reviews Neuroscience*, *11*(10), 697–709. doi:10.1038/nrn2889

Tamietto, M., Castelli, L., Vighetti, S., Perozzo, P., Geminiani, G., Weiskrantz, L., & de Gelder, B. (2009). Unseen facial and bodily expressions trigger fast emotional reactions. *Proceedings of the National Academy of Sciences of the United States of America*, *106*(42), 17661–17666. doi:10.1073/pnas.0908994106

Tanaka, J. W., & Taylor, M. (1991). Object categories and expertise: Is the basic level in the eye of the beholder? *Cognitive Psychology*, *23*, 457–482.

Tanigawa, H., Lu, H. D., & Roe, A. W. (2010). Functional organization for color and orientation in macaque V4. *Nature Neuroscience*, *13*(12), 1542–1548. doi:10.1038/nn.2676

Tarr, M. J., & Bülthoff, H. H. (1995). Is human object recognition better described by geon structural descriptions or by multiple views? Comment on Biederman and Gerhardstein (1993). *Journal of Experimental Psychology: Human Perception and Performance*, *21*(6), 1494–1505.

Taube, J. S. (2007). The head direction signal: Origins and sensory-motor integration. *Annual Review of Neuroscience*, *30*, 181–207. doi:10.1146/annurev.neuro.29.051605.112854

Taylor, J. S. H., Rastle, K., & Davis, M. H. (2013). Can cognitive models explain brain activation during word and pseudoword reading? A meta-analysis of 36 neuroimaging studies. *Psychological Bulletin, 139*(4), 766–791.

Téglás, E., Girotto, V., Gonzalez, M., & Bonatti, L. L. (2007). Intuitions of probabilities shape expectations about the future at 12 months and beyond. *Proceedings of the National Academy of Sciences of the United States of America, 104*(48), 19156–19159.

Tetlock, P. (2002). Social functionalist frameworks for judgement and choice: Intuitive politicians, theologians, and prosecutors. *Psychological Review, 109*(3), 451–471.

Tetlock, P. E., Kristel, O. V., Elson, S. B., Green, M. C., & Lerner, J. S. (2000). The psychology of the unthinkable: Taboo trade-offs, forbidden base rates, and heretical counterfactuals. *Journal of Personality and Social Psychology, 78*(5), 853–870. doi:10.1037/0022-3514.78.5.853

Tetlock, P., & Mellers, B. A. (2002). The great rationality debate. *Psychological Science, 13*(1), 94–99.

Teufel, C., & Fletcher, P. C. (2020). Forms of prediction in the nervous system. *Nature Reviews Neuroscience, 21*(4), 231–242. doi:10.1038/s41583-020-0275-5

Thagard, P. (2011). Critical thinking and informal logic: Neuropsychological perspectives. *Informal Logic, 31*(3), 152–170.

Thakral, P. P., Benoit, R. G., & Schacter, D. L. (2017). Imagining the future: The core episodic simulation network dissociates as a function of timecourse and the amount of simulated information. *Cortex, 90*, 12–30. doi:10.1016/j.cortex.2017.02.005

Theeuwes, J. (1992). Perceptual selectivity for color and form. *Perception and Psychophysics, 51*(6), 599–606.

Theeuwes, J. (2004). Top-down search strategies cannot override attentional capture. *Psychonomic Bulletin & Review, 11*(1), 65–70.

Theeuwes, J., & Belopolsky, A. V. (2012). Reward grabs the eye: Oculomotor capture by rewarding stimuli. *Vision Research, 74*, 80–85. doi:10.1016/j.visres.2012.07.024

Theeuwes, J., Kramer, A. F., Hahn, S., Irwin, D. E., & Zelinski, G. J. (1999). Influence of attentional capture on oculomotor control. *Journal of Experimental Psychology: Human Perception and Performance, 25*, 1595–1608.

Thelen, A., Cappe, C., & Murray, M. M. (2012). Electrical neuroimaging of memory discrimination based on single-trial multisensory learning. *Neuroimage, 62*(3), 1478–1488. doi:10.1016/j.neuroimage.2012.05.027

Thelen, A., Talsma, D., & Murray, M. M. (2015). Single-trial multisensory memories affect later auditory and visual object discrimination. *Cognition, 138*, 148–160. doi:10.1016/j.cognition.2015.02.003

Thomas, J. C. (1974). An analysis of behavior in the hobbits-orcs problem. *Cognitive Psychology, 6*, 257–269.

Thompson, S. K., Carlyon, R. P., & Cusack, R. (2011). An objective measurement of the build-up of auditory streaming and of its modulation by attention. *Journal of Experimental Psychology: Human Perception and Performance, 37*(4), 1253–1262. doi:10.1037/a0021925

Thompson, V. A., Prowse Turner, J. A., & Pennycook, G. (2011). Intuition, reason, and metacognition. *Cognitive Psychology, 63*(3), 107–140. doi:10.1016/j.cogpsych.2011.06.001

Thomson, J. J. (1976). Killing, letting die, and the trolley problem. *Monist: An International Quarterly Journal of General Philosophical Inquiry, 59*, 204–217.

Thorndike, E. L. (1898). Animal intelligence: An experimental study of the associative processes in animals. *Psychological Review: Monograph Supplements, 2*(4), i–109.

Thornton, T. L., & Gilden, D. L. (2007). Parallel and serial processes in visual search. *Psychological Review, 114*(1), 71–103. doi:10.1037/0033-295X.114.1.71

Thorpe, S., Fize, D., & Marlot, C. (1996). Speed of processing in the human visual system. *Nature, 381*(6582), 520–522.

Tian, B., Reser, D., Durham, A., Kustov, A., & Rauschecker, J. P. (2001). Functional specialization in rhesus monkey auditory cortex. *Science, 292*, 290–293.

Tipper, S. P. (2001). Does negative priming reflect inhibitory mechanisms? A review and integration of conflicting views. *The Quarterly Journal of Experimental Psychology, 54*(2), 321–343. doi:10.1080/713755969

Tipples, J. (2002). Eye gaze is not unique: Automatic orienting in response to uninformative arrows. *Psychonomic Bulletin & Review, 9*(2), 314–318.

Toates, F. (1986). *Motivational systems.* Cambridge, MA: Cambridge University Press.

Todd, R. M., Miskovic, V., Chikazoe, J., & Anderson, A. K. (2020). Emotional objectivity: Neural representations of emotions and their interaction with cognition. *Annual Review of Psychology, 71*, 25–48. doi:10.1146/annurev-psych-010419-051044

Todorovic, D. (2009). The effect of the observer vantage point on perceived distortions in linear perspective images. *Attention, Perception, & Psychophysics, 71*(1), 183–193. doi:10.3758/APP.71.1.183

Tolman, E. C. (1948). Cognitive maps in rats and men. *Psychological Review, 55*(4), 189–208.

Tong, E. M. (2010). Personality influences in appraisal-emotion relationships: The role of neuroticism. *Journal of Personality, 78*(2), 393–417. doi:10.1111/j.1467-6494.2010.00620.x

Tononi, G. (2004). An information integration theory of consciousness. *BMC Neuroscience, 5*, 42. doi:10.1186/1471-2202-5-42

Tononi, G., & Edelman, G. M. (1998). Consciousness and complexity. *Science, 282*, 1846–1851.

Tootell, R. B. H., Hadjikhani, N., Hall, E. K., Marrett, S., Vanduffel, W., Vaughan, J. W., & Dale, A. (1998). The retinotopy of visual spatial attention. *Neuron, 21*, 1409–1422.

Toplak, M. E., West, R. F., & Stanovich, K. E. (2011). The cognitive reflection test as a predictor of performance

References

on heuristics-and-biases tasks. *Memory & Cognition, 39*(7), 1275–1289. doi:10.3758/s13421-011-0104-1

Toplak, M. E., West, R. F., & Stanovich, K. E. (2013). Assessing miserly information processing: An expansion of the cognitive reflection test. *Thinking & Reasoning, 20*(2), 147–168. doi:10.1080/13546783.2013.844729

Tottenham, N., Hare, T. A., & Casey, B. J. (2011). Behavioral assessment of emotion discrimination, emotion regulation, and cognitive control in childhood, adolescence, and adulthood. *Frontiers in Psychology, 2*, 39. doi:10.3389/fpsyg.2011.00039

Tracey, I., & Mantyh, P. W. (2007). The cerebral signature for pain perception and its modulation. *Neuron, 55*(3), 377–391. doi:10.1016/j.neuron.2007.07.012

Tranel, D., Damasio, A. R., Damasio, H., & Brandt, J. P. (1994). Sensorimotor skill learning in amnesia: Additional evidence for the neural basis of nondeclarative memory. *Learning & Memory, 1*, 165–179.

Trapp, S., O'Doherty, J. P., & Schwabe, L. (2018). Stressful events as teaching signals for the brain. *Trends in Cognitive Sciences, 22*(6), 475–478. doi:10.1016/j.tics.2018.03.007

Treisman, A. (1996). The binding problem. *Current Opinion in Neurobiology, 6*, 171–178.

Treisman, A. (1998). Feature binding, attention and object perception. *Philosophical Transactions of the Royal Society B-Biological Sciences, 353*, 1295–1306.

Treisman, A. M. (1960). Contextual cues in selective listening. *The Quarterly Journal of Experimental Psychology, 12*(4), 242–248.

Treisman, A. M. (1964). Monitoring and storage of irrelevant messages in selective attention. *Journal of Verbal Learning and Verbal Behavior, 3*, 449–459.

Treisman, A. M., & Davies, A. (1973). Divided attention to ear and eye. In S. Kornblum (Ed.), *Attention & performance iv* (pp. 101–117). Cambridge, MA: Academic Press.

Treisman, A. M., & Gelade, G. (1980). A feature-integration theory of attention. *Cognitive Psychology, 12*(1), 97–136.

Treisman, A., & Schmidt, H. (1982). Illusory conjunctions in the perception of objects. *Cognitive Psychology, 14*, 107–141.

Tremblay, C., Robert, M., Pascual-Leone, A., Lepore, F., Nguyen, D. K., Carmant, L. … Théoret, H. (2004). Action observation and execution: Intracranial recordings in a human subject. *Neurology, 63*(5), 937–938.

Tremblay, S., Sharika, K. M., & Platt, M. L. (2017). Social decision-making and the brain: A comparative perspective. *Trends in Cognitive Sciences, 21*(4), 265–276. doi:10.1016/j.tics.2017.01.007

Tresilian, J. R. (1991). Empirical and theoretical issues in the perception of time to contact. *Journal of Experimental Psychology: Human Perception and Performance, 17*(3), 865–876.

Tresilian, J. R. (1999). Visually timed action: Time-out for 'Tau'? *Trends in Cognitive Sciences, 3*(8), 301–310.

Troiani, V., Price, E. T., & Schultz, R. T. (2014). Unseen fearful faces promote amygdala guidance of attention. *Social Cognitive and Affective Neuroscience, 9*(2), 133–140. doi:10.1093/scan/nss116

Troy, A. S., Shallcross, A. J., & Mauss, I. B. (2013). A person-by-situation approach to emotion regulation: Cognitive reappraisal can either help or hurt, depending on the context. *Psychological Science, 24*(12), 2505–2514. doi:10.1177/0956797615627417

Tsapkini, K., & Rapp, B. (2010). The orthography-specific functions of the left fusiform gyrus: Evidence of modality and category specificity. *Cortex, 46*(2), 185–205. doi:10.1016/j.cortex.2009.02.025

Tsetsos, K., Moran, R., Moreland, J., Chater, N., Usher, M., & Summerfield, C. (2016). Economic irrationality is optimal during noisy decision making. *Proceedings of the National Academy of Sciences of the United States of America, 113*(11), 3102–3107. doi:10.1073/pnas.1519157113

Tsuchiya, N., & Koch, C. (2005). Continuous flash suppression reduces negative afterimages. *Nature Neuroscience, 8*(8), 1096–1101. doi:10.1038/nn1500

Tsujii, T., & Watanabe, S. (2009). Neural correlates of dual-task effect on belief-bias syllogistic reasoning: A near-infrared spectroscopy study. *Brain Research, 1287*, 118–125. doi:10.1016/j.brainres.2009.06.080

Tuckey, M. R., & Brewer, N. (2003a). How schemas affect eyewitness memory over repeated retrieval attempts. *Applied Cognitive Psychology, 17*(7), 785–800. doi:10.1002/acp.906

Tuckey, M. R., & Brewer, N. (2003b). The influence of schemas, stimulus ambiguity, and interview schedule on eyewitness memory over time. *Journal of Experimental Psychology: Applied, 9*(2), 101–118. doi:10.1037/1076-898x.9.2.101

Tuholski, S. W., Engle, R. W., & Beylis, G. C. (2001). Individual differences in working memory capacity and enumeration. *Memory & Cognition, 29*(3), 484–492.

Tulving, E. (1972). Episodic and semantic memory. In E. Tulving & W. Donaldson (Eds.), *Organisation of memory*. London: Academic Press.

Tulving, E. (2002). Episodic memory: From mind to brain. *Annual Review of Neuroscience, 53*, 1–25.

Tulving, E., & Thomson, D. M. (1973). Encoding specificity and retrieval processes in episodic memory. *Psychological Review, 80*(5), 352–373.

Tulving, E., Schacter, D. L., & Stark, H. A. (1982). Priming effects in word-fragment completion are independent of recognition memory. *Journal of Experimental Psychology: Learning, Memory, and Cognition, 8*(4), 336–342.

Turner, L. H., Solomon, R. L., Stellar, E., & Wampler, S. N. (1975). Humoural factors controlling food intake in dogs. *Acta Neurobiologiae Experimentalis, 35*, 491–498.

Turner, M. L., & Engle, R. W. (1989). Is working memory task dependent? *Journal of Memory and Language, 28*, 127–154.

786

Turpin, S. M., & Marais, M. A. (2004). Decision-making: Theory and practice. *Orion*, *20*(2), 143–160.

Tversky, A. (1972). Choice by elimination. *Journal of Mathematical Psychology*, *9*, 341–367.

Tversky, A., & Kahneman, D. (1973). Availability: A heuristic for judging frequency and probability. *Cognitive Psychology*, *5*, 207–232.

Tversky, A., & Kahneman, D. (1981). The framing of decisions and the psychology of choice. *Science*, *211*, 453–458.

Tversky, A., & Kahneman, D. (1983). Extensional versus intuitive reasoning: The conjunction fallacy in probability judgment. *Psychological Review*, *90*(4), 293–315.

Tversky, A., & Koehler, D. J. (1994). Support theory: A nonextensional representation of subjective probability. *Psychological Review*, *101*(4), 547–567.

Tversky, A., & Shafir, E. (1992). Choice under conflict: The dynamics of deferred decision. *Psychological Science*, *3*(6), 358–361.

Tyler, L. K., & Moss, H. E. (1997). Imageability and category-specificity. *Cognitive Neuropsychology*, *14*(2), 293–318.

Tzovara, A., Murray, M. M., Michel, C. M., & De Lucia, M. (2012). A tutorial review of electrical neuroimaging from group-average to single-trial event-related potentials. *Developmental Neuropsychology*, *37*(6), 518–544. doi:10.1080/87565641.2011.636851

Ucros, C. G. (1989). Mood state-dependent memory: A meta-analysis. *Cognition & Emotion*, *3*(2), 139–169. doi:10.1080/02699938908408077

Uddin, L. Q., Kelly, A. M., Biswal, B. B., Castellanos, F. X., & Milham, M. P. (2009). Functional connectivity of default mode network components: Correlation, anticorrelation, and causality. *Human Brain Mapping*, *30*(2), 625–637. doi:10.1002/hbm.20531

Uhlhaas, P. J., & Singer, W. (2006). Neural synchrony in brain disorders: Relevance for cognitive dysfunctions and pathophysiology. *Neuron*, *52*(1), 155–168. doi:10.1016/j.neuron.2006.09.020

Umilta, C., Kohler, E., Gallese, V., Fogassi, L., Fadiga, L., & Keysers, C. (2001). I know what you are doing: A neurophysiological study. *Neuron*, *31*, 155–165.

Ungerleider, L. G., & Haxby, J. V. (1994). 'What' and 'Where' in the brain. *Current Opinion in Neurobiology*, *4*, 157–165.

Ungerleider, L. G., & Mishkin, M. (1981). Two cortical visual systems. In D. J. Dingle, M. A. Goodale, & R. J. W. Mansfield (Eds.), *Analysis of visual behavior*. Cambridge, MA: MIT Press.

Ungerstedt, U. (1971). Adipsia and aphagia after 6-hydroxydopamine induced degeneration of the nigro-striatal dopamine system. *Acta Physiologica Scandinavia*, *82*, 95–122.

Urbantschisch, V. (1880). Über den einfluss einer sinneserrugun auf die Übrigen sinnesempfindungen. *Archiv Für Die Geschamte Psychologie*, *42*, 155–175.

Ursino, M., Cuppini, C., & Magosso, E. (2013). The formation of categories and the representation of feature saliency: Analysis with a computational model trained with an Hebbian paradigm. *Journal of Integrative Neuroscience*, *12*(4), 401–425. doi:10.1142/S0219635213500246

Ursino, M., Cuppini, C., & Magosso, E. (2014). Neurocomputational approaches to modelling multisensory integration in the brain: A review. *Neural Networks*, *60*, 141–165. doi:10.1016/j.neunet.2014.08.003

Uzer, T., Lee, P. J., & Brown, N. R. (2012). On the prevalence of directly retrieved autobiographical memories. *Journal of Experimental Psychology: Learning, Memory, and Cognition*, *38*(5), 1296–1308. doi:10.1037/a0028142

Vaina, L. (1998). Complex motion perception and its deficits. *Current Opinion in Neurobiology*, *8*, 494–502.

Vaitl, D. (1996). Interoception. *Biological Psychology*, *42*, 1–27.

Valenstein, E. S., Cox, V. C., & Kakolewski (1970). Reexamination of the role of the hypothalamus in motivation. *Psychological Review*, *77*(1), 16–31.

Valentine, T., Pickering, A., & Darling, S. (2003). Characteristics of eyewitness identification that predict the outcome of real lineups. *Applied Cognitive Psychology*, *17*(8), 969–993. doi:10.1002/acp.939

Van Atteveldt, N., Murray, M. M., Thut, G., & Schroeder, C. E. (2014). Multisensory integration: Flexible use of general operations. *Neuron*, *81*(6), 1240–1253. doi:10.1016/j.neuron.2014.02.044

Van Boxtel, J. J., & Lu, H. (2013). A predictive coding perspective on autism spectrum disorders. *Frontiers in Psychology*, *4*, 19. doi:10.3389/fpsyg.2013.00019

Van Damme, S., Legrain, V., Vogt, J., & Crombez, G. (2010). Keeping pain in mind: A motivational account of attention to pain. *Neuroscience & Biobehavioral Reviews*, *34*(2), 204–213. doi:10.1016/j.neubiorev.2009.01.005

Van de Cruys, S., Evers, K., Van der Hallen, R., Van Eylen, L., Boets, B., de-Wit, L., & Wagemans, J. (2014). Precise minds in uncertain worlds: Predictive coding in autism. *Psychological Review*, *121*(4), 649–675. doi:10.1037/a0037665

Van den Berg, R., Shin, H., Chou, W.-C., George, R., & Ma, W. J. (2012). Variability in encoding precision accounts for visual short-term limitations. *Proceedings of the National Academy of Sciences of the United States of America*, *109*(22), 8780–8785.

Van den Brink, D., Van Berkum, J. J., Bastiaansen, M. C., Tesink, C. M., Kos, M., Buitelaar, J. K., & Hagoort, P. (2012). Empathy matters: ERP evidence for inter-individual differences in social language processing. *Social, Cognitive, and Affective Neuroscience*, *7*(2), 173–183. doi:10.1093/scan/nsq094

Van den Brink, R. L., Cohen, M. X., van der Burg, E., Talsma, D., Vissers, M. E., & Slagter, H. A. (2014). Subcortical, modality-specific pathways contribute to multisensory processing in humans. *Cerebral Cortex*, *24*(8), 2169–2177. doi:10.1093/cercor/bht069

References

Van der Burg, E., Alais, D., & Cass, J. (2013). Rapid recalibration to audiovisual asynchrony. *The Journal of Neuroscience, 33*(37), 14633–14637. doi:10.1523/JNEUROSCI.1182-13.2013

Van der Burg, E., Olivers, C. N., Bronkhorst, A. W., & Theeuwes, J. (2008). Pip and pop: Nonspatial auditory signals improve spatial visual search. *Journal of Experimental Psychology: Human Perception and Performance, 34*(5), 1053–1065. doi:10.1037/0096-1523.34.5.1053

Van der Burg, E., Olivers, C. N., Bronkhorst, A. W., & Theeuwes, J. (2009). Poke and pop: Tactile-visual synchrony increases visual saliency. *Neuroscience Letters, 450*(1), 60–64. doi:10.1016/j.neulet.2008.11.002

Van der Burg, E., Talsma, D., Olivers, C. N., Hickey, C., & Theeuwes, J. (2011). Early multisensory interactions affect the competition among multiple visual objects. *Neuroimage, 55*(3), 1208–1218. doi:10.1016/j.neuroimage.2010.12.068

Van Der Hulst, M., & Geurts, S. (2001). Associations between overtime and psychological health in high and low reward jobs. *Work & Stress, 15*(3), 227–240. doi:10.1080/026783701110.1080/02678370110066580

Van der, L., Frese, D., & Sonntag, M. (2003). The impact of mental fatigue on exploration in a complex computer task: Rigidity and loss of systematic strategies. *Human Factors, 45*(3), 483–494.

Van der Lubbe, R. H., Buitenweg, J. R., Boschker, M., Gerdes, B., & Jongsma, M. L. (2012). The influence of transient spatial attention on the processing of intracutaneous electrical stimuli examined with ERPS. *Clinical Neurophysiology, 123*(5), 947–959. doi:10.1016/j.clinph.2011.08.034

Van der Veen, F. M., Van Der Molen, M. W., & Jennings, J. R. (2001). Selective attention and response inhibition alter phase-dependent cardiac slowing. *Psychophysiology, 38*, 896–902.

Van der Werf, J., Jensen, O., Fries, P., & Medendorp, W. P. (2010). Neuronal synchronization in human posterior parietal cortex during reach planning. *The Journal of Neuroscience, 304*(7), 1402–1412.

Van Duijvenvoorde, A. C., Peters, S., Braams, B. R., & Crone, E. A. (2016). What motivates adolescents? Neural responses to rewards and their influence on adolescents' risk taking, learning, and cognitive control. *Neuroscience and Biobehavioral Reviews, 70*, 135–147. doi:10.1016/j.neubiorev.2016.06.037

Van Gompel, R. G. P., Pickering, M. J., & Traxler, M. J. (2000). Unrestricted race: A new model of syntactic ambiguity Resolution. In A. Kennedy, R. Radach, D. Heller, & J. Pynte (Eds.), *Reading as a perceptual process* (pp. 621–648). Oxford: Elsevier.

Van Gompel, R. G. P., Pickering, M. J., & Traxler, M. J. (2001). Reanalysis in sentence processing: Evidence against current constraint-based and two-stage models. *Journal of Memory and Language, 45*, 225–258. doi:10.1006/jmla.2001.2773

van Harreveld, F., Wagenmakers, E.-J., & van der Maas, H. L. (2007). The effects of time pressure on chess skill: An investigation into fast and slow processes underlying expert performance. *Psychological Research, 71*(5), 591–597. doi:10.1007/s00426-006-0076-0

Van Horn, J. D., Irimia, A., Torgerson, C. M., Chambers, M. C., Kikinis, R., & Toga, A. W. (2012). Mapping connectivity damage in the case of Phineas Gage. *PLoS One, 7*(5), e37454. doi:10.1371/journal.pone.0037454

Van Oeffelen, M. P., & Vos, P. G. (1982). A probabilistic model for the discrimination of visual number. *Perception & Psychophysics, 32*(2), 163–170.

Van Orden, G. C. (1987). A rows is a rose: Spelling, sound, and reading. *Memory & Cognition, 15*(3), 181–198.

Van Overwalle, F. (2009). Social cognition and the brain: A meta-analysis. *Human Brain Mapping, 30*(3), 829–858. doi:10.1002/hbm.20547

Van Pelt, S., & Medendorp, W. P. (2008). Updating target distance across eye movements in depth. *Journal of Neurophysiology, 99*(5), 2281–2290. doi:10.1152/jn.01281.2007

Van Petten, C., Coulson, S., Rubin, S., Plante, E., & Parks, M. (1999). Time course of word identification and semantic integration in spoken language. *Journal of Experimental Psychology: Learning, Memory, and Cognition, 25*(2), 394–417.

Van Schie, H. T., Mars, R. B., Coles, M. G., & Bekkering, H. (2004). Modulation of activity in medial frontal and motor cortices during error observation. *Nature Neuroscience, 7*(5), 549–554. doi:10.1038/nn1239

Van Steenbergen, H., Band, G. P., & Hommel, B. (2012). Reward valence modulates conflict-driven attentional adaptation: Electrophysiological evidence. *Biological Psychology, 90*(3), 234–241. doi:10.1016/j.biopsycho.2012.03.018

Van Turennout, M., Hagoort, P., & Brown, C. R. (1998). Brain activity during speaking: From syntax to phonology in 400 milliseconds. *Science, 280*(5363), 572–574. doi:10.1126/science.280.5363.572

Van Voorhis, S., & Hillyard, S. A. (1977). Visual evoked potentials and selective attention to points in space. *Perception & Psychophysics, 22*(1), 54–62.

Van Wassenhove, V., Grant, K. W., & Poeppel, D. (2005). Visual speech speeds up the neural processing of auditory speech. *Proceedings of the National Academy of Sciences of the United States of America, 102*(4), 1181–1186. doi:10.1073/pnas.0408949102

Vanlessen, N., De Raedt, R., Koster, E. H. W., & Pourtois, G. (2016). Happy heart, smiling eyes: A systematic review of positive mood effects on broadening of visuospatial attention. *Neuroscience and Biobehavioral Reviews, 68*, 816–837. doi:10.1016/j.neubiorev.2016.07.001

Vanrie, J., Béatse, E., Wagemans, J., Sunaert, S., & Van Hecke, P. (2002). Mental rotation versus invariant features in object perception from different viewpoints: An fMRI study. *Neuropsychologia, 40*, 917–930.

VanRullen, R. (2016). Perceptual cycles. *Trends in Cognitive Sciences*, *20*(10), 723–735. doi:10.1016/j.tics.2016.07.006

Vargha-Khadem, F., Gadian, D. G., Watkins, K. E., Connelly, A., Van Paesschen, W., & Mishkin, M. (1997). Differential effects of early hippocampal pathology on episodic and semantic memory. *Science*, *277*, 376–380.

Vaughan, T. M. (2003). Guest editorial brain-computer interface technology: A review of the second international meeting. *IEEE Transactions on Neural Systems and Rehabilitation Engineering*, *11*(2), 94–109. doi:10.1109/tnsre.2003.814799

Vecera, S. P., Flevaris, A. V., & Filapek, J. C. (2004). Exogenous spatial attention influences figure-ground assignment. *Psychological Science*, *15*(1), 20–26.

Verbruggen, F., & De Houwer, J. (2007). Do emotional stimuli interfere with response inhibition? Evidence from the stop signal paradigm. *Cognition & Emotion*, *21*(2), 391–403. doi:10.1080/02699930600625081

Verbruggen, F., & Logan, G. D. (2008). Response inhibition in the stop-signal paradigm. *Trends in Cognitive Sciences*, *12*(11), 418–424.

Verfaelllie, M., LaRocque, K. F., & Keane, M. M. (2012). Intact implicit verbal relational memory in medial temporal lobe amnesia. *Neuropsychologia*, *50*(8), 2100–2106. doi:10.1016/j.neuropsychologia.2012.05.011

Verguts, T., & Chen, Q. (2017). Numerical cognition: Learning binds biology to culture. *Trends in Cognitive Sciences*, *21*(12), 913–914. doi:10.1016/j.tics.2017.09.004

Verguts, T., & Notebaert, W. (2009). Adaptation by binding: A learning account of cognitive control. *Trends in Cognitive Sciences*, *13*(6), 252–257. doi:10.1016/j.tics.2009.02.007

Verschuere, B., & Kleinberg, B. (2016). Id-check: Online concealed information test reveals true identity. *Journal of Forensic Science*, *61*(Suppl 1), S237–240. doi:10.1111/1556-4029.12960

Ververs, P. M., & Wickens, C. D. (2000). *Designing heads-up displays (Huds) to support flight path guidance while minimizing effects of cognitive tunneling*. Paper presented at the Human Factors & Ergonomics Society, Santa Monica, CA.

Verwey, W. B. (1996). Buffer loading and chunking in sequential keypressing. *Journal of Experimental Psychology: Human Perception and Performance*, *22*(3), 544–562.

Verwey, W. B. (2010). Diminished motor skill development in elderly: Indications for limited motor chunk use. *Acta Psychologica*, *134*(2), 206–214. doi:10.1016/j.actpsy.2010.02.001

Verwey, W. B., & Eikelboom, T. (2003). Evidence for lasting sequence segmentation in the discrete sequence-production task. *Journal of Motor Behavior*, *35*(2), 171–181.

Verwey, W. B., Lammens, R., & van Honk, J. (2002). On the role of the SMA in the discrete sequence production task: A TMS study. *Neuropsychologia*, *40*, 1268–1276.

Vetter, P., Goodbody, S. J., & Wolpert, D. M. (1999). Evidence for an eye-centered spherical representation of the visuomotor map. *Journal of Neuophysiology*, *81*, 935–939.

Vetter, P., Smith, F. W., & Muckli, L. (2014). Decoding sound and imagery content in early visual cortex. *Current Biology*, *24*(11), 1256–1262. doi:10.1016/j.cub.2014.04.020

Viard, A., Desgranges, B., Eustache, F., & Piolino, P. (2012). Factors affecting medial temporal lobe engagement for past and future episodic events: An ale meta-analysis of neuroimaging studies. *Brain and Cognition*, *80*(1), 111–125. doi:10.1016/j.bandc.2012.05.004

Vigliocco, G., & Hartsuiker, R. J. (2002). The interplay of meaning, sound, and syntax in sentence production. *Psychological Bulletin*, *128*(3), 442–472. doi:10.1037/0033-2909.128.3.442

Vigliocco, G., Antonini, T., & Garrett, M. F. (1997). Grammatical gender is on the tip of the tongues. *Psychological Science*, *8*(4), 314317.

Villemure, C., & Bushnell, M. C. (2002). Cognitive modulation of pain: How do attention and emotion influence pain processing? *Pain*, *95*, 195–199.

Vingerhoets, G. (2014). Contribution of the posterior parietal cortex in reaching, grasping, and using objects and tools. *Frontiers in Psychology*, *5*, 151. doi:10.3389/fpsyg.2014.00151

Vingerhoets, G., de Lange, F. P., Vandemaele, P., Deblaere, K., & Achten, E. (2002). Motor imagery in mental rotation: An fMRI study. *Neuroimage*, *17*(3), 1623–1633. doi:10.1006/nimg.2002.1290

Vo, M. L., & Wolfe, J. M. (2012). When does repeated search in scenes involve memory? Looking at versus looking for objects in scenes. *Journal of Experimental Psychology: Human Perception and Performance*, *38*(1), 23–41.

Vogel, E. K., & Machizawa, M. G. (2004). Neural activity predicts individual differences in visual working memory capacity. *Nature*, *428*, 748–751.

Vogel, E. K., McCollough, A. W., & Machizawa, M. G. (2005). Neural measures reveal individual differences in controlling access to working memory. *Nature*, *438*(7067), 500–503. doi:10.1038/nature04171.

Vohs, K. D., Mead, N. L., & Goode, M. R. (2006). The psychological consequences of money. *Science*, *314*(5802), 1154–1156. doi:10.1126/science.1132491

Volle, E., Gilbert, S. J., Benoit, R. G., & Burgess, P. W. (2010). Specialization of the rostral prefrontal cortex for distinct analogy processes. *Cerebral Cortex*, *20*(11), 2647–2659. doi:10.1093/cercor/bhq012

Volz, H.-P., Gaser, C., Häger, F., Rzanny, R., NMentzel, H.-J., Kreitschmaan-Andermahr, I. … Sauer, H. (1997). Brain activation during cognitive stimulation with the Wisconsin card sorting test - A functional MRI study on healthy volunteers and schizophrenics. *Psychiatry Research: Neuroimaging*, *75*, 145–157.

References

von Bastian, C. C., Schwaninger, A., & Michel, S. (2008). *Do multi-view X-ray systems improve X-ray image interpretation in airport security screening.* https://irf.fhnw.ch/bitstream/handle/11654/3291/BasSchMic2008.pdf

von Kriegstein, K., & Giraud, A. L. (2006). Implicit multisensory associations influence voice recognition. *PLoS Biology, 4*(10), e326. doi:10.1371/journal.pbio.0040326

von Kriegstein, K., Dogan, O., Gruter, M., Giraud, A. L., Kell, C. A., Gruter, T. … Kiebel, S. J. (2008). Simulation of talking faces in the human brain improves auditory speech recognition. *Proceedings of the National Academy of Sciences of the United States of America, 105*(18), 6747–6752. doi:10.1073/pnas.0710826105

Von Neumann, J., & Morgenstern, O. (1947). *Theory of games and economic behavior.* Princeton, NJ: Princeton University Press.

Vroomen, J., & Baart, M. (2009). Phonetic recalibration only occurs in speech mode. *Cognition, 110*(2), 254–259. doi:10.1016/j.cognition.2008.10.015

Vroomen, J., Bertelson, P., & De Gelder, B. (2001). The ventriloquist effect does not depend on the direction of automatic visual attention. *Perception & Psychophysics, 63*(4), 651–659.

Vroomen, J., Keetels, M., de Gelder, B., & Bertelson, P. (2004). Recalibration of temporal order perception by exposure to audio-visual asynchrony. *Cognitive Brain Research, 22*(1), 32–35. doi:10.1016/j.cogbrainres.2004.07.003

Vuilleumier, P. (2005). How brains beware: Neural mechanisms of emotional attention. *Trends in Cognitive Sciences, 9*(12), 585–594. doi:10.1016/j.tics.2005.10.011

Vuilleumier, P., Schwartz, S., Clarke, K., Husain, M., & Driver, J. (2002). Testing memory for unseen visual stimuli in patients with extinction and spatial neglect. *Journal of Cognitive Neuroscience, 14*(6), 875–886.

Vuvan, D. T., Zendel, B. R., & Peretz, I. (2018). Random feedback makes listeners tone-deaf. *Scientific Reports, 8*(1), 7283. doi:10.1038/s41598-018-25518-1

Wacongne, C., Changeux, J. P., & Dehaene, S. (2012). A neuronal model of predictive coding accounting for the mismatch negativity. *The Journal of Neuroscience, 32*(11), 3665–3678. doi:10.1523/JNEUROSCI.5003-11.2012

Wade, A. R., Brewer, A. A., Rieger, J. W., & Wandell, B. A. (2002). Functional measurements of human ventral occipital cortex: Retinotopy and colour. *Philosophical Transactions of the Royal Society B-Biological Sciences, 357*(1424), 963–973. doi:10.1098/rstb.2002.1108

Waechter, R. L., Goel, V., Raymont, V., Kruger, F., & Grafman, J. (2013). Transitive inference reasoning is impaired by focal lesions in parietal cortex rather than rostrolateral prefrontal cortex. *Neuropsychologia, 51*(3), 464–471. doi:10.1016/j.neuropsychologia.2012.11.026

Wagemans, J., Elder, J. H., Kubovy, M., Palmer, S. E., Peterson, M. A., Singh, M., & von der Heydt, R. (2012). A century of gestalt psychology in visual perception: I. Perceptual grouping and figure-ground organization. *Psychological Bulletin, 138*(6), 1172–1217. doi:10.1037/a0029333

Wagenaar, W. A. (1986). My memory: A study of autobiographical memory over six years. *Cognitive Psychology, 18*, 225–252.

Wagenmakers, E. J., Beek, T., Dijkhoff, L., Gronau, Q. F., Acosta, A., Adams, R. B. Jr. … Zwaan, R. A. (2016). Registered replication report: Strack, Martin, & Stepper (1988). *Perspectives on Psychological Science, 11*(6), 917–928. doi:10.1177/1745691616674458

Wagenmakers, E.-J., Morey, R. D., & Lee, M. D. (2016). Bayesian benefits for the pragmatic researcher. *Current Directions in Psychological Science, 25*(3), 169–176. doi:10.1177/0963721416643289

Wager, T. D., Rilling, J. K., Smith, E. E., Sokolik, A., Casey, K. L., Davidson, R. J. … Cohen, J. D. (2004). Placebo-induced changes in fMRI in the anticipation and experience of pain. *Science, 303*(5661), 1162–1167. doi:10.1126/science.1093065

Wagner, U., Gais, S., Haider, H., Verleger, R., & Born, I. N. (2004). Sleep inspires insight. *Nature, 427*, 352–355.

Wagner, V., Jescheniak, J. D., & Schriefers, H. (2010). On the flexibility of grammatical advance planning during sentence production: Effects of cognitive load on multiple lexical access. *Journal of Experimental Psychology: Learning, Memory, and Cognition, 36*(2), 423–440. doi:10.1037/a0018619

Wagner, M. J., & Luo, L. (2020). Neocortex-cerebellum circuits for cognitive processing. *Trends in Neuroscience, 43*(1), 42–54. doi:10.1016/j.tins.2019.11.002

Wagner, A. D., Maril, A., Bjork, R. A., & Schacter, D. L. (2001). Prefrontal contributions to executive control: fMRI evidence for functional distinctions within lateral prefrontal cortex. *Neuroimage, 14*(6), 1337–1347. doi:10.1006/nimg.2001.0936

Wahlheim, C. N., & Jacoby, L. L. (2013). Remembering change: The critical roll of recursive reminding in proactive effects of memory. *Memory & Cognition, 41*, 1–15.

Wallace, M. T., Roberson, G. E., Hairston, W. D., Stein, B. E., Vaughan, J. W., & Schirillo, J. A. (2004). Unifying multisensory signals across time and space. *Experimental Brain Research, 158*(2), 252–258. doi:10.1007/s00221-004-1899-9

Wallas, G. (1926). *The art of thought.* New York, NY: Harcourt, Brace.

Wallis, G. (2013). Toward a unified model of face and object recognition in the human visual system. *Frontiers in Psychology, 4*, 497. doi:10.3389/fpsyg.2013.00497

Walls, G. L. (1962). The evolutionary history of eye movements. *Vision Research, 2*, 69–80.

Walsh, V. (2003). Time: The back-door of perception. *Trends in Cognitive Sciences, 7*(8), 335–338.

Walsh, J. J., McNally, M. A., Skariah, A., Butt, A. A., & Eysenck, M. W. (2015). Interpretive bias, repressive coping, and trait anxiety. *Anxiety Stress Coping, 28*(6), 617–633. doi:10.1080/10615806.2015.1007047

Walter, W. G., Cooper, R., Aldridge, V. J., McCallum, W. C., & Winter, A. L. (1964). Contingent negative variation:

An electric sign of sensori-motor association and expectancy in the human brain. *Nature, 203*(4943), 380–384.

Walton, D. (2010). Why fallacies appear to be better arguments than they are. *Informal Logic, 30*(2), 59–184.

Wang, X. T. (1996a). Domain-specific rationality in human choices: Violations of utility axioms and social contexts. *Cognition, 60*, 31–63.

Wang, X. T. (1996b). Framing effects: Dynamics and task domains. *Organizational Behavior and Human Decision Processes, 68*(2), 145–157.

Wang, J., Conder, J. A., Blitzer, D. N., & Shinkareva, S. V. (2010). Neural representation of abstract and concrete concepts: A meta-analysis of neuroimaging studies. *Human Brain Mapping, 31*(10), 1459–1468. doi:10.1002/hbm.20950

Wang, S., Fukuchi, M., Koch, C., & Tsuchiya, N. (2012). Spatial attention is attracted in a sustained fashion toward singular points in the optic flow. *PLoS One, 7*(8), e41040. doi:10.1371/journal.pone.0041040

Ward, L. M. (2011). The thalamic dynamic core theory of conscious experience. *Conscious and Cognition, 20*(2), 464–486. doi:10.1016/j.concog.2011.01.007

Warren, J. D., & Griffiths, T. D. (2003). Distinct mechanism of processing spatial sequences and pitch sequences in the human auditory brain. *The Journal of Neuroscience, 23*(13), 5799–5804.

Warren, R. M. (1970). Perceptual restauration of missing speech sounds. *Science, 167*, 392–393.

Warren, W. H., & Hannon, D. J. (1988). Direction of self-motion is perceived from optical flow. *Nature, 336*, 162–163.

Warrington, E. K. (1982). The fractionation of arithmetical skills: A single case study. *The Quarterly Journal of Experimental Psychology, 34A*(1), 31–51.

Warrington, E. K., & Shallice, T. (1969). The selective impairment of auditory verbal short-term memory. *Brain, 92*, 885–896.

Wason, P. C. (1960). On the failure to eliminate hypotheses in a conceptual task. *The Quarterly Journal of Experimental Psychology, 12*(3), 129–140.

Wason, P. C. (1966). Reasoning. In B. M. Foss (Ed.), *New horizons in psychology*. Harmondsworth: Penguin.

Wason, P. C. (1968). Reasoning about a rule. *The Quarterly Journal of Experimental Psychology, 20*(3), 273–281.

Waszak, F., & Pholulamdeth, V. (2009). Episodic S-R bindings and emotion: About the influence of positive and negative action effects on stimulus-response associations. *Experimental Brain Research, 194*(3), 489–494. doi:10.1007/s00221-009-1745-1

Waszak, F., Wenke, D., & Brass, M. (2008). Cross-talk of instructed and applied arbitrary visuomotor mappings. *Acta Psychologica, 127*(1), 30–35. doi:10.1016/j.actpsy.2006.12.005

Watkins, K. E., Strafella, A. P., & Paus, T. (2003). Seeing and hearing speech excites the motor system involved in speech production. *Neuropsychologia, 41*(8), 989–994. doi:10.1016/s0028-3932(02)00316-0

Watson, D., & Tellegen, A. (1985). Toward a consensual structure of mood. *Psychological Bulletin, 98*(2), 219–235.

Wattendorf, E., Westermann, B., Fiedler, K., Kaza, E., Lotze, M., & Celio, M. R. (2013). Exploration of the neural correlates of ticklish laughter by functional magnetic resonance imaging. *Cerebral Cortex, 23*(6), 1280–1289. doi:10.1093/cercor/bhs094

Webb, T. L., Miles, E., & Sheeran, P. (2012). Dealing with feeling: A meta-analysis of the effectiveness of strategies derived from the process model of emotion regulation. *Psychological Bulletin, 138*(4), 775–808. doi:10.1037/a0027600

Weber, A., & Cutler, A. (2004). Lexical competition in non-native spoken-word recognition. *Journal of Memory and Language, 50*(1), 1–25. doi:10.1016/s0749-596x(03)00105-0

Wegner, D., & Wheatley, T. (1999). Apparent mental causation. *American Psychologist, 54*(7), 480–492.

Weingarten, H. P. (1983). Conditioned cues elicit feeding in sated rats: A role for learning in meal initiation. *Science, 220*(4595), 431–433.

Weisberg, D. S., Keil, F. C., Goodstein, J., Rawson, E., & Gray, J. R. (2008). The seductive allure of neuroscience explanations. *Journal of Cognitive Neuroscience, 20*, 470–477.

Weiskrantz, L. (1986). *Blindsight: A case study and implication*. Oxford: Oxford University Press.

Weiss, Y., Simoncelli, E. P., & Adelson, E. H. (2002). Motion illusions as optimal percepts. *Nature Neuroscience, 5*(6), 598–604. doi:10.1038/nn858

Weissman, D. H., Roberts, K. C., Visscher, K. M., & Woldorff, M. G. (2006). The neural bases of momentary lapses in attention. *Nature Neuroscience, 9*(7), 971–978.

Welch, R. B. (1972). The effect of experienced limb identity upon adaptation to simulated displacement of the visual field. *Perception & Psychophysics, 12*(6), 453–456.

Welch, R. B., & Warren, D. H. (1980). Immediate perceptual response to intersensory discrepancy. *Psychological Bulletin, 88*(3), 638–667.

Welch, R. B., & Warren, D. H. (1986). Intersensory interactions. In K. R. Kauffman & J. P. Thomas (Eds.), *Handbook of perception and human performance volume 1: Sensory processes and perception* (pp. 1–36). New York, NY: Wiley.

Welford, A. T. (1952). The 'Psychological refractory Period' and the timing of high-speed performance- A review and a theory. *British Journal of Psychology: General Section, 43*(1), 2–19.

Weller, J. A., Levin, I. P., Shiv, B., & Bechara, A. (2007). Neural correlates of adaptive decision making for risky gains and losses. *Psychological Science, 18*(11), 958–964.

Wells, H. (1972). Effect of intertrial interval duration on component processes in concept learning. *Journal of Experimental Psychology, 94*(1), 49–51.

Wender, K. F., & Rothkegel, R. (2000). Subitizing and its subprocesses. *Psychological Research, 64*, 81–92.

West, R. L. (1996). An application of prefrontal cortex function theory to cognitive aging. *Psychological Bulletin, 120*(2), 272–292.

Westheimer, G., & McKee, S. P. (1975). Visual acuity in the presence of retinal-image motion. *Journal of the Optical Society of America, 65*(7), 847–850.

Whalen, J., Gallistel, C. R., & Gelman, R. (1999). Nonverbal counting in humans. *Psychological Science, 10*(2), 130–137.

Whalen, P. J. (1998). Fear, vigilance, and ambiguity: Initial neuroimaging studies of the human amygdala. *Current Directions in Psychological Science, 7*, 177–188.

Wheeler, M. E., & Treisman, A. M. (2002). Binding in short-term visual memory. *Journal of Experimental Psychology: General, 131*(1), 48–64. doi:10.1037//0096-3445.131.1.48

White, L. K., Suway, J. G., Pine, D. S., Bar-Haim, Y., & Fox, N. A. (2011). Cascading effects: The influence of attention bias to threat on the interpretation of ambiguous information. *Behaviour Research and Therapy, 49*(4), 244–251. doi:10.1016/j.brat.2011.01.004

Whorf, B. L. (1956). *Language, thought, and reality.* New York, NY: John Wiley and Sons, Inc.

Wickens, C. D. (2008). Multiple resources and mental workload. *Human Factors, 50*(3), 449–455. doi:10.1518/001872008X288394

Wicker, B., Keysers, C., Plailly, J., Royet, J.-P., Gallese, V., & Rizzolatti, G. (2003). Both of us disgusted in my insula: The common neural basis of seeing and feeling disgust. *Neuron, 40*, 655–664.

Wild, C. J., Davis, M. H., & Johnsrude, I. S. (2012). Human auditory cortex is sensitive to the perceived clarity of speech. *Neuroimage, 60*(2), 1490–1502. doi:10.1016/j.neuroimage.2012.01.035

Wilf, M., Holmes, N. P., Schwartz, I., & Makin, T. R. (2013). Dissociating between object affordances and spatial compatibility effects using early response components. *Frontiers in Psychology, 4*, 591. doi:10.3389/fpsyg.2013.00591

Wilkie, R. M., & Wann, J. P. (2003a). Controlling steering and judging heading: Retinal flow, visual direction, and extraretinal information. *Journal of Experimental Psychology: Human Perception and Performance, 29*(2), 363–378.

Wilkie, R. M., & Wann, J. P. (2003b). Eye-movements aid the control of locomotion. *Journal of Visualized, 3*(11), 677–684. doi:10.1167/3.11.3

Wilkie, R. M., & Wann, J. P. (2006). Judgments of path, not heading, guide locomotion. *Journal of Experimental Psychology: Human Perception and Performance, 32*(1), 88–96. doi:10.1037/0096-1523.32.1.88

Wilkie, R. M., Kountouriotis, G. K., Merat, N., & Wann, J. P. (2010). Using vision to control locomotion: Looking where you want to go. *Experimental Brain Research, 204*(4), 539–547. doi:10.1007/s00221-010-2321-4

Wilkinson, L., & Shanks, D. R. (2004). Intentional control and implicit sequence learning. *Journal of Experimental Psychology: Learning, Memory, and Cognition, 30*(2), 354–369.

Williams, J. M. G., Watts, F. N., MacLeod, C. M., & Mathews, A. (1997). *Cognitive psychology and emotional disorders* (2nd ed.). Chichester: Wiley.

Wilson, M. A., & McNaughton, B. L. (1994). Reactivation of hippocampal ensemble memories during sleep. *Science, 265*, 676–679.

Wilson, S. M., Saygin, A. P., Sereno, M. I., & Iacoboni, M. (2004). Listening to speech activates motor areas involved in speech production. *Nature Neuroscience, 7*(7), 701–702. doi:10.1038/nn1263.

Wimmer, H., & Perner, J. (1983). beliefs about beliefs: Representation and constraining function of wrong beliefs in young children's understanding of deception. *Cognition, 13*, 103–128.

Winawer, J., Witthoft, N., Frank, M. C., Wu, L., Wade, A. R., & Boroditsky, L. (2007). Russian blues reveal effects of language on color discrimination. *Proceedings of the National Academy of Sciences of the United States of America, 104*(19), 7780–7785. doi:10.1073/pnas.0701644104

Wing, A. M. (2000). Motor control: Mechanisms of motor equivalence in handwriting. *Current Biology, 10*, R245–R248.

Wise, R. A. (2004). Dopamine, learning and motivation. *Nature Reviews Neuroscience, 5*(6), 483–494. doi:10.1038/nrn1406

Witek, M. A., Clarke, E. F., Wallentin, M., Kringelbach, M. L., & Vuust, P. (2014). Syncopation, body-movement and pleasure in groove music. *PLoS One, 9*(4), e94446. doi:10.1371/journal.pone.0094446

Withagen, R., de Poel, H. J., Araújo, D., & Pepping, G.-J. (2012). Affordances can invite behavior: Reconsidering the relationship between affordances and agency. *New Ideas in Psychology, 30*(2), 250–258. doi:10.1016/j.newideapsych.2011.12.003

Wittmann, B. C., Schott, B. H., Guderian, S., Frey, J. U., Heinze, H. J., & Duzel, E. (2005). Reward-related fMRI activation of dopaminergic midbrain is associated with enhanced hippocampus-dependent long-term memory formation. *Neuron, 45*(3), 459–467. doi:10.1016/j.neuron.2005.01.010

Wixted, J. T. (2004). The psychology and neuroscience of forgetting. *Annual Review of Psychology, 55*, 235–269. doi:10.1146/annurev.psych.55.090902.141555

Wixted, J. T., & Squire, L. R. (2011). The medial temporal lobe and the attributes of memory. *Trends in Cognitive Sciences, 15*(5), 210–217. doi:10.1016/j.tics.2011.03.005

Woldorff, M. G., Gallen, C. C., Hampson, S. A., Hillyard, S. A., Pantev, C., Sobel, D., & Bloom, F. E. (1993). Modulation of early sensory processing in human auditory cortex during auditory selective attention. *Proceedings of the National Academy of Sciences of the United States of America, 90*(18), 8722–8726.

Woldorff, M. G., Hillyard, S. A., Gallen, C. C., Hampson, S. A., & Bloom, F. E. (1998). Magnetoencephalographic recordings demonstrate attention modulation of mismatch-related neural activity in human auditory cortex. *Psychophysiology*, *35*, 283–292.

Wolf, S., & Wolf, H. G. (1949). *Human gastric function: An experimental study of a man and his stomach*. London: Oxford University Press.

Wolfe, J. M. (2003). Moving towards solutions to some enduring controversies in visual search. *Trends in Cognitive Sciences*, *7*(2), 70–76.

Wolfe, J. M., Alvarez, G. A., Rosenholtz, R., Kuzmova, Y. I., & Sherman, A. M. (2011). Visual search for arbitrary objects in real scenes. *Attention, Perception, & Psychophysics*, *73*(6), 1650–1671. doi:10.3758/s13414-011-0153-3

Wolfe, J. M., Cave, K. R., & Franzel, S. L. (1989). Guided search: An alternative to the feature integration model for visual search. *Journal of Experimental Psychology: Human Perception and Performance*, *15*(3), 419–433.

Wolfe, J. M., Horowitz, T. S., & Kenner, N. M. (2005). Rare items often missed in visual searches. *Nature*, *435*, 439–440.

Wolfe, J. M., Horowitz, T. S., Van Wert, M. J., Kenner, N. M., Place, S. S., & Kibbi, N. (2007). Low target prevalence is a stubborn source of errors in visual search tasks. *Journal of Experimental Psychology: General*, *136*(4), 623–638. doi:10.1037/0096-3445.136.4.623

Wolfe, J. M., Vo, M. L., Evans, K. K., & Greene, M. R. (2011). Visual search in scenes involves selective and nonselective pathways. *Trends in Cognitive Sciences*, *15*(2), 77–84. doi:10.1016/j.tics.2010.12.001

Wolff, P., & Holmes, K. J. (2011). Linguistic relativity. *Wiley Interdisciplinary Review in Cognitive Science*, *2*(3), 253–265. doi:10.1002/wcs.104

Wolpaw, J. R. (1980). Correlations between task-related activity and responses to perturbation in primate sensorimotor cortex. *Journal of Neurophysiology*, *44*(6), 1122–1138.

Wolpaw, J. R., Birbaumer, N., Heetderks, W. J., McFarland, D. J., Peckham, P. H., Schalk, G. ... Vaughan, T. M. (2000). Brain-computer interface technology: A review of the first international meeting. *IEEE Transactions on Rehabilitation Engineering*, *8*(2), 164–173.

Wolpert, D. M., Doya, K., & Kawato, M. (2003). A unifying computational framework for motor control and social interaction. *Philosophical Transactions of the Royal Society B-Biological Sciences*, *358*(1431), 593–602. doi:10.1098/rstb.2002.1238

Wolpert, D. M., Gahahramani, Z., & Jordan, M. I. (1995). An internal model for sensorymotor integration. *Science*, *269*(5232), 1880–1882.

Wong, K. F., Yik, M., & Kwong, J. Y. (2006). Understanding the emotional aspects of escalation of commitment: The role of negative affect. *Journal of Applied Psychology*, *91*(2), 282–297. doi:10.1037/0021-9010.91.2.282

Woolf, C. J., Bennett, G. J., Doherty, M., Dubner, R., Kidd, B., Koltzenburg, M. ... Torebjork, E. (1998). Towards a mechanism-based classification of pain? *Pain*, *77*, 227–229.

Woollett, K., & Maguire, E. A. (2009). Navigational expertise May compromise anterograde associative memory. *Neuropsychologia*, *47*(4), 1088–1095. doi:10.1016/j.neuropsychologia.2008.12.036

Woollett, K., & Maguire, E. A. (2011). Acquiring 'the knowledge' of London's layout drives structural brain changes. *Current Biology*, *21*(24), 2109–2114. doi:10.1016/j.cub.2011.11.018

Wright, G. (1984). *Behavioral decision making*. New York, NY: Plenum Press.

Wu, L. L., & Barsalou, L. W. (2009). Perceptual simulation in conceptual combination: Evidence from property generation. *Acta Psychologica*, *132*(2), 173–189. doi:10.1016/j.actpsy.2009.02.002

Wübben, M., & Wangenheim, F. (2008). Instant customer base analysis: Managerial heuristics often 'Get it right'. *Journal of Marketing*, *72*, 82–93.

Wymbs, N. F., Bassett, D. S., Mucha, P. J., Porter, M. A., & Grafton, S. T. (2012). Differential recruitment of the sensorimotor putamen and frontoparietal cortex during motor chunking in humans. *Neuron*, *74*(5), 936–946. doi:10.1016/j.neuron.2012.03.038

Xu, Y. (2010). The neural fate of task-irrelevant features in object-based processing. *The Journal of Neuroscience*, *30*(42), 14020–14028. doi:10.1523/JNEUROSCI.3011-10.2010

Xu, F., & Garcia, V. (2008). Intuitive statistics by 8-month-old infants. *Proceedings of the National Academy of Sciences of the United States of America*, *105*(13), 5012–5015.

Yamamoto, S., & Kitazawa, S. (2001). Reversal of subjective temporal order due to arm crossing. *Nature Neuroscience*, *4*(7), 759–765.

Yamane, Y., Carlson, E. T., Bowman, K. C., Wang, Z., & Connor, C. E. (2008). A neural code for three-dimensional object shape in macaque inferotemporal cortex. *Nature Neuroscience*, *11*(11), 1352–1360. doi:10.1038/nn.2202

Yantis, S., & Egeth, H. E. (1999). On the distinction between visual salience and stimulus-driven attentional capture. *Journal of Experimental Psychology: Human Perception and Performance*, *25*(3), 661–676.

Yates, M. (2005). Phonological neighbors speed visual word processing: Evidence from multiple tasks. *Journal of Experimental Psychology: Learning, Memory, and Cognition*, *31*(6), 1385–1397. doi:10.1037/0278-7393.31.6.1385

Yates, M. (2013). How the clustering of phonological neighbors affects visual word recognition. *Journal of Experimental Psychology: Learning, Memory, and Cognition*, *39*(5), 1649–1656.

Yates, M., Friend, J., & Ploetz, D. M. (2008). The effect of phonological neighborhood density on eye movements during Reading. *Cognition*, *107*(2), 685–692. doi:10.1016/j.cognition.2007.07.020

793

Ye, L., Cardwell, W., & Mark, L. S. (2009). Perceiving multiple affordances for objects. *Ecological Psychology, 21*(3), 185–217. doi:10.1080/10407410903058229

Yechiam, E., & Hochman, G. (2013). Losses as modulators of attention: Review and analysis of the unique effects of losses over gains. *Psychological Bulletin, 139*(2), 497–518.

Yeshurun, Y., Nguyen, M., & Hasson, U. (2021). The default mode network: Where the idiosyncratic self meets the shared social world. *Nature Reviews Neuroscience, 22*(3), 181–192. doi:10.1038/s41583-020-00420-w

Yeung, N., Holroyd, C. B., & Cohen, J. D. (2005). ERP correlates of feedback and reward processing in the presence and absence of response choice. *Cerebral Cortex, 15*(5), 535–544. doi:10.1093/cercor/bhh153

Yilmaz, E. H., & Warren, W. H. (1995). Visual control of braking: A test of the tau-dot hypothesis. *Journal of Experimental Psychology: Human Perception and Performance, 21*(5), 996–1014.

Yon, D., Heyes, C., & Press, C. (2020). Beliefs and desires in the predictive brain. *Nature Communications, 11*(1), 4404. doi:10.1038/s41467-020-18332-9

Yoshida, W., Seymour, B., Koltzenburg, M., & Dolan, R. J. (2013). Uncertainty increases pain: Evidence for a novel mechanism of pain modulation involving the periaqueductal gray. *Journal of Neuroscience, 33*(13), 5638–5646. doi:10.1523/JNEUROSCI.4984-12.2013

Young, P. T. (1966). Hedonic organization and regulation of behavior. *Psychological Review, 73*(1), 59–86.

Young, M., Brooks, L., & Norman, G. (2007). Found in translation: The impact of familiar symptom descriptions on diagnosis in novices. *Medical Education, 41*(12), 1146–1151. doi:10.1111/j.1365-2923.2007.02913.x

Young, A. W., Fruhholz, S., & Schweinberger, S. R. (2020). Face and voice perception: Understanding commonalities and differences. *Trends in Cognitive Sciences, 24*(5), 398–410. doi:10.1016/j.tics.2020.02.001

Young, J. P., Herath, P., Eickhoff, S. B., Grefkes, C., Zilles, K., & Roland, P. E. (2004). Somatotopy and attentional modulation of the human parietal and opercular regions. *The Journal of Neuroscience, 24*(23), 5391–5399. doi:10.1523/jneurosci.4030-03.2004

Zacks, J. M., Kurby, C. A., Eisenberg, M. L., & Haroutunian, N. (2011). Prediction error associated with the perceptual segmentation of naturalistic events. *Journal of Cognitive Neuroscience, 23*(12), 4057–4066.

Zacks, J. M., Speer, N. K., Swallow, K. M., Braver, T. S., & Reynolds, J. R. (2007). Event perception: A mind-brain perspective. *Psychological Bulletin, 133*(2), 273–293. doi:10.1037/0033-2909.133.2.273

Zago, L., Pesenti, M., Mellet, E., Crivello, F., Mazoyer, B., & Tzourio-Mazoyer, N. (2001). Neural correlates of simple and complex mental calculation. *Neuroimage, 13*(2), 314–327. doi:10.1006/nimg.2000.0697

Zeki, S. (1980). The response properties of cells in the middle temporal area (Area MT) of owl monkey visual cortex. *Proceedings of the Royal Society B-Biological Sciences, 207*(1167), 239–248.

Zeki, S. (1983). *The relationship between wavelength and color studied in single cells of monkey Striate cortex proceedings of the 9th meeting of the International Neurobiology Society* (pp. 219–227).

Zeki, S. (1990). A century of cerebral achromatopsia. *Brain, 113*(Pt 6), 1721–1777.

Zeki, S. (2001). Localization and globalization in conscious vision. *Annual Review of Neuroscience, 24*, 57–86.

Zeki, S. (2003). The disunity of consciousness. *Trends in Cognitive Sciences, 7*(5), 214–218. doi:10.1016/s1364-6613(03)00081-0

Zetsche, U., & Joormann, J. (2011). Components of interference control predict depressive symptoms and rumination cross-sectionally and at six months follow-up. *Journal of Behavior Therapy and Experimental Psychiatry, 42*(1), 65–73. doi:10.1016/j.jbtep.2010.06.001

Zhang, J., Zhou, X., Chang, R., & Yang, Y. (2018). Effects of global and local contexts on chord processing: An ERP study. *Neuropsychologia, 109*, 149–154. doi:10.1016/j.neuropsychologia.2017.12.016

Ziemann, U., Muellbacher, W., Hallett, M., & Cohen, L. G. (2001). Modulation of practice-dependent plasticity in human motor cortex. *Brain, 124*, 1171–1181.

Zihl, J., Von Cramon, D., & Mai, N. (1983). Selective disturbance of movement vision after bilateral brain damage. *Brain, 106*, 313–340.

Zoccolan, D., Kouh, M., Poggio, T., & DiCarlo, J. J. (2007). Trade-off between object selectivity and tolerance in monkey inferotemporal cortex. *The Journal of Neuroscience, 27*(45), 12292–12307. doi:10.1523/JNEUROSCI.1897-07.2007

Zogg, J. B., Woods, S. P., Sauceda, J. A., Wiebe, J. S., & Simoni, J. M. (2012). The role of prospective memory in medication adherence: A review of an emerging literature. *Journal of Behavioral Medicine, 35*(1), 47–62. doi:10.1007/s10865-011-9341-9

Zotterman, Y. (1939). Touch, pain and tickling: An electro-physiological investigation on cutaneous sensory nerves. *Journal of Physiology, 95*, 1–28.

Zurif, E. B., Caramazza, A., Myerson, R., & Galvin, J. (1974). Semantic feature representations for normal and aphasic language. *Brain and Language, 1*, 167–187.

Zwaan, R. A., & Madden, C. J. (2004). Updating situation models. *Journal of Experimental Psychology: Learning, Memory, and Cognition, 30*(1), 283–288.

Zwaan, R. A., Langston, M. C., & Graesser, A. C. (1995). The construction of situation models in narrative comprehension: An event-indexing model. *Psychological Science, 6*(5), 292–297.

Zwitserlood, P. (1989). The locus of the effects of sentential-semantic context in spoken-word processing. *Cognition, 32*, 25–64.

Index

Note: Page references in *italics* denote figures and in **bold** tables.